Great North American Indians

Great North American Indians

Profiles in Life and Leadership

Frederick J. Dockstader

A Norback Book

VNR VAN NOSTRAND REINHOLD COMPANY

NEW YORK   CINCINNATI   ATLANTA   DALLAS   SAN FRANCISCO
LONDON   TORONTO   MELBOURNE

Van Nostrand Reinhold Company Regional Offices:
New York   Cincinnati   Atlanta   Dallas   San Francisco

Van Nostrand Reinhold Company International Offices:
London   Toronto   Melbourne

Copyright © 1977 by Litton Educational Publishing, Inc.

Library of Congress Catalog Card Number: 77-23733
ISBN: 0-442-02148-8

Manufactured in the United States of America

Published by Van Nostrand Reinhold Company
450 West 33rd Street, New York, N.Y. 10001

Published simultaneously in Canada by Van Nostrand Reinhold Ltd.

15 14 13 12 11 10 9 8 7 6 5 4 3 2 1

Library of Congress Cataloging in Publication Data

Dockstader, Frederick J
    Great North American Indians.

    Bibliography: p.
    Includes index.
    1. Indians of North America—Biography.
I. Title.
E89.D55   920′.0092′97   77-23733
ISBN 0-442-02148-8

Dedicated to the memory of

FREDERICK WEBB HODGE

warm friend, wise teacher and gentle critic.
Upon whose work so much of this book is based.

Contents

Introduction 1
Abomazine, Abnaki 9
Adario, Tionantati 9
Thomas Wildcat Alford, Shawnee 10
American Horse, Oglala Sioux 11
Annawan, Wampanoag 13
Juan Antonio, Kawia 14
Arapoosh, Crow 17
Spencer Asah, Kiowa 18
Atsidi Sani, Navajo 19
Attakullakulla, Cherokee 20
James Auchiah, Kiowa 21
Awa Tsireh, San Ildefonso 23
Bacon Rind, Osage 24
Amos Bad Heart Bull, Oglala Sioux 25
Barboncito, Navajo 25
James Bear's Heart, Cheyenne 27
Charles Albert Bender, Chippewa 27
Big Bow, Kiowa 29
Big Foot, Miniconjou Sioux 29
Big Mouth, Brûlé Sioux 31
Big Tree, Kiowa 32
Black Beaver, Delaware 33
Black Elk, Oglala Sioux 33
Black Hawk, Sauk 34
Black Kettle, Cheyenne 36
Blacksnake, Seneca 37
Acee Blue Eagle, Creek 39
Bogus Charley, Modoc 40
Gertrude Simmons Bonnin, Yankton Sioux 40
Elias Boudinot, Cherokee 41
Bowl, Cherokee 42
Billy Bowlegs, Seminole 43
Joseph Brant, Mohawk 44
Molly Brant, Mohawk 46
Dennis Wolf Bushyhead, Cherokee 47
Canonchet, Narragansett 48
Canonicus, Narragansett 49
Charlot, Kalispel 49
Jesse Chisholm, Cherokee 50
Henry Roe Cloud, Winnebago 51
Cochise, Chiricahua Apache 53
William Cohoe, Cheyenne 54
Colorow, Moache Ute 55
Comcomly, Chinook 58
George Copway, Ojibwa 59
Cornplanter, Seneca 59
Cornstalk, Shawnee 60
Crazy Horse, Oglala Sioux 61
Crazy Snake, Creek 63
Crow Dog, Brûlé Sioux 65
Curly, Crow 66
Charles Curtis, Kansa 67
Datsolalee, Washo 68

Angel DeCora Dietz, Winnebago 71
Dekanawida, Huron 71
Dekanisora, Onondaga 72
Delaware Prophet, Delaware 73
Ella Carla Deloria, Yankton Sioux 74
Henry Chee Dodge, Navajo 75
Dohasan, Kiowa 76
Edward Pasqual Dozier, Santa Clara 78
Dragging Canoe, Cherokee 79
Dull Knife, Cheyenne 80
Charles Alexander Eastman, Santee Sioux 82
Charles Edensaw, Haida 83
Eskaminzim, Coyotero Apache 84
Flat Mouth, Chippewa 85
Stephen Foreman, Cherokee 86
Herbert Burwell Fowler, Santee Sioux 87
Gall, Hunkpapa Sioux 88
Ganado Mucho, Navajo 89
Daniel Garakonthie, Onondaga 91
Spokane Garry, Spokane 91
Gelelemend, Delaware 92
Geronimo, Chiricahua Apache 93
William Thomas Gilcrease, Creek 96
Francis Godfroy, Miami 98
John Grass, Teton Sioux 98
Haiglar, Catawba 99
Half King, Oneida 101
Handsome Lake, Seneca 102
Ned Hatathli, Navajo 103
Ira Hamilton Hayes, Pima 105
Hendrick, Mohawk 106
John N. B. Hewitt, Tuscarora 107
Hiawatha, Mohawk 108
High Horn, Shawnee 109
Jack Hokeah, Kiowa 110
Hole in the Day, Chippewa 110
Hollow-Horn Bear, Brûlé Sioux 111
Hooker Jim, Modoc 113
Hopocan, Delaware 115
Howling Wolf, Cheyenne 115
Hump, Miniconjou Sioux 116
George Hunt, Kwakiutl 117
Ignacio, Wiminuche Ute 119
Inkpaduta, Wahpekute Sioux 119
Irateba, Mohave 121
Iron Tail, Oglala Sioux 122
Ishi, Yahi 123
Isparhecher, Creek 124
Emily Pauline Johnson, Mohawk 125
Peter Jones, Ojibwa 126
William Jones, Fox 127
Chief Joseph, Nez Percé 128
Charles Journeycake, Delaware 130

John Jumper, Seminole 131
Kamaiakin, Yakima 132
Kénakuk, Kickapoo 133
Keokuk, Sauk 134
Kicking Bird, Kiowa 136
Kintpuash, Modoc 138
Hosteen Klah, Navajo 140
John Konkapot, Mahican 142
Joseph LaFlesche, Omaha 143
Susette LaFlesche, Omaha 143
Francis LaFlesche, Omaha 144
Susan LaFlesche, Omaha 145
Roberta Campbell Lawson, Delaware 145
Lawyer, Nez Percé 146
Leatherlips, Wyandot 148
Little Crow, Mdewakanton Sioux 148
Little Raven, Arapaho 150
Little Turtle, Miami 151
Little Wolf, Cheyenne 152
Logan, Cayuga 154
Lone Wolf, Kiowa 155
Will West Long, Cherokee 156
Looking Glass, Nez Percé 157
Fred Lookout, Osage 160
Alexander McGillivray, Creek 161
William McIntosh, Creek 162
Mangas Coloradas, Mimbreño Apache 163
Manuelito, Navajo 165
Mungo Martin, Kwakiutl 167
Crescencio Martínez, San Ildefonso 168
Julián Martínez, San Ildefonso 169
Massasoit, Wampanoag 171
Mato Tope, Mandan 172
Menewa, Creek 173
Metacom, Wampanoag 174
Miantonomo, Narragansett 176
Micanopy, Seminole 177
Carlos Montezuma, Yavapai 178
Waldo Mootzka, Hopi 180
Stephen Mopope, Kiowa 181
Moses, Sinkiuse Salish 181
Mountain Chief, Blackfoot 183
Mountain Wolf Woman, Winnebago 184
Mary Musgrove, Creek 185
Naiche, Chiricahua Apache 186
Gerald Nailor, Navajo 187
Nampeyo, Hopi 187
Nana, Chiricahua Apache 189
Daniel Ninham, Mahican 190
Ninigret, Niantic 191
Peta Nocona, Comanche 193
Samson Occom, Mohegan 194
Oconostota, Cherokee 195
Opechancanough, Powhatan 196
Opothleyaholo, Creek 197

Oqwa Pi, San Ildefonso 198
Osceola, Seminole 199
Oshkosh, Menomini 200
John Otherday, Wahpeton Sioux 201
Ouray, Uncompaghre Ute 202
Arthur Caswell Parker, Seneca 203
Ely Samuel Parker, Seneca 204
Quanah Parker, Comanche 206
Passaconaway, Pennacook 207
Pawhuska, Osage 208
Payepot, Cree 209
Tonita Peña, San Ildefonso 210
Petalésharo, Skidi Pawnee 211
Peter Perkins Pitchlynn, Choctaw 213
Plenty Coups, Crow 214
Pocahontas, Powhatan 215
Leo Pokagon, Potawatomi 215
Simon Pokagon, Potawatomi 216
Pontiac, Ottawa 217
Popé, San Juan 219
Popovi Da, San Ildefonso 220
Pleasant Porter, Creek 221
Alexander Lawrence Posey, Creek 222
Poundmaker, Cree 223
Poweshiek, Fox 224
Powhatan, Powhatan 225
Pushmataha, Choctaw 226
Queen Anne, Pamunkey 227
John W. Quinney, Mahican 227
Ben Quintana, Cochití 228
Rain in the Face, Hunkpapa Sioux 229
Ramona, Kawia 230
Red Bird, Winnebago 231
Red Cloud, Oglala Sioux 231
Red Jacket, Seneca 234
Red Shoes, Choctaw 236
Red Tomahawk, Teton Sioux 236
Red Wing, Mdewakanton Sioux 238
Major Ridge, Cherokee 238
John Ridge, Cherokee 239
Louis Riel, Cree 241
Rollie Lynn Riggs, Cherokee 242
Rocky Boy, Chippewa 243
Will Rogers, Cherokee 243
Roman Nose, Cheyenne 245
John Ross, Cherokee 246
Sacajawea, Shoshoni 248
Sadekanakte, Onondaga 249
Sagaunash, Potawatomi 249
Sakarissa, Tuscarora 250
Samoset, Pemaquid 250
Sassacus, Pequot 251
Satanta, Kiowa 252
Scarface Charlie, Modoc 253
Schonchin, Modoc 254

Hart Merriam Schultz, Blackfoot 255
Seattle, Duwamish 258
Sequoyah, Cherokee 259
Setangya, Kiowa 261
Shábona, Potawatomi 262
Shakes, Tlingit 263
Shikellamy, Oneida 264
Short Bull, Brûlé Sioux 265
Sitting Bull, Hunkpapa Sioux 266
Sitting Bull, Oglala Sioux 269
Skenandoa, Oneida 272
Redbird Smith, Cherokee 272
Smohalla, Wanapum 274
Spotted Tail, Brûlé Sioux 275
Ernest Spybuck, Shawnee 277
Squanto, Pautuxet 278
Standing Bear, Ponca 279
Stumbling Bear, Kiowa 281
Carl Sweezy, Arapaho 282
Sword Bearer, Crow 282
Quincy Tahoma, Navajo 283
Taimah, Fox 284
Tall Bull, Cheyenne 285
Tammany, Delaware 285
Tarhe, Wyandot 286
Tavibo, Paiute 287
Louis Tawanima, Hopi 288
Tawaquaptewa, Hopi 288
Tecumseh, Shawnee 290
Teedyuscung, Delaware 292
Kateri Tekakwitha, Mohawk 294
Ten Bears, Comanche 294
Tendoy, Bannock 295
Tenskwátawa, Shawnee 297
Jim Thorpe, Sauk 298
Jerome Richard Tiger, Creek 299
Clarence Leonard Tinker, Osage 300
Tomah, Menomini 302
Tomochichi, Creek 302
Toohulhulsote, Nez Percé 304
Monroe Tsatoke, Kiowa 305
Tuekakas, Cayuse 306
Two Guns White Calf, Blackfoot 307
Two Leggings, Crow 308
Two Moon, Cheyenne 310

Two Strike, Brûlé Sioux 311
Tyhee, Bannock 312
Uncas, Mohegan 313
Victorio, Mimbreño Apache 314
Walkara, Timpanagos Ute 315
Walk in the Water, Huron 317
Waneta, Yanktonai Sioux 318
Wannalancet, Mahican 318
Wapasha, Mdewakanton Sioux 319
Nancy Ward, Cherokee 320
War Eagle, Santee Sioux 321
William Whipple Warren, Chippewa 322
Washakie, Shoshoni 323
Washunga, Kansa 325
Stand Watie, Cherokee 326
Wa-Wa-Chaw, Luiseño 327
William Weatherford, Creek 328
Weetamoo, Pocasset 329
White Bird, Nez Percé 329
White Cloud, Chippewa 331
White Eyes, Delaware 331
White Man Runs Him, Crow 332
Wildcat, Seminole 333
Eleazar Williams, Mohawk 335
Winema, Modoc 336
Winnemucca, Paiute 337
Sarah Winnemucca, Paiute 337
Wooden Lance, Kiowa 339
Wooden Leg, Cheyenne 340
Wovoka, Paiute 341
Allen Wright, Choctaw 342
Wyandanch, Montauk 344
Yellow Hand, Cheyenne 345
Chauncey Yellow Robe, Yanktonai Sioux 345
Yellow Thunder, Winnebago 346
Yellow Wolf, Nez Percé 347
Youkioma, Hopi 348
Young Bear, Fox 350
Young Man Afraid of His Horses, Oglala Sioux 351
Zotom, Kiowa 353

For Further Reading 355
Tribal Listing 371
Chronology 373
Index of Names 375

Great North American Indians

Introduction

As an interest in minorities has grown, so has the desire to know more about the people who make up the divers elements of America, and the individuals who were prominent in these cultures. But while many written accounts are available concerning sociopolitical aspects of Indian life, and ethnographic descriptions abound, few comprehensive studies of Indian individuals have yet emerged—those biographical sketches which have been published have been largely concerned with one, or very few, persons. Often, unfortunately, these are only repetitive accounts copied from earlier writings, and involve a nuclear core of less than 50 of the hundreds of important Native North American leaders of the past. In an effort to broaden the degree of information available, as well as increase the variety of subjects, the following sketches are offered.

We know a great deal about some tribes, and almost nothing of others; we also know in depth the careers of some Indian individuals, and know very little about others. Many Indian groups seem to have possessed a talent for developing outstanding individual leaders in abundance, while other equally advanced peoples seem not to have enjoyed such a proportionate number. The reasons for this imbalance are difficult to answer—in some instances, the tribal customs offered little outlet to individual growth; in others, outstanding talent was stifled, or at best temporarily tolerated. One other reason for this apparent paucity may, of course, have been a simple lack of reportage by outside writers.

Persons familiar with Indian–White culture contact writing often note how faceless many of these accounts are, in such statements as ".... the Indians do...." as though these were monolithic robots performing their daily tasks automatically. To cite a truism, "some Indians do, and some Indians don't"—it is necessary to particularize by tribal area, life-style, or person when discussing Indian culture.

A further step towards obscurity is demonstrated in the vast quantity of photographs preserved in collected archives scattered throughout the country, portraying Indian people about whom absolutely nothing is known. Many of these are superb photographic documents, but lack even the most elementary ethnographic or historic information. It is extremely frustrating to try to learn: Who is the person? To what tribe did he belong? Where did he live? When did he live? What did he accomplish? Many of these men and women must have had interesting, even important careers to have warranted the painstaking attention of the early photographer. But today they are only nameless although fascinating, faces.

The difficulties of obtaining precise data concerning individual Indian people are tremendous. Much of the available information amounts to a repetition of earlier accounts, with little new information added; earlier errors also remain uncorrected. Indian people were rarely accorded individual dignity by White authors of early historical accounts—one flagrant example of this is to be found in the large number of multitomed state and county histories which frequently include one or more volumes of local biography. Only a handful of these histories include Indian people among those listed as having settled in the region involved.

Tribal affiliations were not always carefully recorded; some were guesses at best, or so imprecise as to be meaningless today. Others actually represented the tribe of the spouse, rather than that of the individual concerned; this is particularly true where home residence changed with marriage, as was a custom common to many groups. In some instances the "tribe" listed was, in fact, simply a small village or band. And as for the correct age of the person, this is rarely possible to establish with any degree of accuracy. Age, as such, was not important to a majority of Indian people, and the strict recording of birth data, or the observance of birthdays, so momentous in White society, had little relevance to most North American Indians. Older people were respected for their wisdom and experience, but numerical scoring of their years was relatively immaterial.

Indeed, it is the names themselves which present the greatest difficulty in any effort to compile an accurate biographical study. Most Indian people have more than one name during a lifetime, and some make use of several, depending upon the customs of the particular tribe. These are perfectly suitable for a specific period, but can and usually do change as the individual matures; thus, it is often important to know when a given name was recorded, since that fact may have a considerable bearing upon the identity of a given person.

The high incidence of child mortality also had a bearing upon the problem: many babies were not named until some time after their birth, thereby remaining "in limbo" until they had safely passed the critical early period of life. This practice of delaying the naming of the baby may have grown out of a recognition of nature's harsh world; but whatever the reason, most name bestowing in a formal sense occurred some time later.

Some names were used only once, and at the death of the individual were never mentioned again, nor applied to any subsequent persons; other names were put "in storage," to be reapplied after two or three generations had passed. In many tribes, certain names were hereditary, to be handed on from one generation to another—thereby making it difficult today to know which of several similarly named individuals is involved. Some names were ritually, religiously, or historically important—to be bestowed only as individuals took on a given role in the society. Names would be given, sold, or even traded—sometimes as an honor, sometimes as a gesture of friendship or social relationship. A few groups "threw away" their names, others were extremely secretive, never mentioning a name once it was given; this was particularly true in those instances where names had a religious character. Thus, while some names were public, more often they were private, and closely guarded, to be used only under specific circumstances. It is obvious that these customs created a sometimes impassable barrier to the outside questioner.

Not infrequently, the individual Indian would supply a name selected at random when asked—simply to accommodate the visitor or official, largely to get the question answered, provide a courteous reply, and get rid of the nuisance. And the common practice of "opposite acting" also created problems, since translations of names were frequently exactly contrary to the true meaning; these, solemnly entered into the historical record, often caused later confusion. And in some tribes, names per se were not regarded as of particular importance, being treated with a mild vagueness when considered at all. This makes it difficult for the outsider to understand what seems to be an indifference towards self on the part of the individual Indian. And lastly, while Indian memory in general is excellent, it is not infallible, and all vital statistics based upon such personal recall must be regarded with extreme caution. To facilitate reference among these conflicting terms, the varieties of names and their alternate forms and spellings are listed in the Index.

An additional, although perhaps less significant problem is that of "Indian chiefs," i.e., the designation of given individuals as chiefs of the tribe. In some groups, chiefs were truly rulers: authoritative persons who held dominant positions by selection, heredity, or conquest. In other groups, leaders had no other function than to represent the temporary interests of that group. Many tribes had more than one chief at a time—a peace chief, who governed more or less completely during times of tranquility, and a war chief whose military skills were needed at times of stress. And still others had religious chiefs, whose ritual knowledge made their role a particularly important one. Each of these chiefs yielded to the other as the situation demanded.

Not infrequently a tribe would "appoint" a given individual to represent the group for a particular purpose, even though he might not be actually regarded as a leader in daily life. The reason for such a designation was usually oratorical skill, the ability to speak English, particular knowledge of a situation, or clearly recognized wisdom or diplomatic abilities.

These varying responses gave rise to complicated personnel designations which the White men never really understood completely. And this dilemma led in turn to a practice whereby "chiefs" were appointed by Indian Agents, military authorities, and occasionally religious or civil governors. Usually these "chiefs" were the more amenable or cooperative individuals. This practice only added to the number of chiefs, with the result that on occasion a given tribe might have a half dozen or more chiefs at one time. Another confusing early custom was the colonial attitude toward native tribes; the tribes were considered as nations and their leaders as royalty. From this came such names as King Hendrick, Queen Anne, and the myriad "Indian Princesses" which are still in use today.

The translation of Indian language names was a major problem; many of the names were unintelligible to non-Indians, albeit perfectly rational to the native. The logic used in choosing the Indian name was not always evident to the White man who recorded it, and he often twisted the meaning in order to arrive at a "sensible" connotation—in the process losing much or all of the colorful poetry, subtle humor, or shrewd evaluation of character so frequently found. The difficulty of determining the meaning, mastering the pronunciation, or under-standing the reasoning behind a name often resulted in incorrect or absurd transliterations. One example will suffice: the name of Wah-bahnse is usually given as "Dawn of the Day," or "He Causes Brightness"—suggesting a poetic reference to enlightenment, or a bright beginning. But in his own words, the term came from "When I killed the enemy, he was pale, like the light of the early morning." And other, equally complex origins are legion, thus giving rise to much confusion. It must also be added that at times there was a deliberate effort to make the name sound ridiculous, to demean the individual as well as the culture of the people. Some of these were foolish, others simply derisive—and many were outright obscene.

The net result was that names were often wholly invented by Whites solely to attach meaningful or linguistically comfortable labels to a given individual for recording purposes, regardless of the significance or accuracy of the name in the native society. The requirements of the bureaucratic record system, and missionary insistence upon baptismal names in the Christian fashion, often forced a solution whose outcome was largely dependent upon the good taste, sensitivity, knowledge, or bias of the person doing the recording. This was particularly true in those instances where names were imposed by school teachers, Army personnel, Indian Agents, or missionaries whose backgrounds were often betrayed by the assignment of such appellations as Noah, Sam-son, Sarah, or Alexander, to mention only a few.

Furthermore, many Indians went by European *and* native names, i.e., Wovoka, also known as Jack Wilson; Oqwa Pi, or Abel Sánchez; or Galegína, known as Buck Watie, who adopted the name of his patron Elias Boudinot. These names were either taken on by the Indian from neighbors, friends, or employers, were given to them by Whites, or were part of a dual-name system—as in the Pueblos, where tribal names were bestowed ritually, but for daily purposes, baptismal European names were regularly used.

A final problem has been the fact that biographies of Indian people have by and large been undertaken by authors of children's books; rarely has this effort been directed towards adult readers. There is, of course, absolutely nothing wrong with this; but it does affect the treat-ment of the subject, the depth of detail covered, and most regrettable of all, the place it occupies in the minds of most readers. Unfortunately, juvenile writings have never received their due respect in American literature, earning at best a secondary role in critical consideration. All too often this attitude also affects the quality of that writing, thereby perpetuating a vicious circle.

In an effort to grapple with these difficulties, improve the reading consciousness of the literate public, and to come up with a volume which will be useful to most of the general reference needs of today's readers, this collection of 300 of the most sought after Indian biog-raphies from North America has been compiled. This is not to claim that these are "the most important" native American leaders; there are some extremely influential persons omitted, due either to the dif-ficulty of obtaining sufficient information concerning their careers, of the inflexible limitations of space. It must also be stated that in the desire to expand coverage in some areas as opposed to a redundancy of roles in others, it was felt that too much duplication would be less helpful than the introduction of other perhaps lesser known careers. Any work of this nature must represent an arbitrary selection, and today's economics of publishing only emphasize the problem. I deeply regret this limitation, but I trust that the total number of biographies will prove sufficiently balanced to serve most general reference needs.

The biographical sketches themselves are in no sense regarded as complete; within each will be omissions of detail. The ambition to provide a volume complete in coverage and detail would require a book far larger than presently possible. This work is simply intended to bring together the basic information concerning a large number of Native North American leaders for most quick-reference purposes, and to guide the reader to further reading. This brevity will be found particularly for those persons of general familiarity, such as Geronimo, Red Cloud, Sitting Bull, et al. There are so many book-length accounts of their lives that it seemed wiser to restrict their profiles, simply placing them in relationship to their own people, thereby providing more space to include a larger selection of many lesser known and more recent individuals.

Several ground rules were established in organizing this volume. All individuals included were clearly of Indian ancestry, which made it necessary to eliminate a few extremely important persons active in Indian history, such as Madame Montour, Blue Jacket, and Eleazar Wheelock, who were not of Indian parentage. All individuals included are dead; thus avoiding the problem of whom to include among living North American Indians today, for this volume is not intended as an Indian *Who's Who*. A further consideration was the importance of the individual to the Indian people, rather than the evaluation of a career from the White point of view; and in this regard, it must be made clear that not all of the persons included in this work were admired by Indians—several are regarded as betrayers of their own people—yet their importance in history cannot be disregarded.

Sources for the information used in these sketches include the usual historical summaries, personal accounts, and biographical notes; they are all listed in the Bibliography. An effort has been made to examine many of the writings of those who knew—or were—Indian participants, or who wrote about them at the time they were still living. Special attention has also been given to the mention of the families, both spouses and children, many of whom were, or became, important in their own right. All dates and vital statistics have been based upon the best available authority and where these are uncertain—which is not infrequent—that questionable situation is appropriately indicated. Tribal affiliations are those accepted by most scholars of Indian history, or by the individuals themselves at some point in their careers.

Portraits have been used where available. Unfortunately, this is a particularly uncharted sea, and some of these have questionable identification—these are presented only as the reputed likeness of a given individual. Accompanying many of these profiles is a selection

of many of these people will be revealed with the inclusion of these which would have been in common use at the time the person was active. Such inclusion is not only "for art's sake," although the esthetic quality of many of these objects provides a pleasing cultural complement; it is also hoped that a more vivid understanding of the life-style of many of these people will be provided with the inclusion of these objects. To separate these persons from their material world is often to remove much of the vitality and color from the account of their lives. Sources for all of these illustrations are indicated for further reference as desired.

A glance at the Bibliography for this volume will provide a fair indication of the limited number of biographical writings which have been published, in proportion to the vast literature on the general subject of the North American Indian. Many of these writings are now extremely difficult to obtain, and most of them were written after the fact, usually with a White-oriented bias. Others were written at the time the individual was active, and while this has the value of being a firsthand account, it often reflects the racial or social feeling which colored so much of the earlier writings about the Indian—attitudes which still exist today. Military, religious, or economic motivation can be readily detected in many of the evaluations of the role of a given person in such works.

Of paramount value, of course, has been the work of Frederick Webb Hodge, dean of ethnohistorians. His two-volume *Handbook of American Indians North of Mexico* remains the only major volume in which an extensive number of individual profiles can be found. The author is indebted to this one source perhaps more than any other. Two other books of major significance were the biographical compilations by Benjamin B. Thatcher and the *History* prepared by Thomas L. McKenney and James Hall. Without these similar publications any attempt of substance would not be possible today.

A particular effort has been made to include men and women in every field of endeavor, rather than simply presenting the careers of military leaders who have figured so prominently in most biographical collections. Unfortunately, it must be admitted that the latter were the examples which attracted the attention of most writers and their readers, and the peaceful or less dramatic careers of medical, political, artistic, and social leaders often escaped notice. This has resulted in an unbalanced portrayal of the success which Indian people have achieved over the years, which only served to perpetuate the stereotype of the militant, uneducable, intransigent savage. It is hoped that this volume will help somewhat to erase that image.

I am deeply grateful to many people and institutions who have assisted in the preparation of this book. Initially, Craig and Peter Norback provided the organizational inspiration for the project; the contributions of John S. Berseth and John Hawkins, who undertook much of the legwork in running down many of the basic details, is equally appreciated, as is the support and encouragement of Eugene M. Falken and Robert Ewing of Van Nostrand Reinhold Co., since this materially strengthened my belief in the viability of the book. The careful editorial eyes of Alberta Gordon and Nancy Budde Deitch are responsible for the pulling together of the manuscript into a presentable work.

In the data-gathering process, the biographical work of the late Marion Gridley was an inspiration, and the contributions of such friends as Ida Mae Fredericks, David L. Harner, Harry C. James, Jeanne Owen King, and Sallie Wagner were invaluable. Professional courtesies generously provided by Jeanne Engerman, Paula Fleming, Marc Gaede, Carmelo Guadagno, Nancy O. Lurie, Arthur L. Olivas, Ann Reinert, and Melodie A. Rue have strengthened the quality of this book immeasurably.

Lastly, I cannot overlook the cheerful cooperation of the many Reference Librarians and Photographers who provided assistance; a list of all these would take more space than is available. The staffs of Columbia University Library, and the Huntington Free Library, of New York City, were particularly cordial in their assistance to me. And in the final "writer's isolation booth," no one was more patient and supportive than my wife Alice. I can only thank them here, and hope that this final product will justify the support and time spent in researching needed information and illustrations.

To penetrate the curtain of obscurity at this late date is difficult, yet it is to be hoped that *Great North American Indians* will serve the needs of its readers, allowing them to place a large number of major Indian figures in their proper niche in North American history. That this information is so elusive is a further sad testimonial to the confrontation between Indian and White, and the long refusal of one people to recognize the equality of importance of outstanding individuals in the other.

As a final suggestion, resulting from the day-to-day preparation of this book: any reader who will read this work from beginning to end without skipping to better known persons, will find it a surprising narrative of Indian–White relations—and in so doing, will perhaps encounter a fresh approach to an understanding of the problems which confronted both peoples during the resettlement of North America. While this is certainly not a literary novel, the following pages will reveal many moments of high dramatic impact.

FREDERICK J. DOCKSTADER

Abomazine (ca. 1675–1724)

Also Bomazeen, or Bombazine, of unknown derivation, meaning "Keeper of the Ceremonial Fire." A prominent Abnaki sachem who early suffered from the treachery of the colonial authorities. His home was at Kennebec, Maine, and he came to prominence during the last decade of the 17th century, when he went to visit Governor William Phips. In 1693 he made a treaty with Governor Phips, but the next year became involved in disputes with the settlers over land ownership.

Proceeding to the fort at Pemaquid, Maine, in 1694, under a flag of truce, he was seized by the authorities and imprisoned at Boston, then the "capital" of the combined Maine–Massachusetts colony. After his release, Abomazine swore vengeance for the treachery, and raided local settlements from Chelmsford south to Sudbury in 1707; three years later, he went north to attack Saco, in Maine. Hostilities continued until early in 1713, and he finally agreed to a treaty with the Whites at Portsmouth, New Hampshire on July 13.

But this was not a long-lived period of tranquility. Continued friction between Indians and Whites resulted in raids and counterraids, until finally a party of soldiers under Captain Moulton came upon the Abnaki at Taconnet, Maine, killing Abomazine and several of his warriors, early in 1724. The Whites then proceeded to Norridgewock, where they captured Abomazine's wife, and killed his daughter.

Birch Bark Container (and cover); Penobscot
(*Museum of the American Indian*)

Adario (ca. 1650–1701)

Also called Kondiaronk, or Sastaretsi, "The Rat," a Tionantati chief who was famed throughout the Montreal region for his shrewd strategy in dealing with the Whites, as well as with other Indian tribes. Little is known of his birth, but in 1688 he is recorded as having made a treaty with the French whereby he agreed to lead an expedition against his hereditary enemies, the Iroquois. Undertaking the project in good faith, he was astounded to learn that the French had already begun to deal with the Iroquois for peace, and that the latter were preparing to dispatch representatives to go to Montreal to negotiate.

Adario determined to ambush the group of Iroquois chiefs; and after appearing to agree with the instructions of the French commander at Cataracouy not to interfere, departed with his men, and later captured the Iroquois, who were led by Dekanisora, a prominent Onondaga warrior and diplomat. Adario told the latter that the French had instructed him to waylay and murder the Iroquois; and then, in a gesture of generosity, set the party free, with the exception of a hostage who was held in retaliation for a Huron warrior who had been killed during the affray.

Returning to Michilimackinac with his hostage, Adario turned him over to the French commander, who had him executed for murder, not knowing of the background of intrigue involved. Subsequently, the

9

Iroquois set forth with over 1200 warriors in an attack upon Montreal on August 25, 1689. The French, who had been comfortable in the feeling that peace was imminent, were taken completely by surprise, and hundreds were killed, or taken captive. The town was burned, and the carnage was so great that only the existence of a few strong fortifications saved the Whites from being forced entirely out of the country.

Adario later led a delegation of Huron chiefs to Montreal to conclude a treaty, and died in that city on August 1, 1701. He was buried with military honors conducted by the French authorities in the Montreal cemetery, apparently maintaining his dual role to the end.

Thomas Wildcat Alford (1860–1938)

Gaynwawpiahsika, "The Leader," often called Gaynwah, a Shawnee leader who was an outstanding Indian Service worker and teacher in the late 19th and early 20th centuries. He was born in the region of the Canadian River near Sasakwa, Oklahoma on July 15, 1860. His father

Thomas Wildcat Alford (1860–1938) and Family
(*Oklahoma Historical Society*)

was Gaytahkipiahsikah, "Wildcat"; his mother was Waylahskise, "Graceful One," the great-granddaughter of Tecumseh. Both parents were members of the Absentee Shawnee, a small band which had left the main body of that tribe. As a boy he was taught tribal legends and traditions, and then, at the age of 12, was enrolled in mission school. In 1879 he won a scholarship to Hampton Institute in Virginia.

Before he left for the east, the tribal elders told him to be careful about adopting the White man's ways, especially in religion, and to guard against losing his Indian heritage. But only part of their warnings were heeded, and when the young man returned home a confirmed Christian, and something of an eastern dude, he was shunned by his compatriots. He thereupon left to take up a teaching position, and the next year was appointed the principal of a new school which the Federal Government had built for the Shawnee tribe; he stayed there for the next five years. Then he began to work toward helping the older and more conservative Shawnee adults to understand the changes which were taking place in their lives.

Every Indian had to register in order to get a land allotment, but many in the tribe wanted absolutely nothing to do with the White man and his preoccupation with paperwork. In 1893 the United States formed a "Business Committee" of Shawnees to supersede the old tribal government. Alford became chairman of this group, and tried to make the best of an impossible job.

Some unscrupulous operators tried to take advantage of the reluctance of the tradition-minded Indians to sign up for their land allotments. By getting such land for themselves, the Whites hoped to amass large holdings. Alford was generally able to prevent injustices, but not always; his knowledge of White law helped him, but the political position in which many of his adversaries were placed often overcame his arguments. He also spent some time in Washington, D.C., pressing the Shawnee claims for a more equitable settlement. He married Mary Grinnell, by whom he had five children.

Becoming more deeply involved in Indian matters, he became a full-time employee of the U.S. Bureau of Indian Affairs. In 1907, when Oklahoma was admitted to the Union, many problems remained from the earlier Indian Territory days, and Alford was active in helping his people solve what to many were perplexing and often tragic dilemmas. He died at Shawnee, Oklahoma on August 3, 1938 at the age of 78, and was buried in the family plot.

American Horse (1840–1908)

Wasechun Tashunka, an important Oglala Sioux chief, was born in the Black Hills country of South Dakota in 1840. He was the son of Sitting Bear. There were two well-known Sioux people by the name of American Horse; the older was killed at Slim Buttes, South Dakota on September 5, 1875 and was apparently the uncle of the present individual.

American Horse (1840–1908)
(*Huntington Free Library*)

As a young man he was originally named Manishee "Cannot Walk," and did not particularly distinguish himself as a warrior. He was no coward, but for one reason or another advocated peace with the Whites.

That he was acting out of genuine concern for the lives of his people and not as a paid servant of the United States is perhaps demonstrated by the fact that he retained a strong influence in tribal councils throughout the troubles of the latter part of the century. American Horse was known as an outstanding orator and a skilled diplomat; he went to Washington many times as a tribal representative.

In 1887, General George Crook and a federal commission visited the Oglala to try to convince them to sign away most of their South Dakota lands in return for a new reservation and other promised benefits. American Horse tried to talk the treaty to death—even the exasperated Crook had to admit that "He's a better speaker than any of us"—but after two weeks, advocated accepting the terms because he felt that this was the best (or least worst) settlement the Sioux could obtain.

Many of his brother chiefs did not agree, however, and tension rose as the followers of Wovoka's Ghost Dance religion gained more converts as they prepared to dance the White man into oblivion. As reservation conditions worsened, with the Indian Agents failing to fulfill the various agreements which had been made, the Sioux situation became desperate, and people were actually starving; confrontations became commonplace, and it was obvious that sooner or later bloodshed would result. At one point, American Horse stepped between the Indian Police and a group of angry young men, to whom he said, "You are brave today . . . but what will you do tomorrow? The soldiers will pour in, and it will be the end of your people." The son of Red Cloud sharply replied in anger and frustration, "It is you, and men like you, who have reduced our race to slavery and starvation!"

Shortly after this came the climax of the Ghost Dance outbreak which was put down brutally in 1890. American Horse, sensing disaster, had brought his people to the reservation headquarters at Pine Ridge, where they escaped the violent slaughter at Wounded Knee Creek. The very next year, he headed a united Sioux delegation to Washington seeking fairer treatment for the tribe. They returned after mixed success, but the Wounded Knee tragedy had left a bitter aftermath, and the delegation returned to the reservation, in the words of one historian, "to wait for yesterday."

American Horse died at Pine Ridge, South Dakota on December 16, 1908 at the age of 76, a colorful, well-known representative of the Sioux people. He had two daughters, and one son, Samuel, who he sent to Carlisle Indian School.

Beaded Horse's Head Cover; Sioux
(*Museum of the American Indian*)

Annawan (?-1676)

Also spelled Annawon, from Algonquian, "commander; chief," a Wampanoag sachem who became War Captain to Metacom, the leader in King Philip's War (1675–1676). Nothing is known of his parents or his date of birth; he first comes into public mention just before the outbreak of King Philip's War. Totally loyal to Metacom, Annawan must be given credit for much of the success of the Wampanoag campaigns.

Although Massasoit had maintained friendly relations with the Whites throughout his long life, conditions changed abruptly after his death in 1662. Metacom set about forming a confederacy among many of the New England tribes, and relied heavily upon the diplomatic skills of Annawan, his trusted lieutenant. However, Sassamon, the secretary of Metacom, treacherously informed the English of these efforts, and King Philip's War began.

At first, largely because of Annawan's leadership and military tactics, the Indians won a number of victories. Unable to defeat them militarily, the White settlers began to destroy Indian crops and villages, a strategy which proved to be far more effective. The Indian alliance began to fall apart slowly as the various bands drifted away to seek food and rebuild their homes. Historians tend to agree that, had the Indian confederation held fast, the colonists would have been entirely wiped out.

In the final battle of King Philip's War on August 12, 1676 near Kingston, Rhode Island, the colonists obtained the support of a large number of Mohegan Indians; with this assistance, they decisively defeated Metacom and his warriors in The Great Swamp Fight. Annawan and Philip and some of their followers escaped into the Swamp, but Metacom was later betrayed and killed. Annawan rallied the rest of the forces and managed to successfully lead them out of the trap. He continued fighting in the area of Swansea and Plymouth, playing a deadly game of hide-and-seek for a long time, relentlessly pursued by Captain Benjamin Church, who was determined to capture or kill every hostile Indian.

Annawan managed to elude Church by moving continuously, never camping twice in the same spot, although some of his followers were captured from time to time. Finally, one of the captive Indians revealed Annawan's hiding place. Church deployed a small group of Indians to divert Annawan, while at the same time closing in on the rear; in the confusion he seized the Wampanoag's weapons. Thinking themselves surrounded by a larger force than there actually was, the Indians surrendered. Church was given Metacom's wampum belts and other possessions in token of victory, and the prisoners were taken to Plymouth Colony for trial.

After admitting that he had personally killed several English soldiers, Annawan was condemned to death. Church, however, having successfully stamped out the Indian rebellion, felt compassion for the great warrior, and interceded to save him, out of respect for his military qualities. However, while he was absent from the Colony in 1676, a small group of revengeful colonists seized Annawan and beheaded him.

Juan Antonio (ca. 1783–1863)

Cooswootna, also known as Yampoochee, "He gets Mad Quickly," a major figure in the early Indian history of southern California and a chief of the Kostakiklim lineage of the Cahuilla (Kawia) tribe. He was born in the Mount San Jacinto country around 1783, and came into historic notice on July 4, 1842 when he met with Daniel Sexton at San Gorgino Pass; the latter had come into California via the Santa Fe Trail, and celebrated the American holiday by erecting a flagpole.

The abolition of mission rule in the coastal area in the 1840s left a chaotic governmental situation; many speculators flooded into the area, and colonists from Mexico sought to take over mission lands. In 1845 Juan Antonio was recorded as the leader of the Mountain clan groups, active at Rancho San Bernardino. He assisted Lieutenant Edward F. Beale during the U.S. Army explorations of the period, defending them against raiding Ute war parties led by the redoubtable

Walkara. On several occasions, Juan Antonio forced Walkara to retreat, and his courage and strategy led Lieutenant Beale to present him with a pair of military epaulets, which the chief wore from then on at every ceremonial occasion.

By 1852, Juan Antonio had become titular chief of the Cahuilla through his ability as a leader, although he was never the hereditary chief of the tribe, which numbered about 3000 people at that time. He established his home at Politana, where he remained until forced out by Mormon encroachment. A short, stocky man not over 5' 5" in height, he was always known as a severe disciplinarian controlling his own people completely, if on occasion somewhat brutally.

In 1851, the renegade outlaw John Irving invaded the area with 11 companions, stealing cattle and killing local people. Juan Antonio lead a party of Indian warriors against the band, finally killing all but one member. While the Californios applauded the swift pace of justice, the Americans—although equally approving of the removal of the outlaws—were nevertheless unable to reconcile themselves to the fact that Indians had taken upon themselves the execution of the law, and in so doing, had killed White men; accordingly, they deposed Juan Antonio. The authority of the Whites to remove the Indian chief apparently was never questioned. But the Indian people ignored the deposition "manifesto," and continued to accept Juan Antonio as chief.

This was but one of many irritations operating at the time, and the sale of Rancho San Bernardino to the Mormons in 1851 was a further annoyance, since it meant that the Indians who had been living there were forced to move. Juan Antonio himself moved his quarters to Sahatapa. Things grew from bad to worse; and the imposition of taxes by the Americans following the successful outcome of the Mexican War, although based upon the assumption that Indians were citizens, further outraged these original owners of the land—this was something which neither the Mexicans nor the Spaniards had ever done. And lastly, the invasion of thousands of gold-seekers increased the restlessness and outrages on all sides. A ferry was established to convey the newcomers across the Colorado River; the Indians not only envied the profits of the White operators, but resented their monopoly and high charges. They struck against the monopoly, temporarily putting the ferry out of operation.

Out of this turmoil came a local Cupeño leader and rival to Juan Antonio, named Antonio Garra (or Garrá). He attempted to establish an alliance against the Whites with the Quechan, Cócopa, and northern Tulareño peoples; the latter refused, having just made a peaceful arrangement with the Whites in their own region. Incorporating mysticism into his political efforts, Garra promised his followers that his powers would turn the American bullets to water. While there seems no doubt that he was trying to sincerely protect the interests of his own people, it is equally certain that much of his effort was impelled by jealousy of Juan Antonio.

Meanwhile, the U.S. War Department had dispatched a trio of commissioners to negotiate with the California Indians, in hopes of cementing peaceful relations. In the northern part of the territory, George W.

Barbour was successful in making several agreements, notably with the Tulare people, and promised that he would next visit the south California tribes. For mixed reasons, he failed to do so, and this set the stage for further discontent. A feeling of neglect, combined with the rivalries between Garra and Antonio, plus the determination of the former to unite the southern Indians, all fed upon the frustrations of the Indians. Despite the efforts of Pauline Weaver, a part-Cherokee mountain man from Taos who had settled in the region, and a trusted friend of Juan Antonio, a major Indian uprising occurred which resulted in attacks upon Jonathan W. Warner, a leading rancher in the area, and other Whites in the San Bernardino region. Some of the Californios, led by the prominent Lugo family, were successful in getting Antonio to remain neutral in the exploding confrontation, and finally induced him to go on the offensive against his rival. On December 8, 1851 he captured Antonio Garra, and the latter, after receiving a summary court martial, was executed for murder.

At the end of the year, a treaty of friendship was signed on December 20 with General J. H. Bean who was one of the commissioners sent to negotiate for peace with the California Indians. In 1852, Commissioner O. N. Wozencraft sought a treaty which would allow the Cahuilla control of their own lands, as well as recognition of Juan Antonio for his assistance. But the California Senate would not ratify the treaty, thereby setting the scene for further bloodshed. Land greed proved the critical factor—as it had throughout the continent—and combined with an unwillingness to yield any control of land to Indians. When Juan Antonio complained that he and his people had never been compensated for their help in putting down the several uprisings, his pleas went ignored. Eventually, violence broke out in 1854–1855, with sporadic attacks upon local White citizens. Then Juan Antonio went to the Quechan people, requesting their cooperation against the ever-increasing American demands; they refused to cooperate with him. The Mohave, while willing, were hesitant, and the effort failed. This collapse in unity apparently convinced the chief that the road to survival would not succeed along the war route.

By 1856, anti-Mormon feelings in the Southwest were at fever pitch; Bishop Nathan Kinney had gone among the tribal groups trying to convert them, and this aroused the already strong feelings of the non-Mormons throughout San Bernardino County. The result was a diversion of interest in Indian problems; an atmosphere of neglect made them vulnerable to predatory Whites, and they were moved off their land, refused sufficient water for irrigation of their crops, and became literally starving paupers in their own country. Squatters cut off the water supply and raided the Indian families for food which they refused to pay for.

In this atmosphere of desperation, a smallpox epidemic broke out, introduced by White settlers coming into the area. On February 28, 1863 Juan Antonio died of the plague in San Timoteo Cañon, the last of the great Cahuilla leaders.

In 1956, during an archeological excavation in the area, a shallow grave was uncovered in which a skeleton was encountered. It was located approximately 100 yards south of the El Casco Schoolhouse in San

Timoteo. On the shoulders were the remains of a pair of military epaulets—conclusive evidence of the identity of the deceased. After measurements and photographs were taken, the body was reverently reburied.

Arapoosh (ca. 1790–1834)

Known to the Whites as Rotten Belly, or Sour Belly, this great chief of the River Crow was one of the most important early leaders of his people against their traditional enemies. The Crow territory was a large area, extending almost from the Black Hills to the Rocky Mountains. Arapoosh (also Arrapooish or Eripuass) was born probably in the mountains which today bear his name sometime around the end of the 18th century. He is said to have received his name from his disposition. He was known as a surly, decisive, but brave, leader who asked for—and gave—no quarter in battle. The account claiming that he appeared at Pierre's Hole, Idaho, suffering from a gut wound apparently has him confused with a Nez Percé warrior named Tackensuatis, later also called Rotten Belly.

Whatever the source, Rotten Belly was regarded as having extraordinary spirit power which made him virtually unbeatable in war. One example is the source of his medicine. He had a vision that the "Man in the Moon" came to him and offered to be his guardian spirit; accordingly, Arapoosh painted the symbolic design on his medicine shield. Whenever the village planned to undertake a major project, the shield would be rolled along the row of tepees; if the design was uppermost when the shield stopped, success was predicted; but if the design fell "face down," the project was doomed, and thereby abandoned.

Painted Medicine Shield of Arapoosh; Crow
(*Museum of the American Indian*)

In 1825 the Crow nation concluded a treaty of friendship with the United States, but Arapoosh refused to sign it. He was already suspicious that the Whites had come to take more than they gave, and that his people's welfare was in jeopardy. Furthermore, he did not like the idea of being confined to a reservation. As he said to a fur trader, "The Crow country is in exactly the right place. Everything good is to be found there. There is no place like the Crow Country." And he spent much of his warrior life defending his tribal territory, but unfortunately, the White man felt the same way about the lush mountain land inhabited by the Crow nation.

Arapoosh was chief when the Crow warriors won their war against the Blackfoot in the late 1820s. He met William Sublette at Pierre's Hole in 1832 and he was greatly impressed by the stately bearing of the chief and his great reputation. The Crow were later defeated by the Cheyenne, but in June 1833, led by Arapoosh, they gained revenge and an important victory.

But in August 1834, according to Jim Beckwourth, shortly before a battle with the Blackfoot, Arapoosh placed his shield on a pile of buffalo chips, saying "If it rises, I shall die before I return to the village." The shield then appeared to rise to the height of his head, without any visible cause. The chief went off to attack a makeshift Blackfoot fort, and he was killed in one of the assaults.

Spencer Asah (ca. 1908–1954)

Lallo, "Little Boy," was one of the leading Kiowa artists who developed his talents during the first half of the 20th century, to become a leading portrayer of the esthetics of the Southern Plains Indians. He was born about 1908 near Carnegie, Oklahoma, the son of a Buffalo medicine man, thereby growing up deeply affected by the traditions and rituals of his people.

He was educated in local government Indian schools, and graduated from the St. Patrick's Mission School at Anadarko. As a teenager he joined a fine arts club which had been organized by an Indian Service employee, Mrs. Susie Peters. Her strong support resulted in the development of several young Kiowa artists who were eventually invited to join special classes at the University of Oklahoma in 1926–1927.

Enthused by what he saw, Dr. Oscar B. Jacobson, head of the University Art Department, obtained funds from Lewis Ware, a Kiowa member of the state legislature, and Lew H. Wentz, a local oil man. This enabled the five Kiowa men in the group to devote most of their time to the perfection of their own individual style of painting. Eventually their work was shown at several exhibitions, including the First International Art Exhibition at Prague in 1928. The work received a warm welcome by the critics; one commented, "Full of the dark forces of the universe; full of the age of metaphysical symbolism and awe." The exciting watercolors were eagerly sought after by museums and individuals.

Painting essentially from memory, using no models, Asah's work was similar in many respects to that of some of the Pueblo artists who were painting at the time, yet there seems to have been little or no influence exerted upon the work of either group. Most of his characters were individual portraits, which can often be identified, rather than the conventionalized forms so prevalent among Pueblo painters. The Kiowa art form also incorporated foreshortening and perspective—in part an introduction from the instruction gained in classes. Asah created a large number of dance subjects, usually painted on small sheets of paper supplied by Dr. Jacobson; he also painted murals for numerous institutions, including Indian schools, federal buildings, and the University.

He married Ida, a Comanche woman, by whom he had three children. A rotund, placid, and apparently happy man, Spencer Asah died just before his fiftieth birthday on May 5, 1954 at Norman, Oklahoma, just a year after the death of his son, Kay.

Atsidi Sani (ca. 1830–ca. 1870)

Old Smith, from *atsidi*, "smith," *sani*, "old," also known as Herrero Delgadito, "Slender Little Ironworker," and Beshiltheeni, "Metal Worker," or "Knife Maker," was a Navajo medicine man and artist who is regarded as the first to introduce silversmithing to his people. He was born in the vicinity of Nazlini (Wheatfields, in northeastern Arizona), about 1830; little is known of his parents, but he was of the Dibélizhini (Black Sheep People) clan.

By the middle of the 19th century, Atsidi Sani had become friendly with a Mexican ironsmith named Nakai Tsosi, "Thin Mexican," who taught him the basic principles of the craft. At about this same time, Captain Henry Linn Dodge brought a blacksmith, George Carter, with him to Fort Defiance to teach ironsmithing to the Navajo people when he was appointed Indian Agent in 1853; Dodge's interpreter, Juan Anea, was also said to be a skilled silversmith.

Just when the first Navajo silver was produced is open to some argument, but general agreement is that around 1853 Atsidi Sani executed his first silverwork—probably bracelets, conchas, or similar jewelry pieces. He was certainly producing silver before the Navajo people were transported to Bosque Redondo (Fort Sumner) in 1863. It is equally accepted that the slightly over four years' internment there exposed them to Mexican ironworkers, and that several Indians returned from the harrowing experience with a knowledge of metalsmithing which they later put into practice on silver.

Atsidi Sani was a minor headman who was elected one of the head Navajo chiefs at Fort Defiance in 1858. From then on, he enjoyed a major role in Navajo affairs, not only due to his political position, but undoubtedly also owing much of his preeminence as a silversmith. Following the Fort Sumner experience, he was the sixth chief to sign the Treaty of 1868 at Bosque Redondo allowing the Navajo to return to their homeland.

Whatever the date—and 1853 has received almost unanimous acceptance by scholars—Atsidi Sani learned the art from local Mexican ironworkers, at first copying their methods of ironworking; the Mexicans, recognizing his interest and aptitude, named him Herrero Delgadito. At first, he made bridle ornaments and similar iron objects; then he apparently began using silver coins, improvising his tools from whatever he could pick up. Many other Navajo became interested, and he taught them what he knew. He also apprenticed his four sons in ironworking, and one of them, Red Smith, became an excellent silversmith later on. From this simple beginning came a tradition of simple, fine design in rich silver which has persisted to the present day.

Atsidi Sani was equally famous among his people as a medicine man and ceremonial singer, performing many of the rituals with skill and great fidelity to traditional detail. Possessed of an excellent memory, he was widely sought after to perform curing chants, and he became as valued a ceremonial figure as he was honored for the introduction of

Silver Bridle made by Atsidi Sani; Navajo
(*Museum of the American Indian*)

what has become the single most important source of individual income to the tribe today. His workmanship as well as the intrinsic value of his product were of great concern to him—and this pride in fine craftsmanship is still important today to the better smiths among the Navajo. Atsidi Sani died at his home not far from Chinle, Arizona about 1870, one of the honored elders of the Navajo people.

Attakullakulla (ca. 1700–1778)

More accurately, Atagulkalu, "Leaning Wood," from *atá*, "wood" *gal kalú*, "something leaning"; hence, the "Little Carpenter," a reference to his small, slender stature. His real name was Onacona, or Oukounaka, "White Owl." He was a major Cherokee leader born about 1700 in the Cherokee country of Carolina who came into prominence in the years leading up to the American Revolution. The first mention of Attakullakulla refers to his being taken to England in 1730 by Sir Alexander Cuming (or Cumming), an indication that by this time he had become an important Cherokee leader; he was listed in 1738 as a Peace Chief, with Oconostota as the leading war chief. There is ample evidence that the two men worked in complete unison during their long lives; indeed, Attakullakulla married Oconostota's daughter.

Attakullakulla (second from right) and Creek Chiefs in London, 1730 (*Smithsonian Institution, National Anthropological Archives*)

20

The Little Carpenter was an able orator and became the speaker for Old Hop (Kana gatoga), Standing Turkey, the principal chief of the Cherokee. His oratorical skill was so effective, indeed, that he was the principal speaker at the peace council held in 1750 with Governor James Glen, even though he was not the highest authority of the Cherokee. However, he did provide a measure of friendship with the Whites—on one occasion he saved the life of Colonel William Byrd from Cherokee plotters who hated the treaty commissioners and had planned their assassination. Five years later, he was able to effect the signing of a treaty with Governor Glen, and also saw to the building of Fort Dobbs—projects which resulted in the cession of territory to the English, as well as the establishment of a garrison in Cherokee territory. For this and other services, he was commissioned an officer in the Colonial Army by the English.

Attakullakulla was an active protagonist for the Treaty of Broad River, South Carolina, in 1756, and seems to have long continued a friendship with the Whites—even after the fall of Fort Loudon, when most of the garrison was killed. During this battle he saved the life of Colonel Stuart, the commander and a long-time friend, and was active at the peace conferences of September 23, 1761.

But this attitude changed considerably during the next decade. During the Revolutionary War, he raised a regiment of 500 Cherokee warriors which he offered to the Americans—this in spite of the long history of Cherokee loyalty to the British. The reasons are unclear, but this offer seems to suggest that there was little give and take between the Indians and the British, and also there was the continual pressure to cede land. Personal relationships between the Whites and Indians had likewise become increasingly hostile.

Attakullakulla was a major figure in the negotiations and activities of the British and French peoples in Cherokee country, until his death at Natchez Town, on Natchez Creek, in Tennessee in 1777 (some say he died at Tukabatchee in 1778). His son was Dragging Canoe, who became a famous leader in his own right; his niece was Nancy Ward, the famed "Beloved Woman" of the Cherokee.

James Auchiah (1906–1974)

While not officially one of the original "Five Kiowa Artists" who are so well known in Indian art annals, Auchiah was born in 1906 near Medicine Park, Oklahoma. He was the son of Mark Auchiah and the grandson of the great chief Satanta. Eighty-five years after the death of his grandfather, James was able to win the right, after a firm court battle, to remove the remains from a prison grave to a more honored interment in Oklahoma. This was not a hollow gesture, but an indication of the deep spiritual quality held by Auchiah, and most Kiowa people.

This same sense of fitness showed itself in his later art work, and his marriage as a youth to Celia Lonewolf, the great-granddaughter of

Lone Wolf, a warrior-in-arms with Satanta, which united a long history and furthered the efforts of the ambitious young artist to portray the lives and history of his people. He seems to always have been artistically inclined, although he did not achieve early recognition.

As a child in government schools, he received no encouragement in following traditional lore; United States policy of the day was to discourage any effort to perpetuate Indian culture—even to the extent of preventing tribal ceremonies by military force. Indeed, in his own words:

> I shall never forget a classroom experience . . . in 1918, when my teacher discovered I was drawing and painting [an] Indian village with turkeys walking around tepees. I guess I was inspired because it was near Thanksgiving Day and I wanted to take my picture to mother. Of course teacher would not understand my Kiowa art expression, and as routine, did punish me after school to finish my picture without supper, which I was glad to do because I would rather paint than eat.[1]

He attended Rainy Mountain School in western Oklahoma, which fostered so many Indian artists, yet was never able to completely overcome official public hostility to Indian esthetic growth. By 1919, however, the strength of the work of these young people had become so pronounced that recognition could no longer be denied, and the determination of such teachers as Olivia Taylor of St. Patrick's Mission School, and Susie Peters, field matron at the Kiowa Agency, made it possible for many of the more gifted young artists to expand their work by attending outside schools. One of the most successful developments came at the hands of Dr. Oscar B. Jacobson, head of the art department at the University of Oklahoma. In 1927, he invited a small group of selected Kiowa people to attend the University as special students; shortly afterwards, Auchiah became one of this party, and from then on worked with them.

Dr. Jacobson encouraged them to paint in their own way and not to be influenced or dissuaded by White esthetic concepts—nor the ideas of other Indian artists. Out of this came a unique style for the period, and following several successful art exhibitions, the group traveled throughout the United States and Europe, where they received a warm welcome. Even more important than their welcome in Europe was the respect they received as artists back home among their own people; this acceptance was crucial, if they were to survive, once the initial excitement of their achievements subsided.

Commissions followed rapidly, and they were assigned the task of painting several murals in Oklahoma; the WPA employed all of them as prime practitioners in a traditional art form. Perhaps the largest project was the newly built Department of Interior building in Washington, D.C., where Auchiah worked with Steve Mopope in 1939 and which gained for both men the recognition that their work deserved.

In 1940, Auchiah retired to Oklahoma to paint and teach at the Riverside Indian School in Anadarko. But with the outbreak of World War II, he enlisted in the Coast Guard; in 1945, following the end of the war, he entered the civil service, working as a painter for the De-

[1]Pate, J'Nell, "Kiowa Art from Rainy Mountain . . ." pp. 193–200.

partment of Interior. He retired in 1967 to serve as curator at Fort Sill, Oklahoma, where his knowledge of Kiowa culture was invaluable. Poor health forced him to leave this job six years later. He died of a heart attack at his home in Carnegie, Oklahoma on December 28, 1974 at the age of 68.

Awa Tsireh (1898–1956)

Awa Tsireh, "Cat-Tail Bird," also known as Alfonso Roybal, was one of the first successful artists produced by the Santa Fe Indian Art School. He was born February 1, 1898 at San Ildefonso Pueblo, New Mexico; his mother was Alfoncita Martínez, and his father was Juan Estevan Roybal. His uncle was Crescencio Martínez, perhaps the first artist of note at that pueblo. Young Awa Tsireh began drawing animals and figures based on tribal legends and ceremonies at a very early age, carrying the paintings to Santa Fe to sell to a circle of rapidly widening admirers.

Awa Tsireh (1898–1956)
(*Museum of New Mexico; photo by T. Harmon Parkhurst*)

One of the most influential collectors of the day was Alice Corbin Henderson, who provided steady encouragement. Awa Tsireh shared the early years of development with Fred Kabotie and Ma-pe-wi, who also achieved equal success in later years. In 1920, he enjoyed his first important recognition with a showing at the annual exhibition of the Society of Independent Artists in New York City. Five years later he had progressed to a one-man show at the Newberry Library in Chicago.

"Antelope and Fawn" Watercolor Painting by Awa Tsireh (*Museum of the American Indian*)

While still in his twenties, Awa Tsireh was overtaken by tragedy when his wife and infant son both died; although he continued to work, these losses had a great impact upon his personality. In 1931 his paintings were included in the Exposition of Indian Tribal Arts in New York—perhaps the first major exhibit of American Indian art to be held in the United States; the show went on to a resounding success in Europe. His work was shown at the Corcoran Gallery in Washington, and in 1933 at the Century of Progress in Chicago.

In the early thirties, he also produced some important murals, all of which reflected his technique of using striking color, careful attention to detail, and clean, sure lines. Like most of the Indian painters of the period, his figures were two-dimensional and primarily decorative; his subjects were frequently fantastic animals inspired by mythology, or from his own fertile imagination. He was equally gifted with a refreshing sense of humor which was often employed in whimsical combinations of zoomorphic designs. In 1954, in recognition of his talent, he received the award of the *Palmes d'Académiques* presented by the French Government. His paintings had become prized possessions of museums and galleries throughout the world.

Awa Tsireh turned to silversmithing in his later years, but ill health forced him to abandon active art work, and he died in San Ildefonso on March 12, 1956 at the age of 58.

Watercolor painting; "Turkey Chasing a Clown," by Awa Tsireh (*Museum of Northern Arizona*)

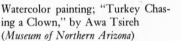

Bacon Rind (1860-1932)

Wahshehah, "Fat on Skin," was a well-known Osage leader who was prominent in tribal affairs in turn-of-the-century Oklahoma. He was also known as "Star That Travels." Bacon Rind was born on January 1, 1860, at Claremore, Indian Territory, the son of Okepasah, an Osage subchief. His mother was Warahumpah, also Osage. He came to prominence in 1900 as a leading Osage politician and representative of his people.

In 1909 he was elected Principal Chief of the tribe, and in 1922 became a member of the Osage Council. In 1924, he went to Washington, D.C., to negotiate with government officials on Osage matters; while there he met with President Calvin Coolidge. Always a picturesque figure, standing some 6'4" in height, Bacon Rind was painted by How-

Bacon Rind (1860-1932) (*Oklahoma Historical Society*)

24

ard Chandler Christy and other leading artists of the day, and became a sought after image of the romantic ideal of the American Indian.

He married twice, the first time to Wakohihekah, and later to Lizzie Mekojah, a Kaw woman. He had five children, of whom four survived. Bacon Rind took an active part in Oklahoma Indian affairs, and was to be seen at almost all of the Osage and neighboring ceremonies and public meetings. He lived at Pawhuska, where he died of cancer on March 28, 1932 at the age of 72.

Amos Bad Heart Bull (1869–1913)

Amos Bad Heart Bull (1869–1913)
(*University of Nebraska Press*)

Also known as Eagle Lance, this Oglala Sioux artist and historian was the creator of a remarkable pictographic history. During the years 1890–1913 he drew over 400 pictures, and, of even greater importance, wrote thousands of words of captions related to the history; these were done in a large ledger book which in effect amounted to a history of his people throughout the 19th century.

As holder of this record, as his father had been, he was in the honored role of tribal historian. It was the duty of Bad Heart Bull to compile a narrative of such famous events in tribal activity as the Battle of the Little Bighorn, the Ghost Dance troubles, and the massacre at Wounded Knee. In addition, he recorded the usual everyday events in Oglala life; he also made note of the Wild West shows which were popular at the time, and the observances of such tribal ceremonies as the Sun Dance.

Amos was essentially a self-taught artist who drew in the style common to all other Sioux artists. What made his pictographs outstanding was his excellent technical skill, his genius for observing even the smallest details, his feeling for decorative elements employed in a unified composition, and his objectivity in recording events which he did not see, but was told about by many different people. All of this was portrayed in a dynamic style outstanding in Indian art.

When Bad Heart Bull died in 1913, there was no male historian to whom the record could pass; it was given, therefore, to his sister Dolly Pretty Cloud. The record became Dolly's most valued possession. In 1926, a graduate student at the University of Nebraska, Helen Blish, heard of the record and persuaded Mrs. Pretty Cloud to allow her to study it, and photograph the illustrations. These were subsequently used for the publication *A Pictographic History of the Oglala Sioux*. Published in 1967, this pictographic history remains the only record we now have of the history and artistry of this remarkable individual. The original ledger lies buried with Dolly Pretty Cloud in accordance with her request.

Barboncito (ca. 1820–1871)

Barboncito, or Hastín Dagha (Daagii), "Man With the Whiskers," also known as Bisahalani, "The Orator," was a major Navajo war chief and

Barboncito (1820–1871)
(*Navajo Tribal Museum*)

one of the leaders who guided his people back from the period of despair at Fort Sumner, New Mexico. He was born about 1820 into the Ma'iideeshgiizhnii (Coyote Pass) clan at Canon de Chelly, Arizona and soon showed the promise that his later career fulfilled. He was also known as Hozhooji Naatá, "Blessing Speaker."

He was one of the chiefs who signed the Doniphan Treaty of 1846, agreeing to peaceful coexistence and mutually profitable trading relationships with the Whites. But the warfare between the Navajo and the Mexicans, which had been traditional, continued, and the Army did not have sufficient strength to control the vast areas which the United States gained following the Mexican War. Despite the efforts of leaders on both sides, battles between Whites and Indians were regular occurrences, with both sides equally at fault.

Apparently Barboncito took little part in these skirmishes; he lived at Canon de Chelly, a respected leader and religious "singer" who was in great demand at tribal ceremonies, widely known for his eloquence. In the late 1850s he argued with both sides to put an end to the escalating warfare, and in 1861 he was one of the signers of the treaty at Fort Fauntleroy, New Mexico.

But when the Civil War broke out, and the Army had to divert manpower elsewhere, the Navajo took advantage of the vacuum; in an effort to contain them, Kit Carson was employed to force their subjugation and remove them to Fort Sumner, New Mexico. Although Barconcito, Manuelito, and other leaders resisted, a lack of food and supplies eventually forced their surrender. In 1864 the infamous "Long Walk" began, between the Navajo homeland and the new reservation area at Bosque Redondo, 350 miles distant. At one point, over 8000 Indians were en route on foot. Barboncito was the last major leader to surrender, bringing his 21 followers into the fort on November 7, 1866; later, finding conditions worse than promised; he escaped and returned home, but was recaptured.

The disastrous effect of imprisonment and neglect was so tragic that the United States finally relented. A delegation was selected, which included Barboncito, to negotiate with General William Tecumseh Sherman; out of these deliberations came a proposal from the United States that all of the Navajo go to Indian Territory (now Oklahoma). Barboncito strongly objected, saying: "I hope to God you will not ask us to go to another country except our own. It might turn out to be another Bosque Redondo. They told us this was a good place when we came here, but it is not." In 1868 a new treaty was drawn up whereby an area was set aside, bounded by the four sacred mountains. Although this was but one-fifth of their former territory, the Navajo were glad to accept it, and their descendants remain there to this day.

Although Barboncito was never head chief of the Navajo, he is still remembered as being one of the most eloquent speakers in council, and his voice, always one of the strongest, was a major influence in all of the deliberations of the tribe. He died March 16, 1871 at Cañon de Chelly, never having lost the respect or affection of his own people, and of his White adversaries.

James Bear's Heart (1851-1882)

Known to his people as Nockkoist, this Cheyenne artist, warrior, and farmer was one of the group of Plains Indians confined at Fort Marion, Florida. Nothing is known of his early life other than the year of his birth, 1851; he was a noted warrior who fought against the Ute enemy, the Texans, the U.S. Army, and on occasion even raided into Mexico. He was captured in 1874, accused of being an accomplice in the murder of some Whites, and was sentenced to a term at Fort Marion.

At this prison located near St. Augustine, Bear's Heart developed a skill which he had learned as a boy—drawing. He was not alone in this pursuit: Howling Wolf, Cohoe, Zotom, and others were active in visually recreating the days of their Plains adventures. There was a wide variation in technical skill and sensitivity among the "Florida Boys" as they were known; but all of them knew the meaning and use of Indian symbolism, as well as the conventions of their art which had been handed down for generations. Bear's Heart was among the more prolific artists, whose work was more technically advanced, and he came to enjoy an unusually receptive audience for his drawings.

Following his three-year prison term at Fort Marion he was enrolled at Hampton Institute in Virginia on April 14, 1878 where he learned to read, write, and speak English, and to master some of the tools of White industrial society. Taking a further step away from Kiowa culture in March of 1879, he became a Christian, baptized in the name of James Bear's Heart.

Although he was not a handsome man—he fell far short of the romantic "noble savage" ideal of the day—standing only 5'9" in height, weighing about 135 pounds, he was nevertheless one of the most popular and respected students at Hampton. He was selected as color-bearer for the inaugural ceremonies marking the opening of Hampton to Indian students. After a brief trip to Lee, Massachusetts in 1880, Bear's Heart returned to the reservation in April of 1881, to work as a carpenter and driver. Shortly afterwards he fell victim to the tuberculosis which had afflicted him for several years, and died at the Cheyenne-Arapaho Agency at Darlington, Indian Territory on January 25, 1882. He is buried in the Reservation cemetery.

Charles Albert Bender (1883-1954)

"Chief" Bender was a well-known part-Chippewa figure in the baseball world who was elected to the Baseball Hall of Fame in 1953. He was born near Brainerd, Minnesota, into the Bad River Band of Chippewa on May 5, 1883, and was educated in local Brainerd schools, and at Carlisle, in Pennsylvania; he later took a degree at Dickinson College. Bender began his major league career in 1903 with the Philadelphia Athletics; during his years with the team, they won the American League pennant five times, and the World's Series on three occasions.

Charles Albert Bender (1883–1954)
(*Frank Rollins Photo*)

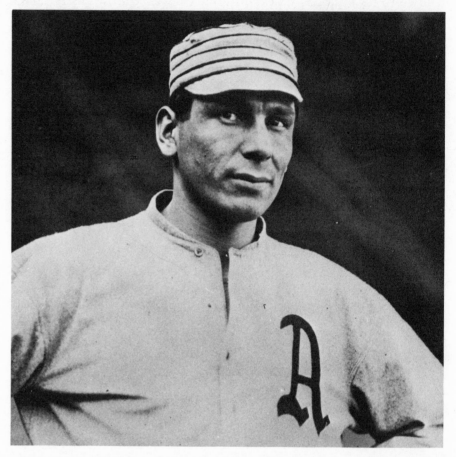

Man's Beaded Bandolier Pouch;
Chippewa
(*Museum of the American Indian*)

Bender's fast ball was judged by many to be the equal of Walter Johnson's, and he soon became the team's leading pitcher. In 1910, 1911, and 1914, he led the League in strike-outs. Indeed, Connie Mack, the Athletic's legendary manager, said, "If everything depended on one game, I just use Albert."

After Mack broke up his "unbeatable team" in 1914, Chief Bender played for the Baltimore entry in the Federal League in 1915, and the Philadelphia Nationals for two years. He retired following that period, having won 200 games and lost 111. During his career as a "superstar" of the day, his top salary was $2400 per year. His favorite title was given him by sports writers, who termed him "Connie Mack's meal ticket."

Chief Bender was a proud man who, when fans of opposing teams gave derisive imitations of the Indian "war whoop," would walk over to the stands and shout, "Foreigners!" He had many interests outside of baseball—everything from precious gems to trapshooting—but he stayed with the game for most of his life. For a time he was a coach at the U.S. Naval Academy, and later for the Chicago White Sox. He returned to the Philadelphia Athletics in 1939, first as a scout for young talent, and then as a coach. The year after his election to the Hall of Fame he died of cancer at his home on May 22, 1954.

28

Big Bow (ca. 1830-1900?)

Zipkiyah (also Zipkoheta and Zepko-eete), a Kiowa chief who was regarded as one of the most strongly anti-White leaders of his tribe. His origin and parentage is not recorded, but he early made a mark in warfare on the Central Plains. With Big Tree, Satanta, Satank, and Lone Wolf, he made the early settlers of Texas, Oklahoma, and Kansas pay dearly for their invasion into his homeland area. According to the missionary Thomas Battey, Big Bow "probably killed and scalped more White people than any other living Kiowa."

When the leaders of the Plains tribes gathered at Medicine Lodge in 1867 to sign a treaty that called for their acceptance of removal to reservation life, Big Bow refused to attend. He was unwilling to give up his traditional, free-roaming life, and kept his people withdrawn in the back country, emerging only for raids and occasional visits to Indian agencies or Army forts—slipping back onto the endless Plains before they could be captured.

Although he was generally friendly with his fellow Kiowa leaders, there was occasional trouble. One of the more serious clashes occurred following his taking of Satanta's wife, and peace was not restored until he agreed to give him five horses in payment for her. Then, in 1870–1871 the U.S. Army mounted a strong effort to subdue the Kiowa, and by 1874 Big Bow was the only major chief who had not been brought into the reservation. Under pressure, the respected old peace chief, Kicking Bird, was persuaded to track him down and point out the odds that were hopelessly stacked against him, and urge him that his best course was to surrender.

Big Bow retired to consider the matter, discussing it with his people, and finally agreed to lead them onto the reservation. The United States was willing to grant him amnesty for all of his past deeds; he was even appointed a Sergeant in the Indian Scouts forces. He served well, and lived out the balance of his life on the reservation, where he died about 1900.

Big Bow (1830-1900)
(*Smithsonian Institution, National Anthropological Archives*)

Big Foot (1825?-1890)

Si Tanka, also known as Spotted Elk, was a Miniconjou Sioux chief who was one of the central figures in the tragic massacre at Wounded Knee Creek, in South Dakota. He was the son of Long Horn, born sometime around 1825 (authorities are reluctant to give a date). He was not known as a warrior or a great leader in his youth, but succeeded to the leadership when his father died in 1874. Big Foot aligned his people with his fellow Sioux during the wars of 1876, but apparrently did not take any noteworthy role in the military acrion. Soon after, he settled down and became one of the first Sioux to raise a corn crop on the Cheyenne River. During this period he also went to Washington, D.C. as a tribal delegate, and worked to establish schools throughout the Sioux territory.

Big Foot (1825-1890) Frozen in Death, at Wounded Knee
(*Smithsonian Institution, National Anthropological Archives*)

Tomahawk of Big Foot; Sioux
(*Museum of the American Indian*

Big Foot's Band at a Grass Dance, Four Months Before Their Annihilation at Wounded Knee
(*U. S. Signal Corps; National Archives*)

The year 1889 was tragic for the Sioux; weather conditions prevented a good harvest and diminished the herds. Even worse, the authorities in Washington were considering taking over much of the Sioux territory and putting the tribe on much smaller reservations. The future looked bleak, until Wovoka's Ghost Dance religion came out of the west to offer new hope. This messiah declared that the White man would soon disappear, all dead Indians would be resurrected, and the Earth Mother would be restored to her original condition. Kicking Bear, who had been part of the delegation visiting Wovoka in 1889, went even further, assuring his people that wearing a Ghost Shirt with its symbolic protection would make a warrior impervious to the White man's bullets and devout performance of the Ghost Dance would hasten the departure of the settlers. In the camps of Big Foot and several other chiefs, the people embraced the new religion with desperate fervor.

The Indian Agents and the Army became alarmed; Indian police were sent to arrest Sitting Bull, who was believed by the Whites to be the real force behind the Ghost Dance. In the ensuing melee Sitting Bull was shot to death and several other Indians were wounded or killed. Over one half of the U.S. Army, under the command of General Nelson Miles, was in the area, ready for action—the memory of the Custer disaster still fresh on their minds. The Indians were equally unsettled, and Hump decided to bring his people into the reservation headquarters for their own safety, as did several other chiefs.

As Big Foot and his group were deciding what to do, a force under Colonel Edwin V. Sumner moved in and arrested them. Big Foot promised to go to the agency peacefully and Sumner withdrew. The Indians had not been on the trail long when they came upon 38 ragged, almost-frozen refugees from Sitting Bull's camp with news of Army atrocities. Big Foot halted the march there, but agreed to continue after

Sumner reminded him of his promise. The Sioux were apprehensive, and when they came to one of their old camps, the families went into the several cabins and locked the doors. Sumner again came forward, but realized pressing the Indians would lead to bloodshed. He trusted Big Foot, even though his orders were to arrest and bring in the Indians without delay.

Not long after Sumner pulled back, Big Foot and his fear-ridden people fled south into the Badlands. Although the Agent claimed that they were going into the back country to join a remnant group of Ghost Dancers, the fact is that most of them headed straight for the Pine Ridge Agency. Soldiers were sent in pursuit and the Sioux were soon recaptured. Big Foot fell ill with pneumonia, and he and most of his people were content to settle down on the banks of Wounded Knee Creek under the watchful eyes of Seventh Cavalry soldiers commanded by Colonel George A. Forsyth.

But the fanatical Ghost Dancers in the group were restless, especially when the troopers moved in to disarm them. As weapons were gathered and stacked in piles near the tepee in which Big Foot lay ill, a medicine man, Yellow Bird, began a Ghost Dance, and his followers fingered their magic Ghost Shirts hidden under their blankets. As the women and children waited fearfully, movements became confusing, and suddenly shots were fired. A few minutes later, 146 Indian men, women, and children, and 25 soldiers were dead; many others were wounded. Big Foot died that fateful day, December 29, 1890, and with him perished the Ghost Dance movement.

Big Mouth (ca. 1830–1873?)

Ehton'ka glala, a Brûlé Sioux chief who was important among his own people as a fearless warrior. He was a major figure at Whetstone Agency in South Dakota, and is recorded by Whites there as being one of the principal Indian chiefs. He steadily gained influence with his people, and his role in tribal relations with the Whites alienated him with the "head chief," Spotted Tail, who favored a more friendly stance.

When Spotted Tail returned from a visit to Washington, reporting a failure of his efforts to exact a greater price for the Black Hills, but still favoring an agreement with the Whites, Big Mouth seized this opportunity to belittle his rival at every occasion His criticism grew stronger, and the Sioux, already confused by the events whirling rapidly around them, began to question the policies adopted by Spotted Tail.

Finally, Spotted Tail realized he would have to take steps to protect his position, since the people were turning slowly to Big Mouth for leadership, and away from him. Accordingly, in 1873 or early 1874, he went with two warriors to the tepee of his rival, called him out to talk, and while they held Big Mouth, Spotted Tail killed him with his rifle.

Big Tree (ca. 1847–1929)

Adoeette, from Kiowa *ado*, "tree," and *e-et*, "great" or "large," was a Kiowa chief who participated in many raids on both Indian and White travelers on the Texas Plains during the active years of Kiowa raiding from 1853 until the death of the great war chief Dohasan in 1866. He was followed by Lone Wolf, who continued the attacks against the increasing White migration into the West, which lead to countermeasures under General Philip Sheridan, and the Kiowa were forced to move onto a reservation set up for them in 1878.

Big Tree (1847–1929)
(*Smithsonian Institution, National Anthropological Archives*)

Painted Buckskin Ceremonial Shield; Kiowa
(*Museum of the American Indian*)

These people were too proud and self-confident to be thus confined, and continued their warfare against the settlers in Texas; and in May 1871, Big Tree, Satank, and Satanta led a band of several hundred warriors in an attack on the Warren wagon train in Young County, Texas. They killed seven men, and escaped with the party's mules.

Returning to the reservation, the Kiowa made little secret of their participation, even boasting of the affair while in the trading post at Fort Sill. Big Tree and some of the others were arrested, imprisoned, and then sent to Texas with Satanta to stand trial. They were convicted and sentenced to life in prison, but in 1873 both men were pardoned and paroled on promise of good behavior.

During a new outbreak of violence in 1874 and 1875 the Army "confiscated" some of the Kiowa horses. Big Tree, together with several other Kiowa warriors still believed to be hostile to the Whites, were briefly imprisoned at Fort Sill. Big Tree, although he apparently did not take an active role in the affair, settled down after this episode and ran a supply train from Wichita to Anadarko for many years. Subsequently, he married a Kiowa woman named Omboke and converted to Christianity, serving as a deacon for the Rainy Mountain Indian Mission for the next 30 years. The couple took up farming on his allotment at Mountain View, in Kiowa County, Oklahoma, and he became a model of peaceful serenity in his old age.

Big Tree died at Fort Sill, Oklahoma on November 13, 1929.

Black Beaver (1806–1880)

Sucktum Mahway, or Sekettu Maquah, a Delaware scout and trapper, was born in 1806 at Belleville, Illinois. Little is known of his youth, but he is known to have spent several years as a young man in the Rocky Mountains, hunting and trapping, and acquiring a familiarity with the territory. In 1834 he was the interpreter for the expedition of General Henry Leavenworth and Colonel Henry Dodge to the upper Red River country, the home of the Comanche, Kiowa, and Wichita tribes. He continued from time to time in the service of the U.S. Government, and during the Mexican War he led a company of Indian scouts and guides under the command of General William S. Harney; from then on he was known as Captain Black Beaver.

During the Gold Rush in 1849 he guided a large party of White miners going from Fort Smith, Arkansas to Albuquerque, New Mexico en route to California. He also frequently undertook trading expeditions into the Southern Plains country in the 1850s, thereby extending his knowledge of the region and its inhabitants.

At the beginning of the Civil War, Black Beaver guided the garrisons of Forts Smith, Arbuckle, Washita, and Cobb in their retreat from Indian Territory to Fort Leavenworth. After the war he became a major spokesman for the Delaware Indians who had moved west, negotiating on their behalf with the Washington authorities. He was highly respected by the neighboring Comanche and Kiowa people, and frequently served them as a mediator with the Whites.

Black Beaver became a legend in his own time, due largely to the tremendous area of the continent which he had covered, his wide experiences with both races, and his own personality as a skilled negotiator, interpreter, scout, and guide—all of which demanded bravery, endurance, and a sound sense of judgment. He died at Anadarko, Indian Territory, on May 8, 1880 at the age of 74, and is buried there.

Black Beaver (1806–1880)
(*Smithsonian Institution, National Anthropological Archives*)

Black Elk (1863–1950)

Ekhaka Sapa, an Oglala Sioux mystic and medicine man who witnessed the great Battle of the Little Bighorn in 1876, when he was 13. He was born on the Little Powder River in December 1863, the son of Black

Elk and Sees the White Cow. Following the end of the Sioux wars, his family joined Crazy Horse (a distant cousin) in initially refusing to go onto the reservation; after they finally capitulated, Crazy Horse was killed. Black Elk and his family immediately fled to Canada where they joined Sitting Bull and his followers. The harshness of the winters and near starvation drove them back to the United States where they settled.

Black Elk is remembered for his many dreams and mystical experiences. The first of these occurred at the age of nine when he fell ill and lay unconscious for several days. He had a vision that seemed to predict the future of his tribe and his own role as a medicine man; he was disturbed by some of the things he saw, but told no one. Even more visions came, however, and he finally told his father about them. By the time he returned from Canada, his reputation had preceded him as a gifted medicine person, and he was sought after as a healer. Black Elk had an uncanny ability to predict certain aspects of the future, and it is said that many times he saved his people from tragedy by timely warning.

He traveled to Europe with Buffalo Bill's Wild West Show, and appeared before Queen Victoria during the celebration of her Diamond Jubilee in 1897. In Paris he fell ill and stayed with a French family. While recuperating there, he had a vision of his people back in America that compelled him to return to them. Back on the reservation, he found that Wovoka's new Ghost Dance religion was gaining firm hold among the Sioux. Initially skeptical of the claims of invulnerability gained by wearing the decorated costumes, Black Elk subsequently had visions which seemed to support the Dancers, and he became a supporter.

Black Elk was not directly involved in the massacre at Wounded Knee Creek in South Dakota, but it had a powerful impact on him. "I can still see the butchered women and children lying heaped and scattered all along the crooked gulch . . . and I can see that something else died there in the bloody mud . . . a people's dream died there. It was a beautiful dream."

In 1932 Black Elk told his story in graphic detail to John G. Neihardt, a major figure in American literature. The vision of the Indian and the literary skill of the White combined to produce a classic work in *Black Elk Speaks; the Life Story of a Holy Man of the Oglala Sioux*. Black Elk died on August 17, 1950 at Manderson, South Dakota, at the age of 87. He had two wives: Kate and Angelina Bissonette, by whom he had two sons, Nick, and Ben Black Elk.

Black Hawk (1767–1838)

Makataimeshekiakiak, from Sauk *makatawi-mishi-kaka*, "Big Black Chest," a reference to the black sparrow hawk, was a Sauk chief who was born in 1767 near present-day Rock Island, in northwest Illinois. His father was Pyesa (or Piasa), a Sauk leader. Famed as a warrior from the age of 15, when he took his first scalp, Black Hawk led early expeditions against the Cherokee and Osage tribes.

In 1804 the Sauk and Fox chiefs ceded all of their lands east of the Mississippi River (about 50,000,000 acres) to the United States for a guaranteed permanent annuity of $1000 per year. Black Hawk and others repudiated this agreement, saying that the chiefs did not have proper tribal authority; he also charged that William Henry Harrison, the chief negotiator, had seen to it that the chiefs became so intoxicated that they did not realize what they were signing.

In the War of 1812, Black Hawk quickly joined the British side, hoping for Canadian support; while his tribal rival Keokuk remained neutral. Briefly discouraged by his defeats in the War of 1812, Black Hawk then signed the Treaty of 1816 which ratified the sale of Sauk lands, and White settlers began to move in promptly. Keokuk, recognizing the inevitable, moved his own band west of the Mississippi River, but Black Hawk and his followers refused to join them.

As did Tecumseh, Pontiac, and others before him, Black Hawk envisioned a vast confederation of Indian tribes that would be strong enough to withstand the Whites. In an effort to unite the tribes he sent emissaries to all neighboring tribes of the region, and particularly sought the alliance of the Winnebago, Kickapoo, and Potawatomi people; he also tried to involve the British in Canada.

Black Hawk (1767–1838) and Whirling Thunder. Painting by Jarvis. (*Thomas Gilcrease Institute of American History and Art*)

In 1831, when American settlers began to plow up the Sauk lands, Black Hawk urged defiance. Accordingly, the governor of Illinois promptly called out the militia, and the Indians were forced to retreat west of the Mississippi River. In 1832, Black Hawk returned with an estimated 2000 followers, including at least 500 warriors. He sent envoys under a flag of truce to confer with General Henry Atkinson who led the federal troops which had been summoned. Fearful of treachery, the Illinois regulars shot most of the envoys—and thus brought on the Black Hawk War.

Wood Burl Medicine Bowl; Bear Effigy Decoration; Sioux (*Museum of the American Indian*)

The Indians were initially successful in defeating the federal troops and devastating the frontier settlements. They suffered heavy losses, however, and when help from other tribes was not forthcoming, Black Hawk retreated north through the Rock River Valley, where he sustained a major defeat on July 21. With the survivors, he attempted to cross the Mississippi River at the mouth of the Bad Axe River in Wisconsin, on August 2. Cut off by the steamer *Warrior* and pursued by Atkinson's men on land, most of the Indians were slaughtered, drowned, or captured. Black Hawk himself escaped, but subsequently was captured and turned over to the Whites by two Winnebago. He was imprisoned in St. Louis, Missouri and as punishment the Indians were forced to cede their lands in Iowa under the euphemism of "The Black Hawk Purchase" of September 21, 1832.

In 1833 he was freed from prison, and accompanied by Keokuk, was taken east to meet President Andrew Jackson in Washington, after which he toured a number of cities where he was an object of much curiosity; his bearing aroused considerable admiration and sympathy. In that same year he dictated *The Autobiography of Black Hawk*, which remains a classic statement of Indian life and White confrontation. He died near Iowaville, on the Des Moines River in Iowa on October 3, 1838 at the age of 71. He married once, to Asshewequa (Singing Bird), and had three children: a daughter Nauasia (or Namequa) known to Whites as Nancy; and two sons, Nasheakusk and Nasomsee, known as Tom Black Hawk.

Black Kettle (ca. 1803–1868)

Moketavato was a Southern Cheyenne chief whose career demonstrated tragically the difficulty many Indian leaders had in living peaceably with the Whites on the frontier. He was born about 1803 near the Black Hills in Dakota country, and joined with the Southern Cheyenne at the time of the great tribal rupture about 1832. Little is known of him until 1861, by which time he had become an important leader of his people, representing them at the signing of the Treaty of Fort Wise, Colorado, which set the terms for peace in that area.

Following a series of skirmishes between some of his younger hotheaded warriors and equally excitable White settlers, he went to Denver in 1864 to sue for peace once again, but was rebuffed by Governor John Evans, who was also the Superintendent of Indian Affairs for Colorado Territory at that time. As head of the Cheyenne–Arapaho delegation, Black Kettle then turned to the authorities at Fort Lyon, Colorado, and was successful in reaching an amicable agreement with the commander of the fort, Major Edward M. Wynkoop, who recognized that such a move would narrow the rapidly increasing state of warfare. The Indians were willing to surrender their rifles and horses to prove their sincerity, apparently not realizing how serious the situation had become. The War Department, in the meantime, had authorized Evans to raise a regiment of volunteers to pacify the Indians. The men were to enlist for a period of 100 days, and were commanded by Colonel John Chivington, an ambitious, fanatical Indian hater. Complaining to his superiors that Wynkoop was too lenient with the Indians, Chivington seems to have been able to secure Wyncoop's replacement with Major Scott N. Anthony. Major Anthony returned the horses and rifles to the Indians and sent them to camp at Sand Creek, about 40 miles distant. There seems to be no doubt that this was a deliberate effort to put the Indians in a place vulnerable to attack. Trusting in the good faith of the Army, the Cheyenne did as they were instructed.

Knowing that his 100 days were running out, Chivington with approximately 1000 men made a forced march early in the morning of November 29, 1864 and reached the Indian encampment of about 100 tepees, housing perhaps 200 warriors and 500 women and children. Apprehensive, yet confident that he had fulfilled the Army stipulations, Black Kettle raised a large American flag and a white flag outside his tepee, and faced the soldiers, with his wife and another chief, White Antelope, by his side. Ignoring the peaceful atmosphere, the troops fired point-blank, killing White Antelope and Black Kettle's wife. In the savage massacre which followed, 161 men, women, and children were slaughtered, the camp was burned, and the bodies of the Indian dead were scalped and badly mutilated.

In spite of this outrage, Black Kettle continued to seek peace, and the next year a treaty was signed at the Little Arkansas near present-day Wichita, Kansas, in which the government disavowed the "gross and wanton outrage" at Sand Creek, and promised to pay reparations to the survivors. In 1867, the Cheyenne and other tribes signed the Treaty of Medicine Lodge, and Black Kettle moved his people to the reservation at Fort Larned, Kansas.

During this time many of the tribes, including the Cheyenne, resented the building of the transcontinental railroad across their territory, because it was driving away the buffalo, as well as bringing in an increasing number of White settlers into their lands. Minor outbreaks continued, involving individual groups, but Black Kettle kept his own band at peace. In the summer of 1868, against the advice of Indian Agent Wynkoop, he moved west to Washita Valley.

When he visited Fort Cobb, about 100 miles away, to reassure the commander there that he desired only to live in peace, he was told that the Army had already begun a major campaign to subjugate all of the local tribes. The Indian Agent told him that the only safe place for his people was the immediate area around the fort. Black Kettle hastened back to the Washita Valley and immediately began preparations to go to Fort Cobb. On the morning of November 27, 1868, the day they were to move, General G. A. Custer and the Seventh Cavalry attacked the camp, destroying it, and killing most of the Indian people, including Black Kettle.

Blacksnake (ca. 1760–1859)

Thaonawyuthe (also Thaowanyuths, Tenwaneus, or Twyneash) "Chain Breaker," was an important Seneca chief during the turbulent period following the American Revolution. He was born about 1760

Blacksnake (1760–1859)
(*New York State Museum*)

at Cattaraugus, New York, about a mile north of Cold Spring. He was a nephew of Cornplanter and of Handsome Lake, and took part in many major tribal council meetings early in his life, due largely to his oratorial skills. In his youth he was known as Dadgayadoh, "The Boys Betting"; he was given the Wolf clan name Thaonawyuthe when he became war chief. During the American Revolution he served on the British side—as did most of the Iroquois—and figured prominently in many battles, most particularly at Oriskany and in the Wyoming Valley.

After the war, Blacksnake was among the Indian leaders who met with officials of the newly formed United States in an attempt to establish firm boundaries and to obtain better treatment for the Indians of the frontier. George Washington and other White leaders were sympathetic, but the tide of settlers refused to be turned back. While there were no more full-scale battles between the two people in Iroquois country, there were many local incidents of violence.

The Indians were also aware that their traditions and heritage were being destroyed by advancing White civilization. In 1799 Blacksnake's uncle, Handsome Lake, had a series of visions which led him to found a new religion which was, in essence, a return to the old tribal culture; this so impressed Blacksnake that he became an early disciple of *Gaiwiio*, the "Good Word." Like many other people, he believed that drunkenness and other aspects of the White man's immorality had to be eliminated from Indian life. He remained a believer, even when he disagreed with Handsome Lake's often dictatorial methods of dealing with political problems.

In the War of 1812, Blacksnake fought on the side of the United States, particularly at the Battle of Lake George in 1813. After the War of 1812, when he became the principal leader of the Seneca people, he was popularly known as Governor Blacksnake. From his home on the Allegheny River, he continued his efforts to secure justice for the Iroquois from both the state and federal governments. He also took a leading role in preaching the religion of Handsome Lake following the latter's death in 1815.

Although Blacksnake remained a staunch traditionalist and leader of the so-called "pagan party," his was a strong voice in favor of improved education for tribal youths, the use of modern agriculture, and of other changes in Indian life—but in a way that would not mean the end of the traditional Indian life-style. His oral version of the *Code of Handsome Lake* was followed by many Seneca people. He is remembered today as having kept the Seneca people together in the critical period following the death of Handsome Lake, when the religion, which was so effective in binding the people into one strong force, could have collapsed, thus destroying their unity and vitality. Blacksnake died at Coldspring, New York on December 26, 1859, at the astonishing age of 99 years.

Feather and Silver Ornamented Headdress; Iroquois (?)
(*Museum of the American Indian*)

Acee Blue Eagle (1909-1959)

Acee Blue Eagle (1909-1959)
(*Alan Ross*)

Alex C. McIntosh, or Chebona Bula, "Laughing Boy," an important Creek artist who devoted much of his life to the preservation of American Indian art and tradition. He was born August 9, 1909 on the Wichita Reservation near Anadarko, Oklahoma, the son of Solomon McIntosh, a Creek descendant of Chief William McIntosh, and Mattie Odom, a Pawnee woman. Both parents died when he was about five years old, and he was adopted by his grandparents, who also died shortly afterwards. W. R. Thompson of Henryetta, Oklahoma, thereupon took on the responsibility of his education as his legal guardian, sending him through Bacone College and the University of Oklahoma.

Acee's talents as an artist were recognized early in his life, and he received strong encouragement from those around him. In the early 1930s he exhibited his work at the Chicago Century of Progress, and painted his first large canvas, *Indian Buffalo Hunt*, for the U.S.S. Oklahoma. At about this time he adopted the name Acee Blue Eagle (Lumhee Holatee) from his initials, and combined it with the name of his grandfather, using this for the rest of his life. In 1935 he was invited to lecture on Indian art at Oxford University in England after which he toured Scotland and France. This gave him considerable confidence in his work, and a name; in 1935 he was able to establish the Art Department at Bacone College, and became its Director for many years during which time he not only continued painting, but also created many murals for buildings throughout the country.

He was very active during World War II, serving in the Air Corps, painting and teaching, and continuing to grow in his art work. After World War II, he became Art Director at Oklahoma State Technical Training School, and lectured throughout the Midwest. His interest in the historical record was furthered by wide travel; he based much of his painting upon his people's descriptions of ancient rituals and traditions, and he often visited Indian ruins, tribal archives, and museums in pursuit of sources for accurate information and inspiration.

Acee's work is notable for its rich natural color and the time-honored Indian silhouette treatment of the subjects. He was among the first of the small number of Indian artists who gained worldwide recognition and he won many prizes in local and national exhibitions. But perhaps even more impressive were his colorful lectures and demonstrations in which he appeared in full costume. He was an eloquent and persuasive speaker with a natural ability to hold an audience's attention. He married twice: to Loretta T. Kendrick, a Cherokee girl, and later to Devi Dja, a Javanese dancer; both ended unhappily in divorce. He died on June 18, 1959 at the age of 49, in the Veteran's Hospital at Muskogee, Oklahoma and was buried in the U.S. National Cemetery at Fort Gibson.

"Stand Up Dancer" painting by Acee Blue Eagle
(*Alan Ross*)

Bogus Charley (ca. 1850–ca. 1880)

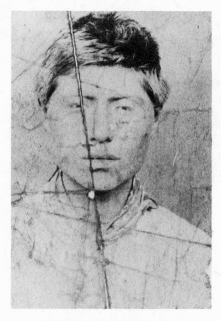

Bogus Charley (1850–1880)
(*Smithsonian Institution, National Anthropological Archives*)

Bogus Charley was a Modoc warrior and was the most Americanized of the Indians in the Modoc War. He had learned to speak English as well as most of the men in the United States troops and thus was an accomplished interpreter. He received his name from the place of his residence, on Bogus Creek, California. He was an ally of Kintpuash and Hooker Jim, and was the individual who eventually made arrangements for the peace conference between the Modoc and General Edwin Canby in 1873.

The conflict escalated when Kintpuash killed Canby. Within a month, Bogus Charley changed from a hawk to a dove, surrendering with Hooker Jim and some others on May 22. He volunteered to act as a bloodhound for the army to ferret out the rebellious Modoc warriors from their Lava Beds stronghold. Kintpuash surrendered in July 1873 and was brought to trial. Bogus Charley and some other Modoc people testified for the prosecution during the affair and Kintpuash was hanged on October 3.

Scarface Charley was appointed the Modoc chief, but when he refused to follow government orders, Bogus Charley replaced him. The tribe was removed to Indian Territory where Bogus Charley remained a leader for many years. He died en route to visit his sister in Walla Walla on October 25, 1880 or 1881.

Gertrude Simmons Bonnin (1875–1938)

Gertrude Simmons Bonnin (1875–1938)
(*Ella C. Deloria Project; Agnes Picotte*)

Zitkala-sa, "Red Bird," a Yankton Sioux reformer and writer was one of a number of White-educated Indians who fought to obtain fairer treatment of her people by the federal government. She was born on the Pine Ridge Reservation, South Dakota on February 22, 1875, the daughter of John Haysting Simmons and Ellen Tate'Iyohiwin, "Reaches for the Wind." Educated on the reservation until the age of 8, she was sent to White's Institute, a Quaker school in Wabash, Indiana. At the age of 19, against her family's wishes, she enrolled at Earlham College, in Richmond, where she won an oratorical contest, then graduated to become a teacher at the Carlisle Indian School in Pennsylvania.

She wanted to become a professional writer but was also interested in music. In following this latter interest, she studied at the Boston Conservatory and went to Paris in 1900 as a chaperone and leader with the Carlisle Band. She became an excellent violinist and enjoyed playing the instrument as a hobby. She also composed an Indian opera based upon the Plains Sun Dance. *Harper's* published two of her stories at the turn of the century, and three of her autobiographical essays appeared in the *Atlantic Monthly*. In 1901, her first book, *Old Indian Legends*, appeared and received a cordial reception.

By this time, Zitkala-sa was back on the reservation, where in 1902 she married a Sioux employee of the U.S. Indian Service, Raymond T. Bonnin; they had one male child. That same year the couple moved to the Uintah and Ouray Reservation in Utah, where they lived for the next 14 years, and where she worked as a teacher for the Indian Service. In 1911 she became active in the Society of American Indians, an organization of educated Native Americans dedicated to the improvement of the conditions of their people. The group was basically interested in the integration and assimilation of the Indian, favoring equal rights for all people, and strongly opposed to the continuance of the Bureau of Indian Affairs.

In 1916, when she was the society's secretary, the Bonnins moved to Washington, D.C. She lobbied for her people among the various officials in the Capitol, and also helped persuade the General Federation of Women's Clubs to take an active interest in Indian welfare. Roberta Campbell Lawson, a part-Delaware woman from Oklahoma, was also prominent in the club's hierarchy at this time, and the two women worked together closely.

Under pressure from the Women's Clubs and others, the federal government agreed to the appointment of a commission to investigate the Indian situation. In 1928, this group, of which Gertrude Bonnin was an advisor, turned in its noted *Report*, under the supervision of Lewis Meriam. The following year President Hoover appointed two Indian Rights Association leaders to head the Bureau of Indian Affairs, and President Franklin Roosevelt's New Deal Administration took even more significant steps to reform United States Indian policy.

In 1926, Zitkala-sa founded the Council of American Indians, and continued to work tirelessly for the rights and welfare of Indians until her death in Washington January 25, 1938 at the age of 61. She was buried in Arlington Cemetery.

Woman's Painted Hide Robe; Sioux
(*Museum of the American Indian*)

Elias Boudinot (ca. 1803–1839)

Also called Buck Watie, or Galegína (Kulakinah, Kilakina, Kullageenah, and similar spellings), meaning "Male Deer," was an important Cherokee leader during the period of Indian removal to Oklahoma. He was born near Rome, Georgia about 1803 (some writers say 1805), the son of David Oowatie (or Uwati), a major figure in Cherokee history; his mother was Susannah Reese, one-half Cherokee. His younger brother was Stand Watie, the famous Confederate General.

As a youngster, Galegína was sent to the foreign mission school at Cornwall, Connecticut in 1818, a school which educated so many Indian leaders in the early 19th century. He was sponsored by a wealthy White philanthropist named Elias Boudinot, from Princeton, New Jersey, and the young Cherokee adopted the name of his patron. While at Cornell, he met and subsequently married Harriet Ruggles Gold, a young White girl of the town. The marriage was violently opposed

Elias Boudinot (1803–1839)
(*Oklahoma Historical Society*)

"The Cherokee Phoenix," edited by
Boudinot
(*Western History Collection, University
of Oklahoma Library*)

by most of the citizens, and Harriet's brother burned the two in effigy,
but to no avail; the young woman showed herself to be firm in her
devotion to her marriage.

By the time his education was completed, Sequoyah, a fellow tribesman, had invented the alphabet for which he is famous, and thousands
of Cherokee could read and write their own language. In 1828 the
Cherokee Council established a national newspaper, the *Cherokee
Phoenix*, which was printed in both English and Cherokee; Elias Boudinot was appointed the first editor. By 1834 the Georgia state legislature had suppressed the newspaper because of its editorial stance,
which insisted on Cherokee land rights and the sanctity of treaties
made legally with the United States Government.

Boudinot, together with a small number of Cherokee people, supported John Ridge and the 1835 Treaty of New Echota (Georgia),
the terms of which included the surrender of Cherokee lands and the
removal of the people to Indian Territory. As a result of his support
for this treaty he was hated by his own people. Because of their roles
in signing the treaty, during the turbulence of the removal period
Boudinot and Ridge were murdered by a small group of Indians at
Park Hill, Indian Territory on June 22, 1839. As far as it can be determined, the Cherokee Council did not know about nor approve of
the killing of the two men.

During his lifetime Boudinot published a novel called *Poor Sarah; or,
the Indian Woman* (1833), in both Cherokee and English. From 1823
until his death he co-translated, with the Reverend Samuel A. Worcester, parts of the *Bible* from English into Cherokee. His wife Harriet
died and he married Delight Sargent; at his death he had six children.
A son, Elias Cornelius Boudinot, is often confused with the father.

Bowl (1756–1839)

"The Bowl," a translation of his Cherokee name, Diwali, referring to
the bowl used for drinking the black drink; he was also known as Colonel Bowles. He was born in 1756, probably in North Carolina, the
son of a Scotch-Irish trader named Bowles, and a Cherokee mother.
Little is known of his childhood, but in maturity he became leader of
a large band of Cherokee militants. After the American Revolution,
during which his group supported the British, he thought that life
would be more comfortable for his people away from the seats of
power of the new nation. In 1794 he led his tribesmen in a massacre
of all of the males in a party of White emigrants at Muscle Shoals, on
the Tennessee River. This act was disavowed by the Eastern Cherokee Tribal Council which also offered to assist in his capture. Bowl
accordingly lost no time in heading farther west to the St. Francis
River in present-day Arkansas.

When the United States purchased the Louisiana Territory in 1803,
there were many delays and misunderstandings in fixing the boundaries for the Western Cherokee Territory. Finally, in late winter 1819–

1820, Bowl led some 60 men and their families into Texas, in response to an invitation from the Mexican authorities who saw them as a buffer between Mexico and increasing Texan militancy. Bowl was commissioned as a Lieutenant Colonel by Mexico in 1827, and in concert with a number of refugees from other tribes, negotiated a land grant from Mexico in an area near present-day Overton, in Rusk County.

Another upheaval in the life of this small band of Cherokees came after 1835 when the Mexican rule in Texas was overthrown. Although President Sam Houston signed a treaty at Grand Shawnee Village on February 23, 1836 guaranteeing Indian land rights, the Texas Senate refused to approve it. In 1838 an ex-Georgian, Mirabeau B. Lamar, took over as president, determined either to drive all Indians out of Texas or simply to exterminate them. Acting on the pretense that the Indians were forming a conspiracy with the Mexicans, several regiments of troops attacked the Cherokee on July 15–16, 1839. Bowl and his warriors managed to hold off the Texans the first day, but on the following morning, he was killed along with most of his people; only a few survivors escaped into Mexico.

He married three times, and had two children, Rebecca, and John, also known as Standing Bowles. He is described as tall in stature, with red or sandy hair, and gray eyes.

Billy Bowlegs (ca. 1810–1859)

Holata Micco, also Halpatter-micco, or Halpuda mikko, "Alligator Chief," a hereditary Seminole war chief, was the leader of one of the last bands of his tribe to remain in Florida against the will of the United States authorities. The exact date of his birth is not certain; he was born on the Alchua Savannah, near Cuscowilla, Florida. His father Secoffee, and his mother were both full-blooded Seminole; his English name is said to be derived from Bowleck, or Bolek, a White trader in the area. The claim that he was bowlegged (hence the name) from riding horseback seems not to be accepted by most writers, although General Howard claimed that his name derived from *Piernas Corvas*, and that he was commonly known as Guillermito. He is said to have been the nephew of Chief Micanopy.

Bowlegs was a skilled warrior who fought in the Seminole Wars of the 1830s when the U.S. Army was continually frustrated in its efforts to round up the Florida Indians for deportation to Indian Territory. He signed the first Treaty of Payne's Landing in 1832, but evaded all attempts to move his people west; Osceola, Wildcat, and many others were captured, while he and his little band of about 100 warriors remained free. They knew the Everglades better than any outsider, and were able to sustain themselves for years without very much interference from White forces.

Micanopy, the head chief of the Seminole, had finally surrendered in 1837, and left for Indian Territory with most of his people in 1838, but Bowlegs continued to hold out. His name is mentioned in con-

Billy Bowlegs (1810–1859)
(*Smithsonian Institution, National Anthropological Archives*)

43

Beaded Cloth Pouch; Seminole
(*Museum of the American Indian*)

nection with an attack on Camp Harney on July 22, 1839. This was but the first of many successful raids made by the new chief of the Florida Indians; he continued to harass the Army and the settlers wherever he could. Continuing the pressure on the Whites, he was able to achieve a peace treaty on August 14, 1842, which terminated the seven years' warfare.

That same year, Bowlegs and a group of Seminole chiefs were taken to Washington, D.C., to see the strength of the nation's capital, and to impress them politically. From 1842 until 1855, relative peace was observed throughout Florida, only to be broken by a small group of Corps of Army Engineers who invaded the home area of Bowlegs, destroying property and cutting down banana trees, simply "to see how old Billy would react." They found out quickly. Two years of sporadic raiding followed, and the settlers increased their pressures upon the United States to remove all of the Indians. Some leaders of the Western Seminole, who had settled in Indian Territory, were also brought back to relate their experiences in their new home. But Bowlegs, upon hearing that Wildcat was coming to talk peace, said, "Tell him not to come out to our country until I send for him." He was offered $10,000 and his people almost $1000 per person if they would go peacefully to the Territory, but they still refused—many of the accounts of life in the west included stories of bad treatment and failure of the Whites to live up to their agreements.

Finally, in 1858, Bowlegs gave in to the demands, and most of the other Seminole followed his lead. They traveled to the west, and shortly thereafter he was asked by Colonel Elias Rector to return to the Everglades to try to persuade Black Warrior and the remaining holdouts to join the rest of the tribe. He was successful in this mission, and the long struggle between the Seminole people and the Army over the occupation of the Everglades came to an end. However, there were still a few small scattered bands (families, really) who remained hidden in the swamp country and refused to emerge. Estimates of their number vary from 250 to 400 persons, and these Indians formed the basis of today's Seminole tribe, presently divided into the Hitchiti and the Mikasuki bands.

After his departure to Indian Territory, Bowlegs seems to have settled down to a more sedentary life, and he died there on April 2, 1859. He had two wives, five daughters, and one son.

Joseph Brant (1742-1807)

Thayendanégea, from Iroquois *thayeñdane-kẽ*, "He Places Two Bets," was an important Mohawk chief who was born while his parents were on a hunting trip along the Ohio River in 1742. His father was Tehowaghwengaraghkwin, a Mohawk Wolf clan chief, and his mother was a full- or half-blooded Indian. The father died, and his mother remarried an Indian, Nicklaus Brant, hence the English name. Young Joseph grew up at Canajoharie Castle, the family home in the Mohawk Valley. His older sister Molly married Sir William Johnson, an English trader who later became the British Superintendent of Indian Affairs. After his marriage to Molly, Johnson adopted the boy and assumed the responsibility of his education.

Joseph was educated at Eleazar Wheelock's Indian Charity School in Lebanon, Connecticut, the forerunner of Dartmouth College. There he became a Christian convert, learned to read and write English, and began translating the *Bible* into the Mohawk language—a project that occupied him intermittently over the balance of his life.

At the age of 13 he joined Johnson's forces in the Battle of Lake George against the French in 1755, and four years later proved himself an able fighter in the Niagara campaign. In 1763, shortly after leaving school, Brant fought with the British in the war against Pontiac, and by the 1770s he was recognized as a prominent leader in the Iroquois League. He married the daughter of an Oneida chief in 1765.

As the American Revolution began, Brant became secretary to Guy Johnson, appointed as British Superintendent of Indian Affairs following the death of his uncle William. He accompanied Guy Johnson to England in 1775, where Brant was presented at court and had his portrait painted by George Romney. He came home more devoted than ever to the English cause, and ironically, his influence was a contributing factor in the disunity of the Iroquois League during and after the American Revolution. After long debate, the Six Nations divided; the Seneca, Cayuga, Onondaga, and Mohawk faction joined Brant and the Oneida and Tuscarora people sided with the Americans. Brant was commissioned a British colonel and participated in devastating raids throughout the Mohawk Valley, particularly in the Cherry Valley and at Minisink; he was also a leader at the Battle of Oriskany.

At the end of the war, Brant used his influence to keep peace on the Mohawk frontier and to protect his people from American reprisal. He also tried, although unsuccessfully, to resolve the Iroquois land claims against the new American government. While still a British officer on half pay, Brant returned to England for a visit during which he was rewarded for his efforts with a land grant at Anaquaqua, along the Grand River in Ontario, Canada. He retired at Anaquaqua with his Mohawk followers; other Indians from the League joined the group, and the area subsequently became the Six Nations Reserve.

Brant built the first Episcopal Church in Upper Canada at Brantford (named for him), and devoted his remaining years to translation work. His first wife died, leaving him two children; he married her half-sister, who was childless, and his third wife gave him seven children. He died at Grand River on November 24, 1807, and was buried near the church he built.

While the forces of the American Revolution caused a rupture in the Iroquois League which was never healed, Brant took the course in which he believed, and his loyalty to the British never faltered. He was a complex man—a scholar, translator, man of religion, a highly respected leader of his people, and a courageous, ferocious warrior in wartime.

Joseph Brant (1742–1807)
(*Museum of the American Indian*)

Ceremonial False Face Society Mask Belonging to Joseph Brant
(*Museum of the American Indian*)

Molly Brant (ca. 1735–1795)

Degonwadonti, the older sister of Joseph Brant, was born around 1735 at Canajoharie, New York, the daughter of a Mohawk man named Tehowaghwengaraghkwin, and a full- or half-blooded Iroquois woman. The mother later remarried following the death of her husband; the husband, an Iroquois named Aroghyadeeka, or Nicklaus Brant, gave his English name to the children. Molly grew up with her brother Joseph at Canajoharie Castle, the family home in the Mohawk Valley.

Little is known of her life before her eventful meeting with William Johnson, the famous British trader who later became Superintendent of Indian Affairs. She is mentioned in passing as a beautiful, somewhat playful tomboy. As the story has it, in 1753 the English were holding a mustering and field play at Fort Johnson; Molly, then 17 years of age, was challenged by one of the young officers to ride. She immediately responded, and the sight of the lovely Mohawk lass apparently caused Johnson to fall in love with her. In time she moved into his home, and became his wife and the father of nine children. He had been married to a White woman previously, by whom he had a son John. The matter of actual wedding ritual has long been a matter of pointless debate; the fact remains that they were married in Indian eyes and custom, and accepted by all of the valley people as husband and wife. While there is little doubt that the political value of having a Mohawk wife did not escape Johnson, it seems equally certain that love was a paramount reason for the marriage. She apparently ran the Johnson household with a firm hand, efficiently managing the needs of the inhabitants and fully devoted to the well-being of her husband.

It must be realized that Molly was not an untutored girl of the forest. She had lived among White neighbors for several years, and had as good an education as was available to girls—Indian or White—at that time. Her native ability and personality helped her to achieve a position of equality with the men around her.

Molly always presided at the table, and in every way fulfilled the role of wife and hostess of Johnson Castle, which enabled her husband to receive guests with decorum, and helped him further the political and diplomatic needs of his office as Superintendent of Indian Affairs. After the successful outcome of the Battle of Lake George, when her husband received the title of "Sir," Molly took on the position of Lady Johnson with grace and dignity, even though she was still "Miss Molly" to the people who had known her as a young woman.

The family lived at Johnstown, where she became a strong link between her own Mohawk people and the British; there is no doubt that she deserves major credit for helping Sir William attain the remarkable success in Indian diplomacy for which he is noted. She seems to have been close to her brother Joseph, even after he left the Johnson household to follow his own career.

On July 11, 1774 death came to Warraghiyagey, as Sir William was known to the Mohawk. He had carefully listed Molly in his will to re-

Carved Wooden Cradle Board; Mohawk
(*Museum of the American Indian*)

ceive land, monies, and other valuables to take care of herself and their children; John was bequeathed the baronetcy, and William's brother Guy became the new Superintendent. Joseph Brant was appointed as secretary to Guy, and the trio held the Mohawk loyal to the Crown, although they were less successful with some of the other Iroquois people; thus the American Revolution ended much of the earlier solidarity of the League of the Iroquois.

With the increasing success of the American troops, Molly fled to Canada with the family, and disappears from history. Little is known of her life following her settlement at the family home at Brantford, where she lived for some two decades and died around 1795.

Dennis Wolf Bushyhead
(1826–1898)

Unáduti, from *unádena*, "woolly," and *duti*, "head," was an important Cherokee leader who flourished in tribal politics during the latter half of the 19th century. He was born on Mouse Creek, near Cleveland, Tennessee on March 18, 1826, the son of Reverend Jesse Bushyhead, an outstanding Cherokee Presbyterian clergyman. Young Dennis attended mission schools in the East until his people were removed to Indian Territory. His father led a detachment of 1200 Indians on the tragic "Trail of Tears"; yet despite the hardships thrust upon the Indian people by U.S. policy. Reverend Bushyhead remained a strong tribal influence in favor of peaceful accommodation to White society.

After his father's death, Dennis returned from school in New Jersey and opened a small business at Fort Gibson, on the Cherokee Reservation. In 1848 he became clerk of the Cherokee National Committee. The next year, like thousands of Americans who heard of the discovery of gold in California, he rushed west to make his fortune. He remained near the mines until after the Civil War; and although he did not make a fortune, he was more successful than most. In 1871, three years after his return to Fort Gibson, he was elected tribal treasurer. After eight years in that position, he was elected Principal Chief, a responsibility he carried out from 1879 to 1887.

Dennis Wolf Bushyhead (1826–1898) (*Smithsonian Institution, National Anthropological Archives*)

This was a period when the U.S. Government was again beginning to intervene in Cherokee life. In the 1830s, when the Indians had been forced to exchange their homes east of the Mississippi for a reservation in Indian Territory, Secretary of War Lewis Cass promised that the western lands would be theirs "as long as the grass grows and the rivers run." In the 1880s, Cass was dead, and his words were forgotten. The settlers pressed even further west, and the Territory, named by the Choctaw Allen Wright *Okla* (people) *homa* (red), had become too desirable a property to be left to its owners. At the same time, White reformers believed it would help the Indian if he were granted United States citizenship, rather than have him remain a citizen of separate tribes or "nations" living in a kind of colonial state.

Accordingly, both desires were served by the passage in 1887 of the Dawes Act, providing for Indian citizenship and also for the breakup of the reservations into individual land allotments. The mixed-blood people, like Bushyhead, were generally in favor of the Dawes Act, but the more tradition-minded full-bloods were not. Though there were some protests and scattered uprisings, Washington went ahead with its plan. In 1889 and 1890 Bushyhead was a delegate at the negotiations between the Cherokee and the United States. He served with distinction, but his efforts were largely defeated by opposition from the Keetoowah Society, a group of militant Cherokee traditionalists. Bushyhead died at Talequah, Oklahoma on February 4, 1898, at the age of 72, a respected leader of his people.

Canonchet (ca. 1630–1676)

From Quanonshet, or Quananchit, this famous Narragansett chief did not at first join in King Philip's War, but the indiscriminate attacks by the colonists on all Indians, regardless of which side they were on, soon turned him into one of the White's chief antagonists. The son of Miantonomo, he succeeded to tribal leadership following the death of his uncle; at that time he was known as Nauntenoo, or Nanuntenoo, "The Dry Man."

In 1675 he signed a treaty with the English agreeing to turn over to them any of Philip's people who might flee into his Rhode Island territory. But it was difficult for him to uphold such an agreement which, in effect, condemned his fellow Indians to death. When the colonists found out that the Narragansett had been sheltering some hostile Wampanoag warriors, they sent a punitive expedition under Captain Michael Pierce against the Narragansett at Patuxet. In a hand-to-hand battle, almost all the colonial soldiers were killed on March 26, 1676.

The shock of this defeat caused the English to immediately gather a far larger force which was dispatched against the Indians, gaining a crushing victory over them, and forcing Canonchet to flee from the battlefield. Some time later, he was surprised in his wigwam near the Patucket River; warned of the danger, he fled, but slipped on the rocks in crossing the river and was captured by an Indian scout who was ahead of the main body of pursuing troops. He was offered his freedom if he would agree to work for peace, but he refused, for by now he realized there could be no lasting peace between the Indian land owners and the White land seekers. Others would carry on the fight, and he asked, simply, "Have not the English buried my people in their own homes?"

Thereupon, Canonchet was taken to Stonington, Connecticut where the Pequot and Mohawk warriors shot, and then beheaded him. That same year, 1676, Metacom was also killed; the war was over, and the era of Indian sovereignty over the New England region was ended.

Canonicus (ca. 1565–1647)

Ca-non-i'-cus, a Latinized form of his own name, Qunnoune, meaning "high, tall," in the sense of elevated, was the sachem of the powerful Narragansett tribe when the Pilgrims landed at Plymouth Rock. He sent the colonists a war challenge: a bundle of arrows tied with a snakeskin, the traditional greeting of sovereignty. They responded by returning the bundle filled with powder and bullets—and thus an uneasy truce was established between Indians and Whites.

When Roger Williams was banished from the Massachusetts Bay Colony in 1635, Canonicus gave him and his followers refuge and a grant of land where the city of Providence, Rhode Island was built. Williams had always been friendly to the Indians and a bond of goodwill and mutual trust was formed between him and Canonicus. When the Massachusetts colonists mounted a punitive expedition against the neighboring Pequots, Williams was able to convince the chief that it was in his own interests to remain neutral. Williams also helped to settle a war between the Wampanoags and the Narragansetts at this same time.

In 1638, Canonicus and his nephew Miantonomo were among the signers of a three-way treaty between the English of Connecticut, the Pequots, and the Narragansetts. Five years later war broke out between the Mohegans led by Uncas, and Canonicus' tribe. When Miantonomo was captured by the Whites, they turned him over to Uncas, who promptly had him executed. Canonicus was deeply wounded by this act of treachery as a reward for his years of friendship toward the colonists. Some scholars regard this as simply a way of striking at Roger Williams through his Indian allies.

Following the death of Canonicus on June 4, 1647—he was then about 82 years old—he was succeeded by his son, Mixan (also spelled Mexam). Relations between the Narragansetts and Whites remained peaceful until the outbreak of King Philip's War in 1675. Canonicus is recorded as being a peace-loving man, prudent in his dealings with the Whites, wise in his relations with his own people, and possessed of a high moral character.

Charlot (ca. 1831–1900)

Slem-hak-kah, from *slum-xi-ki*, "Bear Claw," a Kalispel chief who held tenaciously to his tribe's homelands as long as he possibly could. His father was Victor, the hereditary tribal chief, whose son was born about 1831 in the Bitteroot country of northern Idaho. The name Charlot was taken from a French trader in the region (it also appears as Charlos). Almost nothing is known of the young man's life prior to his succeeding his father as tribal leader.

Charlot (1831–1900)
(*Smithsonian Institution, National Anthropological Archives*)

In August 1872, an agreement had been signed between the Kalispel and the Whites which committed the Indians to remove themselves from the Bitteroot area to Jocko Reservation in western Montana. Charlot adopted a policy of procrastination, putting off the actual move for as long as he possibly could. He hoped that pressures in other areas would divert White attention, and that he might thereby escape removal. But Indian Agent Shanahan interpreted this attitude as one of contempt for the Agency, and incensed, deposed Charlot and appointed his rival Arley (Arlee) to replace him as chief. Obligingly, Arley moved onto the reservation with 81 followers.

Most of the people stayed with Charlot, and in 1884 he is recorded as having 342 followers, representing perhaps two-thirds of the Kalispel at that time. Realizing this disproportion, and hoping to work out a compromise settlement of the impasse, the new Agent, Peter Ronan, took Charlot to Washington, D.C. in January 1884. While the Agent was sympathetic with the Kalispel position, he could do nothing to help them in the face of a government determined to remove then from the fertile valley.

Upon his return, Charlot found that the situation had changed somewhat, and his followers were less determined in their willingness to stay. Reservation life, while not particularly desired, did offer greater accessibility to traders, more protection from raiding Indian enemies, as well as a certain degree of comfort in winter. Moreover, the steadily increasing number of settlers was making hunting more difficult. His own bitterness, together with his stubborn attitude, resulted in a decline in his adherents to a level where, by 1888, he could count on only 189 still living in the region.

Things came to a head in 1889, when Charlot adamantly refused to move, feeling perhaps that he was sufficiently far enough away from Washington to take a defiant stand. To his surprise, Colonel Carrington was ordered to proceed to the Bitteroot area and remove the Kalispel to the reservation by force in 1890. This was successfully accomplished, and a bitter, defeated Charlot led his remaining band onto the Jocko Reservation, where he lived until his death in 1900.

Jesse Chisholm (1805–1868)

A famous Cherokee guide and trader, Chisholm laid out the well-known Chisholm Trail from a point south of present San Antonio, Texas to Abilene, Kansas. He was born in 1805 in Tennessee, the son of a Scottish trader, John D. Chisholm, and a Cherokee mother, the daughter of Chief James Rogers. The family moved to Arkansas in 1816, and around 1825 young Chisholm became a guide and interpreter for many expeditions. He went to Oklahoma in 1826, then was called to serve as an interpreter with the Leavenworth-Dodge party at the peace conference with the Wichita, Kiowa and Comanche Indians at Wichita, Kansas in 1834. He was in great demand for this service, and is said to have had a knowledge of 14 Indian languages.

In 1846 Chisholm again served as interpreter at a large council at Fort Concho, Texas and over the next two decades participated in almost all of the peace meetings between the U.S. Government and the various Southern Plains tribes. In so doing, he built up a reputation for integrity and straight dealing which, in time, made him one of the most prosperous and respected traders in the area.

During his career, Jesse Chisholm built and maintained three trading posts in Indian Territory, at Lexington, Oklahoma City, and at his home at Camp Holmes on the Canadian River. He was often on the trail with wagon trains of goods to supply the needs and desires of the Indian bands scattered throughout the region. At different times during these expeditions he ransomed a total of nine children who had been captured by the Indians. In 1858 he guided Lieutenant Edwin F. Beale from Fort Smith to the Colorado River, after Black Beaver refused to undertake the long trek.

As one of the most admired leaders in the Indian Territory, Jesse Chisholm was asked by both the northern and southern agents to aid their cause in the Civil War. His basic attitude was one of neutrality, but late in 1861 he was with Opothleyaholo's band as they went northwest into Kansas to escape the factionalism then dividing the Indian Territory. He settled near Wichita, which became the base for his trading activities. He married the daughter of James Edwards, another trader; the couple had 13 children.

Early in 1865 he first traveled over the route that later became famous during the days of the great cattle drives, and was named after him. It started south of San Antonio, Texas and wound through Oklahoma to Abilene, Kansas. During its heyday from 1867–1880, over 1,500,000 head of cattle moved over the 800-mile Chisholm Trail; the completion of the railroad spurred travel over the trail for a brief period, but ultimately it died out for lack of need.

Chisholm continued his work of mediating between the Whites and Indian tribes; respected by both sides, he was of great assistance in the negotiations leading to the treaties signed at the Little Arkansas in 1865, and at Medicine Lodge in 1868. He died in his trading camp near Norman, Indian Territory on March 4, 1868 and was buried on the banks of the Canadian River on the homesite of Chief Left Hand, in Canadian County. He is often confused with John Chisum, a later and less well-known Oklahoma cattleman.

Jesse Chisholm (1805–1868)
(*Western History Collections, University of Oklahoma Library*)

Henry Roe Cloud (1884–1950)

Wonah'ilayhunka, "War Chief," a Winnebago teacher and Presbyerian clergyman, played a leading role in expanding educational opportunities for Indian youth. He was born Henry Cloud in a wigwam on the banks of the Missouri River in Thurston County, Nebraska on December 28, 1884. His father was Nah'ilayhunkay, and his mother was "Hard to See," both full-blooded Winnebago. A member of the Bird clan, young Henry lived a wholly Indian life, knowing little of the White world until he was a teenager. He then attended the Genoa Indian School, and the Santee Mission School; at the latter he learned to play the cornet in the school band. In 1901, through the influence and support of Reverend William T. Findley, he left Nebraska and enrolled as a student in Dwight Moody's Academy at Mount Hermon, Massachusetts.

Six years later he met Reverend and Mrs. Walter C. Roe, who took him into their family and induced him to continue his education at Yale University, where, in 1910, he was the first American Indian student to earn the B.A. degree; four years later he returned to receive the M.A. degree. In the meantime, he briefly attended Oberlin College, and then went on to the Auburn School of Theology, graduating with the Bachelor of Divinity degree in 1913, following which he was ordained by the Presbyterian Church. This educational record was attained in a time when it was almost unknown for Indians to achieve such advanced educational status.

His close ties with the Roe family caused him to adopt their name, and from that time on, he went by the name Henry Roe Cloud. Joining his mentor in Oklahoma, young Henry soon found that the greatest need for his abilities was in the field of education, and in 1915 he founded the American Indian Institute at Wichita, Kansas where he worked with Indian boys for the next 13 years, gaining the respect of his colleagues and the gratitude of his students and their families. During this same period, he married Elizabeth G. Bender, the sister of "Chief" Bender of baseball fame, and raised four daughters.

Henry Roe Cloud served effectively on numerous committees and study groups concerned with Indian rights, including the 1926 Brookings Institution survey, which resulted in the Meriam Report—a shocking expose of the condition of the Indian tribes in the early part of this century. He was an active member of the President's Committee of 100, and in 1931 was appointed special representative for the Bureau of Indian Affairs. In 1932 he became Suprintendent of Haskell Institute, in Lawrence, Kansas and in 1936 he was appointed U.S. Supervisor of Indian Education, where he worked to carry out New Deal policies for reform in Indian matters, in response to many of the findings of the Meriam survey.

In the 1940s he undertook his last responsibility—that of Superintendent of the Umatilla Reservation Agency, in Pendleton, Oregon. At the time of his death on February 9, 1950 at Siletz, he was promoting the tracing of family histories for the Indians of the Northwest Coast, to provide the basis for the divisions of a court award of $16,000,000 which had been adjudicated in reparation for illegal land seizures in the 19th century.

Wooden Feather Container with Pictographic Writing; Chippewa
(*Museum of the American Indian*)

Cochise (1812?–1874)

From the Apache meaning "Hardwood," Cochise was the son of a Chiricahua Apache chief; he in turn became leader of the band following the death of his father. He married a daughter of Magnas Coloradas, the celebrated chief of the Mimbreño Apache. The Apaches lived in southern Arizona and western New Mexico, where they had been brutally victimized by Spanish and Mexican scalp hunters and slave traders. Although the enmity between the peoples was intense, the Chiricahua were initially friendly toward the newly arrived Americans in the 1850s. Feeling that they could obtain a certain degree of help from the well-armed Whites, Cochise met with Major Enoch Steen in 1856, and agreed to permit Americans to pass through his country en route to California. Shortly afterwards, some of the Apaches worked regularly for a stagecoach station at Apache Pass, cutting firewood and exchanging it for supplies.

This harmonious situation was upset by stupidity. In 1861 Cochise was summoned to see Lieutenant George N. Bascom at Apache Pass. When he arrived, under a flag of truce, with five other Chiricahua warriors, he was accused of having kidnapped the child of some White settlers. He denied any guilt: the child in fact had been abducted by another band. Refusing to believe him, Bascom arrested the Indians; in the melee, Cochise was badly wounded. He managed to escape from confinement by cutting through the side of the tent with his knife. Some days later he captured three White settlers whom he offered to exchange for his companions. Bascom stubbornly refused and demanded the return of the kidnapped child unharmed. Furious that Bascom would not believe him, Cochise killed his prisoners; whereupon, the Lieutenant hanged the Chiricahua warriors in retaliation.

With this savage action, the long and bitter hatred for Mexicans was broadened to include Americans. Cochise and his father-in-law joined forces to destroy the White settlers and drive them from Apache lands. Over the next ten years this action resulted in an appalling loss of life on both sides. But even worse, the warfare could not resolve the problem of the Apache rights to their own land, nor even provide an acceptable reservation in territory to which they were accustomed.

Cochise and Mangas Coloradas began attacking settlements and quickly succeeded in closing off Apache Pass, the only ready route to the west in southern Arizona. They very nearly forced the Americans out of Arizona altogether, particularly during the Civil War period, when troops were recalled to the east. In 1862, General James Carleton arrived from California, determined to reopen the southern route. At Apache Pass, some 500 Apaches were able to hold off 3000 California Volunteers, until they were finally forced to withdraw after Carleton brought in the artillery. In a skirmish the next day, Mangas Coloradas was badly wounded in the chest. Cochise, determined to save him, placed him in a sling and traveled 100 miles south to Janos, Mexico, where a surgeon lived. Cochise is reputed to have demanded that the surgeon make Mangas Coloradas well, or the town would die. Both Mangas Coloradas and the town were saved, although the next

Warrior's Cap with Antelope Horns;
Apache
(*Museum of the American Indian*)

53

year the older man was murdered while in a military camp flying a truce flag. After the death of Coloradas, Cochise became the principal war chief of the Apache nation.

Although forced deeper and deeper into the fastness of the Dragoon Mountains in southern Arizona, Cochise and some 200 warriors were able to resist all efforts of the Army to capture or exterminate them. They continued their relentless raids on White settlements, and in 1871 General George Crook was given command of the Army's Department of Arizona. He was an experienced Indian fighter who realized the senselessness of annihilatory warfare; he refused to use such actions, trying instead to satisfy the needs of both peoples.

Recognizing that the only way to conquer was to make peace with each Apache band individually, and use these bands to scout the rest, he developed a highly effective group of Apache scouts who soon became famous throughout the territory. Again the White goals were defeated by their own politics; peaceful groups of Apache's were being sent to reservations far from their native country—Bosque Redondo, or Fort Tularosa, in New Mexico. When Cochise learned of the government's intention to remove his band from Cañada Alamosa to Tularosa, he once more went into hiding in the Dragoon mountains. He emerged only when he met with General Oliver O. Howard in 1872 from whom he secured assurance that the Apache would have their own reservation in the Chiricahua Mountains.

When Cochise met with the White authorities, he promised that there would be no more raids if the Chiricahua were guaranteed a reservation in their own territory. He kept his word and brought his 200 people onto the reservation in the fall of 1872. Shortly after, 600 more Indians joined him there, and he continued to live peacefully until his death from dyspepsia on June 8, 1874. He was buried near Bowie, Arizona, leaving his sons Taza (who succeeded him as chief) and Naiche, a younger man.

All who dealt with Cochise regarded him with respect. He was measured at one time, and was 5'9½" tall, weighing 169 pounds, and recorded as being a broad-shouldered, powerfully built man who carried himself with dignity. While gentle in manner during normal occasions, he was capable of extreme cruelty in warfare, torturing his victims as he and his people had learned to do from their Mexican enemies. But he was intelligent and sensitive as well, recognizing from the start that peace was the only possible insurance for the survival of his people—he simply wanted a just and lasting peace.

William Cohoe (1854-1924)

Mohe, "The Elk," or Maspera Mohe, "Water Elk [moose]," was a famous Cheyenne artist, soldier, and farmer. His common name, William Cohoe, is derived from Spanish *cojo*, "crippled," a reference to his physical handicap. He was also known as Nonicas, "Lame Man," or "Broken Leg." Cohoe was born in 1854 in Colorado, the son of Sleeping Bear, and Plain Looking, both Cheyenne people. In his

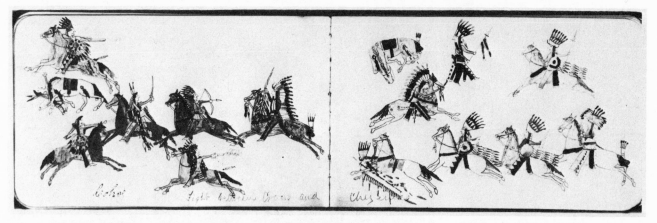

Painting by William Cohoe
(*Western Americana Collection, Yale University Library*)

youth he was a warrior, fighting against the White settlers with other Cheyennes, particularly Bear's Heart, also destined to fame as an artist. The Cheyennes were forced to surrender in December 1874; judged responsible for the killing of several White families during the period, the entire warrior group of 72 men were sent to prison at Fort Marion, off St. Augustine, Florida. Here Captain Richard Pratt encouraged the inmates to develop their skills and talents, providing them with art materials for the purpose. Cohoe, Bear's Heart, Howling Wolf, and others produced sketchbooks which have become treasured examples of Native American art.

In 1878, Cohoe left the prison and became a student, first at Hampton Institute in Virginia, and the next year at Pratt's new Carlisle Indian School. In 1880 he returned west to Indian Territory, determined to abandon traditional Indian life and accept the White man's ways. He wanted to "work hard and succeed." Half of his wish came true; in the next three decades he toiled as a laborer, mill hand, and clerk. In 1881, following the receipt of a farm allotment, he worked as a farmer. The rewards were few, and success never came. He lamented his life: "I have nothing to go ahead and work with. I work hard and try to make a living, at the same time I am getting poor."

Cohoe thereupon abandoned his adopted Christianity, whose tenets he felt had been false to his people, and sought comfort in the traditions of his father. He was a member of the Native American Church, and became Chief of the War Dancers' Society, putting all his energy into efforts to maintain the old ways. He did no more painting, and died on March 18, 1924 on his farm near Bickford, Oklahoma. A small man, about 5′9″ tall, weighing about 130 pounds, he married twice: to Small Woman, and later to Surprise Woman (also known as Vister), both Cheyenne women. He had two sons.

Colorow (ca. 1810–1888)

From Colorado, "The Red," an important chief of the Moache Ute people, was a leader in the fight against White takeover of tribal lands in Colorado and Utah. His own name was Toop'weets, "Rock," a reference to his stolid nature; the source for the name by which he is

commonly known is lost today. His origins are not clear; although he was captured as a child by Ute raiders attacking the Comanche between 1810–1813; his mother was apparently a captive Jicarilla Apache woman. Subsequently, he was adopted into the Ute tribe, and as he grew into manhood, his strong, courageous nature made him a natural leader. He became skilled in battle strategy, and led the Ute warriors in many victories over the Arapaho and other neighboring enemies. His favorite tactic was to make the best use of high ground in combat, and he was often able to surround his enemies in the valley countryside almost before they were aware of what was happening.

As the Whites entered Colorado in increasing numbers, conflicts between Indian tribes virtually ceased. Colorow seems to have met Colonel John C. Frémont during the latter's expedition of 1849, and was at first generally friendly to the White people. But it soon became more and more evident that with each succeeding peace treaty made with the emigrants, the Ute territory and rights diminished. He began to have doubts concerning Chief Ouray's policy of peaceful accommodation, which eventually developed into strong opposition.

For a time, Colorow and his people lived outside Denver, where the Agency was established, and where they were paid their allotments. They camped in a large cave outside the town, and learned the White man's customs of gambling, drinking, and eating—so much so that Colorow himself ballooned up to over 300 pounds, making his six foot, lean, athletic frame a gross caricature. The Whites enjoyed having the Ute perform for them, enacting various social dances; but one time, the band came in to perform the Bear Dance, and followed it up with a Scalp Dance—incorporating fresh, bloody Cheyenne scalps, collected just a day or two earlier. This shocked the Whites into stopping the performances, and subsequently closing the Denver Agency.

After the Agency closed, Colorow moved his people onto the Ute Reservation in the White River country. He became an Indian policeman, employed by the government to uphold law and order on the reservation. About this same time, Ouray began his policy of evicting settlers who had squatted on Indian lands. This was not felt acutely until the people gathered at Hot Sulphur Springs in 1876 to bathe in the curing waters, and were warned away, informed that the property now belonged to a White settler; three years later, troopers began to fence off the Ute holy ground at Medicine [Steamboat] Springs—a sacrilege which shocked the Indians.

As it became increasingly apparent that the Ute had to fight for survival on their native homeland, tensions rose, and hostile incidents were frequent. An undercurrent during this same period was a move in Washington urging the removal of the entire Ute people to Indian Territory (Oklahoma).

In 1878 Nathan C. Meeker became the U.S. Indian Agent for the Ute Reservation. A well-meaning but moralistic, dogmatic man, his early intentions of helping the Indians were fatally affected by a fierce determination that they would have to do everything his way. The result was inevitable: discord became obvious, Indians performed "threatening" war dances in the streets of the Agency, frightened Indian women took their children and disappeared into the countryside. Feeling that Colorow was responsible for much of the increasing hostility, Meeker deposed him, and appointed Sanovick tribal chief in his place. The latter was a hated rival of Colorow, and the incident only intensified the feelings between two key figures in the coming tragedy. Ultimately, fearing for his life, the Agent called in the troops for protection. Some scholars feel that Meeker had been selected as scapegoat, in the thought that his stubborn attitude would inevitably cause the Ute to rebel, thereby providing an excuse for their removal.

Whatever the reason, Major Thomas Thornburgh was dispatched from Fort Steele with 175 men. Colorow intercepted him, and warned him not to attempt to cross Milk Creek into the Ute Reservation territory. Feeling he had sufficient strength behind him, the Major ignored the warning; anticipating just such a step, the Indians were prepared, and trapped his troops in Red Canyon, using their well-proven tactics. The siege lasted for a week, until 1000 fresh troops arrived, and Colorow with his 70 warriors had to surrender after killing 14 soldiers and wounding 43. During the battle, Ute warriors at the reservation headquarters attacked the Agency, burning the buildings and killing Mecker, his family, and seven Whites.

Subsequently, the tribe was moved by force of arms to the Uintah Reservation in Utah. To prevent resistance, Colonel Mackenzie was dispatched to supervise the removal of some 1500 people with their livestock; in desperation, Colorow made a futile attack with about 50 followers, which was easily put down. He was the last to leave his homeland, and although he went to the reservation, he became homesick, going later to Ignacio on the Southern Ute Reservation in Colorado.

The only happy time of these years were the brief periods in the summer when some of the Ute men were allowed off the reservation to hunt in their old homeland. During one of these ventures, Colorow and ten men became involved in a brief confrontation with Sheriff Jim Kendall, who hysterically called for military help to put down a "Ute uprising"; out of the fear-ridden atmosphere, shots were fired, resulting in the deaths of three Whites and seven Indians. In bitter despair, Colorow returned to his home, where he died on December 11, 1888. He left one son, Gus Colorow.

Comcomly (ca. 1765–1830)

One of the wealthiest leaders on the Northwest Coast, Comcomly was a Chinook chief who provided assistance at a time critical in the fortunes of several American explorers and traders. He was friendly to the Lewis and Clark expedition when it arrived at the mouth of the Columbia River in 1805. Six years later, when an American fur-trading party from the shipwrecked *Tonquin* required aid, he provided it; his help to John Jacob Astor during the founding of the Astoria trading post was also an obvious gesture of friendship.

Yet it is also true that he nearly took part in a planned massacre of all the Whites at that post following its erection, an indication that he was well aware of the problems involved in the intrusion of such outsiders. His position as a leader of his people—responsible for their best interests—conflicted with his personal desire for aggrandizement, and he was continually caught between the two roles. He apparently felt that his future lay with the Americans, for he offered to lead some 800 warriors to help defend them against the British in 1812. However, somewhat to his dismay, the Americans saw no profit in a fight, and arranged for the peaceful sale of their property.

Happily for Comcomly, the British also proved to be generous in their relations with the Indians, and gave them presents, with promises of more profitable trade in the future. Indeed, to cement his relations with the Americans and to balance his position, he married his daughter to Duncan M'Dougal, the leader of the Astor Expedition.

Although afflicted by the loss of sight in one eye, Comcomly was a noted sailor, and served for many years as the first pilot on the Columbia River. He had at least three wives, although there is no record of the number of his children. Comcomly was a man who frankly enjoyed the trappings of his position—on his visits to Vancouver, he invariably traveled with a large retinue of slaves, often numbering as many as 300, and he habitually carpeted the ground he had to travel from the ship to a building (a distance of several hundred feet) with beaver and otter fur.

He died in 1830 at the age of 65 during an epidemic of smallpox, and was buried in the traditional stately canoe burial of the Chinook. Following this ceremony, the grave was surreptitiously opened, and his head was secretly removed by a White man who sold it in Edinburgh, Scotland.

George Copway (ca. 1818–ca. 1863)

George Copway (1818–1863)
(State Historical Society of Wisconsin)

Kahgegwagebow, from *kagigegabo*, "he who stands forever," familiarly known as "Stands Fast," was one of the first American Indians to have his writings published and widely read by Whites. He was born near the mouth of the Trent River, in Ontario, Canada in the fall of 1818, and was educated in the Ojibwa tradition. His parents were both full-blooded Ojibwa; his father was a hereditary chief of the tribe, and a medicine man. In his youth, the young man was frequently called upon to help in maintaining the family; there were many difficult times, and during one winter the family came very close to starving to death.

Methodist missionaries in the area converted the parents and young Copway to Christianity, and also took charge of the boy's education; by 1834 he had become actively concerned with Wesleyan missionary work among his fellow Indians. From 1838–1839 he studied at Ebenezer Academy in Illinois, during which time he helped translate into Ojibwa the *Book of the Acts* as well as the *Gospel of St. Luke*. Following this service, he toured the eastern United States, returning home to Toronto in 1840, where he married Elizabeth Howell.

He was employed by the religious presses in New York City for many years, and during the period 1847–1851 turned to his own writing as a full-time activity. Out of these years came *The Life, History, and Travels of Kah-Ge-Ga-Gah-Bowh* (1847), revised in 1850 as *Recollections of a Forest Life: The Traditional History and Characteristic Sketches of the Ojibway Nation*, and even later reissued as *Indian Life and Indian History* (1858); *The Ojibway Conquest* (1850); *The Organization of a New Indian Territory East of the Missouri River* (1850), and *Running Sketches of Men and Places in England, Germany, Belgium, and Scotland* (1851).

Copway's writings were very well received during his lifetime, and he met Longfellow and other literary men of the time. He lived for a time in New York City, but returned eventually to his native homeland to continue his missionary work. He died near Pontiac, Michigan, in 1863, around the age of 45.

Cornplanter (ca. 1735–1836)

From Iroquoian, *gaiant-wa'ka*, "by what one plants," hence, "The Planter," also known as John O'Bail. There are several variants of his

Cornplanter (1735–1836)
(*Smithsonian Institution, National Anthropological Archives*)

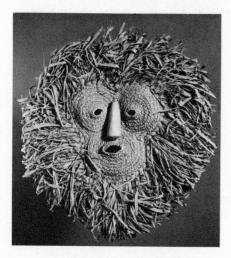

Braided Cornhusk Mask; Seneca
(*Museum of the American Indian*)

name: Garganwahgah, Gyantwaia, Kaiiontwa'ko, Gyantwaka, John Abeel, and John Obeil. He was a Seneca chief born at Ganawagus on the Genesee River in New York, around 1735; his father was a White trader, John O'Bail, and his mother was a Seneca woman. The father soon deserted his wife, and the child was raised by Indian relatives. As a youth, Cornplanter took part in French raids against the British on the frontier, but at the start of the American Revolution he joined the British side, along with most of the other Iroquois tribes. Through his military ability, he became an outstanding fighter, and led his warriors against settlements all along the frontier in New York and the Wyoming Valley. At one point he captured his own father, and offered to accept him into the tribe, to "cherish your old age with plenty of venison." The older White man refused; however, and the son gave him an escort back to the American lines.

Cornplanter, Red Jacket, and Joseph Brant formed an important triumvirate of Iroquois chiefs at this time, and even though they had all been on the British side during the American Revolution, they were able to adjust somewhat to the new American government. Cornplanter supported many treaties which ceded Indian lands, including the 1784 Treaty of Fort Stanwix, and the Treaty of Fort Harmar five years later. In 1790 he visited President Washington to plead for his people who were being treated unfairly. He also acquiesced in some land transfers which were not to the advantage of his own people, as with Governor Denny in Pennsylvania in 1794; this action made many of his erstwhile followers distrust him. But he seems to have been able to hold the respect of enough of the Seneca to secure their support on the American side during the War of 1812.

He and Red Jacket occasionally quarreled, apparently due to Cornplanter's almost fanatical advocacy of temperance—an attitude perhaps shaped by the fate of his favorite son Henry, a former Army major who became a drunkard. In his old age, Cornplanter is said to have had a vision ordering him not to have anything more to do with the White man; whereupon he destroyed the souvenirs and gifts which he had received over the years. He died February 7, 1836 at Cornplantertown, on the banks of the Allegheny River, around the age of 100 years. His last years were spent on a 900-acre farm in Warren County, Pennsylvania. The Cornplanter Reservation in Pennsylvania was named for him.

Cornstalk (ca. 1720–1777)

Wynepuechsika, a Shawnee leader of major importance in the 18th century, was born in western Pennsylvania around 1720. As a young boy, in 1730, he moved with his parents to the Scioto River area of Ohio. He allied himself with the French against the English, and in 1763 he first came into prominence during Pontiac's War, when he launched a series of raids against settlers in West Virginia. Although the French made peace and retreated from the advancing settlers, the Indians did not; they remained on their lands and frequently clashed with the English.

After increasing violence, Cornstalk tried to initiate peace talks in 1774, but was rebuffed by the officials in the region. Instead, Lord Dunmore, the governor of Virginia, called out the militia and advanced into the disputed western territory. It was a foolish move, and Cornstalk with about 1000 warriors met them at Point Pleasant, on the border between Ohio and West Virginia. After a day-long battle on October 10, in which both sides suffered heavy casualties, the Indians withdrew. A peace treaty was signed at Chillicothe in November—a move which Cornstalk had sought many months earlier—but many Shawnees bitterly opposed what they regarded as a capitulation.

Peace came, but the White settlers did not go away—and neither did the Indians. Cornstalk was respected as a warrior and a statesman by people on both sides; he tried to keep the peace, but found this an impossibility in the face of the fear, violence, and determined hatred which existed. In 1777 he went to Point Pleasant to discuss the rapidly worsening situation with the local people but Cornstalk and his party were seized and held as hostages. Shortly afterwards, a White man was killed by marauding Indians, and on November 10, 1777 the infuriated militia men, led by Captain Hall, stormed the jail, and executed Cornstalk, his son Elinipsico, and Red Hawk. Some of the murderers were later brought to trial, but all were acquitted. The Shawnees vowed revenge, and remained at war with the Whites until the Treaty of Greenville was signed on August 3, 1795. As a result of this, the Shawnees were forced to move west out of the way of the ever-advancing settlers.

Cornstalk is remembered as a skillful warrior, an excellent general, and an orator of great ability. His premature removal from the scene of conflict caused the unnecessary deaths of many people on both sides.

Beaded Medicine Pouch; Shawnee
(*Museum of the American Indian*)

Crazy Horse (ca. 1841–1877)

Tashunka Witco, regarded by most Indian people as the greatest of the Sioux leaders, held an implacable hatred for all Whites throughout his short life. Little is known of his early years—even the date of his birth is uncertain. It was most likely in the winter of 1841–1842, although some say 1839; and even 1844 has been suggested. His mother was the sister of Spotted Tail, the Brûlé chief, and his father was an Oglala medicine man who passed on his mystical gifts to his son. Crazy Horse was a solitary youth, given to meditation and visions. In one vivid dream he saw a young man—himself—on horseback with a smooth stone behind his ear, and long, unbraided hair with the feather of a red hawk in it. He took this to be his talisman against the weapons of the Whites, and he appeared so attired in battle thereafter. Indeed, this medicine seems

Medicine Bonnet Belonging to Crazy Horse
(*Museum of the American Indian*)

61

to have been effective; although Crazy Horse was one of the most daring of warriors, he was never wounded in battle.

One account maintains that the behavior of the horse he was riding in a vision was so unusual that he described it as "crazy," hence the name. Another account is that he rode so recklessly into battle that the name became appropriate, and still a third account says that a wild pony dashed through the camp at the time of his birth. It is more likely that his father, also named Crazy Horse, passed his own name along when he learned of the vision and witnessed his son's battle exploits.

Crazy Horse participated in all of the major battles fought by the Sioux—especially the restless, proud Oglala—to protect the holy Black Hills area from White intrusion. As a young man he fought in Red Cloud's War and in the Fetterman massacre in the 1860s. When Red Cloud finally retired to the reservation, Crazy Horse became war chief of the Oglala Sioux. He was also able to call upon his wife's people, the Cheyenne, for warriors in united attacks against the common foe. In the early 1870s he led many successful raids against surveying parties for the Northern Pacific Railroad. In 1876 General George Crook began a campaign to subdue rebellious Indians who refused to be part of the reservation system. Crazy Horse's first meeting with Crook's forces was on March 17, when they launched a surprise attack on his Powder River camp. The soldiers succeeded in capturing most of the Sioux mounts, but Crazy Horse was able to regroup his warriors and, in a blinding snowstorm, stampede the herd back into Indian hands. Three months later another battle was fought on the Upper Rosebud and Crook was forced to withdraw. Then, on June 25, Crazy Horse and Gall annihilated Custer at the Battle of the Little Bighorn.

After this battle the Indian tribes split up. Crazy Horse and his warriors headed for Rosebud, where they hoped to pick up recruits and ammunition, but they were relentlessly pursued by troops under General Nelson Miles. After a long hard winter and a battle in which the Army used artillery with stunning effect, Crazy Horse surrendered on May 6, 1877 with about 1000 Indians. They were reassured by General Miles' promise that they would be given a new reservation in territory familiar to them.

Meanwhile Crazy Horse had married an Oglala girl, Tasina Sapewin, "Black Blanket" (or Black Shawl), who bore him a baby daughter. Life behind boundaries did not agree with him, but there is no strong evidence that he was considering a new Indian rebellion. It is more accurate to say that as the most talented military leader among the Sioux, he was a potential threat to the Army's plans for containment of the Northern Plains people, if he decided to leave the reservation and begin raiding White settlements again.

His wife fell ill from disease, and Crazy Horse married Nellie Larrabee, the daughter of a trader at the Post. Reservation life bored him, and he finally agreed to join as a scout to go to the Yellowstone region; jealousy among his own people, and the enmity of a few Sioux leaders built against him, and these combined with the White fear of this strong leader. Crazy Horse heard of the unhealthy situation, and fled to the Spotted Tail Agency with his wife; he was pursued by Captain Clark and his Indian scouts, and finally agreed to return.

Although he had submitted peaceably, he was taken to a stockade rather than being given his freedom among his people. Amid the confusion of contemporary accounts, it is difficult to know exactly what happened. Apparently, while being led to the stockade, he realized that it meant confinement, and tried to break away. He grabbed a knife from his belt, and lunged through the door; Captain Kennington seized his left arm and Little Big Man seized his right arm. In the ensuing melee, Swift Bear and other Brûlé Indian policemen rushed to help Little Big Man, and suddenly one of the soldiers thrust a bayonet into Crazy Horse's body.

Shocked by the act, the Indians released him, but the damage had been done; he was mortally wounded. Crazy Horse died that night on September 7, 1877 after asking his parents that his heart be returned to his homeland. The next day, his parents were given his body, and they vanished into the hills. To this day, no one knows where the body of the great Oglala warrior lies buried; two White hunters later said that they had seen two elderly Indians carrying an empty litter. They were near Wounded Knee.

Crazy Snake (1846–1912)

Chitto Harjo, from *chitto*, "foolhardy, recklessly brave," *harjo*, "snake," also known as Wilson Jones; a Creek chief who was the leader of the Snake Uprising in Oklahoma in 1901. He was born in 1846 in Creek Territory, near Boley, Oklahoma, the son of Aharlock Harjo. Throughout most of his life, Chitto Harjo and his people had been on relatively friendly terms with the U.S. Government. The Creek people had been moved into the Indian Territory by the Treaty of 1832, which guaranteed them common ownership of their lands and self-government. In the Civil War, some Creek slave owners supported the South, and in 1866 a Reconstruction Treaty was signed which abrogated some of the original terms of the 1832 agreement. As time went on, many in the Five Civilized Tribes became more and more assimilated into the White American cultural life. This was particularly true of the offspring of Indian–White marriages.

Yet there were many full-blooded Indians, like Chitto Harjo, who distrusted Whites, and had as little to do with them as possible. Many of these Indians refused to enroll with the Government authorities, and thereby became "nonpersons" in the eyes and the records of the bureaucracy. This became an increasingly serious problem as plans were made to combine the Indian Territory into the Territory of Oklahoma as a new state, to be known as Oklahoma. The land that had belonged, in common, to the Creek Indians and other tribes was to be divided among all of the enrolled members of the tribes, and separate tribal governments would no longer exist.

The full-blooded Indians did not like this, for several obvious reasons, and Chitto Harjo became their representative in negotiations with the U.S. Government. In 1897, he had set up his own organiza-

Chitto Harjo (1846–1912)
(*Oklahoma Historical Society*)

tion, known as the Snake Government, composed of full-blooded northern Creeks; their capitol was set up at Hickory Ground, Oklahoma, a legislature and judicial system was organized, and every effort was made to create a complete, if parallel, Indian government. Continued pressure caused a full-fledged rebellion in January 1901, known in history as the Crazy Snake Uprising. It was hardly a major rebellion, and lasted for only a few weeks, but it did attract something over 5000 followers. Captured and brought to trial, Crazy Snake and his group were tried on February 2, 1901, found guilty, and after a scolding by a somewhat understanding judge, allowed to go home.

Further encroachments on Creek political freedom continued to give rise to discontent, and although Chitto Harjo made several trips to Washington and hired White lawyers to plead the Creek case, he was ultimately unsuccessful. In 1906 he made an impassioned and widely published speech at Tulsa to the Senate Committee on Land Treaties. Oklahoma became a state in 1907 and the terms of the land legislation came into effect. Some of the nonenrolled Indians did not get the land to which they felt entitled and conflict was inevitable.

Shortly thereafter, an episode occurred which is still not clear in history; it involved the loss of 1000 pounds of smoked bacon. There is confusion as to whether the meat was stolen by Chitto Harjo's people, by outsiders, or involved the overturning of a smokehouse by dogs getting at the bacon. But the fact remains that when police arrived to arrest the alleged thief at the Harjo home in Hickory Hills in the midst of a conference of full-blooded Indians, fighting broke out. One Indian was killed, a White was wounded, and 40 Indians were arrested. Publicized as the Smoked Meat Rebellion, the minor riot was enlarged into rumors of a full-fledged "war." The police returned in force in response to White hysteria; shots were fired, and Chitto Harjo and a small band of followers escaped into the back country. But the edge had been taken off the violence; the next two years he lived in the hills, only occasionally emerging into nearby towns. In one attempt to capture him, he was wounded but finally made his way back into the hills. He took refuge in the home of a friend near Smithville, where he died on April 11, 1912.

A remarkable orator, staunch advocate of traditional ways, and intransigent opponent of White encroachment, Chitto Harjo may never have seemed successful in the eyes of his White adversaries, but he did his best to establish what he believed to be justice for his people.

Crow Dog (ca. 1835–1910?)

Kangi Sunka, a Brûlé Sioux chief and the murderer of chief Spotted Tail. This important figure in the Ghost Dance troubles of 1890 appears never to have taken a prominent role in the Sioux battles of the 1870s and 1880s, but he does seem to have been looked upon as a major leader. He was a cripple, but had won an unusually attractive woman as a wife. According to one story, Spotted Tail stole her from him. On August 6, 1881 he rode up and shot the chief—it is open to question whether Crow Dog murdered Spotted Tail because of his feud over the woman, or for political reasons. It is likely that their rivalry had its roots not only in domestic jealousy, but was also involved in a contest for tribal leadership which included the ambitions of Black Crow, a notorious troublemaker.

Crow Dog was jailed, tried, convicted of the murder, and sentenced to death. However, on appeal, the Supreme Court freed him in a landmark decision, saying that the United States had no jurisdiction over crimes committed on land which belonged to the Indians by treaty right. This decision was to haunt Indian–White relations for many years, since it was never wholly observed by both parties equally.

A defiant enemy of the Whites throughout his life, Crow Dog was one of those who stiffened Indian resistance to further concessions when it became clear in the 1880s that the Whites were greedy for more land. In one way or another, however, the Whites gained the necessary approval from over three-fourths of the adult male Sioux for the cession of additional land. This, together with a drastic reduction

Crow Dog (1835–1910)
(*Smithsonian Institution, National Anthropological Archives*)

65

of Sioux food allotments at a time when there had been a great crop failure in the region, set the stage for the Ghost Dance uprising of 1890. In the fall of that year the Brûlé medicine man, Short Bull, preached Wovoka's message of salvation and miraculous revival of autonomy to the Sioux. As more and more people joined the Ghost Dancers, the Whites in the Northern Plains grew increasingly fearful, and called on the Army for help.

Late in November, Crow Dog gathered his people together and followed Short Bull into the Badlands. They went to a remote area called the Stronghold to dance and wait for the messiah to come and save them. The Army sent emissaries who promised the Sioux better treatment if they returned, warning them of the danger of war if they did not. As the day wore on, a split developed among the Indians; Crow Dog was finally convinced to lead his band back to the Pine Ridge Reservation, and was joined by Two Strike and his people.

In December, both Sitting Bull and Big Foot were killed; the Ghost Dance faded as quickly as it had blossomed. Crow Dog participated in some of the negotiations in the 1890s which somewhat improved the well-being of the Sioux, but his day of glory had passed. He died on the Pine Ridge Reservation, South Dakota about 1910.

Painted Rawhide Bonnet Case; Crow
(*Museum of the American Indian*)

Curly (ca. 1859–1923)

Ashishishe, or Shishi'esh, "The Crow," was a Crow Indian scout for the U.S. Army during the Sioux Wars. He was born about 1859 on the Rosebud River in Crow country, in Montana. His wife was Takes a Shield, a Crow woman. There is little knowledge of his childhood or earlier activities until he became a member of the Indian scouts serving under Captain Thomas Custer, with the Seventh Cavalry.

In late June 1876 Curley was attached to General George Custer's troops as they moved toward the Little Bighorn in search of hostile Indian forces under Crazy Horse, Gall, Sitting Bull, and Two Moons. During the battle which followed, Custer and his entire force were annihilated. Curly, although wounded, managed to disguise himself as a Sioux by braiding his hair, concealing his Crow garments beneath a dead Sioux's blanket, and slipping through the encircling ring of hostile warriors. About two days after the attack, he reached the fork of the Yellowstone and Bighorn Rivers, where he encountered Custer's supply riverboat, the *Far West*.

Although he could not speak English, Curly was able to describe the affair in sign language and diagrams, thereby providing the first word to the outside world of the defeat of Custer and his entire force. In later years, although he was generally reluctant to discuss the battle or his part in it, he was frequently sought out by historians seeking to get greater detail on the famous battle. Charges that he had turned tail and run away from the fight were leveled at him, but were never satisfactorily established; but in the bitter heat of the argument he once even denied having been on the Little Bighorn that fateful day.

Curly (1859–1923)
(*Smithsonian Institution, National Anthropological Archives*)

He later became involved in a long dispute with the government, involving eligibility for retirement pay, which had been denied him for many years. Finally, in April of 1923 he won his case, and was awarded a pension "for the rest of his life." He died a month later on May 22, 1923 at the age of 70. He was buried in the National Cemetery on the Custer Battlefield in Montana.

Charles Curtis (1860–1936)

Curtis, a Kansas lawyer who became Herbert Hoover's vice-president, was born in North Topeka on January 25, 1860. His father was Orren Arms Curtis, and his mother, Hélène Pappan Curtis, a quarter-blood Kansa. Though only one-eighth Indian, he received his early education at an Indian Mission school. In his early twenties he was the first prosecuting attorney of Shawnee County ever to enforce the local prohibition laws. In 1892 he was elected to the U.S. House of Representatives as a regular Republican, where he served eight terms. He gained a seat in the Senate in 1906, which he held (except for two years) until his term as thirty-first Vice-President from 1928–1933.

Many of his legislative achievements were related to Indian and rural affairs. The Curtis Bill of 1898 improved the boundaries of Indian territories and granted the residents thereon the right to elect mayors and other local officials. Although he opposed the Chickasaw and Choctaw claims on so-called leased land, he was also the prime mover in defeating a railroad land grab in the Territory.

Curtis was a conservative, convivial, articulate, sensible man; he was a born politician who was liked by members of both parties. When he retired from government service in 1932, he had served longer in the Capitol than anyone else at that time. He married Anna Elizabeth Baird, by whom he had two daughters and one son. He died in Washington, D.C., on February 8, 1936.

Datsolalee (ca. 1835–1925)

Dabuda, "Wide Hips," commonly known as Datsolálee, Datsolali, Datsalálee, or Louisa Keyser, was recognized throughout the art world as by far the greatest designer and weaver of baskets among the Washo people, among whom this craft had become a fine art. She

Datsolalee (1835–1925)
(*Smithsonian Institution, National Anthropological Archives*)

was born in November 1835, near Sheridan, in the Carson Valley, Nevada, and from her girlhood days was known for her "magic fingers." Little is known of her parentage, but she seems to have lived a usual Indian life of the time; she met Colonel John C. Frémont in 1844 on his way to California.

Religion was an important part of Washo life; from childhood on, members of the tribe were encouraged and trained to seek visions and mystical experiences. Datsolalee's religion was an integral part of her art. It is said that she saw many of her very best designs in dreams and visions before incorporating them into her prized baskets. She was a serious woman; and although she married twice and had several children, she devoted most of her life to her art. Her first marriage, to Assu, a Washo man, produced two children; he died a few years later.

The basketry of the Washo people is composed of cured fern fibers and willow reed in natural colors of red-brown, black, and light tan. The quality of technique, design, and form varies from weaver to weaver, but it has been universally acknowledged that Datsolalee combined these qualities to a superlative degree. Her sense of design, coupled with exceptional technical skill, created works of art which are still prized as some of the loveliest treasures of human handicraft. One of her most famous baskets, to which she applied the title, "Myriads of Stars Shine Over the Graves of Our Ancestors," contains 56,590 stitches—something over 36 stitches to the inch—and required more than a year to weave.

While some of the titles of these baskets sound fanciful, the fact remains that the geometrical designs incorporated into them reflected her view of tribal history and life, together with a conscious effort to record something of her own involvement with her art. Many artists have equaled her technical skill, or come very close to it; very few have taken their art as seriously, in a definite desire to develop it to its greatest potential. This is the more surprising when it is realized that at the crest of Washo basket weaving, the tribe became involved in a disastrous war with the Paiute in 1851; one of the penalties imposed by the victors was a prohibition on Washo basket weaving, in order to improve the income of the Paiute basket weavers.

In the 1860s, Dabuda had become associated with a Dr. S. L. Lee of Carson City. Out of this friendship and patronage came the name by which she was known for the rest of her life—Datsolalee. In 1888 she married a Washo man, Charley Keyser (or Kaiser), and took the name Louisa. But by 1895, her financial situation had become critical—as it had for most of the Washo, still under the Paiute yoke; without basketry, there was nothing they had to offer for sale or in trade. In desperation, Datsolalee took a few glass bottles which she had covered with basketry, to Abram Cohn, proprietor of The Emporium, a clothing store in Carson City. He and his wife were modest basket collectors, and immediately recognized the fine quality of her work. But more importantly, they had lamented the decline in fine Washo basketry, and were astonished to find that some of the women had kept the art alive over the almost half-century of prohibition. They bought all of her baskets, and urged her to produce other types, all of which they guaranteed to purchase.

From then on, her entire output seems to have been handled by Cohn, who fortunately kept a remarkable written catalog of her work—a listing involving 120 objects. It is quite true that she may have made and sold a few objects to other collectors, but the total number of baskets she is known to have produced in her lifetime seems to have been between 275 and 310; the uncertainty lies in the fact that a few baskets, so recorded, may have been made by other weavers. Of the so-called "great treasures," the unusually large and well made pieces, she is recorded as having woven approximately 40. One of the "great treasures" which was started on March 26, 1916 was completed almost exactly one year later; as an indication of the value which collectors placed on her artistry, it sold for $10,000 in 1930.

Datsolalee was a large woman physically; weighing well over 250 pounds, with plump physique and large rounded fingers, she was nevertheless capable of interweaving her work with incredibly minute stitches, pulling them tightly into the coiling. For tools she used only a piece of sharp stone or glass, a bone or iron awl, her teeth, and her fingers.

Few basket-weaving artists have enjoyed the recognition by name and reputation as did Datsolalee; in this she shares prominence with some of the painters, sculptors, and silversmiths of America. In achieving such recognition, she also exalted her art, and her masterpieces are to be found today throughout the world in public and private collections. Although she was almost blind in her old age, Datsolalee continued to work until she died at Carson City, Nevada on December 6, 1925 at the age of 90. She was buried in the Stewart School Cemetery, Nevada.

Angel DeCora Dietz (ca. 1871–1919)

Hinookmahiwi-kilinaka, "Fleecy Cloud Floating Into Place," also known as "The Word Carrier," was a Winnebago artist who became influential in the early years of the 20th century in Indian art and affairs. She was born on the Winnebago Reservation in Nebraska on May 3, 1871. Her mother was a member of the LaMère family; her father was David DeCora (Hagasilikaw), a descendant of the famous Dakaury family who traced their lineage back to a French settler, Sabrevois DesCarris. Following the death of her parents, the young girl was raised by the LaMère family, who put her in the Reservation School in Santee, and at the age of 12 sent her to Hampton Institute from which she graduated in 1891. She later studied in the art departments at Smith College and Drexel Institute, where she studied with Dwight Tryon and Howard Pyle, famed illustrators of the day. Pyle recognized her talent and made it possible for her to attend the Boston Museum of Fine Arts School.

Angel DeCora Dietz (1871–1919)
(*"The Southern Workman"*)

Following this experience, Angel set up her own studio in New York City, illustrating many books, and lecturing on Indian problems. In 1906, U.S. Indian Commissioner Francis E. Leupp offered her the new position as head of the Art Department at Carlisle Indian School in Pennsylvania, where she introduced the then-new philosophy of using Indian design. She enthusiatically accepted, and was at Carlisle for nine years, during which time she met William Dietz (Wicahpi Isnala, "Lone Star") a Sioux teacher whom she married in 1908; also an artist, the two collaborated for some time on Carlisle projects.

The two became extremely active in Indian affairs and activities. Angel also worked with Gertrude Bonnin (Zitkala-sa) for many years, illustrating her books and collaborating in the many interests the two women held jointly in improving Indian conditions. She met President Roosevelt and tried to interest him in the problems facing the Native American, and became a well-known lecturer and protagonist in the Indian movement of the day. With the outbreak of World War I, she worked at the New York State Museum in Albany, replacing a draftsman who had enlisted. In 1918 her marriage ended, and following a divorce, she returned to New York City after the War ended, where she renewed her art work and interest in Indian needs. She was stricken by influenza during the great flu epidemic and died in New York City on February 6, 1919, bringing a premature end to one of the major early influences on American Indian art.

Dekanawida (1550?–1600?)

Also Deganawidah, "Two Rivers Flowing Together," an Iroquois prophet known primarily through legend as the great leader who, with Hiawatha, founded the League of the Iroquois. The exact dates of his life are not known, although he seems to have been active during

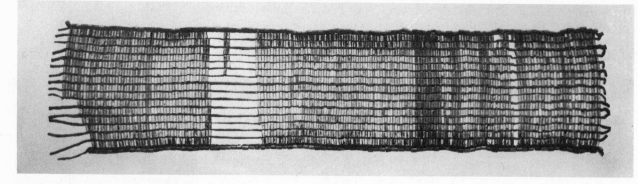

The Great White Belt of Dekanawida;
Huron
(*Museum of the American Indian*)

the middle or last half of the 16th century. He was reputedly one of seven brothers born near Kingston, Ontario, to Huron parents. Though much of what is known of his life is mythical, there seems no question that he actually existed. According to legend, his mother was told in a vision that the new baby should be called Master of Life, and that he would indirectly cause the ruin of her people. The mother and grandmother thereupon tried three times to drown the ill-omened baby in the icy water, but each effort failed.

When he grew up, he left his family and went south to carry out his mission among the Iroquois. There are many different versions of his meeting with Hiawatha; in any case the two men united in an effort to bring together in a great confederation the Oneida, Cayuga, Onondaga, Seneca, and Mohawk. In this effort, Dekanawida, who is said to have had a serious speech impediment, was the silent (although certainly dominant) partner; Hiawatha became the principal spokesman and diplomat who actually put the union into effect. Dekanawida also tried to bring the Erie and neutral tribes into the League. They were more friendly toward his Huron peoples than were most of the other Iroquois; indeed, after his death, the united Iroquois fulfilled the ancient prophecy by attacking and destroying the Huron nation.

The Iroquois Confederacy was an attempt to bring peace to all the tribes in the area of what is now upper New York State. As the code of the League said, "I, Dekanawida and the Confederate Chiefs, now uproot the tallest pine tree and into the cavity thereby made we cast all weapons of war . . . we bury them from sight and we plant again the tree. Thus is The Great Peace established." And thus, too, were created the Pine Tree Chiefs, of whom Dekanawida was one.

The League was completely successful, lasting into the 19th century; being essentially democratic, and one of the few political entities in which women had a major voice—the hereditary chiefs were nominated by the matrons and elected by the village—it remained closer to the aspirations of its members than did many other regimes. The major credit for establishing this unique, sophisticated, political system must go to Dekanawida.

Dekanisora (ca. 1650–1730)

Also Dekanisoura, Dekanasourie, an Onondaga chief and noted orator who participated in many conferences and treaties with French and English colonial authorities. His birth and origin are not known, but he came to notice in 1682 when he visited the explorer Pierre Charlevoix as a member of the Iroquois ambassadors meeting with the French at Montreal.

In 1688, en route to a later meeting with the French, he and his party were captured by Adario, a Tionantati chief bent upon creating trouble between the Iroquois and the French. He claimed that they had instructed him to effect the kidnapping, and then released Dekanisora in a gesture of generosity and friendship.

Apparently the ruse worked, for Dekanisora was involved in later hostilities between the two peoples, going to Albany in 1726 to participate in an extended conference with the Whites, and died there about 1730, while conducting treaty negotiations.

Dekanisora is generally regarded as having been selected by the Iroquois as their speaking representative due to his oratorical talents, as well as his fluent command of French, English, and several Iroquois dialects.

Carved Wooden False Face Mask;
Onondaga
(*Museum of the American Indian*)

Delaware Prophet (ca. 1725–ca. 1775)

Neolin, the "Enlightened One," was an important Delaware religious leader in the mid-18th century, who lived most of his life in the vicinity of Lake Erie. Little is known of his early life; he first came into prominence around 1760, during the formative years of Pontiac's efforts to unify the tribes against the Whites.

Like many Indian prophets, he had a mystical experience which had profound results. He had journeyed to Heaven, he said, and had met with the Master of Life. Somewhat like the Hebrew prophet Moses, he was given a written prayer and laws to bring back to his people. In the beginning, according to Neolin, life was good; the Indians had lived in harmony with nature until the White man arrived. Then it became difficult for the Indians not only to make a good life upon the earth, but also to move along the pathway to Heaven. The Europeans had brought so many bad influences and evil ways to North America that it was almost impossible to live according to the ancient laws.

The Prophet's prescription for salvation was twofold. First, there must be a renunciation of all White influences, customs, and products—especially liquor, and there must be no trade with the invaders. Second, there must be a return to the traditional ways, but such evil practices as war dances and medicine-making must be shunned. The essence of his message was a kind of Puritanism and self-denial that struck a responsive chord among many Indians who were disturbed by the rapid, and seemingly irresistible, spread of White influence among the tribes. He carried with him a map of the soul's progress from birth to death to Heaven; and he taught the lessons of this new preaching throughout the Delaware Indian territory. Like Kenakuk and some other Indian holy men, he devised a prayer stick for his followers to use.

He also predicted that there would be a great war against the Whites—a revelation which bore tremendous fruit. One of his converts was Pontiac, who felt his purposes were greatly strengthened by this religious support; incorporating the work of the Delaware Prophet into his own call for action, he was able to increase the number of his followers, and the prophecy was fulfilled with the coordinated attack upon the British forts along the frontier in 1763.

Although Neolin had promised that the Master of Life would help the Indian drive out the White, this did not happen. Defeated, Pontiac retired from active battle, and was murdered shortly thereafter. The Delaware Prophet, suffering the oblivion which comes to all prophets whose claims fail, disappeared from history, and little more is known of him after about 1770. He is important as one of the several major religious leaders in the rearguard action to preserve traditional customs against the ravages of the onrushing tide of White settlement.

Ella Carla Deloria (1888–1971)
(*Ella C. Deloria Project; Agnes Picotte*)

Ella Carla Deloria (1888–1971)

Anpetu Wastéwin, from *anpetu* "day," *wasté* "good," *win* "woman," was a Yankton Sioux scholar, interpreter, and lecturer who became a nationally famous linguist and ethnologist. She was born January 3, 1888 at Wakpala, South Dakota, the daughter of Reverend and Mrs. Philip Deloria (Tipi Sapa). Her father was an influential Episcopal clergyman who was well known throughout the Plains Indian community in his own right.

Ella attended local schools, then went on to Oberlin College and Columbia University, where she graduated with the B.S. degree in 1915. After graduation she taught school for a brief period, and then became the national Health Education Secretary of Indian Schools conducted by the YWCA. In 1929 she returned to Columbia to begin working with Dr. Franz Boas on a study of the Siouan language; they were coauthors of two major technical studies of Dakota grammar.

Her first book, *Dakota Texts*, published in 1932, is still the primary authority on the subject. During this period she wrote for many periodicals, scholarly journals, and lectured widely on Sioux ethnology. In 1944 her book *Speaking of Indians* appeared, intended primarily for the use of church groups in their missionary work, and included an interest in Indian culture and customs. Her background in religious work, which she inherited from her parents, was always a major influence in her professional and personal life. In that same year, she was invited to present a major lecture for the American Philosophical Society in Philadelphia—the same organization which had also supported her studies of Dakota language and social customs.

In later years, Ella Deloria devoted her time to writing, lecturing, and mission school work, most particularly in efforts to record the Dakota language in its most complete form so that it would not join the host of other Native American tongues which have so tragically disappeared into oblivion. From 1955–1958 she was the principal of St. Elizabeth's School at Wakpala, but returned again to her major interest—linguistics—to which she devoted her full energies until she died of pneumonia at the Tripp Nursing Home in Vermillion, South Dakota on February 12, 1971. She left a great archive of Siouan language notes, ethnological observations, and a legacy of devotion to her people which was formalized as the Ella C. Deloria Project at the

University of South Dakota, as an ongoing effort to preserve the culture of the Dakota people.

Henry Chee Dodge (1860–1947)

Henry Chee Dodge (1860–1947)
(*Museum of Northern Arizona; Fronske Photo*)

Chee Dodge, "The Interpreter," from his Navajo name Adits'aii, literally, "one who hears and understands," or Ashkihih Diitsi, "Boy Interpreter," was one of the best known contemporary Navajo leaders. He was born at Fort Defiance, Arizona on February 22, 1860; his mother was Bisnayanchi, a Navajo-Jémez woman of the Coyote Pass clan; his father was Juan Anea, or Anaya (some say Cocinas, or Cosonisas), known as *Gohsinahsu*, the Mexican silversmith and interpreter for Captain Henry Linn Dodge, the Indian Agent to the Navajo. Following the death of his father in 1862, Bisnayanchi named her son after Captain Dodge; as a youth he was commonly called *Kilchii*, Red Boy, whence the common name Chee. He came to know Kit Carson, and when the latter was retained to aid the U.S. Army in rounding up the Indian people for transportation to Bosque Redondo (Fort Sumner), Bisnayanchi fled to the Hopi country for food, and to escape the troops. She died shortly thereafter, and the orphaned Chee wandered from family to family until he was eventually taken in.

From the age of four to about eight years of age, Kilchee and his adopted family were at Bosque Redondo; he was eventually adopted by Perry H. Williams, an Agency employee who taught him English. With an education, he was able to qualify as the official Navajo interpreter. His fluency with languages and his diplomatic skills served him well; on April 19, 1884, he became the political successor to the great war chief Manuelito, and was appointed "tribal chief" by Superintendent of Indian Affairs Dennis M. Riordan. In 1884 he went to Washington, where he met President Chester A. Arthur. He also recognized the importance of Navajo crafts, and sponsored Atsidi Sani, the first influential silversmith. Around 1890, he took his accumulated savings and invested in a trading post and sheep ranch. He was successful in both ventures; and became one of the area's leading, as well as wealthiest, citizens. He built his home *Tso Tsela*, "Stars Lying Down," not far from Crystal, New Mexico where he lived for the rest of his life.

In 1923 Chee Dodge was the popular choice as the first Chairman of the newly formed Navajo Tribal Council, which had been established to represent and protect the tribe's interests, not only with the U.S. Government, but also with the several corporations that were making investments in the area. He stepped down in 1928, but kept a strong interest in tribal affairs. In 1934 he and other Navajo were forced to dispose of over one-half of their livestock due to a program initiated by the Bureau of Indian Affairs, asserting that the reservation was being overgrazed. In the violence which followed this drastic program, many Indian sheep owners were jailed.

The grim irony of this penalty for success—the slaughtering of healthy flocks of sheep, and herds of horses and cattle which were

Classic "Chief's Blanket"; Navajo
(*Museum of the American Indian*)

raised from a few head of sheep, horses, and cattle in 1868 to the thousands of animals to be seen everywhere on the reservation in the mid-1930s—was not lost on Chee Dodge, but there was nothing to be done. Animals were killed by the hundreds, and the shock of this animal slaughtering still remains vivid to the Navajo.

In 1942, Chee Dodge was elected tribal Chairman for another term; although he was now an old man, he continued to labor for his people, and journeyed many times to Washington to plead their cause. He was reelected in 1946, but was never able to take office. He had contracted pneumonia, and died on January 7, 1947 in the hospital at Ganado, Arizona at the age of 87, a respected and admired figure known throughout the southwest. He was buried at Fort Defiance.

He had four wives: Adzaan Tsinajinnie, whom he divorced to marry both Nanabah and her younger sister; following Nanabah's death he married K'eehabah. Of five children, one girl died; the others—Tom, Ben, Mary and Annie—are well-known prominent people in the Navajo tribe today.

Dohasan (ca. 1805–1866)

Also Dohá, Tohausen, or Tohosa, from *dohăsan*, "Little Bluff," or *dohăte*, "Bluff," was an important Kiowa leader during the mid-19th century. The name actually was applied to several Kiowa leaders—father, son, and nephew. After a band of Kiowa warriors led by Adate was defeated and massacred in 1833 by the Osage, Dohasan (the son) was selected to replace the disgraced and deposed chief. One of his first efforts was to establish peace between the two tribes.

In a short time, he built the strength of the tribe back to a position of key importance in the Southern Plains, and he proved to be such a successful leader that the name became a hereditary title among the people. In 1862, the Indian Agent met with the Kiowa, Comanche, Arapaho, and other groups at the Arkansas River to disperse treaty annuities; provoked by his inability to stop the raiding parties, the Agent threatened to punish the Indians. Dohasan listened to him, and then exploded: "The White man is a fool . . . there are three chiefs—the White chief, the Spanish chief, and myself. The Spanish chief and myself are men. We do bad toward each other sometimes—stealing horses and talking scalps—but we do not get mad and act the fool. The White chief is a child, and like a child, gets mad quick. . . ."

In 1840, after a treaty was signed granting Americans safe passage through Kiowa territory, the travelers brought smallpox to the Indians, and in 1849 a devastating cholera epidemic swept through the country. The Kiowa had little natural immunity to these foreign diseases, and thousands of people lost their lives. In addition to this catastrophe, Dohasan and his warriors became increasingly opposed to the growing flood of Whites going through their hunting grounds, and in the 1840s they mounted many raids against the intruders.

Dohasan (the Younger) and his Wife
Amkima, 1893
(*Smithsonian Institution, National Anthropological Archives*)

The Army was called in to protect the citizens, and in 1853 Dohasan signed the Treaty of Fort Atkinson. In return for an annuity of $18,000, the Kiowa agreed not to take up arms against either the Mexicans or the Americans. But custom, and the temptation offered by all the richly laden wagon trains coming through—as well as the resentment the Indians felt at being pushed off their lands—proved too strong, and the raids continued. Many times, Dohasan seemed to regard them as simply his tribe's private business. As he said at one council, ". . . When my young men, to keep their women and children from starving, take from the White man passing through our country, killing and driving away our buffalo, a cup of sugar or coffee, the White chief is angry and threatens to send his soldiers. I have looked for them for a long time, but they have not come. He is a coward. His heart is a woman's. I have spoken. Tell the great chief what I have said."

Fools or not, the Americans wanted the Kiowa kept to strictly limited areas, and in 1865, Dohasan agreed to the Treaty of the Little Arkansas, by which the Kiowa accepted a reservation in the area of the present-day Oklahoma panhandle. Although Dohasan believed it was outrageous that foreigners should come in and tell his tribe what to do in their own territory, he was now too old and too weary—and too well aware of Army power—to do more than make a token protest. He died on the reservation in 1866 and was succeeded by Lone Wolf (Guipago).

Edward Pasqual Dozier (1916–1971)

Edward Pasqual Dozier (1916–1971)
(*Arizona State Museum*)

Awa Tside, "Cattail Bird," was one of the earliest scholars of Indian blood to make his way into the forefront of modern anthropology as an outstanding teacher, scholar, and writer. He was born at Santa Clara Pueblo on April 23, 1916, son of Thomas Sublette Dozier, of Anglo-Hispano descent, and Leocadia Gutiérrez, a Santa Clara woman. By the age of 12, the young boy was fluent in Tewa, Spanish, and English—languages which were to serve him well in later life.

He attended BIA government school and St. Michaels, in Santa Fe, New Mexico. In 1930 he went to the University of New Mexico, intending to study medicine; there he became acquainted with Dr. W. W. Hill, who saw in the young man an ideal assistant and interpreter. Out of this relationship came a major change in his goal, and Dozier transferred to anthropology as his life work.

His education was interrupted by World War II, and he served in the Air Force Pacific theater, returning to the University of New Mexico after the war, where he earned the B.A. and M.A. degrees at the University in 1946–1949, specializing in Pueblo linguistic studies. In 1952 he received the Ph.D. degree from the University of California at Los Angeles. His dissertation concerned the Tewa people who had migrated to Arizona in the late 17th–18th centuries and moved into the Hopi pueblo, where they subsequently developed a unique community. This subject remained a favorite research interest throughout his life.

Dozier's first teaching position was at the University of Oregon, after which he received a Wenner-Gren Fellowship; he then taught for several years, and was invited to the University of Arizona in 1961, where he became one of the most popular anthropology teachers. Just prior to this assignment he had undertaken field work in the Philippines, as something of a "change of pace," looking for similarities and differences in the lifeways of the Kalinga people of Luzón. Nine years later he returned to restudy their culture, and taught at the University of the Philippines; unfortunately, it was during a time of considerable unrest in Mindanao, and this seriously handicapped his research, although he saw a great deal of militant activism at first hand.

He had accepted an invitation to join the faculty at the University of Minnesota, but was prevented from joining due to a brain tumor which was successfully operated upon. He subsequently succumbed to a heart attack in Tucson, on May 2, 1971. He was married twice: his first wife was Claire Butler, a BIA staff member, in Washington, D.C., by whom he had a daughter, Wanda; this marriage ended in divorce. While at the University of New Mexico, he married Marianne Fink, a psychologist, who survived him with their two children, Miguel and Anya.

Dr. Dozier was a gregarious, generous person, with wide interests and enthusiasms. Professionally, he was an intense man, deeply involved in Indian affairs. His cultural background gave him an unusual combination and understanding of Indian, Anglo, and Hispano matters which enabled him to move effectively into these cultures with equal ease. He was wholly objective in his judgments of each of the three peoples, yet he was undoubtedly most deeply concerned with Pueblo problems. Although he had already made major contributions to Amerindian studies, and many honors had come to him, there is no question but that he would have become one of the nation's major anthropological scholars had his life not been so tragically cut short.

Dragging Canoe (ca. 1730–1792)

Tsíyu-gunsíni, from *tsíyi*, "canoe," and *gunsíni*, "he is dragging it," also Tsungunsini, Cheucunsene, or Kunmesee, was a Cherokee leader who violently opposed the White man's expansion into Indian lands. Born about 1730 at Running Water village (or Natchez Town), on the Tennessee River, his father was the celebrated Chief Attakulla-kulla; his mother was a Cherokee woman whose name is unknown. In 1775 the Cherokee had sold all of what is now Kentucky and part of Tennessee; furious, Dragging Canoe prophetically declared that, "Finally, the whole country which the Cherokee and his fathers have for so long occupied, will be demanded; and the remnant of the *Ani-Yunwiya*, "The Real People," once so great and formidable, will be obliged to seek refuge in some distant wilderness . . . until they again behold the advancing banners of the same greedy host. . . ." He ended his speech by promising, "You will find the settlement of this land dark and bloody."

This huge land sale took place on the eve of the American Revolution. Although most of the Cherokee did not choose sides in that conflict, Dragging Canoe cast his lot with the British. They provided guns and ammunition to him and to his warriors, who used Chickamauga Creek as a base from which to attack settlers in Tennessee. In 1782 the Cherokee were driven out of this region and moved down river to the Chickamauga Lower Towns. He established his own home, *Mialaquo*, near Chickamauga, Tennessee.

The Cherokee people had signed the Treaty of Hopewell in 1785, which set up formal boundaries for the Cherokee Nation and abandoned all lands outside this area. By that treaty, no White settlers could occupy any lands allotted to the Indians; but when they began to encroach upon the reserved areas, the government did nothing to prevent this violation of the agreement. Dragging Canoe tried to enforce the restriction by making constant raids on settlers and land speculators.

The friction of these attacks, and the bloodshed which resulted, caused both sides to attempt to find a peaceful settlement in the Treaty of Halston in 1791. This treaty reaffirmed the United States' guarantees of Cherokee claims and provided for additional compensation for Indian losses by way of a small annual stipend and the turning over to them of "useful implements of husbandry," which would allow them to advance their goal of developing a viable agricultural economy.

But the squatters and the land grabbers kept coming. Dragging Canoe died at Running Water, Tennessee on March 1, 1792, still fighting the invasion. Over the next four decades treaties were made and broken, until finally in 1838 the Cherokee nation was forced to "remove" to Indian Territory in Oklahoma over the appalling "Trail of Tears," an episode which still haunts American history. Thus the sad prophecy of Dragging Canoe was fulfilled: that his people would have to "seek refuge in some distant wilderness," and that the settlement of Kentucky would indeed prove to be a "dark and bloody ground."

Dull Knife (1810–1883)
(*Oklahoma Historical Society*)

Dull Knife (ca. 1810–ca. 1883)

Tamela Pashme, was a nickname given him by the Sioux, and by which he was most commonly known. It was applied following a combat he had with an enemy who was carrying a buffalo-hide shield. His knife would not pierce the tough hide; and although he was badly wounded, he won the battle. He was born about 1810 on the Rosebud River, in Montana, and given the name Wahiev (also Wo-hiev), meaning "Morning Star."

Dull Knife was the leader with Little Wolf of the epic 1500-mile journey of the Northern Cheyenne from their exile in Indian Territory back to their northern homeland. He became a noted warrior and a respected chief who remained at peace with the Whites during most of his life. In 1851 the Cheyenne had signed a treaty ceding their rights to east–west routes through their territory. Although the United States did not live up to some of its pledges made in that treaty, the Indians did not take to the warpath until 1865, following the massacre of Black Kettle's villages by forces led by Colonel Chivington the previous year. In 1868 Dull Knife signed the Treaty of Fort Laramie, and for a few years there was a time of fitful peace.

The settlers kept coming into and through the Plains country, however, and there were increasing raids and conflicts. The Cheyenne were ordered to settle on the Red Cloud Reservation—Sioux territory which offered no welcome and little food. The Cheyenne situation could only go from bad to worse; although historians disagree over whether the Cheyenne participated on the side of the Sioux in the War of 1876, there is general consensus that in the Army's reaction to Custer's disastrous defeat on the Little Bighorn, the Cheyenne were savagely attacked. They lost hundreds of their ponies and suffered the destruction of most of their village. Most of Dull Knife's own people escaped the attack, but they soon surrendered rather than face a winter on the open prairies.

In spite of a promise that they would be located on a reservation in their own homeland in the north, they were soon shipped south to Indian Territory. In the White view, the Northern Cheyenne were supposed to rejoin the Southern branch of the tribe, and become a peaceful agricultural people—thereby staying out of the White man's way. But once they had sampled the desolate Indian Territory countryside, most of the Northern Cheyenne hated it and resolved to escape. In September 1878, led by Dull Knife and Little Wolf, a desperately homesick band of about 300 Cheyenne men, women, and children started north toward home.

Initially, the Army was confident that they would almost immediately capture the refugees; but the Indians were able to elude their pursuers, living off food and horses taken from settlers. Eventually, the Army had almost 10,000 soldiers on the trail of the elusive Cheyenne. As they neared their home country, a split developed in the group. Dull Knife and his people pressed on in an attempt to reach the Sioux at Red Cloud Agency; Little Wolf persuaded his followers to remain where they were, in hiding from the troops that now were on all sides. Dull Knife still had faith in the "good" soldiers—those who had been his friends and who had promised him a reservation in the north; he felt that if he could find them, they would see to it that the Cheyenne were given a fair deal.

Most of Dull Knife's band were captured and imprisoned at Fort Robinson, Nebraska, prior to resettlement back at the Indian Territory area assigned to them. In a desperate move borne of months of hardship, disillusionment at the White man's failure to keep his word, and uncertainty as to their future, they made one last attempt to reach home. In a carefully synchronized effort, many Cheyenne people, men as well as women, lost their lives in an escape from the fort, but Dull Knife managed to elude the soldiers and escape. He and some others reached the Sioux and were given refuge.

The Army soon caught up with them, but by that time common sense interposed, and a decision was made: the Northern Cheyenne were to have their own reservation in the Rosebud Valley. Dull Knife died in 1883 and was buried on the high ground of his native land. He had one son, Bull Hump.

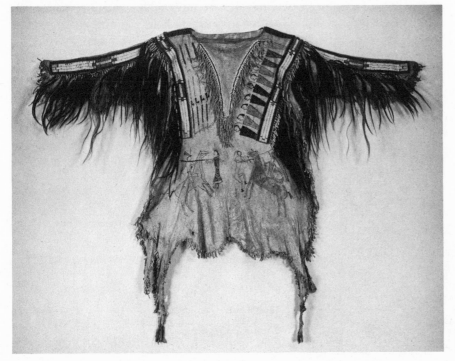

Painted War Shirt; Cheyenne
(*Museum of the American Indian*)

Charles Alexander Eastman (1858-1939)
(*Smithsonian Institution, National Anthropological Archives*)

Charles Alexander Eastman
(1858–1939)

Ohiyesa, "the Winner," a famed Santee Sioux physician and author, served his own people and the United States during a distinguished and varied career. He was born in 1858 in Redwood Falls, Minnesota, the son of Jacob Eastman, "Lightning," a Santee Sioux, and Mary, a half-blood Sioux. His childhood name was Hakadah, "the Last One"; he knew little about the White man until he was 15 years of age. Encouraged by his father to seek an education, he attended mission schools and Beloit College before going east to Dartmouth College, where he obtained the B.S. degree in 1887. He subsequently attended Boston University, graduating in 1890 with one of the first M.D. degrees granted to an Indian student.

His first position was that of physician at the Pine Ridge Agency, South Dakota, where he treated the victims of the massacre at Wounded Knee. Shocked by what he saw, he became determined to improve the life of the Indian people. As traveling secretary for the Young Men's Christian Association he established 32 Indian YMCA groups throughout the country. He then went to Washington, D.C., as a representative of the Santee Sioux, pleading their claims before the courts and in Congress.

During these early years, he also found the time to write, eventually producing nine books, including *Indian Boyhood* and *The Soul of the Indian*. His work contributed greatly to a better understanding of the Sioux by Whites who were disturbed over the obvious wrongs which had been suffered by the Indian. In 1903 President Theodore Roosevelt appointed Dr. Eastman to revise Sioux allotments so that all members of the tribe would receive a fair share of the funds voted by congress. He also lectured extensively on Indian life, both in the United States and in England. He was instrumental in helping to found the Boy Scouts and the Campfire Girls of America, and remained active in Scouting for most of his life. In the 1920s he was appointed U.S. Indian Inspector, and was assigned the task of verifying the burial place of Sacajawea. He was also a member of the Secretary of the Interior's *Committee of 100*, formed to survey Indian affairs.

He married Elaine Goodale, a prominent poet of the early 20th century, by whom he had six children. In 1933 Dr. Eastman was awarded the first Indian Achievement Award. He died at his home in Detroit, Michigan on January 8, 1939, at the age of 80.

Wooden Courting Flute; Sioux
(*Museum of the American Indian*)

Charles Edensaw (1839–1924)

Also spelled Edenshaw, from Tlingit *edensaw* "glacier," or *itinsa*, "waterfall," a prosperous and talented professional Haida carver and chief of Yatza Village, on Graham Island (of the Queen Charlotte group), British Columbia, Canada. The name Edensaw, or Idansu, is attached to several important leaders, one of the most important being Albert Edward Edensaw, *Gwaigu-unithin*, the uncle of Charles. The latter was born in 1839 at Cape Ball, Graham Island, into the Stistas clan; his mother was a member of the Eagle people. His father was a Raven man of the Kwaduwawas clan; both parents were from Skidegate.

The baby was named Takayren, "Noise in the House," perhaps a reference to his powerful lungs; the family settled at Skidegate, where he grew up. Upon reaching adulthood, he was encouraged by his mother to move to Massett, following the death of the father. He did so, and a story is told of an occasion when his mother gave him a small pistol; he held it to his head, and pulled the trigger, but nothing happened. He repeated this twice more, and the gun exploded, wounding him slightly in the face. In celebration of his survival, he gave a potlatch, repeating the episode to demonstrate his near miss with death.

Young Charles was a skilled artist, and showed his talent at an early age, being greatly influenced by his uncle. He married, and shortly afterwards turned his attention to carving and silversmithing, becoming one of the few full-fledged professional artists of the region. The increasing interest in Northwest Coast Indian culture, sculptural arts, and the popularity of argillite, the black slate material found near Skidegate, gave an impetus which developed this into a unique art, and Eden-

Charles Edensaw (1839–1924)
(*National Museums of Canada*)

"The Bear Mother"; Argillite Carving of Caesarian Birth; by Charles Edenshaw
(*Museum of the American Indian*)

saw became one of the major carvers of the material. His heritage and prosperity caused him to become selected as the chief of the small village of Yatza on Graham Island; his knowledge of the iconography of the Haida people made him a greatly sought after person by visitors, anthropologists, and art collectors. This reputation gave him a pre-eminence among his people, and until his death he was easily the best known of Haida artists.

Many of his finest carvings were collected by museums and art patrons and today serve as indicia of the intricacies of Northwest Coast iconography; he did many of the model totem poles collected by John R. Swanton in 1900–1901, as well as drawings and crayon sketches made for Franz Boas a decade earlier. These provide an important key to the meanings of much of the visual symbology of Haida (and other tribes of the Northwest Coast) art. He was equally talented in metal working, and enjoyed silver crafting as much as wood carving.

Charles Edensaw had four daughters and one son; the death of the latter, Gyinawen (Robert), while still a young man, was a blow from which the father never quite recovered. He died at Masset on September 12, 1924, at the age of 85, the most highly regarded carver of the Haida people.

Eskaminzim (ca. 1825–1890)

Big Mouth, head chief of the Coyotero Apache, was a peaceful leader who was forced to violence by the actions of White settlers. The date of his birth is unknown, but was probably about 1825 in the Gila country. The background to Apache–White relations is succinctly and frankly stated in an 1871 report of the Board of Indian Commissioners to President Ulysses S. Grant: "Until about 10 years ago the Apache were the friends of the Americans. Much of the time since then, the attempt to exterminate them has been carried on, at a cost of from three to four million dollars per annum." And yet, the Apache persisted in living.

Warrior chiefs like Magnas Coloradas and Gerónimo continued their raiding parties throughout the southwest, defending their homelands. Others, like Eskaminzim and his Aravaipa group, lived peacefully as farmers and hunters. Both manufactured the proscribed *tulepah* (called *tizwin* by the Whites)—a potent brew which often provided the preliminary to trouble.

As more settlers came into the Territory, the friction increased and gave rise to greater antagonism, resulting in more and more hostile confrontations. Early in 1871, Eskaminzim and his people journeyed to the Army's old Camp Grant, near Tucson, Arizona to seek peace. Lieutenant Royal E. Whitman, a veteran officer, and the camp commander, was favorably disposed towards the Indians and tried to help them. But on April 30 a combined band of American–Mexican–Indian self-appointed vigilantes arrived, attacked the camp, murdering over 118 Apache men, women, and children—including eight members of Eskaminzim's own family. Bitterly, he abandoned his quest for peace and became an Apache raider, terrorizing the countryside. After his band killed several Whites, the United States forces pursued him actively, until, in 1874, bedraggled and recognizing the impossible situation, Eskaminzim and his band surrendered at San Carlos.

Fortunately, the Indian Agent at the time was John P. Clum, a man genuinely concerned with the welfare of the Apache people. He and Eskaminzim became friends and peace was maintained. But in September 1876, after Eskaminzim returned from a trip to Washington with Clum, trouble again broke out between settlers and Indians. Taza, the son of Cochise, had died in Washington from pneumonia while on the trip, and Eskaminzim was blamed by Naiche, the brother, for not properly taking care of Taza. In an effort to keep out of fighting, and to avoid further friction with the Chiricahua Apache, Eskaminzim moved off the reservation to a ranch.

Caught between the anger of the Apache clan and the settlers intent upon driving all Apache people out of the region, Eskaminzim continued to exhort his people to stay out of trouble. But as the unrest continued, many on both sides found the aging chief a convenient scapegoat, and eventually a band of local citizenry destroyed his home. He fled back to the reservation, but eventually returned to rebuild his ranch, helped by some of his Army friends. But the suspicions of the White settlers would not die out, and he was soon arrested and sent to prison in Arkansas. In 1889 he returned home again, and disappointed and dejected, died at the San Carlos Agency, Arizona, in 1890. His wife, the daughter of Chief Santos, survived him.

Eskaminzim (1825–1890)
(*Smithsonian Institution, National Anthropological Archives*)

Flat Mouth (1774–1860)

Eshkebugecoshe (also Eskeebucecose, Aishkebogekoshe, or Ashkebuggecoash), "Flat Mouth" or "Wide Mouth," was an important Chippewa chief during the first half of the 19th century, when the young American nation was establishing itself in the eastern United States. The French knew him as Guelle Plat. He was born in 1774 into the Awausee clan on the Plains west of the Red River. His father was Wasonaunequa (Yellow Hair), a notorious medicine man who was widely feared by the people because many of his opponents met untimely deaths—by witchery, some said; others claimed they had been poisoned. Poisoning was a common practice at the time, and was the reason for the disappearance of many Indians around the Great Lakes area. The fear in which he was held gave Wasonaunequa a power which made him, in essence, a village chief, although he did not have the hereditary right to such a role.

In his youth, Flat Mouth traveled widely, visiting many other tribes, and even living for some time among the Cree, Hidatsa, and Assiniboin peoples—experiences which served him well in later life. At the

Evil Medicine Effigy; Chippewa
(*Museum of the American Indian*)

death of his father, Flat Mouth became a chief of the Pillager Chippewa band, but he was quite different from his father. Flat Mouth was friendly to the Whites throughout his lifetime, and yet was able to retain the loyalty and respect of the other Indian people, most of whom did not share his feelings.

When the Shawnee prophet Tenskwátawa visited his village at Leech Lake, his message apparently made a great impression upon Flat Mouth, who followed his prophecies closely, and put a stop to some of the more reprehensible practices current among the Chippewa, including the wide use of poison. He was one of the major war leaders when the warfare broke out against the Sioux, which eventually resulted in the Sioux being driven from the headwaters of the Mississippi River out onto the Plains. Although his own village at Leech Lake, Minnesota was leveled, he still was able to attract enough warriors to his side to keep it functioning, as new structures were built on the same location.

In 1812, the British Indian Agent visited the village in an effort to enlist the support of the Pillager band. Flat Mouth felt that wisdom dictated continuing his policy of peaceful relations with the Americans, and returned the proffered wampum belts, saying that just as he would not want the British to interfere in his wars, he would not interfere in their war.

During the War of 1812, his people remained neutral, or active supporters of the Americans, depending upon local circumstances. Later, they were able to retain most of their lands, and are one of the few Indian nations east of the Mississippi River who still live on their own homelands—due in no small part to the role played so carefully by Flat Mouth. He died at Leech Lake around 1860.

Stephen Foreman (1807-1881)

A mixed-bood Cherokee leader, educator, and Presbyterian clergyman who was a staunch supporter of Chief John Ross during the difficult days of forced removal from Georgia and resettlement in Indian Territory. He was born October 22, 1807 to Anthony Foreman, a Scotchman, and Elizabeth Gurdaygee, a Cherokee woman, at Rome, Georgia. The Foremans later moved to Cleveland, Tennessee where he started his education; but the father died shortly after their survival, and the large family—there were 12 children—was too poor to continue the luxury of education. Fortunately, young Stephen was rescued by the missionary to the Cherokees, Reverend Samuel Worcester, at New Echota, Georgia, who saw to his educational needs.

Foreman went on to study at the College of Richmond, in Virginia, and at the Princeton Theological Seminary, where he graduated and received authorization to preach by the Tennessee Presbytery in September 1835. He preached for a time at Brainard Mission. His graduation from the Seminary came just at the time the Georgia authorities and the U.S. Government were applying tremendous pressures on the Cherokee to surrender their lands east of the Mississippi in exchange for territory in the west.

Although he believed that the White man's greed for land was immoral and completely unscrupulous, he did not forsake his religious faith, and continued to work as an active missionary to the Cherokee and cooperated with Worcester in the translation of several books of the *Bible*. He was gifted linguistically, serving as associate editor of the *Cherokee Phoenix* for many years, and later provided translations for the *Cherokee Advocate*. In 1838 he was imprisoned for a brief period when the U.S. Army was crushing the last Cherokee resistance to removal. Shortly afterwards, along with Jesse Bushyhead, Stephen Foreman led one of the last detachments of Indians west, and in 1841 he organized the Cherokee Nation's Public School system, becoming their first superintendent of public instruction. He remained closely allied with Chief John Ross who made every effort to secure the best possible treatment for the Cherokee people, short of going to war.

His abilities caused him to be elected to the Supreme Court of the Cherokee Nation on October 11, 1844 and from 1847–1855 he was the Executive Councilor of the tribe. This prominence placed him in a position of major influence, and in 1846 he, with several other leaders, petitioned Washington for the redress of past wrongs, saying, "We have not used the language of humble supplicants, but that of men who know their rights, however unable they may be to maintain them—of men conscious of having suffered great wrongs, and apprehending still greater [wrongs] which have been threatened."

During the Civil War years, Stephen Foreman spent much of his time in Texas, vigorously pursuing his missionary work. When he returned to Indian Territory, he purchased the former home of Elias Boudinot, and rebuilt it into "The Church in the Woods," creating a house of worship which he used as the basis for his religious work during the rest of his life.

He married twice: to Sarah Watkins Riley, by whom he had ten children; following her death, he married Ruth Riley Candy, who bore him four more children. He died at Park Hill, Indian Territory on December 8, 1881 at the age of 74, and was buried at the Park Hill Cemetery.

Stephen Foreman (1807–1881)
(*Oklahoma Historical Society*)

Herbert Burwell Fowler
(1919–1977)

Ohiyesa, "The Winner," a Santee Sioux psychiatrist whose work in the field of Indian medicine earned him widespread recognition. He was born in Cheyenne, Wyoming on April 14, 1919, the son of Herbert B. Fowler, Sr., and Mary Eastman, a half-blooded Sioux woman. He was educated in local schools, then attended the University of Wyoming, where he obtained the B.S. degree in 1942. He continued his education at the University of Michigan, where he gained the M.D. degree in Medicine and Surgery in 1946.

Herbert Burwell Fowler (1919-1977)
(*Julia Hanson Fowler*)

Following a period of internship at Harper Hospital in Detroit, Dr. Fowler was a resident physician at the University of Utah College of Medicine from 1957–1962. During that period of service, he traveled to Europe to study various psychiatric installations for the National Institute of Mental Health. He was active throughout his life in mental health programs, specializing in the field of American Indian needs.

The clinic which he established in 1958 on the Ute Reservation in Utah was the first mental health clinic on an Indian reservation. He acted as a psychiatric consultant to many organizational and tribal groups, and became nationally recognized as an authority on the mental health problems of the Native Americans.

One of Dr. Fowler's major interests was in the expanding field of Alaskan Native problems, and in this capacity, he visited Alaska on many speaking and consulting occasions. He was deeply concerned with the relationship between Native Americans and the local police forces in those cities where the two frequently came into conflict, and many of his public-speaking engagements and professional writings reflected this concern. One of his major contributions to the subject was the textbook, *Police and the Emotionally Disturbed* (1975).

In 1975 the National Tribal Chairman's Association established the Whitecloud Center at the University of Oregon Health Sciences Center and Dr. Fowler was appointed director, a position he held until his death. He was the recipient of many fellowships and awards, including the NIMH Career Teacher Award in 1960–1962, and was named to receive the $50,000 Lenin Prize Laureate in Science in May 1977.

He did not live to participate in the award ceremony, succumbing to a massive hematoma on January 2, 1977, in Portland, Oregon at the age of 58. He left a wife, Julia M. (Hansen) Fowler, three daughters, and four sons. He was buried at the Sunset Hills Cemetery in Spokane, Washington.

Gall (1840–1895)
(*Smithsonian Institution, National Anthropological Archives*)

Gall (ca. 1840–1895)

Pizí, "Man Who Goes in the Middle," a Hunkpapa Sioux chief, was one of the major Indian field commanders at the Battle of the Little Bighorn. He was born around 1840 on the Moreau River in South Dakota; little is known of his parents, both of whom died, and the boy was raised as an orphan. He earned his name when, as a hungry youngster, he tried to eat the gall bladder of an animal for nourishment. Later in his youth he had the name Matohinsda, "Bear Shedding His Hair," but the name Pizí was the one by which he was best known throughout his life.

As a young man he took part in the many battles fought by the Dakota bands in Red Cloud's War of the 1860s. When the Treaty of 1868 was signed, Gall and many others refused to comply with the provision that all Dakota Indians return to their reservations. Sitting Bull adopted him as a younger brother, and later he became the Dakota war chief. A price was put on his head by the Army; charged with a murder he did not commit, he came into Fort Berthold to protest. He was seized, bayoneted, and left for dead. He was able to crawl away, and survived, later preying upon the Bozeman Expedition with several disastrous raids.

In 1876, Sitting Bull, Gall, and their warriors were grouped in a huge encampment on the Little Bighorn River; it was perhaps the largest single gathering of Indian forces yet seen in the Northern Plains area. On June 25, troops under General Custer and Major Reno attacked. Gall sprang into action, and turned the flank of Reno's men, forcing them to retreat. Then he and Crazy Horse surrounded Custer's cavalry and wiped them out.

Gall at first pursued Reno's detachment, but he returned to the main camp when it became apparent that the main body of the United States force was en route to the scene. The encampment broke up and the various bands began a retreat to the north. After several skirmishes with the Army, Gall, Sitting Bull, and their followers escaped into Canada. Winters there were harsh, and many became discouraged; after four years, Gall, Crow Chief, and others denounced Sitting Bull and returned to the United States where they settled at Standing Rock Reservation. In 1881 he reconciled himself to White authority and became a farmer, eventually becoming a friend of the Indian agent, James McLaughlin, who convinced him that the Dakota Indians should send their children to school.

When Sitting Bull returned from Canada in 1881, Gall opposed the policies of his erstwhile mentor, accusing him of cowardice, since he had by now come to realize the futility of any further armed resistance. It was a time of relative peace, and Gall grew to be highly regarded by Whites for his wisdom and honesty. He was appointed a judge of the Court of Indian Affairs in 1889, and in that same year he was instrumental in gaining the ratification of the last agreement with the Dakota Indians, by which the Sioux reservation was broken up into several smaller parcels, and some of the lands were ceded to the Whites.

During his last years he was an envoy to Washington, D.C., in behalf of his tribe, and enjoyed a place of considerable prestige until his death at Oak Creek, South Dakota on December 5, 1895 at the age of 54.

Long-Tailed Eagle Feather Bonnet; Sioux
(*Museum of the American Indian*)

Ganado Mucho (ca. 1809–1893)

Also Ganados Muchos, Mucho Ganado, and Hastín Totsohnii, or Tótsoni, "Big Water Man," an important Navajo headman and rancher who was a firm proponent of peace on all sides in the mid-19th century southwest. His popular name, Ganado Mucho (Spanish for "many cattle") refers to the large herds which he accumulated early in life. Two other names by which he was known are Aguas Grandes ("Big Water" in Spanish), and as a young man, Bitsoo Yeiyaa'tii,

Ganado Mucho (1809–1893)
(*Museum of New Mexico*)

Woven Wool Blanket; Navajo
(*Museum of the American Indian*)

"The Lisper," or "Tongue Talker." He was born about 1809 in the Ganado area near Klagetoh, in Arizona, into the Tótsoni (Big Water) clan. The names of his parents are not reported, although one of them was part Hopi.

The period from 1850 to 1875 in New Mexico was one of violence and turbulence. The fact that Ganado Mucho owned such large herds of cattle caused many Whites to accuse him and other Navajo of cattle theft. While there were certainly raids on cattle all during the period, he denied participating in such thefts, and there seems no evidence to contradict him. The continuing friction between Mexicans and Americans, with the Navajo caught in the middle, led Ganado Mucho to sign a treaty in 1858 along with other headmen whereby they agreed to return any stolen livestock. But the restlessness and turmoil continued, and when Major O. L. Shepherd had a Navajo flogged unjustly, in frustration at his inability to control the situation, the bitter hatred of the Navajo people against the Whites exploded.

Raid led to counterraid, and in 1859 the Navajo under Manuelito attacked Fort Defiance. Ganado Mucho was sympathetic to the attackers, but continued to counsel patience and peace; the Indian Agent at the time, Silas Kendrick, recognized the dangerous situation that was building up. He sided with the Navajo, but was helpless in the face of prejudice. Infuriated at Shepherd's one-sided attitude, he resigned in February 1860, leaving the Navajo without a supporter among the Whites.

Ganado Mucho tried to keep the peace, but the violence continued, and in 1861, Colonel Edward R. S. Canby called for a peace treaty. Manuelito attended the conference, saying that he would keep the peace as long as the Whites did, but the open antagonism of the Army against the Navajo only stirred the Ute and Mexican raiders to greater activity. Finally, in 1863, "The Rope Thrower" (Kit Carson) was dispatched to carry out a scorched-earth policy which drove most of the Navajo into hiding—or into United States forts for shelter. Ganado Mucho retreated with his people into the Black Mountain area for safety, hiding from Whites and Mexicans alike.

In the fall of 1865, seeing his small group slowly starving to death, he led them to Bosque Redondo, a desolate region southeast of Albuquerque, which had been selected for Navajo resettlement. The Civil War had reduced the number of soldiers available for protection of the confined Indians, and Utes and Mexicans made the most of their opportunity, skirmishing with impunity. On one such occasion, Ganado Mucho's son was killed, and his two daughters were kidnaped and eventually sold as slaves. But the misery and deplorable conditions suffered by the Navajo finally moved the United States to take remedial action, and in 1868 a treaty was signed allowing the surviving Indians—now numbering about 6000 wretched individuals—to return to their homeland.

The Navajo rejoiced, and for a time all was well. But White cattlemen continued to encroach on Navajo territory with virtual immunity from penalty—although Ganado Mucho and other Indian ranchers were severely punished if their herds strayed beyond the reservation boundaries. Indian Agent W. F. M. Arny became so obsessed with restricting the Navajo to the reservation area that Mormons in the area, frightened by the hostility which this caused, petitioned President Grant for Arny's removal, and in 1875 he did resign, but left a wake of ill-feeling behind him.

Despite his advancing age, Ganado Mucho never gave up the fight for fair treatment for himself and his people, although the atmosphere of distrust continued well into the 20th century. He died in his eighties, in 1893, at his home near Klagetoh, with honor and the respect of all the Navajo people.

Daniel Garakonthie (ca. 1600–1676)

From *gara kontie*, "moving sun," this early Iroquois chief was a great friend of the French settlers and missionaries in the 17th century. He was born at Onondaga, probably around 1600, and lived the usual life of his time. He first came into notice around 1654. He had been living in Montreal for some time, gaining an increasing interest in, and respect for, French customs and religion. In 1657, partly as a move toward peace, some 50 missionaries and others settled near the Onondaga village. Tension between the two races broke out in open hostility, and the missionaries were forced to flee for their lives the next year; in this effort they were probably aided by Garakonthie.

Subsequently he became an open and articulate advocate of the Whites, and in 1661 welcomed the Jesuit Father Simon LeMoyne by converting his cabin into a chapel for the missionary. He also went back and forth to Montreal several times on missions for the exchange of prisoners; it is estimated that he was responsible for the release of more than 60 captive Indians.

In 1662 he was able to check almost single-handedly the war group intent upon assassinating LeMoyne. Five years later, peace of sorts was established, and in 1669 Garakonthie was baptized a Christian in the cathedral of Quebec, taking the name Daniel. Although many of his fellow tribesmen thought him a fool, and something less than a man for his pacific support of the French, he was able to maintain his influence over them due to his superb oratorical skill.

He often undertook major missions, not only to the French, but also to the British, trying to maintain peaceful relations for his own people, as well as protecting the Whites. As he felt his own death was approaching, he held a great feast to which all Indians were invited. As a climax to the occasion, he stood up strongly and exhorted all of his people to embrace the White man's Christianity and customs, arguing that the Whites were far too many, and their war powers were too strong. He urged the Indians to reject liquor and to seek education as the key to survival. He died at Onondaga, New York in 1676, asking for a Christian burial.

Spokane Garry (1811–1892)

Spokan Garry—as he always spelled it—from *spokein*, "sun children," or perhaps "sun people" (also *spikani*, or *spokan-ee*), the Indian for whom the city of Spokane, Washington, is named. The distinction of being the first person to use the *Book of Common Prayer* for public worship in the Pacific Northwest goes to this Salish chief. He was born in 1811 near the junction of Latah Creek and the Spokane River in Washington, the son of Chief Illim Spokanee of the Central Spokane tribe.

In 1825, Governor George Simpson directed Alexander Ross to select two young Indian boys to attend the Red River Settlement (Anglican missionary) school to receive an education. The Salish and Kutenai tribes were asked to make such a choice, and each picked the son of a chief for the purpose. Both boys were then about 14 years of age; they were baptized and given the English names of Directors of the Hudson's Bay Company—Spokane Garry, for Nicholas Garry, and Kootenai Pelly, for another Director.

Four years later. Garry traveled in the Northwest, preaching to his people, and in 1830, he took four young Indian boys back to the Red River Settlement, where they were also baptized and given English names. But the next year, Kootenai Pelly died, leaving Garry to carry on his work alone. The two had been very close, and the loss of his companion had a strong impact upon Garry.

Garry was selected as chief by his people because of his educational training. He carried over to his new role as chief some of the organizational qualities which had so impressed him at Red River; he built a church and a schoolhouse, both within what is today downtown Spokane. There he taught English and agriculture, and conducted Sunday services using the *Book of Common Prayer* as a guide. At first, he was a zealous, effective preacher, and Indian people from throughout the region attended his services; but in time, he came to realize more and more that not all of the Christian message was of equal value to his people, and he became more selective and less dogmatic.

Several times he requested that the church leaders send a teacher to the community, but received no response. This lack of concern for his appeal, coupled with the eventual arrival of other White missionaries who made no effort to associate their work with him, gradually caused him to abandon his own preaching, and turn his attention instead to tribal matters. And indeed, the times had changed; settlers were moving into the Northwest in increasing numbers; the village of Spokane Falls was growing, and Indian lands were being overrun. Garry himself was driven from his home and fertile farmlands in 1888 by selfish Whites, who felt their needs overshadowed his rights. In 1890, the city of Spokane was incorporated—and, ironically, named for the very tribe whose lands had been so unceremoniously appropriated.

Spokane Garry died a bitter, impoverished old man on January 14, 1892 at his home in Indian Canyon, near Spokane. He married twice: Lucy, his first wife, died sometime after bearing him a daughter. He subsequently married Nina, by whom he had two sons and one daughter. He was buried in the Greenwood Cemetery in Spokane.

Gelelemend (ca. 1722–1811)

"The Leader," also known as Killbuck, a Delaware chief who achieved a remarkable education and put it to good use in defense of his people.

He was born about 1722 in Pennsylvania, the son of Killbuck, whose name he adopted in later years. In 1778, following the death of White Eyes, Gelelemend was selected as the chief of the Delaware people due to his reputation for wisdom and diplomatic ability. At this time he joined the Christian faith, and was baptised William Henry.

Gelelemend was always an advocate for peace with the colonists, and apparently recognized the growing strength of the Americans, for he firmly opposed war with them. In this stance, he was challenged by Hopocan, the leader of the war faction of the Delaware. The persuasive oratory of the latter finally won over most of the chiefs on the council. This forced Gelelemend to leave with a small band of followers; in recognition of his friendship, the officer in charge of the local American garrison invited Gelelemend to bring his people on to an island in the Allegheny River, where they would be protected from the hostile Indians under Hopocan.

However, it was not Hopocan and his followers who proved to be the most serious enemy. In 1782, a small party of Whites, who had raided the nearby Christian Indian settlement at Gnadenhütten, massacring almost 100 men, women, and children, returned via the Allegheny River; they attacked Gelelemend's group, killing and wounding several people. Gelelemend saved himself by plunging into the river and swimming to safety, but he lost all of the treaty documents which had been given to him by William Penn.

Although his services in the cause of peace were widely recognized, his Christian conversion and many White friends made him suspect. Most of the Munsee Delaware held him responsible for the many White attacks upon them, and he was eventually forced to flee to Pittsburgh, where he remained until his death in January of 1811.

Geronimo (1829-1909)

Goyathlay (The Yawner; One Who Yawns), with the possible exception of Sitting Bull, the most famous Indian of the late 19th century. A Chiricahua Apache war chief who was a feared opponent of both the Americans and the Mexicans in the Southwest. He was born into the Bedonkohe clan, in No-doyohn Canyon along the Gila River in southern Arizona in June of 1829, the son of Taklishim "The Gray One," and Juana, a part Mexican woman. Goyathlay was the fourth in a family of eight children; little is known of his boyhood beyond the fact that his father died when he was young. "Jerónimo" or "Geronimo" meaning Jerome, was a transliteration of the Spanish attempt to pronounce Goyathlay.

The great Mimbreño leader, Mangas Coloradas, was war chief at the time, and had formed an alliance with Cochise. By 1872, Cochise had established a period of relative peace which most Apache people observed, until, in 1876, the Americans decided to remove the Chiricahua from Apache Pass to San Carlos, following border raids against Mexican settlements. Only about half of the tribe made the move. The rest, led by Geronimo, fled into Mexico where they continued to raid

Geronimo (1829-1909)
(*Arizona Historical Society*)

their ancient enemies, selling stolen livestock to American traders in New Mexico.

The Apache base of operations was near Ojo Caliente, close to the Mexican border in Arizona. In 1877 the Indian Police were ordered to bring the band into San Carlos. Surprisingly, they succeeded, but once they were settled at San Carlos, friction between the other people and restlessness made them dissatisfied, and they constantly left the reservation to take part in raiding parties. In September 1881, Geronimo and about 70 Chiricahua warriors left for Sierra Madre, Mexico; after about six months of raiding, they returned to San Carlos and succeeded in freeing all the Apaches there who wanted to escape military rule. But after they crossed the border, Geromino and his band were cut off by a Mexican regiment which killed most of the women and children, who were grouped for safety in the vanguard. After this disaster, the life of the Apaches in Mexico became a war of attrition as they tried to maintain their independence and survive in a hostile environment.

In 1883, the United States sent a detachment under General George Crook to deal with the Chiricahua; Crook was an able soldier with the patience and integrity to try to settle Indian problems fairly. At this point Mexico and the United States had agreed that soldiers of either country could cross the border in pursuit of marauding Apache. Crook took advantage of this; and in May, while Geronimo was off on a raid, he captured Geronimo's base camp, together with all of the women and children. This forced Geronimo to meet with Crook to arrange peace. Most of the Indians returned to San Carlos on Crook's guarantee of his support and aid. In February 1884, Geronimo and his subchiefs joined their people and began developing profitable ranches.

Unfortunately, Geronimo's fame and the panic his name evoked among the Whites caused an irresponsible press to turn this peaceful development into a *cause célèbre* in which Crook, the hero, became the victim; while Geronimo, seeking peace, was assigned the role of a monstrous villain. Crook, according to this press, had "surrendered" to Geronimo. Although this version was grossly inaccurate, it was true that the Apache were bored with reservation life and often turned to alcohol for solace—creating a fertile atmosphere for trouble.

The authorities recognized the potential danger of the situation and attempted to stop the Indians from brewing *tizwin*, a native intoxicant. New trouble began on May 17, 1885 when Geronimo and 134 warriors left on what was to become their most spectacular series of raids. Crook was again sent in pursuit, and caught up with him in May of 1886, warning Geronimo that this time all of the offenders would be exiled to Florida. Shortly thereafter, Geronimo and his followers fled into their old hideout, Mexico, causing a wave of hysteria to explode in the United States. General Nelson A. Miles was assigned to replace Crook, and with 5000 soldiers, 400 Apache scouts, the large civilian militia, and the active support of the Mexican army, Miles undertook a vigorous campaign against Geronimo and his band, variously estimated at between 24 to 35 warriors. It took 18 months for Miles to succeed in his attempt to effectively subdue the Apache. Finally, Geronimo was induced to surrender on September 4, 1887. True to the warning, 340 Apache were shipped to Fort Marion, Florida, and later were transferred to Mount Vernon Barracks, Alabama. Through the efforts of Crook and Clum, many of them were allowed to return to San Carlos, but Arizona refused to admit Geronimo and his closest associates, including Naiche, the hereditary chief.

But finally, help came from an unexpected quarter. The ancient enemies of the Apache—the Comanche and Kiowa—offered part of their reservation at Fort Sill, Oklahoma, to Geronimo. He accepted, and the Apache took up farming and livestock farming with considerable success. In further demonstration of a peaceful attitude, he even embraced the Christian faith, joining the Dutch Reformed Church. He also dictated his memoirs, *Geronimo's Story of His People*, which was published in 1905. He later appeared at the national expositions in St. Louis and Omaha, and rode in Theodore Roosevelt's inaugural parade. Four years later he developed pneumonia and died on February 17, 1909; he was buried in the Apache cemetery at Cache Creek, near Fort Sill, Oklahoma. The alleged removal of his body seems not to have been true.

The name of Geronimo to this day is a fierce battle cry; in his own time it caused terror in the settlements of the Southwest. While his final capitulation meant the end of murderous raids, it also marked the close of the ancient freewheeling lifestyle of the Apache people.

William Thomas Gilcrease
(1890–1962)

William Thomas Gilcrease (1890–1962)
(*Thomas Gilcrease Institute of American History and Art*)

Thomas Gilcrease, a one-eighth Creek Indian, gathered one of the nation's largest and most important collections of paintings, sculptures, books, documents, and artifacts relating to Indian and White history in the Americas. He was born at Robeline, Louisiana on February 8, 1890, the oldest of 14 children. His father was William Gilcrease and his mother was Elizabeth Vowell Gilcrease.

When Thomas was only a few months old the family moved to Eufaula, in Indian Territory. The father was of mixed Scotch–Irish–French ancestry and his wife was one-fourth Creek; accordingly, they took advantage of her land rights to settle on a farm in the Creek Nation. Subsequently they moved to Twin Mounds, where the young boy was taught to read and write English by Alexander Posey, the famous Creek poet, who lived nearby. About this time he dropped the name William, preferring to be known simply as Tom Gilcrease from then on.

Tom picked cotton, worked in a gin, and when his father opened a grocery store in Wealaka, he was the clerk. In 1899, as the result of the Dawes Act land allocation, William Gilcrease received one of the 160-acre tracts for each of his children. In 1905, oil was discovered on Thomas Gilcrease's allotment in the midst of the Glen Pool field—the first oil well in Oklahoma Territory.

The young man attended school from 1907 to 1908 at Bacone, near Muskogee, and the State Teachers College in Emporia, Kansas. It was during this time that he had his first oil well on his tract, and by 1910 he owned 32 wells. From this time on he made Tulsa his home, while traveling throughout the world on oil business. Much of his free time during these trips was spent in museums and libraries, and he developed a growing interest in and concern for the preservation of historic records relating to the United States, and more particularly the American Indian—an obvious outgrowth of his Indian ancestry.

By 1925 he had married Belle M. Howell, a part Osage girl, had sired two sons, Thomas Obed Gilcrease and Barton Gilcrease, and was divorced. The Gilcrease Oil Company was prospering, and he embarked on a trip around the world to consider the best way in which to further his new-found interest and passion for the field of history. Unfortunately, he never finished the trip; the sudden illness of a close friend called him back to the United States in mid-journey.

His first thought of establishing a writer's colony was discarded as he became increasingly aware that Oklahoma had no museum, library, or cultural institutions of significance in contrast to the rich strength in such bodies that he found elsewhere. Accordingly, he was determined to build a library and museum and started to seriously collect whatever he could acquire in the historical Americana field. He bought mainly in London, for he had discovered that much of America's past had been taken to England and Europe by colonial traveler–collectors.

The Gilcrease Museum, Tulsa, Oklahoma
(*Thomas Gilcrease Institute of American History and Art*)

By 1942 his collection was of sufficient merit to have become established as The Thomas Gilcrease Foundation, and in 1949 the Thomas Gilcrease Museum was opened to house the many objects he had accumulated. The library was rich in books, documents, and manuscripts relating to the history and growth of the country, and the paintings and sculpture had grown to a point where no serious study of American art could be carried on without recourse to its holdings.

By this time it is said that he had spent perhaps $12,000,000 on his collecting activities and there seemed to be no end in sight. In 1953 disaster struck, when the levying of controls in the oil industry caused a drastic cutback not only in production, but in his income as well. At this time he owed about $2,500,000 to dealers for objects and paintings which he had bought, and the threat of what might happen to the magnificent collection induced the City of Tulsa to issue bonds to pay off the debt and assume responsibility for the museum. In August 1954, the bond issue was approved by the citizenry and title to the collection passed to the City of Tulsa. Four years later, he deeded the title to the land and the building over to the City, which has maintained the institution ever since.

Thomas Gilcrease married a second time, to Norma DesCygne Smallwood, the Miss America of 1926. This marriage lasted only a short time before he divorced her; they had one daughter, DesCygne Gilcrease. He died in Tulsa, Oklahoma on May 6, 1962 at the age of 72, and was buried in a crypt adjacent to his beloved museum. He left behind him a remarkable monument to American history and a record of American Indian life which remains unique in its range and importance. As he often said, "Every man should leave his mark"—his is one of America's outstanding collections of Americana.

Francis Godfroy (ca. 1790–1840)

Francis Godfroy (1790–1840)
(*State Historical Society of Wisconsin*)

A Miami chief and trader who was an influential war leader and who later became a wealthy businessman. Godfroy (or Godfrey) led his tribe in their last great battle on December 18, 1812; Tecumseh had rallied the frontier Indians to form a unified defense against the White invasion and preparations were under way for battle.

However, General William Henry Harrison decided to strike first, and sent troops to attack the Miami villages along the Mississinewa River in Indiana. The destruction went according to plan until the soldiers set up camp for the night near Jalapa. Godfroy had gathered about 300 of his warriors there, and they attacked at dawn. A huge, powerful leader, he led his men in a direct assault with stunning ferocity. The Army quickly retreated, believing that all of the might of Tecumseh had descended upon them. Eight soldiers were lost, however, while the Miami forces counted 30 slain.

Godfroy pulled back his men and reconsidered his position. Despite his victory, the Americans still outnumbered and outgunned him. The younger warriors were eager to continue the war, but Godfroy had had enough. He retired from the battlefield and accommodated himself to the White man's customs by taking over the trading post on the Wabash River which his father had established several years earlier.

He became a prosperous, even rich man, by providing a trading center for a wide area in north central Indiana, and lived the rest of his life in comfort—indeed, at one point he weighed over 400 pounds. He agreed to the cession of tribal lands by signing several treaties between 1818 and 1840; the last treaty was signed the year of his death.

John Grass (ca. 1837–1918)

John Grass (1837–1918)
(*American Museum of Natural History*)

Commonly known as Pezi ("grass"), but also frequently called Mato Watakpe, Charging Bear, he was a Teton Sioux chief of the Sihasapa band who came to prominence as a diplomat and political leader of the Sioux in their long struggle against the United States. He was the son of Grass, one of the important Sioux of the early 19th century. Although John Grass probably took part in some of the Sioux battles in the 1860s and 1870s, he is not mentioned anywhere as a war leader. He spoke a number of Sioux dialects and also learned English; thus he was able to communicate with almost all of the people of the Western Plains in one way or another. On the Standing Rock Reservation he was trusted by Indian and White alike, and provided a great degree of intercommunication between both peoples. The Whites approved of his success as a farmer using this success to prove that their policy of turning nomadic hunters into settled farmers actually worked.

Although Grass was known as a "progressive" by Indian Agents, thereby gaining their approval, he was suspicious of them and of the government's plans for his people. He only went along with most of

Pictographic Record Stick; Sioux
(*Museum of the American Indian*)

the United States programs because he was too well aware of the Army's power. In 1882 a commission arrived to discuss trading cattle for some Sioux reservation land which settlers and speculators were interested in acquiring. The Indians rejected the offer and the Whites went away empty handed. However, the Whites were determined to try again since the terms of the 1868 treaty stipulated that any further disposal of Sioux lands had to be ratified by three-quarters of the tribe's adult males. In 1889, commissions led by General George Crook and Richard H. Pratt, the founder of the Carlisle Indian School, arrived determined to get the signatures necessary to achieve their goal.

With great oratorical skill, Grass almost talked the commission into oblivion; at this juncture, the Indian Agent, James McLaughlin, convinced him that the government was going to take the land with or without Sioux consent. This was probably not true, since the Indian Rights Organization and other similarly founded groups in the east had developed an effective lobby in Congress. But the threat rang true to Grass, who had seen the United States take whatever it wanted throughout his life; when he lost heart, the Standing Rock people were equally dispirited, and signed away some of their land with a feeling of helpless apathy. This attitude, held by Grass that the United States would take whatever it wanted appeared to be justified, when, not long after the ratification of the treaty by all of the Sioux people, Congress greatly reduced the Sioux food allotment. This action led to renewed violence which culminated in the Ghost Dance Uprising and Wounded Knee.

John Grass was one of the chiefs who negotiated a settlement after the tragedy at Wounded Knee. He occupied a respected place in Sioux life and his death at Standing Rock on May 10, 1918 was mourned by all of his people.

Haiglar (ca. 1690–1763)

Arataswa, also Erretaswa, or Oroloswa, of unknown meaning; his more familiar name was apparently taken from German–Swiss settlers in the region named Heigler, or Hegler. The name also appears as Haigler, and he was also referred to occasionally as William Bull, although this may be a different person. He was an important leader in Catawba history who witnessed the decline of his people from a thriving, populous society spread throughout the Carolinas to what one historian called "a pitiful remnant." The Catawba were extremely warlike, being occupied almost continuously in battle against the Iroquois, Shawnee, and Cherokee people. Ranging widely in their warfare, they often traveled as far north as the Ohio Valley in pursuit of raiding parties. Although they were excellent fighters, this unceasing combat inevitably took its toll in their numbers, and with the outbreak of two disastrous smallpox epidemics in 1738 and 1759 their earlier important position was lost as the most populous tribe in the Southeast, second only to the Cherokee.

The early history of Haiglar is not known; his name was first mentioned by Governor John Glen in a historical document in 1748. He was referred to as "King" Haiglar—this being a term used by the settlers to mean the head of the tribe. King Haiglar assumed his position of leadership following the death of his predecessor. It is likely that he was born and grew to adulthood in the vicinity of the Catawba River in northern South Carolina.

Haiglar was friendly toward the Whites and at their urging attended a peace conference held with many of the hostile tribes at Albany, New York in 1751. The English hoped that the Indians friendly to them would cease fighting among themselves and would concentrate their energies against the French who were coming down into New York, Ohio, and Pennsylvania in increasing numbers. Although there were many expressions of ill-suppressed anger and bitterness, the pipe of peace was finally shared by all of the participants. Haiglar himself led a party of warriors against Fort Duquesne in support of the British, and thus was partially responsible for the fall of this fort in 1759. Later that year warfare broke out with the Cherokee who were strongly resisting White expansion; Haiglar aided Colonel Grant, providing the decisive strength at the crucial battle of Etchoe.

Mold-decorated blackware bowl; Catawba
(*Museum of the American Indian*)

Haigler had long been dismayed at the effect English liquor had on his people, and he used his position to initiate protests against the practice of selling liquor to the Indians. In a memorable letter dated

May 26, 1756, to Chief Justice Henley, his strong words were successful in getting the authorities to limit, if not entirely eliminate the sale of liquor to the Indians.

He was also successful in getting the English to build forts to protect the Catawba from attack and in obtaining supplies of food and other trade goods. The English, in turn, were able to induce him to sign a treaty in 1762 agreeing that the tribe would live on a reservation—the first to be established in the Southeast. Haiglar was greatly beloved and respected by his people, and widespread sadness resulted from the news of his murder. He was killed by a band of Shawnee raiders at Twelve Mile Creek on August 30, 1763 while en route to his home in Catawba Old Town from a visit to the Waxhaw people, attended only by a single servant.

In 1826, the state of South Carolina erected a statue at Camden, sculptured by J. B. Mathieu; it is said to be the first memorial statue to an Indian erected in the United States.

Half King (ca. 1700–1754)

Tanacharison, also known as Tannghrishon, Tenachrisan, Scruniyatha, or Seruniyattha, was an important Oneida chief who played an important role in the French versus English wars on the western Pennsylvania frontier in the mid-18th century. He was born about 1700 on the eastern shore of Lake Erie in a village not far from Buffalo. At this time the powerful Five Nations of the Iroquois had extended their sphere of influence from upper New York into the Ohio River Valley. To supervise those alien Indian tribes living on lands claimed by right of conquest, the Iroquois developed the practice of appointing a deputy or "vice regent" who exercised considerable power over the subject tribes. The Whites recognized this custom, and called such individuals "Half King"; Tanacharison was perhaps the best known. The Iroquois strongly supported the British cause and, together with the Virginia colonists, actively opposed French attempts to build forts and trading posts along the Ohio River.

In 1747, Tanacharison was dispatched to establish his headquarters near Logstown, south of where Fort Duquesne (now Pittsburgh) was to be built. Here he received many representatives from Governor Robert Dinwiddie of Virginia, including George Washington and the interpreter Conrad Weiser. In 1752 he and other Indian leaders signed a treaty of mutual friendship with the Virginians which tacitly acknowledged the right of the Virginia colonists to move into the region, as well as the Indian intention of resisting the French. However, the firm determination of the French was demonstrated when the English were prevented from building a fort at the point where the Monongahela and the Allegheny Rivers join to form the Ohio, and the French rather than the British established Fort Duquesne. This fort was to remain an important French outpost all through the early period of the French and Indian Wars.

Half King participated in many of the military actions of the time, and claimed responsibility for the victory over Joseph Coulon, Sieur de Jumonville, a French leader on advance patrol. On July 4, 1754 Coulon's brother, Sieur de Villers, accepted George Washington's surrender at Fort Necessity, not far from Logstown; it is likely that Half King was among the Indian leaders present at the scene.

The increasing power of the British slowly forced the French into strengthening many of their outpost garrisons—thus weakening the forces of Half King and his followers, who retreated to the east. Half King died of pneumonia on October 4, 1754 at Aughwick, the home of John Harris, on the site of Harrisburg and was succeeded by Scarouady. A staunch supporter of the British, Half King never lived to see the combined British–Iroquois forces defeat the French—and then lose, in turn, just 20 years later in the American Revolution.

Tanacharison is often confused with another "Half King," known as Dunquad, or Pomoacan.

Handsome Lake (ca. 1735–1815)

From Iroquoian *ganio'dai-io*, Kaniatario, or Ganeodiyo, "Beautiful Lake," this great leader and prophet was born at the Seneca village of Conawagas on the Genesee River near Avon, New York around 1735. He was born into the Wolf clan, with the name Hadawa'ko, "Shaking Snow," but was subsequently raised by the Turtle clan people; he was a half-brother to Cornplanter. He is reported as slim of build with an unusually attractive appearance; little is known of his parents. Later in his career he was given the title Skaniadariyo when he became a chief of the League.

At the time of his birth, the Seneca were at the height of their power, living in what is now upper New York State; in his old age, the Seneca were losing more and more of their reservation land to the invading White settlers. Handsome Lake participated in many of the battles fought by his tribe during the French and Indian Wars, and in the American Revolution. The Seneca were among the tribes that had joined forces with the British during the Revolution, and after the peace was signed, the great League of the Iroquois was demoralized and shaken to its foundations.

The people began searching for an answer. In 1799, after a period of illness following a long drinking bout, Handsome Lake had a series of visions. He was visited by four messengers from the supernatural world who took him on a heavenly journey during which he learned many things. Many important Indian leaders, including his nephew Blacksnake, and Cornplanter saw him at this time and testified to the power of his revelations. As he regained his health, Handsome Lake began bringing *Gai'wiio*, the "Good Word," to his people. As with many Indian prophets, he preached against drunkenness and other evil manifestations of the White man's world, contending that if the people were to survive, they would have to follow the highest moral standards. He also taught that the Great Spirit was grieved by the sale of Indian lands to the Whites.

This was not a new religion that Handsome Lake offered; as with many messiahs, he preached a revival of the traditional customs of sharing, innocence, goodness, and truth. He soon came to regard himself as the fifth angel, or messenger of the Great Spirit. He saw enemies among the many practitioners of witchcraft, and over the years participated in the persecution and murder of many "witches." Word of his teaching spread throughout the region, and he quickly won many converts to his cause. During this same period, he also gained political power; in 1801 he was elected a Seneca leader, and in the following year headed the tribal delegation to confer with President Thomas Jefferson and other officials in Washington, D.C. Alternately threatening and pleading, he urged Jefferson to guarantee Iroquois land boundaries, and to cut off the liquor traffic in the reservation area.

Handsome Lake brought hope and comfort to many of his people who still suffered from military defeat and maltreatment at the hands of the Whites. He used his influence to convince many of the men to abandon their increasingly fruitless hunting on dwindling lands, and to make modern farming a respectable and acceptable occupation. Yet, his often high-handed methods also made enemies; soon Red Jacket and others who had opposed his rise to power were able to argue with increasing success that the Prophet was not a good temporal leader. His political troubles, combined with the backlash resulting from his intense opposition to witchcraft—and some of the excessive methods he resorted to in combatting it—caused his prestige to decline, and in 1809 he went into a brief exile.

Following the outbreak of the War of 1812, Handsome Lake was able to restrain most of the men from joining the conflict, and all during this period his preaching enjoyed increasing popularity; he gained many new converts. He was particularly effective in reducing drunkenness among his followers, and in returning to them a sense of the value of their traditional culture. He died August 10, 1815 at Onondaga and was buried beneath the Council House. His religious doctrines were carried on by Blacksnake and his other disciples.

The principles of Handsome Lake's teachings were published around 1850 as *The Code of Handsome Lake*. It is difficult to analyze at this late date the degree to which this work reflects the thinking of Handsome Lake, since it is based largely on the interpretations of many of his followers who were influenced by the Quaker faith to which they had been exposed.

Today, Handsome Lake is referred to with respect as *Sedwa'gowa'ne*, "Our Great Teacher," and his teachings and oral traditions remain a strong force in Iroquois country.

Pictographic Prayer Stick of Handsome Lake; Seneca
(*Milwaukee Public Museum*)

Ned Hatathli (1923-1972)

One of the most important contemporary Navajo leaders, Ned Hatathli was born at Coalmine Mesa, near Tuba City, Arizona on October 11, 1923. He was brought up in the traditional manner until, at the urging of his uncle who was an Indian Police officer, he was sent away to boarding school. Ultimately he attended Tuba City High School, graduating as class valedictorian. On a class trip to the coast, he was amazed at the world he saw outside the reservation—most particularly the limitless ocean. Illness in his early teens brought him home again for a period, during which time he learned more of the Navajo traditions, which were to affect him deeply during the balance of his life.

In the late 1930s he attended Haskell Institute in Lawrence, Kansas but left to join the U.S. Navy in World War II—the ocean still held a fascination for the desert lad, and it proved far vaster than he had ever dreamed. After the war the young veteran was part of the tremendous explosion of energy and determination which so changed Native American culture in the postwar years. Working his way through Arizona State University at Flagstaff, he graduated with a B.S degree (cum laude), and subsequently became one of the first Navajo to earn a Ph.D. degree. Following his academic study, he returned to the reservation to become a leader in the tribe's movement towards economic and social equality.

Ned Hatathli (1923–1972)
(*Wheelwright Museum*)

He was one of the founders of the Navajo Arts and Crafts Guild, and exerted a tremendous influence upon the development of better quality crafts production. He felt strongly that art was an important part of the life of a people, and spent much time and effort in improving the quality of weaving and upgrading the quality of silversmithing which significantly increased tribal income. He was elected to the Navajo Tribal Council in 1955, and was appointed Director of Tribal Resources; in this latter post, it is notable that he regarded people as much of a "tribal resource" as were coal, oil, and uranium. In the exploitation of these mineral riches, Ned was instrumental in establishing a measure of control. A huge coal-fired power plant was built and a network of sawmills and uranium processing plants were also established to use the local resources wisely—and for the profit of the Indian. Vast land acreage was also purchased by his department, which saw to its irrigation and use for raising livestock.

When the Tribal Council decided to improve educational opportunities for its young people in the mid-1960s, the Navajo Community College was established, with Ned Hatathli as executive vice-president. After classes began in 1969, he became its first president; and in 1971 he saw the passage of a bill through Congress which provided federal support for the construction and operating expenses of the college.

He died from an accidental gunshot wound at Many Farms, near Chinle, Arizona on October 16, 1972 at the age of 49, which left his tribe without the leadership of one of its most energetic, able, and ambitious men. His wife Florence and four children survive him.

Ira Hamilton Hayes (1932–1955)

Ira Hayes, one of the genuine heroes of World War II, was born on January 12, 1923, at Sacatón, Arizona, on the Pima Reservation. His father was Joe E. Hayes and his mother was Nancy W. Hayes, both full-blooded Pima farming people. Ira's life was uneventful until he entered the armed services. Early in 1945 he was part of the invading Marine Corps force on the Japanese stronghold of Iwo Jima. His life was completely changed as a result of photographer Joe Rosenthal, who took a picture of Hayes and five other Marines raising the American flag atop Mount Suribachi on February 23, 1945. In the effort, three of the six were killed.

The photograph caught the nation's fancy and President Roosevelt called the survivors back from combat to participate in a war bond drive. A postage stamp was issued, with the design derived from the photograph, and a huge bronze statue of the event was erected in Washington, D.C. The young men were bewildered by the grossly overdone acclaim they received—especially Hayes, who thought himself no more a hero than thousands of his comrades-in-arms who were still back in front-line action. He was shuttled from one city to another, and always there was the ostentatious display, the questionable sincerity, the public hoopla—and the inevitable free liquor. He asked to be sent back to the combat zone, saying, "Sometimes I wished that guy had never made that picture."

When the war was over he returned to the reservation; restless and

Ira Hamilton Hayes (1932–1955) (*Bureau of Indian Affairs, National Archives*)

105

Iwo Jima Monument—U.S. Marine
Corps Memorial Statue
(*Official USMC Photograph*)

disturbed by what he felt was unwarranted adulation, and unable to
really deal with it, he became a drifter and an alcoholic. He was arrested 51 times in 13 years and almost every arrest was the result of
well-meaning friends who offered him a drink in token of his Marine
service.

Ira Hayes was never again able to get his life back on an even keel.
He died of exposure at the age of 23 on January 24, 1955. He was a
young man who was "a hero to everyone but himself," memorialized
in bronze in Washington, and in the hearts of the Pima people at
Sacaton. He was buried in Arlington Cemetery. He never married.

Hendrick (ca. 1680–1755)

Tiyanoga or Aroniateka, a Mohawk chief who figured importantly
in the pre-Revolutionary period, was born around 1680. He was the
son of Hunnis, a Mohawk chief's daughter, and a Mohegan named
The Wolf. There were two men called Hendrick, and considerable
confusion is caused by this fact. The name Aupamut is often used to
refer to Hendrick, and Henry Rowe Schoolcraft called "Captain Hendrick" by still another name, Soiengarata. He was adopted as a brother
by his mother's tribe, and was elected a chief while still a young man;
at this same time, Hendrick became a Christian, and an ally of the
British.

In 1710 he visited England and was presented to Queen Anne; this
visit, and his importance as the major Mohawk leader of the time led
to his being called "King Hendrick," a title which stayed with him

the rest of his life. He was a strong voice for his tribe at the various councils between the English and the Six Nations; during this period one of the major points for discussion and action was the presence of the French on the frontier. Hendrick and his allies, such as Sir William Johnson, maintained a common front against the French located in the north and west, and Hendrick and his warriors participated in many raids and scouting expeditions.

In 1751 Hendrick journeyed to Stockbridge, Massachusetts where he met with Jonathan Edwards with whom he talked over the possibility of the Mohawks settling in that area and being taught the European techniques of agriculture and the domestic arts. While this idea enjoyed an enthusiastic response, the real site of Indian–White cooperation was to be the battlefield. In 1754, at the Congress of Albany, Hendrick bitterly castigated the English for their lack of military spirit which manifested itself in an inadequate defense of the frontier against the inroads of the French forces. He was particularly critical of their lack of a united attack; picking up three sticks, he said, "Put them together and you cannot break them. Take them one by one, you can break them easily." His speech was widely quoted, his advice was taken, and the English military became a more effective body.

The next summer Hendrick, although now about 70 years of age, led the Mohawk as part of Johnson's Expedition against the French under Baron Dieskau. The French were defeated at the crucial Battle of Lake George, September 8, 1755, but Hendrick lost his life. His remarks to Colonel Williams as he surveyed the battlefield are still remembered as evidence of his oratorial skills: "If my warriors are to fight, they are too few; if they are to die, they are too many."

King Hendrick (1680–1755)
(*New York State Museum*)

John N. B. Hewitt (1859-1937)

John Napoleon Brinton Hewitt was a part-Tuscarora scholar who became one of the nation's major Iroquois authorities. He was born in Lewiston, Niagara County, New York on December 16, 1859, the son of a Scotch physician. His mother was Harriet Brinton, of French–English–Tuscarora lineage. Young John was educated in Niagara schools, later at the Wilson Union Academy, and the Lockport Union Academy; subsequently he attended a private school at Mt. Hope District, in Lewiston.

He studied medicine, intending to follow his father's career, but in 1880 he met Erminie A. Smith, an outstanding scholar of the day. She retained him to assist her in collecting Iroquois myths for the next four years. At her death in 1886, Hewitt was called to Washington to aid the Bureau of American Ethnology in finishing up the work she had not completed. He so thoroughly enjoyed the task that he stayed there for the next half-century. He proved to have a remarkable aptitude for languages, becoming fluent in Tuscarora, Onondaga, and Mohawk, as well as being well-versed in several other Indian tongues.

His research provided the definite link needed to trace the origin of the Cherokee language to a relationship with the Iroquois, which was until then only a speculative theory. Most of his work was in the linguistic, mythological, and ethnohistorical field, in which he was paramount during his lifetime. Very religious, he combined a Christian upbringing with a deep respect for Iroquoian religious beliefs.

He was one of the founders of the American Anthropological Association as well as being very active in many of the other anthropological and scientific societies of the time. He was always a quiet, unassuming person, and if he had a scholarly fault it was in his desire for perfection. At his death in Washington, D.C., on October 14, 1937, he left over 12,000 pages of unpublished manuscript, much of which remains extremely important to this day. That it was unpublished is unfortunate for it could have had a great influence upon the anthropologists of the time. Hewitt could never quite "let go" of a manuscript, and his restless search for "one more fact" denied many of his major works a justified publication.

Hiawatha (1525?–1575?)

Hiawatha (or Heowenta), from Iroquois *Haio-hwa'tha*, "he makes rivers," co-founder of the League of the Iroquois. He was born into the Turtle clan of the Mohawk tribe sometime early in the 16th century. Nothing is known of his childhood or early youth.

Apparently he became deeply impressed by the divine message of Dekanawida and joined with him in his effort to unite the Iroquois tribes in a League to insure peace. His skill as a diplomat and an orator made him vitally important to Dekanawida, who suffered from a severe speech impediment. As a disciple of the latter, Hiawatha brought the message of peace to the tribes, but at first had little success in overcoming their suspicion and intratribal hatred. He met especially strong resistance from Atotarho, the Onondaga chief, who was jealous of the role of Hiawatha in the great design to unite the Iroquois tribes.

Around 1550, Hiawatha apparently succeeded in convincing the Cayuga, Mohawk, and Oneida of the wisdom of Dekanawida's plan, and induced them to band together, leaving the Onondaga and the Seneca alone and isolated. Eventually, around 1570, the Seneca joined, and pressure was put on Atotarho to acquiesce for the common good. Special considerations were offered to him, most particularly that the Onondaga would be regarded as the "central fire" of the League, that their village would be the "capitol," and that all League meetings would be held there, with the Onondaga enjoying certain political powers. To further mollify his defiance, Atotarho himself was placed at the head of the roll of hereditary chiefs. Despite the fact that many concessions were made to Atotarho to persuade him to join the League, Hiawatha was credited with possessing remarkable magical powers in overcoming the obstinate opposition of the formidable chief.

The League was democratic in many of its principles. Power flowed

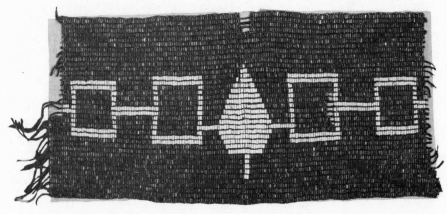

The Hiawatha Wampum Belt
(*New York State Museum*)

up from the small local units, hereditary chiefs were nominated by clan matrons and elected by villages, and all member groups were given a representative voice. Built on such a firm foundation with obvious demonstrated values, it is not surprising that the organization which became established provided something of a model for later American political planning.

When Henry Wadsworth Longfellow wrote his classic epic poem *Hiawatha*, he confused Indian history by basing most of his narrative upon Chippewa legend rather than Mohawk legend, the tribe from which Hiawatha actually came. Hiawatha himself seems to have disappeared in antiquity; the date and place of his death are not recorded, and he, along with Dekanawida, became almost godlike beings to the Iroquois, and their memories continue to be revered today as major figures in history.

High Horn (ca. 1775–1812)

Spemicalawba or Spamagelabe, from *spumuk*, "high," *alaba*, "horn," was a prominent Shawnee chief whose mother was the sister of Tecumseh. He was born about 1775 in Ohio, at Wapakoneta, and was captured as a young boy by General James Logan, of Kentucky. The latter raised and educated him, and gave him his own name; from that time on, the boy was known to the Whites as Captain Logan. The latter was often confused in historical accounts with Logan, the Mingo (Tahgahjute).

Upon his return to his own people, High Horn was a lifelong friend of the Whites. He met and married a young Indian woman who, like himself, had also been captured and raised by a White family. During the efforts by Tecumseh to unite the Indians against the settlers, High Horn tried, in vain, to dissuade the older man. In the War of 1812, High Horn enlisted on the side of the Americans, serving as a scout and a spy. His courage and loyalty to the Indian people came under question at one time, and he set out with two companions to prove himself. They ran into a small British party under Captain Elliott, with five Indian soldiers. Although High Horn himself was badly wounded in the ensuing encounter, Elliott and two of his men were killed. The Shawnee group made their way back to the camp of General Winchester where High Horn died of his wounds two days later, on November 24, 1812.

He was buried with full military honors, and the town of Logansport, Ohio was subsequently named in his honor. High Horn was described as a tall man of firm physique, intelligent, and with a fine sense of humor.

Watercolor Painting by Jack Hokeah (*Museum of Northern Arizona; Marc Gaede Photo*)

Jack Hokeah (1900-1969)

One of the most remarkable of the Five Kiowa artists, he was born in Caddo County, Oklahoma around 1900. He was orphaned as a boy, and raised by his grandmother; his grandfather was Tsen T'ainte "White Horse," a famous Kiowa warrior.

He was educated at St. Patrick's school through the primary grades and then went to Santa Fe Indian School, where his painting enjoyed some initial interest. As with the other Kiowa youths with whom he grew up, he was selected by Dr. Oscar Jacobson for further training at the University of Oklahoma art department, and became one of that special team of influential artists in the Southern Plains area.

However, Hokeah was also an exceptional dancer, and became perhaps better known for his dancing ability than for his painting. He did not produce the quantity of paintings that his colleagues did, in part because he was in demand as a dancer. He was on the stage as a performer for a time in New York City and then went to work for the Bureau of Indian Affairs. He traveled widely—possibly more than any other young Kiowa of his generation. He was a lithe, handsome man, providing the perfect image of the Indian ideal to most Whites; the excitement which his performances evoked had a powerful effect upon both Indians and Whites alike.

His paintings were published in several books, notably those portfolios by Jacobson and d'Ucel, which were the first to feature the work of the Kiowa artists. His mural in the Santa Fe Indian School is still maintained as an example of early Kiowa work. He died at Fort Cobb, Oklahoma on December 14, 1969.

Hole in the Day (1825-1868)

Bugonegijik (also Bagwunagijik, Bugonaykishig), "Opening in the Sky," was the name given to a father and a son who were successive chiefs of the Noka (Bear) clan of the Chippewa from 1825–1868. The elder was a warrior who fought on the American side in the War of 1812. He devoted his life, after becoming chief in 1825, to fighting against the Sioux, who for centuries had contested with the Chippewa over the prized hunting and fishing grounds around Lake Superior. Hole in the Day had an advantage early in his efforts because the Chippewa were able to obtain firearms from the Whites; but even after the Sioux achieved a near parity in weapons, he was still able to end the struggle by driving the Sioux west of the Mississippi. To avert further bloodshed, the U.S. Army intervened to establish boundary lines between the warring tribes and hostilities decreased to sporadic individual clashes.

The younger Hole in the Day became chief when his father died in 1846, and like his father, he saw the advantage of being friendly to the Whites and wary of the Sioux. He visited Washington, D.C., several times, and became known as a man with whom some sort of an agreement could always be made. Some called him "the betrayer of his people," while others thought of him simply as a lady's man with a taste for high living. Indeed, he married a White woman reporter, whom he met during one of his Washington visits.

There seems no question that most of the agreements he made on behalf of his people also brought him personal benefit, and he soon became very wealthy. In the 1860s, however, new officials in the Department of the Interior declined to look after his interests in the traditional way he had come to expect, and he became uncooperative with them. They tried to arrest him at one point, but many of the Chippewa rallied to his defense. Like many good politicians of the era, he had prudently distributed benefits among his constituency, and as a result had a reservoir of popular support which forced the government men to back down in their attacks against him.

At this time, the White settlers, eager for Indian land, were expanding into the region. The treaties of 1864, 1867, and 1868 forced the Chippewa to remove to the White Earth reservation in Minnesota. At first, Hole in the Day refused to move and defied the government to force him to go. He was accused of planning a revolt in 1862, like the Sioux uprising of that year; if it was true that such a revolt was planned it never came about. Eventually the issue came to a head and just as it seemed he was willing to capitulate, he was murdered by members of his own tribe at Crow Wing, Minnesota on June 27, 1868. It seems certain that they had become convinced that he had betrayed his trust in the negotiations.

His career was a complex one; while he benefited personally from many of his political activities, it is equally true that he protected his people against the inroads of White settlers. He was a strong political and psychological force and although full justice for his people was not always obtained at least time was gained for the Chippewa to adjust to the new pressures being thrust upon them.

Hole in the Day (1825–1868)
(*Smithsonian Institution, National Anthropological Archives*)

Hollow-Horn Bear (1850–1913)

Mati-he-hlogeco, a prominent Brûlé Sioux chief who was a respected leader on the warpath and at the negotiating table. He was born in

Hollow-Horn Bear (1850-1913)
(*Huntington Free Library*)

1850, in present-day Sheridan County, Nebraska, the son of chief Iron Shell. At the age of 16 he accompanied his father in battle against the Pawnee, achieving considerable notice in his prowess as a warrior. Subsequently he participated in many raids against the Whites in Montana, Wyoming, and the Dakotas. His most notable victory was over Lieutenant Fetterman in 1866 and raids on the Pacific Railroad labor camp workers.

In 1873, in order to prevent more killing, Hollow-Horn Bear accompanied Spotted Tail onto the reservation. Hollow-Horn Bear was appointed a Captain of the Indian Police at Crow Agency on the Rosebud Reservation, and was acknowledged by his people as one of the best of that distrusted group. In 1881, Spotted Tail was murdered by his rival Crow Dog, and Hollow-Horn Bear was dispatched to arrest the assassin.

In 1889, the United States sent General George Crook and a commission to negotiate with the Sioux for the purpose of breaking up the large reservations. As one of the major orators of the Sioux, Hollow-Horn Bear was chosen as the chief spokesman for his people. Crook was trusted by the Indians because of his earlier fair dealings with them, but he felt that the only way to achieve the desired result was to play upon the internal frictions which were particularly intense among the Brûlé people. Crook's strategy was essentially to divide and conquer, taking advantage of the Indian weakness to factionalize. But Hollow-Horn Bear asked that all the chiefs meet together with the commissioners, observing that, "You want to make everything safe here, and then go on to the others and tell them we have signed."

But Crook brushed aside these objections, and continued with his original plan. After a huge feast of beef and many professions of friendship and loyalty, he succeeded in getting most of the Brûlé to agree to his proposals. Crow Dog, the murderer of Spotted Tail, was the first to sign. Crook went from tribe to tribe, eventually completing most of the initial assignment.

Hollow-Horn Bear continued to be an important conciliator between Indians and Whites, although he repeatedly found himself protesting to the authorities for their continued flouting of the basic rights of the Indian people. In 1905 he was selected as one of the Native Americans to ride in President Theodore Roosevelt's inaugural parade in Washington, D.C.

He died of pneumonia on March 15, 1913 and was buried in the nation's capitol. His portrait was used on the 14¢ blue postage stamp issued in 1922 as part of our regular postal series as representative of the American Indian.

Hollow-Horn Bear; on U.S. postage stamp.

Hooker Jim (ca. 1825–1879)

Hakar Jim, from *hakar* "let me see," was one of the principal, and perhaps the most influential, leaders in the Modoc War of 1872–1873. Little is known of his youth, but with the outbreak of hostilities between Indians and Whites in northern California, his name became known throughout the west. The Modoc people lived on the California-Oregon border in an area without very much contact with the Whites until the Gold Rush of 1848–1849 brought large numbers of prospectors into the region. Always a warlike people, the Indians attacked the settlers who tried to take their lands. In time, however, resistance seemed futile in the face of the unceasing flow of invaders, and the Modoc tried to live in peace with their unwelcome neighbors. They traded primarily at Yreka, California where the townspeople gave them the colorful (and sometimes derogatory) names by which they became known.

Finally, in the 1860s, the government decided to move them onto a reservation in Oregon which was already settled by a related tribe, the Klamath. Relations between the two peoples were not friendly; the

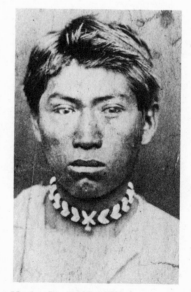

Hooker Jim (1825–1879)
(*Smithsonian Institution, National Anthropological Archives*)

113

government had allotted no money for needed supplies and the land resources of the reservation were so limited that friction was unavoidable. Several groups of the Modoc eventually fled from the reservation to return to their California homeland. Hooker Jim was the leader of one of these bands, and one of the most outspoken opponents of reservation confinement.

The Army pursued them in an attempt to force them to return. Kintpuash, the subchief who was the leader of the rebellious Modoc, vascillated, and considered surrendering to the visibly superior military forces of the Army, but was convinced by Hooker Jim and others not to yield. More outbreaks of violence followed, and in 1872, Hooker Jim and his band were attacked by vigilantes who killed several Indians. The Modoc retreated to the Lava Beds, killing 12 settlers en route. There they met with Kintpuash, who had made up his mind to make peace. Hooker Jim was fearful of being hanged for the murder of the Whites; thus he cajoled, berated, and finally forced Kintpuash into unyielding resistance.

When the peace commission arrived, Hooker Jim and his group said that the only way Kintpuash could prove he was not a coward and a traitor was to murder General Edward S. Canby, the leader of the peace party. At a conference on April 11, 1873 Kintpuash shot Canby; Reverend Thomas was also killed, and the Indian Superintendent, Meacham, was badly wounded. The war was on in earnest. The Modoc forces used the guerrilla tactics of ambush, constantly moving around in the impregnable lava bed country and avoiding full confrontation with the soldiers.

Nonetheless, although the Modoc forces continued to effectively hold off the Army, inflicting severe losses daily, the Indian casualties steadily increased—and proportionately, they could not afford this attrition. Hooker Jim disagreed with Kintpuash's strategy; shortly thereafter he deserted the chief and eventually surrendered. In exchange for amnesty, Hooker Jim and his band offered to help find Kintpuash, and on May 27 they confronted him, demanding that he give up. Furious, Kintpuash refused, and condemned them for their betrayal after he had refused to desert them earlier, and assured Hooker Jim that he would shoot him on sight if he came to him again. The pursuit continued for a few more days before Kintpuash finally surrendered, ending the war on June 1. Fifty-three Indians had held off more than 1000 Whites for over nine months—militarily successful, but certainly a Pyrrhic victory, for in the end they had to give up the land for which they were fighting.

In July, the Modoc leaders were tried by a court martial for the murder of the peace commissioners. Hooker Jim testified for the prosecution in a desperate and successful effort to save his life. Six men were condemned to death, but eventually the sentences of two were commuted. The remaining quartet was executed at Fort Klamath on October 3, 1873. The surviving 153 Modoc people, including Hooker Jim and his band, were sent to Indian Territory. He died at the Quapaw Agency in 1879.

Hopocan (ca. 1725-1794)

Hopokan, from a reference to "Tobacco Pipe," this Delaware chief was born into the Wolf clan in Pennsylvania around 1725. His name became translated into "Pipe" in English, and he was commonly known as Captain Pipe by the colonists. He was a hereditary war chief and led the Delaware warriors valiantly against other tribes; he was particularly effective in opposing the English during their war with the French. He tried unsuccessfully to capture Fort Pitt in 1763 and found himself captured during the assault on that stronghold.

Following the establishment of peace, his people gave him the name Konieschguanokee, "Maker of Daylight" and he seems to have been known by that name from then on. He settled on the upper Muskingum River in Ohio and participated in many councils with other tribes and with the Americans. During the Revolutionary War he sided with the British but he refused to take part in many of the battles. He said that he was more interested in the welfare of his people than in the quarrels of the White man. He recognized quite clearly that with the establishment of peace there would be no safety for the Indian regardless of which side emerged victorious.

In 1782, following the defeat of American forces at Sandusky, Hopocan captured Colonel William Crawford, whose Ohio volunteer regiment included some members who had been involved in a savage massacre of a number of Christian Indians. In retaliation, Crawford was mercilessly tortured to death, an act which was reported throughout the east in published journals of the day, and became something of a *cause célèbre*.

As a widely respected orator and diplomat, Hopocan was called upon to participate in many treaty councils, most notably those at Fort Pitt in 1778 and Fort Harmer in 1787. He resided at Walhonding Creek in northern Ohio, later moved to Cranestown, and finally to Captain Pipe's Village located on the Upper Sandusky, where he died in 1794.

Howling Wolf (ca. 1850-1927)

Honanisto (Honanist-to), a Cheyenne warrior, artist, and war chief, was born about 1850, the son of Eagle Head (Minimic), the principal chief of the tribe, and Shield (Hohanonivah). He joined with other warriors early in his youth, counting his first coup in 1867, and in time became a respected war leader.

In 1874, the U.S. Army began an intensive campaign against the tribes of the Middle Plains in an effort to force them onto reservations and lessen the disastrous raiding which had been so prevalent throughout the region. Eventually a combination of winter weather and the

Army's campaign against the tribes of the Middle Plains forced the Indians to surrender; but Howling Wolf held out until 1875. He was imprisoned at Fort Marion in St. Augustine, Florida along with many other Cheyenne warriors. While at Fort Marion he began work on a series of unique drawings of Cheyenne life. The finished product was a sketchbook of 12 portrayals of traditional Cheyenne life as he had lived it from the coming of the first Whites to the death of Roman Nose.

Howling Wolf was released from Fort Marion in 1878 and returned to Darlington Agency, Oklahoma where he worked at the school as a janitor. Shortly thereafter, he became a Christian convert, cut his hair, and adopted the White man's life, turning to farming for a livelihood. He urged his fellow Cheyenne to do the same. But frontier life was particularly hard at the time and the U.S. Government being insensitive to Indian needs failed to provide the supplies which had been promised in the many treaties. The death of his father in 1881 further influenced Howling Wolf to veer away from his recently adopted life, and he became anti-White once again, returning to traditional Indian customs. In 1884 he was elected chief of the Dog Soldiers—young warriors who attempted to run Indian life on the reservation without interference from the Army or Indian Agents. They were traditionally a form of Cheyenne "police force," as the Indians saw it, and accepted on that basis; but the White man saw these Dog Soldiers as a direct, unacceptable challenge to White authority.

The passage of the Dawes Act in 1887 represented an effort to take land away from the several tribes and to give part of it back in individual allotments to each person. Steps were taken to put the act into effect in 1892—followed by an opening up of the "surplus" Cheyenne lands to White settlement. Like Redbird Smith and several other Indian leaders, Howling Wolf saw this as an attempt to break up tribal organization, make the Indian Territory a state (eventually called Oklahoma), and to take even more land from the Indian for the benefit of the new wave of White settlers. And this is precisely what happened.

Howling Wolf opposed the implementation of the Act as long as he could, but in the end was powerless against the White juggernaut. He was a strong man, about 5'9" in height, weighing about 161 pounds. He was divorced twice: from Bear Woman and Magpie Woman, and then married Curly Hair (Mamakiaeh), who died. He had at least 8 children (some say 10), and lived well into the 20th century, dying as a result of an automobile accident in Waurika, Oklahoma on July 2, 1927 at the age of 77.

Hump (ca. 1848–1908)

Etokeah, a Miniconjou Sioux war chief, was a great leader during the battles between the Sioux and the Whites in the second half of the 19th century. His exact birthdate and the facts of his parentage seem not to be recorded. He first came into public notice in 1866 when he led the charge against Captain William Fetterman's soldiers outside Fort Phil Kearney in Wyoming.

Hump did not sign the Treaty of Fort Laramie in 1866, thereby earning for himself the designation of a hostile or "nontreaty" chief. He was a comrade-in-arms of Crazy Horse, Red Cloud, and other great Sioux chiefs of the period. In 1876 he led his warriors into battle against Generals George Crook and George Custer, and for a time after the defeat of the Sioux in the 1880s he lived in Canada.

He eventually returned to the United States but remained hostile to the Whites. In company with most of the Sioux, his band was aroused by the Ghost Dance religion, which culminated in the massacre at Wounded Knee Creek in 1890. Although Hump seems never to have become a true believer he did lead his people in the Ghost Dance raids until early December of that year. The Army had become alarmed that the Sioux were planning a group insurrection and they sent emissaries to all of the major chiefs to try to forestall that action. Hump was visited by an old friend, Captain Ezra Ewers, who convinced him of the futility of armed resistance; whereupon Hump carefully separated his band from the Dancers and led them into the protective custody of the Pine Ridge Agency. As Hump was breaking camp, refugees from Sitting Bull's group arrived and related how their leader had been killed during an attempt to arrest him. They were eager to find allies to help them gain revenge. Hump refused to join in with these warriors who were off to join Big Foot, then encamped near Wounded Knee Creek. After the infamous massacre and subsequent action in 1890, Hump and several other Sioux chiefs went to Washington, D.C. to plead for fair treatment for their people. Although they won some of their points, they failed to gain concessions in others; reservation confinement continued, effectively ending the old way of life. Hump died at Cherry Creek, South Dakota in December 1908 at the age of 70. He is buried in the Episcopal Cemetery near there.

George Hunt (1854-1933)

Hau was a Kwakiutl ethnologist and tribal informant who had a major role in anthropological and linguistic research during the late 19th and early 20th centuries. He was born in 1854 at Fort Rupert, British Columbia, into the Kyinanuk Tlingit people. His father was Robert Hunt, the Scottish factor of the Hudson's Bay Company trading post in British Columbia and his mother was Mary Ebbetts, a Tlingit (some say Tsimshian) woman from Tongass. Young Hunt grew up speaking Kwakwala, the Kwakiutl tongue, as well as Tlingit, and was raised as an Indian, without very much formal schooling. He first came into notice as a guide and interpreter for Adrian Jacobsen's expedition to the North Pacific Coast in 1881–1883.

Carved Wooden Octopus Spirit Mask;
Kwakiutl
(*Museum of the American Indian*)

But it was with the anthropologist Franz Boas, whom he first met in 1886, that he made his major contribution to the recording of Kwakiutl lore and custom. He did not work with Boas initially, but following a trip to the World Columbian Exposition in Chicago he began a formal relationship with him. Boas taught Hunt to write Kwakiutl in phonetic script and to translate it into English with scientific care—Hunt seems to have been particularly skilled in linguistic subtleties. For some time, his "outside" work was interrupted for periods of cannery labor, but in 1897 he was employed to accompany the Jesup Northwest Expedition. From 1897 on most of his time was spent in ethnological research and tending to Boas' demanding inquiries.

Hunt's name appears as coauthor with Boas on *Kwakiutl Texts*, published in 1905–1906, and *The Ethnology of the Kwakiutl*, which appeared in 1921. He was acknowledged as the major source of Boas' information on many other books and articles. He was an indefatigable investigator and selfless student of the culture of his people. He always went directly to the source—when he wanted to know about shamanism, he became a shaman. When he wanted to know about cookery, he wrote down the recipes he obtained from the Kwakiutl women. Over the years he was associated with Boas, he is known to have written down and sent on to his mentor over 6000 pages of manuscript material, carefully inscribed in the form he had been taught.

George Hunt (1854–1933) and his
Wife
(*American Museum of Natural History*)

George Hunt held a unique position in anthropology. He was trusted by Boas and his staff, and looked upon respectfully by the Indian people as a "real man"—an important figure in whom they could confide. He earned, in time, the right to potlatch ceremonies, became a real chief, and had the right to perform in Hámatsa rites—all because of the position he held in Kwakiutl society. This was even more remarkable in view of the role he had in recording Indian religious and social customs for the White man.

Although Hunt lived all of his adult life with his people at Fort Rupert, he did travel to the United States on occasion. In 1903 Hunt spent many months in New York City, working on the newly organized

Northwest Coast Indian exhibits at the American Museum of Natural History. After he returned to his home in Fort Rupert, he continued to work for many years on the Kwakiutl studies which Boas had started. He died on September 5, 1933 at Fort Rupert. George Hunt lived astride two cultures to the benefit of both.

Ignacio (1828-1913)

Ignacio (1828–1913)
(*State Historical Society of Colorado, Library*)

Ignacio, from Spanish St. Ignace, was chief of the Wiminuche Ute people in southwestern Colorado. He was born in the San Juan area in 1828 and was not heard of until the death of Ouray, at which time he succeeded to the chieftainship of all of the Southern Ute at Cimarrón; he was also called John Lyon, after a local citizen. He was normally a quiet, peaceful person, but was relentless in purpose; in his youth, his father, a medicine man, was retained to cure a sick Indian; when he could not do so, he was killed—a not uncommon practice in early days. In revenge, Ignacio went on a rampage and wiped out the whole family of 12 persons. He was a large man, about 6′2″ in height, weighing about 225 pounds.

Ignacio died at the Ute Mountain Reservation on December 9, 1913. The town of Ignacio, Colorado was named after him.

Inkpaduta (ca. 1815–ca. 1878)

Scarlet Point, from Sioux *inka* "point," and *duta*, "red [scarlet]," was the Wahpekute Sioux leader of a bloody outbreak in Iowa in 1856–1857. He was born on a camping trip about 1815 at Watonwan River, South Dakota. His father was Wamdesapa, a minor Wahpekute chief; his mother was a Lower Sisseton woman. The life of Inkpaduta demonstrates how a major tragedy can grow out of a minor incident, particularly when there are underlying emotions of distrust and dislike.

Inkpaduta lived during a time when the Sioux were beginning to feel the increasing pressure of advancing White settlers. The Indian land was taken by force, by squatters settling on the land, or by political treaties sometimes secured by less-than-honorable negotiations. The Indians were being slowly compressed from all sides—and to make matters worse, the Chippewa, newly armed with guns supplied by the White traders were overwhelming the Sioux and forcing them to retreat towards the west.

Following the Sauk–Fox Treaty of 1825, Wamdesapa left the main Wahpekute band because he was dissatisfied with the treaty settlement. He moved to the Vermilion River, and in 1828, in a clash over personal rivalries, he killed Tasagi, the Wahpekute head chief. In effect, this made him an outlaw in Indian eyes; from that time on, the small band was rejected by the major tribes. In 1848 Wamdesapa died, thereby making Inkpaduta the chief of the band. He seems to have embarked early on a career of violence; one of his first acts in 1849 was an attack upon the new Wahpekute chief, Wamundeyakapi, in which he killed the chief and 17 of his warriors without injury to his own force. He was hunted by both Indian and White, but he seems to have lived a charmed life with a remarkable ability to elude capture.

Inkpaduta seems not to have participated in any treaty meetings or other political or diplomatic gatherings, always operating on the fringe of the groups. His band of about a dozen warriors and their families was continually on the move, although the area around Lake Herman and Lake Thompson seems to have been their main home base.

His raiding on his own people changed radically in 1854 when a few Whites, apparently led by Henry Lott, a bootlegger and renegade, killed Inkpaduta's brother without provocation. This event seems to have turned Inkpaduta into an implacable enemy of the White man. Suffering was universal in the winter of 1856–1857 and the Indians were forced to beg or steal food when government rations failed to appear. On one such occasion, Inkpaduta appeared at the farm of a settler; in the squabble which developed over food, one of the Indians was bitten by the farmer's dog. The Indian killed the animal, prompting a posse to hunt down the band and take all of their guns, thereby leaving them without weapons with which to hunt.

In retaliation, on March 8–9, 1856, Inkpaduta began an orgy of murder at Spirit Lake and the Okoboji country in northern Iowa, which ended in the death of 47 Whites and the kidnapping of 4 women. Although the troops were called out, the Indians were able to hold them off in several skirmishes and then escape into the forest cover. Little Crow was employed to capture Inkpaduta; with a force of some 106 warriors he traveled to Lake Herman, then tracked Inkpaduta to Lake Thompson, where he killed three members of his band. Inkpaduta and the rest escaped. Feeling that he had carried out his assignment, Little Crow returned, expecting that the White troops would pursue the band on their own. But this did not happen; after a brief foray into the forest, the soldiers turned to other matters, and Inkpaduta was never captured. This failure on the part of the White man to pursue and capture Inkpaduta seems to have made a major impression upon Little Crow and may well have paved the way for the New Ulm outbreak. The Indians saw this apparent lack of concern as a weakness of the White man, suggesting that they could embark upon such murderous adventures with impunity.

Inkpaduta and his band continued on their trail of terror throughout the frontier; their exploits turned the Whites against all Santee Sioux, and coupled with the 1862 massacres, had a major influence upon subsequent White–Sioux relationships. He played only a minor role in the 1862 attacks, although it is assumed that he communicated closely with Little Crow during the height of the uprising and continued his hit-and-run tactics, always turning up in unexpected spots throughout the entire Sioux country.

His last major notice was at the Little Bighorn, where his band was among those opposed by Major Reno. Subsequently, he went north to Canada and disappeared from historic note. He died around 1878 (some accounts say 1882) in obscurity.

Irateba (ca. 1814–1878)

Also Irataba, Arateva, or Yaratev, from *eecheyara ɪav*, "beautiful bird," an important leader of the Mohave people at the time the White settlers were first entering the Mohave territory in southeastern California. Little is known of his early life; he was of the Neolge (Nyoltc) or Sun Fire clan, and is said to have been born around 1814 not far from present-day Needles, California. He was a subchief under Cairook, the headman, and in time became the hereditary leader of the Huttoh-pah band in the Mohave Valley. His first known experience with the White man seems to have been in 1849–1850, when he served as a guide for Lieutenant Joseph C. Ives on his exploration up the Colorado River; in 1851 he was with Lieutenant Lorenzo Sitgreaves, and he later guided Lieutenant Amiel W. Whipple; subsequently, he aided the overland exploring party of Ives. In all of these efforts he provided an indispensable source of information on the geography, topography, animal life and food resources of the region.

At this same time, from 1857–1859, Lieutenant Edwin F. Beale was commissioned to lay out wagon roads from Fort Smith, Arkansas through Fort Defiance to the Colorado River, during which time he introduced camels in an experiment to determine their suitability to the Southwest. As the wagon trains came west, the Mohave people began to worry that they would be overwhelmed by the increasing number of Whites. In August 1858 they attacked a band of emigrants and in December a small detachment of troops arrived to establish a fort. The Mohave immediately opposed the force; the Army soldiers were greatly outnumbered and thus they retreated. They returned the following spring with many more soldiers and established Fort Mohave. At a conference with the six Mohave chiefs led by Cairook, and Irateba, whose experience with the Whites gave him an important role, the United States negotiators demanded that those Indians responsible for the December attack surrender, and that the chiefs themselves become hostages against further outbreaks by the tribe.

Astounded and dismayed by this turn of events, the Indians, including Cairook, nevertheless went to Fort Yuma, where they were imprisoned; Irateba seems not to have been with them. It appears that the chiefs never really understood why they were being confined nor how long this confinement might last. Maltreatment at the hands of the prison guards, combined with the confinement, caused them to attempt to escape; in the ensuing melee five of the Mohave, including Cairook, were killed. This placed Irateba at the head of the tribe and introduced a period of relative peace. He went to Los Angeles in 1861 in an attempt to improve the conditions of his people, but the discovery of gold in the area in 1862 resulted in a swarm of prospectors coming into the region, which led to inevitable conflict.

As more Whites came into the Mohave country, the Army was increasingly concerned about keeping the peace. The situation was further aggravated by the presence of a large number of Mormons who had been stirring up the Indians in an effort to counteract the Army and to establish themselves as the dominant White group in the west. Tension reached critical proportions and as a gesture of friendship—as well as to show him where the balance of power resided—the federal authorities took Irateba on a trip to New York, Philadelphia, and then to Washington in 1863–1864. During his travels Irateba met President Lincoln and many other important people.

When Irateba returned home, it was as a major advocate for peace with the Whites. In an effort to relay what he had seen in the east, and hoping to make his people understand the futility of violent opposition, he graphically described his experiences. Some of his people deserted his leadership, deriding what they regarded as fanciful tales of the huge cities on the other coast—accounts which to them were unbelievable, and which they felt to be untruthful exaggerations. Although there was relative peace between Indians some intertribal strife developed. This rupture was caused mainly by the widening split between Irateba and his pacific efforts and the militant stand of a subchief, Homoseah Quahote and his followers, who felt that the only solution was violent opposition. At one point Irateba was captured and held prisoner for a period of time.

This humilitation and a continuing series of defeats caused the Mohave to look elsewhere for leadership. At the time of his death on June 17, 1878 he was no longer the once-powerful Mohave chief that he had been in the past. He had been repudiated by his people who could not see the wisdom of his efforts at trying to maintain a balance between a small number of ill-equipped warriors opposed by an overwhelming force implacably bent upon the settlement and eventual possession of their homeland.

Irateba is described as a handsome man, about 6′4″ tall, with a powerful physique, charismatic personality, and great political ability. His death is variously ascribed to old age, or to smallpox; the actual cause is uncertain. He was cremated according to Mohave custom, along with his personal possessions, his horses, papers, and the silver-headed cane given to him by Abraham Lincoln as a symbol of his chieftainship. Faced with the dual odds of internal strife and external power, he staved off the inevitable for as long as possible.

Painted Clay Effigy Vessel; Mohave
(*Museum of the American Indian*)

Iron Tail (ca. 1850–1916)

Sinte Maza was a famous Oglala Sioux war chief who holds a well-known place in history. He was born around 1850 in South Dakota and received his name at his birth. His mother saw a band of Indian hunters pursuing a herd of buffalo—the animals' tails stood upright, "as if they were shafts of iron."

An outstanding warrior in the early days of fighting against both Indian and White enemies, Iron Tail was a respected leader by the time Buffalo Bill Cody came onto the prairies. They became friends and in 1889 he went to Europe with the Wild West Show where he was lionized by French and English society.

Iron Tail was a handsome man, physically well-built, and the "ideal Indian" type. When James Earle Fraser was commissioned to design the

Iron Tail (1850–1916)
(*Smithsonian Institution, National Anthropological Archives*)

122

"Indian head nickel," Iron Tail was one of the three models he used for the composite portrait which appeared on the coin.

In 1916, Iron Tail was at St. Luke's Hospital in Philadelphia, ill of pneumonia. Not wishing to remain in the hospital he took the train headed west to his home in South Dakota. He died of the illness, still on the train, at Fort Wayne, Indiana on May 29, 1916 at the age of 65.

Ishi (ca. 1860–1916)

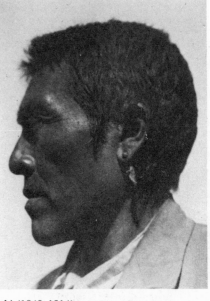

Ishi (1860–1916)
(*Lowie Museum of Anthropology, University of California*)

Renowned as "the last wild Indian in the United States," Ishi was the sole survivor of the Yahi tribe, a subdivision of the Yana. The Yahi band once numbered around 1500 persons and lived a relatively peaceful existence in an isolated section of northern California not far from Mount Lassen. The arrival of the Whites, particularly during the Gold Rush of 1849, caused such wholesale annihilation that by 1872 only a half-dozen persons remained alive of the Yahi band. Ishi was one of the survivors of this tribe of Indians. Ishi, and the few remaining Yahi, spent the daytime in hiding, only venturing out at night to forage for food, maintaining their native way of life as best they could.

Following the deaths of their respective grandparents, Ishi and another young man, Timawi, traveled north in search of a better refuge. After Timawi was killed by a settler Ishi fled back to the south. In 1908, when some surveyors finally discovered them, his mother was seriously ill. Ishi remained out of sight while the surveyors, seemingly friendly, approached her. An uncle and a cousin drowned in their attempt to escape down a nearby river. Although she was cared for, the mother subsequently died. Ishi was no longer part of the "ending people" but was the sole survivor of his tribe. He lost track of time, wandering off aimlessly in his grief, spending the winter in a bear cave.

Finally, on August 29, 1911, close to starvation, he collapsed by the corral of a slaughterhouse at Oroville. He was picked up and placed in jail where it was felt that he would be cared for. The local people got in touch with the Director of the Museum of Anthropology at Berkeley, Dr. Alfred L. Kroeber, who immediately went to see the bewildered man. He arranged to have Ishi brought to Berkeley and to live at the museum, where the two became fast friends. There was also a linguist at the museum who knew some of the Yahi–Yana language; the astonishment at hearing his own tongue spoken by a White man was profound, but it did put the Indian's fears to rest, assuring him of their friendly intentions.

Ishi spent the rest of his life at the museum, describing his tribal customs, religious beliefs, traditions, and language. He became very close to the museum staff, and the friendship which grew as a result provides a unique chapter in Indian–White relations. Ishi's Indian reluctance to reveal his given name posed a problem, but Kroeber solved it by giving his friend the name *Ishi*, "man," by which he was always known. Once during his years at the museum he returned to his own country, but the effect was traumatic, and he seemed not to wish to stay, His visit to his own country did convince him, however, that his decision to preserve the records of his people in the White man's museum was acceptable to his ancestors.

Unfortunately, he contracted tuberculosis and died on March 25, 1916, after having lived for four years and seven months in the midst of a totally different world from that into which he was born. His remains were cremated in accordance with Yahi custom. Ishi was a gentle and sensitive man, beloved by all who knew him—and with him passed the last of the Stone Age people in North America.

Isparhecher (1829–1902)

Isparhecher (1829–1902)
(*Oklahoma Historical Society*)

Isparhecher, also known as Ispaheche or Spahecha, was an important Creek chief who was the leader of the full-blooded faction which held fast to tribal tradition and customs as Americanization took place in Oklahoma at the turn of the 20th century. He was born in Alabama in 1829 into the Tiger clan. His father was Tardeka Tustanugga and his mother was Kecharte, both Lower Creeks. Isparhecher and most of his people were forced to move to Indian Territory in the late 1830s; both parents died along the way—two of the thousands of victims of the United States enforced removal of Indians to the west.

As he grew to young manhood, Isparhecher became a farmer and tribal leader simply through the force of his ability and personality. In 1861, at the outbreak of the Civil War, he served as a Sergeant in the Creek Mounted Volunteers for the Confederate Army; but in 1863, as he and many others lost confidence in the South, he volunteered in the Kansas Infantry Indian Home Guards for the Union side. He and many others thus came to be known as the "Loyal Creek faction."

He was elected to the Creek House of Warriors in 1867. During his term there, the tribe adopted its new constitution. In the 1870s while serving as a local judge, Isparhecher was attracted to the growing conservative party within the tribe, which was led by Lochar Harjo, and drew most of its strength from the Loyal farmers west of Okmulgee. When Lochar Harjo died, and Isparhecher succeeded to his position, the split within the tribe widened. In 1881 warriors for both sides gathered to support the two opposing points of view, though no blood was shed. In 1882, Isparhecher became Principal Chief of the Loyal Creek people, but pressures led to political attacks upon him, and he was impeached that same year. There were armed clashes between the factions which led to open warfare. The major battle took place in an orchard of green peaches near Okmulgee, hence the name, The Green Peach War (also called Ispaheche's War). Several men were killed before General Pleasant Porter's forces succeeded in controlling the rebels in February 1883. Peace was not fully restored, however, until the resignation of Chief Checote of the major Creek group, and a new election was held. The contest narrowed down to Isparhecher and Progressive Joseph M. Prettyman, in which Isparhecher gained a tenuous victory. After serving for a few weeks, he waived his office, feeling that he could not effectively administer such a closely divided group. Secretary of the Interior Teller thereupon decided the vote in favor of Prettyman, whom he believed to be more sympathetic to United States interests.

The U.S. Government was planning to break up the great reservation lands in Indian Territory into individual allotments for each Indian. Isparhecher became the Creek representative in Washington and also ran for office in 1887 and again in 1891. By the time of the election on September 3, 1895, the Oklahoma Indians were facing complete Americanization. Most of the voters wanted no part of this prospect, and Isparhecher was elected Principal Chief.

Nothing could stop the bureaucratic mill, however, and in 1899 the Dawes Commission opened a Land Office at Muskogee for the purpose of allotting Creek lands to individual members of the tribe. That same year Pleasant Porter was elected Principal Chief. Isparhecher was the Creek delegate to the Dawes Commission and strenuously opposed the plan, but to no avail.

Defeated and dejected Isparhecher died of a stroke on December 22, 1902. He was buried in the cemetery near Beggs, Oklahoma. He was married four times—his first wife was Pollkissut, the daughter of Poskofa, by whom he had a son, Washington. At her death, he married Lucy Barnett, a Creek, who bore him four children. His third wife was Alma Harrover who abandoned him for another man and his last wife was Cindoche Sixkiller, a Creek woman who survived him.

Emily Pauline Johnson (1861–1913)

Emily Pauline Johnson (1861–1913)
(*National Museums of Canada*)

Known as Tekahionwake, "Double Wampum," this Mohawk poet enjoyed both critical and popular acclaim for her writing around the turn of the century. She was born near Brantford, Ontario on March 10, 1861, the daughter of Mohawk chief Henry Martin Johnson (Onwanonsyshon) and his English wife, Emily S. Howells. An older cousin on her mother's side was the writer William Dean Howells.

Pauline was a precocious youngster, and by the age of 12 had read most of Scott, Longfellow, Shakespeare, Byron, and other classic English writers. She had also begun to write verse of her own, although for several years she was too shy to present it for publication. When, in her mid-teens, she submitted a poem to the local newspaper, the editor advised her to send her work to more widely circulated publications. This she did, and during those early years her poetry appeared in *Harper's Weekly*, *Smart Set*, *The Atheneum*, and similar literary publications of the period.

Another turning point in her life occurred in 1892 when the Young Liberals Club of Toronto sponsored an evening program devoted to the presentation of Canadian literature. In Mohawk costume, Pauline Johnson read one of her most recent poems entitled, "A Cry From an Indian Wife," which relates the story of the Northwest Rebellion from the Indian point of view:

> O! coward self I hesitate no more;
> Go forth, and win the glories of the war.
> Go forth, nor bend to greed of white men's hands,
> By right, by birth, we Indians own these lands.

The audience was deeply moved and called for more of her writing. The next morning's press spread the word of her triumph and she soon gave full evening readings of her work. It was for this presentation that she wrote what was probably her most famous work—*The Song My Paddle Sings*.

Her first book—*Songs of the Great Dominion*—appeared in 1889. The success of her early recitals was such that she soon embarked on a tour of Canadian cities and then, in 1894, gave several readings in London. The timing was just right for the general tone of her compositions, and she was able to meet most of the English literary world. She was favorably reviewed by most of the critics and arranged for the publication in 1895 of *White Wampum*, a book which received equally warm acceptance.

She was on tour for a large part of the next 15 years, from Vancouver to Halifax and from Boulder, Colorado to Birmingham, England. In 1903 a volume of her poetry, *Canadian Born*, was quickly sold out of its first edition. When she finally retired from the exhausting schedule of public appearances, she settled in Vancouver, British Columbia.

She gathered a collection of *Legends of Vancouver*, published in 1911, which one critic hailed as "an imaginative treatment of Indian folklore . . . the beginning of a new literature." But for the now famous poet it was close to the end. Her final books, *The Shaganappi*, appeared in 1913, followed closely by *Flint and Feathers*. She died of cancer on March 7, 1913 at her home in Vancouver and was buried at Stanley Park in that city. In commemoration of her role in Canadian literature, the government issued a 5¢ postage stamp in 1961 celebrating the centenary of her birth, and featuring her portrait—the first such issue honoring an author to appear on a Canadian postage stamp—and the first Indian so recognized.

Peter Jones (1802-1856)

Kahkewaquonaby or Kahkewagonnaby was an Ojibwa writer who figured prominently in missionary efforts to help his people in the early 19th century. He was born January 1, 1802 at Burlington Heights, on the western end of Lake Ontario, near Hamilton. His father, a government surveyor, was a Welshman named Augustus Jones, and a close friend of Joseph Brant. His mother was Tuhbenahneeguay, the daughter of Missisauga chief Wahbanosay.

Kahkewaquonaby lived "in the Indian way" until he was about 16 years of age, at which time his father had him baptized into the Episcopalian faith at Brantford, where he was given the name Peter. Subsequently, the young man took an active role in the Wesleyan Methodist evangelical services, and in 1827 was sent on a missionary tour throughout western Ontario, even though he was not ordained until 1830, when the Wesleyan Conference made him a deacon. In 1833 he became a full-fledged minister and entered into his lifetime work as a writer of hymnbooks, religious tracts, and preaching to the Missisauga and related people of the Ontario region.

Out of these efforts came several extensive writings, perhaps the most important of which was *The Life and Journals of Kah-ke-wa-quona-by*, published in 1860; and *A History of the Ojebway Indians*, which since its appearance in 1861 has been a major source of information about the life of these people. He married an English woman who bore him four sons; his seventh child, Peter E. Jones, assumed his father's name, and published *The Indian*, a local journal devoted to Indian affairs of the day.

Peter Jones came to be regarded as the ruling chief of the Missisauga, was their chief pastor, and made many visits to New York, London, Toronto, and other large cities in behalf of his people. He worked diligently in the political arena as well as in religious activities, particularly striving to protect the land titles of the Indian. His continual work to the point of exhaustion took its toll and his health finally gave out. He died at Brantford on June 29, 1856. A monument was erected in his memory by the Ojibwa people in 1857.

William Jones (1871-1909)

William Jones (1871-1909)
("*The Southern Workman*")

Mesasiáwa, "Black Eagle," was a member of the Fox tribe who became an outstanding Indian ethnologist. He was born on March 28, 1871 on the Sac-Fox Reservation in Indian Territory. His father was Henry Clay Jones, "Bald Eagle," a Welsh–Fox blacksmith and interpreter; his mother was Sarah Penny, an English woman. In his early years, William was brought up by his grandmother in the Indian tradition. He attended Indian schools in Kansas and Indiana before going East to Hampton Institute in 1889, and then to Phillips Academy in Massachusetts. In 1896 he entered Harvard, where he came under the aegis of Frederic Ward Putnam, the leading anthropologist of the day. Six years later he received the M.A. degree from Columbia University, and in 1904, the Ph.D. degree; both degrees were obtained under the tutelage of Franz Boas, who was deeply interested in the young man, and urged him to continue with his interest in American Indian language study.

During his undergraduate and graduate years, Jones had become engrossed in the culture of his people. In appearance and manner he was a full-blooded Indian and he was able to talk easily with tribal leaders to gain access to many old papers and records. He had a gift for linguistics; his *Fox Texts*, published in 1907, was "the first considerable body of Algonquian lore published in accurate and reliable form in the native tongue, with translation rendering faithfully the style and the contents of the original. [They are] among the best North American texts that have ever been published."

William Jones also wrote many other articles for both scholarly and popular publications. In 1906 he was sent to the Philippine Islands on an ethnological expedition for the Field Museum of Chicago to study some of the native tribes. On March 29, 1909, while in camp along

White Buffalo Story-Telling Effigy; Fox
(*Museum of the American Indian*)

the Cagayan River, on the island of Luzón, he was attacked by head-hunters and killed. He had just turned 38.

He was buried in the Manila Municipal Cemetery; in his honor, the town of Jones was named, just south of Echague, near where he died. With his passing America lost one of its most gifted ethnological scholars.

Chief Joseph, The Younger
(ca. 1832–1904)

Chief Joseph (1832-1904)
(*Smithsonian Institution, National Anthropological Archives*)

Hinmaton Yalatkit, "Thunder Rolling in the Heights," a Nez Percé chief, was an essentially peaceful man who came to be known as one of the greatest Indian military commanders of the 19th century. He was born at the mouth of Joseph Creek, in the Wallowa Valley, Washington, sometime between January and April 1832, the third child of Khap-khaponimi, a Nez Percé woman, and her husband, Tuekakas, a Cayuse man also known as Old Joseph. Baptized Ephraim as a lad, as was common missionary practice, he later took the name Joseph, by which he was known throughout his life. He had two brothers, Ollokot (Frog) and Smuguiskugin or Shugun (Brown) and two sisters, Celia, also known as Sarah, and Elawmonmi.

Joseph was a tall, heavyset man, handsome and dignified in bearing. He became chief around the age of 30 after the death of his father. While courageous, he was not a warrior chief; he relied upon diplomacy and passive resistance in his relations with Whites. Following the establishment of the reservation in 1835, White settlers began to move onto the beautiful fertile land—especially after gold was discovered. Accordingly, a new treaty was signed in 1863 which reduced the reservation to about 550 square miles. The reservation no longer included the land of many of the leaders of the tribe, including Joseph's father. These leaders refused to sign the treaty and also rejected an amended treaty in 1868. Although the government maintained that the treaties covered all Nez Percé, those who had refused to sign continued to occupy their homeland in the Wallowa Valley in relative peace with their White neighbors. The split between treaty and nontreaty Nez Percé was never reconciled.

Finally, in 1877, under pressure from settlers, squatters, and prospectors, the government decided to take action against Joseph and the rest of the nontreaty Nez Percé. General O. O. Howard met with Joseph and his fellow chiefs in an attempt to reach a peaceful settlement. But negotiations were disrupted because of trouble which broke out between some of the young Nez Percé and a number of Whites, in which casualties were suffered by both groups. Howard was then determined to subdue the tribe and Joseph was forced into a state of war.

In the first major battle, at White Bird Canyon, the federal forces were all but annihilated. The Nez Percé won 18 more battles, but Joseph clearly realized that he had but three ways to end the war: annihilation, surrender, or retreat; he chose the latter. At first he planned to join the Crow people in Montana, but when they refused to assist him, his goal was to reach Canada—to join Sitting Bull and the Sioux who had fled there in 1876.

The retreat of Joseph and his people is generally acknowledged as one of the most brilliant in United States military history. They eluded the pursuing troops, often by adroit rearguard actions in which a few sharpshooters were able to hold off a large number of attackers. Their speed and flexibility amazed the Army; they even managed to maintain good relations with the Whites they encountered along the way. Joseph was the undisputed leader, but all chiefs participated in decisions and were free to go their own way. Joseph led about 750 of his people twice over the Rocky Mountains, through Yellowstone Park (it had been established in 1872), and across the Missouri River.

The journey covered four states and over 1500 miles. Less than 40 miles from the Canadian border, at Bear Paws, Montana, the Nez Percé made camp, exhausted and near starvation. Some chiefs advocated moving on into Canada immediately, but most felt that without rest only the strongest could make it. Joseph agreed, unaware that fresh troops under the command of General Nelson Miles were rapidly approaching. They attacked the camp early the next morning on September 30. Amid the fierce fighting Joseph had his men dig in, and they were able to beat off the soldiers and entrench themselves for a long siege; but Joseph clearly realized that defeat was inevitable for his small, weakened band.

On October 5, 1877 he surrendered, saying "I am tired of fighting. Our chiefs are killed . . . It is cold and we have no blankets. The little children are freezing to death. My people, some of them, have run away to the hills and have no blankets, no food. No one knows where they are, perhaps freezing to death. I want time to look for my children and see how many I can find. Maybe I shall find them among the dead. Hear me, my chiefs: I am tired; my heart is sick and sad. From where the sun now stands, I will fight no more forever."

Although General Miles and Joseph had agreed that the Nez Percé would be returned to the west, the pledge was ignored in Washington. Instead, they were sent to Indian Territory, where in an alien environment, homeless and dispirited, many died or grew weak. Joseph made every appeal possible to get his people to an area that at least resembled their homeland. He went twice to Washington D.C., where he won many supporters, but the leaders of the western states were adamant. They feared that the dissidents would stir up trouble among the peaceful Nez Percé on the reservation. In 1885, however, some of the exiles were sent to the Lapwai Reservation in Idaho, and the others, including Joseph, went to the Colville Reservation in Washington.

Joseph was regarded with high esteem by his enemies as well as his friends. He was about 6'2" tall, strong, with piercing black eyes; he was an excellent orator. True to his pledge, he fought no longer, though he continued working for the betterment of his people and for his dream that they would one day be allowed to return to their beloved Wallowa Valley, where the bones of their ancestors were. In 1897 he went east and met President McKinley, General Miles, and General Howard, and in 1903 he again visited the Capitol, meeting President Roosevelt

Rifle of Chief Joseph
(*Museum of the American Indian*)

129

and escorted by Miles. He died on September 21, 1904. His first wife died, and he married two widows. When White authorities demanded that he take only one, he replied, "I fought all through the war for my country and these women. You took away my country; I shall keep my wives."

Charles Journeycake (1817–1894)

Neshapanasumin, or Johnny-cake, a Delaware chief and later a Baptist preacher, was born on December 16, 1817, on the upper Sandusky River in the Delaware settlement of Ohio. His father was Solomon Journeycake, a Delaware chief. His mother Sally was a French–Indian interpreter; her illness caused the young boy to become a Christian and he was baptized in 1833. His religious predisposition and training induced him to remain faithful to this act for the rest of his life.

Young Charles could read and write English and was comfortable living in both Indian and White society. Like many Indian Christians of the day, he was a temperance advocate who influenced many Delaware people to abstain from liquor. He was also a skilled hunter and trapper. The story is told that he agreed to guide a group of Indian men on a beaver-trapping trip if they would worship with him during the journey. They did, and the success of the venture caused several of the men to become members of his Baptist congregation. He also induced John Conner, who became the tribe's principal chief, to attend the church, but Conner was too faithful to the Indian tradition to give up the faith of his ancestors. In 1855 Journeycake became head of the Wolf clan.

In 1861 the United States government chose Journeycake to be one of the Delaware subchiefs—a practice imposed upon the Indians by the Washington authorities at this time. The appointment was favored by almost everyone—as one Indian Agent said, "He is beyond the reach of bribery and would look after and protect the interests of the people, and particularly the industrial and moral interests of the tribe." During this time White settlers were coming into Kansas in increasing numbers and the Delaware decided that it would be best for them to move to Indian Territory. In 1866, Journeycake and six others were selected to represent the tribe in negotiations with the United States. After it was agreed that the Delaware would have a reasonable choice of location in the area, the seven began an inspection tour. They decided to settle in what is now northeastern Oklahoma, on land belonging to the Cherokee.

Washington then arranged a meeting between the two tribes which was attended by Journeycake and his brother Isaac, who was an interpreter. On April 8, 1867 a treaty was signed by the two Indian Nations, whereby the Delaware bought Cherokee land and became a part of the Cherokee Nation, although they still kept their own separate tribal government. The United States' officials reassured the worried

Charles Journeycake (1817–1894)
(*Western History Collections, University of Oklahoma Library*)

Delaware that they would guarantee the satisfaction of both sides in this treaty.

Subsequently, Journeycake and his French–Delaware wife, Jane Sosha, settled down in Nowata County to a life of farming and preaching. He became the principal Delaware representative in dealings with the United States, and from a small house on his farm, each Delaware family was paid its small annuity. In 1883 the Cherokee Council refused to allow the Delaware to share in the proceeds of land sales to White settlers. At this same time, many Delaware were wondering what had happened to the money the government had paid them for their Kansas holdings and for their resettlement among the Cherokee.

Finally, in 1890, Journeycake was empowered by tribal leaders to bring suit against the Cherokee and the United States government to redress these wrongs. In the midst of the long-drawn-out litigation, Journeycake died on January 3, 1894—just ten months before the U. S. Supreme Court upheld his case in a landmark decision that called for the Delaware to be paid their past-due compensation. That same year his wife died; they left eight daughters and two sons. He was buried in the cemetery at Lightning Creek, Indian Territory.

Jumper (ca. 1820–1896)

John Jumper, Hemha Micco, also known as Otee Emathla, "He Makes Sense," was a Seminole chief who led his people on the Confederate side during the Civil War. He was born in Florida around 1820 and moved with his people to Indian Territory in 1840–1841. As a young man he did not, as far as is known, participate to any great extent in the battles that preceded the Seminole move west. A large, strong man, 6'4" in height, and weighing over 200 pounds, John Jumper was also a man dedicated to peace. When he became chief following the death of Micanopy's nephew Jim Jumper, John worked for the betterment of his tribe.

A major issue was the unpopular union between the Seminole and the Creek which had been forced upon the Indians by the government when both tribes were resettled in Indian Territory. Finally, in 1856, a treaty was signed in Washington by which the ties between these two tribes were severed and both tribes were given new lands and annuities. Around this same time tensions between the North and South over the slavery issue were near the breaking point. In 1861, the Confederate authorities sent General Albert Pike to negotiate a treaty with Jumper, who was persuaded to raise a small force to join the Southern forces already in Indian Territory.

Since both Creek and Seminole people were more sympathetic to the slave-owning traditions of the South, they naturally sided with the Confederacy. Jumper himself was in command of the Seminole forces at the battle with the Union Indian regiment led by Opothleyaholo, where Lower Creeks under McIntosh and General Stand Watie's Cherokees forced the Unionists to retreat to Kansas.

John Jumper (1820–1896)
(*Oklahoma Historical Society*)

After the Union victory, however, Reconstruction came to the Territory. The Seminole were forced to sell their 2,000,000 acres of land to the government for 15 cents per acre—then had to purchase from the Creek new homelands of 200,000 acres for $.50 per acre. Jumper and other leaders protested against this and other equally harsh injustices, but only occasionally with success. Throughout most of his life he was a devout Christian, and in 1877, when he resigned as chief of the Southern Seminole, he became pastor of the Spring Baptist Church.

He served in that capacity for several years, but returned to public life in 1881 when he was elected chief of the united Seminole Nation to replace his old Northern rival John Chupco, who had recently died. John Jumper continued to serve in the Baptist church until 1894, just two years before his death.

Kamaiakin (ca. 1800–ca. 1877)

Also Kamiakin, Kamiakan, or Camaekin, meaning "He Won't Go," from *ka* "no," *miah* "to go," *kamman* "to want"; an important war leader of the Yakima and related Northwestern tribes in the mid-19th century. He was born about 1800 at Ahtanum Creek near Tampico, Washington, the son of Kiyiyah (Howling Wolf), a Nez Percé chief, and Kaemoxmith, a Yakima woman. He first came into prominence when he went to Waiilatpu in 1839 to request the American missionaries for a teacher; refused because of personal jealousy between two of the Whites there, he turned to Catholic priests in the vicinity—an act which was to have major consequences for the Protestant group. In 1841, he met Captain Charles Wilkes of the U.S. Exploring Expedition, who referred to him in his *Journal* as "Kamaiyah."

Relations between Indians and Whites in the Washington Territory had long been tense, although active fighting was usually confined to individual clashes. But when surveyors for a railroad route came through in 1853, and reports of the discovery of gold began to attract large numbers of Whites, conflict became inevitable. Most of the gold seekers were rough miners and ruffians far more savage than the Indian landowners, who had already learned of the inroads of White civilization and its cost to the neighboring Nez Percé people. Consequently, when the Superintendent of Indian Affairs, Isaac Stevens, called for a meeting in 1855 to negotiate treaties with the several tribes—a step which many fully realized meant loss of land—the Yakima, Palouse, Cayuse, and Wallawalla found themselves united in their opposition to any such treaty.

Kamaiakin emerged as the strong leader of the people who refused to consider any treaty which would deny the Indians the right to their lands and freedom of travel, but White pressure, combined with indecision on the part of some of the chiefs eventually overcame his resistance, and treaties were forced through. But long before the treaties were ratified or put into effect locally, White settlers and miners began to swarm into the areas that were designated to be surrendered.

Kamaiakin (1800–1877)
(*Washington State Historical Society*)

132

In September 1855, A. J. Bolon, a special Indian Agent appointed by Stevens, was murdered by some young Yakima men; troops were immediately dispatched to the scene, since Stevens had been informed that Kamaiakin and his people were talking of war. Although the chief did not condone the murder of the Agent, he had become thoroughly antagonized by the events of the past year, and when Major Haller appeared with armed men, he led a force of some 500 Yakima warriors against him. Even with the assistance of a howitzer, the troops were not able to overcome the Indians in a two-day battle, and had to retreat to The Dalles.

The victory excited the Indian people who were hostile to Stevens, to all treaty making, and to Whites in general. Many of the tribes combined in an effort to force the White man out of the country. For three years fighting between Indian and White forces took place throughout the area—at one time even Seattle was under attack, saved only by the timely intervention of a naval force then in the harbor. But time was against the Indians; Stevens' reliance upon and condoning of the undisciplined volunteer forces combined with the increasing number of Army troops coming into the region slowly forced the tribes to break into smaller and smaller units. The smaller units were eventually overcome, the leaders hanged, and the people put on reservation lands. In a final, savage 30-day campaign, Colonel George Wright slaughtered Indians indiscriminately throughout the central Washington area, finally putting an end to their resistance on October 5, 1868.

Kamaiakin himself was the only major Yakima figure to survive the holocaust. He had fled to Kutenai country in British Columbia with his family following the victory of the Whites, and lived there for some time. He eventually returned to his homeland where he lived in obscurity for another ten years. He is described as a tall man, 6'1" in height, proud of bearing, an eloquent speaker with a keen mind, and a strong, dominating personality. He married Salkow, the daughter of Teias, a Yakima chief, and later also took as wives two daughters of a Klikitat leader named Tennaks.

But the White man was not finished with his bitter enemy. Kamaiakin died at his camp at Rock Lake about 1877 or 1878; some time after his burial at the south end of the Lake, the grave was opened and his head was twisted off his body for public exhibition as a curiosity.

Kénakuk (ca. 1785–1852)

Kénakuk, or Kanakuk, "Putting His Foot Down," also called Pakaka, or Pah-kah-kah, the Kickapoo Prophet, was for many years chief of a peaceful, agricultural, Northern branch of the tribe. Little is known of his early life; he first came into prominence around 1812 as the leader of pacifist, religious Indians who had settled along the Osage River in Illinois. Like many Indian holy men, he had been visited by spirits who gave him a vision in which he saw the secrets of life. Inspired by the same ideas as Tenskwátawa, he taught his people the way of fasting and meditation and carved small wooden sticks which he

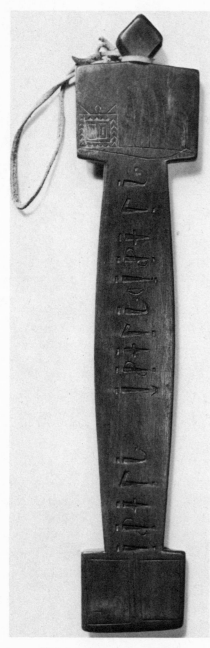

Kénakuk Prayer Stick; Kickapoo
(*Museum of the American Indian*)

sold them to support himself. These sticks were engraved with wooden symbols for use in their worship.

For many years the Kickapoo had been wanderers; the men were hunters and the women took care of the children and the homes. Kénakuk taught his followers that the days of the wandering hunter were over and that agriculture was an occupation worthy of the most valiant men. Whether it was coincidence or not, the farming type of life that Kénakuk encouraged fit in with United States government policy of the time, and he was given considerable assistance from Washington in setting up farms. Although the occupation of farming earned the contempt of the Southern Kickapoo and other more traditional Indians, Kénakuk's people soon became a relatively prosperous stable community.

But as White settlers moved into the region, the government wanted all Kickapoos to move out, particularly in view of the excellence of their farms. Ultimately these farms caught the eyes of the land-greedy Whites and a treaty was signed in 1819 ceding all Kickapoo lands in Illinois. It was hard for the people to face the loss of their fertile farms, and Kénakuk delayed his departure, as did other members of the Kickapoo. During the 1820s Kénakuk frequently went to St. Louis to reason with the Indian Agent, William Clark, and explained to him why it was impractical for his people to move. "The Great Spirit . . . has give our nation a piece of land. Why do you want to take it away and give us so much trouble?" he asked.

For a time the Illinois settlers were content to live side by side with the Indians, especially Kénakuk's peaceful Kickapoo. But the Whites continued to covet the fertile acreage next door, and finally in 1832, the Treaty of Castor Hill was signed, exchanging the tribe's Illinois territory for an area in Brown County, Kansas, along the Missouri River. After making the move some years after the treaty was signed, the Kénakuk band of 350 persons rebuilt their homes, living much as they had in Illinois, even though their village was only about a mile away from their old enemies, the warring Kickapoo, headed by Kishko, who was hostile to Kénakuk.

Kénakuk contracted smallpox and died in 1852, just as the problem of squatters on Indian lands was becoming intolerable, and as the government was again demanding that the tribe sacrifice more land. He promised to revive in three days; but when he failed to return to life, his teachings suffered a loss of belief, and without the strong hand of their leader, the band declined and eventually died out. He left one son, John Kénakuk.

Keokuk (ca. 1783-1848)

Nicknamed "The Watchful Fox," from *kiyo'kaga*, "One Who Moves Warily," he was born at Saukenuk about 1783 (some claim 1788) of an Indian–French father and a Sauk mother near Rock Island, Illinois. Although he held no inherited position, he established his leadership by the persuasiveness of his words and by his heroism as

Keokuk (1783–1848)
(*Smithsonian Institution, National Anthropological Archives*)

a warrior. He was particularly effective on horseback against his people's long-time enemies, the Sioux. In recognition of this he was given the privilege of attending ceremonies mounted on his horse. He was eventually appointed chief of the Sauk and Fox confederacy by the United States government—an awkward role which was never fully accepted by many of the Indians.

Keokuk was ambitious—some say greedy—and worked tirelessly to advance his own interests. The Sauk loyalties were split by the War of 1812. Black Hawk led a faction to the British side, while Keokuk advocated neutrality. Remaining with the main body of the tribe, Keokuk took advantage of the absence of his hated rival to gain a seat on the Council. When Black Hawk returned, defeated, the rivalry was intensified; Keokuk advocated compliance with most White demands, but Black Hawk staunchly opposed any collaboration.

Earlier in the 19th century, the Sauk chiefs had been manipulated into ceding all of their lands east—and some of the western territory as well—to the federal government. In 1823 Keokuk and Black Hawk agreed that they should make a mutual effort to retain the traditional tribal villages in exchange for ceding additional lands. Keokuk went to Washington to plead the case, but failed. The land was ceded for money and some minor concessions, but the matter of the villages was not resolved. Keokuk was then given a tour through the East, which convinced him of the inevitability of White domination over the Indians, and he returned to his people advocating alliance. Black Hawk was determined to defend the villages and tried to form a union

Tomahawk of Chief Keokuk; Sauk
(*Museum of the American Indian*)

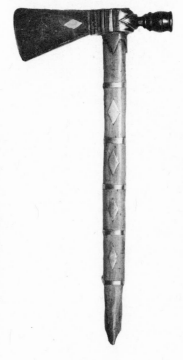

135

with other tribes in the Northwest Territory to resist further White expansion; but when in 1831 the government put up the villages for sale, Keokuk was able to persuade most of the Sauk people that resistance would be futile.

Months after the agreement was signed, fighting broke out between the Menomini and the Fox. Black Hawk sided with the latter, and decided, under this pretext, to activate the alliance which he had tried to form earlier, thus giving rise to the short-lived Black Hawk War of 1832. But the Indians were badly divided, and were routed by White troops at the Battle of Bad Axe, Wisconsin. Continuing his intrigue during the final peace negotiations at Rock Island, Illinois, Keokuk was able to maneuver his appointment as chief of the Sauk-Fox, and was given administration of the $20,000 annuity which the government paid for the Sauk lands, and further, his faction was given 40 square miles of territory on the Iowa River. The terms of the treaty so outraged Black Hawk that he whipped off his breechclout and whipped Keokuk across the face to show his contempt for what he felt was a sellout.

While Keokuk was never a popular chief, he did gain some prestige by his success in debating against United States and Sioux representatives over the ownership of lands in Iowa. But the White migration continued west, and in 1845 Keokuk was forced to give up the recently acquired Iowa lands in exchange for a reservation in Kansas. In April 1848, shortly after the Sauk had been removed there, he died near Pomona, Kansas of unknown causes; some say he was murdered by a supporter of Black Hawk. By the time of his death, Keokuk was alienated from Indian and White alike. The Sauk distrusted him because of his willingness to agree to every White wish; the latter no longer found him useful because of his loss of influence among his own people.

While it is clear that unity between the Sauk and Fox could not have prevented White settlement on their lands, the split between Keokuk and Black Hawk only exacerbated the problem. That Keokuk recognized the inevitable and dealt with it as best he could, although personally benefiting from the situation, does not necessarily lessen his role as a leader who could manipulate a peaceful accommodation which otherwise would have certainly ended in bloodshed.

In 1883 his remains were taken from Kansas to Keokuk, Iowa (which was named for him), and buried in Rand Park. A bronze bust was placed in the Capitol in Washington—indicative of his significance in White land politics, if not in Sauk affection.

He was married twice: to Emma, and later to Hannie, by whom he had one son, Moses Keokuk, who succeeded him as chief.

Kicking Bird (ca. 1835–1875)

Tene-angop'te, "The Kicking Bird," or "Eagle Striking," also known as Watohkonk, "Black Eagle," was a Kiowa chief widely known for his wisdom as a leader and his courage and strength as a warrior. Little is known of his early life; his grandfather was a Crow captive who had been adopted into the tribe. As a leader, Kicking Bird advocated

Kicking Bird (1835–1875)
(*Oklahoma Historical Society*)

peace with the Whites, realizing the ultimate hopelessness of military resistance, and tried to persuade his people to accept what he felt was inevitable. Accordingly, at Wichita, Kansas, he signed the first Kiowa Treaty in 1865; this set up a reservation whose boundaries were subsequently established in the Treaty of Medicine Lodge in 1867.

Kicking Bird and his people did not participate in the militant opposition of many of the Indian people against a move to the reservation, and he was a strong force for peace; yet his friendliness towards the Americans bore little fruit. In 1873 the government failed to keep a promise to free Kiowa chiefs who had been captured earlier. This, together with the theft of Indian horses and cattle by Whites, and the continued encroachment of buffalo hunters on the reservation land, caused many of the tribe to doubt the wisdom of his policies. At one point, taunted by his people for a lack of courage, he proved he had not lost his warrior spirit or ability by leading a victorious war party against a detachment of troops in Texas.

When another Kiowa chief, Lone Wolf, began gathering a force to war against the White buffalo hunters, the decision as to which side to support was difficult and dangerous. Kicking Bird still believed in the ultimate wisdom of peace, however, and was able to persuade more than one-half of the tribe to keep out of the hostilities. He was eventually head chief of all of the Kiowa, and continued a project of improving education among his people. He prevailed upon Thomas C. Battey, the Indian Agent, to open the first school for the tribe; as this work was proceeding, he died suddenly at Cache Creek—his friends say he was poisoned—on May 3, 1875, and was buried at Fort Sill, Oklahoma in the post cemetery. He is known to have had one wife named Guadalupe.

Tomahawk of Kicking Bird; Kiowa
(*Museum of the American Indian*)

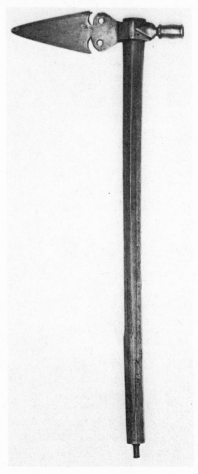

Kintpuash (ca. 1837–1873)

Also spelled Kintpoos, Peintposes, and Keintpoees, from *kintpuas*, "He Has Water Brash [pyrosis]," more commonly known as Captain Jack; one of the major participants in the Modoc War. A full-blood, he was born at Wa'chamshwash Village on Lower Lost River near the California–Oregon border around 1837, the son of a Modoc chief who was killed by Whites in the Ben Wright massacre. Little is known of his life until he was about 25 years of age.

The Modoc tribe had few dealings with the Whites prior to the Gold Rush of 1848–1849. Whereas most California Indians did

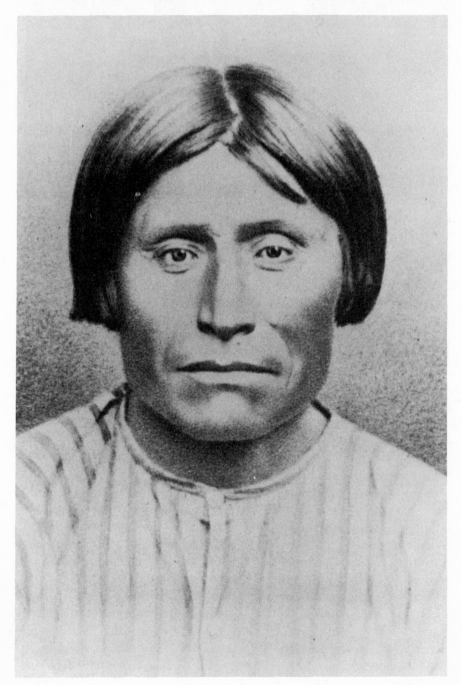

Kintpuash (1837–1873)
(*Smithsonian Institution, National Anthropological Archives*)

138

not resist the influx of the gold seekers, the more militant Modoc people fought regularly with the White settlers rather than let them take their best lands. Kintpuash, who was inclined towards peace at the time, befriended the settlers at Yreka, California, and often traded there. He got the nickname "Captain Jack" from his habit of wearing a uniform coat decorated with brass buttons which had been given to him by the military.

But the friction increased, resulting in hostilities between the two races, and finally in 1864, Schonchin, the head chief of the Modoc tribe, signed a treaty which agreed to their removal onto a reservation in Oregon. The latter area was already occupied by the Klamath people, and although they were distant cousins of the Modoc, they did not welcome the newcomers. Kintpuash realized that the land was insufficient to support two large treaty provisions, and he led a group back to their native California, where he asked that they be given their own reservation. The United States refused, and the settlers began to demand the removal of the Indians. On November 28, 1872 troops invaded the Modoc camp, forcing Kintpuash to consent to removal. During the confrontation a fight broke out, and when both sides stopped firing, 8 soldiers and 15 Indians were dead. Fearing retaliation, the Modoc band fled into the neighboring Lava Beds, a desolate area where they thought they would be left alone.

But this was not to be. Hooker Jim and some other Modoc warriors camped across the Lost River had been attacked by White settlers; in retreating to the Lava Beds they had killed 12 of their attackers in revenge for their own losses. Everyone assumed that the Whites would pursue them; accordingly, they prepared for an attack. On January 13 the troops moved into the vast, almost inaccessible volcanic area. Initially, Kintpuash wanted to surrender, realizing that the government would eventually win, but he was outvoted by Hooker Jim, Schonchin John, and their followers—all of whom comprised the most militant division of the Modoc group.

On February 28, Kintpuash's cousin Winema, who had married a settler named Frank Riddle, arrived with her husband and three Whites on a peace mission. When Kintpuash agreed to a conference with government authorities, he was called a coward by Hooker Jim and Schonchin John. They insisted that he prove his mettle by killing General Edward S. Canby, the head of the United States delegation. Reluctantly, Kintpuash agreed to kill him if Canby did not agree to giving them amnesty and land in their rightful home in California. At the fateful meeting Kintpuash drew a pistol and shot Canby. In the confusion another peace commissioner, Reverend Eleazer Thomas was also killed and the Indian Superintendent Albert Meacham was badly wounded. Winema and her husband escaped with the other members of the party.

The government quickly brought in heavier weapons and more troops. Initially, the Indians' knowledge of the terrain worked in their favor, but as the Modoc situation became more untenable, many surrendered. Hooker Jim even offered to bring in his chief in exchange for amnesty. "You intend to buy your liberty and freedom by running me to earth . . . you realize life is sweet, but you did not think so when

Painted Wooden Bow; Modoc
(*Museum of the American Indian*)

139

you forced me to promise that I would kill that man, Canby . . ." charged Kintpuash. It was not until the Modoc quarreled among themselves, split up, and left the protection of the Lava Beds that they were finally overcome. Kintpuash was forced to surrender in late May, and after a military trial in which Hooker Jim testified for the prosecution, Kintpuash, Schonchin John, Boston Charley, and Black Jim were hanged on October 3, 1873. Kintpuash is known to have had two wives; one named Lizzie, and one whose name is not recorded.

In an action aggravated by Indian betraying Indian, White prejudice, greed for land and a sensation-seeking press, the Army employed over 1000 soldiers to conquer a Modoc force which never numbered more than 53 warriors. During the nine-month campaign, the Army lost 7 officers, 39 soldiers, 2 scouts, and 16 civilians, while the Modoc force suffered 7 men and 11 women killed. The cost in Army humiliation and public money was hardly offset by the capture and transportation to Indian Territory of 153 Modoc Indians. Out of this brief and all-too-bloody encounter, no one emerged with glory. Perhaps the only direct profit was a melodrama entitled *Captain Jack*, which appeared on the stage for a brief time in 1873, in a last attempt to capitalize upon the tragedy.

Hosteen Klah (1867–1937)

Klah, "Left Handed," was a Navajo medicine man, sand painter, and weaver who was responsible for several innovations in opening up Navajo religious practices to permanent record. He was born at Bear Mountain, near Fort Wingate, New Mexico in late October 1867. His father was Hoskay Nolyae; his mother was Ahson Tsosie of the Tsithahni clan. He was born just before the Navajo were allowed to leave the misery of the Bosque Redondo concentration center for the return to their homeland in New Mexico. As a child he was named Ahway Eskay, the usual term for a youngster before puberty.

One of the most formative experiences of his early life occurred while he was living with an uncle. He was severely injured when the pony he was riding fell into an arroyo, and for many months the young lad was on crutches. His uncle was a medicine man, and to help the boy's recovery, performed the Wind Chant over his body. Following this five-day ritual, the Fire Ceremony was held. The impressionable boy was thrilled by these ancient ceremonies and he began to learn all he could from the knowledgeable older religious leaders.

At about this same time he was found to be a hermaphrodite. In some warrior cultures this would have earned him contempt, but the Navajo honored him for combining the best qualities of both sexes. In the early 1890s the New Mexico exhibit at the World's Columbian Exposition in Chicago was looking for a male weaver. Klah had already had a modest amount of experience as a weaver, contrary to usual Navajo practice where women do the weaving, and he was able to secure the position. He worked hard at the craft and eventually became one of the tribe's outstanding craftsmen. He wove his first complete rug in 1892–1893.

Hosteen Klah (1867–1937)
(*Wheelwright Museum*)

140

He continued studying with medicine men to improve his spiritual education and was able to provide invaluable data to Dr. Washington Matthews for *The Night Chant*, a classic in the field of American Indian ceremonial practices. This relationship may have increased Klah's fascination with the *Yeibichai* ritual, for he concentrated on the sequences of the ceremony for well over a quarter of a century. In 1917 he became a full-fledged medicine man and performed his first Night Chant, a nine-day religious ceremony held for curing purposes.

The unique art of creating designs with finely ground earth, commonly known as "sand painting," plays an important role in the *Yeibichai* ritual. The many materials used provide the colorful pigments for these highly ritualized designs, which are by nature impermanent and traditionally scattered outside the *hogán* following the completion of the ceremony. As one method of making a permanent record, he began to experiment with figurative designs, and was able to master the difficult technique of figure weaving. In 1916 he completed his first *Yei*-dancer rug. By 1919 he had developed his skills to a point where he was able to undertake actual reproductions of dry-sand ritual designs; that same year, he wove a "Whirling Logs" rug which has become a famous example of the art. Although many conservative Navajo deplored his weaving as sacreligious, there were no dire consequences, contrary to their forewarnings; and over the next 18 years he wove 25 permanent records of these motifs which were centuries old. He trained two of his nieces in the same art and between them another 25 textiles were produced.

His work with Franc J. Newcomb and Dr. Gladys Reichard of Columbia University was important in further establishing a body

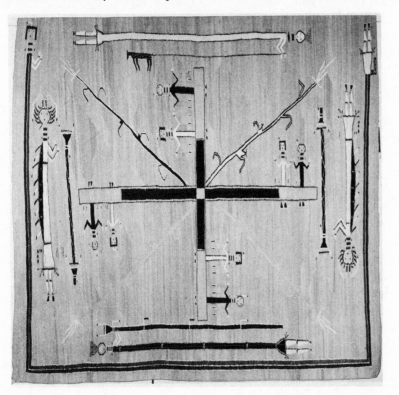

Sand Painting Blanket Woven by Hosteen Klah; Navajo (*Wheelwright Museum*)

of permanent record. His efforts have been memorialized in the Wheelwright Museum in Santa Fe, New Mexico, founded by Mary Cabot Wheelwright, a long-time friend. He died at the age of 70 on February 27, 1937 and was eventually buried on the Museum grounds. A thoroughly tradition-minded Navajo, he was successful in enlightening the outside world to the dignity, beauty, and vitality of Navajo ritual art.

John Konkapot (ca. 1700–ca. 1775)

Konkapot was a Mahican chief who was a major force in the conversion of a large number of his people to Christianity in the early 18th century. In 1724 he was among the signers of a treaty ceding to the colonial authorities the land in the Housatonic River Valley in what is today western Massachusetts. The settlers promply moved in, eventually forcing the Indian people out of their home village of Westenhuck, where the Mahican council fire (in effect, the capitol of the tribe) had been located since around 1664. Although this was a traumatic move, it did not result in uprisings as had similar invasions by Whites elsewhere.

Little is known of the early life of Konkapot. He was given the name "Captain" by Governor Belcher of Connecticut in 1634, by which time he had come into historical prominence and was known as Captain Konkapot (later Captain John) from that time on. The Indians invited the Moravian missionaries to move into their town, where Konkapot was converted to Christianity and baptized under the name John. Meanwhile, John Sergeant had founded the town of Stockbridge, New York in 1836, as a model community for dispossessed Indians. The colonial government had set this land aside for the exclusive use of the Mahican tribe, and the Indians left Westenhuck, moving to Stockbridge where they took the name "Stockbridge Indians" by which they were commonly known from then on. One segment of the group moved farther west to join the Christian Indians in Pennsylvania.

Around 1774, John Konkapot became chief of the Stockbridge and his people increasingly joined the Christian faith. With the help of Jonathan Edwards, who taught at Stockbridge from 1750 to 1757, the Stockbridge Indians became introduced to the White man's culture. Konkapot became the recognized spokesman for the Mahican and related Housatonic tribes, and figures prominently in the history of the Connecticut–New York area. All during the French and Indian Wars the Stockbridge people remained on the side of the English, despite the occasional attack they suffered from other tribes and the slow attrition of their land.

His leadership was respected by both groups in the New England region, and he protected his people to the best of his ability, often standing between them and the avaricious settlers who were steadily increasing in the Valley area. He died around 1775 on the eve of the American Revolution as the patriarch of the Stockbridge community. His death saved him from the experience of being forced to leave the reserved area, a fate which befell his people shortly afterward.

The LaFlesche Family

One of the more unusual American Indian families was that sired by Inshtamaza (also Estamaza), Iron Eye, more commonly known as Joseph LaFlesche. He was the son of a French fur trader and Waoo-winchtcha, an Osage woman. He was chosen by Big Elk to succeed him and became the last of the Omaha chiefs.

Joseph believed that the White man had come to stay, and that only realistic course for Indians was to adjust to this fact, however, unfortunate. Accordingly, while teaching his children to know and respect traditional life, he raised them in the White fashion. Following Omaha custom, he had several wives: Mary Gale, Hinnuaganun "The One Woman," a part Iowa woman, was the mother of five children, including Rosalie, a businesswoman; Susan, a physician; Mary, a teacher; and Susette, a worker for Indian rights. The second wife, Tainne (Elizabeth Esau), bore him five children, four who stayed on the reservation, and Francis, who became an outstanding anthropologist.

The three best known children follow in chronological order.

Susette LaFlesche (1854–1903)

Inshtatheumba (also Inshta Theaumba), "Bright Eyes," called familiarly "Yosette," was born on the Omaha reservation in Nebraska around 1854 and attended the Omaha Presbyterian Mission School; she was then sent to the Elizabeth (New Jersey) Institute for Young Ladies. After graduation, she taught in the reservation school, during which time she became increasingly involved in Indian affairs. In 1877 the government gave the Sioux all Ponca lands in Dakota and Nebraska and moved the Ponca by force to Indian Territory. About one-fourth of the Ponca people died in this new and unfertile land and in 1879 Chief Standing Bear and a group of his people set out on the journey back to their homeland. When the military arrested them, a local newspaperman, Thomas H. Tibbles, of the *Omaha Herald* publicized the tragedy and at a landmark trial, the Poncas were given their freedom.

Susette and her father had been very active in their support of the Ponca and when Standing Bear and Tibbles went east to plead their case, she and her brother Francis went along as interpreters. The contingent received tremendous popular support, especially in Boston, where an Indian Citizenship Committee was formed. In 1881 Susette delivered a paper before the Association for the Advancement of Women on "The Position, Occupation, and Culture of Indian Women." She also edited *Ploughed Under; the Story of an Indian Chief*, by Standing Bear. These several efforts put her in close daily relationship with Tibbles, and that same year they were married.

Susette and her husband made several tours of the United States and England to lecture on Indian rights and White wrongs. She was a remarkable speaker, presenting her arguments with clarity, force,

Susette LaFlesche (1854–1903) (*Smithsonian Institution, National Anthropological Archives*)

143

and dignity, and made a strong impression on her audience. They both appeared before Congressional committees that were at that time trying to deal with the Indian issue, and played a major role in achieving a fair hearing for Indian needs. They were both in favor of education and assimilation into the American mainstream, but not at the price of ignoring the Indian desire to retain some of their traditional cultural values. During the 1890s the couple lived in Washington, D.C., where they continued to lecture and write, and then returned to Lincoln, Nebraska.

Susette continued to lecture and write until her health began to fail. She died at the age of 49 on May 26, 1903 in Lincoln, Nebraska, just one year before Thomas Tibbles ran for Vice-President of the United States on the Populist ticket. She was buried at Bancroft, Nebraska. The couple had no children.

Francis LaFlesche (1857–1932)

Francis LaFlesche (1857–1932)
(*Nebraska State Historical Society*)

An anthropologist and writer, Francis lived in two worlds as a boy. Named Zhogaxe, "Woodworker," from *zho*, "wood," *gaxe*, "one who works," he was born in Omaha, Nebraska on December 25, 1857, the son of Iron Eye and Tainne. He attended the Presbyterian Mission School in Bellevue, Nebraska, learning the White man's language and ways. But back on the reservation, his father taught him to know and respect the traditional Indian culture. The boy participated in tribal dances and ceremonies, and in some of the last buffalo hunts on the Great Plains. He wrote vividly of this experience in *The Middle Five: Indian Boys at School*, published in 1900, which became a minor classic about the life and problems of adjustment of Indian pupils in White schools.

In 1881, Alice C. Fletcher, a noted anthropologist of the day, began her study of the Omaha Indians. Francis became her interpreter, and in time, her collaborator, and for the next 25 years the two worked at compiling one of the most thorough studies of an Indian tribe ever made. Most of the research was done by Francis; the organizing and writing was done by Alice. Coincidental to this study, Francis joined the staff of the U.S. Senate Committee on Indian Affairs, in Washington, as interpreter and advisor. Living in Washington, he also attended the National University School of Law, graduating with the degrees of Bachelor of Jurisprudence and Master of Laws.

In 1910, he joined the Bureau of American Ethnology, at which post he remained until his retirement in 1930. During this period he completed the second part of his lifework—the monumental study of the rituals and ceremonies of the Osage tribe. He also worked on language studies, publishing an *Osage Dictionary* in 1932. He was deeply interested in music, working with Alice Fletcher on *A Study of Omaha Music*, published in 1893, and on his own created an opera *Da-o-ma* in 1912, although it was never performed. Later he collaborated with Charles Wakefield Cadman, whose famous composition *From the Land of the Sky-Blue Water* was based upon Omaha themes introduced to him by LaFlesche.

All of this work was characterized by careful attention to detail and sensitive appreciation for the Indian heritage which was such an important part of his life. And although this achievement brought professional acclaim—he was awarded an honorary LLD by the University of Nebraska in 1926—he remained a modest, kindly person.

In his social life Francis was less successful. He married Alice Mitchell, an Omaha girl, but divorced her shortly after the birth of a child which he regarded as not his own, and later married Rosa Bourassa, a part Chippewa woman. They separated following a brief time together and he never married again. He died at the age of 75 near Macy, Nebraska on September 5, 1932, back home on his beloved reservation lands.

Susan LaFlesche (1865–1915)

The youngest of the three most famous LaFlesche children, Susan was born in Omaha, Nebraska on June 17, 1865. She followed her sister's path at the Elizabeth Institute for Young Ladies and then graduated in 1886 from Hampton Institute. But she undertook a quite different career by entering the Women's Medical College of Pennsylvania, where she graduated in 1889, becoming the first female Indian physician. For the next five years she was the government physician to the Omaha, traveling around the reservation on horseback. In 1894 she married Henri Picotte, who was half Sioux and half French, and moved to Bancroft, Nebraska, where her practice included both Indian and White patients. They had two boys, Caryl and Pierre; her husband died in 1905.

In 1905, Susan acted upon her strong religious interest, and became a missionary, working with the Omaha Blackbird Hills Presbyterian Church. She moved to the town of Walthill soon after its founding in 1906 and quickly became one of its leading citizens. She headed a delegation to Washington to fight for a prohibition on the sale of liquor, arguing successfully that such a proscription should be written into every deed of sale of Omaha property.

But her health was failing, and she became deaf; by the time of her premature death at the age of 50, on September 18, 1916, she had treated almost every member of the Omaha tribe. She died in the hospital at Walthill which she had founded, and in her honor it was renamed for her. She was buried at Bancroft, Nebraska.

Susan LaFlesche (1865–1915)
(*Smithsonian Institution, National Anthropological Archives*)

Roberta Campbell Lawson
(1878–1940)

Roberta Lawson was a part Delaware–part White woman who became a leader in many spheres of activity in Indian Territory and a social figure following Oklahoma statehood. She was born at Alluwe,

Roberta Campbell Lawson (1878–1940)
(*Oklahoma Historical Society*)

Indian Territory, on October 31, 1878. Her father was J. E. Campbell, a White rancher who had emigrated from Virginia; her mother Emmaline, was the daughter of Delaware chief Journeycake. Roberta was first educated at home and then left home to attend Hardin College near Independence, Missouri.

In 1901 she married Eugene Lawson, a banker, who later became involved in the Lawson Petroleum Company, the success of which allowed her certain financial independence and the opportunity to participate actively in many civic and educational enterprises. She served as trustee in many Oklahoma organizations, notably the Oklahoma Historical Society, the Tulsa University, and the Oklahoma College for Women. In 1931, she took upon herself the responsibility of administering drought relief funds for the state. She was especially active in the women's club movement; these clubs provided one of the few avenues open to women who were interested in public life—and in many states proved a potent force for social and political change.

Roberta Lawson was president of the Oklahoma State Federation of Women's Clubs from 1917 to 1919 and of the General Federation of Women's Clubs from 1935 to 1938.

Her several personal interests included the improvement of a woman's role in politics; a concern for the better education of future civil servants, much as West Point trained young men for the Army; and education for Indian people in the state. She died of leukemia at Nowata, Oklahoma on December 31, 1940, at the age of 62, leaving one son Edward. Throughout much of her life she had been an active collector of Indian art and books on Indian culture. At her death, these were bequeathed to Philbrook Art Center in Tulsa, Oklahoma, where they today form the Roberta Campbell Lawson Collection.

Lawyer (1795–1876)
(*Washington State Historical Society*)

Lawyer (ca. 1795–1876)

Hallalhotsoot, or Hollolsotetote, from Salish "The Talker," was a major leader of the Nez Percé from 1858 until 1871, at the time the Whites were attempting to confine the tribe to a reservation. As with most Nez Percé people, he was friendly to the early White explorers and settlers who came into the Pacific Northwest. As a young man, he was often a guide to such parties, and he first comes into mention when he was wounded in a fight with the Blackfoot at Pierre's Hole in Idaho, on August 7, 1832.

He was an intelligent man and a persuasive speaker, and when someone referred to him as "The Lawyer," following an especially moving speech, the name fit so well that he retained it for the rest of his life. He heard Spokane Garry preach, and out of curiosity welcomed the missionaries into the Nez Percé region. Since he had already learned some English through his earlier contacts with White explorers, he was at first the interpreter and then instructor to the missionaries in both the

Nez Percé and Flathead languages. Although he was sympathetic to their message, at this stage of his life he did not become a Christian.

In 1855 there was a great gathering of the tribes at Walla Walla to talk peace and settle reservation boundary problems with the United States negotiators. The old chief, named Ellis, had just died from smallpox, and because of divided feelings within the tribe, the Indians asked Superintendent of Indian Affairs Henry A. G. Lee to name a new chief. He selected a man named Richard, whom he felt would be most malleable to White interests, but Richard died shortly after he was selected as the new chief. He was succeeded by Lawyer, a far more able leader; he and Chief Joseph lead the Nez Percé at the negotiations, and Lawyer was the only chief to eventually sign his name in writing, rather than with the usual X.

His ability to read and write was notable again when in later negotiations, the Indians persisted in their efforts to force the commissioners to recognize the fact that the government had completely failed to honor the terms of the previous treaty. Following a rereading of the treaty by Commissioner Hale, and his attempts to gloss over some of the more glaring discrepancies, Lawyer pulled out a small notebook from his pocket, and proceeded to read some of his notes which he had made during the original council eight years before. His words, quoting the White negotiator's professions of law, permanence and truth, completely silenced the discomfited Hale, who abruptly adjourned the session.

The treaty was signed, essentially, because of many of the Treaty Chiefs (as those chiefs were named who agreed to the pact) lived on lands which would not be affected by its terms. Indeed, when word came to him that a group of hostile Cayuse warriors planned to kill some of the Whites, Lawyer moved his tent next to the tent of the latter, effectively quelling the plot. But in 1861, gold was discovered in the Northwest, and a flood of settlers poured into the area in such numbers that within the year Nez Percé culture was completely overwhelmed by the newcomers, and never wholly recovered. In 1863, after the settlers had continuously violated the reservation boundaries and the Whites refused to take any effective action—other than to dispatch a new United States commission to force the further diminishing of those boundaries—many of the Nez Percé, including Joseph, lost their patience.

Lawyer, now a Christian and still disposed to have faith in the Whites, also protested against the unfair treatment of his tribe, and finally went to Washington in 1868 to negotiate a new agreement. Although the words on paper seemed to guarantee the Nez Percé people an honorable arrangement, as with so many prior compacts, the actions of the authorities were essentially unchanged. However, by this time the chief had fallen into disrepute with his people, due in no small part to his support of the Whites and the continued role he played as middleman during many confrontations. In 1871 he was forced to relinquish his leadership, and he died at his home on Jaunuary 3, 1876, just a year before the Nez Percé tribe set out on its history-making flight under the leadership of Chief Joseph and Looking Glass.

Typical Cornhusk "Sally Bag"; Nez Percé
(*Museum of the American Indian*)

Leatherlips (ca. 1732–1810)

The origin for the name Leatherlips is not known; his Huron name is recorded as Shateyaronyah (or Shateiarônhia) "Two Equal Clouds." He was a Wyandot chief of the Sandusky band and was a signer of the Treaty of Greenville, Ohio in 1795. His birthdate is not known, although he was said to be 63 years of age at the time of the Treaty signing.

Leatherlips was always friendly to the Whites, although he was aware of the danger to his people from their increasing settlement of the Ohio region. He was noted throughout the area as having a remarkable character and personality; apparently his outstanding qualities—and perhaps more importantly, his strong friendship for the Americans and his influence among them—aroused the jealousy or hostility of Tecumseh (some say Tenskwátawa), for it is alleged that he was responsible for the plot to remove the Wyandot chief.

Whatever the origin, it seems clear that Leatherlips was charged with practicing witchcraft—an accusation which, in those days, was tantamount to subjecting the victim to a sentence of death. In this accusation, Tecumseh seems certainly to have assented, and was able to secure the nomination of another Huron, named Roundhead, as the executioner.

The sentence was handed to Leatherlips by his own brother in the form of an inscribed birchbark token bearing the design of a tomahawk. The chief made no effort to resist, nor to escape; the site of the execution was near his home north of Columbus, on the Scioto River. He was executed on June 1, 1810, in front of several witnesses, including some Whites—one of them a justice of the peace who tried to save him without success. After he sang his death song, the old man knelt in front of his executioner, who then killed him by a blow of his war club. The calm manner in which Leatherlips met his fate impressed the Whites and many accounts of the episode were published in the journals of the time. In 1888 a memorial was erected on the spot by The Wyandot Club of Columbus.

Little Crow (ca. 1820–1863)

Taheton Wakawa Mini, "Crow Hunts Walking," or Tahatan Wakuwa Mini, "Hawk That Hunts Walking"; also Tahetan Wakan Mani, "Sacred Pigeon-Hawk Which Comes Walking," a Mdewakanton Sioux leader who was a major figure in the uprising at New Ulm, Minnesota in 1862. His name is recorded in many forms; another common title is Taoyateduta (or Taoyatechata), "His Red People." The term Little Crow seems to derive from a Chippewa appellation referring to a dried crow skin charm which he regularly wore as a talisman; from this the French called him Le Petit Corbeau.

Little Crow was born around 1820 at the Kapoosia Village near south St. Paul, Minnesota. His mother was the daughter of a chief of the Leaf Dweller clan and his father was Cetanwakuwa, "Charging Hawk." Other accounts give his mother as Minneokadawin, "Empties Into Water," and his father as Wakoyantanke, "Big Thunder." Little Crow had two brothers who, in his youth, became jealous of him, and on May 10, 1846, tried to assassinate him. The shot broke both of his arms and the Agency surgeon advised amputation. He refused to suffer such a loss and was able to save his hands, although they were badly injured and he never had full use of them for the rest of his life.

Little Crow had six wives during his life, two of whom were "political," in the sense that they were taken by him to firm up relationships with neighboring tribes or bands. He had at least 22 children by these marriages. Physically, he is described as tall, deliberate in manner, and possessed of a powerful, dominating personality, yet one who changed his mind frequently.

He seems never to have been very friendly to the Whites, although he used them to suit his purposes from time to time. In 1846 he requested that the Indian Agent at Fort Snelling send a missionary to remove the scourge of liquor, in response to which Reverend Thomas S. Williamson was sent to the tribe. He was a signer of the Treaty of Mendota on August 5, 1851, which ceded most of the Sioux territory in Minnesota. In spite of this earlier indication of agreement, Little Crow used every occasion to argue against yielding Indian lands, and supported resistance against the settlers who sought to occupy the area. He was retained by the Agency authorities to hunt down Inkpaduta after the massacre at Okoboji and Spirit Lake in 1856–1857. He took a force of 106 warriors with him, and caught up with Inkpaduta in late July 1857; three of the major warriors were killed, although Inkpaduta himself escaped. Little Crow returned, feeling that he had carried out his commission but Major Cullen, the Superintendent of Indian Affairs, failed to follow up on this escape, which in essence allowed Inkpaduta to remain unpunished for the murders. Many critics cite this failure as the direct cause of the later outbreak by Little Crow at New Ulm, since the Indians interpreted the reaction as one of weakness on the part of the White man.

The people of Kapoosia had been moved some years earlier to a reservation set aside for them on the Upper Minnesota River. They had lived there in relative peace until the outbreak on August 18, 1862, at which time Little Crow led a large force in an attack on Fort Ridgely on August 20–22. Although the attack was unsuccessful and he was wounded, the Indians roamed throughout the region, attacking settlements and settlers without mercy, culminating finally in a bloody raid on the frontier town of New Ulm. In all, over 1000 Whites were killed during the brief outbreak, which was subsequently brought to an end by a victory of the Army forces at Wood Lake on September 23, 1862, under General Henry Sibley.

Little Crow fled into the forest with several hundred warriors; some were captured, but a military party of over 6000 soldiers failed to find the main party, and Little Crow fled into Canada with about 250 men. They later returned to Minnesota, attacking isolated settlers, and killing some 40 more, venturing as far as within sight of St. Paul. Thirty-two of the Indians who were captured were executed

Little Crow (1820–1863)
(*State Historical Society of Wisconsin*)

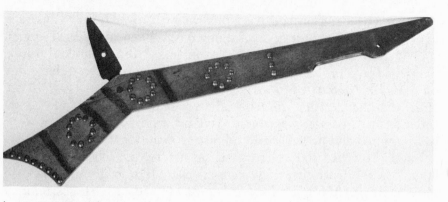

Gunstock Warclub with Iron Blade;
Sioux
(*Museum of the American Indian*)

in a mass hanging, but the fear of further attack overshadowed the settlements for many years afterwards.

Little Crow and his son, while foraging for food in the forest near St. Paul, were encountered by surprise by a settler named Nathan Lampson and his son Chauncey. In the brief encounter, Little Crow was killed on July 3, 1873, near Hutchison, Minnesota. The son, Woinapa, was wounded but escaped. The body of the Sioux was brought back to town and thrown on the garbage dump of the local slaughterhouse, as a token of the hatred which the settlers felt towards him. Later, the skeleton was placed on public exhibit by the Minnesota Historical Society; but in 1971, the remains were turned over to the descendants of the chief for burial in the Santee Sioux cemetery, near Flandreau, South Dakota. The repercussions of the New Ulm attacks culminated in the complete removal of the Sioux from Minnesota.

Little Raven (ca. 1817–1889)

Hosa, meaning "Young Crow," was the most articulate and successful spokesman of the Arapaho tribe for peace with neighboring tribes and with the incoming Whites. He was born on the Platte River in central Nebraska about 1817, the son of the hereditary chief of the tribe. Little Raven became chief when his father died in 1855. A born leader, admired for his intelligence, oratorical skill, and impressive appearance, he guided his people through one of the most difficult periods of their history.

In 1861 he signed the Treaty of Fort Wise, Colorado, but shortly afterwards became disillusioned with the failure of the White men to keep their promises, and he joined with the Cheyenne war parties as the leader of the Southern Arapaho on the Kansas border. The odds against the Indian forces were too great, however, and he was one of the nine signers of the Treaty of Medicine Lodge, Kansas on October 28, 1867, by which the Arapaho and others agreed to move to reservations. That Little Raven was not an ignorant signer, however, is indicated by a comment he made two years earlier, at the Little Arkansas River: "Boone came out and got them [the Indians] to sign a paper, but they did not know what it meant. The Cheyennes signed it first, then I; but we did not know what it was. That is why I want an interpreter, so that I can know what I sign." He continued to follow this practice

Painted Sun Dance Buffalo Skull;
Arapaho
(*Museum of the American Indian*)

150

in all his future signings, although it proved of little help in the face of White determination to separate the Indian from his land.

Many of the Plains tribes, especially the younger warriors, grew restless at confinement on the reservations. They longed for the old days of buffalo hunting and freedom to raid on the open prairies. Skirmishes and battles became common as they stole away from the agencies from time to time. Little Raven was able to keep most of his warriors away from the soldiers' guns, but recognized the ever-present danger. In 1871 he was one of a number of Indian leaders who visited the Eastern cities. He told an enraptured audience at Cooper Union in New York City: "I have been waiting many years for Washington to give us our rights. The government sent agents and soldiers out there to us, and both have driven us from our lands. We do not want to fight [but] the White man has taken away everything."

When Little Raven returned west, he told his people that the White Father in Washington would take care of them all, would raise their corn and feed their livestock, and tend the sick. He stayed at peace during the Kiowa–Cheyenne wars of 1874–1875, secure in the knowledge that he had met with the Principal Chief of the Whites; he himself had been to the mint where the great presses printed more than enough money for all of the needs of his tribe. When the Indian Agent protested that there simply was not enough money to do all of the things he claimed, he simply laughed at such ignorance.

The days of warfare were over for him, and he lived out the rest of his days peacefully. He died at Cantonment, in Indian Territory, in 1889 at the age of 72, fulfilling a reputation of having maintained leadership of the progressive group of the Southern Arapaho for over 20 years. He was succeeded by Nawat, "Left Handed Man."

Little Raven (1817–1889)
(*Museum of the American Indian*)

Little Turtle (1752–1812)

Michikinikwa, or Mishekunnoghwuah, Meshikinnoquah, was born in Little Turtle Village on the Eel River near Fort Wayne, Indiana, of a Mahican mother and Acquenacke, a Miami chief. The exact date is unknown, but it was sometime in 1752; his name refers to his size at birth. The boy apparently received some education among the Jesuits. According to tribal custom he belonged to his mother's tribe, but the Miami elders recognized his talents and welcomed him into council discussion. He was friendly to the British in his youth and participated in the massacre of a French detachment on the frontier in 1780. Ten years later he was a leader in the defeat of the American Brigadier General Josiah Harmar on the Miami River, and in 1791 at St. Mary's, took a similar toll of the forces under General Arthur Sinclair.

The newly independent American government refused to relinquish its claim to the Northwest Territories, however, and in 1792 General "Mad Anthony" Wayne took over from Sinclair. This new commander was called "the chief who never sleeps" by Little Turtle, who now advised his people to seek peace. However, other chiefs wanted to press

Little Turtle (1752–1812)
(*Smithsonian Institution, National Anthropological Archives*)

151

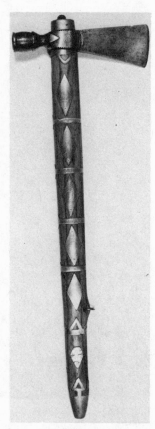

Tomahawk of Little Turtle; Miami
(*Museum of the American Indian*)

on to more victories, and Little Turtle was present, but not in command, at the Battle of Fallen Timbers. The Indians were decisively defeated and in 1795 Little Turtle and the other leaders signed the Treaty of Greenville, Ohio. Reminded of his long record of warfare against the Americans, he said, "I am the last to sign the treaty; I will be the last to break it."

In 1797 he was invited to Washington, D.C., where he met President Washington, General Kosciusko, and other American leaders. General Kosciusko presented him with his own brace of beautifully worked pistols. After his return to what was to become Indiana, he signed many of the treaties involved in William Henry Harrison's speedy (some thought overbearing) desire to acquire most of the Indian lands. The Miami began to distrust his leadership, but he was able to convince most of them that the course of acquiescence was best under the circumstances. When Tecumseh urged the Indians in the area to join his confederation and oppose American expansionism militarily, Little Turtle's influence kept most of the Miami neutral. His efforts to turn his people to peaceful agricultural pursuits were only partially successful, and his battle to induce the government to control liquor smuggling was wholly defeated by White interference.

Like many other Indian chiefs who had been active warriors in youth, Little Turtle came to accept the White man's presence and even to adopt some of his customs. He had one wife, who gave him a daughter, Manwangopath, "Sweet Breeze," and in his old age he was supported somewhat comfortably on a government pension. He died at Fort Wayne on July 14, 1812, under the care of an Army surgeon.

Little Wolf (ca. 1820–1904)

Ohkom Kakit, a famed Northern Cheyenne chief who was the leader with Dull Knife of the epic 1500-mile journey of the Cheyenne from their exile in Indian Territory back to their northern home. He was born around 1820 in Montana near the juncture of the Eel and Blue Rivers.

Known in his youth as Two Tails, he had gained a reputation as a warrior by the middle of the 19th century, mostly in battles with other tribes—at a time when only a few White men had come to disturb the Indian way of life. In 1851 the Cheyenne signed the famous Big Treaty, as it was known to the Indians, but recorded by the Whites as the Treaty of Horse Creek. This agreement gave the Americans the right to cross Cheyenne territory with their wagon trains, and relations between the two were mostly peaceful.

In 1864, however, the Army killed many of the people in the camp of Black Kettle, a Cheyenne chief seeking peace. This changed the feelings of many of the Indians, and the next year Little Wolf and many of his warriors took to the warpath to avenge this unnecessary slaughter. A brief period of peace followed when the Army withdrew from their territory by the terms of the Treaty of Fort Laramie in 1868. Little

Little Wolf (1820–1904)
(*Oklahoma Historical Society*)

152

Wolf and his people were even given possession of Fort Phil Kearney, which had been built just a few years earlier at the cost of many lives. But they could not stay in one place for very long, and when the Cheyenne left to follow the buffalo herds, they burned the fort to the ground.

In 1876, after Custer's defeat at the Little Bighorn, the Army began an all-out campaign against the Plains Indians. In November, a force of about 1100 cavalrymen destroyed Dull Knife's village, capturing all of their ponies. Many of the people escaped, but agreed to surrender to General George Crook who promised them a reservation in their own country. However, it was not long before Little Wolf and most of the other Cheyenne were sent to Indian Territory where they were expected to unite with the Southern Cheyenne and start life anew.

Most of the Northern Cheyenne found Indian Territory a poor place to live; it was not like their home. It was desolate and impossible for agricultural or hunting activities and many of the people became ill with fever and pneumonia. Of some 1000 people who arrived at the Agency near Darlington in August 1877, more than 600 became ill within two months, and during the ensuing winter, 43 died. Accustomed to life on the high dry Montana plains, the Cheyenne people readily fell victim to malaria, the scourge of the Oklahoma region. Rations and medicine promised from Washington failed to arrive and the Agency physician could not cope with the widespread problem, although he expended every effort.

Sick in body, heart, and mind, the Cheyenne wanted only to leave, or die. Early in July, Little Wolf went with a group of his men to the Agent, asking either to be allowed to return to their homeland, or to go to Washington to plead their cause. The Agent tried to get them to put off their complaint until the following year, when they would become more accustomed to the region, but they refused, feeling that only more deaths would ensue. In September 1878, after several attempts to convince the Agent that they had to return home or perish, Little Wolf, Dull Knife, and about 300 Cheyenne people started the long trek towards Montana. Although he was now about 57 years old, Little Wolf still had the stamina of his younger days. It was he who made most of the decisions and planned the strategy which enabled the small band to elude the thousands of soldiers dispatched to bring them back.

After crossing the Platte River, the two forces split, in part to make it more difficult for the soldiers to follow them, but in part due to some disagreement between Dull Knife and Little Wolf as to the wisest strategy to follow on the trip. The band following Little Wolf was followed by several different bodies of soldiers, but always refused to shoot first; in four major encounters, the number of people killed on both sides was remarkably few, considering the desperate circumstances. At last, on the west side of the Little Missouri River, not far from the mouth of the Powder River, Lieutenant W. P. Clark met with Little Wolf and induced him to surrender and return to Fort Keogh.

At Fort Keogh General Nelson Miles met with the Cheyenne and convinced them that he would find them a reservation in their home region. The long trip had caused great suffering for the Cheyenne but they were successful in achieving their goal. Little Wolf had managed

Little Wolf's Tomahawk; Cheyenne
(*Museum of the American Indian*)

to elude his pursuers with slight loss of life, while Dull Knife and his band were far less successful; they had been captured shortly after separating, and many were killed in an abortive attempt to escape from confinement at Fort Robinson.

Subsequently, when General Miles suggested that Little Wolf and his warriors should enlist in the Army as Indian Scouts, they quickly agreed; life on the reservation was monotonous and scouting paid well. Besides, it offered a certain amount of excitement, as well as an occasional taste of the old days. Little Wolf lived on for almost 30 years on the Tongue River Reservation. He became blind in his old age, still a respected figure with an alert mind. He died in 1904, about 84 years of age.

Logan (ca. 1723–1780)

James Logan was an important Iroquois leader born in Shamokin (now Sunbury), Pennsylvania about 1723 (some say at Auburn, New York about 1725). His Cayuga name, Tahgahjute, meaning "His Eyelashes Jut Out" is perhaps a reference to his prominent brows, or possibly to a habit of peering sharply at others (some say "Short Dress"). His mother was a Cayuga woman; his father was Shikellamy, a part-French man raised by the Oneida. The son was named for Quaker James Logan, colonial secretary and Acting Governor of the Pennsylvania Colony. He was popularly known as "Logan the Mingo."

Logan was a strong friend of the Whites, both in Pennsylvania and later in Ohio where he became a leader among the Mingo people (a term referring to those Iroquois who left the main group in New York and settled outside the home area), at which time he was given the name Sayughdowa. But in 1774 his attitude changed radically; White settlers killed some of his people in an unprovoked attack, including his wife and other members of his family. This treacherous act turned him implacably against the colonists; with Mingo and Shawnee supporters who were determined to drive the Whites out, he sought revenge throughout the area from the Allegheny River to Cumberland Gap.

The Shawnee chief Cornstalk had also become involved in driving out the Whites, but was defeated, and a peace parley was planned in November 1774. Logan was invited to attend the conclave by John Gibson, an emissary of Lord Dunmore, the governor of Virginia. The Indian replied in a memorable statement which was read at the conference, and subsequently reprinted in newspapers throughout the colonies and in Europe. Although it is a translation into English, and thereby somewhat altered, it has become a highly regarded standard of Indian oratory:

> I appeal to any white man to say if he ever entered Logan's cabin hungry and he gave him not meat; if he ever came cold and naked he clothed him not. During the course of the last long and bloody war, Logan remained idle in his cabin, an advocate for peace. Such was my love for the whites that my countrymen pointed as I passed and said, 'Logan is a friend of the white man.' I had even thought to have lived with you but for the injuries of one man. Colonel Cresap,

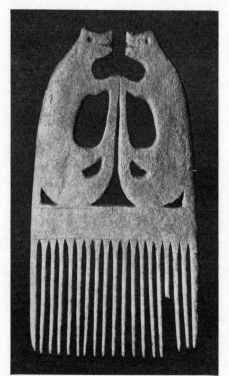

Carved Bone Hair Comb; Iroquois
(*Museum of the American Indian*)

the last spring, in cold blood and unprovoked, murdered all the relatives of Logan, not even sparing his wives and children. There runs not a drop of my blood in the veins of any living creature.

This calls on me for revenge, I have sought it; I have killed many; I have fully glutted my vengeance. For my country I rejoice at the beams of peace; but do not harbor a thought that mine is the joy of fear. Logan never felt fear. He will not turn his heel to save his life. Who is there to mourn for Logan? Not one.

Although believed by Logan to have been responsible, Cresap was later found innocent of the murders; these were charged to another lawless group of settlers led by one Daniel Greathouse. But the result was the same: the Revolution came and Logan and most of the frontier Indians allied with the English. The outcome left him frustrated, and in his later years he became dissolute and quarrelsome, and was murdered near Detroit in 1780, probably by a nephew named Todkados.

He is described as being about 6′ tall, of calm and distinguished appearance, with a quality of character which was at once commanding, yet considerate of those around him. He was a determined leader of his people, but was unable to stem the ever-increasing flood of settlers.

Lone Wolf (ca. 1820–1879)

Lone Wolf (1820–1879)
(*Smithsonian Institution, National Anthropological Archives*)

Guipago was a Kiowa chief who was active at the time the U.S. Army was fighting the Indians in Texas. He was, in general, opposed to the peaceful policy of Kicking Bird and in favor of the sometimes belligerent independence of Big Tree, Satank, and Satanta. He was one of the nine who signed the Treaty of Medicine Lodge of 1867 which placed the Kiowa on a reservation.

After the death of Satank and the imprisonment of Big Tree and Satanta, Lone Wolf became the principal chief of the Kiowa living around Fort Sill. He was regarded with great respect, for it was known that he had considerable medicine power—during a tremendous lightning storm, his tepee had been struck by a bolt which killed his wife and child, but left him unharmed.

He made two trips to Washington, D.C., to talk peace and to secure help from the authorities there, but although he was exposed to the city and its resources, he seems not to have been impressed either by the government's power, or its treaty guarantees. In 1873 he was able to gain the release of Satanta and Big Tree from prison by promising that his tribe would remain at peace.

That same year, however, his son and nephew were killed by a party of raiding Texans; embittered by this action, Lone Wolf led a group of warriors south to recover the bodies and to avenge their deaths. During the following year he became feared throughout the Southern Plains as the leader of the hostile portion of the Kiowa tribe; he joined Quanah Parker and his Comanche in their attack on Adobe Walls, and fought the Army to a standstill at the Anadarko Agency on August 22, 1874. He was engaged in several running battles with the Texas

Rangers, finally heading south to escape Army capture.

The order went out for his arrest at all costs, and in the spring of 1875 General Ranald S. Mackenzie succeeded in forcing him to surrender at Fort Sill. Lone Wolf and about 75 of his warriors were sent to Fort Marion, in Florida, where he remained until May 1878. The long imprisonment broke the chief's health, however, and he died in 1879, just a year after his release, and was buried on Mt. Scott, in Indian Territory. He was succeeded by Mamaday (Mamanti), his adopted son, who was also known as Lone Wolf. The older man had given the younger warrior his name—and right of succession—in gratitude for a feat of bravery in battle during the Texas raiding expedition of 1874. The gesture proved not to have been in vain—in time, Mamaday proved fully capable of walking in the moccasins of his foster father.

Will West Long (1870–1947)

Wili Westi, a well-known Cherokee informant and farmer, was born in the Big Cove, North Carolina, about 1870. His father was John Long, a Cherokee Baptist preacher; his mother was Sally Terrapin, a traditionalist Cherokee woman. Will grew up in one of the most conservation Indian communities isolated in the Smoky Mountains. The community was composed of several Cherokee families who had hidden in the back country at the time the Indians were being rounded up for removal to Oklahoma in 1838.

Although the father was a Christian, the Long household was basically pagan, and the extensive knowledge which the mother had of traditional customs was especially influential in the future career of the young man. However, throughout his life, this split in religious and philosophical outlook was to greatly affect him. His early introduction to White schools was at High Point, North Carolina, and proved an unhappy experience which lasted only a short time. He did eventually learn English and was also taught the Cherokee syllabary by a schoolmate—skills which enabled him later to become a professional interpreter and translator. In 1887 the noted ethnologist James Mooney came to study Cherokee life, and soon found an excellent interpreter and scribe in Will. Some seven years later Mooney urged him to enroll in an experiment in higher education being conducted at Hampton Institute, after which he spent several years in Massachusetts where he absorbed more and more of White civilization.

In 1904 he returned to the reservation because of his mother's death and found to his surprise that the "old ways" still had a strong hold on his emotions. For a long time he had been in poor health, but the environment and Cherokee medical cures restored him to good health—and with his restored health his faith in Indian culture increased. His relationship with Mooney, who was still working in the area, became closer and the two became good friends, working in harmony until about 1920. During this time, and subsequently, Will served as informant and interpreter for many of the nation's leading scholars.

Carved Wooden Mask by Will West Long; Cherokee
(*Museum of the American Indian*)

The swift changes to which the Cherokee were now exposed were demoralizing; there were simply not enough people numerically to withstand many of the social and political pressures. Disease had seriously affected the health of almost all of the people, and their isolated location tended to work against their efforts to secure a voice in support of better living conditions. Will seems to have sensed that such knowledge as existed should be permanently stored in books, documents, and museums if it were to survive. To this end he devoted most of his mature years, even though he was troubled by occasional doubts as to the propriety of his work, and interrupted by the needs of his farm.

Will West Long continued work on translations and the preservation of Cherokee data, particularly in the fields of medicine and curing. He had learned to carve ceremonial masks from his cousin, Charley Lawson, and his products were eagerly sought after by museums and collectors throughout the country, many of which today own examples of his skill. He died on March 14, 1947 of a heart attack at Qualla, North Carolina, at the age of 77.

Looking Glass (1823?-1877)

Allalimya Takanin, the leading war chief during the dramatic 1600-mile flight of the Nez Percé towards Canada in 1877. He was born about 1823 in the Wallowa country, the son of chief Apash Wyakaikt (Flint Necklace), the head of the Asotin band, also known as Looking Glass. The name came from a small trade mirror which the father wore around his neck on a thong. At his death in 1863, the son took the glass for himself, adopting at the same time the name by which he was known for the rest of his life.

The Nez Percé tribe had always had a peaceful relationship with the Whites in their region, even after the discoveries of gold on their lands in 1855 and 1862. In 1863, however, a treaty was signed at Lapwai, Idaho which forced them to accept life on a comparatively small reservation there. This was in clear violation of an earlier agreement, and the Indians were quick to point this out to the U.S. Commissioners, but the latter impatiently waved the argument aside. The White population in the area totaled almost 19,000 people and the government had determined that the Indians would have to move out to make room for them.

Looking Glass and several of the other chiefs refused to sign the treaty; these Indians became known as the "nontreaty Nez Percés." In May 1877, General Oliver O. Howard delivered an ultimatum to the Nez Percé: move voluntarily onto the reservation or be forced to do so by the Army. The chiefs, conscious of the superior military forces arrayed against them, reluctantly consented, and were given 30 days in which to leave their homes and move to the new area. The abrupt move, combined with the already existing bitterness between Indians and settlers only increased the tension of the time. Two of the young Nez Percé warriors killed some White settlers and Howard

Looking Glass (1823–1877)
(*Smithsonian Institution, National Anthropological Archives*)

decided to move the Indians out at once, instead of allowing them further time.

Accordingly, in July, a force of troops under Lieutenant Stephen C. Whipple approached Looking Glass's encampment. The chief had moved his people away from the Lapwai Agency area, feeling that they would be safer and less involved with the increasing hostilities; in truth, the Nez Percé were engaged in passive resistance and were not activists for either approach. The chief came out of his dwelling and asked that Whipple leave his people in peace. What happened demonstrated much of the difficulty between Indian and White in the early days. Whipple not only had trained, well-disciplined soldiers with him, but also a number of volunteer militia—settlers who had no love for the Indians. One of the settlers fired at a warrior against whom he had a grudge and then firing broke out all around. The soldiers attacked the camp without reason, looted and burned the village, turning once-neutral people into active hostiles. Looking Glass and his people escaped, united with Joseph and the other militant nontreaty Indians, and The Nez Percé War was on.

Looking Glass became the major military influence in the battles that followed. As war chief, his advice was listened to and usually followed, even though it proved disastrous on two critical occasions. The first was on August 9, 1877 at Big Hole, where he assured everyone that it would be safe to rest. He felt that they were safe from pursuit, and when two Flathead scouts came into the camp urging the Nez Percé to take a short route into Canada via their country he argued successfully against the idea. He did not trust the Flatheads, did not feel the route would offer game, and also thought that they might be forced to fight their way north.

But their leisurely travel proved their undoing. The government forces launched a surprise attack early in the morning of August 9, killing and wounding many Indians. Although the Nez Percé rallied and successfully drove off the forces, the damage was serious. Joseph took over, for Looking Glass had fallen from grace due to his bad strategy and it was clear that now the Indians would have to run and fight.

Although Looking Glass had been replaced by Lean Elk as the war leader, while Joseph took on the overall command of the Nez Percé retreat, his influence remained very strong. He was still regarded as one whose voice was important in war councils. Some six weeks later when the Nez Percé reached Bear Paw Mountains, seeking the pass which would lead through that range and into Canada, Looking Glass once again advocated a slower pace although they were only 40 miles south of the Canadian border. The trip had taken a tragic toll of the older people and he felt that they had outdistanced the Army, now under General Nelson A. Miles.

But for a second time, Looking Glass underestimated the persistence of the military men pursuing him, even though, as earlier, the medicine leader warned of impending defeat. Cheyenne scouts had picked up the trail, discovered the camp, and reported back to Miles of their nearby location; on September 30, 1877 he attacked. Initially the Indians outfought the Army, holding off Miles for four days and inflicting a tremendous number of casualties on the troops. But the freezing weather, combined with their fewer numbers, the arrival of badly needed reinforcements under General Howard for the Army and—perhaps most critically—the numbing psychological effect of the constant pursuit to demoralize the already exhausted warriors, forced the Nez Percé to consider the need to surrender, so short of their goal.

Looking Glass still opposed yielding, having lost all trust in the White man's word. He was determined to press on with his band to Canada and Sitting Bull's group. Several other chiefs agreed to accompany him on a desperate flight north; but he was destined never to know the outcome. Shortly after noon on October 5, 1877, he was called out to see what was believed to be an Indian courier from the Sioux approaching in the distance. As he jumped up to see for himself he was struck in the head by a bullet. His was the last fatality in the Nez Percé War.

Fred Lookout (ca. 1860–1949)

Wahtsake Tumpah, "The Eagle Who Sits Thinking," was an Osage chief who led his people through a period during which the exploitation of oil deposits on their reservation made them the richest people in the world for a time. Born about 1860 near Independence, Kansas, Fred Lookout's father, Wahkasetompahpe, was a great chief who had united the two families of the Osage in Indian Territory and who kept them together during the early days of marginal survival. Fred's mother was Metsahehum, an Osage woman.

The young man was sent off the reservation for an education and attended the Osage Boarding School at Pawhuska, Oklahoma and then went on to Carlisle Indian School. Returning to the reservation, he was elected to the Osage Tribal Council in 1896. By the time Lookout became head chief of the Osage Nation following the death of his father in 1913, he was able to deal with the White man on equal terms.

Grizzly Bearclaw Necklace, Otter Fur Trim; Osage
(*Museum of the American Indian*)

Fred Lookout (1860–1949)
(*Western History Collections, University of Oklahoma Library*)

160

The discovery of oil near the Osage capital at Pawhuska brought an influx of boomers, prospectors, and fortune hunters greedy to take what they could from the Indian owners of the lands. Boomtowns sprang up overnight on the Southern Plains and the Osage people became incredibly prosperous—in 1925 the average Osage family had an annual income of over $50,000.

But Lookout and other tribal leaders succeeded in holding fast to the tribe's mineral rights in the face of overwhelming pressure and they also managed to keep most of the Osage people from being cheated by the scavenging Whites. He was reelected nine times as principal chief and led many delegations to Washington, D.C., to ensure that the rights of the Osage were not violated. As a member of the Native American Church, he was deeply knowledgeable in the peyote ritual. He married Julia Pryor Mosechehe of Pawhuska, by whom he had two sons and one daughter. Known throughout the Oklahoma area for his dignity, integrity, and kindliness, he was widely mourned at his death at the age of 88 on August 28, 1949 at his home in Pawhuska, Oklahoma.

Alexander McGillivray
(ca. 1759–1793)

Hippo-ilk-mico, "The Good Child King," was born in 1759 in what is now Elmore County, Alabama, at the trading post of his father, Lachlan McGillivray, a wealthy Scotch trader. His mother was Sehoy Marchand, the daughter of a French army captain, and a Creek matron of the influential Wind clan. He lived at the family home until he, was about 14 and then went to Charleston, South Carolina and Savannah, Georgia to pursue his education. Shortly after his return home, his talents and training led to his being elected as head chief of the Creek Nation.

As the American Revolution drew closer, Lachlan, a Loyalist, returned to Scotland, and Alexander became a British agent with the rank and pay of colonel. The subsequent confiscation by Georgia of property inherited from his father embittered him, and caused him to embark upon active hostility. At one time he was said to have had 10,000 warriors at his command from the Creek, Chickamauga, and Seminole tribes. He led many attacks against the White settlements, particularly in eastern Tennessee and the Cumberland Valley.

After the war McGillivray worked to build a united Indian front against further White settlement and to promote his own trading interests. In 1784, as "Emperor of the Creeks and the Seminoles," he signed a treaty with the Spanish in Florida, along with his long-time partner, William Panton, assuring Spanish monopoly on trade with the Creek confederacy. He used arms acquired from Spain to supply his warriors in their continuing war of attrition against American settlers in Georgia and along the Cumberland River.

McGillivray himself was not known as a warrior, but as a skilled diplomat, a shrewd trader, and a respected leader of his people.

The United States repeatedly tried to make peace with McGillivray, and in 1790 he was persuaded to go to New York. He met with President Washington and signed a peace treaty that gave up some disputed Creek lands, assured him of a $1200 annual salary, and the rank of brigadier general in the Army. But two years later, back in the South, he repudiated the treaty and repledged his allegiance to the Spanish, who had offered him a remuneration of $3500 per year. Though he held four somewhat contradictory positions—Indian chief and Emperor, British general, Spanish colonel, and American brigadier general—he was able to skillfully manipulate them all for his own and his tribe's best interests. His last years were marked by illness and he died on February 17, 1793 at Panton's home in Pensacola, Florida. At his death he owned his home, Little Tallase, near Wetumpka, Alabama, several plantations, 60 slaves, 300 head of cattle, and many horses. He married twice; once to the daughter of Joseph Curnell, and his second wife who was the mother of a son, Alexander, and two daughters.

A tall, handsome man, McGillivray was said to have "the polished urbanity of the Frenchman, the duplicity of the Spaniard, the cool sagacity of the Scotsman, and the subtlety and inveterate hatred of the Indian." Although always mindful of his own interests, he held an equal concern for the needs of his Indian people.

William McIntosh (1775-1825)
(*Smithsonian Institution, National Anthropological Archives*)

William McIntosh (1775-1825)

A Creek chief who played a major role in relations between the Creek Indians and the Whites in the post-Revolutionary era of the Southeast. McIntosh (some spelling show MacIntosh, although he usually signed his name as used here) was born in Coweta, Carroll County, Georgia in 1775. His mother was a Creek woman; his father, William MacIntosh, was a Scotch Captain in the British Army, at that time Agent to the Creek. He had a half-brother, Rolly, who was also called Chilly. Young William was carefully educated and soon became a tribal leader by virtue of his abilities. At the turn of the century the federal government arranged for the state of Georgia to cede the Mississippi territory in exchange for million of acres of Creek lands within the state's borders.

Most Indians were unhappy at losing their homes in this manner. The government had ignored their needs to foster White ambitions and thus the Creek sided with the British in the War of 1812. However, sensing the weakness of the British position, McIntosh persuaded his Lower Creek people to join the Americans. He was commissioned a Major General in the U.S. Army and helped to defeat his Indian rivals at the battles of Atasi in 1813, and at Horseshoe Bend in 1814, where Menewa and the Upper Creek opposition were crushed.

After the war he remained on friendly terms with the Americans, fighting in the Seminole War of 1817–1818. Georgia continued to occupy Indian territory despite the opposition of many chiefs—but not the opposition of McIntosh, whose name was signed to many of the treaties, even though he spoke for less than one-tenth of the Indians affected. In 1824, by which time about 15,000,000 acres of the total Creek holding of 25,000,000 acres had been ceded, the Tribal Council decreed the death penalty for any Creek who transferred any lands to the Whites.

In 1825, after some chiefs had broken off treaty negotiations, McIntosh persuaded some other chiefs to agree to the American terms saying, "The White man is growing. He wants our lands; he will buy them now—by and by he will take them." Since only a few chiefs signed, Secretary of War John C. Calhoun refused to recognize the agreement but the U.S. Senate ratified it and the Creek lost their lands.

The Creek took their revenge on McIntosh, whom many now saw as a traitor, by sentencing him to death. A war party led by his long-time rival, Menewa, carried out the execution on the morning of May 1, 1825, shooting him and a companion as they tried to escape from their home. McIntosh was buried on the banks of the Chatta-hoochee River near Whitesburg, Georgia. He had three wives—Susanna Coe, a Creek; Peggy, a Cherokee woman; and Eliza Haw-kins, who survived him, as did one son, David.

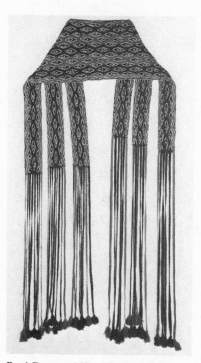

Bead-Decorated Wool Sash, made for William McIntosh in 1825 by his Daughter; Creek
(*Museum of the American Indian*)

Mangas Coloradas (ca. 1791–1863)

Also called Mangus Coloradus, Mangos Colorados, and similar corruptions of the Spanish term for "Red Sleeves." His Apache name was Dasoda-hae, "He Just Sits There." He was the leader of the Mimbreño Apache band and·an important war chief during the era of the so-called Apache Wars. He was related by marriage to both the White Mountain and Chiricahua bands and Cochise was his son-in-law. He was born in New Mexico around 1791.

The Mimbreño people lived near the Santa Rita copper mines in southwestern New Mexico, hence an inevitable position for contest with miners subsequently coming into the region. But the initial contact between American settlers and miners with the Apaches was friendly—the major source of Indian hostility was directed towards their hereditary Mexican enemies. The state of Chihuahua, Mexico offered a $100 bounty for each Apache scalp, regardless of sex or age. Seeing an easy profit, some American trappers invited the Mim-breño people to a great feast at Santa Rita in 1837, and then suddenly began slaughtering them for their scalps. In retaliation, Mangas Coloradas and his warriors wiped out most of the miners and raided nearby settlements. Of such greed were born many tragic conflicts.

In 1846, again willing to try living at peace with the Whites, Mangas Coloradas pledged his friendship to General Stephen W. Kearny who had just been put in charge of the New Mexico Territory. But there was conflict: a boundary commission at Santa Rita forced the Mimbreño to return some Mexican captives, while it refused to punish a Mexican who had murdered an Apache. Furious at this obvious

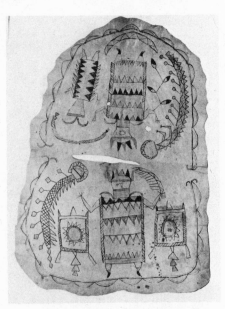

Painted Buckskin Medicine Shirt;
Apache
(*Museum of the American Indian*)

prejudice, the Mimbreño retaliated by stealing livestock from the commission. The pendulum swung again in 1852 when Mangas Coloradas signed yet another treaty of friendship with the Americans. Shortly afterwards, however, he was seized by some gold miners at Pinos Altos, bound, and lashed with a whip until his back was in ribbons.

The so-called "warning" for the Indians to stay away outraged Mangas Coloradas, finally convincing him that Whites were no good and that their word simply could not be trusted in any relationship with Indian people. He thereupon gathered a large band of warriors together and became the scourge of White settlements in the Southwest until the end of his life.

This raiding became even more serious when he joined forces with Cochise, who had been treated in an equally vicious manner by the Whites in Arizona. Aided by the fact that United States troops had been returned east to fight in the Civil War, they were initially completely successful in their campaign against the Americans whom they raided and plundered mercilessly.

The situation became so critical that General James H. Carleton was dispatched to Apache Pass with 3000 California Volunteers to reopen the east–west route which had been blocked by the Apache forces. The combined strength of 500 Mimbreño and Chiricahua warriors led by Mangas Coloradas and Cochise was sufficient to hold off the Californians until Carleton brought up the artillery. Though the Indians were helpless against the howitzers, any small group of soldiers was an easy victim. One day when a platoon headed west, Mangas Coloradas and 50 warriors attacked, and during the battle he was shot in the chest. His warriors quickly picked him up and retreated to their camp; determined to save Mangas Coloradas, Cochise carried him on a litter 100 miles south to Janos, Mexico where a surgeon lived. Cochise simply told the surgeon that if Mangus Coloradas died the town would die. Months later Mangas Coloradas returned to his Mimbres Mountains.

Now an old man in his seventies, he tried once again to effect a reconciliation between the Americans and the Apache. There are several versions of the episode, but the most reliable recounts that on January 19, 1863 he was approached by a Mexican carrying a flag of truce with a message asking him to meet with Captain Edmond Shirland of the California Volunteers. His followers warned of a trap, but Mangas Coloradas was determined and went alone to meet the Americans. They immediately seized him and took him as a prisoner to Fort McLane, where the commander, General Joseph West, made it clear to his guards that he did not want to see the Apache alive the next day. Around midnight, the guards began heating their bayonets in the campfire, casually touching them against the arms and legs of their prisoner. Mangas Coloradas tried to avoid the torture, but finally stood up, berating the soldiers in Spanish. His protest was cut short as they shot him to death. The official report charged that he was killed while trying to escape.

Mangas Coloradas was a very tall man, well over 6′ and had a commanding presence. Huge shouldered, with powerful back and arms, he had enormous strength and stamina. Even in his seventies he was able to outwrestle, outride, and outshoot his younger warriors. Little is known for certain of his family; it is said that he married once, to Carmen, by whom he had three sons, Chie, Ponce, and Salvador, and three daughters whose names are not known.

Manuelito (ca. 1818–1894)

Spanish for "Little Manuel," or Hastín Ch'ilhajinii, also Childhajin, "The Man of the Black Weeds," was the major Navajo war leader in the 19th century; another early name for him was Ashkii Dighin, "Holy Boy." His war name, Hashkeh Naabah, "The Angry Warrior," aptly described him. Little is known of his life before he was selected headman in 1855 to succed Zarcillas Largas (Long Earrings). He is thought to have been born near Bear's Ears, in southeastern Utah, about 1818, (some say 1820), into the Bit'ahni (Folded Arms People) clan. The Navajo at that time lived in the vast region including much of Arizona, New Mexico, Utah, and Colorado; they ranged widely throughout the Southwest and were responsible more to clan leaders than to single "head chiefs." Each headman was responsible for the acts of his own people. The inability of Whites to recognize this political limitation was the basis for many of the misunderstandings between the two peoples.

By the end of the 1850s, many Navajo leaders, including Manuelito, had become wealthy through livestock, agriculture, and raids on Mexican and neighboring Indian tribes. But as the western territories became part of the United States after the Mexican War, this all changed. The Mexicans automatically became American citizens; but the Indians, although native occupants, did not. And when the Mexican–Americans made frequent raids on Navajo homes, kidnapping women and children to be sold as slaves, the U.S. Army seldom intervened; but when the Navajo retaliated, the government speedily punished them. In fact, Manuelito's own home, crops, and livestock had been destroyed by soldiers in a "punishment raid" in 1859.

The next year he made several attacks on Fort Defiance, Arizona, the major military outpost at the time, and Colonel Edward R.S. Canby unsuccessfully pursued him. The Navajo knew their vast country so well that direct confrontation in battle rarely took place. In January 1861, Manuelito and other important leaders met with Canby and again agreed to try to keep the peace, even though Manuelito did not believe this was possible. By this time, the Civil War had erupted, and Army strength was greatly diminished. Many of the Navajo went to Fort Fauntleroy, New Mexico, to trade, and with the loose control, incidents and confrontations between Indian and White became commonplace.

In 1863, the situation was so critical that General James Carleton was sent from California with orders to remove all the Indians to a new reservation at Fort Sumner, New Mexico—a desolate area called Bosque Redondo, which was completely unable to support very many people. The Navajo were given a short time to surrender; when they

Manuelito (1818–1894) and his Wife, Juana
(*Museum of New Mexico; Ben Wittick Photo*)

defied his order, Carleton sent Kit Carson and his troops to destroy crops, livestock, and homes. The waste was so tremendous that the end was inevitable; Delgadito was the first to surrender in October 1863. Others followed, and this was the beginning of the traumatic "Long Walk" of the Navajo from their homelands 350 miles southeast to Fort Sumner. Carleton had shrewdly arranged ample provisions and good treatment for this first group, and Delgadito was quite willing to return and try to persuade other chiefs to surrender.

Carson increased the pressure upon the outlying groups, raiding the Canyon de Chelly, a Navajo heartland, and by March, Navajo were surrendering by the thousands. Barboncito, one of the most important leaders, was captured, but Manuelito held out until late April, hoping that he and his people would be able to remain near the fort. His wish was refused, and Carson sent four Navajo to try to persuade him to surrender, without success. Then, in February 1865, Carleton sent six other Navajo headmen to plead with Manuelito, now the very last hold out, to surrender for the sake of his starving people. Still Manuelito refused, saying, "I have nothing to lose but my life, and they can come and take that whenever they please . . . if I am killed, innocent blood will be shed." But finally, in September, Manuelito and 23 of his warriors surrendered, their emaciated bodies clad only in rags

But in the meantime, the plight of the Navajo now living at Bosque Redondo was appalling; there was no food or clothing, and the people were dying from starvation and disease. It was recognized that the harsh policies of Carleton were wrong and he was removed. In 1868 a new treaty was signed granting the Navajo a reservation back in their vast territory, along with livestock and food supplies. Manuelito served as head chief from 1870 to 1884, when he was succeeded by Henry Chee Dodge. He was also selected in 1872 to head the Indian Police force on the reservation.

He continued to be a strong force for the balance of his life, ever conscious of the needs of the Navajo. In 1876 he traveled to Washington where he met with President U. S. Grant to intervene for his people. He died in 1876 at the age of 75, one of the most respected figures in Navajo history.

He is known to have had two wives; the first was the daughter of Narbona, the great Navajo war chief from whom Manuelito learned so much. The second wife was a Mexican captive. He had several children but nothing is known of their careers.

Woven Wool "Chief's Blanket"; Navajo
(*Museum of the American Indian*)

Mungo Martin (ca. 1879–1962)

Naqapenkim, a major Kwakiutl chief and artist, who was instrumental in the preservation and restoration of many of his tribe's totem poles. He was born at Fort Rupert, in British Columbia, in 1879 or 1880. He

Mungo Martin (1879–1962)
(*British Columbia Government Photograph*)

167

Totem Pole Carved by Mungo Martin in Beacon Hill Park
(*British Columbia Government Photograph*)

was the son of Yanukwalas (some say Kwuksutinuk), a leading Kwakiutl man, and Sarah Finlay, the daughter of a Hudson's Bay Company employee. After the death of Yanukwalas, his mother married Charlie James, who taught young Mungo the sculptor's art.

Traditionally, the Kwakiutl were world famous for their wood-carving skills, creating magnificent totem poles, food utensils, musical instruments, and ceremonial objects which were used in the elaborate rituals and pageants. Painted designs were often applied to these carvings, using earth pigments mixed in a fish-oil base, until the introduction of the White man's commercial paints. As the European came into the area to settle, many of the old tribal customs died or were radically changed. Work for artists declined, and Mungo Martin was forced to turn to fishing to make a living.

Then in 1949, a change in attitudes resulted in the University of British Columbia becoming interested in the preservation of many of the old totem poles which were decaying from lack of care. Mungo Martin was selected to supervise the repair of the poles which were to be placed in a special park on North Vancouver Island.

In addition to restoration work, he also carved many new and original poles. He worked at Thunderbird Park from 1952 until his death, producing powerful designs which in some instances were copies of traditional designs, and other designs which were of his own creation. He used cedar logs 40′ or more in length, carving just as the old sculptors worked, with traditional tools, supplemented by modern equipment. The city of Victoria commissioned a tremendous pole in 1956 for Beacon Hill Park. Standing 127′ 6″ high, it is the tallest totem pole in existence.

Martin also made a 100′ centennial pole as a gift for Queen Elizabeth II in 1958. He remained as curator at the Park in Vancouver, and was also important in assisting the University's Department of Anthropology in building up a major collection of Kwakiutl material culture. Before his death, he was careful to instruct his great-grandson in the technique of carving totem poles, so that the ancient art could continue.

He drowned on August 16, 1962 at the age of 83, while on a fishing trip off the coast of Victoria. He was buried at Alert Bay, as he had requested, with full naval honors.

Crescencio Martínez (ca. 1890–1918)

Te E, "Home of the Elk," one of the very first Pueblo artists on record, was born at San Ildefonso, New Mexico around 1890. He was the uncle of Awa Tsireh, another important Pueblo artist. As far as is recorded, Crescencio started his career by painting pottery, then ultimately turned to watercolors as early as 1910. As these new materials became available, almost everyone at San Ildefonso started to use them, and the more capable and imaginative people were able to help and influence each other. Crescencio was a talented and imaginative artist, and even aided some of his less successful friends by signing their works after

Painting of Eagle Dancers, by Crescencio Martínez; San Ildefonso (*Museum of New Mexico; Mildred Tolbert Photo*)

he became well known, thereby making their paintings more salable.

It was Dr. Edgar Lee Hewett of the Museum of New Mexico who started Crescencio off on an art career by giving him his first paper and watercolors after he saw him drawing with difficulty on cardboard box ends. Subsequently, Dr. Hewett gave Crescencio a commission to paint a series of tribal Winter and Summer ceremonial dances for the Museum collection. At about the same time, he was also requested to paint a similar series for the School of American Research, which was also located in Santa Fe. His art was included in the 1918–1919 show of the Society of Independent Artists in New York, and some of his work was exhibited in 1920 at the American Museum of Natural History in New York, under the sponsorship of the writer Mary Austin.

Tragically, Martínez contracted pneumonia during an influenza attack, and died on June 20, 1918, never living to complete the series of paintings. He married Maximiliana, the sister of María Martínez. Although his career lasted only a few years, he had a tremendous influence on many of his colleagues. His sharp lines, vivid colors, and two-dimensional scenes of tribal ceremonies established a style which lasted for decades after his death. Perhaps of even greater significance was the impact his painting had upon Europeans. Many White men had never been aware of the existence of "Indian painting" until the time of these displays and the favorable response it received was due in part to the enthusiasm of Hewett, Henderson, Austin, and a small group of devoted artists in Santa Fe.

Julián Martinez (1897–ca. 1943)

Pocano, "Coming of the Spirits," one of the most famous Pueblo artists, was born at San Ildefonso, New Mexico in 1897. His name is inseparably linked with his equally important wife, María Montoya (1884–). Both Julián and María levied a tremendous influence upon the course of ceramic artistry in the Southwest.

Julián Martínez (1897–1943) and his
Wife, María
(*Museum of New Mexico; Wyatt Davis
Photograph*)

In his youth, Julián was active as an artist, working primarily on
paper and animal hides; but his marriage to María, and their honeymoon
spent at the St. Louis World's Fair in 1904, where he helped organize
the Indian Village exhibit, enabled him to find his true milieu. When
the two returned to New Mexico, Julián was very unhappy as a farmer,
and he shortly found a job as a laborer at an archeological excavation
being conducted in the area. He thoroughly enjoyed this work, particularly the opportunity it gave him to examine the examples of prehistoric artifacts which were uncovered. Together, the two studied the
ancient objects and Julián attempted to repair and sometimes copy them.
He also collected large numbers of potsherds in order to study the
designs and art styles.

In time, Julián was offered a job as janitor at the New Mexico State
Museum in Santa Fe, which he eagerly accepted, and the couple went
to the Museum to live and study. Although María became homesick
for San Ildefonso and they stayed only three years at the Santa Fe
Museum, they made great artistic progress. They spent hours studying
the collection of pottery in the museum storage, and experimenting
with the many techniques displayed there. During this time, Julián
continued painting, and created several murals for government buildings. The couple were also finding considerable success in selling their
art work, which convinced them that they could indeed make a living
at San Ildefonso.

María spent hours working with the various shapes she had seen
and applied the techniques to her own pottery making. Julián was intrigued by many of the old designs, particularly the Plumed Serpent,
avanyu, and the sun symbol which he would use repeatedly in his later
work. In the course of their experiments, about 1919–1920, they
rediscovered the ancient method of producing a satiny black finish which
became their hallmark, although it was eventually developed by other
potters in the Pueblo, and in neighboring Santa Clara and Nambé. This

pottery with its polished surface became an immediate success, and it was developed into a thriving industry which continues to this day, bringing the Pueblo of San Ildefonso more income than its farm produce.

Two of the men who had a most profound influence on their work were Dr. Kenneth Chapman and Dr. Edgar Lee Hewett, both from the Museum of New Mexico. They urged the pair to continually improve their quality and to sign their pieces for the benefit of museums and collectors. In this atmosphere of success, the only speck on the horizon to mar their happiness was Julián's increasing alcoholism. The couple made many trips throughout the United States and abroad, exhibiting their works, and educating others to the qualities inherent in Indian art. They demonstrated at the Century of Progress in 1933 in Chicago, where they were awarded many honors. In the late 1930s, Julian was elected Governor of the Pueblo of San Ildefonso, a post he held until his death. Unfortunately, he was never able to conquer alcoholism, and it continued to affect his artistic success; finally, he wandered away from the Pueblo and was later discovered on March 6, 1943, dead from exposure.

The couple had several children, all of whom have made a major mark in the art world. But the influence of the revival of the matte-finished blackware, the perfection of designs by Julián, and the magnificent modeling of the basic pottery by María have made the Martínez work prized possessions of museums and collectors throughout the world. Through this innovation, Julián and María transformed pottery into ceramics.

Painting on Deerskin by Julián Martínez; San Ildefonso
(*Museum of the American Indian*)

Massasoit (ca. 1580–ca. 1662)

"Great Chief," also known as Ousamequin, from Algonquian *wusáme-quin*, "Yellow Feather," was a staunch friend of the Plymouth Colony. Born around 1580, he became chief in 1607 largely due to his prowess as a warrior. His tribal territory included much of eastern Massachusetts including Cape Cod, and Rhode Island, and his home was Pawkunnakut (Pokanoket), in Bristol County, Rhode Island. Shortly before the Pilgrims landed, the Wampanoag were ravaged by a plague in 1617 (perhaps yellow fever) brought by early explorers. Reduced in number from 18,000 to about 7000, the tribe was threatened by its powerful neighbors the Narragansett, who had not been touched by the disease. Massasoit saw the superior arms of the English settlers as a good defense and was quick to befriend them. He gave them a large tract of land, and on March 22, 1621, entered into a treaty of friendship which included a mutual protection clause. As a further gesture of alliance, he and his people helped the colonists by introducing them to new foods and planting methods. His influence was important in the area, and during his lifetime, relatively peaceful relations existed between Indian and White.

In 1623 Massasoit fell seriously ill, and Governor Bradford sent a party to attend him. At his bedside were Indians from as far away as

100 miles who came to pay their last respects. However, the Pilgrims administered their own medicine, and he recovered, now even friendlier than before. He warned them of an Indian plot against the Weymouth Colony in time for them to take defensive action; Miles Standish trapped the leaders of the plot and killed them. This strengthened Massasoit's position among those tribes who wished to live peaceably with the colonists, but alienated him from those Indians who considered him a traitor and who subsequently allied themselves with the Narragansett. In 1632, Massasoit was forced to flee to Plymouth to escape capture by the Narragansett. Peace was restored three years later through the efforts of Standish and especially of Roger Williams.

Massasoit died in Rhode Island in 1662, survived by two daughters and three sons. The two oldest boys were sent to Plymouth Court for education; in the custom of the day, they were given "English" names: Wamsutta, who died shortly after his father's death, was renamed Alexander, and Metacom (or Pometacomet) was known as Philip. He later became chief and led the confederation which sought to oust the Whites during King Philip's War. The youngest boy, Sunsonewhew, or Suconewhew, briefly attended Harvard College.

Portrait Sketch of Mato Tope by George Catlin
(*American Museum of Natural History*)

Mato Tope (ca. 1800–ca. 1861)

From *mato* "bear," *tope* "four," better known as "Four Bears," the name by which two Mandan chiefs, father and son, are known. Little is known of the elder man. except that he was Second Chief of the Mandan people at the time George Catlin visited the tribe in 1832 and painted his portrait. Catlin called him Mah-to-toh-pa, and was apparently tremendously impressed by him, for he devoted a great deal of attention to his portraits and his role among his people; few other Upper Missouri people of the time had such an impact upon the artist.

Later, when Karl Bodmer visited the Mandan in 1834, Mato Tope was again a figure of interest, and was the subject of one of Bodmer's best remembered portraits. These have become some of the most popular masterpieces of frontier art and were reproduced widely; to this day they play an important part in the basic understanding of many non-Indians concerning the "Noble Savage" of the Western Plains.

Mato Tope led his people in battles against many of the neighboring tribes, and in 1837 was selected as a chief—but in that same year the Mandan were stricken by an epidemic of smallpox. The impact of this disease among the Mandan, Hidatsa, and Arikara cannot be fully understood even today—one report lists only 31 survivors out of the 1600 Mandan—and it left an indelible imprint upon the Indians of the Upper Missouri which is still keenly felt. Mato Tope succumbed July 30, 1837 at the age of 37—only one out of the thousands of Mandan who died a horrible death. It was such an emotional event that Eastern Whites were even caught up in the tragedy of the moment; one account has him accusing the Whites on his deathbed of genocide, charging his descendents to not rest until the score was settled: ". . . all that you hold dear are all dead or dying, with their faces all rotten, caused by those dogs, the Whites . . . Rise together and do not leave one of them alive."

This episode does not seem to enjoy acceptance today, although there is no question as to the annihilation of the Mandan tribe by the disease. It is thought that the charge was surreptitiously entered into the historical record by persons intent upon discrediting the establishment agencies of the period.

Following the death of the elder Four Bears, his son became a chief, but the Mandan did not embark upon a campaign against the Whites. Instead, they began to make plans for their own defense and security against any further White incursions. In concert with the Hidatsa, the young Four Bears convinced the Arikara and several other small bands to join him in establishing a strong unified settlement at Like-a-Fishhook Bend on the Missouri River in North Dakota.

This region became the center for a large reservation in time, and finally became Fort Berthold, founded as an Army outpost. This site continues today to be the combined reservation area of the several Upper Missouri Plains tribes. Four Bears signed the Treaty of Fort Laramie in 1851, and continued to serve his people well until his death in 1861 at his village.

Menewa (1765?–1865)

Also Menawa, "Great Warrior," a Lower Creek chief who was born along the Tallapoosa River in central Alabama about 1765. It is probable that his father was White and his mother a Creek; little is known of his childhood until his appearance in history as Hothlepoya, "Crazy War Hunter," because of his daring horse-stealing expeditions as a young man against the White settlements in southern Tennessee. He became something of a legendary figure in the region, hated, admired, and feared. His wealth and influence among the Lower Creek people grew year by year.

His great rival was William McIntosh, another mixed-blood Creek chief, who instigated a murder for which Menewa (as he had become known) was blamed by the Whites. A Creek village was burned in retaliation and both sides grew tense. It was about this time that Tecumseh came south looking for allies against the settlers, and Menewa readily agreed with the need for mutual trust and support. With the Indians' faith strengthened by this measure of unity with their brothers, the Creek Wars began in 1812.

Menewa (1765–1865)
(*Smithsonian Institution, National Anthropological Archives*)

At this time, the Creek head chief was a medicine man, more concerned with spirits and visions than battle tactics and strategy; hence Menewa was chosen to be the war chief. Yet one of his first acts was to follow the visions of the medicine chief and deploy his warriors to meet the White forces at Horseshoe Bend, Alabama in 1814. It left a fatally weak position wide open: General Andrew Jackson's troops clearly had the superior position, and Menewa saw his mistake even before the battle began, but it was too late to draw back. The odds were impossible: of

Beaded Trade-Cloth Pouch; Seminole
(*Museum of the American Indian*)

the almost 1000 Indian warriors at Horseshoe Bend, more than 800 were killed, and the rest were almost all wounded. Menewa himself was left for dead, but revived during the night and crawled back to the base camp hidden in the swamps. Soon after this the Americans took vengeance. Menewa's village was completely destroyed and his wealth and most of the possessions of his followers were confiscated.

Despite these defeats, Menewa continued to hold the respect and trust of his people. McIntosh, on the other hand, was now engaged in the illegal sale to Whites of millions of acres of tribal land. Accordingly, the Creek elders met and condemned him to death, selecting Menewa to carry out the sentence; in 1825 he led the execution party. The next year, Menewa was in Washington, attempting to convince the federal authorities of the illegality of McIntosh's disposal of the most fertile Creek lands. Unlike most other Indian missions of this nature, he met with some success. By compromising and maneuvering he managed to get the government to agree to return to certain Creek people land that they could use for subsistence farming—the Indians might live off the land, but not make a profit from it—and that it would pass into the ownership of these farmers after a probationary period of five years. Not everyone got his own land back (including Menewa), but the arrangement was the best that could be negotiated at the time. Before the Great Warrior left Washington, he smoked the pipe of peace and had his portrait painted for the art gallery of the War Department.

Almost ten years later, when some of the Creek warriors joined their Seminole cousins in a war against the Whites, Menewa and some of his loyal troops served on the Federal side. For this service he was promised that he could remain on his native land until his death. Yet, when the Creek tribe was removed by force to Indian Territory in 1836–1840 to make room for an advancing White population, Menewa was forced to accompany the rest. Another promise to the Indian had been broken by the government.

No longer a Great Warrior, Menewa died in his new home in Indian Territory in 1865, never reconciled to the move.

Metacom (ca. 1639?–1676)

Met'a-com, Metacomet, or Pometacom, was more familiarly known as King Philip. The meaning of *Metacom* is unclear. It may refer to "the far away place" while others have suggested that it refers to his home, "The Chief's House." He had several other names, most commonly Philip of Pokanoket, from the place where he was born around 1639, and the nickname, Wagwises, "The Circling Fox." This Wampanoag chief was the sachem of Pokanoket and the leader of the most savage war ever fought in New England, a war which proved conclusive in the struggle between Indian and White for the possession of that region. In a gesture of friendship, his father, Massasoit had requested the colonists to give names to his older two sons. When Massasoit and his eldest son Alexander died in 1661–1662, Philip, so named (and the second son) inherited the leadership of the Wampanoag tribe.

By the time Metacom became chief, life had changed greatly from the days when the early colonists were dependent upon the local Indians for survival. More and more settlers had arrived, slowly enlarging the English territory as the Indians traded their lands for the White man's goods—muskets, trinkets, and liquor. Conflicts were common, since even though the Indians had given up land, they did not have the same sense of trespass as the White man, believing that land really belonged to all people who were free to roam it at will and make use of it as the need arose, especially if it were not being used. But by this time the English were able to enforce their views of property rights through force of arms; they made the Indians subject to their own harsh laws and justice.

The friction intensified, overshadowing the ancient rivalries between the various tribes of the area. Metacom saw this and became the first Indian leader to realize that only a united Indian front could withstand the Whites. At the same time there was continuing division; some tribes were eager to join against the hated colonists, while others were cool, even hostile to unifying, having become economically dependent upon the English. Some tribes were jealous of Metacom assuming a leading role in the opposition. The Christian Indians, of course, remained loyal to the English.

In June 1675, the first hostilities broke out at Swansea. After nine years of planning, and well before Metacom was completely prepared, the war began—as it was to end—in an act of betrayal. Metacom's personal secretary, a Christian Indian named John Sassamon, warned Governor Josiah Winslow of Plymouth Colony of the conspiracy. Shortly thereafter Sassamon was found dead; the colonists tried three Indians for the crime and hanged them. This infuriated Metacom's people, who felt that the Whites had no jurisdiction over intra-Indian affairs. One confrontation led to another, and finally hostilities broke out on June 23 with a skirmish in the village of Swansea. It spread, and while the Indians initially were completely victorious, the tide of war began to turn slowly in favor of the Whites, who greatly outnumbered and outgunned the Indians. Crops were destroyed, the colonists captured Indian women and children, sold them into slavery, and offered amnesty to all Indians who would abandon Metacom.

During June and July 1676, several decisive battles were fought. The colonists, joined by enemies of Metacom, tracked down the various bands, killing hundreds of warriors. Finally, on August 12, 1676, a group of Whites was led by a disloyal Wampanoag to Metacom's hideout; in the ensuing ambush he was killed by an Indian named Alderman. His body was quartered and his head was displayed for over a year in

Metacom (1639–1676), from an Early Engraving
(*Smithsonian Institution, National Anthropological Archives*)

Carved Steatite Pipe from Warren, Rhode Island. Known Popularly as "King Philip's Pipe"
(*Museum of the American Indian*)

the Plymouth public square—a common practice in those days to serve as a warning. Metacom's wife Nanuskooke (or Wootonekanuske), the daughter of the sachem of Pokanoket, and their son were both sold as slaves in Bermuda.

Although the colonists suffered may casualties in the War, and 12 of the 52 towns were completely destroyed by Indian attacks, they managed to survive. In so doing, they also demolished the intertribal unity which Metacom had created. Following his death, there was no further effective resistance to White domination of southern New England, yet the name and career of this able, cautious leader has not been lost in history.

Halberd-Type Tomahawk, Used in Early New England
(*Museum of the American Indian*)

Miantonomo (ca. 1600–1643)

From Narragansett, *miantónimi*, "He Wages War" (?), was the ruler of that tribe, with his uncle, Canonicus. Although the Indians were regarded as being friendly to the English, the Massachusetts authorities were often unfriendly and suspicious. This is probably due to the welcome the Indians extended to Roger Williams and his people when they fled from the Massachusetts Bay Colony to Rhode Island, seeking religious freedom. In time, Williams became a trusted friend and advisor to both of the Narragansett chiefs.

Certainly Miantonomo himself was wary of English intentions. In 1642 he is said to have visited Wyandanch and the Montauk people on Long Island to discuss common problems, saying: "Brothers, we must be as one as the English are, or we shall all be destroyed . . . Since these Englishmen have seized our country, they have. cut down the grass with scythes, and the trees with axes . . . All the sachems to the east and the west have joined with us, and we are resolved to fall upon them . . ." It must not be overlooked that the old enmity between the Narragansett and Pequot peoples had continued, in spite of the peace agreement which the English had forced upon Uncas and Miantonomo in 1638; indeed, there is some evidence to support the feeling that Uncas encouraged the colonists in their suspicions of Miantonomo's loyalty.

For whatever reason, in 1642 the English called Miantonomo to Boston to answer charges of plotting against the White government, after which he was released with stern warnings. And in the next year Uncas and his Mohegan followers, supported by the still-suspicious colonists, went to war against the Narragansett. In the ensuing battle, Miantonomo was captured and brought to the English authorities at Hartford. They regarded him not only as guilty of treachery, but also saw an opportunity to retaliate against Roger Williams. Metacom was tried in Boston and condemned to death; abandoning any legal responsibility, the colonists turned Miantonomo over to Uncas, who quickly saw to the removal of his hated rival. He was executed by the latter's brother, Wawequa, in September 1643. The Narragansett people marked the grave with a stone monument and honored their slain chief's memory for many years thereafter. He had one son, Nanutenoo.

Micanopy (ca. 1780–1849)

Micanopy (1780–1849)
(*Oklahoma Historical Society*)

Micanopy was also known as Micconopy, Micco-nuppe, and Michenopah—from *micco*, "chief," *nopi* "head," "Head Chief," or "Chief Over Chiefs." This major Seminole leader was the grandson of King Payne who had united the Florida Indians into one tribe. He was also occasionally known as Halputta Hadjo, "Crazy Alligator," although there is some confusion with the use of this name. The place and date of Micanopy's birth is not known; it was probably around 1780 in the general St. Augustine region of Florida. Micanopy was growing old at the time of the Seminole Wars and left most of the fighting to the younger warriors such as Osceola and Wildcat.

Though many Whites found this short, fat, seemingly indolent person to be far from their romantic ideal of a great Indian chief, the Seminole respected him, and generally followed his leadership. As did many of his fellow tribesmen, he employed runaway slaves to till the soil and tend his livestock; at one point he had over 100 Negroes in his service. Though they were called slaves, they had considerably more freedom than most of their brothers in Georgia and the other colonies. There was also a large amount of inbreeding; so much so, that they came to have a great deal of influence in the Seminole councils (a few Negroes even became war chiefs), and the proportion of Negro blood in the Seminole population today is extremely high. The net result was a surprisingly large number of wealthy Seminole people, among whom Micanopy was a leading example.

After Spain sold Florida to the United States in 1819, and Andrew Jackson was appointed governor in 1821, settlers from the North began to come into the territory. Inevitably, there was conflict between Whites and Indians; United States–Spanish treaty provisions ignored Indian rights, and the latter withdrew from the coastal lands in an effort to avoid confrontation, but the Whites wanted more. The issue was also complicated by the slavery question, since the Whites wanted to recapture refugee slaves who had fled to the Seminole lands for safety.

Some measure of the passions of the time towards anything like a peaceful settlement may be seen in the statement of the U.S. Indian Agent to Thomas McKenny in 1824, commenting upon the unwillingness of the Indians to give up their homeland:

> . . . The only course, therefore, which remains for us to rid ourselves of them, is to adopt such a mode of treatment toward them, as will induce them to acts that will justify their expulsion by force.

Finally, the government gave in to the pressures for removal of the Indians to the west; and on May 9, 1832, some Seminole chiefs were induced to sign a treaty at Payne's Landing agreeing to cede their

Man's Cotton Appliqué Councillor's
Robe; Seminole
(*Museum of the American Indian*)

Florida lands for new homes in the Creek area in Indian Territory. The treaty also provided for "the Creeks to reunite with the Seminoles as one people." Although Micanopy was opposed to removal and refused to sign the treaty, he did not at first advocate violent resistance. But at later negotiations at Fort King, involving efforts by the United States to obtain the immediate removal of the Indians, he refused to sign, and supported Osceola and the other young leaders as they prepared to defend themselves.

As passions grew on both sides, the Army moved in, and many of the White civilians withdrew from their plantations in December 1835. General Wiley Thompson, the Indian Agent for Florida, was killed by Osceola in retaliation for his earlier mistreatment of Seminole people, and Micanopy led an ambush in which Major Francis Dade and 100 soldiers were annihilated. The Seminole Wars, thus begun, did not end for almost seven years.

Whether due to advanced age or to a feeling of the inevitable outcome, Micanopy was one of the first Indian leaders to lose heart and agree to leave Florida. In June 1837, shortly after he signed a supplementary treaty to this effect, he was kidnapped by some of his young warriors. Later that same year he came in for a peace treaty with General Thomas S. Jesup; and, although he was under a flag of truce, Jesup had him taken prisoner. This brutal violation of honor did not go unnoticed, and gave rise to strong support for the Seminole people in the cities of the East. Nevertheless, Micanopy was sent to Charleston, South Carolina, and from there, on to Indian Territory with about 200 others.

The War continued, but by 1842 most of the Seminole had been removed. Only Billy Tiger and Billy Bowlegs remained isolated in the Everglades, resisting all efforts to capture them. Of all of the tribes forced to move to Indian Territory, none were more unhappy and faced more hardship than the Seminole. They found the climate and the landscape totally alien to the way of life which they had developed, and they camped near the Army forts, living miserably on meager government rations.

Micanopy and many of the other Indians took refuge in liquor as a means of escape. He sought to reestablish his control over his people, and while he met with some success, he was never the clear-cut Head Chief he had once been. In 1845 he was one of the signers to a treaty which gave the Seminole some measure of independence from the Creek Nation, but they did not achieve total self-government in Indian Territory until 1855, six years after Micanopy's death. He died at his home there in 1849; he had two wives, one of whom was named Futtatike.

Carlos Montezuma (ca. 1867–1923)

Wassaja, or Wasagah, from Yavapai, "signaling; beckoning," was a Yavapai orphan who became a well-known physician and Indian

178

rights leader. He was born in the Superstition Mountains of central Arizona about 1867, the son of Cocuyevah; the name of his mother is not recorded. Five years after he was born, he was captured by a band of Pima warriors avenging a Yavapai raid. They took him with about a dozen other captives to their Gila River home and later to Florence, where he ws sold for $30 to a White photographer–prospector named Carlos Gentile.

Carlos Montezuma (1867–1923)
(*Arizona Historical Society Library*)

His mother had determined to find her son, and asked permission of the Indian Agent to leave the reservation for the purpose. He refused, but she left secretly, and was shot by an Indian scout in the nearby mountains. The young Wassaja was taken to Santa Fe by Gentile, then to Pueblo, where they departed for the East by railroad. He was baptized as a Christian, and renamed Carlos for his foster father, and Montezuma for the famous prehistoric ruin in Arizona—and what Gentile regarded as part of his heritage. Subsequently, young Carlos received an excellent primary and secondary education in Chicago, attended Carlisle, and returned to Chicago. Unfortunately, Gentile's photography business failed, and he committed suicide.

Montezuma earned enough money to go to the University of Illinois, graduating *cum laude* with a B.S. degree in 1884. In 1888, he received his M.D. degree from the Chicago Medical School (a part of Northwestern University), and then accepted a one-year appointment as physician–surgeon at the United States Indian School at Fort Stevenson, North Dakota. Later he went on to serve at Indian agencies in Nevada and Washington, and at the Carlisle Indian School in Pennsylvania.

Throughout his professional career, Carlos Montezuma was a strong opponent of the reservation system and the Bureau of Indian Affairs. His memory of the humiliation of his mother having to ask permission to leave the land theoretically given to her, and her subsequent death, coupled with the position in which Indians were then put by government fiat, combined to make him an active fighter for Indian needs. He was infuriated by the fact that Negroes had been made citizens of the United States in 1888, while the original inhabitants of the country were still regarded as aliens.

Accordingly, in 1896, he quit to undertake an active effort to have the BIA abolished; he opened up his own private practice in Chicago in gastroenterology. He was very successful in this effort, and was invited to teach at the College of Physicians and Surgeons, as well as in the Postgraduate Medical School. In 1906 his work led to public recognition, and President Theodore Roosevelt offered him the position as head of the Bureau of Indian Affairs, but he declined. In 1916 he started an Indian affairs magazine entitled *Wassaja*, which he supported from his personal funds. In this publication, he used the slogan, "Let My People Go," so popular today. The next year he was jailed for opposing the drafting of American Indians in World War I, but was released by the intervention of President Woodrow Wilson, who subsequently reoffered him the Commissioner of Indian Affairs post; he still refused, knowing that it would compromise his crusade.

Meanwhile, he had married a Roumanian woman, joined the Masonic Order, of which he attained the rank of Master Mason, and continued to participate actively in Indian affairs, lecturing passionately against the maintenance of the federal Indian Bureau system. During this entire period he was also working full-time as a physician, which taxed his strength markedly. In a second marriage, he took as his wife Marie Keller, who worked with him. Soon after this marriage, his debilitated physique—already suffering from a chronic diabetic condition—fell victim to tuberculosis, and the two returned to Arizona in 1922. But Carlos could no longer continue his fight, and on January 31, 1923, he died at the age of 55, and was buried in the Indian Cemetery at Fort McDowell, Arizona.

Although his publication *Wassaja* had ceased, the name was revived when a similar newspaper was founded in California in 1972 in honor of his long fight for Indian rights.

Waldo Mootzka (1910–1940)

Also known as Mootska, "Point of Yucca," (Waldo = Walter) was a major Hopi painter who was especially noted for his imaginative representations of tribal ceremonies and mythological scenes. He was born in 1910 at New Oraibi, Arizona; his father was Tom Mootzka, his mother was a member of the Badger clan. The boy went to school in Albuquerque, and returned to Oraibi before settling in Santa Fe, New Mexico. Like most of the early Pueblo painters, he was self-taught. And though he was strongly influenced by another Hopi artist, Fred Kabotie, Mootzka tended to experiment with other styles and modes more than most of his contemporaries. Some of his work suggests a European influence in its three-dimensional quality which he achieved through modeling with colors, while some of his works are reflective of the flat, bright colors so common to Indian art of the Southwest.

Waldo Mootzka had a great feeling for color, and used a full palette to achieve a wide range of hues; his work is also marked by fine attention to detail. Much of his artistry is concerned with the mystical and symbolic elements in Pueblo life, and in common with most major Hopi artists, he returned again and again for inspiration to the subject of *Kachinas*—portrayals of men wearing elaborate costumes and masks who represent various supernatural beings in the Pueblo spirit world. He also portrayed village scenes and animals, although the latter tend to be stiff and formal.

Perhaps the best period of Waldo Mootzka's work was in the mid-1930s, even though at this time he had become increasingly debilitated by tuberculosis. In later years, in Santa Fe, he was sponsored by Frank Patania, who taught him silversmithing, an activity in which he had become involved almost full-time until he died in an automobile accident in Phoenix, in 1940, at the age of 38. He is buried at his home in Oraibi, Arizona.

"Kachina and Mana" Watercolor Painting by Waldo Mootzka; Hopi (*Museum of Northern Arizona; Marc Gaede Photo*)

Stephen Mopope (1898-1974)

Qued Koi, or "Painted Robe," was one of the Five Kiowa Artists who attained a major position in Indian painting in the 1930s and 1940s under the tutelage of Susie Peters and Oscar Jacobson. He was born August 27, 1898, near Red Stone Baptist Mission, on the Kiowa Reservation in Oklahoma. His grandfather was a Mexican captive, and his maternal grandparent was Apiatan, a noted Kiowa warrior.

During his childhood he was educated by his grandmother, who gave him much of his traditional knowledge and background. As a child he often spent his time drawing; on one occasion his great-uncle Silverhorn discoverd the child sketching; delighted with the ability of the youngster, in concert with another uncle, Hakok, he taught him the technique and style of painting on tanned hide in the old way. This training was invaluable to him later in life, and he never abandoned the traditional approach.

He was encouraged by Susie Peters and Edith Mahier, who had taken a strong interest in the artistic skills of the younger Kiowa people, and when Miss Peters appealed to Dr. Jacobson at the University of Oklahoma Art Department, Mopope was one of the five youths selected for such training as was deemed to be desirable. Along with Tsatoke, Hokeah, Asah, Smoky and later, Auchiah, Mopope entered a life of artistic activity marked by exhibitions in various museums and galleries throughout the country.

Along with Jack Hokeah, Mopope proved to be an exceptional dancer, and the pair figured prominently in exhibitions and gatherings wherever the opportunity presented itself. He spent many of his younger days painting, and was commissioned to do murals in several United States federal buildings, as well as municipal and business buildings in Oklahoma.

In later years, he was not as active as some of the other Kiowa artists because he spent much of his time farming. He married Janet Berry, by whom he had two daughters. His work is highly prized in many museum and private collections, and he was awarded a Certificate of Appreciation by the Indian Arts and Craft Board in 1966. He died on February 3, 1974 at Fort Cobb, Oklahoma, a highly respected artist whose work graces many gallery walls throughout the world.

"The Eagle Dancer" by Stephen Mopope; Kiowa
(*Museum of the American Indian*)

Watercolor Painting of a Buffalo Hunt, by Stephen Mopope; Kiowa
(*Museum of Northern Arizona; Marc Gaede Photo*)

Moses (ca. 1829-1899)

Quelatikan, or Quelatican, "The Blue Horn," from his headdress, a major Sinkiuse Salish leader, was an essentially peaceful chief who managed for most of his life to keep his people from confinement on a reservation. He was born at Wenatchee Flat in central Washington about 1829. His father was a great leader of the Salish named Sulktalths-

Moses (1829–1899)
(*Washington State Historical Society*)

cosum (Sulktashkosha), "Half Sun," and his mother was Karneetsa, "Beneath the Robes," one-half Spokane. As a boy his name was Loolowkin, "The Head Band," but when he attended Henry M. Spalding's mission school, he was baptized Moses.

During the early part of his life, Moses lived peacefully, as did his people, simply because there were not very many Whites in the Salish territory. But as settlers moved into the Northwest in increasing numbers, confrontation between the two races became more frequent and more serious. Finally, in 1855, the Treaty of Walla Walla was signed, by which the leaders—or alleged leaders—of some of the tribes in the Eastern Washington area agreed to move to reservation lands, in return for government guarantees of safety.

Many warriors did not want to leave, feeling that they had not been fairly represented, and this led to the wars of 1855–1858. There is no record of the number of battles in which Moses participated, but according to General O. O. Howard he was the war chief in the Battle of the Yakima River against troops commanded by General George Wright. About 1854 he took the name of his father, Sulktalthscosum, meaning "Half Sun," or "Piece Split From the Sun," following the death of the latter in battle. In 1858, Moses became the leader of his tribe after the old chief, Quiltenock, had been killed by miners, and two younger chiefs, Ouhi and Qualchiah, had met the same fate at the hand of soldiers.

Moses was a big, handsome, ambitious man who set out to become the principal leader of all of the tribes in the area. He was also something of a successful diplomat, and although he fought no more major battles against the Americans, he was able to stave off the demands of the Whites that the Indians be put on a reservation. The Big Bend country of the Columbia River offered plenty of room to roam, hunt, and fish without disturbing the settlers, but in the mid-1870s the government brought pressure to move the Indians onto more restricted land. The result was inevitable: in 1877 open warfare broke out between the Army and Chief Joseph and his Nez Percés; the next year, the Bannock War began.

Moses kept his people away from these conflicts, insisting to General O. O. Howard that he was a man of peace who should not be confined to the Yakima Reservation with a lot of Indians whom he and his people did not know. Finally, in 1879 he was arrested, then paroled and sent to Washington to negotiate directly with the Department of the Interior officials. He won most of his points and was given a reservation near his home territory, next to the Colville Reservation. His people, however, never became firmly established there because of continued White pressure, and in 1884, under General Nelson Miles, troops moved in to force the band to move onto the Colville Reservation in spite of the earlier agreements; they live there today.

Moses continued to live peacefully as a farmer for the rest of his life, supported by a government annuity of $1000 per year. He married several times—to Silpe, a Flathead woman, whom he left shortly following the marriage; later he married Quemollah and Kittitas, the daughter of Chief Ouhi; Mali (Mary) Shantlahow; and lastly, Peotsenmy, a Nez Percé woman. On March 25, 1899, he died at his home near Wilbur, Washington, and was buried in the Chief Moses cemetery on the Colville Reservation, near Nespelem, Washington.

Carved Horn Rattle with Wool Decoration; Salish
(*Museum of the American Indian*)

Mountain Chief (1848–1942)

Ninastoko or Nin-na-stoko, the last hereditary chief of the Blackfoot people, was born on Old Man River in southern Alberta, Canada in 1848. At the age of 18 he led the Blackfoot warriors against the Crow and Atsina at Cypress Hills, and a year later was the war chief in a great battle against the Kutenai, where he nearly lost his life in a hand-to-hand fight with Cut Nose. He was badly wounded in the leg in 1873, when he fought against the Crow, and limped for the rest of his life as a result of this injury.

Mountain Chief (1848–1942)
(*Museum of the American Indian*)

During the negotiations with the Whites which led to the signing of the Treaty of 1886 ceding lands east of the Sweet Grass Hills, Mountain Chief was an active participant and signer, and in 1895 he signed the treaty which transferred the land which is now Glacier Park.

An active representative of his people, Mountain Chief made several trips to the East, where he met with four different Presidents, including McKinley, Taft, Roosevelt, and finally Woodrow Wilson. During a somewhat theatrical ceremony, he officiated in 1922 at the "adoption" of Queen Marie of Roumania while she was visiting Glacier National Park, thereby nobly continuing one of the ceremonial responsibilities of the later Indian leaders living in the White man's world.

One of his more colorful activities was assisting General Hugh L. Scott who had worked for several decades in the recording of the Plains sign language. Mountain Chief was skilled in the art, and took a leading role in the council which was filmed in motion picture by General Scott.

He was a remarkably colorful person, who made a striking figure when in costume, and became well known in the Glacier Park area. He went blind in his old age and died in his home on the reservation on February 2, 1942 at the age of 94. He was buried in the cemetery at Browning, Montana. He had one son, Walter, and a daughter, Rosa Mad Wolf.

Mountain Wolf Woman
(1884–1960)

Kéhachiwinga, "Wolf's Mountain Home Maker," was a Winnebago woman who was the subject of a remarkable autobiographical account written down by Nancy Lurie in 1958, and subsequently published in book form as *Mountain Wolf Woman*—a notable contribution to the literature of culture change and personality. She was selected by Dr. Lurie, in part, because her brother Hágaga had been interviewed by Paul Radin, and that account was published in an equally well-received book, *Crashing Thunder*. The comparison and contrast between the two provided a valuable insight into the life of one Indian family.

Kéhachiwingwa had a life which was typical in many ways of Indian women at the turn of the century. She was born into the Thunder clan in April 1884 at East Fork River, Wisconsin, the daughter of Charles Blowsnake and Lucy Goodvillage, both full-blooded Winnebago. She was forced by her strong-willed brothers to marry a man for whom she did not care, and later, when she had left him, was forced into yet another marriage. She had a total of 11 children, three of whom died. At the time of her interview, she had 39 grandchildren and 11 great-grandchildren; she was proud of her family and content with her life.

She was a conventional Christian for a time in her youth, but subsequently joined the Peyote religion, staying with this group for the rest of her life. Wherever she traveled—the Dakotas, Nebraska, Wisconsin—there were meetings of the members of this society, which found its adherents among many strata of Indian culture. Peyote is a hallucinogenic cactus plant (*Lophophora williamsii*), which brought intense religious and mystical experiences to those who consumed the small "button." It has since become better known as the sacrament used by members of the Native American Church.

Mountain Wolf Woman's account provided many White Americans with their first understanding and insight into this religious practice, as well as the life of a contemporary Indian woman. It was "the record of a great old lady recalling a memorable life," commented the Chicago *Sun Times*. And it was indeed just that; Mountain Wolf Woman lived to enjoy her fame, succumbing to pneumonia at the age of 76, in Black River Falls, Wisconsin on November 9, 1960.

Mary Musgrove (ca. 1700–ca. 1763)

Coosaponakeesa, a Creek interpreter, trader, and political leader, was an important figure in the founding and development of the colony of Georgia by James Oglethorpe. She was born at Coweta, Alabama in Creek territory around 1700, and lived on the Chattahoochee River until about the age of seven, at which time her White father took her to South Carolina to be educated. During her stay there she was baptized into the Church of England and given the name Mary. She returned to Alabama about 1716 and soon met and married a young White trader, John Musgrove; the couple moved to Georgia in 1732 and opened a trading post at Yamacraw Bluff on the Savannah River, exchanging trade goods purchased in Charleston for deer skins gathered by the local Creek hunters.

In 1733, Oglethorpe and ten others arrived with a charter from King George II allowing him to establish a new English colony south of the Carolinas and north of Spanish Florida. They found the Musgroves already there, operating a prosperous enterprise, and Mary soon became Oglethorpe's main interpreter and a trusted emissary in his dealings with the Indians of the area. Her influence among the tribes helped the English to establish their colony with minor difficulty. The Creek warriors fought on the British side in several battles against the Spanish, including Oglethorpe's attack on San Augustín in 1740, and the Battle of Bloody Marsh on Isla San Simón in 1742.

The next year Oglethorpe left Georgia, but Mary Musgrove continued to work for the English among her people. A second trading post was established at Mount Venture, on the Altamaha River, which became something of a "listening post" for the British, and her efforts there went far to prevent the land north of Florida from becoming a Spanish possession. It was at Mount Venture that John Musgrove died in 1739, and that Mary eventually married Captain Jacob Matthews of the ranger forces stationed at the Post. Subsequently, the couple went to Savannah because of Jacob's poor health, and he died there in 1742.

Mary remained loyal to the British, but was faced with increasing pressures from both the French and the Spanish to join their side as they exhorted the Creeks to desert the British. She continued to be effective as a negotiator between the several contestants, however, and at the age of 49 married Thomas Bosomworth, the chaplain of the colony and a Church of England clergyman. Unfortunately, Bosomworth seems to have been something of a scoundrel who was more interested in profit than piety; he abandoned his clerical duties and took up cattle raising on St. Catharine's Island in Georgia, which was among the properties Mary had induced the Creek council to grant her, along with Ossabaw and Sapelo Islands.

Bosomworth also managed to obtain appointment as Agent to the Creek Indians. But, as a climax to his persuasive efforts, he got Mary to title herself "Empress of the Creek Nation,"—an entirely fictitious role, since the Creek people at no time had established any royalty. But Mary seemed unable to retain any sense of independence or realization of these manipulations of her position. Bosomworth had purchased his cattle on credit, and to pay for them, he got Mary to enter a claim against the English colonists for her past services. She claimed that, as Empress she was the sovereign ruler of the Creek Indians and not a subject of the King of England; in 1749 she brought a band of warriors to Savannah to press her claims in a more forceful way. The terrorized population of colonists prepared for battle, but managed to get the Indians to agree to a council, during which they were able to demonstrate how absurd Bosomworth's position really was.

The Creek listened, and finally withdrew, realizing that they had been used by Mary and her husband for selfish purposes. Abandoned, the couple stormed and threatened, but to no avail; the colonists refused the claim, but did allow them to go to England to present their case to the Crown in person. At that distance, Mary had an easier time, and in 1759 was paid a modest compensation, and allowed to sell Ossabaw and Sapelo. The pair returned to St. Catharine's, where Mary tried to reestablish her earlier good relations with the Indians and the colonists, but she died shortly afterwards, in 1763, and was buried on the island.

Naiche (1857–1921)
(*Arizona Historical Society Library*)

Naiche (ca. 1857–1921)

Also known as Natchez, or Nache, from *na-ai-che*, meaning "meddlesome; a mischief-maker," was an important Chiricahua Apache chief who was active during the period of the Apache Wars. He was the second son of Cochise; his mother was a daughter of Mangas Coloradas. As a youth, Naiche was the leader of many raiding parties, and following the death of his older brother, Tazi, he became chief of the Chiricahua.

In 1897, Naiche refused to be confined to the reservation established by the United States near San Carlos, Arizona. Instead, he fled into Mexico, along with Geronimo and a number of other warriors. Hiding out in the Sierra Madre Mountains, the band was able to carry out many raids on their traditional enemies, the Mexicans, as well as on American settlements in New Mexico. As to which man was actually "head" of the band, there is some disagreement among historians; Naiche was certainly the hereditary chief, but the greater reputation of Geronimo (especially among Whites), as well as his age, seems to have strongly influenced the younger Naiche to defer to him.

For several years the Apaches were hunted relentlessly by the Army, until they were finally caught by cavalry under the command of Captain Emmett Crawford. On May 25, 1883, Naiche surrendered to General George Crook. He and his band were then sent to San Carlos where they lived for a short time; but they soon became restless. In 1885 Naiche, Geronimo, and over 100 Indians left on what was

186

to be their last spectacular attempt at freedom. As usual, they headed
south into the rugged country where the Army found it almost impossible to operate with any effectiveness. However, with the wise use
of Apache scouts, the troops caught up with the little band in Mexico,
and forced them to surrender. Geronimo, Naiche, and the band of
warriors were sent to Fort Marion, Florida, then west to Mount
Vernon Barracks in Alabama. The continued efforts in their behalf
by General Crook and John Clum to allow their return to Arizona
were to no avail; the hostile climate in that territory prevented any
generous consideration, and finally the Apache group was invited
by the Comanche and Kiowa people to share part of their reservation.

On October 4, 1894, Naiche, with 295 other Apache people, arrived
At Fort Sill, Oklahoma, remaining there until 1913, still as nominal
prisoners of war under Captain Hugh L. Scott. Naiche eventually
returned to the Southwest, living in peace until 1921, when he died
of influenza at Mescalero, New Mexico.

Buckskin Saddle-Bag with Cut-Out
Decoration; Apache
(*Museum of the American Indian*)

Gerald Nailor (1917-1952)

Toh Yah, "Walking by the River," was one of the most gifted artists
of his day. He was born in 1917 at Pinedale, near Crownpoint, New
Mexico, of Navajo parents. He attended Santa Fe Indian School,
where he received his early training and encouragement; he was later
assisted by Olaf Nordmark at the University of Oklahoma. In 1942
Nailor was selected to paint the mural decorating the interior of the
Navajo Tribal Council house at Window Rock, and also created several
murals in Washington, D.C.

Living as a rancher, Gerald married a Picuris girl, Santana Simbola,
and had three children. In a tragic episode at the age of 35, he became
involved in an altercation with a Picuris man who was savagely beating
his wife. Nailor interceded to try to help the woman, but was brutally
beaten himself. Taken to the Taos Hospital, he never recovered, and
died on August 13, 1952, thus ending a career which had already proven
itself—but which was destined to become far greater had it not been
so tragically curtailed. His home was at San Lorenzo, Picuris, New
Mexico.

Watercolor Painting of Stylized Yeibi-
chai Dancers, by Gerald Nailor;
Navajo
(*Museum of Northern Arizona; Marc
Gaede Photo*)

Nampeyo (ca. 1859-1942)

Also known as Nampayo, Nampayu, this Hopi potter revolutionized
her tribe's ceramic art by bringing back the use of ancient forms and
designs. She was born at Hano, Arizona about 1859, the daughter
of Qotsvema, a member of the Snake clan, and Qotcakao, a Tobacco
clan woman. Her name Nampeyo means "Snake Girl" in Tewa (*Tcu
Mana*, with the same meaning in Hopi). The young girl began her

Nampeyo (1859–1942)
(*Southwest Museum; Vroman Photo*)

career by watching her grandmother make the large *ollas*, for carrying water, and other vessels which were used in everyday activities. Nampeyo lived at Hano, a small village adjacent to Walpi on the first of the three mesas where the Hopi had lived for several hundred years. Hano had been established around 1700 by members of the Tewa people who had come as refugees from Spanish oppression from New Mexico, and though they had intermarried and lived with Hopi people since that time, still retained their own speech and ritual practices.

As she progressed in her art, Nampeyo noted that many of the Hopi pottery techniques were superior to the methods that had been in use at Hano in recent times. She was a particularly attractive girl, and her first husband, Kwivioya, who married her in 1879; left simply because he feared that he would not be able to keep other men away from her. In 1881 she married Lesou, a young man from neighboring Walpi.

Her early departures from the traditional work of her Hano neighbors disturbed them; but when they saw that White traders were paying higher prices for her work, they began more and more to copy her. Sometime around 1892 she became interested in the ancient work of the tribe and began to search out old pieces that she might study. In 1895, her husband was hired by Dr. Jesse W. Fewkes, who had begun the excavation of Sikyatki, an early Pueblo ruin in the vicinity. Lesou was himself interested in the ancient forms, and told Nampeyo about the objects which the expedition was uncovering. She began to visit the camp, and also journeyed to nearby Awátovi, Tsukuvi and Payupki, where there were other ruins. The couple looked diligently for sherds, and in the abundant pieces of broken pottery which lay on the surface, found many old pieces which seemed particularly suited for their use.

In so doing, however, Nampeyo realized that she also had to adapt her forms to the old Awátovi and Sikyatki shapes, in order to give them the best representation. Although some traders deliberately sold her work as antique, Nampeyo herself was not a copier; she simply took the elements of the prehistoric designs which appealed to her and incorporated them into her own work.

As she improved in her design, her ceramics took on the bold, fluid designs which introduced the background as an essential element, becoming a part of the whole creation. Even today, although many of her colleagues have adopted her techniques and forms, Nampeyo's work is still recognizable as a unique achievement.

Painted Clay Bowl by Nampeyo; Hopi
(*Museum of the American Indian*)

Like many Indian artists "discovered" in the Southwest by Whites, she became a favorite, and was taken on several trips away from home to demonstrate her skill. In 1898 and 1910 she was in Chicago, and in 1904 she was employed by the Fred Harvey Company at the Grand Canyon, the first of several such long-time sponsorships by that firm. The Harvey alliance was instrumental in gaining a market for her pottery beyond the traditional White traders in the immediate area and her fame became truly worldwide.

Although she continued to work into her old age, the great intensity of her efforts affected her eyes, and she began to go blind; she could still form the pottery, but could no longer execute the remarkably fine, precise and fluid linear decoration for which she was famous. Her husband helped her, duplicating her artistry with surprising skill; following his death in 1932, her daughter Fannie carried on the tradition. Nampeyo died in her home at the age of 82 on July 20, 1942.

The role of Nampeyo in the revival of ceramics among the Hopi people is better realized when it is recalled that at the time she began to change from the traditional forms, there were almost no women producing pottery at Second or Third Mesa villages; only a few were still working at Walpi. Not only was she responsible for improving the quality of the ware itself, but today pottery is the major income-producing craft followed by the women, and the esthetic superiority of the designing is at once obvious in any comparison with older work.

Nampeyo and Lesou had four daughters—Annie, Cecilia, Fannie, and Nellie, all of whom have carried on the art to some degree, although Fannie seems to have most closely achieved the success of her mother.

Nana (ca. 1810–1895?)

Also known as Nané or Nanay, Nana was a minor Chiricahua Apache chief who had perhaps the longest fighting career of any of the Apache warriors. He was a companion-in-arms with Mangas Coloradas, and was closely allied with Victorio until the latter died in Mexico in 1880. Nana had sustained many injuries in battle, and in his later years was so crippled that it was difficult for him to mount a horse.

However, he was always steady and reliable in battle, and implacable in his determination to seek justice or revenge. After the death of Victorio, he vowed to avenge the loss, and rallied the band as well

Nana (1810–1895)
(*Arizona State Historical Society Library*)

189

Buckskin Dance Skirt; Apache
(*Museum of the American Indian*)

as other Chiricahua and Mescalero Apache warriors. In July 1881, they began a campaign of terror, at first attacking only isolated settlers. As they gained in strength and equipment, they picked larger, more ambitious targets, including an Army supply train.

The Ninth Cavalry was dispatched to apprehend Nana and his warriors and settlers formed posses to increase the pressure, but the Apaches either eluded or defeated them in battle. Nana seems to have been an excellent strategist who knew every hill and valley of the rugged New Mexico country in which he fought. By the time he had retreated into the Sierra Madre Mountains in Mexico in late August, his band had traveled over 1200 miles, killed between 75–100 enemies, and captured several hundred livestock.

The next year, Nana was captured in a surprise attack, and brought into the San Carlos Reservation located in southern Arizona. But again he escaped, this time in 1885, accompanied by Geronimo, Naiche, several other chiefs, and about 144 Chiricahua Apache. The band headed for the Sierra Madre range, where they separated, and Nana kept his people out of the hands of the Army for about a year. Finally, in March 1886, he attended a council at which several other Apache chiefs met with General George Crook, Lieutenant John G. Bourke, and other Army officials, to discuss a surrender.

The Apache were eventually sent back to San Carlos, and a large body of them were later shipped to Florida, finally ending up at Fort Sill, Oklahoma, where they were given land. It was there that Nana, now an old man of perhaps eighty years or more, ended his career, still hostile to White controls. He died about 1895 and was buried in the Apache cemetery near Fort Sill.

Daniel Ninham (ca. 1710–1778)

Ninham was a Mahican chief and member of the Wappinger Conferation who led his forces on the colonial side during the American Revolution. The place and exact date of his birth are not known, but he first came to public notice when he was mentioned as an important member of the "Wappinoes" tribe in a document dated October 13, 1730. He became chief in 1740, after which he established his home at Westenhuck, and was apparently a force to be reckoned with in the area of western New England and east–central New York during the Indian Wars of 1746 and 1754.

In 1755, Ninham joined the English side under Sir William Johnson, and proved to be a loyal, valiant fighter. With some of the other chiefs in the Confederacy, he sailed to England around 1762. They were greeted with a great deal of popular acclaim, interest, and curiosity, as would be expected in those days. Their testimony that most of their lands on the east side of the Hudson River had been taken from them forcibly and illegally during British warfare was received with sympathy and promises of fair restitution.

But when Ninham returned to the colonies, the authorities there were not so quick to correct injustice. He found that what had already angered the colonial White settlers applied equally to the Native American inhabitants of the land. Their case languished in the courts, while the people grew restless on the reservations. In fairness, it should be noted that the American Revolution intervened, distracting all such legal matters.

With the outbreak of hostilities, Ninham led his fighting men on the side of the colonists in an effort to improve the relationship between the two races, and to prove loyalty to the citizens in the New York area. His warriors fought well and valiantly, and on August 30, 1778 he led some 30 men on a scouting expedition toward Yonkers. At Cortlandt's Ridge, he encountered Colonel Eminck, who tried to entrap Ninham and his party, but failed. On the next day, in a desperate effort, the Mahican band made a "last stand" at Kingsbridge against the British, but was defeated; Daniel Ninham himself was killed in the fighting on August 31, 1778. He is buried at Pelham's Neck, in Westchester County, New York.

Ninigret (ca. 1600–1678)

His name is also spelled Ninicraft, Nenekunat, and Niniglud (of unknown meaning); this Niantic sachem was a brother-in-law or brother, of Miantonomo. No details exist concerning his birthplace or parentage, but he is known to have maintained a home at Wequapaug in Rhode Island, where he managed to establish irregularly peaceful relationships with the Whites for most of his life. Owing to the times, and the incessant hostilities between the colonists and the several Indian tribes in the southern New England region, this balance was achieved only by dextrous diplomacy.

During the Pequot–Narragansett War of 1632, Ninigret remained independent; indeed, this attitude was expressed in such firm terms that it annoyed the Boston authorities and adversely affected their mutual relations. In 1637 Ninigret was called to the colonial court to defend himself against charges of harboring some of the refugee Pequot warriors–a claim apparently brought against him by Uncas, who was jealous of his position. While he was able to clear himself somewhat, the next year he was forced into a treaty which also involved the payment of a large annual tribute of wampum. Later, in May 1645, he was again charged with faithlessness, and because he had not fulfilled the payment of wampum due from the earlier agreement, he and the other Narragansett chiefs had a further fine of 2000 fathoms of wampum added, which was to be paid within 20 months. An annual tribute in wampum was also charged for those Pequots held by the Niantic and Narragansett peoples. Until the total amount was settled, the sons of several of them, including the son of Ninigret, were to be kept in Boston as hostages.

It must be realized that this amounted to a string of handmade shell beads almost 2½ miles in length—an amount far beyond the ability of the impoverished people to pay. Completely aside from the greed this levy reflected, the matter of payment of wampum fines was a perpetual cancer in the relationship between the English and the New England Indians, and one which was never completely resolved. Nor could it hope to be settled peacefully; the time-consuming process of bead manufacture took Indians from their food-raising and hunting pursuits, stripped them of any surplus wealth, and added further resentment to the injustices they suffered daily.

In 1652, Ninigret visited Manhattan, where he spent the winter with the Dutch. Uncas charged that he had secretly engaged in negotiations against the English; this aroused the paranoia of the colonists who accused Ninigret of treachery—apparently without justification—and summoned him to Boston in September 1653 to defend himself. Nothing came of the affair, but the false charges deepened his antagonism towards the Whites, just as his own proud and haughty behavior infuriated them. During the intervening summer, Ninigret had turned his attention to intertribal frictions, which had become increasingly serious. He attacked the forces of the eastern Long Island sachem, Ascassasotick, who was emboldened by his English friends; the assaults increased back and forth, culminating in the death of Ninigret's nephew. Ninigret thereupon raised a large army, with the intent of destroying the Long Island tribe, hiring warriors from surrounding tribes to assist him.

There seems to be little doubt that he would have succeeded in his purpose, had the English not interfered. Claiming that the Long Island people were under their protection, that he had failed to pay the tribute due, and that he was still harboring some of the Pequots sought by the English, they sent a force under Major Willard with some 300 men against him. While some of the charges may have been specious, it seems true that Ninigret was protecting those few Pequot in his band; but it is equally certain that much of the colonial concern had more to do with the prospect of such a large armed force on their frontier than any defense pact with subject Indian tribes.

The Niantic chief did not defend himself, but gathered his forces and abandoned his village, taking refuge in a large swamp nearby. Willard was able to achieve the surrender of some 150 Pequot refugees, destroy crops and wigwams, but there was little direct combat in the desultory campaign. Eventually Ninigret was forced to agree to a humiliating peace treaty on October 18, 1654, which required further payments of wampum.

But conflicts between the tribes did not come to the same peaceful conclusion. The pressures of the times were too great, and the aggravations caused by the White-imposed government did not allow any truce. The Niantic and the Narragansett continued to harass the eastern Long Island peoples, repeatedly attacking them and keeping tensions high in the southern New England region. At the same time, Uncas took full advantage of the situation to further his own interests, accusing Ninigret and the others of transgressions whenever possible.

On one occasion, some Indians [probably Narragansett] fired into a colonist's home, setting it ablaze. Out of this episode came the command in 1660 for Ninigret and other chiefs to deliver the guilty parties to Boston for punishment, failing which they would be forced to pay a 500-fathom wampum fine, plus another 500 fathoms punitive levy. Further, a bill was presented to him, requiring reimbursement of the past wampum debt which was still outstanding—with the threat that if the payments were not made, the Indians would be sold into slavery in the Barbados Islands.

Wooden Warclub with Iron Blade and Incised Decoration; Mahican (*Museum of the American Indian*)

The complete outcome is not known, and apparently the English were not strong enough to secure complete fulfillment of this staggering penalty. The Connecticut authorities did agree to accept a mortgage on Niantic land—an agreement which was signed by Neneglud [probably Ninigret] and two other sachems.

After this episode, Ninigret seems to have declined in power; he remained occasionally active in his pursuit of the eastern Long Island peoples, but had little contact with the Whites. He took little, if any part, in King Philip's War of 1675–1676, due perhaps to his advanced age. He died at his Wequapaug home shortly after, in 1678, still holding the allegiance of the Niantic and Narragansett peoples. He was never a convert to Christianity, although he did not seem to have been opposed to the religious doctrines so much as to have been offended by the actions of those who claimed to be Christians. When asked by Dr. Mayhew why he was not a convert, he said, simply, "Go and make the English good first, and then I will consider it."

His son, Thomas Ninigret, recorded as an important Narragansett chief in the first quarter of the 18th century, is often confused with the father.

Peta Nocona (ca. 1825–ca. 1861)

Usually known as Nocona, or Nokoni, "The Wanderer," from *peta nokona*, "lone camper," or "one who camps alone," this Comanche chief was one of the most feared raiders on the early Southwestern Plains. Little is known of his birth or parentage, but he was the leader of a band of Quahadi Comanche who raided Fort Parker, Texas, in

1836, kidnapping several White settlers, including a nine-year old girl named Cynthia Ann Parker.

She was eventually adopted by the Comanche and given the name Preloch, growing up as a member of the tribe and apparently quite content with the Indian way of life. Nocona married the young girl, who bore him several children, including the great Comanche leader Quanah Parker. There seems ample evidence that this was a love match, for contrary to Comanche custom, Nocona took no other wife during the rest of his life. They lived the traditional Comanche life, moving from camp to camp, with the men often leaving on extended hunting and raiding expeditions.

In December of 1860, a group of Texas Rangers under Captain Sul Ross invaded Nocona's camp while the warriors were away hunting. Many of the women and children in the camp were killed outright by the Rangers, but a few, including Cynthia Ann Nocona, were captured. She was returned to the Parker family, who tried to get her to return to the White way of life. But she refused, and was imprisoned in her own home—for her own good, said her parents—after she had tried to escape back to her Indian family. She died in the home of her parents about a year later, literally of a broken heart.

Peta Nocona never saw his wife after the kidnapping, and died from an infected wound about 1861 in the Antelope Hills, having established a romantic frontier legend.

Bead-Decorated Cloth Pouch; Mohegan
(*Museum of the American Indian*)

Samson Occom (1723-1792)

The son of Benoni Ocum, or Occum ("On The Other Side"), he was a Mohegan clergyman born in New London, Connecticut in 1723, and educated by Reverend Eleazar Wheelock, the noted missionary and teacher. Samson was christianized in 1741 and in 1749 he moved to Long Island, where he married a young woman, Mary Fowler (or Mary Montauk), by whom he had ten children. In 1759, without the benefit of much formal education, he was ordained by the Long Island Presbytery, and became a preacher to the Montauk people. Throughout this period he maintained his contact with Wheelock, and in 1765 sailed to England to help raise money for Wheelock's new Indian Charity School. He was the first Indian known to preach in England, and this trip, lasting over two years, attracted wide interest He was an impressive orator and his appearances were well-staged; he raised £12,026—sufficient funds for the school to move to new quarters in New Hampshire, where it evolved into Dartmouth College.

When Occom returned to the colonies, he became estranged from Wheelock, who had turned his school from teaching Indians to the education of Whites who were to become missionairies to the Indians. Occom accused him of "turning an Alma Mater into an Alba Mater," and began traveling among the New England tribes, preaching and teaching. He was not so much interested in theology as he was in personal morality, and he became a popular orator among many Indians.

Another of his concerns was the effects of the burgeoning White population on his people. In 1773 he developed a plan to settle some hard-pressed New England Indians in New York State on land belonging to the Oneida tribe. After the turbulent Revolutionary War years and other difficult times, the Brotherton Community was formed in Oneida County, New York in 1786.

Samson Occom served as minister at Brotherton, but turned more and more to drinking, brought on primarily by frustration with his efforts to obtain a fair hearing for his community. He died a bitter, tired man at New Stockbridge, New York on August 2, 1792 at the age of 69.

Oconostota (ca. 1710–1783)

His name is derived from *áganu-státa*, "groundhog sausage," the major Cherokee war chief of the 18th century, who was in turn an ally and then an enemy of the English during the early days of colonization in the Southeast. Little is known of his birth or parentage, but he is believed to have been one of the six Indian leaders invited to visit King George II around 1730; Attakullakulla was also in that party, and the two worked together throughout their long careers.

During the early days of the English frontier wars against the French, Oconostota was helpful to the British, but the spread of settlements, and increasing friction between Indians and Whites, aggravated by poorly concealed contempt of the latter towards the original owners of the land, threatened to explode in an all-out war. The Cherokee began to take revenge for savage attacks upon them by some of the settlers, and when Oconostota headed a party of 32 chiefs to Charlestown to talk peace with Governor William H. Lyttleton in 1759, the latter demanded that the Indians guilty of one of the attacks be surrendered for trial. When the Cherokee refused on grounds of justified defense, he had them all thrown into jail.

Although Oconostota was shortly released through the strong intercession of Attakullakulla, the peace chief of the tribe, who gave up one of the fugitives sought by the British, Oconostota returned home a bitter enemy of the Whites. In alliance with his Creek neighbors, his forces besieged Fort Prince George in 1760. In reprisal for the humiliation of being jailed, Oconostota killed Lieutenant Richard Cotymore; thereupon the garrison executed the Cherokee hostages who were still being held. This touched off a series of attacks upon settlers throughout the area, culminating in a major assault on Fort Loudon in Tennessee, and the massacre of over 200 Whites. English reinforcements moved into the area under Colonel Archibald Montgomery, who, with 1600 men relieved Fort Prince George and attacked and destroyed most of the Lower Towns of the Cherokee tribe. However, he was completely defeated in his efforts to help Fort Loudon, was forced to retreat, and was ultimately replaced by Colonel James

Grant the next year. The latter headed a strengthened force of 2600 men and laid waste to all of the Middle Towns, finally forcing the Indians to sue for peace and a treaty in 1763 which set the stage for even greater encroachment upon their lands.

In 1768 another war ended the ancient conflict between the Cherokee and the Iroquois—when Oconostota and several other chiefs went to New York to seal a pact to that effect. In the Revolutionary War the Cherokee lands were under increasing pressure from White settlers. Largely because of this, the Indians allied themselves with the English against the colonists. Unsupported by the former, however, the Cherokee suffered defeat after defeat, and Oconostota was finally forced to give up the tribal leadership; his age and physical infirmity had made him no longer the daring, skillful war strategist that he had once been. He relinquished command to his son Tuksi (the Terrapin), and shortly thereafter died at Echota in 1783.

Opechancanough (ca. 1545–1644)

O-pe-chan-can'ough, also called Mangopeomen, was a Powhatan chief and the brother of Powhatan. The meaning of the names is not known. He was born about 1545, apparently at Powhatan village. He was a bitter enemy of the English and in 1608 captured Captain John Smith, whose life was saved by Powhatan's daughter (and niece of Opechancanough), Pocahontas. After his release, Smith wanted to develop better relations between the colonists, whose food supply was always in jeopardy, and the Indians. He made arrangements to meet with Opechancanough to negotiate a trade; the contemptuous refusal of the latter to supply any food and Smith's determination to show the Indians that he and the colonists were a force to be respected, caused him to seize the chief by the hair, at pistol point, and hold him for ransom. There was no bloodshed and Opechancanough was ransomed by his people; but he never forgave the Whites for the humiliation he suffered.

Animosity and distrust between the two peoples continued with only a brief period of relative calm following the marriage of Pocahontas and John Rolfe, during which time Powhatan was able to contain the strong passions. At the death of Powhatan however, Opechancanough dominated the tribe even though his elder brother Opitchipan became chief. Plans were immediately laid by Opechancanough to destroy the Jamestown colony, and despite the fact that a Christian Indian, Chanco, revealed the plot to the English, 347 settlers were massacred on March 22, 1622. For many years thereafter, intermittent warfare continued between Whites and Indians.

Opechancanough grew old, but never relented in his firm determination to drive the English out of Indian country. Although he was in his nineties, and confined to a litter by his infirmities, he led his forces in a climactic battle on April 18, 1644, during which both sides suffered heavy casualties; the Whites lost over 300 men. The Indians finally retreated, and in the flight following their defeat, Opechancanough was captured and taken to Jamestown, where he was shot by one of his guards.

Opothleyaholo (ca. 1798–1862)

Opothleyaholo (1798–1862)
(*Oklahoma Historical Society*)

Hupuehelth Yaholo, from *huhuewa*, "child," *hehle* "good," *yaholo*, "hallooer," or Hupuihilth Yahola, and Apothleyahola, best known as Opothleyaholo—the variety of spellings is a good indication of the difficulty early historians had in the transcription of Indian names. This Creek chief was an important leader of the Muskhogean people in Indian Territory who supported the Union in the Civil War. He was born in the Creek Nation in Georgia about 1798 and very quickly became one of his people's leading warriors.

He fought against Andrew Jackson in the Creek War of 1813–1814, which ended in defeat for the Indians at Horseshoe Bend. In peacetime he became the Speaker of the Upper Creek Council and participated in many of the land negotiations with the Whites. In the 1820s William McIntosh and his Lower Creeks ceded their lands and moved west to Indian Territory. Opothleyaholo went to Washington, D.C., to protest removal, but encountered only deaf ears; the Creeks were forced to sign a series of agreements which required them to leave their homeland.

By the terms of the Treaty of March 1832, the Creek were given five years to complete the cession of all lands east of the Mississippi in exchange for a reservation in Indian Territory. In 1832 Opothleyaholo accompanied Benjamin Hawkins, the Indian Agent, to Texas to purchase lands for the Alabama Creeks, for which they paid $20,000. In 1826 he lead about 2700 of his people on a harrowing journey to the west; almost 400 died en route. The Creek refugees eventually settled into their new territory, and under the honest, intelligent administration of Opothleyaholo, many of them prospered. His philosophy of leadership was perhaps summed up in a speech which he gave on education: "We Indians are like an island in the middle of the river. The White man comes upon us as a flood. We crumble and fall . . . Let us save our people by educating our boys and girls and young men and young women in the ways of the White man. Then they may be planted and deeply rooted about us and our people may stand unmoved in the flood of the White man."

The Lower and Upper Creek peoples in Indian Territory had little to do with each other. When the Civil War came, the South enlisted many of the Lower Creek in their cause, while most of the Upper Creek remained loyal or joined the Union. In 1861 the Confederates moved into Indian Territory, and undertook several battles in an effort to establish their control, most of which were successful; in December, after suffering several defeats, Opothleyaholo retreated, leading a band of refugees across the border into Kansas. He lost all his livestock, his land, and most of his once-impressive wealth. Age, earlier experiences, and the shock of the defeat caused his early death in 1862, near Leroy Creek, Kansas. He had one wife, two daughters, and a son.

Stroud Cloth Bag; Seminole
(*Museum of the American Indian*)

Oqwa Pi (ca. 1900–1971)

From Tewa *oqwa pi*, "Red Cloud," also known as Abel Sánchez, one of the earliest Pueblo Indian artists, was one of the major influences during the formative years of watercolor painting in the Southwest. He was born at San Ildefonso Pueblo, New Mexico, about 1900, the son of full-blooded Tewa parents.

He began painting about 1919, after his education in Santa Fe schools, but was untrained in art. Shortly afterwards, his talent was recognized and he was encouraged by local art patrons. He was a hard worker, who turned out a large amount of painting throughout his life. He made a good living at painting, and is one of the few Southwest artists who never succumbed to liquor or any other illnesses induced by hardship and neglect.

He served as lieutenant governor of his Pueblo, and was later elected governor of San Ildefonso, an honor accorded many Pueblo artists during their careers. Indeed, it is probable that more artists have become major political figures in Indian life than in White culture.

His work has been published widely, most notably in journals and books dealing with Indian art. He first exhibited in a major show at the Exposition of Indian Tribal Arts, in New York City in 1931, and was later included in almost every primary Indian art show in the United States. Oqwa Pi has been honored by awards from many exhibitions, as well as by his own colleagues; he worked quietly but energetically until his death in March 1971, at his home in Santa Fe, New Mexico.

"Koshares." Watercolor Painting by Oqwa Pi
(*Museum of New Mexico*)

Oqwa Pi (1900–1971)
(*Museum of New Mexico; Wes Bradfield Photo*)

198

Osceola (ca. 1804–1838)

He was also called Assiola, from *asi-yaholo*, "Black Drink Crier," referring to *asi*, the purifying emetic used in the busk ritual, and *yaholo*, the long-drawn-out cry of attendants at the ceremony. Some accounts derive the name from Hasse Ola (*háshay* "sun," *ola* "rising"), "The Rising Sun," but this is not generally accepted; even less accepted is the name Ossiolachih, "Singing Eagle." His ceremonial name was Talassee Tustenuggee, whence the nickname "Talcy" sometimes applied to him. His birthplace is unclear; most accounts say that he was born about 1804 east of the Chattahoochee River in Georgia. An equally early source attaches his origin to the Tallapoosa River in Alabama, sometime between 1800–1806.

Osceola (1804–1838)
(*Museum of the American Indian*)

His ancestry is equally controversial. Most records agree that his mother was a full-blooded Creek woman (perhaps Polly Coppinger), but the ancestry of his father is less certain. One account claims that he was an English trader named William Powell (hence the common boyhood name Billy Powell applied to the lad). However, Osceola always claimed to be full-blooded, and it is more generally thought that Powell was the mother's second husband.

Following the Creek War of 1813–1814 many Creek people fled from Georgia seeking refuge with other tribes; Osceola and his mother seem to have been among this group, going into the Seminole country of northern Florida. Subsequently they were caught up in the First Seminole War of 1819, and it is quite possible that even as a teenager he participated in combat against the forces under General Andrew Jackson in 1819. There is a report that he was captured in 1818 by Jackson during the campaigns against the Spaniards in Florida, but was quickly released because of his age.

Although not a hereditary chief—nor, as far as is known, ever elected to that position—Osceola soon achieved a position of leadership by virtue of his abilities. Like most Seminole, he opposed the treaties of Payne's Landing in 1832 and of Fort Gibson in 1833, by which certain chiefs had agreed to move to Indian Territory within three years. He had married two young sisters, in accordance with Creek custom, and moved into the Big Swamp, Ouithlocko, which became his home. He had two sons as a result of his marriage.

One of the sisters was called Chotter, or Chechoter ("Morning Dew"), the daughter of a Creek chief and a fugitive slave mother. By the laws of the day, if the mother was a slave the daughter was also considered a slave. One day, Osceola took her to Fort King, where two professional slave catchers who were talking to General Wiley Thompson, commander of the fort, recognized the girl and claimed her under the law. Thompson told the men to take her and Osceola was unable to prevent her being dragged away in irons for shipment to the slave states. Shocked at the barbarity of the White man's law, Osceola vowed to spend the rest of his life revenging this savage act.

In 1835, when General Thompson brought together many of the Indian leaders to gain their consent for a confirmation of the terms of the earlier treaties, most silently refused to touch the pen proffered

Fringed Buckskin Coat of Osceola;
Seminole
(*Museum of the American Indian*)

for the purpose. Osceola, however, is said to have expressed his feeling more vividly, plunging a hunting knife through the document. He was arrested and imprisoned but was released when he promised to support the impending emigration. Instead of keeping his promise to support the emigration he organized active Seminole resistance and achieved the revenge he had sought by killing Thompson, and also Charlie Amathla, one of the leading Seminole forces behind the agreement to the Fort Gibson Treaty.

Thus began the Second Seminole War, from 1835–1842, in which the 30-year-old Osceola was clearly recognized as the most important Indian military leader involved, and government efforts focused on his elimination. On Christmas eve of 1825, Major F. L. Dade and a force of about 100 men left Fort King to achieve this end. Within three days all but three of his troops had been killed by Osceola and his warriors. Many soldiers were sent on missions to capture or kill Osceola but the Seminole engaged in one of the great early guerrilla campaigns, employing elusive tactics with remarkable success. The humiliated Army began to hear criticism from politicians and the public for its failure to end the costly war; at the same time there was a great ground swell of respect and sympathy for Osceola, for the Seminole people, and the cause for which they were fighting.

Generals succeeded one another in a vain effort to gain a decisive victory, and finally in October 1837, the area commander General Thomas S. Jesup, frustrated by his troop's failures and infuriated by the criticism from politicians and the public called for a conference with Osceola under a flag of truce. Flagrantly betraying the truce promise, Jesup had Osceola seized and bound. There was a public outcry at this wanton treachery, but Jesup had the famous leader imprisoned in Fort Moultrie, South Carolina.

Within three months, Osceola was no longer a problem; he died on January 30, 1838. There are varying accounts as to the cause of his death—poison, maltreatment, or malaria—but all agree that lack of freedom and disillusionment at the treachery of the Whites had a devastating effect upon his will to live. He was buried just outside of Fort Moultrie, on Sullivan's Island, in the harbor at Charleston. Even at his death there was no rest from White invasion; his head was cut off and for many years was on display in the "Medical Museum" of Dr. Valentine Mott, until it was destroyed by fire in 1866.

The war continued sporadically for another four years, but with the loss of their great leader Seminole determination to resist also seemed to erode. In 1842 most of the remaining Seminole moved to Indian Territory, although some remained hidden in the swamps and are the forefathers of the contemporary Seminole people in Florida.

Oshkosh (1795–1858)

His name is also spelled Oskashe and Oiscoss, from *uskasha* or *osh-kushi*, meaning "hoof," or "nail," which is actually a reference to a major tribal social division and symbolic of a brave animal; from the name comes the occasional interpretation of "The Brave" for this important warrior who fought against the United States in his youth, but eventually changed sides in later years. He was a Menomini leader who was born at the Old King's Village on the Fox River near Green Bay, Wisconsin in 1795. Little is known of his parents, although he is known to have been a member of the Owasse clan. He first came to public notice in the War of 1812 when he and about 100 warriors joined the British forces, fighting under Chief Tomah. He helped capture Fort Mackinaw from the Americans and earned the name by which he was permanently known.

The next year he participated in an unsuccessful attack on Fort Sandusky, Ohio and demonstrated his skill as a warrior in many battles thereafter. Though he was a descendant of a family of important chiefs, Oshkosh himself did not become a leader until the U.S. Indian Agent Lewis Cass appointed him head chief of the Menomini on August 11, 1827—the Whites needed a leader to negotiate and sign the Treaty of Butte des Morts, and Oshkosh was acceptable to both parties. This treaty involved an attempt to solve the dispute between the Menomini and a group of Iroquois led by Eleazar Williams who desired to settle in the region.

Oshkosh eventually became adjusted to American sovereignty in the Great Lakes area and after British efforts to stir up the Indians against the new country subsided he fought on the American side in the Black Hawk War of 1832. Following the success of that campaign, he seems to have made every effort to keep the peace with the United States and to try to get his people to adjust to White authority as much as he possibly could. Perhaps his greatest test in this effort was at the time he signed the Treaty of Lake Powahekone in 1848, whereby the Menomini ceded lands in Wisconsin; that he was not overthrown by his people is indicative of his position and strength.

Oshkosh was effective in his dealings with the Whites and was respected by his tribe as a great orator and wise spokesman. Not a large man, he was affable and possessed of singular common sense; unfortunately, he had a terrible temper which he frequently was unable to control. More serious was his addiction to liquor; he often had problems with intoxication, which earned him the contempt of the Whites in the area and he died in a drunken brawl at Keshena, Wisconsin on August 20, 1858. His son succeeded him as tribal chief.

Oshkosh (1795–1858)
(*State Historical Society of Wisconsin*)

Woven Yarn Medicine Bag; Chippewa
(*Museum of the American Indian*)

John Otherday (1801–1871)

Also known as Other Day and Angpetu Tokecha, this Wahpeton Sioux missionary and interpreter figured prominently in the Sioux uprisings at Spirit Lake and New Ulm. He was born at Swan Lake, Minnesota in 1801. His father was Red Bird (Zitkaduta) and his mother was a Sioux woman from Minnesota.

In his youth, Otherday was apparently a headstrong young man given to strong outbursts of temper; on one occasion, he killed two

German Silver Cross with Engraved
Designs; Sioux
(*American Museum of Natural History*)

of his companions during a drunken brawl. With the advent of White settlers into the area, however, he seems to have changed remarkably. He eventually converted to the Christian faith and joined Dr. Thomas S. Williamson's church, and was baptized under the name of John. He abandoned most of his people's customs and adopted the habits and clothing of the White man.

He married a White woman and settled on the Sioux Reservation in Minnesota. During the Spirit Lake outbreak led by Inkpaduta in 1857, Otherday rescued one of the captives, and tried to track down some of the culprits. And later, when Little Crow attacked New Ulm in 1862, Otherday warned the settlers of their danger, guiding a band of 62 to safety at St. Paul, and then aided others to escape the attacks of the Sioux raiders. He subsequently served as a scout for General Sibley in efforts to capture Little Crow and his warriors.

These exploits made him a hero to the White settlers, and in 1867 he traveled to Washington, where he was received with ceremony, awarded a grant of $2500 by Congress, and figured in the signing of the Wahpeton–Sisseton treaty on February 19, 1867. Returning to Minnesota, he built a new home with the money, occupying a farm near Henderson, Minnesota for a few years. His attempts at farming did not succeed, however, and he sold his home, moving to the Sisseton Sioux Reservation in South Dakota.

Another house was built for him on the Sioux Reservation and he lived out the rest of his days in peace. He suffered from tuberculosis and in 1871 succumbed to the disease. He was buried a few miles south of Peever, South Dakota.

Ouray (1820–1880)
(*Colorado Historical Society*)

Ouray (ca. 1820–1880)

"The Arrow," also known as Willie Ouray, was a famous chief of the Uncompaghre Ute. The year of his birth is a matter of uncertainty; he was born about 1820 (some say 1833) in Taos, New Mexico, the son of a Ute father and a Jicarilla Apache mother (one account claims that his father was Guera Mura, a Jicarilla captive). He learned Spanish as a boy and used that language for most of his life. In his youth, in southern Colorado, he fought with the Kiowa and the Sioux, and lost his only son; the latter was taken as a captive and never given up by the warriors.

At his father's death in 1860, Ouray became chief. He was actually appointed in Washington, where he was given the title, medals, and a $1000 annuity. He was also appointed government interpreter. He was known then, and continued throughout his life, to be a staunch friend of the White man, although he was equally firm in defending the interests of his people. He signed "U-ray, the Arrow," to the Treaty of Conejos, in Colorado, in 1863. At this time he was closely associated with Kit Carson, then a military officer, and in the summer of 1867 the two took a strong hand in suppressing the revolt of another Ute leader, Chief Kaniatse.

Ouray journeyed to Washington again in 1872 to give strong resistance to the governmental takeover of lands which had been permanently granted to the Ute. Though his manner was generally acknowledged to be dignified, at one point in the arguments he lost his temper with an official who accused the Ute of laziness: "We work as hard as you do. Did you ever try skinning a buffalo?" Although the next year he was forced to accept a compromise settlement, he did manage to secure a better award for his tribe than many others enjoyed.

In 1879 the Ute people around White River became embroiled in a dispute with the Indian Agent, one Nathan Meeker. When he called for military aid, the Indians in the area killed him and seven other Whites and held some Agency women as hostages. When the Army troops arrived, the conditions were set for a savage, bloody conflict, but Ouray intervened and was able to capitalize upon the respect held by both sides for him, and effected a peaceful solution.

Ouray married at least twice; his earlier wives are not known, but in 1859 he married Chipeta, a Ute woman who was at his side when he died at Ignacio, Colorado on August 27, 1880, a victim of Bright's disease. They had no children. He was secretly buried south of the town, and in 1925 was reburied at Montrose, Colorado. He was succeeded as Ute chief by Shavanaux (Shavano).

Arthur Caswell Parker (1881-1955)

Gawasowaneh, "Big Snowsnake," a major Seneca figure in New York State anthropology and museum professional activities, was born on April 5, 1881 at Cattaraugus, New York to Frederick Ely, a part Iroquoian father, and Geneva H. Griswold Parker, of Scotch-English ancestry. He was probably about one-quarter Iroquoian blood. His grandfather was a brother of General Ely S. Parker, the noted Army officer and Indian Commissioner. Young Arthur studied at Dickinson Seminary in Pennsylvania and then entered Harvard University, where he came under the influence of the leading anthropological museum director of the day, Dr. Frederick Ward Putnam. Unfortunately, he never completed his Ph.D. degree, which was to be a cause of permanent regret to him, although he was awarded an honorary degree by Union College in 1940.

Parker became a field archeologist for Harvard's Peabody Museum in 1903-1904, also working part-time at the American Museum of Natural History during that period. In 1906 he was appointed state archeologist for the New York State Museum at Albany. During this period he participated in excavations in Iroquois country and wrote many articles and books, including *The Archaeological History of New York*, which was the leading study of the subject for many years. He organized the New York State Archaeological Survey and built the Museum into a major anthropological facility; it was a great

Arthur Caswell Parker (1881-1955)
(*Rochester Museum & Science Center*)

accomplishment, but also became the scene of one of the major tragedies of his life. In 1911, a disastrous fire struck the west end of the Capitol building, destroying most of the irreplaceable Indian paintings and objects collected before 1850 by Lewis Henry Morgan, as well as much of Parker's own collection, equally unique, although perhaps less ancient.

As a founder of the *American Indian Magazine*, 1911–1916, and an officer in many ethnic societies and organizations, Parker was a leading force in Indian affairs of the period. He served as an advisor to several federal commissions and a number of Presidents and other federal officers. In 1925 he was appointed director of the Rochester Museum of Arts and Sciences, where he remained until his retirement in 1946. At the time of his death at Naples, New York on January 1, 1955, he was one of the world's leading authorities on museum administration, Indian affairs, and Iroquois culture in general. His oft-quoted principle was, "It is not what a museum has, but what it does with what it has, that counts." His lifetime bibliography included 350 titles, of which 14 were major books. He married twice; the first time was to Beatrice Tahamont, by whom he had two children; and later to Anna T. Cook, the mother of one more child.

Ely Samuel Parker (1828–1895)

Hasanoanda (or Hasonnoanda), "The Reader," or as some say, "Coming to the Front," was a famous Seneca chief, U.S. Army officer, and the first Indian Commissioner of Indian Affairs. He was a member of the Wolf clan and was born in 1828 at Indian Falls near Pembroke, New York. His father, William Parker, Jonoesdowa, was a Tonawanda Seneca chief; his mother Elizabeth, Gaontgwutwus, was a descendant of Skaniadario, an important Huron figure; his grandfather was Red Jacket. He grew up on the reservation and was educated in mission school and local academies.

Ely was a bright young man, interested in many things. He helped his friend, the ethnologist Lewis Henry Morgan, prepare the classic study, *League of the Ho-Dé-No-Sau-Nee or Iroquois*, which was published in 1851. In the next year, he became a sachem, taking the title Donehogawa (or Deioninhogawen), "He Holds the Door Open." He studied law, but was refused admission to the bar because, as an Indian, he was not a United States citizen. He also studied at the Rensselaer Polytechnic Institute, and then went to work for the federal government as a civil engineer. From 1858 to 1861 he was in charge of the construction of several government buildings at Galena, Illinois. There he met a former Army officer, Ulysses S. Grant, forming a friendship which lasted throughout his life.

When the Civil War began, Parker confidently expected to be commissioned in the Corps of Engineers on the basis of his vast experience. But the old racial prejudices which had earlier prevented his legal career were still alive, and no one to whom he applied would help. Secretary of State William H. Seward reputedly told him that "the

Ely Samuel Parker (1828–1895)
(*Smithsonian Institution, National Anthropological Archives*)

whites would win the war without Indian help." Parker persisted, however, and in May 1863 was commissioned a captain and assigned to the Seventh Division. Soon after that he joined Grant at Vicksburg, shortly becoming a lieutenant general; his friendship with Grant, his education, and excellent penmanship caused the latter to appoint him as his military secretary. At Appomattox Court House, Colonel Bowers, the adjutant general, was so nervous that he could not write clearly and Parker was requested to write out the final copy of the agreement by which General Robert E. Lee surrendered the Confederate Army to the Federal forces. After the war he remained in the Army, becoming a brigadier general at the age of 39. Two years later, in 1869, Grant appointed his old comrade-in-arms the first Indian Commissioner of Indian Affairs. That same year he married Minnie Sackett Wast.

When Parker began to administer his office in a manner designed to secure justice for the Indians of the country, he ran into powerful White opposition; this post had long been a haven for political appointees who had little interest in the corruption which was widespread on the Indian frontier. In 1871 a Committee of the House of Representatives brought him to trial on charges of defrauding the government. He was completely exonerated of all charges but the injustice and obvious racial malice he suffered disheartened him completely, and he resigned his post and returned to New York.

After several ill-fated business ventures, Parker became superintendent for buildings and supplies of the New York City Police Department in 1876, holding the post until his death on August 31, 1895. He died at his country home in Fairfield, Connecticut and was buried in the Red Jacket lot at Forest Lawn Cemetery, in Buffalo.

Quanah Parker (ca. 1845-1911)

The name Quanah was derived from Comanche *kwaina*, meaning "fragrant" or "sweet smelling." Quanah was the son of Peta Nocona, a chief of the warlike Quahadi band, and Cynthia Ann Parker the daughter of a Texas settler who had been captured on May 19, 1836 at the age of nine. Adopted by the band and named Preloch, she lived happily with the Indian people, grew to maturity, and married Nocona. She was recaptured by Texas Rangers in a raid and forcibly returned to her home, where she died (of a broken heart, most accounts say) four years later, still yearning to return to her Comanche world. Quanah himself was born at Cedar Lake, Texas in May 1845.

Quanah Parker (1845-1911) and his Wife, Tonarcy
(*Smithsonian Institution, National Anthropological Archives*)

206

A strong, fearless youth, Quanah became tribal leader after the death of his father. He formed his own band of raiders, some of whom were the best warriors in the region. They refused to accept the terms of the Medicine Lodge Treaty of 1867 which decreed that the Comanche, along with the Kiowa, Apache, Cheyenne, and Arapaho people, were to be settled in Indian Territory. For the next seven years Quanah lived in open rebellion, raiding frontier towns and White settlers. In 1874 he was in command of a united Indian force of about 700 that attacked a party of buffalo hunters who had been decimating the herds in the area. The hunters were securely protected by the stout fortification of Adobe Walls in the Texas Panhandle, and though badly outnumbered, they had a cannon which enabled them to turn the tide against the Indians. Quanah and his band were then pursued by General Ranald Mackenzie, and after a two-year harassment, finally surrendered.

At this point, Quanah Parker changed his life remarkably. Setting aside his enmity toward the Whites, he accommodated himself to their civilization, and became a prosperous, settled farmer in Indian Territory. Although he remained loyal to the Comanche traditions of his fathers, he encouraged his people to seek education and to learn the White man's ways. Through his influence, the confederated tribes leased surplus pasture lands to stock raisers, and thereby gained substantial income. He was appointed judge of the Court of Indian Affairs in 1886 and helped build it into a major force. Indeed, he was successful to a point where factionalism and jealousy within the tribe and White pressures against polygamy combined to cause him to lose his judgeship in 1898.

Quanah traveled widely as a representative of his tribe, and along with Geronimo and several other famed Indian personages of the day, rode in Theodore Roosevelt's inaugural parade. He had seven wives, two of whom survived him, and three sons and four daughters. He died on February 21, 1911 at the age of 64, in Cache, Oklahoma and was buried beside his mother Cynthia Ann, whose body he had earlier reinterred in Cache.

Passaconaway (1565?–1665?)

Pa-sa-con'a-way, from *papisse-conwa*, "bear cub," was a Pennacook chief who controlled a vast area of New England at the time the first White settlers arrived. The date of his birth is uncertain, but he is known to have resided at Pennacook on the Merrimack River, near Concord, New Hampshire. In 1629 his daughter married Winnepurget, the sachem of Saugus; this love affair became the basis of the romantic poem *The Bridal of Pennacook* by John Greenleaf Whittier.

Passaconaway was a powerful chief, and one of the few to withstand any invasion of his territory by the Mohawk; on the other hand, he found it impossible to remain independent of English rule. After several battles and minor skirmishes, the colonists decided to disarm the Indians to prevent future outbreaks. In 1642 soldiers were sent to deal with

Passaconaway; however, he was absent, and instead they shot at and kidnapped his wife and son, Wannalancet.

The Pennacook were outraged by the incident, and the authorities in Massachusetts apologized for the brutal action of their men, making certain that both the woman and the boy were returned unharmed. But Passaconaway recognized the inevitable and in 1644 he signed a treaty placing himself and his tribe under the authority of the colonists.

He was not only an outstanding political and military leader, but Passaconaway was regarded as a powerful medicine man whose magical powers were deeply respected by his people. It is said that he had visions of the future under English rule, in which he saw that those who refused to submit were ruthlessly exterminated. When he died at Pennacook in 1665, at about 100 years of age, he advised his son and his people, "never to contend with the English, nor to make war with them." His burial place is unknown.

Pawhuska (1760–1825)
(*Oklahoma Historical Society*)

Painted Buckskin Medicine Shield Osage
(*Museum of the American Indian*)

Pawhuska (1760?–1825)

He was also known as Pahuska, Pauhuska, Pahhueska, "White Hair," Cahaga Tonga, or Teshuhimga, and known to the French as Cheveaux Blancs. He was a well-known Osage leader who figured prominently in the early 19th century history of his tribe. Little is known of his early life. He is thought to have been born about 1760 in Great Osage Village (often called White Hair's Village) on the Little Osage River in what is now Missouri. He was headman of the tribe in 1806 at the time Lieutenant Zebulon Pike established Camp Independence—an ironic name in view of the 1808 cession of all Osage lands in the Missouri area at the Treaty of Fort Clark. The name White Hair stems from an incident when he snatched the wig from General St. Claire during battle, thinking he had captured the White man. General St. Claire escaped from the ignominious episode relatively intact, and from then on the Osage wore the wig as "war medicine," as a scalp ornament.

The hereditary chief of the Osage was Tawagahe, "Town Builder," more commonly known as Clermont (or Clermore), who was evidently a great warrior and capable person; however, Pawhuska usurped his position while Tawagahe was still a youth. He was able to hold the chieftainship in spite of the greater abilities of the younger man due to the support of influential Whites, most notably Pierre Chouteau, the noted Indian trader. It seems, in fact, that both Pawhuska and another Osage chief, Cashesegra (Koshisigré) "Big Tracks," were actually maintained, if not created, by Chouteau. Since they owed their positions to him, neither man opposed the economic or political desires of the Chouteaus, nor could they effectively control their own people, thereby becoming puppets.

This seems even more evident in viewing the large number of treaties which Pawhuska signed, ceding Osage rights to their own territory. He was unable to prevent the Osage warriors from taking the warpath against the Whites on the Arkansas River, and continually appears to have been largely a figurehead in Indian eyes. The prominence of his name in White accounts of the period may well be explained by his willingness to accommodate their demands in land negotiations.

Pierre Chouteau took Pawhuska to Washington where he met President Thomas Jefferson and other notables of the day. During his life in the Osage area, the chief worked closely with the founding and development of the Harmony Mission. He died about August 25, 1825 at his home in Vernon County, Missouri, and was buried in a large tomb on Blue Mound. Some time later his grave was vandalized by White looters who stole the skull and most of the bones. Later the mound was rebuilt by some Osage people, although the bones were not reinterred. The town of Pawhuska, Oklahoma is named for him, as is the present Osage Agency.

Payepot (1816-1908)

Payepot, also known as Piapot, was an important Cree war chief who was active on the Western Canadian Plains during the period of White expansion in that region. Soon after his birth in 1816 he was named Kikikwawason, "Flash in the Sky." A smallpox epidemic struck his tribe and everyone scattered from the scourge which had been introduced by incoming explorers. He and his grandmother were captured by the Sioux, with whom they remained for 14 years, until a party of raiding Cree warriors freed them. The young man had become known by that time as Payepot or "One Who Knows the Secrets of the Sioux." Shortly after his rescue from the Sioux by the Cree warriors, he became an important person in Cree life due to his knowledge of the Sioux people and the area in which they lived.

Following his selection as chief, he led many successful attacks on the Sioux and Blackfoot people—traditional enemies of the Cree. Then, in 1870, he led about 700 warriors into Blackfoot territory and destroyed some lodges. In retaliation, the Blackfoot and their southern cognates, the Piegan, mounted a swift and bloody counterattack, killing over one-half of the Cree attackers. This made a major readjustment in the relative position of the two tribes in western Canada.

At about this time, Whites were coming into the area in increasing numbers. Payepot rejected a treaty in 1874 which would have moved his people onto a reserve; a year later, he was forced by the threat of military action to sign the agreement. He and his tribe moved west, refusing to accept confinement, and for a time they disrupted the construction of the Canadian Pacific Railroad by pulling up the surveyor's stakes and using them for firewood.

In 1883 there was a confrontation between the Cree and the railroad men; Payepot and several hundred of his warriors camped on the right-of-way, directly in the path of the advancing construction crews who refused to push them aside for fear of starting a battle. The Royal Canadian Mounted Police were called on for help and when they told Payepot that he had 15 minutes to move, he turned his back on them in contempt.

Payepot (1816-1908)
(*Glenbow-Alberta Institute*)

Beaded Cloth "Fire Bag": Cree
(*Museum of the American Indian*)

When the deadline passed, the police moved in and pulled up the stakes of the chief's tepee.

The onlookers expected shots to be fired, but Payepot only smiled and moved his people away. Like most Plains Indians he respected courage—perhaps more to the point, he knew that if he killed the Mounties, their comrades and the Army would move in and kill many more of his own people. And so he moved out of the path of the White advance and onto the barren reserve land. Here, a quarter of the Cree residents perished before they ignored government orders and moved, in desperation, to the verdant Qu'appelle Valley near Regina.

Eventually the authorities agreed to this move and the Cree lived on in peace. Though he neither admired nor trusted the Whites, Payepot did respect their power, and he kept the hotheaded young bloods from joining in such adventures as the Riel Rebellion in 1885. But he was finally deposed as chief by the Whites after the tribe held a Sun Dance which had been expressly forbidden by the authorities. Most Cree paid little attention to the White directive, however, and remained loyal to their old chief until his death in 1908 at the age of 92 years.

Tonita Peña (1895-1949)

Tonita Peña (1895-1949)
(*Museum of New Mexico; T. Harmon Parkhurst Photo*)

Quah Ah (White Coral Beads) was the first Pueblo woman artist to throw off the traditional restrictions that were usually imposed upon women in Pueblo culture, and paint just as freely as her esthetic sensitivity directed. She was born Tonita Vigil, at San Ildefonso Peublo, New Mexico on June 13, 1895, the daughter of Ascensión Vigil and Natividad Peña. Following the death of her mother, she was brought up by her aunt, Martina Vigil, of Cochiti, who saw to her education at the San Ildefonso Pueblo and then at St. Catherine's in Santa Fe. Her early life was much the same as any Pueblo child.

At the age of 14 she married Juan Rosario Chávez of Cochiti. He died two years later in 1911 and she married Felipe Herrera. Of her three children, one, Joe Hilario Herrera (See Ru) became one of the leading figures in Pueblo art; still living, he has become increasingly active in Indian political affairs, and no longer paints actively.

Largely due to the fact that many of her realtives were artists in their own right, Tonita began painting at a very early age, and by 21 was selling and exhibiting her work throughout the Southwest. She had little formal training, but was encouraged and somewhat guided by Dr. Edgar Lee Hewett and Dr. Kenneth M. Chapman, both of whom recognized her talent, and were attracted by the fact that she was the only female painter at the time to advance beyond relatively casual experimentation.

Her own determination to succeed, combined with her very remarkable talent, enabled her to make a substantial contribution to the world of Indian art. She taught at the Santa Fe Indian School and at Albuquerque Indian School, where she inspired her students to produce fine works, yet not fall into the practice of copying the teacher. She

210

was so highly regarded that she was chosen among those artists who were commissioned to make precise copies of the newly excavated murals at Pajarito for preservation, prior to their restoration. At the introductory Exposition of American Indian Tribal Arts in 1931, her painting *Spring Dances* was labeled "the best in the show." Her works were reproduced in many publications and are in many museum and private collections throughout the world. She was also active in mural painting, producing many murals which grace buildings in Arizona and New Mexico.

She later married Epitacio Arquero, who was elected Governor of Cochití Pueblo; by him she had three children. At her death in September 1949, she had probably advanced the cause of Pueblo art more than any other female artist, and was justifiably "the Grand Old Lady of Pueblo Art," as Oscar Jacobson so aptly lauded her.

Watercolor Painting of the "Hunting Dance" by Tonita Peña, San Ildefonso (*American Museum of Natural History*)

Petalésharo (1797–1832?)

He was also known as Pitalésharu, "Man Chief," and Pitarésharu, "Chief of Men." This famous Pawnee chief was born about 1797 and was the son of the noted Skidi Pawnee chief, Letalesha (Old Knife). A great deal of legend has grown up around this handsome, remarkably brave young man, and it is difficult to separate fact from fancy.

In 1816 or 1817, while he was still a young warrior, the Skidi kidnapped a young Comanche girl. The next year, after she had been treated like a royal guest, the priests began preparing her for one of their religious customs—the Sacrifice to the Morning Star. It is doubtful that the girl herself realized what was about to happen, in view of the past year's benevolent treatment, until her lovely costume was stripped from her body and she was carried to a wooden scaffold in the middle

Petalésharo (1797–1832)
(*Smithsonian Institution, National Anthropological Archives*)

211

of the village. There she was bound, outstretched, to the wooden framework.

At the climax of the ceremony, as the warriors fitted their sacred arrows to their bows in preparation for the volley that would end the girl's life, Petalésharo stepped in front of the priests and offered his own life in place of hers. Both he and his father had long wished to end what they regarded as a brutal custom, and this seemed like the time to act. Stunned, the people watched as he cut the thongs binding her ankles and wrists, put her on his horse, then mounted and rode off toward her home, some 400 miles away. The feared gods did not strike him down, did not destroy their crops—in fact, they did nothing. When Petalésharo returned to his village, he was greeted as a hero who had liberated the tribe from an old and foolish fear, rather than the violator of an ancient tabu.

In the winter of 1821, coincidental to a trip to Washington, D.C., with other chiefs who were conferring with United States officials, a newspaperman found an account of this exploit in an Indian Affairs report. He wrote a somewhat embellished and romanticized story for the *National Intelligencer*, and Petalésharo became an overnight hero to the citizens of the nation's capital. The girls at Miss White's School gave him a silver medal inscribed, *To the Bravest of the Brave*, which he kept around his neck.

There is considerable disagreement concerning the remainder of his years, caused principally by the fact that the name Petalésharo, or a variant, was held by at least four Pawnee chiefs. There is no doubt that he and his father signed the Pawnee Treaty of 1825, which promised that the tribe would not harass travelers en route to and from Santa Fe; but authorities differ sharply on whether or not he was the *Petahlays-hahrho* who signed the Treaty of Grand Pawnee Village, Nebraska on October 9, 1833. In 1830 the Skidi Pawnee were struck by an outbreak of smallpox and some reports from Indian agents claimed that over half of the total population of Skidi Pawnee—and almost everyone over the age of 30—died from the disease. If this were the case, it would suggest that Petalésharo would have been one of the victims. A later treaty signed *Petanésharo*, at Table Creek, Nebraska, made in September 1857, would almost certainly not have been the same person under such circumstances.

Silver Medal Presented to Petalésharo in 1821
(*American Numismatic Society*)

Peter Perkins Pitchlynn
(1806–1881)

Peter Perkins Pitchlynn (1806–1881)
(*Oklahoma Historical Society*)

Also known as Hatchootucknee, "The Snapping Turtle," Pitchlynn was an important Choctaw leader during the removal period. He was born at Hushookwa, Noxubee County, Mississippi on January 30, 1806. His father was John Pitchlynn, the son of a White interpreter for the federal government; the name refers to pitch workers in Lynn, England. His mother was Sophia Folsom, a half-Choctaw, half-White woman. As a boy, young Peter attended schools in Tennessee and then graduated from the University of Nashville. As an indication of his future career, his first public act was a strong reaction against the Choctaw Treaty, which he felt to be a fraud; upon meeting President Jackson, he refused to shake hands with him.

He returned home after graduation to settle down as a farmer, and married a half-blooded Choctaw woman, Rhoda Folsom. His people soon recognized his talents and education and he emerged as a natural leader, convincing the Choctaw to abandon the practice of polygamy. In 1824 he was elected to the Choctaw Council, where he was a strong advocate in enforcing the ban against the liquor traffic. Realizing the need for education among the young people, he got the tribal leaders to establish and support a school near Georgetown, Kentucky.

The Choctaw were a peaceful, agricultural tribe; even when their chiefs signed a series of onerous treaties ceding their lands to the United States, only a few people thought of active rebellion. In 1828, preparing for the move to the west away from the greedy White settlers, Pitchlynn and some others formed an advance party to select suitable lands for resettlement. He was able to make peace with the local Osage tribe and to obtain some fertile farmland, which enabled the Choctaw to move west with less difficulty than most of the other removed tribes. In the early 1830s he established his own farm and raised his family in Indian Territory. He continued to be active in tribal affairs, signed the Treaty of Dancing Rabbit Creek in 1830, saw to the establishment of the first Choctaw school in 1842, and in his travels met many important people of the day, including Henry Clay and Charles Dickens. The latter described him as "a handsome man with black hair, a sunburnt complexion, and bright, piercing eyes."

Pitchlynn became increasingly important in tribal affairs and in 1846 was elected principal chief of the Choctaws. With the outbreak of the Civil War, although he felt loyal to the Union—despite the fact that he owned a 600-acre plantation and 100 slaves—he was unable to keep many of the Choctaw from joining the Confederacy. At the end of the Civil War he moved his home to Washington, D.C., in order to more effectively represent the tribe and to press his case that the cession of Choctaw lands earlier in the century had certainly been immoral and probably illegal. In this undertaking he failed; but he did succeed in gaining the attention and the respect of many in the government.

He was a member of the Masonic Order and was also active in the Lutheran Church. He was widely noted as a remarkable orator, being eagerly sought after as a speaker. His wife Rhoda had died, after bearing him two sons and a daughter, and for several years he lived with Mrs. Carolyn Eckloff Lombardi, as a common-law wife; by her he had five more children and married her in 1869. On January 17, 1881, he died in Washington, and was buried with honors in the Congressional Cemetery, near the grave of his fellow tribesman Pushmataha.

Plenty Coups (1849–1932)
(*Smithsonian Institution, National Anthropological Archives*)

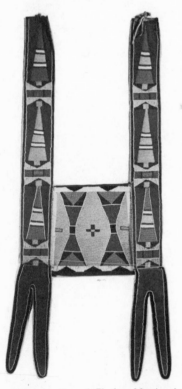

Beaded Stroud-Cloth Martingale; Crow
(*Museum of the American Indian*)

Plenty Coups (ca. 1849–1932)

A translation of his Crow name, Aleekchea'ahoosh, "Many Achievements," he was a noted Mountain Crow warrior who "never fought against the White man." He was born in the Crazy Mountains near Billings, Montana about 1849. He was the son of Otter Woman, a Crow, and Medicine Bird, a part-Shoshoni warrior. He gained his name in his youth by performing 80 feats of valor in combat. Earlier he had been known by the boyhood names of Faces the Buffalo North and also Swift Arrow. His war exploits were such that he became a chief when he was about 25 years of age.

In 1876 Plenty Coups was the leader of General George Crook's Indian Scouts during the campaigns against the Sioux; it is said that he kept Crook's forces from the fate suffered by Custer that same year on the Little Bighorn River. Certainly the sight of the uniformed cavalry of the day and their tight discipline made an indelible impression on the Crow scout.

He was active, and apparently responsible for, the successful negotiations with the Northern Pacific Railroad in gaining the right to construct the line through the Crow country; the payment made to the Crow was larger than the settlement usually made in such transactions. In 1883 he led the delegation conferring with the Dawes Commission, and shortly thereafter went to Washington, D.C., to strengthen the Crow claims for land payments.

Plenty Coups became one of the first of his tribe to take up farming and ranching, by which he grew prosperous, and by 1890 he was regarded as one of the most respected Crow leaders. In 1904, when Pretty Eagle died, Plenty Coups became the principal chief of all of the Mountain Crow people.

Despite occasional friction, the Whites remained high in his esteem, and during World War I he urged his young men to join the U.S. Armed forces. He was chosen to be the Indian representative at the tomb of the Unknown Soldier at Arlington, Virginia on November 11, 1921. Though reputed to have had 11 wives, among whom were Magpie, Strikes the Iron, and Kills Together, Plenty Coups had no children. On March 4, 1928, he and his wife deeded their home and the surrounding 40 acres to the United States to serve as a reminder of friendship between Indian and White. Today it is maintained as a museum of Crow culture and history.

He died at Pryor, Montana on May 3, 1932. As an indication of Crow regard for Plenty Coups, it was decided that after his death, there would be no more Crow "chiefs."

Pocahontas (ca. 1595?-1617)

From Algonquian *pocahántesu*, "She is Playful," although another, but dubious, translation suggests "Bright Stream Between Two Hills." Her Pamunkey name was Mataoaka (also Matoax, and Matowaka), "She Plays with Things"; both names apparently referring to her vivacious disposition. The exact date of her birth is not clear; it is said to have been between 1595-1597, but the earlier date is preferred by most writers. It is certain that she was the favorite daughter of Powhatan, the powerful chief of the Virginia confederacy. In 1608, Captain John Smith of Jamestown was captured and sentenced to death. According to Smith, the girl successfully pleaded with her father to spare him. Although historians have some doubts about the account, it has become a lasting legend of early colonial life.

Pocahontas (1595–1617), Painted While She was in London (*Smithsonian Institution, National Anthropological Archives*)

Smith left for England in 1609, and relations between Indians and colonists deteriorated. In 1613 Pocahontas was taken as hostage by the Jamestown settlers, who demanded and eventually received a large ransom, including English prisoners held by the Indians. The English had treated their captives well, and Pocahontas liked Jamestown; she became a Christian and was baptized Rebecca. During her stay in Jamestown, John Rolfe, a young English widower who had introduced tobacco cultivation into the colony, fell in love with her, and she with him. Sir Thomas Dale, the Governor, hoping that the union of the two might bring Indians and Whites closer together, granted permission for their marriage which took place on April 5, 1613. It is probable that Pocahontas may have been married at the time to Kocoum, a minor chief, but this is uncertain. The expected result of the marriage was that Powhatan kept the peace until his death.

In 1616, Pocahontas, John Rolfe, and several others went to England, where she was received as a princess, presented to King James I and Queen Anne, and generally lionized. On March 20 or 21, 1617, she caught smallpox while on board ship at Gravesend, England, just before returning to America, and died. She is buried in the chancel of St. George's Parish Church in England. Her son Thomas Rolfe was raised in England by an uncle, later returned to America, acquired considerable wealth, and through his only daughter founded the Randolph family of Virginia. While she seems not to have been a particularly beautiful woman, Pocahontas captured the romantic mood of the period, and has become the idealized American Indian woman, with all of the attendant realities and misconceptions.

Leo Pokagon (ca. 1775-1841)

The two Pokagons—Leo and Simon—contributed equally to the Potawatomi people, and it seems appropriate to treat them similarly.

Leopold Pokagon, or Pocagin, from Potawatomi *pugegin*, "rib," was a lifelong friend of the Whites, even after they seized much of the tribal lands near the southern tip of Lake Michigan. The exact

215

date and place of his birth is not known, but was probably around 1775 in the vicinity of Bertrand, Berrien County, Michigan. He was born a Chippewa, but was captured by Chief Zawnk and adopted by the Potawatomi. He eventually married Elizabeth, daughter of Sawawk, a minor chief.

In time, as testimonial to his abilities, Pokagon became the civil chief of the tribe, at the same time Topenebee was the war chief. While both faced the inroads of White settlers into the southern Lake Michigan area, Topenebee preached war, and Leo tried to maintain peaceful relations as best he could, feeling this was the only road to survival in the face of overwhelming power and numbers.

Living quietly in their village just north of South Bend, Indiana, the Pokagon band were a very religious people, and when the Jesuit "black robes" came as missionaries, many of them converted quickly to Christianity. Father Stephen Badin, in fact, wrote that "The respectable Chief Pokagon summons his band morning and evening for their prayers." But this cordial welcome meant little when it came to ownership of land; despite the awarding of $150,000 to the Pokagon band by the U.S. Government for land fraud, Leo never lived to see the fulfillment of the debt; it remained for his son to receive the delayed compensation.

As far as is known, Leo Pokagon always tried to keep his people from the battlefield, in the belief that they would only lose. When fighting broke out between the followers of Black Hawk and the United States in 1832, Pokagon, an eloquent orator, persuaded most of his people to stay out of the conflict, although Topenebee and others of his band were allied with Black Hawk. He was fully vindicated by the outcome of the war, but enjoyed little solace as the peace terms were disclosed.

Pokagon signed many treaties with the United States, including that of Tippecanoe River, transferring a large amount of territory to the White government, including the site which later became Chicago. In 1833 the Potawatomi ceded their village area to the United States; Pokagon, reluctant to sign the treaty, finally did so, saying, "I would rather die than do this." In 1837 he and his people were resettled in the area of Dowagiac, in Cass County, Michigan—a move which they undertook with heavy hearts.

Leo Pokagon never quite recovered from the loss of his band's territory, realizing the relentless pressure of the Whites paid no attention to the loyalty of the Potawatomi. He died on July 8, 1841 at the age of 66, and was succeeded by his son Paul, who died soon after, and then his son Francis, who also did not live long.

Simon Pokagon (1830–1899)

Simon Pokagon, the youngest son of Leo, was 10 when his father died. He was born in St. Joseph Valley, Michigan in the spring of 1830; he went on to gain a good education, and eventually to equal his father as chief of the Potawatomi tribe. He was also a major Indian writer. He studied at Notre Dame, Indiana and Oberlin and Twinsberg, in Ohio. He emerged with an excellent educatio guages, a gifted organist, and was widely regarded Indian of his generation."

His writings on Indian culture and lore were p magazines and he became well known through his travels. In 1861 and 1864 he journeyed to Washington on behalf of his tribe, where he met President Lincoln; in 1874 he met President Grant. During a summer hunting and vacation trip, he met Lonidaw Sinagaw, known to the Whites as "Angela," a daughter of the Potawatomi chief of a distant band, named Chief Sinagaw. They were married and had four children before her premature death. Simon then married Victoria, who joined him at the Long Lake home of the Pokagons.

The story of the Pokagon courtship, which is also a picture of Potawatomi social customs, was written and published in book form as *Ogimawekive Mitigwaki; Queen of the Woods*, and upon its publication in 1899, caused a stir as a remarkable product of American Indian literature. Included in the book is a section on Indian music, with selections composed by Simon Pokagon.

Simon, the "last Potawatomi chief in the Midwest," died at his home near Hartford, Michigan on January 28, 1899 at the age of 68. He was buried at Rush Lake Cemetery. A monument to Leo and Simon Pokagon was erected in Jackson Park, Chicago.

Pontiac (ca. 1720–1769)

The name Pontiac is derived from Ottawa *obwendiyag*, but is of unknown meaning. This Ottawa chief was the leading force behind a coordinated attack on English outposts in the Great Lakes area. Although little is known of his early years, it is believed that he was

Carved Wooden Warclub; Ottawa
(*Museum of the American Indian*)

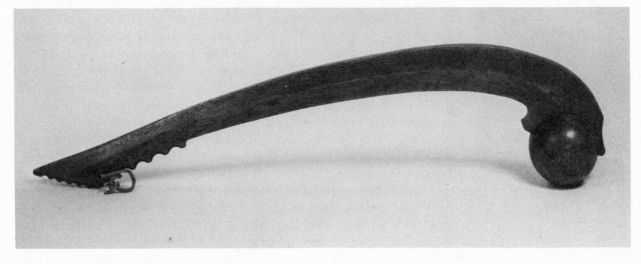

born of an Ottawa father and Chippewa mother around 1720, along the Maumee River near the mouth of the Auglaize, in Ohio. (Some accounts say the Ottawa River near the Michigan-Ohio boundary.) During Pontiac's youth, most of the Midwestern tribes sold hides to the French fur traders in the area. The French and Indian relationship was mutually beneficial—the French wanted furs and the Indians wanted arms and other European goods—so both sides were content. But when the English came, they wanted the land, and they took it.

With the defeat of the French following the French and Indian Wars, the British assumed dominance in dealing with frontier Indians. Pontiac's first experience with them was in 1760 when he was forced to surrender Detroit to the British and retreat into the woods. Pontiac was a natural leader, respected among the Indian people for his eloquence, wisdom, and his achievements as a warrior and military strategist. While at first disposed to be friendly toward the English after their victory in the French and Indian War, their tactless conduct towards him, his increasing sensitivity toward the British ambitions for Indian lands, and, perhaps most importantly, a mistaken belief that the French were about to take up war again, led him to plan an offensive coup.

Like many other foresighted Indian leaders, Pontiac's idea was that the tribes west of the Appalachians should unify, take advantage of the general confusion of the times, and in one surprise attack overwhelm the British forts and settlements. To this end, he sent red wampum belts to all tribes, and received in return indications of encouragement and support. Following a general War Council on April 27, 1763, the alliance was formed, and in May the general attack began. Pontiac and his men entered Fort Detroit wearing blankets to cover their guns and knives; however, the fort commander, Major Henry Gladwin, had been forewarned by a half-breed girl, and the Ottawa found themselves surrounded. They left the fort peaceably, but shortly after, returned and laid siege. They were unable to prevent the fort from being resupplied and the standoff dragged on. Elsewhere, Pontiac's allies were more successful: in the course of the war, which lasted until the fall of 1764, the Indians captured eight British forts and forced the abandonment of a ninth.

Early reinforcements sent to aid Detroit were defeated, but the Indian alliance began to split up, nevertheless. It became clear that no help could be expected from the French; greater numbers of troops began to come from the East to help the British; and the traditional Indian occupations—hunting and fishing—suffered, greatly affecting native survival. Protracted techniques were contrary to Indian warfare practices.

Finally, with the knowledge that peace had been established between the French and the British in the Louisiana Territory, the disillusioned Pontiac abandoned his siege and withdrew West. His failure to defeat the British diminished his influence, and the Indians perceived that their once great leader had become a liability to their future, since now they had to deal with the Whites, who saw him as a continuing threat. Earlier jealousies and tribal hatreds began to surface again, and on April 20, 1769, while visiting a trading post at Cahokia, Illinois, Pontiac was murdered by a Peoria warrior. The motive for the killing is not known, but it is possible that the British, fearing Pontiac, may have bribed his Indian executioner.

The idea of Indian unity against the White man suffered a setback, but did not die with him. What had started with Popé in 1680 was to be revived again and again all over the country during the next 125 years, to end only with the culminating tragedy at Wounded Knee in 1890.

Pontiac was tall, powerfully built, with an imposing grace and personality—a man of great eloquence and forthright demeanor. He is known to have had one wife, Kantuckeegan, and at least two sons, Otussa and Shegenaba. His character and abilities have been so strained through historic accounts, some presenting him as an "Indian saint," and others portraying him as a Machiavellian monster, that we little realize the potential of his skills.

Popé (?–1690)

From Tewa *po'pñ*, "Pumpkin Mountain," Popé was a San Juan medicine man who led the group of men responsible for the successful revolt of the Indians of the Southwestern Pueblos against the Spanish in 1680. When the Spanish first arrived in the 1540s, the Pueblo people were prepared to accept them as new deities, but soon found themselves abused by the Spanish. As later colonists arrived in increasing numbers, they claimed the territory for the Spanish King, moved into the Indians' homes, and created a feudal state, using the Indians as slaves to farm the lands for the profit of the Spanish under the *encomienda* system. Furthermore, every exploring party was accompanied by Catholic priests who insisted that the Indians abandon their old ways and convert to Christianity. Any Indian found practicing traditional ceremonies was cruelly punished.

This oppression became so brutal that the Pueblo people became desperate. Around 1675, Popé became influential as a leader of the dissident forces. An older, aggressive man, he had always opposed White settlement and the forced abandonment of Indian customs. In secret meetings, he told the people that their own gods disapproved of the message of the Spanish priests, and that White rule must be ended. The Spanish feared his growing influence, and on three occasions had him seized and flogged in the public plaza in Santa Fe. On the last occasion, 47 medicine men were arrested—three were hanged, and the others, including Popé, were savagely flogged and jailed. The Indian people were furious at this treatment and also feared that without the protection of their religious leaders, they would be overwhelmed by the evils of sickness and death. A delegation of more than 70 Christianized Indians threatened a revolt unless the medicine men were released; the Spanish governor reluctantly consented.

Popé then went into hiding at Taos Pueblo and began to methodically

Carved Figurine Representing Hilili Kachina, One of the Warrior Beings; Hopi
(*Museum of Northern Arizona; Marc Gaede Photo*)

organize an insurrection. The uprising was to include all Indians of the Southwestern Pueblo area, and was to take place August 13, 1680. It actually started on August 10, probably because Popé feared that informers would warn the Spanish. The Indians quickly killed almost 500 Spaniards and on August 14 put the capital at Santa Fe under siege. They demanded that the Whites leave; the Whites refused, retreating to fortified buildings. On August 20, a decisive battle was fought, forcing the remaining Spanish to retreat into Texas, accompanied by a small force of loyal Indians. Popé then began to eliminate every trace of the White man's presence, and tried to return the people to their traditional way of life. The success of the revolt led the Indians to give the credit to their Kachinas—the masked beings who provided the supernatural protection and guidance for the Pueblos—who they felt had won the confrontation with the Christian god.

But old problems remained, as well as some new ones. There were severe droughts, political disorganization, and tribal rivalries which led to fragmentation. Without Spanish military protection, the Pueblos were increasingly vulnerable to attack by the Apaches and other Indian marauders. Following the uprising, Popé himself began to abuse his power, ruling arbitrarily and executing those who disputed his decisions. Dissension arose and intratribal hatreds surfaced more and more. Popé was deposed at one time, and then reelected in 1688. He died two years later, leaving an unsettled political situation in the Pueblos.

In 1692, the Spaniards returned under the leadership of Diego de Vargas, and the Pueblo people were once again forced to adjust to colonial life. Although Popé became a despot and thus lost much of his public support, he remains the only person who successfully welded a large group of Western Indians from many tribes into a single force powerful enough to defeat their oppressors and drive them from Indian lands for such a long period of time.

Popovi Da (1923-1971)

Tony Martínez was a famous San Ildefonso artist, the eldest son of Julián and María Martínez of that Pueblo. He was born April 10, 1923 into the Summer phratry of his mother, and quickly showed the promise of his gifted parents. As did his father, he directed his efforts towards painting instead of ceramics, but with the death of Julián in 1943, the young man worked with his mother, designing and decorating her pottery for many years. His special skill was in beautifully balanced geometrical and symbolic designs.

He was educated in much the same manner as were almost all Pueblo children of the period: at San Ildefonso School, then at St. Catherine's School in Santa Fe. In 1939 he graduated from Santa Fe Indian School, where he had enrolled in art classes. With the outbreak of World War II, he served in the Army, first in Tennessee, and then finally at Los

Popovi Da (1923-1971)
(*Museum of New Mexico; Photo by Tyler Dingee*)

220

Alamos, just a few miles from his home. After his discharge from the Army, he opened his own arts and crafts studio in 1948, in the San Ildefonso plaza; this was under the name Popovi Da (Red Fox), which he legally adopted as his own.

San Ildefonso soon became an exciting center for fine art from the whole Pueblo region. He continued his experiments in ceramics, developing a unique combination of black-and-sienna matte ware, and also produced some excellent silver jewelry. His role in the Southwestern art field is marked by his being selected as the Pueblo art representative at many national and international conferences on the subject, and his being recognized by museum curators, collectors, and his peers as an innovative, sincere and gifted master craftsman.

He was elected governor of San Ildefonso Pueblo in 1952, a post in which he served for eight years, and he was also elected Chairman of the All-Indian Pueblo Council. He married Anita Cata Montoya, a Santa Clara classmate from his Santa Fe school days. They had two daughters, Janice and Joyce, and two sons, Bernard and Tony. Following a short illness, Popovi Da died in Santa Fe on October 17, 1971. The elder son Tony Da has carried on the family name and artistic tradition in an equally gifted manner.

Pleasant Porter (1840–1907)

Pleasant Porter (1840–1907)
(*American Museum of Natural History*)

Talof Harjo, "Crazy Bear," was the last chief of the Creek Nation before it became part of Oklahoma state in 1907. He was born on September 26, 1840, at Clarkesville, Alabama, the son of Benjamin Edward Porter, and Phoebe Porter who was the daughter of Tulope Tustunuggee, a Creek chief. Although he had a limited education, young Porter's native ability and extensive reading enabled him to become a widely respected tribal leader. During the Civil War, the Creek were divided in their allegiances; Porter sided with the majority in support of the Southern cause, and became a lieutenant in the Confederate Second Creek Regiment. He was wounded in combat at Pea Ridge, and walked with a slight limp for the rest of his life.

After the War, he returned to his home and took an active part in tribal affairs, which had been thrown into turmoil by the divisions of the conflict. The tribal elections of 1871 proved to be a crucial test between predominantly full-blood conservatives, who wanted a return to the traditional tribal government, and the mostly mixed-blood progressives, who favored the political system prescribed by the 1876 Constitution.

A third group, composed of Indian and Negro ancestry (the latter was no small force in the Creek Nation), tended to favor the Conservative side. Pleasant Porter was a dedicated progressive, however, and when there were threats of a civil war during the election, he was appointed General of the progressive warriors. Although the dispute was settled without bloodshed, more controversy arose between the two factions when a railroad was built through part of their land and White speculators attempted to cash in on the new development. The con-

221

tinuing contention died down when the U.S. Government intervened to guarantee constitutional government in the tribe. In the meantime, Porter had served a period as school superintendent, and is credited with establishing an outstanding educational system for the Creek people.

As a prominent member for almost 20 years of the Council of the Creek Nation, Porter was often a delegate to Washington. As more and more White settlers entered the area, it became difficult to hold onto Indian land, and in 1889 he was one of the leaders who worked out an agreement with the Dawes Commission to cede some Creek territory to the United States for the new settlers. He also had a significant role in the negotiations of 1902 which led to the cession of all Creek territory to the U.S. Government in return for individual allotments of land for each enrolled member of the tribe.

One of the most successful leaders of his people during the confusing period of transfer from tribal self-government to control by the U.S. Government, Porter was a member of the House of Kings, the House of Warriors, and was Principal Chief during the years when the Indian Territory was merged into the newly formed State of Oklahoma in 1907. A tall man, approximately 6' in height, weighing about 225 pounds, he was an impressive figure. He married Mary Ellen Keys, a Cherokee woman. His duties caused him to travel widely, and while en route by train to a meeting in Missouri, he suffered a stroke and died on September 3, 1907. He is buried at Wealaka, Oklahoma.

Alexander Lawrence Posey (1873-1908)
(*Oklahoma Historical Society*)

Alexander Lawrence Posey
(1873-1908)

Chinnubie Harjo, a name taken from a mythological character in Muskhogean legend, was a famous Creek writer and educator. He was born near Eufaula, Oklahoma on August 3, 1873, the son of Lewis H. Posey, a Scotch-Irish father and Nancy Phillips, a Creek woman. She raised him as an Indian, filling his childhood years with stories of Creek folklore and history. He spoke no English until he was 12 years old. Subsequently he went off to study at Bacone Indian University, where he acted as librarian, and learned to set type for a small paper, *The Instructor*, which served to establish his lifetime interest in literary work.

Upon graduation in 1895, his abilities were quickly recognized as an asset by his fellow Creek people, and he was elected to the House of Warriors; he also became the Superintendent of Public Instruction of the Creek Nation. In 1901 he resigned his position to return home and devote full time to writing. He became editor of the *Indian Journal*, in which the popular "Fux Fixico Letters" were first published—a series of satirical dialogues between a cast of fictitious Creek characters who spoke in humorous dialect, commenting upon White politics of the day.

He also continued his interest in politics, striving to represent Indian interests in the planning for Oklahoma statehood, and working for the Dawes Commission by enrolling as citizens all those members of his tribe, many of whom wanted as little to do as possible with the White man's government. Perhaps his greatest contribution at this time was his role as a delegate in 1905 to the Sequoyah Constitutional Convention at Muskogee, where he was elected as secretary, and was responsible for the excellent wording of the final document. Not too long afterwards, en route from Muskogee to Eufaula, he was accidentally drowned in the Oktahutchee River on May 27, 1908, at the age of 34.

In the eyes of most Creek people, Alexander Posey is best remembered as a literary figure of major importance, a great poet, and a staunch defender of Creek interests in education and politics.

Poundmaker (1842–1886)

Poundmaker (1842–1886)
(*Museum of Man; National Museums of Canada*)

Opeteca Hanawaywin was a powerful, peaceful Cree leader in Canada at a time when that country was attempting to place Indians on reservations. Poundmaker received his name as a young man because of his ability to conceal himself in buffalo robes and entice many of the animals into corrals or pounds. Little is known of his youth until he became chief, soon after the Cree moved onto a reservation at Battleford, in Saskatchewan in 1879.

At first the people accepted their fate, but with more and more promises left unfulfilled, unrest developed in 1880. Not only were the men restricted in their hunting grounds, but the buffalo herds grew too small to provide sufficient food and hides. Faced with starvation, and the need for clothing and coverings for the dwellings, they began to venture into forbidden territory to obtain provisions, occasionally raiding nearby White settlers. Poundmaker counseled peace during this time, even in 1884 when the Mounted Police invaded a tribal ceremony during an attempt to arrest a wanted man.

But the next year, tribes all over western Canada were desperate, ready for an all-out struggle against the Whites. Despite his best efforts, Poundmaker found it impossible to control his young men, and when they raided a nearby settlement, he abandoned the effort and joined with them. A detachment of about 300 Canadian soldiers pursued the Indians and attacked their camp at Cut Knife Creek. Led by Poundmaker, the Cree defeated the troops, who were able to retreat through an area that the chief may well have deliberately left open, to allow their escape.

Eventually, however, reinforcements were dispatched from the East, strengthening the local forces, and as the leaders of other, more hostile tribes, surrendered, Poundmaker himself came in and was tried in court. But no account was taken of his peaceful past, nor of his history of friendship with the Whites, and he was found guilty and sentenced to prison. He died at the age of 44 in June 1886, at Cut Knife Hill in Saskatchewan.

Poweshiek (ca. 1813–ca. 1845)

"Round Bear," or "Aroused Bear," more accurately Pawishik'—"he who shakes something off himself," was a major Fox (Mesquakie) chief who figured prominently in the period of the Black Hawk War. He was born into the Bear clan, a ruling group of the Fox people, at Musquawkenuk (Davenport), Iowa, about 1813. His parents were full-blooded Fox Indians; his grandfather was Black Thunder, an early famed Fox leader.

Although Keokuk has often been blamed for the weakening of Black Hawk's military strength, it seems more likely that it was due to the separation of Poweshiek from the main Sauk–Fox confederation. There had long been tension between the two tribes, and when Sauk leaders gave up some of the Rock Island territory in Illinois without the approval of the tribe, he took his people to Iowa.

With the outbreak of the Black Hawk War in 1832, Poweshiek fought along with Black Hawk at Bad Axe River, and participated in several other minor clashes, but he seems never to have really entered into the fray wholeheartedly. Following the defeat of the Indians by General Henry Atkinson, they were forced to cede some of their lands as a penalty. In 1833, Poweshiek went to Washington, D.C., with Keokuk, Black Hawk, and other chiefs to intercede with the authorities for better treatment. Late that same year, he effectively frustrated attempts of the Indian Agent at Rock Island, who had hoped to defraud the Fox people of the $20,000 payment due them. He also demonstrated his integrity in internal affairs by refusing a proffered bribe from Keokuk.

About 1836, Poweshiek was invited to Nauvoo, Illinois to meet with Joseph Smith, the Mormon leader, who was interested in the Indian people of the area. He was shown four metal tablets which Smith in-

Yarn Medicine Bag Woven with Thunderbird Designs; Fox
(*Museum of the American Indian*)

formed him were sacred writings. Poweshiek asked for an explanation of the markings which would indicate any benefit to the Indian people; Smith was apparently unable to supply a satisfactory answer, and Poweshiek left, unimpressed with the new religion—thereby ending Mormon efforts at conversion.

Poweshiek continued to work in the defense of his tribe for the balance of his life, and while he signed several treaties which ceded Indian land, he seems never to have benefited personally from the transactions, but was always hoping to appease the appetite of the White man. He died at DesMoines, Iowa (one account claims he died in Kansas) sometime around 1843–1845.

Powhatan (ca. 1550–1618)

From the Algonquian, *pau't-hanne*, or *pauwau-atan*, earlier translated as "Falls in a Current," but more acceptably today rendered as "Hill of the Pow-Wow," this important leader was also known by his correct name, Wahunsonacock, but the more popular form derives from his tribal affiliation, and became commonly used. He was the ruling chief, and probably the founder, of the Powhatan Confederacy in Virginia. He is the first Indian leader known to have any important contact with the English colonists. According to Captain John Smith of the Jamestown colony, in 1610 Powhatan was about 60 years old and was "a tall, well-proportioned man, with a sour look." Powhatan's father had been forced north from Florida by the Spaniards, and had conquered six tribes; after the father's death, the son enlarged the Confederacy to include 30 tribes with more than 100 villages inhabited by some 9000 peoples. His dominion extended from the Potomac River to Albemarle Sound in North Carolina.

Almost from the beginning Powhatan was suspicious of the White colonists. When Smith was captured in 1608, he was inclined to execute the intruder, but the chief's "dearest daughter," Pocahontas, interceded and saved the Englishman's life. In 1609, in an attempt at friendship, the colonists crowned Powhatan "emperor"; but he seems not to have been impressed by this honor, and the very next year they tried to capture and imprison him. In 1613 they succeeded in taking Pocahontas as a hostage, and Powhatan was forced to ransom her with some English prisoners. But in the meantime, Pocahontas and a young widower, John Rolfe, had fallen in love, and in 1614, were married. Powhatan did not attend the marriage ceremony, but he did fulfill the hopes of the English by restraining his people from further attacks on the settlers.

When Powhatan died in 1618, and was succeeded by his brother Opitchipan, the peace that had prevailed quickly disintegrated. Warfare between the Jamestown colonists and the Powhatan tribes erupted with renewed vigor, with massacres and hundreds of deaths on both sides. By 1634 the Confederacy created by Powhatan and his father had been

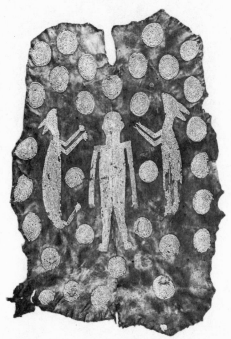

Buckskin Mantle Decorated with Shells, Worn by Powhatan (*The Ashmolean Museum*)

wiped out by the strife and suffering of 15 years of savage hostility. Besides Pocahontas, Powhatan had three sons: Namontack, Nantahoack, and Pochins.

Pushmataha (ca. 1764-1824)

Pushmataha (1764-1824)
(*Smithsonian Institution, National Anthropological Archives*)

His name was derived from Choctaw *apushim-alhtaha*, "Sapling is Ready for Him." He was a Choctaw chief of the Kinsahahi clan, born in June 1764 at Noxubee Creek, Mississippi. The identity of his parents is unknown; he said of himself, "I had no father. I had no mother. The lightning rent the living oak, and Pushmataha sprang forth"—and thus a legend was born. He was a courageous warrior in his youth, known as Hochifoiksho (a term meaning that he was nameless until he earned his own name). In an expedition against the Osage, he disappeared early, and when he came back to the war party, the others all called him a coward and mocked him. Quietly, he replied, "Let those laugh who can show more scalps than I can," and threw five scalps on the ground. This gave him the name Eagle, and for a time he lived in Texas, where he led many raids against enemy Indian villages. His accounts of his own exploits earned him the name Ishtilawata, "The Bragger."

In 1805 he was elected principal chief of the Choctaw, and became known as Pushmataha; he always claimed it meant "Oak Tree." Soon after he became principal chief, he signed the treaty at Mount Dexter which ceded a large tribal area in Alabama and Mississippi to the United States in return for $500 cash and an annuity for himself of $150. He became quite friendly with the Whites, and when Tecumseh came south looking for support of his Indian Confederacy, Pushmataha eloquently, and successfully, urged his people not to join. In 1811, some of the neighboring Creek allied themselves with the British, but Pushmataha remained loyal to the Americans. He led about 500 of his warriors in the defeat of the Creek under Weatherford, at Kantchati (Holy Ground) in Alabama, and became known to the Americans as "The Indian General."

After the Civil War, Pushmataha signed more treaties ceding tribal lands; and at Doak's Stand in 1820, he was credited with displaying "as much diplomacy and a business capacity equal to that of General Jackson, against whom he was pitted." During this same period he invested a great deal of his own and of tribal money in the education of Choctaw youth. In 1824 he journeyed to Washington to negotiate another treaty. After meeting President Monroe, General Lafayette, and other leaders, he suddenly fell ill, and died at midnight on December 23–24, 1824 at the age of 60. He was given a military funeral and was buried in the National Cemetery.

The prevailing attitude toward Pushmataha was summed up by Andrew Jackson as: "The greatest and bravest Indian I have ever known." Since Jackson was not particularly noted as being an advocate of Indian people, this is perhaps faint praise; but others who knew of his abilities agreed with the high estimate of Pushmataha. He left one son, Johnson Pushmataha, known as Mingo.

Queen Anne (ca. 1650–ca. 1725)

The widow of Totopotomoi, the Pamunkey chief, Queen Anne became the chief of the tribe following the death of her husband during a battle in which he supported the English against other Indian warriors. Due to her authoritative position, she was always called "Queen Anne" by the colonists. In 1675 she was called upon to furnish warriors to fight with the Whites during Bacon's Rebellion; this was her first appearance in colonial history. Her appearance at the colonial Council, in which she scornfully rejected the request to furnish warriors for the Whites on the grounds that her people had been neglected for the past 20 years, in spite of their friendship to the Whites, was a dramatic confrontation between Indian and White.

It was only after strong promises of better treatment by the colonists that Queen Anne agreed to provide the needed assistance. Following the end of the Rebellion, a silver headband, or coronet, inscribed *Queen of Pamunkey* was presented to her by King Charles II. Little more is heard about her following this period, beyond an appearance in 1715, when she visited the colonial authorities to request fair treatment for her people.

Queen Anne (1650–1725)
(*Association for the Preservation of Virginia Antiquities*)

John W. Quinney (1797–1855)

John Waunnacon Quinney, Waun-na-con, or Quinequan, from *quinnequant*, "The Dish," was an important Mahican (or Stockbridge) leader who figured prominently in the life of his people in the East, and led them to a new home in the Great Lakes region. He was born in 1797 in New Stockbridge, New York to a family which had been prominent in tribal affairs for generations. After an education in Yorktown, New York schools, under United States patronage, and mostly White teachers, he returned to his people and soon became one of their outstanding young men. In 1822, at the age of 25, he accompanied the representatives of other tribes, including Eleazar Williams, to negotiate with the Menomini for the purchase of lands around Green Bay, Wisconsin.

The Indians of New York were being increasingly hard pressed by the influx of White settlers, while at the same time they were being offered what seemed to be a good price for their homes by land speculators. A move west would get them out into the open area, away from the Whites. The negotiations were successful but after the Indians had paid for the land the U.S. Government steeped in to claim the Green Bay land for its own. In vain, the purchasers tried to set the decision aside, and in 1825 the State of New York even took the unprecedented action of admitting the injustice, by paying a portion of the amount "just to give full value." But the land was never returned to the original purchasers. In 1828, Quinney went to Washington to plead with Congress for justice, but he was able to recover only a token payment of $25,000 for improvements.

John Waunnacon Quinney (1797–1855)
(*State Historical Society of Wisconsin*)

Deerskin Coat Belonging to John W. Quinney; Mahican
(*Museum of the American Indian*)

Almost four years later, the tribe moved to Lake Winnebago, where Quinney drew up a Constitution which called for the replacement of the hereditary chief by elected leaders. The tribe settled down in peace, only to be harassed again by the United States to move west. Quinney took part in most of the negotiations, and in 1852 his tribesmen elected him head sachem. After a major effort he convinced the United States to cede to him and the tribes an area of 460 acres back at Stockbridge, New York. This success marked the last of his nine trips to Washington in behalf of his people; shortly afterwards, the tribe moved east, and he died at Stockbridge, New York on July 21, 1855.

Although John Quinney was always able to deal with the Whites, he respected and held his major allegiance to the traditional Indian life. Indeed, in 1846 he was even able to secure the repeal of an act making citizens of his tribe, thereby enabling them to maintain their own customs and government again. His speech in 1852 to Congress in support of Indian self-government may have been the first public use of the term *Native American* in political context:

> I am a true Native American, descended from one of those characters whose memory every true American reveres. My grand-father, David Nau-nai-nuk-nuk, was a warrior, and he assisted your fathers in their struggle for liberty.

He married once, to Lucinda Lewis, a Stockbridge–Munsee woman, by whom he had a son, Osceola. The latter married Phoebe Ann Doxtator (or Dockstader), an Oneida who became a major influence in the political activities of the tribe.

Watercolor Painting of a Clown with Food, by Ben Quintana; Cochití
(*Museum of Northern Arizona; Marc Gaede Photo*)

Ben Quintana (ca. 1925–1944)

Ha-a-tee, an outstanding young Pueblo artist, was born at Cochití, New Mexico about 1925; little is known of his parentage or early background. He was a contemporary of another important artist from the same pueblo, Joe Herrera; and like him, Ben was taught by Joe's artist mother, Tonita Peña. Later, Po-tsunu (Gerónima Montoya), a famed artist and art teacher, saw something of the promise in the young boy, and gave him her encouragement and support.

Quintana was something of a teen-age prodigy, and at the age of 15 won first prize out of 80 entrants in the New Mexico State Coronado Quadricentennial Competition, in 1940. Two years later he won the first prize in a poster contest held by *American Magazine*, which attracted over 50,000 entries. He also painted several murals for the Cochití Day School, and for the Santa Fe Indian School, New Mexico. As he entered young manhood in the early 1940s he was recognized among the most promising young artists of the day.

Like most of his contemporaries, he served in the U.S. Armed Forces, but lost his life in combat on November 9, 1944 in action in the Philippines, for which he was awarded the Silver Star for heroism posthumously. Although virtually all of Ben Quintana's paintings were done while he was still in his teens, they reflect the talent and promise of a truly gifted artist. His works have been acquired by museums and private collectors throughout the world, and had he lived long enough to fulfill the early predictions held by critics, it seems certain that he would have been among the greatest of contemporary American Indian painters.

Rain In The Face (ca. 1835–1905)

Rain in the Face (1835–1905) (*Smithsonian Institution, National Anthropological Archives*)

Iromagaja, from *ite amaraju-lit*, "Face Raining," was also called Iromagaju or Amarazhu. He was a Hunkpapa Sioux war chief who was a leading warrior in many battles with the White man, including the celebrated Battle of the Little Bighorn. He was born at the forks of the Cheyenne River in North Dakota about 1835. His parents were not important people, so that he had to make his reputation by his own efforts. His name apparently originated from two episodes, which he related himself: during a fight with a Cheyenne boy his face was bloodied by blows from his opponent. The blood streaked his face paint, creating a memorable sight. Another time, he stated that before a raid on the Gros Ventres, he painted his face half black and half red, as was commonly done, to represent the setting sun. The battle lasted all day in the rain, and his face became streaked with color.

Iromagaja was often on the warpath during the turbulent 1860s. In 1866 he was one of the leaders in the annihilation of Captain William Fetterman and his troops at Fort Phil Kearny, Wyoming, when the officer foolishly led his men into an ambush. Two years later, Iromagaja participated in a daring raid on Fort Totten, North Dakota in which he was badly wounded. In this period he also took part in many raids on the expeditions passing through Sioux country en route to the Black Hills gold mines.

His home was at Standing Rock Reservation. In 1873, one of the Indians on the reservation accused him of the murder of a White surgeon. He was jailed at Fort Abraham Lincoln, also in North Dakota. Though he admitted his guilt, and was imprisoned for a while, he was allowed to escape by a friendly guard. Back on the warpath, he joined in attacks on the Northern Pacific Railroad work crews and on other Whites in the region, joining with Sitting Bull and his hostile forces in 1874. And in 1876 Iromagaja was one of the leading participants in the Battle of the Little Bighorn; indeed, some accounts say that he was the warrior who killed General George Custer, but he never made such a claim himself. Most historians doubt the statement, feeling that in the melee

Rifle Taken from Rain in the Face (*Museum of the American Indian*)

it would have been impossible for any individual to have been certain of such a coup.

Though he was badly wounded during the battle and walked with a limp thereafter, he followed Sitting Bull and others who retreated into Canada. He remained there until 1880, when a number of the Sioux went south. In 1880, feeling that further resistance was fruitless, he surrendered with them at Fort Keogh, Montana to General Miles.

Later, he said, "When we were conquered, I remained silent, as a warrior should. Rain in the Face was killed when he put down his weapons before the Great Father. His spirit was gone then." Iromagaja was evidently difficult to live with; he is known to have had seven wives, the last of whom was found in his tepee with her throat cut. He died at Standing Rock, North Dakota on September 14, 1905 at the age of 70, and was buried near Aberdeen, South Dakota.

Cave Where Ramona Was Born; Cary Ranch, Anza, California
(*Harry C. James*)

Ramona (ca. 1865–1922)

This legendary figure, primarily the product of American literature, figured as a part-fiction, part-fact woman who was picked out of obscurity and lifted to national attention when Helen Hunt Jackson published her book *Ramona* in 1884. Mrs. Jackson had written a polemic attack upon the Indian Bureau and the general Indian situation in *A Century of Dishonor*, appearing in 1881. Her interest was further stimulated when she visited Southern California and heard of a Mission Indian girl whose life had the elements of a novel in it. The central character seems to have been loosely based upon a Cahuilla girl, Ramona Lubo, or Lugo (some sources claim she was Ramona Gonzaga Ortega (or Ortegna), who lived near Mission San Diego. She seems to have been born in a cave on the Cary Ranch at Anza, California, about 1865.

Accordingly, Mrs. Jackson sought out Ramona, and eventually wrote a novel which was part truth, but largely fiction, involving an elopement with Alessandro, who was a wholly created character. While the book is based upon the social atmosphere and interracial relations of the period, a majority of the episodes were fictional.

For many years after the publication of the book, Ramona was a celebrity, sought out by readers and lionized by southern California society—albeit at a safe distance. She had a small souvenir stand at the Mission, at which she sold her photographs and many of her own baskets (she was actually a very skilled basket weaver), and was briefly publicized at the time the motion picture *Ramona* was made. The theme song from the film remains a standard to this day. Needless to say, the Cahuilla exemplar enjoyed very little of the financial rewards from all this publicity.

Ramona lived an otherwise uneventful life, and died on July 21, 1922 near Hemet, California, and was buried in the old Cahuilla cemetery west of Anza, adjacent to her husband, Juan Diego.

Red Bird (ca. 1788-1828)

Wánig Suchka, a noted Winnebago war chief, was friendly to the Whites who came to settle in his native land until a misunderstanding caused all-out warfare. He was born near the mouth of the Wisconsin River about 1788, the son of a hereditary war chief. His name has been given two origins: one claiming that it derived from his custom of always wearing a red coat, perhaps acquired from English soldiers; while the other, and perhaps more likely account refers to his habit of wearing a preserved red bird on each shoulder in lieu of an epaulet. Whatever the truth, the farmers in the Prairie du Chien (Wisconsin) region had long regarded Red Bird and his people as their friends and protectors.

But they seem to have taken his goodwill too much for granted—or perhaps their treatment of the Indians was not always what it might have been. In 1827, two Winnebago men were arrested and charged with the murder of a local farming family. Through an error in communication, the Indians were rumored to have been turned over by the authorities to the Chippewa—hereditary enemies of the Winnebago—and beaten to death. Acting upon the false report, the Winnebago council met and determined to obtain revenge, electing Red Bird as the person to carry out the council decision. He promptly visited the home of a local White farmer and murdered him and his hired men. He then rejoined his tribe and led them in an attack upon a Mississippi riverboat. In the ensuing conflict, four Whites and about ten Indians were killed.

In the meantime, the alarm had been spread, and a detachment of soldiers arrived to quell the so-called "Red Bird War." Faced by formidable armed might, Red Bird and his followers surrendered and were subsequently tried and convicted of murder. In the general confusion of the times, the court sentence somehow was not well-handled, and apparently was never actually made public. Red Bird was imprisoned at Prairie du Chien, where he died on February 16, 1828, never having been sentenced; later that same year, the other Indians involved in the affair were pardoned by President John Quincy Adams after a delegation of Winnebago leaders went to Washington to plead in their behalf. In 1923, William Leonard wrote a short-lived play *Red Bird* which dramatized this incident.

Red Cloud (1822-1909)

His name is derived from Siouan *Makhpiya-luta*, Scarlet Cloud (also *Makhpia-sha*, Red Cloud). He was a courageous nonhereditary Oglala Sioux chief at Pine Ridge, South Dakota who led his people in several important victories over the forces of the United States. He was born in Nebraska on September 20, 1822, near the Platte River to the distinguished Snake family; his father was Lone Man (*Ishna Witca*), and his mother was Walks as She Thinks, a Saone Teton. He had a twin brother, Roaring Cloud, also known as "Sky," about whom almost

Red Cloud (1822–1909)
(*Smithsonian Institution, National Anthropological Archives*)

nothing is known. The intelligence, strength, and bravery of Red Cloud became widely known throughout the tribe, and he was credited with 80 coups, or individual feats of bravery. He was eventually chosen as tribal chief over the hereditary claimant to the title, Young Man Afraid of His Horses.

His name has been the source of considerable controversy, and several "origins" are recorded. One account claims that his name came from the wave of red flannel blankets of his warriors sweeping over the Plains; a more likely source stems from the great red meteorite which is known to have struck the Plains region the day of his birth. Sioux winter counts record this event, and it is true that there were many babies named Red Cloud who were born that day.

The Oglala were the largest division of the Sioux Nation, and Red Cloud became perhaps the most important field commander among both Sioux and Cheyenne. He was strongly opposed to the westward expansion of the Whites, and believed that it was his mission to defend the Indians' last and best hunting grounds. In the 1860s his warriors succeeded in virtually closing down the Bozeman Trail and other overland routes from Fort Laramie, Wyoming, and the east, to the Montana goldfields and the northwest. A peace conference was held at Fort Laramie in 1866, but when it became apparent that the United States intended to bring in more troops and expand their system of fortifications, Red Cloud stormed out of the meeting and took to the warpath. Soon afterwards, his forces surrounded the troops and laborers building Fort Phil Kearny, and skirmishes became a daily threat. In December, Captain William Fetterman foolishly pursued a band of Indians with a detachment of 80 soldiers, ran into an ambush, and he and his troops were annihilated.

Throughout 1867 the war of attrition continued, and not a single wagon moved along the trail to the goldfields. Finally, in 1868, the United States requested another peace council. In return for Red Cloud's pledge to live in peace, the government promised to abandon all forts along the trail, and accept the territorial claims of the Sioux. However, Red Cloud stayed away until the last troops had actually been withdrawn and the forts were left standing unoccupied; only then did he sign the treaty at Fort Laramie on November 6, 1868. This event is frequently cited as one of the few times when Indian military power was able to force the United States to completely carry out the provisions of a peace treaty. Red Cloud kept his word, refusing to lead his younger men, impatient and hostile, when they demanded retaliatory action for the skirmishes which came in ever-increasing numbers. Two years later he headed a party of other Sioux leaders, visiting Washington and New York, to plead the Indians' cause, asking why "Commissioners are sent out to us who do nothing but rob us."

Although he was critical of the White representatives and of their continuing expansionism, he counseled peace during the troubles of 1876, when Crazy Horse, Gall, and Sitting Bull gathered their armies for battle. Five years later, Red Cloud was again on the offensive—this time demanding the removal of Indian Agent V. T. McGillicuddy. But times had changed, and this time the White man won. Red Cloud was removed as chief, and not long afterwards the tribe was removed to the Pine Ridge Reservation in South Dakota. Here, blind and ailing, he lived with his wife—contrary to usual Indian practice, he had married but once—in a house the government built for him until his death on December 10, 1909.

Buckskin War Shirt Belonging to Red Cloud
(*Museum of the American Indian*)

As a man, Red Cloud is described as being of tall, slender build, with courteous manners and quiet, yet firm, demeanor. He was highly respected by his people, and could claim equal rank with any contemporary general, statesman, or patriot in the country.

Red Jacket (1756–1830)
(*New-York Historical Society*)

Red Jacket (ca. 1756–1830)

Sagoyewátha, from Iroquois *sa-go-ye-wa'tha*, "He Causes Them to Be Awake," was a Seneca chief of the Wolf clan born at Canoga (some say Seneca Old Castle, near Geneva), New York. He was named Otetiani, "He is Prepared" or "Always Ready," but took the name Sagoyewatha when he became a chief. The Whites knew him commonly as Red Jacket from his habit of wearing a colonial military garment given him by the British during the American Revolution. Red Jacket did not always distinguish himself in battle; indeed, Cornplanter accused him of cowardice in retreating before the American forces, and Brant gave him the name "Cow Killer" from an episode when he was absent from battle, and was found slaughtering a cow. This epithet remained with him for the rest of his life.

After the Revolution the Americans still had to deal cautiously with the Iroquois League; the nation was weak, the League was still powerful, and most of the Indian people had sided with the British. England still had trading posts in upper New York, as well as many military forces in Canada. This placed Red Jacket in a key position; through oratory and political skill he had become a Seneca chief and a major influence in the tribe. He advocated peace with the Americans, but at the same time rejected any inroads of White culture, religion, or settlement. He was particularly opposed to missionaries, even though many Indians were Christianized by this time. Although he argued hotly against land sales, he also ratified many agreements disposing of Iroquois land.

In the spring of 1792, the 50 chiefs of the Iroquois League were invited to Philadelphia, then the seat of the new American government. There, Red Jacket met George Washington, who gave him a silver medal. His views toward the Whites softened somewhat, but he still remained a staunch advocate of Indian cultural and territorial integrity. In the War of 1812, he sided with the Americans, and although he did take part in some minor skirmishes, his battle record and loyalty remain ambiguous.

After 1815, Red Jacket was at the height of his power among his people. A commanding figure, 6' 2" tall, and possessed of both a remarkable memory and eloquent oratorical skills, he turned his talents toward driving the White man out of Indian country. In 1821 he succeeded in persuading the New York legislators to pass a law protecting the state reservation lands. Yet the tide of change was against him; he was not a constructive thinker, many of his people were opposed to his intransigence, and others were disturbed by his increasing dependence upon liquor. In 1827 he was deposed as chief, and his second wife became a Christian.

"The Trial of Red Jacket," painting by John Mix Stanley
(*Buffalo & Erie County Historical Society*)

Through the intervention of the Office of Indian Affairs he was briefly restored to his political position and reconciled to his wife, but he subsequently resorted again to excessive drinking, and died on January 20, 1830 at Seneca Village, New York. He had two wives, and at least 17 children; all but one of them, however, died in infancy or early youth. In sum, Red Jacket was an egotist who required center stage at all times. While he never occupied a major place in Indian esteem, he did fulfill a useful role to both peoples as intermediary between Iroquois and White groups.

The Red Jacket Medal
(*Buffalo & Erie County Historical Society*)

Red Shoes (ca. 1700–1748)

Shulush Homa or Shulush Humma, was a Choctaw (some scholars say Chitimacha) chief who was the war leader of his people during the early struggles for power between the French and the English in the lower Mississippi Valley. He was of the Okla Hunnah (Six People) clan, with his home village in Jasper County, Mississippi. Soon after their occupation of Louisiana, the French established an alliance with the powerful Choctaw Nation which was maintained by the regular presentation of honors and gifts to the tribal chiefs.

At first, Red Shoes supported this alliance, and in the 1730s warred against the Natchez; later, he attacked the Chickasaw. The English assisted the Chickasaw and the French brought in reinforcements from Canada to help the Choctaw. But more and more English traders came in from the East, and slowly convinced many of the Indians that a wiser course lay in supporting the English. Red Shoes held fast to his French loyalty until about 1734, when he abruptly changed sides; his disaffection had nothing to do with the war effort, but was caused by the rape of his favorite wife by a Frenchman.

By about 1740 a so-called peace party became active, led by Red Shoes. Undoubtedly, the fact that the English were obviously becoming stronger in the area had something to do with his decision—as did the influence of better goods being offered by the English traders. In the end, although many of the Indians still favored the French, Red Shoes sought to persuade them as to the advantages of an English relationship. He opened peace negotiations with the Chickasaw, but French Governor Marquis de Vaudreuil was able to break them up and thereby divide the uneasy Choctaw alliance; 32 villages went over to the French, while 10 villages remained loyal to the English.

In 1748 a violent civil war broke out, in which both pro-French and pro-British groups suffered heavy losses. At a peace council the leaders decided to stop fighting the White man's battles and to reconcile their differences; otherwise, they realized they would eventually be totally destroyed. But the pro-French party felt that much of the fault for the split lay at Red Shoes' door, and they refused to include him in any new tribal agreement. Some of the English sympathizers felt the same way, and in the end, the council consented to his removal, which by Choctaw custom of the day, meant a death sentence. Not long afterwards, in 1748, Red Shoes was assassinated while conveying a shipment of British goods to his village.

Red Tomahawk (ca. 1853–1931)

Tacanhpi-luta (also Onspecannonpa-luta) was a Teton Sioux responsible for the death of Sitting Bull in 1890. He was born around 1853 near the Cheyenne River in South Dakota, but little is known of his early life. He had been appointed a Sergeant of Indian Police at Standing Rock Agency in South Dakota, a position which he filled effectively.

Red Tomahawk (1853–1931)
(*Smithsonian Institution, National Anthropological Archives*)

In 1890 Wovoka's Ghost Dance religion swept through the camps of the bitter, frustrated Sioux. Violent rebellion seemed imminent, and the panicky United States authorities decided to jail Sitting Bull, whom they considered to be the leader of the dissidents. In the belief that jailing Sitting Bull would put an end to any such uprising, the order was given to the Indian Police to gather their forces and bring him in.

Sergeant Red Tomahawk rode 40 miles in four hours to give the necessary orders, and on December 15, 1890, Lieutenant Bull Head and Red Tomahawk led 43 Indian Police out to take in the old medicine man. At first, Sitting Bull agreed to the arrest peacefully, but tempers flared, shots blazed, and Sioux blood flowed. The affair lasted only a few minutes, but in the melee, six policemen, including Bull Head, were killed, as was Sitting Bull and eight of his followers.

Army troops quickly appeared and began to attack the Indians indiscriminately—policemen and prisoners alike. Red Tomahawk, now in command, swiftly fashioned a white flag and ran fearlessly toward the charging soldiers. They pulled up, and the question of an outbreak was temporarily ended, to be permanently and tragically settled one week later at Wounded Knee Creek.

Red Tomahawk died at Standing Rock Agency on August 7, 1931 at the age of 82, and was buried at Bismarck, North Dakota. He had two wives, three daughters, and one son.

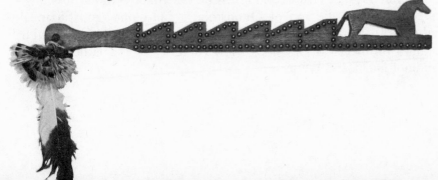

Wooden Dance Club Decorated with Feathers and Brass Tacks; Sioux
(*Museum of the American Indian*)

237

Red Wing (ca. 1750–ca. 1825)

Tatank'amimi was a Mdewakanton Sioux chief who was first an ally of the British, and then shifted easily into friendship with the Americans after the War of 1812. The name Red Wing derives from a family charm—a swan wing dyed or painted red—and was held by a long line of Sioux chiefs, whose lands were on the west shore of Lake Pepin in Minnesota. The best known individual who bore the name was Tatank'amimi, Walking Buffalo; each member of the lineage had more than one name.

Although less influential than his contemporaries Little Crow and Wapasha, Red Wing was nevertheless an important leader of the Minnesota Sioux. As were most of his people, he was a friend of the Whites. It was easy to be friendly in those early days—the settlers had not yet come into the area in large numbers, there was still more than enough meat for the hunters, and the goods introduced by the White traders were highly valued and eagerly sought after.

Red Wing was greatly admired by his own people, as well as by the White neighbors. Besides being a successful warrior, he had also proved himself to be something of a prophet and seer. During the War of 1812 he fought on the British side, notably at Sandusky, Mackinaw, and Prairie du Chien. But one day, while engaged in a particularly brisk battle, he had a vision that the British would be driven out by the Americans. He compared the style of battle tactics followed by both sides, and the adaptability of the Americans, and was disturbed by what he saw. He lost no time in returning to a British commander his Royal George medal and proclaiming a policy of peace with all sides. He faithfully followed this neutral stance for the rest of his life.

He retired from the battlefield, never having suffered a defeat. By 1820, he was regarded as a firm friend of the United States, and in articles of the day his name was mentioned as such a staunch supporter that the town of Red Wing, along the Mississippi River in Minnesota, was named in honor of him and his forebears. He died about 1825 and was buried on Barn Bluff, overlooking the town. The name Red Wing continued on for another generation, but died out in the 1860s.

Major Ridge (ca. 1770–1839)

Also known as The Ridge, the title Major derives from his rank in a Cherokee unit of the American Army during the Creek Wars. Together with his son, they were leading figures in the Cherokee removal to Indian Territory during the first half of the 19th century. Ridge was born about 1770 at Hiwassee, in the Old Cherokee Nation (now Tennessee). He was the son of Ogonstota, a full-blood, and Susannah Catherine, a half-Cherokee, half-Scot woman of the Deer clan. His younger brother was David Oowatie (or Uwati) the father of Elias Boudinot and Stand Watie.

Ridge was named Nunna Hidihi, from *nungno huttarhee*, "Man on the Mountain Top." He had little formal education; when the family moved to Georgia, he learned most of what passed for an education from his parents and neighbors. But his native abilities soon commanded attention and by the age of 21 he had been elected to the Cherokee Council, in time becoming the Speaker, with the name Kanuntaclagee, "Big Speaker," a compliment to his oratorical talent. From these political activities he gained an important position in the community and considerable prosperity. He owned a large farm, which he managed well and was in partnership with George Lavendar, a prominent trader of the time. In 1792 he married Susie Wickett ("Princess Sehoya"), a full-blooded Cherokee woman.

Major Ridge (1770–1839)
(*Oklahoma Historical Society*)

From this marriage came a son, John, who is frequently confused with the father; indeed, the careers of the two are so closely intertwined that separate treatment is almost impossible. The son, known as Ganun'dalegi, from *gahna tahltlegi*, "One Who Follows the Ridge," was born in May 1803 at Rome, Georgia. In 1819 his father sent him to school in Cornwall, Connecticut, where he received an excellent education along with his cousin, Elias Boudinot. He suffered from a hip disease, which affected his walk. The two young Cherokee men did well at Cornwall, and were very popular until they announced their engagements to two local girls. Ridge eventually married Sarah Bird Northrup, and both young men brought their brides back to Georgia, but only after a year of bitterness and rancor from the bigotry of the Cornwall people. In time he sired a son, John Rollin Ridge.

Although Major Ridge served temporarily as a General under Andrew Jackson during the Creek Wars, he, his son John, and his nephew Elias Boudinot were unhappy at the way the American authorities—especially the Georgia Legislature—were dealing with the rights of the Cherokee people. White settlers were moving onto tribal lands and in many cases were treating the Indians as animals to be driven back deeper into the back country. Unfortunately, the breed of Georgia settler at the time was far inferior to the Indian people who were being challenged, and this fact only served to increase the interracial hatred and contempt. Recognizing the problem, the two young Cherokee men embarked on a speaking tour of the North in an effort to turn the tide of national opinion in their favor. Although they met with some success, it was not easy—there were far too many vested interests involved in the ownership and development of land at the time.

Woven River Cane Basket; Cherokee
(*Museum of the American Indian*)

Early in the 1830s, Major Ridge, his son, and Boudinot became prime movers in the Treaty Party—the group which favored an accommodation with the United States. Some whispers were heard charging bribes and deals, but most scholars today believe that the trio honestly believed that the Cherokee people had no hope of winning, and that if the tribe appeared reasonable they might be able to strike a better bargain. There does seem to be some truth in the belief that John Ridge was restless under the rule of the principal chief at the time, John Ross, and hoped to replace him. In any event, they ultimately proposed what is known as The Ridge Treaty on June 19, 1834. This treaty was never ratified by the U.S. Senate because most of the members were inflexibly

John Ridge (1803–1839)
(*Oklahoma Historical Society*)

determined to move the Indians west.

In December 1835, the members of the Treaty Party were forced to sign the Treaty of New Echota, which traded their Georgia farms and forests for the sterile plains of Indian Territory (now Oklahoma). The fact that only 500 out of 17,000 Cherokee people agreed to the treaty was meaningless in the tenor of the times; John Ross and most of the other leaders refused to sign, and fought bitterly against removal with all of their energy. But, as Ridge foresaw, the Indians could not halt the tide, and forcible removal was put into effect.

Accordingly, in 1838, Army troops were moved into the Southeast with orders to round up all Cherokee people and move them to Indian Territory. They were forced to leave their homes and possessions, taking only what they could hastily gather together; families were separated and property was stolen, abandoned, or sold for a pittance to obtain food. General Winfield Scott and 7000 soldiers placed the Indians in stockades and the sad Trail of Tears began. Most of the people walked the whole distance from North Carolina to Oklahoma; only the old, sick, or infirm rode in wagons over the frozen, snow-covered land. It is estimated that of approximately 18,000 Indians who were removed, over 4000 died in the stockades or along the trail.

Major Ridge recognized the inevitable when he signed the treaty, saying, "With this treaty, I sign my death warrant"—and so it came to be. In 1829 the Cherokee Council had decreed that any person found guilty of selling land without the consent of the people would suffer the death penalty. On June 20, 1839, he, his son John, and Elias Boudinot were killed in their homes, executed by Council fiat. Only Stand Watie escaped—he had been forewarned of the impending attack by the enforcers of the death penalty. The Treaty Party was no more.

Carved Steatite Pipe Bowl; Design of a Man Seated, Reading a Book; Cherokee
(*Museum of the American Indian*)

Louis Riel (1844-1885)

Riel was the mixed-blood Cree leader of the famous *métis* rebellion in Manitoba, Canada. He was born along the Seine River, near St. Boniface, in lower Assiniboia on October 22, 1844. His father was Louis Riel, a French settler and trader, and his mother was Julie Lagimodière, a part-French–part-Cree woman. The young boy was baptized Louis, but later took the name Louis David Riel.

In his youth he was apparently a religious boy; although unsuited for the priesthood, as his father had hoped, young Louis grew up in the Red River *métissage* world. He was educated at the Collège de Montréal, and in 1869, feeling the weight of the battle then going on between the Hudson Bay Company and the Government, which was having a disastrous effect upon the local *métis* population, Louis took upon himself the leadership of the *métis* and Indian people. He was elected—or assumed, since he had previously been secretary—presidency of the provisional government of Assiniboia which had been set up by the *métis*. By terms of a treaty in 1870, Assiniboia entered the Canadian confederacy as part of Manitoba, but Riel continued to oppose the settlement, and when troops were dispatched to control the inflammatory situation, he fled. He was later elected to the Parliament as the representative from Provencher from 1873–1874, but in 1875 he was expelled for his militancy.

The weight of emotional strain seems to have affected Riel's mental balance and from 1876–1878 he was committed to the asylum at Longue Port, and later at Beauport, Québec. Following his release, he went to Keeseville, New York, where he eventually became a United States citizen, and then went west to Montana, where he taught for a time at a mission school.

The *métis* and Indian population continued to suffer discrimination and mistreatment, just as their fellow Indians in the United States, and in June 1884, Riel was back in Manitoba, in answer to an invitation to head a protest mission. He responded, and in March 1885, the political militancy turned into open rebellion, in which Riel appealed to the Indian people for their support. Troops were called out, and in a campaign lasting slightly over three months, finally succeeded in bringing the rebellion to an end on July 2, 1885. Several of the leaders were captured, and Riel himself surrendered peaceably. After a trial which attracted widespread attention, he was found guilty of treason and hanged on November 16, 1885 at Regina, Northwest Territories. At the same trial, 18 *métis* were imprisoned, 8 Indian participants were hanged, and 2 Whites were tried but discharged.

The battle was not really a French-English clash, so much as it was a farmer–hunter war. The coming of the European people threatened the survival of the nomadic hunting-trapping culture of the *métis* and the Indians. The arrival of large numbers of settlers, surveyors, and a governing group which did not include any local people, made the *métis* feel that their lands had been sold without any consideration being given to them in the matter. Much of the bloodshed could have been avoided by more intelligent diplomacy. The execution of Riel had traumatic and widespread political effects, for he became a martyr to French-English hostility. In 1886, amnesty was granted to all of the participants still in prison.

Rollie Lynn Riggs (1899-1954)

Rollie Lynn Riggs (1899-1954)
(*Western History Collections; University of Oklahoma Library*)

An outstanding dramatist and poet, Rollie Lynn Riggs was born near Claremore, Indian Territory on August 31, 1899. His father was W. G. Riggs and his mother was Ella Riggs, a Cherokee. He was educated at the local public school and Eastern University Preparatory School in Claremore, following which he attended the University of Oklahoma.

Following graduation, young Riggs clerked for the Adams Express Company in Chicago, then traveled to New York City where he became a reporter for the *Wall Street Journal*, which sharpened his writing skills. He sought work in Hollywood for a brief time as an extra in motion pictures, then returned to the University of Oklahoma in 1920 to continue his writing and poetry studies. His first book of poetry *Fandango; Ballads of the Old West* appeared in 1922, and that same year he became an instructor in the English Department of the University of Oklahoma.

A period of illness followed due to a nervous breakdown and he recuperated in Santa Fe, New Mexico. During this time he appears to have written a variety of plays and poems which appeared in various literary magazines and anthologies, including *The American Mercury*, *The Nation*, and *The New Republic*. All of these plays and poems reflected in one sense or another the Texas-Oklahoma region, primarily using folk themes of the west. Among these were other works, such as *Borned in Texas*, a comedy he had written while he was in Paris on a Guggenheim Fellowship. It appeared on Broadway as *Broadside* in 1930.

But certainly nothing he wrote created the lasting effect of his major play, *Green Grow the Lilacs*, produced in 1931 by The Theater Guild in New York City. The play became an overnight success, and was acclaimed widely as having caught the early American spirit more successfully than anything of a similar nature. It was swept on to even greater recognition when Richard Rodgers and Oscar Hammerstein II collaborated with Riggs in weaving it into the musical comedy *Oklahoma!* which was first produced in 1943 and remains one of the standard classics of the musical stage. A healthy timing with a wave of nostalgic interest in the country, combined with superb musical and theatrical presentation, resulted in a revolution in the American musical theater.

In 1936, Riggs wrote *The Cherokee Night*, a play based upon the tragedy of the Cherokee people, but it was not a lasting success, perhaps because of the unpleasant memories it stirred up at a time when such views of the past were not welcome. A measure of his personal feelings about his work can be realized when, on the opening night of one of his plays, the publisher delivered the initial copy of *The Iron Dish*, a book of poems. He missed the curtain of the play in order to enjoy the book.

Although he continued to work in the theater and to produce poems,

Oklahoma! was always the peak of his success. He died of cancer in New York City on June 30, 1954, and was subsequently buried in Woodland Cemetery in his native Claremore.

Rocky Boy (ca. 1860-1914)

Stone Child was the leader of a group of about 350 Chippewa nomads who belonged to that class of "forgotten Indians," provided for neither by the United States government nor by their own tribe. In the 19th century the band had left the main Chippewa tribe in Wisconsin to hunt in Montana; they never returned home, preferring to live off-reservation.

But as more and more land became plowed under for farms or fenced in for pasture, it became difficult for them to support themselves by traditional hunting methods. As the years passed, these Chippewa people became completely nomadic, living more and more on charity—and sometimes at the whim—of local White settlers. While the home tribe was given reservation land and assistance in setting up farms, these Indians did not share in any of this largess.

Living conditions became critical for this nomadic band of Chippewa, and in an effort to obtain assistance, Stone Child emerged as their leader; most of his White neighbors translated his name as "Rocky Boy," and the group soon came to be known as Rocky Boy's Band. He was eventually successful in bringing their desperate situation to the attention of the Bureau of Indian Affairs. At first Congress granted the Rocky Boy Band a small annual appropriation, barely sufficient to sustain life. There was a strong feeling of opposition to the action—this was long before today's welfare state atmosphere—due in part to the attitude held by some that the people had brought their plight on themselves by leaving Wisconsin. With skillful eloquence, Rocky Boy was able to counter these attacks, and finally, in 1914, the government was persuaded to grant the Indians part of the Fort Assiniboin military reserve in north central Montana, along with farm equipment and breeding stock.

Shortly thereafter, Rocky Boy died in 1914 secure in the knowledge that due to his efforts, the wandering days of his people had ended.

Will Rogers (1879-1935)

Christened William Penn Adair Rogers, this great humorist, actor, and writer was born at Oologah, near Claremore, Indian Territory on November 4, 1879. His parents were both part-Cherokee; his father, Clement Vann Rogers, was a former Confederate army officer and a prosperous rancher and banker and his mother was Mary A. Schrimsher. Clement Rogers was a member of the Federal Commission set up in 1893 to administer the affairs of the Five Tribes in the Territory and was a leader in Cherokee affairs throughout the region.

William Penn Adair Rogers (1879–
1935)
(*Oklahoma Historical Society*)

Will was educated at schools in Vinita, Oklahoma and the Kemper
Military Academy in Missouri; he became an expert cowhand on the
family ranch. In 1902 he sold some cattle his father had given him,
and traveled to England, Argentina, and on to South Africa, where he
joined a traveling Wild West Show as the rope-tossing "Cherokee Kid."
He continued to appear in these shows after returning to the United
States in 1904.

The next year he began his career in vaudeville at Hammerstein's
Roof Garden in New York City, where he met with indifferent success.
Slowly, however, his popularity increased as he added his unique brand
of self-deprecating homespun humor to his act. The times were right
for his style of monologue; audiences loved his Oklahoma drawl and
his diffident plainsman's manner, and he began to appear in musical
shows on Broadway and in London. In 1914 he joined Ziegfeld's Follies,
and until 1924 he appeared in several editions of the show, as well as
acting in motion pictures.

His humor became more and more topical, and a newspaper column that he had started as a weekly in 1922 grew into a daily satirical commentary on the nation's foibles and fancies which reached over 35 million readers at its peak. As the "Cowboy Philosopher," whose famous comment, "Well, all I know is what I read in the papers," his nonpartisan humor, often directed at government officials and congressmen, made a real hit with his readers.

With the advent of talking pictures, his career reached its zenith; the Rogers family settled in Hollywood and Will became perhaps the highest paid actor of the time. *A Connecticut Yankee in King Arthur's Court* and *David Harum* were among the 17 pictures in which he starred, pretty much playing himself, the down-to-earth cowboy-humorist the nation had grown to love. As the Depression wore on, Rogers gave of his own funds, and appeared at many benefit performances for relief and charitable organizations.

He was an early booster of air travel, and often flew to his engagements around the country. In August 1935, Will Rogers and his Oklahoma friend, Wiley Post, set off on a flight to the Orient in Post's airplane. Near Point Barrow, Alaska, the plane developed engine trouble and crashed; both men were killed on August 15, 1935.

He wrote many books between 1919–1927, including *Rogerisms*, *The Illiterate Digest*, and *Letters of a Self-Made Diplomat to His President*. He married Betty Blake by whom he had two sons and one daughter.

Roman Nose (ca. 1830–1868)

Woquini or Wokini, from *wokinih*, "Hook Nose," a common name applied to him by Whites, was a famous Southern Cheyenne warrior who remained at peace with the Whites until the 1860s. The exact date and place of his birth are not known, nor is information about his parentage. His correct name was Sauts, meaning "Bat," but he was usually referred to by the more descriptive name. At first, he did not attack any of the growing number of wagon trains on the Bozeman and Oregon trails which ran through Cheyenne country. However, as more and more Americans came into the area, skirmishes and battles broke out, and after the massacre of Black Kettle's camp in 1864, the Cheyenne became convinced that the soldiers were intent upon exterminating them.

Tall, handsome, strong, and courageous, Roman Nose was a powerful leader; however, he was not an actual "chief." He headed the War Society which was important to the Cheyenne and his prowess made him a natural leader in combat. He put great faith in his magnificent feathered war bonnet, which he firmly believed would protect him in battle as long as no one else ever touched it. In the year 1865 he fought in many battles against Whites, fearlessly charging into the thick of the enemy, often in hand-to-hand combat, but no bullet ever brought him down. He allied himself with Red Cloud in the united effort to hold back the White man and his warriors became the scourge of the Plains.

In 1866, at a council in Fort Ellsworth, Kansas, Roman Nose bitterly protested against the location of the Union Pacific railroad on the Indian hunting grounds. He told General Innis N. Palmer: "If the palefaces come farther into our land, there will be scalps of your brethren in the wigwams of the Cheyenne." But the railroad pushed on and the Indians continued to defend their territory. In 1867 Roman Nose led his forces in scattered forays on wagon trains, the derailment of a freight train on the main line, and the annihilation of a gang of track layers. These attacks were sporadic and of minimal effect, for the White man continued to push forward.

Finally, in 1868, a climax was reached for the Cheyenne in a battle at Beecher's Island on the Arikaree River in Colorado. On September 16, a force of 52 picked troops, most with considerable experience, were headed by Colonel George A. Forsyth, an able commander, to try to subdue the Indians in that general area. He was suddenly surrounded by no less than 600 Cheyenne warriors, and in the nine days of the siege, valiantly held off the horde of Indians, emerging on September 25, when he was relieved by a company of cavalry—himself badly wounded, and his forces depleted by 23 casualties, six of which were fatal.

The Cheyenne lost nine warriors by death. Proportionately, this would be considered a resounding victory, in view of the greater firepower of the Whites (few of the Cheyenne had firearms at the Beecher's Island battle, although the Whites were well armed and supplied), but it was in fact a disaster, for one of the nine was Roman Nose himself.

At the feast, the night before encountering the Whites, the food had been prepared by a woman who, unknowingly, broke the medicine taboo—whether she touched the bonnet or used a metal fork in preparing the meat is not clear—but upon hearing of the episode, Roman Nose held back from the fight at first, in the certain knowledge that his bonnet no longer could protect him. Finally, in response to the demands of his warriors to lead them as he always had in the past, he simply said, "My medicine be broken. I know that I shall be killed today." Tying his bonnet strings firmly under his chin, he mounted his horse, and galloped into the battle, towards the men on the island. He was shot as he dashed past a small group of soldiers concealed in the high grass, and died the first night of the battle on September 17, 1868.

John Ross (1790–1866)

Coowescoowe, "The Egret," was the son of Daniel Ross, a Scotsman, and a Scotch-Cherokee woman, Mary (Molly) McDonald. John was born on the Coosa River at Tahnoovayah, Georgia (some accounts say Rossville), near Lookout Mountain on October 3, 1790. As a boy he was known as Tsan-usdí, "Little John," and was brought up as an Indian among Indians. He was educated at home by White tutors, and then at Kingston Academy in Tennessee. Although only one-eighth blood, he always considered himself a Cherokee, and at the age of 23 married Elizabeth Brown Henley, known as Quatie, an almost full-blood Cherokee widow.

In the War of 1812, Ross was an adjutant of a Cherokee regiment under General Andrew Jackson, and saw action in the Creek War of 1813 at the Battle of Horseshoe Bend; his action in providing a diversion is credited with saving the day for Jackson's troops. After the war the Cherokees formed a government patterned on the model of the United States and young Ross emerged as a leader becoming a member of the National Council in 1817. He was the president of the National Council from 1819 until 1826 and helped draft the Cherokee Constitution in 1827. From 1828 to 1839 he was principal chief of the Cherokee Nation.

During these years the strong voice of John Ross rose in opposition to federal and state encroachments on the tribal lands of his people. He headed several delegations to Washington, resisting the claim of the state of Georgia that the Cherokees were merely tenants on state lands. Between 1828 and 1831 when the Georgia legislature stripped the Cherokee of all civil rights the Indians refused to yield. They took their case to the Supreme Court and won. Chief Justice John Marshall's opinion was a scathing denunciation of Georgia's violation of treaty rights, but President Jackson refused to implement the decision and enforce the treaties as evidenced by his notorious comment, "John Marshall has made his decision. Now let him enforce it."

In 1835 a dispirited minority of Cherokee leaders signed the Treaty of New Echota, Georgia, which called for the surrender of Cherokee lands and the removal of the tribe west of the Mississippi River. Ross and most Cherokees did not sign and refused to move from their fertile homelands. Georgia continued to press, and a small group under Major Ridge did go west. Ross, continuing the opposition for three more years, finally led the Cherokee majority in 1838–1839 on the infamous Trail of Tears. More than 4000 Cherokee people, one-fourth of the entire number, perished from exposure, starvation, and disease; among them, Quatie, Ross's wife.

Upon arriving in Indian Territory, Ross joined the Western Cherokees, consisting of about 3000 people who had moved west several years earlier. He helped to write a Constitution for the United Cherokees, and was chief of the entire Nation from 1839 until his death. Despite his ownership of numerous slaves and a large plantation, he counseled against any Cherokee alliance with the South during the Civil War. He was overruled and in 1861 the tribe joined the Confederacy. In 1862 Federal troops invaded Indian Territory, and the next year the Cherokee repudiated their ties with the Southern cause. During this period the government deposed Ross from his office.

In 1866, growing old, but still laboring for justice for his people, Ross headed a delegation to Washington to work out a new treaty which would protect the Cherokee and their Constitution. He died on August 1, 1866 in Washington while negotiations were in progress and was buried in Park Hill, Oklahoma. Following the death of his first wife, by whom he had five children, he married Mary Bryan Stapler in 1844, who bore him two girls and one son.

John Ross (1790–1866)
(*Oklahoma Historical Society*)

Blackware Pottery Bowl with Stick-Impressed Design; Cherokee
(*Museum of the American Indian*)

247

Sacajawea (1784–1812?)

Sacajawea (more accurately Sacagawea), from Hidatsa (?) *tsakakawía*, "Bird Woman," was an interpreter and the only woman on the Lewis and Clark Expedition of 1804–1806. She was born into the Shoshoni tribe in the Rocky Mountains. The exact date has been variously reported as 1784 and 1788. Her Shoshoni name was Boinaiv, meaning "Grass Maiden." The matter of an accurate rendition of the name by which she is popularly known has long been a matter for argument. Today, an exact translation is impossible; a more accurate meaning seems to be "Boat Traveler," a reference to her appearance in the longboats which were being dragged through the shallows. In an effort to indicate the use of long oars, the Indians flapped their arms; Clark thought this meant birds or "Bird Woman," hence the name which has come into common use.

Around the age of 12, Boinaiv was captured by some Crow warriors and sold to the Hidatsa on the Missouri River in North Dakota. Then she and another Indian girl were sold to a French-Canadian fur trader, Toussaint Charbonneau, who married them both. In 1804 Lewis and Clark hired him as a guide and interpreter for their western journey. Charbonneau took Sacajawea and her newborn baby, Baptiste, along; she proved to be a valuable intermediary between the explorers and the several Indian tribes they encountered, particularly in view of her knowledge of the Shoshoni language. When the expedition came to the Rockies and her home village, she had a joyous reunion with her people, and especially with her brother, now chief, Cameahwait, who greeted her as *Wadze-wipe*, "Lost Woman." This relationship was particularly helpful to the party. Although Cameahwait was initially hostile, intending to kill the Whites for their goods, he was dissuaded by the intercession of his sister, and eventually was willing to provide horses and supplies to the expedition in barter. At this time, Sacajawea adopted the son of her dead sister and named him Basil.

Sacajawea, as she was known by now (Lewis called her "Jenny" throughout his journal) accompanied the expedition across the Rockies and down the Columbia River to the Pacific, arriving there on November 7, 1805. Both Lewis and Clark testified to her fortitude, endurance, and serenity; Clark was especially fond of her and her son. Eventually he transported the Charbonneau family to St. Louis in 1809 and helped them to set up a farm. In 1811 they left their son Baptiste with Clark, to return west with an expedition led by Manuel Lisa; Clark adopted the son as his own.

The death of Sacajawea remains one of history's great mysteries. One account records Lisa's clerk thusly: "This evening [December 20, 1812] the Wife of Charbonneau, a Snake Squaw, died . . . aged about 25 years." However, some other sources indicate that Sacajawea spent most of her life with her own people, moving with them to the Wind River Reservation and finally dying at Fort Washakie on April 9, 1884, aged about 100 years. In an effort to settle the question, Commissioner Charles H. Burke dispatched Inspector Charles A. Eastman

(Ohiyesa) to locate the burial place. In a report sent to Burke on March 2, 1925, Eastman reported that he had interviewed many surviving Indian people, had found the site, and felt that it was indeed the resting place of "the real Sacajawea." However, at the present writing, the 1812 date seems to have stronger support.

Whatever the truth, and this may never be conclusively proven, there is no doubt that Sacajawea was a major key to the success of the Lewis and Clark Expedition. Her role, however, has been less clearly perceived; she was not a guide, as is often claimed. Rather, she was particularly effective in providing help through her interpreting services with Indians along the way—serving, as Lewis put it, as ". . . the inspiration, the genius of the occasion." She has been honored with many plaques and monuments throughout the Western states.

Sadekanakte (ca. 1640–1701?)

Carved Wooden False Face Society Mask; Onondaga
(*American Museum of Natural History*)

He was also known as Sadakanaktie, Sudagunachte, and Sadaganacktie; another form is Adaquarande, Adaquarondo, and Aqueendera. He was a major Onondaga chief who was particularly famous for his eloquent oratory. He was probably born around 1640 at Onondaga, New York and is first mentioned as attending a council at this village on June 29, 1690, where he was the principal speaker for the tribe. In 1693, he again filled the role of a major participant, indicating the power of his oral delivery.

He figures throughout Iroquois history of the 18th century as an orator and leader of the Onondaga, although he seems never to have been a war chief. In 1693 he was brought into a council on a litter carried by four men, indicating how greatly the people felt the need for his presence, in spite of his illness. He died in 1701 at Onondaga and another man was named in his place with the same title; he died in the mid-1800s. This practice of continuing a name as a title is responsible for the frequent confusion in trying to identify Indian personalities.

Sagaunash (ca. 1780–1841)

Also known as Saganash, he was called Billy Caldwell or "The Englishman." He was a Potawatomi chief and interpreter in the 19th century and was born about 1780 in southern Ontario, Canada, the son of an Irish officer in the Colonial Army and a Potawatomi woman. He was educated in Catholic schools, where he learned to read and write, and mastered English and French—all skills which later served him well. Since he also knew several local native dialects, he was superbly placed to serve as an interpreter and a middleman.

He seems to have grown up in a mixed-culture world, where he touched almost daily with various Indian and White groups, which sharpened his knowledge of both. In 1807 he became an active worker for the British Crown, and served those interests faithfully until the defeat of Tecumseh in 1813. Since he had served as secretary to the great Shawnee leader, his death affected Sagaunash tremendously, and the subsequent victory of the Americans over the British in the War of 1812 further convinced him that the better wisdom lay in switching to United States support.

Accordingly, he moved to Chicago in 1820, where he lived for a time. He was elected a Justice of the Peace in 1826; and this role, plus his own wise actions, made him a powerful influence during the Winnebago uprisings of 1827. At that time, he joined with Shabona to help control the Indian militants as much as possible.

He married the daughter of Chief Neescotnemeg and lived out a peaceful life with her. He died at Council Bluffs, Iowa on September 28, 1841, at the age of 60.

Sakarissa (ca. 1730–1810?)

Sakarissa was also known as Sagarissa, Sequareesa, Shequallisere, Achsaquareesory (and many similar forms), meaning "Spear Dragger." He was a leading Tuscarora chief who was born about 1730 at Niagara Landing, New York, and was known as Oghshigwarise or Osequirison in his youth. In 1752 he was one of the chiefs who represented the Tuscarora at Ganatisgoa, and appeared in Pennsylvania the next year. The Moravians called him Segwarusa, chief of the Tuscarora when he met with them in 1755. He met with Sir William Johnson in 1761 at Oneida Lake, and was one of the signers of the Treaty of Fort Stanwix in 1768.

In short, he was an extremely active leader of his people, traveling restlessly to further their interests. He was at Canandaigua in 1794, where he not only represented the tribe, but requested that the Quakers send some teachers to him for the education of the young people. He went to North Carolina in 1802, accompanied by Solomon Longbeard, where the two negotiated for the settlement of land claims connected with Tuscarora holdings.

A final mention of Sakarissa seems to have been in 1805, when, as an old man, he was one of the founders of the Tuscarora Congregational Church. While much of this activity seems genuine, it is not impossible that his name covers the activities of several individuals, all of whom bore the same name. This was a common practice, particularly when White recorders were transliterating Indian names. The date of his death is unknown, but was probably sometime around 1810.

Samoset (ca. 1590–ca. 1653)

Sam'o-set, also known as Samaset, from Algonquian *osamoset*, "He Walks Over Much," perhaps referring to his long journeys by land was the Pemaquid sagamore of the Moratiggon (Monhegan Island) band. He was the first man to greet the Pilgrims on their arrival in the New World. Almost nothing is known of his early life, but on Friday, March 16, 1621, he walked into Plymouth Plantation and to the utter astonishment of the colonists, called out, "Welcome, Englishman!" He had learned some English from the fishermen with whom he had traded along the Maine coast.

Samoset was a tall man, and even though the weather was cold, he was wearing only a fringed loincloth; in pity, the settlers gave him a blanket and some food. He told them that for the past eight months he had been visiting his friend Massasoit, the Wampanoag chief, into whose territory the colonists had ventured. Samoset stayed the night in Plymouth, departing with assurances that he would try to arrange a meeting with the great chief for them. A few days later he returned with Squanto, a Patuxet man who spoke good English, and Massasoit himself. This meeting marked the beginning of friendly relations between the Plymouth residents and the Wampanoag chief which lasted throughout the chief's long life.

Little more is known of Samoset, aside from an occasional mention of his trading with the Whites. In July 1625, he and another Indian, Unongoit, signed the first deed between Indians and English, selling 12,000 acres of Pemaquid territory to a John Brown of New Harbor, Maine. In 1653, he signed another deed which conveyed 1000 acres to three colonists. He is believed to have died around 1653, shortly after this last sale, and is buried in Bristol, Maine. He had one son.

Considerable controversy existed for a time over a seeming derivation of his name from the English "Somerset." However, since both Captain John Somerset and Christopher Levett Somersett are recorded as having visited his area in 1623–1624, it would seem likely that this name is attributed to him after the fact.

Sassacus (ca. 1560–1637)

His name is derived from Massachuset *sassakusu*, "Wild; Fierce Man." He was the last Pequot leader when the tribe was virtually wiped out by the English. He was born near Groton, Connecticut about 1560, the son of Wopwigwoot, the first Pequot chief to come into contact with the Whites. As a young warrior he was the scourge of New England, ranging far and wide in his efforts to push back the invaders. Many thought that he had magical power because of his invincibility in battle, even under great odds. He became chief about 1632, after his father was killed by the Dutch in a war which materially weakened the tribe.

In 1634, in order to protect his people from further depredations, Sassacus offered to surrender all the land the Pequot had conquered, in exchange for the establishment of a plantation, peace, and mutual protection. The basis of this proposal is not clear, for he remained bitterly hostile to the Whites, and the exchange completely alienated his young son-in-law Uncas, who was thereupon banished, leaving with a group of equally antagonistic followers to form the rival Mohegan Nation.

As the Pequot regrouped and slowly gained new strength, they raided both neighboring tribes and colonists. In 1637, in Connecticut, they attacked the English fort at Saybrook, killed several people at Wethersfield, and kidnapped two young girls. The Whites mounted an expedition under John Mason, who enlisted the help of the Narragansett tribe and on July 5, 1637 he led his forces in a surprise attack on the overconfident Sassacus and his Pequot settlement located on the Mystic River. Sassacus, who did not believe his warriors were in any danger from the colonists, found that about 700 Indians were killed in that surprise attack.

The once powerful Sassacus, his nation shattered and his enemies triumphant, slipped off to the west with about 20 warriors and a great load of wampum representing the tribal treasury. But they were soon in the hands of the Mohawk, who stole their wampum and killed all of them. A few months later, in June 1637, the English governor of Massachusetts was presented with the scalps of Sassacus, his brother, and five Pequot chiefs. So ended the Pequot nation; the few survivors were absorbed into neighboring tribes.

Satanta (1830–1878)
(*Oklahoma Historical Society*)

Satanta (1830–1878)

Set-tainte, "White Bear," from *set* "bear," *tain* "white," *te* "person," was a noted Kiowa chief who enjoyed the reputation of being "The Orator of the Plains." His boyhood name was Gúaton-bain, "Big Ribs." He was born about 1830 and came into prominence as one of the major Kiowa leaders to sign the Medicine Lodge Treaty of 1867 by which the Kiowa ceded their lands in the valleys of the Canadian and Arkansas Rivers, abandoned their nomadic life, and agreed to move to a reservation in Indian Territory. Besides being a fearless warrior, he was an eloquent and persuasive speaker in tribal councils and in treaty negotiations with the White man.

Only a few of the tribe really agreed to the terms of the treaty, but after the Army took Satanta and Lone Wolf as hostages more of the Kiowa came onto the reservation lands to settle. Reservation life still did not prevent many of the young warriors from continuing their raids into Texas and Mexico. The Kiowa were the most hostile opponents of White incursion into Indian lands and they simply could not or would not give up the exciting life of the hunter and warrior for the prosaic agricultural existence prescribed by White precept.

In 1871, Satanta, Setangya, and Big Tree led a group of warriors in an attack on the Warren wagon train, in Texas, which culminated in the death of seven teamsters. Back at Fort Sill, Setangya—or Satanta—unwisely boasted to the Indian agent of their role in the murders, and were subsequently arrested by the Army troops, and transported to Texas for trial. On the way, Setangya made a suicidal attempt to escape; Satanta and Big Tree were tried, convicted, and sentenced to life imprisonment. Two years later they were paroled on a pledge of good behavior not only for themselves, but for the entire Kiowa tribe.

But trouble broke out again in 1874, and Satanta was sent back to prison for violating the terms of the parole, although the general impression seems to be that he did not take part in the violence at that time. A proud, dignified and daring Plains warrior, he did not adjust to life behind bars, and on October 11, 1878, committed suicide by jumping from an upper floor of the prison hospital at Huntsville, Texas. He is still remembered by his tribe as being one of their greatest war leaders.

Scarface Charlie (ca. 1837–1896)

Scarface Charlie (1837–1896)
(*Denver Public Library, Western History Dept.*)

Chichikam Lupalkuelatko (also Chikchackam Lilalkuelatko) "Wagon Scarface," or "Run Over By a Wagon and Scarred," was a Modoc warrior born on the Rogue River in California about 1837. He hated Whites as the result of a traumatic childhood experience. When he was about ten years old, he and his father, Tipsoe Tyee, encountered four White emigrants. The boy was able to hide in a lava cave, but the father was captured, chained by the feet to the rear of a wagon, and dragged over eight miles to his death. Later, climbing out of his hiding place, Charlie tore his face on a piece of jutting lava—other accounts say that he was accidentally run over by a wagon, permanently scarring his face; the Modoc form of his name seems to support this latter story. He was later named Scarface Charlie by the Whites with whom he often traded.

In the 1860s hostility erupted between the Modoc people and the United States authorities who wanted them to move onto the Klamath Reservation in Oregon. A subchief named Kintpuash, to whom Charlie was loyal, left the reservation with his followers in 1872, but the Army pursued and caught up with them. In one fateful confrontation, a soldier was ordered to disarm Charlie, who only laughed at him; the soldier then drew his pistol and they both fired, each missing. After a brief melee the soldiers backed off and the Modoc retreated into a remote area of lava formation. At the same time, another band of Modoc warriors, led by Hooker Jim, escaped into the beds after they had killed 12 settlers in revenge for a vigilante attack on their camp.

Kintpuash wanted to sue for peace, feeling that the superior forces of the Army made the outcome inevitable, and he wanted to spare his people bloodshed. Although Scarface Charlie thought this was a foolish decision, he respected the decision of his leader. On occasion, however, he had to be restrained by Kintpuash from attacking White emissaries. In 1873 the government appointed a peace commission led by General Edward Canby to try to settle the increasing violence. Hooker Jim and some of the other Modoc accused Kintpuash of cowardice for agreeing to meet with the commission, demanding that he kill Canby. On the other hand, the chief's sister, Winema, was urging him to make peace.

On April 11, 1873, Kintpuash took the fateful step and shot Canby; Reverend Thomas was also killed and Indian Superintendent Meacham was badly injured, but was saved by Winema. All-out war had begun. In one battle where the Modoc were led by Scarface Charlie, two-thirds of the soldiers were killed or wounded. But by this time Charlie had grown tired of the slaughter, and is said to have shouted to the survivors, "You who are not dead had better go home. We don't want to kill you all in a day." Later, he said, "My heart was sick at seeing so many men killed." Modoc losses increased as food became scarce in this war of attrition. Hooker Jim and his band deserted, and in late May, Kintpuash surrendered. In a court martial held in July, Hooker Jim testified for the prosecution in order to save himself; Kintpuash and five others were found guilty and condemned to death. Two had their sentences commuted, but the four remaining were hanged at Fort Klamath in October 1873.

Scarface Charlie and the surviving 152 Modoc people were first sent to Wyoming, then to Nebraska, and finally to Indian Territory, where he was eventually appointed chief of the band. He became a Christian convert, and accompanied Winema and several other Modoc participants in the rebellion East, where they participated in a successful play, *Winema*, written by Albert Meacham (who had been saved by Winema). He died of tuberculosis on December 3, 1896 at Seneca Station on the Shawnee land given to the Modoc which had been carved out of the Quapaw Agency.

He was regarded as the most impulsive, but also the wisest military strategist among the Modoc forces. Certainly his ability enabled Kintpuash to more successfully withstand the superior numbers and equipment of the Whites, and his knowledge of the terrain made successful pursuit impossible. At no time was he ever accused of ignoble warfare against his enemies.

Schonchin (ca. 1815–1873)

Schonchin, from *skonches*, "He Who Goes with His Head Down (or out-thrust)" commonly known as Schonchin Jim (or Sconchin Jim), was a Modoc leader who tried to protect his people and their lands against White invasion during the Gold Rush in 1849, but capitulated peacefully when he became precariously outnumbered. He had a younger brother, John, who became one of the major figures in the Modoc War. Early records indicate that Schonchin was head chief by about 1846; he was not a hereditary chief and had to arrive at his position through native ability. When the White goldseekers poured into northern California after the discovery of gold in 1848, Schonchin and his approximately 600 warriors attempted to fight them off. The Modoc were a traditionally warlike tribe, and they made settlement in their territory difficult and dangerous.

By the 1860s, however, Schonchin realized that there were but two choices open: fight and face probable annihilation, or try to accommodate

White demands. He chose the latter course and in 1864, signed a treaty ceding tribal lands to the government in exchange for a reservation. Many of his people were unhappy with this Hobson's choice, especially when it became very apparent that the Klamath, who were already established in superior numbers on the Oregon reservation intended for the Modoc, had no intention of welcoming their distant cousins.

Largely stimulated by John Schonchin, the old chief's younger brother, Kintpuash and some others led a dissident group to leave the reservation and return to their true home in California. Old Schonchin tried to convince them that it was suicidal to resist the U.S. Army, but he did not interfere when they rejected his advice and left Oregon. Subsequently, when the Army attempted to force them back to the reservation, hostilities broke out, and the Modoc War began in 1872. Old Schonchin remained at peace, but John Schonchin became one of the primary leaders of the resistance movement. He was militant in his opposition, and combined with Hooker Jim, Boston Charley, and others to resist all efforts of the Whites to establish a peaceful solution.

Perhaps one of the leading influences toward this strong feeling of Modoc invulnerability was the foolish initial effort of the Army to return them to Oregon by force. At dawn on November 28, troops entered the camp, and in the confusion firing broke out from both sides, and the Modoc fled into the nearby Lava Beds, leaving a large number of soldiers killed or wounded. The sense of military success was so strong—there were very few Indians killed in the exchange—that, combined with the protection offered by the impenetrable lava flows and tunnel-like caves, the Indians initially felt they could withstand any amount of White onslaught.

And indeed they did hold out remarkably, in view of the total numbers involved on both sides. But, after a series of skirmishes and a peace council during which two United States government commissioners were killed, and one was badly wounded, the Modoc finally capitulated on June 1.

General Davis was determined to hang the rebellious leaders at once, but he received orders from Washington that the condemned men must be tried by court martial. This only delayed a foregone conclusion, for the warriors were formally tried and found guilty, with six of their number being condemned to death for the murder of the two commissioners and assault upon the third. Eventually, the sentences of two were commuted, and on October 3, 1873, Schonchin John, Kintpuash, Boston Charley, and Black Jim were hanged at Fort Klamath.

The hostile Modoc were transported to Indian Territory, where many of their descendants live today; the balance of the tribe was returned to their permanent home in Oregon.

Schonchin Jim (1815–1873) (*Smithsonian Institution, National Anthropological Archives*)

Hart Merriam Schultz (1882–1970)

Nitoh Mahkwi, "Lone Wolf," as he signed his work, was a Blackfoot artist whose paintings and bronzes of the Old West were often compared

Hart Merriam Schultz (1882–1970)
(*Paul Dyck Photo*)

"Buffalo Hunt" Bronze Sculpture by
Lone Wolf Schultz; Blackfoot
(*Paul Dyck Photo*)

with those of Frederic Remington. He was born on February 18, 1882 at Birch Creek, on the Blackfoot Reservation in Montana. He was the son of the White writer James Willard Schultz and his wife Natahki or Mutsiawotan Ahki (Fine Shield Woman), a full-blooded Blackfoot woman. The boy was named for C. Hart Merriam, a well-known author and professor of osteology at Yale University.

The young man grew up on the reservation in Montana, attended Indian schools and riding the range, he learned to be a cowboy. He began to draw and paint around the age of 10. In 1910 he went to Los Angeles to study at the Art Students League and four years later he attended the Chicago Art Institute. He enjoyed the encouragement of many artists of the period, particularly Thomas Moran, who had a great influence on him. Another early supporter was Harry Carr, the art critic of the *Los Angeles Times*.

Hart painted both in oils and watercolors, drawing on his boyhood memories for the Western scenes which made him famous. Cowboys and Indians, buffalo and horses, hunters and scouts—all of these subjects evoked a life and a time that was forever gone, yet continued to stir the imagination of Americans. In 1904, long afflicted with poor health, he went to the Southwest for his health, and from 1914 until his death, divided his time between his father's home "Butterfly Lodge"

256

Oil Painting by Lone Wolf Schultz;
Blackfoot
(*Paul Dyck Photo*)

in the White Mountains of Arizona. Later, he maintained a studio in Tucson, and spent his winters there, traveling north to Montana during the summers.

Like Remington, Hart was also a sculptor, working effectively in bronze, and it is perhaps in this medium that he gained his greatest success. In 1916, he had his first major show in Los Angeles, out of which came many commissions. One particularly important collector of his work was August Heckscher of New York City, who introduced him to the Eastern art world, and during the 1920s provided the avenue whereby Hart was able to place his work in many of the galleries of New York City. It was perhaps the decade of the 1920s in which his work flourished the most remarkably, and during this time he was also at the height of his creative abilities in sculpture; many of the bronzes which come from this period grace the collections of major museums today.

Lone Wolf did some commercial illustration during his career, including drawings for his father's many books. He died at Tucson, Arizona on February 9, 1970 and was subsequently buried near Browning, Montana, leaving behind him a great legacy of Western art. He married only once, to Naomah Tracy, who survived him.

Seattle (ca. 1788–1866)

Seattle (1788–1866)
(*Washington State Historical Society*)

Seattle, more correctly Seathl or Sealth, the chief of the Suquamish, Duwamish, and allied Salish-speaking tribes, was born near the present location of the city named for him. He was the son of Suquamish leader named Schweabe and a Duwamish woman named Scholitza (or Wood-sholitsa); therefore, he is usually regarded as Duwamish. The date of his birth is uncertain; it was sometime between 1786–1790. As a young man, Seathl was an active warrior widely known for his daring. Then he became convinced that peace was preferable to war, largely due to the influence of Catholic missionaries who were coming into the Northwest Territory in the 1830s. In time, he converted to Christianity, taking the name Noah from his favorite biblical character; at the same time, many of his tribesmen also converted.

Following the peak of the California Gold Rush, more Whites came into the Northwest to settle in the Puget Sound region. They were warmly received by the Indians, and in 1852 the name of the local settlement was changed to "Seattle" in honor of the chief.

During this time, however, there was increasing conflict between Indian and White. Some Indians rebelled against the oppressive weight, and were led by Kamiakin and Leschi; but Seathl and his people remained at peace. Finally, in the spring of 1855, Governor Isaac Stevens called a series of councils to try to persuade all of the tribes to move onto reservations which had been set aside for them. The Indians were given a voice in establishing the boundaries of these reservations, and were thereby able to include some of their favorite lands.

Although Seathl was the first to sign the Port Elliott Treaty of 1855 accepting a reservation, he declared, "The red man has ever fled the approach of the White man as morning mist flees the rising sun. It matters little where we pass the remnant of our days. They will not be many. The Indian's night promises to be dark . . . a few more moons . . . a few more winters."

The reservations were not readily accepted by many tribes, and warfare continued for over 15 years, until the military superiority of the U.S. Army finally crushed all Indian resistance in the area. Seathl had continuously refused to let his people become enmeshed in the conflict, realizing that only bloodshed would result, with the certain extinction of his small band. They moved to the Port Madison Reservation and lived in relative peace despite the chaos whirling around them. There he lived in Old Man House, just across from northern Bainbridge Island; this was a "community house," measuring some 60 × 900 feet—easily the largest Indian-made wooden structure in the region.

In his old age, Seathl asked for and received a small tribute from the citizens of the town named after him—advance compensation against the tribal belief that the mention of a man's name after his death disturbed his spirit. He died at Port Madison on June 7, 1866 and was buried in the Suquamish Indian cemetery near Seattle. He married twice; his first wife, Ladaila, a Duwamish woman, died after bearing one daughter, Kiksomlo, known as "Angeline." The second, Oiahl, had three daughters all of whom died young, and two boys, George and Seeanumpkin.

Sequoyah (1776–1843)

Also known as Sogwili or Sikwaji, from *tsikwaya*, "Sparrow" (some say "Principal Bird"), Sequoyah was one of the most remarkable people in United States history. He was the son of Wurteh (or Wurtee), a half-blood Cherokee matron of the Paint clan and the daughter of a chief, and Colonel Nathaniel Gist, an important White participant in the American Revolution. He was born in 1776 (some records say 1760) at Taskigi, near Fort Loudon, Tennessee. An injury to his leg while on a hunting trip developed into a form of arthritis, leaving him permanently crippled and with the nickname "The Lame One." He had a quick mind and a fertile imagination, which served him well when he became intrigued with the "talking leaves" of the Whites, although he neither spoke nor wrote English at the time. Through the perpetuation of early errors in transliteration, he has been known as George Guess, or Guest; neither form is accepted as correct today.

Sequoyah (1776–1843)
(*Museum of the American Indian*)

He was raised as a traditional hunter and trader, but became a drunkard in early youth, perhaps out of frustration with his physical condition. Realizing what drinking was doing to him, he seems to have resolutely turned away from liquor, deliberately seeking a new way of life. He chose metal work and in time developed into a fine craftsman, emerging as an outstanding silversmith. This latter skill was an important asset in his effort to reproduce the written language of the Whites, when he worked to devise a means of writing the Cherokee language. He began in 1809 with pictorial symbols, but quickly realized the impracticability of this means of communication, and subsequently developed a syllabary of 86 characters derived from Greek, Hebrew, and English. His sources were mission school books. His effort did not initially meet with tribal approval; he was suspected of practicing witchcraft, and at one time all of his papers were burned. But he persevered, and in 1821, in order to demonstrate the practical value of his system, as well as to overcome tribal obstruction, he gave a demonstration to the assembled Cherokee leaders by writing a message which his six-year-old daughter read and independently, understood and answered. By such means he was able to convince his people that his writing system was viable. The Tribal Council formally adopted the syllabary in 1821.

More impressively, he went to Arkansas in 1824, where some of the Cherokee had previously migrated. He sent back written messages to his Eastern tribesmen, and to many of the friends of the Arkansas Indians. This so astonished the Eastern Cherokee that in a very few months literally thousands of Cherokee people, both east and west, were able to read and write in their own language. This was the first tribe north of Mexico to have its own universally intelligible writing system.

By 1824 parts of the *Bible* had been translated into Cherokee, thus gaining the assistance of the White missionaries, who had previously been hostile or lukewarm to its development. In 1828 the Cherokee Tribal Council established its own publication, *Cherokee Phoenix and Indian Advocate*, a weekly newspaper which flourished until its suppression by the State of Georgia in 1835 because of its advocation of Cherokee rights to their lands.

Cherokee Alphabet.

The Cherokee Alphabet
(*American Museum of Natural History*)

In the meantime, he married a Cherokee woman, Sarah (or Sally), by whom he had a son, Chusaleta. He was awarded a lifetime pension in recognition of his work—the first ever granted by an Indian tribe—and was selected as an envoy to Washington to represent the tribe in its continuing efforts for justice in the unceasing land issue. In an effort to expand the use of his syllabary, he moved to Indian Territory, where he taught large numbers of Cherokee the new system. He also became interested in the fate of a group of "lost Cherokee" people who had wandered west during the American Revolution, but had disappeared into the wilderness. He hoped to find them by discovering peoples who spoke Cherokee.

In his search for the "lost Cherokee" people he was accompanied by his son Tessee and seven loyal followers. The search proved to be a long and far more difficult trip than had been realized; the party traveled to the border of Mexico, where they were told of a mysterious band of Indians who were reputedly from the North, and who spoke a strange language. Crossing the Mauluke River, they went south to San Cranto, but became aware of the need for more supplies. Sequoyah remained in the area, sick from dysentery, while most of his companions went back to obtain the needed food. When Tessee returned, accompanied by one of the party named The Worm, they found Sequoyah in very bad condition; he died in August 1843. He was buried near San Fernando, Tamaulipas, Mexico, along with his treasured papers, in a still-undiscovered grave.

Cherokee Shoe Repair Shop; Tahlequah, Oklahoma
(*Museum of the American Indian*)

Sequoyah's inventiveness, intelligence, and humanity were respected by Indians and Whites equally. He had been an educator and political envoy, but was first and foremost a man of intellectual curiosity and integrity, concerned for the betterment of his people. Although a statue to his honor was placed in the Capitol's Statuary Hall by the State of Oklahoma after his death, it somehow seems even more fitting that the name of a species of giant redwood trees—the oldest living objects in the country—were given the name Sequoia in remembrance of this remarkable genius.

Setangya (ca. 1810–1871)

Known to the Whites as Satank, from *Set-angia*, "Sitting Bear," this Kiowa chief was for many years the principal war chief of his tribe. He was born in the Black Hills around 1810, and was part Sarsi; nothing is known of his parentage. He saw his people move south from Dakota, eventually going as far as the Comanche country in Texas; at first the two tribes fought each other, but eventually made peace, even becoming allies. The unrelenting hostility of the Kiowa to White settlement of the Southern Plains was a continuing barrier to the westward movement of the emigrants.

Setangya belonged to the Kiowa Dog Soldier Society and was always in the forefront of military activities; he is thought to have been the main force behind the agreement between the Kiowa and the Cheyenne forces, which strengthened the Indian resistance to the Whites. In 1846, an arrow struck his upper lip in a battle with the Pawnee, resulting in a bad scar which marked him for the rest of his life.

Setangya (1810–1871)
(*Oklahoma Historical Society*)

Setangya was one of the principal Kiowa signers of the Treaty of Medicine Lodge in 1867. By the terms of this treaty the Kiowa agreed to live in peace on a reservation assigned to them in Indian Territory. But this was no life for an aggressive, militaristic society and they continued to raid into neighboring Texas territory, and in 1870 Setangya's son was killed. The father went south, collected the young man's bones, and from then on carried them with him wherever he went, bundled in a buckskin sack on a separate horse.

Thoroughly disillusioned by promises made but not kept, increasingly conscious of the narrowing of their lands, and the visible diminishing of the great buffalo herds, it was impossible for the Indian people to remain tranquil, and in 1871 Setangya, accompanied by Satanta, Big Tree, Mamanti, and other important Kiowa chiefs attacked a wagon train in Texas, killing seven White teamsters and capturing 41 mules. They then returned to Fort Sill, adjacent to their reservation, exultant over their triumph.

Shortly after arriving, the Kiowa boasted of the raid to the Indian Agent Lawrie Tatum, who was astonished at their public admission of responsibility for the deaths of the Whites. The Army lost no time in arresting the raiders and sent them to Texas for trial in late May 1871. But Setangya was an unwilling prisoner; on the route west, in a last gesture of defiance he sang his death song, slipped the handcuffs from his wrists, then drew a concealed knife and attacked one of the guards. The escorting soldiers immediately shot and killed him. He was subsequently buried in the military cemetery at Fort Sill, Oklahoma.

Shábona (1775–1859)
(*State Historical Society of Wisconsin*)

Shábona (ca. 1775–1859)

Shábona was a Potawatomi leader who was born along the Maumee River in Ohio (some say the Kankakee River in Will County, Illinois). His name has many variants: Shabonee, Shaubena, Shabbona, and even Chambly—probably derived from Captain Jacques de Chambly. The meaning of the name is unclear; the best evidence suggests it is from Potawatomi, "Built Like a Bear," perhaps due to the fact that he was hunchbacked. His father, an Ottawa, was related to Pontiac, making Shábona the great-nephew of the latter. Shábona married Spotka, the daughter of the Potawatomi chief, following whose death he inherited the tribal leadership. The area in which the band lived is known today as Shabbona Grove, in DeKalb County, Illinois.

Around 1807 Shábona became a supporter of Tecumseh, and during the next five years he visited many villages in northern Illinois, trying to induce the people to join Tecumseh's united confederacy. When the War of 1812 commenced, Shábona hesitated to follow his leader to the British side, and in August 1812 he and Sauganash helped to save the lives of some White families in the Chicago massacre. Yet, at the Battle of the Thames, he fought side-by-side with Tecumseh, and mourned his death deeply.

From that time on, Shábona was a staunch friend of the federal government, and was able to persuade most of the Potawatomi not to join the Winnebago in their revolt of 1827. The militants took him prisoner and threatened his life, but he remained firm in his support of peaceful accommodation with the Whites. Though many Indians turned against him as a result, his influence continued to be an important force among most of his tribe, and he was able to keep them from entering into the Black Hawk War, although he was unable to convince Black Hawk and his followers that it was futile, and probably suicidal, to challenge the federal military forces. Following a last conference with Black Hawk, Shábona, his son, and his nephew rode out to warn the White settlers of the impending attack. This gained him new enemies among the Sauk–

Fox; in revenge, the latter ambushed the trio, killing all but Shábona.

In 1836, Shábona led the Potawatomi in the move to new lands west of the Mississippi, following the refusal of the government to honor a pledge to allow his people to settle on two sections of land near their old village. When he returned to claim his acreage, he found that it had been sold to White land speculators because it had been "abandoned." He was never able to reestablish his claim, but some grateful settlers bought him a small farm near Seneca, Illinois. He died on July 17, 1859 at Morris, Illinois, at the age of 84; he was buried in Evergreen Cemetery in that city. Following the death of his first wife, he married Miomex Zebequa, and later Pokanoka; he had several children with both wives. His son Smoke died before 1859, so Shábona was succeeded by his grandson, also named Smoke. The names of two sons are known: Bill Shaubena, also known as Pypegee; and the youngest, Mamas.

Shábona is described as being over 6′ in height, with a large head, and of graceful movement in spite of his deformity.

Shakes (ca. 1800–ca. 1944)

Also known as Shaikes, the name applied to several chiefs of the Tlingit tribe living along the Stikine River of Alaska in the 19th–20th centuries. Sir George Simpson encountered the first-mentioned Chief Shakes during his expedition in 1841–1842 and he mentioned, in particular, the cruelty that the chief displayed toward his slaves, writing that he killed five of them during the dedication of a new house, and on another occasion shot a slave simply to reestablish his own prestige.

Little is known of the early ancestry of the Shakes family, but the fur trade which established Tlingit wealth seems also to have secured a preeminent position for the Shakes name around the area of Wrangell, where Chief Shakes had his home. Indeed, he seems to have been powerful enough to retain his control over the Tlingit even after the bombardment of Wrangell following the purchase of Alaska in 1867.

Carved Wooden Rattle Belonging to Shakes; Tlingit
(*Museum of the American Indian*)

Visitors to Alaska, from missionaries to United States government Indian Agents all describe the majesty and pomp which characterized the home life of Chief Shakes. But it must be borne in mind that this was quite typical of Northwest Coast culture in general at the time; position was based upon wealth, prestige, and power, and the demonstration of status was a mandatory part of everyday life.

In his relations with the United States government, Chief Shakes was able to obtain promises that a modern educational system and economic advantages would be established for the Tlingit people. However, many of these freely made promises failed to materialize, and Indians in the area became greatly disillusioned. Nevertheless, despite this dissatisfaction, there were no important battles between the Tlingit and the White settlers. Although Shakes came to accept the presence of Americans in his territory, he did not welcome the missionaries, saying, "I am too old to learn a new religion, and besides, many of my people who have died were bad . . . and must be in your Hell; and I must go there also, for a Stikine chief never deserts his people in time of trouble."

In the early 20th century, the last of the Chief Shakes line accommodated himself to White civilization by establishing his own "Museum of Indian Curiosities," displaying many fine old sculptural objects of Tlingit origin. The great wealth of the chief had made it possible for him to acquire large numbers of such objects, which were sold from time to time to collectors, dealers, and museum curators, with the result that mementos of Chief Shakes are to be found in many of the large museums throughout the world. He died at Wrangell in February 1944.

Shikellamy (?-1748)

Ongwaterohiathe, "He Lightens the Sky for Us," also known as Swateny or Swataney, from *onkhiswathetani*, "Our Enlightener," was an important Oneida chief who acted as Iroquois proconsul over the conquered lands in Pennsylvania. His birthdate is not known; he claimed to have been born a Cayuga, the son of a French White and a Cayuga woman; some have claimed that he was a Frenchman from Canada who was later adopted into the Oneida tribe. It seems certain that he was captured at the age of two by Oneida warriors and was raised by that tribe. His home was on the upper Schuylkill River in Pennsylvania.

Around 1727 he moved into the Susquehanna Valley to look after his people's interests in the area; as the Iroquois realized the value which the White men placed on the land they controlled, they saw that it would be vital to their own interests to have an Iroquois representative conduct all business with the colonists. All tributary tribes were cautioned never to sign any papers on their own.

Accordingly, representatives or vice regents were appointed to conduct business in behalf of the Six Nations with all Whites—Shikellamy was one of these individuals, often called "Half Kings" by the colonists. He established his center at Shamokin (now Sunbury) where he received negotiators. He was noted for his friendliness to the Whites, especially the missionaries, and is credited with having saved many lives on the frontier. In accordance with Iroquois policy and because of his own convictions, he was friendly to the English but wary of the French. His skills and dignified mien made him a natural diplomat, and he soon became the major channel for negotiations with the Whites in the Pennsylvania region. He got along well with the local authorities, and was able to convince them to recognize Iroquois dominion over all tribes and Indian lands in the area.

But of far greater significance was his success in getting the Whites to control the liquor traffic among the tribes—a problem which had been causing havoc among the Indians. And in 1736 he negotiated two major treaties whereby the colonists agreed to pay the Iroquois for lands already ceded by other tribes and to acknowledge their claims on the lower Delaware River. The Six Nations also sold to the Whites certain Delaware lands in the Blue Mountains—a remarkable step in expropriation.

By participating in these arrangements, it is felt that Pennsylvania "brought upon herself after many years a Delaware War, but escaped a Six Nations War, a French alliance with the Iroquois, and the threatening possibility of the destruction of all of the English colonies on the coast." It was in recognition of the importance of ironmongering following the Iroquois acquisition of firearms which led him to agree to permit the establishment of a Moravian mission only upon the simultaneous settlement of a forge at Shamokin in 1747. Shortly afterwards, David Zeisberger became an assistant missionary at the mission, and in time, a major influence upon the old chief. He nursed him through his final illness, attending him at his death at Shamokin on December 6, 1748. He left four sons—Arahpot (Unhappy Jake); Tachnechdorus (John Shikellamy), John Petty (Petit), and Tahgahjute, or James Logan. His wife was a Cayuga woman.

Short Bull (ca. 1845–1915)

Short Bull was a Brûlé Sioux medicine man who was one of the leaders of the Ghost Dance religion among the Sioux. He was born about 1845 on the Niobrara River in Nebraska. Very little is known of his early childhood, and he first came into public notice when he was one of the Rosebud Sioux leaders selected when the Sioux decided to send a delegation to Nevada for an audience with Wovoka, the newly proclaimed "Indian Messiah." Short Bull made the trip west, along with Kicking Bear and several others.

When he returned home, Short Bull claimed that he had been chosen to bring a special message from Wovoka to the Sioux—a message which they were delighted to hear after a long winter of starvation rations: the White man was going to leave Indian country, and the great buffalo

Short Bull (1845–1915)
(*U.S. Signal Corps, National Archives*)

Muslin Ghost Dance Shirt, Painted
with Sacred Designs; Sioux
(*Museum of the American Indian*)

herds would return, if the Indians would celebrate the Ghost Dance
and obey the Creator's will.

The Sioux, however, interpreted Wovoka's message as being more
warlike than it was intended, and soon they were dancing with a reckless, rebellious abandon which alarmed the Whites. The warriors gained
renewed confidence as they wore the specially painted Ghost shirts,
which Kicking Bear had assured them would turn aside the White man's
bullets. In October 1890, Short Bull told his Rosebud people that the
White man's day was soon over, and that they had nothing to fear from
the soldiers.

The next month, the Army yielded to demands from the Indian
Agents and settlers in the area for protection from the swelling frenzy
which they saw all around them. The officers demanded that the dancing stop; but the Indians were not going to cease just as the final victory
was close at hand, and they left the reservation for Pass Creek, where
Short Bull had claimed a Sacred Tree was sprouting in symbol of the
truth of his promises. At the site, he had a vision calling upon him to
lead all of the Sioux to the Bad Lands, where the Indian Christ would
descend from Heaven to meet his people.

Over 1000 people made the trip to a remote place called The Stronghold, where they began the dancing and waiting for the promised appearance. On December 7 the mixed-blood scout Louis Shaugreau
delivered a message to Short Bull, telling him that if he gave up dancing
and returned to the reservation, the tribal rations would be generously
increased. The Sioux preacher's reply was a brave one: "If the Great
Father would allow us to continue the dance, would give us more rations,
and would quit taking away pieces of our reservation, I would favor
returning"—but three days later, two of the chiefs, Crow Dog and Two
Strike, announced that they were abandoning the dance and that their
people were accompanying them back to the reservation. Within a few
days only about 200 Indians were left.

Although he was now assumed to be the Messiah himself, Short
Bull faced other problems. Before the month of December was over,
Sitting Bull had been murdered, Big Foot and his band had been mas-
sacred at Wounded Knee Creek, and Short Bull's group had left The
Stronghold. The next year, he and other Sioux Indians joined Buffalo
Bill's Wild West Show, fascinating and terrifying audiences all over
the world for more money than they had ever seen in their lives. Short
Bull lived on for many years, even joining the Congregational Church
in his later years, and died peacefully on the reservation around 1915.

Sitting Bull (1834-1890)

Tatanka Iyotanka (Yotanka), a Hunkpapa Sioux leader, was born on
March 31, 1834 at Many Caches on the Grand River near Bullhead,
South Dakota. He was the son of Tatanka Psica, Jumping Badger
(sometimes known as Jumping Bull or Sitting Bull), a Sioux war chief.
In his early years, the lad was known as Hunkesni, "Slow," but soon

became more widely acclaimed for his courage and strength in battle. He was head of the Strong Hearts, a warrior society, and became an important medicine man and tribal councillor, although he was never a true "chief" of his people.

Sitting Bull was implacably opposed to the White man's continual encroachment on Indian land. Always something of a militant, in the 1860s he was active in the Plains Indian wars, and his camp became a meeting place for many tribes in the area who staunchly opposed the Whites. In 1868, following Red Cloud's war, the United States government signed a treaty guaranteeing the Plains Indians a reservation north of the Platte River, plus the right to hunt buffalo off the reservation. The territory included Paha Sapa (the Black Hills), an area traditionally regarded as sacred by the Sioux. But the authorities did little to prevent the Whites from coming onto the reservation; and when gold was discovered in 1874, thousands of prospectors poured onto the land, ignoring land ownership and Indian rights. The Indian people were particularly incensed by the desecration resulting from miners' digging into the sacred area, and in the following year, Sitting Bull, as head of the Sioux war council, made plans with the Cheyenne and Arapaho to force them out.

Recognizing the dangerous situation, the government ordered all Indians to return to their reservations by the end of January 1876. When the Indians defied the order, the Army was moved into the area; the Indians also gathered their own forces and upwards of 3000 warriors

Sitting Bull, the Hunkpapa (1834–1890)
(*Smithsonian Institution, National Anthropological Archives*)

readied themselves for the coming battle. In early June, Sitting Bull performed a Sun Dance to determine the outcome; he danced for more than a day and a half before receiving a vision. In his vision he saw many White soldiers falling upside down from the sky into the Indian camp; this was clearly a good sign and the Indians were confident of victory.

On June 16, at the Battle of the Rosebud, Crazy Horse defeated the troops under General George Crook, but the vision was not fulfilled until June 25, when General George Custer and several hundred soldiers were wiped out when they attacked the Indian camp on the banks of the Little Bighorn. Aroused and humiliated by these and other defeats, the Army concentrated on a relentless pursuit of the Sioux. Many surrendered, but Sitting Bull and his followers escaped into Canada. While they were not welcomed by the Canadians nor helped through the severe winter, their unwilling hosts did resist United States efforts to have the Indians returned. Many Indians died, or went back to the reservation during the bitter winter, and finally on July 19, 1881, Sitting Bull and the remaining holdouts surrendered at Fort Buford, Montana. He was imprisoned for two years before being allowed to return to Standing Rock; but by that time he had become a legend to the Whites, and in 1885 was the star attraction in Buffalo Bill's Wild West Show which traveled throughout the East.

Sitting Bull's heart remained with the Indian needs. He trusted no Whites, and expected only deceit and lies from them, especially in any treaty negotiation, for that is all that he had ever experienced. When the government tried to break up the Sioux reservation, he cautioned his people against being tricked again into selling their heritage. But the Federal Commission, sent out in 1889 to negotiate the matter, was able to bypass his influence by meeting individually with tribal leaders, or in very small groups away from tribal council meetings.

This divide-and-conquer technique had long been successful in dealing with Indians, and Sitting Bull was perhaps the last Sioux leader whose influence was strong enough to unite the people under one person. When he enthusiastically supported the adoption of the Ghost Dance movement which had just been introduced by Kicking Bear, some Indian Agents panicked; they feared that the Ghost Dancers and their strange ceremonies—so highly charged with emotion—would lead to an uprising, not recognizing the essentially pacifistic nature of the movement. Indian Police were sent to arrest Sitting Bull on December 15, 1890, in the hope that this would end the Ghost Dance. In the melee which ensued, Sitting Bull, his son Crow Foot, and several others were shot to death by Red Tomahawk and Bullhead, of the Police group. A few days later, the tragic massacre at Wounded Knee took place, and the Ghost Dance did indeed cease.

Sitting Bull was a man of many dimensions, whose actions aroused as mixed emotions as did his personality. He had several wives—some accounts record nine—of whom perhaps Pretty Plume, *Wiyaka-wastewin*, and Zuzela are best known. He is said to have sired nine children, among whom Crow Foot and Standing Holy are most frequently mentioned. His intransigeance in the face of White aggression, his courage in defending his people, and his refusal to step aside in an impossible struggle, have made him into an almost mythical figure in American history. Among Indian people his organizational ability, medicine power, and willingness to lead have made him a figure of respect, even among some who denigrate him as a glory seeker or for not being a "true chief."

Sitting Bull the Minor (1841–1876)

While most readers interested in Indian history know that there were many persons named Sitting Bull, few recognize that there were two whose prominence overshadowed all the others during the period from 1860 to 1890. The famous Hunkpapa leader who captured White imagination and is by far the best known Indian today, was not alone in his Plains career.

Just ten years after the birth of Sitting Bull, the northern Sioux, another baby was born in 1841 to an Oglala family near Deer Creek, just north of Fort Laramie. Named Drum Packer, this young man became an avid student of the White man's customs, learning to read and write from the Overland Trail telegrapher, a friendly man named Oscar Collister. In time the young Sioux learned to use the talking wire, and became a fluent speaker of English.

He seems always to have had a voracious curiosity for the written word, poring over books, newspapers, and anything else he could get his hands on. Once he grew to manhood he became no longer the Drum Packer, but Sitting Bull, Tatanka Iotanka, the leader of Little Wound's cutoff band of Oglala Sioux warriors. This was a group of individuals who had gathered together to form a unit to hold off the Pawnee, who occupied southern Nebraska.

At this time, Sitting Bull, the Oglala, was friendly to the Whites—a sentiment which lasted only until the outrage at Sand Creek in 1864. At that time, he and Crazy Horse, with whom he had always had a close relationship, answered the Cheyenne call for help. Both men recognized that, in the long run, it was always the friendly Indians who seemed to suffer more from the Whites than the hostile Indians. Sand Creek showed that no longer could one remain neutral; one must take sides.

Sitting Bull fought under Little Wound from 1865 to 1868, until the Treaty at Fort Laramie was signed. In January 1865, he attacked at Julesburg, Colorado to avenge the outrage at Sand Creek; from there his warriors went on to destroy Overland Trail stations, scourging the countryside of White men, women, and children. He attacked wherever he found White soldiers, and took part in the Fetterman affair. Eventually, he joined the forces of Red Cloud, performing so effectively that no White group dared cross the lands unless accompanied by a heavily armed Army escort. Confusion inevitably arose from his name, and many exploits of the Hunkpapa Sitting Bull were credited to (or charged against) the Oglala Sitting Bull.

But Sitting Bull also recognized the signs as he roamed the country:

Sitting Bull, the Oglala (1841–1876)
(*Smithsonian Institution, National Anthropological Archives*)

there were fewer buffalo, people were going without food and clothing, reservations were slowly growing all over the Indian lands, and fences were beginning to appear. There was a need for skillful negotiations and knowledgeable headmen. He decided to abandon the fight and go on the reservation in an effort to more effectively help his people.

He enrolled on the Red Cloud Agency, and by 1870 had become so highly regarded that he was selected as one of 20 men to go to Washington to represent the Oglala. He was only 29 years old, but he impressed everyone with his dignity, diplomatic skill, and knowledge. Then the government decided to move the Red Cloud Agency from the Platte to the White River, Nebraska. In 1872 an outbreak was threatened by young, hotheaded warriors, following the murder of two Indians at the Platte by Whites. Sitting Bull and 14 men held off the frenzied warriors arguing the fruitlessness of such an act, until troops arrived to establish a precarious calm.

But the Agency was moved to the White River anyway, and tension continued throughout the rest of the year; the stockade, which in time came to be known as Camp Robinson, was the scene of many small clashes, each contributing to a general buildup of hostility between Indian and White. It was a time to test any leader, and although Sitting Bull no longer trusted the White man, his greater concern was for the safety and well-being of his own people. He frequently rose to the defense of the Whites, especially when he protected a small contingent of troops led by Lieutenant Crawford when a council was held at Lone Tree, near the camp, to consider the sale of land in the Black Hills. In the spring of 1875, Sitting Bull, the Oglala, accompanied Red Cloud and Spotted Tail to Washington to discuss the plague of gold seekers overrunning the Black Hills, and the hungry people, whose rations had been diverted to the pockets of the agents. The Whites, however, were interested only in discussing the sale of lands, not the problems of rations or starving Indians. An investigation into the matter of ration withholding was started but nothing came of it.

After the quarreling was over—involving arguments between Red Cloud and Spotted Tail, as well as between all the others—Sitting Bull, who had kept aloof from the bickering, was presented with a fine Winchester carbine on June 7, 1875 with a special brightly polished brass breech, upon which was engraved:

Sitting Bull, from The President
for Bravery & True Friendship

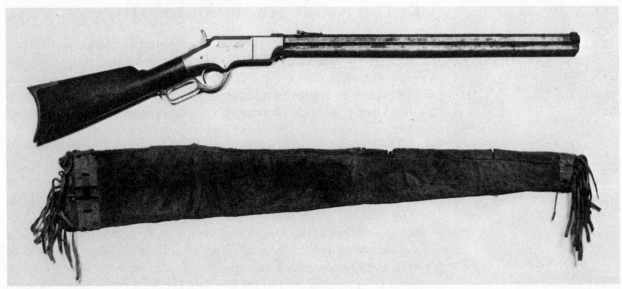

It was a token of acknowledgment for his courageous protection of Lieutenant Crawford and his 22 soldiers at Camp Robinson.

The Golden Winchester of Sitting Bull, the Oglala
(*Museum of the American Indian*)

His luck ran out in 1876. In September, following the victory of the Sioux over Custer at the Little Bighorn, a commission was sent to buy the Black Hills. By this time, the Whites had lost their patience and were determined to win the coveted gold-bearing region. A few chiefs' were brought into the stockade, and the terms of sale were read to them: unless they signed, there would be no more rations; they must go south to Indian Territory, or to smaller reservation areas. Meanwhile, they were being kept in "protective custody" in the stockade.

Outraged at the duplicity in the terms of the sale, Sitting Bull charged out of the gates, daring the soldiers to shoot. None did, and he started for the war camp of Crazy Horse, carrying his golden rifle. There he saw the poor conditions of the people, the sick and dying women and children, and the lack of proper food and medicine.

Discouraged, he returned home to find that the rest of the chiefs had signed away the Black Hills during his absence. He realized that no longer would the Sioux hold out; everywhere the soldiers were picking up more and more refugees or shooting them on sight. He was asked to go north with a message to Crazy Horse, to induce him to come into the Agency and sue for peace. He clearly recognized that the result would be long imprisonment for Crazy Horse, but he felt it would be better than death on the frozen plains.

So he went, with four other chiefs and a small party of men bringing back stray ponies, carrying the white flag of truce given to him by General Crook. As they passed the camp of Crow Indian scouts located just outside the fort parade ground, 12 of the Crow attacked without warning, killing Sitting Bull and his four companions, as Crazy Horse and General Miles watched from the distance, helpless in averting the slaughter. It was December 17, 1876, a bad day to die.

Skenandoa (ca. 1706–1816)

The name Sken-an-do'a was derived from Iroquoian *skennon'do*, "Deer." He was an Oneida chief about whom little is known today. He apparently led a dissolute life as a young man, drinking heavily and unable to settle down to a worthwhile career. On one occasion, while on business in Albany, he drank too much and found himself out on the street the next morning with everything of value stolen from him. The disgrace caused him to change his ways, and from then on he seems to have led a more sober life. In 1755, influenced by Reverend Samuel Kirkland, a prominent Congregational missionary to the Oneida, he became an enthusiastic convert. At this same time, he was also an ally of the English and fought on their side during the French and Indian War.

At the outbreak of the American Revolution, Kirkland was able to win Skenandoa over to the Colonial cause, and his influence was sufficient to keep the Oneida and Tuscarora people from joining the rest of the Iroquois nation in support of the English. He apparently never wavered in this loyalty, and was instrumental in preventing the massacre of a group of Whites at German Flats, New York. He also had a leading role in the issuance of the Oneida Declaration of Neutrality in May 1775, in which he was joined by 11 other chiefs. He was described as a tall man, 6'3" in height and graceful in bearing. In his old age he lost his sight, observing that he "had become an old hemlock, dead at the top." He died at Oneida Castle, New York on March 11, 1816, and was buried, at his own request, beside Kirkland at Clinton, in the Hamilton College graveyard. One son survived him.

Redbird Smith (1850–1918)

Chea Sequah (?), "Red Bird," was the leader of the Cherokee traditionalists who resented and resisted the Americanization of their tribe. He was born on July 19, 1850, near Fort Smith, Arkansas, the son of Pig Redbird Smith (so named by White neighbors, because he was a blacksmith), a Cherokee farmer; his mother was Lizzie Hildebrand, part-Cherokee. The Keetowah Society, named after *kituwha*, "key," had been formed by Evan Jones and his son John, for the protection of the Cherokee people during the period following the Civil War when their

Redbird Smith, in Turban (1850–1918), with Three Followers Displaying Keetowah Society Wampum Belts (*Smithsonian Institution, National Anthropological Archives*)

territory had been overrun by Northern armies. The society fell apart in the relatively stable era of the 1870s and 1880s, but was revived ten years later when the Dawes Commission arrived in Indian Territory to negotiate the return to United States control land that had been ceded to the Five Civilized Tribes (Cherokee, Choctaw, Chickasaw, Creek, and Seminole) when they were removed from the East.

White settlers who had come into the area in increasing numbers—some had, in fact, been sold land by the Indians—were agitating for the protection of Washington's laws. The Commission proposed that the tribes give up their common ownership of territory, that the people be given individual 160-acre plots of land, and that all tribal members become citizens of the United States, and of a new state, to be called Oklahoma. Many full bloods felt that this would spell the end of their traditional way of life, and they united to talk about ways to fight statehood and all that it represented.

The Keetowah Society was revived, but there was now a split in its ranks; some members were resigned to losing their autonomy, while others remained steadfastly opposed to any capitulation. Redbird Smith soon came forward to effect a cementing of the two groups. He also helped form the Mothers Society, which welcomed members from all five tribes; they tried every means possible to dissuade the government from its avowed purpose. Their small monthly dues payments were used to hire lawyers and lobbyists in Washington, and many delegations were sent to the capitol to plead their case.

But too many powerful interests were allied against them. Oklahoma was beginnning to boom, and no one could keep the land speculators and businessmen from what they wanted. Then, too, many mixed bloods felt that the best interests of all the people would be served if they accepted statehood and individual property rights.

As passions increased, Redbird Smith and his followers became known as the Nighthawk Keetowahs, for they worked day and night with fanatic concentration on their cause; indeed, most of their planning meetings were held secretly at night to avoid the premature revealing of their plans. They convinced many of the Indians of the justice of their "movement," and got them to refuse to enroll with the U.S. Census of 1900—thereby causing considerable bureaucratic confusion. In 1902 Smith was arrested and forced to enroll. He soon went to Washington to make one last appeal, saying, "I can't stand and live and breathe if I take this allotment," but he met with little success. Disheartened, he returned to Indian Territory and advised his followers that further resistance was futile.

In 1905 the Cherokee decided to sign the allotment agreement—the last tribe to do so. Redbird Smith became Principal Chief in 1908, and the next year almost 42,000 Indians signed for their allotments; of these, less than 9000 were full bloods. Redbird and the Nighthawks withdrew to the hills, where they hoped to live in their traditional way without further interference from the Whites. In this hope, alas, he was again doomed to disappointment. He died in the new state of Oklahoma on November 8, 1918, survived by his wife, Lucy Fields Smith. With him ended the Redbird Smith Movement.

Smohalla (ca. 1815–1907)

Smohalla, more correctly called Smóqula, "The Preacher" (also Smokeller), was an Indian religious leader and preacher born at Wallula, on the upper Columbia River in Washington, around 1815. He was a member of the Wanapum (or Sokulk) tribe. Little is known of his family background but he is known to have been a hunchback. As a young man he frequented a nearby Roman Catholic mission, where he absorbed a great deal of the Catholic ritual and faith. He distinguished himself as a warrior, gaining the name Waipshwa, "Rock Carrier," and subsequently became renowned as a gifted medicine man and visionary.

By the 1850s his fame aroused the enmity of Moses, chief of a nearby Sinkiuse band. The two men met on the battlefield, and Smohalla was left for dead although, in fact, he survived and quickly left the area, unseen by anyone. For several years he went on what he would later describe as a visit to the Spirit World; in reality, he wandered south, traveling as far as Mexico. Then he returned to his own people, seemingly back from the dead.

Capitalizing on the emotional and psychological shock of his reappearance, Smohalla told his followers that he had a message from the "Other Side." In essence, he said that all things were immortal and that the essential goodness of life was to be found in the simple things. He advocated a return to the primitive Indian verities and the rejection of all things related to the White man. Smohalla prophesied that the corrupting influence of the Whites would eventually disappear and that the land and its true children, the Indian, would return to the pristine state that existed before the Europeans had intruded.

This message formed the basis of the so-called Dreamer religion, or *Washani*, a spiritual belief which flourished among the tribes of the Pacific Northwest well into the 20th century. Based on teachings of Sowapso, an earlier prophet from the area, its ceremonies had Mormon, Christian, and Indian overtones. The ritual, as developed by Smohalla, a rival of Sohappy, the son of Sowapso, sought to induce visions and spiritual experiences through the use of such sensual and hypnotic devices as drums, bells, and rhythmic dancing. In many ways the Dreamer religion was parallel to the later and more famous Ghost Dance religion, and certainly the common appeal of both was the vision of a land free from the presence of the White man, and a return to the "Good Old Days."

Perhaps the most influential convert to the Dreamer religion was Tuekakas (Old Joseph) of the Nez Percé. When some of his Christian co-chiefs signed the Treaty of Lapwai in 1863, ceding his lands to the Whites, he and his son rejected its terms. Disillusioned with the Americans and their religion, Tuekakas rejected his lifelong Christianity and became a Dreamer.

All of the followers of Smohalla continued to look down on White influence and the appendages of the new "civilization," even after they had been moved onto reservations. Smohalla was looked upon as a Messiah; the name Yúyunipi-tqana, "Shouting Mountain," was used in reference to his oratory. His preaching gave comfort and hope to besieged Indians of many tribes. The Whites regarded Smohalla's religion as a barrier to civilizing influences and the acceptance of land restrictions—and, of course, the efforts of the Christian missionaries.

The Dreamer religion continued to flourish even after the death of Smohalla in 1907. He was buried at Satus graveyard in Washington, but his work was carried on by his nephew Puckhyahtoot, "the Last Prophet." He was married ten times but had only one son, Yoyouni, who froze to death while hunting. His last wife, Stongkee, survived him.

Spotted Tail (ca. 1823–1881)

Sinte Gleska (also Sinte Galeska or Zintalah Galeshka), from Sioux *sinte*, "tail," *gleska* "spotted," was a Brûlé Sioux leader who became one of the most important individuals in the Northern Plains country. Known as Jumping Buffalo in his youth, the name Spotted Tail was applied in reference to a striped raccoon which was given to him by a

Spotted Tail (1823–1881)
(*Museum of the American Indian*)

beaver trapper. He was born about 1823 or 1824 along the White River in South Dakota (some accounts say near Fort Laramie, Wyoming). He was the son of a Saone man named Cunka (Tangled Hair) and a Brûlé woman, Walks with the Pipe. He was not a hereditary chief and gained his eminence through is integrity and ability. Renowned as a man of his word, he astounded Army officials on one occasion when he and two other Indians accused of murder walked into Fort Laramie to give themselves up, in order to spare the rest of the tribe.

They were imprisoned for a period, during which time he learned to read and write English. Shortly after being freed, the head chief Little Thunder died, and the tribal leaders passed over the hereditary candidate and selected Spotted Tail as chief. Although he favored the Treaty of 1865, feeling that White settlement in the region was unavoidable, he and the other leading chiefs did not sign the document, holding out for better terms. Later, he signed the more important Treaty at Fort Laramie on April 29, 1868, whereby the Sioux permitted the building of a railroad with the assurance that they would be given a permanent reservation including all of present-day South Dakota, among other provisions.

He made several trips to Washington during his lifetime, on each occasion learning more of the White man's customs. When gold was discovered in the Black Hills, Spotted Tail and Red Cloud were designated to go to Washington to negotiate the sale of the mineral rights. Before leaving for Washington, Spotted Tail determined to examine the land in question to learn the true value of the minerals. He listened carefully to the talk of the miners and realized that the mines were indeed of great value. When negotiations were opened, and $6,000,000 was offered to the Indians, Spotted Tail demanded an amount ten miles that for the mineral rights. This sum was unacceptable to the Government and no treaty resulted. Instead, the miners were allowed to enter

Quilled Buckskin War Shirt of Spotted Tail; Sioux
(*Museum of the American Indian*)

the Black Hills without Army interference, and shortly thereafter, the Sioux found themselves overrun without any recourse save warfare.

During this period, Spotted Tail was appointed chief of all the Sioux at Rosebud and Spotted Tail Agencies, since the redoubtable Red Cloud was out of favor with the White authorities. He was able to negotiate a peaceful arrangement which resulted in the surrender of his nephew, Crazy Horse, in 1877. But another force had been at work over several years, i.e., a plot by several subchiefs, notably Black Crow, Crow Dog, and a few other minor Brûlé men who were jealous of the chief, and eager to supplant him. There also seems to have been the matter of one of the wives of Thigh—or perhaps Crow Dog—who had been "stolen" by Spotted Tail, which added fuel to the flames of the rivalry. In any event, inspired by Black Crow, and inflamed over the loss of the woman, Crow Dog shot and killed Spotted Tail on August 5, 1881 at the Agency.

He was eventually tried for the murder, and in a landmark decision by the court, was freed on the grounds that the courts had no jurisdiction over crimes committed on Indian reservation land. However, neither he nor Spotted Tail's son, Little Spotted Tail, were capable of leading the Sioux, and the tribe was left without strong leadership at a critical time in their history.

Spotted Tail was buried at the Episcopal Cemetery at Rosebud, South Dakota. One daughter, Peheziwi, survived him.

Ernest Spybuck (1883-1949)

Mahthela, one of the few Shawnee artists of record, was born in 1883 near Tecumseh, Oklahoma on the Pawnee-Shawnee Reservation. He was the son of John Spybuck and Peahchepeahso, both Shawnee. Young

"Delawares at Annual Ceremony in Oklahoma," painted by Ernest Spybuck; Shawnee
(*Museum of the American Indian*)

Ernest Spybuck (1883–1949)
(*Museum of the American Indian*)

Mahthela never studied art but began drawing when he was about six years old. He was educated at the Shawnee Boarding School and the Sacred Heart Mission. One of his early teachers, Harriet Patrick Gilstrap, noticed his work, and apparently was responsible for giving him considerable encouragement.

As with most Indian artists, he drew his inspiration from tribal life and traditions, painting what he saw, remembered, or heard about from the older people around him. He always seems to have been engrossed in his work. In the 1920s his paintings came to the attention of Dr. George G. Heye, who commissioned him to paint a large number of genre paintings of Shawnee life of the period for the Museum of the American Indian Collection. Other examples of his work are in museums and collections in several cities in Oklahoma. He did a few murals during his career, but most of his work was in watercolor on paper.

He died at his home west of Shawnee, Oklahoma in 1949 at the age of 66, never having traveled outside of Pottawatomie County during his life.

Squanto (ca. 1580–1622)

Squanto, a contraction of the name Tisquantum, "door or entrance," was a member of the Patuxet tribe who was recorded as having been kidnaped by Captain George Weymouth in 1605, and was among 27 (some say 24) Indians later taken to Málaga, Spain and sold into slavery by Captain Thomas Hunt. Squanto eventually escaped and made his way to England; from there he made his way to America in 1618–1619 with the help of John Slanie. Other versions claim that he was brought directly to England, and became the protégé of a merchant, Sir Fernando Gorges, who was interested in finding out as much as he could concerning the new lands across the sea. In any event, he spent some 14 years, which involved two round trips to Europe, before returning to his homeland, where he found to his dismay that his tribe had been virtually wiped out by a plague in 1617—probably yellow fever or some similar disease—introduced by European explorers.

During his years away from home he became fluent in English. With no tribe of his own, Squanto became associated with the Wampanoag people, and became an interpreter for their chief, Massasoit, the dominant leader of the region, in meetings with the Pilgrims. On March 21, 1621, Squanto arranged an initial conference which had far-reaching effects; one of the Plymouth colony's early governors, William Bradford, wrote, "Squanto continued with them, was their interpreter, and was a special instrument sent of God for their good beyond their expectation. He directed them how to set their corn, where to take fish, and to procure other commodities."

Some Indians were suspicious of Squanto's friendship with the colonists. Having no tribe of his own, it was thought, he might be in collusion with them against the other Indians. It was generally suspected that he was trying to usurp the power of Massasoit, and at one time the latter demanded that the English turn Squanto over to him as a prisoner.

Governor Bradford refused, sensing the importance of the latter as an interpreter. During this period of personal attack, Caunbitant, a local chief, allied himself with the Narragansetts to force Massasoit out, and also to drive out the hated English from the land. Squanto learned of this effort and intended to warn the English; he was captured by Caunbitant but was rescued by Captain Miles Standish, and the plot never succeeded. But there did seem to be every indication that Squanto hoped in some way to replace Massasoit as the great sachem of the region.

With the arrival of more colonists, the problem of food became critical. In the fall of 1622 it was decided to sail one of the ships, the *Swan*, around Cape Cod and into Narragansett Bay to barter with the Indians of that area for food. Squanto volunteered his services as pilot and interpreter, since he had made the trip twice before. Bad weather forced the expedition to seek the safety of what is now Chatham Harbor on the Cape, where Squanto introduced the English to the local Indians. Ample provisions for the coming winter were secured, but as the *Swan* was preparing to leave, Squanto fell "sick of an Indian fever," and died in November or early December 1622.

Squanto was long remembered, and deservedly so, by the residents of Plymouth Colony for his invaluable help in getting them through their first difficult years in the New World. While there is no doubt that he could be charged with having played "both ends against the middle" in his efforts to make himself an important person in colonial life, there is no evidence that he was maliciously, nor indeed, evilly guilty of anything beyond inordinate ambition.

Painted Oak Splint Basket and Cover; Mohegan
(*Museum of the American Indian*)

Standing Bear (ca. 1829–1908)

Mochunozhin was a celebrated Ponca chief who became famous during his long fight against the United States when the government attempted to transfer Ponca tribal lands to the Sioux. Little is known of his early life prior to this time.

The Ponca tribe had lived at the mouth of the Niobrara River in Nebraska for many years, and welcomed the Lewis and Clark expedition in 1804 when the Whites passed through on their way west. When settlement of the Plains began in earnest a half century later, they remained at peace, and in 1858 boundaries were set up between them and the neighboring Sioux, who often raided the prosperous Ponca people. A treaty was signed which guaranteed the latter a permanent home on the Niobrara.

But in 1868, in a treaty which established boundaries for the Sioux, the government surveyors inadvertently included the Ponca lands within this area. The Sioux began raiding Ponca villages, demanding tribute and threatening to drive the Ponca off "Sioux land." The Ponca and their White supporters protested many times, and finally in 1875 the government agreed to correct the error—but instead of restoring the land to the Ponca, Washington appropriated money to compensate for the Sioux attacks.

Buckskin Tobacco Bag, Decorated with Beads and Quillwork; Ponca
(*Museum of the American Indian*)

After the defeat of General Custer in 1876, Congress decided to send the northern tribes to Indian Territory, and the peaceful Ponca were included in the groups to be relocated. In February 1877, Standing Bear and eight other chiefs went to Indian Territory to inspect the new lands, and were dismayed at the alien climate and inhospitable geography. They refused to designate any area as appropriate for their people, and asked to be returned home. The. U.S. Indian Inspector, Edward C. Kemble told them that if they wished to return, they would have to walk. The party reached the Niobrara 40 days later, having traveled the 500-mile distance on foot with one blanket each and a few dollars among them. They found the Indian Agent unwilling to listen to their protests; determined to force the Indians off their lands, he called on the military for support.

Under such threats, Kemble was able to persuade 170 Ponca men, women, and children to journey south to Indian Territory in late April, but Standing Bear remained adamant, and the Agent had him imprisoned. Shortly thereafter, a new Agent, E. A. Howard arrived to replace Kemble and released the now bitter chief. Fruitless negotiations continued into May, and finally armed soldiers were moved into the area to force the removal of the 500 remaining Ponca. The journey to Indian Territory took 50 days, during which time bad weather and disease severely debilitated the people; in the following year, on the Quapaw Reservation, almost a fourth of the tribe died. They were given new and better land 150 miles away, but the high death rate continued, and included the children of Standing Bear himself.

In January, desiring to bury his son on the old Ponca land, Standing Bear set out for the Niobrara with 66 followers. They managed to reach the Omaha Reservation safely, where they asked to borrow seed and land. The Ponca were about to put in a crop when forces under the command of General George Crook arrived with orders to return them to Indian Territory. They were placed under guard at Fort Omaha, where Crook and a newspaper correspondent, Thomas H. Tibbles, visited them and were appalled at their physical condition and the history of their troubles.

Accounts of their tragic story appeared in the Omaha newspapers, citizens became interested, and Standing Bear was given an opportunity to tell his story in a local church, where he repeated his narrative to a crowded audience. Two lawyers, A. J. Poppleton and John L. Webster, offered their services and Judge Elmer S. Dundy served Crook with a writ of habeas corpus to determine by what authority he was holding the Ponca group. The United States attorney protested that the Indians had no right to habeas corpus, because they were not "persons within the meaning of the law." Thus began the great civil rights case, *Standing Bear vs. Crook*, on April 18, 1879.

It was a short trial. Standing Bear's speech to the bench climaxed the trial: "I want to save myself and my tribe. . . . If a White man had land, and someone should swindle him, that man would try to get it back, and you would not blame him. . . . My brothers, a power which I cannot resist crowds me down to the ground. I need help." Judge Dundy ruled not only that "an Indian is a person within the meaning of the law," but also that in peacetime there was no authority to force Indians to move, or to be confined against their will. General Crook was the first to congratulate Standing Bear after the decision was read. Then the chief and his followers set out for the Niobrara, where they were allotted a few hundred acres of land. Upon hearing the decision in thier case, the other Ponca people asked to return north to their old homes Fearful that a precedent would be set that any tribe could leave any reservation—and uneasily conscious that a majority did not like the areas to which they had been assigned and could not make a living on them—the Commissioner of Indian Affairs ruled that Dundy's decision applied only to Standing Bear and his people. *Sic transit juris.*

In the winter of 1879–1880, Standing Bear went on a lecture tour of the East, accompanied by Tibbles and Susette and Francis LaFlesche, who translated his history of the Ponca. He was enthusiastically received, and the government finally appropriated funds to improve the lot of the Ponca people; nevertheless, those in Indian Territory were never allowed to return home.

Standing Bear died in September 1908, around the age of 80. He is remembered as one of the first leaders to advocate nonviolent resistance to military force, to fight illegal acts through the courts, and to use the power of an informed and aroused public opinion to achieve some element of justice for his people.

Stumbling Bear (ca. 1832–1903)

Stumbling Bear (1832–1903)
(*Smithsonian Institution, National Anthropological Archives*)

Setimkia, more accurately translated as "Charging Bear," meaning an animal pressing down or bearing down upon one, was an early Kiowa foe of the White man who worked for peace in his later years. He was a cousin of the celebrated chief Kicking Bird and was renowned as a warrior in his youth. As did most Kiowa at the time, Stumbling Bear participated equally in raids on both neighboring Indian tribes and Whites. In 1854, he sought to avenge his brother's death by leading a war party against the Pawnee, but instead, met with some Sauk and Fox warriors who drove them off with superior firepower.

The Kiowa quickly learned that they would have to acquire a good supply of the wonderful new "smoke sticks" if they were to maintain their position on the Plains and much of their subsequent raiding of White wagon trains was with that purpose in mind. In 1856, Stumbling Bear led an expedition against the Navajo which was successful in obtaining a large amount of loot; and throughout the 1860s he led his band into battle on many separate occasions throughout the Kiowa territory. With Big Bow, Big Tree, Satanta, and Satank he was the scourge of the Southern Plains, and in 1865 he was the major force uniting the Kiowa against Kit Carson.

But shortly after the signing of the Treaty of Medicine Lodge in 1867, Stumbling Bear joined with Kicking Bird as an all-out advocate of peaceful accommodation with the White man. In 1872 he served on a delegation of Kiowa chiefs visiting Washington, and in 1878 the government built a home for him on the reservation in which he lived until his death. He died at Fort Sill in 1903, the last surviving Kiowa chief from the old Plains days.

Carl Sweezy (ca. 1880–1953)

Carl Sweezy (1880–1953)
(*Oklahoma Historical Society*)

Wattan (also Waatina), meaning black, was an Arapaho artist who was one of the best Indian painters of the turn-of-the-century era. He was born sometime between 1879 and 1881 near Darlington, on the old Cheyenne–Arapaho Reservation in Oklahoma. His father was Hinan Ba Seth (Big Man); his mother died when he was very young. The boy was raised as an orphan in mission schools in Indian Territory, and then went on to high school in Halstead, Kansas.

While at the Mennonite School in Kansas, his older brother took the name of Fieldie Sweezy, after the railway agent there; the other children of the family took the same surname, and Wattan became Carl Sweezy. Returning home to Washington Crossing, in Oklahoma, he began to draw. When anthropologist James Mooney arrived to record the customs and arts of the Arapaho, he could not find any experienced person to serve as an artist. Fortunately, he saw some of Carl's work and proceeded to train the young man to "paint only what is Indian and to paint it accurately."

This collaboration, lasting from 1900–1910, was a great success and by far the most prolific period in Sweezy's life; to the end of his career, Carl Sweezy said that he painted "in the Mooney way." After finishing his work with Mooney, Carl went off to attend Carlisle Indian School, but returned to the reservation due to illness. He began playing professional baseball once his strength was regained, first in Enid, Oklahoma and then with an all-Indian team that toured throughout the country. In Portland, Oregon, he saw some of his unsigned paintings, work he had done for Mooney, displayed at the Lewis and Clark Exposition. From then on, he valued his work more highly and signed most of it.

Although he retired in 1920 to paint full-time, he really never made a living from his art. For many years he was a farmer and a dairyman, as he and his wife Hattie Powless, an Oneida, raised two sons and a daughter. Yet he still continued to paint and his works began to appear in museums and private collections. He produced Indian scenes which reflected both the contemporary and historic periods in Indian life; his work was done in vivid color with careful attention to detail.

His traditional two-dimensional drawings, orderly and balanced in design, were drawn from his own experiences, and from the rich heritage of the Arapaho. He spent many long hours listening to the stories the elders told of the hunts and the battles, the freedom and the glory of the days gone by. After the death of his wife in 1944, he retired to Oklahoma City, where he lived with friends until his death at Lawton, Oklahoma on May 28, 1953. A book of his paintings, *The Arapaho Way*, was published in 1966.

Sword Bearer (1863–1887)

Sword Bearer was also called "Man Who Carries a Sword," Cheeztah-paezh, Chesetopah, or Sheetapah, "Wraps His Tail." He was a part-Crow–part-Bannock war leader of the Crow tribe in the last part of the 19th century. His name comes from an occasion when the Cheyenne gave him a red-painted cavalry saber which he carried into battle from that time on. He was also known as the Crow Messiah, due to his magical skills.

On one occasion when the Crow were facing the United States troops, Sword Bearer went forward, boasting that with his sword he would silence their fire. Astonishingly, the single cannon which the troops had either misfired or the powder failed to ignite. The result of this seemingly magical power caused the troops to retreat in disarray.

He participated in the great 1887 Sun Dance, after which he engaged in a skirmish with the Army on November 5, 1887 at the Crow Agency; taunting the troops and charging them with his sword in hand, he was killed at the age of 24.

Quincy Tahoma (1920–1956)

He was also known as Tohoma from *tahoma*, "Water Edge." He was a Navajo artist who was one of the most successful products of the Santa Fe Indian School Studio in New Mexico. He was born in 1920 near Tuba City, Arizona and was raised by his mother. As a boy he learned many of the traditional Navajo religious chants and practiced the ancient art of sand painting. From this background came many of his inspirations.

"Deer Family," Watercolor Painting by Quincy Tahoma; Navajo (*Museum of Northern Arizona; Marc Gaede Photo*)

After studying at Santa Fe, from 1936–1940, he served overseas during World War II in the Signal Corps. Returning home, he turned all of his energies into his art, and became a full-time painter. In 1946 his first published work appeared in the *Encyclopaedia Britannica Junior*. The clean precise lines, brilliant colors, and two-dimensional character of his work was typical of much of the Navajo painting done at that time in the Southwest. His work was simply more imaginative and his elegance of design and remarkable animal forms set him apart from others. He also broke away from the more formal patterns to some extent in his portrayal of dynamic movement—his subjects were not posed, but were caught in midaction.

He established a studio in which he welcomed other young Indian artists, many of whom have become well established as major exponents of painting. His most popular subjects were Indians of traditional times engaged in their everyday pursuits of hunting, fighting, and riding. He also produced many memorable landscape designs in a style which became his hallmark. One of his more individual idiosyncrasies, for which he became very well known, was his use of a small signature design which varied from painting to painting. Each signature design was in itself a miniature painting, depicting what he called "the end of the story"—a fancied termination of the narrative in the major painting itself.

Unfortunately, the disease which has affected so many gifted Indian artists, alcoholism, also contributed to his own destruction and he died in Santa Fe in November 1956, at the age of 35. He left behind him a legacy of Indian art which has never been forgotten by those familiar with the field.

Taimah (ca. 1790–ca. 1830)

Taimah was also known as Tama, Tamah, or Taiomah, from *taima*, "Thunderclap," referring to the sudden sound of thunder. He was an important Mesquakie (Fox) Thunder clan leader born about 1790. Little is known of his early life, but he became the principal chief of the Mesquakie village after that tribe moved south to the area near Burlington in Des Moines County, Iowa.

Taimah was a prominent medicine man, noted for his curing ability, as well as for being a strong, courageous warrior. He was a firm friend of the White settlers in the region and is credited with saving the life of the Indian Agent at Prairie du Chien. When an embittered Wisconsin Indian set out to murder the agent, Taimah warned him ahead of time.

He was one of the signers of the Treaty between the Sauk and Fox people on August 4, 1824, involving the combining of the two tribes, and he subsequently became a major participant in Indian affairs in Iowa. He died in the Mesquakie village about 1830, a respected leader of his people. The name of the present-day Indian Reservation near Tama, Iowa, as well as the county of that name, were both established in his honor. He is also known as Faimah, the Bear, through an early error in transliteration.

Tall Bull (ca. 1830–1869)

Hotóakhihoois (also Hotúaeka'ash Tait or Otóah-hastis) was a major leader of the Cheyenne fighting society, the famed Dog Soldiers, during the period of Plains warfare in the 1860s. There were several other Cheyenne men who held the name Tall Bull, but this Dog Soldier chief was the most noted. His men were among the most feared warriors on the frontier, and many historians have since applied the term "Dog Soldiers" to fighters of all tribes in error. Tall Bull was allied with Roman Nose in many battles—especially during 1867 and 1868 near the Kansas–Nebraska border.

The Cheyenne feared and resented the White policy of forcing Indians to abandon their traditional hunting grounds to settle on reservations established for their use. Greatly encouraged by the successes of Red Cloud in the North, they determined to fight the United States soldiers rather than accept confinement. Many battles were fought during the next several years towards that goal, sometimes with Indian victories, but more often in vain—slowly, little by little, the attrition of Cheyenne military strength increased. A great loss occurred in September 1868 when Roman Nose, the great war leader, was killed, adding to the burden of Cheyenne losses.

Tall Bull continued to lead his Dog Soldiers with valor and brilliance, but more and more soldiers were being sent against the tribe. At the same time, some bands were more friendly than others, even to the point of being willing to come in and settle on reservations. But the repeated attacks by Whites against friendly Indians, brought to a head by the savage destruction of Black Kettle and his village on the Washita River by General Custer destroyed any further trust.

Now implacably turned against the White troops, the Cheyenne began raiding along the border area even more violently, and in the early summer of 1869, General Eugene A. Carr was sent with a troop of soldiers and Pawnee scouts to try to bring the area under military control. They camped near the Republican River, not far from where a small party of Sioux and Cheyenne Dog Soldiers were located. The latter attacked the soldiers, hoping to drive off their horses, but the Pawnee scouts learned of their presence and frustrated the effort.

The next day, Tall Bull moved with his people to Summit Springs, intending to camp and then attack the soldiers in force the next day. However, the Pawnee scouts had located the village and General Carr determined to strike first. On July 11, 1869, he attacked early in the morning, surprising the Indians; in the savage battle which followed, Tall Bull was killed, and the Cheyenne were completely defeated.

Tammany (ca. 1625–ca. 1701)

Tam'ma-ny or Tamanend, "The Affable," (and many variant spellings) was the chief of the Unami (Turtle clan) Delaware, a greatly admired and written-about figure of the late 17th and early 18th centuries. He

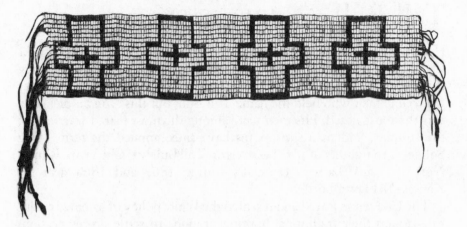

Wampum Belt Given to William Penn
by Tammany, 1683
(*Museum of the American Indian*)

lived along the Delaware River, probably somewhere in what is now Bucks County, Pennsylvania. There are few facts known about his life but there are many legends and tales that flourished long after his death. He is supposed to have welcomed William Penn to America on October 27, 1682. His name certainly appears as one of the signers of two treaties made at Shackamaxon with Penn on June 23, 1683, and a third treaty signed on July 5, 1697.

At a meeting between Indian leaders and the Provincial Council of Pennsylvania held in 1694, Tammany pledged his friendship to the colonists and historians seem to be in general agreement that he remained loyal to the Whites for the rest of his life. The colonists, in turn, endowed him with "every good and noble quality that a human being may possess," according to an account of the era. People were fascinated by the tale that Tammany fought and drove out of his country an evil spirit who had tried to become a ruler of the Lenni Lenape (Delawares). The duel that they fought lasted for many days, during which whole forests were trampled into prairies.

Many of the societies that flourished during the early years of the American Revolution adopted the name of the Lenni Lenape chief as a symbol of American resistance to British rule for one reason or another, and he became known as Saint Tammany, patron saint of America. Of the many organizations which bore his name, only two survived into the 19th century: "The Improved Order of Red Men" which was a social, fraternal, and benevolent organization and "The Society of St. Tammany" which was founded in 1789, and eventually became the Democratic party organization of New York.

Tammany lived into the 18th century, and while the exact date of his death is unknown, it was before July 1, 1701, at which time a comment upon his career was published. He was buried in the Tammany Burial Grounds near Chalfonte, Pennsylvania.

Tarhe (1742-1818)

Tar'he was a major Wyandot chief commonly known as "The Crane," from the supposed meaning of his Indian name; the term *tarhe* literally refers to "the tree" or "at the tree." His name actually seems to have come from the French appellation *Chef Grue*, a reference to his tall, slender build. He was born near Detroit in 1742 and was a member of the Porcupine clan. As a youth, Tarhe fought against American settlers, staunchly resisting the frontier movement in the late 18th century. He was at Cornstalk's side at Point Pleasant in 1774, and was one of the 13 chiefs who took part in the Battle of Fallen Timbers when General Anthony Wayne led the victorious American forces; wounded in the arm, he was reportedly the only chief who managed to escape. Recognizing the overwhelming strength of the Americans, Tarhe became a major influence in support of the Treaty of Greenville in 1795, even though he knew it meant that the Indians would have to abandon their homelands and move farther west.

Early in the 19th century, when Tecumseh began forming his confederation to resist White encroachment, Tarhe counseled his people not to join. In the War of 1812, although he was then 70 years old, he led his warriors in several battles against the English; they were active at the Battle of the Thames when Tecumseh was killed. Although in some respects in this period he could be regarded as a White Man's Indian—indeed, William Henry Harrison judged him to be "Intelligent and upright, the noblest of all the chiefs"—he was still able to maintain the respect and affection of most of the Indians in the Northwest Territory.

Tarhe was the primary priest of the Wyandot and Keeper of the Calumet, a symbol of the coalition which bound the tribes north of the Ohio River in a loose alliance for mutual benefit and protection. He died at Crane Town, near Upper Sandusky, Ohio, in November 1818, at the age of 76. His funeral was attended by both Indians and Whites who came from hundreds of miles around. He is recorded as being a lithe, wiry man of great endurance. He was mild in temperament, yet stern and determined.

Carved Wooden Ladle Belonging to Tarhe; Wyandot
(*Museum of the American Indian*)

Tavibo (ca. 1810–1870)

Távibo or Táb-be-bo, "Sun Man," also known as "The Paiute Prophet," was an important medicine man, and the father of Wovoka, founder of the Ghost Dance religion. He was born around 1810 in Mason Valley, near Walker Lake, in the territory which eventually became part of the state of Nevada. During his lifetime the Indians began to be forced out of the valleys by a slow but steady flow of armed, often dangerous, Whites. Though there were occasional raids and battles, most of the Indians either tried to adjust to the White man's civilization or moved farther back into the mountains.

As they witnessed their way of life being destroyed, and nothing of value replacing it, the Paiute looked to their religious leaders for help. Tavibo had a vision that an earthquake would swallow up the Whites and leave the Indians to inherit the earth. However, it seemed unbelievable that a quake would take only White people and leave all of the Indians unscathed, so Tavibo sought another vision. It was then revealed to him that the earthquake would destroy all men but that the

Indians alone would be resurrected. With this correction, his prophecy attracted many Paiute and members of other tribes, all of whom were desperate to believe anything which offered the promise of a better life.

Tavibo became a respected and powerful man but when the earthquake did not materialize, many people lost their faith in his powers. Subsequently, he had another vision, again an earthquake which told him that only his followers would be saved. Somehow, he managed to retain a body of faithful followers, although never the number of believers which he enjoyed at first. He died in 1870 with his prophecies unfilled, leaving to his teen-age son his mystic gifts, little realizing what the far-flung results of Wovoka's work would actually be within the next 20 years.

Louis Tawanima (ca. 1879–1969)

Tawanima, from Hopi *tawa* "sun," and *nima* "how measured," was one of the first American Indians to participate in Olympic Games competition. He was born at Shungopovi, Second Mesa, Arizona, about 1879 into the Sand clan. His early life is not recorded; he attended Carlisle where he was coached by Glenn S. "Pop" Warner. He participated along with Jim Thorpe in many track and field contests, particularly the 1908 Olympic Games in London, where he was successful in the 26-mile run, and in the 1912 Olympics at Stockholm, in which he took a silver medal in the 10,000-meter run.

Tawanima also competed in many races in the United States, winning a 12-mile marathon in New York City in January 1910, and the famed "Bunion Derby" from New York to California in 1925. Louis came in first, but was disqualified for infraction of the rules—he ran too fast, thereby injuring the audience show which the promoter had relied upon to pay the costs.

Louis returned home and retired to a life of farming. In 1957 he was enshrined in the Arizona Hall of Fame. In his old age he became blind and on January 18, 1969, while returning home at night following a religious ceremony, he apparently misjudged the path and suffered a fatal fall off of the mesa cliff at Shungopovi. The name Tawanima is also commonly spelled Tewanima.

Tawaquaptewa (ca. 1882–1960)

Also spelled Tewaquoptiwa, "Sun in the Horizon," was one of the best known Hopi leaders. He was born about 1882 at Oraibi, Third

Mesa, Arizona; his father was Cheauka, "clay" or "adobe," of the Bear clan. Until about 1902 when he was selected as village chief by the clan elders, he seems not to have been prominent in public affairs. "I paid more attention to girls than to politics, since I never expected to be chief," he said. But once he succeeded his uncle Lolóloma following Lolóloma's death from smallpox in 1901, he represented his people to the best of his ability.

Unfortunately, these were the most troubled times in recent Hopi history, and Tawaquaptewa was destined to endure an equally troubled period of leadership. For more than three centuries the tribe had been relatively untouched by the world swirling around outside their isolated mesas, save for occasional visits from Whites—or raids by enemy Indians. But with exploring and surveying parties coming into the village more frequently, the pressures which had been suffered elsewhere by Indians inexorably descended upon the Hopi. These pressures, in turn, levied an increasing impact upon the traditional Hopi way of life.

As with most tribes, the Hopi were divided between militant opposition to and passive acceptance of the Whites. Tawaquaptewa initially supported the role of his uncle in welcoming the Whites. On the other hand, Lolóloma's rival Lomahongyoma had steadfastly opposed any White inroads whatsoever; he was succeeded by a younger man, Youkioma, who continued this policy. Both of the young men were bold and impatient, eager to show their new authority—worse, the situation was exacerbated by stubborn and ill-advised interference from missionaries and government agents. Finally, dissension got to the point where the village was split down the middle. In September 1906, a tug-of-war game was held, and the losers—in this instance, those hostile to the Whites—were forced to leave and establish a new settlement, which eventually became Hotevilla. This is one of the few such violent schisms in human history solved without bloodshed.

Although Tawaquaptewa had emerged triumphant from this clash, he was not prepared for the next event. The Indian Agent Leupp, perhaps with the misguided intention of having the village chief become accustomed to American ways, bundled him off in October 1906 to Riverside Indian School in California to learn English and the Christian religion. This was disastrous, coming as it did at a crucial time when the village was in need of all the leadership it could possibly assemble. (One wonders if this suggests an ulterior motive as well.) Tawaquaptewa protested that his people needed him—as they did—but in vain. Indeed, during his absence, Lomahongyoma, the dissenter, tried to return to Oraibi, perhaps to make himself chief. But the people refused to support him, and he eventually left, to establish still a third village at Bakabi in 1907.

Upon his return to Oraibi in 1910, Tawaquaptewa was furious at the effort made to unseat him, and even more bitter at the actions of the Agent who had acted in such a high-handed manner, and whom he felt had supported his opponents. He turned abruptly from his former

Tawaquaptewa (1882-1960)
(*Southwest Museum*)

289

Kwewu, "Fox" Kachina Doll Made by Tawaquaptewa
(*Frederick J. Dockstader*)

friendly attitude toward the Whites to one of bitter, unbending antagonism to everything White.

Much of this bitterness was passed on to his people, and he changed from a somewhat paternal leader to a suspicious, sour, and jealous man who seemed to take out his frustrations on the village residents. Many of them turned away from him, became Christian, and moved to the lower village, Kiaktsomovi (New Oraibi), thereby weakening the old village fabric even more. Some residents who wanted to "stay Hopi" migrated to the satellite colony village of Moenkopi, near Tuba City. Thus, although Oraibi could justly claim to be the oldest continuously inhabited village in the United States, having been founded around 1125–1150 A.D., the annual residency declined from about 600 in 1900 to 350 at the time of the split. By 1950, half a century later, fewer than 100 still maintained residence there.

One of the activities by which Tawaquaptewa became best known to Whites who visited the village was his craftwork. He became a well-known carver of the small wooden Kachina dolls, in which he established a monopoly, thereby protecting his economic base. At first his products were typical of the traditional forms and designs, but in later years he developed an individual style based upon sheer invention.

Tawaquaptewa died on April 30, 1960 at Oraibi, a lonely old man; his wife Naninonsi (Nasingonsi) of the Parrot clan had died in 1955. They had one adopted daughter, Betty. Public claims that he was 106 years old at the time of his death seem not to be substantiated by any existing records.

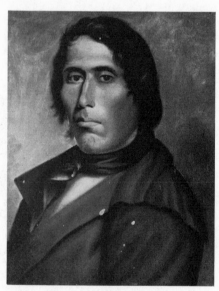

Tecumseh (1768–1813)
(*Field Museum of Natural History*)

Tecumseh (1768?–1813)

Tecumtha or Tikamthi, "Goes Through One Place to Another," a reference to the "Shooting Star," by which name he was also known was a famous Shawnee chief considered by many to have been the most effective Indian opponent of the United States. He was born into the Crouching Panther clan in March 1768 at Piqua, on the Mad River near Springfield, Ohio. He was one of eight children born to Puckeshinwa (or Pukeesheno), an important Shawnee war chief, and Methoataske (or Meetheetashe), a part-Creek–Cherokee woman. His brother, said to be his twin, was Tenskwátawa, "The Shawnee Prophet."

The Shawnee at this time were nomadic, living on the frontier of Ohio during the Revolutionary War period. After Lord Dunmore's War in 1774, officials ceded the land north of the Ohio River to the Indians, but settlers nevertheless continued to move into the region. Chief Cornstalk tried to maintain peace, but in 1777 he was murdered by the Whites while meeting with them to discuss the increasing conflicts. In revenge, the Shawnees embarked on a war of retaliation in 1780, in which Tecumseh took part. He was a brave, skilled fighter, but was always known as a leader who would not stand for barbarism or arbitrary, unnecessary killing—a code which made him respected throughout his life.

290

By his early twenties, Tecumseh had already become a recognized leader of his people. He and his warriors attacked the encroaching settlers throughout the Indian lands, often in alliance with Creek and Cherokee neighbors. A climactic battle took place on August 20, 1794, when troops under General Anthony Wayne defeated the Indians at Greenville, Ohio. The following spring most of the Indian leaders signed the Greenville Treaty, which ceded a large portion of land to the Whites; however, Tecumseh refused to sign and with a large number of followers who also resented White encroachment, he moved to Indiana. There, in the late 1790s, he met a White woman, Rebecca Galloway, who taught him English and read to him from various history books, including the *Bible*. These studies and his own observations led to the final development of a conviction he had long held: all Indian land belonged to Indians as a whole and not to one particular tribe. Historically, tribes had been free to roam at will, limited only by the occupancy and use by other Indians. There were no boundaries, fences, or border guards—these were all the creations of the Whites. As owners of the land in common, all tribes had the right and the obligation to defend their territory against White invasion. As a corollary, no one tribe could dispossess the other tribes by signing away this land. If in unity there could be strength, then perhaps an Indian Nation could be established to deal with the United States as an equal.

This was a very heady doctrine, and one which gained him many enthusiastic followers. In 1805, Tecumseh's twin brother, then named Lauliwásikau, had a vision which fit beautifully into this program. He took the name Tenskwátawa (The Open Door), and preached a return to the traditional Indian ways and the rejection of all White things. He soon attracted a large following and allied himself with Tecumseh. In May 1808, the two brothers established a Shawnee village on the west bank of the Tippecanoe River where it joins the Wabash. Tecumseh then set out on the first of several pilgrimages to persuade other tribes that his plan held their only hope for survival. He eventually visited all of the tribes in the Midwestern region; and although he was rejected by some, he nonetheless succeeded in rallying many groups to his cause. In this effort, Tenskwátawa's reputation and religious influence as a powerful preacher was important, and since Tecumseh was a stirring orator in his own right, the two made an extremely effective pair. The initial successes of this drive for converts enabled Tecumseh to establish an alliance with the British, who were an important source of arms for Indians in the area.

Tension was increasing between the Americans and the British, who looked upon Tecumseh's Indian Confederacy as perhaps the nucleus of a buffer state between United States expansion and the territorial integrity of Canada. The Americans also recognized the potential threat to their own plans, and became concerned over the brothers' activities. At first they thought the prime mover was Tenskwátawa, whom they called The Shawnee Prophet, but soon came to realize that Tecumseh was the greater threat. In 1809, William Henry Harrison, Governor of the Northwest Territory, induced some of the weaker chiefs to accept $7000 and an annuity of $1750 in exchange for 3,000,000 acres of

Indian land. Tecumseh was enraged at this maneuver. The next year he gathered a huge force of warriors from many tribes at Tippecanoe, and accompanied by his brother, went to meet with Harrison at Vincennes, the United States territorial headquarters. There he insisted that land sales were invalid unless Indians as a whole agreed to them. The Whites rejected this notion, and the conference eventually ended in mutual hostility. Harrison later wrote: "The implicit obedience and respect which the followers of Tecumseh pay him is really astonishing and . . . bespeaks him as one of those uncommon geniuses, which spring up occasionally to produce revolutions."

Tecumseh recognized that the time had finally come to activate the Indian Confederacy he had been trying to establish. Harrison knew he must strike a major blow before the alliance could be formalized. On November 6, 1811, while Tecumseh was away, Harrison maneuvered Tenskwátawa into a battle outside the village of Tippecanoe. Both sides fought to a standstill, but by the next day most of the Indians had vanished; Harrison's troops moved into the village and destroyed it. While this was hardly the major victory he sought, Harrison had managed to throw the Indian union fatally off balance.

As Tecumseh tried to rally his forces in the wake of the battle, the War of 1812 broke out. Both the British and the Americans tried to persuade the Indians to join them, which further disintegrated the Confederation, as each tribe chose sides. Tecumseh and many others joined the British and played a key role in many subsequent battles. Eventually, however, the British began to retreat, and Tecumseh grew worried as he saw many of the British, especially commanders like General Crocker, lose heart. Finally, on October 5, 1813, the Indians took a firm stand at the Battle of the Thames against what turned out to be vastly superior American forces. Tecumseh and many other Indians were killed, and his dream of an Indian Nation united against the Whites died with him. He was 44 years old at his death.

Tomahawk Presented to Tecumseh by Col. Henry Proctor
(*Museum of the American Indian*)

Teedyuscung (ca. 1705–1763)

Friendship Wampum Belt Exchanged by Teedyuscung with Gov. William Denny, 1756
(*Museum of the American Indian*)

Derived from *kekeuskung* or *kikeuskund*, "The Healer," (some say "Earth Trembler") was an important Delaware chief of the Turtle clan born around 1705 in the area of present-day Trenton, New Jersey. His father was a well-known Delaware man known to the colonists as

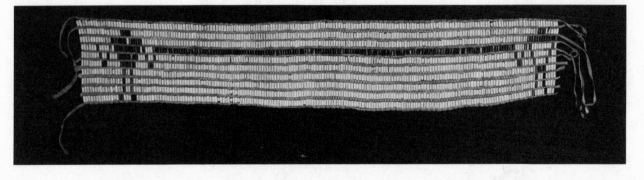

"Old Captain Harris." Around 1730 Teedyuscung and part of his tribe moved to the upper Delaware River in eastern Pennsylvania. His early years were spent in making and selling brooms and baskets, which built him a reputation for integrity and gave him the nickname, "Honest John." In 1737 he was one of the most outspoken Indians protesting the infamous "Walking Purchase" by which the Indians lost much of their Pennsylvania lands.

Under the influence of Moravian missionaries at Gnadenhütten, he became a Christian in 1750, being baptized as Gideon, "War Trumpet;" his wife was named Elizabeth. He was loyal for a period, but his links to his people were too strong to be easily broken; in 1763 he turned away from the mission when the Delaware called for leadership in their battle with the Iroquois and the westward moving White settlers. He became war chief in 1754.

For many years, the Delaware, who had ceded their lands relatively peacefully, had been looked down upon by both Indian and White. The Iroquois had sold their [Delaware] land, and ignored their protests, calling them "women." The tribe had moved away meekly in the past but were now ready to take a stand. Teedyuscung rallied the Delaware, Mahican, and Shawnee peoples, all of whom were pressed between the English and the French, to attack the settlers in the Wyoming Valley. He proved to be a strong and effective leader and by 1756 had forced the English to begin negotiations for peace and fair treatment. Announcing that "The Delawares are no longer the slaves of the Six Nations," Teedyuscung pressed the British to agree that his people would never again be deprived of their land. Hoping to win this accord with the British, he helped to persuade the tribes living farther to the west to desert the French cause and to side with the British.

This strength and control of the several Indian tribes gained him the title, "King of the Delawares," by which he was known throughout the Pennsylvania region. Eventually his efforts, as well as the termination of French rule in the west—in part due to the efforts of the missionary, Christian Post—made possible the British victory at Fort Duquesne in 1758. As a reward for his service, a town was built for him and his followers in the Wyoming Valley.

Teedyuscung was a heavy drinker like many of the Indian and White leaders of the time. According to Conrad Weiser, a colonial interpreter and mediator, "Though he is a drunkard and a very irregular man, yet he is a man that can think well, and I believe him to be sincere. . . ." He was a strong and able negotiator, and in his several dealings with Governor Denny of Pennsylvania, frequently convinced the latter of the justice of his claims. He was able to persuade many of the colonial authorities that stolen Indian lands should be returned or that fair compensation should be made. But towards the end of his life, the old chief accepted £400 to withdraw the charges of fraud which he had maintained throughout his life in connection with the Walking Purchase of Delaware lands. This abrupt reversal of a lifelong claim has never been explained.

On April 16, 1763, he was burned to death in his house at Wajomick when it was set afire, presumably by some of his enemies among the Iroquois. He had one son, Tachgokanhelle, who survived him.

Kateri Tekakwitha (1656–1680)

Tegaquitha, "The Lily of the Mohawks," as she was popularly known, was the first recorded Indian Roman Catholic nun in North America. She was born in 1656 at Gandawague Castle, near Fonda, New York, to a Mohawk father and a Christianized Algonquin mother of the Turtle clan. During her childhood, her parents and a younger brother died from smallpox, and she was left a badly scarred and pockmarked orphan. Never a pretty child, she was adopted by her uncle, a Mohawk chief, but left largely to herself. She was always a "loner" who was apparently quite religiously inclined, and at about the age of ten became strongly influenced by Jesuit missionaries. Eventually on Easter Sunday, in 1635, she was baptized despite the strong opposition of her uncle and took the name Kateri (Catherine).

After this event, she was shunned by most of her tribe, especially when she refused to work in the fields on Sundays. In 1677 she escaped from her village and traveled the 200 miles by canoe to join a colony of Christian Indians at Sault St. Louis, not far from Montreal. Here, her life was one of deep asceticism and piety. She sought to establish a convent on Heron Island on the St. Lawrence River, but her plans were rejected by Church authorities; as a result she abandoned the project and became a nun.

It was a time of perfervid piety at Sault St. Louis, and in her zeal to obtain complete penance, Kateri persuaded a friend to whip her, in the custom of the day—a practice which she followed every Sunday for a year. Although the savage whippings became too much for her body to withstand, she resolutely continued the practice. Refusing any aid, she persevered in this mortification until she died at the age of 24 on April 17, 1680 at the Ville Marie of St. Francis Xavier. She was buried near La Prairie, Quebec. Her devotions and self-denial were so remarkable that many miraculous visions and cures were claimed in her name, and in 1884 she was proposed as a candidate for canonization, and in 1932 her name was formally presented to the Vatican for consideration.

Ten Bears (1792–1873)

Also known as Ten Elks, Paria Semen (also Parra-wa-semen, Pariasea-men, Parooway Semehno, Parrywasaymen, or Parywahsaymen) was an eloquent, poetic speaker and adroit negotiator who effectively represented his Comanche followers. Although he was apparently never active as a great warrior, he was still held in high esteem by the tribe, who chose him to be their delegate at many peace conferences with the Whites. His early years were seemingly uneventful; he was born about 1792 on the Southwestern Plains and by middle age had come to be a leading speaker for the Comanche.

He visited Washington, D.C., in 1863, but failed to win any significant concessions from the authorities. He signed the 1865 treaty at the Little Arkansas River and two years later was present as a speaker at the Council at Medicine Lodge, Kansas, which resulted in a treaty whereby the Comanche agreed to go on a recently established reservation in the southwestern section of the Indian Territory.

Though he was always a peacemaker, Ten Bears was equally determined as an Indian patriot who resented the White man's intrusion. During a long and eloquent address at the Medicine Lodge conference, he stated, "You said you wanted to put us upon a reservation. . . . I was born upon the prairie, where the wind blew free and there was nothing to break the light of the sun. I was born where there were no enclosures and where everything drew a free breath. . . I want to die there, and not within walls."

But the Whites were not there to negotiate; they were there to dictate. Previous treaties had "not made allowance for the rapid growth of the White race," and the Comanche, Kiowa, and other tribes of the Central Plains were forced to sign a treaty whereby they gave up most of their lands in exchange for a reservation. The days of free hunting were over and the Indians were expected to become peaceful farmers.

Ten Bears set off on another futile journey to Washington, D.C., with other leaders from the Southern Plains, always hoping that this time it would be different, that the White man would honor his promises, but it was not to be. He returned home to the hated reservation, where he died at Fort Sill a few weeks later, in 1873.

Ten Bears (1792–1873)
(*Museum of the American Indian*)

Tendoy (ca. 1834–1907)

Also known as Tendoi, "The Climber," he was a celebrated Lemhi Bannock chief who was primarily noted for his friendliness toward Whites. He was born in the Boise River area in Idaho, about 1834, the son of Kontakayak (also Tamkahanka), a Bannock war chief, and a Tukyudeka woman related to Washakie. As a boy he was known as Untendoip, "He Likes Broth," a reference to his healthy appetite. After his father died in combat with the Blackfoot, Tendoy became the war chief of a band of Bannock, Shoshoni, and Tukuarika people inhabiting the Lemhi Valley area in Idaho.

Tendoy and a few of his close associates kept themselves relatively well-off economically by maintaining astute trading relations with the Whites in western Montana; they were mostly active in keeping the miners supplied with their various needs. Most of the other Bannock people lived in poverty, however, until the United States established an Indian Agency at Fort Hall, Idaho, in 1868.

As more and more settlers moved into the valley, Tendoy kept to his policy of friendship, observing a peaceful stance even during the Bannock War and the Nez Percé troubles in 1878. He was even urged to kill a few Whites in order to impress Washington with his potential for trouble; it was thought that his people could thereby gain greater

Shoshoni Delegation at Washington, D.C. (Tendoy and Tyhee)
(*Idaho State Historical Society*)

consideration and appropriations from Congress. His reply was vigorous: "I have not the blood of a single White man in my camp, nor do I intend such."

As far as is known, the people never opposed his leadership and policy of accommodation—perhaps because they were permitted to live in peace and prosperity alongside relatively few White settlers. In that region, at the time, there was land enough for all. He worked closely during his life with Tyhee, another important Bannock leader.

In February 1875, President Grant issued an Executive Order which allowed the Bannock to remain in the Lemhi Valley, one of the few times such permission was achieved by Native inhabitants. A few years later, he went to Washington to represent the Bannock people, and on May 14, 1880, he expressed the appreciation of his people for their being allowed to stay in their homeland; but on February 23, 1892, the inevitable pressure again caused removal. This time a treaty was signed whereby the Bannock moved to Fort Hall, Idaho, where they remain today.

When the Treaty of 1892 was signed, Tendoy was awarded a lifetime pension of $15 per month by the government. He settled down to farming in the area, and died at Fort Hall on May 9, 1907, at the age of 73. He had one son, Topamby. Some years later a monument to his memory was erected by local residents.

Tenskwátawa (ca. 1768–ca. 1837)

Originally named Lauliwásikau, "Loud Voice," from *lalawéthika*, "Rattle," this famous Shawnee visionary and preacher was commonly called "The Shawnee Prophet" by White neighbors. He was born in March 1768, at Piqua, on the Mad River near Springfield, Ohio, and is said to have been the twin brother of Tecumseh. His father was Puckeshinwa, a Shawnee war chief and his mother was Methoataske, a part-Creek–Cherokee woman.

Until about 1805, Lauliwásikau led a relatively ordinary life; some accounts indicate that he was a drunkard. But in that year he had a vision which shocked him out of his old dissolute ways: he had been taken to the spirit world, where he saw his past ills and had a view of the future. He was called upon to use his remarkable talents as an orator and a teacher to bring a message of hope to the Shawnee people: the Indian must return to the ways of his forefathers, must reject all White customs and products (especially liquor), and must honor the ancient system of common ownership of property among all tribes. This was a time of trouble for the Indians, who saw their traditional way of life being ruthlessly destroyed by the White settlers; like all tribes, the reversion to the past was an inevitable reaction. Many Shawnee people became devout followers of his preaching and soon word of his inspirational guidance spread to other tribes. When he predicted the eclipse of the sun in 1806, his fame as a prophet was assured.

At this time he took on the name Tenskwátawa, "The Open Door," from *tenskwátawaskwate* "a door," and *thénui*, "to be open." He also began to work more closely with his brother; whether by design or by coincidence, the ideas and messages of the two complemented and reinforced each other. Both taught that the White ways should be shunned and that the way to preserve the Indian heritage was for all tribes to unite as common owners of the land against the westward movement of the frontier settlements. As Indian unrest spread, the Whites—especially William Henry Harrison and other influential officials of the Northwest Territory—became alarmed. At first they

Prayer Stick Belonging to Tenskwátawa; Shawnee
(*Cranbook Institute of Science*)

Tenskwatawa (1768–1837)
(*Thomas Gilcrease Institute of American History and Art*)

thought the prime leader of the movement was The Shawnee Prophet, but soon it became apparent that Tecumseh was the man to really fear. Governor Harrison met with Tecumseh several times, but without success.

In 1811, while Tecumseh was away persuading other tribes to join in a great Indian Confederation, both sides back in Indiana made ready for battle. Tenskwátawa, as his brother's deputy, was in command; though he was not a skilled nor particularly brave war leader, the Battle of Tippecanoe took place on November 7, 1811. Tenskwátawa kept back from the field of battle, making medicine, and predicting the imminent defeat of Harrison's forces. But the Indians were not yet prepared for the battle, their leadership was weak, and after a day of fighting they retreated into the forest. The soldiers advanced, destroyed the Indian village at Tippecanoe, and Tenskwátawa's prestige as a prophet and effective leader collapsed. He eventually moved to Canada, where he lived on a British government pension until 1826. Then he returned to Ohio, but soon moved west with the rest of the Shawnee people. The exact date of his death is uncertain; he apparently died in November 1837, at Argentine, Wyandotte County, Kansas.

Jim Thorpe (1888–1953)

James Francis Thorpe, Wathohuck, or "Bright Path," and his twin brother Charles were born near Prague, Oklahoma on May 28, 1888. Their father was Hiram Thorpe, a half-Sauk–Fox Indian and half-Irish farmer, and their mother was Charlotte View, the part-French granddaughter of the Sauk chief Black Hawk. The two boys were raised on a farm and lived and played in the outdoors, until Charles died at the age of nine. Young Jim was educated at the Sauk–Fox Reservation School and at Haskell Institute, before going on in 1904 to Carlisle Indian School. At that time the athletic coach was the great Glenn S. "Pop" Warner, who subsequently went on to coach at Pittsburgh, Stanford, and Temple Universities.

Warner recognized the inherent ability of the young man, and developed his talents to the point where Thorpe and his teammates defeated the best collegiate teams of the day, including Harvard, Army, and Pennsylvania. Thorpe was far more than just a fine football player. He was an all-round athlete and spent two summers playing semiprofessional baseball. Under Warner's tutelage, he prepared for the 1912 Olympic track and field contests. At the Stockholm games he stunned the Western world by winning both the pentathlon and the decathlon, a feat never accomplished before or since. King Gustav of Sweden presented him with a trophy and called him "the greatest athlete in the world."

But in 1913, the Amateur Athletic Union virtuously pointed to his semiprofessional baseball activity and revoked his amateur standing.

298

"I was simply an Indian schoolboy, not wise to the ways of the world," Thorpe wrote the AAU. "On the same teams I played with were several college men . . . all considered as amateurs." The simon-pure AAU made no allowance for naïveté however, and ordered him to return all Olympic medals and trophies—the greatest feats of the century were thus expunged from the Olympic record books.

Thorpe joined the New York Giants; unfortunately, he never learned to hit a curve ball and ended his baseball career in the minor leagues in 1919. The next year, at the age of 32, he helped organize the American Professional Football Association, and played for the Canton (Ohio) Bulldogs. He was still a spectacular attraction for the fans, and his team went undefeated in 1922 and 1923. "If he were playing today," remarked one contemporary sportswriter, Thorpe would be as rich as Joe Namath." But those were easier times, and Thorpe was a happy-go-lucky, hard-living "good sport," rather similar in personality to his near-contemporary, Babe Ruth. When he left professional football in 1929, he was far from wealthy.

The Thorpe name lived on, but the man himself fell into obscurity and hard times. He made occasional celebrity appearances and had a few stunt roles in the movies, but his athletic career had begun a slow decline. In 1937 he returned to Oklahoma and took part in Sauk–Fox tribal matters, opposing the new constitution that many Indians felt gave too much power to the federal government.

In the early 1940s he was a popular lecturer and in 1945 he joined the Merchant Marine. After the War, he was in California where the biographical motion picture, *Jim Thorpe—All-American*, was produced in 1950–1951. He died at the age of 64 in Lomita, California on March 28, 1953, and was buried near Carlisle Institute. Thorpe married three times—to Iva Miller, then Frieda Kirkpatrick, and lastly to Patricia Gladys Askew; in all, he had eight children. Physically, he was a large man, 6'1" tall, weighing 188 pounds.

In 1954, the towns of Mauch Chunk and East Mauch Chunk, in Pennsylvania, united and were renamed Jim Thorpe. In 1955, in his honor, the National Football League established the Jim Thorpe Memorial Trophy as a most valuable player award. Ironically, 20 years after his death, the AAU relented and replaced his records in the Olympic books.

An Associated Press poll of sportswriters in 1950 ranked Jim Thorpe as the "greatest American athlete of the first half of this century" . . . a fitting tribute to this magnificent Sauk sports champion.

James Francis Thorpe (1888–1953)
(*Pro Football Hall of Fame*)

Jerome Richard Tiger (1941-1967)

Köcha, as he signed a few of his early works, was a remarkably talented artist whose flowering career was ended abruptly by his death at the age of 26. He was born July 8, 1941 at Tahlequah, Oklahoma, the son of Reverend John M. Tiger, a Seminole, and Lucinda Lewis, a Creek.

Jerome Tiger (1941–1967)
(*Bjorne Holm Photo*)

He attended public school in Eufaula and Muskogee, and had a year's training at the Cleveland (Ohio) Engineering Institute.

Jerome Tiger, as he was usually known, served in the U.S. Naval Reserve from 1958 to 1960, but seems not to have worked seriously at painting until about 1962, when he submitted a few examples of his work to the Philbrook Indian Art Annual. His work was in a style which came to be recognizably original and effective with him. While in the so-called "traditional Indian style," his paintings were unique in their delicacy, strong color values, precise, miniaturized detail, and contained an unusual sense of depth perception. His scenes of Indian life and traditional mythology proved to be extraordinarily popular, and in the few short years he was active, he became one of the most sought-after Indian artists in the country.

In 1960 he married Margaret (Peggy) Lois Richmond, and had three children. Always something of a happy-go-lucky young man, he was playing with a small revolver on the night of August 13, 1967, when it suddenly went off, cutting short one of the most promising lives in the field of Indian art.

"The Intruders," Watercolor Painting by Jerome Tiger; Creek
(*Museum of the American Indian*)

Clarence Leonard Tinker
(1887–1942)

Clarence Tinker, a one-eighth Osage, became a major general in the U.S. Air Force, the highest ranking officer of Indian ancestry in the nation's military history. He was born near Elgin, Kansas on November 21, 1887; his father was George Ed Tinker, a part-Osage Indian, and his mother was Rose Jacobs Tinker. As a youth he attended

Clarence Leonard Tinker (1887–1942)
(*Western History Collections, University of Oklahoma Library*)

Wentworth Military Academy in Lexington, Missouri, and in 1908 was commissioned a second lieutenant in the Philippine constabulary, where he served for five years. In 1913 he was commissioned in the regular U.S. Army forces.

After service in World War I, Tinker became interested in the then rapidly developing arm of military aviation. He soon earned his wings and by 1927 was serving on the Air Corps staff. During the next 12 years he commanded various bases in the United States, notably Mather Field and March Field, both in California. He advanced in rank as he became increasingly experienced. While on duty in London, he effected the rescue of a flier downed by an air crash, for which he received the Soldier's Medal.

In December, 1941, Major General Tinker was commander of the entire U.S. Air Forces in Hawaii. Exactly seven months after the Pearl Harbor attack, Tinker was shot down on June 7, 1942, while leading his bomber squadron during the Battle of Midway. His body was never recovered. He married while on duty in the Philippines and had one daughter and two sons; his son Clarence Jr., was lost in a flight over the Mediterranean Sea, and like his father, his body was never recovered. The Tinker Air Force Base near Oklahoma City, Oklahoma, was named in his honor in October 1942.

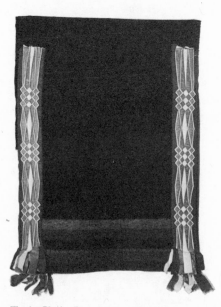

Trade-Cloth Breechclout Decorated with Ribbonwork; Osage
(*Museum of the American Indian*)

301

Tomah (ca. 1752–1817)

Tomah, Tomau, or Thomas Carron was a Menomini chief who was a friend of the Americans, yet later fought on the British side during the War of 1812. He was born about 1752 near the present-day city of Green Bay, Wisconsin, and early in life gained recognition as a tribal leader of importance, due mainly to his eloquence and intelligent handling of Indian affairs. When the hereditary claimant to tribal leadership, Chakaucho Kama, was regarded as incompetent to assume the role, Tomah was chosen as acting chief. His wisdom in this position placed him in the forefront of Menomini activities.

In 1805, Tomah served as a guide for Lieutenant Zebulon Pike, who judged him to be a great hunter and a true friend of the White man. When Tecumseh came to the Menomini to urge them to join his united Indian front against White encroachment, Tomah counseled against any such involvement. Fearful that his small tribe would be overwhelmed by the Americans—and also conscious that they would not count for much in any subsequent all-Indian government, in the event of success—he responded to Tecumseh's stories of Indian victories in the East by saying, "It is my boast that these hands are unstained with human blood."

Yet he was certainly aware of the injustices his people had suffered, and when it appeared that the British had a chance to win the War of 1812, driving the Americans out of Indian lands around the western Great Lakes, he decided to join forces with them. With about 100 of his warriors, including his protégé, the young future chief Oshkosh, he helped in the capture of Forts Mackinaw and Sandusky. But, in the end, Tomah lost his hope for the future with the British defeat.

He died on July 8, 1818 according to the inscription on his tombstone; however, several persons who attended his funeral placed the date as in the summer of 1817. With his passing, the Menomini resistance to White advance crumbled as they mourned their fallen leader—the only man they thought capable of holding them together in the face of that flood.

Tomochichi (ca. 1650–1739)

He was also called Tomo Chachi Mico, from Creek *Tomo-chee-chee*, "The One Who Causes to Fly Up," perhaps a reference to his "causing a stir" wherever he went. He was a Creek chief born about 1650 at Apalachukla on the Chattahoochee River in Alabama. Around the turn of the century he moved to Yamacraw, in the Savannah area, and eventually became known as The King of Yamacraw. He met the English colonists led by James Oglethorpe in Yamacraw when they landed in 1733. He was friendly to the colonists, and not only signed a treaty with them, but negotiated another in their behalf with a neighboring tribe of Lower Creek people.

Tomochichi (1650–1739) with his Nephew Toonahowi
(*Smithsonian Institution, National Anthropological Archives*)

In 1734 Tomochichi, his wife Scenanki, and several other Creek Indians sailed to England with Oglethorpe. While there they were treated as visiting royalty, presented at the court of King George II and Queen Caroline, and introduced to the Archbishop of Canterbury and other notables. The famous portrait of Tomochichi and his nephew Toonahowi was painted by Cornelis Verelst during this visit.

Tomochichi and his group were the objects of wonder and attention in London at this time. He took advantage of this interest to plead the Native American cause eloquently, asking for fair trade agreements, favored-nation status, standardized prices, free repair of firearms, and the prohibition of rum. Although these requests were not immediately granted, the Chief made a deep impression on British officials and the general public, many of whom became very sympathetic to the Indian position.

Another result of his visit and of his friendly invitation to visit the New World was that English traders began to come to Indian lands for commercial purposes. Thus began an era of prosperity for both the Creek people and the White traders which lasted throughout most of the 18th century, and which without doubt so closely allied the Creek Nation with the English that it had a lasting effect upon relationships between the two during the whole period of the American Revolution.

Tomochichi lived to an old age, remaining loyal to the colonists. At his death at Yamacraw on October 15, 1739, he was given an impressive public funeral at Savannah, and was buried in the city square.

Toolhulhulsote (ca. 1810–1877)

Also called Toohoolhoolzote, meaning "Sound," this Nez Percé chief was one of the leaders who refused to sign the Treaty of 1863 which ceded much of the Nez Percé land to the Whites. Little is known of his birth and childhood; he lived at Pikunan, an area along the Snake River south of the mouth of the Salmon River. As a youth he was a skilled warrior and a hunter, and was so strong that he could carry a deer on each shoulder. In his later years he was a fiery, tough-minded adversary of the incoming White authorities, haughty in manner, and determined to seek the best possible solution for his people. After 1863 Toolhulhulsote and a number of other Nez Percé leaders, including the legendary Joseph, refused to move to the new reservation area and stayed on their ancient tribal lands.

But trouble came in 1877 when the United States government began to press the enforcement of the treaty terms among the holdouts. In the arguments which ensued, Toolhulhulsote was the speaker for the nontreaty Indians, and while at first he spoke calmly, he became infuriated at the open attitude of contempt which General O. O. Howard displayed toward him. Feeling that he was simply fighting for the same liberty of person and property which the Americans had long supported, he argued, "I have heard about a trade. We never made a trade. Part of the Indians gave up their lands; I never did. I belong to the land out of which I came. The Earth is my mother, and I never gave up the earth." But Howard insisted upon compliance, saying, "The Indians did make such an agreement, and as Washington told you last year, the minority Indians must be bound by that agreement."

Toolhulhulsote exploded: "You are always talking about Washington. I would like to know who Washington is? Is he a chief or a common man, or a house, or a place? Leave Mr. Washington, if he is a man, alone. He has no sense. He does not know anything about our country. He never was here. You are chief, Howard, and I am elected by my people to speak for them and do the best I can for them. Let us settle the matter between you and me." He was a Dreamer—a follower of the visionary Smohalla—and believed that the Indians would soon rule their lands again with no interference from the Whites. To General Howard the chief seemed arrogant, rude, and perhaps dangerous, so he arrested him. Jailed, Toolhulhulsote indeed advocated war, but the other leaders, although outraged, elected to go along with the government plans. The old chief was released but he was more intense in his hatred of the Whites than ever.

Coming to the conference as equals, expecting an opportunity to prove to General Howard the injustice of his demands, the Indians departed in humiliation, realizing that they had indeed lost all of their traditional homelands, and could expect no fair treatment from the Whites. This sense of misunderstanding and intransigence had much to do with the development of hatred and implacable hostility which soon emerged. Trouble broke out between some young Nez Percé men and the Whites; the Army moved in, the Indians resisted, and the Nez Percé War was on.

In the battle at Clearwater River on July 11, the old war chief proved that he was still a skilled warrior. Howard's troops attacked the Indians from an embankment across the river from their camp. Toolhulhulsote quickly led 24 sharpshooters across the water and up the embankment to where they would be on a level with the soldiers. The accuracy of their fire kept the Whites at bay until the rest of the Nez Percé could join the fray. By afternoon of the second day of the battle, the main force of the Indians had left the scene, protected by the expert shooting of a small number of warriors—who also escaped in their turn.

This became the pattern of the war. Amply supplied, and with good rifles, the skill of the warriors was easily equal to that of their pursuers. As the Nez Percé retreated toward Canada and freedom, they held off their foe by strategic skill and superior marksmanship. Toolhulhulsote was killed around September 30, 1877, during the final battle of the war, at the Bear Paw in Montana. He did not live to see the surrender of his people, their exile to Oklahoma, or their eventual return to the reservation—but not to their ancestral homeland.

Monroe Tsatoke (1904–1937)

From *tsa-tokee*, "Hunting Horse," this Kiowa artist was one of a group of five young men who was sent to the University of Oklahoma in 1926 to develop his artistic talents. He was born September 29, 1904, of mixed-blood parents, near Saddle Mountain, Oklahoma, attended local schools, and finished his education at Bacone College. Like his father, Tsa-To-Ke, who had been a scout for General Custer, young Monroe settled down to the life of a farmer. He liked to draw, however, and spent a great deal of his time improving his art.

The first contact he had with formal art instruction was in the early 1920s, when Mrs. Susie Peters organized a Fine Arts Club at Anadarko for Indian boys and girls who showed artistic promise. Mrs. W. B. Lane also assisted in this informal training, and when it was observed that several of the young men seemed to possess unusual ability, Mrs. Peters was able to induce Dr. Oscar J. Jacobson, then head of the Art Department at the University of Oklahoma, to enroll five of the Kiowa boys in an unofficial art program. They were not regular students, but were allowed to sketch and paint in an art atmosphere under the guidance of a remarkable teacher.

Watercolor Painting of Three Kiowas, by Monroe Tsatoke *(Museum of Northern Arizona; Marc Gaede Photo)*

Out of this environment emerged an unusual art expression, and Monroe Tsatoke has usually been regarded as the major force of the group. He responded to the opportunity with great enthusiasm and hard work, developing rapidly and dramatically into an important painter. Jacobson had encouraged the five to paint what they knew—their heritage, their legends, and their experiences. Tsatoke worked feverishly at his art and his paintings seemed to throb with energy and dynamism. He also loved to sing—he was chief singer at many Kiowa dances—and some of his paintings are based on tribal songs. While still a young man, he contracted tuberculosis, but refused to allow this to interfere with his career.

Tsatoke and the other Kiowas enjoyed the support and patronage of many collectors, most particularly Lewis Ware, Lew Wentz, and Leslie Van Ness Denman. Out of this backing developed a school of art which became the dominant art force in the Plains Indian world for three decades. Monroe, in particular, had always had a strong degree of spirituality, which had been demonstrated in many of his paintings. He joined the Native American Church and participated in the hallucinogenic properties of the peyote sacraments, which deepened his religious feelings.

He created a series of paintings based upon these mystical experiences, but was never quite satisfied with the fidelity, feeling that he was unable to even come close to capturing the splendor of his visions. He never finished all of the series he had planned, succumbing to tuberculosis on February 3, 1937 at the age of 32. He was survived by his wife, Martha Koomsataddle, a Kiowa, and four children. He was buried on Saddle Mountain in Oklahoma.

Tuekakas, or Old Joseph (1790–1871)
(*Washington State Historical Society*)

Tuekakas (ca. 1790–1871)

Also spelled Ta-wait-akas and known as Old Joseph, he was a Cayuse chief of the Wallowa Valley people and the father of the famous Nez Percé Chief Joseph. He is sometimes called Wallamootkin, but this is actually a reference to his band, known as the "Cropped Forehead" people, from the way they wore their hair. Tuekakas was born sometime between 1785 and 1790 near Wawawai on the Snake River, the son of a Nez Percé woman and a Cayuse chief of the Wallamootkin band. The tribe was basically peaceful during the early 19th century, living quietly in Idaho, eastern Oregon, and Washington. In 1836 they welcomed the missionaries Henry Spalding and his wife to their land. Three years later, Spalding performed the marriage ceremony for Tuekakas, whom he christened Joseph, and baptized their third son Ephraim, who in time became the younger Joseph.

In 1847 the neighboring Cayuse killed another missionary, Marcus Whitman and his wife, forcing the Spaldings to temporarily leave the region. Because of the government's punitive expedition against the Cayuse, many of the latter joined with the Nez Percé, who retired to their native Wallowa Valley in Oregon. By the middle of the century the Cayuse had indeed become almost completely merged with the Nez Percé and were almost regarded as one tribe.

In 1855, federal representatives, including Isaac Stevens, met with the Northwest Indians in Walla Walla, Washington to draw up boundaries for a reservation to accommodate the Indians. The Yakima, Umatilla, Walla Walla, Cayuse, and the Nez Percé were all present and three huge reservation tracts were delineated. Tuekakas returned to the Wallowa country and erected poles to indicate his tribe's boundaries, but White settlers began to intrude, particularly after gold was discovered there. In 1863 a new commission headed by Superintendent Calvin Hale arrived from Washington to draw up new, more constricted boundaries, reflecting the unwillingness of the United States govern-

Quill-Decorated Buckskin War Shirt;
Nez Percé
(*Museum of the American Indian*)

ment to support Indian claims against the White squatters. Out of this meeting, the Lapwai Treaty was signed by most of the chiefs whose lands were already within the new reservations, but those who were dispossessed, including Tuekakas, refused to sign and went home to their people, furious and disillusioned.

The elder Joseph never again reconciled himself to White rule and rejected his adopted Christianity in favor of the new Dream religion which had been founded by Smohalla. The nontreaty Nez Percé, as they were called, did not move during Tuekakas' lifetime, and before his death he told his son, "Always remember that your father never sold his country. You must stop your ears whenever you are asked to sign a treaty selling your home. This country holds your father's body. Never sell the bones of your father and your mother."

Tuekakas married twice. His Walla Walla wife died early; his Cayuse wife Khapkhaponimi (Bark Scrapings), baptized Asenoth by Spalding, bore him five children: Celia, also known as Sarah; another daughter Elawmonmi; Young Joseph; and two boys, Smuguiskugin (Brown), also called Shugin, and Ollokot (Frog). Old Joseph was blind at his death in August 1871 and was buried at the fork of the Lostine and Wallowa Rivers; later his body was reburied at the foot of Lake Wallowa.

Two Guns White Calf
(ca. 1872–1934)

John Two Guns, also known as John Whitecalf Two Guns, a well-known Pikuni Blackfoot chief, was probably the Indian whose face was most familiar to White Americans in the early 20th century. His picture as the archetypal Indian appeared in thousands of newspapers, magazines, and other publications throughout the world. His brooding,

U.S. Indian Head Nickel Issued in
1913
(*American Numismatic Society*)

Two Guns White Calf (1872–1934)
(*Smithsonian Institution, National Anthropological Archives*)

handsome visage, which suggested the life of the romantic Noble Savage to non-Indians, became a symbol of the Vanishing American to many viewers.

He was born near Fort Benton, Montana about 1872, the son of White Calf, the last chief of the Pikuni Blackfoot, and lived a quiet boyhood on the northern Plains. He was not part of the old buffalo days—these days had long vanished—but he did participate in many of the post-buffalo-day activities of the region.

He is one of three Indians who was part of the composite "American Indian" used by James Earl Fraser in his preparation of the design for the Indian head nickel (the so-called "buffalo nickel"), although Fraser often asserted that there was no single Indian whose actual profile adorned that coin. As Fraser emphasized, many physical types went into the shaping of the head as it finally emerged on the finished coin. Other Indians who sat for Fraser at the time were John Big Tree, a Seneca and Iron Tail, a Sioux—each contributing some physical feature to the final result.

If John Two Guns was not the complete model for the nickel, he certainly posed for tens of thousands of tourists who snapped his picture at the Glacier Park Hotel in Montana, where for many summers he was a major attraction. He also traveled a great deal for the publicity department of the Great Northern Railroad, and it was this agency that originated the name Two Guns White Calf by which he was most familiarly known.

John Two Guns died of pneumonia on March 12, 1934 at Blackfoot Indian Hospital, at the age of 63. He was buried in the Catholic Cemetery in Browning, Montana.

Two Leggings (ca. 1844–1923)

Two Leggings, a River Crow warrior, was a minor war chief during the time when the U. S. Army was campaigning against the Plains Indians. He was born in 1844 along the Bighorn River in Montana, the son of Four (or No Wife), and Strikes at Different Camps. A member of the Not Mixed clan, his baby name was Big Crane. As a young man he participated in several horse-stealing raids against the neighboring Dakota; at the time, the Crow were not involved in combat against the Whites. In fact, many of the Crow young men, such as Curly and White Man Runs Him, became well-known scouts for the Army.

The origin of his name is accounted for by an episode in which he came into a trader's store wearing a badly torn pair of buckskin leggings; around these leggings he had wrapped some red trade cloth, which he stuffed with grass for warmth against the winter cold. The appearance was humorous to the other Indians, and he was given the nickname, "Two Leggings, " which he was called for the rest of his life. At one time he was named "His Eyes are Dreamy," during an intense search for a vision.

Two Leggings (1844–1923)
(*Smithsonian Institution, National Anthropological Archives*)

From 1919 to 1923 the old man told the story of his life to a Montana businessman, William Wildschut, who had been collecting Crow lore for many years. These notes became the basic manuscript for the book *Two Leggings; the Making of a Crow Warrior* (1967), edited by Peter Nabokov.

The significance of the life of Two Leggings lies in the fact that the observations are made by a man, who, by Crow standards, may never have quite made it to the top. Most records of Indian careers which have been preserved concern only those remarkably successful leaders. Lost to us are the stories of the lives of the far greater number of people who led equally "Indian" lives, but because they were not at the top of the hierarchy, passed unnoticed into history. But with this book on Two Leggings we are left with a story of the ambitions, problems, and difficulties of an unsuccessful vision seeker.

Such average talents ignore the ability of an individual to record the ambitions, hopes, accomplishments, and life cycle which can make our understanding of old-time Indian life more balanced, and perhaps more human. It is this quality which makes the career of Two Leggings worthy of note—and rare in contemporary annals.

Two Leggings married Ties Up Her Bundle; they had no children, but adopted a girl, Red Clay Woman, and a boy, Sings to the Sweat Lodge, also known as Amos Two Leggings. Two Leggings died at his home south of Hardin, Montana on April 23, 1923.

Two Moon (1847–1917)

Two Moon (1847–1917)
(*Smithsonian Institution, National Anthropological Archives*)

Ishi'eyo Nissi (also Ishaynishus), meaning "Two Moons," (i.e., months), was the name of two prominent Cheyenne chiefs who flourished in the 19th century. Their identities are often confused in historical records and it is sometimes difficult to distinguish which individual is meant by the writer. The name appears with equal frequency as Two Moon.

The elder Two Moon, the uncle of the younger man, was an important warrior chief who led his warriors in many battles against the Whites, as well as against traditional tribal enemies. In late 1866 he commanded the Cheyenne forces in the attack on Fort Phil Kearney in Wyoming. The Cheyenne had joined with the Sioux in an effort to drive the White soldiers out of their country, and thereby close off the trails to the West. When Captain William Fetterman foolishly led a force of 80 troopers in pursuit of one of the Indian bands, his men were surrounded and annihilated. This defeat shocked the nation, resulting in the dispatching of larger forces leading to the Treaty of Fort Laramie, in 1868. Although this agreement was considered to be fair to both sides leading many to hope that there would be peace on the Plains, it was not to be. As more and more settlers kept coming into the area, the Indians felt increasingly hemmed in and their freedom threatened.

The younger, and better known, Two Moon began to take an increasingly significant role in the skirmishes between Whites and Indians

Painting on Buckskin Showing the Battle of the Little Bighorn; Custer is Standing at the Left; Cheyenne
(*Museum of the American Indian*)

in the region. In 1876 the U.S. Army began a full-scale effort to defeat the Cheyenne and the Sioux, in order to permanently remove the barrier to westward travel. In March of that year Two Moon was one of the leaders of the camp on Powder River which was attacked by soldiers under Colonel Joseph J. Reynolds. Although the Indians did not suffer great losses in lives, most of their possessions and ponies were captured. Two Moon was able to retrieve the horses later that night.

The Cheyenne warriors were an important part of the Indian forces at the Little Bighorn when Custer attacked, and Two Moon took a major role in leading his people in the defeat of the Seventh Cavalry forces. Later, he described the famous battle to the writer Hamlin Garland, who published the account in *McClure's* magazine in 1898.

After the battle, as United States reinforcements came into the area seeking revenge, the various Indian bands dispersed in various directions. Sitting Bull led a group to southern Canada, while Two Moon eventually brought his people down the Tongue River to Fort Keogh, where he was induced to surrender to General Nelson Miles. Subsequently, several of the Cheyenne warriors, including Two Moon, were recruited to service as U.S. Army scouts. In late 1878, when Little Wolf brought his Cheyenne people on their long trek north from Indian Territory, it was Two Moon and other Cheyenne scouts who first made contact with them. No blood was shed, and the tired band of homesick wanderers was brought peacefully into the fort.

Two Moon remained on the White man's path for the rest of his life, and was chief of the Northern Cheyenne on the reservation, acting in their best interests. He went to Washington on several occasions, and in 1914 he met with President Woodrow Wilson. He died at home, around 1917 at the age of 70.

Two Strike (1832–1915)

Two Strike, also Two Strikes, or Nomkahpa (also Nom-pa-ap'a), "Knocks Two Off," was named from an occasion when he dispatched two enemy Ute warriors from their horses by blows from his war club. He was a war leader of the Brûlé Sioux who played a major role in many of the events during the latter part of the 19th century. He was born near the Republican River in southern Nebraska in 1832. In the 1860s, Two Strike participated in several raids, including a major attack on the Union Pacific Railroad in 1868. During the 1870s he became a supporter of Spotted Tail, who advocated a middle course in dealing with the Whites

After Crow Dog murdered Spotted Tail in 1881, Two Strike became the leader of a small band of Brûlé who followed his leadership in his devotion to tradition and efforts to insulate them from involvement with the Whites. A strong adherent to the Ghost Dance religion, he pulled his scattered people together and, after some hesitation, followed the advice of Crow Dog and led them to the camp of Short Bull, one of the most fervent Ghost Dance disciples.

Two Strike (1832–1915)
(*Smithsonian Institution, National Anthropological Archives*)

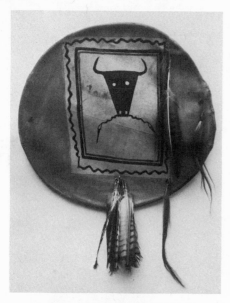

Painted Muslin Dance Shield; Sioux
(*Museum of the American Indian*)

Early in December 1890, General John Brooke sent envoys to the Ghost Dancers, and Two Strike was one of those who agreed to come in to discuss peace terms. He had decided that he wanted to bring his people to the Pine Ridge Agency, but he was afraid of both the fanatic Indians and of the vengeful soldiers. Assured that the latter would not harm him if he remained peaceful, he returned to his tribe and led them away from the Dancers; Crow Dog shortly thereafter followed the same course.

But trouble began anew when the Brûlé heard of the savage massacre of Big Foot and his people at Wounded Knee Creek. Two Strike's warriors and many other Sioux left Pine Ridge and went on a rampage of anger and grief. They rejoined the Ghost Dance people and talked of all-out war, but to no avail; the Army outnumbered and outgunned them. General Nelson Miles pledged that no harm would come to any Indian who came into the Agency; he had fulfilled his promises in the past, and so the Indians believed him.

Two Strike surrendered on January 15, 1891, and shortly after went to Washington, D.C., as part of a delegation seeking improved conditions for his people. He seems to have dropped out of public activity after that date, and continued to live quietly on the reservation until his death about 1915. He was buried on Pine Ridge Reservation.

Tyhee (ca. 1825–1871)

Taihee, Tag-hee, or Taighe, from *taghee*, "Chief," was a Bannock leader who fought the Whites during his early life, but later became an advocate of peace. Little is known of his childhood in the early 19th century, when the Bannock homeland was in the eastern Idaho and western Washington territory. His world was comparatively undisturbed by White emigrants, and he seems to have lived the carefree life of most young Indians of the period.

As time went on, however, more and more settlers, traders, trappers, and missionaries came from the East. The tribe began to find itself slowly hemmed in, as it lost its hunting grounds, the game slowly disappeared, and even Indian survival itself was challenged. The people resisted, and several battles took place in the area, but in 1863, the Bannock were defeated and forced to sign the Treaty of Fort Bridger in 1869.

Most of the tribe moved onto the reservation, including Tyhee. Although his fellow tribesmen all remembered the days of their warrior fathers, who felt it was a disgrace to work on the land, Tyhee settled down and became a successful farmer. In 1873, after squatters had invaded Indian land, another treaty was signed which guaranteed reservation borders against White encroachment. This agreement was not enforced, however, and when Tyhee became tribal chief in 1874, he called on the United States to live up to its bargain.

But the situation grew worse as the buffalo declined and the government failed to provide the tribe with food from any other sources. In

1877 there were several confrontations between the desperate Bannock people and the Army troops. Tyhee counseled peace, but as tensions increased, he found his authority diminished. Many of the Indians looked to Buffalo Horn and others who urged war as a way to lead them out of the crisis.

A period of irresolution was broken in the spring of 1878 when several thousand Bannock people left the reservation for the Camas prairie, in search of food and freedom. The alarmist Eastern newspapers headlined the event as the Bannock War, but it was far less sensational. Troops under General O. O. Howard were dispatched in pursuit, and in August most of the Indians were rounded up and returned to their reservation. Unfortunately, the so-called Bannock War ended in senseless tragedy when troopers killed all of the women and children in a small Bannock encampment at Clark's Ford on September 5, 1878.

Tyhee resumed his primary role in tribal affairs, and to some extent, tribal conditions improved. In 1887 he was involved in negotiations for the sale of a railroad right-of-way through Bannock lands. Some Shoshoni chiefs resisted the sale, since they also inhabited the reservation lands concerned, but were eventually forced to accept the treaty.

In 1888, perhaps as a reward for his compliance, Tyhee was invited to Washington, D.C., where he was given the usual medals, reception, and meetings with government officials. Although some critics charge that he was a coward and a traitor to his people, Tyhee insisted that he was a realist and simply recognized the hopeless position of the Indian, and was working for his tribe's welfare against insuperable odds. He died in the winter of 1870–1871, still bearing the mixed regard of his people.

Uncas (ca. 1606–ca. 1682)

Un'kas, from *Wonkas*, "The Fox," also known as Poquiam, was an important and controversial Mohegan leader among the Indians of New England during the period of its early colonial development. The exact date of his birth is not known; it is generally accepted as around 1606. He was the son of Owenoco, a Pequot sachem, and in his late teens, he married the daughter of the principal Pequot chief, Sassacus. Uncas soon rebelled against his father-in-law but was defeated and banished from the territory. Displaying the resourceful qualities for which he later became famous, he returned and placed himself at the head of a group of dissidents who called themselves "Mohegans," and lived in what is now northern Connecticut and southern Massachusetts. Uncas often fought with the neighboring tribes, but was friendly toward the English, whom he saw as powerful allies and as a source of trade goods and political support.

Uncas and Miantonomo, the Narragansett chief, were bitter rivals. In 1643 a force of 1000 Narragansetts were defeated by Uncas and about 500 of his warriors, who captured Miantonomo and brought him to the English authorities at Hartford. The latter turned him over to Uncas for execution and pledged their help in future conflicts. In 1656 this promise was fulfilled when the colonists, led by Captain Leffingwell, came to the aid of the Mohegans in another battle with the Narragansett chief Pessacus, who almost succeeded in avenging the death of their great chief.

All historical accounts indicate that Uncas never strayed too far from the warpath, fighting with equal vigor against the Mohawk, Narragansett, Pequot, Pocomtuc, and other tribes of the region. During King Philip's War of 1675-1676, Uncas remained on the side of the colonists—whether by coercion, bribery, or conviction is not clear— and was a major force in saving them from almost certain defeat. Although the now-aging warrior did not himself take part in any of the battles so far as is known, his son Oneco and several hundred Mohegans fought in support of the colonists at Brookfield and Hadley, Massachusetts.

Perhaps, were it not for James Fenimore Cooper's *The Last of the Mohicans*, Uncas would not have become as well known in colonial history. In view of his role in establishing the Mohegan group, he could more properly be termed The First Mohegan. Certainly in his last years, he seems to have deteriorated considerably, and lost many of the more admirable qualities which had earlier balanced off his quarrelsome nature. Indeed, when he died in 1682 or 1683, Uncas was remembered by the Whites more for being "old and wicked . . . a drunkard" than for his having been one of their oldest Indian allies.

Victorio (ca. 1825-1880)

Victorio (1825-1880)
(*Arizona Historical Society*)

Victorio was a famed Mimbreño Apache war leader, held in high regard by the Apache, along with Cochise and Mangas Coloradas, whom he succeeded as head of the Ojo Caliente band. He was probably born about 1825 in Chihuahua, Mexico, and fought under Mangas Coloradas as a youth, where he quickly distinguished himself as a brave warrior and skilled strategist. He was known as Bidu-ya, or Beduiat.

In 1863 the Apache took advantage of the Civil War, which required the bulk of the Army to move East. They raided throughout the border area with relative impunity, not subject to serious control because sufficient forces were not available to carry out the effort. It should not be thought that the soldiers did not try to control the Indian raids; there simply were too few soldiers for the requirements of the vast country and an elusive foe. There were numerous attacks and counter-attacks, and the Army troops were victorious in many; but the raids went on.

After the death of Mangas Coloradas in 1863, Victorio became chief, and battled both Mexicans and Americans with equal force. During the next several years, he harassed frontier settlers in both the United States and Mexico until General George Crook was assigned to the area in 1871. Even the presence of this doughty warrior did not wholly quell the raiding, and it was not until 1877, after years of warfare alternating with peace, that Victorio agreed to the government proposal to settle the band on a 600-square-mile reservation area in southwestern New Mexico, at Ojo Caliente. Since this was their home territory, Victorio and his people were contented to go there.

But in May 1877, the bureaucracy decided that the band should be moved to the San Carlos Reservation in Arizona. The Ojo Caliente lands were to be placed in public domain for settlement by Whites. Enraged at what they felt was duplicity, 300 Apache people left the reservation in September 1877, and promptly began renewed raiding in the area. They were pursued and captured, then they escaped, and the warfare went on, until finally they were again brought to a point of surrendering, upon condition that they could go back to Ojo Caliente. The Army agreed but distrust caused few Indians to believe the promise. In April 1878, when it was finally decided to take the group to the Mescalero Reservation instead, they broke away once more.

Basketry Bowl; Apache
(*Museum of the American Indian*)

Following a short period, Victorio agreed to settle down, tired of the unceasing warfare and the effect constant movement had upon his people, and it seemed that peace was finally at hand. But no sooner had they come onto the reservation than Victorio was indicted in July 1879 for horse stealing. The fear of the consequences caused him to escape once more and resume hostilities. In that same month, they attacked the U.S. Calvary and ran off 46 horses. Back in Mexico, they raided the surrounding settlers almost at will; one posse that pursued the Apache into their mountain retreat never returned. In early 1880, Victorio and his warriors were in the mountains some 40 miles from the Mescalero reservation, and in constant touch with the Indians on that reservation, who came and went with relative freedom. Exasperated, Colonel Edward Hatch took a large force and surrounded the reservation, and proceeded to collect all of the weapons his soldiers could find. But it was too late; more than 200 Indians had left the reservation to join with Victorio's forces, bringing his fighting total to about 250.

Finally, increasing the pressure began to pay off for the Army, which now had almost 2500 men actively pursuing the elusive Indians. They forced Victorio's band into Mexico, where they retreated into the Tres Castillos Mountains in Chihuahua, and on October 14, 1880, a large force of Mexican soldiers under Colonel Joaquín Terrazas attacked the group in force. In the battle which followed, Victorio and about 80 warriors were killed, and the rest of the band was captured.

There are conflicting accounts of the actual battle but the end result is the same. Victorio's abilities as a military general, his tactics, endurance, and perseverance in the face of such tremendous odds, gained him the respect of even his most hostile adversaries. He had managed to survive and even flourish despite the great odds against him.

Walkara (ca. 1808–1855)

Wal-ka-ra, or Wakara ("Yellow," referring to his fondness for yellow-dyed buckskin and yellow face paint) was also known to the Whites as Walker. This major Ute chief was influential during the Mormon settlement of Utah. He was born in 1808 at Spanish Forks, Utah, one of five sons of a Timpanogos Ute chief, and like most Ute Indians at this time, he was essentially hostile to outsiders. In his youth, Walkara was an expert horseman, and in time became the leader of a band of young men in horse-stealing raids which were greatly feared by American and Mexican horse ranchers. He formed alliances with Pegleg Smith and Jim Beckwourth, both renegades, who supplied him with weapons, whiskey, and supplies for horses.

In 1840, Walkara and his warriors reached the height of their career when they stole over 3000 horses from the Mexicans. The Mexicans angrily pursued him but were defeated at Cajón Pass in California after several bloody skirmishes. This encouraged the Ute men, and by the time the Mormons arrived in 1848, Walkara was a formidable power in the region. Brigham Young was firmly committed to peace, however, and eventually established friendly relations with Walkara, based in no small measure on the gifts (seen as tribute) and promises of profitable trade which would come to the Indians. This friendship developed to a point where Walkara was even willing to be baptized in 1850.

However, as towns began to spring up along his favorite springs, and as the Mormons came to expect the Indians to obey their laws, Walkara and the Ute people became restive. In 1850, while Walkara was ill, the Shoshoni attacked his people and made off with many horses. Walkara asked his White friends to cure him and join him on an expedition of revenge. The Mormons did what they could medically but refused to go to war in support of him. In anger, he threatened to attack, but was dissuaded by some of the older men. He finally attacked the Shoshoni on his own but the Mormon refusal to support him in warfare was the start of increasing tension between Indians and Whites. When the Mormons also refused to supply liquor or to trade in weapons, Walkara no longer saw any value in continuing a friendly relationship. The breaking point came when he asked a Mormon woman to marry him; the indignant refusal of the girl and the reaction by the Mormons against what they made plain was regarded as an insult, turned him to the war trail in 1853. The hit-and-run raids which followed soon terrorized the countryside; homes and settlements were burned and settlers were killed, but Brigham Young succeeded in restraining his people. They moved off of their scattered farmsteads into forts and makeshift stockades.

Walkara seems to have realized that he could not continue his war successfully under such circumstances, and with winter approaching, agreed to settle for peace. The relieved Whites welcomed him with a gift of 20 acres of land, thinking this would mollify their erstwhile enemy.

Instead, Walkara felt this gesture to be a small return to someone who had once lived free on his ancestral lands, and indignantly spurned the offer. When he was rejected for the second time in his courtship of another Mormon woman, he saw that the White assurances of equality were as false as the claims of peaceful side-by-side occupancy of land, and he turned away from them for the last time. On January 29, 1855, he died at Meadow Creek, not having reached his fiftieth birthday. At his request, and in keeping with Ute custom, his two Indian wives were killed and buried with him, as were two captive Indian children. It was the last recorded sacrificial burial, and perhaps a symbolic, tragic close to an era.

Walk In The Water
(ca. 1775–ca. 1825)

Myeerah was a Huron chief who was one of the principal Indian leaders in the wars against the Whites in the Old Northwest Territory. He was an ally of Tecumseh in the early 19th century, and provided considerable strength to the proposed Confederacy, from the Indian people in the Northeast. Like many other chiefs in the area, he was a strong advocate of an independent Indian state which would be free to trade with the English in Canada and the newly emerged Americans in the East. Although the English supported this concept of a separate state, which they realized would provide a buffer between themselves and the United States, the latter opposed it vigorously, perhaps with the feeling that it would set a bad precedent at a time when individual "state's rights" feelings ran high in the country.

Walk in the Water signed treaties in Detroit in 1807 and 1808, joining his people with the Chippewa, Potawatomi, and Ottawa in an effort to keep peace with the Americans. Relations became more strained, however, as additional settlers moved into Indian Territory and as the British persuaded many tribes that the United States was ultimately going to take all of their lands, and completely destroy their way of life. Accordingly, when the War of 1812 broke out, many Indians, including Walk in the Water, allied themselves with the British.

Deerskin Pouch Decorated with Moosehair, Huron
(*Museum of the American Indian*)

In January 1813 he and Roundhead were in command of the Indian forces that combined with Colonel Henry Proctor's British soldiers to defeat the Americans at the Raisin River south of Detroit, and was also involved in winning the battle at Fort Malden. But these victories came to nothing following the victory of United States Captain Oliver H. Perry on Lake Erie, which ushered in a change in the direction of the war. Americans under William Henry Harrison drove the British and Indian forces back into Canada, and the final blow—from the Indian point of view—was the Battle of the Thames, in October 1812, where the great Tecumseh lost his life.

Walk in the Water survived the battle, and crossed Lake St. Clair to Detroit, where he sued for peace with the victorious Americans. Accounts of the time describe him as a handsome, noble figure, "the sight of whom few will forget," striding through the settlement to the military headquarters. After the war he settled on a reservation near Brownstone, Michigan, where he lived for the remainder of his days, avoiding public activities. The exact date of his death is not known, although it was presumably about 1825.

317

Waneta (ca. 1795–1848)

Also known as Wanotan, Wahnaataa, Wahnahtah, "The Charger," from Nakota *wanata*, "He Who Rushes On," was an important Yanktonai Sioux chief who figured prominently in the early history of South Dakota. He was born about 1795 on the banks of the Elm River in the northern part of that state. He was the son of Red Thunder (Shappa) and came into prominence early in his life when he enlisted in the British army during the War of 1812. He and his father are recorded as having performed with outstanding courage at Sandusky and Fort Meigs. They both apparently fought with reckless bravery, and Waneta himself was badly injured at Sandusky. He was later commissioned a captain and invited to visit London.

Waneta continued in his loyalty to the English for another eight years, at one time attempting to wipe out Fort Snelling; this enterprise did not succeed, however, and the outcome led to a change in his feelings toward the American forces. From that time on, he allied his people with the Americans and became one of the major American adherents in the Dakota region. He signed the treaty of Fort Pierre in 1825, and more importantly, was a signer of the Treaty of Prairie du Chien which established the boundaries of the Sioux Territory on August 17, 1825.

His name appears in many connections during the following two decades as the major leader of the Sioux forces in Dakota country. He died in 1848 at the age of 53, at the mouth of Beaver Creek, near Standing Rock Reservation in North Dakota.

Wannalancet (1625?–1700?)

Wa-na-lan'set was an important Mahican chief, who succeeded his father, Passaconaway, as one of the most powerful Indian leaders in northern New England and one of the most unfortunate in his dealings with the Whites. Throughout his life he followed the advice of his father never to contend with the power of the English colonists, who were flowing into the area in ever increasing numbers.

Beyond the fact of his having been imprisoned for debt in 1659, little is known of his life prior to the outbreak of King Philip's War in 1675. The colonists, alarmed at the Indian unity against them, proceeded to attack many of the local bands, most of which were, in fact, friendly. About 100 Whites marched up to Wannalancet's village on the Merrimack River, the Indians fled at the approach of this obviously hostile group, and the latter burned down the empty village.

Wannalancet did not retaliate for this act of war, perhaps because he was aware of the defeats suffered by other tribes, due to the superior firepower of the English. In 1676 he took about 400 of his people to Dover, to seek refuge from the War, but they were tricked by the English into a position whereby they became prisoners. About 200 of the most able-bodied were put aboard a ship and taken to be sold as slaves; Wannalancet bitterly protested at the deceit but met only deaf ears.

Increasing pressures were put on him; in response, and to prove his friendly intentions, he agreed to sign a treaty at Dover which re-affirmed the right of the colonists to be the final authority in the governing of the tribe. As the War came to an end, and relative peace was once again established, he returned to his homeland with the remnants of his band. After several skirmishes with White squatters who had moved into the area in his absence, Wannalancet decided to accept an invitation from some friendly English in the North to move there. He settled in Canada, and it is presumed that he remained there until his death around the end of the century.

Wapasha (c. 1718–1876)

Wapasha (1718–1876)
(*State Historical Society of Wisconsin*)

Wapasha, Wabasha, or Wapusha, "Red Leaf," from *wape* "leaf," and *sha*, "red," was the name of a succession of chiefs of the Mdewakanton Sioux active during the last half of the 18th century and through most of the 19th century. The first known Wapasha was born around 1718 in what is now Minnesota. During his lifetime, the Chippewa were the great enemies of his tribe, and he spent much of his time either negotiating peace or leading his people into battle against them. He also tried to reestablish trade relations with the English after their withdrawal from Mdewakanton territory after one of their traders was murdered there. Wabasha captured the killer and set off to deliver him to the authorities at Quebec. The murderer escaped en route, but Wapasha did not turn back; instead, he continued on, and offered himself in reparation for the crime.

The English refused the gesture, but thereafter counted on him as one of their great friends. He was an ally during the American Revolution, although he did not participate in any significant battles. His success at winning back the English with their valuable trade gave the Mdewakanton a good measure of wealth and the period of relative peace which was established allowed him to move his people to a new and better located home at Winona, on the Mississippi River. He died near Hokah, in Houston county, Minnesota, on January 5, 1806.

His son, Wapasha the Second, usually known as "The Leaf" was born around 1799, probably at Winona, and grew up in an atmosphere of relative friendliness with the Americans. He met the explorer Zebulon M. Pike during Pike's 1805 expedition searching for the source of the Mississippi River. He helped the Whites negotiate with other tribes in the area. In the War of 1812, he was nominally on the British side, but was actually more sympathetic to the American cause— so much so, that his son-in-law, Rolette was charged with acting in collusion with Wapasha in behalf of the Americans, and was tried by an English court-martial.

At the council held at Prairie du Chien in August 1825, Wapasha played an important role, supporting the Americans in their dealings with the Midwestern tribes. His benevolent personality impressed the Whites, who generally accorded him the reputation as being one of the most honorable, intelligent, and diplomatic leaders in the region. Whether this point of view was due to his cooperative attitude, or because of his consistent support of American interests is difficult to say; indeed, it was probably a combination of these factors. He died of smallpox in 1836, aged about 63 years, and was succeeded by his son (some authorities claim his nephew).

The third Wapasha, more commonly known as Joseph Wapasha, continued the friendly relationship with the Whites which had been established by his predecessors. Details as to his birth are not known, but it was probably around 1825 in the vicinity of Winona or Wabasha, Minnesota. He was principal chief in 1862, and became increasingly active in Indian–White relations as the temper of the times slowly began to change. It was the period of ever-expanding White settlement, with all of the accompanying troubles which marked that expansion throughout the country. No longer could even the most friendly Indian tribes rely upon that friendly attitude to protect their lives and their permanent occupancy of homelands. Wapasha took part in some battles between the Sioux and the Whites but in the attack by Little Crow on New Ulm, Minnesota, he played a reluctant role. He was, in fact, opposed to the outbreak but was forced into the affair by pressures from his people.

The public reaction against all Indians in Minnesota following the New Ulm attacks impartially included Wapasha's people along with all of the others, and he was helpless to prevent the removal of his band to a reservation on the Upper Missouri River; subsequently, the Sioux were moved again to Santee Agency, Nebraska, where he died April 23, 1876. He was succeeded by his son, Napoleon Wapasha, who became chief of the Santee Sioux on the Niobrara Reservation, and became the first of the Wapasha line to become a United States citizen.

Nancy Ward (ca. 1738–ca. 1824)

From the English rendition of Nanye-hi, "One Who Goes About," named from the mythological Spirit People, she was a major Cherokee figure of the Southern frontier who became an almost legendary person, due largely to her queenly manner and resolute personality. She was born into the Wolf clan about 1738 at Chota, near Fort Loudon, Tennessee; her father was Fivekiller, a Cherokee-Delaware man, and her mother was Tame Deer (Tame Doe) the sister of Attakullakulla, known popularly as Catherine. In her youth, Nanye-hi had the nickname Tsistunagiska, "Wild Rose," from the delicate texture of her skin which was likened to rose petals.

She married Kingfisher, a Cherokee of the Deer clan, and showed her mettle early. In a skirmish against the Creek forces at the Battle of Taliwa in 1755, she aided her husband as he was firing from behind a bulwark, chewing on the bullets to make them more deadly; he was killed and she seized his musket, continuing the fire. Her participation was credited by the Cherokee with helping to turn the tide of battle in their favor, and she was given the title of Ghighau (or Agigau), "Beloved Woman." This title traditionally gave her a lifetime voice in all tribal councils, as well as the power to pardon condemned captives.

Yet she was not a bloodthirsty person; she went behind her people's backs to warn the settlers in the Holston and Watauga Valleys that they were going to be attacked by the pro-British Cherokee. When the Whites mounted a devastating counterattack, her home was among those spared. She followed the same pattern in 1780, although this time she met the White attackers and urged them to talk peace with the Cherokee chiefs. They refused to halt their advance, however, and went on to defeat the Indians. The "queenly and commanding" Nancy Ward took an active role in the peace talks of the 1780s, continually exhorting the two groups to friendship and peaceful coexistence.

Although there were many on both sides who thought her ideas were foolish and even dangerous, there were few, if any—of either race—who did not respect her. As more and more settlers came into eastern Tennessee, she apparently became disenchanted with her views on friendship with Whites. She advised the Cherokee Council of 1817 not to cede any more tribal lands to them, but they rejected her counsel, and within a few years she and many other Cherokee people were forced to move away from their homes.

She married Briant (Bryant) Ward, a White trader, and moved to Womankiller Ford, on the Ocowee River, where she conducted a well-known inn for many years. The inn prospered and she became a wealthy person before her death in the Spring of 1824. She had three children: Catherine, Fivekiller, and Elizabeth. For many years after her death she was the center of many legends known for her friendship, beauty, power, and wisdom. Even today she is remembered with deep affection by the Cherokee people.

War Eagle (ca. 1785–1851)

Also known as Little Eagle, or Huya-na, this Sioux chief was one of the last of his tribe to live in the area around Sioux City, Iowa. He was born into the Santee tribe in what is today Wisconsin (perhaps Minnesota); little is known of his parents. Even as a youth he was a friend of the Whites, and is not known to have taken to the warpath, in spite of his militant name. A tall, strong young man, he often served as a guide for steamboats on the Upper Mississippi River.

During the War of 1812, when Colonel Robert Dickson succeeded in persuading many of the Santee Sioux to join the British side, War Eagle remained loyal to the Americans, serving as an Army courier and interpreter. He eventually convinced many of his fellow tribesmen that their best interests lay with the United States. After the War, there was a

War Eagle (1785–1851)
(*State Historical Society of Wisconsin*)

struggle for leadership among the Santee and War Eagle left his home to go to St Louis.

In St. Louis he met Manuel Lisa, an important trader who had employed Sacajawea and many other Indian people; through Lisa, War Eagle became a scout and messenger for the American Fur Company. He took great pride in his ability to traverse long distances in a relatively short time, and continued to go on such missions even after he settled among the Yankton Sioux in Iowa. His leadership and his skills as a diplomat and orator soon earned him election as chief of this tribe in spite of his origin in a different, although related group.

In 1837, he went to Washington, D.C., to participate in a conference which resulted in the Sioux having to cede to the United States all of their lands east of the Mississippi. The unwillingness of the White man to consider Indian needs and the fact that they were being forced to leave their ancestral homelands was a tremendous emotional shock to War Eagle, and he returned home totally disillusioned, despite his earlier loyalty to the United States. He stayed near Sioux City for the remainder of his life, living in the home of his son-in-law, Théophile Bruguier, a local trader. He never advocated resistance or warfare against the United States, recognizing the futility of the Indian position. Following his death in 1851, a memorial was erected by local citizens over his grave on a bluff overlooking the Missouri River.

Considerable confusion exists due to the fact that there were several important people with the name War Eagle from many different tribes, including the Sioux, Winnebago, Osage, Comanche, and Cayuse.

William Whipple Warren
(1825–1853)

This remarkable young Chippewa writer was one of the first Indians to record the traditional history of his people in a classic volume published posthumously in 1885. He was born at LaPointe, Minnesota on May 27, 1825, the son of Lyman M. Warren, a fur trader, blacksmith, and Indian Agent. His mother was Mary Cadotte, a part-French–part-Chippewa woman. The young boy was educated at the LaPointe Indian School, and later attended Mackinaw Mission School. He traveled to New York and furthered his education at Clarkson and the Oneida Institute, returning home with an excellent education, fluent in English, and imbued with a desire to learn more and to write.

Once home, William found that he had lost some of his proficiency in the Chippewa language, and he spent a major portion of his time with the older people, to regain fluency and to increase his knowledge of the traditional stories of his forebears. He became a superb speaker of the language, impressing even the most learned Indian people with his command of Chippewa. Raised in a devout Christian household, his reading habits were fixed, and he apparently fit smoothly into the missionary world around him at the time.

In 1842 he married Matilda Aitken, and continued his work as an interpreter and student of Indian ways. Shortly after his marriage, however, he bagan to suffer from tuberculosis, brought on by exposure during the long winters spent out in the wilderness. In 1845 the family moved to Crow Wing, Minnesota, where William continued his work as an interpreter, and also pursued his studies of Chippewa life. In 1850 he was elected to the Minnesota State Legislature, where he quickly became known for his ability and hard work.

In 1851 he began to write brief sketches about the life of his people, one of which appeared in the local newspaper. Well received by its readers, these sketches apparently started him on what was to engage him for the rest of his short life: the history of the Chippewa Indian people. By now, Warren knew almost all of the older Indians in the area, and was able to obtain from them first-hand accounts of their own lives and experiences. These first-hand accounts, combined with his sensitive command of the Chippewa language, enabled him to accumulate and record in English a tremendous store of knowledge concerning the traditions and customs of the Indian people, at that time universally called the Ojibway.

In the winter of 1852 he completed the manuscript of his major work, *History of the Ojibways, Based Upon Traditions and Oral Statements*, and took it to New York, where he hoped to see it published. Unfortunately, his failing health and the disinterest of the publishers of the day caused him to abandon his efforts and return home. He got as far as St. Paul, where exhaustion forced him to stop over with his sister Charlotte. He began to hemorrhage and died on June 1, 1853, at the age of 28.

With his passing, American history lost a great student and recorder. Warren had planned two other works, and it is certain that he would have contributed significantly to our knowledge of Great Lakes Indian life had he lived on. He was buried in the cemetery at St. Paul, Minnesota.

Washakie (ca. 1804-1900)

The name Wa'sha-kie is derived from Shoshonean *wus'sik-he*, "A Gourd Rattle," referring to his practice of stampeding Sioux horses by creeping up and rattling a gourd or hide rattle furiously. He was an Eastern Shoshoni chief whose father was Paseego, a Umatilla man, and his mother was a Shoshoni. Originally named Pinquana ("Sweet Smelling), he grew up with his mother's people in the Green River Valley in eastern Utah and southern Wyoming; later he took the name Washakie by which he is better known. These Indians welcomed and aided the White fur trappers and traders who arrived in the early 1800s. By the 1840s, when Washakie became chief of his tribe, waves of settlers had started crossing the tribal lands, heading west. He and his Shoshoni people assisted

Painted Hide Depicting the Sun Dance,
by Washakie; Shoshoni
(*Museum of the American Indian*)

them in many ways, such as recovering lost stock and helping them cross dangerous rivers. Of equal importance was Washakie's refusal to allow Indian reprisals against settlers whose stock destroyed—inadvertently or otherwise—the Indian herding and root grounds. This remarkable forbearance and assistance was attested to by a document signed by 9000 settlers, commending Washakie and the Shoshoni for their kind treatment.

Washakie (1804–1900)
(*Western History Collections, Denver Public Library*)

If Washakie insisted on peace with the Whites, he exercised no restraint in fighting the traditional Indian enemies of the Shoshoni, and his feats of valor made him a popular leader. However, in 1862, against his wishes a large number of Shoshoni warriors joined the Bannock in raids on emigrant trains and settlements. Rather than be drawn into the conflict, Washakie took his loyal followers to Fort Bridger, Wyoming, for protection. In 1863, General Patrick Connor's troops defeated the rebels in the Battle of Bear River. In 1868, Washakie, representing his own people and the Bannock, signed a treaty giving a right-of-way through the Green River Valley to the Union Pacific Railroad in exchange for a reservation at Wind River, Wyoming. In the wars between the Army and the Sioux (and other Western tribes), Washakie joined the Whites both as a scout and warrior, to fight his traditional enemies the Sioux, Blackfoot, and Cheyenne. He and his warriors also fought under the command of General George Crook in 1876.

A very tall man, Washakie was a commanding presence even into his old age. It is said that when he was about 70 years old, some of the younger men wished to depose him. He disappeared from camp, returning two months later with six enemy Indian scalps; he was no longer opposed as chief. However fierce he might be toward his Indian enemies, he maintained a consistent friendship with the Whites. He died at Flathead Village in Bitterroot Valley, Montana on February 10, 1900, and was buried at Fort Washakie, Wyoming. He had at least two wives: a Shoshoni woman whose name is not known, and Ahawhypersie, a Crow captive. Of his reported 12 children, the names of two daughters are recorded as Enga Peahroa and Naunangai. Of the sons, the following are known: Cocoosh (Dick Washakie) who succeeded him as chief, Connayah (Bishop Washakie), Wobaah (Charles Washakie), and George Washakie.

Washunga (ca. 1830–1908)

Washunga was a Kansa chief who led his tribe during the period when the United States government was breaking up reservation lands into individual allotments. He was a full-blood non-Christian conservative, and like most of those who shared his background at this time, he was suspicious of the White man's intentions. He came into prominence about 1885, when he was selected as the tribal chief councilor.

At about this same time, the mixed-blood Kansas politician Charles Curtis was emerging as a figure of national importance in Republican political life. Curtis had entered Congress in 1892, and because of his familiarity with local reservation life and his own Indian blood, he became influential in Indian affairs. He eventually convinced his friend Washunga that the best solution for the Indian was to accept the individual land allotments which resulted from the enactment of the Dawes Act, and to become landed citizens of the United States.

As a result, Washunga and a delegation of Kansa headmen arrived in Washington in 1902 to sign an allotment treaty, the details of which had

Washunga (1830–1908)
(*Smithsonian Institution, National Anthropological Archives*)

been worked out with Curtis during the preceding months. Each individual was to receive about 450 acres—meaning that some families enjoyed substantial acreage.

Although Washunga was an old man by this time, he was still mentally alert, and his personal force was sufficient to steer the negotiations successfully through to completion. But once the agreement was signed, he felt that he had done his work, and retired from active participation in tribal affairs.

He died in 1908, at about the age of 78, and with no strong successor Kansa fortunes tended to drift for many years until his adopted daughter, Mrs. Lucy Tayiah Eads, became principal chief.

Stand Watie (1806–1871)

Stand Watie (1806–1871)
(*Oklahoma Historical Society*)

Degataga, "Standing Together," (immovable), also known as Takertawker, was a famed Cherokee leader and Confederate general who supported the Ridge faction during the days of the Cherokee removal. He was born at Coosawalee, near Rome, Georgia (then the Cherokee Nation) on December 12, 1806. He was a member of the Deer clan; his father was David Oowatie (or Uwati), an important Cherokee leader, and his mother was Susannah Reese, the part-Cherokee daughter of Charles Reese, an English trader. Dagataga was the younger brother of Buck Watie, better known as Elias Boudinot.

He attended school at Brainerd Mission, in eastern Tennessee, and early in his youth took an active role in Cherokee affairs. He signed the Treaty of New Echota, thus becoming one of the members of the "Treaty Party," and a supporter of the stand taken by Major Ridge and his son John, both of whom were strongly opposed to John Ross. As a member of the Treaty Party, Stand Watie left himself open to attack by the conservative Cherokee faction.

Stand Watie was forewarned of the assassination attack upon Elias Boudinot and the Ridges and managed to escape, but he opposed John Ross for the rest of his life. After the arrival of the Cherokee people in Indian Territory in 1846, following the tragic journey over the Trail of Tears, Stand Watie reorganized tribal affairs, and became a member of the Cherokee Council from 1845 to 1861. He was elected speaker of the Council from 1857 to 1859.

With the outbreak of the Civil War, Stand Watie supported the Confederate side, as did so many Cherokee people. In time he commanded two regiments of the Cherokee Mounted Rifles, whose wartime record was remarkable. It is said that they participated in more battles west of the Mississippi than did any other unit. This was in keeping with the general record of the Five Tribes throughout the Civil War: they lost more men per proportion of population than any Southern State in support of the Confederacy.

In 1864, Stand Watie was commissioned a brigadier general and commanded his regiment at the Battle of Pea Ridge in Arkansas, in which the Union forces, although victorious, suffered great losses. He went on to lay waste to federal lands throughout the Missouri–Kansas area, and is generally credited with being the last Confederate general to surrender.

Following the Civil War, Stand Watie took up farming at Grand River near Bernice, in Indian Territory, where he continued his interest in Cherokee affairs. He married Sarah Caroline "Betsy" Bell, by whom he had three sons and two daughters, and in 1864 he was elected principal chief of the Southern band of Cherokee.

A man of small stature but firm physique, Stand Watie was possessed of considerable personality and dignified bearing. He was a quiet man, not given to demonstrative or emotional excess; yet when the occasion demanded, he was vibrant and could effectively inspire others. Perhaps his name "Immovable" best describes his character: when he felt he was right, he was unyielding, yet he was always open to argument.

He had a sound knowledge of Cherokee culture and served as the source for most of the Cherokee ethnological information included in Henry Rowe Schoolcraft's *Information Respecting the History, Condition, and Prospects of the Indian Tribes of the United States* which was published in 1855. Stand Watie died at his home on Honey Creek on September 9, 1871, and was buried in the Ridge Cemetery in Delaware County, Oklahoma.

Wa-Wa-Chaw (1888–1972)

Wawa Calac Chaw, "Keep From the Water," was a writer, artist, and lecturer on Indian and feminist matters. She was born on December 25, 1888 at Valley Center in the Tule River area of California. She was a member of the Rincón division of the Luíseño tribe, and was taken at infancy to protect her health by Dr. Cornelius Duggan and his sister Mary Duggan, both of New York, and raised as their own child.

She was something of a child prodigy; her early artistic talent showed itself in medical and scientific sketches she did of early radium and cancer experiments during the work of Pierre and Marie Curie. An ardent activist in behalf of Indian and feminist causes, she gave a talk while still in her teens at a meeting at the Astor Hotel sponsored by Carrie Chapman Catt.

Never at a loss for expression, she painted huge canvases in oil, many of which were portraits of people important at the time, or subjects involving social problems which deeply concerned her. She was a co-worker and fund raiser for Dr. Carlos Montezuma and his *Wassaja* project; as his close friend, she planned many of his campaigns and spoke out for the needs he represented.

During her life, Wa-Wa-Chaw came in contact with many White intellectuals and leaders of the day, including Sir Oliver Lodge, Arthur C. Parker, General Richard H. Pratt, Arthur Conan Doyle. These people had a profound influence upon her work, as she did upon them.

She was a colorful person—outspoken, yet with a childlike quality which endeared her to all who knew her. She was vain about her art

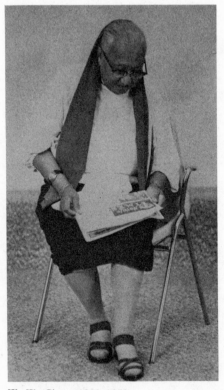

Wa-Wa-Chaw (1888–1972)
(*Stan Steiner Photo*)

work, yet modest about herself and her accomplishments in the social field. She wrote for many publications of the day up until the time of her death. She sold her paintings in the sidewalk shows in Greenwich Village, but was even more interested in "selling" her message of equality for Indian women.

She married Manuel Carmonia-Núñez, the Puerto Rican "son of the last Spanish Lieutenant," a businessman and organizer for the Cigar Workers' Union. From then on, she went by the name of Benita Núñez; they had at least one child, who died in infancy. Wa-Wa-Chaw was well known throughout the Indian community and a familiar figure on the lecture platform in the first quarter of the 20th century. She died in New York City on May 12, 1972 at the age of 83.

William Weatherford
(ca. 1780–1822)

Lumhe Chati or "Red Eagle," was a half-blood Creek chief who led his people against the Whites in the wars inspired by the great advocate of Indian unity, Tecumseh. Scholars do not agree on his parentage, but it seems most likely that he was the son of Charles Weatherford, a prosperous Scotch trader, and Sehoy, the half-sister of Alexander McGillivray. He was raised on the Alabama River near the site of the present city of Montgomery and became a handsome, eloquent, and brave adult.

Despite his European blood the young Weatherford came to realize that the Indian had to fight against White domination or go under, so when Tecumseh called for united action, he began to prepare for conflict. The so-called Creek War did not begin until 1812, months after the battles farther north, but it was the hardest fought. On August 30, 1813, Weatherford's 1000 Creek warriors killed over 500 Whites, both soldiers and civilians, at Fort Mims, in Alabama. In the famous "Thirty Battles" that followed, both sides saw thousands of their comrades die. Finally, in the Battle of Horseshoe Bend on the Tallapoosa River, on March 29, 1814, General Andrew Jackson defeated the Indians.

Weatherford surrendered, having no other choice, and expected to be executed because of the hatred many Whites had for him. But many recalled his courage and ability, and especially his calls for restraint at the Fort Mims attack. Jackson pardoned him on the condition that he work for peace. Weatherford agreed, provided that the Indian women and children, camped in the nearby woods, be given safe conduct and protection. Both men lived up to the bargain.

Weatherford took up life on a plantation, and soon became a prosperous and respected member of both Indian and White communities. He had a large family, with many children, and exerted his influence in the years following as an advocate of peaceful relations with the ever increasing White population. He died on March 9, 1822, at his home in Polk County, Tennessee, just before the United States removed the Creek from their tribal lands and shipped them west to Indian Territory. He was buried about five miles from Benton, Tennessee.

Weetamoo (ca. 1650–1676)

Also known as Wetamoo, Weetamoe, Wetemoo, Weetamore, meaning "Sweetheart," she was commonly known as the Squaw Sachem of Pocasset. She was born about 1650 at the mouth of the Taunton River, near present-day Fall River, and was the daughter of Chief Corbitant of Pocasset. She became the leader of the Pocasset, a small tribe living around Tiverton, Rhode Island. Her sister was Wootonekauske, who became the wife of Metacom; Weetamoo herself married his brother Wamsutta. Until the death of her husband in 1662, Weetamoo was known as Namumpum, or Tatapanum.

She believed that Wamsutta had been poisoned by the English, and as a result became bitterly hostile to the Whites, joining with her brother-in-law against the Whites throughout King Philip's War. Following the death of her husband, Weetamoo married Petonowowett (Peter Nunnuit or "Ben"), from whom she later separated, due to his friendliness with the colonists. She then married Quinapin (or Quequequamanchet), the son of Ninigret. He had captured a White woman, Mary Rowlandson, in 1675, and her account of her experiences in captivity form one of our important sources of information concerning the life of Weetamoo and her court.

Weetamoo ruled regally, demonstrating skill in diplomacy and apparently thoroughly enjoying the physical trappings of her position. She was conscious at all times of the needs of her people and worked for fair treatment at the hands of the English. At the height of her power, she commanded 300 warriors, and was widely respected as a capable leader and fighter. She was apparently a tall, well-built woman, physically attractive, with considerable personal charm. She is recorded as taking great care with her person and making a beautiful appearance which deeply impressed the Whites.

During King Philip's War, she deployed her warriors with skill; but following the disastrous Great Swamp Fight in 1675, she was forced to move about to escape capture. She remained completely loyal to Metacom during the last months of the War, but drowned on August 6, 1676 while crossing the Teticut River, closely pursued by colonial troops. Her body was recovered and the Whites cut off her head and set it up on display at Taunton.

White Bird (ca. 1807–1882?)

Pepeo Kiskiok Hihih, literally "White Goose," also known as Penpenhihi, was a Nez Percé leader who was one of the major forces of effective defiance against the White man during the Nez Percé War. His name is derived from the white goose wing fan which he always carried as a badge of his role as a shaman. White Bird was already an elderly man when the hostilities broke out. His importance was due not only to his skill as a negotiator but also to his skill as an excellent marksman, a leading position in the military strategy of the campaign.

White Bird had refused to sign the Treaty of 1863, thereby becoming one of the "nontreaty chiefs," along with Joseph, Looking Glass, and Toolhulhulsote. They all continued to live in areas outside the new reservation at Lapwai in Idaho. Having lived longer than most of the others, he had seen the problems that faced the Indian in dealing with the White settlers, and was firmly convinced that the best course was to have as little to do with the emigrants as possible.

In May 1877, General O.O. Howard held a meeting with the Nontreaty Chiefs to inform them that the time had come when they would have to move onto the reservation—either voluntarily or by force. After considerable argument, the Nez Percé reluctantly agreed to move, but Howard's hostility exposed itself when he allowed them only 30 days to carry out the move. Unfortunately, during the last days of the removal, the Indians paused for a last free conclave. As the younger men sat talking about the old days and the injustices their people had suffered at the hands of the White men, a few rash warriors went on a foray during which some White settlers were killed. Howard then determined to move on the Nez Percé immediately, and the war was on.

Although he was openly and firmly hostile to White encroachment on Nez Percé lands, White Bird was opposed to war, feeling it would inevitably bring disaster. Nonetheless, once war broke out, he accepted his role as a leader in council and a protector of the women and children. However, the accuracy of White Bird and his sharpshooting warriors meant that he also played a significant role in the military defense of the tribe as well. Usually outnumbered, it was a typical battle pattern for the Nez Percé to surround the enemy and accurately pick them off one by one, allowing the tribe as a whole to escape in the confusion.

One of the major battles was at Big Hole in Montana, where, believing they were safe from attack, the people had stopped to rest. On the morning of August 9, 1877, the troops launched a surprise attack on the sleeping camp. In the confusion, it was White Bird who rallied the warriors for counterattack, crying, "Why are we retreating? Fight! Shoot them down! We can shoot as well as any of these soldiers!" And indeed they could; though there was great loss of life on both sides, the Indians managed to escape.

After a historic retreat, the Nez Percé managed to reach Bear Paw, Montana, 40 miles from the Canadian border. They were cut off, and in a six-day battle, held off the forces of Colonel Nelson A. Miles, but the result was inevitable. White Bird wanted to fight to the death; others counseled surrender, and some advised individual efforts to escape. One by one the major leaders were killed off, leaving the tribe without many of its greatest leaders.

Rather than surrender, White Bird and some other Nez Percé leaders managed to escape to Canada with about 200 men, women, and children, many of whom were badly wounded. Once there, they were received warmly by Sitting Bull and his Sioux who had fled north earlier. Although earlier the two tribes had been enemies, they lived together harmoniously in common adversity. The presence of so many Indians in Canada intensified United States fears of dissident Indians at large who might stir up trouble. Delegations were sent to try to persuade them to return, and many did, although the promises made to induce their return were rarely kept.

White Bird remained in Canada for almost five years, adamant in his refusal to be lured onto a reservation. He died there, under obscure and bizarre circumstances: apparently he ministered to two young Indian men who subsequently died, in spite of his skill as a medicine man. Their father then killed White Bird in retribution; the year was probably 1882.

White Cloud (ca. 1830–1898)

Wabanaquot, from *waban* "white" and *aquot* "cloud," was a noted Chippewa chief who conducted himself in a manner which detracted from the good image of his people—a reminder that not all "important" chiefs were necessarily working for the good of their tribe. He was born at Gull Lake, near Brainerd, Minnesota about 1830, the son of Wabojeeg, a chief appointed by the United States government. Following the death of his father, White Cloud became the head chief of the Minnesota Chippewa, and led them to the White Earth Reservation in 1868, where they settled down to an agricultural life.

White Cloud had many of the attributes needed at the time: he was a man of peace, a master politician, an excellent diplomat, and a leader who made the most of his extraordinary oratorical gifts. However, he also became a connoisseur of the White man's whiskey, and although he converted to Christianity in 1871, he always looked with warm favor upon those who could supply him with liquor.

In the 1870s White Cloud became involved in a bitter fight against three Indian Agents who were serving the Chippewa faithfully and effectively. Their policies, while beneficial to the Indians, were detrimental to the selfish interests of an influential trader in the area. White Cloud took the side of the trader in this dispute, largely due to the generous supply of liquor he received from the latter.

In the tribal council debates which followed, heated verbal battles ensued in which the oratory of White Cloud was severely tested. He eventually succeeded in silencing all of the other chiefs except Wendjima-dub, a courageous and independent chief whose oratorical eloquence rivaled White Cloud. He was the only leader who spoke out against the trader, defending the good work of the agents, and pointing out the selfish bias of White Cloud.

The controversy lasted almost ten years, and although neither side really "won," the bitterness weakened the tribal unity severely. White Cloud lived out his days on the reservation, and died at White Earth in 1898. Shortly after his death, the State of Minnesota in a surprising gesture, erected a monument over his grave—the only Indian so honored.

White Eyes (1730?–1778)

Koquethagechton, also known as Kuckquetackton, was an important Ohio Lenni Lenape (Delaware) chief who was a great friend of the

Whites. He was murdered by American soldiers during the Revolutionary War. The place and date of his birth are not recorded, nor are details of his parentage; he was probably born around 1730 of full-blood Lenni Lenape heritage in the tribal homeland in western Pennsylvania, near the traditional lands of the Shawnee. At this time both tribes were dominated by the Iroquois, who took charge of most important negotiations by virtue of their military superiority.

White Eyes had achieved sufficient importance among his people to have been recognized as their chief around 1776, following a period of service as chief counselor. He was friendly to the Moravian missionaries who were then working among the Indians, although he never himself became a Christian. He believed that the best interests of the Lenni Lenape would be served by friendship with all Whites, and always advocated a policy of strict neutrality. One result of this practice was that in 1774, during Lord Dunmore's War, he alienated the once friendly Shawnee, who were quite literally fighting for their lives.

The next year, at the signing of the Treaty of Fort Pitt, White Eyes declared his nation independent of the Iroquois, and refused to follow their orders to fight as allies of the English against the American revolutionaries. He said, "I am no woman; I will do as I please." But later, when his rival, the Lenape war chief Hopocan (also known as Captain Pipe), had almost succeeded in inducing the Lenni Lenape to take to the warpath in 1778, he said that if they insisted, he would accompany the warriors—but that he would try to be the first to die in battle, so that he would not have to witness the complete destruction of his people.

However, he was finally forced to choose sides, and he declared himself for the Americans, even though many, if not most, of the tribe favored the English. Accordingly, in November 1778, he guided General Lachlin McIntosh and his troops through the forest in their expedition against Sandusky. The circumstances surrounding the episode have never been clarified, but along the way he was shot by the soldiers; apparently in an effort to avoid responsibility, the Americans sent word back to his tribe that he had died of smallpox at Pittsburgh.

White Man Runs Him
(ca. 1855–1925)

Miastashedekaroos (also Mahrstahsheedahkuroosh, Batsida Karoosh, and Mars-che-coodo), was a Crow warrior who was chief of Custer's Seventh Cavalry Indian Scouts during the Battle of the Little Bighorn. His boyhood name was Beshayeschayecoosis, "The White Buffalo That Turns Around." He inherited his adult name from his father, who had been pursued by a White man armed with a rifle which he kept firing to force the Indian to run. Later, referring to his activity as an Army scout against the Indians, the name was sometimes applied in derision by his enemies. As with many Crow warriors, White Man Runs Him was a warrior against the Sioux in his youth, and participated

Rawhide Cut-Out Elk Effigy, Used as Love Medicine; Crow
(*Museum of the American Indian*)

White Man Runs Him (1855–1925)
(*Smithsonian Institution, National Anthropological Archives*)

in many successful horse-stealing forays against his tribal hereditary enemies.

In 1876, he and three or four other Indian scouts, including Curly, were with Lieutenant Charles A. Varnum, the Army Chief of Scouts, out in front of the cavalry troopers as they searched for Sioux who had left the reservation. From a high peak in the Wolf Mountains they saw the enemy camp on the Little Bighorn. After they reported its position to Custer, the Indian scouts were ordered to the rear of the Army lines.

There is some disagreement among historians concerning the actions of the Indian scouts during the battle which followed. White Man Runs Him always claimed that Curly disappeared before the battle—yet it was Curly who first brought news of Custer's defeat to the outside world. Both men lived into the 20th century and were interviewed many times about their roles at the Little Bighorn. White Man Runs Him died about 1925, and was reburied four years later in the National Cemetery at Little Bighorn Battlefield, Montana, in 1929.

Wildcat (ca. 1810–1857)

Coacoochee (also Coocoochee, Cowacoochee, or Cooacoochee), was a major Seminole leader during the period of hostilities against the U.S. Army in the early 19th century. He was born about 1810 in the Seminole

Wildcat (1810–1857)
(*State Photographic Archives; Strozier Library, Florida State University*)

village of Yulaka, along the St. Johns River in Florida, the son of a famous chief, Emathla, also known as King Philip. His uncle was the powerful Chief Micanopy. Wildcat had a twin sister who died in her youth.

Wildcat's lifetime encompassed the whole range of major troubles between the Seminole and the United States government. The First Seminole War lasted from 1817 to 1818 and had a somewhat inconclusive ending. Then, after 1822 when Florida became an organized territory, there were many incidents which gradually developed into a complex situation involving land ownership, the White desire to get Indians off the lands and gain control of the region, and the Seminole policy of welcoming as laborers runaway slaves from Georgia. In 1835, at the beginning of the Second Seminole War, Wildcat was only about 19 years old, but he had already emerged as the leader of a large band of Indians and Negroes.

When the American forces under General Hernández captured King Philip in 1837, they asked Wildcat to come in and talk peace—and removal to Indian Territory (Oklahoma). Wildcat was suspicious and retreated into the back country. When he finally emerged later, it was as an emissary of the great Osceola, who was willing at that time to begin peace discussions under a flag of truce. The Army agreed, but General Thomas S. Jesup took advantage of the situation to capture and imprison the Seminole leaders, including Osceola and Wildcat. By fasting so they could slip between the bars of the jail, Wildcat and his party made a successful and daring escape from Fort Marion, and he soon became a key figure in the Seminole resistance movement. He held General Zachary Taylor to a qualified "draw" at the Battle of Lake Okeechobee on Christmas Day in 1837, but found the continued pressures hopeless.

The constant fighting and moving about in the Everglades began to take their toll, and during this period most of the Seminole gave up the fight and moved west; in 1841 Wildcat and his band of 200 people were forced to journey to Fort Gibson in Indian Territory, arriving in November. Downcast at his defeat, he said, "I was in hopes I should be killed in battle, but a bullet never reached me." The Seminole found Oklahoma to be very different from Florida, and they became wholly demoralized. In 1843 Wildcat and a delegation went to Washington to ask for help, but they were unsuccessful. Upon their return home they found that their lands had been devastated by floods—and another problem had emerged: the Creek neighbors were eager to bring the Seminole Negroes into their tribe as slaves, to profit from their labor.

Wildcat saw the need for a solution, and during a hunting and trading expedition into Comanche country in Texas the idea occurred to him of establishing an Indian colony in the south near the Mexican border, which would combine the Seminole and the Texas Indian people in an alliance. In 1849 he suggested to Indian agents that Bowlegs and the remaining Seminole holdouts in Florida would be willing to join him and his followers if the government cleared the way for them to found a settlement near the Rio Grande. Although this plan never came to a head, Wildcat gathered a group of over 100 Negroes and Indians—men, women, and children—in late 1849 and moved into Texas. Along the way he picked up more recruits and allies, including about 1000 Kickapoo; but he ran into trouble with the Creek people and some Whites who thought he was luring away their slaves.

In 1849, Micanopy died, but Wildcat was not appointed chief in his place; disappointed, he abandoned any thought of remaining in the Territory. In 1850 he tried to persuade the rest of the Seminole to join him in Texas, but failed. Then the Comanche and other tribes captured many of Wildcat's Negroes, holding them for ransom. Creek slave hunters paid the tribute and brought them back to Indian Territory, but not before a slave revolt had taken the lives of several men on both sides.

Wildcat persevered, however, and was eventually given a grant of land by the Mexican authorities, in return for military service against the Apache and Comanche raiders who were plaguing the region. He was given a commission as Colonel in the Mexican Army, and his followers settled down just south of the border. An energetic, vigorous man of about 5′ 10″ in height, Wildcat fell ill of smallpox in 1857, on an expedition mounted by the Mexican forces and died at Alto, near the town of Muzquiz, in Coahuila, Mexico at the age of 47. His son was known as Gato Chiquito, "Young Wildcat."

Cloth Turban, Decorated with Egret Feather and Silver Band; Seminole
(*Museum of the American Indian*)

Eleazar Williams (1788–1858)

Williams was an 18th century Mohawk preacher and many-sided missionary who was the center of a major controversy because he claimed to be the Lost Dauphin of France. He was born in May 1788 at St. Regis, near Lake George, New York; one of 13 children of Thomas Williams (Tehoragwarregen), and Mary Ann Rice (Konwatewenteta); some sources claim his mother was Eunice Williams, a White woman. He was badly scarred as a child, particularly on his arms and legs. In 1800, he was taken with his brother John to Long Meadow, Massachusetts to be educated and was sponsored by Nathaniel Ely until Ely's death in 1807.

In 1809 Williams studied with Reverend Enoch Hale, intending to become a missionary to the Indians, and followed this program at East Hampton until the outbreak of the War of 1812. His knowledge of English, and his role in Indian–White relations earned him the position of Superintendent General of the North Indian Department. He served as a scout during the War and was wounded at the Battle of Plattsburg. He was elected a sachem at Caughnawaga by the Iroquois Council in 1812, with the name Onwarenhiiaki, "Tree Cutter."

His remarkable oratorical skill in Iroquois served him well in inducing Indian people to convert to Christianity—but more importantly, placed him in a key position to manipulate the sale of lands. In time, he became involved in a scheme with the Ogden Land Company to move the

Eleazar Williams (1788–1858)
(*Smithsonian Institution, National Anthropological Archives*)

Indians west of Lake Michigan, where a new Iroquois Empire was to be set up under a single, supreme head (perhaps Williams himself, who did not lack for ambition). Indeed, he apparently forged the signatures of the Oneida chiefs on a document purporting to approve the sale, and presented it to Jedediah Morse in 1820, although the Oneida chiefs had actually strongly opposed the plan. Williams entered into negotiations with the Ogden Company in 1821, but the plan finally failed in 1827 when the promised schools and other facilities did not materialize. The Oneida did move west in 1832, but the other Iroquois people refused to cede their lands.

Williams seems to have disappeared from public activity for a period following the land scheme, but surfaced again in 1852, when he claimed to be the Lost Dauphin of France, saying that his father was Louis XVI and his mother was Marie Antoinette. He said that he had been kidnapped, imprisoned in the Tower for a period—showing the scars on his arms and legs as confirmation—and that he had been secretly carried to Canada. His remarkable physical similarity in appearance to the Bourbon line coincided with a romantic period in United States history, and he found many willing believers. One believer in particular, Dr. John H. Hanson, wrote a book *The Lost Prince*, supporting the story, and this, with an article in *Putnam's Magazine* in 1853, gave his claim some popularity, although it was quickly challenged by others, and subsequently shown to be false.

In 1823 he married Mary Magdeline Jourdain, a half-Menomini girl; they had two daughters who died in infancy, and one son, John Lowe Williams. Eleazar Williams died on August 28, 1858, near Hogansburg, New York, after one of the most remarkable and controversial careers in early Indian history.

Winema (ca. 1848–1932)

Kaitchkona Winema, "The Strong Hearted Woman," or less accurately, "The Little Woman Chief," from the Modoc *kitchkani laki shnawedsh*, "female subchief," was an important figure in the Modoc War of 1872–1873, and in other affairs of her tribe. The name *Winema* was apparently applied by Joaquin Miller. Born on the Link River in northern California in September 1848, she was early known as *Nonooktowa*, the "Strange Child"; her father was a Modoc man named Secot, but her mother's name is not recorded. Her early life was adventurous, and her fearless exploits, such as shooting a grizzly bear and fighting alongside the men in battle, were greatly admired. She seems to have been something of a tomboy, and once when she and some other girls who were canoeing got caught in the rapids, Winema manipulated the canoe brilliantly and all were saved. In late youth she fell in love with, and eventually married, a White miner from Kentucky named Frank Riddle, and the admiration of her people turned to scorn; only her brother Kintpuash and a warrior named Scarface Charlie remained loyal to her. Following her marriage she became known familiarly to Whites as Toby Riddle.

Winema (1848–1932)
(*Smithsonian Institution, National Anthropological Archives*)

The 1860s saw growing friction between the Modoc people and the White Settlers moving into northern California in ever-increasing numbers. Winema served as an interpreter, with her husband, in the negotiations between the government and the Modoc which shortly led to the removal of the Indians to a reservation in Oregon. Many of the Modoc never agreed willingly to this move, and Kintpuash and a group of followers frequently left the reservation to return to their traditional homelands. When they were finally pursued by government forces in an effort to round up the band and end the intermittent resistance, they fled to the nearby lava beds. Winema tried to act as a peacemaker between the warring parties, since she was trusted by both sides, and was fluent in Modoc and English. In February 1873, a peace commission attempted to resolve the situation and Winema was able to persuade Kintpuash to meet with them. However, other Modoc opposed the move, and convinced Kintpuash that the leader of the delegation, General Edward Canby, could not be trusted and must be killed.

Woven Basket; Modoc
(*Museum of the American Indian*)

Winema learned of the plot, and warned Canby, but he decided to go ahead with the peace talks. On April 11, 1873, Kintpuash and several warriors attacked the camp, and killed Canby and another commissioner, Eleazar Thomas; a third commissioner, Albert Meacham, was badly injured, but Winema intervened and saved his life. With these murders, all-out war began, and although the Modoc held off the vastly superior Army forces for many months, they were finally defeated. Kintpuash and five other leaders were tried, convicted, and executed. Meacham, still a champion for the Indian position in spite of the attack upon him, took the story East in the form of a lecture-play entitled *Winema;* this play told of the War and reasons which led to the uprising. The troupe included Winema, Frank Riddle, and their son Jeff, and several other Modoc participants and toured during 1874–1881.

Following the successful tour of the group, Winema returned to Oregon where she lived quietly for many years. She died on the reservation on May 30, 1932, and was buried in the Modoc Cemetery. The Winema National Forest is named for her.

Sarah Winnemucca
(ca. 1844–1891)

Thocmetony, Tocmetone, "Shell Flower," known as Sarah or Sallie, was a Paviotso Paiute woman who struggled throughout most of her life to secure fair treatment for her people. She was born in 1844 near Humboldt Lake in northern Nevada at a more peaceful time before the arrival of many White outsiders. Her grandfather, the elder Chief Winnemucca, "The Giver," was known as Captain Truckee to the Whites; he had guided Captain John C. Frémont across the mountains into California in 1845–1856. In 1860, he took Thocmetony and some others to the San Joaquín Valley for a brief visit. By the time they returned home, the young girl had learned a fair amount of English

Sarah Winnemucca (1844–1891)
(*Nevada State Museum*)

Old Winnemucca
(*Nevada State Museum*)

which she improved by staying for a year with the family of Major William Ormsby, a stagecoach agent; later she enrolled at St. Mary's Convent, but was forced to leave within a month when White parents objected to the presence of an Indian child at the school.

The origin of the name Winnemucca is uncertain; most accounts refer to *one-e-mucca* (or *winnamuck*), to an incident during the visit of Frémont, when the chief was observed wearing only one moccasin (*muck*, "moccasin"), having taken the mate off to relieve his foot. The term "one muck," combining English and Paiute, seems to have stuck, resulting in the peculiar name.

Meanwhile, her father, younger Chief Winnemucca (Wobitsawah-kah), had become a tribal leader and was having difficulty controlling his people in the face of the increasing number of White settlers flowing into Nevada, and finally tension between the two brought on the so-called Paiute War of 1860, which resulted in the establishment of the Paiute Reservation at Pyramid Lake. But in 1865, aggression against Indian people increased; they were killed at random and their homes were destroyed by raiding soldiers.

In an effort to avoid further bloodshed, and to help her people, Sarah became an interpreter between Indians and Whites, but in the relentless harassment, her mother, sister, and brother were killed, and she developed a lifelong hatred for the people she felt were primarily responsible for the lack of understanding between the two peoples—the Indian Agents. She went to live with her brother, Natchez, in 1866, at Pyramid Lake; along with many other Paiute people, she applied to the Army Post at Camp McDermitt for food. Her knowledge of English impressed the Army officers and she stayed on to serve as official interpreter.

Although she was a government employee, she protested vigorously against the treatment accorded the Paiute, and in 1870 went to San Francisco to present her case to General John Schofield. Although sympathetic, he could not help her, pointing out that he had no jurisdiction over the area. She then went to Gold Hill, Nevada to Senator John P. Jones, a wealthy railroad man and state politician, whom she felt would have the necessary authority. He gave her moral advice and a $20 gold piece.

In 1872 the Paiute were moved to Oregon, where they found a brief respite on the Malheur Reservation with Agent Samuel Parrish. Sarah became his interpreter and then taught at the local school. But after only four years, Parrish was replaced by William Rinehart, whose policies were such that the Paiute began to leave the Reservation in large numbers. Many of them, including Chief Winnemucca, joined the Bannock in their 1878 war against the Whites. Sarah rejected the violence and offered her services to the Army as an interpreter and peacemaker; she undertook a dangerous mission into the heart of the Bannock country and successfully persuaded her father and his band to return to a neutral position.

After this experience, and what she considered to be the unjustified removal of all the Paiute to Washington, Sarah stepped up her campaign against the Indian Agents. Some of them retaliated, attempting to discredit her with charges that she was a liar and a "drunken prostitute"; but her message aroused a wave of popular sympathy. At this time she married Lieutenant Edward Bartlett, but the two were divorced after a year together, and she married a Paiute man.

In 1879-1880 the Government paid for Chief Winnemucca and his daughter to go to Washington to argue the Paiute claims. But although President Hayes and Interior Secretary Carl Schurz both agreed that the tribe should be returned to their own Malheur Reservation, the Indian Agent at Yakima, Washington, did nothing to follow through on the decision. Many Indians drifted south—but even those who made the trip safely were not given the land allotments which the Winnemuccas had been promised. Even an 1884 Act of Congress had no effect whatsoever upon the independent conduct of Indian Agents isolated in the Far West.

Sarah went on several lecture tours throughout the East, soliciting support for the Paiute struggle for justice. In 1881 she married Lieutenant Lambert H. Hopkins, and with his support, wrote the book, *Life Among the Paiutes*, published in 1884, which is a vivid account of Indian life of the period, despite its sometimes uneven presentation. In the middle 1880s she taught at a reservation school in Nevada.

But time, and her continuing struggle and its emotional impact were taking their toll; she began to deteriorate mentally and psychologically, and she retired to her sister's home in Monida, Montana, where she died of tuberculosis on October 16, 1891. The woman who was called "The Princess" by Whites, and "Mother" by her tribe, was also surely "the most famous Indian woman on the Pacific Coast." The city of Winnemucca, in Humboldt County, Nevada, was named for Chief Winnemucca.

Wooden Lance (ca. 1860-1931)

Wooden Lance (1860-1931)
(*Smithsonian Institution, National Anthropological Archives*)

A'piatan, Ahpeatone, or Ahpiatom, "Wooden Lance," the last Kiowa chief, was a young man of partly Sioux ancestry who was living with his fellow Kiowa in Indian Territory when the Ghost Dance religion of Wovoka swept across the Plains like prairie fire. He was born in the Canadian River area about 1860 (some accounts say 1856), and became recognized as a major force among his people while he was still quite young.

The Sioux medicine man High Wolf had brought the word of the new Messiah and his message of hope for the Indian to the Kiowa people. The tribal chiefs were interested, but cautious, and finally decided to send an emissary to look into these mystic accounts. Accordingly, they dispatched A'piatan to accompany High Wolf north in February 1891, to find out more about this new faith that everyone was talking about. They were excited about the many rumors they had heard—not only that all of the dead Indians would be resurrected to live in a Paradise on earth, but more particularly the teaching that the White man would return whence he had come, and leave the Indian country in peace.

A'piatan found great hope in these prophecies, for he had just lost his child; the teachings suggested that he might see him again, and this helped ease his grief. He set out for the Sioux country, where he hoped he might see the Messiah for himself, and perhaps also be reunited with his beloved son. Instead, he found only bloodshed and sorrow, climaxed by Sitting Bull's murder and the news of the massacre at Wounded Knee Creek. Finally, he turned toward the West, and eventually arrived in Mason Valley, Nevada, the home of Wovoka.

But the Messiah had also lost heart; he had never realized that his preaching would bring such bloodshed to the Indian people, nor had he understood the extremes to which the frustrated and bitter people would be driven in their desperation. He told A'piatan that the hope which had been offered to the Ghost Dancers was false, and that he should return home. Dispirited, the Kiowa envoy rode back to the south, and told his people what he had learned, and that there indeed seemed no way to avoid the increasing pressures of the waves of White settlers.

Instead of totally giving up, however, A'piatan felt that he could help his people in other ways, and turned to active participation in tribal affairs. He went to Washington with General Hugh Scott in 1894 to represent the tribe in negotiations with the White leaders, and was elected as the last principal chief of the Kiowa tribe. He died in Oklahoma on August 8, 1931, an honored and widely respected man who had seen and survived the transition from the buffalo days to the modern era.

Wooden Leg (1858–1940)
(*Smithsonian Institution, National Anthropological Archives*)

Wooden Leg (1858–1940)

Kummok'quiviokta was a Cheyenne leader who lived as a young man in the midst of some of the most important events of his tribe's history; he subsequently told of these times in his autobiography which was published in 1931. He was born in 1858 at the Cheyenne River, in the Black Hills of Dakota; his mother was Eagle Feather on the Forehead and his father was Many Bullet Wounds (also called White Buffalo Shaking Off the Dust), both Northern Cheyenne people. The boy, at first called "Eats from the Hand," in reference to his good appetite, grew to be an unusually tall, strong young man; he was 6'2" tall and weighted about 235 pounds. This physique gave rise to his name: a tireless walker; he was said to have "wooden legs which never tire" hence another name for him: Good Walker.

In March 1876, he and his family were camped with a mixed band of Cheyenne and Sioux people near the Powder River when they were attacked by troops under Colonel Joseph J. Reynolds. Led by the redoubtable Two Moon, most of the Indians escaped; Wooden Leg found shelter in the Sitting Bull encampment, and was at that camp on the Little Bighorn River when Custer attacked and was annihilated. Subsequently, Army reinforcements poured into the area and established a restive peace.

It was ordered that the Cheyenne people would be exiled to Indian Territory. Although he was at first content to go south, anticipating the freedom to roam the Plains and hunt the buffalo, Wooden Leg was unhappy after they finally reached the alien country—it proved to be clearly a land no one would want to live in.

But he and his family did not join the group led by Dull Knife and Little Wolf on their tragic flight back to the northern homeland in 1878. After the tragedy of that exodus, the government relented and allowed the Cheyenne to settle in the Tongue River country of Montana.

Wooden Leg traveled the White man's road from then on, albeit with reluctance. For a time he was an Army scout, and was partially involved with the Ghost Dance troubles of 1890. In time, he was prevailed upon to become a judge of the Indian Court, but there were times when he disliked imposing White man's laws upon his own people, particularly their strange insistence upon monogamy. Although he set a good example by giving up his second wife, he and his fellow Indians soon learned that they could live comfortably in the traditional way, out of sight of the missionary censors: it was simply family courtesy to have one's sister-in-law live at home.

At the age of 50, Wooden Leg was baptized into the Christian faith, in company with his wife and two daughters. Neither an intransigent holdout, nor a bought-off traitor, he perhaps summed up the attitude of the average Indian towards reservation life when he said, "Yes, it is pleasant to be situated where I can sleep soundly at night without fear . . . but I like to think about the old times when every man had to be brave. I wish I could live again through some of the past days of real freedom."

He became a tribal historian, enjoying the role of a "last link" with the days when the buffalo roamed the Plains in great herds, and at his death in Montana in 1940, was a widely respected figure.

Wovoka (ca. 1858–1932)

Wovoka (1858–1932)
(*Smithsonian Institution, National Anthropological Archives*)

Wo-vo'ka, "The Cutter," also known as Wanekia, "One Who Makes Life," was a Paiute visionary responsible for the birth and expansion of the Ghost Dance religion. He was born on the Walker River, in Mason Valley, Nevada about 1858, the son of Tävibo (The White Man), a medicine man and Paiute mystic. After the death of his father, the teen-aged Wovoka was taken in by a local rancher named David Wilson, and given the name Jack. The Wilsons were devout Christians and nurtured Wovoka's religious nature, which he inherited from his father.

When Wovoka was about 30, he had a mystical experience which had a profound effect upon him—and the subsequent history of the western Indians as well. He fell ill from a fever at the same time as the solar eclipse of January 1, 1889 took place. During this illness he had a vision which offered new hope to the beleagured western tribes and which became the core of the Ghost Dance movement. Wovoka's vision was that the former Indian lands would revert to their ancient owners; the buffalo, elk, deer, and other game which had once been so plentiful would reappear and the land would again be a Paradise. The Messiah would return, all Whites would disappear, and all of the dead Indians would be resurrected. This vision would be realized—perhaps as early as 1891—if all of the Indians lived peaceably and practiced the Ghost Dance while wearing a prescribed costume. Because of Wovoka's mystical personality, the manner in which the vision appeared, and because the

Tule-and-Feather Duck Decoy; Paiute
(*Museum of the American Indian*)

Indian people yearned nostalgically for the return of their lost homelands they devoutly believed in the prophecy.

The Ghost Dance itself was a simple ritual. Participants formed a circle, joined hands, and moved slowly to the left while singing songs of Wovoka's dreams for the future; these were specifically composed for each dance. The costumes were generally shirts or dresses made of buckskin or muslin, and painted with symbolic designs. Some of the more extreme followers believed and spread the idea that these painted shirts were actually impervious to the bullets of the White man.

Wovoka was not a naïve actor in this drama; indeed, much of his mystical qualities were more accurately the result of skillful legerdemain, and so mesmerized his audiences that in time he came to be regarded as The Messiah himself. Emissaries came from other tribes to meet the man some called The Red Man's Christ. The Sioux in particular, perhaps because the Ghost Dance came at such a critical time in their history, were especially moved by his preaching. On the other hand, the Whites regarded the new religion with antipathy and fear, seeing in it a strong unifying movement of resistance among the Indians; accordingly, they determined to arrest the man whom they considered to be its most dangerous fomentor—Sitting Bull. The old chief fought back, but was murdered along with his son and several other Sioux.

The Whites continued their campaign against the Ghost Dance and rounded up many of its adherents, including Big Foot, the leader of a small Hunkpapa Sioux band. Shortly before Christmas in 1890, most of them were massacred by trigger-happy soldiers at Wounded Knee Creek, South Dakota. Wovoka's dream of a green, peaceful land was buried in blood-soaked bodies.

Although countless Indians had subscribed to his vision, Wovoka was stunned at the tragedy which had grown out of such a temperate faith. He had never advocated a physical uprising as a means of realizing his vision, nor did he imagine it would cause violence to others. The dream which he believed—somewhat naïvely—would come about naturally through ritual and faith. While many of the Indians continued to keep faith with him for many years, the impact of the vision was decisively lost in the slaughter of innocent Indians.

Wovoka, recognizing the inevitable, advocated reconciliation with the Whites from that time on, although he never denied his original vision as the eventual future hope of the Indian. He died at Schurz, on the Walker River Reservation in Nevada, on September 20, 1932, at the age of 74, and was buried in the little cemetery there. During his life he had only one wife, Mary, by whom he had three daughters, Daisy, Ida, and Alice and one son who died in his teens.

Allen Wright (1825–1885)

Kiliahote or Kilihote, "Let's Kindle a Fire," was a famous Choctaw preacher and political leader. He was born along the Yaknukni (Yockanookany) River in Attala County, Mississippi on November 28, 1825.

His parents were almost full-blooded Choctaw; his father was Ishtema-hilubi and his mother was of the Hayupatuklo clan. Wright regarded himself as 7/8 Choctaw.

Preparing for emigration to Indian Territory, the mother died, but the family arrived in 1832; a few years after their arrival to Indian Territory the father died, and young Kiliahote was taken in by Reverend Kingsbury, a Presbyterian missionary who was responsible for his profound religious leanings. He have the young Kiliahote the name "Allen Wright" after an early Choctaw missionary, by which he was known for the rest of his life. A good student, Allen attended several local schools, including Pine Ridge and the Spencer Academy; subsequently he was selected to go east to complete his education. In 1852 he graduated from Union College in Schenectady, New York, with an A.B. degree, and three years later completed the M.A. degree at Union Theological Seminary in New York.

Allen Wright (1825–1885)
(*Oklahoma Historical Society*)

In 1856 he was ordained by the Presbyterian Church and returned to work among his own people. He had become widely recognized as a scholar in Latin, Greek, and Hebrew due to his remarkable linguistic aptitude. In addition to ministering to his people, he was also elected to the Choctaw House of Representatives, and later, to the Senate. In 1862 he served briefly in the Confederate Army. After the Civil War he was elected as Principal Chief of the Choctaw Nation in 1866, and was re-elected for another term in 1868.

At the time of the planning of the Choctaw and the Chickasaw Treaties of 1866, he was an active force in the wording of the terms, and suggested the name Oklahoma, from *okla* "red," *homma* "people," as a suitable name for the region. In time, this became the official name for the 46th state. He married a missionary, Harriet Newell Mitchell, of Dayton, Ohio, by whom he had four sons and four daughters.

Continuing with his linguistic interests, Wright published his *Chahta Leksikon*, or Choctaw dictionary, in 1880, and later translated the Choctaw and Chickasaw constitution, code of laws, and also did several hymnals, all of which have become the standard forms of these works. He died on December 2, 1885 at Boggy Depot, Oklahoma, and is buried there near his home.

Wyandanch (1600?-1659)

Also called Wyandance or Wiantance, "The Wise Speaker," was a Montauk chief who is regarded as the last major Indian leader on Long Island, New York. He was the sachem of Montauk, and at the death of his brother Pogattacut in 1653 became the Great Sachem of Paumanack. Like most of the Indians in the area, he was essentially peaceful, and is not known to have fought any major battles with the Dutch or the English. His home was on Montauk Point.

Wyandanch became a friend of Lion Gardiner, an Englishman who purchased the island of Manchonack from him on May 3, 1639 for trade cloth and other supplies; the land today is known as Gardiner's Island, in Suffolk County, New York.

In 1653, the Niantic chief Ninigret invaded the Montauk village during the wedding of Wyandanch's daughter Quashawam (also known as Momone, "Heather Flower"), kidnapped her, and held her captive until Gardiner provided the ransom which freed the girl. As a reward, Wyandanch gave the English the area of Smithtown in 1655, totaling 7000 acres, with the right to graze cattle on the land for seven years. In the late 1650s, a smallpox epidemic struck the region; lacking any immunity to the White man's diseases, most of the Indian population died, and the Long Island tribes lost almost one-third of their people.

Wyandanch at first escaped the malady, but in 1659, he too succumbed to the dread scourge; his wife Witchikittawbut survived him. There were reports that he had been poisoned, although this seems unlikely. His young son Wyancombone became tribal chief in his place, but three years later, he too, died from the disease which ended the family line.

Yellow Hand (ca. 1850–1876)

Nape-zi, from *nape*, "hand," and *zi*, "yellow," was a Cheyenne war leader about whom very little is known with the exception of one dramatic—and final—episode in his career. He was the eldest son of Chief Cut Nose.

On July 17, 1876, less than a month after Custer's defeat at the Little Bighorn, approximately 500 troops under the command of General Wesley Merritt were en route to Fort Fetterman to join General George Crook. At War Bonnet Creek, the force intercepted a band of approximately 800 Cheyenne warriors who were headed for the camp of Sitting Bull. Although no fighting immediately resulted, both sides refused to yield; there ensued a goodly amount of bluff-and-bluster by each, without any solution. Each group was trying to convince the other of their respective strength and determination to proceed.

Finally, as the eyewitness accounts testify, the Army scout and frontier hunter, "Buffalo Bill" Cody was challenged by Yellow Hand to engage him in single combat. This grew largely out of the back-and-forth defiance which had gone on for some time. Cody accepted, and the two men mounted their ponies to begin the duel.

The initial circling, looking for an opening, went on for several minutes, and suddenly Yellow Hand fired his rifle, but missed. Cody returned the fire, killing the Cheyenne's pony, and the combat continued on foot. Circling warily, each man fired again, and Cody's bullet struck his opponent, but did not kill him. The Army scout closed in, drew his knife, and stabbed the wounded Indian; Yellow Hand dropped to the ground and died. Then the warriors and soldiers who had been watching the fight jumped into action, and shortly afterwards, following desultory fighting, both sides withdrew by mutual agreement.

Chauncey Yellow Robe
(1870–1930)

Tashinagi was a Yanktonai Sioux educator who was a link between the buffalo days and the modern-day Plains Indian. He was born near Rapid City, South Dakota, about 1870, the son of Tasi Nagi (Yellow Robe); his mother was Tahcawin, "The Doe," a niece of Sitting Bull. As a boy, he was known as Canowicakte, "Kills in the Woods," a reference to his having killed a buffalo during a hunting trip.

Tashinagi was raised in the traditional way for the period, and in 1891 was taken to Carlisle Indian School by Captain Richard H. Pratt, where he proved to be an excellent pupil. He attended the Columbian Exposition in 1892, as Cadet Captain from Carlisle. Upon graduation in 1895, he was employed in Indian Schools, and in 1903 was appointed Disciplinarian at Rapid City Indian School, a post he held for most of his life.

Yellow Robe presided at the ceremonies in which President Calvin Coolidge was "adopted" into the Sioux Tribe in 1927, during the *Days of '76* celebration at Deadwood, South Dakota. The famous presentation of the feather war bonnet to Coolidge became a newsworthy photograph which was featured throughout the world.

In 1913, he spoke out angrily against a motion picture written around the Wounded Knee affair, featuring "Buffalo Bill" Cody, criticizing the making of a movie based upon such a tragedy. He was a member of the Masonic Order in Rapid City, and frequently appeared as a speaker. A notable orator, in 1920 he was invited to relate some episodes from his early life over the newly opened radio station WCAT. As he talked, he became more and more animated, and suddenly exploded in a great war whoop, blowing out the transmitter tube, and completely shutting down the infant station.

He was always active in Indian affairs, seeking a better understanding between White and Indian, and in an effort to present a truer picture, he participated in *The Silent Enemy*, sponsored by the American Museum of Natural History in 1929. During the filming of the picture, he caught a bad cold and died at Rockefeller Institute Hospital from pneumonia on April 6, 1930. He had married a French Canadian nurse, by whom he had four children—Evelyn, Rosebud, Chauncina, and Chauncey, Jr.

Chauncey was buried at Mountain View Cemetery, in Rapid City, South Dakota.

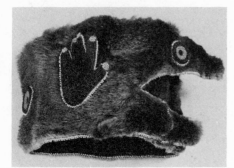

Man's Otter-Fur Turban, Decorated with Beadwork; Winnebago
(*Museum of the American Indian*)

Yellow Thunder (ca. 1774–1874)

Wakunchakukah or Waunkauntshawzeekau was an important Winnebago leader who figured prominently in the disposal of tribal lands in the Green Bay area of Wisconsin. He was born near Lake Winnebago about 1774, and seems to have led a relatively quiet life during his early youth.

During the early part of the 19th century, the Winnebago owned all of the land surrounding Lake Winnebago and Green Bay, inhabiting several small villages scattered throughout the region. Following the War of 1812 and White expansion into the Midwest, the United States government determined to settle the Indians in the Great Lakes onto reservations, negotiating with them for land cessions. A new reservation was set aside for the Winnebago in Iowa and another in Minnesota.

There was considerable dissent among the Indians, since most of them did not want to leave their lush, fertile homeland to move to less hospitable, unknown regions. The Black Hawk War, although an unsuccessful Indian effort, had stirred many of the people to hostility, and the authorities took considerable pains to try to achieve peaceful settlement of land purchases.

Accordingly, Yellow Thunder and several other Winnebago chiefs were invited to travel to Washington to meet the leading politicians of the day, and to try to influence their feelings about disposing of their lands. On November 1, 1837, the group was induced to sign a treaty which abandoned their claims to all of their Wisconsin lands, and to move west of the Mississippi River within eight months.

When pressed to move, the Indians protested bitterly, charging that they had been lied to—that they had been told they would have eight years to move, instead of eight months. But in 1840, troops were dispatched to remove them by force, rumors flew that Yellow Thunder was intending to lead a revolt in protest against the action, and he was put in chains. This was not true, and he was later released; but the troops proceeded with the removal to the reservations which are inhabited today by the Winnebago in the two states designated as their new homes.

Shortly afterwards, Yellow Thunder appeared with his wife at their old home, where he quietly entered a homestead claim to 40 acres, as was prescribed by the terms, north of Portage, Wisconsin. He lived there until his death in February 1874. It has been suggested that he was allowed to remain unmolested on his homestead in recognition of his original role in the negotiations for the land treaty. He was respected as a major tribal figure by his people and his advice was heeded in council. Following his death, a monument was erected in his memory on July 27, 1909, north of Baraboo, Wisconsin.

Yellow Wolf (1856–1935)

Hermene Moxmox, a nephew of the Nez Perce Chief Joseph, was a warrior and scout during the Nez Percé War. But more important, he was to tell in vivid detail the story of that war and its aftermath from the Indian point of view. In 1877, when the War took place, Yellow Wolf was 21 years old; he had already established a reputation as a hunter and a marksman. Also, like many of his tribe, he was superb at breaking and training horses. Because mobility and sharpshooting were two key elements in the 1600-mile Nez Percé success in their retreat toward Canada, Yellow Wolf played an important role.

Woven Cornhusk Wallet; Nez Percé
(*Museum of the American Indian*)

One essential facet to Nez Percé philosophy was respect for individual choice. Though the majority might prefer a particular choice of action, the individual or band which elected an alternate solution was neither held in disrespect nor prevented in any way from following it through. Thus, at the final, crucial battle of the war in Bear Paws, Montana, between September 30 and October 5, 1877, councils were held to decide on a course of action. While Joseph and the majority of the surviving Indians surrendered, some chose to escape to refuge in Canada and find Sitting Bull's group, Yellow Wolf was among them. Those who surrendered were sent to Indian Territory (Oklahoma), which violated the surrender agreement. In Indian Territory the climate, malaise, and malaria devastated the tribe.

The United States government was disturbed by the dissident Nez Percé who had amicably joined their former Sioux enemies who were also in exile in Canada. Delegations were sent to try to induce them to return to the United States, but, as the Indians were to discover, the promises made in this effort were rarely honored later.

With a band of 13 men, 9 women, and several children, Yellow Wolf capitulated, and returned to the United States in 1888, hoping to settle with his people on the Lapwai Reservation in Idaho. In spite of his efforts to avoid Whites en route, skirmishes occurred, and government forces were sent to capture the small band. The result was that Yellow Wolf and his people were sent to Indian Territory, where they joined Joseph and the others who had surrendered earlier at Bear Paws.

In 1895, after six years of pleading with the government, the Nez Percé were divided, and some were indeed sent to the Lapwai Reservation; but Joseph, Yellow Wolf, and others were sent to the Colville Reservation in Washington. This action was taken partly for punishment, and partly out of fear that a new uprising might be generated. Joseph never lived on his homeland again; he died at Colville Reservation in 1904.

In 1908, a White man, Lucullus McWhorter, became acquainted with Yellow Wolf and urged him to tell the Nez Percé story. His accurate descriptions and keen insight into the extraordinary ordeal faced by his people provided a moving history of the event, which was published as *Yellow Wolf* in 1940, five years after the death of the old warrior. McWhorter described Yellow Wolf as a tall, handsome man of somber bearing and sensitive demeanor. His seriousness would no doubt be due to the history of his people which he was narrating. And, too, it was perhaps due to his contrasting memories of the War and his early life in his beloved Wallowa Valley home. He evoked the latter beautifully, when comparing it to his life in Indian Territory: "No mountains, no springs, no clear running rivers. Thoughts come of the Wallowa where I grew up. Of my own country when only the Indians were there. Of tepees along the bending river. Of the blue water lake, wide meadows with horse and cattle herds. From the mountain forests, voices seemed calling. I felt as dreaming. Not my living self."

Shortly after completing his narrative, Yellow Wolf died at Colville in 1935, one of the last of those who had taken a major part in the Nez Percé War of the Pacific Northwest.

Youkioma (ca. 1880–1929)

Yukioma, Yukeoma, or Youkeoma, from Hopi "Nearly Complete," or "Almost Perfect," was an Oraibi chief who was one of the key participants in a historic confrontation which resulted in the complete division of that village. He was born at Old Oraibi about 1880, a member of the Kokop clan.

Toward the end of the 19th century the Hopi people on Third Mesa had become deeply divided between those who opposed cooperation with the White man—commonly termed the Hostiles or Conservatives—and those who felt that accommodation was inevitable, and were known as the Friendlies or Progressives. Lolóloma, the hereditary chief in 1891, tended to follow a Progressive policy. He was opposed by many of his people, led primarily by Lomahongyoma, who split from the Friendly faction that summer, and claimed to be the "real chief" of Oraibi, since more people agreed with him than with Lolóloma.

The ceremonial life of the village was split as was the whole social and economic pattern. Children were withdrawn from school, troops were brought in to capture them and take them back to the new school established at Keams Canyon, by force. The chief, Lolóloma, was taken as a prisoner to Fort Wingate, along with several subchiefs, thereby antagonizing some of the very people who had been sympathetic to the Whites.

Youkioma comes into prominence at the time of the actual split, at the turn of the century. The rift between Lolóloma and Lomahongyoma had widened, and had become so bitter as to be insoluble. Harassed on all sides by internal factionalism, well-meaning civilians, missionary intrigue, and military force, the Hopi become so confused and antagonized that every suggestion, no matter how intelligent or sound, was rejected. In 1902 Lolóloma died, and his rival, Lomahongyoma, now an old man, retired from the front lines of political action.

Into this arena stepped two new, young antagonists: Tawaquaptewa, the nephew and successor of Lolóloma, and Youkioma, who became the head of the Conservative faction. Both were remarkably similar: small in stature, ambitious, somewhat devious, and tenacious in their personalities. They sharpened and renewed the conflict, giving it a more pointed focus. In 1904 religious rivalry caused a clash between the two forces, with the result that in 1906, two, instead of one, vital ceremonies were conducted by the rival parties—an unprecedented departure from the usual Hopi practice.

This brought the bitter feelings to a head. Tawaquaptewa sent to the outlying Oraibi colony of Moenkopi for support, while Youkioma planned his own strategy to gather strength for the coming battle, which was now recognized as inevitable. In late August, the Hostile people were scheduled to hold the celebrated Snake Dance; to allow more time, they postponed the rites until September 5, 1906. On the night of September 6, 1906 meetings were held in the rival headquarters to plan for the approaching clash. While everyone wanted to avoid bloodshed, no one was willing to abandon their strong position. A few Whites tried to intervene, threatening to bring troops in if the situation got out of hand.

On the morning of September 7, 1906 a few minor skirmishes took place, during which Youkioma was physically ejected from the house of one of the Progressives. Finally, late in the afternoon, a large group of men, divided more or less evenly, faced each other on level ground near the village. Youkioma faced his rival, Tawaquaptewa, and drew a long line in the earth with his foot, saying, "If your people force us away from the village and are strong enough to pass me over this line, it will be done. But if we pass you over the line, it will not be done." He then placed himself exactly in the center of the line, facing Oraibi.

The struggle was on. Observers say that it was a general push-of-war, in which Youkioma was seen to be forced back and forth over

Youkioma (1880-1929)
(*Museum of Northern Arizona*)

Carved Wooden Kachina Doll Representing Masau'u Kachina; Hopi
(*Museum of the American Indian*)

the line several times, on occasion "squirted" up into the air over the shoulders of his backers. He was badly mauled in the effort, and in the end, the Hostiles were clearly forced back away from the village.

After catching his breath, Youkioma admitted defeat, and with his followers gathered up their possessions, and walked away from Oraibi to the north. They stopped about seven miles distant, where there were good springs, and eventually established the village of Hotevilla, starting with a population of about 400 people. Although the new village had a difficult birth, it eventually prospered, in time becoming even larger than its parent; it is still known as one of the most conservative Hopi villages.

The surprising reaction of White authorities further deteriorated Indian relations: Youkioma and several of his leaders were jailed, in spite of the fact that a peaceful, bloodless solution had been worked out by the Indian people themselves. This deprived the exiled Hopi of their leadership just at a time when such direction was needed most. This foolish action only embittered Youkioma even more. He became a sour, bitter old man, so obstinate in any dealings with the Whites that he was jailed eight times, sent to Carlisle for a brief period of "rehabilitation," and once went to Washington, D.C., with Indian Agent Lawshe in 1911 in an effort to win him over by a show of government power. He met President Taft and was photographed with several of the leading political figures of the day.

There seems little question that Youkioma was a difficult man to live with, let alone deal with. But he supported the best interests of his people as he saw them—no doubt with some degree of self-interest—and he was a key figure in one of the most remarkable examples of Indian factional dispute in history. Rarely has there been an opportunity to establish a permanent record of what must have happened many times in the prehistoric past. As he grew older, Youkioma retired more and more from active participation in village affairs, and continued to live at Hotevilla until his death in 1929.

Young Bear (ca. 1868–1933?)

Maqui-banasha was a Mesquakie (Fox) chief who was one of several individuals in the same lineage to carry the name. He was the oldest son of Pushetonequa, one of the most prominent leaders of the Fox people in the 19th century.

After the tribe settled on a new reservation in Iowa, Young Bear became chief. He was interested in preserving as much of the traditional culture as he could, and became a major exponent of that effort, promoting the revival of arts and crafts, recording myths and other tribal accounts, in the recognition that this was one of the few ways the declining morale of his people could be lifted. Their population was dwindling and intermarriage was threatening the integrity of the Fox blood line which resulted in general malaise among the people.

In an interview published in the *Annals of Iowa* in 1928, Young Bear brooded: "Our race will soon be no more . . . we are losing our customs, habits, and many of our arts are past and gone. The government is educating our people, and when our children come back to our homes they are not as we have taught them."

Young Bear continued to work to overcome that negative effect, and his work, in fact, did stimulate a certain degree of renaissance in Fox cultural activities, which he was fortunately able to see before his death at Tama in 1933.

Young Man Afraid of His Horses
(ca. 1830–1900)

Tasunka Kokipapi was a subchief under Red Cloud, who counseled his Oglala Sioux people during the turbulence of the last half of the 19th century. His name is usually misunderstood by most Whites: it translates as "The Young Man of Whose Horses They Are Afraid," or perhaps more accurately, "Young Men Fear His Horses"—a reference to his being so powerful in war that his enemies even fear his horses.

Although he was, in fact, a hereditary chief and therefore in line to seniority over his people, he yielded—by force or by conviction— to the superior abilities of Red Cloud. During the 1860s he was one of the warrior chiefs who led the Oglala Sioux in holding back White expansion for many years.

By the treaty of 1868 the United States solemnly agreed not to take any more land without the consent of three-quarters of the tribe's adult males. In the 1870s gold seekers and settlers often encroached upon Sioux lands, but even then Red Cloud and his chiefs did not join in the battles against Custer and other Army troops in 1876. Young Man Afraid of His Horses was a strong friend of the Whites all during this period. He broke with Red Cloud to side with Indian Agent Valentine T. McGillicuddy in a struggle for power on the reservation—yet he was stoutly opposed to proposals advanced by the United States for further acquisition of Sioux lands. During this period he was installed by the White authorities as President of the Pine Ridge Indian Council and was taken on several trips to Washington, D.C., but still refused to change his position on land sales.

In 1890, the climax of Wovoka's new Messiah message—the Ghost Dance—captured the imagination and kindled the hopes of the Sioux. The events of the last 20 years—forced land sales, unfulfilled treaties, decreased or diverted food allotments, political duplicity—all made him as unhappy as most Sioux, but he did not believe in the supposed power of the Ghost Dance. Accompanied only by American Horse, he tried to convince his people that to follow the Dancers meant disaster.

After the massacre at Wounded Knee Creek, Young Man Afraid of His Horses realized that Sioux resistance was finished, and that no longer was any help possible from that direction. He got in touch with as many of the Sioux camps as he could, telling them to trust General Miles and to make whatever terms of peace they could, and to surrender. He was convinced that this was the only way to save the lives of his people. He was opposed primarily by Short Bull and Kicking Bear, who threatened to shoot any Indian who left the prairies for reservation life.

Actually, it was indeed all over. The defiance of the few holdouts was based more upon fear of punishment if captured than of true conviction. Their followers were of even less confidence; they had seen their fellow Dancers lying dead in the snow, the much-touted Ghost Shirts full of bullet holes and stained with the blood of the warriors. It took two weeks, but finally, some 3500 Sioux swelled the population at Pine Ridge Agency, finished with fighting, and concerned only with caring for the wounded, sick, and starving men, women, and children, refugees from the tragedy of the past December.

Young Man Afraid of His Horses took a leading role in the subsequent negotiations during the early 1890s which led to a somewhat fairer treatment of the Sioux, but even at the time of his death in 1900.

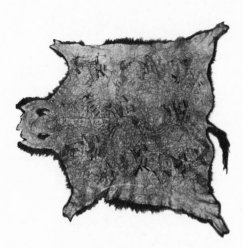

Buffalo Hide Robe, Painted by Young Man Afraid of His Horses; Sioux (*Museum of the American Indian*)

Young Man Afraid of His Horses (1830–1900) (*Nebraska State Historical Society*)

352

he realized that the day of equal justice had not arrived. To some Indians he was an apologist for the White authorities who regarded him with respect and showered him with attention. But to many other Indian people, he was protecting the best interests of the Sioux in the only way he felt would succeed. He was about 70 when he died at Pine Ridge Reservation in South Dakota.

Zotom (1853-1913)

"The Biter," or "Hole Biter," also called Podaladalte, "Snake Head," was a Kiowa warrior, artist, and missionary who was one of the group of Indian prisoners transported to Fort Marion, Florida, in 1875. Little is known of his birth; he was apparently born in 1853 to Keinti-kead, "White Shield," and his mother was Sahpooly, "Owl"; both parents were full-blooded Kiowa. As a young man Zotom participated in many Kiowa raids into Texas and Mexico, stealing horses and whatever other booty could be obtained.

He was captured in 1875, and with some 71 other Plains warriors was sent to Fort Marion for imprisonment and rehabilitation. There, he was initially sullen and rebellious; however, he eventually emerged from his angry shell, and very quickly developed as one of the most promising inmates of the Fort. His special talents as a painter became evident, and his decorated ladies' fans were in great demand. A strong man with a graceful body, he was also a gifted dancer. He was the camp bugler in addition to being one of the hardest workers.

In 1878, Zotom and some others went off to study at Hampton Institute in Virginia, but after a few months he moved on to Paris Hill, near Utica, New York. There he was sponsored by Reverend and Mrs. John B. Wicks, who supported his study for the Episcopalian ministry. He had embraced Christianity in October of that year, and was baptized Paul Caryl Zotom. After three years of study he was ordained a deacon on June 7, 1881, and sent to Indian Territory to establish an Episcopal mission to the Kiowa. This was not an easy task, and Zotom was not really prepared to handle it. It was easy and natural to be a Christian in the midst of the faithful, fervent church-goers of the East; but on the Plains of the West, where people were suspicious of all things White, the young Kiowa must have felt something like a traitor.

Yet his White sponsors were patient and generous for a time, continuing his allowance even after he had participated in a forbidden Sun Dance. When their support lagged—and especially during a period when he was the sole Episcopal worker in the field—he appealed to the bishop for help, and a replacement for the missing personnel. Caught between two cultures, the mercurial, brilliant Zotom was unable to sense just where he belonged. In 1889 the bishop paid him a visit, and was outraged to find him in Indian clothing—choosing to see this as an outward sign of an inward fall from grace. As a result, he was dropped as a missionary, and in 1894 he lost his position as deacon.

Because of his many unanswered pleas for help which had gone unanswered, Zotom felt let down by his church, and the next year he joined the congregation of Isabel Crawford, a local Baptist missionary, but this also did not live up to his expectations. He ultimately joined the Native American Church, where the peyote-based rituals more completely answered his spiritual needs.

He also turned more and more to art for economic support. One of the more interesting projects he completed was the painting of model tepee coverings for the Omaha Exposition of 1898, and a series of buckskin shield covers, which provided important ethnological and artistic materials. He died in Oklahoma on April 27, 1913, at the age of 60. He married three times—to Keahpaum, "Prepared Meat," a Kiowa from whom he was divorced after having one son; Mary Yeagtaupt, "Thrusting the Lance to Both Sides," a Crow-Comanche, whom he also divorced; and his last wife was Mary Aungattay (also known as Mary Buffalo), "Standing in the Track," a Kiowa woman who bore him several children.

Scene at Fort Sill, Indian Territory;
by Zotom
(*Museum of the American Indian*)

For Further Reading

The following sources were consulted in the preparation of this book. They offer further background information and are of value to those readers interested in expanding their knowledge of the lives and careers of individual Indian people, and the world in which they lived. This listing is by no means complete, and it should be borne in mind that most of these volumes will include their own individual bibliographies.

ABBOTT, JOHN S. C., *History of King Philip.* New York: Harper (1957) 410pp.

ABEL, ANNIE H., *The American Indian as Participant in the Civil War.* Glendale: A. H. Clark (1919) 408pp.

ABEL, ANNIE H., *The American Indian as Slave-Holder and Secessionist.* Glendale: A. H. Clark (1915) 394pp.

ADAIR, BEVERLY, Messiah Figures in Nativistic Religious Cults. *Univ. Arizona, MA Thesis* (1966) 105pp.

ADAIR, JAMES, *The History of the American Indians.* London: Edward & Charles Dilly, (1775) 464pp.

ADAMS, ALEXANDER, *Geronimo: A Biography.* New York: Putnam (1971) 381pp.

ADAMS, M. N., The Sioux Outbreak in the Year 1862. *Minnesota Historical Society Collections* **9**: 431–52 (1901).

ALDEN, TIMOTHY, *An Account of Sundry Missions Performed Among the Senecas and Munsees.* New York: J. Seymour (1827) 180pp.

ALFORD, THOMAS W., *Civilization; as Told to Florence Drake.* Norman: Univ. Oklahoma (1936) 203pp.

ANDERSON, JOHN A., *The Sioux of the Rosebud: A History in Pictures.* Norman: Univ. Oklahoma (1971) 320pp.

ANDERSON, MABEL W., *The Life of General Stand Watie; and Contemporary Cherokee History.* Pryor, Okla.: Published by the author (1931) 86pp.

ANDREWS, RALPH W., *Indian Leaders Who Have Helped Shape America.* Seattle: Superior (1971) 184pp.

ANDREWS, RALPH W., *Indians, as the Westerners Saw Them.* Seattle: Superior (1963) 176pp.

ANONYMOUS, Death of Ben Quintana. *El Palacio* **52**: 9 (1945).

APPLETON, MARION B., *Index of Pacific Northwest Portraits.* Seattle: Univ. Washington (1972) 210pp.

ARMSTRONG, PERRY A., *The Sauks and the Black Hawk War.* Springfield, Ill.: H. W. Rokker (1887) 726pp.

ARNOLD, ELLIOTT, *Blood Brother.* New York: Duell, Sloan & Pearce (1947) 558pp.

ARNOLD, OREN, *Savage Son.* Albuquerque: Univ. New Mexico (1951) 273pp.

AVERILL, ESTHER H., *King Philip, the Indian Chief.* New York: Harper (1950) 147pp.

BAD HEART BULL, AMOS, *A Pictographic History of the Oglala Sioux.* Lincoln: Univ. Nebraska (1967) 530pp.

BAHOS, CHARLES LEE, John Ross; Unionist or Secessionist in 1861? *Tulsa Univ., MA Thesis* (1968) 141pp.

BAILEY, LYNN R., *The Long Walk: A History of the Navajo Wars, 1846–68.* Los Angeles: Westernlore (1964) 252pp.

BAILEY, PAUL, *Walkara, Hawk of the Mountains.* Los Angeles: Westernlore (1954) 185pp.

BAILEY, PAUL, *Wovoka, the Indian Messiah.* Los Angeles: Westernlore (1957) 223pp.

BAIRD, W. DAVID, *Peter Pitchlynn, Chief of the Choctaws.* Norman: Univ. Oklahoma (1972) 238pp.

BALL, EVE, *In the Days of Victorio; Recollections of a Warm Springs Apache.* Tuscon: Univ. Arizona (1970) 222pp.

BARBEAU, MARIUS C., *Haida Carvers in Argillite.* Ottawa, Canada: National Museum Bulletin 139 (1957) 214pp.

BARRETT, STEPHEN M., *Geronimo's Story of His Life.* New York: Duffield (1906) 216pp.

BATTEY, THOMAS C., *The Life and Adventures of a Quaker Among the Indians.* Boston: Lee & Shepard (1875) 339pp.

BEAL, MERRILL D., *"I Will Fight No More Forever"; Chief Joseph and the Nez Percé War.* Seattle: Univ. Washington (1963) 366pp.

BEARSS, EDWIN C., The Civil War Comes to Indian Territory, 1861: The Flight of Opothleyaholo. *Journal of the West* 11: 9–42 (1972).

BEAUCHAMP, WILLIAM, *A History of the New York Iroquois, Now Commonly Called the Six Nations.* Albany: N. Y. State Museum Bulletin 78, Part 9 (1905) pp. 125–461.

BEAUCHAMP, WILLIAM, *Shikellimy and His Son Logan.* Albany: N. Y. Historical and Preservation Society (1916) pp. 599–611.

BELOUS, RUSSELL R., AND WEINSTEIN, ROBERT A., *Will Soulé, Indian Photographer at Fort Sill, Oklahoma, 1869–1874.* Los Angeles: Ward Ritchie (1969) 120pp.

BERTHRONG, DONALD J., *The Southern Cheyennes.* Norman: Univ. Oklahoma (1963) 446pp.

BETZINEZ, JASON, AND NYE, WILBUR S., *I Fought With Geronimo.* Harrisburg: Stackpole (1959) 214pp.

Biography Index. New York: H. W. Wilson Co. (1946–).

BISHOP, HARRIET E., *Dakota War-whoop; Indian Massacres and War in Minnesota.* Chicago: Lakeside (1965) 395pp.

BLACK ELK, BENJAMIN, *Notes on the Teton Sioux.* Vermilion, South Dakota: *W. H. Over Museum News; XIII #3* (1962) pp. 1–6.

BLODGETT, HAROLD, *Samson Occom.* Hanover: Dartmouth College (1935) 230pp.

BOAS, FRANZ, *Kwakiutl Ethnology* (Codere, Helen, Ed.) Chicago: Univ. of Chicago (1966) 439pp.

BOAS, FRANZ, Obituary of William Jones, *American Anthropologist* 11: 137–39 (1909).

BOAS, FRANZ, AND HUNT, GEORGE, *Kwakiutl Texts.* New York: American Museum of Natural History, Memoir VI (1905) 532pp.

BODGE, GEORGE, *Soldiers in King Philip's War.* Boston: Published by the author (1891) 369pp.

BOLSTER, MEL H., The Smoked Meat Rebellion. *Chronicles of Oklahoma* 31: 37–55 (1953).

BONFANTI, LEO, *Biographies and Legends of the New England Indians.* Wakefield, Mass.: Pride (1970) 3 vols.

BORDEAUX, WILLIAM J., *Conquering the Mighty Sioux.* Sioux Falls: Published by the author (1929) 211pp.

BOURASSA, JOSEPH N., The Life of Wah-bahn-se, The Warrior Chief of the Pottawatamies. *Kansas Historical Quarterly* 38: 132–43 (1972).

BOWSFIELD, HARTWELL, *Louis Riel, the Rebel and the Hero.* Toronto: Oxford Univ. (1971) 160pp.

BOYD, GEORGE A., *Elias Boudinot, Patriot and Statesman, 1740–1821.* Princeton: Princeton Univ. (1952) 321pp.

BOYD, MARK F., Asi-yaholo, or Osceola. *Florida Historical Quarterly* 33: 249–305 (1955).

BRADLEY, J. H., History of the Sioux. *Montana Historical Contributions* 9: 29–140 (1923).

BRADY, CYRUS T., *Indian Fights and Fighters.* New York: Doubleday Page (1923) 423pp.

BRADY, CYRUS T., *Northwestern Fights and Fighters.* New York: McClure (1907) 373pp.

BRAGG, WILLIAM F., JR., Sacajawea's Role in Western History. *Univ. Wyoming, MA Thesis* (1953) 88pp.

BRECK, JAMES, *An Apostle of the Wilderness.* New York: Whittaker (1903) 195pp.

BRIMLOW, GEORGE F., *The Bannock Indian War of 1878.* Caldwell: Caxton (1938) 231pp.

BRIMLOW, GEORGE F., The Life of Sarah Winnemucca; the Formative Years. *Oregon Historical Quarterly* 53: 103–34 (1952).

BRININSTOOL, EARL A., Crazy Horse, his Career and Death. *Nebraska History* 12: 78pp. (1929).

BRININSTOOL, EARL A., *Crazy Horse, the Invincible Oglalla Sioux Chief.* Los Angeles: Wetzel (1949) 87pp.

BRININSTOOL, EARL A., *Dull Knife, a Cheyenne Napoleon.* Hollywood: Published by the author (1935) 31pp.

BRININSTOOL, EARL A., *Fighting Indian Warriors* (originally *Fighting Red Cloud's Warriors*). Harrisburg: Stackpole (1953) 353pp.

BRITT, ALFRED, *Great Indian Chiefs*. New York: McGraw-Hill (1938) 280pp.

BROWN, DOUGLAS S., *The Catawba Indians: The People of the River*. Columbia: Univ. South Carolina (1966) 400pp.

BROWN, EVELYN H., *Kateri Tekakwitha, Mohawk Maid*. New York: Vision (1958) 190pp.

BROWN, JOHN P., *Old Frontiers: The Story of the Cherokee Indians*. Kingsport: Southern (1938) 570pp.

BROWN, VINSON, *Great Upon the Mountain; The Story of Crazy Horse*. New York: Macmillan (1975) 169pp.

BRUSH, EDWARD H., *Iroquois Past and Present*. Buffalo: Baker, Jones (1901) 104pp.

BRYANT, CHARLES, AND MURCH, ABEL B., *A History of the Great Massacre by the Sioux Indians in Minnesota*. Cincinnati: Rickey & Carroll (1864) 504pp.

BUECHNER, CECILIA B., The Pokagons. *Indiana Historical Society Pubs.* **10**: 279–340 (1933).

BULLA, CLYDE R., *Squanto, Friend of the White Man*. New York: Crowell (1954) 106pp.

CARLEY, KENNETH, As Red Men Viewed It: Three Indian Accounts of the Uprising. *Minnesota History* **38**: 126–49 (1962).

CARLEY, KENNETH, *The Sioux Uprising of 1862*. St. Paul: Minnesota Historical Society (1961) 80pp.

CARLSON, FRANK, Chief Seattle. *Univ. Washington Bulletin III #2* (1903).

CARLSON, VADA, *Cochise, Chief of the Chiricahuas*. New York: Harvey House (1973) 174pp.

CARPENTER, FRANCES, *Pocahontas and Her World*. New York: Knopf (1957) 241pp.

CARTER, ANTHONY, In Memory of Mungo Martin. *The Beaver #301* pp. 44–45 (1970).

CASWELL, HARRIET S., *Our Life Among the Iroquois Indians*. Boston: Congregational (1892) 321pp.

CATLIN, GEORGE, *Letters and Notes on the Ceremonies, Customs and Condition of the North American Indians*. London (1841) 2 vols.

CAUGHEY, JOHN W., *McGillivray of the Creeks*. Norman: Univ. Oklahoma (1938) 385pp.

CERBELAUD SALAGNAC, GEORGES, *La Révolte des Métis; Louis Riel, Héros ou Rebelle?* Tours: Mame (1971) 205pp.

CHALMERS, HARVEY, AND MONTURE, ETHEL B., *Joseph Brant, Mohawk*. East Lansing: Michigan State Univ. (1955) 364pp.

CHAPIN, HOWARD M., *Sachems of the Narragansetts*. Providence: Rhode Island Historical Society (1931) 117pp.

CLARKE, MARY W., *Chief Bowles and the Texas Cherokees*. Norman: Univ. Oklahoma (1971) 154pp.

CLUM, WOODWORTH, *Apache Agent; the Story of John P. Clum*. Boston: Houghton Mifflin (1936) 296pp.

COCHRAN, GEORGE M., *Indian Portraits of the Pacific Northwest: Thirty of the Principal Tribes*. Portland: Binfords & Mort (1959) 62pp.

COE, CHARLES H., The Parentage and Birthplace of Osceola. *Florida Historical Quarterly* **17**: 304–11 (1939).

COE, CHARLES H., *Red Patriots; the Story of the Seminoles*. Cincinnati: The Editor (1898) 290pp.

COE, STEPHEN HOWARD, Cornplanter (Kaiiontwa'/Kan) ca. 1750–1836: Seneca Chief. *American Univ., MA Thesis* (1962) 105pp.

COHOE, WILLIAM, *A Cheyenne Sketchbook*. Norman: Univ. Oklahoma (1964) 96pp.

COLLIER, PETER, *When Shall They Rest? The Cheyenne's Long Struggle With Americans*. New York: Holt, Rinehart & Winston (1973) 167pp.

COLLINGS, ELLSWORTH, Roman Nose: Chief of the Southern Cheyennes. *Chronicles of Oklahoma* **42**: 429–57 (1964).

COLLINS, JOHN, *Nampeyo, Hopi Potter*. Flagstaff: Northland (1974) 52pp.

CONOVER, GEORGE S., *The Birth-place of Sa-go-ye-wat-ha, or the Indian Red jacket*. Waterloo, N.Y.: Seneca (1884) 22pp.

COOKE, DAVID C., *Apache Warrior*.   New York: Norton (1963) 212pp.

COOKE, DAVID C., *Fighting Indians of America*.   New York: Dodd Mead (1966) 266+206pp.

COOKE, DAVID C., *Tecumseh, Destiny's Warrior*.   New York: Messner (1959) 192pp.

COPWAY, GEORGE, *The Life, Letters and Speeches of Kah-ge-ga-gah-bowh*.   New York: Benedict (1850) 224pp.

COPWAY, GEORGE, *The Traditional History and Characteristic Sketches of the Ojibway Nation*.   London: C. Gilpin (1851) 298pp.

CORSON, E. F., Long Hair, Chief of the Crows. *Archives of Dermatology and Syphilology* **16:** 443–47 (1947).

CORWIN, HUGH D., *The Kiowa Indians*.   Lawton, Okla.: Published by the author (1959) 221pp.

COTTERILL, ROBERT S., *The Southern Indians*.   Norman: Univ. Oklahoma (1954) 255pp.

CRAWFORD, ISABEL A. H., *Kiowa: The History of a Blanket Indian Mission*.   New York: Revell (1915) 242pp.

CROCCHIOLA, STANLEY F. H., *Satanta and the Kiowas*.   Borger, Tex.: Hess (1968) 391pp.

CROOK, GEORGE, *The Autobiography of General George Crook*.   (Schmitt, Martin F., Ed.) Norman: Univ. Oklahoma (1946) 326pp.

CROOKS, MAURICIA DALE, Dennis Wolfe Bushyhead and His Influence on Oklahoma History. *Univ. Oklahoma, MA Thesis* (1937) 126pp.

CROSS, HENRY H., *The T. B. Walker Collection of Indian Portraits*.   Madison: Historical Society of Wisconsin (1948) 164pp.+125 plates.

CROWDER, DAVID, *Tendoy, Chief of the Lemhis*.   Pocatello: Univ. Idaho (1966) 120pp.

Current Biography.   New York: H. W. Wilson Company (1940–).

CURTIS, EDWARD S., *The North American Indian*.   Seattle Cambridge: Curtis (1907–1930) 20 vols.

CUSHMAN, HORATIO B., *History of the Choctaw, Chickasaw and Natchez Indians*.   Greenville, Texas: Headlight (1899) 504pp.

DALE, EDWARD E., *Cherokee Cavaliers*.   Norman: Univ. Oklahoma (1939) 319pp.

DANIELS, A. W., Reminiscences of Little Crow. *Minnesota Historical Society Collections* **12:** 513–30 (1908).

DAVID, JOHN BENJAMIN, The Life and Works of Sequoyah. *George Peabody College, MA Thesis* (1929) 102pp.

DAVIDSON, JOHN N., *Muh-he-kan-ne-ok: A History of Stockbridge*.   Milwaukee: S. Chapman (1893) 64pp.

DAVIS, CARLYLE C., *The True Story of "Ramona."*   New York: Dodge (1914) 265pp.

DAVIS, RUSSELL G., AND ASHABRANNER, BRENT K., *Chief Joseph, War Chief of the Nez Percé*.   New York: McGraw-Hill (1962) 190pp.

DEARDORFF, MERLE H., The Religion of Handsome Lake; its Origin and Development. Washington: *Bureau of Amer. Ethnol. Bulletin 149 Pt. 5*, pp. 77–107 (1951).

DEBO, ANGIE, *A History of the Indians of the United States*.   Norman: Univ. Oklahoma (1970) 386pp.

DEBO, ANGIE, *And Still the Waters Run*.   Princeton: Princeton Univ. (1940) 417pp.

DEBO, ANGIE, *Rise and Fall of the Choctaw Republic*.   Norman: Univ. Oklahoma (1934) 314pp.

DEBO, ANGIE, *The Road to Disappearance*.   Norman: Univ. Oklahoma (1941) 399pp.

DEFOREST, JOHN W., *History of the Indians of Connecticut: From the Earliest Known Period to 1850*.   Hartford: Hamersley (1851) 510pp.

DENIG, EDWIN T., *Five Indian Tribes of the Upper Missouri* (Ewers, John C., Ed.) Norman: Univ. Oklahoma (1961) 217pp.

DENNIS, HENRY C., *The American Indian: A Chronology and Fact Book*.   Dobbs Ferry: Oceana (1971) 137pp.

DEUR, LYNNE, *Indian Chiefs*.   New York: Lerner (1972) 103pp.

DICKASON, DAVID H., Chief Simon Pokagon: The Indian Longfellow. *Indiana Magazine of History* **57:** 127–40 (1961).

DICKERSON, PHILIP J., *History of the Osage Nation: its People, Resources and Prospects*.   Pawhuska, Okla. (1906) 144pp.

Dictionary of American Biography.   New York: Scribners (1928–).

DIXON, JOSEPH K., *The Vanishing Race; The Last Great Indian Council*.   New York: Doubleday Page (1913) 231pp.

DOCKSTADER, FREDERICK J., AND DOCKSTADER, ALICE W., The American Indian in Graduate Studies; a Bibliography of Theses and Dissertations. New York: Museum of the American Indian, Contributions XXV (1974) 362+426pp.

DODDRIDGE, JOSEPH, *Notes on the Settlement and Indian Wars of the Western Parks of Virginia and Pennsylvania from 1763 to 1783, Inclusive.* Albany: J. Munsell (1876) 331pp.

DOLLAR, CLYDE D., The High Plains Smallpox Epidemic of 1837–38. *Western History Quarterly* **8**: 15–38 (1977).

DONALDSON, THOMAS C., *Extra Census Bulletins from 11th U. S. Census.* Washington, D.C.: U.S. Census Office (1887–1894) 5 vols.

DORSEY, JAMES O., *A Study of Siouan Cults.* Washington: *Bureau of Amer. Ethnol. Annual Report XI*, pp. 351–544 (1894).

DOWNEY, FAIRFAX D., *Indian-Fighting Army.* New York: Scribners (1941) 329pp.

DRAKE, BENJAMIN, *The Life of Tecumseh and of His Brother the Prophet.* Cincinnati: E. Morgan (1841) 235pp.

DRAKE, FRANCIS S., *Indian History for Young Folks.* New York: Harper (1885) 479pp.

DRAKE, SAMUEL G., *The Book of the Indians; or Biography and History of the Indians of North America.* Boston: H. B. Massey (1851) 784pp.

DUNN, DOROTHY, Awah Tsireh, Painter of San Ildefonso. *El Palacio* **43**: 108–15 (1956).

DUNN, JACOB P., *Massacres of the Mountains: A History of the Indian Wars of the Far West.* New York: Harper (1886) 784pp.

DUSENBERRY, VERNE, The Rocky Boy Indians; Montana's Displaced Persons. Helena: *Montana Heritage Series 3* (1954) 16pp.

EASTMAN, CHARLES A., *Indian Heroes and Great Chieftains.* Boston: Little Brown (1918) 241pp.

EASTMAN, ELAINE G., *Pratt, the Red Man's Moses.* Norman: Univ. Oklahoma (1935) 285pp.

EATON, RACHEL S., *John Ross and the Cherokee Indians.* Muskogee: Star (1921) 153pp.

EELLS, MYRON, *Ten Years of Missionary Work Among the Indians at Skokomish, Washington Territory, 1874–1884.* Boston: Congregational (1886) 271pp.

EGGLESTON, EDWARD, *Tecumseh and the Shawnee Prophet.* New York: Dodd Mead (1878) 332pp.

ELLIS, EDWARD S., *The Indian Wars of the United States.* Grand Rapids, Mich.: R. D. Farrell (1892) 516pp.

EMMITT, ROBERT, *The Last War Trail; the Utes and the Settlement of Colorado.* Norman: Univ. Oklahoma (1954) 333pp.

Encyclopedia Americana. New York: Americana Corporation.

EVANS, STEVEN ROSS, Chief Joseph and the Red Napoleon Myth. *Washington State Univ., MA Thesis* (1969) 90pp.

EVANS, WILLIAM E., The Garra Uprising. *California Historical Quarterly* **45**: 339–49 (1966).

EWY, MARVIN, Charles Curtis of Kansas: Vice-President of the United States, 1929–1933. *Kansas-Emporia Univ., MA Thesis* (1960) 167pp.

FARRELL, R. C., The Burial of Sitting Bull. *W. H. Over Museum Bulletin* **15**: 1–2 (1954).

FAULKNER, COLLEELA, The Life and Times of Reverend Stephen Foreman. *Univ. Oklahoma, MA Thesis* (1949) 254pp.

FELTON, HAROLD W., *Nancy Ward, Cherokee.* New York: Dodd Mead (1975) 89pp.

FELTON, WILLIAM R. AND BROWN, MARK H., *The Frontier Years: L. A. Huffman, Photographer of the Plains.* New York: Holt (1955) 272pp.

FERGUS, MABEL ELIZABETH, Alexander McGillivray and William Augustus Bowles: Two Characters in the Early History of the South. *Columbia Univ., MA Thesis* (1913) 35pp.

FIELDER, MILDRED, *Sioux Indian Leaders.* Seattle: Superior (1975) 160pp.

FINLEY, JAMES B., *Life Among the Indians.* Cincinnati: Hitchcock & Walden (1857) 548pp.

FISKE, FRANK B., *The Taming of the Sioux.* Bismarck: Tribune (1917) 186pp.

FISKE, FRANK B., *Life and Death of Sitting Bull.* Fort Yates: Pioneer-Arrow (1933) 72pp.

FLOOD, EDITH LYLE, Alexander Posey in Oklahoma History. *Univ. Oklahoma, MA Thesis* (1938) 108pp.

FORDE, LOIS ELIZABETH, Elias Cornelius Boudinot. *Columbia Univ., PhD Dissertation* (1951) 265pp.

FOREMAN, CAROLYN, *Indians Abroad, 1493-1938.* Norman: Univ. Oklahoma (1943) 247pp.

FOREMAN, CAROLYN, *Indian Woman Chiefs.* Muskogee: Star (1954) 86pp.

FOREMAN, CAROLYN, John Jumper, *Chronicles of Oklahoma* **29**: 137–52 (1951).

FOREMAN, CAROLYN, The Jumper Family of the Seminole Nation. *Chronicles of Oklahoma* **34**: 272 85 (1956).

FOREMAN, GRANT, *The Five Civilized Tribes.* Norman: Univ. Oklahoma (1934) 456pp.

FOREMAN, GRANT, *Indian Removal: The Emigration of the Five Civilized Tribes of Indians.* Norman: Univ. Oklahoma (1956) 415pp.

FOREMAN, GRANT, *The Last Trek of the Indians.* Norman: Univ. Oklahoma (1946) 382pp.

FOREMAN, GRANT, *Sequoyah.* Norman: Univ. Oklahoma (1938) 90pp.

FOSTER, ANNIE, *The Mohawk Princess; Being Some Account of the Life of Tekahion-wake (E. Pauline Johnson).* Vancouver: Lions Gate (1931) 216pp.

FOSTER, GEORGE E., *Se-quo-yah, the American Cadmus and Modern Moses.* Philadelphia: Indian Rights Association (1885) 244pp.

FOWLER, DON, D., Notes on the Early Life of Chief Washakie. *Annals of Wyoming* **36**: 36–42 (1964).

FOX, HETTIE MARIE, Tecumseh and His Indian Wars. *Univ. Oklahoma, MA Thesis* (1936) 112pp.

FUNDABURK, EMMA LILA, *Southeastern Life Portraits: a Catalog of Pictures, 1564–1860.* Luverne, Ala.: Published by the author (1958) 135pp.

GABRIEL, RALPH H., *Elias Boudinot, Cherokee, and His America.* Norman: Univ. Oklahoma (1941) 190pp.

GARD, WAYNE, *The Chisholm Trail.* Norman: Univ. Oklahoma (1954) 296pp.

GARLAND, HAMLIN, *The Book of the American Indian.* New York: Harper (1923) 274pp.

GARLAND, HAMLIN, General Custer's Last Fight as Seen by Two Moon. *McClure's* XI (1898).

GARST, DORIS S., *Chief Joseph the Nez Percés.* New York: Messner (1953) 184pp.

GARST, DORIS S., *Sitting Bull, Champion of his People.* New York: Messner (1946) 189pp.

GEHM, KATHERINE, *Sarah Winnemucca: Most Extraordinary Woman of the Paiute Nation.* Phoenix: O'Sullivan, Woodside (1975) 196pp.

GHENT, WILLIAM J., *Road to Oregon.* New York: Longman Greens (1929) 274pp.

GIBSON, ARRELL M., *The Chickasaws.* Norman: Univ. Oklahoma (1971) 312pp.

GIBSON, ARRELL M., *The Kickapoos: Lords of the Middle Border.* Norman: Univ. Oklahoma (1963) 391pp.

GIFFORD, JOHN C., *Billy Bowlegs and the Seminole War.* Coconut Grove, Fla.: Triangle (1925) 79pp.

GILPIN, LAURA, In Memorium: Popovi Da of San Ildefonso. *El Palacio* #78 (1972) p. 45.

GOGGIN, JOHN M., Osceola. *Florida Historical Quarterly* **23**: 161–92 (1955).

GOLDENWEISER, ALEXANDER, The Rites of New Religions Among the Native Tribes of North America. *Columbia Univ., MA Thesis* (1904) 85pp.

GOODE, WILLIAM H., *Outposts of Zion; With Limnings of Mission Life.* Cincinnati: Poe & Hitchcock (1863) 46pp.

GRANGE, ROGER T., JR., Fort Robinson, Outpost on the Plains. *Nebraska History* **39**: 151–240 (1958).

GRAY, WILLIAM H., *A History of Oregon, 1792–1849.* Portland: Harris & Holman (1870) 706pp.

GRAYMOUNT, BARBARA, *The Iroquois in the American Revolution.* Syracuse: Syracuse Univ. (1972) 359pp.

GREEN, NORMA KIPP, *Iron Eyes Family; the Children of Joseph LaFlesche.* Lincoln: Johnson (1969) 225pp.

GREENMAN, EMERSON F., *Chieftainship Among Michigan Indians. Michigan History* **24**: 361–79 (1940).

GRIDLEY, MARION, *American Indian Women.* New York: Hawthorn (1974) 178pp.

GRIDLEY, MARION, *America's Indian Statues.* Chicago: The Amerindian (1966) 104pp.

GRIDLEY, MARION, *Contemporary American Indian Leaders.* New York: Dodd Mead (1972) 201pp.

GRIDLEY, MARION, *Indians of Today.* Chicago: Indian Council Fire (1936–1971) 504pp.

GRINNELL, GEORGE B., *The Cheyenne Indians; Their History and Ways of Life.* New Haven: Yale Univ. (1923) 2 vols.

GRINNELL, GEORGE B., *The Fighting Cheyennes*.   New York: Scribners (1915) 431pp.

GRINNELL, GEORGE B., *The Indians of Today*.   Chicago: H. S. Stone (1900) 185pp. + 55 plates.

GROVES, GLENWOOD I., *Famous American Indians*.   Chicago: Published by the author (1944) 272pp.

HABER, GRACE S., *With Pipe and Tomahawk; the Story of Logan the Mingo Chief*.   New York: Pageant (1958) 126pp.

HAFEN, LEROY R., *Fort Laramie and the Pageant of the West, 1834–1890*.   Glendale: Clark (1938) 429pp.

HAGAN, WILLIAM T., Quanah Parker, Indian Judge. *El Palacio* **49**: 30–39 (1962).

HAGAN, WILLIAM T., *The Sac and Fox Indians*.   Norman: Univ. Oklahoma (1958) 287pp.

HAINES, FRANCIS, *The Nez Percês; Tribesmen of the Columbia Plateau*.   Norman: Univ. Oklahoma (1955) 329pp.

HARRINGTON, LYN, The Last of the Haida Carvers. *Natural History* **58**: 200–205 (1949).

HARRISON, CHARLES, *Ancient Warriors of the North Pacific*.   London: Witherby (1925) 222pp.

HARRISON, MICHAEL, Chief Charlot's Battle With Bureaucracy. *Montana* **10**:(4): 27–33 (1960).

HATHAWAY, WORTEN MASON, Brigadier General Stand Watie, Confederate Guerilla. *Univ. Oklahoma, MA Thesis* (1966).

HAYNE, COE, *Paths to Forgotten Folk*.   Philadelphia: Judson (1921) 206pp.

HEARD, ISAAC V. D., *History of the Sioux War and Massacres of 1862 and 1863*.   New York: Harper (1865) 354pp.

HEBARD, GRACE, *The Bozeman Trail*.   Glendale: Clark (1922) 2 vols.

HEBARD, GRACE, *Sacajawea*.   Glendale: Clark (1933) 340pp.

HEBARD, GRACE, *Washakie*.   Glendale: Clark (1930) 337pp.

HECKEWELDER, JOHN G. E., *History, Manners and Customs of the Indian Nations*.   Philadelphia: Pennsylvania Society (1876) 465pp.

HECKEWELDER, JOHN G. E., *A Narrative of the Mission of the United Brethren Among the Delaware and Mohegan Indians*.   Philadelphia: M'Carty & Davis (1820) 429pp.

HEIDERSTADT, DOROTHY, *Indian Friends and Foes*.   New York: McKay (1958) 130pp.

HEIDERSTADT, DOROTHY, *More Indian Friends and Foes*.   New York: McKay (1963) 146pp.

HENRY, THOMAS R., *Wilderness Messiah; the Story of Hiawatha and the Iroquois*.   New York: W. Sloane (1955) 285pp.

HEUMAN, WILLIAM, *Famous American Indians*.   New York: Dodd Mead (1972) 138pp.

HINES, GUSTAVUS, *Oregon; Its History, Condition and Prospects*.   Auburn, N.Y.: Derby & Miller (1851) 437pp.

HIRSCHFELDER, ARLENE, *American Indian and Eskimo Authors*.   New York: Interbooks (1973) 99pp.

HODGE, FREDERICK WEBB, Handbook of American Indians North of Mexico. Washington: *Bureau of Amer. Ethnol., Bulletin 30, 2 vols.* (1910).

HODGE, FREDERICK WEBB, Pitalesharu and his Medal. *Masterkey* **24**: 111–19 (1950).

HODGE, FREDERICK WEBB, AND ORCHARD, WILLIAM C., John Quinney's Coat. *Indian Notes* **6**: 343–51 (1929).

HODGES, BERT, Notes on the History of the Creek Nation and Some of its Leaders. *Chronicles of Oklahoma* **43**: 9–18 (1965).

HODGES, DEWEY WHITSETT, Colonel E. C. Boudinot and His Influence on Oklahoma History. *Univ. Oklahoma, MA Thesis* (1929) 60pp.

HOEL, WILLIAM BAKER, Little Turtle, the Miami Chieftain. *Miami Univ., MA Thesis* (1938) 56pp.

HOFFMAN, VIRGINIA, AND JOHNSON, BRODERICK H., *Navajo Biographies*. Rough Rock: Diné (1970) 342pp.

HOFFMAN, WALTER J., The Menomini Indians. Washington: *Bureau of Amer. Ethnol. Annual Report 14, Pt. 1*, 328pp. (1897).

HOPKINS, SARAH WINNEMUCCA, *Life Among the Piutes: Their Wrongs and Claims*.   Boston: Putnam (1883) 268pp.

HORAN, JAMES J., *The McKenney-Hall Portrait Gallery of American Indians*.   New York: Crown (1972) 373pp.

HOWARD, HELEN A., Indians and an American Indian Agent: Chief Charlot and the Forged Document. *Journal of the West* 5: 379–97 (1966).

HOWARD, JAMES J., *The Kenekuk Religion.* Vermillion: Univ. South Dakota Museum (1965) 48pp.

HOWARD, OLIVER O., *Famous Indian Chiefs I Have Known.* New York: Century (1908) 364pp.

HUBBARD, JOHN N., *An Account of Sa-go-ye-wat-ha or Red Jacket and His People, 1750–1830.* Albany: J. Munsell (1886) 356pp.

HUBBARD, WILLIAM, *The History of the Indian Wars in New England.* Roxbury, Mass.: Woodward (1865) 292 + 303 pp.

HUDEN, JOHN C., *Indian Place Names of New England.* New York: Museum of the American Indian, Contributions XVIII (1962) 408pp.

HUDSON, CHARLES M., JR., *The Catawba Nation.* Athens: Univ. Georgia (1970) 142pp.

HUFFORD, DAVID A., *The Real Ramona of Helen Hunt Jackson's Famous Novel.* Los Angeles: Hufford (1900) 57pp.

HUGGINS, ELI L., Smohalla, the Prophet of Priest Rapids. *Overland Monthly* 17: 208–15 (1891).

HUGHES, THOMAS, *Indian Chiefs of Southern Minnesota.* Mankato: Published by the author (1927) 131pp.

HUGHES, WILLIS BOLDT, Indian Messiahs in United States History. *Univ. Oregon, MA Thesis* (1948) 170pp.

HULBERT, ARCHER B., *David Zeisberger's History of Northern American Indians.* Columbus: F. J. Heer (1910) 189pp.

HULBERT, WINIFRED, *Indian Americans.* New York: Friendship (1932) 161pp.

HYDE, GEORGE, *A Sioux Chronicle.* Norman: Univ. Oklahoma (1956) 334pp.

HYDE, GEORGE, *Red Cloud's Folk; A History of the Oglala Sioux Indians.* Norman: Univ. Oklahoma (1937) 331pp.

HYDE, GEORGE, *Spotted Tail's Folk; A History of the Brulé Sioux.* Norman: Univ. Oklahoma (1937) 331pp.

The Indian's Friend. New Haven: The National Indian Association.

The Indian Leader. Lawrence, Kans.: Haskell Institute.

Indian Office Reports. Washington, D.C.: U.S. Govt. Printing Office. Reports of the Commissioner of Indian Affairs.

Indian School Journal. Chilocco, Okla.: U.S. Indian Service.

The Indian Sentinel. Washington, D.C.: Bureau of Catholic Indian Missions.

JACKSON, DONALD, *Ma-kai-me-she-mia-kiak; Autobiography of Black Hawk.* Urbana: Univ. Illinois (1955) 206pp.

JACKSON, WILLIAM H., *Descriptive Catalogue of Photographs of North American Indians.* Washington, D.C.: U.S. Govt. Printing Office (1877) 124pp.

JACOBS, WILBUR R., *Indians of the Southern Colonial Frontier.* Columbia: Univ. South Carolina (1954) 108pp.

JACOBSON, OSCAR B., *Kiowa Indian Art.* Nice: C. Szwedzicki (1929) 30 plates.

JAMES, EDWARD T., JAMES, JANET W., AND BOYER, PAUL S., *Notable American Women, 1607–1950.* Cambridge: Harvard Univ. (1971) 3 vols.

JAMES, HARRY C., *The Cahuilla Indians.* Los Angeles: Westernlore (1960) 184pp.

JARRETT, CHARLOTTE JEAN, The Influence of General Stand Watie on the History of Oklahoma. *Univ. Oklahoma, MA Thesis* (1929) 64pp.

JOHNSON, OLGA W., *Flathead and Kootenay.* Glendale: Clark (1969) 392pp.

JOHNSON, WILLIS FLETCHER, *Life of Sitting Bull and the History of the Indian War of 1890–91.* Philadelphia: Edgewood (1891) 606pp.

JOHNSTON, CHARLES H. L., *Famous Indian Chiefs.* New York: Page (1909) 463pp.

JOHNSTON, JEAN, Ancestry and Descendants of Molly Brant. *Ontario History* 43: 86–92 (1971).

JOHNSTON, JEAN, Molly Brant, Mohawk Matron. *Ontario History* 56: 105–24 (1964).

JONES, CHARLES C., *Historical Sketch of Tomo-chi-chi, Mico of the Yamacraws.* Albany: J. Munsell (1868) 133pp.

JONES, HESTER, Gerald Nailor, Famous Navajo Artist, 1917–1952. *El Palacio* 59: 294–95 (1952).

JONES, PETER, *History of the Ojebway Indians, 1802–1856.* London: A. W. Bennett (1861) 278pp.

JOSEPHY, ALVIN M., JR., *The Nez Percé Indians and the Opening of the Northwest.* New Haven: Yale Univ. (1965) 704 pp. + 24 plates.

JOSEPHY, ALVIN M., JR., *The Patriot Chiefs.* New York: Viking (1961) 364pp.

JUERGENS, ISABEL, *Wigwam and Warpath.* New York: Grosset (1969) 91pp.

KAHO, NOEL, Green Grow the Lilacs. *The American Scene* **4**: 52–53 (1962).

KELLOGG, LOUISE P., Angel DeCora Dietz. *Wisconsin Archeologist* 18 (1919).

KINGSBURY, GEORGE W., *History of Dakota Territory.* Chicago: S. J. Clark (1915) 5 vols.

KINZIE, JULIETTE A., Chicago's Indian Chiefs. *Chicago History Society. Bulletin 1,* pp. 105–16 (1935).

KLINCK, CARL F., *Tecumseh, Fact and Fancy in Early Records.* Englewood Cliffs: Prentice-Hall (1961) 246pp.

KOLECKI, JOHN HENRY, Red Jacket: the Last of the Senecas. *Niagara Univ., MA Thesis* (1950) 109pp.

KRAUSE, AUREL (Erna Gunther, Trans.), *The Tlingit Indians; Results of a Trip to the Northwest Coast of America and the Bering Straits.* Seattle: Univ. Washington (1956) 310pp.

KRIEG, FREDERICK C., Chief Plenty Coups: The Final Dignity. *Montana* **16**: 28–39 (1966).

KROEBER, CLIFTON B., The Mohave as Nationalist, 1859–1874. *American Philosophical Society Proc.* 109 (3): 173–80 (1965).

KROEBER, THEODORA, *Ishi in Two Worlds: A Biography of the Last Wild Indian in North America.* Berkeley: Univ. California (1961) 255pp.

KROEBER, THEODORA, *Ishi, Last of His Tribe.* Berkeley: Univ. California (1964) 209pp.

LAIN, GAYLE RAYMOND, Sitting Bull, Orator of the Plains. *Univ. Wyoming, MA Thesis* (1969) 76pp.

LAWSON, MARIE A., *Pocahontas and Captain John Smith; the Story of the Virginia Colony.* New York: Random House (1950) 185pp.

LECKIE, WILLIAM H., *The Military Conquest of the Southern Plains.* Norman: Univ. Oklahoma (1963) 269pp.

LEIPOLD, L. EDMOND, *Famous American Indians.* Minneapolis: Denison (1967) 79pp.

LEWIS, ANNA, *Chief Pushmataha, American Patriot.* New York: Exposition (1959) 204pp.

LEWIS, GEORGE E., *Black Beaver, the Trapper.* Chicago: Law (1911).

LEWIS, WILLIAM S., The Case for Spokane Garry, *Spokane Historical Society Bulletin, 1 #1 (1917).*

LINDERMAN, FRANK B., *American: Plenty Coups, Last of the Crows.* London: Faber & Faber (1930) 318pp.

LITTON, GASTON, The Principal Chiefs of the Cherokee Nation. *Chronicles of Oklahoma* **45**: 253–70 (1937).

LOCKWOOD, FRANK C., *The Apache Indians.* New York: Macmillan (1938) 348pp.

LOCKWOOD, FRANK C., *Pioneer Days in Arizona.* New York: Macmillan (1932) 388pp.

LOGAN, JOHN H., *History of the Upper Country of South Carolina.* Charleston: S. G. Courtenay (1859) 521pp.

LURIE, NANCY O., *Mountain Wolf Woman, Sister of Crashing Thunder.* Ann Arbor: Michigan Univ. (1961) 142pp.

McCARTHY, J. E., Portraits of Osceola and the Artists who Painted Them. *Jacksonville History Society Papers, II,* pp. 23–44 (1949).

McCLARY, BEN HARRIS, The Last Beloved Woman of the Cherokees. *Tennessee Historical Society Quarterly* **21**: 352–64 (1962).

McCLURE, DAVID, *Memories of the Reverend Eleazar Wheelock, D. D.* Newburyport (1911) 336pp.

McCOY, ISAAC, *History of Baptist Indian Missions.* New York: Raynor (1840) 611pp.

McCREIGHT, ISRAEL, *The Wigwam: Puffs From the Peace Pipe.* Dubois, Penn.: published by author (1944) 58pp.

McKENNEY, THOMAS, AND HALL, JAMES, *History of the Indian Tribes of North America* (Hodge, Frederick W., Ed.) Edinburgh: John Grant, 1933, 3 vols.

McLAUGHLIN, JAMES, *My Friend the Indian.* Boston: Houghton Mifflin (1910) 412 pp.

McLEOD, KEN, The Beginnings of the Modoc War. *Pacific Historian, III,* p. 73–80 (1959).

McRAYE, WALTER, *Pauline Johnson and Her Friends.* Toronto: Ryerson (1947) 182pp.

McREYNOLDS, EDWIN C., *The Seminoles.* Norman: Univ. Oklahoma (1957) 412pp.

McSpadden, Joseph W., *Indian Heroes*. New York: Crowell (1928) 305pp.

McWhorter, Lucullus V., *Hear Me, My Chiefs!* Caldwell: Caxton (1952) 640pp.

McWhorter, Lucullus V., *Yellow Wolf; His Own Story*. Caldwell: Caxton (1940) 324pp.

Madsden, Brigham D., *The Bannock of Idaho*. Caldwell: Caxton (1958) 382pp.

Mahon, John K., *History of the Second Seminole War, 1835–1842*. Gainesville: Univ. Florida (1967) 387pp.

Marquis, Thomas B., *Rain in the Face and Curly the Crow*. Hardin, Mont.: Custer Battle Museum (1934) 8pp.

Marquis, Thomas B., *Sitting Bull and Gall the Warrior*. Hardin, Mont.: Custer Battle Museum (1934) 8pp.

Marquis, Thomas B., *Wooden Leg, a Warrior Who Fought Custer*. Minneapolis: Midwest (1931) 384pp.

Marriott, Alice, *María, the Potter of San Ildefonso*. Norman: Univ. Oklahoma (1948) 294pp.

Marriott, Alice, *Sequoyah; Leader of the Cherokees*. New York: Random House (1956) 180pp.

Mason, Edwin C., The Bannock-Piute War of 1878; The Letters of Major Edwin C. Mason. *Journal of the West* 11: 128–42 (1972).

Matson, Nehemiah, *Memories of Shaubena*. Chicago: Grainger (1878) 252pp.

Matthews, Washington, Two Mandan Chiefs. *American Antiquarian and Oriental Journal* 10: 269–72 (1888).

Mayer, Brantz, *Tah-gah-jute; or Logan and Captain Michael Cresap*. Baltimore: J. Murphy (1851) 124pp.

Mayhew, Experience, *Indian Converts*. London: S. Gerrish (1727) 310pp.

Meacham, Albert B., *Wi-ne-ma (the Woman Chief) and Her People*. Hartford: American (1876) 168pp.

Meany, Edmond S., Chief Joseph, the Nez Percé. *Wisconsin Univ., MA Thesis* (1901) 63pp.

Meeker, Ezra, *Pioneer Reminiscences of Puget Sound*. Seattle: Lowman & Hanford (1905) 554pp.

Methvin, John J., Apheahtone, Kiowa—a Bit of History. *Chronicles of Oklahoma* 9: 335–37 (1931).

Mille, David H., Sitting Bull's White Squaw. *Montana* 14:(2): 54–71 (1964).

Milling, Chapman J., *Red Carolinians*. Chapel Hill: Univ. North Carolina (1940) 438pp.

Milroy, Thomas W., A Physician by the Name of Ohiyesa: Charles Alexander Eastman, M.D., *Minnesota Medicine* 54: 569–72 (1971).

Mitchell, S. H., *The Indian Chief Journeycake*. Philadelphia: American Baptist (1895) 108pp.

Montgomery, Elizabeth R., *Chief Seattle, Great Statesman*. Champaign: Garrard (1966) 80pp.

Mooney, James, Calendar History of the Kiowa Indians. Washington: *Bureau of Amer. Ethnol., Annual Report XVII, Pt. 1*, pp. 129–445 (1898).

Mooney, James, The Ghost Dance Religion and the Sioux Outbreak of 1890. Washington: *Bureau of Amer. Ethnol., Annual Report XIV, Pt. 2*, pp. 641–1100 (1896).

Moorehead, Warren, K., The Passing of Red Cloud. *Kansas State Historical Society, Transactions.* 10: 294–311 (1908).

Moorehead, Warren K., *Wanneta the Sioux*. New York: Dodd Mead (1890) 285pp.

Morgan, Lewis H., *League of the Hodénosaunee, or Iroquois*. Rochester: Sage & Bro. (1851) 477pp.

Morse, Jedediah, *A Report to the Secretary of War of the United States on Indian Affairs*. New Haven: S. Converse (1822) 400pp.

Morse, Marian Frances, Alexander McGillivray, Who Put Not His Trust in Princes. *Florida State Univ., MA Thesis* (1936) 56pp.

Mulkearn, L., Half King, Seneca Diplomat of the Ohio Valley. *Western Pennsylvania Historical Magazine* 37: 65–81 (1954).

Murray, Keith, *The Modocs and Their War*. Norman: Univ. Oklahoma (1959) 346pp.

Myers, J. Jay, *Red Chiefs and White Challengers*. New York: Simon & Schuster (1972) 282pp.

Myers, Sandra L., *Reflections on the Indian Way*. Forth Worth: Westerners (1973) 13pp.

NABOKOV, PETER, *Two Leggings; The Making of a Crow Warrior.* New York: Crowell (1967) 226pp.

NEET, J. FREDERICK, JR., Stand Watie: Confederate General in the Cherokee Nation. *Great Plains Journal* **6**: 36–51 (1966).

NEIHARDT, JOHN G., *Black Elk Speaks.* New York: Morrow (1932) 280pp.

NEQUATEWA, EDMUND, Nampeyo, Famous Hopi Potter. *Plateau* **5**: 40–42 (1943).

NEWCOMB, FRANC J., *Hosteen Klah, Navaho Medicine Man and Sand Painter.* Norman: Univ. Oklahoma (1964) 227pp.

Newsweek Obituary sections.

NICHOLS, PHEBE J., I Knew Chief Oshkosh. *Wisconsin Indian Research Institute Journal* **1**: 24–32 (1965).

NICHOLS, PHEBE J., *Oshkosh the Brave, Chief of the Wisconsin Menominees, and His Family.* Oshkosh: Castle-Pierce (1954) 145pp.

NORWOOD, JOSEPH W., *The Tammany Legend (Tamenend).* Boston: Meador (1938) 248pp.

O'BEIRNE, HARRY F., *Leaders and Leading Men of the Indian Territory.* Chicago: American (1891) vol. 1

O'DONNELL, JAMES H., Alexander McGillivray: Training for Leadership, 1778–1783. *Georgia Historical Quarterly* **49**: 172–186 (1965).

OEHLER, C. M., *The Sioux Uprising.* New York: Oxford Univ. (1959) 272pp.

OLSON, JAMES C., *Red Cloud and the Sioux Problem.* Lincoln: Univ. Nebraska (1965) 375pp.

OSKISON, JOHN M., *Tecumseh and His Times.* New York: Putnam (1938) 244pp.

OVERTON, JACQUELINE, *Indian Life on Long Island.* Port Washington: Friedman (1963) 150pp.

OWEN, M. B., Alabama Indian Chiefs, *Alabama Historical Quarterly* **13**: 5–90 (1951).

PALLADINO, LAWRENCE B., *Indian and White in the Northeast.* Lancaster: Wickersham (1922) 512pp.

PARKER, ARTHUR C., *The Code of Handsome Lake.* Albany: N.Y. State Museum Bulletin 163 (1912) 140pp.

PARKER, ARTHUR C., *The Life of General Ely S. Parker.* Buffalo: Buffalo Historical Society (1919) 346pp.

PATE J'NELL, Kiowa Art from Rainy Mountain; the Story of James Auchiah. *American Indian Quarterly*, pp. 193–200 (1975).

PECKHAM, HOWARD H., *Pontiac and the Indian Uprising.* Princeton: Princeton Univ. (1947) 346pp.

PETERSEN, KAREN, *Howling Wolf: A Cheyenne Warrior's Graphic Interpretation of His People.* Palto Alto: American West (1968) 63pp.

PHILLIPS, GEORGE H., *Chiefs and Challengers: Indian Resistance and Cooperation in Southern California.* Berkeley: Univ. California (1975) 226pp.

PHISTER, NATHAN P., The Indian Messiah. *American Anthropologist* **4**: 105–108 (1891).

PIERCE, EBENEZER W., *Indian History, Biography and Geneaology.* North Abington, Mass.: Mitchell (1878) 261pp.

PITEZEL, JOHN H., *Lights and Shades of Missionary Life.* Cincinnati: Western (1857) 431pp.

PORTER, C. FAYNE, *Our Indian Heritage; Profiles of Twelve Great Leaders.* New York: Chilton (1964) 228pp.

PORTER, KENNETH W., Billy Bowlegs (Holata Micco) in the Seminole Wars. *Florida Historical Quarterly* **45**: 391–401 (1966).

PORTER, KENNETH W., Wildcat's Death and Burial. *Chronicles of Oklahoma* **21**: 41–43 (1943).

POTTER, WOODBOURNE, *The War in Florida.* Baltimore: Lewis & Coleman (1836) 184pp.

POWERS, MABEL, *The Indian as Peacemaker.* New York: Revell (1932) 223pp.

RAND, CLAYTON, *Opoyotheyola, Son of the South.*

RATHKE, WILLIAM C., Chief Waubonsie and the Pottawattamie Indians. *Annals of Iowa* **35**: 81–100 (1959).

The Red Man. Carlisle, Penna.: Carlisle Indian School.

REED, GERARD ALEXANDER, Stand Watie, the Cherokee Nation, and the War of Rebellion. *Univ. Oklahoma, MA Thesis* (1964) 141pp.

REID, RUSSELL, Sakakawea. *North Dakota History* **30**: 101–13 (1963).

RELANDER, CLICK, *Drummers and Dreamers.* Caldwell: Caxton (1956) 345pp.

REYNOLDS, CHARLES R., JR., *American Indian Portraits From the Wanamaker Expedition of 1913.* Brattleboro: Stephen Green (1971) 123pp.

RICHARDSON, RUPERT A., *The Comanche Barrier to Southern Plains Settlement.* Glendale: Clark (1933) 424pp.

RIDDLE, JEFF C., *The Indian History of the Modoc War, and the Causes That Led To It.* San Francisco: Marnell (1914) 295pp.

RIDEOUT, HENRY M., *William Jones, Indian, Cowboy, American Scholar, and Anthropologist in the Field.* New York: Stokes (1912) 212pp.

RIGHTS, DOUGLAS, *The American Indians in North Carolina.* Durham: Univ. North Carolina (1947) 318pp.

RISTER, CARL C., *Border Captives: The Traffic in Prisoners by Southern Plains Indians. 1835–1875.* Norman: Univ. Oklahoma (1940) 220pp.

RISTER, CARL C., Satanta. *Southwest Review,* Autumn (1931).

RITZENTHALER, ROBERT E., AND NEIHOF, ARTHUR, *Famous American Indians.* Milwaukee: Milwaukee Public Museum (1958) 28pp.

ROARK, HARRY M., *Chief Journeycake; Indian Statesman and Christian Leader.* Dallas: Taylor (1970) 133pp.

ROBINSON, DOANE, A History of the Dakota or Sioux Indians. *South Dakota History Collections #2* (1904) 523pp.

ROLAND, ALBERT, *Great Indian Chiefs.* New York: Collier (1966) 152pp.

RONAN, PETER, *Historical Sketch of the Flathead Nation From the Year 1813 to 1890.* Helena (1890) 85pp.

RUBY, ROBERT, AND BROWN, JOHN A., *Half-Sun on the Columbia: A Biography of Chief Moses.* Norman: Univ. Oklahoma (1965) 377pp.

RUSKIN, GERTRUDE M., *John Ross, Chief of an Eagle Race.* Chattanooga: John Ross House (1963) 88pp.

RUTTENBER, EDWARD M., *History of the Indian Tribes of Hudson's River.* Albany: J. Munsell (1872) 415pp.

SAARINEN, ALINE B., *The Proud Possessors.* New York: Random House, (1958)423pp.

SABIN, EDWARD L., *Boys' Book of Indian Warriors and Heroic Indian Women.* New York: Jacobs (1918) 349pp.

SALISBURY, ROBERT, Chief Hole-in-the-Day, the Younger, and the Chippewa Disturbance of 1862. *St. Cloud Univ., MA Thesis* (1967).

SANDERS, JOHN, *Who's Who Among Oklahoma Indians, 1927.* Oklahoma City: Trave (1928).

SANDOZ, MARI, *Cheyenne Autumn.* New York: McGraw-Hill (1953) 282pp.

SANDOZ, MARI, *Crazy Horse, the Strange Man of the Oglalas.* New York: Knopf (1942) 428pp.

SANDOZ, MARI, *Hostiles and Friendlies.* Lincoln: Nebraska Univ. (1959) 250pp.

SARGENT, DANIEL, *Catherine Tekakwitha.* New York: Longmans Green (1937) 246pp.

SASS, HERBERT R., *Hear Me, My Chiefs!* New York: Morrow (1940) 256pp.

SAWLER, RUBY ETHEL, Emily Pauline Johnson, the Indian Woman of Letters. *Acadia Univ., MA Thesis* (1950) 78pp.

SCHAFER, JACK W., *Heroes Without Glory.* New York: Houghton Mifflin (1965) 323pp.

SCHMITT, MARVIN, AND BROWN, DEE, *Fighting Indians of the West.* New York: Scribners (1955) 384pp.

SCHOOLCRAFT, HENRY R., *Information Concerning the History, Condition and Prospects of the Indian Tribes of the United States.* Philadelphia: Lippincott, Grambo (1851–1857) 6 vols.

SCHOOR, GENE, *The Jim Thorpe Story: America's Greatest Athlete.* New York: Messner (1951) 186pp.

SCOTT, HUGH L., *Some Memories of a Soldier.* New York: Century (1928) 673pp.

SCRIVNER, FULSOM C., *Mohave People.* San Antonio: Naylor (1970) 144pp.

SEAGLE, WILLIAM, The Murder of Spotted Tail. *Indian Historian* **III** (4): 10–22 (1970).

SELDEN, SAMUEL WARD, The Legend, Myth and Code of Deganaweda and Their Significance to Iroquois Cultural History. *Indiana Univ., PhD Dissertation* (1966) 247pp.

SEYMOUR, FLORA W., *Indian Agents of the Old Frontier.* New York: Appleton Century (1941) 402pp.

SEYMOUR, FLORA W., *Women of Trail and Wigwam.* New York: Women's Press (1930) 112pp.

SHERA, JOHN W., Poundmaker's Capture of a Wagon Train. *Pioneer West* **1**: 7–9 (1969).

SIMMONS, LEO W., *Sun Chief: The Autobiography of a Hopi Indian.* New Haven: Yale Univ. (1942) 460pp.

SIPE, CHESTER H., *The Indian Chiefs of Pennsylvania.* Butler: Ziegler (1927) 569pp.

SLUMAN, NORMAN, *Poundmaker.* Toronto: Ryerson (1967) 301pp.

SMITH, GERALD A., Juan Antonio, Cahuilla Indian Chief; A Friend of the Whites. *San Bernardino Museum Qtly.* **8** (1):(1960) 40pp.

SMITH, WILLIAM R. L., *The Story of the Cherokees.* Cleveland, Tenn.: Church of God (1928) 229pp.

SNEVE, VIRGINIA DRIVING HAWK, *They Led A Nation.* Sioux Falls: Brevet (1975) 46pp.

SNODGRASS, JEANNE O., *American Indian Painters: A Biographical Directory.* New York: Museum of the American Indian, Contributions 21, Pt. 1 (1968) 269pp.

SOMMER, CHARLES H., *Quanah Parker; Last Chief of the Comanches.* St. Louis: Published by the author (1945) 48pp.

SPLAWN, ANDREW J., *Ka-mi-akin, the Last Hero of the Yakimas.* Portland: Binfords & Mort (1944) 500pp.

SPRAGUE, JOHN T., *The Origin, Progress and Conclusion of the War With Florida.* Gainesville: Univ. Florida (1964) 597pp.

STACHER, SAMUEL F., Ouray and the Utes. *Colorado* **27**: 134–40 (1950).

STANDING BEAR, LUTHER, *My People the Sioux.* Lincoln: Univ. Nebraska (1975) 288pp.

STANLEY, JOHN M., Portraits of North American Indians. Washington: *Smithsonian Miscellaneous Collections, #11*, 76pp. (1852).

STARKEY, MARION L., *The Cherokee Nation.* New York: Knopf (1946) 355pp.

STARR, EMMET, *History of the Cherokee Indians.* Oklahoma City: Warden (1921) 680pp.

STARR, EMMET, *Old Cherokee Families: Old Families and Their Genealogy.* Norman: Univ. Oklahoma (1972) 303 + 476pp.

STEMBER, SOL, *Heroes of the American Indian.* London: Fleet (1971) 124 pp.

STEVENSON, JAMES F., Stand Watie in the Civil War. *Tulsa Univ., MA Thesis* (1948) 74pp.

STONE, WILLIAM L., *Life of Joseph Brant, Thayendenegea.* Albany: J. Munsell (1838) 2 vols.

STONE, WILLIAM L., *The Life and Times of Red Jacket, or Sa-go-ye-wat-ha.* New York: Wiley and Putnam (1841) 484pp.

SUTTON, FELIX, *Indian Chiefs of the West.* New York: Messner (1970) 96pp.

SWANTON, JOHN R., Early History of the Creek Indians and Their Neighbors. Washington: *Bureau of Amer. Ethnol. Bulletin 73*, 492pp. (1922).

SWANTON, JOHN R., The Indians of the Southeastern United States. Washington: *Bureau of Amer. Ethnol. Bulletin 137*, 943pp. (1946).

SWEETSER, KATE D., *Book of Indian Braves.* New York: Harper (1913) 184pp.

SWEEZY, CARL, *The Arapaho Way: A Memoir of an Indian Boyhood.* New York: Potter (1966) 80pp.

SYLVESTER, HERBERT M., *Indian Wars of New England.* Boston: Clarke (1910) 3 vols.

TANNER, CLARA LEE, *Southwestern Indian Painting.* Tucson: Univ. Arizona (1973) 478pp.

TAYLOR, JOSEPH H., Inkpaduta and Sons. *North Dakota Historical Quarterly* **4**: 153–64 (1930).

TAYLOR, MORRIS T., Kicking Bird; a Chief of the Kiowas. *Kansas Historical Quarterly* **38**: 295–319 (1972).

TAYLOR, THOMAS U., *Jesse Chisholm.* Bandera, Tex: Frontier Times (1939) 217pp.

TEAKLE, THOMAS, *The Spirit Lake Massacre.* Iowa City: Iowa State Historical Society (1918) 336pp.

TERRELL, JOHN U., AND TERRELL, DONNA, *Indian Women of the Western Morning: Their Life in Early America.* New York: Dial (1974) 214pp.

THATCHER, BENJAMIN B., *Indian Biography; or, An Historical Account of Those Individuals Who Have Been Distinguished Among the North American Nations.* New York: Harper (1832) 326 + 320pp.

THOBURN, JOSEPH B., AND HOLCOMB, ISAAC M., *A History of Oklahoma*. Oklahoma City: Warden (1914) 123pp.

THOMAS, ROBERT K., The Redbird Smith Movement. *Bureau of Amer. Ethnol. Bulletin 180, Pt 16* (1961).

THOMPSON, ERWIN M., *The Modoc War: Its Military History and Topography*. Sacramento: Argus (1971) 188pp.

THOMPSON, J. R. E., Thayendenega the Mohawk and his Several Portraits. *Connoisseur 170*, pp. 49–53 (1969).

THORNTON, MILDRED V., *Indian Lives and Legends*. Vancouver: Mitchell (1966) 301pp.

THRAPP, DAN, *Victorio and the Mimbres Apaches*. Norman: Univ. Oklahoma (1974) 393pp.

THURMAN, MILBURN D., A Case of Historical Mythology; the Morning Star Sacrifice of 1833. *Nebraska History* **51**: 269–80 (1970).

THURMAN, MILBURN D., The Skidi Pawnee Morning Star Sacrifice of 1827. *Plains Anthropologist* **15**: 309–11 (1970).

TIBBLES, THOMAS H., *Buckskin and Blanket Days*. New York: Doubleday (1957) 336pp.

TIBBLES, THOMAS H., *The Ponca Chiefs: an Account of the Trial of Standing Bear*. Lincoln: Univ. Nebraska (1972) 143pp.

TILGHMAN, ZOE A., *Quanah, the Eagle of the Comanches*. Oklahoma City: Harlow (1938) 196pp.

TIME obituary sections.

TITIEV, MISCHA, A Historic Figure, Writ Small. *Michigan Alumni Quarterly Rev.* **42**: 359–80 (1959).

TRAVIS, RALPH, Reminiscences of Fort Rupert. *The Beaver*, pp. 32–34 (1946).

TRELEASE, ALLEN W., *Indian Affairs of Colonial New York: The Seventeenth Century*. Ithaca: Cornell Univ. (1960) 379pp.

TRENHOLM, VIRGINIA C., *The Arapahoes: Our People*. Norman: Univ. Oklahoma (1970) 372pp.

TUCKER, GLENN, *Tecumseh, Vision of Glory*. New York: Bobbs Merrill (1956) 399pp.

TUCKER, NORMAN, Nancy Ward, Ghighau of the Cherokees. *Georgia Historical Quarterly* **53**: 192–200 (1969).

TURPIN, MADELEINE, Peter Pitchlynn and His Role in Choctaw History. *Tulsa Univ., MA Thesis* (1964) 135pp.

TYLER, BARBARA ANN, Apache Warfare Under the Leadership of Cochise. *Texas Christian Univ., MA Thesis* (1965) 229pp.

UNDERWOOD, LARRY D., The Other Sitting Bull. *American History Illustrated*, pp. 26–27 (1973).

URQUHART, LENA M., *Colorow, the Angry Chieftain*. Denver: Golden Bell (1968) 51pp.

U.S. DEPT. INTERIOR, *Biographical and Historical Index of American Indians and Persons Involved in Indian Affairs*. Boston: G.K. Hall (1966) 6600pp., 8 vols.

U.S. GOVT. PRINTING OFFICE, *Famous Indians: a Collection of Short Biographies*. (1966) 30pp.

VAN VALKENBURGH, RICHARD, Navajo Naat'aani. *Kiva*. **13**: 14–23 (1948).

VERRILL, A. HYATT, *The Real Americans*. New York: Putnam (1954) 310pp.

VERWYST, CHRYSOSTOM A., *Life and Labors of Rt. Reverand Frederic Baraga*. Milwaukee: Wiltzius (1900) 476pp.

VESTAL, STANLEY, *Sitting Bull: Champion of the Sioux*. Norman: Univ. Oklahoma (1957) 349pp.

VESTAL, STANLEY, *Warpath and Council Fire*. New York: Random House (1948) 338pp.

VUILLEUMIER, MARION, *Indians on Olde Cape Cod*. Taunton: Sullwold (1970) 96pp.

WAGNER, GLENDOLIN, *Blankets and Moccasins*. Caldwell: Caxton (1933) 304pp.

WALKER, ROBERT S., *Torchlights to the Cherokees: the Brainerd Mission*. New York: Macmillan (1931) 339pp.

WALKER, THOMAS B., *Descriptive Catalog With Reproduction of Life-Size Bust Portraits of Famous Indian Chiefs*. Minneapolis: Hahn & Hamon (1909) 69pp.

WALLACE, ANTHONY F. C., *The Death and Rebirth of the Seneca*. New York: Knopf (1970) 384pp.

WALWORTH, ELLEN H., *The Life and Times of Kateri Tekakwitha, the Lily of the Mohawks, 1656–1680*. Buffalo: Paul (1893) 314pp.

WALLACE, ANTHONY F. C., *King of the Delawares: Teedyuseung, 1700–1763*. Philadelphia: Univ. Pennsylvania (1949) 305pp.

WALLACE, ERNEST, AND HOEBEL, E. ADAMSON, *The Comanches: Lords of the Southern Plains*. Norman: Univ., Oklahoma (1952) 400pp.

WALLACE, PAUL A. W., *Indians in Pennsylvania*. Harrisburg: Pennsylvania Historical and Museum Commission (1961) 194pp.

WALLACE, PAUL A. W., *White Roots of Peace*. Philadelphia: Univ. Pennsylvania (1946) 57pp.

WALTRIP, LELA AND RUFUS, *Indian Women*. New York: McKay (1964) 169pp.

WARD, M. M., The Disappearance of the Head of Osceola. *Florida Historical Collections* **5**: 21–394 (1885).

WARREN, WILLIAM W., History of the Ojibway Nation. St Paul: *Minnesota Historical Collections* **5**: 21–394 (1885).

WATETCH, ABEL, *Payepot and His People*. Saskatoon: Saskatchewan History and Folklore Society (1959) 66pp.

WAYNE, BENNETT, *Indian Patriots of the Great West*. Champaign: Garrard (1974) 166pp.

WEEKS, ALVIN G., *Massasoit of the Wampanoags*. Fall River: Plimpton (1920) 270pp.

WELLMAN, PAUL I., *Indian Wars and Warriors*. New York: Houghton Mifflin (1959) 2 vols.

WELLS, WILLIAM ALVA, Osceola and the Second Seminole War. *Univ. Oklahoma, MA Thesis* (1936) 186pp.

WESLAGER, CLARENCE A., *The Delaware Indians: a History*. New Brunswick: Rutgers Univ. (1972) 546pp.

WEST, RUTH T., Pushmataha's Travels. *Chronicles of Oklahoma* **37**: 162–74 (1959).

WHARTON, CLARENCE R., *Satanta, The Great Chief of the Kiowas and His People*. Dallas: Banks Upshaw (1935) 246pp.

Who's Who in America. Chicago: A. N. Marquis (1899–).

Who Was Who in America. Chicago: A. N. Marquis (1963–).

WILKINS, THURMAN, *Cherokee Tragedy: the Story of the Ridge Family*. New York: Macmillan (1970) 398pp.

WILSON, DOROTHY C., *Bright Eyes: the Story of Susette LaFlesche*. New York: McGraw-Hill (1974) 397pp.

WILTSEY, NORMAN B., Plenty Coups: Statesman Chief of the Crows. *Montana* **13**: 28–39 (1963).

WIMER, JAMES, *Events in Indian History*. Lancaster, G. Hills (1841) 633pp.

WINCH, FRANK, *Thrilling Lives of Buffalo Bill: Colonel William F. Cody, Last of the Great Scouts*. New York: S. L. Parsons (1911) 224pp.

WINCHELL, NEWTON H., *The Aborigines of Minnesota*. St. Paul: Pioneer (1911) 761pp.

WINFREY, DORMAN H., Chief Bowles and the Texas Cherokee. *Chronicles of Oklahoma* **32**: (1): 31–41 (1954).

WITTHOFT, JOHN, Will West Long, Cherokee Informant. *American Anthropologist* **50**: 355–59 (1948).

WOLDERT, ALBERT, The Last of the Cherokees in Texas, and the Life and Death of Chief Bowles. *Chronicles of Oklahoma* **I** (3): 179–226 (1921).

WOLFE, LOUISE, *Indians Courageous*. New York: Dodd Mead (1956) 236pp.

WOOD, NORMAN B., *Lives of Famous Indian Chiefs*. Aurora, Ill.: American Indian Historical Publ. (1906) 771pp.

WOODWARD, ARTHUR, Irateba—Chief of the Mohave. *Plateau* **25**: 53–68 (1953).

WOODWARD, GRACE S., *The Cherokees*. Norman: Univ. Oklahoma (1963) 359pp.

WOODWARD, GRACE S., *Pocahontas*. Norman: Univ. Oklahoma (1969) 227pp.

WRIGHT, MURIEL H., *A Guide to the Indian Tribes of Oklahoma*. Norman: Univ. Oklahoma (1951) 300pp.

WRIGHT, PETER M., The Pursuit of Dull Knife From Fort Reno in 1878–1879. *Chronicles of Oklahoma* **46**: 141–54 (1968).

WYATT, EDGAR, *Cochise: Apache Warrior and Statesman*. New York: McGraw-Hill (1953) 192pp.

YOUNG, CALVIN, *Little Turtle, Me-she-kin-no-quah; the Great Chief of the Miami Indian Nation*. Indianapolis: Sentinel (1917) 249pp.

ZINER, FEENIE, *Dark Pilgrim: the Story of Squanto*. New York: Chilton (1965) 158pp.

ZO-TOM, *1877: Plains Indian Sketch Books of Zo-Tom and Howling Wolf*. Flagstaff: Northland Press (1969) 25pp. + 64 plates.

Tribal Listing

ABNAKI
Abomazine

APACHE
Chiricahua
Cochise
Geronimo
Naiche
Nana
Coyotero
Eskaminzim
Mimbreño
Mangas Coloradas
Victorio

ARAPAHO
Little Raven
Carl Sweezy

BANNOCK
Tendoy
Tyhee

BLACKFOOT
Mountain Chief
Hart M. Schultz
Two Guns White Calf

CATAWBA
Haiglar

CAYUSE
Tuekakas

CHEROKEE
Attakullakulla
Elias Boudinot
Bowl
Dennis W. Bushyhead
Jesse Chisholm
Dragging Canoe
Stephen Foreman
Will West Long
Oconostota
John Ridge
Major Ridge
Rollie Lynn Riggs
Will Rogers
John Ross
Sequoyah
Redbird Smith
Nancy Ward
Stand Watie

CHEYENNE
James Bear's Heart
Black Kettle
William Cohoe
Dull Knife
Howling Wolf
Little Wolf

Roman Nose
Tall Bull
Two Moon
Wooden Leg
Yellow Hand

CHINOOK
Comcomly

CHIPPEWA
Charles A. Bender
Flat Mouth
Hole in the Day
Rocky Boy
William W. Warren
White Cloud

CHOCTAW
Peter P. Pitchlynn
Pushmataha
Red Shoes
Allen Wright

COMANCHE
Peta Nocona
Quanah Parker
Ten Bears

CREE
Payepot
Poundmaker
Louis Riel

CREEK
Acee Blue Eagle
Crazy Snake
Thomas Gilcrease
Isparhecher
Alexander McGillivray
William McIntosh
Menewa
Mary Musgrove
Pleasant Porter
Alexander L. Posey
Jerome R. Tiger
Tomochichi
William Weatherford

CROW
Arapoosh
Curly
Plenty Coups
Sword Bearer
Two Leggings
White Man Runs Him

DELAWARE
Black Beaver
Delaware Prophet
Gelelemend
Hopocan

Charles Journeycake
Roberta C. Lawson
Tammany
Teedyuscung
White Eyes

FOX
William Jones
Poweshiek
Taimah
Young Bear

HAIDA
Charles Edensaw

HURON
Dekanawida
Walk in the Water

IROQUOIS
Cayuga
Logan
Mohawk
Joseph Brant
Molly Brant
Hendrick
Hiawatha
Emily Pauline Johnson
Kateri Tekakwitha
Eleazar Williams
Oneida
Half King
Shikellamy
Skenandoa
Onondaga
Dekanisora
Daniel Garakonthie
Sadekanakte
Seneca
Blacksnake
Cornplanter
Handsome Lake
Arthur C. Parker
Ely S. Parker
Red Jacket
Tuscarora
John N. B. Hewitt
Sakarissa

KALISPEL
Charlot

KANSA
Charles Curtis
Washunga

KAWIA
Juan Antonio
Ramona

KICKAPOO
Kenakuk

KIOWA
Spencer Asah
James Auchiah
Big Bow
Big Tree
Dohasan
Jack Hokeah
Kicking Bird
Lone Wolf
Stephen Mopope
Satanta
Setangya
Stumbling Bear
Monroe Tsatoke
Wooden Lance
Zotom

KWAKIUTL
George Hunt
Mungo Martin

LUISEÑO
Wa-Wa-Chaw

MAHICAN
John Konkapot
Daniel Ninham
John W. Quinney
Wannalancet

MANDAN
Mato Tope

MENOMINI
Oshkosh
Tomah

MIAMI
Francis Godfroy
Little Turtle

MODOC
Bogus Charley
Hooker Jim
Kintpuash
Scarface Charlie
Schonchin
Winema

MOHAVE
Irateba

MOHEGAN
Samson Occom
Uncas

MONTAUK
Wyandanch

NARRAGANSETT
Canonchet
Canonicus
Miantonomo

NAVAJO
Atsidi Sani
Barboncito
Henry Chee Dodge
Ganado Mucho
Ned Hatathli
Hosteen Klah
Manuelito
Gerald Nailor
Quincy Tahoma

NEZ PERCÉ
Chief Joseph
Lawyer
Looking Glass
Toohulhulsote
White Bird
Yellow Wolf

NIANTIC
Ninigret

OJIBWA
George Copway
Peter Jones

OMAHA
Francis LaFlesche
Susan LaFlesche
Susette LaFlesche
Joseph LaFlesche

OSAGE
Bacon Rind
Fred Lookout
Pawhuska
Clarence L. Tinker

OTTAWA
Pontiac

PAIUTE
Tavibo
Winnemucca
Sarah Winnemucca
Wovoka

PAMUNKEY
Queen Anne

PAUTUXET
Squanto

PAWNEE
Petalésharo

PEMAQUID
Samoset

PENNACOOK
Passaconaway

PEQUOT
Sassacus

PIMA
Ira H. Hayes

POCASSET
Weetamoo

PONCA
Standing Bear

POTAWATOMI
Leo Pokagon
Simon Pokagon
Sagaunash
Shábona

POWAHATAN
Opechancanough
Pocahontas
Powhatan

PUEBLO
Cochití
Ben Quintana
Hopi
Waldo Mootzka
Nampeyo
Louis Tawanima
Tawaquaptewa
Youkioma
San Ildefonso
Awa Tsireh
Crescencio Martínez
Julián Martínez
Oqwa Pi
Popovi Da
Tonita Peña
San Juan
Popé
Santa Clara
Edward P. Dozier

SALISH
Duwamish
Seattle
Sinkiuse
Moses

Spokane
Spokane Garry

SAUK
Black Hawk
Keokuk
Jim Thorpe

SEMINOLE
Billy Bowlegs
John Jumper
Micanopy
Opothleyaholo
Osceola
Wildcat

SHAWNEE
Thomas W. Alford
Cornstalk
High Horn
Ernest Spybuck
Tecumseh
Tenskwátawa

SHOSHONI
Sacajawea
Washakie

SIOUX
Brûlé
Big Mouth
Crow Dog
Hollow-Horn Bear
Short Bull
Spotted Tail
Two Strike
Hunkpapa
Gall
Rain in the Face
Sitting Bull
Mdewakanton
Little Crow
Red Wing
Wapasha
Miniconjou
Big Foot
Hump
Oglala
American Horse
Amos Bad Heart Bull
Black Elk
Crazy Horse
Iron Tail
Red Cloud
Sitting Bull
Young Man Afraid of
his Horses

Santee
Charles A. Eastman
Herbert B. Fowler
War Eagle
Teton
John Grass
Red Tomahawk
Wahpekute
Inkpaduta
Wahpeton
John Otherday
Yankton
Gertrude S. Bonnin
Ella C. Deloria
Yanktonai
Waneta
Chauncey Yellow Robe

TIONANTATI
Adario

TLINGIT
Shakes

UTE
Colorow
Ignacio
Ouray
Walkara

WAMPANOAG
Annawan
Massasoit
Metacom

WANAPUM
Smohalla

WASHO
Datsolalee

WINNEBAGO
Henry Roe Cloud
Angel DeCora Dietz
Mountain Wolf Woman
Red Bird
Yellow Thunder

WYANDOT
Leatherlips
Tarhe

YAHI
Ishi

YAKIMA
Kamaiakin

YAVAPAI
Carlos Montezuma

Chronology

1525–1575	Hiawatha
1545–1644	Opechancanough
1550–1600	Dekanawida
1550–1618	Powhatan
1560–1637	Sassacus
1565–1647	Canonicus
1565–1665	Passaconaway
1580–1622	Squanto
1580–1662	Massasoit
1590–1653	Samoset
1595–1617	Pocahontas
1600–1643	Miantonomo
1600–1659	Wyandanch
1600–1676	Daniel Garakonthie
1600–1678	Ninigret
? –1676	Annawan
1606–1682	Uncas
? –1690	Pope
1625–1700	Wannalancet
1625–1701	Tammany
1630–1676	Canonchet
1639–1676	Metacom
1640–1701	Sadekanakte
1650–1676	Weetamoo
1650–1701	Adario
1650–1725	Queen Anne
1650–1730	Dekanisora
1650–1739	Tomochichi
1656–1680	Kateri Tekakwitha
1675–1724	Abomazine
? –1748	Shikellamy
1680–1755	Hendrick
1690–1763	Haiglar
1700–1748	Red Shoes
1700–1754	Half King
1700–1763	Mary Musgrove
1700–1775	John Konkapot
1700–1778	Attakullakulla
1705–1763	Teedyuscung
1706–1816	Skenandoa
1710–1778	Daniel Ninham
1710–1783	Oconostota
1718–1876	Wapasha (*family*)
1720–1769	Pontiac
1720–1777	Cornstalk
1722–1811	Gelelemend
1723–1780	Logan
1723–1792	Samson Occom
1725–1775	Delaware Prophet
1725–1794	Hopocan
1730–1778	White Eyes
1730–1792	Dragging Canoe
1730–1810	Sakarissa

1732–1810	Leatherlips
1735–1795	Molly Brant
1735–1815	Handsome Lake
1735–1836	Cornplanter
1738–1824	Nancy Ward
1742–1807	Joseph Brant
1742–1818	Tarhe
1750–1825	Red Wing
1752–1812	Little Turtle
1752–1817	Tomah
1756–1830	Red Jacket
1756–1839	Bowl
1759–1793	Alexander McGillivray
1760–1825	Pawhuska
1760–1859	Blacksnake
1764–1824	Pushmataha
1765–1830	Comcomly
1765–1865	Menewa
1767–1838	Black Hawk
1768–1813	Tecumseh
1768–1837	Tenskwátawa
1770–1839	Major Ridge
1774–1860	Flat Mouth
1774–1874	Yellow Thunder
1775–1812	High Horn
1775–1825	William McIntosh
1775–1825	Walk in the Water
1775–1841	Leo Pokagon
1775–1859	Shábona
1776–1843	Sequoyah
1780–1822	William Weatherford
1780–1841	Sagaunash
1780–1849	Micanopy
1783–1848	Keokuk
1783–1863	Juan Antonio
1784–1812	Sacajawea
1785–1851	War Eagle
1785–1852	Kénakuk
1788–1828	Red Bird
1788–1858	Eleazar Williams
1788–1866	Seattle
1790–1830	Taimah
1790–1834	Arapoosh
1790–1840	Francis Godfroy
1790–1866	John Ross
1790–1871	Tuekakas
1791–1863	Mangas Coloradas
1792–1873	Ten Bears
1795–1848	Waneta
1795–1858	Oshkosh
1795–1876	Lawyer
1797–1832	Petalésharo
1797–1855	John W. Quinney
1798–1862	Opothleyaholo
1800–1861	Mato Tope

1800–1877	Kamaiakin
1800–1944	Shakes (*family*)
1801–1871	John Otherday
1802–1856	Peter Jones
1803–1839	Elias Boudinot
1803–1839	John Ridge
1803–1868	Black Kettle
1804–1838	Osceola
1804–1900	Washakie
1805–1866	Dohasan
1805–1868	Jesse Chisholm
1806–1871	Stand Watie
1806–1880	Black Beaver
1806–1881	Peter P. Pitchlynn
1807–1881	Stephen Foreman
1807–1882	White Bird
1808–1855	Walkara
1809–1893	Ganado Mucho
1810–1857	Wildcat
1810–1859	Billy Bowlegs
1810–1870	Tavibo
1810–1871	Setangya
1810–1877	Toolhulhulsote
1810–1883	Dull Knife
1810–1888	Colorow
1810–1895	Nana
1811–1892	Spokane Garry
1812–1874	Cochise
1813–1845	Poweshiek
1814–1878	Irateba
1815–1873	Schonchin
1815–1878	Inkpaduta
1815–1907	Smohalla
1816–1908	Payepot
1817–1889	Little Raven
1817–1894	Charles Journeycake
1818–1863	George Copway
1818–1894	Manuelito
1820–1863	Little Crow
1820–1871	Barboncito
1820–1879	Lone Wolf
1820–1880	Ouray
1820–1896	Jumper
1820–1904	Little Wolf
1822–1909	Red Cloud
1823–1877	Looking Glass
1823–1881	Spotted Tail
1825–1853	William W. Warren
1825–1861	Peta Nocona
1825–1868	Hole in the Day
1825–1871	Tyhee
1825–1879	Hooker Jim
1825–1880	Victorio
1825–1885	Allen Wright
1825–1890	Big Foot
1825–1890	Eskaminzin

1826–1898 Dennis W. Bushyhead	1848–1908 Hump	1871–1909 William Jones
1828–1895 Ely S. Parker	1848–1932 Winema	1871–1919 Angel DeCora Dietz
1828–1913 Ignacio	1848–1942 Mountain Chief	1872–1934 Two Guns White Calf
1829–1899 Moses	1849–1932 Plenty Coups	1873–1908 Alexander L. Posey
1829–1902 Isparhecher		1875–1938 Gertrude S. Bonnin
1829–1908 Standing Bear	1850–1876 Yellow Hand	1878–1940 Roberta C. Lawson
1829–1909 Geronimo	1850–1880 Bogus Charley	1879–1935 Will Rogers
1830–1868 Roman Nose	1850–1913 Hollow-Horn Bear	1879–1962 Mungo Martin
1830–1869 Tall Bull	1850–1916 Iron Tail	1879–1969 Louis Tawanima
1830–1870 Atsidi Sani	1850–1918 Redbird Smith	1880–1929 Youkioma
1830–1873 Big Mouth	1850–1927 Howling Wolf	1880–1953 Carl Sweezy
1830–1878 Satanta	1851–1882 James Bear's Heart	1881–1955 Arthur C. Parker
1830–1898 White Cloud	1853–1913 Zotom	1882–1960 Tawaquaptewa
1830–1899 Simon Pokagon	1853–1931 Red Tomahawk	1882–1970 Hart M. Schultz
1830–1900 Big Bow	1854–1903 Susette LaFlesche	1883–1949 Ernest Spybuck
1830–1900 Young Man Afraid	1854–1924 William Cohoe	1883–1954 Charles A. Bender
of His Horses	1854–1933 George Hunt	1884–1950 Henry R. Cloud
1830–1908 Washunga	1855–1925 White Man Runs Him	1884–1960 Mountain Wolf Woman
1831–1900 Charlot	1856–1935 Yellow Wolf	1887–1942 Clarence L. Tinker
1832–1903 Stumbling Bear	1857–1921 Naiche	1888–1953 Jim Thorpe
1832–1904 Chief Joseph	1857–1932 Francis LaFlesche	1888–1971 Ella C. Deloria
1832–1915 Two Strike	1858–1932 Wovoka	1888–1972 Wa-Wa-Chaw
1834–1890 Sitting Bull, *Hunkpapa*	1858–1939 Charles A. Eastman	1890–1918 Crescencio Martínez
1834–1907 Tendoy	1858–1940 Wooden Leg	1890–1962 Thomas Gilcrease
1835–1875 Kicking Bird	1859–1923 Curly	1895–1949 Tonita Peña
1835–1905 Rain in the Face	1859–1937 John N. B. Hewitt	1897–1943 Julián Martínez
1835–1910 Crow Dog	1859–1942 Nampeyo	1898–1956 Awa Tsireh
1835–1925 Datsolalee	1860–1914 Rocky Boy	1898–1974 Stephen Mopope
1837–1873 Kintpuash	1860–1916 Ishi	1899–1954 Rollie L. Riggs
1837–1896 Scarface Charlie	1860–1931 Wooden Lance	
1837–1918 John Grass	1860–1932 Bacon Rind	1900–1969 Jack Hokeah
1839–1924 Charles Edensaw (*family*)	1860–1936 Charles Curtis	1900–1971 Oqwa Pi
1840–1895 Gall	1860–1938 Thomas W. Alford	1904–1937 Monroe Tsatoke
1840–1907 Pleasant Porter	1860–1947 Henry Chee Dodge	1906–1974 James Auchiah
1840–1908 American Horse	1860–1949 Fred Lookout	1908–1954 Spencer Asah
1841–1876 Sitting Bull, *Oglala*	1861–1913 Emily P. Johnson	1909–1959 Acee Blue Eagle
1841–1877 Crazy Horse	1863–1887 Sword Bearer	1910–1940 Waldo Mootzka
1842–1886 Poundmaker	1863–1950 Black Elk	1916–1971 Edward P. Dozier
1844–1885 Louis Riel	1865–1915 Susan LaFlesche	1917–1952 Gerald Nailor
1844–1891 Sarah Winnemucca	1865–1922 Ramona	1919–1977 Herbert B. Fowler
1844–1923 Two Leggings	1867–1923 Carlos Montezuma	1920–1956 Quincy Tahoma
1844–1911 Quanah Parker	1867–1937 Hosteen Klah	1923–1971 Popovi Da
1845–1915 Short Bull	1868–1933 Young Bear	1923–1972 Ned Hatathli
1846–1912 Crazy Snake	1869–1913 Amos Bad Heart Bull	1925–1944 Ben Quintana
1847–1917 Two Moon	1870–1930 Chauncey Yellow Robe	1932–1955 Ira H. Hayes
1847–1929 Big Tree	1870–1947 Will West Long	1941–1967 Jerome R. Tiger

Index of Names

The following includes all of the people—Indian and non-Indian—who are mentioned in the text, together with the many variants of their names and alternative English translations of the native forms. Those not found in the biographies are included for reference purposes, as well as to indicate the extremely wide range of spellings found in the literature; to have printed all of them in the text would have made the work unwieldy.

Those persons whose relationship may seem only peripheral are included simply in an effort to demonstrate the scope of their world, and the many people with whom they came into contact in the course of their careers.

Abeel, John, 60
Abomazeen, 9
Abomazine, 9
Abombazine, 9
Achsaquareesory, 250
Acquenacke, 151
Adams, John Quincy, 231
Adaquarande, 249
Adaquarondo, 249
Adario, 9–10, 72
Adate, 76
Addo Eto, 32
Adits'aii, 75
Adoeete, 32
Adooeette, 32
Adzaan Tsinajinnie, 76
Affable, The, 285
Agigau, 321
Aguas Grandes, 89
Aharlock Harjo, 63
Ahawhypersie, 325
Ahpamut, 106
Ahpeatone, 339
Ahpiatom, 339
Ahpiaton, 339
Ahson Tsosie, 140
Ahway Eshkay, 140
Aishebogekoshe, 85
Aitken, Matilda, 323
Alderman, 175
Aleekchea'ahoosh, 214
Alessandro, 230
Alexander, 172, 174
Alford, Thomas Wildcat, 10–11
Allalimya Takanin, 157
Alligator, Chief, 43
Almost Perfect, 348
Always Ready, 234
Amarashu, 229
Amathla, Charlie, 200
Amaya, Juan, 75
American Horse, 11–13, 351
—, Samuel, 13
Anaya, Juan, 19
Anea, Juan, 19
Angeline, 258
Angpetu Tokecha, 201
Angpetu Wastéwin, 74
Angry Warrior, The, 165
Annawan, 13–14
Annawon, 13–14
Anthony, Maj. Scott N., 37
Antonio, Juan, 14–17
Apash Wyakaikt, 157
Apiatan, 181, 339, 340
Apothleyahola, 197
Aqueendera, 249
Arahpot, 265
Arapooish, 17
Arapoosh, 17–18
Arataswa, 99

Arateva, 121
Aripooish, 17
Arlee, 50
Arley, 50
Arny, William F. M., 90
Aroghadecka, 46
Aroniateka, 106
Aroused Bear, 224
Arquero, Epitacio, 211
Arrapooish, 17
Arrow, The, 202
Arthur, Chester A., 75
Asah, Spencer, 18, 181
—, Ida, 18
—, Kay, 18
Ascassasotick, 192
Asenoth, 307
Ashishishe, 66
Ashkebuggecoash, 85
Askew, Patricia Gladys, 299
Ashkikihih Diitsii, 75
Ashkii Dighin, 165
Asshewequa, 36
Assiola, 199
Assu, 69
Astor, John Jacob, 58
Atagulkalu, 20
Atkinson, Genl. Henry, 35, 224
Atotarho, 108
Atsidi Sani, 19–20, 75
Attakullakulla, 20–21, 79, 195, 320
Auchiah, James, 21–23, 181
—, Mark, 21
Aungattay, Mary, 354
Aupamut, 106
Awa Tside, 78
Awa Tsireh, 23–24, 168

Babe Ruth, 299
Bacon Rind, 24–25
Bad Heart Bull, Amos, 25
—, Dolly, 25
Badin, Stephen, 216
Bagwunagijik, 110
Baird, Elizabeth, 68
Bald Eagle, 127
Barboncito, 25–26, 166
Barbour, George W., 15–16
Bark Scrapings, 307
Barnett, Lucy, 125
Bartlett, Lieut. Edward C., 339
Bascom, Lieut. George W., 53
Bat, The, 245
Batsida Karoosh, 332
Battey, Thomas C., 29, 137
Beale, Lieut. Edward F., 14–15, 51, 121
Bean, Genl. J. H., 16
Bear Claw, 49
Bear Cub, 207
Bear's Heart, James, 27, 55
Bear Shedding His Hair, 88

Bear Woman, 116
Beautiful Bird, 121
Beautiful Lake, 102
Beckwourth, Jim, 17, 316
Beduiat, 314
Belcher, Gov., 142
Bell, Sarah Caroline, 327
Beloved Woman, 21, 321
Bender, Charles A., 27–28, 52
—, Elizabeth G., 52
Beneath the Robes, 182
Berry, Jane, 181
Beshayeychayecossis, 332
Beshiltheeni, 19
Bidu-ya, 314
Big Black Chest, 34
Big Bow, 29, 281
Big Crane, 308
Big Elk, 143
Big Foot, 29–31, 66, 117, 266, 312
Big Man, 282
Big Mouth, 31, 84
Big Ribs, 252
Big Snowsnake, 203
Big Speaker, 239
Big Thunder, 149
Big Tracks, 208
Big Tree, 29, 32–33, 155, 252, 262, 281
Big Tree, John, 308
Big Water Man, 89
Billy Tiger, 178
Bird Woman, 248
Bisahalani, 25
Bisnayanchi, 75
Bissonette, Angelina, 34
Biter, The, 353
Bitsoo Yeiyaa'tii, 59
Black, 282
Black Beaver, 33, 51
Black Blanket, 62
Black Crow, 65, 277
Black Drink Crier, 199
Black Eagle, 127, 136
Black Elk, 33–34
—, Angelina, 34
—, Ben, 34
—, Kate, 34
—, Nick, 34
Black Hawk, 34–36, 135, 136, 216, 224, 262, 298
—, Asshwequa, 36
—, Namequa, 36
—, Nanasia, 36
—, Nancy, 36
—, Nasheakusk, 36
—, Nasomsee, 36
—, Tom, 36
Black Jim, 140, 152, 255
Black Kettle, 36–37, 80, 152, 285
Black Shawl, 62
Blacksnake, 37–38, 102, 103

Black Sparrow Hawk, 34
Black Thunder, 224
Blake, Betty, 245
Blessing Speaker, 26
Blish, Helen, 25
Blowsnake, Charles, 184
Blue Eagle, Acee, 39
—, Devi Dja, 39
—, Loretta T., 39
Blue Horn, The, 181
Bluff, 76
Boas, Franz, 74, 84, 117, 127
Boat Traveler, 248
Bodmer, Karl, 172
Bogus Charley, 40
Boinaiv, 43
Boleck, 43
Bolek, 43
Bolon, A. J., 133
Bomazeen, 9
Bomazine, 9
Bombazeen, 9
Bombazine, 9
Bonnin, Gertrude S., 40–41, 71
—, Raymond T., 41
Bosomworth, Mary, 185–186
—, Thomas, 185
Boston Charley, 140, 255
Boudinot, Elias, 41–42, 87, 238, 239,
    240, 326
—, Cornelius, 42
—, Delight, 42
—, Harriet, 41
Bourassa, Rosa, 145
Bourke, Lieut. John G., 190
Bowers, Col., 205
Bowl, The, 42–43
—, Col., 42
—, John, 43
—, Rebecca, 43
Bowleck, 43
Bowlegs, Billy, 43–44, 178
Bowles, 42
—, Col., 42
—, Standing, 43
Boy Interpreter, The, 75
Boys Betting, The, 38
Bradford, Gov. William, 171, 278, 279
Bragger, The, 226
Brant, Joseph, 44–45, 46, 47, 60, 126
—, Molly, 45, 46–47
—, Niklaus, 44, 46
Brave, The, 201
Bright Eyes, 143
Bright Path, 298
Bright Stream Between Two Hills, 215
Brinton, Harriet, 107
Broken Leg, 55
Brooke, Genl. John, 312
Brown, 128
Brown, John, 251
Brughier, Théophile, 322
Buck Watie, 41
Buffalo Bill (Cody), 34, 266, 268, 345,
    346
Buffalo Horn, 313
Buffalo, Mary, 354
Bugonegijig, 110
Built Like a Bear, 262
Bull, Amos Bad Heart, 25
Bull, William, 99
Bullhead, 237, 269
Bull Hump, 81

Burke, Charles H., 248
Bushyhead, Dennis W., 47–48
—, Elizabeth A., 48
—, Jesse, 47, 87
—, Eloize P., 48
Butler, Claire, 78
Butler, Eloize P., 48
Byrd, Col. William, 21

Cadman, Charles W., 144
Cadotte, Mary, 322
Cahaga Tonga, 208
Cairook, 121
Caldwell, Billy, 249
Calhoun, John C., 163
Camaekin, 132
Cameahwait, 248
Campbell, J. E., 146
—, Emmaline, 146
Canby, Genl. Edwin R. S., 40, 90
    114, 139, 140, 337
Candy, Ruth R., 87
Cannot Walk, 12
Canonchet, 48
Canonicus, 49, 176
Canowicakte, 345
Captain Jack, 140
Captain John Konkapot, 142
Captain Truckee, 337
Carleton, Genl. James H., 53, 164, 165,
    166, 167
Carr, Genl. Eugene A., 285
—, Harry, 256
Carmen, 165
Carmonia-Núñez, Manuel, 328
Carrington, Col., 50
Carron, Thomas, 302
Carson, Christopher (Kit), 26, 75, 90,
    166, 202, 281
Carter, George, 19
Cashesegra, 208
Cass, Gov. Lewis, 47, 201
Catherine, 320
Catlin, George, 172
Catt, Carrie Chapman, 327
Cattail Bird, 23, 78
Cat Tail Bird, 23
Caunbitant, 279
Celia, 128
Cetan Wakuwa, 149
Chain Breaker, 37
Chakaucho Kama, 302
Chambly, 262
—, Capt. Jacques de, 262
Chanco, 196
Chapman, Kenneth M., 171, 210
Charbonneau, Baptiste, 248
—, Basil, 248
—, Jenny, 248
—, Toussaint, 248
Charger, The, 318
Charging Bear, 98, 281
Charging Hawk, 149
Charles II, King, 227
Charlevoix, Pierre, 72
Charlos, 50
Charlot, 49–50
Chávez, Juan Rosario, 210
Chea Sequah, 272
Cheauka, 288
Chebona Bula, 39
Chechoter, 199
Checote, 124

Chee, 75
Chee Dodge, Henry, 75
Cheeztahpaezh, 282
Chef Grue, 287
Cherokee Kid, The, 244
Chesetopah, 282
Cheucunsene, 79
Cheveaux Blancs, 208
Chichikam Lupalkuelatko, 253
Chikchacham Lilalkuelatko, 253
Chie, 165
Chief Over Chiefs, 177
Chief of Men, 211
Childhajin, 165
Chinnubie Harjo, 222
Chipeta, 203
Chisholm, Jesse, 50–51
—, John D., 50
Chisum, John, 51
Chito Hadjo, 63
Chito Harjo, 63
Chitto Harjo, 63
Chivington, Col. John, 36–37, 80
Chotter, 199
Chouteau, Pierre, 208, 209
Christy, Howard C., 25
Chupsco, John, 132
Church, Capt. Benjamin, 14
Chusaleta, 260
Cindoche Sixkiller, 125
Circling Fox, The, 174
Clark, Capt., 62, 248
Clark, Capt. William, 62, 134, 248
Clarke, Lieut. William P., 58, 153
Clay, Henry, 213
Clermont, 208
Clermore, 208
Climber, The, 295
Cloud, Henry Roe, 51–52
—, Elizabeth Bender, 52
Clum, John P., 85, 95, 187
Coacoochee, 333
Cochise, 53–54, 85, 163, 164, 186, 314
Cocinas, Juan, 75
Cocoosh, 325
Cocuyevah, 179
Cody, William F., 34, 122, 268
Coe, Susannah, 163
Cohoe, William, 27, 54–55
Cohn, Abram, 70
Collister, Oscar, 270
Colorado, 55
Colorow, 55–58
—, Gus, 58
Comcomly, 58–59
Coming of the Spirits, 169
Coming to the Front, 204
Commander, The, 13
Connayah, 325
Conner, John, 130
Connor, Genl. Patrick, 325
Cooacoochee, 333
Coochoochee, 333
Cook, Anna T., 204
Coolidge, Calvin, 24, 346
Cooper, James Fenimore, 314
Coosaponakeesa, 185
Cooswootna, 14
Coowescoowe, 246
Coppinger, Polly, 199
Copway, George, 59
—, Elizabeth Howell, 59
Corbitant, Chief, 329

Cornplanter, 38, 59–60, 102, 234
Cornstalk, 60–61, 154, 287, 290
Cosonisas, Juan, 75
Coytmore, Lieut. Richard, 195
Coulon, Joseph, 102
Cowacoochee, 332
Cowboy Philosopher, The, 245
Cow Killer, 234
Crane, The, 286
Crawford, Lieut., 271
Crawford, Capt. Emmett, 186
Crawford, Col. William, 115
Crazy Alligator, 177
Crazy Bear, 221
Crazy Horse, 34, 61–63, 66, 89, 117, 173, 233, 268, 270, 271, 272, 277
Crazy Snake, 63–65
Crazy War Hunter, 173
Cresap, Col. Michael, 154, 155
Crocker, Genl., 292
Crook, Genl. George, 12, 54, 62, 95, 99, 113, 117, 153, 186, 187, 190, 214, 268, 272, 280, 281, 291, 314, 325, 345
Crow, The, 66
Crow Chief, 89
Crow Dog, 65–66, 112, 113, 266, 277, 311, 312
Crow Foot, 269
Crow Hunts Walking, 148
Crow Messiah, The, 283
Cullen, Maj., 149
Cumming, Sir Alexander, 20
Cunka, 276
Curie, Marie, 327
—, Pierre, 327
Curley, 66
Curly, 66–67, 308, 333
Curly Hair, 116
Curnell, Joseph, 162
Curtis, Charles, 67–68, 325, 326
—, Anna Elizabeth Baird, 68
—, Hélène Pappan, 67
—, Orren Arms, 67
Custer, Genl. George A., 30, 37, 66, 80, 89, 117, 214, 229, 268, 271, 280, 285, 305, 311, 332, 345, 351
—, Capt. Thomas W., 66
Cut Nose, 183, 345
Cutter, The, 341

Da, Popovi, 220–221
—, Anita, 221
—, Tony, 221
Daagii, 25
Dabuda, 68
Dade, Maj. Francis L., 178, 200
Dagayadoh, 38
Dale, Gov. Thomas, 215
Dasoda-hae, 163
Datsalalee, 68
Datsolalee, 68–71
Datsolali, 68
Davis, Genl., 255
DeCora, Angel, 70
—, David, 71
Deer, The, 272
Deganawedah, 71
Deganawida, 71
Degataga, 326
Degonwadonti, 46
Deioninhogawen, 204
Dekanasourie, 72
Dekanawida, 71–72, 108

Dekanawidah, 71, 108, 109
Dekanisora, 9, 72–73
Dekaury (DeKaury), 70
Delaware Prophet, The, 73–74
Delgadito, 166
Deloria, Ella Carla, 74–75
—, Philip, 74
Denman, Leslie Van Ness, 306
Denny, Gov. William, 60, 293
Des Carris, Sabrevois, 71
De Vargas, Diego, 220
Dickens, Charles, 213
Dickson, Col. Robert, 321
Diego, Juan, 230
Dieskau, Baron Ludwig August, 107
Dietz, Angel DeCora, 71
—, William, 71
Dinwiddie, Robert, 101
Dish, The, 227
Diwali, 42
Dja, Devi, 39
Dockstader, Phoebe Ann, 228
Dodge, Chee, 75–76, 167
—, Annie, 76
—, Ben, 76
—, Mary, 76
—, Tom, 76
Dodge, Capt. Henry Linn, 19, 33, 75
Doe, The, 345
Doha, 76
Dohasan, 32, 76–77
Dohasen, 32
Do-hauson, 32
Donehogawa, 204
Door, The, 278, 296
Double Wampum, 125
Doxtator, Phoebe Ann, 228
Doyle, Arthur Conan, 327
Dozier, Edward Pasqual, 78–79
—, Anya, 78
—, Leocadia Gutiérrez, 78
—, Marianne, 78
—, Miguel, 78
—, Thomas Sublette, 78
—, Wanda, 78
Dragging Canoe, 21, 79–80
Drum Packer, The, 270
Dry Man, The, 48
d'Ucel, Jeanne, 110
Duggan, Cornelius, 327
—, Mary, 327
Dull Knife, 80–81, 152, 153, 154, 341
Dumquad, 102
Dundy, Elmer S., 280
Dunmore, Lord John, 61, 154, 190, 331

Eads, Lucy Tayiah, 326
Eagle Feather on the Forehead, 340
Eagle Head, 115
Eagle Lance, 25
Eagle Striking, 136
Eagle Who Sits Thinking, 160
Earth Trembler, 292
Eastman, Charles Alexander, 82, 248
—, Jacob, 82
—, Mary, 82, 87
Eats From the Hand, 340
Ebbetts, Mary, 117
Edensaw, Albert Edward, 83
Edensaw, Charles, 83
Edenshaw, Charles, 83–84
Edwards, James, 51
Edwards, Jonathan, 107, 142

Egret, The, 246
Ehton'ka Glala, 31
Ekaha Sapa, 33
Elamonwi, 307
Elarmonmi, 307
Elawmonmi, 307
Elinipsico, 61
Elk, The, 54
Elliott, Capt., 109
Ellis, Chief, 147
Ely, Frederick, 203
Ely, Nathaniel, 335
Emathla, 333
Eminck, Col., 191
Empress of the Creek Nation, 185, 186
Empties into Water, 149
Enga Peahroa, 325
Englishman, The, 249
Enlightened One, The, 73
Ephraim, 128
Eripuass, 17
Erretaswa, 99
Esau, Elizabeth, 143
Eshkebugecoshe, 85
Eskaminzim, 85–85
Eskeebucecose, 85
Eskiminzim, 84
Estamaza, 143
Etokeah, 116
Evans, Gov. John, 36
Ewers, Capt. Ezra, 117

Face Raining, 229
Faces the Buffalo North, 214
Faimah, 284
Fat on Skin, 24
Falls in a Current, 225
Fetterman, Capt. William J., 112, 117, 229, 233, 310
Fewkes, Jesse Walter, 188
Fields, Lucy, 256
Fierce Man, The, 251
Findley, Rev. William T., 52
Finlay, Sarah, 168
Fivekiller, 320
Flash in the Sky, 209
Flat Mouth, 85–86
Fleecy Cloud Floating into Space, 71
Fletcher, Alice, C., 144
Flint Necklace, 157
Folsom, Rhoda, 213, 214
—, Sophia, 213
Foreman, Stephen, 86–87
—, Anthony, 86
Forsyth, Maj. George A., 31, 246
Four, 172, 308
Four Bears, 172, 173
Fowler, Herbert B., 87–88
—, Julia M., 88
—, Mary, 194
Fox, The, 313
Fraser, James Earle, 122, 308
Frémont, Genl. John C., 56, 69, 337, 338
Frog, 128, 307
Futtatike, 178

Gaiantwaka, 60
Gale, Mary, 143
Galegina, 42
Gall, 62, 66, 88–89, 233
Galloway, Rebecca, 291
Ganado Mucho, 89–91
Ganados Muchos, 89

Ganeodiyo, 102
Ganio'dai-io, 102
Ganun'dalegi, 239
Gaontgwutwus, Elizabeth, 204
Garakonthie, Daniel, 91
Gardiner, Lion, 344
Garganwahgeh, 60
Garland, Hamlin, 311
Garra, Antonio, 15
Garry, Nicholas, 92
—, Spokan, 91
—, Spokane, 91–92, 146
Gatewood, Lieut. Charles B., 95
Gato Chiquito, 335
Gáwasowneh, 203
Gaynwah, 10
Gaynwawbiahsika, 10
Gaytahklipiahsikah, 10
Gelelemend, 92–93
—, William Henry, 93
Gentile, Carlos, 179
George II, King, 185, 195, 303
Geronimo, 84, 93–96, 186, 187, 190, 207
Gess, George, 259
Ghigau, 321
Gibson, John, 154
Gideon, 292
Gilcrease, Thomas, 96–97
—, Barton, 96
—, Belle Howell, 96
—, DesCygne, 97
—, Elizabeth Vowell, 96
—, Norma Smallwood, 97
—, Thomas Obed, 96
—, William Thomas, 96
Gilstrap, Harriet Patrick, 278
Gist, George, 259
—, Col. Nathaniel, 259
Giver, The, 337
Gladwin, Maj. Henry, 218
Glen [Glenn], Gov. John, 21, 100
Godfrey, Francis, 98
Godfroy, Francis, 98
Gohsinahsu, 75
Gold, Harriet Ruggles, 41
Goodale, Elaine, 82
Good Child Crier, The, 197
Good Child King, The, 161
Goodvillage, Lucy, 184
Good Walker, 340
Gorges, Sir Fernando, 278
Gourd Rattle, 323
Goyahkla, 93
Goyakla, 93
Goyathlay, 93
Graceful One, The, 11
Grant, Col. James, 100, 195, 196
Grant, Ulysses S., 84, 91, 167, 204, 217, 296
Grass, John, 98–99
Grass Maiden, 248
Gray One, The, 93
Great Chief, The, 171
Greathouse, Daniel, 155
Great Sachem of Paumanack, 344
Great Warrior, The, 173
Grinnell, Mary, 11
Griswold, Geneva H., 203
Guadalupe, 137
Guelle Plat, 85
Guaton-bain, 252
Guera Mura, 202
Guest, George, 259

Guillermito, 43
Gui'pago, 77, 155
Gurdaugee, Elizabeth, 86
Gustav, King, 298
Gutiérrez, Leocadia, 78
Gwaigo-unithin, 83
Gyantwaia, 60
Gyantwaka, 60
Gyinawen, 84

Ha-a-tee, 228
Hadawa'ko, 102
Hágaga, 184
Hagasilikaw, 71
Haiglar, 99–101
Haigler, 99
Haio-hwa'tha, 108
Hakadah, 82
Hakar Jim, 113
Hakok, 181
Hale, Calvin, H., 147, 306
Hale, Rev. Enoch, 335
Half King, 101–102, 265
Half Sun, 182
Hall, Capt., 61
Hallalhotsoot, 146
Haller, Maj., 133
Halpatter Micco, 43
Halpuda Mikko, 43
Halputta Hadjo, 177
Hammerstein, Oscar II, 242
Handsome Lake, 38, 102–103
Hansen, Julia M., 88
Hanson, Dr. John H., 336
Hard to See, 52
Hardwood, 53
Harmer, Genl. Josiah, 151
Harney, Genl. William S., 33
Harris, John, 102
Harris, Old Captain, 292
Harrison, Genl. William H., 35, 98, 291, 29
Harrover, Alma, 125
Hasanoanda, 204
Hashkeh Naabah, 165
Hasonnoanda, 204
Hasse Ola, 199
Hastín Chilhajinii, 165
Hastín Dagha, 25
Hastín Ditsii, 75
Hastín Totsohnii, 89
Hatathli, Ned, 103–105
—, Florence, 105
Hatch, Col. Edward, 315
Hatchootucknee, 213
Hau, 117
Hawk That Hunts Walking, 148
Hawk Which Comes Walking, 148
Hawkins, Benjamin, 197
—, Eliza, 163
Hayes, Ira Hamilton, 105–106
—, Joe E., 105
—, Nancy W., 105
Hayes, Rutherford B., 339
Head Band, The, 182
Head Chief, 177, 178
Healer, The, 292
Heather Flower, 344
He Causes Them to be Awake, 234
Hecksher, August, 257
He Gets Mad Quickly, 14
He Has Water Brash, 138
Hegler, 99
Heigler, 99

He Holds the Door Open, 204
He is Prepared, 234
He Just Sits There, 163
He Lightens the Sky for Us, 264
He Likes Broth, 295
He Makes Rivers, 108
He Makes Sense, 131
Hemha Micco, 131
Henderson, Alice Corbin, 23
Hendrick, 106–107
Henley, Chief Justice, 101
—, Elizabeth Brown, 247
Henry, 60
Heowenta, 108
He Places Two Bets, 44
Hermene Moxmox, 347
Hernández, Genl. Joseph M., 333
Herrera, Felipe, 210
Herrera, Joe, 210, 228
Herrero Delgadito, 19
He Wages War, 176
He Walks Over Much, 250
Hewett, Edgar Lee, 169, 171, 210
He Who Goes With His Head Down, 254
He Who Rushes On, 318
He Who Stands Forever, 59
Hewitt, John Napoleon B., 107–108
He Won't Go, 132
Heye, George G., 278
Hiawatha, 72, 108–109
High Horn, 109–110
High Wolf, 339
Hildebrand, Lizzie, 272
Hill of the Pow-Wow, 225
Hill, W. W., 78
Hinan BaSeth, 282
Hinmaton Yalatkit, 128
Hinnuaganun, 143
Hinookmahiwi-klinaka, 71
Hippo-ilk-mico, 161
His Eyes are Dreamy, 308
His Red People, 148
His Scarlet People, 148
Hochifoiksho, 226
Hohanonivah, 115
Hokeah, Jack, 110, 181
Holata Mico, 43
Holatta Micco, 43
Hole Biter, 353
Hole in the Day, 110–111
Holds the Door Open, 204
Hollolsotetote, 146
Hollow-Horn Bear, 111–113
Holy Boy, 165
Home of the Elk, 168
Homoseah Quahote, 122
Honanisto, 115
Honest John, 292
Hoof, 200
Hook Nose, 245
Hooker Jim, 40, 113–114, 139, 140, 253, 254, 255
Hoover, Herbert C., 41, 67
Hopkins, Lieut. Lambert H., 339
Hopocan, 93, 115
Hopokan, 115
Hoppocan, 115, 332
Hosa, 150
Hoskay Nolyae, 140
Hosteen Klah, 140–142
Hothlepoya, 173
Hotóakhihoois, 285
Hotúaeka'ash Tait, 285

Houston, Samuel, 43
Howard, E. A., 280
—, Genl. O. O., 43, 54, 128, 157, 159, 182, 304, 305, 313, 330
Howell, Belle M., 96
—, Elizabeth, 59
Howells, Emily S, 125
—, William Dean, 125
Howling Wolf, 27, 55, 115–116, 132
Hozhoii Naatá, 26
Hump, 29, 116–117
Hunkesni, 266
Hunnis, 106
Hunt, George, 117–119, 278
—, Robert, 117
—, Capt. Thomas, 278
Hunting Horse, 305
Hupuehelth Yaholo, 197
Hupuihilth Yahola, 197
Huya-na, 321

Ida, 18
Idansu, 83
Ignacio, 119
Illim Spokanee, 92
Indian General, The, 226
Inkpaduta, 119–120, 149, 202
Inshta Maza, 143
Inshtamaza, 143
Inshta Theaumba, 143
Inshta Theumba, 143
Interpreter, The, 75
Irataba, 121
Irateba, 121–122
Iromagaja, 229, 230
Iromagaju, 229
Iron Eye, 143, 144
Iron Shell, 112
Iron Tail, 122–123, 308
Irving, John, 15
Ishaynishu, 310
Ishi, 123–124
Ishi'eyo Nissi, 310
Ishna Witca, 231
Ishtematulubi, 344
Ishtilawata, 226
Ispaheche, 124
Ispaheches, 124
Isparhecher, 124–125
—, Lucy Barnett, 125
—, Alma Harrover, 125
—, Pollkissut, 125
—, Cindoche Sixkiller, 125
Ives, Lieut. Joseph C., 121

Jack, Captain, 138, 139
Jackson, Genl. Andrew, 36, 173, 177, 197, 199–226, 239, 247, 328
—, Helen Hunt, 230
Jacobsen, Adrian, 117
Jacobson, Oscar B., 18, 22, 110, 181, 211, 305
James, Charlie, 168
James I, King, 215
Jefferson, Thomas, 103, 209
Jenny, 248
Jerome, 93
Jerónimo, 93
Jesup, Genl. Thomas S., 178, 200, 333
John Two Guns, 307, 308
Johnny-cake, 130
Johnson, Emily Pauline, 125–126
—, Guy, 45, 47

—, Henry Martin, 125
—, John, 46
—, Walter, 28
—, Sir William, 45, 46, 107, 190, 250
Jones, Augustus, 126
—, Evan, 272
—, Henry Clay, 127
—, John, 272
—, Sen. John P., 338
—, Peter, 126–127
—, Peter E., 127
—, William, 127–128
—, Wilson, 63
Jonoesdowa, 204
Joseph, Chief, 128–130, 147, 158, 159, 182, 304, 306, 330, 347, 348
—, Old, 128, 306–307
Jourdain, Mary Magdeline, 336
Journeycake, Charles, 130–131
—, Emmaline Lawson, 146
—, Isaac, 130
—, Jane Sosha, 131
—, Sally, 130
—, Solomon, 130
Juana, 93
Jumper, 131–132
—, Jim, 131
—, John, 131
Jumping Badger, 266
Jumping Buffalo, 275
Jumping Bull, 266

Kabotie, Fred, 23, 180
Kaemoxmith, 132
Kahgegwagebow, 59
Kahkewagonnaby, 126
Kahkewaquonaby, 126
Kaiiontwa'ko, 60
Kaiser, Charley, 70
Kaitchkona Winema, 336
Kamaiakan, 132, 133
Kamaiakin, 132–133
Kamaikan, 132
Kamiakan, 132
Kamiakin, 132, 258
Kamaiyah, 132
Kanakuk, 133
Kana gatoga, 21
Kanakukm, 133
Kanekuk, 133
Kangi Sunka, 65
Kaniatse, Chief, 202
Kantuckeegan, 239
Kanuntaclagee, 239
Karneetsa, 182
Kearny, Col. Stephen W., 163
Kecharte, 124
Keehabah, 76
Keep From the Water, 327
Kehachiwinga, 184
Keintpoees, 138
Keintposes, 138
Kekeuskung, 292
Keller, Marie, 180
Kemble, Edward C., 280
Keintikead, 353
Kenakuk, 73, 133–134
—, John, 134
Kendall, Jim, 58
Kendrick, Loretta, 39
Kendrick, Silas, 90
Kenekuk, 133
Kennington, Capt., 63

Keokuk, 35, 36, 134–136, 224
—, Emma, 136
—, Hanna, 136
—, Moses, 136
Keys, Mary Ellen, 222
Keyser, Charley, 70
—, Louisa, 68
Khapkhaponimi, 128, 307
Kickapoo Prophet, The, 133
Kicking Bear, 30, 265, 266, 269, 352
Kicking Bird, 29, 136–137, 155, 281
Kikeuskund, 292
Kikikwawason, 209
Kiksomlo, 258
Kilakina, 41
Kilchii, 75
Kiliahote, 342, 343
Kilihote, 342
Killbuck, 92–93
Kill in the Woods, 345
Kills Together, 214
Kingfisher, 320
King Haiglar, 100
King Hendrick, 106
King Payne, 177
King Philip, 13–14, 174, 193, 332, 333
King of Yamacraw, The, 302
Kingsbury, Rev., 343
Kinney, Bishop Nathan, 16
Kintpoosh, 138
Kintpoos, 138
Kintpuash, 40, 114, 139–140, 253, 254, 255, 336, 337
Kirkland, Rev. Samuel, 272
Kirkpatrick, Frieda, 299
Kishko, 134
Kittitas, 182
Kiyiyah, 132
Kiyókaga, 134
Klah, 140
Knife Maker, 19
Knocks Two Off, 311
Knows the Secrets of the Sioux, 209
Köcha, 299
Kocoum, 215
Koquethagechton, 331
Kondiaronk, 9
Konieschguanokee, 115
Konkapot, 142
—, Capt. John, 142
Kontaikayak, 295
Konwatewentata, Mary Rice, 335
Koomsataddle, Martha, 306
Kootenai Pelly, 92
Koquethagechton, 331
Kosciusko, Genl. Thaddeus, 152
Kóshisiaré, 208
Kroeber, Alfred L., 123
Kuckquetackton, 331
Kulakinah, 42
Kullageenah, 42
Kummok'quiviokta, 340
Kunmesee, 79
Kwaina, 206
Kwivioya, 188
Kwuksutinuk, 168

Lachlan, 161
Ladaila, 258
Lafayette, Marquis de, 226
LaFlesche, Joseph, 143
—, Elizabeth, 143
—, Francis, 143, 144–145, 281

—, Mary, 143
—, Rosalie, 143
—, Susan, 143, 144
—, Susette, 143–144, 281
—, Tainne, 143, 144
Lagimodière, Julie, 241
Lallo, 18
Lamar, Mirabeau B., 43
LaMère Family, 71
Lame Man, 54
Lame One, The, 259
Lampson, Chauncey, 150
—, Nathan, 150
Lane, Mrs. W. B., 305
Larrabee, Joe, 62
—, Nancy, 62
Last One, The, 82
Last Prophet, The, 275
Laughing Boy, 39
Lauliwásikau, 291, 297
Lavendar, George, 239
Lawshe, 350
Lawson, Charley, 157
—, Edward, 146
—, Eugene, 146
—, Roberta C., 41, 145–146
Lawyer, 146–147
Leader, The, 10, 92
Leaf, The, 319
Lean Elk, 159
Leaning Wood, 20
Leatherlips, 148
Leavenworth, Genl. Henry, 33
Lee, Henry A. G., 147
Lee, Genl. Robert E., 205
Lee, Dr. S. L., 70
Leffingwell, Capt., 314
Left Hand, 140
Left Handed, 51
Left Handed Man, 151
LeMoyne, Simon, 91
Leonard, William, 231
Le Petit Corbeau, 148
Leschi, 258
Lesou, 188
Let's Kindle a Fire, 342
Letalesha, 211
Leupp, Francis E., 71, 289
Lewis, Lucinda, 228, 299
—, Capt. Meriwether, 58, 248
Lightning, 82
Lily of the Mohawks, 294
Lincoln, Abraham, 122, 217
Lisa, Manuel, 248, 322
Lisper, 90
Little Bluff, 76
Little Boy, 18
Little Carpenter, The, 20
Little Crow, 120, 148–150, 202, 238, 320
Little Eagle, 321
Little John, 246
Little Manuel, 165
Lttle Raven, 150–151
Little Spotted Tail, 277
Little Thunder, 276
Little Turtle, 151–152
Little Wolf, 80, 81, 152–154, 311, 341
Little Woman Chief, 336
Little Wound, 270
Lizzie, 140
Lochar Harjo, 124
Lodge, Sir Oliver, 327
Logan, 154–155

—, Capt., 109
—, James, 109, 154, 265
— the Mingo, 109, 154
Lolóloma, 289, 348, 349
Lomahongyoma, 288, 289, 349
Lombardi, Carolyn Eckloff, 214
Lone Camper, 193
Lone Man, The, 231
Lone Star, 71
Lone Wolf, 21, 22, 29, 32, 77, 137, 155–156, 252, 255, 257
—, Celia, 21
Long Horn, 29
Long, John, 156
—, Will West, 156–157
Longbeard, Solomon, 250
Long Earrings, 165
Longfellow, Henry W., 59, 109
Lookout, Fred, 160–161
Looking Glass, 147, 157, 159, 330
Loolowkin, 182
Lost Dauphin, The, 335
Lost Maiden, 248
Lost Woman, 248
Lott, Henry, 120
Loud Voice, 297
Louis XVI, King, 336
Lubo, Ramona, 230
Lucy, 92
Lugo, Ramona, 230
Lumhe Chati, 328
Lumhee Holatee, 39
Lumhi Holati, 39
Lurie, Nancy O., 184
Lyon, John, 119
Lyttleton, Gov. William H., 195

MacIntosh, William, 162
Mackenzie, Col. Ranald S., 57, 156, 207
M'Dougal, Duncan, 58
McDonald, Mary (Molly), 246
McGillivray, Alexander, 161–162, 328
—, Alexander, Jr., 162
—, Lachlan, 161
McGillicuddy, Valentine T., 233, 351
McIntosh, Alex C., 39
—, Chilly, 162
—, David, 163
—, Eliza Hawkins, 163
—, Lachlin, 332
—, Peggy, 163
—, Rolly, 162
—, Solomon, 39
—, Susanna Coe, 162
—, William, 39, 162–163, 173, 197
McKenny, Thomas, 177
McKinley, William, 129, 183
McLaughlin, James, 89, 99
McWhorter, Lucullus V., 348
Machunahzha, 279
Mack, Connie, 28
Mad Wolf, Rosa, 184
Magpie, 214
Magpie Woman, 116
Mahier, Edith, 181
Mahrstahsheedahkuroosh, 33⁄
Mahthela, 277, 278
Mahtotohpa, 172
Makataimeshkiakiak, 34
Maker of Daylight, 115
Makhpia-sha, 231
Makhpiya-luta, 231
Male Deer, 42

Mamaday, 156
Mamakiah, 116
Mamanti, 156, 262
Mamas, 263
Man Chief, 211
Man of the Black Weeds, 165
Mangas Coloradas, 53, 84, 93, 163–165, 186, 189, 314
Mangos Colorados, 163
Mangopeonen, 196
Mangus Coloradus, 163
Manishee, 12
Man of the Black Weeds, 165
Man on the Mountain Top, 239
Manuelito, 26, 75, 90, 165–167
Manwangopath, 152
Man Who Carries a Sword, 282
Man Who Goes in the Middle, 88
Man With Whiskers, 25
Many Achievements, 214
Many Bullet Wounds, 340
Many Cattle, 89
Ma-pe-wi, 23
Maqui-banasha, 350
Marchand, Sehoy, 161
Marie Antoinette, 336
Mars-che-coodo, 332
Marshall, Justice John, 247
Martin, Mungo, 167–168
Martínez, Alfoncita, 23
—, Crescencio, 23, 168–169
—, Janice, 221
—, Joyce, 221
—, María, 169, 170, 171, 220
—, Maximiliana, 169
—, Julián, 169–171, 220
—, Tony, 220
Mary Buffalo, 354
Mason, John, 252
Maspera Mohe, 54
Massasoit, 13, 171–172, 174, 251, 278, 279
—, Alexander, 172, 174
—, Metacom, 13–14, 172
—, Philip, 172, 174, 175
—, Sunsonewhew, 172
Master of Life, 72
Mataoaka, 215
Mathieu, J. B., 101
Mati-he-hlogeco, 111
Matoax, 215
Matohinsda, 88
Mato Tope, 172–173
Matowaka, 215
Mato Watakpe, 98
Matthews, Capt. Jacob, 185
Matthews, Dr. Washington, 141, 185
Mayhew, Rev. Experience, 193
Meacham, Albert, 114, 139, 254, 337
Meddler, The, 186
Medicine Bird, 214
Meeker, Nathan, 57, 203
Meethetashe, 290
Mekojah, Lizzie, 25
Menawa, 173
Menewa, 173
Meriam, Lewis, 41
Merriam, C. Hart, 256
Merritt, Genl. Wesley, 345
Mesasiawa, 127
Meshikinnoquah, 151
Metacom, 13, 48, 172, 174–176, 329
Metacomet, 174

Metal Worker, The, 19
Methoataske, 290, 297
Metsahehum, 160
Mexam, 49
Miantonomo, 48, 49, 176–177, 191, 313
Micanopy, 43, 177–178, 333, 335
Micconopy, 177
Micco-nuppe, 177
Michenopah, 177
Michikinikwa, 151
Mikanopy, 177
Miles, Genl. Nelson, 30, 62, 95, 129, 130,
   153, 154, 159, 182, 272, 311, 312, 330,
   352
Miller, Iva, 299
Miller, Joaquín, 336
Mingo, 226
Minimii, 115
Minneokadawin, 149
Miomex Zebequa, 263
Mishekunnoghwah, 151
Mitchell, Alice, 145
Mitchell, Harriet Newell, 344
Mixan, 49
Mochunozhin, 279
Mohe, 54
Moketavato, 36
Momone, 344
Monroe, James, 226
Montauk, Mary, 194
Montezuma, Carlos, 178–180, 327
Montgomery, Col. Archibald, 195
Montoya, Anita Cata, 221
—, Gerónima, 228
—, María, 169, 170
Moody, Dwight, 52
Mooney, James, 156, 282
Mootska, Waldo (Walter), 180
—, Tom, 180
Mopope, Stephen, 22, 181
Moran, Thomas, 256
Morgan, Lewis Henry, 204
Morning Dew, 199
Morning Star, 80
Morse, Jedediah, 336
Mosechehe, Julia Pryor, 161
Moses, 73, 181–182, 274
—, Walter, 184
Mott, Dr. Valentine, 200
Moulton, Capt., 9
Mountain Chief, 183
—, Walter, 184
Mountain Wolf Woman, 184
Moving Sun, 91
Moxmox, Hermene, 347
Mucho Ganado, 89
Musgrove, John, 185
—, Mary, 185–186
Mutsiawotan, Ahki, 256
Myeerah, 317

Nabokov, Peter, 309
Nache, 186
Nachez, 186
Nah'ilayhunkay, 52
Naiche, 54, 85, 95, 186, 190
Nail, The, 200
Nailor, Gerald, 187
Nakai Tsosi, 19
Namath, Joe, 299
Namequa, 36
Namontack, 225
Nampayo, 187

Nampayu, 187
Nampeyo, 187–189
—, Annie, 189
—, Cecilia, 189
—, Fannie, 189
—, Nellie, 189
Namumpum, 329
Nana, 189–190
Nanabah, 76
Nanasia, 36
Nanay, 189
Nancy, 36
Nancy Ward, 320
Nané, 189
Nane-yih, 320
Naninonsi, 290
Nantahoack, 225
Nanu-hi, 320
Nanuntenoo, 48, 177
Nanuskooke, 176
Nape-zi, 345
Naqapenkim, 167
Narbona, 167
Nasheakusk, 36
Nasingonsi, 289
Nasomsee, 36
Natahki, 256
Natchez, 186, 338
Nauasia, 36
Naunangai, George, 325
Naunainuknuk, David, 228
Nauntenoo, 48, 177
Nauasia, 36
Nawat, 151
Nearly Complete, 348
Neescotnemeg, 250
Neihardt, John G, 34
Neneglud, 191, 193
Nenekunat, 191
Neolin, 73
Neshapanasumin, 130
Newcomb, Franc J., 141
Nina, 92
Ninastoko, 183
Ninham, Daniel, 190–191
Ninicraft, 191
Niniglud, 191
Ninigret, 191–193, 329, 344
—, Thomas, 193
Ninna-stoko, 183
Nitoh Makwi, 255
Noah, 258
Nockkoist, 27
Nockoist, 27
Nocona, Peta, 193–194, 206
Noise in the House, 83
Nokona, 193
Nokoni, 193
Nomkahpa, 311
Nompaapa, 311
Nonicas, 54
Nonooktowa, 336
Nordmark, Olaf, 187
Northrup, Sarah Bird, 239
No Wife, 308
Núñez, Benita, 328
—, Manuel Carmonia, 328
Nunna Hidihi, 239
Nunnuit, Peter, 329

Oak Tree, 226
O'Bail, John, 59, 60
Obeil, John, 60
Occom, Samson, 194–195

Occum, Samson, 194
Oconostota, 20, 195–196
Ocum, Benoni, 194
Odensu, 83
Odom, Mattie, 39
Oghshigwarise, 250
Oglethorpe, Gov. James, 185, 302, 303
Ogonstota, 238
Ohiyesa, 82, 87, 249
Ohkom Kakit, 152
Ohkum Kakit, 152
Oiahl, 258
Oiscoss, 200
Old Hop, 21
Old Joseph, 128, 275
Old Knife, 211
Old Smith, 19
Ollokot, 128, 307
Omboke, 33
Onacona, 20
Oneco, 314
One Who Moves Warily, 134
Ongwaterohiathe, 264
One Who Causes to Fly Up, 302
One to Follows the Ridge, 239
One Who Goes About, 320
One Who Makes Life, 000
One Who Moves Warily, 134
One Who Yawns, 93
One Woman, The, 143
Onongoit, 251
Onspecannonpa-luta, 236
On The Other Side, 194
Onwanonsyshon, 125
Onwarenhiiaki, 335
Ookoonaka, 20
Oowatie, David, 41, 238, 326
Opechancanough, 196
Open Door, The, 290, 297
Opening in the Sky, 110
Opeteca Hanawaywin, 223
Opetheyaholo, 131, 197
Opitchipan, 196, 225
Opothleyaholo, 51, 131, 197
Oqwa Pi, 198
Orator, The, 25
Ormsby, Maj. William, 338
Oroloswa, 99
Ortega, Ramona Gonzaga, 230
Ortegna, Ramona Gonzaga, 230
Osceola, 43, 177, 178, 199, 200, 228, 333
Osequirison, 250
Oshkosh, 200, 302
Oskashe, 200
Ossiolachih, 199
Otee Emathla, 131
Oteemathla, 131
Otherday, John, 201–202
Other Day, John, 201–202
Otóah-hastis, 285
Otter Woman, 214
Otussa, 219
Ouabasha, 319
Ouhi, Chief, 182
Ouray, 56, 119, 202–203
—, Willie, 202
Our Enlightener, 264
Our Great Teacher, 103
Ousamequin, 171
Owenoco, 313
Owl, 353

Packs His Drum, 270
Pahueska, 208

Pahuska, 208
Pah-kah-kah, 133
Painted Robe, 181
Paiute Prophet, The, 287
Pakaka, 133
Palmer, Genl. Innis N., 246
Panton, William, 161, 162
Pariaseamen, 294
Paria Semen, 294
Parker, Arthur Caswell, 203, 204, 327
—, Cynthia Ann, 194, 206, 207
—, Ely Samuel, 203, 204–206
—, Quanah, 155, 194, 206–207
—, William, 204
Paroway Semehno, 294
Parrawasemen, 294
Parrish, Samuel, 338
Parrywahsaymen, 207–208, 294
Parrywasaymen, 294
Pasaconaway, 207
Paseego, 323
Passaconaway, 207, 318
Patania, Frank, 180
Pauhuska, 208
Pawhuska, 208–209
Pawishik, 224
Payepot, 209–210
Peahchepeahso, 277
Peggy, 163
Peheziwi, 277
Peña, Natividad, 210
Peña, Tonita, 210–211, 228
Penn, William, 93, 286
Penny, Sarah, 127
Penpenhihi, 329
Peopeo Kiskiok Hihih, 329
Peotsenmy, 182
Perry, Capt. Oliver H., 317
Pessacus, 314
Petahlayshahahrho, 212
Petalésharo, 211–212
Petanésharo, 212
Peters, Susie, 18, 22, 181, 305
Petit, John, 265
Petopowowett, 329
Petty, John, 265
Pezi, 98
Philip, King, 48, 49, 314, 318, 329
Philip of Pokanoket, 174
Phillips, Nancy, 222
Phips, Sir William, 9
Piapot, 209
Piasa, 34
Picotte, Caryl, 145
—, Henri, 145
—, Pierre, 145
—, Susan, 145
Piece Split from the Sun, 182
Pierce, Capt. Michael, 48
Piernas Corvas, 43
Pike, Genl. Albert, 131
Pike, Lieut. Zebulon, 208, 302, 319
Pinquana, 323
Pipe, Capt., 115, 332
Pitalésharu, 211
Pitarésharu, 211
Pitchlynn, John, 213
—, Peter Perkins, 212–213
Pizí, 88
Plain Looking, 55
Planter, The, 59
Playful, 215
Plenty Coups, 214

Pocagin, 215
Pocahontas, 196, 215, 225
Pocano, 169
Pochims, 225
Podaladalte, 353
Pogattacut, 344
Point of Yucca, 180
Pokagon, Angela, 217
—, Elizabeth, 216
—, Francis, 216
—, Leopold, 215–216, 217
—, Paul, 216
—, Simon, 215, 216–217
—, Victoria, 217
Pokanoka, 263
Pollkissut, 125
Pometacom, 174
Pometacomet, 172
Pomoacan, 102
Ponce, 165
Pontiac, 35, 45, 61, 73, 217–219, 262
Popé, 219–220
Pópñ, 219
Popovi Da, 220–221
Poppleton, Andrew J., 280
Poquiam, 313
Porter, Benjamin E., 221
—, Phoebe, 221
—, Pleasant, 124, 221–222
Posey, Alexander L., 96, 222–223
—, Lewis H., 222
Poskofa, 125
Post, Christian, 292
Post, Wiley, 245
Potsunu, 228
Poundmaker, 223
Poweshiek, 223–224
Powhatan, 196, 215, 225
Powell, Billy, 199
—, William, 199
Powless, Hattie, 282
Pratt, Capt. Richard H., 55, 99, 327, 345
Preacher, The, 274
Preloch, 194, 206
Prepared Meat, 354
Pretty Cloud, Dolly, 25
Pretty Eagle, 214
Pretty Plume, 269
Prettyman, Joseph, 124
Princess, The, 339
Principal Bird, 259
Proctor, Col. Henry, 317
Puckeshinwa, 290, 297
Puckhyatoot, 275
Pukeesheno, 290
Pumpkin Mountain, 219
Pushetonequa, 350
Pushmataha, 226
—, Johnson, 226
Putnam, Frederick W., 127, 203
Putting His Foot Down, 133
Pyesa, 34
Pyle, Howard, 71
Pypegee, 263

Qotcakao, 187
Qotsvema, 187
Quah Ah, 210
Qualchiah, 182
Quananchit, 48
Quanonshet, 48
Quashawam, 344
Quatie, 247

Qued Koi, 181
Queen Anne, 106, 215, 227
Queen Caroline, 303
Queen Marie, 183
Queen of Pamunkey, 227
Queen Victoria, 34
Quelatican, 181
Quelatikan, 181
Quemollah, 182
Quequequamanchet, 329
Quiltenoche, 182
Quiltenock, 182
Quinapin, 329
Quinequan, 227
Quinney, John Waunnacon, 227–228
—, Lucinda Lewis, 228
—, Osceola, 228
—, Phoebe Ann, 228
Quintana, Ben, 228–229
Qunnone, 49
Qunnoune, 49

Radin, Paul, 184
Rain in the Face, 229–230
Ramona, 230
Rat, The, 9
Rattle, 297
Reaches for the Wind, 40
Reader, The, 204
Rector, Col. Elias, 44
Red, The, 55
Red Bird, 40, 201, 231, 272
Red Boy, 75
Red Clay Woman, 309
Red Cloud, 13, 62, 88, 117, 198, 231–233, 245, 267, 270, 271, 276, 277, 285, 351
Red Eagle, 328
Red Fox, 221
Red Hawk, 61
Red Jacket, 60, 103, 204, 234–235
Red Leaf, 319
Red Man's Christ, The, 342
Red Shoes, 236
Red Sleeves, 163
Red Thunder, 318
Red Tomahawk, 236–237, 269
Red Wing, 238
Reese, Charles, 326
—, Susannah, 41, 326
Reichard, Gladys, 141
Remington, Frederic S., 256, 257
Reno, Maj. Marcus, 89, 120
Reynolds, Col. Joseph, 311, 340
Rice, Mary Ann, 335
Richard, Chief, 147
Richmond, Margaret Lois, 300
Riddle, Frank, 139, 336, 337
—, Jeff, 337
—, Toby, 336
Ridge, John, 42, 239, 240, 326
—, John Rollin, 239
—, Major, 238–240, 326
—, Susannah, 238
—, The, 238
Riel, David, 241
—, Louis, 241–242
Riggs, Ella, 242
—, Rollie Lynn, 242–243
—, W. G., 242
Riley, Sarah Watkins, 87
Rinehart, William, 338
Riordan, Dennis, 75
Rising Sun, 199

Roaring Cloud, 231
Rock, 55
Rock Carrier, 274
Rocky Boy, 243
Rodgers, Richard, 242
Roe, Rev. Walter C., 52
Rogers, Clement Vann, 243
—, Betty Blake, 244
—, James, 50
—, Will, 243–244
Rolette, 319
Rolfe, Catherine, 215
—, John, 196, 215, 225
—, Rebecca, 215
—, Thomas, 215
Roman Nose, 116, 245–246, 285
Ronan, Peter, 50
Roosevelt, Franklin, 41, 105
—, Theodore, 71, 82, 95, 113, 129, 179, 183, 207
Rope Thrower, The, 90
Rosenthal, Joe, 105
Ross, Alexander, 92
Ross, Daniel, 246
—, John, 86, 87, 239, 240, 246–247
—, Capt. Sul, 194
Rotten Belly, 17
Round Bear, 224
Roundhead, 148, 317
Rowlandson, Mary, 329
Roybal, Alfonso, 23
—, Juan Esteván, 23
Run Over by a Wagon and Scarred, 253
Rushing Eagle, 149

Sacagawea, 248
Sacajawea, 82, 248–249, 322
Sacargarweah, 248
Sacred Pigeon, 148
Sadaganacktie, 249
Sadagunachte, 249
Sadakanaktie, 249
Sadekanakte, 249
Sagarissa, 250
Sagaunash, 249–250
Sagoyewatha, 234
Sahpooly, 353
St. Claire, Genl. Arthur, 208
Saint Tammany, 286
Sakarissa, 250
Salkow, 133
Salvador, 165
Samaset, 250
Samoset, 250–251
Samuel, 13
Sánchez, Abel, 198
Sanovick, 57
Santana Simbola, 187
Santos, 85
Sapling is Ready, 226
Sargent, Delight, 42
Sassacus, 251–252, 313
Sassakusu, 251
Sassamon, John, 13, 175
Sastaretsi, 9
Satank, 29, 32, 155, 261, 281
Satanta, 21, 22, 29, 32, 155, 252–253, 262
Sauganash, 245
Sauts, 245
Sawawk, 216
Sayughdowa, 154
Scarface Charlie, 40, 253–254, 336
—, Charley, 253

Scarlet Cloud, 231
Scarlet Point, 119
Scenanki, 303
Scholfield, Genl. John, 338
Scholitza, 258
Schonchin John, 254–255
—, Jim, 139, 140, 254–255
Schoolcraft, Henry Rowe, 106, 327
Schrimscher, Elizabeth A., 48
Schrimsher, Mary A., 243
Schultz, Hart Merriam, 255–257
—, James W., 256
—, Naomah Tracy, 267
Schurz, Carl, 339
Schweabe, 258
Sconchin John, 254
—, Jim, 254
Scott, Genl. Hugh L., 183, 184, 187, 340
Scott, Genl. Winfield, 240
Scruniyatha, 101
Sealth, 258
Seathl, 258
Seattle, 258
—, George, 258
—, Oiahl, 258
Secamumpkin, 258
Secoffee, 43
Secot, 336
Sedwagowane, 103
See Ru, 210
Sees the White Cow, 34
See-ti-toh, 252
Segwarusa, 250
Sehoy, 328
Sehoya, Princess, 239
Sequareesa, 250
Sequioa, 259
Sequoyah, 42, 259–261
—, Sarah (Sally), 260
Sergeant, John, 142
Serunyattha, 101
Set-t'ainte, 252
Set Tainte, 252
Setangaia, 261
Setangia, 261
Setangya, 252, 261–262
Setimkía, 281
Setumkía, 281
Seward, William H., 204
Sexton, Daniel, 14
Shabbona, 262
Shabona, 262–263
Shabonee, 262
Shaikes, 263–264
Shakes, 263–264
Shaking Snow, 102
Shantlahow, Mali, 182
Shappa, 318
Shateiaronhia, 148
Shateyaronyah, 148
Shaubena, 262
—, Bill, 263
Shaugreau, Louis, 266
Shavanaux, 203
Shavano, 203
Shawnee Prophet, The, 290, 291, 296, 297
Sheetapah, 282
Shegenaba, 219
She is Playful, 215
Shell Flower, 337
Shepherd, O. L., 90
She Plays With Things, 215

Shequallisere, 250
Sheridan, Genl. Philip, 32
—, Genl. William T., 26
Shield, 115
Shikellamy, 154, 264–265
—, John, 265
Shirland, Capt. Edmond, 164
Shishi'esh, 66
Shooting Star, 290
Short Bull, 66, 265–266, 311, 352
Short Dress, 154
Shouting Mountain, 275
Shugin, 128, 307
Shuhsheeohsh, 66
Shulush Homa, 236
—, Humma, 236
Sibley, Genl. Henry, 149, 202
Sieur de Jumonville, 102
Sieur de Villers, 102
Signaller, The, 178
Sikwaj'i, 259
Silpe, 182
Silverhorn, 181
Simmons, John Haysting, 40
Simpson, George, 92, 263
Sinagaw, 217
—, Lonidaw, 217
Sinclair, Genl. Arthur, 151
Singing Bird, 36
Singing Eagle, 199
Sings to the Sweat Lodge, 309
Sinte Galeshka, 275
Sinte Gleska, 275
Sinte Maza, 122
Sitanka, 29
Si Tanka, 29
Sitgreaves, Lorenzo, 121
Sitting Bear, 11, 261
Sitting Bull (Hunkpapa), 30, 66, 88, 93, 129, 229, 233, 236, 238, 266–269, 270, 271, 311, 330, 340, 342, 345, 347
Sitting Bull (Oglala), 269–272
Sixkiller, Clndoche, 125
Sitting Bull the Minor, 269–272
Skaniadario, 102, 204
Skenandoa, 272
Sky, 231
Slanie, John, 278
Sleeping Bear, 55
Slemhakkah, 49
Slender Little Ironworker, 19
Slow, 266
Small Woman, 55
Smallwood, Norma DesCygne, 97
Smith, Capt. John, 196, 215, 224, 225
Smith, Erminie A., 107
—, Joseph, 224, 225
—, Lucy Fields, 274
—, Pegleg, 316
—, Pig Redbird, 272
—, Redbird, 116, 272–274
Smohalla, 274–275, 304, 307
Smohallah, 274
Smoke, 263
Smokeller, 274
Smoky, Louise, 181
Smóqula, 274
Smuguiskugin, 128, 307
Snake Girl, 187
Snake Head, 353
Snapping Turtle, The, 213
Sogwili, 259
Sohappy, 275

Soiengarata, 106
Somerset, Christopher L., 251
—, Capt. John, 251
Sosha, Jane, 131
Sound, 304
Sour Belly, 17
Sowapso, 275
Spahecha, 124
Spalding, Rev. Henry M., 182, 306
Spamagelabe, 109
Sparrow, The, 259
Spear Dragger, The, 250
Spemicalawba, 109
Spemicalawbe, 109
Spokan Garry, 91
Spokane Garry, 91–92
Spotka, 262
Spotted Elk, 29
Spotted Tail, 31, 61, 65, 112, 113, 271, 275–277, 311
Spybuck, Ernest, 277–278
—, John, 277
Squanto, 251, 278–279
Squaw Sachem of Pocasset, 329
Standing Bear, 143, 279–281
Standing Bowles, 43
Standing Holy, 269
Standing in the Track, 354
Standing Together, 326
Standing Turkey, 21
Standish, Capt. Miles, 172, 279
Stands Fast, 59
Stand Watie, 240, 326–327
Stapler, Mary Bryan, 247
Star That Travels, 24
Steen, Maj. Enoch, 53
Stevens, Gov. Isaac, 132, 133, 258, 306
Stone Child, 243
Stongkee, 275
Strange Child, 336
Strike at Different Camps, 308
Strikes the Iron, 214
Strong Hearted Woman, The, 336
Stuart, Col., 21
Stumbling Bear, 281
Sublette, William, 17
Sucktum Mahway, 33
Suconewhew, 172
Sudagunachte, 249
Sulktalthscosum, 181, 182
Sulktashkosha, 182
Sumner, Col. Edwin V., 30
Sun in the Horizon, 288
Sun Man, 287, 341
Sunsonewhew, 172
Surprise Woman, 55
Swanton, John R., 84
Swataney, 264
Swateny, 264
Sweet Breeze, 152
Sweetheart, 329
Sweet Smelling, 323
Sweezy, Carl, 282
—, Fieldie, 282
Swift Arrow, 214
Swift Bear, 63
Sword Bearer, 282–283
Sword Carrier, 282

Tabbebo, 287
Tacanhpi-luta, 236
Tachgokanhelle, 293
Tachnechdorus, 265
Tackensuatis, 17

Taft, William H., 183, 350
Tag-hee, 312
Tahamont, Beatrice, 204
Tahatan Wakuwa Mini, 148
Tahcawin, 345
Tahetan Wakan Mani, 148
Taheton Wakawa Mini, 148
Tahgahjute, 109, 154, 265
Tahoma, Quincy, 283–284
Taighe, 312
Taihee, 312
Taimah, 284
Taiomah, 284
Takayren, 83
Takertawker, 326
Takes a Shield, 66
Talasse Tustenuggee, 199
Taklishim, 93
Talcy, 199
Talker, The, 146
Tall Bull, 285–286
Talof Harjo, 221
Tangled Hair, 276
Tamah, 284
Tamanend, 284
Tame Deer, 320
Tame Doe, 320
Tamela Pashme, 80
Tamkahanka, 295
Tammany, 285–286
Tanacharison, 101
Tannghrishon, 101
Taoyatechata, 148
Taoyateduta, 148
Tardeka Tustanugga, 124
Tarhe, 286
Tarhee, 286
Tasagi, 119
Tashinagi, 345
Tashunka Kokipapi, 351
Tachunka Witco, 61
Tasi Nagi, 345
Tasina Sapewin, 62
Tasunka Kokipapi, 351
Tatanka Iotanka, 270
Tatanka Iyotanka, 266
Tatank'amimi, 238
Tatanka Psica, 266
Tatanka Yotanka, 266
Tatapanum, 329
Tate Iyohiwin, Ellen, 40
Tatum, Lawrie, 262
Tavibo, 287–288, 341
Tawagahe, 208
Tawaitakas, 306
Tawanima, 288
Tawaquaptewa, 288–290, 349
—, Betty, 290
Tawaquoptewa, 288
Taylor, Olivia, 22
Taylor, Genl. Zachary, 334
Taza, 54, 85
Tecumseh, 11, 35, 98, 109, 148, 152, 173, 226, 250, 262, 287, 290–292, 296, 297, 302, 317, 328
Tecumtha, 290
Tcu Mana, 187
Te E, 168
Teedyscung, 292–293
—, Elizabeth, 292
Tegaquitha, 294
Teh-toot-sah, 77
Tehoragwarregen, 335
Tehowaghwengaraghkwin, 44, 46

Teias, 133
Tekahionwake, 125
Tekakwitha, Kateri, 294
Teller, Henry M., 124
Tenachrisan, 101
Ten Bears, 294–295
Tendoi, 295
Tendoy, 295–296
Tene'angopte, 136
Ten Elks, 294–296
Tennaks, 133
Tenskwátawa, 86, 133, 143, 290, 291, 297–298
Tenwaneus, 37
Terrapin, Sally, 156
Terrapin, The, 196
Terrazas, Col. Joaquín, 315
Teshuhimga, 208
Tessee, 260, 261
Tewanima, Louis, 288
Tewaquaptewa, 288
Tewaquoptiwa, 288
Thaowanyuthe, 28, 37
Thaowanyuths, 37
Thayandanégea, 44
Thigh, 277
Thin Mexican, 19
Thocmetone, 337
Thocmetony, 337
Thomas, Rev. Eleazer, 114, 139, 254, 337
Thompson, Genl. Wiley R., 39, 178, 199
Thornburgh, Maj. Thomas, 57
Thorpe, James F., 298–299
—, Charles, 298
—, Frieda, 299
—, Hiram, 298
—, Iva, 299
—, Patricia, 299
Thrusting the Lance to Both Sides, 354
Thunderclap, 284
Thunder in the Mountains, 128
Thunder on the Mountain Top, 128
Thunder Rolling in the Heights, 128
Tibbles, Thomas H., 143, 144, 280, 281
Ties Up Her Bundle, 309
Tiger, Billy, 178
Tiger, Jerome, 299–300
Tiger, Rev. John M., 299
Tikamthe, 290
Tikamthi, 290
Timawi, 123
Tinker, Clarence, 300–302
—, Clarence, Jr., 301
—, George, 300
—, Rose, 300
Tionantati, 72
Tipi Sapa, 74
Tipsoe Tyee, 312
Tisquantum, 278
Tiyanoga, 106
Tobacco Pipe, 115
Todkados, 154
Tohausen, 76
Tohoma, 283
Tohosa, 76
Toh Yah, 187
Tomah, 201, 302
Tomau, 302
Tomo Chachi Mico, 302
Tomochichi, 302
Ton-a-enko, 136
Tonarcy, 206
Tongue Talker, 90

Tonicy, 206
Toohoolhoolzote, 304
Toohulhulsote, 304, 330
Toonahowi, 303
Toop'weets, 55
Topamby, 296
Topenebee, 216
Totankiotanka, 270
Totanka Psica, 266
Totanka Yotanka, 266
Totopotomoi, 227
Tótsoni, 89
Town Builder, The, 208
Tracy, Naomah, 257
Tree Cutter, 335
Truckee, Captain, 337
Trumpet, The, 292
Tryon, Dwight, 71
Tsakakawía, 248
Tsan-usdí, 246
Tsatoke, Monroe, 181, 305–306
Tsa-To-Ke, 305
Tsen T'ainte, 110
Tsi yu-gunsini, 79
Tsikwaya, 259
Tsistunagiska, 320
Tubbenahneeguay, 126
Tuekakas, 275, 306
—, Celia, 307
—, Ephraim, 306
—, Sarah, 307
Tuekukas, 128
Tuhbenahneeguay, 126
Tuksi, 196
Tulope Tustenuggee, 221
Two Equal Clouds, 148
Two Guns, John, 307
Two Guns White Calf, 307–308
Two Leggings, 308–309
—, Amos, 309
Two Moon, 310–311, 340
Two Moons, 66, 310
Two Rivers Flowing Together, 71
Two Strike, 66, 266, 311, 312
Two Strikes, 311
Two Tails, 152
Twuneash, 37
Tyhee, 295, 312–313

d'Ucel, Jeanne, 110
Unaduti, 47
Uncas, 176, 191, 192, 251, 313–314
Unhappy Jake, 265
Unkas, 313
Unongoit, 251
Untendoip, 295
U-ray, 202
Uwati, 41, 326
Uwatie, 238

Varnum, Lieut. Charles A., 333
Vaudreuil, Marquis de, 236
Verelst, Cornelius, 303
Victor, 49
Victorio, 189, 314–315
View, Charlotte, 298
Vigil, Ascensíon, 210
—, Martina, 210
—, Tonita, 210
Vister, 55

Waatina, 282
Wabanaquot, 331

Wabasha, 319
—, Joseph, 319
—, Napoleon, 320
Wabojeeg, 330
Wadze Wipe, 248
Wagon Scarface, 253
Wagwises, 174
Wahbanosay, 126
Wahiev, 80
Wahkasetompahhe, 160
Wahnaataa, 318
Wahnatah, 318
Wahshehah, 24
Wahtsake Tumpah, 160
Wahunasonacock, 225
Waipashaw, 274
Wakara, 315
Wakohihekah, 25
Wakoyantanke, 149
Wakunchakukah, 346
Walkara, 15, 315–317
Walker, 315
Walking Buffalo, The, 238
Walking by the River, 187
Walk in the Water, 317
Walks as She Thinks, 231
Walks With the Pipe, 276
Wallamootkin, 306
Walter, 184
Wamdesapa, 119
Wamsutta, 172, 329
Wamundeyakapi, 120
Wanderer, The, 193
Wanekia, 341
Waneta, 318
Wanig Suchka, 231
Wannalancet, 208, 318–319
Wannalanset, 318
Wanotan, 318
Waoowinchtcha, 143
Wapasha, 238, 319–320
—, Joseph, 320
—, Napoleon, 320
—, the Second, 319
Wapusha, 319
Warahumpah, 24
War Chief, 51
Ward, Bryant (Briant), 321
—, Catherine, 321
—, Elizabeth, 321
—, Fivekiller, 321
—, Nancy, 21, 320–321
War Eagle, 321–322
Ware, Lewis, 18, 306
Warner, Glen S., 288
—, Jonathan W., 16
Warraghiyagey, 46
Warren, Charlotte, 323
—, Lyman M., 322
—, William W., 322–323
War Trumpeter, 292
Warsaja, 178
Wasagah, 178
Wasechuntashunka, 11
Wasechun Tashunka, 11
Washakie, 295, 323–325
—, Bishop, 325
—, Charles, 325
—, Dick, 325
—, George, 325
Washington, George, 38, 60, 101, 102,
    152, 162, 234
Washunga, 325–326

Wasonaunequa, 85
Wassaja, 178
Wast, Minnie Sackett, 205
Watchful Fox, The, 134
Water Edge, 283
Water Elk, 54
Wathohuck, 298
Watie, Buck, 42, 326
—, Stand, 41, 131, 238, 326–327
Watohkonk, 136
Wattan, 282
Waunkauntshawzeekau, 346
Waun-na-con, 227
Wa-Wa-Chaw, 327–328
Wawa Calac Chaw, 327
Wawequa, 176
Waylahskise, 11
Wayne, Genl. Anthony, 151, 287, 291
Weatherford, Charles, 328
—, Sehoy, 328
—, William, 226, 328
Weaver, Pauline, 16
Webster, John L., 280
Weetamoe, 329
Weetamoo, 329
Weetamore, 329
Weiser, Conrad, 101, 293
Wendjimadub, 331
Wentz, Lewis H., 18, 306
West, Genl. Joseph, 164
Westi, Wili, 156
Weymouth, Capt. George, 278
Wheelock, Eleazar, 45, 194
Wheelwright, Mary C., 142
Whipple, Lieut. Amiel, 121
Whipple, Lieut, Stephen C., 158
White Antelope, 37
White Bear, 252
White Bird, 329–331
White Buffalo Shaking Off the Earth, 340
White Buffalo That Turns Around, 332
White Calf, 308
White Calf Two Guns, John, 307
White Cloud, 331
White Coral Beads, 210
White Eyes, 93, 331–332
White Goose, 329
White Hair, 208
White Horse, 110
White Man Runs Him, 308, 332–333
White Owl, 20
White Shield, 353
Whitman, Marcus, 306
—, Lieut. Royal E., 84
Whittier, John Greenleaf, 207
Wiantance, 344
Wicahpi Isnala, 71
Wickett, Susie, 239
Wicks, Rev. John J., 253, 353
Wide Mouth, 85
Wide Hips, 68
Wildcat, 11, 43, 177, 333–335
Wild Man, The, 251
Wild Rose, 320
Wildschut, William, 309
Wili Westi, 156
Wilkes, Capt. Charles, 132
Willard, Maj., 192
Williams, Eleazar, 201, 227, 335–336
—, Eunice, 335
—, John, 335, 336

—, Perry H., 75
—, Roger, 49, 172, 176
—, Thomas, 335
Williamson, Rev. Thomas S., 149, 202
Wilson, Alice, 342
—, Daisy, 342
—, David, 341
—, Ida, 342
—, Jack, 341
—, Mary, 342
—, Woodrow S, 179, 183, 311
Winchester, Genl., 110
Winema, 139, 253, 254, 336–337
Winnemucca, 337–338
—, Old, 337
—, Sarah (Sally), 337–339
Winnepurget, 207
Winner, The, 82, 87
Winslow, Genl. Josiah, 175
Wise Speaker, The, 344
Witchikittawbut, 344
Wiyaka Wastewin, 269
Wobaah, 325
Wobitsawahkah, 338
Wo-hiev, 80
Woinapa, 150
Wokini, 245
Wolf, The, 106
Wolf's Mountain Home Maker, 184
Wonah'ilayhunka, 51
Wonkas, 313
Wooden Lance, 339–340
Wooden Leg, 340–341
Woodsholitsa, 258
Woodworker, The, 144
Woohkinih, 245
Wootenekanuske, 176

Wootonekauske, 176
Woquini, 245
Worcester, Rev. Samuel A., 42, 86
Word Carrier, The, 71
Worm, The, 261
Wovoka, 13, 30, 34, 66, 237, 265, 266, 287, 288, 339, 341–342, 351
—, Jack, 341
Wozencraft, O. N., 16
Wraps His Tail, 282
Wright, Allen, 47, 342–344
—, Ben, 138
—, Col. George, 133
—, George, 182
Wuhtee, 259
Wurteh, 259
Wyancombone, 344
Wyandance, 344
Wyandanch, 176, 344
Wynepyechsika, 60
Wynkoop, Maj. Edward M., 36, 37

Yamacraw King, The, 302
Yampoochee, 14
Yanukwalas, 168
Yaratev, 121
Yawner, The, 93
Yeagtaupt, Mary, 354
Yellow, 315
Yellow Bird, 31
Yellow Feather, 171
Yellow Hair, 85
Yellow Hand, 345
Yellow Robe, Chauncey, 345–346
—, Chauncey, Jr., 346
—, Chauncina, 346

—, Evelyn, 346
—, Rosebud, 346
Yellow Thunder, 346–348
Yellow Wolf, 347–348
Yosette, 143
Youkeoma, 348
Youkioma, 348
Young Bear, 350–351
Young, Brigham, 316
Young Crow, 150
Young Joseph, 128
Young Man Afraid of His Horses, 232, 351–353
Young Man of Whose Horses They Are Afraid, 351
Young Men Fear His Horses, 351
Yoyouni, 275
Yucca Point, 275
Yukeoma, 348
Yukioma, 348
Yuyunipi-tqana, 275

Zarcillas Largas, 165
Zawnk, Chief, 216
Zebequa, Miomex, 263
Zeisberger, David, 265
Zepko-eete, 29
Zhogaxe, 144
Zintalah Galeshka, 275
Zintalah Galeska, 275
Zipkiyah, 29
Zipkoheta, 29
Zitkaduta, 201
Zitkala-sa, 40–41, 71
Zotom, 27, 353–354
—, Paul Caryl, 353
Zuzela, 269

TEXTBOOK OF
DIABETES

TEXTBOOK OF
DIABETES

EDITED BY

JOHN C. PICKUP MA, BM, DPhil, MRCPath
DIVISION OF CHEMICAL PATHOLOGY
UNITED MEDICAL AND DENTAL SCHOOLS OF
GUY'S AND ST THOMAS'S HOSPITALS
GUY'S HOSPITAL, LONDON
AND

GARETH WILLIAMS MA, MD, MRCP
DEPARTMENT OF MEDICINE
THE UNIVERSITY OF LIVERPOOL
ROYAL LIVERPOOL HOSPITAL, LIVERPOOL

IN TWO VOLUMES
VOLUME ONE

OXFORD

BLACKWELL SCIENTIFIC PUBLICATIONS

LONDON EDINBURGH BOSTON

MELBOURNE PARIS BERLIN VIENNA

© 1991 by
Blackwell Scientific Publications
Editorial Offices:
Osney Mead, Oxford OX2 oEL
25 John Street, London WC1N 2BL
23 Ainslie Place, Edinburgh EH3 6AJ
3 Cambridge Center, Cambridge,
  Massachusetts 02142, USA
54 University Street, Carlton
  Victoria 3053, Australia

Other Editorial Offices:
Librairie Arnette SA
2, rue Casimir-Delavigne
75006 Paris
France

Blackwell Wissenschaft-Verlag
Meinekestrasse 4
D-1000 Berlin 15
Germany

Blackwell MZV
Feldgasse 13
A-1238 Wien
Austria

First published 1991
Reprinted 1991

Set in Palatino by Setrite Typesetters, Hong Kong
Printed and bound in Hong Kong by
China Translation & Printing Services

DISTRIBUTORS

Marston Book Services Ltd
PO Box 87
Oxford OX2 oDT
(*Orders*: Tel: 0865 791155
        Fax: 0865 791927
        Telex: 837515)

USA
Blackwell Scientific Publications, Inc.
3 Cambridge Center
Cambridge, MA 02142
(*Orders*: Tel: 800 759−6102)

Canada
Times Mirror Professional Publishing, Ltd
5240 Finch Avenue East
Scarborough, Ontario M1S 5A2
(*Orders*: Tel: 416 298−1588)

Australia
Blackwell Scientific Publications
(Australia) Pty Ltd
54 University Street
Carlton, Victoria 3053
(*Orders*: (03) 347−0300)

British Library
Cataloguing in Publication Data

Textbook of diabetes.
  1. Man. Diabetes
  I. Pickup, John C. (John Christopher).
  II. Williams, Gareth
  616.462

ISBNs
  Vol. 1   0−632−03056−9
  Vol. 2   0−632−03058−5
  The set   0−632−025948−1

Contents

List of Contributors, xi

Foreword, xvii
HARRY KEEN

Preface, xix

Section 1: The History of Diabetes

1 The Millenia Before Insulin, 3
IAN A. MACFARLANE

2 The Discovery of Insulin, 10
MICHAEL BLISS

Section 2: Introduction to the Clinical Problems of Diabetes

3 Insulin-Dependent Diabetes Mellitus, 17
GEOFFREY V. GILL

4 Non-Insulin-Dependent Diabetes Mellitus, 24
GEOFFREY V. GILL

5 Public Health Problems of Diabetes Mellitus and its Cost to the Community, 30
D. R. R. WILLIAMS

Section 3: Classification and Diagnosis of Diabetes Mellitus

6 Classification and Diagnosis of Diabetes Mellitus and Impaired Glucose Tolerance, 37
PETER H. BENNETT

Section 4: Epidemiology of Diabetes

7 The Epidemiology of Diabetes Mellitus, 47
R. JOHN JARRETT

Section 5: Non-Diabetic Insulin Biosynthesis, Secretion and Action

8 The Anatomy, Organization and Ultrastructure of the Islets of Langerhans, 57
ANNE E. BISHOP AND
JULIA M. POLAK

9 Insulin Biosynthesis and Secretion, 72
SIMON L. HOWELL

10 The Structure and Phylogeny of Insulin, 84
STEVEN P. WOOD AND
ALASDAIR MCLEOD

11 The Insulin Receptor, 90
RICHARD H. JONES

12 Insulin Action and Responses: The Biochemistry of Postreceptor Events, 99
D. GRAHAME HARDIE AND
PHILIP COHEN

Section 6: Pathogenesis of Insulin-Dependent Diabetes Mellitus

13 Histology of the Islet in Insulin-Dependent Diabetes Mellitus, 107
ALAN K. FOULIS

14 Genetics of Insulin-Dependent Diabetes Mellitus, 113
GRAHAM A. HITMAN AND BRENDAN
MARSHALL

15 Immune Factors in the Pathogenesis of Insulin-Dependent Diabetes Mellitus, 122
GIAN FRANCO BOTTAZZO AND
EZIO BONIFACIO

V

16 Viruses in the Pathogenesis of Insulin-Dependent Diabetes Mellitus, 141
TERESA M. SZOPA AND
KEITH W. TAYLOR

17 Animal Models of Insulin-Dependent Diabetes Mellitus, 151
ADRIAN J. BONE

Section 7: Pathogenesis of Non-Insulin-Dependent Diabetes Mellitus

18 The Pathology of the Pancreas in Non-Insulin-Dependent Diabetes Mellitus, 167
PER WESTERMARK

19 Genetics in Non-Insulin-Dependent Diabetes Mellitus, 172
GRAHAM A. HITMAN

20 Obesity, Body Fat Distribution and Diet in the Aetiology of Non-Insulin-Dependent Diabetes Mellitus, 181
MIKE E. J. LEAN AND JIM I. MANN

21 The Pathogenesis of Non-Insulin-Dependent Diabetes Mellitus: The Role of Insulin Resistance, 192
DONALD J. CHISHOLM AND
EDWARD W. KRAEGEN

22 Pancreatic Abnormalities in Non-Insulin-Dependent Diabetes Mellitus, 198
LUIS C. RAMIREZ AND PHILIP RASKIN

23 Neuroendocrine Factors in the Pathogenesis of Non-Insulin-Dependent Diabetes Mellitus, 205
GARETH WILLIAMS

24 Animal Models of Non-Insulin-Dependent Diabetes Mellitus, 228
CLIFFORD J. BAILEY AND
PETER R. FLATT

Section 8: Other Types of Diabetes Mellitus

25 Maturity-Onset Diabetes of the Young (MODY), 243
ROBERT B. TATTERSALL

26 Malnutrition-Related Diabetes Mellitus, 247
V. MOHAN, A. RAMACHANDRAN AND
M. VISWANATHAN

27 Diabetes Mellitus and Pancreatic Disease, 256
CHI KONG CHING AND
JONATHAN M. RHODES

28 Diabetes Mellitus and Endocrine Diseases, 263
IAN A. MACFARLANE

29 Hereditary and Acquired Syndromes of Insulin Resistance, 276
C. RONALD KAHN, BARRY J.
GOLDSTEIN AND S. SETHU K. REDDY

30 Insulinopathies, 286
HOWARD S. TAGER

31 Genetic and Other Disorders Associated with Diabetes Mellitus, 291
AH WAH CHAN

Section 9: Biochemical Abnormalities in Diabetes Mellitus

32 Mechanisms of Hyperglycaemia and Disorders of Intermediary Metabolism, 303
PATRICK SHARP AND
DESMOND G. JOHNSTON

33 Glucagon and Gut Hormones in Diabetes Mellitus, 313
BERNHARD KREYMANN AND
STEPHEN R. BLOOM

34 The Concept and Measurement of 'Control', 325
DAVID R. MCCANCE AND
LAURENCE KENNEDY

35 Assay of Insulin, 335
PENELOPE M. S. CLARK AND
C. NICK HALES

36 C-Peptide and B-Cell Function in Diabetes Mellitus, 348
CHRISTIAN BINDER

Section 10: Management of Insulin-Dependent Diabetes Mellitus

37 Insulin Manufacture and Formulation, 357
TERENCE CHADWICK

38 The Pharmacokinetics of Insulin, 371
BIRGITTA LINDE

39 Insulin Injection Treatment for Insulin-
    Dependent Diabetic Patients, 384
    JOHN C. PICKUP AND
    GARETH WILLIAMS

40 Insulin Antibodies, 397
    ANTONY KURTZ

41 Diet in the Management of Insulin-
    Dependent Diabetes Mellitus, 407
    MIKE E. J. LEAN AND JIM I. MANN

42 Continuous Subcutaneous Insulin Infusion
    (CSII), 416
    JOHN C. PICKUP

43 The Artificial Pancreas and Related
    Devices, 427
    A. MICHAEL ALBISSER

44 Implantable Insulin Pumps, 431
    KARL IRSIGLER

45 Insulin Precipitation in Insulin Infusion
    Devices: Mechanisms and Possible
    Remedies, 437
    WILLIAM D. LOUGHEED AND
    A. MICHAEL ALBISSER

46 Alternative Methods, Systems and Routes of
    Insulin Delivery, 442
    PHILIP D. HOME

**Section 11: Management of Non-Insulin-
Dependent Diabetes Mellitus**

47 Dietary Management of Non-Insulin-
    Dependent Diabetes Mellitus, 453
    MIKE E. J. LEAN AND JIM I. MANN

48 Oral Agents and Insulin in the Treatment
    of Non-Insulin-Dependent Diabetes
    Mellitus, 462
    RURY R. HOLMAN AND
    ROBERT C. TURNER

Section 12: Acute Metabolic Complications

49 Diabetic Ketoacidosis, Non-Ketotic
    Hyperosmolar Coma and Lactic
    Acidosis, 479
    A. J. KRENTZ AND
    MALCOLM NATTRASS

50 Hypoglycaemia and Diabetes Mellitus, 495
    BRIAN M. FRIER

51 Problems with Overnight Glycaemic
    Control in Insulin-Treated Diabetic
    Patients, 507
    GEREMIA B. BOLLI

Section 13: Chronic Diabetic Complications

*Part 13.1: General Mechanisms of Diabetic
Complications*

52 The Determinants of Microvascular
    Complications in Diabetes: An
    Overview, 519
    KRISTIAN F. HANSSEN

53 Pathophysiology of Microvascular
    Disease: An Overview, 526
    JAMES D. WALKER AND
    GIAN CARLO VIBERTI

54 Biochemical Basis of Microvascular
    Disease, 534
    CATHLEEN J. MULLARKEY AND
    MICHAEL BROWNLEE

55 The Regulation of Microvascular Function
    in Diabetes Mellitus, 546
    JOHN E. TOOKE AND
    ANGELA C. SHORE

Part 13.2: Diabetic Eye Disease

56 The Epidemiology of Diabetic
    Retinopathy, 557
    RONALD R. KLEIN

57 The Pathogenesis of Diabetic Retinopathy
    and Cataract, 564
    EVA M. KOHNER, MASSIMO PORTA
    AND STEPHEN L. HYER

58 The Lesions and Natural History of
    Diabetic Retinopathy, 575
    EVA M. KOHNER

59 The Surgical Management of Diabetic
    Eye Disease, 589
    PETER J. BARRY

60 Psychological, Social and Practical Aspects of Visual Handicap for the Diabetic Patient, 605
JACQUELINE N. JONES

Part 13.3: Diabetic Neuropathy

61 Diabetic Neuropathy: Epidemiology and Pathogenesis, 613
P. K. THOMAS

62 Clinical Aspects of Diabetic Somatic Neuropathy, 623
JOHN D. WARD

63 Autonomic Neuropathy, 635
DAVID J. EWING

Part 13.4: Diabetic Nephropathy

64 Epidemiology and Natural History of Diabetic Nephropathy, 651
TORSTEN DECKERT,
KNUT BORCH-JOHNSEN AND
ANASUYA GRENFELL

65 Aetiology and Pathogenesis of Diabetic Nephropathy: Clues from Early Functional Abnormalities, 657
JAMES D. WALKER AND
GIAN CARLO VIBERTI

66 The Relationship between Structural and Functional Abnormalities in Diabetic Nephropathy, 671
RUDOLF W. BILOUS

67 Clinical Features and Management of Established Diabetic Nephropathy, 677
ANASUYA GRENFELL

Part 13.5: Macrovascular Disease and Hypertension

68 The Heart and Macrovascular Disease in Diabetes Mellitus, 701
ROGER H. JAY AND
D. JOHN BETTERIDGE

69 Hypertension in Diabetes Mellitus, 719
GARETH WILLIAMS

Part 13.6: Other Diabetic Complications

70 The Diabetic Foot, 735
MICHAEL E. EDMONDS AND
ALI V. M. FOSTER

71 Gastrointestinal Problems in Diabetes Mellitus, 745
BASIL F. CLARKE

72 The Skin in Diabetes Mellitus, 753
SUSAN HALL AND
GARY R. SIBBALD

73 Connective Tissue and Joint Disease in Diabetes Mellitus, 762
ADRIAN J. CRISP

74 Bone and Mineral Metabolism in Diabetes, 771
RAYMOND BRUCE AND
JOHN C. STEVENSON

75 Sexual Function in Diabetic Women, 775
JUDITH M. STEEL

76 Sexual Function in Diabetic Men, 779
JOHN D. WARD

77 Psychological Problems and Psychiatric Disorders in Diabetes Mellitus, 784
GREG WILKINSON

Section 14: Diabetes and Intercurrent Events

78 Exercise and Diabetes Mellitus, 795
VEIKKO A. KOIVISTO

79 Drugs and Diabetes, 803
ROY TAYLOR

80 Infection and Diabetes Mellitus, 813
R. MALCOLM WILSON

81 Surgery and Diabetes Mellitus, 820
GEOFFREY V. GILL

82 Eating Disorders and Diabetes Mellitus, 827
JUDITH M. STEEL

Section 15: Diabetes in Special Groups

83 Pregnancy and Diabetes Mellitus, 835
CLARA LOWY

84 Mechanisms of Teratogenesis in
Diabetes Mellitus, 851
CAROLINE J. CRACE

85 Contraception for Diabetic Women, 856
JUDITH M. STEEL

86 Genetic Counselling in Diabetes
Mellitus, 861
DAVID LESLIE

87 Diabetes Mellitus in Childhood and
Adolescence, 866
STEPHEN A. GREENE

88 'Brittle' Diabetes Mellitus, 884
JOHN C. PICKUP AND
GARETH WILLIAMS

89 Diabetes Mellitus and Old Age, 897
ROBERT W. STOUT

90 Diabetes Mellitus in the Third World, 905
JEAN-MARIE EKOÉ

91 Diabetes Mellitus in Ethnic Communities in
the UK, 909
HUGH M. MATHER

Section 16: Living With Diabetes

92 Employment, Life Insurance, Smoking and
Alcohol, 915
ANDREW MACLEOD

93 Driving and Diabetes Mellitus, 919
BRIAN M. FRIER

94 Travel and Diabetes Mellitus, 922
JUDITH M. STEEL

95 Adjustment to Life with Diabetes
Mellitus, 926
JOHN L. DAY

96 A Patient's View of Diabetes, 929
TERESA MCLEAN

**Section 17: The Organization of Diabetes
Care**

97 Diabetes Education, 933
JOHN L. DAY

98 Organization of Diabetes Care in the
Hospital, 940
ANTHONY H. KNIGHT

99 General Practice and the Community, 948
PETER R. W. TASKER

100 The Role of the Diabetes Specialist
Nurse, 952
PATRICIA M. JOHNS

101 Computers in Diabetes Management, 958
PETER H. WISE

102 Helping People with Diabetes to Help
Themselves: A History of the Diabetic
Associations, 965
JAMES G. L. JACKSON

**Section 18: Future Directions for Diabetes
Research and Management**

103 Prevention of Insulin-Dependent Diabetes
Mellitus, 971
JOHN DUPRÉ, J. L. MAHON AND
C. R. STILLER

104 New Drugs in the Management of
Diabetes Mellitus, 977
GARETH WILLIAMS AND
JOHN C. PICKUP

105 Glucose Sensors, 994
JOHN C. PICKUP

106 Transplantation of the Endocrine
Pancreas, 1001
PETER J. MORRIS, DEREK W. R.
GRAY AND ROBERT SUTTON

Index

List of Contributors

A. MICHAEL ALBISSER, BEng, MA, PhD, *Director, Loyal True Blue and Orange Research Institute, P.O. Box 209, Richmond Hill, Ontario, L4C 4YZ, Canada*

CLIFFORD J. BAILEY, BSc, PhD, *Senior Lecturer, Department of Pharmaceutical Sciences, Aston University, Aston Triangle, Birmingham B4 7ET, UK*

PETER J. BARRY, FRCS, FCOphth, *Consultant Ophthalmic Surgeon, Royal Victoria Eye and Ear Hospital and St Vincent's Hospital, Dublin, Ireland*

PETER H. BENNETT, MB, FRCP, FFCM, *Chief, Phoenix Epidemiology and Clinical Research Branch, National Institute of Diabetes and Digestive and Kidney Diseases, 1550 East Indian School Road, Phoenix, Arizona 85014, USA*

D. JOHN BETTERIDGE, BSc, MD, PhD, FRCP, *Reader in Medicine and Honorary Consultant Physician, Department of Medicine, University College and Middlesex School of Medicine, The Rayne Institute, 5 University Street, London WC1E 6JJ, UK*

RUDOLF W. BILOUS, MD, MRCP, *Senior Registrar in Diabetes and Endocrinology, Department of Medicine, The Medical School, Framlington Place, Newcastle upon Tyne NE2 4HH, UK*

CHRISTIAN BINDER, MD, *Chairman, Steno Memorial and Hvidøre Hospital, Niels Steensensvej 2, DK-2820 Gentofte, Denmark*

ANNE E. BISHOP, PhD, *Principal Research Officer, Department of Histochemistry, Royal Postgraduate Medical School, Hammersmith Hospital, London W12 0HS, UK*

MICHAEL BLISS, MA, PhD, FRSC, *Professor of History, History Department, University of Toronto, Toronto, Ontario, Canada M5S 1AI*

STEPHEN R. BLOOM, DSc, MD, FRCP, *Professor of Endocrinology, Department of Medicine, Royal Postgraduate Medical School, Du Cane Road, London W12 0NN, UK*

GEREMIA B. BOLLI, MD, *Associate Professor of Diabetology, Istituto Patologica Medica, Via E Dal Pozzo, 06100 Perugia, Italy*

ADRIAN J. BONE, BSc, DPhil, *Lecturer in Molecular Endocrinology, Professorial Medical Unit, Room LD 68, Level D, South Laboratory and Pathology Block, Southampton General Hospital, Tremona Road, Southampton SO9 4XY, UK*

EZIO BONIFACIO, BSc, PhD, *Research Fellow, Department of Immunology, University College and Middlesex School of Medicine, Arthur Stanley House, 40–50 Tottenham Street, London W1P 9PG, UK*

KNUT BORCH-JOHNSEN, MD, *Senior Research Assistant, Steno Diabetes Centre, Niels Steensenvej 2, DK-280, Gentofte, Denmark*

GIAN FRANCO BOTTAZZO, MD, FRCP, *Professor of Clinical Immunology, Department of Immunology, University College and Middlesex School of Medicine, Arthur Stanley House, 40–50 Tottenham Street, London W1P 9PG, UK*

MICHAEL BROWNLEE, MD, *Anita and Jack Salts Chair of Diabetes Research, Professor of Medicine and Pathology, Albert Einstein College of Medicine, 1300 Morris Park Avenue, The Bronx, New York, NY 10461, USA*

RAYMOND BRUCE, MB, ChB, *Clinical Research Fellow, Wynn Institute for Metabolic Research, 21 Wellington Road, London NW8 9SQ, UK*

TERENCE CHADWICK, BSc, MB, ChB, MRCP, MFPP, *Head of Medical Affairs, Fisons PLC, Bakewell Road, Loughborough, Leicestershire LE11 0RH, UK (Former Programme Director for New Insulins, NOVO Industrials)*

AH WAH CHAN, MB, BCh, MRCP (UK), *Registrar, Professorial Medical Unit, Royal Liverpool Hospital, Prescot Street, Liverpool L7 8XP, UK*

CHI KONG CHING, MB, ChB, MRCP, *Senior Registrar, Derbyshire Royal Infirmary, London Road, Derby, DE1 2QY, UK*

DONALD J. CHISHOLM, MB, BS, FRACP, *Assistant Director, Garvan Institute of Medical Research, St Vincent's Hospital, Sydney 2010, Australia*

PENELOPE M. S. CLARK, PhD, MRCPath, *Principal Biochemist, Department of Clinical Biochemistry, Addenbrooke's Hospital, Hills Road, Cambridge CB2 2QR, UK*

BASIL F. CLARKE, MB, FRCPE, *Consultant Physician and Senior Lecturer, The Royal Infirmary, Edinburgh EH3 9YW, UK*

PHILIP COHEN, BSc, PhD, *Royal Society Research Professor, Department of Biochemistry, University of Dundee, Medical Sciences Institute, Dundee DD1 4HN, UK*

CAROLINE J. CRACE, PhD, *Formerly Research Assistant, Clinical Sciences Centre, University of Sheffield, Department of Paediatrics, Northern General Hospital, Sheffield S5 7AU, UK*

ADRIAN J. CRISP, MA, MD, MRCP (UK), *Consultant Rheumatologist, Addenbrooke's Hospital, Hills Road, Cambridge CB2 2QQ, UK*

JOHN L. DAY, MD, FRCP, *Consultant Physician, Department of Medicine, The Ipswich Hospital, Heath Road Wing, Ipswich, Suffolk IP4 5PD, UK*

TORSTEN DECKERT, MD, DMSc, *Chief Physician, Steno Memorial Hospital, Niels Steensensvej 2, DK-2820, Gentofte, Denmark*

JOHN DUPRÉ, FRCP (Lond.), FRCP (C), *Chief of Endocrinology and Metabolism, University Hospital London, Ontario N6A 5A5, Canada*

MICHAEL E. EDMONDS, MD, MRCP, *Senior Lecturer, Diabetic Department, King's College Hospital, Denmark Hill, London SE5 9RS, UK*

JEAN-MARIE EKOÉ, MD, *Visiting Professor of Medicine, Department of Medicine and Epidemiology Research Unit, Hôtel-Dieu de Montréal, University of Montréal, 3840 Rue St-Urbain, Montréal, Québec H2W 1T8, Canada*

DAVID J. EWING, MD, FRCP, *Wellcome Trust Senior Lecturer, Department of Medicine, The Royal Infirmary, Edinburgh EH3 9YW, UK*

PETER R. FLATT, BSc, PhD, *Professor of Biological and Biomedical Sciences, Biomedical Sciences Research Centre, Department of Biological & Biomedical Sciences, University of Ulster, Coleraine, Co. Londonderry BT52 1SA, Northern Ireland, UK*

ALI V. M. FOSTER, BA (Hons), DPodM, SRCh, *Chief Chiropodist, Diabetic Clinic, King's College Hospital, Denmark Hill, London SE5 9RS, UK*

ALAN K. FOULIS, BSc, MD, MRCPath, *Consultant Pathologist, Department of Pathology, Royal Infirmary, Glasgow G4 0SF, UK*

BRIAN M. FRIER, BSc, MD, FRCP, *Consultant Physician and Senior Lecturer, The Royal Infirmary, Edinburgh EH3 9YW, UK*

GEOFFREY V. GILL, MSc, MD, FRCP, DTM & H, *Consultant Physician, Arrowe Park Hospital, Arrowe Park Road, Upton, Wirral, Merseyside L49 5PE, UK*

BARRY J. GOLDSTEIN, MD, PhD, *Assistant Professor of Medicine, Harvard Medical School, and Investigator, Research Division, Joslin Diabetes Center, One Joslin Place, Boston, Massachusetts 02215, USA*

DEREK W. R. GRAY, DPhil, FRCS, MRCP, *Clinical Reader and Consultant Surgeon, Nuffield Department of Surgery, John Radcliffe Hospital, Headington, Oxford OX3 9DU, UK*

STEPHEN A. GREENE, MB, BS, MRCP, *Consultant Paediatrician and Paediatric Endocrinologist, Department of Child Health, Ninewells Hospital & Medical School, Dundee DD1 9SY, UK*

ANASUYA GRENFELL, MA, MD, MRCP, *Senior Medical Registrar, Ipswich Hospital, Heath Road Wing, Ipswich, Suffolk IP4 5PD, UK*

C. NICK HALES, MA, MD, PhD, FRCPath FRCP, *Professor of Clinical Biochemistry, Department of Clinical Biochemistry, Addenbrooke's Hospital, Hills Road, Cambridge CB2 2QR, UK*

KRISTIAN F. HANSSEN, MD, *Consultant Physician, University Department of Medicine, Aker Hospital, 0514 Oslo 5, Norway*

D. GRAHAME HARDIE, MA, PhD, *Reader, Department of Biochemistry, University of Dundee, Medical Sciences Institute, Dundee DD1 4HN, UK*

SUSAN HALL, *Department of Dermatology, Toronto General Hospital, 101 College Street, Toronto, Ontario M5G 1L7, Canada*

GRAHAM A. HITMAN, MB, FRCP, *Senior Lecturer and Honorary Consultant Physician, Department of Medicine, The Royal London Hospital, Whitechapel, London E1 1BB, UK*

RURY R. HOLMAN, MB, ChB, MRCP (UK), *Honorary Consultant Physician, Diabetes Research Laboratories, Radcliffe Infirmary, Woodstock Road, Oxford OX2 6HE, UK*

PHILIP D. HOME, MA, DPhil, FRCP, *Senior Lecturer and Consultant Physician, University of Newcastle upon Tyne, Freeman Diabetes Unit, Freeman Hospital, Newcastle upon Tyne NE7 7DN, UK*

SIMON L. HOWELL, BSc, PhD, DSc, *Professor of Endocrine Physiology, Biomedical Sciences Division, King's College, Campden Hill Road, London W8 7AH, UK*

STEPHEN L. HYER, MD, MRCP, *Senior Registrar (Diabetes and Endocrinology), St George's Hospital, Blackshaw Road, London SW17 0QT, UK*

KARL IRSIGLER, MD, *Professor of Medicine, 3rd Medical Department with Metabolic Diseases and Luolwig Boltzmann Research Institute for Metabolic Diseases and Nutrition, City Hospital Vienna-Lainz, Wolkerbergenstraße 1, A-1130 Vienna, Austria*

JAMES G. L. JACKSON, MD, (h.c.) *Formerly Executive Director, European Association for the Study of Diabetes, 'Cobbles', 10 Fam Court, Longcross Road, Chertsey, Surrey KT16 0DJ, UK*

R. JOHN JARRETT, MD, FFCM, *Professor of Clinical Epidemiology, Department of Public Health Medicine, United Medical and Dental Schools, Guy's Campus, London SE1 9RT, UK*

ROGER H. JAY, MA, MB, BS, MRCP, *Associate Research Fellow and Honorary Clinical Lecturer, Department of Medicine, University College and Middlesex School of Medicine, The Rayne Institute, 5 University Street, London WC1E 6JJ, UK*

PATRICIA M. JOHNS, RN, RM, *Dip Nursing, Diabetes Nurse Specialist, Maidstone Hospital, Hermitage Lane, Barming, Maidstone, Kent ME16 9QQ, UK*

DESMOND G. JOHNSTON, FRCP, PhD, *Professor of Clinical Endocrinology, Alexander Simpson Laboratory for Metabolic Research, St. Mary's Hospital Medical School, London W2, UK*

JACQUELINE N. JONES, BSc, SRN, *Research Nurse, Diabetic Day Care Centre, Greenwich District Hospital, Vanbrugh Hill, London SE10 9HE, UK*

RICHARD H. JONES, MA, MB, FRCP, *Senior Lecturer, Department of Medicine, United Medical and Dental Schools of Guy's and St Thomas's Hospitals, Medway Hospital, Gillingham, Kent ME7 5NY, UK*

C. RONALD KAHN, MD, *Mary K. Iacocca Professor of Medicine, Harvard Medical School, Chief, Division of Diabetes and Metabolism, Brigham and Women's Hospital, and Director, Research Laboratory, Joslin Diabetes Center, One Joslin Place, Boston, Massachusetts 02215, USA*

HARRY KEEN, MD, FRCP, *Professor of Human Metabolism, Unit for Metabolic Medicine, United Medical and Dental Schools (Guy's Campus), London SE1 9RT, UK*

LAURENCE KENNEDY, MD, FRCP, *Consultant Physician, Sir George E. Clark Metabolic Unit, Royal Victoria Hospital, Belfast BT12 6BA, Northern Ireland, UK*

RONALD KLEIN, MD, MPH, *Professor of Ophthalmology, Department of Ophthalmology, University of Wisconsin—Madison, F4/334 Clinical Sciences Center, 600 Highland Avenue, Madison, Wisconsin 53792, USA*

ANTHONY H. KNIGHT, FRCP, *Consultant Physician, Stoke Mandeville Hospital, Aylesbury, Bucks HP21 8AL, UK*

EVA M. KOHNER, MD, FRCP, *Professor of Medical Ophthalmology and Consultant Physician, Royal Postgraduate Medical School, Hammersmith Hospital, Du Cane Road, London W12 0HS, and Moorfields Eye Hospital, City Road, London EC1V 2PD, UK*

VEIKKO A. KOIVISTO, MD, *Senior Lecturer, Department of Medicine, Helsinki University Second Hospital, 00290 Helsinki Central, Finland*

EDWARD W. KRAEGEN, BSc, PhD, *Head, Diabetes Research Group, Garvan Institute of Medical Research, St Vincents Hospital, Sydney 2010, Australia*

BERNHARD KREYMANN, MD, *ii. Medizinische Klinik und Poliklinik Der Technischen Universität München, Ismaninger Strasse 22, 8000 München 80, Germany*

A. J. KRENTZ, MB, ChB, MRCP, *Senior Registrar, The General Hospital, Steelhouse Lane, Birmingham B4 6NH, UK*

ANTONY KURTZ, PhD, FRCP, *Reader, University College and Middlesex School of Medicine, London W1N 8AA, UK*

MIKE E. J. LEAN, MA, MD, FRCP, *Senior Lecturer, University of Glasgow Department of Human Nutrition, Royal Infirmary, Queen Elizabeth Building, Alexandra Parade, Glasgow G12 2ER, UK*

DAVID LESLIE, MD, FRCP, *Senior Lecturer, Department of Medicine, Charing Cross and Westminster Medical School, Westminster Hospital, 17 Horseferry Road, London SW1P 2AR, UK*

BIRGITTA LINDE, MD, PhD, *Assistant Professor and Consultant Physician, Department of Clinical Physiology, Karolinska Hospital, Box 60500, 104 01 Stockholm, Sweden*

WILLIAM D. LOUGHEED, PEng, *Biomedical Engineer, Loyal True Blue and Orange Research Institute, PO Box 209, Richmond Hill, Ontario, L4C 4YZ Canada*

CLARA LOWY, MB, MSc, FRCP, *Reader in Medicine, Division of Medicine, St Thomas's Campus, United Medical and Dental Schools, Unit of Endocrinology and Diabetes, Diabetic Day Center, St Thomas's Hospital, Lambeth Palace Road, London SE1 7EH, UK*

DAVID R. MCCANCE, BSc, MD, MRCP, *Senior Registrar, Sir George E. Clark Metabolic Unit, Royal Victoria Hospital, Belfast BT12 6BA, Northern Ireland, UK*

IAN A. MACFARLANE, MD, MRCP, *Consultant Physician, The Diabetes Centre, Walton Hospital, Rice Lane, Liverpool L9 1AE, UK*

TERESA MCLEAN, MA (Oxon), *Writer and Cricket Journalist, 31 Newmarket Road, Cambridge CB5 8EG, UK*

ANDREW MACLEOD, MA, MRCP, *Lecturer, Department of Medicine, United Medical and Dental Schools, St Thomas's Hospital, London SE1 7EH, UK*

ALASDAIR MCLEOD, BSc, BDS, *Research Fellow, Laboratory of Molecular Biology, Department of Crystallography, Malet Street, London WC1E 7HX, UK*

J. L. MAHON, MD, FRCP (C), *Research Fellow, Endocrinology and Metabolism, University Hospital London, Ontario N6A 5A5, Canada*

JIM I. MANN, MA, DM, PhD, *Professor of Human Nutrition, University of Otago, and Consultant Physician, Dunedin Hospital, Dunedin, New Zealand*

BRENDAN MARSHALL, PhD, *Postdoctoral Fellow, Department of Medicine, The London Hospital, Whitechapel, London E1 1BB, UK*

HUGH M. MATHER, MD, FRCP, *Consultant Physician, Ealing Hospital, Uxbridge Road, Southall, Middlesex UB1 3HW, UK*

V. MOHAN, MD, MNAMS, PhD, *Deputy Director, Diabetes Research Centre, 4 Main Road, Royapuram, Madras 600–013, India*

PETER J. MORRIS, PhD, FRCS, FRACS, FACS (Hon.), *Nuffield Professor of Surgery, University of Oxford, John Radcliffe Hospital, Headington, Oxford OX3 9DU, UK*

CATHLEEN J. MULLARKEY, MD, *Instructor, Department of Medicine, Albert Einstein College of Medicine, 1300 Morris Park Avenue, The Bronx, New York 10461, USA*

MALCOLM NATTRASS, MB, ChB, PhD, FRCP, *Consultant Physician, The General Hospital, Steelhouse Lane, Birmingham B4 6NH, UK*

JOHN C. PICKUP, MA, BM, DPhil, MRCPath, *Reader and Honorary Consultant Physician, Division of Chemical Pathology, United Medical and Dental Schools of Guy's and St Thomas's Hospitals, Guy's Hospital, London SE1 9RT, UK*

JULIA M. POLAK, DSc, MD, FRCPath, *Professor of Endocrine Pathology; Head, Histochemistry Unit and Deputy Director, Department of Histopathology, Royal Postgraduate Medical School, Du Cane Road, London W12 0NN, UK*

MASSIMO PORTA, MD, PhD, *Associate Professor of Medicine, University of Sassari, Italy, and Honorary Clinical Assistant, Diabetic Retinopathy Unit, Hammersmith Hospital, Du Cane Road, London W12 0NN, UK*

A. RAMACHANDRAN, MD, MNAMS, PhD, *Deputy Director, Diabetes Research Centre, 4 Main Road, Royapuram, Madras 600–013, India*

LUIS C. RAMIREZ, MD, *Assistant Professor of Medicine, Department of Internal Medicine, University of Texas Southwestern Medical Center at Dallas, 5323 Harry Hines Boulevard, Dallas, Texas 75235, USA*

PHILIP RASKIN, MD, *Professor of Medicine, Department of Internal Medicine, University of Texas Southwestern Medical Center at Dallas, 5323 Harry Hines Boulevard, Dallas, Texas 75235, USA*

S. SETHU K. REDDY, MD, FRCPC, *Department of Medicine, 5303 Morris Street, Gerard Hall, Camp Hill Medicine Centre, Dalhousie University, Halifax Nova Scotia, Canada*

JONATHAN M. RHODES, MA, MD, FRCP, *Senior Lecturer in Medicine and Gastroenterology, Royal Liverpool Hospital, Prescot Street, Liverpool L7 8XP, UK*

PATRICK SHARP, MD, MRCP, *Lecturer in Endocrinology, St. Mary's Hospital Medical School, Norfolk Place, Paddington, London W2 1PG, UK*

GARY R. SIBBALD, BSc, MD, FRCP (C), ABIM, DAAD, *Acting Head, Division of Dermatology, Department of Medicine, Women's College Hospital, University of Toronto, 76 Grenville Street, Toronto, Ontario M5S 1B2, Canada*

ANGELA C. SHORE, BSc, PhD, *Research Fellow, Diabetes Research (Microvascular Studies), Postgraduate Medical School, Royal Devon & Exeter Hospital, Exeter, Devon EX2 5DW, UK*

JUDITH M. STEEL, MB ChB, FRCPEd, *Associate Specialist, Department of Diabetes, Edinburgh Royal Infirmary, Lauriston Place, Edinburgh EH3 9YW, UK*

JOHN C. STEVENSON, MB, MRCP, *Consultant Endocrinologist, Wynn Institute for Metabolic Research, 21 Wellington Road, London NW8 9SQ, UK*

C. R. STILLER, MD, FRCP (C), *Professor of Medicine, University of Western Ontario; Director of Immunology, Robarts Research Institute; Chief, Multi-organ Transplant Service, University Hospital, 339 Windermere Road, London, Ontario N6A 5A5, Canada*

ROBERT W. STOUT, MD, DSc, FRCP, FRCPEd, FRCPI, *Professor of Geriatric Medicine, Department of Geriatric Medicine, The Queen's University of Belfast, Whitla Medical Building, 97 Lisburn Road, Belfast BT9 7BL, Northern Ireland, UK*

ROBERT SUTTON, MB, BS, FRCS, DPhil (Oxon), *Lecturer in Surgery, Nuffield Department of Surgery, John Radcliffe Hospital, Headington, Oxford OX3 9DU, UK*

TERESA M. SZOPA, BSc, PhD, *Research Fellow, Medical Unit, London Hospital, Whitechapel, London E1 1BB, UK*

HOWARD S. TAGER, PhD, *Louis Block Professor, Department of Biochemistry and Molecular Biology, The University of Chicago, 920 East 58th Street, Chicago, Illinois 60637, USA*

PETER R. W. TASKER, MB, BS, DCH, FRCGP, *General Practitioner, Doomsday House, Hall Lane, South Wootton, King's Lynn, Norfolk PE30 3LQ, UK*

ROBERT B. TATTERSALL, MD, FRCP, *Professor of Clinical Diabetes, University Hospital, Queen's Medical Centre, Nottingham NG7 2UH, UK*

KEITH W. TAYLOR, MA, PhD, MRCP, *Emeritus Professor of Biochemistry, Medical Unit, London Hospital, Whitechapel, London E1 1BB, UK*

ROY TAYLOR, BSc, MD, FRCP, *Consultant Physician and Senior Lecturer, Royal Victoria Infirmary, Queen Victoria Road, Newcastle upon Tyne NE1 4LP, UK*

P. K. THOMAS, DSc, MD, FRCP, FRCPath, *Professor of Neurological Science, Royal Free Hospital School of Medicine, Rowland Hill Street, London NW3 2PF, UK*

JOHN E. TOOKE, MA, MSc, DM, MRCP, *Consultant Physician and Senior Lecturer, Diabetes Research (Microvascular Studies), Postgraduate Medical School, Royal Devon and Exeter Hospital, Exeter, Devon EX2 5DW, UK*

ROBERT C. TURNER, MD, FRCP, *Clinical Reader, Diabetes Research Laboratories, Radcliffe Infirmary, Woodstock Road, Oxford OX2 6HE, UK*

GIAN CARLO VIBERTI, MD, FRCP, *Professor of Diabetic Medicine, Unit for Metabolic Medicine, 4th Floor, Hunts House, United Medical and Dental Schools, Guy's Hospital Campus, London SE1 9RT, UK*

M. VISWANATHAN, MD, FAMS, *Director, Diabetes Research Centre, 5 Main Road, Royapuram, Madras 600-013, India*

JAMES D. WALKER, BSc, MRCP, *Senior Medical Registrar, 4th Floor, King George V Block, St Bartholomew's Hospital, West Smithfield, London EC1, UK*

JOHN D. WARD, BSc, MD, FRCP, *Consultant Physician, Royal Hallamshire Hospital, Glossop Road, Sheffield S10 2JF, UK*

PER WESTERMARK, MD, *Professor of Pathology, University of Uppsala, Department of Pathology, University Hospital, S-751 85 Uppsala, Sweden*

GREG WILKINSON, FRCP (Edin.), MRCPsych, *Director, Academic Sub-Department of Psychological Medicine, University of Wales College of Medicine, North Wales Hospital, Denbigh, Clwyd LL16 5SS, UK*

D.R.R. WILLIAMS, MA, PhD, MFPHM, *University Lecturer in Community Medicine, Level 5, Addenbrooke's Hospital, Hills Road, Cambridge CB2 2QQ, UK*

GARETH WILLIAMS, MA, MD, MRCP, *Senior Lecturer, Department of Medicine, University of Liverpool, PO Box 147, Liverpool L69 3BX, and Honorary Consultant Physician, Royal Liverpool Hospital, Prescot Street, Liverpool L7 8XP, UK*

R. MALCOLM WILSON, DM, MRCP, *Senior Lecturer, Department of Medicine, Royal Hallamshire Hospital, Glossop Road, Sheffield S10 2JF, UK*

PETER H. WISE, MB, BS, PhD, FRCP, FRACP, *Consultant Physician, Charing Cross Hospital, Fulham Palace Road, London W6 8RF, UK*

STEVEN P. WOOD, BSc, DPhil, *Senior Research Fellow, Laboratory of Molecular Biology, Department of Crystallography, Birkbeck College, Malet Street, London WC1E 7HX, UK*

Foreword

The diabetic state commands more attention now than ever before. At a time when in all branches of medicine, indeed in all branches of science, the engagement generally with the problem becomes increasingly demanding and technologically complex, understanding diabetes occupies a continuingly prominent place. Diabetes has always stood out in the history of medicine and science. The graphic descriptions by ancient observers must put the severe, insulin-deficient diabetic state among the earliest of the readily recognized clinical conditions, the paradigm of the 'clinical syndrome'. Exploration of the nature of diabetes claimed the attention of the father of experimental medicine, the great Claude Bernard, so much of whose thought and perception remains with us today. He understood the importance of the balance between glucose production and glucose consumption in determining the level of glucose concentration though he had little conception of the factors which regulated them. He saw diabetes essentially as the outcome of a disturbance of relationships, a distortion of a homeostatic system, a disorder of adaptation.

Bernard shared the scientific stage with the other giant of 19th century biomedical science, Louis Pasteur, whose discoveries promoted a quite different model of disease, one that was more direct and simple. The disease process resulted from a single, well-defined causal agency — a germ. If the germ was not present, the disease could not occur, though having the germ did not guarantee the appearance of the disease. The Pasteurian notion of disease in the present day context can be extended to include the abnormal gene or a toxic substance as the causal agency of disease. Had Pasteur ever pronounced upon diabetes, he might well have wondered about some specific enzymatic abnormality in the pathways of glucose metabolism, an area not unfamiliar to him.

In the contemporary world of diabetes, the Bernardian and the Pasteurian views contend. A pure Bernardian would regard the diabetic state as a disorder of adaptation, a breakdown in the interrelation and regulation of the balance of factors determining glucose production and disposal. It is perhaps best exemplified in the debates in the 1990s by the Reaven concept of glucose intolerance and non-insulin-dependent diabetes mellitus (NIDDM). His construct of the conditions resulting in the diabetic state introduces the interaction of regulatory mechanisms unknown in their nature to Bernard and Pasteur. This construct is compatible with the observed 'continuous distribution' of glucose tolerance/intolerance in most populations, showing no clear break between the normal and the abnormal.

The scientific advances of recent decades might seem to promote the Pasteurian view of the diabetic state. We have witnessed an explosive expansion of knowledge and understanding of the genetic control of cell structure and function, and its role in the causation of disease. The search for a diabetes (susceptibility) gene has excited much research interest and is best established in the insulin-dependent variety of diabetes. An environmental trigger which initiates a process culminating in the destruction of the pancreatic B cell is also sought and fulfils the Pasteurian expectation of a single causal factor of major effect operating in a genetically susceptible setting.

It becomes likely that these two major views of the causation of the diabetic state are not mutually incompatible and indeed both operate to explain the occurrence of diabetes in man. Thus, genetic factors contribute to the adaptive disorder of NIDDM (though their nature remains far from clear) while the process affecting the B cell in the insulin-dependent variety of the disease may fall far short of complete destruction of insulin-producing cells in many of the people it affects and is itself presumably modulated by other genetic and environmental factors.

The diabetic state impacts upon mankind in many ways. At the 'macro' level, it throws up the question of the adequacy of provision of medical services, the question of prescriptive screening, and the social and emotional predicament of the diabetic individual. For the individual, it carries a variety of clinical and therapeutic problems, often complicated in the long course of the disease by damage to the eye, the kidney, the peripheral nerves, and the arterial wall. It is these delayed 'complications' which provide most of the burden of diabetes upon the individual and upon society. While the diabetic state appears to be the *sine qua non* of their appearance, other individual factors, some probably genetic, will also determine their time of onset, their rate of progression and their ultimate severity.

For clinical and basic scientists, diabetes is the point of departure for research enquiries in many fields. The history of the discovery of insulin, its characterization, structure and synthesis have contributed much to broaden understanding of biochemistry and genetics. Research into the insulin receptor is telling us about the mechanisms of hormonal signals. Immunological mechanisms are bound up with some forms of the diabetic state; their understanding and control may well lead to the prevention of insulin-dependent diabetes in the foreseeable future.

These and many other aspects of the diabetic state are dealt with in the chapters that follow. Clear answers as to 'the cause' of diabetes and its complications are not yet available. However, the growing pace of research and its increasingly prompt application to the patient make the lot of the person with diabetes progressively easier to bear. The comprehensive account of our knowledge of the disease in this book will make a substantial contribution to improving both our understanding of the disease and the care of patients suffering from it.

HARRY KEEN
London, July 1990

Preface

Our main intention in producing this book was to disseminate information about diabetes mellitus amongst the many different people involved in tackling the scientific, medical and social problems of the disease. The ramifications of diabetes extend into so many areas that it demands a truly multidisciplinary approach. Its clinical management depends on an integrated team of specialists as diverse as physicians, chiropodists, nurses, psychiatrists and general practitioners, and research into the disease and its treatment requires the combined skills of immunologists, physiologists, pathologists, chemists and many others. The problems of diabetes will only be identified and solved if there is understanding and effective communication between these various groups.

We therefore set out to summarize the key clinical and scientific topics of diabetes in a form which would be useful to the specialist in a given area and yet readily accessible to the non-specialist who wishes to learn about the main principles and challenges of disciplines beyond his or her own. The 'clinical' chapters are intended to provide a clear and up-to-date guide to the features, diagnosis and treatment of diabetes and its complications, which will be of real practical value to those concerned with the everyday management of the disease. In the 'scientific' (non-clinical) sections, we have aimed to cover the major aspects of metabolism and what is known of the disease processes which result in diabetes; we hope that these are both comprehensive and, for the most part, interesting and intelligible to those who are not career scientists. Throughout the book, we have attempted to highlight recent clinical and scientific advances, and their impact on the understanding and treatment of diabetes, as well as the questions which remain unanswered.

Overall, we have tried to cater for a wide range of interests and requirements. The book should also be useful for those preparing for postgraduate examinations.

Each chapter is constructed as a self-contained essay prepared by an expert in the field and, as such, should stand alone; we therefore make no apologies for the reiteration of important concepts in more than one chapter. At the same time, the book is designed as an integrated text and we have tried to avoid unnecessary repetition through extensive cross-referencing. We have edited each chapter according to a common format, beginning with a summary of its major points, and have made extensive use of figures, flow-charts and tables where these usefully illustrate important points in the text. If we have managed to produce an integrated book, we hope that this has been achieved without stifling the individuality of the contributors.

Every textbook runs the risk of various criticisms, some of which we have tried to anticipate. The first is that any book of this size will inevitably be out of date by the time it appears. We have tried to incorporate new and important material at all stages up to the final proofs, and can only hope that the great distress which this has caused our publishers has been justified. Secondly, every textbook is parochial to some extent. We have aimed to encompass a wider view of diabetes than that encountered in our own practice by including contributions from authors in a dozen or so countries, which cover topics such as diabetes in the Third World, malnutrition-related diabetes and diabetes in ethnic groups in the UK. Finally, the scope of a book such as this is sometimes questioned. We hope that our choice of chapters reflects both the breadth and the excitement of diabetes and that, for example, those dealing with the historical background of diabetes and the short but thought-provoking personal view of the disease will not be neglected.

This book's gestation slightly exceeded that of the blue whale and, at times, the book seemed likely to join the whale on the list of endangered species. Fortunately, several groups of people have fought to ensure its survival. We are profoundly grateful for their contributions to the book, which range from the obvious to the invisible. The first, of course, is the 120 authors who have provided the substance of the book with skill and authority. We would like to thank them, not only for the quality of their contributions, but also for their stoical and (mostly) gallant tolerance of editorial interference with their work. We are particularly indebted to those who, through efficiency or intimidation, managed to meet or even beat our deadlines. The second group is the team at Blackwell Scientific Publications, who have distinguished themselves by their endless support, enthusiasm and ability to apply firm but generally painless pressure at crucial moments. Karen Anthony and Rachel Nalumoso deserve special mention for having served so nobly (and indeed survived) in the frontline skirmishes between publishers, authors and editors. Peter Saugman initiated the project and provided constant support and encouragement throughout. Thirdly, many friends and colleagues have helped in various ways, particularly by providing clinical photographs and other material, hounding elusive references and making suggestions — sometimes kind but always constructive — about the content of the book. We have especially valued the help of Ian MacFarlane, Geoff Gill and Paul Drury in this respect, and also acknowledge the assistance of Charles Bodmer and Alan Patrick in struggling through the proofs, and of Jackie Williams and Adrian Brown in drawing up the tables for Chapter 79. The fourth group is our secretariat, namely Caroline Williams, Luine Weir and Denise Janson, whose skills in typing, organization and cryptography are fortunately underpinned by the rare virtues of patience and good humour.

Finally, we are indebted to our families for having tolerated the book's relentless invasion of evenings, weekends and holidays, and for having accepted so many times our increasingly flimsy assurances that it would be finished one day.

JOHN C. PICKUP
GARETH WILLIAMS
London and Liverpool, July 1990

SECTION 1
THE HISTORY OF
DIABETES

1　The Millenia Before Insulin

Summary

- Polyuric states, clinically resembling diabetes mellitus, were described as early as 1550 BC by the ancient Egyptians.
- The sweet taste of diabetic urine was noted in the 5–6th century AD by Indian physicians, and in the 17th century by Thomas Willis who distinguished 'diabetes mellitus' from other polyuric states.
- In the mid-18th century, Matthew Dobson discovered that diabetic serum as well as urine contained sugar and concluded that diabetes was a systemic condition rather than a disease of the kidneys.
- Claude Bernard made numerous discoveries in the field of metabolism and diabetes in the mid- to late 19th century, describing the storage of glucose in the liver as glycogen and acute hyperglycaemia following damage to the medulla oblongata (*piqûre* diabetes).
- In 1889, Minkowsky and von Mering observed that total pancreatectomy produced diabetes in dogs.
- In 1893, Laguesse named the pancreatic islets after Langerhans, who had described them in 1869 and suggested that they produced a glucose-lowering substance. This then hypothetical hormone was named 'insulin' by de Meyer in 1909, over a decade before its discovery.
- Various workers, including Zülzer, isolated active but impure hypoglycaemic extracts from the pancreas before the discovery of insulin in 1921 by Banting, Best, Collip and Macleod.

Diabetes mellitus is a disease which was recognized in antiquity but its history has been characterized by numerous cycles of discovery, neglect and rediscovery. For the purposes of this brief review, the history of diabetes mellitus up to the time of the discovery of insulin can be conveniently divided into three sections: the *ancient* period, during which the clinical features of the disorder were described; the *diagnostic* period, from the 16th century onwards, in which diabetes mellitus was distinguished as a disease entity; and the *experimental* period which began in the mid-19th century, during which the gluco-regulatory role of the pancreas became clear and the biochemical disturbances of diabetes were initially characterized (see Table 1.1).

The ancient period

The Ebers papyrus, dating from about 1550 BC, testifies to the long history of diabetes (Fig. 1.1). This papyrus, found in a grave in Thebes in 1862 and named after the Egyptologist, Georg Ebers, contains descriptions of various diseases, including a polyuric state resembling diabetes mellitus. The treatment recommended — which was no more bizarre and no less successful than some prescribed over 3000 years later — was a 4-day course of a decoction of bones, wheat, grain, grit, green lead and earth.

The term 'diabetes', which is Ionian Greek and means 'to run through' or 'a siphon', was first used by Aretaeus of Cappadocia in the 2nd century AD as a generic description for conditions causing increased urine output. Aretaeus wrote an accurate factual description of the condition which is instantly recognizable today (Table 1.2) and concluded that it was due to a fault in the kidneys. Despite the clarity of his account, however, Aretaeus would not have been able to distinguish the various non-diabetic disorders presenting with polyuria.

3

Table 1.1. Milestones in the history of diabetes mellitus.

Date	Source	Observation
15th century BC 2nd century AD	Ebers papyrus (Egypt) Galen (Rome) Aretaeus (Cappadocia)	Clinical descriptions of polyuric conditions resembling diabetes mellitus
5th century	Susruta and Charuka (India)	Clinical descriptions including sugary urine; obese and thin patients distinguished
10th century	Avicenna (Arabia)	Clinical descriptions including sugary urine; gangrene and impotence described as complications
17th century	Thomas Willis (England)	Diabetic urine contains sugar
18th century	Matthew Dobson (England) Thomas Cawley (England)	Diabetic serum contains sugar Diabetes may follow pancreatic damage
19th century	Claude Bernard (France)	Glucose stored as hepatic glycogen *Piqûre* diabetes Ligation of pancreatic duct causes exocrine degeneration
	Paul Langerhans (Germany) Oskar Minkowski and Josef Von Mering (Germany)	Identified pancreatic islets Pancreatectomy causes diabetes
20th century	Jean de Meyer (Belgium)	Hypothetical pancreatic glucose-lowering hormone named 'insulin'
	Georg Zülzer (Germany) Nicolas Paulesco (Romania) Israel Kleiner (USA)	Isolated hypoglycaemic extracts from pancreas

The Roman physician, Galen (AD 131−201), like Aretaeus, thought diabetes to be a rare disease and apparently encountered only two cases. Galen employed alternative terms for diabetes, including 'diarrhoea urinosa' and 'dipsakos', the latter emphasizing the cardinal symptoms of excessive thirst and drinking.

The association of polyuria with a sweet-tasting substance in the urine was first reported in Sanskrit literature dating from the 5−6th centuries AD at the time of two notable Indian physicians, Susruta and Charuka. The urine of polyuric patients was described as tasting like honey, being sticky to the touch and strongly attracting ants. Indian descriptions of this time appear to distinguish two forms of diabetes, one affecting older, fatter people and the other thin people who did not survive long. During the same era, Chinese and Japanese physicians also described diabetes and the sweetness of diabetic urine, which apparently attracted dogs. They also observed that

Table 1.2. Clinical description of diabetes by Aretaeus of Cappadocia (2nd century AD). (Adapted from Papaspyros NS, 1964[10].)

'Diabetes is a dreadful affliction, not very frequent among men, being a melting down of the flesh and limbs into urine. The patients never stop making water and the flow is incessant, like the opening of aqueducts. Life is short, unpleasant and painful, thirst unquenchable, drinking excessive, and disproportionate to the large quantity of urine, for yet more urine is passed. One cannot stop them either from drinking or making water. If for a while they abstain from drinking, their mouths become parched and their bodies dry; the viscera seem scorched up; the patients are affected by nausea, restlessness and a burning thirst, and within a short time, they expire.'

Fig. 1.1. The Ebers papyrus. (Reproduced by kind permission of the Wellcome Institute of the History of Medicine.)

people with diabetes were prone to develop boils and an affliction which clinically resembles tuberculosis.

The fact that diabetic urine tasted sweet was subsequently emphasized by Arabic medical texts during the 9th−11th centuries, when Arabic medicine was at its peak of achievement. Avicenna (AD 960−1037) described accurately the clinical features of diabetes and mentions two specific complications of the disease, namely, gangrene and the 'collapse' of sexual function.

The diagnostic period

The recorded advances during this period were largely made in Europe, although some centuries apparently elapsed before European physicians made the key observation that diabetic urine was sugary. The 16th century Swiss physician, Von Hohenheim (who accorded himself the name 'Paracelsus' in recognition of his own scientific achievements) reported that diabetic urine contained an abnormal substance which remained as a white powder after evaporation. He concluded, however, that this substance was salt and that diabetes was due to the deposition of salt in the kidneys, causing 'thirst' of the kidneys and polyuria. Von Hohenheim's observations on diabetic urine, incidentally, were made at a time

when 'uroscopy' (inspection of the urine) was a highly developed art.

It was not until the 17th century that Thomas Willis (1621−75) (Fig. 1.2) made reference to the sweet taste of diabetic urine [1] and thereby duplicated the observation which had first appeared in Eastern medical writings over one thousand years previously. Willis made several other astute observations about the disease, which still ring true today. He wrote that diabetes had been rare in classical times 'but in our age, given to good fellowship and gusling down chiefly of unallayed wine, we meet with examples and instances enough, I may say daily, of this disease ... wherefore the urine of the sick is so wonderfully sweet, or hath an honied taste ... As to what belongs the cure, it seems a most hard thing in this disease to draw propositions for curing, for that its cause lies so deeply hid, and hath its origin so deep and remote' [1].

Another celebrated physician of the 17th century was Thomas Sydenham (1624−89), who speculated that diabetes was a systemic disease arising in the blood where 'chyle' was incompletely digested and its non-absorbed residue had to be excreted. This concept was elaborated a century later by Matthew Dobson (1735−84), a physician in Liverpool. Dobson was a gifted natural philosopher

Fig. 1.2. Thomas Willis (1621−75), Fellow of the Royal Society and physician to Charles II. (Reproduced by kind permission of the Wellcome Institute of the History of Medicine.)

and experimental physiologist and a skilled clinical observer with a wide range of interests. He had treated nine patients with diabetes — a modest clinical load in comparison with diabetic clinics in present-day Liverpool — when he published in 1776 a series of experiments showing that the serum of a diabetic patient, as well as his urine, contained a substance with a sweet taste (Fig. 1.3) [2]. Moreover, he proved that this substance was sugar and concluded that this had previously existed in the serum rather than being formed in the kidneys. He wrote, 'this idea of the disease explains its emaciating effects, from so large a proportion of the alimentary matter being drawn off by the kidneys, before it is perfectly assimilated and applied to the purpose of nutrition'. This was the first evidence that diabetes might be a generalized disorder.

A few years after Dobson's important paper, another English physician, John Rollo (*d.* 1809), published a study entitled, 'An account of two cases of the diabetes mellitus, with remarks as they arose during the progress of the cure' [3]. He was one of the first to use the adjective 'mellitus' (from the Latin and Greek roots for 'honey') used to distinguish the condition from other polyuric diseases in which glycosuria was absent and the urine tasteless (Latin, *insipidus*). Rollo made other contributions to the study of diabetes, including descriptions of diabetic cataracts and the odour of acetone (which he likened to decaying apples) on the breath of some diabetic subjects. Another important observation made at this time was the report by Thomas Cawley in 1788 that diabetes may follow damage to the pancreas, such as through calculus formation [4].

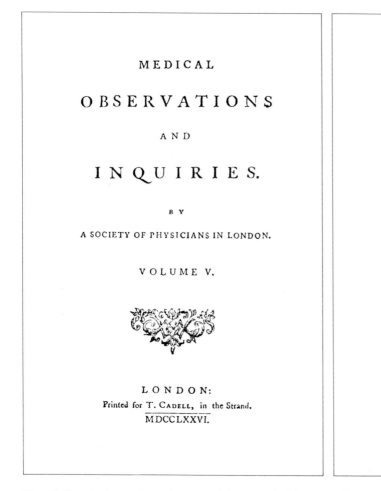

Fig. 1.3. Frontispiece and opening page of the paper by Matthew Dobson [2], in which he described the presence of sugar in both diabetic serum and urine (1776).

The experimental period

The 19th century was extremely important for most branches of medicine; it is no exaggeration to suggest that the science and practice of medicine gained more during these hundred years than they had during all the previous centuries together.

Among the physiologists who contributed much to the understanding of diabetes at that time, a special place must be given to Claude Bernard (1813–78) (Fig. 1.4). Bernard made numerous discoveries, including the observation that the sugar which appears in diabetic urine was stored in the liver in the form of glycogen. He also demonstrated that the central nervous system was involved in controlling the blood glucose concentration when, during attempts to stimulate the vagal motor nuclei, he induced transient glycosuria and hyperglycaemia by transfixing the medulla of a conscious rabbit with a blunt needle [5]. The significance of this observation, rather euphemistically named 'piqûre' diabetes (French, piquer = to prick), was soon eclipsed by discoveries implicating the pancreas as the likely seat of diabetes. Bernard performed many systematic experiments on the pancreas [6] and, although he himself did not attribute any endocrine activity to the gland, he developed the technique of ligating the pancreatic duct which was subsequently shown by others to cause degeneration of the exocrine tissue while leaving its endocrine function intact.

Other notable discoveries were made in the study of diabetes during the mid-19th century. Coma was first recognized as a complication of diabetes by W. Prout (1785–1859) of Guy's Hospital; Prout made other contributions in the field of clinical chemistry, including the introduction of iodine to treat goitre. In 1869, an American ophthalmologist, H.D. Noyes, observed that a form of 'retinitis' occurred in glycosuric patients and in 1874, Professor A. Kussmaul (1822–1902) of Freiburg University described the 'air hunger' of ketoacidosis.

The endocrine, blood-glucose-lowering properties of the pancreas began to be clarified in the second half of the 19th century. Important studies were performed in Strasbourg in 1889 by Oskar Minkowski (1858–1931) and Josef Von Mering (1849–1908) (Fig. 1.5). They removed the pancreas from a dog in order to discover whether the organ was essential to life. After the operation, the animal unexpectedly displayed the typical

Fig. 1.4. Claude Bernard (1813–78). (Reproduced by kind permission of the Wellcome Institute of the History of Medicine.)

signs of severe diabetes, with polyuria and incontinence, insatiable thirst, hyperphagia and wasting. Minkowski found the dog to be glycosuric and hyperglycaemic [7]. This observation firmly established the role of pancreatic disorders in causing diabetes and stimulated many workers to try to isolate the active pancreatic principle as a possible treatment for the disease.

The source of the blood-glucose-lowering substance remained a mystery for some years. In 1869, while working in Berlin for his doctorate, Paul Langerhans (1847–1888) (Fig. 1.6) had noticed small clusters of cells in teased preparations of pancreas which stood out against and could be separated from the surrounding exocrine and ductal tissue [8]. Langerhans simply described these structures, without speculating as to their possible function. It was only in 1893 that Edouard Laguesse (1861–1927) suggested that these clumps of cells, which he named the 'islets of Langerhans', might constitute the endocrine tissue of the pancreas. This theme was continued by the Belgian

Fig. 1.5. Josef Von Mering (1849–1908, left) and Oskar Minkowski (1858–1931, right).

Fig. 1.6. Paul Langerhans (1847–1888). (Reproduced by kind permission of the Wellcome Institute of the History of Medicine.)

physician, Jean de Meyer, who in 1909 gave the name 'insulin' (Latin, *insula* = island) to the glucose-lowering hormone, whose existence at that time was still hypothetical, which he postulated was produced by the islet tissue.

On the threshold of the discovery of insulin

Sadly, the accelerating pace of scientific discoveries leading into the 20th century was not matched by improvements in the treatment of diabetes. The outcome remained particularly gloomy for those patients unfortunate enough to develop insulin-dependent diabetes. In the first two decades of this century, they faced a short and harrowing future not very different from that described by Aretaeus (Table 1.2) and comparable with the prognosis associated nowadays with advanced malignancy or AIDS. Those patients who opted for active treatment were subjected to starvation diets which extended their lives — and their misery — for only a few months. Others simply resigned themselves to their fate; after learning his diagnosis, Dr Robin Lawrence (who later founded the Diabetic Clinic at King's College

Hospital, London, and the British Diabetic Association — see Chapter 102) set off on a European tour which he fully expected to be the last journey of his life.

Nonetheless, as recounted in the next chapter, several workers were actively searching for the elusive 'insulin' during the early years of this century and one, Georg Zülzer, had even tested a pancreatic extract in man and had taken out an American patent on his preparation. All these early preparations, however, were of low and variable potency and often highly toxic, and none was consistently useful in treating the disease.

The widening gap between the increasing theoretical knowledge of diabetes and the lack of any effective treatment is apparent from the diabetes textbooks of this period. In retrospect, these books are fascinating historical documents as they reflect the last few years of the defeatist approach to diabetes which was soon to be dramatically and irrevocably overturned. The textbook by Professor M. Labbé of Geneva [9] makes particularly interesting and sometimes moving reading, as it was published in the Spring of 1922 at the time when the first hesitant clinical trials of insulin were being undertaken in Toronto.

IAN A. MACFARLANE

References and further reading

1 Willis T. *Pharmaceutica rationalis sive diatriba de medicamentorum operationitus in humano corpore*, 2 vols. London. 1674–5.

2 Dobson M. Experiments and observations on the urine in diabetes. *Med Obs Inq* 1776; **5**: 298–316.

3 Rollo J. An account of two cases of the diabetes mellitus, with remarks as they arose during the progress of the cure. London, 1797.

4 Cawley T. A singular case of diabetes, consisting entirely in the quality of urine; with an inquiry into the different theories of that disease. *London Med J* 1788; **9**: 286–308.

5 Bernard C. *Leçons de physiologie*. Paris: J.B. Ballière, 1855, p. 289.

6 Bernard C. *Mémoire sur le pancréas*. Paris: J.B. Ballière, 1856. (Published as a monograph of the Physiological Society, Academic Press, London, 1985.)

7 Mering J Von, Minkowski O. Diabetes mellitus nach pankreasextirpation. *Arch Exper Path Pharm Leipzig* 1890; **26**: 371–87.

8 Langerhans P. *Beiträge zur mikroskopischen Anatomie der Bauchspeicheldrüse*. Inaugural dissertation. Berlin: Gustave Lange, 1869.

9 Labbé M. *A Clinical Treatise on Diabetes Mellitus*. London: William Heinemann (Medical Books), 1922.

10 Papaspyros NS. *The History of Diabetes Mellitus*, 2nd edn. Stuttgart: Georg Thieme Verlag, 1964.

2   The Discovery of Insulin

Summary

• The discovery of insulin at the University of Toronto resulted from a collaborative effort involving Frederick G. Banting, Charles H. Best, James B. Collip and J.J.R. Macleod.
• Work was begun by Banting in Toronto in the summer of 1921, supervised by Macleod and with Best as student assistant.
• Chilled extracts of both atrophied and whole pancreas lowered blood glucose levels in depancreatized dogs, thus disproving Banting's original hypothesis that ligation of the pancreatic ducts to cause atrophy of acinar tissue was essential to prevent breakdown of insulin within the gland.
• Collip joined the team in late 1921 and developed an extraction procedure which yielded more potent and pure preparations suitable for clinical use.
• The first diabetic patient treated by insulin, in January 1922, was a 14-year-old boy, Leonard Thompson.

Before the discovery of insulin at the University of Toronto in 1921–2, there was no effective treatment for insulin-dependent diabetes mellitus. At best, it was possible by systematic undernutrition through the 'starvation' diet promoted by F.M. Allen to abolish glycosuria and prolong life by some months. With rigid adherence to diet, some insulin-dependent diabetic patients survived for 2 or 3 years after onset before being overcome either by the diabetes or by the effects of starvation.

The idea of treating diabetes with pancreatic material dated from Minkowski's and Von Mering's discovery in 1889 at the University of Strasbourg that dogs developed severe diabetes immediately after pancreatectomy [1]. Although initially over-simplistic, the rationale for pancreatic replacement therapy was supported by speculation that an internal or endocrine secretion of the pancreas was active in regulating carbohydrate metabolism. The development of the concepts of hormones and endocrine regulation reinforced this notion, but the pancreas' supposed internal secretion remained remarkably elusive.

Many researchers reported negative or inconclusive results. A few, such as G.L. Zülzer in Germany (1906), E.L. Scott in America (1911–12), and Nicolas Paulesco in Romania (1921), claimed to have isolated pancreatic extracts which reduced glycosuria and/or glycaemia when administered to diabetic subjects. None, however, was able to convince the scientific community of his claims, treat human diabetes effectively, or even to repeat his own experiments conclusively. The man who came closest to success, as indicated in his brilliant paper published in 1919 [2], was Israel Kleiner, working at the Rockefeller Institute. Kleiner was one of the first to perform serial blood sugar estimations which permitted a much clearer understanding of the effects of administering pancreatic extracts. However, he abandoned his work, apparently on moving to a university which was poorly equipped for major animal experimentation. Many of the European researchers, including Zülzer and Paulesco, similarly suffered from lack of resources as well as the disruptive impact of the Great War.

At 2 a.m. on 31 October, 1920, Frederick Grant Banting (1891–1941) (Fig. 2.1), a practising physician and surgeon in London, Ontario, jotted down the following entry (reproduced verbatim) in his notebook: 'Diabetus. Ligate pancreatic ducts of

Fig. 2.1. The discoverers of insulin. *Top left*: C.H. Best; *top right*: J.J.R. Macleod; *lower left*: F.G. Banting; *lower right*: J.B. Collip; *bottom*: N. Paulesco.

dog. Keep dogs alive till acini degenerate leaving islets. Try to isolate the internal secretion of these to relieve glycosurea.'

The idea that this procedure might protect the internal secretion against destruction by pancreatic juices had come to Banting in the course of background reading about the pancreas. He was a well-trained surgeon with no experience in either diabetes or serious research, but was enthusiastic at the thought of making useful discoveries and approached J.J.R. Macleod (1876–1935) (Fig. 2.1), then Professor of Physiology at his *alma mater*, the University of Toronto. Macleod promised him laboratory space, dogs and a student assistant to conduct experiments in the summer of 1921. Banting's notebook indicates that he was exploring the feasibility of transplanting healthy islet-cell tissue from ligated, atrophied pancreas into a pancreatectomized diabetic subject. Macleod, a Scots-born scientist with an international reputation, supervised the research and advised Banting from the beginning. One of Macleod's student assistants, Charles H. Best (1899–1978) (Fig. 2.1), won the toss of a coin for the right to help Banting in the experiments.

Banting and Best began work on 17 May, 1921. At the end of July, they abandoned the transplantation proposal and began injecting chilled extracts of atrophied pancreas, prepared according to Macleod's suggestions, into pancreatectomized diabetic animals. They were greatly encouraged by the frequent finding of declines in blood glucose levels after injection and tended to interpret all of their data favourably. Macleod, who had been in Scotland during the summer's experiments, encouraged them to repeat and amplify their findings that autumn. By December, the team had realized that extracts of chilled whole pancreas would produce the same results, making Banting's ligation procedures superfluous (and thereby disproving his working hypothesis). At Banting's request, Macleod invited a trained biochemist, James B. Collip (1892–1965) (Fig. 2.1), to join the team later that month.

The first public presentation of the research results, at a meeting of the American Physiological Society on 30 December, was received with considerable scepticism. Banting and Best's paper (later published in the *Journal of Laboratory and Clinical Medicine* [3]) was open to severe criticism on many counts, not least their failure to check for fever and other symptoms of toxicity which had bedevilled other researchers. Indeed, Banting's and Best's results were arguably not as good as those of Paulesco or Kleiner.

Collip, however, was already engaged in a vital series of buttressing experiments, the most important of which were the discoveries that the pancreatic extract enabled diabetic liver to mobilize glycogen and that it could clear ketonuria. On 11 January, 1922, an extract made by Banting and

Fig. 2.2. Leonard Thompson, the first patient to be treated by insulin in January 1922.

Best was injected into Leonard Thompson (Fig. 2.2), a 14-year-old boy dying of diabetes in Toronto General Hospital. It failed to relieve his symptoms, caused a sterile abscess to form, and was judged a failure. On 23 January, however, a separate extract made by Collip reduced Thompson's blood sugar to normal, abolished his glycosuria and ketonuria, and thereby inaugurated the use of insulin in the treatment of diabetes mellitus.

Collip had developed an extraction technique which removed the toxic contaminants from Banting and Best's crude and variable extract, and so was able to isolate the active principle effectively and convincingly. On 3 May, 1922, the Toronto group delivered a paper to the Association of American Physicians in Washington, DC, entitled *The Effect Produced on Diabetes of Extracts of Pancreas*. They were given a standing ovation for what the audience acclaimed as one of the greatest achievements of modern medicine. By then, the group had accepted Macleod's suggestion to name the extract 'insulin' after the Latin root for the islet cells in the pancreas. It was later learned that others had earlier suggested the same name for the then-hypothetical secretion (Chapter 1); insulin is therefore a substance which was named before it was discovered.

Collip's technique was crude and sometimes ineffective. The team's problems in producing insulin — which continued while desperate diabetic patients flocked to Toronto — were not finally solved until chemists at Eli Lilly and Company of Indiana, with whom the group decided to collaborate, developed commercially viable extraction techniques involving isoelectric precipitation. Under licence from the University of Toronto, which held the patents on manufacturing techniques, Danish and other scientists (including a group at the Medical Research Council in England), soon became involved in the development and use of insulin. By October 1923, insulin was widely available in North America and Europe.

In one of the Nobel Committee's quickest ever recognitions, Banting and Macleod were awarded the 1923 prize in physiology or medicine for the discovery of insulin. Banting announced that he would share his prize money equally with Best; Macleod shared his with Collip. At the time, and for many years afterwards, there was much controversy about the awards and the relative contributions of the Toronto team. Banting and Best, who were both deeply insecure, suspicious men, believed that they had discovered insulin while working on their own in the summer of 1921. With rather more justification, Macleod and Collip believed that Banting and Best's interesting but inconclusive studies could not have led to insulin without their own work.

In fact, insulin was discovered at the University of Toronto through a truly collaborative effort, directed by Macleod, and based on experiments initiated by Banting with the help of Best. The greatest single breakthrough in the research was made by Collip, who perhaps deserved a formal share of the Nobel Prize. The University of Toronto and its financial supporters contributed substantially to the discovery by providing this team with what, at the time, were first-rate research facilities and techniques together with unlimited supplies of experimental animals.

The controversy was secondary to the wonder of the discovery. As a speaker said at a dinner to honour the Nobel laureates, 'in insulin there is glory enough for all'. No one knew this better than the starving diabetic children and their parents, who were experiencing one of the most dramatic reprieves in the history of medicine. Suddenly in 1922, the question of the speed of death in diabetes was replaced by that of the quality of life with insulin. Leonard Thompson lived until 1935; at least two of the 'doomed' children who were first treated in Toronto in 1922 outlived all four of insulin's discoverers. One of the children, Ted Ryder (Fig. 2.3), was alive and in good health when this text first went to press in 1990. The great American diabetologist, Elliot Joslin, graphically described the impact of the discovery of insulin when he compared the 'near

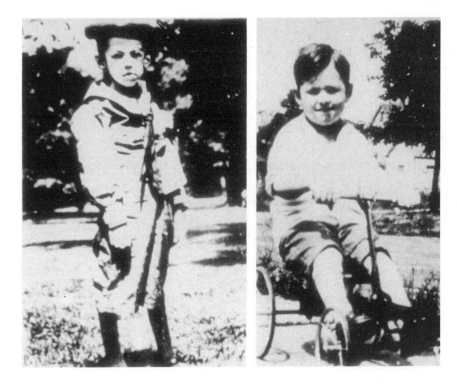

Fig. 2.3. Ted Ryder, one of the first children to be treated by insulin. Before (left) and after (right) insulin therapy.

resurrections' he had witnessed to the effect of the prophecies of Ezekiel in the valley of dry bones: '. . . and the breath came into them, and they lived, and stood up upon their feet, an exceeding great army.'

MICHAEL BLISS

References

The notebooks and personal papers of the discoverers of insulin are preserved at the Fisher Rare Book Library at the University of Toronto. A full account of their work and that of their predecessors has been published [4].

1 Mering J Von, Minkowski O. Diabetes mellitus nach pankreasextirpation. *Arch Exp Pathol Pharmacol, Leipzig* 1890; **26**: 371–87.
2 Kleiner IS. The action of intravenous injections of pancreas emulsions in experimental diabetes. *J Biol Chem* 1919; **40**: 153–70.
3 Banting FG, Best CH. The internal secretion of the pancreas. *J Lab Clin Med* 1922; **7**: 256–71.
4 Bliss M. *The Discovery of Insulin*. Toronto: McClelland and Stewart, 1982; and Edinburgh: Paul Harris Publishing, 1983.

SECTION 2
INTRODUCTION TO THE CLINICAL PROBLEMS OF DIABETES

3 Insulin-Dependent Diabetes Mellitus

Summary

- Insulin-dependent diabetes mellitus (IDDM), generally synonymous with Type 1 diabetes, identifies patients who cannot survive without insulin replacement.
- The prevalence of IDDM in the UK is about 0.25%; there is marked geographical variation in its prevalence world-wide.
- Patients mostly present young but over 10% of diabetic subjects aged over 65 years require insulin.
- IDDM usually presents acutely with hyperglycaemic symptoms (polyuria, thirst, polydipsia), tiredness and weight loss. Nausea, vomiting and drowsiness usually denote impending ketoacidosis. Minor symptoms include cramps, blurred vision and superficial infections.
- The acute presentation of IDDM is probably the culmination of chronic autoimmune destruction of the pancreatic B-cells. Subtle abnormalities of insulin secretion and glucose tolerance can be detected during this 'pre-diabetic' phase.
- Some IDDM patients experience a temporary remission ('honeymoon period') after starting insulin, with good glycaemic control and low insulin requirements. This is due to correction of hyperglycaemia, which directly damages the B-cells. Remission ends when continuing autoimmune damage has destroyed a critical mass of B-cells.
- Long-standing IDDM patients are susceptible to 'microvascular' complications (nephropathy, retinopathy and neuropathy) specific to diabetes, and to non-specific macrovascular disease (coronary heart and peripheral vascular disease).
- Mortality in IDDM is increased 4- to 7-fold over the matched non-diabetic population; nephropathy and coronary heart disease are the main causes of death.
- A proportion of IDDM patients survive without significant complications for many years; the factor(s) protecting them against complications are unknown.

Definitions: insulin-dependent versus insulin-treated

In a clinical setting, 'insulin-dependent diabetes' and 'Type 1' diabetes are generally used synonymously, and generally correspond to the outdated term, 'juvenile-onset' diabetes. The complexities of the classification of diabetes are discussed in Chapter 6; for the purposes of this book, insulin-dependent diabetes (IDDM) will be the preferred nomenclature. The important point of 'insulin-dependent diabetes' is the word *dependent*, which emphasizes that, without insulin replacement, these patients will die. They must be distinguished from those who are better controlled with insulin, but who can survive without it. The latter are usually non-insulin-dependent diabetic (NIDDM) patients who have failed to respond to maximal oral hypoglycaemic agent treatment.

IDDM is the 'classical', life-threatening form of diabetes, the treatment of which was revolutionized by the discovery of insulin by Banting and Best [1]. It remains the type of diabetes which excites most clinical and research interest and, to most members of the public, it is the *only* form of the disease. In numerical terms, however, it constitutes a minority of the total diabetic population.

Magnitude of the problem of IDDM in Britain

The prevalence of diabetes mellitus in Britain is traditionally taken to be 1%. This remains broadly true, with overall prevalence rates in three recent large British surveys quoted as 9.5/1000 (Poole, in Dorset) [2], 10.4/1000 (Oxford) [3] and 10.5/1000 (Southall, in West London) [4]. Only about one-quarter of these patients are truly insulin-dependent [5], but the relative complexity of their treatment and their increasing risk of serious complications with the passage of time, make the management of IDDM a considerable logistic health problem. Moreover, the community prevalence of IDDM [5] is not usually reflected in the hospital diabetic clinic population, which generally has a considerably higher proportion of IDDM patients [6]. There is also some evidence that the incidence of IDDM in childhood is increasing, perhaps as much as two-fold each decade [7]. This increase may be related to relative affluence, as IDDM seems to be associated with the higher socio-economic classes [8]. The above factors, together with the increasing number of NIDDM patients being transferred to insulin treatment, all contribute to the major health care problem posed by insulin-treated diabetes in the UK.

In other countries, IDDM may impose a different burden. The striking differences in prevalence between so-called 'developed' and 'underdeveloped' countries [9] are described in Chapter 7.

Some epidemiological features of IDDM

There is a well-described seasonal variation in the presentation of IDDM patients, 'clustering' tending to occur in autumn and winter [10] (see Chapter 7). The disease affects a slight excess of males, but this becomes less marked at older ages

Table 3.1. Prevalence of IDDM with age, including proportion of insulin-treated patients (Neill *et al.* 1987, [3]).

Age group (y)	Prevalence (per 1000)	% Insulin treated
0−9	0.5	100.0
10−19	2.4	100.0
20−29	3.9	91.7
30−39	3.2	78.6
40−49	3.9	51.2
50−59	4.8	37.6
60−69	5.6	28.1
70−79	8.2	23.2
80+	8.5	26.9

of presentation [5]. Although IDDM is predominantly 'juvenile-onset', it can present at all ages of life; indeed, a significant number of new elderly diabetic patients (up to 10% of those over 65 years [11]) may require insulin, which poses special problems in this group [12]. Table 3.1 demonstrates clearly the generally *rising* diabetic prevalence with increasing age, but the *falling* proportion of patients treated with insulin. These data again show that a substantial minority of elderly patients are insulin-treated, although many will not be truly insulin-dependent.

Clinical features of IDDM

The classical symptoms of IDDM are thirst, passage of large amounts of urine (polyuria), overwhelming tiredness and weight loss, often dramatic (Table 3.2). Other minor symptoms — which are nevertheless quite common if specifically sought — include muscular cramps (usually in the legs), skin infections, penile or vulval pruritis due to candidiasis, and blurred vision due to osmotic changes in the lens. Nausea, vomiting and drowsiness usually denote impending ketoacidosis and possible coma.

It is unusual to find specific abnormal physical signs in newly presenting patients with IDDM, although they tend to look ill and may show evidence of recent weight loss and sometimes mild dehydration. Skin sepsis or candidiasis may be present. In contrast to NIDDM, evidence of established diabetic microvascular complications is extremely rare.

The duration of symptoms is short, usually only 2−3 weeks or less. Some patients may present in ketoacidosis, although this is now relatively rare (5−10% of cases). The chances of detecting early, asymptomatic IDDM are exceedingly remote because of the relatively acute clinical onset of the disease.

The typical acute presentation of IDDM is illustrated in the Case History, which also emphasizes the current policy to return newly diagnosed patients to their normal routine as soon as possible after they have started insulin treatment and learned 'first-aid' rules for managing their diabetes.

The causes and natural history of IDDM

The aetiology of IDDM is complex but major contributory factors probably include a genetic

Table 3.2. Symptoms of insulin-dependent diabetes (IDDM). NB: Symptoms due to diabetic microvascular complications are extremely rare at presentation.

Major symptoms	Minor symptoms	Features of ketoacidosis
Thirst	Cramps	Nausea
Polyuria	Constipation	Vomiting
Weight loss	Blurred vision	Drowsiness
Fatigue	Candidiasis	Abdominal pain
	Skin sepsis	

predisposition (identified by specific HLA antigens) together with environmental 'trigger' factors (possibly viral infections). B-cells are apparently destroyed by autoimmune damage. There is now no doubt that, although the clinical onset of IDDM is abrupt, circulating antibodies to the pancreatic islet-cells may have been present for many years previously. During this 'pre-diabetic' phase, there may be subtle abnormalities in insulin secretion in response to intravenous glucose challenge but symptoms are absent and oral glucose tolerance is normal [13]. Loss of B-cell mass accelerates markedly in the 6 months or so before clinical presentation. During this phase, which is still asymptomatic, abnormalities in oral glucose tolerance or fasting hyperglycaemia frequently appear.

After starting insulin treatment, many patients enjoy excellent glycaemic control with only small doses of insulin. This 'honeymoon period', long recognized in clinical practice [14], lasts from 2−3 months to a year or more. The honeymoon period in a teenager is illustrated in Fig. 3.1 (overleaf), which shows the evolution of insulin requirements and glycaemic control (measured by glycosylated haemoglobin — see Chapter 34) in the months following diagnosis. In pathophysiological terms, the honeymoon corresponds to a temporary improvement in B-cell function caused by the lowering of high glucose levels, which directly impair B-cell function and insulin release [15]. Insulin requirements during the honeymoon may be remarkably low and occasionally true 'remissions' occur, when insulin can be com-

---

Case history: insulin-dependent diabetes

TB, 19-year-old motor mechanic.

1 April
Presented to family doctor with 2-week history of:
• Unusual thirst (drinking several bottles of fizzy glucose drinks per day).
• Passing large volumes of urine several times day and night.
• Weight loss of about 7 kg.
• Feeling increasingly tired and unwell.
Family doctor tested urine and measured blood glucose using test-strips:
• Urinalysis: 2% glucose, +++ ketones.
• Blood glucose: greater than 17 mmol/1.
Patient sent immediately to local hospital:
• Plasma glucose 19.4 mmol/1.
• Plasma bicarbonate 16.0 mmol/1
• Plasma urea 10.6 mmol/1.
Patient admitted to hospital because of risk of ketoacidosis.
• First insulin injection given by patient himself.

• Initial discussion about diabetes.

2 April
• Patient shown how to measure his blood glucose level.
• Further discussion about diabetes with diabetes specialist nurse.

3 April
• Symptoms settling.
• Blood glucose levels stabilizing with twice-daily intermediate plus short-acting insulins; ketonuria +.
• Self-monitoring technique checked.
• Discussion with dietitian.

4 April
• Fasting blood glucose 8 mmol/1, ketonuria absent.
• Injection and self-monitoring technique checked.
• 'First-aid' knowledge checked and contact telephone number given in case of emergencies.
• Discharged home, with follow-up home visit by the diabetes nurse in 2 days.

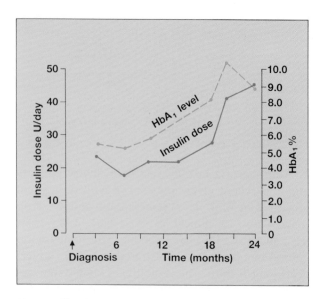

Fig. 3.1. The 'honeymoon period' in a teenager with IDDM. The graph shows daily insulin dose and glycosylated haemoglobin (HbA$_1$) levels in an 18-year-old girl during the first two years after diagnosis. Glycaemic control was probably deteriorating from the end of the first year, but this was not clinically apparent until 15–18 months, when insulin doses were progressively increased.

pletely withdrawn. This is, however, always a temporary state of affairs: ultimately, the continuing autoimmune destruction of the remaining B-cells reaches the point where endogenous insulin secretion falls below the level necessary to prevent hyperglycaemia. Because of this, most diabetologists prefer to maintain standard insulin therapy, albeit in very small doses, in order to avoid disappointment when deteriorating glycaemic control and increasing insulin requirements herald the end of the honeymoon.

A proportion of patients with IDDM appear to retain some endogenous insulin production in the long-term (i.e. they remain 'C-peptide positive' — see Chapter 36), thus in effect maintaining their honeymoon [16]. There is evidence that these patients have better blood glucose control, and

they might therefore be less prone to diabetic complications, than their 'C-peptide negative' counterparts [17].

These observations have recently stimulated considerable interest as to whether the honeymoon period can be prolonged, or indeed a true remission of IDDM secured. As hyperglycaemia itself may damage remaining B-cells [15], one approach has been to impose intensive blood glucose control immediately after diagnosis. Attempts have also been made to control the autoimmune process held responsible for B-cell destruction, using various immunosuppressive agents. Most interest so far has centred on cyclosporin [18, 19], which has given provisionally encouraging results (Chapter 103). It appears, however, that the drug must be given very early to have maximum benefit, and its potentially serious side-effects (which unfortunately include a toxic effect on the B-cell) must be weighed against its possible advantages. For the time being, immunosuppressive treatment of newly diagnosed IDDM patients must remain experimental and confined to specialist centres.

The outcome and prognosis of IDDM

The longer term natural history of diabetes (both IDDM and NIDDM) is darkened by the appearance in some patients of potentially serious complications. These include the specific diabetic problems of retinopathy, nephropathy and neuropathy, which are often termed diabetic 'microangiopathic' or 'microvascular' complications even though the cause of neuropathy is probably not strictly microvascular disease. Atheromatous disease of the larger arteries (particularly coronary heart and peripheral vascular disease), which is not specific to diabetes, also occurs. Although both major types of diabetes are affected by both groups of complications, the IDDM patient of early onset is particularly susceptible to microvascular

Duration of DM (y)	Neuropathy (%)	Retinopathy (%)	Nephropathy (%)
0	8	5	0
5	15	16	2
10	26	26	5
15	31	40	8
20	40	48	10
25	49	50	14

Table 3.3. Percentage of patients affected by different diabetic complications with increasing duration of diabetes (after Pirart, 1978 [20]).

problems. Table 3.3 demonstrates the cumulative prevalence of these complications with increasing duration of diabetes. The figures come from the well-known study by Pirart of a large cohort of Belgian patients [20], which included all types of diabetes. The early complication figures therefore probably reflect predominantly NIDDM patients (some of whom have microvascular disease at presentation) whereas the later data most likely represent those with IDDM. For IDDM patients, the risk of developing diabetic complications as time progresses is high. This study, and many others, has suggested strongly that the complication risk in IDDM is related not only to the duration of disease, but also to the degree of glycaemic control. Absolute proof that good control can retard or prevent the development of complications has not yet been obtained, but the assumption is accepted by most diabetologists and indeed is almost an article of faith in the current approach to achieve the best possible diabetic control.

The ultimate index of disease severity is the risk of premature death. For diabetic patients overall, the mortality risk is about twice that in the age-matched, non-diabetic population [21]. For IDDM patients in particular, the risks are considerably greater, being about 4−5 times normal [22] and up to 7 times normal for those whose disease presents in childhood [23]. Overall life expectancy is reduced by about 25%. The

Table 3.4. Causes of mortality in insulin-dependent (IDDM) and non-insulin-dependent (NIDDM) diabetes (Marks & Krall 1971, [24]).

	IDDM (%)	NIDDM (%)
Cardiovascular disease	15	58
Cerebrovascular disease	3	12
Nephropathy	55	3
Diabetic 'coma'	4	1
Malignancy	0	11
Infections	10	4
Others	13	11

major causes of premature death are shown in Table 3.4, which also highlights the different causes of death in IDDM and NIDDM [24]. Nephropathy and heart disease together account for 70% of deaths in IDDM whereas in NIDDM, 70% of deaths are due to cardiac and cerebral arteriosclerosis. Interestingly, mortality rates peak at about 15−25 years duration of IDDM, and decrease thereafter [25]. To some extent, the pattern of appearance of complications with the duration of diabetes is similar: prevalence rates tend to 'plateau' at around 20 years after diagnosis (Table 3.3).

At first sight, these statistics seem rather depressing, but there are grounds for guarded optimism. Only a minority of patients develop complications and in most cases, these are asymptomatic or cause little trouble: blindness

Fig. 3.2. Long-standing insulin-dependent diabetes. These six patients have all had IDDM for over 50 years and between them represent 320 years of the disease. They are all clinically well and only two have diabetic complications, which do not interfere with their lives.

and renal failure affect only a small proportion. Furthermore, virtually all our present data are derived from cohorts of patients who were diagnosed and initially treated during the 'dark ages' when glycaemic control was not considered important. Today's patients with IDDM are likely to be considerably better controlled than their counterparts 25 years ago, and it is our hope that this will be reflected in reduced complication and mortality rates in the future.

Long-standing IDDM

Despite the potential problems of IDDM, some patients do remarkably well in the long-term. Figure 3.2 shows six IDDM patients, all looking extremely fit and all of whom hold the Nabarro Medal of the British Diabetic Association (awarded after 50 years of insulin treatment). The ages of this group range from 59–77 years, and their duration of diabetes is 51–56 years — a total of 320 years of insulin-dependent diabetes. Despite over half a century of IDDM, only two have complications: one has background retinopathy and early nephropathy (both asymptomatic), and another proliferative retinopathy (successfully managed with laser treatment and vitrectomy).

Patients such as these provide useful inspiration for younger people with diabetes and also present an intriguing challenge to the accepted concepts concerning the development of diabetic complications. Studies on long-standing IDDM patients are necessarily uncontrolled and to some extent anecdotal. Nevertheless, reports from Britain [26], Denmark [27] and the USA [28] do show some common features, notably normal body weight, normal blood pressure and regular diabetic clinic contact. A family history of longevity may also contribute. Retrospective long-term glycaemic control is difficult or impossible to assess in these patients but control generally seems to be satisfactory or better than average; when photographed, the mean glycosylated haemoglobin (HbA$_1$) of the group was 8.5% (range 7.3–9.7%; non-diabetic range, 5.0–8.0%). Whatever the protective factors — and there are undoubtedly many which remain unknown — these long-standing IDDM patients remain remarkably well and free from complications until their eventual demise at an advanced age from non-diabetic causes.

GEOFFREY V. GILL

References

1 Banting FG, Best CH. The internal secretion of the pancreas. *J Lab Clin Med* 1922; **7**: 251–66.
2 Gatling W, Houston AC, Hill RD. An epidemiological survey: the prevalence of diabetes mellitus in a typical English community. *J R Coll Physicians Lond* 1985; **4**: 248–50.
3 Neill HAW, Gatling W, Mather HM, Thompson AV, Thorogood M, Fowler GH, Hill RD, Mann JI. The Oxford Community Diabetes Study: evidence for an increase in the prevalence of known diabetes in Great Britain. *Diabetic Med* 1987; **4**: 539–43.
4 Mather HM, Keen H. The Southall Diabetes Survey: prevalence of known diabetes in Asians and Europeans. *Br Med J* 1985; **291**: 1081–4.
5 Gatling W, Mullee M, Hill R. General characteristics of a community-based diabetic population. *Pract Diabetes* 1988; **5**: 104–7.
6 Hardy KJ, Gill GV. Social aspects of diabetes — what do the patients know? *Diabetic Med* 1987; **4**: 576A.
7 Stewart-Brown S, Haslum M, Butler N. Evidence for increasing prevalence of diabetes mellitus in childhood. *Br Med J* 1983; **286**: 1855–7.
8 Ardron M, MacFarlane I, Robinson C. Educational achievements, employment and social class of insulin dependent diabetes: a survey of a young adult clinic in Liverpool. *Diabetic Med* 1987; **4**: 546–8.
9 Gill GV. Diabetes and the third world. *Pract Diabetes* 1988; **5**: 148.
10 Leslie RDG. Causes of insulin-dependent diabetes. *Br Med J* 1983; **287**: 5–6.
11 Kilvert A, Fitzgerald MG, Wright AD, Nattrass M. Newly diagnosed, insulin dependent diabetes mellitus in elderly patients. *Diabetic Med* 1984; **1**: 115–8.
12 Bates A. Diabetes in old age. *Pract Diabetes* 1986; **3**: 120–3.
13 Eisenbarth GS. Type 1 diabetes mellitus. A chronic autoimmune disease. *N Engl J Med* 1986; **314**: 1360–8.
14 Ireland JT, Thomson WST, Williamson J. *Diabetes Today.* Chichester: HM & M Publishers, 1980.
15 Madsbad S, Faber OK, Binder C, McNair P, Christiansen C, Transbol I. Prevalence of residual beta cell function in insulin-dependent diabetics with relation to age at onset and duration of diabetes. *Diabetes* 1978; **27** (suppl 1): 262–4.
16 Grajwer LA, Pildes RS, Horwitz DL, Rubenstein AH. Control of juvenile diabetes mellitus and its relationship to endogenous insulin secretion as measured by C-peptide immunoreactivity. *J Pediatr* 1977; **90**: 42–8.
17 Bonner-Weir S, Trent DF, Weir GC. Partial pancreatectomy in the rat and subsequent defect in glucose-induced insulin release. *J Clin Invest* 1983; **71**: 1544–53.
18 Leading article. Cyclosporin for diabetes? *Lancet* 1986; **2**: 140.
19 Herold KC, Rubenstein AH. Immunosuppression for insulin-dependent diabetes. *N Engl J Med* 1988; **318**: 701–3.
20 Pirart J. Diabetes mellitus and its degenerative complications: a prospective study of 4,400 patients observed between 1947 and 1973. *Diabetes Care* 1978; **1**: 168–88.
21 Gatling W, Mullee M, Hill RD. A comparison of mortality in a diabetic population and age/sex matched controls. *Diabetic Med* 1987; **4**: 574A.
22 Goodkin G. Mortality factors in diabetes. *J Occup Med* 1975; **17**: 716–21.
23 Dorman JS, Laporte RE, Kuller LH, Cruickshank KJ,

Orchard TJ, Wagener DK, Becker DJ, Cavender DE, Drash AL. The Pittsburgh insulin-dependent diabetes (IDDM) morbidity and mortality study. Mortality results. *Diabetes* 1984; **33**: 271–6.

24 Marks HH, Krall LP. Onset, course, prognosis and mortality in diabetes mellitus. In: Marble A, White P *et al.*, eds. *Joslin's Diabetes Mellitus* 12th edn. Philadelphia: Lea & Febiger 1988: 209–54.

25 Green A, Borch-Johnsen K, Andersen PK, Hougaard P, Keiding N, Kreiner S, Deckert T. Relative mortality of Type 1 (insulin dependent) diabetes in Denmark: 1933–1981. *Diabetologia* 1985; **28**: 339–42.

26 Oakley WG, Pyke DA, Tattersall RB, Watkins PJ. Long term diabetes. *Q J Med* 1974; **43**: 145–56.

27 Deckert T, Poulsen JE, Larsen M. Prognosis of diabetics with diabetes onset before the age of thirty one. II Factors influencing the prognosis. *Diabetologia* 1978; **14**: 371–7.

28 Cochran HA, Marble A, Galloway JA. Factors in the survival of patients with insulin-requiring diabetes for 50 years. *Diabetes Care* 1979; **2**: 363–8.

4 Non-Insulin-Dependent Diabetes Mellitus

Summary

- Non-insulin-dependent diabetes mellitus (NIDDM; Type 2) denotes diabetic patients who can survive long-term without insulin replacement, although many receive insulin to improve their glycaemic control.
- NIDDM affects about half a million people in the UK, about 75% of the diabetic population. NIDDM is extremely common in certain communities (e.g. 50% of Pima Indians in the USA).
- Patients are mostly older and obese and present with insidious hyperglycaemic symptoms; many cases are diagnosed incidentally or because of the presence of diabetic complications.
- NIDDM is apparently due to a combination of impaired insulin secretion (especially in non-obese subjects) and insensitivity of the target tissues to insulin (especially in obese subjects). There is a strong genetic predisposition to the disease.
- Specific microvascular complications are less common than in IDDM, where the onset is earlier and exposure to the disease generally longer. However, retinopathy (especially with maculopathy rather than proliferative changes), nephropathy (sometimes with renal failure) and neuropathy all occur.
- NIDDM carries a high risk of large-vessel atherosclerosis; commonly associated hypertension, hyperlipidaemia and obesity may contribute. Myocardial infarction is also common and accounts for 60% of deaths.
- NIDDM is not 'mild' diabetes: overall mortality is increased 2−3 fold and life expectancy reduced by 5−10 years.

Definition

Similar problems of definition and classification apply to non-insulin-dependent (NIDDM), also known as 'Type 2' diabetes, as to the insulin-dependent variety (IDDM) — see Chapter 6. NIDDM is taken as the large subgroup of diabetic patients whose life is not dependent on exogenous insulin. Although there is evidence for a relative deficit in insulin secretory capacity in NIDDM, these subjects generally have peripheral insulin resistance and many are obese [1]. Most patients are treated by dietary restriction with or without oral hypoglycaemic agents, but some will come to need insulin treatment for adequate metabolic control. This is thought to be due either to diminishing pancreatic insulin reserves, or to the patients' failure to comply with dietary or oral treatment. Even with insulin treatment, however, these patients remain part of the NIDDM spectrum.

'Maturity-onset diabetes of the young' (MODY) ([2], Chapter 25), and gestational diabetes (Chapter 83) are both variants of NIDDM. The outmoded concepts of 'stress diabetes' and 'steroid diabetes' probably represent early sub-clinical stages of NIDDM, clinically 'unmasked' by temporary excesses of circulating counter-regulatory hormones.

Magnitude of the problem of NIDDM

As patients with NIDDM do not die without insulin treatment, they have commonly been regarded as having a 'mild' form of the disease [3]. It is now recognized that in terms of natural history, the disease is anything but mild [4]. Large-vessel disease in particular is severe and accelerated in NIDDM, leading to early mortality (often from ischaemic heart disease), and considerable morbidity from angina, claudication, stroke and foot problems. The importance of these complications is compounded by the considerably larger number of patients with NIDDM as compared with IDDM. Of the 1% or so of the British population who are diabetic, some 75% have NIDDM, amounting to nearly half a million people [5–8]. This figure represents 'true' NIDDM, i.e. not simply those receiving diet and/or drug treatment. Classification by treatment alone is likely to yield erroneous proportions of the two types of diabetes. Patterns of insulin treatment in NIDDM are extremely variable and indeed, many NIDDM patients may be quite wrongly treated with insulin [9, 10].

In other parts of the world, the prevalence of NIDDM is considerably different (Chapter 7). The disease is generally less common in Africa, whereas the Pima Indians of Arizona and the inhabitants of the Micronesian island of Nauru are celebrated examples of especially high NIDDM rates (50% and 30% of these populations, respectively). Other examples are shown in Table 4.1, demonstrating also the increased risk of developing diabetes when populations become urbanized. Immigrant populations are also at high risk — for example, Asian immigrants in the UK may have NIDDM rates 4 times those of their home populations [6] (Chapter 91), the prevalence being similar or even greater amongst Asian immigrants elsewhere [13].

Clinical features of NIDDM

An important feature of NIDDM is that it comprises two distinct subgroups, differing in both pathophysiology and management. These are *obese* and *non-obese* NIDDM (Fig. 4.1). Obesity is certainly a major problem in NIDDM; some 54% of males and 73% of females are over 120% of their ideal body weight at presentation [14]. Reduced insulin secretory capacity is thought to be the major defect in non-obese NIDDM, whereas insulin resistance is generally considered to be the hallmark of obese NIDDM [1]; indeed, such patients are often actually hyperinsulinaemic as measured by conventional radioimmunoassay — but see Chapters 22 and 35. The therapeutic consequences are that the non-obese patient should be initially treated with a normo-caloric diet excluding refined carbohydrate; if this gives inadequate control, a

Table 4.1. Prevalence rates of NIDDM in different geographical locations (after Zimmet 1982 [12]).

Ethnic group	Prevalence (%)
Pima Indians (Arizona)	50
Nauru (Micronesians)	30
Fiji (Melanesians)	2 rural
	7 urban
Fiji (Indians)	13 rural
	15 urban

sulphonylurea drug is added. For the obese patient, initial treatment is a weight-reducing diet (also sugar-free), with metformin often used as second-line drug treatment.

A second major consideration is that NIDDM usually (but by no means always) presents later in life. About 70% of patients are over 55 years of age [15]. In a British community-based survey of 640 patients with established NIDDM, the mean age was 67 years and the age at diagnosis 59 years [8]. Table 3.1 shows that, with increasing age, the proportion of the diabetic population treated with insulin falls. In absolute terms, the total prevalence of diabetes rises with age, some 3–5% or more of the population over 75 years of age having the disease [16]. An overall male preponderance of NIDDM has been described (approximately 3:2, male:female) [14] and strong genetic factors are demonstrated by some 40% of patients having a first-degree relative with NIDDM [14]. These important clinical and epidemiological features of NIDDM are summarized in Table 4.2.

The classical symptoms of NIDDM are those of hyperglycaemia (thirst, polyuria) and fatigue. The onset is, however, more insidious than in IDDM, and marked weight loss is not a frequent feature. The major forms of presentation are shown in Table 4.3. It is of particular interest that only just over half of the patients present because of classic diabetic symptoms. The rest are discovered indirectly — for example, because of the incidental finding of glycosuria (at insurance or work medical examinations, or during hospital admissions or clinic visits), intercurrent infections (usually genital candidiasis or urinary tract infections), or established microvascular complications of diabetes (usually retinopathy detected by ophthalmic opticians, but sometimes foot ulceration and/or neuropathy).

A typical presentation is illustrated by the Case History (overleaf).

• Very common	75% of all diabetic patients (500 000 in UK)
• Disease of ageing	Most patients >60 years
• Obesity common	Two-thirds are overweight
• Genetic factors	40% have family history
• Male predominance	3:2 male excess

Table 4.2. Some important statistics concerning NIDDM.

Table 4.3. Modes of presentation of NIDDM (UK Prospective Diabetes Study 1988 [14]).

Diabetic symptoms	53%
Incidental finding (usually glycosuria)	29%
Infections (e.g. candidiasis)	16%
Complications (e.g. retinopathy) detected by an optician	2%

The natural history of NIDDM

NIDDM is a heterogeneous condition affecting predominantly older people with relatively short life expectancies. It is therefore difficult to define the natural history of this disease. There is, however, little clinical doubt that, in general, B-cell function tends to deteriorate in NIDDM as the years go by. Consequently, some patients initially controlled by diet will eventually progress to oral hypoglycaemic agents, and similarly some who start with oral agents will eventually require insulin for satisfactory glycaemic control (even though most remain strictly non-insulin-dependent). Study of these treatment changes might give important information as to the natural history of NIDDM, although other factors affect treatment patterns. In particular, poor patient compliance (especially with diet) will greatly affect glycaemic control and may necessitate transfer from diet to oral agents or from these to insulin. There is also considerable variability in medical opinion as to when and whether to initiate drug or insulin therapy. The decision to use insulin is particularly difficult, as this may be associated with weight gain and possibly increased atherogenic risk; there may be little or no improvement in eventual glycaemic control [17]. Bearing in mind the limitations

Case history: Non-insulin-dependent diabetes mellitus

JT, 57-year-old publisher.

1 April
Attended surgical vascular clinic for assessment of intermittent claudication of 3 months duration.
• Weight 88 kg (ideal body weight = 72 kg).
• Routine urinalysis showed 2% glucose, no ketones.
• Random blood glucose 13 mmol/l.
• Femoral and carotid bruits noted.
• Referred to diabetic clinic.

3 April
Attended diabetic clinic.
• Urine: 2% glucose, no ketones.
• Random blood glucose 12.1 mmol/l; HbA_1 14% (HbA_1 non-diabetic range 5.0–8.0%).
• On direct questioning, admitted to minor thirst and nocturia for several months.
• Weight-reducing diet prescribed by dietitian.
• Discussion about diabetes with diabetes nurse, shown how to measure blood glucose.

10 April
Attended diabetic clinic.
• Following diet rigidly (on his admission); blood glucose levels at home 11–17 mmol/l.
• 1% glycosuria; fasting blood glucose 9.8 mmol/l.

30 June
• Weight 80 kg; home blood glucose levels 7–9 mmol/l.
• Fasting blood glucose 9.5 mmol/l; HbA_1 11%.
• Claudication distance unchanged.

2 August
• Weight 74 kg, home blood glucose levels 7–9 mmol/l.
• Fasting blood glucose, 8.2 mmol/l; HbA_1 9.5%.
• Prescribed glibenclamide 2.5 mg with breakfast.

14 September
• Weight 75 kg; home blood glucose levels around 7 mmol/l.
• Fasting blood glucose, 7.1 mmol/l; HbA_1 8.0%.
• For shared-care, transferred to family doctor; next out-patient appointment in 12 months.

Table 4.4. Causes of mortality in non-insulin-dependent (NIDDM), compared with insulin-dependent (IDDM) diabetes (Marks & Krall 1971 [20]).

	NIDDM (%)	IDDM (%)
Cardiovascular disease	58	15
Cerebrovascular disease	12	3
Nephropathy	3	55
Diabetic 'coma'	1	4
Malignancy	11	0
Infections	4	10
Other	11	13

of data related to the treatment of NIDDM, a recent British survey suggests that about 15–20% of NIDDM patients are receiving insulin treatment [5, 8].

The outcome and prognosis of NIDDM

As mentioned in Chapter 3, both IDDM and NIDDM carry the risk of long-term diabetic com-

Fig. 4.1. The size of the problem: two distinct clinical subgroups of NIDDM, the non-obese and the obese. Aetiological factors differ, as does their management.

plications, including the specific microvascular diseases (retinopathy, nephropathy and neuropathy) and the non-specific macrovascular problems of occlusive atherosclerotic disease affecting heart, brain and legs. The patient with NIDDM is more likely to be troubled by large-vessel disease, partly because NIDDM generally appears at a time of life when arteriosclerotic problems are frequent even in the non-diabetic population. In addition, these patients frequently have many other adverse arteriosclerotic risk factors such as obesity, hyperlipidaemia, hypertension (which is more common in diabetic people [18]) and smoking (at least as frequent amongst diabetic as non-diabetic subjects [19]).

Peripheral vascular disease may cause intermittent claudication and gangrene, sometimes requiring amputation. Together with neuropathy, it is a major cause of the diabetic foot syndrome, a source of considerable morbidity and cost to the health services. Cerebrovascular disease presents as transient ischaemic attacks or stroke, which is commoner amongst diabetic patients and carries a higher mortality than in the non-diabetic population [20, 21] (see Table 4.4). It is coronary artery disease, however, which is the main scourge of NIDDM. Angina afflicts 17% or more of patients [4] and ultimately nearly 60% die from ischaemic heart disease as compared with 15% of patients with IDDM [20] (see Table 4.4). As with stroke, myocardial infarction is more common in diabetes [22] and also carries a worse prognosis [23]: the mortality is about double the rate in non-diabetic subjects. Overall mortality in NIDDM is increased 2–3 fold and life expectancy is reduced by 5–10 years compared with the general population [24, 25].

Interestingly, the mortality risk does not seem particularly related to the duration of the disease [15]; indeed, for NIDDM patients diagnosed over the age of 75 years, mortality is similar to that of their age-matched non-diabetic counterparts [24].

Table 4.5. Medical problems and diabetic complications in NIDDM (Gill 1986 [4]).

Retinopathy	17%
Cataracts	14%
Painful neuropathy	8%
Foot ulcers	3%
Angina	17%
Claudication	12%

It is hoped that the present treatment strategies in diabetes and greater efforts to correct other atherogenic risk factors will improve the prognosis of NIDDM in the future.

As mentioned, the specific microvascular complications of diabetes are less prominent in NIDDM than in IDDM, but they still provide cause for concern. The major problems are summarized in Table 4.5. Retinopathy and cataracts each affect about 15% of patients. Maculopathy is an especially common form of retinopathy in NIDDM and may threaten vision [26]; by contrast, proliferative retinopathy (the commonest cause of blindness in IDDM) is rare. Nephropathy is probably as likely to develop in NIDDM as it is in IDDM [26], although its prevalence is lower because NIDDM patients usually have a shorter exposure to diabetes and less opportunity to progress to end-stage nephropathy with renal failure. Finally, neuropathy is a common complication and causes serious morbidity in a substantial proportion of NIDDM patients, about 8% of whom have painful (rather than asymptomatic) neuropathy [4]. At least one-third of male NIDDM patients, when directly questioned, have some degree of impotence [27].

The challenge of NIDDM

The error in regarding NIDDM as 'mild diabetes' [4] is now well recognized, as is its importance as a major cause of disability and premature death. These problems are accentuated by the very large numbers of patients concerned — considerably more than those with the insulin-dependent variety of the disease. The particularly high prevalence of NIDDM in the elderly [16], and in immigrant populations [6], poses a particular logistic challenge to the organization of diabetic care. Fortunately, these challenges are now being met, with increasing devolution of the care of NIDDM patients to the community, usually in a well-structured 'shared-care' system combining the resources of the hospital diabetic clinic and the family doctor [28].

Significant numbers of NIDDM patients are asymptomatic [14], and many undiagnosed patients are present in the community [29]. This raises a controversial issue as to whether widespread screening programmes should be introduced to detect and treat the disease before it is clinically apparent. Such strategies may be difficult to justify as there remains fundamental disagreement as to whether early treatment of NIDDM reduces the risk of future complications and improves the ultimate outcome of the disease [30].

GEOFFREY V. GILL

References

1 Cahill GF. Beta cell deficiency, insulin resistance, or both? N Engl J Med 1988; **318**: 1268–9.

2 Tattersall RB. Mild familial diabetes with dominant inheritance. Q J Med 1974; **43**: 339–57.

3 Pirart J. Diabetes mellitus and its degenerative complications: a prospective study of 4,400 patients observed between 1947 and 1973. Diabetes Care 1978; **1**: 168–88.

4 Gill GV. Type 2 diabetes — is it 'mild diabetes'? Practical Diabetes 1986; **3**: 280–2.

5 Gatling W, Houston AC, Hill RD. An epidemiological survey: the prevalence of diabetes mellitus in a typical English community. J R Coll Physicians Lond 1985; **4**: 248–50.

6 Mather HM, Keen H. The Southall Diabetes Survey: prevalence of known diabetes in Asians and Europeans. Br Med J 1985; **291**: 1081–4.

7 Neill HAW, Gatling W, Mather HM, Thompson AV, Thorogood M, Fowler GH, Hill RD, Mann JI. The Oxford Community Diabetes Study — evidence for an increase in the prevalence of known diabetes in Great Britain. Diabetic Med 1987; **4**: 539–43.

8 Gatling W, Mullee M, Hill R. General characteristics of a community-based diabetic population. Practical Diabetes 1988; **5**: 104–7.

9 Rendell M. C-peptide levels as a criterion in the treatment of maturity-onset diabetes. J Clin End Metab 1983; **57**: 1198–206.

10 Cohen M, Crosbie C, Cusworth L, Zimmet P. Insulin — not always a life sentence: withdrawal of insulin therapy in non-insulin dependent diabetes. Diabetes Res 1984; **1**: 31–4.

11 Gill GV. Metabolic diseases. In: Manson-Bahr PEC, Bell DR, eds. Manson's Tropical Diseases, 19th edn. Baillière-Tindall, 1987: Ch. 66.

12 Zimmet P. Type 2 (non-insulin dependent) diabetes — an epidemiological overview. Diabetologia 1982; **22**: 399–411.

13 Campbell GD. Diabetes in Asians and Africans in and around Durban. S Afr Med J 1963; **37**: 1195–208.

14 Multi-centre study. UK Prospective Diabetes Study. IV. Characteristics of newly presenting type 2 diabetic patients: male preponderance and obesity at different ages. Diabetic Med 1988; **5**: 154–9.

15 Nathan DM, Singer DE, Godine JE, Perlmuter LC. Non-insulin dependent diabetes in older patients. Complications and risk factors. Am J Med 1986; **81**: 837–42.

16 Petri MP, Gatling W, Petri L, Hill RD. Diabetes in the elderly — an epidemiological perspective. Pract Diabetes 1986; **3**: 153–5.

17 Tattersall RB, Scott AR. When to use insulin in the maturity onset diabetic. Postgrad Med J 1987; **63**: 859–64.

18 Barrett-Connor E, Criqui MH, Klauber MR, Holdbook M. Diabetes and hypertension in a community of older adults. Am J Epidemiol 1981; **113**: 276–84.

19 Kyne DA, Gill GV. Management deficiencies in Type 2 diabetes. Practical Diabetes 1987; **4**: 57–8.

20 Marks HH, Krall LP. Onset, course, prognosis and mortality of diabetes mellitus. In: Marble A, White P et al., eds.

Joslin's Diabetes Mellitus, 11th edn. Philadelphia: Lea & Febiger, 1971: 209–54.

21 Oppenheimer SM, Hoffbrand BI, Oswald GA, Yudkin JS. Diabetes mellitus and early mortality from stroke. *Br Med J* 1985; **291**: 1014–5.

22 Rytter L, Troelsen S, Beck-Nielsen H. Prevalence and mortality of acute myocardial infarction in patients with diabetes. *Diabetes Care* 1985; **8**: 230–4.

23 Gwilt D. Why do diabetic patients die after myocardial infarction? *Practical Diabetes* 1984; **1**: 36–9.

24 Panzram G. Mortality and survival in Type 2 (non-insulin dependent) diabetes mellitus. *Diabetologia* 1987; **30**: 123–31.

25 Goodkin G. Mortality factors in diabetes. *J Occup Med* 1975; **17**: 716–21.

26 Watkins PJ, Grenfell A, Edmonds M. Diabetic complications of non-insulin dependent diabetes. *Diabetic Med* 1987; **4**: 293–6.

27 McCulloch DK, Campbell IW, Wu FC, Prescott RJ, Clarke BF. The prevalence of diabetic impotence. *Diabetologia* 1980; **18**: 279–83.

28 Home P, Walford S. Diabetes care: whose responsibility? *Br Med J* 1984; **289**: 713–4.

29 Simmons D, Williams DRR, Powell MJ. Prevalence of diabetes in a predominantly Asian community: preliminary findings of the Coventry diabetes study. *Br Med J* 1989; **298**: 18–21.

30 Moses RG, Colagiuri S, Shannon AG. Effectiveness of mass screening for diabetes mellitus using random capillary blood glucose measurements. *Med J Aust* 1985; **143**: 544–6.

5 Public Health Problems of Diabetes and its Cost to the Community

Summary

• The economic costs of diabetes, which include effects on morbidity, employment, productivity, premature mortality and the use of Health Service resources, render the disease a major influence on the provision of world health care.

• Hospital admission rates for diabetes were recorded as 2.8% of all admissions in the UK (1981) and 7.2% in the USA (1983).

• The acute bed occupancy for diabetic patients is about 5–6 times higher than for non-diabetic subjects, and it is particularly high in the elderly and in children (diabetic girls are 15–20 times more likely to occupy a bed).

• In developed countries, the cost of diabetes to society may be estimated to be about 4–5% of the total health care costs; the burden for developing countries is unknown and is an important area for future research.

The impact of diabetes on personal and public health is already considerable [1] and, in several areas of the world, is increasing. In most countries for which data exist, the disease is sufficiently common and its adverse effects on morbidity, employment, productivity and premature mortality sufficiently great for diabetes to rank as one of the most important influences on world health. In order to appreciate the clinical significance of diabetes and the importance of its prevention, the effects of diabetes on society must be fully understood. Yet, in many respects, the public health problem of diabetes is underestimated.

Other chapters consider the incidence, prevalence and mortality rates for diabetes (Chapter 7) and its complications. Chapter 92 will deal with employment and productivity. These issues are not considered here except where relevant to estimates of cost. Such data, however, enable only part of the financial and social burden of diabetes to be measured, as diabetic individuals need frequent and sometimes intensive contact with health services.

The use of health services by patients with diabetes

Hospital admissions

In England and Wales in 1981, patients with diabetes accounted for 2.8% of the total hospital admissions recorded [2]. The admission rates for diabetes as the principal diagnosis vary geographically within England and Wales, with higher figures in the North and West, and such rates rose generally in the decade 1968–78 [3].

Equivalent admission rates in North America are considerably higher, possibly because of differences in data collection, disease definition and clinical practice. In 1983, the United States National Hospital Discharge Survey recorded 2.8 million hospital admissions in diabetic patients, with diabetes given as the primary diagnosis in 675 000 cases. Diabetic patients accounted for 7.2% of total admissions, the hospitalization rate being 2.4 times that for the non-diabetic population [4].

The impact of diabetes on hospital in-patient facilities is better gauged by hospital bed occupancy rather than admission rates. This is partly because many diabetes-related disorders such as ketoacidosis or peripheral vascular disease require relatively long hospital stays, and also because diabetes itself, even when not directly related to the main cause of admission, tends to prolong hospital stays, especially for children and the elderly.

Studies of IDDM patients in Denmark [5] and of all forms of diabetes in the UK [6] have suggested that patients with diabetes have around 5–6 times the acute hospital bed occupancy of non-diabetic patients. Absolute rates for bed occupancy are high for the diabetic elderly (especially women) [6, 7] but the contrast between diabetic and non-diabetic usage is most marked for children aged under 15, where rates for the general population are low. Compared with their non-diabetic peers, diabetic girls are 15–20 times and boys 7–10 times more likely to occupy an acute hospital bed [6].

Out-patient services and primary care

Hospital admission data are very difficult to collect and assess, but the situation is even worse for out-patient services and for primary care. Information on the use of out-patient services has been used to evaluate the costs described below [8, 9, 10]. However, reliable data on the use of these facilities are lacking for many countries and, as geographical variations in the pattern of diabetes care and referral are likely to be considerable, extrapolation from local studies cannot usually be justified.

Limited data on primary care are available but, in most countries, derive from a relatively small number of volunteer, 'sentinel' practices which cannot be taken as representative of primary care as a whole. In the UK, 48 such practices contributed data to the 1981–2 survey of general practice morbidity [11]. 'Disease episode' rates for diabetes are compared with those for myocardial infarc-

tion and cerebrovascular disease in Table 5.1. A 'disease episode' was defined in this survey as 'an instance or period of sickness during which there was one or more [general practitioner] consultation'. The incidence of diabetes-related episodes was greater than those for the two comparison diseases for most age groups. However, rates for all three were considerably lower than those for the two groups of disorders which dominate in general practice in the UK, namely depressive disorders (72 episodes/1000 persons at risk; all ages, both sexes) and upper respiratory tract infections (124/1000).

Studies of primary care in the UK have consistently shown that the proportion of diabetic patients attending hospital clinics for the care of their diabetes is low — around 50% for inner city practices and between 20 and 30% for suburban and rural practices [2]. Less well documented, although of more interest, is the number of patients who do not regularly attend any clinic, either in hospital or in general practice. The effect which this may have on prognosis is completely unknown. These areas of unmet need have important economic consequences for any attempt to improve diabetes care.

In the USA in 1980, consultations for diabetes care (visits to physicians' consulting rooms, hospital out-patient clinics or casualty departments, or contacts by telephone) made up 1.6% of total consultations [12]. National, self-reported information on the frequency of care in the USA suggests that about 50% of patients with diabetes had seen a physician for that condition during the month prior to interview and a further 30% within the previous 2–6 months. Around 10% had not seen a physician regarding their diabetes within the previous year [12].

Table 5.1. Frequency of diabetes-related disease 'episodes' (see text) in general practice compared with those for two comparison diseases. Rates are per 1000 persons at risk/year and are given here for selected age groups only [11].

Disease group	All ages	25–44 y	45–64 y	65–74 y	75 y and over
Diabetes (ICD* 250)	7.7	3.3	12.6	24.9	25.1
Myocardial infarction (ICD 410, 411)	4.3	1.0	8.1	13.6	16.6
Stroke (ICD 430–4, 436–8, except 437.2)	4.3	0.2	3.5	14.5	36.7

* ICD: International Classification of Diseases, 9th revision.

Studies of the economics of diabetes and diabetic health care

This section will describe attempts to estimate the costs of diabetes to the individual or to society. Recently, Songer [13] has extensively reviewed studies based in the USA (reference [10], for example), Canada [14], Sweden [9] and Australia [15]. Other workers have addressed the same questions in the UK [8, 16, 17] and in France [18]. All these published studies relate to developed countries, in which the prevalence of diabetes lies between 1 and 5%. The large and growing economic burden of diabetes on the health of developing countries, where the prevalence of NIDDM may be considerably greater (Chapter 7), is largely undocumented and must be regarded as a priority for future research in this field.

Songer lists five main approaches appropriate to explore aspects of the cost of diabetes [13], of which the 'human capital' model, usually attributed to Rice [19], has been most commonly used to assess its cost to society rather than to the individual. Using published statistics (hospital admissions, absence from work, mortality, etc.), this method calculates expenditure on health care (hospital admissions, out-patient and primary care) and estimates certain 'indirect costs' (such as productivity lost through sickness and premature death, and the costs of sickness and invalidity benefits attributable to the disease and its complications). The human capital approach has several limitations. First, it assumes that productivity losses during, for example, sickness absence equals the sum which would have been paid to the employee for work done during the lost time. Other assumptions have to be made in the apportionment of hospital costs between diagnostic categories [3, 8]. Another important drawback of this method in assessing the cost of multisystem diseases such as diabetes is that contributions to the cost of other chronic diseases (for example, ischaemic heart disease) are not included. Most categories of cost are therefore underestimated.

Isolated figures for the costs of any one disease are difficult to interpret unless set against similar estimates for other diseases, or compared with the country's current total health care budget. Figure 5.1 compares Laing's human capital estimate of the cost of diabetes (total M£161.3) with those for ischaemic heart disease (M£732.7 — including a large contribution from sickness absence from work) and cerebrovascular disease

(M£476.7 — including a large contribution from health care costs) [14]. These estimates were for England and Wales in 1979/80, at a time when the total health care budget was around M£4600. Separate figures were given for estimated numbers of years lost (before the age of 65) as a result of premature death. These cost estimates can be updated, at least to take account of inflation, but there are many reasons why it might be misleading to do so. In particular, a number of important changes — the wider use of disposable syringes, home blood glucose monitoring and the availability of testing strips on prescription — have been introduced since these estimates were compiled, and their influence on health care costs have not yet been fully assessed.

Entmacher et al. [10], using similar methods, estimated that the costs of diabetes in North America rose from M$2589 in 1969 to M$13750 in

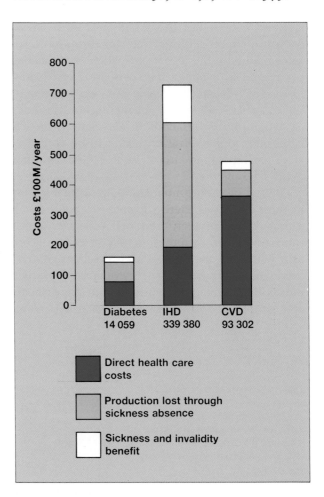

Fig. 5.1. Comparative costs of diabetes, ischaemic heart disease (IHD), and cerebrovascular disease (CVD) as assessed by Laing (1979/80 data [8]). Figures under each condition are estimated years of life lost through premature mortality (under 65 years).

1984. The relative contribution (5.4%) of diabetes health care costs to the 1984 total for diabetes is similar to that calculated by Laing for the UK, as is the total for diabetes when expressed as a percentage of the national health care budget (4%). Jönsson, in his estimate for Sweden [9], was able to apportion diabetic health care costs to individual complications, and found that the contribution of peripheral vascular disease was particularly important, making up 15% of total diabetic health care costs.

Relatively little work has been carried out on the personal costs of diabetes to patients and their relatives. Recent unpublished work from the USA (T.J. Songer et al., personal communication) suggests that a child diagnosed with IDDM at the age of seven will face costs of around $52 000 as a result of diabetes from the time of diagnosis until the age of 40. The health-care component of this total is substantial ($25 000), although the extent to which the individual and the family have to pay this from their own resources will clearly depend on the health-care system of the country in which they live. The methods employed in this study (ascertainment of cases from a diabetes register and direct enquiry about hospital admissions, insulin use, blood and urine monitoring, etc.) merit wider application.

The importance of economic analysis

To some, attempts to assess the costs of diabetes or evaluate the cost effectiveness of various methods of diabetes care will seem, at best, irrelevant or, at worst, distasteful. It should be appreciated, however, that the term 'costs' as used in this context includes, rather than excludes, the inconvenience and suffering caused to the patient by diabetes and its consequences. Attempts have not been made to quantify such costs but this is because of methodological difficulties and not because they are, in any way, considered irrelevant.

Studies concerning the cost-effectiveness of various approaches to diabetes care (such as screening, education and treatment programmes) are beyond the scope of the present discussion, but will undoubtedly help in deciding how to provide this care in the future.

It is useful to make assessments, however crude, of the economic consequences of a disease such as diabetes. Decisions about attempts to prevent diabetes or improving diabetes care are more soundly made if some estimate of the economic consequences of the disease is available. The cost of diabetes care in an average NHS district has been estimated at M£1.44 per year at 1988 prices [20]. Such estimates can, and should, become part of the reasoning behind attempts to improve diabetes management and so reduce the extent to which consequences of the disease consume scarce health-care resources. Economic analyses of diabetes are an additional dimension to our appreciation of the magnitude of the problems of the disease and an aid rather than a hindrance in our attempts to solve them.

D.R.R. WILLIAMS

References

1 Keen H. Diabetes mellitus: a problem in personal and public health. In: *Oxford Textbook of Public Health*, Vol 4. Oxford: Oxford Medical Publications, 1986: 268–78.

2 Williams DRR. Health services for patients with diabetes. In: Jarrett RJ, ed. *Diabetes Mellitus*. London: Croom Helm, 1986: 57–75.

3 Robinson N, Edmeades SP, Fuller JH. Recent changes in diabetic mortality and morbidity in England and Wales. *Health Trends* 1984: **16**: 33–7.

4 Sinnock P. Hospital utilization for diabetes. In: *Diabetes in America*. NIH: US Department of Health and Human Services, 1985: XXVI-1–XXVI-11.

5 Green A, Solander F. Epidemiological studies of diabetes mellitus in Denmark: 6. Use of hospital services by insulin-treated diabetic patients. *Diabetologia* 1984; **26**: 195–8.

6 Williams DRR. Hospital admissions of diabetic patients: information from Hospital Activity Analysis. *Diabetic Med* 1985; **2**: 27–32.

7 Damsgaard EM, Frøland A, Green A. Use of hospital services by elderly diabetics: the Frederica study of diabetic and fasting hyperglycaemia patients aged 60–74 years. *Diabetic Med* 1987; **4**: 317–22.

8 Laing WA. The cost of diet-related disease. In: Turner MR, ed. *Preventive Nutrition and Society*. London: Academic Press, 1981: 55–76.

9 Jönsson B. Diabetes — the cost of illness and the cost of control. An estimate for Sweden 1978. *Acta Med Scand Suppl* 1983; **671**: 19–27.

10 Entmacher PS, Sinnock S, Bostic E, Harris MI. Economic impact of diabetes. In: *Diabetes in America*. NIH: US Department of Health and Human Services, 1985: XXXII-1–XXXII-13.

11 Royal College of General Practitioners, Office of Population Censuses and Surveys, Department of Health and Social Security. *Morbidity Statistics from General Practice 1981–82*. London: HMSO, 1986. Series MB5, No. 1.

12 Harris MI. Ambulatory medical care for diabetes. In: *Diabetes in America*. NIH: US Department of Health and Human Services, 1985: XXXV-1–XXXV-13.

13 Songer TJ. The economics of diabetes care. In: Alberti KGMM, DeFronzo RA, Keen H, Zimmet P, eds. *International Textbook of Diabetes*, John Wiley, in press.

14 Bain M, Ross SA. Socio-economic impact of diabetes mellitus. In: Chiasson L-P, Hunt J, Hepworth HP, Ross S, Tan

M, Zinman B, eds. *Status of Diabetes in Canada*. A project of the Association du Diabète du Québec, the Canadian Diabetes Association and the Juvenile Diabetes Foundation Canada, 1987.

15 Australian Diabetes Foundation. *Diabetes in Australia*. A statement by the Australian Diabetes Foundation, 1986.

16 Office of Health Economics. *The Pattern of diabetes*. London: Office of Health Economics, 1964.

17 Office of Health Economics. *The costs of medical care*. London: Office of Health Economics, 1964.

18 Triomphe A, Flori YA, Costagliola D, Eschwège E. The cost of diabetes in France. *Health Policy* 1988; **9**: 39−48.

19 Rice DP, Hodgson TA, Kopstein AN. The economic costs of illness: a replication and update. *Health Care Financing Rev* 1985; **7**: 61−80.

20 Alexander WD. Diabetes care in the South East Thames Region of the United Kingdom. *Diabetes Med* 1988; **5**: 577−8.

SECTION 3
CLASSIFICATION AND DIAGNOSIS OF DIABETES MELLITUS

6 Classification and Diagnosis of Diabetes Mellitus and Impaired Glucose Tolerance

Summary

• The diabetic syndrome is characterized by chronic hyperglycaemia. Clinical features include symptoms and signs primarily related to the severity of the metabolic disturbance.

• The syndrome has several well-defined causes but those of the more common types are only partially understood.

• The WHO classification (1980 and 1985), based on the US National Diabetes Data Group recommendations, is now generally accepted. Individuals fall within a single class (defined by simple clinical and biochemical descriptions) at any one time, but their classification may change in the course of time.

• *Insulin-dependent diabetes mellitus* (IDDM) and *non-insulin-dependent diabetes mellitus* (NIDDM) are distinguished by the propensity to develop ketosis and the dependency on insulin treatment for survival in the former class.

• *Malnutrition-related diabetes mellitus* occurs primarily in tropical developing countries, and is associated with nutritional deficiency and the absence of spontaneous ketosis.

• *Other types of diabetes mellitus* are associated with well-defined conditions such as chronic pancreatitis, haemochromatosis, endocrine disorders, drug administration, mutant insulins and insulin receptor abnormalities.

• *Gestational diabetes* is that which occurs for the first time during pregnancy.

• *Impaired glucose tolerance* (IGT) describes hyperglycaemia during an oral glucose tolerance test (OGTT), but below the levels diagnostic of diabetes. These subjects have an increased risk of developing diabetes subsequently and are vulnerable to macrovascular disease.

• *Statistical risk classes* describe currently normoglycaemic individuals who either have had a previous abnormality of glucose tolerance (e.g. gestational diabetes or IGT), or have a potential abnormality (e.g. normal subjects with islet cell antibodies, or HLA identical siblings of diabetic patients). Both classes are at increased risk of developing diabetes.

• Diabetes can be diagnosed in symptomatic patients by a grossly elevated random blood or plasma glucose concentration, or by two fasting values above a specified range (whole blood glucose >6.7 mmol/l, or plasma glucose >7.8 mmol/l).

• When doubt exists, a formal 75-g OGTT must be performed. The WHO diagnostic criteria applied to the venous plasma glucose level 2 h after the load define diabetes as >11.1 mmol/l, IGT as between 7.8 and 11.1 mmol/l, and normal glucose tolerance as <7.8 mmol/l.

• Urinary glucose, or HbA_1 or other glycated protein measurements, should not be used to diagnose diabetes.

Diabetes is characterized by chronic hyperglycaemia and disordered carbohydrate, lipid and protein metabolism and is associated with the development of specific microvascular complications and of non-specific macrovascular disease. In the vast majority of cases, the diagnosis can be made with reasonable certainty but the underlying aetiology and pathogenesis remain largely obscure.

Historical background

That diabetes is a syndrome rather than a single disease was recognized in 1875 by Bouchardat [1], who distinguished 'diabète maigre' and 'diabète gras' as two types carrying different prognoses and requiring different management. Early in the present century, diabetes was classified according to age of onset or severity of the metabolic disturbance, using terms such as 'juvenile-onset' and 'maturity-onset', 'brittle' and 'stable' diabetes. In the 1930s, the term 'secondary diabetes' was introduced to define the relatively rare cases associated with specific disorders such as haemochromatosis, acromegaly and chronic pancreatitis.

The view that the commoner forms of diabetes were not a single disease then slowly re-emerged. In 1936, Himsworth characterized diabetes as 'insulin sensitive' or 'insulin resistant' [2], and he later stated that 'diabetes is not one disease entity, but a syndrome which includes a group of disorders differing in their clinical features, biochemistry and causes' [3]. R.D. Lawrence [4] identified two main classes of diabetic patient, namely those who were insulin-deficient and those who probably were not. In addition to the common 'lipoplethoric diabetes' (associated with obesity and without ketosis) and insulin-deficient diabetes (characterized by ketosis and, in the absence of insulin treatment, coma), he further distinguished secondary forms due to primary pancreatic destruction, primary endocrine disease and disorders of fat storage (notably lipoatrophic diabetes) [4]. Lawrence's classification was supported by Harris [5], who suggested that 'the insulin deficient type and the lipoplethoric type tended to run separately in families and may be due to separate genetic influences'.

In 1955, Hugh-Jones [6] distinguished Type 1 and Type 2 diabetes by clinical criteria. Type 1 diabetes affected 'young people who are often underweight; it is severe in that the patient depends on the administration of insulin to prevent ketosis'. By contrast, Type 2 diabetes was 'mild and characteristically arises in middle age patients who are often obese (lipoplethoric diabetes of Lawrence) and seldom requires insulin except during added infection'. Hugh-Jones also described 'J-type' diabetes in Jamaica affecting young adults or children who required high insulin dosages but were not prone to ketosis (see Chapter 26).

In the meantime, the terms 'juvenile-onset' and 'adult-' or 'maturity-onset' diabetes came into general use as clinical diagnoses with therapeutic implications, but the concept that they might have different causes had not yet developed. Various other terms (e.g. potential diabetes, prediabetes, latent diabetes, asymptomatic diabetes, chemical diabetes, subclinical diabetes and overt diabetes) were used inconsistently, causing confusion rather than clarification; they are now obsolete.

In 1976, the late Andrew Cudworth recognized that diabetes is a clinically heterogeneous disorder and suggested discarding the rigid terms 'juvenile-onset' and 'maturity-onset' in favour of 'Type 1' and 'Type 2' diabetes, respectively [7]. He justified the classification by pointing out that insulin-dependent (Type 1) patients were distinguished by the then recently established HLA associations [8] and by the occurrence of islet-cell antibodies, implying a specific aetiology (see Chapters 14 and 15). Bottazzo and Doniach [9] supported Cudworth's classification but emphasized that insulin requirement is sometimes delayed in individuals who are islet-cell antibody positive and that Type 1 diabetes is not necessarily insulin-dependent at the time of diagnosis (even though it usually becomes so later). Irvine [10] later subdivided Type 1 diabetes according to whether the islets were destroyed by genetically determined autoimmune disease (Type 1a), a viral infection or other agent (Type 1c), or a combination of the two (Type 1b); this subclassification reflected the then-current notion that viral

Table 6.1. 1985 WHO classification of diabetes mellitus and allied categories of glucose intolerance.

A. CLINICAL CLASSES

Diabetes mellitus
- *Insulin-dependent diabetes mellitus (IDDM)*
- *Non-insulin-dependent diabetes mellitus (NIDDM)*
  (a) Non-obese
  (b) Obese
- *Malnutrition-related diabetes mellitus (MRDM)*
- *Other types of diabetes mellitus* associated with specific conditions and syndromes (see Table 6.2 for details)
- *Gestational diabetes mellitus (GDM)*

Impaired glucose tolerance (IGT)
(a) Non-obese
(b) Obese
(c) Associated with certain conditions and syndromes

B. STATISTICAL RISK CLASSES
Previous abnormality of glucose tolerance
Potential abnormality of glucose tolerance

infection might frequently cause insulin-dependent diabetes.

By 1978, the frequent association of insulin-dependent diabetes with certain HLA antigens and islet-cell antibodies was widely recognized. The National Diabetes Data Group (NDDG) in the USA published a provisional consensus classification [11], which became the basis for that recommended by the World Health Organization Expert Committee on Diabetes in 1980 [12].

The WHO classification represented a landmark by providing standardized diagnostic criteria for diabetes and a uniform terminology suitable for clinical and epidemiological research, which have now been widely adopted. A subsequent WHO Study Group Report in 1985 [13] introduced a further major class of diabetes, malnutrition-related diabetes mellitus (Chapter 26).

The WHO classification of diabetes

The current WHO classification is shown in Table 6.1. The first two major clinical classes of diabetes mellitus are distinguished primarily by dependency for survival on insulin treatment.

IDDM

Insulin-dependent diabetes mellitus (IDDM) is judged to be present when the classical symptoms of diabetes (thirst, polyuria, wasting and stupor, or coma) are associated with readily detectable concentrations of glucose and ketone bodies in the blood and urine. Insulin treatment is necessary, not only to control hyperglycaemia, but to prevent spontaneous ketosis and death.

NIDDM

Non-insulin-dependent diabetes (NIDDM), although often asymptomatic, may also present with classical hyperglycaemic symptoms (thirst, polyuria, weight loss), but despite hyperglycaemia, ketone bodies are present in only low concentrations in the blood and urine. Coma is rare in NIDDM but may result from extreme hyperglycaemia and hyperosmolarity; lactic acidosis or ketoacidosis can also occur in fulminating illness (e.g. severe infection or mesenteric artery thrombosis) due to an acute increase in insulin requirements, but *spontaneous* ketosis does not occur. Some NIDDM patients later progress to a state of absolute insulin deficiency.

The categorization into these two classes is based on clinical characteristics, rather than on any information concerning their aetiology or pathogenesis. In most cases, the clinical distinction between IDDM and NIDDM is usually clear, although it may be easier at the time of diagnosis than in retrospect.

Malnutrition-related diabetes mellitus

Malnutrition-related diabetes mellitus (MRDM), the third major class, also has a heterogeneous aetiology and pathogenesis. It occurs primarily in tropical developing countries, typically in malnourished adolescents or young adults, as hyperglycaemia without spontaneous ketosis. The two distinct subclasses, fibrocalculous pancreatic diabetes and protein-deficient pancreatic diabetes, are described in detail in Chapter 26.

Other types of diabetes

The class of 'other types of diabetes' includes those associated with various specific conditions and syndromes outlined in Table 6.2.

Gestational diabetes mellitus

Gestational diabetes mellitus (GDM, see Chapter 83) is defined as diabetes which first presents or is recognized during pregnancy (thus excluding diabetic women who become pregnant). Many women will revert to normoglycaemia after parturition but are at increased risk of subsequently developing NIDDM or IDDM. Some will remain diabetic after pregnancy and there is some evidence that the incidence of IDDM is truly increased in pregnancy (Chapter 83). Women with GDM must therefore be reclassified following the conclusion of pregnancy.

Impaired glucose tolerance

Impaired glucose tolerance (IGT) is not diabetes mellitus *per se*, but describes glucose tolerance outside the range normally found in young healthy adults. These subjects are at higher risk than the general population for the future development of diabetes, and IGT may represent a stage in the natural history of NIDDM: if followed up, 10–25% will develop NIDDM within 5 years. Many will return, apparently spontaneously, to normal glucose tolerance, although their risk of subsequent

Table 6.2. *Other types of diabetes mellitus.*

1 Diabetes due to pancreatic disease
  - Chronic or recurrent pancreatitis (Chapter 27)
  - Haemochromatosis (Chapter 31)

2 Diabetes due to other endocrine disease (Chapter 28)
  - Cushing's syndrome
  - Hyperaldosteronism
  - Acromegaly
  - Thyrotoxicosis
  - Phaeochromocytoma
  - Glucagonoma

3 Diabetes due to drugs and toxins (Chapters 17 and 79)
  - Glucocorticoids and ACTH
  - Diazoxide
  - Diuretics
  - Phenytoin
  - Pentamidine
  - Vacor (rodenticide)

4 Diabetes due to abnormalities of insulin or its receptor
  - Insulinopathies (Chapter 30)
  - Receptor defects (Chapter 29)
  - Circulating antireceptor antibodies (Chapter 29)

5 Diabetes associated with genetic syndromes (Chapter 31)
  - DIDMOAD syndrome
  - Myotonic dystrophy and other muscle disorders
  - Lipoatrophy
  - Type 1 glycogen storage disease
  - Cystic fibrosis

(Table adapted from the WHO classification; see references [11−13] for further details.)

diabetes remains increased. A brief phase of IGT is occasionally identified in subjects who later develop IDDM.

Individuals with continuing IGT do not develop significant microvascular (renal, neuropathic or retinal) complications but have increased prevalences of coronary heart and arterial disease associated with premature death, as compared with age-matched normoglycaemic subjects. As a group, IGT subjects show increased frequencies of hypertension, hyperlipidaemia, obesity and fasting hyperinsulinaemia; insulin resistance may underlie the impaired glucose tolerance and possibly some of the associated abnormalities.

The WHO classification contains three subcategories of IGT, namely non-obese, obese and that associated with specified conditions including those listed under other types of diabetes (Table 6.2) and certain drugs.

A major concern in persons with IGT is whether or not the progression to diabetes and its complications can be arrested. Several studies have indicated that dietary restriction with even modest weight loss and increased exercise can achieve short-term improvement in glucose tolerance in subjects with IGT and one report suggests that treatment with tolbutamide prevented the development of diabetes [14].

Statistical risk classes

The WHO classification also contains two 'statistical risk classes', first proposed by the NDDG [11], which have not been used extensively. *Previous abnormality of glucose tolerance* consists of cases where diabetes or IGT previously existed but glucose tolerance is now normal (e.g. women who had gestational diabetes with normoglycaemia *postpartum*); this category carries a substantial risk of developing diabetes in the future. *Potential abnormality of glucose tolerance* defines individuals with normal glucose tolerance but whose risks of developing diabetes are greatly increased. This group includes normoglycaemic subjects who have islet-cell antibodies and the monozygotic-twin or HLA-identical siblings of a diabetic patient.

Justification for present classification

This classification makes it possible to categorize patients with varying degrees of glucose tolerance and provides a uniform basis for clinical research and collection of data concerning the aetiology, natural history and impact of diabetes. The basic system requires only simple clinical or biochemical observations. Subjects can be allocated only to a single class at a given time, although an individual's classification may change in the course of time. The present classification employs aetiological criteria only in the classes of MRDM, 'other types of diabetes' and IGT associated with certain conditions.

The clinical basis for classification is justified because the aetiology and pathophysiology of diabetes are unknown in most cases. The separation of IGT from the various classes of diabetes reflects the heterogeneity of glucose intolerance and emphasizes that these subjects are not inevitably destined to develop diabetes and its specific microvascular complications, although they are vulnerable to non-specific macrovascular disease.

Problems with the present classification

The WHO classification is in general use, but has a number of disadvantages. Firstly, its phenotypic criteria, although simple to apply, lack the specificity of a precise aetiopathological diagnosis.

A second is the difficulty of defining insulin dependency and proneness or resistance to ketosis in a few patients. Typical diagnostic dilemmas are the young patient whose hyperglycaemia is treated promptly with insulin and who has never suffered ketoacidosis; and older non-obese patients, who for many years have not required insulin, but who now receive insulin either to control increasing hyperglycaemia or following an episode of ketosis during intercurrent illness. The latter patients are insulin-treated and may need insulin for glycaemic control, but may or may not require insulin for survival.

A further difficulty relates to the classification of IDDM and the current usage of the term 'Type 1' diabetes. Subjects with the characteristic auto-immune features of IDDM (see Chapter 15) may be initially normoglycaemic and some will first manifest diabetes which is not insulin-dependent; hyperglycaemia may be controlled with diet or oral hypoglycaemic agents for some years before insulin dependency supervenes. Consequently, according to the WHO classification, a patient

developing IDDM may have either a potential abnormality of glucose tolerance, IGT, NIDDM or IDDM. Many authors have adopted the term 'Type 1' to describe this syndrome and, perhaps unwittingly, have introduced a two-dimensional classification, one based on aetiopathological and the other on clinical criteria. The term 'Type 1', by analogy with other disease classifications (e.g. Type 1 glycogen storage disease), tends to imply a single common aetiology. This may not be true in all cases of IDDM. The WHO Study Group in 1985 recognized this dilemma, and also the fact that the immunological and genetic markers associated with IDDM may occur in people with NIDDM. The Study Group deliberately omitted the designations Type 1 and Type 2 from their classification but conceded that, because of widespread usage, these should be regarded as completely synonymous with IDDM and NIDDM respectively and should not carry aetiopathogenic implications [13]. This may have been an unwise decision.

Diagnosis of diabetes

Casual and fasting criteria

The clinical diagnosis of diabetes is often suggested by the presence of classical hypergly-

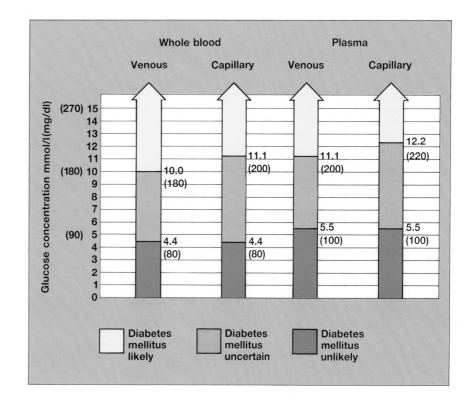

Fig. 6.1. Casual (random) blood glucose values and their interpretations (redrawn from reference [13]).

caemic symptoms and glycosuria, sometimes with drowsiness or coma. If so, the diagnosis can usually be confirmed by fasting blood or plasma glucose determinations without provocative tests. The likelihood of diabetes can also be assessed from casual or random blood glucose concentrations according to values recommended by the WHO Study Group [13] (Fig. 6.1). Single casual estimations carry considerable uncertainty. A value falling within the wide range designated 'diabetes likely' should be followed up by a formal glucose tolerance test.

Diagnostic criteria, based on fasting values and those 2 h after a standard 75-g oral glucose load are shown in Table 6.3. Whole blood glucose values are about 15% lower than the corresponding plasma values in patients with a normal haematocrit, and arterial and capillary concentrations are 7–10% higher than those in venous blood. The diagnostic thresholds therefore differ considerably depending on the source of the sample.

Interpretation of fasting glucose concentration requires care. The values may be unreliable because of incomplete fasting (10–16 h is recommended). Moreover, a fasting glucose level below the limits set in Table 6.3 by no means guarantees a normal glucose tolerance test: indeed, some three-quarters of newly diagnosed diabetic patients have 'normal' fasting glucose values [15]. For these reasons, diabetes is diagnosed when the fasting glucose concentration exceeds the defined limits (at least 6.7 mmol/l for whole venous blood, or 7.8 mmol/l for venous plasma) on more than one occasion. Values which are variable or close to these limits must be clarified by a formal glucose tolerance test.

It is obviously crucial to establish the diagnosis with confidence, as the consequences for the patient are considerable. Unless the patient presents with clear-cut symptoms and/or hyperglycaemia in the obviously diagnostic range, particular care should be taken. Equivocal glycaemic values, a high index of suspicion, or the need to refute the diagnosis all demand further investigation with an oral glucose tolerance test. The possible effects of intercurrent illness, nutritional state and drug treatment on glucose tolerance may also need consideration in individual cases.

Oral glucose tolerance test (OGTT)

The OGTT is the only form of glucose tolerance testing recommended for the diagnosis of diabetes, and is the only test for IGT. Subtle disturbances in glucose tolerance can be detected by measuring the rate of glucose disposal after an intravenous bolus injection (intravenous glucose tolerance test), but this is essentially a research procedure. The use of glycosuria as a diagnostic criterion for diabetes is obsolete, and measurements of HbA_1 or other glycated proteins are not used for diagnostic purposes.

Table 6.3. Diagnostic values for the oral glucose tolerance test.*

	Glucose concentration, mmol/l (mg/dl)			
	Whole blood		Plasma	
	Venous	Capillary	Venous	Capillary
Diabetes mellitus				
Fasting value	≥6.7	≥6.7	≥7.8	≥7.8
or	(≥120)	(≥120)	(≥140)	(≥140)
2 h after glucose load	≥10.0	≥11.1	11.1	≥12.2
	(≥180)	(≥200)	(≥200)	(≥220)
Impaired glucose tolerance				
Fasting value	<6.7	<6.7	<7.8	<7.8
and	(<120)	(<120)	(<140)	(<140)
2 h after glucose load	6.7–10.0	7.8–11.1	7.8–11.1	8.9–12.2
	(120–180)	(140–200)	(140–200)	(160–220)

* For epidemiological or population screening purposes, the 2-h value after 75-g oral glucose may be used alone. The fasting value alone is considered less reliable since true fasting cannot be assured and spurious diagnosis of diabetes may more readily occur. (Reproduced from [13] with permission.)

PROCEDURE

The OGTT should be administered in the morning after an overnight fast of 10−16 h during which only water may be drunk, and following at least three days of unrestricted diet (greater than 150 g of carbohydrate daily). Any concurrent illness or medication should be noted. Smoking and strenuous activity should not be permitted during the test. The patient may drink water to alleviate thirst.

A fasting blood sample should be taken before giving the glucose load. The subject then drinks 75 g of glucose (or a 75-g glucose equivalent load containing starch hydrolysates) in 250−300 ml of water; 235 ml of Lucozade is an acceptable alternative. Although OGTTs are seldom indicated in children, the glucose load should be adjusted to body weight and children should receive 1.75 g per kg body weight to a maximum of 75 g. The glucose load should be consumed over approximately 5 min. A further blood sample must be collected 2 h after the load; values measured at intermediate times are not required to establish the diagnosis but may confirm it.

Blood or plasma glucose concentration should be measured by a formal laboratory procedure (e.g. an autoanalyser based on the glucose oxidase or hexokinase reactions) in samples collected into fluoride−oxalate tubes which prevent the red cells from metabolizing glucose. Due to the great importance of the diagnosis, the less accurate glucose oxidase test strips should not be used. The test results should be compared with the values

in Table 6.3. Schematic examples are shown in Fig. 6.2.

1 *Diabetes* is diagnosed if the fasting values exceed those given *or* the 2-h level exceeds those specified (11.1 mmol/l in venous plasma).

2 *Impaired glucose tolerance* is present when the fasting levels are less than those specified in the table *and* the 2-h values fall within the specified range (7.8−11.1 mmol/l in venous plasma).

3 *Glucose tolerance is normal* when the fasting values are normal and the 2-h value is less than that specified for IGT (7.8 mmol/l in venous plasma).

The criteria for interpretation of the OGTT are the same regardless of the age of the subjects, even though there is evidence that glucose tolerance is relatively reduced in the elderly (Chapter 89).

Diagnosis of diabetes in special groups

Glucose tolerance in pregnancy

There is disagreement about the need to screen all women for glucose intolerance during pregnancy (see Chapter 83). In North America, it is currently recommended that between the 24th and 28th weeks of gestation, all women should receive a 50-g glucose load followed by a blood glucose measurement 1 h later [16]; positively screened subjects should then be given a 100-g OGTT, which is interpreted according to the O'Sullivan and Mahan criteria for gestational diabetes [16]. In other countries, screening for diabetes in preg-

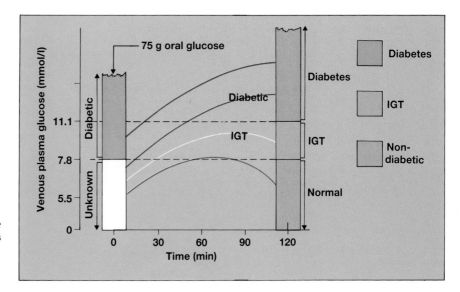

Fig. 6.2. Schematic glycaemic profiles for subjects with normal glucose tolerance, IGT and frank diabetes, during a 75-g oral glucose tolerance test. The diagnostic values are those defined by the WHO for venous plasma glucose concentrations.

nancy is less systematic, but is generally undertaken in women with glycosuria in pregnancy; a history of a stillborn or a large for gestational age infant in a previous pregnancy; evidence of fetal macrosomia or hydramnios in the current pregnancy; or a family history of diabetes.

The WHO recommends that the 75-g glucose load and standard diagnostic criteria (Table 6.3) should be used in pregnancy, exactly as in the non-pregnant state [13], although there is increasing evidence that the diagnostic limits vary both with the stage of pregnancy and the woman's ethnic origin (see Chapter 83). As discussed in Chapter 83, the pregnant woman with IGT should be managed as if she had gestational diabetes.

Diagnosis of diabetes in children

Diabetes in children usually presents with severe symptoms and marked hyperglycaemia and ketonuria, and the diagnosis can usually be confirmed by casual or fasting blood glucose measurements without recourse to the OGTT. However, a small proportion of children and adolescents with less severe symptoms and hyperglycaemia may require an OGTT for diagnosis. Apart from the variation in the recommended glucose load according to body weight, the recommended diagnostic criteria for children are the same as those for adults.

Conclusions

The current classification and diagnostic criteria of diabetes are quite different from those used a decade or more ago. The WHO criteria have gained international recognition and their utility and validity have not been seriously challenged. The category of IGT (which contains many subjects who previously might have been diagnosed diabetic) is now generally accepted.

Continuing research is elucidating the aetiology and pathogenesis of many forms of diabetes and more diabetic subjects will be classified as having a defined cause for their disease. The fact that IGT, NIDDM and IDDM can each occur in the same subject, and hence may sometimes represent different stages of the same disease process, is now widely accepted. This does not in any way invalidate the present classification, but raises the possibility of adding terms describing the cause of the syndrome to the existing classes of diabetes and IGT. To do so without introducing confusion will require the formulation of standardized definitions, criteria and terminology. Given the successful introduction of the present WHO classification and the rapid scientific advances of the past decade, this no longer seems an impossible goal.

PETER H. BENNETT

References

1 Bouchardat A. *De la Glycosurie au Diabète Sucré: son traitement hygiénique*. Paris: Germer-Ballière, 1875.
2 Himsworth HP. Diabetes mellitus: its differentiation into insulin-sensitive and insulin-insensitive types. *Lancet* 1936; i: 117–20.
3 Himsworth HP. The syndrome of diabetes mellitus and its causes. *Lancet* 1949; i: 465–73.
4 Lawrence RD. Types of human diabetes. *Br Med J* 1951; i: 373–5.
5 Harris H. The familial distribution of diabetes mellitus: a study of the relatives of 1241 diabetic propositi. *Ann Eugen* 1950; **15**: 95–119.
6 Hugh-Jones P. Diabetes in Jamaica. *Lancet* 1955; i: 891–7.
7 Cudworth AG. The aetiology of diabetes mellitus. *Br J Hosp Med* 1976; **16**: 207–16.
8 Cudworth AG. Type 1 diabetes mellitus. *Diabetologia* 1978; **14**: 281–91.
9 Bottazzo GF, Doniach D. Pancreatic autoimmunity and HLA antigens. *Lancet* 1976; ii: 800.
10 Irvine WJ. Classification of idiopathic diabetes. *Lancet* 1977; i: 638–42.
11 National Diabetes Data Group. Classification and diagnosis of diabetes mellitus and other categories of glucose intolerance. *Diabetes* 1979; **28**: 1039–57.
12 WHO Expert Committee on Diabetes Mellitus. Second Report, Geneva, Switzerland, 1980 (*WHO Technical Report Series*, No. 646).
13 *Diabetes Mellitus*. Report of a WHO Study Group, Geneva, Switzerland, 1985 (*WHO Technical Report Series*, No. 727).
14 Sartor G, Scherstén B, Carlstrom S *et al*. Ten-year follow-up of subjects with impaired glucose tolerance. *Diabetes* 1980; **29**: 41–9.
15 Harris MI, Hadden WC, Knowler WC, Bennett PH. Prevalence of diabetes and impaired glucose tolerance and plasma glucose levels in U.S. population aged 20–74 yr. *Diabetes* 1987; **36**: 523–34.
16 Summary and Recommendations of the Second International Workshop-Conference on Gestational Diabetes Mellitus. *Diabetes* 1985; **34** (suppl 2): 123–6.

SECTION 4
EPIDEMIOLOGY OF
DIABETES MELLITUS

7   The Epidemiology of Diabetes Mellitus

Summary

IDDM

- The incidence of IDDM peaks at about 11—13 years of age.
- There is a striking seasonal variation in incidence in older children and adolescents, with lowest rates in the spring and summer.
- Incidence varies enormously between countries, being 35 times higher in Finland than in Japan.
- The incidence is increasing in some countries (e.g. Finland and Scotland) but apparently not in others (e.g. USA).

NIDDM

- Prevalence varies greatly between populations, being high in North American Indians and Micronesians of the Pacific and relatively low in the UK.
- Prevalence is high in migrant populations (e.g. Indians in South Africa, Trinidad, Singapore and the UK, Japanese in the USA).
- Prevalence is often higher in urban than in rural communities.
- It is uncertain whether the rising frequency in developed countries is explicable simply by the increasing proportion of older people in the population.

The previous chapter outlines the currently accepted classification of diabetes mellitus. However, as the epidemiological features of most of the minor subdivisions of the disease have not been explored in detail, the present account will be confined to IDDM and NIDDM.

The epidemiology of IDDM

Most studies of the incidence and prevalence of IDDM have been conducted in children, adolescents and young adults. This is partly because older subjects presenting with diabetes are unlikely to have IDDM and so are often omitted from such studies, and partly because of important methodological reasons. Registers of diabetic patients are few, mainly because they are difficult and costly to set up and maintain, and it is usually necessary to use *ad hoc* methods to identify new and existing IDDM patients. In the paediatric age group, this may be done by accessing paediatricians' records and/or by using hospital admission or discharge records; for older subjects, however, routine hospital notes will not usually be adequate to diagnose insulin-dependence with certainty. In those countries having some system of national service, army medical records can be used to identify diabetic patients and thus to calculate the prevalence rates at the age of conscription (around 18 years), usually in males only. Another source of information is insulin prescriptions, which in young people can reasonably be assumed to equate with insulin-dependence. For these reasons, most of the data relating to the incidence and prevalence of IDDM concern the age range between birth and 20 years.

Two striking epidemiological patterns of incidence have emerged from these studies. The first concerns age of onset of IDDM. Incidence rises from birth to 12 years, reaching a peak at age 11—13 years (varying somewhat in different studies) before falling to a much lower rate (Fig. 7.1). The second pattern relates to seasonal variation (Fig. 7.2), the incidence in older children and adolescents (but not in other age groups) being

47

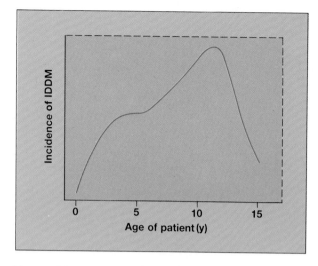

Fig. 7.1. The variation in the incidence of IDDM with age, showing the peak at 11–13 years.

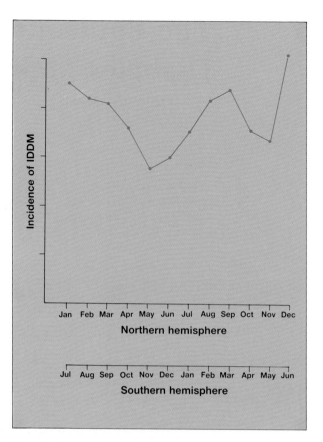

Fig. 7.2. Seasonal pattern of incidence of the clinical onset of IDDM in children and adolescents.

lowest in the spring and summer months. This seasonal dependence has been observed both north and south of the equator. Although these patterns are relatively consistent, explanations remain hypothetical. The seasonal pattern obviously suggests that infections commoner in autumn and winter might be involved in causing or precipitating IDDM (see Chapter 16). However, simple hypotheses implicating specific viral infections seem to be untenable, as it is now apparent that both immunological and biochemical disorders may be present for months or even years before IDDM becomes clinically manifest.

Incidence of IDDM

In recent years, an increasing number of diabetes registries have been established in different countries and many of these are co-ordinated within the group designated Diabetes Epidemiology Research International [1]. Their work has clearly demonstrated an enormous range of incidence rates between populations, with lesser degrees of variation within populations (Table 7.1). Finland has the highest national incidence and its Scandinavian neighbours, Norway and Sweden, also have relatively high rates. Other European countries, such as the German Demo-

cratic Republic, France and Poland, have relatively low rates. Of the economically developed countries, Japan has the lowest reported incidence. Canada provides a notable example of variation in incidence within a population (see Table 7.1).

In some countries, including Finland and Scotland, incidence rates are increasing. However, the registry in Pittsburgh (USA) has shown no significant variation over several years. Mid-West Poland experienced a temporary doubling of incidence between 1982–4, largely confined to younger children, accompanied by an alteration in the pattern of seasonal variation. These changes in incidence lend additional support to the proposed role of environmental factors in the genesis of IDDM [1].

The limited data available on incidence in the age range 15–30 years are presented in Table 7.2. The higher rates in Sweden may represent a secular increase, although methodological differences in ascertainment cannot be ruled out.

Table 7.1. Estimates of incidence (per 100 000) of IDDM in young persons (≤20 years).

Country	Year(s)	Age range	Ethnic group	Incidence rate		
				Male	Female	Total
Canada						
Montreal	1971−8	0−17	French Canadian			7.4
			Other			10.4
Toronto	1976−8	0−18				9.0
Prince Edward						
Island	1975−86	0−14		27.0	20.8	—
Denmark	1970−6	0−14		14.5	13.4	14.0
Finland	1970−9	0−14		29.7	27.3	28.6
France						
All	1975	0−14				3.7
Rhône	1960−79	0−15	French			4.7
			N. African			10.2
Israel	1975−80	0−20	Ashkenazi Jews			6.8
			Non-Ashkenazi Jews			4.3
			Arab			1.2
Japan	1977−80	0−17				0.8
Poland						
Mid-West	1970−81	0−16		3.5	3.6	3.5
	1982−4	0−16		6.7	6.6	6.6
Scotland						
All	1977−83	0−18		21.7	20.2	21.0
Tayside Region	1980−3	0−18		23.5	19.3	21.7
Sweden	1977−80	0−14		21.7	19.8	
USA						
Allegheny						
County	1965−80	0−20	White	16.1	14.8	15.4
			Black	8.9	10.3	9.6

Table 7.2. Estimates of incidence (per 100 000) of IDDM in the age range 15−30 years.

Country	Year(s)	Age range	Incidence rate	
			Male	Female
Norway (Oslo)	1925−54	20−24	8.3	5.9
		25−29	10.1	7.8
Norway (Oslo)	1956−64	20−24	9.6	7.4
			11.2	5.2
Denmark	1970−4	15−29	14.3	10.8
Sweden	1983	15−19	22.5	12.1
		20−24	22.7	12.2
		25−29	24.5	17.7

The epidemiology of NIDDM

Prevalence

A number of problems complicate attempts to compare the prevalence of NIDDM between and within populations over different periods of time, or in different geographical locations during the same period. The principal problem is the use of inconstant diagnostic criteria. Apparent secular trends may be confounded by local differences in methods of population screening. The positive association between age and NIDDM incidence must be taken into account where age-structure differs between populations and it must be remembered that differences in mortality rates can distort prevalence estimates.

Data on NIDDM prevalence and incidence derive from two sources, namely the notification of already-known cases and epidemiological surveys identifying previously and newly diagnosed patients. Both methods present problems in their interpretation. In the first, there is no certain way to estimate the extent of under-diagnosis (due to subjects failing to present to the diagnostic agencies) or to allow for either under- or over-diagnosis because of inappropriate criteria. Furthermore, a variable and unknown proportion of insulin-treated patients should really be categorized as NIDDM. Until recently, epidemiological surveys failed to adopt uniform diagnostic criteria and often omitted to test a representative sample of the study population.

COMPARISONS BETWEEN POPULATIONS

In 1972, West compared the prevalence rates of 'abnormal glucose tolerance' between 12 different populations [2]. Samples were drawn by similar methods from people aged 30 years or more (mean age = 50 years), who were given a 75-g oral glucose load. Venous whole blood glucose concentration was measured 2 h later, and 'abnormal glucose tolerance' was defined as a value of > 8.3 mmol/l (150 mg/dl). Although this value was substantially lower than that suggested by the WHO Study Group (see Chapter 6), West's data (Table 7.3) indicate that there must have been

Table 7.3. Prevalence of abnormal glucose tolerance per 1000 population (blood glucose > 8.3 mmol/l (150 mg/dl) 2 h after 75-g oral glucose) on subjects aged 30 years or more (after West KM, *Acta Diabetol Lat* 1972; **9** (suppl 1): 405−28).

East Pakistan (now Bangladesh)	20
Panama	25
El Salvador	32
Malaya (now Malaysia)	33
Honduras	41
Guatemala	42
Nicaragua	50
Costa Rica	54
Uruguay	69
Venezuela	70
USA	150
North Carolina Cherokees	250

very large differences in the prevalence of NIDDM between the populations studied, with the North Carolina Cherokee Indians heading the league table.

Several North American Indian populations have been observed to have very high rates of NIDDM — much higher than those observed in the descendants of European immigrants to the USA [3, 4]. Notable amongst these are the Pima Indians of Arizona, who have the highest recorded prevalence and incidence of NIDDM in the world (30% of adults are affected) and who have been the subject of long-term studies by a team from the National Institute of Arthritis, Diabetes, and Digestive and Kidney Diseases [3]. These high prevalence rates in North American Indians are a relatively modern phenomenon. Although there are no reliable prevalence data from before World War II, the records of the Indian Health Service indicate that diabetes was an uncommon diagnosis until the 1950s [4]. NIDDM may be a complication of the obesity which is currently prevalent in the Pimas and which may be due to the relative affluence recently acquired by these people, who previously had to survive under the precarious conditions of the desert.

In 1963, Sloan [5] noted variation in the prevalence of diabetes (essentially all NIDDM) in different ethnic groups in Hawaii. Prior and colleagues [6] further documented very high diabetes prevalences in several geo-ethnic groups in the Pacific area. More recently, Zimmet and colleagues [7] have performed a number of diabetes screening programmes, mainly using cluster sampling techniques and applying the WHO diagnostic criteria. Comparative, age-standardized rates for diabetes prevalence in the Pacific Region are shown in Table 7.4. By far the highest rate (approaching that of the Pimas) was observed in the Micronesian population of the small island of Nauru, with a high frequency also observed in the (Asian) Indian population of Fiji [8]. Similarly high rates have also been noted in migrant Indian populations in South Africa [9], Trinidad [10], Singapore [11] and the UK [12] (see Chapter 91). Until recently, this phenomenon was thought to be associated with external migration. However, a household enquiry in an area of New Delhi [13] has also documented relatively high rates of diabetes; migration within countries, i.e. from rural to urban environments, may also be a factor. It is also possible that the prevalence of diabetes in India has increased since the multicentre study

Table 7.4. Age-standardized diabetes prevalence rates per 1000 population* — Pacific region (1975—81) (after Zimmet [7]).

Geo-ethnic group	No. studied (≥20 years)	Diabetes prevalence/ 1000 population
Micronesians		
Nauru	456	303
Polynesians		
Tuvalu	397	39
W. Samoa (r)[†]	745	27
(u)	744	70
Melanesians		
Loyalty	535	20
New Caledonia	172	15
Fiji (r)	477	18
(u)	861	69
New Guinea (u)	184	154
Indians		
Fiji (r)	452	133
(u)	848	148

Notes
* Age standardized to Western Samoa Census of 1976.
[†]r = rural; u = urban.

conducted by the Indian Council of Medical Research in 1975 [14]. In that study, despite using very 'soft' criteria, the overall prevalence of diabetes above age 15 years was only 1.8%, with slightly higher figures in urban (2.1%) than rural (1.5%) areas.

Mexican Americans are another immigrant population with a higher prevalence (at least twice) of NIDDM than the indigenous population [15, 16]. However, there are not yet any data on the risk as compared with Mexican Americans remaining in Mexico.

Other striking racial differences in the USA were demonstrated by the Second National Health and Nutrition Examination Survey [17], conducted in 1976—80. This study, based on oral glucose tolerance testing, found that the rates of both previously diagnosed and newly diagnosed diabetes were substantially higher in Black subjects of both sexes as compared with Whites (Table 7.5).

Japanese migrants to the state of Hawaii and to the United States mainland have been compared with Japanese residents of Hiroshima, the source of much of the migration to Hawaii. The age-adjusted prevalence of diabetes (more accurately, 'abnormal glucose tolerance', as the studies antedated the WHO criteria) was approximately doubled in the migrant Japanese [18, 19].

COMPARISONS WITHIN POPULATIONS

A number of studies have sought regional differences or secular changes in the prevalence of NIDDM within populations with a relatively homogeneous ethnic composition.

As in the Indian study quoted earlier [13], investigations in a number of developing countries have shown urban—rural differences of varying degree, with generally higher rates in urban areas (Table 7.4).

Barker *et al.* [20] studied the incidence of diabetes over a period of 2 years in nine towns selected 'to encompass the range of socioeconomic conditions and spread of latitude in England and Wales'. The age range was limited to 18—50 years and incident cases were only those referred to

Table 7.5. Prevalence of previously diagnosed and of undiagnosed diabetes in the population of the USA aged 20—74 years from National Health and Nutrition Examination Survey II, 1976—80 (after Harris [17]).

Age group	Per cent of population				
	20—74	20—44	45—54	55—64	65—74
Previously diagnosed					
White males	2.8	0.5	4.5	5.3	9.1
White females	3.6	1.4	3.9	6.6	8.8
Black males	4.5	1.8	3.6	9.2	17.2
Black females	5.9	2.6	7.5	16.3	10.8
Previously undiagnosed — WHO criteria					
White males	2.7	0.5	3.3	4.1	10.0
White females	3.7	0.8	4.8	8.6	8.2
Black males	4.1	1.0	7.5	5.4	12.2
Black females	5.1	0.9	7.1	11.6	13.3

hospital. Differences in incidence rates of NIDDM were observed between the towns but these appeared to be related to worse socio-economic conditions. Incidence rates were lower in the upper social classes, but social class distribution alone did not account for the between-town differences.

Although the incidence of NIDDM is obviously increasing in several developing countries and in the Indian populations of North America, it remains uncertain whether there has been any increase in developed countries which is not explicable by the rising numbers of older individuals. In the USA [21], the reported incidence of NIDDM increased between 1935–6 (data from the National Health Survey) and in the early 1970s (National Health Interview Surveys, 1964–81). Between 1964 and 1973, incidence rates increased by about 30% in persons aged 25–54 years, 50% in the group aged 55–64 and 66% in those aged 65 years and above. Since 1973, however, rates have remained stable or have even declined. Interpretation is difficult because the period of the apparent increase coincided with attempts to screen for undiagnosed diabetes by a variety of official and unofficial agencies. Furthermore, given that the oral glucose tolerance test was widely used in screening and that glycaemic diagnostic criteria were lower at that time, an unknown number of those diagnosed as NIDDM would not be so classified today. This uncertainty is highlighted by O'Sullivan and Acheson [22], who compared diabetes prevalence rates from similar surveys of two Massachusetts towns, Oxford and Sudbury, in 1946 and 1964 respectively. They could find no evidence that prevalence had increased over this 18-year interval when age and sex adjustments had been applied, despite the fact that a larger proportion of the population of Sudbury claimed to have diabetes.

Mortality rates in diabetes mellitus

In developed countries, deaths due specifically to the metabolic disorders of diabetes (ketoacidosis, non-ketotic hyperosmolar diabetic coma) or to complications of its treatment (hypoglycaemia) are relatively uncommon. However, both IDDM and NIDDM carry an increased mortality rate compared with the non-diabetic population. In young-onset IDDM patients, the excess mortality is due principally to renal failure (Chapter 64), often complicated by cardiovascular disease (Chapter 68) [23]; this is currently being modified by the increasing availability of renal dialysis and transplantation. In older diabetic patients, excess mortality is attributable mainly to cardiovascular disease, similar in nature to that affecting the non-diabetic population [24].

However, there are deviations from this general pattern. Thus, a large Japanese series of autopsied diabetic subjects [25] cited renal disease as the cause of death in 19.3% of all cases, including 18.5% of those dying between 50–59 years and 17.7% of the group aged 60–69 years. The relatively low proportion of renal failure deaths in NIDDM observed in Europe and North America is probably due to mortality from the 'competing risk' of cardiovascular disease. In Japan, death from ischaemic heart disease is still relatively uncommon, although migrant Japanese who develop diabetes come to resemble North Americans in terms of their mortality statistics [19].

R. JOHN JARRETT

References

1 Diabetes Epidemiology Research International. Preventing insulin dependent diabetes mellitus. *Br Med J* 1987; **295**: 479–81.
2 West KM. Substantial differences in the diagnostic criteria used by diabetes experts. *Diabetes* 1975; **24**: 641–4.
3 Bennett PH, Rushforth NB, Miller M, *et al*. Epidemiologic studies of diabetes in the Pima Indians. *Recent Prog Hormone Res* 1976; **32**: 333–76.
4 West KM. Diabetes in American Indians and other native populations of the New World. *Diabetes* 1974; **23**: 841–55.
5 Sloan NR. Ethnic distribution of diabetes mellitus in Hawaii. *J Am Med Ass* 1963; **183**: 419–24.
6 Prior AM, Davidson F. The epidemiology of diabetes in Polynesians and Europeans in New Zealand and the Pacific. *Aust NZ Med J* 1966; **65**: 375–83.
7 Zimmet P. Epidemiology of diabetes and its macrovascular manifestations in Pacific populations: the medical effects of social progress. *Diabetes Care* 1979; **2**: 144–53.
8 Zimmet P, Taylor R, Ram P, *et al*. Prevalence of diabetes and impaired glucose tolerance in the biracial (Melanesian and Indian) population of Fiji: a rural–urban comparison. *Am J Epidemiol* 1983; **118**: 673–88.
9 Marine N, Vinik AI, Edelstein I, *et al*. Diabetes, hyperglycemia and glycosuria among Indians, Malays and Africans (Bantus) in Cape Town, South Africa. *Diabetes* 1969; **18**: 840–57.
10 Poon A, King T, Henry MV, Rampersad F. Prevalence and natural history of diabetes in Trinidad. *Lancet* 1968; **1**: 155–60.
11 Cheah JS, Tambyah JA, Mitra NR. Prevalence of diabetes mellitus among the ethnic groups in Singapore. *Trop Geog Med* 1975; **27**: 14–16.
12 Mather HM, Keen H. The Southall Diabetes Survey: prevalence of known diabetes in Asians and Europeans. *Br Med J* 1985; **291**: 1081–4.
13 Verma NPS, Mehta SP, Madhu S, *et al*. Prevalence of known

diabetes in an urban Indian environment: the Darya Ganj diabetes survey. *Br Med J* 1986; **293**: 422−3.

14 Ahuja MMS. Epidemiological studies on diabetes mellitus in India. In: Ahuja MMS, ed. *Epidemiology of Diabetes in Developing Countries*. New Delhi: Interprint, 1979: 29−38.

15 Hanis CL, Ferrell RE, Barton SA, *et al*. Diabetes among Mexican Americans in Starr County, Texas. *Am J Epidemiol* 1983; **118**: 659−72.

16 Stern MP, Gaskill SP, Hazuda HP, *et al*. Does obesity explain excess prevalence of diabetes among Mexican Americans? Results of the San Antonio Heart Study. *Diabetologia* 1983; **24**: 272−7.

17 Harris MI, Hadden WC, Knowler WC, *et al*. Prevalence of diabetes and impaired glucose tolerance and plasma glucose levels in U.S. population aged 20−74 years. *Diabetes* 1987; **36**: 523−34.

18 Kawate R, Miyanishi M, Yamakido M, *et al*. Preliminary studies of the prevalence and mortality of diabetes mellitus in Japanese in Japan and on the island of Hawaii. *Adv Metab Dis* 1978; **9**: 202−24.

19 Kawate R, Yamakido M, Nishimato Y. Migrant studies among the Japanese in Hiroshima and Hawaii. In: Waldhäusl WK, ed. *Proceedings of the 10th Congress of the International Diabetes Federation*. Amsterdam, Excerpta Medica, 1980: 526−31.

20 Barker DJP, Gardner MJ, Power C. Incidence of diabetes amongst people aged 18−50 years in nine British towns: a collaborative study. *Diabetologia* 1982; **22**: 421−5.

21 Everhart J, Knowler WC, Bennett PH. Incidence and risk factors for noninsulin-dependent diabetes. In: Harris MI, Hamman RF, eds. *Diabetes in America: diabetes data compiled 1984*. NIH Publication No. 85−1468, 1985: IV-1−35.

22 O'Sullivan JB, Acheson RM. Comparisons of diabetes prevalence rates in Oxford (1946) and Sudbury (1964). *Adv Metab Dis* 1978; **9**: 1−11.

23 Borch-Johnsen K, Andersen PK, Deckert T. The effect of proteinuria on relative mortality in Type 1 (insulin-dependent) diabetes mellitus. *Diabetologia* 1985; **28**: 590−6.

24 Panzram G. Mortality and survival in Type 2 (non-insulin-dependent) diabetes mellitus. *Diabetologia* 1987; **30**: 123−31.

25 Goto Y, Shin-Ichiro S, Masuda M. Causes of death in 3151 diabetic autopsy cases. *Tohoku J Exp Med* 1974; **112**: 339−53.

SECTION 5
NON-DIABETIC INSULIN BIOSYNTHESIS, SECRETION AND ACTION

8 The Anatomy, Organization and Ultrastructure of the Islets of Langerhans

Summary

- The pancreatic islets were discovered in 1869 by Paul Langerhans.
- The normal adult pancreas contains about 1 million islets (each composed of 3000 endocrine cells) which constitute 3% of the total gland mass.
- The islet cells are derived embryologically from the endoderm cell cords which also produce the ducts and exocrine tissue, and can be distinguished morphologically and immunocytochemically by 9–12 weeks of gestation.
- The major islet cell types are B (producing insulin), A (glucagon), D (somatostatin) and PP (pancreatic polypeptide); the products of the minor D_1 and P cells are unknown.
- Each islet consists of a core of B cells surrounded by a cortex of other cell types, in which A cells generally predominate; PP-rich islets are found in the posterior part of the pancreatic head.
- Islet cell types can be distinguished by various histological stains (Gomori or silver-impregnation methods) and the electron-microscopical appearance of their secretory granules. They can be identified by immunocytochemical staining of their peptide hormones at light or electron microscopical level. Like all neuroendocrine cells and nerves, all islet cell types are immunoreactive for neurone-specific enolase.
- Post-translational processing of islet-cell hormones apparently occurs within the secretory granules which mature after their release from the Golgi apparatus.
- Islet cells contain other recently characterized bioactive peptides, including 7B2, GAWK and pancreastatin; the latter inhibits insulin secretion and pancreatic exocrine secretion, but their functional significance is unknown.
- Amylin (islet amyloid polypeptide), a 37-amino-acid peptide structurally similar to calcitonin-gene-related peptide, is synthesized by B cells and is a major component of the amyloid deposits characteristic of NIDDM; amylin is postulated to contribute to the insulin resistance of this condition.
- The islets are densely innervated by adrenergic, cholinergic and peptidergic fibres (including cholecystokinin, substance P and neuropeptide Y), and richly supplied by vessels passing through the cortex into the B-cell-rich core. The secretion of insulin and other islet-cell hormones may be tightly integrated by neural, humoral and paracrine mechanisms.

The islets of Langerhans were first recognized in 1869 as dense clusters of clear cells embedded in the exocrine pancreas and are named after Paul Langerhans, who discovered them while studying for his doctorate in Berlin. The endocrine function of the pancreas was not established until 20 years later [1] and shortly afterwards it became clear that this function is mediated by the islets [2]. The importance of the islets as the body's major centre for the control of glucose homeostasis is emphasized by their remarkably rich vascular and nervous supplies, which convey many metabolic, endocrine and neural stimuli to the different islet cell types.

57

Embryological development of the islets

The human pancreas arises from the gut endoderm during the 5th week of fetal life as two buds, the duodenal and hepatic diverticula. The dorsal bud develops from the dorsal wall of the duodenum and eventually forms the entire body and tail of the pancreas and part of the head. The remaining posterior portion of the head is derived from the ventral bud, which arises from the primitive bile duct. Fusion of the two separate parts occurs early, at about 7 weeks of gestation in man (see Fig. 8.1).

The glandular tissue of the pancreas develops by budding and branching of the primordial epithelial cell cords. This budding results from cell division in a plane perpendicular to the axis of the lumen of the forming ducts, disrupting tight junction complexes and separating the cells from those surrounding them. The islets originate from specialized buds of the same epithelial cords which give rise to the pancreatic ducts and typical acinar exocrine cells. The endocrine cells generally separate at an early stage (around the 3rd month of gestation) and undergo independent differentiation, although some retain their original connection with the ducts; occasional peptide-containing ductal cells occur in the normal adult pancreas.

During embryonic life, the A cells (containing glucagon) are generally the first to develop and the pancreatic polypeptide-containing PP cells the last. In man, A cells have been recognized morphologically at about 9 weeks, D cells (containing somatostatin) at 10 weeks and B cells 1 week later. However, the cells may be functional at an earlier

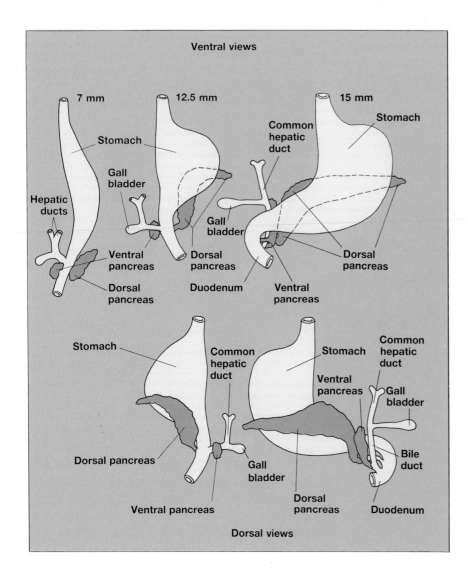

Fig. 8.1. Embryological development of the pancreas, showing outgrowth of the dorsal and ventral pancreatic buds from the duodenum and bile duct. Grown-rump length of the embryo is shown in mm.

stage as hormonal products have been identified up to 3 weeks before the cells can be distinguished morphologically.

The islets are most dense (600–700/cm³ of the pancreas) at about the 30th week of gestation. The normal adult pancreas contains around 1 million islets, which constitute about 3% of the total gland mass. Adult human islets each contain about 3000 polygonal endocrine cells and are scattered irregularly throughout the exocrine parenchyma, most densely in the tail region. Although the bulk of the pancreatic endocrine tissue is organized as islets, single extra-insular endocrine cells can occasionally be found [3]. There is some variation in the cellular composition of the islets. Ninety per cent of the pancreas contains 'B-cell-rich' islets which have a regular spheroidal or ellipsoidal shape. The remaining 10% of the gland, comprising the posterior portion of the head region derived from the ventral pancreatic bud, is known as the 'PP lobe' as it contains 'PP-rich islets' which have a less compact, trabeculated structure. Each islet is partially separated from the acinar parenchyma by an incomplete capsule made up of connective tissue fibres running from the interstitial septa of the exocrine part of the gland.

Morphological features of the islets

Histological and histochemical characteristics

On routine histological staining with haematoxylin and eosin, the islets of Langerhans can be readily identified as they stain less intensely than the surrounding parenchyma (Fig. 8.2). The different islet cell types were originally distinguished histologically [4, 5]. B cells have particularly pale cytoplasm and prominent chromatin in ovoid nuclei, whereas A cells are larger and possess coarse, granular cytoplasm with poorly visible nuclear chromatin.

The different islet cell types can be demonstrated by various histochemical techniques, including staining with safranin and methyl green, which shows A and B cells as red and green respectively. The widely used Gomori's aldehyde fuchsin trichrome stain colours the positive B cells deep violet, whereas the negative A cells appear red and the D cells green.

Various histochemical techniques exploit the finding that certain pancreatic endocrine cell types can be impregnated with silver by virtue of the secretory granules which they contain. These cells are argyrophil, i.e. they will take up silver but cannot reduce it. The silver impregnation method of Grimelius [6] stains A cells (Fig. 8.3), whereas Davenport's technique [7] demonstrates D cells. Different stains can be applied sequentially to a single tissue section to identify specific types, for example Grimelius' silver nitrate stain (A cells), aldehyde fuchsin (B cells) and lead–haematoxylin (D cells) [8].

Immunocytochemistry

LIGHT MICROSCOPY

A major advance in the histological examination of the endocrine system was the development of immunocytochemical procedures, using specific antibodies raised against peptide hormones and labelled with fluorescein or peroxidase, to localize peptides to their sites of production and storage. Immunocytochemical techniques have been greatly refined and are now reliable and sensitive. The use of antibodies to whole, bioactive peptides and to their precursor molecules and cryptic fragments has helped to characterize and localize the intracellular processing of the islet peptides. Controlled antibody reactions have been used to show conclusively that A, B, D and PP cells are the sites of origin of glucagon, insulin, somatostatin and pancreatic polypeptide, respectively. It is also possible, using antibody elutions, to immunostain more than one peptide in a single tissue section (Fig. 8.4), thus defining anatomical relationships between particular endocrine cells and/or nerves.

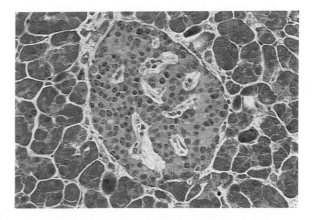

Fig. 8.2. A section of normal pancreas stained with haematoxylin and eosin. The islet in the centre is easily identified by its distinct morphology and lighter staining than the surrounding exocrine tissue.

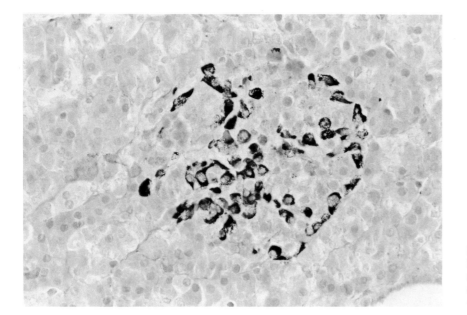

Fig. 8.3. Argyrophil (A) cells in an islet demonstrated by Grimelius' silver impregnation technique. The section has been counterstained with haematoxylin.

DEMONSTRATION OF ENTIRE NEUROENDOCRINE COMPLEXES

The above techniques cannot demonstrate all of the neuroendocrine elements of the pancreas but it is now possible to immunostain two separate proteins which occur in both islet cells and nerves.

One is an isoenzyme of enolase, initially thought to occur only in the nervous system and hence named 'neuron-specific enolase' (NSE) [9]. NSE has subsequently been found in many organs, not only in nerves but also in all identifiable endocrine cells, including those of the pancreas [10, 11]. A more recently characterized protein, present in islet and other endocrine tissue and in all nerves, has been designated 'protein gene product 9.5' (PGP 9.5) (Fig. 8.5 [12]). Immunostaining for either of these antigens is a simple means of identifying endocrine cells and nerves simultaneously.

ELECTRON MICROSCOPY

Endocrine cell types were originally classified by electron microscopy according to the size, shape

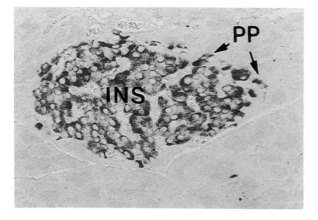

Fig. 8.4. An islet double immunostained for insulin and pancreatic polypeptide using the unlabelled enzyme or peroxidase anti-peroxidase (PAP) method. The use of different coloured couplers in the immunostaining method allows distinction to be made between the two cell types; the B-cell core of the islet is blue and the PP cells at the periphery are brown.

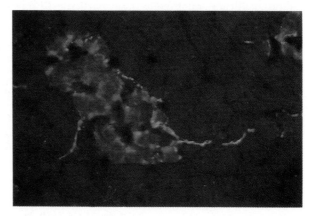

Fig. 8.5. Protein gene product 9.5 immunostained in islet cells and surrounding nerves using the indirect immunofluorescence technique.

and electron density of their secretory granules, combined with examination of serial semi-thin-thin sections [13]. Modern electron immunocyto-chemical methods, using antibodies labelled with colloidal gold particles which are visible on electron microscopy, can localize antigens to individual organelles without obscuring cellular morphology. Multiple immunostaining methods, using specific antibodies labelled with gold particles of different sizes, can characterize more than one antigen within the same cell (Fig. 8.6). This approach, coupled with the application of region-specific antisera, has been particularly successful in investigating the synthetic processing of peptides within islet cells [14–16].

Islet cell types

It was noticed at the turn of the century that the cells of the islets of Langerhans are not homogeneous, and two separate populations, designated A and B cells, were initially described [17]. In man, five different cell types have now been identified histologically: the A, B, D, PP and D_1 cells. The first four have been functionally identified as producing glucagon (A), insulin (B), somatostatin (D) and pancreatic polypeptide (PP) respectively. Their main morphological features are summarized in Table 8.1.

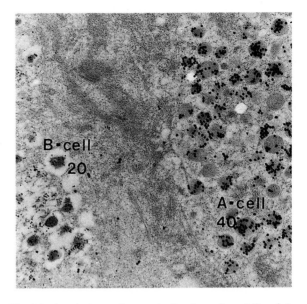

Fig. 8.6. An electron micrograph showing adjacent B and A cells immunostained for insulin (20 nm gold particles) and glucagon (40 nm) using the double immunogold staining method.

B CELLS

B cells are the most numerous islet cell type in all species examined. They were first identified as the source of insulin in 1938 when the B cells of dogs with induced diabetes were found to be

Table 8.1. Main morphological characteristics of pancreatic islet cells.

	Cell type			
	A	B	D	PP
Peptide products	Glucagon, GLP-1, GLP-2, GRPP, Glicentin	Insulin, C-peptide	Somatostatin (rat somatostatin cryptic peptide)	Pancreatic polypeptide
Localization within islet	Cortex	Medulla	Mainly in cortex	Mainly cortex in PP lobe (also outside islet in remainder of gland)
Staining techniques	Grimelius' silver Safranin Orange G Mallory–Azan	Aldehyde fuchsin Aldehyde thionin Methyl green	Davenport's silver lead haematoxylin	
	Immunocytochemistry for specific peptide products			
Secretory granules (diameter in nm)	200–300, eccentric core within halo of proteinaceous material	250–400, heterogenous, polymorphous core within large halo	150–400, moderately electron-dense core with tightly fitting membrane	100–200, round or oval electron-dense core with narrow halo

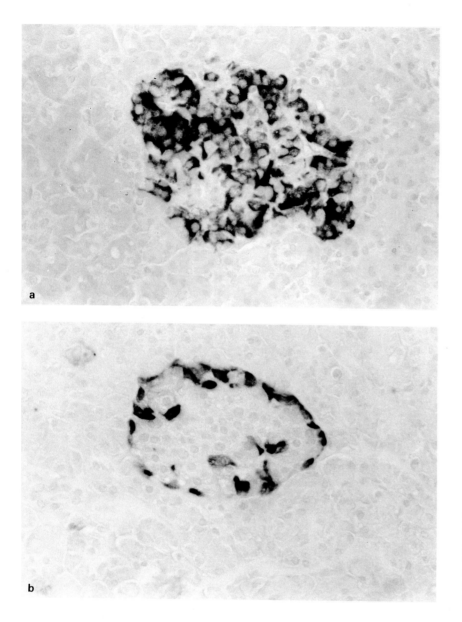

Fig. 8.7. Islets immunostained by the PAP method for the four major pancreatic hormones. (a) Insulin: the B cells are arranged at the core of the islet. (b) Glucagon: the A cells lie at the periphery of the islet (*continues opposite*).

extensively degranulated or destroyed [18]. More direct functional evidence has been obtained by perfusing the pancreas with high-glucose media, when selective degranulation of the B cells occurs with a concomitant increase in insulin concentrations in the venous effluent [19, 20].

B cells are characteristically stained by aldehyde fuchsin, but this reaction is not specific to B cells. The stain probably interacts with sulphonic acid groups [21], possibly formed by breakage of the disulphide bridges in proinsulin. As mentioned earlier, most pancreatic islets are rich in B cells, which form a homocellular medulla (Fig. 8.7a). The arrangement of the other cell types in a hetero-cellular cortex surrounding the B-cell core, where they receive both blood-borne and neural stimuli first, suggests that they process incoming infor-

mation and act accordingly to regulate B-cell function (see below).

Electron microscopy shows that the B cells contain two types of secretory granule (Fig. 8.8). The more abundant consist of a crystalline core surrounded by a halo and a clearly defined limiting membrane, and are scattered throughout the cytoplasm. The less numerous granules are found close to the Golgi apparatus and have a homogeneous core enclosed by a membrane coated externally with bristles consisting of the protein, clathrin. Electron immunocytochemical techniques have shown that the coated granules contain high levels of proinsulin and little cleaved insulin and are therefore probably immature whereas the mature, non-coated granules contain mostly insulin.

Electron immunocytochemistry has also been

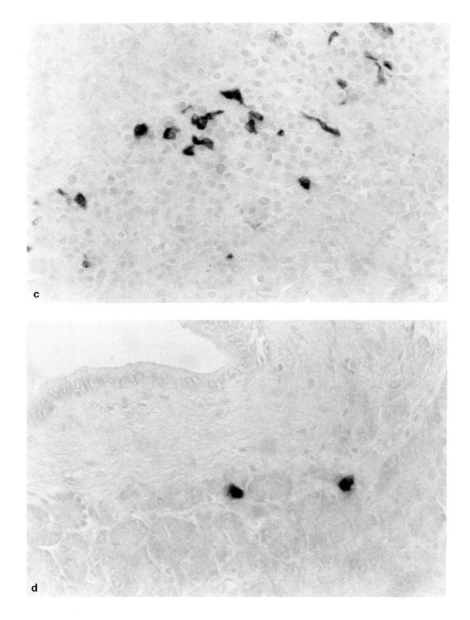

(c) Somatostatin: D cells are scattered in the islet and show typical elongations. (d) Pancreatic polypeptide: an example of the extra-insular location of PP cells with two lying in the exocrine tissue near a duct.

used to study the chemistry of insulin biosynthesis. Immunogold labelling methods have demonstrated that maturation of secretory vesicles is accompanied by a fall in their internal pH [16]. Cultured B cells were incubated with DAMP, a basic dinitrophenol derivative which accumulates in acidic compartments, and immunostained for DAMP, proinsulin and insulin. Insulin-rich, mature secretory vesicles contained more DAMP and thus were more acidic than immature, proinsulin-rich vesicles, suggesting that proinsulin is converted to insulin only when intravesicular pH has fallen to a critical level (Fig. 8.9).

Adult human B cells may contain numerous lipid inclusions, known as ceroid bodies. B cells and A cells are interconnected through both tight- and gap-junctions [22].

A CELLS

Although A and B cells were distinguished over 80 years ago, it was not until 1962 that A cells were shown to produce glucagon [23]. In most species, the A cells lie in the islet cortex together with the other non-B cells (Fig. 8.7b) and can be identified by the Grimelius argyrophil reaction [6] or by immunocytochemical staining for glucagon. A cells, like PP cells, show a distinct topographical predilection. In humans and other mammals, A cells are numerous in the islets of the tail and body of the pancreas but sparser in those of the ventral head portion. This differential distribution, opposite to that of PP cells, probably reflects the development of the pancreas from its two separate primordia. On electron microscopy,

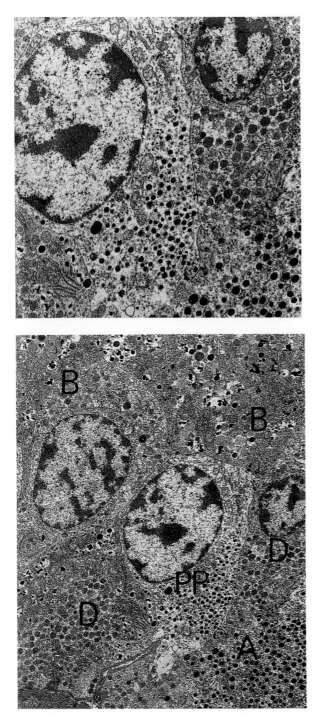

Fig. 8.8. Conventional electron micrographs showing the typical appearances of the four main types of islet endocrine cells. They are distinguished by the differences in size of the granules: see bottom panel.

A cells contain heterogeneous secretory granules, with an outer, clear halo and a prominent electron-dense core [24] (Fig. 8.8). As discussed below, the various peptide products of the A cell are differentially segregated within the granules.

Studies of glucagon have been considerably hampered by the presence of circulating gut-derived peptides cross-reacting with pancreatic glucagon. High-molecular-weight precursors of pancreatic glucagon have now been characterized. The preproglucagon molecule contains pancreatic glucagon (which contains 20 amino-acid residues), together with glicentin, glicentin-related pancreatic peptide (GRPP) and the two glucagon-like peptides (GLP-1 and GLP-2) [25, 26] (see Chapter 33). Glicentin (also known as gut glucagon) is a 69-residue peptide consisting of pancreatic glucagon with a C-terminal extension and is produced by endocrine cells in the gut as well as by A cells. Immunogold staining has revealed that glicentin immunoreactivity is localized to the halo of the A-cell secretory granules, whereas glucagon, GLP-1 and GLP-2 immunoreactivities are found in the granule core [27, 28] (Fig. 8.10). Pancreatic glucagon can be detected by specific antisera in non-coated secretory granules but not in coated immature granules where its immunoreactivity is masked. The level of glicentin-immunoreactivity falls progressively as the granules mature [15], suggesting that final processing of the glicentin precursor to pancreatic glucagon occurs within the granules, after the peptide has passed through the Golgi apparatus.

D CELLS

The D cell, the third endocrine cell type to be described in human islets, was identified in 1931 [29]. D cells can be demonstrated histochemically by modifications of Davenport's silver impregnation technique [7] or by immunocytochemical staining for somatostatin. The rather larger secretory granules of the D cells contain a rounded core of low or moderate electron density enclosed by a tightly fitting membrane (Fig. 8.8). D cells were originally thought to produce a gastrin-like peptide but in 1975 were found to contain somatostatin [13, 30, 31]. This 14-amino-acid peptide, first isolated from the hypothalamus and named for its ability to suppress growth hormone release, is now known to be produced by neurones and endocrine cells at many sites in the body (see Chapter 33). Among its many actions is surprisingly efficient suppression of insulin and glucagon release [32].

Pancreatic D cells, like the somatostatin-producing cells of the gut, are distinguished morphologically by apical and/or basal elongations which apparently project on to adjacent cells or capillaries and may release somatostatin at their terminations [33] (Figs 8.7c and 8.11). Somatostatin is a potent inhibitor of many endocrine and exocrine functions, including the release of all pancreatic hormones [32, 34, 35]. Somatostatin-containing cells may represent an overlap between the classical endocrine and nervous systems, in that somatostatin may act in three separate ways: as an endocrine hormone (when released into the circulation), in a paracrine manner (when secreted to affect adjacent cells) and as a neurotransmitter (somatostatin is found in both central and peripheral neurons) [36]. The possible relevance of somatostatin to the regulation of islet-cell secretion and to the pathophysiology of diabetes is discussed further in Chapter 33.

The biologically active forms of somatostatin, the 14-residue peptide and its N-terminally extended form (somatostatin-28), are both derived from a 92-residue precursor, prosomatostatin [37–9]. In the pancreatic islets, processing to somatostatin-14 predominates and little somatostatin-28 or prosomatostatin can be identified. The pancreas also contains another molecular species of somatostatin, termed somatostatin-28 (1–12), which is liberated in equimolar amounts with somatostatin-14 (together with a cleavage dipeptide) by the splitting of somatostatin-28 [40].

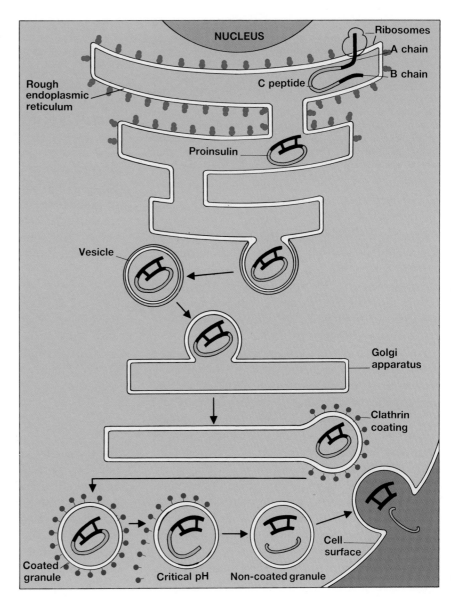

Fig. 8.9. Schematic representation of the processing of insulin within the B cell (adapted from references [16] and [83] with permission of the Rockefeller University Press).

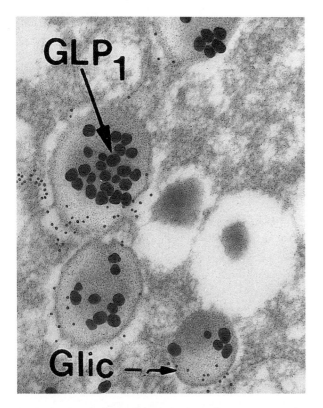

Fig. 8.10. An electron micrograph of A-cell secretory granules immunostained for GLP-1 (40-nm gold particles) and glicentin (5 nm) using the double immunogold staining method. Immunoreactivity for GLP-1 is confined to the electron-dense core of each granule whilst that for glicentin lies in the halo.

PP CELLS

Originally termed F cells, the PP cells produce pancreatic polypeptide (PP), a 36-amino-acid peptide which, in man, is found exclusively in the pancreas [41]. PP appears to be released by eating and other vagal stimuli but has relatively few described metabolic or gastrointestinal effects [42, 43] (see Chapter 33).

Like A cells, PP cells are preferentially localized within the pancreas, being the most frequent cell type in the islets of the ventral, 'PP-rich' portion of the pancreatic head [44]. Phylogenetically, PP cells are the last endocrine cell type to populate the islets and are found not only around the islet periphery but also in ducts and acini (where pancreatic endocrine cell production is thought to take place) and frequently embedded in the acinar tissue (Fig. 8.7d). This extra-insular location contrasts with the distribution of the other islet cell types, which only rarely lie outside the islets and are then confined to the ducts.

On electron microscopy, PP cells are found to contain fairly sparse, small granules and may be

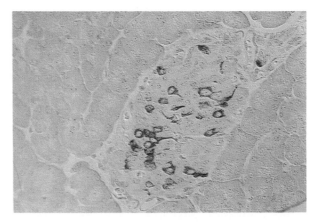

Fig. 8.11. An islet immunostained for somatostatin using the PAP technique. Nomarski interference optics were used to enhance the image of the immunostained cells, which display characteristic elongations.

confused with D cells or degranulated B cells (Fig. 8.8).

OTHER ISLET CELL TYPES

Minor populations of other cells carrying secretory granules are found in the islets. D_1 *cells* resemble the PP cell in that they contain small, round granules with a closely applied membrane or a very thin, clear peripheral space, but are not immunoreactive for PP. They are sparse in the human pancreas but more frequently found in the dog or guinea-pig. Mammalian islets also include the rare *P cells*, which contain very small, round, haloed granules. The peptides secreted by these minor cell types have not been identified.

Recently discovered islet peptides

Several recently characterized bioactive peptides have been localized to the pancreatic islets as well as to other endocrine cells, and some are now known to have experimental effects on islet-cell secretion.

7B2

7B2 (originally known as APPG, or 'anterior pituitary pig peptide') consists of around 180 amino-acid residues and has structural homology with both IGF1 and Rous sarcoma virus [45, 46]. It was first isolated from porcine and human pituitary glands, but is broadly distributed throughout the central and peripheral nervous system and in many endocrine cells [47, 48]. B cells and insulinomas contain particularly high concentrations of 7B2 [48], but the pathophysiological significance of this observation is not known.

GAWK

GAWK is another regulatory peptide originally extracted from the pituitary gland. It was named from the first four amino acids of its 74-residue sequence [49]. Within the islets, GAWK is found mainly in A cells [50]. The sequence of GAWK is now known to lie within the human chromogranin B molecule [51]. The chromogranins are a family of proteins which are widely distributed in endocrine cells [52−4], where they are contained within secretory granules [55]. Chromogranins were originally thought to stabilize the internal matrix of secretory granules but there is now evidence that they constitute a group of prohormones, giving rise to various peptides including GAWK, CCB (C-terminal of chromogranin B) and pancreastatin. The physiological functions of the chromogranins and of GAWK are unknown.

Pancreastatin

The 49-amino-acid peptide termed 'pancreastatin' was first isolated from porcine pancreas and shown to suppress the first phase of glucose-stimulated insulin secretion in the isolated, perfused rat pancreas [56]. It was subsequently also shown to inhibit second-phase insulin release as well as meal-stimulated pancreatic exocrine secretion [57]. A sequence similar to porcine pancreastatin is embedded within that of human chromogranin A [58, 59]. Pancreastatin has been localized by immunocytochemistry, at both light and electron microscopical levels, to all pancreatic endocrine cell types [60].

Amylin

Amylin (also known as 'islet amyloid polypeptide', or IAPP) was recently extracted from the amyloid deposits found in the islets of man and other mammals, and from an insulinoma [61−4] (see Chapter 18). It consists of 37 amino acids [62] and shares more than 40% sequence homology with calcitonin-gene-related peptide (CGRP). Amylin has been localized to B cells [64, 65] and has provoked particular interest as it may play an important role in the pathogenesis of NIDDM [64, 66, 67]. Amylin, or an amylin-related precursor, is synthesized by B cells and may be the monomer

of islet amyloid [62−3]. Deposition of amyloid in the islets occurs in many mammals and increases with age but is further increased in NIDDM, in proportion to the clinical severity of the condition [68−70]. Impaired glucose tolerance in NIDDM stems in part from insulin resistance in skeletal muscle (Chapter 21); as human amylin (and the structurally similar CGRP) has been found to inhibit basal and insulin-stimulated glycogen synthesis in skeletal muscle in vitro [67], it has been suggested that abnormal amylin turnover (increased synthesis or reduced clearance) may contribute to the pathogenesis of NIDDM in man.

Integration of islet secretory activity

The islets are richly supplied with both blood vessels and nerves, both of which may be involved in regulating islet secretion (Fig. 8.13).

Blood supply

Afferent arterioles, arising from the branches of the splenic and pancreatico-duodenal arteries, may supply acinar tissue before reaching the islets; the islets may therefore receive humoral metabolic input from the rest of the pancreas. Within the islets, the arterioles branch to form a dense mesh of wide, anastomosing capillaries, reminiscent of the renal glomerulus. Electron microscopy has shown that the capillary endothelium is fenestrated, consistent with the rapid appearance of peptides in the circulation following islet-cell stimulation. The blood from this dense sinusoidal network drains into 1−6 venules, which in turn feed into an intralobular vein.

The blood flow through the islet appears to be

Fig. 8.12. Vasoactive intestinal polypeptide immunostained in cell bodies of an intrapancreatic ganglion and its associated nerve (indirect immunofluorescence technique).

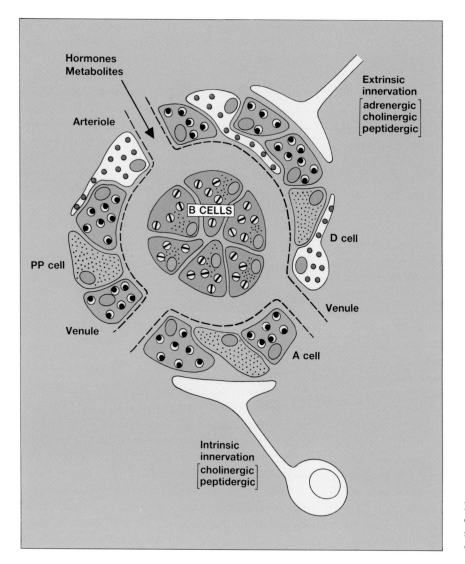

Fig. 8.13. Schematic representation of the structure of a pancreatic islet showing the four major endocrine cell types.

selectively organized. The afferent vessels branch first in the B-cell-poor peripheral zone and then feed the central portion with its dense population of B cells. In this way, peptides secreted by A, D, and PP cells could potentially influence the activity of the B cells; insulin release is known to be stimulated by glucagon [71] and inhibited by somatostatin [32]. This local endocrine mechanism may therefore provide a further opportunity, in addition to paracrine influences, for the integrated control of insulin release by the islet.

Innervation

The close functional relationship between the nervous system and glucoregulation was first revealed by Claude Bernard, who found that experimental transfixing of the medulla in-

duced hyperglycaemia ('piqûre' diabetes), and Langerhans himself described the rich innervation of the islets. The discovery of insulin shifted emphasis to the humoral control of islet secretion but the neural control of the islets is increasingly attracting attention. Bioactive peptides found in peripheral nerves, as well as the classical 'autonomic transmitters', may have important regulatory functions.

The pancreatic islets are innervated by parasympathetic cholinergic, sympathetic adrenergic and various peptidergic nerves, with certain peptides also being found in the cholinergic and adrenergic innervation. The pancreas receives its *extrinsic* innervation from the coeliac plexus. Postganglionic sympathetic fibres (originating in the plexus) and vagal preganglionic efferents (passing through the plexus) enter the pancreas with the arteries. The adrenergic nerves supply blood vessels, and both types branch and innervate the exocrine parenchyma and the islets.

The preganglionic parasympathetic fibres synapse in the *intrinsic* ganglia, which are embedded in the gland's substance and supply a rich innervation to the islets; the juxtaposed units of islets and nerves have been termed 'neuro-insular complexes' [72]. As well as the cholinergic ganglion cells, the intrinsic ganglia also contain frequent peptide-immunoreactive cells, the source of most of the pancreatic peptidergic nerves; a few peptidergic nerves may arise outside the pancreas. Nerves containing enkephalin, substance P, cholecystokinin tetrapeptide [73], CGRP [74, 75], and neuropeptide Y (NPY) [75–8], have all been described in the pancreas of various mammals. The most abundant peptidergic nerves, however, are those containing VIP [79–81], which are scattered in the exocrine parenchyma (Fig. 8.13), around blood vessels and frequently in association with the islets. Cholecystokinin tetrapeptide-immunoreactive nerves are also found in islets, whereas those containing substance P, enkephalian or NPY are not, occurring mainly around non-immunoreactive neuronal cell bodies in the ganglia. VIP is known to stimulate the release of all pancreatic hormones. It seems most likely that this secretion is effected by VIP released locally from nerves rather than circulating in the bloodstream, as the effective concentrations of the peptide far exceed its normal circulating levels: for example, insulin is released by VIP concentrations of 1–50 nmol/l, roughly 100 times its normal plasma levels.

Electron microscopy reveals various nerve terminals in the islets. These appear to correspond to cholinergic (30–50-nm-diameter, agranular vesicles), adrenergic (30–50-nm-diameter, dense vesicles) and peptidergic endings (60–200-nm-diameter, dense vesicles). There seems to be no particular association between each of the three nerve types and the different islet cells, nor any specialized areas of the islet-cell membrane, as seen in neuromuscular junctions. However, endings are found in intercellular spaces; the substances released may diffuse across these spaces and act on the cells, analogous to the way in which autonomic nerves affect smooth muscle cells.

ANNE E. BISHOP
JULIA M. POLAK

References

1 Von Mering I, Minkowsky O. Diabetes mellitus nach Pankreasextirpation. *Zentralblatt Klin Med* 1889; **10**: 393–4.

2 Laguesse E. Sur la formation des îlots de Langerhans dans le pancréas. *Comptes Rendus des Séances de la Société de Biologie et Ses Filiales*, Paris 1894; **46**: 819–20.

3 Rahier J, Wallon J, Henquin J. Cell populations in the endocrine pancreas of human neonates and infants. *Diabetalogia* 1981; **20**: 540–6.

4 Diamare V. Studi comparativi sulle isole die Langerhans del pancreas. *Int Monatschrift Anat Physiol* 1899; **16**: 155–209.

5 Schulz W. *Arch Mikr Anat* 1900; **56**: 491.

6 Grimelius L. A silver nitrate stain for A$_2$ cells of human pancreatic islets. *Acta Soc Med Uppsala* 1968; **73**: 243–70.

7 Davenport HA. Staining nerve fibres in mounted sections with alcoholic silver nitrate solution. *Arch Neurol Psychiatr* 1930; **24**: 690.

8 Kito H, Hosoda S. Triple staining for simultaneous visualisation of cell types in islets of Langerhans of pancreas. *J Histochem Cytochem* 1977; **25**: 1019–20.

9 Marangos PJ, Zomzely-Neurath C, Luk DCM, York C. Isolation and characterisation of the nervous system protein 14-3-2 from rat brain. *J Biol Chem* 1975; **250**: 1884–1901.

10 Schmechel D, Marangos PJ, Brightman M. Neuron specific enolase is a molecular marker for peripheral and central neuroendocrine cells. *Nature* 1978; **276**: 834–6.

11 Bishop AE, Polak JM, Facer P, Ferri GL, Marangos PJ, Pearse AGE. Neuron-specific enolase: a common marker for the endocrine cells of the gut and pancreas. *Gastroenterology* 1982; **83**: 902–15.

12 Thompson RJ, Doran JF, Jackson P, Dhillon AP, Rode J. PGP 9.5 — a new marker for vertebrate neurons and neuroendocrine cells. *Brain Res* 1983; **278**: 224–8.

13 Polak JM, Pearse AGE, Heath CM. Complete identification of endocrine cells in the gastrointestinal tract using semithin-thin sections to identify motilin cells in human and animal intestine. *Gut* 1975; **16**: 225–9.

14 Varndell IM, Tapia FJ, Probert L, Buchan AMJ, Gu J, de Mey J, Bloom SR, Polak JM. Immunogold staining procedure for the localisation of regulatory peptides. *Peptides* 1982; **3**: 259–72.

15 Ravazzola M, Perrelet A, Unger RH, Orci L. Immunocytochemical characterisation of secretory granule maturation in pancreatic A cells. *Endocrinology* 1984; **114**: 481–5.

16 Orci L, Ravazzola M, Amherdt M, Madsen O, Perrelet A, Vassali JD, Anderson RGW. Conversion of proinsulin to insulin occurs co-ordinately with acidification of maturing secretory vesicles. *J Cell Biol* 1987; **103**: 2273–81.

17 Lane MA. The cytological characteristics of the areas of Langerhans. *Am J Anat* 1907; **7**: 409–21.

18 Richardson KC, Young FG. Histology of diabetes induced in dogs by injection of anterior-pituitary extracts. *Lancet* 1938; i: 1098–1101.

19 Anderson E, Long JA. Effect of hyperglycemia on insulin secretion as determined with isolated rat pancreas in perfusion apparatus. *Endocrinology* 1947; **40**: 92–7.

20 Bell ET. The incidence and significance of degranulation of the beta cells in the islets of Langerhans in diabetes mellitus. *Diabetes* 1953; **2**: 125–9.

21 Gomori G. Aldehyde-fuchsin: a new stain for elastic tissue. *Am J Clin Pathol* 1950; **20**: 655–6.

22 Orci L. The microanatomy of the islets of Langerhans. *Metabolism* 1976; **25** (suppl 1): 1303–13.

23 Baum J, Simon BE, Unger RH, Madison LL. Localisation of glucagon in the alpha cells in the pancreatic islets by immunofluorescent techniques. *Diabetes* 1962; **11**: 371–4.

24 Grimelius L, Polak JM, Solcia E, Pearse AGE. The entero-glucagon cell. In: Bloom SR, ed. *Gut Hormones*. Edinburgh: Churchill Livingstone, 1978: 365–8.

25 Bell GI, Sanchez-Pescador R, Laybourn PJ, Najarian RC. Exon duplication and divergence in the human preproglucagon gene. *Nature* 1983; **304**: 368–71.

26 Lopez LC, Frazier ML, Su CJ, Kumar A, Saunders GF. Mammalian pancreatic preproglucagon contains three glucagon-related peptides. *Proc Natl Acad Sci USA* 1983; **80**: 5485–9.

27 Ravazzola M, Orci L. Glucagon and glicentin immunoreactivity are topologically segregated in the alpha granule of the human pancreatic A cell. *Nature* 1980; **284**: 66–7.

28 Polak JM, Buchan AMJ, Probert L, Tapia F, De Mey J, Bloom SR. Regulatory peptides in endocrine cells and autonomic nerves. Electron immunocytochemistry. *Scand J Gastroenterol* 1981; **16** (suppl 70): 11–17.

29 Bloom W. New types of granular cell in islets of Langerhans of men. *Anat Rec* 1931; **49**: 363–71.

30 Polak JM, Pearse AGE, Grimelius L, Bloom SR, Arimura A. Growth-hormone releasing inhibiting hormone (GH-RIH) in gastrointestinal and pancreatic D cells. *Lancet* 1975; i: 1220–2.

31 Orci L, Baetens D, Dubois MP, Rufener C. Evidence for the D-cell of the pancreas secreting somatostatin. *Horm Metab Res* 1975; **7**: 400–2.

32 Alberti KGMM, Christensen NJ, Christensen SE, Hansen AP, Iversen J, Lundbaek K, Seyer-Hansen K, Ørskov H. Inhibition of insulin secretion by somatostatin. *Lancet* 1973; ii: 1299–301.

33 Larsson LI, Goltermann N, de Magistris L, Rehfeld JF, Schwartz TW. Somatostatin cell processes as pathways for paracrine secretion. *Science* 1979; **205**: 1393–4.

34 Gerich JE, Charles MA, Godsley GM. Regulation of pancreatic insulin and glucagon secretion. *Ann Rev Physiol* 1976; **38**: 353–88.

35 Mortimer CH, Turnbridge WMG, Carr D, Yeomans L, Lind T, Coy DH, Bloom SR, Kastin A, Mallinson CN, Besser GM, Schally AV, Hall R. Growth hormone-releasing inhibiting hormone: effects on circulating glucagon, insulin and growth hormone in normal, diabetic, acromegalic and hypopituitary patients. *Lancet* 1974; i: 697–701.

36 Luft R, Efendic S, Hökfelt T. Somatostatin – both hormone and neurotransmitter? *Diabetologia* 1978; **14**: 1–4.

37 Böhlen P, Brazeau P, Benoit R, Ling N, Esch F, Guillemin R. Isolation and amino acid composition of two somatostatin-like peptides from ovine hypothalamus: somatostatin-28 and somatostatin-25. *Biochem Biophys Res Commun* 1980; **96**: 725–7.

38 Pradayrol L, Jørnvall H, Mutt V, Ribert A. N-terminally extended somatostatin: the primary structure of somatostatin-28. *FEBS Lett* 1980; **109**: 55–8.

39 Schally AV, Huang WY, Chang RCC, Arimura A, Redding TW, Millar RP, Hunkapiller MW, Hood LE. Localisation and structure of pre-somatostatin: a putative somatostatin precursor from pig hypothalamus. *Proc Natl Acad Sci USA* 1980; **77**: 4489–93.

40 Benoit R, Böhlen P, Ling N, Briskin A, Esch F, Brazeau P, Ying SY, Guillemin R. Presence of somatostatin-28 (1-12) in hypothalamus and pancreas. *Proc Natl Acad Sci USA* 1982; **79**: 917–21.

41 Larsson LI, Sundler F, Håkanson R. Pancreatic polypeptide – a postulated new hormone: identification of its cellular storage site by light and electron microscopic immunocytochemistry. *Diabetologia* 1976; **12**: 211–6.

42 Adrian TE, Bloom SR, Besterman HS, Barnes AJ, Cooke TJ, Russell CGR, Faber FG. Mechanism of pancreatic polypeptide release in man. *Lancet* 1977; i: 161–3.

43 Schwartz TW, Rehfeld JF, Stadil F, Larsson LI, Chance RE, Moon N. Pancreatic polypeptide response to food in duodenal ulcer patients before and after vagotomy. *Lancet* 1976; i: 1102–5.

44 Orci L, Baetens D, Ravazzola M, Stefan Y, Malaisse-Lagae F. Pancreatic polypeptide and glucagon: non-random distribution in pancreatic islets. *Life Sci* 1976; **19**: 1811–3.

45 Hsi KL, Seidah NG, De Serres G, Chrétien M. Isolation and NH₂-terminal sequence of a novel porcine anterior pituitary polypeptide: homology to proinsulin, secretin and Rous sarcoma virus transforming protein TVFV6o. *FEBS Lett* 1982; **147**: 261–6.

46 Seidah NG, Hsi KL, De Serres G, Rochemont J, Hamelin J, Antakly T, Cantin M, Chretien M. Isolation and NH₂-terminal sequence of a highly conserved human and porcine pituitary protein belonging to a new superfamily. *Arch Biochem Biophys* 1983; **225**: 525–34.

47 Iguchi H, Chan JSD, Seidah NG, Chretien M. Tissue distribution and molecular forms of a novel pituitary peptide in the rat: *Neuroendocrinology* 1984; **39**: 453–7.

48 Suzuki H, Ghatei MA, Williams SJ, Uttenthal LO, Facer P, Bishop AE, Polak JM, Bloom SR. Production of pituitary protein 7B2 immunoreactivity by endocrine tumours and its possible diagnostic value. *J Clin Endocrinol Metab* 1986; **63**: 758–65.

49 Benjannet S, Leduc R, Lezure C, Seidah NC, Marcinkiewicz M, Chrétien M. GAWK, a novel human pituitary peptide: isolation, immunocytochemical localization and complete amino acid sequence. *Biochem Biophys Res Commun* 1985; **126**: 607–9.

50 Bishop AE, Sekiya K, Salahuddin MJ et al. The distribution of GAWK-like immunoreactivity in neuroendocrine cells of the human gut, pancreas, adrenal and pituitary glands and its co-localization with chromogranin B. *Histochem* 1989; **90**: 475–83.

51 Benjannet S, Leduc R, Advouche N et al. Chromogranin B (secretogranin 1), a putative precursor of two novel pituitary peptides through processing at paired basic residues. *FEBS Lett* 1987; **224**: 142–8.

52 O'Connor DT, Burton D, Deftos LJ. Immunoreceptive human chromogranin A in diverse polypeptide hormone-producing human tumours and normal endocrine tissues. *J Clin Endocrinol Metab* 1983; **57**: 1084–6.

53 Wilson BS, Lloyd RV. Detection of chromogranin in neuroendocrine cells with a monoclonal antibody. *Am J Pathol* 1984; **115**: 458–68.

54 Rindi G, Buffa R, Sessa F, Tortora O, Solcia E. Chromogranin A,B and C: immunoreactivities of mammalian endocrine cells. *Histochemistry* 1986; **88**: 19–28.

55 Varndell IM, Lloyd RV, Wilson BS, Polak JM. Ultrastructural localization of chromogranin: a potential marker for the electron microscopical recognition of endocrine cell secretory granules. *Histochem J* 1985; **17**: 981–92.

56 Tatemoto K, Efendic S, Mutt V, Makk G, Feistner GJ, Barchas JD. Pancreastatin, a novel pancreatic peptide that inhibits insulin secretion. *Nature* 1986; **324**: 476–8.

57 Ishizuka J, Asada I, Poston GJ, Lluis F, Tatemoto K, Greeley GH, Thompson JC. A new pancreatic peptide, pancreastatin regulates exocrine and endocrine secretions from the pan-

creas. *Gastroenterology* 1987; **92**: 1148.

58 Eiden L. Is chromogranin a prohormone? *Nature* 1987; **325**: 301.

59 Huttner WB, Benedum UM. Chromogranin A and pancreastatin. *Nature* 1987; 325−405.

60 Bretherton-Watt D, Ghatei MA, Bishop AE, Facer P, Fahey M, Hedges M, Williams G, Valentino KL, Tatemoto K, Roth K, Polak JM, Bloom SR. Pancreastatin distribution and plasma levels in the pig. *Peptides* 1989; **9**: 1005−14.

61 Westermark P, Wernstedt C, Wilander E, Sletton K. A novel peptide in the calcitonin gene-related family as an amyloid fibril protein in the endocrine pancreas. *Biochem Biophys Res Commun* 1986; **140**: 827−31.

62 Westermark P, Wernstedt C, Wilander E, Hayden DW, O'Brien TD, Johnson KH. Amyloid fibrils in human insulinoma and islets of Langerhans of the diabetic cat are derived from a neuro-peptide-like protein also present in normal islet cells. *Proc Natl Acad Sci USA* 1987; **84**: 3881−5.

63 Westermark P, Wernstedt C, O'Brien TD, Hayden DW, Johnson KH. Islet amyloid in Type 2 human diabetes mellitus and adult diabetic cats contains a novel putative polypeptide hormone. *Am J Pathol* 1987; **127**: 414−7.

64 Clark A, Cooper GJS, Lewis CE, Morris JF, Willis AC, Reid KBM, Turner RC. Islet amyloid formed from diabetes-associated peptide may be pathogenic in type-2 diabetes. *Lancet* 1987; ii: 231−4.

65 Johnson KK, O'Brien TD, Hayden DW, Jordan K, Ghobrial HKG, Mahoney WC, Westermark P. Immunolocalization of islet amyloid polypeptide in pancreatic beta cells by means of peroxidase anti-peroxidase and protein A techniques. *Am J Pathol* 1988; **130**: 1−8.

66 Cooper GJS, Leighton B, Dimitriadis GD, Parry-Billings M, Kowalchuk JM, Howland K, Rothbard JB, Willis AC, Reid KBM. Amylin found in amyloid deposits in human type 2 diabetes mellitus may be a hormone that regulates glycogen metabolism in skeletal muscle. *Proc Natl Acad Sci USA* 1988; **85**: 7763−6.

67 Leighton B, Cooper GJS. Pancreastatin, amylin and calcitonin gene-related peptide cause resistance to insulin in skeletal muscle *in vitro*. *Nature* 1988; **335**: 632−5.

68 Westermark P, Wilander E. The influence of amyloid deposition on the islet volume in maturity onset diabetes mellitus. *Diabetologia* 1978; **15**: 417−21.

69 Westermark P, Grimelius L. The pancreatic islet cells in insular amyloidosis in human diabetic and non-diabetic adults. *Acta Pathol Microbiol Scand (A)* 1973; **81**: 291−300.

70 Ehrlich J, Ratner IM. Amyloidosis of the islets of Langerhans: A re-study of islet hyalin in diabetic and non-diabetic individuals. *Am J Pathol* 1961; **38**: 49−59.

71 Samols E, Morris G, Marks V. Promotion of insulin secretion by glucagon. *Lancet* 1965; ii: 415−16.

72 Van Campenhout E. Contribution a l'étude de l'histogénèse du pancréas chez quelques mammifères. *Arch Biol Liège* 1927; **37**: 121−71.

73 Larsson LI. Innervation of the pancreas by substance P, enkephalin, vasoactive intestinal polypeptide and gastrin/CCK immunoreactive nerves. *J Histochem Cytochem* 1979; **27**: 1283−4.

74 Mulderry PK, Ghatei MA, Bishop AE, Allen YS, Polak JM, Bloom SR. Distribution and chromatographic characterisation of CGRP-like immunoreactivity in the brain and gut of the rat. *Reg Peptides* 1985; **6**: 133−43.

75 Su HC, Bishop AE, Power RF, Hamada Y, Polak JM. Dual intrinsic and extrinsic origins of CGRP- and NPY-immunoreactive nerves of rat gut and pancreas. *J Neurosci* 1987; **7**: 2674−87.

76 Carlei F, Allen JM, Bishop AE, Bloom SR, Polak JM. Occurrence, distribution and nature of neuropeptide Y in the rat pancreas. *Experientia* 1985; **41**: 1554−7.

77 Ekblad E, Wahlestedt C, Ekelund R, Hakanson R, Sundler F. Neuropeptide Y in the gut and pancreas. Distribution and possible vasomotor function. *Front Horm Res* 1984; **12**: 85−90.

78 Sundler F, Moghimzadeh E, Håkanson R, Ekelund M, Emson P. Nerve fibres in the gut and pancreas displaying neuropeptide Y immunoreactivity. *Cell Tiss Res* 1983; **230**: 487−93.

79 Bishop AE, Polak JM, Green IC, Bryant MG, Bloom SR. The location of VIP in the pancreas of man and rat. *Diabetologia* 1980; **18**: 73−8.

80 Larsson LI, Fahrenkrug J, Holst JJ, Schaffalitzky de Muckadell OB. Innervation of the pancreas by vasoactive intestinal polypeptide immunoreactive nerves. *Life Science* 1978; **22**: 773−9.

81 Sundler F, Alumets J, Håkanson R, Fahrenkrug J, Schaffalitzky de Muckadell OB. Peptidergic (VIP) nerves in the pancreas. *Histochemistry* 1978; **55**: 173−6.

9   Insulin Biosynthesis and Secretion

Summary

- Insulin biosynthesis proceeds through two intermediates: *preproinsulin*, which is cleaved by protease activity in the endoplasmic reticulum, and the resultant *proinsulin* which is packaged in vesicles and transported to the Golgi apparatus.
- Conversion to insulin by removal of C peptide occurs in the Golgi apparatus and the maturing secretory granules by enzymes with trypsin- and carboxypeptidase B-like activity.
- After removal of C peptide, the insulin co-precipitates with zinc ions as microcrystals within the secretory granules.
- Increases in the extracellular glucose concentration stimulate proinsulin biosynthesis but not enzymatic conversion to insulin. Over-production of insulin can be controlled by fusion of B-cell granules with lysosomes and proteolytic degradation (crinophagy)
- The granule contents are released by fusion of the granule membrane with the B-cell membrane (exocytosis).
- Translocation of granules to the cell membrane involves the cytoskeleton: microtubules composed of polymerized tubulin subunits provide the mechanical framework for transport and microfilaments of actin, together with myosin, produce the motive force.
- Insulin secretagogues may be *initiators* (effective alone, such as glucose and some amino acids) or *potentiators* (which increase the response to initiators, such as glucagon).
- Glucose-stimulated insulin release is biphasic, comprising a rapid first phase lasting 5–10 min and a prolonged second phase lasting for the duration of the stimulus.

- Glucose metabolism is required for insulin release, possibly by generating ATP which closes a K^+ channel in the B-cell membrane, thus reducing K^+ efflux, depolarizing the membrane and promoting Ca^{2+} entry into the cell via a voltage-gated Ca^{2+} channel; increased intracellular Ca^{2+} concentrations stimulate insulin release.
- Sulphonylurea drugs may also close a membrane K^+ channel, causing Ca^{2+} entry into the B cell.
- Vagal stimulation increases insulin release which is blocked by atropine. Sympathetic nerve stimulation inhibits insulin release.
- Gut hormones such as GIP and glucagon-like peptide 1 7–36 amide enhance nutrient-stimulated insulin release.
- Leucine and arginine elicit biphasic insulin release, in the absence of glucose.
- Stimulus-secretion coupling may involve several mechanisms. Cyclic AMP, Ca^{2+} (perhaps acting through the calcium-dependent regulatory proteins, calmodulin and protein kinase C) and phosphoinositide metabolites (inositol trisphosphate and diacylglycerol) may act as messengers in islet B cells.

This chapter summarizes the available information about the cellular events involved in the biosynthesis, storage and secretion of insulin and their regulation under physiological conditions.

Insulin biosynthesis

Insulin biosynthesis proceeds through at least two intermediates, preproinsulin and proinsulin. The genetic information for their biosynthesis is initially encoded by a messenger RNA of 600 nucleotides, transcription of which gives rise to preproinsulin, an 11.5-kDa polypeptide. This is rapidly (within 1 min) discharged into the cisternal space of the rough endoplasmic reticulum, where proteolytic enzymes cleave preproinsulin into proinsulin. Proinsulin is a 9-kDa peptide, containing the A and B chains of insulin joined by a connecting peptide (C peptide) of 30–35 amino acids [1]. The structural conformations of proinsulin and insulin are very similar, and a major function of the C peptide is to facilitate the correct folding of the A and B chains and alignment of their disulphide bridges before eventual cleavage (Fig. 9.1). Proinsulin is then transported by microvesicles to the Golgi apparatus [2], where

it is packaged in vesicles and surrounded by a membrane containing an ATP-dependent proton pump. The conversion of proinsulin to insulin is initiated in the Golgi complex and continues within the maturing secretory granule through the sequential action of proteases which possess trypsin- and carboxypeptidase B-like activities [3]. These enzymes remove the C peptide and two cleavage dipeptides (Fig. 9.1), yielding insulin which has a lower solubility and so co-precipitates with Zn^{2+} to form microcrystals within the secretory granule [4]. Insulin and C peptide are stored together in the granule sac and are ultimately released in equimolar amounts; under normal conditions, 95% of the biosynthetic product is secreted as insulin and less than 5% as

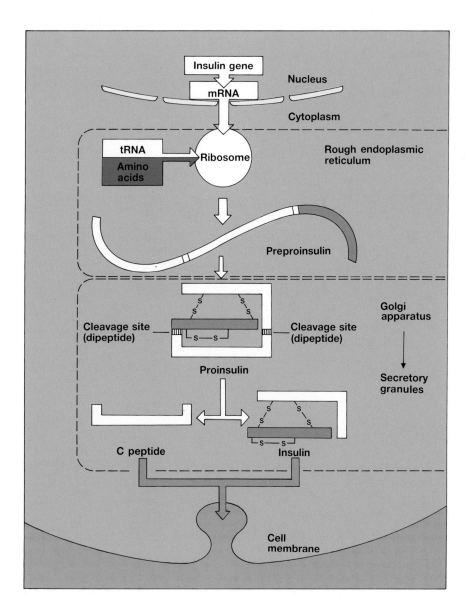

Fig. 9.1. Biosynthesis of preproinsulin and its subsequent conversion to proinsulin and insulin. Preproinsulin conversion occurs within 1 min, and cleavage of proinsulin to insulin within 1 h.

unconverted proinsulin [1]. The cellular processes involved in insulin biosynthesis, storage and secretion and their approximate durations are summarized in Fig. 9.2.

Acute (<2 h) increases in the extracellular concentration of glucose and certain other sugars result in a rapid and dramatic increase in proinsulin synthesis [5]. There is a sigmoidal relationship between glucose concentrations and biosynthetic activity, with a threshold value of 2–4 mmol/l. This is lower than the threshold for stimulation of insulin secretion, possibly to ensure an adequate supply of insulin. Glucose availability has no effect on the rate of conversion of proinsulin to insulin.

In circumstances in which there is overproduction of insulin by the B cells, granules may fuse with lysosomes when their contents are destroyed by proteolytic action [6]; this intracellular degradation of granules is termed *crinophagy*.

Insulin secretion

In normal B cells, insulin is released by the process of exocytosis (Fig. 9.3), in which the granules first move close to the cell membrane and the granule membrane and cell membrane then fuse together, releasing the granule contents. This process has been visualized by scanning and freeze-etching electron microscopy, which has demonstrated that the number of exocytotic profiles observed is increased by stimulation with glucose [7, 8]. In some insulin-secreting tumour lines, however, substantial release may occur through alternative route(s) which do not involve secretory granules.

The translocation of granules: role of the cytoskeleton

The role of cytoskeletal elements, notably microtubules and microfilaments, in the intracellular translocation of insulin storage granules has been extensively studied. However, the ways in which the metabolic signals developed during stimulation of insulin secretion are translated into granule movement and exocytosis remain unknown.

Microtubules are formed by the polymerization of subunits of tubulin (molecular weight, 55 kDa). They were first implicated in the mechanism of insulin secretion with the observation that colchicine and various other 'microtubule (spindle) poisons' all effectively inhibit insulin

Molecular stages	Cellular events	Organelles	
Reduced unfolded preproinsulin	Preproinsulin synthesis and cleavage to proinsulin (10–20 min)	Rough endoplasmic reticulum	
S–S bond formation, proinsulin folding		Microvesicles	
Formation of Zn-proinsulin hexamers	Transfer (20 min)		
		Golgi	
Zn-insulin hexamer with released C peptide. Precipitation begins	Proinsulin conversion begins	Early	Secretory granules
	Conversion completed (30–120 min)		
		Mature	
Crystal formation	Storage (for hours–days)		

Fig. 9.2. The intracellular pathway of insulin biosynthesis, storage and release in the pancreatic B cell. The molecular folding of the proinsulin molecule, its conversion to insulin and the subsequent arrangement of the insulin hexamers into a regular pattern is shown at the left. The time course of the various processes, and the organelles involved are also shown.

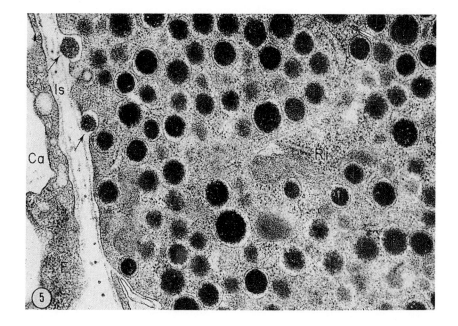

Fig. 9.3. Electron micrograph of insulin storage granules (B granules) in a pancreatic B cell and their secretion by exocytosis. The granule membrane and plasma membrane fuse together and the granule contents then diffuse across the capillary membrane into the bloodstream.

release [9], even though they have quite different effects on microtubule function. Colchicine itself disaggregates microtubules by binding to their tubulin subunits, whereas vinblastine causes formation of paracrystals of microtubular protein and nocodazole produces microtubule disaggregation through a different mechanism. All these drugs have the common effect of inhibiting glucose-stimulated insulin secretion, implying that it is the dynamic turnover of tubulin to microtubules which is important for the mechanism of secretion rather than the total number of microtubules present in the B cell. The localization of microtubules within the B cell has been studied in monolayer cultures [10]. Microtubules normally form a network radiating outwards from the perinuclear region, which is disrupted by prior exposure of the cells to colchicine.

Microtubules could provide a mechanical structure along which secretory granules move in an orientated fashion. However, with increasing knowledge of their biochemistry, it is now clear that the microtubules themselves could not provide the motive force to propel the granules through the cytoplasm. There has thus been increasing interest in the possible role of contractile proteins, actin and myosin, in the secretory process [9].

Actin, the constituent protein of microfilaments, exists in cells in two forms — a globular (g) form of 43 kDa molecular weight and a filamentous (f)

form which associates to form microfilaments. Evidence for the involvement of microfilaments in insulin release derives partly from the anti-secretory actions of two drugs, cytochalasin B and phalloidin, which interfere with microfilament formation.

A combined microtubular–microfilamentous system may drive the intracellular movement of the granules [9]. This possibility is supported by the observations that isolated granules can interact with microfilaments *in vitro*, and that the regulation of microfilament polymerization is governed by factors similar to those which alter rates of insulin secretion [10].

Myosin light and heavy chains have been detected in rat and catfish islets at concentrations which are considerably higher than those found in liver, and have been localized to B and A cells by immunofluorescence. It seems likely that actin (microfilaments), tubulin (microtubules) and myosin might act together to transport granules, the microtubules acting as a network along which the granules are propelled by the interaction of actin and myosin. Possible mechanisms for the regulation of granule movement are outlined in Fig. 9.4.

The movement of granules through the cytoplasm may be regulated independently of the process of granule extrusion; little is known of the biochemical processes involved in this final fusion step.

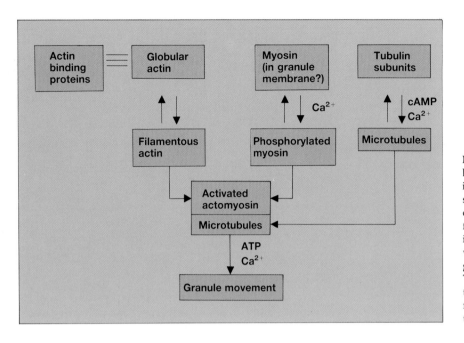

Fig. 9.4. Possible actions of the B-cell cytoskeleton to produce intracellular granule movement on stimulation of secretion. The contractile proteins, actin (in its filamentous form) and myosin, may interact to provide the motive force which propels insulin secretory granules along the microtubules. These consist of polymerized tubulin subunits and may act as mechanical guides for granule transport.

Regulation of insulin secretion

The major physiological determinant of insulin secretion in mammals is glucose availability, although a large number of physiological and pharmacological agents can also act as secretagogues [11]. These can be divided into two groups (Table 9.1): *initiators* or primary stimuli, i.e. agents capable of provoking insulin release alone, such as glucose and certain amino acids; and *potentiators*, i.e. agents which are ineffective alone but will increase the insulin released in response to glucose or amino acids, such as glucagon and phosphodiesterase inhibitors (see Fig. 9.5).

In man, following the ingestion of 50 g of glucose, blood insulin levels rise about five-fold, returning to basal within 2 h. The sluggish absorption of oral glucose obscures rapid events in the pancreas. In the perfused pancreas *in vitro*, raising the extracellular glucose concentration is followed after a delay of 50–100 s by a rapid increase in insulin release, returning towards basal levels in 5–10 min. This *first phase* of secretion is followed by a prolonged *second phase*, which continues for as long as the stimulus persists (Fig. 9.6). A similar rapid rise in insulin release is seen in man following an intravenous injection of glucose. The reason for the biphasic nature of the responses is unclear; not all stimuli evoke such a biphasic response [12].

GLUCOSE

B cells are acutely sensitive to small changes of extracellular glucose within a narrow physiological range. In response to glucose, B cells in isolated islets release insulin in a sigmoidal fashion (Fig. 9.5). Concentrations of glucose below 5 mmol/l do

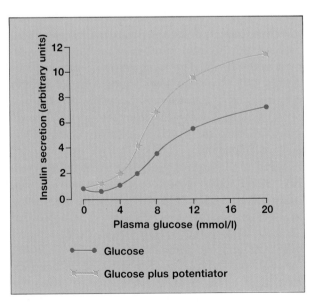

Fig. 9.5. Insulin secretory responses of islets of Langerhans to increasing glucose concentrations. No stimulation is seen below a threshold value of 5 mmol/l. Addition of a potentiator enhances secretion at all glucose concentrations, shifting the dose–response curve to the left. (Redrawn from [34].)

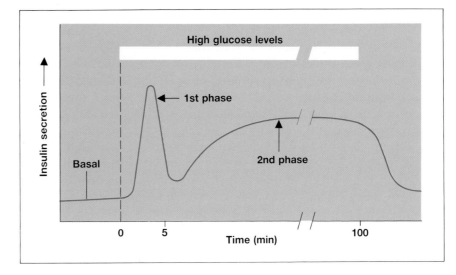

Fig. 9.6. Insulin release *in vitro* from an isolated, perfused pancreas, in response to an increase in the glucose concentration in the perfusing medium. An acute *first phase*, lasting a few minutes, is followed by a sustained *second phase* of secretion, which persists for the duration of the high-glucose stimulus.

not affect rates of release of insulin and the largest increases in secretory rates occur with extracellular glucose concentrations between 5.5 and 17 mmol/l, with half-maximal stimulation at 8 mmol/l [11].

Glucose must apparently be metabolized to affect insulin secretion, as insulin release is only provoked by glucose and sugar analogues that are metabolized, whereas release is prevented by mannoheptulose, an inhibitor of glucose metabolism. A similar sigmoidal relationship to that between the extracellular glucose concentration and insulin release also exists for O_2 consumption, glucose 6-phosphate content, lactate formation, $^{45}Ca^{2+}$ uptake and membrane electrical activity. Certain intermediates of glycolysis have also been demonstrated to induce insulin secretion, e.g. D-glyceraldehyde. Thus it is possible that certain metabolites of glucose may act as coupling factors between raised glucose concentrations and distal events in the regulation of insulin secretion.

Table 9.1. Factors which influence insulin secretion.

	Stimulators		Inhibitors
	Initiators (primary stimuli)	Potentiators	
Metabolites	Glucose Arginine, lysine Ketone bodies Free fatty acids	Cyclic AMP	
Neurotransmitters		Acetylcholine	Adrenaline Noradrenaline Neuropeptide Y Galanin
Gut peptides		Glucagon GLP1 7−36 amide GIP Secretin	Somatostatin
Drugs	Sulphonylureas		Diazoxide

ADENOSINE TRIPHOSPHATE (ATP)

Glucose metabolism increases the ATP content of B cells, the greatest increase apparently occurring in the cytosol. The dose–response curve for glucose-induced changes in ATP is different from that of insulin release, with marked changes in ATP occurring when the glucose concentration is raised from 0 to 5 mmol/l, whereas further increases in glucose concentration result in only small changes in total ATP content [13]. A role for ATP in the overall mechanism of secretion is implied by the observation that inhibitors of oxidative phosphorylation, which lower cellular ATP levels, also inhibit insulin release.

Using the patch-clamp technique, an inhibitory action of ATP has been demonstrated on potassium channel activity in the B-cell membrane [14, 15]. Such an ATP-sensitive potassium channel may provide the link between metabolism and the electrophysiological effects of glucose, as closing the channel will reduce potassium efflux, leading to membrane depolarization which in turn promotes calcium entry into the cell through voltage-dependent channels in the membrane; increased intracellular calcium levels then stimulate insulin secretion. However, the extreme sensitivity of the channel to ATP (even at micromolar concentrations) suggests that it would be closed even under basal conditions, although the channels studied so far in excised patches of B-cell membrane may behave differently in the intact cell.

Stimulation with glucose triggers characteristic electrical activity of the B-cell membrane, consisting of slow waves with superimposed spikes [16]. Raising the glucose concentration is followed by initial depolarization, bringing the membrane potential to a threshold at which electrical activity starts. The subsequent activity has two components, the first composed of continuous spike activity, followed by a partial repolarization without spikes, after which slow waves develop. The current carrier during the electrical bursts consists of Ca^{2+} ions entering the B cell via voltage-dependent channels in its membrane.

SULPHONYLUREAS

Tolbutamide was originally suggested to stimulate insulin secretion by inhibiting islet cyclic AMP phosphodiesterases. It has subsequently been proposed that the sulphonylureas affect Ca^{2+} transport across the plasma membrane, mediated by native ionophores, and that they have ionophoretic properties themselves. This is consistent with observed effects of sulphonylureas on $^{45}Ca^{2+}$ handling and on insulin release in isolated islets. More recently, these drugs have been suggested to act by closing a sulphonylurea-sensitive potassium channel (similar to the ATP-sensitive potassium channel described above). This hypothesis presents an interesting new model for the mechanism of action of these clinically important drugs [17] (see Fig. 9.7).

NEUROTRANSMITTERS

The islets are innervated by the autonomic nervous system, with a sympathetic branch from the middle splanchnic nerves and a parasympathetic branch from the vagus (see Chapter 8). Stimulation of the vagus, or mixed autonomic nerve, entering the pancreas causes insulin release, which can be blocked by atropine. Similarly, insulin secretion can also be evoked by direct stimulation with acetylcholine, which can be blocked by atropine [18], suggesting the involvement of muscarinic receptors. These secretory effects are dependent on the presence of glucose and Ca^{2+} uptake. Insulin secretion is inhibited following stimulation of the sympathetic innervation, and also by adrenaline or noradrenaline. Alpha and beta-adrenergic receptors have been identified and partially characterized in islets [19, 20]. In general, alpha-adrenergic agonists inhibit while beta-agonists stimulate insulin secretion.

In addition to the 'classical' neurotransmitters, several regulatory peptides have been identified within various types of nerves and terminals within the islets and have been found to exert experimental effects on insulin secretion [21] (see Chapter 8). Among these are vasoactive intestinal peptide [21], neuropeptide Y [22] and galanin [23], all of which inhibit insulin release *in vitro*; galanin apparently acts by activating ATP-sensitive channels which are blocked by sulphonylureas [23].

GUT PEPTIDES AND THE ENTERO-INSULAR AXIS

Various gut–pancreas peptides also affect insulin secretion, notably the other islet hormones, glucagon (which is stimulatory) and somatostatin which powerfully inhibits insulin release (see Chapter 33). These actions could be mediated by

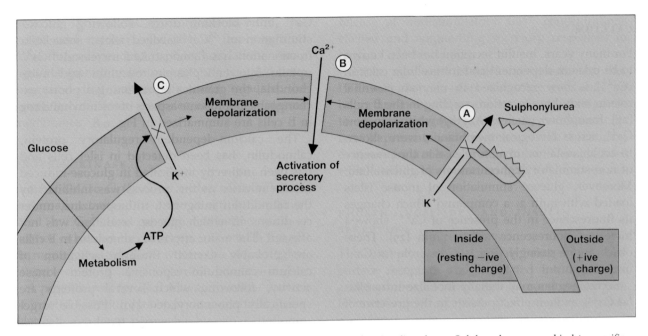

Fig. 9.7. Possible mechanism through which sulphonylureas may stimulate insulin release. Sulphonylureas may bind to specific membrane receptors which act to close K^+ channels in the membrane (A). This reduces K^+ efflux, increasing the net intracellular positive charge and tending to depolarize the membrane, which in turn promotes Ca^{2+} entry into the B cell through voltage-dependent channels in the plasma membrane (B). Increased intracellular Ca^{2+} levels stimulate insulin secretion. Glucose may act similarly, by generating ATP within B cells which acts to close ATP-sensitive K^+ channels (C). By contrast, the peptide galanin apparently inhibits insulin release by opening membrane K^+ channels, an action which is opposed by sulphonylureas [23].

a local paracrine action or by hormones carried in the capillaries within the islet which now seem to be organized in such a way that the secretions of the various islet cell types interact in a specific fashion [24].

Certain gut hormones may mediate the 'incretin' effect (i.e. the augmented insulin release following ingestion rather than parenteral administration of a glucose load) of the so-called 'entero-insular' axis. Possible candidates include gastric inhibitory peptide (GIP) and the recently identified C-terminal fragment of glucagon-like peptide 1 (GLP1 7-36 amide) (see Chapter 33), both of which enhance nutrient-stimulated insulin secretion. GIP is thought to act by activating adenylase cyclase and increasing intracellular cyclic AMP levels.

AMINO ACIDS

Only leucine and arginine, in the absence of glucose, are effective insulin secretagogues *in vitro*. The insulin response is biphasic. The mechanism by which amino acids stimulate the release of insulin is not clear; they do not have to be metabolized but transport alone is not sufficient for stimulation. It has been suggested that the inward movement of amino acid cationic charge may depolarize the B cell and open voltage-gated Ca^{2+} channels [25].

Stimulus−secretion coupling and intracellular messengers

CYCLIC AMP

Cyclic AMP (cAMP) acts as a potentiator of nutrient-induced insulin secretion; the site of action of cAMP is likely to be distal to the site of nutrient recognition.

The major effect of cAMP is thought to be exerted through the activation of protein kinases. cAMP-dependent protein kinase activity has been detected in islet homogenates, 85% of the activity being in the soluble fraction. Activation of the protein kinase follows binding of cAMP, with the release of the catalytic subunit from the cAMP-binding, regulatory subunit [26]. The phosphorylation of a number of cellular proteins by the activated protein kinase has been demonstrated.

In islets, glucose and the muscarinic agonist, carbamylcholine, stimulate the release of lipid-bound radioactivity from PIP_2 (phosphatidyl inositol 4,5 bis-phosphate) and PIP (phosphatidyl inositol 4-phosphate) with the concomitant accumulation of inositol trisphosphate (IP_3) [33]. This may indicate that agonist-induced PI hydrolysis (which is mediated by phospholipase C) could play a role in the stimulation of insulin secretion. Although stimulation of PIP_2 hydrolysis in islets seems to be mediated by activation of the muscarinic cholinergic receptor, the mechanism by which the metabolic secretagogue, glucose, might increase PIP_2 turnover is unclear. The role of IP_3 and related compounds in intracellular signalling is at present the subject of intense investigation. Possible ways in which initiators and potentiators of insulin secretion may interact and various messengers may be involved in stimulus-secretion coupling are shown in Fig. 9.9.

Conclusion

The pathways involved in the recognition of individual secretagogues and in the transduction of the recognized signals into activation of the secretory mechanism have been studied extensively in the last few years. This work has yielded much information about the basic biology of the pancreatic B cell, and will be an important basis for future studies of the role of the endocrine pancreas in the pathophysiology of both IDDM and NIDDM.

SIMON L. HOWELL

References

1 Steiner DF, Kemmler W, Clark AL, Oyer PE, Rubenstein AH. The biosynthesis of insulin. In: Steiner DF, Freinkel N (eds) *Handbook of Physiology*, Section 7, Vol 1. American Physiological Society, 1972: 175–98.

2 Orci L. Patterns of sub-cellular organization in the endocrine pancreas. *J Endocrinol* 1984; 102: 3–11.

3 Orci L, Ravazzola M, Amherdt M, *et al.* Conversion of proinsulin to insulin occurs coordinately with acidification of maturing secretory granules. *J Cell Biol* 1986; 103: 2273–81.

4 Howell SL, Young DA, Lacy PE. Isolation and properties of secretory granules from rat islets of Langerhans. III. *J Cell Biol* 1969; 41: 154–61.

5 Ashcroft SJH, Bunce J, Lowry M, Hanson SE, Hedeskov CJ. The effects of sugars on (pro)insulin biosynthesis. *Biochem J* 1978; 174: 517–26.

6 Halban PA, Wollheim CB. Intracellular degradation of insulin stores by pancreatic islets *in vitro*. *J Biol Chem* 1980; 255: 6003–6.

7 Lacy PE. Beta cell secretion. From the standpoint of a pathobiologist. *Diabetes* 1970; 19: 895–905.

8 Rhodes CJ, Halban PA. Newly synthesised proinsulin/insulin and stored insulin are released from pancreatic B-cells predominantly via a regulated, rather than a constitutive, pathway. *J Cell Biol* 1987; 105: 145–53.

9 Howell SL, Tyhurst M. The pancreatic B cell cytoskeleton and insulin secretion. *Diabetes Metab Rev* 1986; 2: 107–23.

10 Howell SL. The mechanism of insulin secretion (review). *Diabetologia* 1984; 26: 319–27.

11 Hedeskov CJ. Mechanism of glucose-induced insulin secretion. *Physiol Rev* 1980; 60: 442–509.

12 Howell SL, Bird GStJ. Biosynthesis and secretion of insulin. *Br Med Bull* 1989; 45: 19–37.

13 Ashcroft SJH, Weerasinghe LCC, Randle PJ. Interrelationship of islet metabolism, ATP content and insulin release. *Biochem J* 1973; 132: 223–31.

14 Cook DL, Hales CN. Intracellular ATP directly blocks potassium channels in pancreatic B cells. *Nature* 1984; 311: 271–3.

15 Ashcroft FM, Harrison DE, Ashcroft SJH. Glucose induces closure of single potassium channels in isolated rat pancreatic B cells. *Nature* 1984; 312: 446–8.

16 Meissner HP, Schmelz H. Membrane potential of beta-cells in pancreatic islets. *Pflügers Arch* 1974; 351: 185–206.

17 Boyd AE. Sulphorylurea receptors, ion channels and fruit flies. *Diabetes* 1988; 37: 847–50.

18 Gagerman E, Idahl LA, Meissner HP, Taljedal IB. Insulin release, cAMP, cGMP and membrane potential in acetylcholine-stimulated islets. *Am J Physiol* 1978; 235: E493–E500.

19 Fyles JM, Cawthorne MA, Howell SL. The determination of alpha adrenergic receptor concentration on rat pancreatic islet cells. *Biosci Repts* 1987; 7: 17–25.

20 Fyles JM, Cawthorne M, Howell SL. Characterization of beta adrenergic receptors in rat and guinea pig islets of Langerhans. *J Endocrinol* 1986; 111: 263–70.

21 Åhren B, Taborsky GJ, Porte D. Neuropeptidergic versus cholinergic and adrenergic regulation of islet hormone secretion. *Diabetologia* 1986; 29: 827–36.

22 Moltz JH, McDonald JK. Neuropeptide Y: direct and indirect action on insulin secretion in the rat. *Peptides* 1985; 6: 1155–9.

23 de Weiue J, Schmid-Antomarchi H, Fosset M, Lazdunski M. ATP-sensitive K^+ channels that are blocked by hypoglycemia-inducing sulfonylureas in insulin-secreting cells are activated by galanin, a hyperglycemia-inducing hormone. *Proc Natl Acad Sci USA* 1988; 85: 1312–16.

24 Stagner JI, Samols E, Marks V. The anterograde and retrograde infusion of glucagon antibodies suggests that A-cells are vascularly perfused before D-cells within the rat islet. *Diabetologia* 1989; 32: 203–6.

25 Hermans MP, Schmeer V, Henquin JC. The permissive effect of glucose, tolbutamide and high K^+ on arginine stimulation of insulin secretion. *Diabetologia* 1987; 30: 659–65.

26 Montague W, Howell SL. Effects of insulin secretagogues on protein kinase activity in rat islets of Langerhans. *Biochem J* 1974; 134: 321–7.

27 Wollheim CB, Sharp GWG. Calcium regulation of insulin release. *Physiol Rev* 1981; 61: 914–73.

28 Wollheim CB, Blondel B, Trueheart PA, Renold AE, Sharp GWG. Calcium-induced insulin release in monolayer cultures of the endocrine pancreas. Studies with ionophore A23187. *J Biol Chem* 1975; 250: 1354–60.

29 Rorsman P, Abrahamsson H, Gylfe E, Hellman B. Dual

effects of glucose on the cytosolic Ca^{2+} activity of mouse pancreatic B-cells. *FEBS Lett* 170 1984; **196**: 200–5.

30 Sugden MC, Christie MR, Ashcroft SJH. Presence and possible role of calcium dependent regulator (calmodulin) in rat islets of Langerhans. *FEBS Lett* 1979; **105**: 95–100.

31 Jones PM, Stutchfield J, Howell SL. Effects of Ca^{2+} and a phorbol ester on insulin secretion from islets of Langerhans permeabilised by high voltage discharge. *FEBS Lett* 1985; **191**: 102–6.

32 Hii CST, Jones PM, Persaud SJ, Howell SL. Reassessment of the role of protein kinase C in glucose-stimulated insulin secretion. *Biochem J* 1987; **246**: 489–93.

33 Turk J, Wolf BA, McDaniel ML. Glucose-induced accumulation of inositol triphosphates in isolated pancreatic islets. *Biochem J* 1986; **237**: 259–63.

34 Howell SL. Regulation and mechanism of insulin secretion. In: Besser GM, Bodanski HJ, Cudworth AG (eds) *Clinical Diabetes*. Gower Medical, London, 1988.

10   The Structure and Phylogeny of Insulin

Summary

• The insulin molecule consists of two polypeptide chains, the A chain (21 amino-acid residues) and B chain (30 residues), linked by two disulphide bridges.

• Human insulin differs from porcine insulin in a single residue (at position B30) and from bovine insulin by two additional amino-acid substitutions (A8 and A10).

• The tertiary structure of monomeric insulin consists of a hydrophobic core buried beneath a surface which is hydrophilic, except for two non-polar regions which are involved in aggregation of insulin molecules.

• Insulin exists as monomers in dilute solutions (e.g. in the circulation) but as hexamers (consisting of six monomers which self-associate in conjunction with two zinc ions) in crystals and in the B-cell secretory granule.

• The receptor-binding region of the molecule may be centred on the dimer-forming residues (B24–B26).

• Insulin is phylogenetically ancient and belongs to a large family of homologous molecules with different functions, including insulin-like growth factors and ovarian relaxin.

It is now some 35 years since Sanger and colleagues reported the primary amino acid sequence of porcine insulin [1] and 20 years since Dorothy Hodgkin and her colleagues used X-ray diffraction to elucidate its three-dimensional structure [2]. Subsequently, X-ray diffraction studies of the various crystalline forms of insulin have increased our understanding of the ways in which individual insulin molecules may associate with one another [3–5]. Tertiary structures of insulin from several species (including man) and of insulin analogues have also been investigated [6–13]. Primary structures are available for more than 70 insulins and insulin-like molecules. All these molecules share a similar basic design and, despite variations in their primary sequences, they can probably all fold their polypeptide chains to achieve an insulin-like tertiary structure.

This chapter will first describe the structure of insulin and the possible functional importance of specific parts of the molecule. Finally, the structural similarities between insulin and the other members of an expanding family of homologous molecules will be discussed.

Structure of insulin

The insulin molecule consists of two polypeptide chains, designated A and B, linked by two disulphide bridges. The A chain also contains an intrachain disulphide bridge linking residues 6 and 11. The A chain consists of 21 amino-acid residues and the B chain of 30. The derivation of insulin from its precursor, proinsulin, is discussed in Chapter 9.

The primary structure of human insulin is shown in Fig. 10.1, which highlights the sequence differences between the human molecule and those of porcine and bovine insulin. Human insulin differs from porcine only in the last residue of the B chain (Thr in man, Ala in the pig), and from bovine by substitution at two additional residues in the A chain (positions 8 and 10: respectively Thr and Ile in man and Ala and Val in the ox). The secondary structures of the A and B

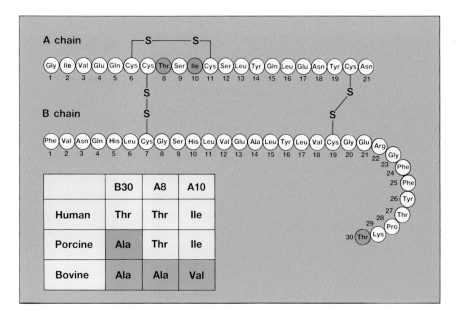

Fig. 10.1. Primary structure (amino-acid sequence) of human insulin. The highlighted residues are those which differ in porcine and bovine insulins, as shown in the inset.

	B30	A8	A10
Human	Thr	Thr	Ile
Porcine	Ala	Thr	Ile
Bovine	Ala	Ala	Val

chains are shown in Fig. 10.2. The A chain contains two helical regions, A1 to A8 and A13 to A19, whose axes are almost antiparallel. These are connected by an extended loop which is bridged by the intrachain disulphide bond (Fig. 10.2a). The dominant secondary structural element of the B chain is the alpha-helical section between residues B9 and B19, followed by a sharp turn to position B23 (Fig. 10.2b). Residues B1−B8 and B23−B30 are in extended conformation, although the region B1−B8 can assume a helical conformation in crystal forms in which four zinc ions, rather than the usual two, or six phenol molecules are associated with each hexamer [4, 30]. This region is considered to be somewhat mobile, its exact conformation being determined by forces of aggregation.

The A and B chains fold together to produce a compact insulin protomer (Fig. 10.3). The disposition of the amino-acid side chains is largely consistent with the pattern found in most water-soluble proteins in which the hydrophobic core is buried within a hydrophilic surface, with the exception of two non-polar regions on the surface. These participate in the interaction between insulin monomers during their aggregation into dimers and hexamers. The B chain provides most of the intermolecular contacts involved in aggregation. In dimer formation, residues B24−B26 of the two associating monomers interact to form an antiparallel beta-pleated sheet (Fig. 10.4). The four participating hydrogen bonds are screened by a cluster of non-polar side chains: B24 and B25 (both

Phe), B16 and B26 (both Tyr), and B12 (Val). The conformations of the two component monomers are similar but not identical when associated in the common two-zinc (2Zn) crystal, but may be identical in other forms [5].

The 2Zn-insulin hexamer is composed of three identical insulin dimers associated in the three-fold symmetrical pattern shown in Fig. 10.5. The dimers are held together by contacts between hydrophobic residues in the helical and N-terminal regions of each monomer's B chain, and by co-ordination of two zinc ions by the B10 His residues which come to lie close to the central axis of the hexamer. Zinc−insulin hexamers are believed to exist in the storage granules of the B cells but because of the massive dilution following secretion, these rapidly dissociate to produce the monomer, which is the dominant species in the circulation. The properties of insulin in solution generally agree with those predicted by its crystal structure, although some spectroscopic measurements on very dilute solutions suggest that the monomer may be less highly organized in isolation than it is when aggregated [10].

In bovine insulin, the sequence differs from those of porcine and human in the A8−A10 loop regions. These areas protrude from the hexamer surface and fit into concavities of adjacent hexamers, leading to a crystal packing disturbance [9]. This may partly explain the slightly altered solubility and crystallization behaviour of bovine insulin, which could affect its pharmacokinetic and therapeutic properties and perhaps explain

(a)

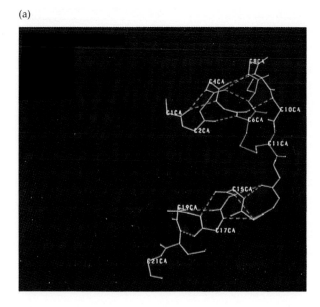

(b)

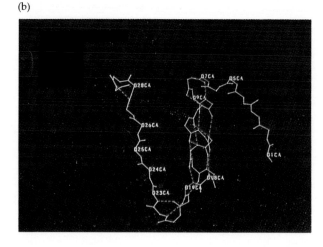

(c)

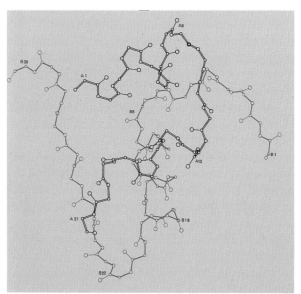

Fig. 10.2. The main chain atoms and hydrogen bonds (dashed lines) of the secondary structure of (a) the A chain (numbered C1−C21CA) and (b) the B chain (numbered D1−D30CA). (c) This shows the position of the two chains in the intact molecule.

the altered glycaemic control shown by some patients when changed to or from bovine insulin preparations.

Proinsulin can also form dimers and zinc hexamers. It is assumed that the C peptide packs against the insulin surface exposed in the hexamer to produce a compact structure, but this awaits confirmation by X-ray structural analysis.

Receptor-binding region of insulin

Since the structure of insulin was first described, much effort has been invested in attempting to identify the surface region of the monomer which interacts with the target-cell receptor. Sites have been identified where sequence variation or chemical modification lead to marked changes in activity, suggesting that they are involved in receptor binding. Attention was initially drawn to a sequence-invariant region which included the N and C termini of the A chain and adjacent B chain residues [11]. This idea has now been extended [12, 13] with the suggestion that receptor binding centres on the dimer-forming residues (B24−B26) but also involves surrounding sites (A1, A19, A21, B12, B16) (Fig. 10.6). The side chains of B24 and B25 (both Phe) are of particular interest as their substitution (by either natural mutation

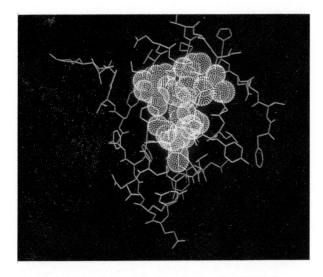

Fig. 10.3. Molecular model of porcine insulin. Highlights indicate van der Waals dot surfaces of the buried residues (A6, A11, A16, B11, B15, A2) of the hydrophobic core.

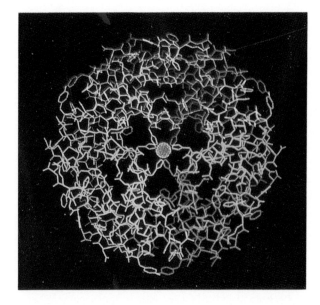

Fig. 10.5. The insulin hexamer viewed along its axis of threefold symmetry, with each of the six molecules coloured differently.

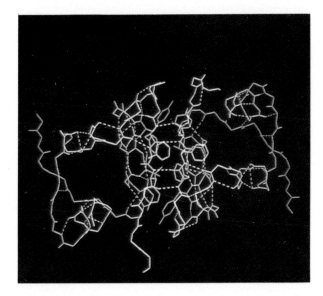

Fig. 10.4. The hydrogen bonds (dashed lines) of the pleated sheet between the two insulin molecules of a dimer, and the cluster of aromatic and apolar residues of the interface, shown in red. These residues are among those implicated in receptor binding.

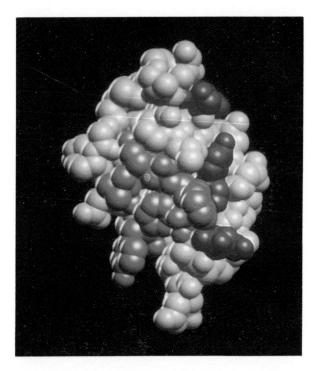

Fig. 10.6. Space-filling model showing the surface area of the insulin molecule which may be presented to the receptor. If residues B26–B30 (centre top) are flexible and move away to allow receptor binding, then underlying residues (such as A3 Val) will become exposed.

or semisynthesis) can dramatically alter biological activity [14–16]. Furthermore, this region has been shown to be important for negative co-operative effects on receptor binding [17] (see Chapter 11). It has been suggested that these effects are mediated at a molecular level by dimerization of bound insulin molecules, implying that the conserved residues of the A chain alone make up the binding surface [18].

These models convey essentially static views of important residues. Under various conditions, however, small structural perturbations can apparently be accommodated by relative movements of the rigid helical sections of the molecule [19]. A more dynamic view of the insulin molecule may have to be taken, as its capacity for conformational change may be important for its biological activity [20]. For instance, insulin which contains a short (seven-carbon) covalent crosslink between A1 (Gly) and B29 (Lys) which restricts the conformation in this region, has low biological activity, despite its structural similarity to porcine insulin [21]. Moreover, analogues lacking five residues from the C terminus of the B chain have recently been described which are fully active or even superactive. This raises further questions about the location of this part of the molecule when intact insulin binds to its receptor, and has renewed speculation about the possible importance of flexibility in this region for the expression of biological activity [22, 23].

Phylogeny of the insulin molecule

Insulin is phylogenetically ancient, being found not only in mammals, but also in birds, reptiles, both teleost and elasmobranch fish, and also the very primitive hagfish. Insulin molecules from many species have now been sequenced (Table 10.1). They show many structural variations, but structurally important residues in the core, the disulphide bridges and glycine residues at bends are generally conserved, suggesting that all insulins can achieve a tertiary structure similar to that of the porcine molecule.

The insulins are members of a larger family of molecules which all have some degree of homology in their sequence and probably in their tertiary structure. The insulin-like growth factors 1 and 2 (IGF-1 and IGF-2), which are responsible for most of the insulin-like activity of serum, are single-chain proteins which contain sequences analogous to the A chain, C peptide and B chain moieties of proinsulin [24] (see Table 10.1). They have close homology with insulin in the structurally important core regions but are quite different throughout much of their surface. Their low, but distinct, insulin-like activity correlates with the possession of certain residues thought to be important for the activity of insulin itself. The presence of additional parts of the molecule (the C-peptide-like region and the A-chain extension) must modify the receptor-binding region and/or the molecule's potential for conformational change, and so specify binding to IGF receptors. On the other hand, ovarian relaxin, which has no insulin-like activity, has a sequence less closely related to that of insulin, although molecular modelling shows that it could fold like the insulin pattern [25, 26].

Recently, two more distant members of the insulin family have been described. These were isolated from the neurones of a mollusc (MIP-molluscan insulin-like peptide) [27] and an insect (bombyxin) [28] and both seem to have roles in growth and development. They both have the essential distribution of disulphide bonds and non-polar residues capable of packing a hydrophobic core of similar volume to that of insulin [29]. The basic architecture of insulin seems, therefore, to be of an ancient design, from which evolution has generated a family of molecules with a wide range of functions.

STEVEN P. WOOD
ALASDAIR MCLEOD

Table 10.1. Primary sequences (designated using the conventional single-letter code for each amino acid) of insulin from several species and other structurally related molecules, to show the extent of homology. (IGF 1 and 2: insulin-like growth factors 1 and 2; MIP: molluscan insulin-like peptide.)

	B CHAIN	C PEPTIDE	A CHAIN	D PEPTIDE
Human insulin	FVNQHLCGSHLVEALYLVCGERGFFYTPKT	RREAEDLQVGQVELGGGPGAGSLQPLALEGSLQKR	GIVEQCCTSICSLYQLENYCN	
Turkey insulin	AANQHLCGSHLVEALYLVCGERGFFYSPKA		GIVEQCCHNTCSLYQLENYCN	
Rattlesnake insulin	APNQRLCGSHLVEALFLICGERGFYYSPRS		GIVEQCCENTCSLYQLENYCN	
Cod insulin	MAPPQHLCGSHLVDALYLVCGDRGFFYNPK		GIVDQCCHRPCDIFDLQNYCN	
Dogfish insulin	LPSQHLCGSHLVEALYFVCGPKGFYYLPKA		GIVEHCCHNTCSLYDLEGYCNQ	
Hagfish insulin	RTTGHLCGKDLVNALYIACGVRGFFYDPTK		GIVEQCCHKRCSIYNLQNYCN	
Human IGF1	GPETLCGAELVDALQFVCGDRGFYFNKPT	GYGSSSRRAPQT	GIVDECCFRSCDLRRLEMYCA	PLKPAKSA
Human IGF2	AYRPSETLCGGELVDTLQFVCGDRGFYFSRPA	SRVSRRSR	GIVEECCFRSCDLALLETYCA	TPAKSE
PTTH-II	XQPQAVHTYCGRHLARTLADLCWEAGVD		GIVDECCLRPCSVDVLLSYC	
MIP	QFSACNINDRPHRRGVCGSALADLVDFACSSSNQPAMV		QGTTNIVCECCMKPCTLSELRQYCP	
Pig relaxin	STNDFIKACGRELVRLWVEICGVWS		RMTLSEKCCEVGCIRKDIARLC	

References

1 Brown H, Sanger F, Kitai R. The structure of pig and sheep insulin. *Biochem J* 1955; **60**: 556–65.

2 Adams MJ, Blundell TL, Dodson EJ, Dodson GG, Vijayan M, Baker EN, Harding MM, Hodgkin DC, Rimmer B, Sheat S. Structure of 2 zinc insulin crystals. *Nature* 1969; **224**: 491–5.

3 Baker EN, Blundell TL, Cutfield JF, Cutfield SM, Dodson EJ, Dodson GG, Hodgkin DMC, Hubbard RE, Isaacs NW, Reynolds CD, Sakabe K, Sakabe N, Vijayan NM. The structure of 2 Zn pig insulin crystals at 1.5 Å resolution. *Phil Trans R Soc London* 1988; **319**: 369–456.

4 Bentley GA, Dodson EJ, Dodson GG, Hodgkin DC, Mercola DA. Structure of 4-zinc insulin. *Nature* 1976; **261**: 166–8.

5 Dodson EJ, Dodson GG, Lewitova A, Sabesan N. Zinc free cubic pig insulin: crystallisation and structure determination. *J Molec Biol* 1978; **125**: 387–96.

6 Pullen RA, Lindsay DG, Wood SP, Tickle IJ, Blundell TL, Wollmer A, Krail G, Brandenburg D, Zahn H, Glieman J, Gammeltoft S. Receptor binding region of insulin. *Nature* 1976; **259**: 369–73.

7 Cutfield JF, Cutfield SM, Dodson EJ, Dodson GG, Emdin SF, Reynolds CD. Structure and biological activity of hagfish insulin. *J Molec Biol* 1979; **132**: 85–100.

8 Chawdhury SA, Dodson EJ, Dodson GG, Reynolds CD, Tolley SP, Blundell TL, Cleasby A, Pitts JE, Tickle IJ, Wood SP. The crystal structures of three non-pancreatic human insulins. *Diabetologia* 1983; **25**: 460–4.

9 Blundell TL, Wood SP. Is the evolution of insulin Darwinian or due to selectively neutral mutation? *Nature* 1975; **257**: 197–203.

10 Pocker Y, Biswas SB. Conformational dynamics of insulin in solution. Circular dichroism studies. *Biochemistry* 1980; **19**: 5043–9.

11 Blundell T, Dodson G, Hodgkin D, Mercola D. Insulin: the structure in the crystal and its reflection in chemistry and biology. *Adv Protein Chem* 1972; **26**: 279–402.

12 Blundell TL, Wood SP. The conformation, flexibility and dynamics of polypeptide hormones. *Ann Rev Biochem* 1982; **51**: 123–54.

13 Blundell TL, Pitts JE, Wood SP. The conformation and molecular biology of pancreatic hormones and homologous growth factors. *CRC Crit Rev Biochem* 1982; **13**: 141–213.

14 Tager H, Thomas N, Assoian R, Rubenstein A, Saekow M, Olefsky J, Kaiser ET. Semisynthesis and biological activity of porcine (Leu B24) and (Leu B25) insulin. *Proc Natl Acad Sci USA* 1980; **77**: 3181–5.

15 Wollmer A, Strassburger W, Glatter U, Dodson GG, McCall M, Danho W, Brandenburg D, Gattner H-G, Danho W. Two mutant forms of human insulin. Structural consequences of the substitution of invariant B24 or B25 phenylalanine by leucine. *Hoppe-Seylers Z Physiol Chem* 1981; **362**: 581–91.

16 Kobayashi M, Ohgaku S, Iwasaki M, Megawa H, Shigeta Y, Inouye K. Supernormal Insulin: [D-Phe B24]-insulin with increased affinity for insulin receptors. *Biochem Biophys Res Commun* 1982; **107**: 392–436.

17 De Meyts P, Van Obberghen E, Roth J, Wollmer A, Brandenburg D. Mapping of the residues responsible for the negative cooperativity of the receptor binding region of insulin. *Nature* 1978; **273**: 504–9.

18 Saunders DJ. Structure–function relationships in insulin. *Diabetologia* 1982; **23**: 386–90.

19 Chothia C, Lesk A, Dodson GG, Hodgkin DC. Transmission of conformational change in insulin. *Nature* 1983; **302**: 500–5.

20 Dodson EJ, Dodson GG, Hubbard RE, Reynolds CD. Insulin's structural behaviour and its relation to activity. *Biopolymers* 1983; **22**: 281–91.

21 Dodson GG, Cutfield S, Hoenjet E, Wollmer A, Brandenburg D. Crystal structure, aggregation and biological potency of beef insulin cross-linked at A1 and B29 by diaminosuberic acid. In: Brandenburg D, Wollmer A, eds. *Insulin. Chemistry, Structure and Function of Insulin and Related Hormones* Berlin: Walter de Gruyter & Co., 1980: 17–26.

22 Nagagawa SH, Tager HS. Role of the Phenylalanine B25 side chain in directing insulin interaction with its receptor. Steric and conformational effects. *J Biol Chem* 1986; **261**: 7332–41.

23 Casaretto M, Spoden M, Diaconescu C, Gattner HG, Zahn H, Brandenburg D, Wollmer A. Shortened insulin with enhanced *in vitro* potency. *Hoppe-Seylers Z Physiol Chem* 1987; **368**: 709–16.

24 Blundell TL, Humbel RE. Hormone families: pancreatic hormones and homologous growth factors. *Nature* 1980; **287**: 781–7.

25 Bedarkar S, Turnell WG, Blundell TL, Schwabe C. Relaxin has conformational homology with insulin. *Nature* 1977; **270**: 449–51.

26 Isaacs N, James R, Niall H. Relaxin and its structural relationship to insulin. *Nature* 1978; **271**: 278–81.

27 Smit AB, Vreugdenhil E, Ebberink RHM, Geraerts WPM, Klootwijk J, Joosse J. Growth-controlling molluscan neurons produce the precursor of an insulin-related peptide. *Nature* 1988; **331**: 535–8.

28 Nagasawa H, Kataoka H, Isogai A, Tamura S, Suzuki A, Mizoguchi A, Fujiwara Y, Suzuki A, Takahashi SY, Ishizaki H. *Proc Natl Acad Sci USA* 1986; **83**: 5840–3.

29 Jhoti H, McLeod AN, Blundell TL, Ishizaki H, Nagasawa H, Suzuki A. Prothoracicotrophic hormone (PTTH) has an insulin-like tertiary structure. *FEBS Lett* 1987; **219**: 419–25.

30 Derewenda U, Derewenda Z, Dodson EJ, Dodson GG, Reynolds CD, Smith GD, Sparkes C and Swenson D. Phenol stabilises more helix in a new symmetrical zinc insulin hexamer. *Nature* 1989; **338**: 594–596.

11   The Insulin Receptor

Summary

• Insulin receptors lie on the target cell surface; when occupied, they are concentrated within coated pits lined by the protein, clathrin.

• The receptor consists of two extracellular alpha-subunits (MW, 130 kDa) linked covalently to two beta-subunits (MW, 95 kDa) which straddle the cell membrane. It has some structural similarities with the receptors for growth factors, LDL and certain oncogene products.

• The gene for the insulin receptor precursor lies on the short arm of chromosome 19.

• Insulin binds to sites on the alpha-subunits and activates a protein kinase within the beta-subunit which phosphorylates several tyrosine residues on the receptor. This change may trigger the intracellular events underlying insulin's metabolic effects.

• The receptor–insulin complex is internalized by the surrounding membrane invaginating to form an endosome. Insulin is degraded intracellularly whereas the receptors are recycled to the cell surface.

• The binding of insulin to its receptor does not conform to the law of mass action, due both to 'negative co-operativity' (by which receptor–insulin complexes reduce the affinity of other binding sites for insulin) and to other receptor interactions which may increase affinity.

• High ambient insulin levels reduce insulin-binding capacity by increasing receptor turnover ('down-regulation').

Peptide hormones circulate in plasma in remarkably small amounts. Only 50 g of insulin are required for a human lifetime and, excluding the contents of the pancreatic islets, euglycaemia and freedom from ketosis in the postabsorptive state are maintained by approximately 10 µg of insulin — roughly 1 part in 7000 million by weight. Highly specialized mechanisms must be invoked to explain how such low concentrations of hormones could exert profound effects on intracellular chemistry, particularly as the bilipid plasma membrane of cells would prevent their access to intracellular sites. During the 1950s, Sutherland developed the idea that target cells would carry specific 'receptor' sites on the cell surface and that the hormonal signal would be carried inside the cell by one or more 'second messengers' [1]. These receptors were conceived as complex molecules with three essential characteristics. First, they should possess high specificity for the hormone concerned with very little ability to recognize any other molecular structure. Secondly, they should have high affinity for the hormone, such that in the presence of very low free hormone concentrations, thermodynamic factors would favour the associated, hormone–receptor complex condition rather than dissociation. Finally, the interaction of the hormone with its specific receptor would result in a physico-chemical change on the inside of the plasma membrane, probably involving part of the receptor structure itself. This in turn would initiate an amplification cascade so that changes in hormone concentration in the picomolar range could induce metabolic events at millimolar concentrations.

Insulin binding to cells

The ability to label insulin with radioactive iodine led rapidly to confirmation that both isolated plasma membranes and intact cells contain sites which bind insulin with high specificity and affinity.

The characteristics of insulin binding to cell membrane preparations are illustrated in Fig. 11.1a. Insulin bound at equilibrium to the receptor preparation increases with rising concentrations of the free hormone in the medium. The non-linear response is characteristic of bimolecular dynamic interactions and can be quantitatively described by deriving values for two variables, the capacity and affinity of the system. The *capacity* is the total quantity of insulin capable of being bound by the preparation at an infinite free insulin concentration. From this value, it should be possible to evaluate the number of binding sites, for example per cell. The *affinity* of the binding reaction is usually expressed as the reciprocal of the Kd, i.e. the free insulin concentration required to produce half-maximal occupation of the receptor population by the hormone.

These theoretically simple calculations do not apply in practice in the case of insulin and its binding sites. Fig. 11.1b illustrates these difficulties. To calculate capacity (i.e. total receptor number) and affinity, it is usual to transform the data graphically as a 'Scatchard plot' [2]. For a classical binding reaction which obeys the law of mass action, plotting the ratio of bound to free hormone (derived at different points along the curve of Fig. 11.1a) against the total mass of bound hormone results in a straight line (Fig. 11.1b). The *x* intercept is equal to the maximal capacity of the system and the slope represents the affinity [2]. Insulin does not conform to this classical binding equation, binding data consistently producing a curve as illustrated in Fig. 11.1b. Owing to experimental variance, it is impossible to assign an accurate value to the *x* intercept and hence to the receptor number and the lack of linearity vitiates attempts to ascribe a single value to the slope of the line and hence calculate the affinity of the binding reaction.

Apart from possible methodological difficulties, two major contending theories have been advanced to explain these observations. First, a system containing at least two functionally distinct types of sites with different affinities will exhibit these properties. Secondly, the insulin binding site complex itself could in some way reduce the binding affinity of the remaining unoccupied sites and/or of other occupied sites. This latter possibility, known as *negative co-operativity*, has been confirmed and extensively explored by Pierre De Meyts [3] and the use of insulin analogues has even defined the sites on the insulin molecule responsible for the phenomenon [4].

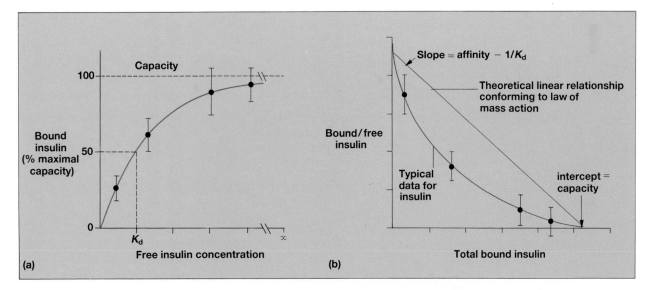

Fig. 11.1. (a) Theoretical set of data depicting increasing quantities of insulin bound at equilibrium to a preparation of cell-surface insulin receptors with increasing concentrations of free insulin in the medium. The saturable system can be regarded as possessing a maximal capacity (insulin bound at infinite free insulin concentration) and an affinity, which is expressed as the reciprocal of the Kd (i.e. the free insulin concentration required for 50% of maximal receptor occupancy). (b) Replotting such data with transformation of the axes as shown here (Scatchard plot) will produce a straight line if the law of mass action for bimolecular reactions applies. The curve illustrated is a typical finding with the insulin receptor (see text).

More recent kinetic studies have suggested further complexities. In addition to the concentration-related negative co-operativity effect (which reduces binding affinity), time-dependent changes may under some circumstances lead to an increase in affinity [5] (Fig. 11.2).

These phenomena may explain why attempts to use these methods to evaluate and compare receptor binding properties in normal and disease states have often led to confusion and uncertainty [6]. Moreover, the anticipated description of insulin−receptor interactions at the molecular level will itself be complex and is likely to involve a number of secondary interactions.

Binding sites are receptor sites

The classical definition of receptor sites demands a clearly established link between the characteristics of binding and the transmission of the hormonal signal. In the case of insulin, this requirement has posed a few problems. Many cells (e.g. erythrocytes) possess specific insulin binding sites but cannot be shown to respond metabolically to the hormone. Some other cell types which do respond (e.g. adipocytes) exhibit a maximal insulin effect (e.g. increasing lipid synthesis) when only a small percentage of identifiable receptor sites are occupied. This apparent divergence between the dose−response relationships for insulin binding and insulin action requires explanation, if the binding sites are true receptors responsible

for signal transmission. It is now clear that the metabolic effects of insulin are indeed mediated via the established binding sites as demonstrated with insulin tracers. Two strands of evidence deserve mention. First, studies involving a wide variety of insulin analogues have shown a parallel relationship between changes in binding affinity and their metabolic potencies. This correlation is in contrast to the very different pattern of specificity displayed by the analogues to insulin antibodies or to insulin-degrading enzymes, both of which are capable of binding to the hormone at different sites. Secondly, destruction of cellular binding sites by, for example, trypsin (to which they are exquisitely sensitive) leads to a parallel loss of insulin action in the treated cells.

It is apparent that, at least for certain rapid metabolic effects of insulin (although perhaps not for effects on growth), the initial interaction of the hormone with the receptor ceases to be the rate-limiting step when only some 10−25% of the available sites are occupied. This fact explains the apparent discrepancies between dose−response relationships for insulin binding and insulin action, and as illustrated in Fig. 11.3 has important physiological implications.

Figure 11.3a defines a series of equilibrium binding curves for insulin to target tissue receptors. In the first condition (A), the total number of receptors present can bind a nominal 100 pmol of insulin and it is presupposed that only 25% of the total number of receptors need be occupied to

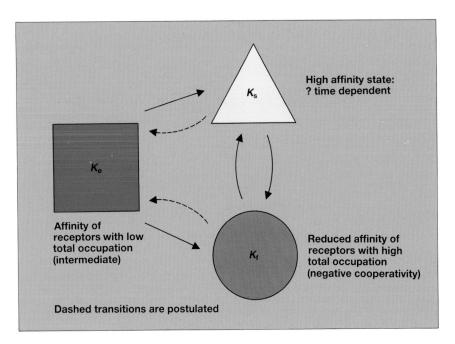

Fig. 11.2. At least three affinity states for insulin−receptor interactions have been described. Insulin−receptor complexes may reduce the binding affinity of remaining unoccupied sites, whereas separate time-dependent changes may result in increased affinity.

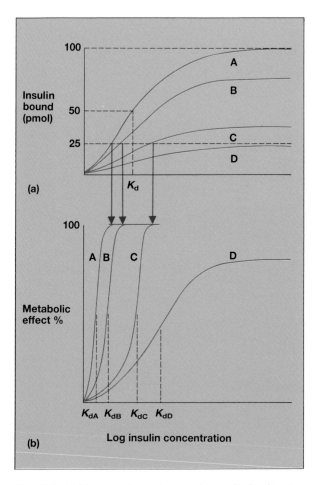

Fig. 11.3. (a) Theoretical set of curves for insulin binding to a target tissue with progressively decreasing (A to D) numbers of receptors present. The Kd for curves A to D is unchanged. (b) Equivalent dose–response curves expected for a metabolic effect for which receptor occupation ceases to be the rate-limiting step when 25% of the original total number of sites are associated with insulin.

achieve a maximum metabolic effect (Fig. 11.3b). The remaining curves (B–D) illustrate the effect of a progressive reduction in the total number of target cell receptors. The affinity of the sites (Kd) remains unchanged. The effect on insulin action is, however, quite different. In conditions B and C, the total number of receptors still exceeds 25% of the original number and the maximal metabolic effect can therefore still be obtained. Only when the total number falls below the threshold (curve D) does a reduced insulin action become apparent. Notably, as Fig. 11.3b illustrates, the effect of altering receptor number changes the Kd of the response although the affinity of the sites for insulin remains unaltered.

This phenomenon has had profound impli-

cations for the interpretation of metabolic studies. The euglycaemic clamp (see Chapter 21) is often used to measure insulin resistance in disease states and defines a dose–response relationship for insulin action. If the curve is shifted to the right of normal (when plotted as in Fig. 11.3b), the subject has been said to display reduced sensitivity to insulin. Reduction in maximal capacity for glucose disposal is defined as reduced responsiveness and is a frequent finding in insulin-resistant states such as obesity and NIDDM [7]. The subtle (and controversial) changes reported for receptor binding in these conditions are insufficient to account for the reduced responsiveness, leading to the conclusion that a 'postreceptor' or more precisely, 'postbinding' step is responsible for insulin resistance.

However, insulin receptor numbers can change under various conditions. High ambient insulin concentrations are known to reduce insulin binding to a variety of isolated cell systems. This phenomenon, known as *down-regulation*, may be due to increased receptor internalization and turnover. It may explain reduced overall insulin sensitivity in hyperinsulinaemia and may function at the tissue level to modulate the sensitivities of individual cells. It is probable that fat or muscle cells in close proximity to a capillary will be exposed to higher ambient insulin levels than other cells sited more distantly. Down-regulation (and the opposite process, 'up-regulation') may serve to 'tune' each cell to produce similar responses to changes in circulating concentrations.

Receptor internalization and recycling

The interaction of insulin with its receptor triggers the hormone's effects on intracellular enzymes from the cell surface. The details of the signalling process are still largely unknown but a crucial early event is apparently the enzymatic phosphorylation, by the receptor itself, of several of its own tyrosine residues [8] (see Chapter 12). In addition, the formation of the complex initiates a process whereby the receptor and its associated insulin are 'internalized', or carried into the cell (Fig. 11.4). This phenomenon displays a more conventional relationship to insulin binding than the metabolic effects in that, in intact cell systems, the velocity of insulin degradation is directly proportional to the total bound insulin [9].

The sequence of internalization and the subsequent fate of the receptor and insulin has been

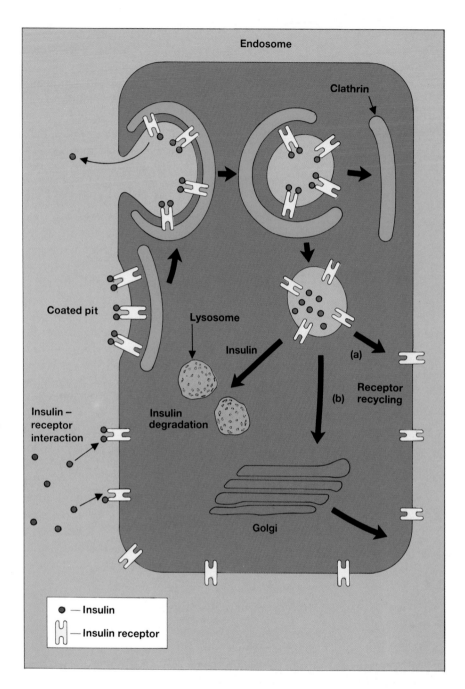

Fig. 11.4. Insulin–receptor itinerary. The complex is internalized by endocytosis in clathrin-coated pits. The bulk of receptors are recycled to the cell surface by one of two routes (a and b) but insulin is completely degraded by lysosomes.

well characterized in microanatomical terms (Fig. 11.4), but the biochemical steps involved remain largely unknown.

Occupied receptors, initially widely spread over the cell surface, cluster together in indentations in the plasma membrane lined on the cytoplasmic surface by the protein, clathrin [10]. These 'coated pits' then invaginate to form endocytotic vesicles (endosomes). During this process, a small proportion of the bound insulin may undergo partial degradation and is released back into the interstitial space in a less active form but with essentially unmodified molecular weight. The majority

of the bound insulin is internalized with the receptors. The low-density endosomes contain a proton pump which lowers the internal pH, causing dissociation of the complex. From this point on, the receptors and the hormone follow different pathways. The insulin is transferred to a lysosomal compartment where complete degradation takes place, whereas the receptors may follow one of two routes back to the cell surface. A proportion may be rapidly returned to the plasma membrane (route a). The majority appear to be transported to the Golgi complex where they join newly synthesized receptors and may undergo some reprocessing before recycling to the cell surface (route b). It has been reported that some insulin–receptor internalization can occur in areas of the plasma membrane lacking in clathrin and that the resulting uncoated vesicles follow a functionally distinct intracellular itinerary [11]. This alternative pathway may be largely responsible for rapid recycling of receptors to the cell surface without reprocessing in the Golgi apparatus.

Receptor-mediated endocytosis accounts for approximately 85% of insulin clearance *in vivo*. It follows that conditions characterized by impaired insulin receptor number or affinity will inevitably reduce the rate at which insulin is cleared from the circulation. The fact that in obesity and NIDDM insulin clearance rates and half-life are similar to those in normal subjects, strongly suggests that abnormalities of the number or affinities of insulin receptors cannot be responsible for the insulin resistance characteristic of these conditions. Similarly, the process of internalization and degradation must be largely unimpaired. The 'post-binding' defect causing insulin resistance could reside in a component of receptor function responsible for signal transmission, perhaps the kinase activity, but is more likely to be due to abnormalities in intracellular metabolic enzymes.

The parallel dependence of both insulin action and metabolism on the same population of receptors also has implications for the pharmacology of newly available insulin analogues. Certain analogues which resist aggregation into hexamers are more rapidly absorbed from subcutaneous depots (see Chapter 37) [12, 13]. Several such compounds are now undergoing clinical assessment. Although in some cases the analogues' affinities for the insulin receptor are markedly reduced, their hypoglycaemic activities are similar to that of insulin itself because receptor-mediated degradation is also reduced and plasma levels are accordingly much higher. It has been shown that the receptor-binding affinity has to fall to 10% or less of that of insulin itself before hypoglycaemic activity is significantly impaired [14]. These considerations serve to clarify on theoretical grounds why only in certain rare syndromes in which there are major receptor abnormalities can the receptor itself be implicated in the disease state (Chapter 29). Indeed, the search for a mechanism of this kind in NIDDM was doomed to failure from the start as subtle alterations in receptor number or affinity are intrinsically self-compensating.

Lesser alterations in receptor characteristics could, however, influence the balance between hepatic and peripheral effects of endogenous insulin. Receptors in the liver are responsible for the extraction of 50–70% of insulin secreted into the portal vein [15]. In this sense, they act as gatekeepers to the peripheral tissues, and the extent to which secreted insulin affects, for example, skeletal muscle is powerfully modulated by hepatic insulin extraction [16]. The extent to which this factor may contribute to peripheral hyperinsulinaemia and its possible ill effects is only now beginning to be explored.

Insulin receptor structure

Classical biochemical methods established that the intact insulin receptor consists of a heterodimer of four glycosylated peptide subunits covalently linked by disulphide bonds. Two identical alpha-subunits (MW 130 kDa), which contain the insulin binding sites, are linked to two beta-subunits (MW 95 kDa) which contain the kinase activity [17]. As described below, the alpha-subunit lies extracellularly, whereas the beta-subunit spans the cell membrane.

The successful cloning of cDNA for the human insulin receptor precursor (by two separate groups in 1985) has provided much more detailed structural information [18, 19, 20]. The human haploid genome contains only one copy of the proreceptor gene, sited on the short arm of chromosome 19 (Fig. 11.5) [19, 21, 22]. The gene itself has not been fully sequenced at the time of writing but is known to be very large — at least 120 kb — with 22 exons.

Transcription yields several mRNA species varying in length from 5.7 to 9.5 kb with most of the differences in the 3' untranslated region. cDNA sequencing has demonstrated two forms of the proreceptor coding sequence which differ by 36 bases; alternative splicing from intron 11 is probably responsible for this difference. The proreceptor consists of a linear sequence of 1370 or 1382 amino-acid residues. At the N terminal, a signal sequence of 27 largely hydrophobic amino acids (to promote insertion into the endoplasmic reticulum) precedes the alpha-subunit of 719 or 731 residues, the two forms of the subunit differing by 12 amino acids close to its C terminal. There follows a tetrapeptide (Arg–Lys–Arg–Arg), typical of proteolytic cleavage sites, and finally the 620 amino acids of the beta-subunit.

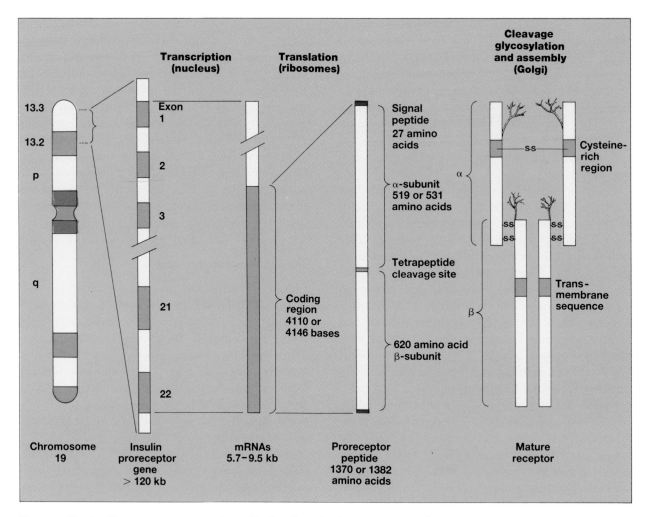

Fig. 11.5. The insulin proreceptor gene and peptide domains, showing processing to the mature receptor.

Both subunits contain glycosylation sites related to asparagine residues, and cysteine residues capable of stabilizing secondary structure and of forming disulphide bridges between subunits. The insulin-binding domain is still unknown although, by analogy with the LDL receptor, a cysteine-rich region between residues 155 and 312 of the alpha-subunit may be implicated. Only the beta-subunit contains a hydrophobic sequence long enough to span the plasma membrane. It follows that the alpha-subunit is entirely extracellular.

After glycosylation and cleavage, the receptor is inserted into the plasma membrane with most, but possibly not all, of the alpha—beta units paired to form mature $\alpha_2\beta_2$ complexes containing two insulin-binding sites and two potentially active intracellular domains. It is not known whether one or both binding sites for insulin need to be occupied to trigger signal transmission or inter-nalization. The intracellular C terminal of the beta-subunit contains an ATP binding site and a sequence homologous with known tyrosine kinases.

Sequencing the receptor has allowed interesting comparisons with other receptor molecules (Fig. 11.6). The receptor for insulin-like growth factor-1 (IGF-1) is particularly similar, with not only 50% sequence homology with the insulin receptor (84% in its tyrosine kinase region) but an entirely comparable relationship between the four subunits and the plasma membrane [23]. The receptor for epidermal growth factor (EGF), although a single polypeptide, also possesses an extracellular binding domain and an intracellular tyrosine kinase. The insulin receptor alpha-subunit displays considerable homology to the extracellular region of the EGF receptor [24]. Comparisons can also be drawn with the LDL receptor (which, consistent with its role as a

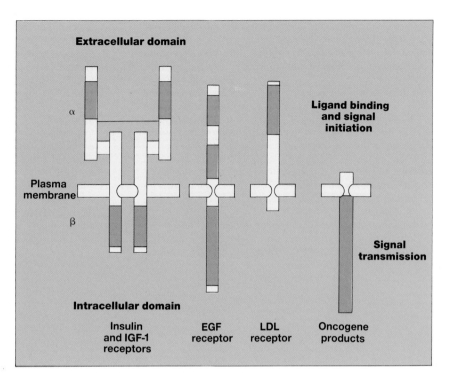

Fig. 11.6. The insulin receptor displays functional and some structural homologies with certain receptors for growth factors, the LDL receptor and some oncogene products.

transporter rather than a signalling protein, does not possess kinase activity) and with certain of the oncogene products which lack extracellular binding domains but possess kinase sequences. Defects in insulin action have recently been ascribed to mutations identified in the insulin receptor gene (see Chapter 19).

It can be expected that further application of molecular biological techniques will now rapidly clarify the role of specific sites within the receptor. A complete description of the binding events and the mechanism of receptor activation will lead to opportunities for pharmacological intervention which could dramatically alter our approach to the treatment of diabetes.

RICHARD H. JONES

References

1 Sutherland EW. Studies on the mechanism of hormone action. *Science* 1972; **177**: 401−408.

2 Scatchard G. The attraction of proteins for small molecules and ions. *Ann NY Acad Sci* 1949; **51**: 660−72.

3 De Meyts P. Insulin receptors: Experimental validation of the negative cooperativity concept. In: Dumont J, Nunez J, eds. *Hormones and Cell Regulation*, Vol 4. Elsevier North Holland Biomedical Press, Amsterdam. 1980: 107−21.

4 De Meyts P, Van Obberghen E, Roth J, Wollmer A, Brandenburg D. Mapping of the residues responsible for the negative cooperativity of the receptor-binding region of insulin. *Nature* 1978; **273**: 504−9.

5 Gammeltoft S. Insulin receptors: binding kinetics and structure−function relationships of insulin. *Physiol Rev* 1984; **64**, No 4: 1321−78.

6 Taylor R. Insulin receptor assays − clinical application and limitations. *Diabetic Med* 1984; **1**: 181.

7 Kolterman OG, Gray RS, Griffin J, Burstein P, Insel J, Scarlett JA, Olefsky JM. Receptor and postreceptor defects contribute to the insulin resistance in non insulin-dependent diabetes mellitus. *J Clin Invest* 1981; **68**: 957−69.

8 Kasuga M, Karlsson FA, Kahn CR. Insulin stimulates the phosphorylation of the 95,000 dalton subunit of its own receptor. *Science* 1982; **215**: 185−7.

9 Terris S, Steiner DF. Binding and degradation of ^{125}I-insulin rat hepatocytes. *J Biol Chem* 1975; **250**: 8389−98.

10 Goldstein JJ, Anderson RG, Brown MS. Coated pits, coated vesicles and receptor-mediated endocytosis. *Nature* 1979; **279**: 679−85.

11 Renston RH, Maloney DG, Jones AL, Hradek GT, Wong KY, Goldfine ID. Bile secretory apparatus: evidence for a vesicular transport mechanism for proteins in the rat using horseradish peroxidase and ^{125}I-insulin. *Gastroenterology* 1980; **78**: 1373−8.

12 Brange J, Ribel U, Harrison JF, Dodson G, Hansen MT, Havelund S, Melberg SG, Norris F, Norris K, Snel L, Sörensen AR, Voigt HO. Monomeric insulins obtained by protein engineering and their medical implications. *Nature* 1988; **333**: 679−82.

13 Vora JP, Owens DR, Dolbien J, Atiea JA, Dean JD, Kang S, Burch A, Brange J. Recombinant DNA derived monomeric insulin analogue: comparison with soluble human insulin in normal subjects. *Br Med J* 1988; **297**: 1239−9.

14 Jones RH, Dron DI, Ellis MJ, Sönksen PH, Brandenburg D. Biological properties of chemically modified insulins. *Diabetologia* 1976; **12**: 601−8.

15 Field JB. Extraction of insulin by the liver. *Ann Rev Med* 1973; **20**: 309−14.

16 Chap Z, Ishida T, Chou C, Hartley CJ, Entman ML, Brandenburg D, Jones RH, Field JB. First-pass hepatic ex-

traction and metabolic effects of insulin and insulin analogues. *Am J Physiol* 1987; **252**: E209−17.

17 Shia MA, Pilch PF. The beta subunit of the insulin receptor is an insulin-activated protein kinase. *Biochemistry* 1983; **22**: 717−21.

18 Ullrich A, Bell JR, Chen EY, Herrera R, Petruzzelli LM, Dull TJ, Gray A, Coussens L, Liao Y-C, Tsubokawa M, Mason A, Seeburg PH, Grunfeld C, Rosen OM, Ramachandran J. Human insulin receptor and its relationship to the tyrosine kinase family of oncogenes. *Nature* 1985; **313**: 756−61.

19 Ebina Y, Ellis L, Jarnagin K, Ederg M, Graf L, Clauser E, Ou J, Masiarz F, Kan YW, Goldfine ID, Roth RA, Rutter WJ. The human insulin receptor cDNA: The structural basis for hormone-activated transmembrane signalling. *Cell* 1985; **40**: 747−58.

20 Goldfine ID. The insulin receptor: Molecular biology and transmembrane signalling. *Endocrine Rev* 1987; **8**: 235−55.

21 Yang-Feng TL, Francke U, Ullrich A. Gene for human insulin receptor: localization to site on chromosome 19 involved in pre-B-cell leukemia. *Science* 1985; **228**: 728−30.

22 Straus SD, Pang KJ, Kull FC, Jacobs S, Mohandas T. Human insulin receptor gene. Data supporting assignment to chromosome 19. *Diabetes* 1985; **34**: 816−20.

23 Ullrich A, Gray A, Tam AW, Yang-Feng TL, Tsubokawa M, Collins C, Henzel W, Le Bon T, Kathunia S, Chen E, Jacobs S, Francke U, Ramachandran J, Fujita-Yamaguchi Y. Insulin-like growth factor I receptor primary structure: comparison with insulin receptor suggests structural determinats that define functional specificity. *EMBO J* 1986; **5**: 2503−12.

24 Ullrich A, Coussens L, Hayflick JS, Dull TJ, Gray A, Tam AW, Lee J, Yarden Y. Human epidermal growth factor receptor cDNA sequence and aberrant expression of the amplified gene in A431 epidermoid carcinoma cells. *Nature* 1984; **309**: 418−25.

12 Insulin Action and Responses: the Biochemistry of Postreceptor Events

Summary

● The major intracellular actions of insulin are stimulation of both nutrient uptake and biosynthetic processes.

● Glucose uptake is enhanced by increasing glucose transporters on the cell surface, probably by promoting their translocation from an intracellular pool.

● The insulin receptor contains a tyrosine kinase which autophosphorylates the receptor's beta-subunit; the kinase activity is essential for many actions of insulin.

● The mechanisms mediating the postreceptor events are not completely understood.

● The insulin receptor functions most likely by directly phosphorylating and altering the activity of protein kinases and other regulatory proteins; however, the possibility that the receptor could trigger production of a 'second messenger' such as the recently identified glycosylated inositol phosphate, cannot yet be excluded.

The last 20 years have seen considerable advances in our understanding of how insulin regulates metabolism. Like other polypeptide hormones, the first step involves its interaction with a specific receptor in the target cell's plasma membrane (Chapter 11) but the nature of the 'postreceptor' events which it triggers and the precise molecular mechanisms underlying its effects are not yet fully understood.

After binding to their receptors, many hormones activate specific signalling systems which bridge the plasma membrane and influence intracellular events by controlling the production (or breakdown) of a specific 'second messenger'. These intracellular mediators include substances as diverse as cyclic AMP (cAMP), cyclic GMP, (cGMP), calcium ions and diacylglycerol, which activate specific enzymes, the second messenger-dependent protein kinases. These in turn phosphorylate serine and threonine residues on regulatory proteins and trigger conformational changes which alter their biological activities [1]. By these simple devices, hormonal stimuli are amplified up to one-million-fold, and many cellular processes can be controlled through the same basic underlying mechanism (Fig. 12.1).

It is clear that insulin can alter the phosphorylation states of many intracellular proteins within minutes. However, the identity of the second messenger for insulin — if indeed one exists — is unknown. This chapter will review current understanding of the postreceptor responses to insulin, with particular emphasis on the role of protein phosphorylation in controlling metabolic processes.

Lowering of intracellular cyclic AMP levels

Cyclic AMP is perhaps the most familiar of the second messengers, and raised intracellular concentrations mediate the actions of the catabolic hormones, glucagon and the catecholamines. Many actions of insulin are antagonistic to those of glucagon and the catecholamines, and it is well established that insulin can suppress the increased cAMP produced by these [2]. A decrease in the level of cAMP reduces the activity of cAMP-dependent protein kinase, leading to decreased phosphorylation of further intracellular enzymes. Insulin appears to lower cAMP concentrations by activating one or more of the membrane-associated

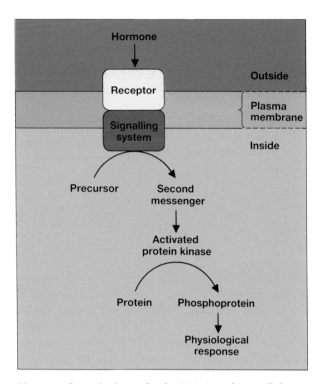

Fig. 12.1. General scheme for the initiation of intracellular events by a hormone which acts via a second messenger system.

phosphodiesterases which hydrolyse cAMP to 5'-AMP (Fig. 12.2). The precise mechanism of activation is unknown but it is likely that a covalent modification (such as protein phosphorylation) is involved [3].

Lowering of cAMP is an important postreceptor action of insulin which underlies a number of its anticatabolic actions, such as inhibition of glycogenolysis and gluconeogenesis in liver and inhibition of lipolysis in adipose tissue. However, it is important to note that all the other metabolic effects of insulin listed below do not involve changes in cAMP concentration.

Stimulation of glucose uptake

The classical hypoglycaemic action of insulin results from its ability to stimulate both the uptake of glucose into cells and its subsequent intracellular metabolism. Insulin dramatically increases glucose uptake into certain tissues, such as fat and muscle, although in most others (e.g. liver), glucose transport is not insulin-dependent. Glucose influx across the plasma membrane is catalysed by the 'glucose transporter', a family of 50–60

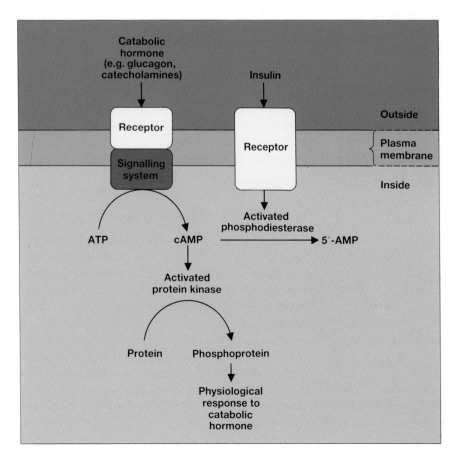

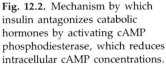

Fig. 12.2. Mechanism by which insulin antagonizes catabolic hormones by activating cAMP phosphodiesterase, which reduces intracellular cAMP concentrations.

kDa proteins which bind tightly to the inhibitor cytochalasin B and are found both on the cell surface and intracellularly. Experiments (using a cytochalasin-B-binding assay) have shown that insulin exerts its effect by increasing the number of glucose transporters exposed on the cell surface, with a corresponding reduction in those located at an intracellular site(s) [4]. This observation has led to the model shown in Fig. 12.3, in which glucose transporters cycle between an intracellular pool (bound to vesicles, or endosomes) and the cell surface via exocytosis and endocytosis. The ability of insulin to increase the numbers of certain other receptors (e.g. those for insulin-like growth factor-2 and transferrin) at the cell surface appears to be mediated by analogous mechanisms [5]. Insulin may therefore have a general effect on membrane cycling, either by activating exocytosis, or inhibiting endocytosis, or both. As well as affecting their distribution, there is now evidence that insulin also modulates the intrinsic activity of the glucose transporters; the molecular mechanisms are un-

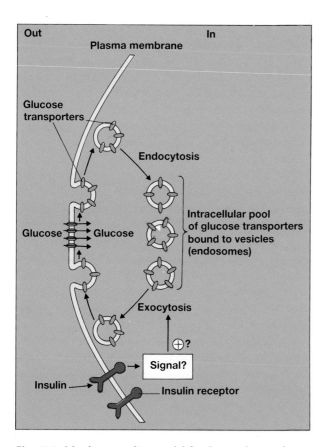

Fig. 12.3. Membrane cycling model for the regulation of glucose transport by insulin which increases the number of glucose transporters on the cell surface. (Redrawn from Tanner and Lienhard 1987 [5] with permission.)

known [4] but insulin does not cause detectable phosphorylation of the 55 kDa protein itself [6].

Activation of glycogen synthesis in skeletal muscle

Much of the glucose taken up by muscle in response to insulin is converted to glycogen. It is well established that insulin stimulates glycogen synthesis by increasing the activity of glycogen synthase, the rate-determining enzyme of this pathway. Activation results from the dephosphorylation of phosphoserine residues which are introduced by glycogen synthase kinase-3 and dephosphorylated by the glycogen-bound form of protein phosphatase-1 [7, 8]. Insulin must exert its effect either by inhibiting the former enzyme or by activating the latter, but these alternatives cannot be distinguished at present and the molecular mechanisms involved are unknown.

Activation of lipogenesis

Following its insulin-stimulated uptake into adipose tissue, glucose is largely metabolized to fatty acids and triglycerides (Fig. 12.4). Several intracellular enzymes in the pathway leading from glucose to fatty acid synthesis are activated acutely by insulin (indicated by the numbers in Fig. 12.4). Carbohydrate becomes committed to either lipid synthesis or oxidation once pyruvate is converted to acetyl CoA by the mitochondrial pyruvate dehydrogenase complex (PDH) (step 2 in Fig. 12.4). PDH is inactivated by a PDH kinase and reactivated by a PDH phosphatase. Insulin acts on adipocytes within minutes to promote the dephosphorylation and therefore activation of PDH, apparently by activating PDH phosphatase [9].

The first step which diverts acetyl CoA to fatty acid synthesis is catalysed by acetyl-CoA carboxylase (step 3 in Fig. 12.4). This enzyme is rapidly activated by insulin in adipocytes [10] and in common with many other insulin-sensitive proteins is regulated by phosphorylation/dephosphorylation mechanisms, notably by an 'AMP-activated' protein kinase, which causes phosphorylation and inactivation [11, 12]. Stimulation by insulin might be expected to involve dephosphorylation of acetyl-CoA carboxylase, yet insulin paradoxically increases phosphorylation; the residues involved are serines, which are also phosphorylated *in vitro* by casein kinase-2 [13]. As casein kinase-2 does not activate acetyl CoA

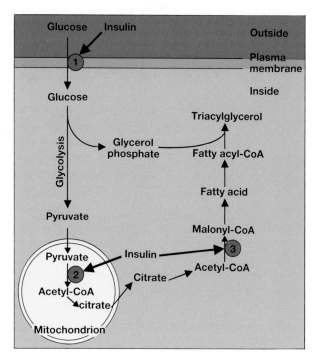

Fig. 12.4. Pathway of conversion of glucose into lipid (lipogenesis) in adipose cells. Major insulin-activated steps are: (1) glucose transport; (2) pyruvate dehydrogenase; (3) acetyl-CoA carboxylase.

carboxylase, insulin must stimulate enzyme activity by some other mechanism.

In other tissues, such as heart muscle, acetyl CoA produced by the PDH reaction is not used for lipid synthesis, but is oxidized for energy. Insulin does not activate cardiac PDH acutely, but long-term food deprivation or experimental alloxan-induced diabetes (both of which reduce circulating insulin levels) produce chronic inactivation which seems to be due to the synthesis of a protein activator of PDH kinase [14].

Insulin-stimulated phosphorylation of intracellular proteins

In addition to acetyl-CoA carboxylase, a variety of other proteins rapidly become phosphorylated on serine or threonine residues in response to insulin. In most cases, the function of the increased phosphorylation is not known. One example is the ribosomal protein S6, whose phosphorylation may be involved in the stimulation of protein synthesis by insulin [15]. In this case, insulin increases phosphorylation by activating specific S6 kinase(s), which are themselves phosphorylated and activated by further insulin-activated, serine-specific protein kinase(s) [16].

Effects on RNA and DNA synthesis

The receptor for insulin is structurally related to those for several growth factors (Chapter 11), and insulin can, in combination with certain growth factors, stimulate DNA synthesis and cell division [17]. It also regulates the synthesis of messenger RNA coding for several proteins, causing induction of the glycolytic enzymes, glucokinase and pyruvate kinase, and repression of the gluconeogenic enzymes, phosphoenolpyruvate carboxykinase and glucose 6-phosphatase [18, 19]. These effects are undoubtedly important in the overall actions of insulin, but they are even less well understood at the molecular level than its short-term metabolic effects.

Does insulin act via a tyrosine kinase cascade or a second messenger?

The interaction of insulin with its receptor in the plasma membrane is followed by activation of the protein tyrosine kinase located on the intracellular domain of the receptor's beta-subunit (Chapter 11). Genetic engineering experiments in which mutations are made in this domain have shown that the tyrosine kinase activity is essential for many actions of insulin [20], and the kinase is known to 'autophosphorylate' the beta-subunit, generating an even more active kinase [21].

What happens next is uncertain. One possibility is that the tyrosine kinase activity of the receptor might phosphorylate intracellular proteins directly. For this mechanism to operate, intracellular targets for the tyrosine kinase would have to include serine/threonine-specific protein kinases and phosphatases, to account for the observation that many of insulin's rapid postreceptor effects involve increases or decreases in the phosphorylation states of intracellular proteins on serine and/or threonine residues. To date, no important target proteins for the receptor tyrosine kinase have been identified.

An alternative possibility is that the beta-subunit is the only important substrate for the receptor tyrosine kinase, and that autophosphorylation allows the receptor to generate a second messenger. Over the years, there have been many claims for the identity of the 'insulin second messenger'; cGMP, small peptides and hydrogen peroxide have all been implicated but none has stood the test of time. The most recent candidate is a glycosylated inositol phosphate (GIP), the exact structure of which is unknown [22]. It is believed to exist in the plasma membrane as a precursor in which a carbohydrate moiety is linked through glucosamine to the phospholipid, phosphatidylinositol. GIP is thought to be released from the plasma membrane by an insulin-stimulated phospholipase C enzyme (Fig. 12.5). It has been reported that GIP is released from isolated membranes treated with insulin and that it activates cAMP phosphodiesterase and pyruvate dehydrogenase in cell-free systems [23, 24]. However, a curious observation is that insulin-stimulated release of GIP from membranes does not require ATP, despite the fact that an active tyrosine kinase is necessary for the insulin receptor to function [19]. Moreover, GIP mimics some effects of insulin when added to intact cells [25, 26], despite its hydrophilic structure which would prevent simple diffusion across the plasma membrane. This suggests that GIP might not function as a true second messenger, but rather as a local hormone

with its own cell-surface receptor, which might act to transmit the effects of insulin to neighbouring cells.

D. GRAHAME HARDIE
PHILIP COHEN

References

1 Cohen P. Protein phosphorylation and hormone action. *Proc R Soc London B* 1988; **234**: 115−44.
2 Butcher RW, Baird CE, Sutherland EW. Effect of lipolytic and antilipolytic substances on adenosine 3', 5'-monophosphate levels in isolated fat cells. *J Biol Chem* 1968; **243**: 1705−12.
3 Degerman E, Belfrage P, Newman AH, Rice KC, Mangianello VC. Purification of the putative hormone-sensitive cyclic AMP phosphodiesterase from rat adipose tissue using a derivative of cilostamide as a novel affinity ligand. *J Biol Chem* 1987; **262**: 5797−807.
4 Simpson IA, Cushman, SW. Hormonal regulation of mammalian glucose transport. *Ann Rev Biochem* 1986; **55**: 1059−89.
5 Tanner LI, Lienhard GE. Insulin elicits a redistribution of

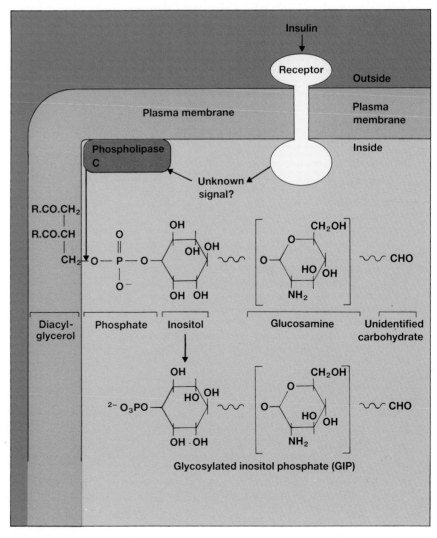

Fig. 12.5. Model for the release of glycosylated inositol phosphate (GIP), a putative second messenger for insulin, from the plasma membrane. The nature of the linkages between inositol, glucosamine, and the unidentified carbohydrate are not known. Although the model shows the GIP being released on the inside of the plasma membrane, available evidence is equally compatible with a model in which GIP is released on the outside. (Redrawn from Saltiel *et al.* 1986 [22].)

transferrin receptors in 3T3-L1 adipocytes through an increase in the rate constant for receptor externalization. *J Biol Chem* 1987; **262**: 8975−80.

6 Gibbs EM, Allard WJ, Lienhard GE. The glucose transporter in 3T3-L1 adipocytes is phosphorylated in response to phorbol ester but not in response to insulin. *J Biol Chem* 1986; **261**: 16 597−603.

7 Cohen P. Muscle glycogen synthase. In: Boyer PD, Krebs EG, eds. Vol 17. New York: Academic Press, 1986: 461−97.

8 Cohen P. The structure and regulation of protein phosphatases. *Ann Rev Biochem* 1989; **58**: 453−508.

9 Thomas AP, Denton RM. Use of toluene-permeabilized mitochondria to study the regulation of adipose tissue pyruvate dehydrogenase *in situ*. Further evidence that insulin acts through stimulation of pyruvate dehydrogenase phosphate phosphatase. *Biochem J* 1986; **238**: 93−101.

10 Halestrap AP, Denton RM. Insulin and the regulation of adipose tissue acetyl-coenzyme A carboxylase. *Biochem J* 1973; **132**: 509−17.

11 Munday MR, Campbell DG, Carling D, Hardie DG. Identification by amino acid sequencing of three major regulatory phosphorylation sites on rat acetyl-CoA carboxylase. *Eur J Biochem* 1988; **175**: 331−8.

12 Sim ATR, Hardie DG. The low activity of acetyl-CoA carboxylase in basal and glucagon-stimulated hepatocytes is due to phosphorylation by the AMP-activated protein kinase and not cyclic AMP-dependent protein kinase. *FEBS Lett* 1988; **233**: 294−8.

13 Haystead TAJ, Campbell DG, Hardie DG. Analysis of sites phosphorylated on acetyl-CoA carboxylase in response to insulin in isolated adipocytes: comparison with sites phosphorylated by casein kinase-2 and the calmodulin-dependent multiprotein kinase. *Eur J Biochem* 1988; **175**: 347−54.

14 Randle PJ. Fuel selection in animals. *Biochem Soc Trans* 1986; **14**: 799−806.

15 Thomas G, Martin-Perez J, Siegmann M, Otto AM. The effect of serum, EGF, PGF$_{2\alpha}$ and insulin on S6 phosphorylation and the initiation of protein and DNA synthesis. *Cell* 1982; **30**: 235−42.

16 Sturgill TW, Ray LB, Erikson E, Maller JL. Insulin-stimulated MAP-2 kinase phosphorylates and activates ribosomal protein S6 kinase. *Nature* 1988; **334**: 715−18.

17 Rozengurt E. Stimulation of DNA synthesis in quiescent cultured cells: exogenous agents, internal signals and early events. *Curr Topics Cell Reg* 1980; **17**: 59−88.

18 Magnuson MA, Quinn PG, Granner DK. Multihormonal regulation of phosphoenolpyruvate and carboxykinase-chloramphenicol acetyltransferase fusion genes. Insulin's effects oppose those of cAMP and dexamethasome. *J Biol Chem* 1987; **262**: 14 917−20.

19 Pilkis SJ, El-Maghrabi MR, Claus TH. Hormonal regulation of hepatic gluconeogenesis and glycolysis. *Ann Rev Biochem* 1988; **57**: 755−83.

20 Rosen OM, Herrera R, Olowe Y, Petruzzelli LM, Cobb MH. Phosphorylation activates the insulin receptor tyrosine protein kinase. *Proc Natl Acad Sci USA* 1983; **80**: 3237−40.

21 Chou CK, Dull TJ, Russell DS, Gherzi R, Lebwohl D, Ullrich A, Rosen OM. Human insulin receptors mutated at the ATP-binding site lack protein tyrosine kinase activity and fail to mediate postreceptor effects of insulin. *J Biol Chem* 1987; **262**: 1842−7.

22 Saltiel AR, Fox JA, Sherline P, Cuatrecasas P. Insulin-stimulated hydrolysis of a novel glycolipid generates modulators of cAMP phosphodiesterase. *Science* 1986; **233**: 967−72.

23 Saltiel AR, Cuatrecasas P. Insulin stimulates the generation from hepatic plasma membranes of modulators derived from an inositol glycolipid. *Proc Natl Acad Sci USA* 1986; **83**: 5793−7.

24 Saltiel AR. Insulin generates an enzyme modulator from hepatic plasma membranes: regulation of cAMP phosphodiesterase, pyruvate dehydrogenase and adenylate cyclase. *Endocrinology* 1987; **120**: 967−72.

25 Kelly KL, Mato JM, Merida I, Jarett L. Glucose transport and antilipolysis are differentially regulated by the polar head group of an insulin-sensitive glycophospholipid. *Proc Natl Acad Sci USA* 1987; **84**: 6404−7.

26 Alemany S, Mato JM, Stralfors P. Phospho-dephospho control by insulin is mimicked by a phospho-oligosaccharide in adipocytes. *Nature* 1988; **330**: 77−9.

Addendum

Since this chapter was written, there have been important developments in the area of glucose transport. This function is now known to be carried out by a family of related transmembrane glucose transporter proteins termed GLUT 1−5 (Gould GW, Bell GI. *Trends Biochem Sci* 1990; **15**:18). GLUT 1 is expressed at low levels in almost all cells, and its expression at the cell surface is stimulated about 3-fold by insulin. Muscle and adipose tissue also express GLUT 4 at much higher levels. In these cells, insulin stimulates GLUT 4 translocation to the cell surface more than 10-fold, which is sufficient to explain the observed stimulation of glucose transport without having to invoke a change in the intrinsic activity of the transporters.

In terms of the mechanism of action of insulin, the protein kinase cascade hypothesis has been gaining ground while there has been little progress in identifying a second messenger. It now appears that insulin activates a family of serine/threonine-specific protein kinases, one of which phosphorylates the glycogen-binding or G subunit which couples the catalytic subunit of protein phosphatase-1 to the glycogen particles in skeletal muscle. This phosphorylation increases the glycogen synthase phosphatase activity of the enzyme, providing an elegant explanation of the dephosphorylation of glycogen synthase by insulin (Dent P *et al. Nature* 1990; in press). Since glucose uptake and its conversion into muscle glycogen is the major mechanism by which insulin reduces blood glucose, these systems are of central importance in diabetes.

SECTION 6
PATHOGENESIS OF INSULIN-DEPENDENT DIABETES MELLITUS

13 Histology of the Islet in Insulin-Dependent Diabetes Mellitus

Summary

• In long-standing IDDM, all islets are insulin-deficient and devoid of B cells, although A, D and PP cells are preserved.

• In recent-onset IDDM, most islets are insulin-deficient, but the rest contain B cells; some islets with residual B cells show 'insulitis', i.e. infiltration with chronic inflammatory cells (mostly cytotoxic/suppressor T cells), thought to be a manifestation of continuing and gradual autoimmune destruction.

• The B cell surface does not normally carry class II major histocompatibility complex (MHC) molecules, without which helper T cells could not recognize B-cell antigens. In IDDM, however, a proportion of B cells display aberrant expression of Class II MHC molecules, which could trigger an autoimmune attack and insulitis.

• IDDM is also characterized by increased expression of class I MHC molecules by B cells and other islet endocrine cells; this may be stimulated by interferon-alpha secreted by B cells and may precede aberrant class II MHC expression, but its significance is unclear.

Insulin-deficient islets and insulitis

The most obvious histological finding in the pancreas of a patient who has had IDDM for many years is an almost total lack of insulin-secreting B cells [1]. Apart from moderate atrophy of the exocrine pancreas and sometimes a mild degree of interstitial fibrosis, there are no other histological abnormalities. In particular, glucagon-secreting A cells, somatostatin-secreting D cells and pancreatic-polypeptide-secreting PP cells have a normal distribution and are present in normal numbers. In contrast to islets in NIDDM (Chapter 18), amyloid is not deposited within the islets. Since B cells constitute the majority of endocrine cells in normal islets, the islets in long-standing IDDM are small (Fig. 13.1) and have been termed 'pseudo-atrophic' [1]. Perhaps a better term is 'insulin-deficient', since their only abnormality is that they have suffered selective destruction of B cells.

There are essentially three types of islet distinguishable histologically in pancreases of patients with recent-onset (less than 1 year's duration) IDDM [1, 2]. The majority (approximately 70%) are insulin-deficient and are identical to those seen in long-standing IDDM. The remaining islets all contain residual B cells, and many may appear quite normal. Finally, a proportion of insulin-containing islets are affected by a chronic inflammatory cell infiltrate. This lesion has been termed 'insulitis' (Fig. 13.2). The finding that insulin-containing islets were over 20 times more likely to be affected by insulitis than insulin-deficient islets provided the first real evidence that B-cell destruction was caused by the insulitis process [2]. The cellular composition of the inflammatory infiltrate is consistent with this concept. Most cells are lymphocytes, mainly T cells. Of these, CD8 (cytotoxic/suppressor) cells out-number CD4 (helper) cells [3].

There has been some disagreement as to the frequency of insulitis in IDDM. In a personal series of 74 cases of recent-onset IDDM, insulitis was present in 59 (80%) [4]. As these cases were part of a retrospective study in which, in many instances, only one piece of pancreas was available for study, even this relatively high figure is liable to be an underestimate.

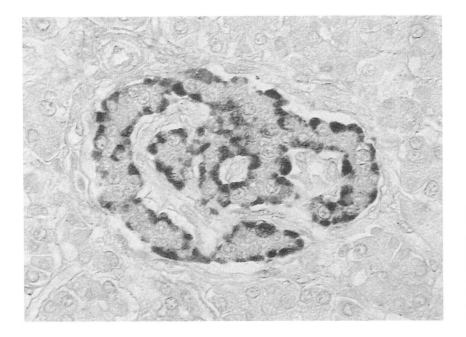

Fig. 13.1. An insulin-deficient islet. The section has been stained for glucagon, somatostatin and pancreatic polypeptide by an immuno-alkaline phosphatase method. All the endocrine cells appear to have been stained, confirming the lack of B cells (×490).

Gepts [1] first drew attention to the fact that the histological features suggested a very slow evolution of IDDM. In keeping with this, clinical evidence of B-cell dysfunction (presumably due to loss of B cells) can be demonstrated up to 3 years before clinical presentation [5] and residual B-cell function persists in three-quarters of IDDM patients years after presentation [6]. Histological evidence of this slow destructive process includes the finding of insulin-containing islets affected by insulitis up to 6 years after the clinical diag-nosis of IDDM [2].

An unexplained histological feature in recent-onset IDDM pancreases is the lobular distribution of islet types [2]. In a given exocrine lobule, all islets may be quite normal; in an adjacent lobule, all may contain insulin and be affected by insulitis, whereas all the remaining lobules in a large area may contain only insulin-deficient islets (Fig. 13.3). Thus, a single section of pancreas can display a spectrum of islet changes, ranging from normal islets to islets where B cells are actively

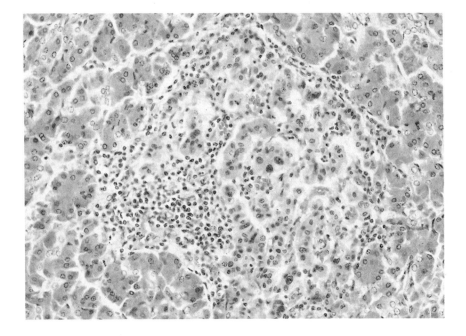

Fig. 13.2. Insulitis. There is a chronic inflammatory cell infiltrate centred on this islet. Haematoxylin and eosin (×300).

Fig. 13.3. Lobular distribution of islet types in recent-onset IDDM. All islets in one lobule contain insulin. Islets in the remainder of the picture are insulin-deficient. Immunoperoxidase staining for insulin (×13).

being destroyed or have been destroyed. It is therefore possible to define events taking place in islets before the onset of insulitis.

Abnormalities of major histocompatibility complex (MHC) product expression

IDDM fulfils the criteria of an organ-specific, autoimmune disease where the B cell is the target [7]. As with other autoimmune diseases, there is a marked genetic predisposition to IDDM which is linked to Class II MHC genes. Thus, up to 98% of patients with IDDM possess the Class II MHC alleles, DR3 or DR4 [8]. Bottazzo *et al.* have proposed a hypothesis to explain this [9] (Chapter 15). T-helper lymphocytes, the cells which initiate an immune response, only recognize the antigen against which they are directed if it is presented to them by a cell expressing the same class II MHC molecule as themselves. Under normal circumstances, antigen-presenting cells in lymph nodes, such as dendritic reticulum cells and

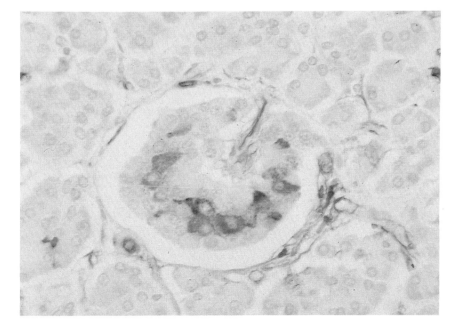

Fig. 13.4. Many endocrine cells in this islet express class II MHC molecules. Double stains show that these cells are B cells. Immunoperoxidase stain for class II MHC (×525).

macrophages, express class II MHC molecules and can thus present foreign antigens to helper T cells. Many cells in the body do not normally express class II MHC products and thus cannot present any cell-specific surface antigens which they may possess. However, should such a cell express class II MHC aberrantly, it may then become an antigen-presenting cell and present its unique antigen to potentially autoreactive T-helper lymphocytes. This may then initiate the autoimmune destruction of that particular cell type.

Since normal islet endocrine cells do not express class II MHC, the question arose as to whether B cells (but not A, D or PP cells) would express class II MHC in IDDM. Following Bottazzo's original observation [3], it has been conclusively shown that a proportion of B cells, but not other islet endocrine cells, in IDDM aberrantly express class II MHC products [10, 11] (Fig. 13.4). This abnormality has not been seen in any other pancreatic disease. The majority of islets where B cells were found to express class II MHC showed no evidence of inflammation. This suggests that, within a given islet, aberrant expression of class II MHC by B cells is an early event which could initiate an autoimmune attack with resulting insulitis.

(a)

(b)

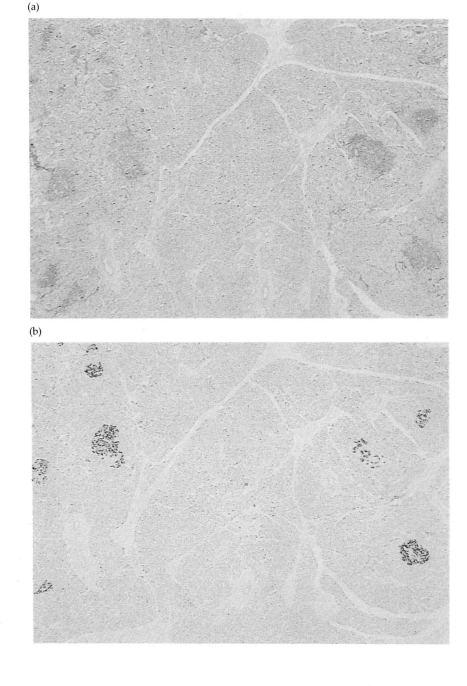

Fig. 13.5. In (a) the section has been immunostained for class I MHC; in (b) the section has been immunostained for insulin. Note that the insulin-containing islets hyperexpress class I MHC. There are many insulin-deficient islets in this field and they do not hyperexpress class I MHC (×33).

A second abnormality of MHC expression in IDDM has now been defined. Class I MHC products (HLA A, B, C in man) are present on most nucleated cells of the body and, using immuno-histochemical techniques, can be demonstrated on normal islet cells. In recent-onset IDDM, however, 92% of residual insulin-containing islets showed markedly increased expression of class I MHC, whereas less than 1% of insulin-deficient islets were thus affected [11] (Fig. 13.5). In contrast to the abnormality of class II MHC expression, all endocrine cell types in a given insulin-containing islet hyperexpressed class I MHC. Thus A, D and PP cells in such islets hyperexpressed class I MHC in insulin-containing islets when they were adjacent to B cells, but not when they were physi-cally divorced from B cells in insulin-deficient islets. Since most of the islets which hyper-expressed class I MHC were otherwise normal and showed no evidence of inflammation, this observation prompted the suggestion that B cells in these islets may be secreting some substance which had a paracrine effect on adjacent A, D and PP cells causing them to hyperexpress class I MHC. One substance known to be capable of doing this *in vitro* is interferon-alpha (IFN-alpha) [12]. Dia-betic pancreases were, therefore, examined for the presence of IFN-alpha in islets. Ninety-three per cent of islets which hyperexpressed class I MHC displayed immunoreactive IFN-alpha within B cells (Fig. 13.6). IFN-alpha was demonstrated in only 0.4% of islets which did not hyperexpress class I MHC [13]. The hyperexpression of class I

MHC, confined to islets, appeared — like the abnormality of class II MHC expression — to be unique to IDDM. However, the presence of IFN-alpha, confined to B cells, was also seen in four cases of acute infantile viral pancreatitis, three of which were known to be caused by Coxsackie B viruses [13].

A possible sequence of events

A hypothetical scheme to explain these histological findings is shown in Fig. 13.7. There is fairly convincing evidence that, within a given islet, hyperexpression of class I MHC by endocrine cells is an earlier event than aberrant expression of class II MHC by B cells [14]. The findings in a presumed 'prediabetic' pancreas are in keeping with this concept [15]. It is suggested that this early islet abnormality is at least partially due to IFN-alpha secretion by B cells. Although such secretion could undoubtedly be initiated by fac-tors other than viruses, the possibility remains that the earliest event in at least some cases of IDDM is a non-cytopathic viral infection which specifically targets B cells. Given a particular genetic predisposition (related to class II MHC genes), this may result in aberrant expression of class II MHC molecules by B cells and hence trigger an autoimmune response. Thus IDDM may be an example of an autoimmune disease initiated, in at least some cases, by a viral infection.

ALAN K. FOULIS

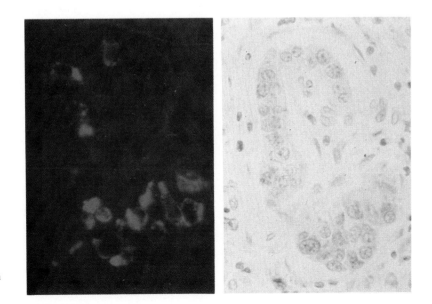

Fig. 13.6. This islet from a patient with IDDM has been stained by immunofluorescence for insulin (left) and by immunoperoxidase for IFN-alpha (right). Note that B cells contain IFN-alpha (×550).

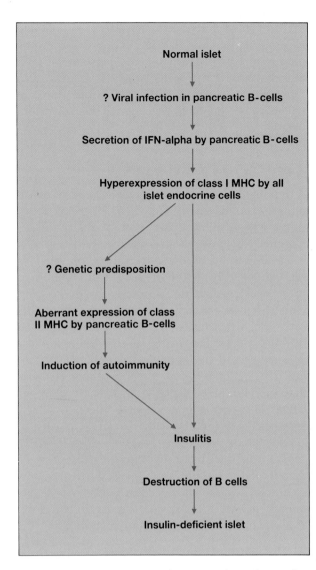

Fig. 13.7. Proposed sequence of events in the evolution of IDDM.

The flowchart shows:

Normal islet
→ ? Viral infection in pancreatic B-cells
→ Secretion of IFN-alpha by pancreatic B-cells
→ Hyperexpression of class I MHC by all islet endocrine cells
→ ? Genetic predisposition
→ Aberrant expression of class II MHC by pancreatic B-cells
→ Induction of autoimmunity
→ Insulitis
→ Destruction of B cells
→ Insulin-deficient islet

References

1 Gepts W. Pathologic anatomy of the pancreas in juvenile diabetes mellitus. *Diabetes* 1965; **14**: 619–33.

2 Foulis AK, Liddle CN, Farquharson MA, Richmond JA, Weir RS. The histopathology of the pancreas in Type 1 (insulin-dependent) diabetes mellitus: a 25-year review of deaths in patients under 20 years of age in the United Kingdom. *Diabetologia* 1986; **29**: 267–74.

3 Bottazzo GF, Dean BM, McNally JM, MacKay EH, Swift PGF, Gamble DR. *In situ* characterisation of autoimmune phenomena and expression of HLA molecules in the pancreas in diabetic insulitis. *N Engl J Med* 1985; **313**: 353–60.

4 Foulis AK. *Pancreatic Pathology in Type 1 (insulin-dependent) diabetes mellitus*. MD Thesis, Glasgow University, 1987.

5 Tarn AC, Smith CP, Spencer KM, Bottazzo GF, Gale EAM. Type 1 (insulin-dependent) diabetes: a disease of slow clinical onset? *Br Med J* 1987; **294**: 342–5.

6 Mustonen A, Knip M, Huttunen NP, Puukka R, Kaar ML, Akerblom HK. Evidence of delayed beta cell destruction in Type 1 (insulin-dependent) diabetic patients with persisting complement-fixing cytoplasmic islet cell antibodies. *Diabetologia* 1984; **27**: 421–6.

7 Bottazzo GF. Beta-cell damage in diabetic insulitis: are we approaching a solution? *Diabetologia* 1984; **26**: 241–9.

8 Wolf E, Spencer KM, Cudworth AG. The genetic susceptibility to Type 1 (insulin-dependent) diabetes: analysis of the HLA−DR association. *Diabetologia* 1983; **24**: 224–30.

9 Bottazzo GF, Pujol-Borrell R, Hanafusa T, Feldmann M. Role of aberrant HLA−DR expression and antigen presentation in induction of endocrine autoimmunity. *Lancet* 1983; **ii**: 1115–18.

10 Foulis AK, Farquharson MA. Aberrant expression of HLA−DR antigens by insulin containing beta cells in recent onset Type 1 (insulin-dependent) diabetes mellitus. *Diabetes* 1986; **35**: 1215–24.

11 Foulis AK, Farquharson MA, Hardman R. Aberrant expression of Class II major histocompatibility complex molecules by B cells and hyperexpression of Class I major histocompatibility complex molecules by insulin containing islets in Type 1 (insulin-dependent) diabetes mellitus. *Diabetologia* 1987; **30**: 333–43.

12 Pujol-Borrell R, Todd I, Doshi M, Gray D, Feldmann M, Bottazzo GF. Differential expression and regulation of MHC products in the endocrine and exocrine cells of the human pancreas. *Clin Exp Immunol* 1986; **65**: 128–39.

13 Foulis AK, Farquharson MA, Meager A. Immunoreactive alpha-interferon in insulin-secreting beta cells in Type 1 diabetes mellitus. *Lancet* 1987; **ii**: 1423–7.

14 Foulis AK. The pathogenesis of beta cell destruction in Type 1 (insulin-dependent) diabetes mellitus. *J Pathol* 1987; **152**: 141–8.

15 Foulis AK, Jackson R, Farquharson MA. The pancreas in idiopathic Addison's disease — a search for a prediabetic pancreas. *Histopathology* 1988; **12**: 481–90.

14 Genetics of Insulin-Dependent Diabetes Mellitus

Summary

• Evidence for an involvement of genetic factors in the aetiology of IDDM comes mainly from studies on animals, human twins, families and populations.

• The NOD mouse and BB rat develop spontaneous diabetes characterized by lymphocytic infiltration of the islets, similar to human IDDM. In both models, disease susceptibility is linked to the MHC genes.

• In experiments with transgenic mice, exogenous genes such as various putative susceptibity genes are inserted into specific tissues in the animal. Hybrid gene constructs of the insulin gene promoter sequence and class I or II MHC genes, or interferon-gamma (IFN-gamma), allow these to be expressed on islet B cells. Class I and II expression is associated with diabetes but not lymphocytic infiltration of islets, and IFN-gamma with diabetes and inflammatory destruction of the islets.

• The concordance rate for IDDM of 30–50% average monozygotic twins further indicates a genetic influence in the aetiology of the disease.

• There is an increased risk of developing IDDM in the family members of those with the disease, e.g. HLA-identical siblings have 90 times the risk of the general population of developing IDDM by the age of 16 years.

• Population studies show an association of IDDM with the HLA genes DR3 and DR4 (on chromosome 6). The maximum risk is for those who possess both DR3 and DR4 ($\times$ 14 relative risk). In Japan, the association is with DR4/DRw9 and in China, with DR3/DRw9.

• Cloning of the class II genes indicates that abnormalities of the DQβ molecule (lack of aspartate residue at position 57) might confer susceptibility to IDDM by altering the ability to present self-antigen to the immune system.

• Several non-HLA gene associations have been identified for IDDM, including those with the hypervariable region near the insulin gene (on chromosome 11) and with polymorphism of the T-cell receptor beta chain (on chromosome 7) although both are controversial.

Insulin-dependent diabetes (IDDM) is thought to be a genetic disease and distinct from non-insulin dependent diabetes mellitus (NIDDM). Formal evidence for the genetic aetiology of IDDM comes from animal, twin and HLA population and family studies.

Animal models of IDDM

Considerable effort has been invested in developing animal models of IDDM in an attempt to produce a simplified system in which the genetics of IDDM can be dissected. Three such models exist: the NOD mouse, the BB rat, and the newer, exciting model of the transgenic mouse (for fuller descriptions of these animals see Chapter 17).

The non-obese diabetic (NOD) mouse

The NOD mouse was first described in 1980 [1] and was subsequently proposed as a model of IDDM. The NOD mouse develops IDDM spontaneously at approximately 12 weeks of age, with a strong predominance of the disease in females. There is progressive invasion of the pancreatic islets by mononuclear cells, followed by B-cell destruction and the development of diabetes, a sequence similar to that observed in human IDDM [2].

Breeding studies have suggested that the propensity of the NOD mouse to develop IDDM is controlled by two [3], or possibly three [4], recessive genes located on separate chromosomes. One of the susceptibility genes has subsequently been shown to be linked to the mouse MHC complex (IDD 1) and, although alone not sufficient to induce insulitis [5], seems to determine its course.

The nature of the MHC susceptibility gene is not clear but its localization to the MHC complex is intriguing as the NOD mouse has an unusual class II MHC. There is no expression of I-E (the murine equivalent of DR) molecules and there is doubt as to whether islet B cells in the NOD mouse express class II molecules (see Chapters 13 and 15) at any time during the development of diabetes, as they are not detected with any available monoclonal antibody or by alloreactive or autoreactive T-cell clones [6, 7]. By backcross experiments, a non-MHC gene (IDD 2) located between the T-lymphocyte marker Thy1 and malic enzyme genes (chromosome 9) has been found to determine insulitis. This acts as an autosomal recessive gene in the development of diabetes but it is dominant with variable penetrance for insulitis. Hence, those animals which inherit only IDD 2 and not IDD 1 develop insulitis but not diabetes, whereas those animals which inherit both IDD 1 and IDD 2 develop IDDM.

BB rat

Disease susceptibility loci have likewise been located within the MHC complex in the BB rat, another animal model of IDDM [8]. Using the restriction fragment length polymorphism (RFLP) technique, it is possible to distinguish BB rats from their BBN control strain using both HLA class I and II probes. Furthermore, a second gene determining T-cell lymphopenia is also required for manifestation of diabetes.

Transgenic mice

Transgenic mice have been described as the mystery tour of immunology [9], and have provided new and somewhat surprising insights into IDDM and also the immune system in general.

The localization of IDDM susceptibility loci to the MHC in NOD mice, BB rats and humans has led to speculation about the role of class I and II MHC molecules in IDDM (see Chapters 13 and 15). One view is that aberrant class II expression results in specific T-helper cell stimulation and lymphocyte infiltration followed by cytotoxic destruction of B cells. However, Dean et al. [10] studied the time course of expression of class II MHC in BB rats before the onset of diabetes and found that the expression of class II molecules by B cells occurs only after the inflammatory response against islet tissue has begun, suggesting that MHC expression is purely a secondary consequence of the autoimmune reaction. Intermediate between these two extremes is the possibility of some sort of deleterious cascade mechanism whereby MHC expression induced as a consequence of an autoimmune reaction could potentiate the reaction by recruiting more T lymphocytes which would in turn release cytokines and interferon-gamma (IFN-gamma) leading to still more MHC expression.

The need to resolve this dilemma stimulated the emergence of transgenic mice as a model for IDDM. Transgenic mice express exogenous genes in a tissue-specific manner and thus offer the opportunity to introduce putative susceptibility genes into experimental animals and observe the in vivo results. Sarvetnic et al. [11] and Lo et al. [12] created lines of transgenic mice carrying hybrid gene constructs which contained the enhancer and promoter sequences of insulin genes (either rat or human) fused to the structural genes for either I-E or I-A class II MHC molecules. The aim was to target specifically the expression of class II MHC antigens to B cells (Fig. 14.1). (The introduced class II genes were from the same mouse strain as the zygotes which gave rise to the transgenic mice and were not mutated or altered in any way).

Transgenic mice expressing both alpha and beta chains of the introduced class II genes became diabetic, but, surprisingly, without evidence of lymphocytic infiltration of pancreatic islets. On the contrary, Lo et al. reported that the mice were tolerant to the introduced transgene products, despite the absence of expression of transgene products in the thymus or any other lymphoid tissue [12]. These observations have since been extended by Allison et al. [13] who performed virtually identical experiments with introduced class I genes. Once again the transgenic mice, whether syngeneic or allogeneic to the transgene, developed IDDM with no evidence of lymphocyte infiltration of the islets. These results suggest a

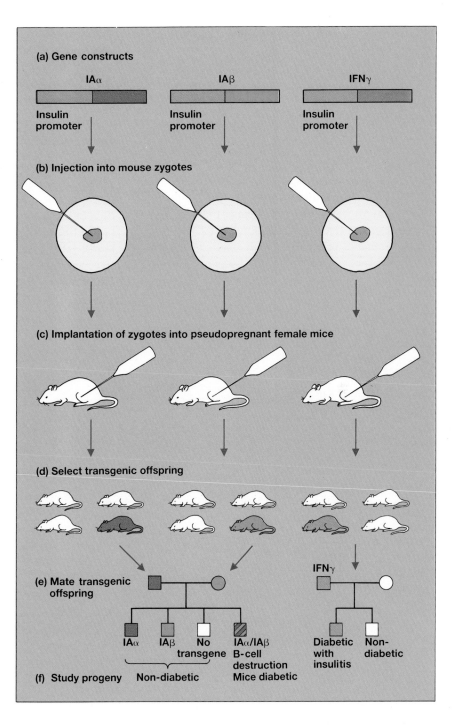

Fig. 14.1. The principle of transgenic mice. Illustrated are the experiments of Sarvetnic *et al.* 1988 [11]. The insulin gene promoter is fused to the coding regions of the gene being studied (in this case IAα, IAβ or IFN-gamma) and injected into mouse zygotes. As the insulin gene promoter contains all the information necessary for tissue-specific expression of insulin, the gene construct will only be expressed in those tissues which normally synthesize insulin, i.e. pancreatic B cells of the resulting transgenic mice. The effect of the expression of the transgenic product can then be studied.

non-immune role for the class I and II genes in the disease process. Therefore, a different picture of the pathogenesis of IDDM seems to be emerging from each of these animal models, although all agree that IDDM at least requires an MHC gene for expression of the disease.

In mice which expressed transgenic IFN-gamma in the B cells [11], a similar diabetic state was produced. However, in the IFN-gamma model,

the disappearance of B cells from the transgenic pancreas was accompanied by inflammatory destruction of the islets, suggesting a condition more akin to that observed for the inheritance of IDD 2 with IDD 1 in the NOD mouse. With regard to the latter, Nishimoto *et al.* [14] have reported that transgenic NOD mice which express I-E molecules fail to develop insulitis. These results suggest that the recessive MHC-linked gene identified by Hattari *et al.* [5] and Wicker *et al.* [4] is involved in the pathogenesis of autoimmune insulitis is I-E.

Studies in man

Twin studies

Amongst monozygotic twins there is a concordance value of 30−50% for IDDM [15]. These figures may overestimate concordance because of ascertainment bias but nevertheless they suggest a significant genetic contribution to IDDM. The high *discordance* rates have been used to suggest that IDDM is a multifactorial disease which is principally environmentally determined. An alter-

native hypothesis proposed by Eisenbarth [16] is that these differences can still be explained genetically by somatic cell gene rearrangements of the immunoglobulin and T-cell receptor genes in response to certain environmental stimuli.

Family studies

The study of siblings with IDDM provides conclusive evidence of the genetic component in the disease: the risk of a sibling of an IDDM patient developing diabetes by the age of 16 is increased by up to 27 times [17]. In the UK multiplex family study [18], families were recruited if there were two siblings with IDDM. By HLA-typing the parents and two affected siblings, it was ascer-

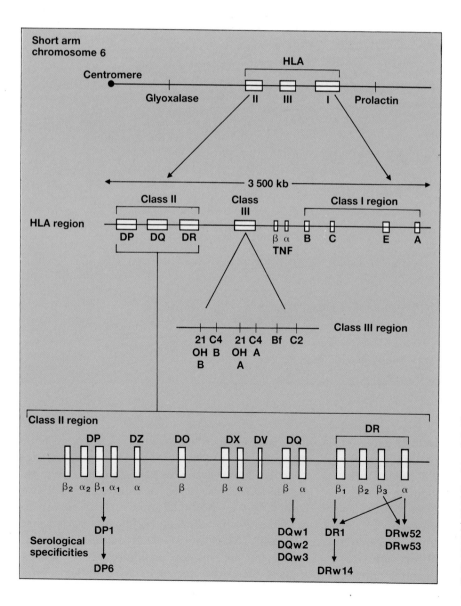

Fig. 14.2. Gene map: short arm chromosome 6. (Modified from Trowsdale and Campbell 1988 [19].) At the Xth HLA International Workshop, the Class II genes were renamed; DRβ$_1$, DRβ$_2$, DRβ$_3$ and DRα are now known as DRB1, DRB2, DRB3 and DRA; DQα, DQβ, DXα and DXβ as DQA1, DQB1, DQA2 and DQB2; DOβ and DZα as DOB and DNA; DPα$_1$, DPβ$_1$, DPα$_2$ and DPβ$_2$ as DPA1, DPB1, DPA2 and DPB2.

tained how frequently the two diabetic subjects shared both parental haplotypes (i.e. HLA identical; expected in 25% of cases), shared one haplotype (HLA haploidentical; expected in 50%) or did not share any parental haplotype (HLA non-identical; expected in 25%). In 376 such families, 57% were HLA identical, 38% haploidentical and 6% non-identical. This skewed distribution demonstrates HLA gene sharing in IDDM siblings: the fact that 6% were non-identical argues for heterogeneity of genetic markers in this disease. From this type of study, empirical values can be derived for the relative risk of IDDM occurring in a sibling of an IDDM subject — by the age of 16 an HLA-identical sibling has 90 times the risk of the general population; a haploidentical sibling 37 times the risk and an HLA non-identical sibling virtually no risk of developing IDDM [17]. These observations are relevant to the subject of genetic counselling in IDDM (Chapter 86).

Population studies

One feature distinguishing NIDDM from IDDM in Caucasoid races is the HLA association present in the latter but not the former [17]. The HLA region is located on the short arm of chromosome 6 (Fig. 14.2) and consists of the class I region (HLA A, E, C and B), the class III region (the complement C4 and C2 genes, the properdin Bf gene and the 21–hydroxylase genes) and the class II region (mainly HLA-DR, DQ and DP) [19]. Additionally, genes for tumour necrosis factors (TNFα and TNFβ) are located between the class I and class III regions. The HLA class I molecules are expressed on the surface of most nucleated cells, whereas the HLA class II molecules are only expressed by B lymphocytes, macrophages and activated T lymphocytes. The function of the HLA molecules is to present processed antigen which is recognized by the T-cell receptor. Not all genes within the human MHC are HLA-related; an example is the 21-hydroxylase gene involved in steroid biosynthesis, which is deleted in certain forms of congenital adrenal hyperplasia.

Associations with IDDM were first described for HLA A1-B8, B18 and B15 and subsequently, with the emergence of HLA DR-typing, for HLA-DR3 and DR4 [17, 20, 21, 22]. The higher relative risks associated with DR3 compared to B8, and with DR4 compared to B15, were cited as evidence that the class II genes were closer to MHC IDDM susceptibility gene(s) than the class I genes. Individuals who possess both DR3 and DR4 have the highest relative risk for IDDM, in contrast to those individuals who are either DR3 or DR4 homozygous or DR3/not DR4 and DR4/not DR3 (Table 14.1). Furthermore, concordant twins are more likely to be DR3/4 than discordant twins (Fig. 14.3). DR2 shows a strong protective effect against IDDM.

These HLA-DR associations are not constant throughout the world. In South India, although there is an increased prevalence of either DR3 or DR4 in IDDM individuals, there is no additional susceptibility in those individuals with both DR3 and DR4 [23]. In Japan, the maximum risk is associated with HLA-DR4, DRw9 and in China, with DR3, DRw9 [24, 25]. These varying HLA associations have led to speculation that the genes specifying DR4, DR3 or DRw9 are not the actual susceptibility genes themselves [26].

These HLA associations have been further re-

Table 14.1. Relative risks associated with HLA-DR in IDDM subjects.

	Diabetic probands (n=122), % positive	Healthy subjects (n=110), % positive	Relative risk	95% confidence limits
DR2	4%	28%	0.1	0.05– 0.3
DR3	70%	32%	5.0	2.9 – 8.8
DR4	78%	34%	6.8	3.8 –12.1
DR3, DR4	51%	7%	14.3	6.3 –32.4
DR3, DRX	20%	25%	0.7	0.4 – 1.3
DR4, DRY	27%	27%	1.0	0.6 – 1.8
DRZ, DRZ	2.5%	50%	0.04	0.01– 0.13

Data have been taken from the Barts–Windsor Study [17].
DRX = any other antigen but DR4.
DRY = any other antigen but DR3.
DRZ = not DR3 or DR4.

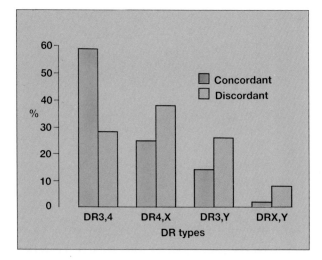

Fig. 14.3. HLA-DR types in concordant and discordant IDDM twin pairs. Key: X = DRX, another antigen apart from DR3; Y = DRY, another antigen apart from DR4. (Redrawn from Johnstone *et al.* 1983 [55] with permission.)

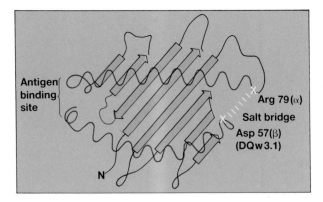

Fig. 14.4. Schematic representation of the foreign antigen site in a class II molecule. Beta strands are shown as thick lines, alpha helices as wavy lines. The model represents the structure of HLA-A2 depicted in Bjorkman *et al.* 1987 [40] on which is superimposed a model by Todd *et al.* 1987 [39]. It is hypothesized that a salt bridge would be formed between position 57 aspartate of the DQβ chain and the arginine at position 79 of the DQα chain. A non-aspartate at position 57 of the DQβ chain would prevent the formation of a salt bridge, thereby facilitating a change in peptide binding and T-cell recognition.(Redrawn with permission from Todd [39].)

fined following the cloning of many of the genes in the class II region. RFLP and sequence variation of DRα, DRβ III, DQβ and DXα genes identifies two subclasses of DR3 associated with DRw52a and DRw52b [27, 28, 29, 30, 31, 32]. The frequencies of the two subclasses differ in different parts of the world; the only common denominator is the serological specificity of DR3 [23, 33]. Other RFLPs of DQβ and DXα determine a subclass of individuals with DR4 who are at high risk of IDDM [31, 34–38].

These studies led Todd, Bell and McDevitt [39] to clone and sequence DR and DQ alleles from haplotypes either associated with, neutral to, or protective against IDDM. As a result they proposed a model of IDDM in which the lack of an aspartate residue at position 57 of the DQβ molecule results in susceptibility to IDDM. They account for the increased susceptibility of DR3/DR4 heterozygotes by proposing that the DQα chain encoded by DR3 forms a heterodimer with the DQβ chain of DR4, thereby stimulating a greater autoimmune response than would a DR3 or DR4 homodimer, presumably because of an enhanced ability to present self-antigen to the immune system. According to recent models of the three-dimensional structure of class I and II molecules [40], the residue at position 57 of HLA β chains could have an important role in peptide binding and T-cell receptor recognition (Fig.14.4). Thus, in the view of Todd *et al.* [39], the scale of diabetes

susceptibility of various HLA haplotypes is due to the differing degrees to which they can present self-antigen to the immune system.

There appear to be several weaknesses in this argument. First, the BB rat which spontaneously develops autoimmune diabetes analogous to the NOD mouse contains serine at position 57 in both IDDM-sensitive and resistant strains. Secondly, I-A (murine equivalent to DQ) transgenes which produced diabetes in recipient mice in the experiments of Sarvetnic *et al.* [11] contained the supposedly protective aspartate at residue 57 of IAβ. Thirdly, approximately 10% of human IDDM patients also carry the aspartate residue.

The intense search in the class II region presupposes that IDDM is primarily an autoimmune disease, in which case differences in the amino-acid sequence of the class II HLA molecules between diabetic and non-diabetic patients assume great importance. On the other hand, if auto-immunity is neither necessary (transgenic mice) nor sufficient (NOD mouse) for the development of IDDM, then alterations in the sequence of HLA molecules which might affect their ability to present self-antigen to the immune system would seem to be less relevant. In this case, it is possible that the currently known HLA genes merely serve as genetic markers for closely associated primary loci determining disease susceptibility.

Non-MHC associations in man

Animal models point to the possibility of a non-MHC gene association in man, which is supported by the estimate that the HLA associations in man account for only 60% of the genetic load to IDDM [41]. Many associations of non-MHC markers have been investigated in IDDM [42] (Table 14.2) but the only one which has stood the test of repeated observation is that of the hypervariable region near the insulin gene on chromosome 11.

The insulin gene

Two alleles of the hypervariable region of the insulin gene, designated class 1 and class 3, have been studied [43]. In Danish, British and American Caucasian subjects, there is an association of the class 1 allele with IDDM (Fig. 14.5) [44–6]. In other racial groups (e.g. Black Americans [47] and Japanese [48]), this association is not seen, whereas one study of Dravidian subjects in South India shows a weak association of the class 3 allele [49]. Therefore, it seems unlikely that the hypervariable region itself is directly involved in the pathogenesis of IDDM. A more likely explanation is that there is a closely linked locus which might be involved in MHC gene regulation and might therefore determine insulitis (as does IDD

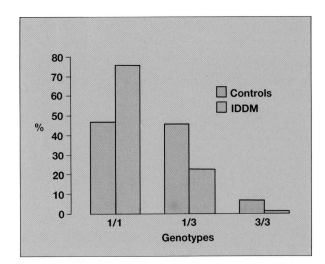

Fig. 14.5. Insulin genotypes distribution in Caucasian IDDM subjects. Key: 1/1 = homozygous for the class 1 allele; 1/3 = heterozygous class 1 and class 3; 3/3 = homozygous class 3 allele. Figures have been pooled from three studies of Danish, American and British Caucasian subjects [44–6].
Relative incidence of possession of homozygous class 1 allele for IDDM = 3.7 (95% confidence limits 2.6–6.0).

2 in the NOD mice). Alternatively, the locus may be involved in some aspect of B-cell metabolism which prevents the islet from surviving an immunological attack.

T-cell receptor

Both Hoover *et al.* [50] and Millward *et al.* [51] have suggested that polymorphism of the constant region of the T-cell receptor β chain (which is encoded by a gene on chromosome 7) may be associated with IDDM, and specifically in at-risk individuals with DR3. Study of the T-cell receptor variable genes of activated T-helper lymphocytes in monozygotic twins might help to test Eisenbarth's hypothesis that somatic cell gene rearrangements [16] could explain discordance of disease between twin pairs.

Other candidate loci

Mouse chromosome 9 is syngeneic with the long arm of human chromosome 11; loci in the Thy 1/ malic enzyme region deserve study to determine whether an association exists with human IDDM as in the NOD mouse. Genes involved in MHC gene modulation may also be of interest, especially in view of the results of the experiments

Table 14.2. Polymorphic non-HLA loci studied in relation to IDDM: no associations found.

ABO blood group
Acid phosphatase I
Adenosine deaminase
Pancreatic amylase
Cholinesterase 2
Esterase D
Duffy blood group
Galactose-1-phosphate uridyl transferase
Group-specific protein
Glutamic–oxaloacetic transaminase
Glutamic–pyruvic transaminase
Haptoglobin
Immunoglobulin heavy chain RFLPs
Kell blood group
Kidd blood group
Lewis blood group
MNSs blood group
P blood group
Phosphogluconate dehydrogenase
Phosphoglucomutase-1 and -2
Phosphoglycollate phosphatase
Rhesus blood group
Transferrin

with IFN-gamma transgenic mice [11]; possible loci include interferons gamma and alpha and tumour necrosis factors. Lastly, genes which determine susceptibility of the B cell to environmental damage — such as those involved in modulating free radical damage — may also be important.

What is the survival advantage of IDDM?

IDDM was recognized some 3000 years ago but, from the evolutionary point of view, it is a recent disease (see Chapter 1). Untreated IDDM is fatal and, by conferring a survival disadvantage, might be expected to be selected against and eventually removed from the population. The continued existence of IDDM suggests that the genes associated with it possess (or possessed) some survival advantage. Perhaps the HLA haplotypes afforded protection against environmental factors or diseases which threatened the survival of the species in the past.

Several studies have demonstrated preferential transmission of certain DR alleles to diabetic and non-diabetic offspring alike [52−4]. Vadheim and colleagues demonstrated that DR4 from non-diabetic fathers was transmitted to 72% of their offspring, compared with 58% from mothers and the 50% expected by Mendelian principles [54]. Additionally, DR3 from both fathers and mothers was transmitted to 62−68% of offspring. It is therefore possible that the IDDM HLA susceptibility alleles confer an advantage for fertility which presumably would outweigh the disadvantage of an HLA-linked susceptibility gene to IDDM. This may also explain how the human MHC confers the risk of IDDM without it actually involving the HLA genes themselves.

Conclusions

The major genetic predisposition to IDDM is determined by genes within the human MHC and in particular is related to DR3, DR4 and DRw9. Sequencing studies of the DQβ gene have suggested a model of IDDM whereby amino acids at position 57 are critical to the pathogenesis of IDDM. On the other hand, evidence from the NOD and transgenic mice suggests that the HLA genes alone do not determine IDDM although they may be primarily or secondarily involved in B-cell de-

struction. The nature of the non-MHC gene still awaits clarification.

GRAHAM A. HITMAN

BRENDAN MARSHALL

References

1 Makino S, Kunimoto D, Muraok D, Mizushima Y, Katagini K, Tochino Y. Breeding of a non-obese, diabetic strain of mice. *Exp Anim (Tokyo)* 1980; **29**: 1−13.
2 Rossini AA, Mordes JP, Like AA. Immunology of insulin-dependent diabetes mellitus. *Ann Rev Immunol* 1985; **3**: 289−320.
3 Makino S, Muraoka Y, Kishimoto Y, Hayashi Y. *Exp Anim (Tokyo)* 1985; **34**: 425−532.
4 Wicker LS, Miller BJ, Coker LZ, et al. Genetic control of diabetes and insulitis in the non-obese diabetic (NOD) mouse. *J Exp Med* 1987; **165**: 1639−54.
5 Hattari M, Buse JB, Jackson RA, et al. The NOD mouse: recessive diabetogenic gene in the major histocompatibility complex. *Science* 1986; **231**: 733−5.
6 Hanafusa T, Fujino-Kurihara H, Miyazaki A, et al. Expression of Class II major histocompatibility complex antigens on pancreatic B cells in the NOD mouse. *Diabetologia* 1987; **30**: 104−8.
7 Signore A, Cooke A, Pozzilli P, Butcher G, Simpson E, Beverley PCL. Class II and IL2 receptor positive cells in the pancreas of NOD mice. *Diabetologia* 1987; **30**: 902−5.
8 Buse JB, Rifae-Haddad R, Lees S, et al. Major histocompatibility complex restriction fragment length polymorphisms define three diabetogenic haplotypes in BB and BBN rats. *J Exp Med* 1985; **162**: 444−58.
9 Parham P. Intolerable secretion in tolerant transgenic mice. *Nature* 1988; **323**: 500−3.
10 Dean BM, Walker R, Bone AJ, Baird JD, Cooke A. Prediabetes in the spontaneously diabetic BB/E rat: lymphocyte subpopulations in the pancreatic infiltrates and expression of rat MHC class II molecules in endocrine cells. *Diabetologia* 1985; **28**: 464−6.
11 Sarvetnic N, Liggitt D, Pitts SL, Hansen SE, Stewart TA. Insulin dependent diabetes mellitus induced in transgenic mice by ectopic expression of Class II MHC and interferon-gamma. *Cell* 1988; **52**: 773−82.
12 Lo D, Burkly LC, Widera G, et al. Diabetes and tolerance in transgenic mice expressing Class II MHC molecules in pancreatic beta cells. *Cell* 1988; **53**: 159−68.
13 Allison J, Campbell JL, Marahan G, Mandel TE, Harrison LC, Miller JFAP. Diabetes in transgenic mice resulting from over expression of Class I histocompatibility molecules in pancreatic B cells. *Nature* 1988; **333**: 529−33.
14 Nishimoto H, Kikutani H, Yamamura K, Kishimoto T. Prevention of autoimmune insulitis by expression of I-E molecules in NOD mice. *Nature* 1987; **328**: 432−4
15 Barnett AH, Eff C, Leslie RDG, Pyke DA. Diabetes in identical twins. *Diabetologia* 1981; **20**: 87−93.
16 Eisenbarth GS. Genes, generator of diversity, glycoconjugates and autoimmune β-cell insufficiency in Type 1 diabetes. *Diabetes* 1987; **36**: 355−64.
17 Cudworth AG, Wolf E. The genetic susceptibility to Type 1 (insulin-dependent) diabetes mellitus. In: *Clinics in Endocrinology and Metabolism*. Vol. 11. WB Saunders Co. Ltd, 1982: 389−407.
18 Gorsuch AN, Spencer KM, Wolf E, Cudworth AG. Insulin

dependent diabetes mellitus. In: Kobberling J, Tattersall R, eds. *The Genetics of Diabetes Mellitus*, Serono Symposium 47. London: Academic Press, 1982: 43–53.

19 Trowsdale J, Campbell RD. Physical map of the human HLA region. *Immunol Today* 1988; **9**: 34–5.

20 Thomsen M, Platz P, Anderson OO, *et al*. MLC typing in juvenile diabetes mellitus and idiopathic Addison's disease. *Transplant Rev* 1975; **22**: 120–47.

21 Cudworth AG, Festenstein H. HLA genetic heterogeneity in diabetes mellitus. *Br Med Bull* 1984; **34**: 285–90.

22 Sachs JA, Cudworth AG, Jaraquemada D, Gorsuch AN, Festenstein H. Type 1 diabetes and the HLA-D locus. *Diabetologia* 1980; **418**: 41–3.

23 Serjeantson SW, Ranford PR, Kirk RL, *et al*. HLA-DR and -DQ genotyping in insulin dependent diabetes mellitus in South India. *Dis Markers* 1987; **5** 101–8.

24 Chan SH, Yeo PPB, Lee SW, Tan SH, Chean JS, Wong HE. HLA and insulin dependent diabetes mellitus in Singaporean Chinese. *Ann Acad Med Singapore* 1985; **14**: 215–18.

25 Bertrams J, Baur MP. Insulin-dependent diabetes mellitus. In: Albert ED, Baur MP, Mayr WR, eds. *Histocompatibility Testing* 1984. Berlin: Springer–Verlag, 1984: 348–58.

26 Hitman GA, Niven MJ. Genes and diabetes mellitus. *Br. Med Bull* 1989; **45**: 191–205.

27 Hitman GA, Sachs J, Cassell P, *et al*. A DR3 related DXα gene polymorphism strongly associates with insulin dependent diabetes mellitus. *Immunogenetics* 1986; **23**: 47–51.

28 Hitman GA, Niven MJ, Festenstein H, *et al*. HLA Class II alpha chain gene polymorphisms in patients with insulin-dependent diabetes mellitus, dermatitis herpetiformis and coeliac disease. *J Clin Invest* 1987; **79**: 609–15.

29 Stetler D, Grumer FC, Erlich HA. Polymorphic restriction endonuclease sites linked to the HLA-DR gene: localisation and use as genetic markers for insulin dependent diabetes. *Proc Natl Acad Sci USA* 1985; **82**: 8100–4.

30 Gorski J, Niven MJ, Sachs JA, *et al*. HLA-DRα, -DXα and DRβ III gene association studies in DR3 individuals. *Hum Immunol* 1987; **20**: 273–8.

31 Cohen-Haguenauer O, Robbins E, Massart C, *et al*. A systematic study of the HLA class IIβ DNA restriction fragments in insulin dependent diabetes mellitus. *Proc Natl Acad Sci USA* 1985; **83**: 3335–9.

32 Bontrop R, Tilanus M, Mikulski M, van Eggermond M, Termijtelen A, Giphert M. Polymorphisms within the HLA-DR3 haplotypes. *Immunogenetics* 1986; **23**: 401–5.

33 Hitman GA, Karir PK, Sachs JA, *et al*. HLA-D region RFLPs indicate that susceptibility to insulin dependent diabetes in South India is located in the HLA-DQ region. *Diabetic Med* 1988; **5**: 57–60.

34 Owerbach D, Lernmark A, Platz P, *et al*. HLA-D region β chain DNA endonuclease fragments differ between HLA-DR identical healthy and insulin dependent diabetic individuals. *Nature* 1983; **303**: 815–17.

35 Michelson B, Lernmark A. Molecular cloning of a polymorphic DNA endonuclease fragment associates insulin dependent diabetes mellitus with HLA-DQ. *J Clin Invest* 1987; **75**: 1144–52.

36 Festenstein H, Awad J, Hitman GA, *et al*. New HLA-DNA polymorphisms associated with autoimmune disease. *Nature* 1986; **322**: 64–7.

37 Sachs JA, Cassell PG, Festenstein H, Awad J, Hitman GA. DQβ restriction fragment length polymorphism and its relationship to insulin dependent diabetes mellitus. *Dis Markers* 1987; **5**: 199–206.

38 Nepom BS, Palmer J, Kim SJ, Hansen JA, Holbeck SL, Nepom G. Specific genomic markers for the HLA-DQ subregion discriminate between DR4+ insulin dependent diabetes mellitus and DR4+ seropositive juvenile rheumatoid arthritis. *J Exp Med* 1986; **164**: 345–9.

39 Todd JA, Bell GI, McDevitt HO. HLA-DQβ gene contributes to susceptibility and resistance to insulin-dependent diabetes mellitus. *Nature* 1987; **329**: 599–604.

40 Bjorkman PJ, Saper MA, Samraoui B, Bennett WS, Strominger JL, Wiley DC. The foreign antigen binding site and T cell recognition regions of Class I histocompatibility antigens. *Nature* 1987; **329**: 512–18.

41 Rotter JI, Landow EM. Measuring the genetic combination of a single locus to a multilocus disease. *Clin Gen* 1984; **26**: 529–42.

42 Niven MJ, Hitman GA. Non HLA associations in type 1 (insulin dependent) diabetes mellitus. In: AH Barnett, ed. *Immunogenetics of Insulin Dependent Diabetes*. MTP Press, 1987: 33–41.

43 Bell GI, Horito S, Karam JH. A polymorphic locus near the human insulin gene is associated with insulin dependent diabetes mellitus. *Diabetologia* 1986; **33**: 176–83.

44 Owerbach D, Nerup J. Restriction fragment length polymorphism of the insulin gene in diabetes mellitus. *Diabetes* 1982; **31**: 275–7.

45 Bell GI, Horito S, Karam JH. A highly polymorphic locus near the human insulin gene is associated with insulin-dependent diabetes mellitus. *Diabetes* 1984; **33**: 176–83.

46 Hitman GA, Tarn AC, Winter RM, *et al*. Type 1 (insulin-dependent) diabetes and a highly variable locus close to the insulin gene on chromosome 11. *Diabetologia* 1985; **28**: 218–22.

47 Elbein S, Rotwein P, Permutt MA, Bell GI, Sanz N, Karam JH. Lack of association of the polymorphic locus in the 5' flanking region of the human insulin gene and diabetes in American blacks. *Diabetes* 1985; **5**: 433–9.

48 Nomura M, Iwama N, Mukai M, *et al*. High frequency of Class 3 allele in the human insulin gene in Japanese Type 2 (non-insulin-dependent) diabetic patients with a family history of diabetes. *Diabetologia* 1986; **29**: 402–4.

49 Kambo PK, Hitman GA, Mohan V, *et al*. The genetic predisposition to fibrocalculous pancreatic diabetes. *Diabetologia* 1989; **32**: 45–51.

50 Hoover ML, Angelini G, Ball E, *et al*. HLA-DQ and T cell receptor genes in insulin dependent diabetes mellitus. *Cold Spring Harbor Symposium on Quantitative Biology* 1986; **51**: 803–9.

51 Millward BA, Welsh KI, Leslie RDG, Pyke DA, Demaine AG. T cell receptor beta chain polymorphisms are associated with insulin dependent diabetes. *Clin Exp Immunol* 1987; **70**: 152–7.

52 Cudworth AG, Gorsuch AN, Wolf E, Festenstein H. A new look at HLA genes with particular reference to type 1 diabetes. *Lancet* 1979; i: 389–91.

53 Awdeh ZL, Raum D, Yarvis EJ, Alper CA. Extended HLA/complement allele haplotypes: evidence for T/t-like complex in man. *Proc Natl Acad Sci USA* 1985; **80**: 259–63.

54 Vadheim CM, Rotter JI, Mclaren NK, Riley WJ, Anderson CE. Preferential transmission of diabetic alleles within the HLA gene complex. *N Engl J Med* 1986 **315**: 1314–18.

55 Johnstone C, Pyke DA, Cudworth AG, Wolf E. HLA-DR typing in identical twins with insulin-dependent diabetes: difference between concordant and discordant pairs. *Br Med J* 1983; **286**: 253–5.

15   Immune Factors in the Pathogenesis of Insulin-Dependent Diabetes Mellitus

Summary

• Several lines of evidence suggest that humoral and cell-mediated autoimmune B-cell damage lead ultimately to IDDM.

• Circulating islet-cell antibodies (ICA) are found in most newly diagnosed IDDM patients. ICA are class IgG and are directed against unknown cytoplasmic antigens in B cells and in the other islet endocrine cells. *In vitro*, ICA are cytotoxic to islet cells and impair insulin release but their *in vivo* actions are unknown.

• Spontaneous autoantibodies to insulin (IAA) also occur in many untreated, newly diagnosed IDDM patients.

• ICA and IAA are present during the prolonged 'prediabetic' period lasting up to several years before the clinical onset of IDDM, suggesting continuing autoimmune B-cell damage. Insulin secretion and glycaemia remain normal until relatively late in the disease process. After presentation, ICA and IAA titres generally fall progressively.

• ICA also occur in close relatives of IDDM patients, especially in high-risk siblings who share one or both HLA haplotypes with the diabetic proband. About 75% of those siblings with complement-fixing or high-titre (>20 JDF units) ICA will develop IDDM within 8 years. IAA may also predict susceptibility to IDDM.

• 'Insulitis' (the mononuclear cell infiltration of islets in newly diagnosed IDDM subjects) consists mainly of cytotoxic/suppressor T lymphocytes and activated T lymphocytes. The presence of these cells, together with penetration of IgG into islet B cells and local complement deposition, strongly suggest an autoimmune process. Only islet B cells are destroyed; the other islet endocrine cells remain intact.

• The major histocompatability (MHC, or HLA) antigens may be critical in modulating the immune response and the predisposition to autoimmunity. HLA class I molecules (A, B, C) are essential to the activation of cytotoxic T lymphocytes and class II molecules (DP, DQ, DR) to the activation of T-helper lymphocytes.

• HLA class II antigens associated with an increased risk of IDDM (DR3, DR4) may optimize the presentation of islet B-cell autoantigens to T-helper lymphocytes and therefore promote autoimmune damage. By contrast, the HLA-DR2 molecule, which carries a reduced risk of IDDM, may have a configuration which impedes B-cell autoantigen presentation and therefore protects against autoimmune destruction.

• Viruses or other environmental agents may induce aberrant HLA class II antigen expression on islet B cells which do not normally display these molecules. B cells could then act as antigen-presenting cells, exposing their own surface antigen to T-helper lymphocytes. Aberrant expression of class I antigens could similarly trigger cytotoxic T-lymphocyte activation. Both mechanisms would lead to autoimmune B-cell destruction.

• Cytokines released by activated lymphocytes and macrophages may enhance autoimmune damage, either by direct islet B-cell toxicity (e.g. interleukin-1) or by inducing aberrant or enhancing normal expression of HLA molecules by islet B cells (e.g. interleukin-2).

• Hypertrophied capillaries surrounding 'diabetic' islets strongly express HLA class I and class II antigens and may represent the portal of entry for the immune cells which invade the islet and destroy the B cells.

For many years, IDDM has been recognized in association with other diseases of presumed auto-immune aetiology and tissue-specific autoanti-bodies, directed against the endocrine cells of the islets of Langerhans, were first identified in the mid-1970s. Since then, our understanding of immune mechanisms in general and of the disease process in IDDM has increased considerably. This chapter will first consider the basic functioning of the immune system (reviewed in detail by Roitt, Brostoff and Male [1]) and then discuss the several lines of evidence which implicate autoimmune damage in the pathogenesis of IDDM.

The immune system: a brief account

Cells of the immune system

The various cell types which contribute to mounting an immune response to a foreign antigen (or autologous self-antigens) are shown in Table 15.1.

LYMPHOCYTES

Several distinct subsets of lymphocytes are involved. All are derived from common precursor cells, the characteristics of the mature lymphocytes being determined by their site of differentiation (thymus for T lymphocytes, bone marrow and liver for B lymphocytes). Other types of lymphocytes are the killer (K) and natural killer (NK) cells. These various subsets have different functions and are distinguished immunologically by their different surface antigens which can be identified using a battery of monoclonal antisera (see Table 15.1).

T lymphocytes are primarily involved in cell-mediated immune responses such as delayed hypersensitivity reactions, allograft rejection, graft-versus-host disease, direct killing of tumour cells and the lysis of virus-infected cells. T lymphocytes are further subdivided into several different types. *T-helper lymphocytes* are activated by being exposed to a foreign antigen together with an HLA class II antigen on the surface of an antigen-presenting cell (see below) [2]. Activated T-helper lymphocytes release various cytokines (see Table 15.2), which are regulatory peptides with a range of paracrine and autocrine effects including the activation of macrophages and cytotoxic T lymphocytes and the stimulation of B lymphocytes to synthesize antibodies [3]. *Cytotoxic T lymphocytes*

[4] are activated by the combination of foreign antigen, particularly viruses, and HLA class I molecules presented on the surface of cells and then lyse these target cells and destroy the attached foreign antigen. *T-suppressor lymphocytes* are apparently activated by T-helper lymphocytes and act to inhibit the latter, apparently providing a 'damping' circuit which prevents an excessive immune response. All T lymphocytes carry a specific receptor (Ti) and other surface markers including the CD3 (T3) antigen which is closely associated with the Ti receptor. In addition, cytotoxic T lymphocytes carry a specific CD8 antigen (also known as T8, OKT8 or Leu 2) and T-helper cells the CD4 (T4, OKT4 or Leu 3) antigen. After activation, all T lymphocytes express two further surface markers, HLA class II antigens and inter-leukin-2 (IL-2) receptors.

B lymphocytes recognize soluble antigens through specific immunoglobulins which they synthesize and transport to their surface where the antibodies bind and act as receptors to the antigen. Complete activation of B lymphocytes depends not only on this mechanism but also on further stimulation by lymphokines produced by activated T-helper lymphocytes. Once activated, B lymphocytes divide and may differentiate into plasma cells, whose main function is the secretion of circulating antibodies.

Killer (K) cells are another subset of lymphocytes which possess membrane receptors for the constant fragment (Fc) of immunoglobulins. K cells interact with antibodies to kill target cells through a mechanism termed 'antibody-dependent cellular cytotoxicity' [5]. *Natural killer (NK) cells* are large granular lymphocytes which provide a more primitive defence mechanism which is only now being elucidated [6]. They are activated by interferon-gamma (IFN-gamma) and produce cytotoxicity without needing antibodies to be attached to the target cell [7].

ANTIGEN-PRESENTING CELLS

These cells are crucial in inducing activation of T-helper lymphocytes in response to foreign antigens. Unlike B lymphocytes, which can recognize intact native proteins, T-helper cells can only react to antigen which has been ingested and chemically modified by antigen-processing cells. Moreover, the antigen fragments must then be transported to the surface of the antigen-processing cell and presented to the T-helper lymphocyte together

Table 15.1. Cells involved in the immune response.

Type	Subgroup	Surface markers	Activated by	Functions
LYMPHO-CYTES	T lymphocytes (all carry CD3 [T3] and Ti markers) — T-helper lymphocytes	CD4 (T4, OKT4)	Ag+class II antigen on antigen-presenting cell	Activate B lymphocytes Activate cytotoxic T cells Activate T-suppressor cells
	Cytotoxic T lymphocytes	CD8 (T8, OKT8)	Surface Ag (virus) + class I antigen on target cell	Lysis of target cell
	T-suppressor lymphocytes	CD8 (T8, OKT8)	Activated T-helper lymphocytes	Inhibit cell-mediated and humoral immune responses
	B lymphocytes	Immunoglobulins	Ag binding to surface immuno-globulin Amplified by T-helper cell lymphokines	Differentiate into plasma cells Synthesize immuno-globulins
	Killer cells	Fc receptors	Antibody-coated target cells	Lysis of target cells
	Natural killer cells	CD2 (some only)	IFN-gamma Immune complexes	Lysis of target cells
ANTIGEN-PRESENT-ING CELLS	Macrophages / Dendritic cells	HLA class II antigens	Recognition and ingestion of Ag	Ingestion and processing of Ag Presentation of Ag + class II antigens to activate T-helper cells Release of IL-1 and TNF-alpha

Note: Ag = foreign antigen.

with HLA class II molecules in order to trigger T-cell activation. Morphologically, antigen-presenting cells are macrophages and the related dendritic cells.

Relevance of the MHC (HLA) molecules

In man, the antigens of the major histocompatability complex (MHC) are also known as the 'human-lymphocyte-associated' (HLA) antigens. These molecules, especially those of class II, may determine the size and target of the immune response and are therefore crucial to the process of autoimmune damage. They are proteins encoded within the MHC (HLA) region which, in man, is located on the short arm of chromosome 6 (Fig. 15.1).

Class I molecules are encoded by three major class I genes, termed A, B and C. Their sequences are highly variable but each has a common dimeric structure consisting of a heavy chain (a 45-kDa protein encoded by the HLA genes) linked covalently to an unrelated protein, β_2-microglobulin, whose gene lies on chromosome 15. Class I molecules occur on the surface of most nucleated cells and their expression is increased by IFN-gamma. They are essential for lysis of virus-carrying cells and are presented together with foreign antigen to activate cytotoxic T lymphocytes (see Fig. 15.1).

Class II molecules are encoded by three related groups of genes, HLA DP, DQ and DR [2]. Each molecule consists of a dimer comprising an alpha and a beta chain, each spanning the cell membrane and having a molecular weight of about 30 kDa. In contrast to the widespread distribution of class I antigens, class II molecules are normally

Table 15.2. Major cytokines involved in the immune response.

	Name	Source	Actions
MONOKINES (produced by monocytes)	IL-1	Macrophages	Induces IL-2 release from T-helper cells Stimulates B-cells maturation
	TNF-alpha	Macrophages	Cytotoxic to tumour cells *in vitro*
LYMPHOKINES (produced by lymphocytes)	IL-2	T-helper cells	Stimulates division of activated T and activated B cells
	IFN-gamma	T-helper and cytotoxic T cells	Activates macrophages Activates NK cells Increases HLA class I and II antigen expression on cell surfaces Inhibits virus replication
	B-cell stimulating factor	Activated T cells	Stimulates division of activated B cells

expressed only on specific cell types, notably antigen-presenting cells, B lymphocytes, activated T lymphocytes, certain capillary endothelial cells and epithelium-lined cavities. Exposure to IFN-gamma may induce the expression of class II molecules on other tissues (thyroid and gut epithelia) and 'inappropriate' or 'aberrant' expression of these antigens has been observed in various tissues undergoing autoimmune damage (Table 15.3). Class II molecules presented together with antigen by an antigen-presenting cell will activate T-helper lymphocytes (see Fig. 15.1).

The specific recognition and antigen-presenting processes involving the HLA class I and class II antigens are known as the 'HLA (MHC) restriction' phenomenon [8].

Mechanism of the normal immune response

A physiological immune response involves a complex interplay of positive and negative regulatory processes. If a foreign antigen enters the body, it is first recognized, ingested and processed by macrophages which, in turn, become activated. Cytotoxic and T-helper lymphocytes are activated as described above by external antigens presented in combination with class I and class II antigens

respectively (Fig. 15.1). When T-helper lymphocytes are activated, they stimulate B lymphocytes to divide and synthesize specific antibodies to the particular antigen, and also enhance the activity of cytotoxic T cells in killing cells bearing foreign antigen. K and NK cells will also be activated to attack target cells. At the same time, T-suppressor lymphocytes will act to stop both antibody production and cell-mediated immune reactions when the antigen has been eliminated.

The physiological activation and expansion of the various limbs of the immune system are also influenced by a variety of lymphokines and monokines, known collectively as cytokines (Table 15.2) [3]. An intricate network of idiotype/anti-idiotype antibody interactions [9] also contributes to the fine tuning in the ultimate modulation of an effective immune response. Other, recently characterized molecules may also be important. These are the so-called 'adhesion' and 'homing' molecules [10]. Studies of their expression on the capillary endothelial cell compartment, lymphocytes and epithelial cells have provided clues to a role for these molecules in immunocyte trafficking and in antigen processing and presentation (Fig. 15.2).

This carefully constructed defence system pro-

inheritance which does not follow classical Mendelian laws [54].

In this study, ICA were found in siblings who were HLA non-identical with the proband as well as in HLA-identical and haplo-identical siblings, and in some parents [55]. However, CF-ICA or high-titre ICA were found in the genetically susceptible groups and approximately 75% of individuals with CF-ICA or ICA titres >20 Juvenile Diabetes Foundation (JDF) units progressed to IDDM within 8 years [56] (Fig. 15.7). Previous family studies and other work on twins [57], schoolchildren [58] and patients with polyglandular autoimmune disease [59] have confirmed both the extended autoimmune prodrome preceding the clinical onset of IDDM and the value of ICA as a predictive marker for the future development of the disease. Recent efforts toward the standardization of ICA measurements, in particular the introduction of reference JDF units, have enabled better comparison of data from different studies [60].

A correlation has been found between the presence of IAA and CF-ICA or high-titre ICA, and the subsequent progression to overt diabetes [61, 62]. The coexistence of these immune markers and impaired metabolic function (e.g. reduced

insulin secretion following intravenous glucose injection) have been reported to increase the predictive value of ICA [25]. Some of the cell-mediated immune abnormalities noted in newly diagnosed IDDM patients have also been detected together with humoral responses against islet cells in non-diabetic subjects who are genetically susceptible to IDDM [63]. The progression to diabetes is also

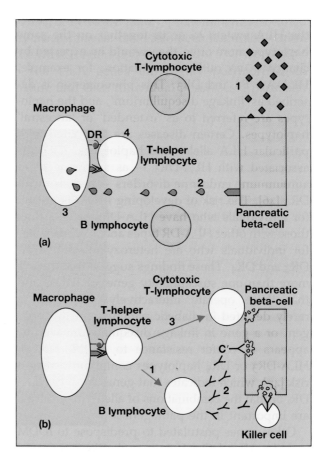

Fig. 15.8. Diagrammatic representation of the hypothetical steps leading to 'activation' of the immune system against the islet B cell. In this scheme, the macrophage plays the central role in antigen presentation. (a) The triggering events: (1) Environmental attack (? viruses). (2) Release of autoantigens from the B cell. (3) The macrophage processes the autoantigens and inserts them into its surface membrane. Class II molecules (DR) present islet autoantigens to the T-helper lymphocyte. (4) Activation of the T-helper lymphocyte. (b) Completing the vicious circle leading to death of the B cell: (1) Activation of B lymphocytes by the T-helper cell. (2) Production of islet-cell antibodies followed by antibody-dependent complement (C') and killer (K) cell-mediated cytoxicity. (3) Activation of the cytotoxic T lymphocyte. (2) and (3) lead to lysis and death of the B cell.
The T-suppressor lymphocyte is not represented in the diagram. The role of this cell in autoimmunity is not clearly understood at present but growing evidence indicates that organ (islet B cell) specific T-suppressor cells may exist, leading to de-repression of autoreactive helper and cytotoxic T lymphocytes.

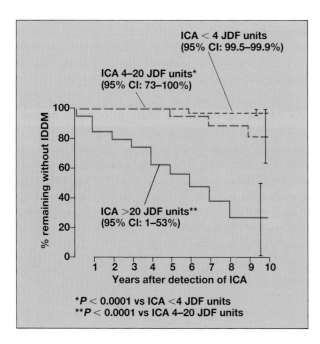

Fig. 15.7. Cumulative risk for developing IDDM over 10 years. The diagram summarizes the data on 719 first-degree relatives of IDDM probands in relation to peak titres of ICA level. The risk was greatest for relatives with the highest levels of ICA (>20 JDF units). 95% CI=95% confidence intervals.

likely to be modified by other factors including age, family history and genetic susceptibility.

Autoimmune pathogenesis of IDDM

How the autoimmune attack against B cells in the islet is initiated and carried out remains, at present, unresolved. Among the several hypotheses advanced [64], one supports the concept that sensitization against the autoantigen expressed on the pancreatic B cells follows a series of events similar to those indicated above for the elimination of foreign antigens (Fig. 15.8a,b). As previously described, physiological immune responses are initiated by HLA class II-positive cells, such as macrophages, which present antigens to T-helper lymphocytes which then trigger the chain of immune reactions. Recently, the 'inappropriate' or 'aberrant' expression of class II molecules has been observed on a variety of cells which are the targets of autoimmune attack (Table 15.3), including the B cells of islets affected by insulitis [65] (see Chapter 13). A and D cells do not express class II products in these islets, which is consistent with the sparing of these cells in the killing process (Fig. 15.9c,d). The exact role of the aberrant expression of class II molecules in the pathogenesis of autoimmune diseases is not yet fully understood. Nevertheless, this phenomenon has concentrated attention on the possibility that the target cell itself may become an antigen-presenting cell which presents its own surface autoantigens [66], and it also provides a clue regarding the association of autoimmune diseases, including IDDM with certain HLA specificities [13].

It has been postulated that as yet unrecognized agents, which could be environmental factors (e.g. viruses), are responsible for triggering class II expression on cells, such as B cells, which subsequently undergo autoimmune destruction. If this phenomenon occurs in genetically susceptible individuals, for example, those who develop IDDM, the configuration of certain class II products (HLA-DR3 or DR4 or both, but not HLA-DR2) may be ideal for presentation of autoantigens which are normally expressed on the surface of B cells (Fig. 15.10a,b). This initial event could lead to activation of T-helper cells which, in turn, stimulate effector B and cytotoxic T lymphocytes. Whether the induction of autoimmune T lymphocytes leads to clinical autoimmune disease may depend upon other regulatory mechanisms, such as T-suppressor cell activity [67] or the production of anti-idiotypic antibodies (antibodies directed against particular clones of autoreactive lymphocytes). Lymphokines, for example interferons (IFN) and tumour necrosis factor (TNF), which are produced by invading lymphocytes and macrophages and are known to be potent modulators of class II product expression in certain cells, might then be responsible for perpetuating the cycle of *in situ* HLA gene activation [68]. It is perhaps unlikely that this cytokine combination is responsible for initiating the process *in vivo*, as these agents can also induce class II molecules on A and D cells *in vitro*, cells which do not express these molecules in the 'diabetic' islet. Interestingly, since the genes coding for TNF were identified on chromosome 6, a DNA polymorphism in TNF genes has been reported in mice [69]. A strain which spontaneously develops an SLE-like syndrome had a particular RFLP pattern and these animals also displayed a reduction in TNF production. The human TNF-alpha gene is also polymorphic and an association of particular TNF RFLPs with certain diabetogenic haplotypes has been reported [70]. It remains to be seen whether

Table 15.3. Inappropriate HLA class II antigen expression and autoimmune disease.

Disease	Cell type
Hashimoto's thyroiditis and Graves' disease	Thyroid epithelial cell
Primary biliary cirrhosis	Bile duct epithelial cell
IDDM	Islet B cell
Alopecia areata	Hair follicle
Sjögren's syndrome	Salivary duct epithelium
Fibrosing alveolitis	Alveolar epithelium
Inflammatory bowel disease	Gut epithelium
Atrophic gastritis	Gastric parietal cell
Autoimmune protracted diarrhoea of infancy	Immature enterocyte

References

1 Roitt I, Brostoff J, Male D, eds. *Immunology*. Edinburgh: Churchill Livingston, and London: Gower Medical, 1985.

2 Unanue ER, Allen PM. The basis of the immunoregulatory role of macrophages and other accessory cells. *Science* 1987; **236**: 551−3.

3 Balkwill FR, Burke F. The cytokine network. *Immunol Today* 1989; **10**: 299−304.

4 Battisto JR, Plate J, Shearer G, eds. In: *Cytoxic T Cells. Biology and Relevance to Disease. Ann NY Acad Sci* 1988; 532.

5 Wigzell H. Antibody-dependent cell-mediated cytotoxicity. In: Milgrom F, Abeyounis CJ, Albini B, eds. *Antibodies: Protective, Destructive and Regulatory Role*. Basel: Karger, 1985: 1−13.

6 Janeway CA. A primitive immune system. *Nature* 1989; 341−108.

7 Ritz J. The role of natural killer cells in immune surveillance. *N Engl J Med* 1989; **320**: 1748−9.

8 Pujol-Borrell R, Todd L. Inappropriate HLA Class II in autoimmunity: is it the primary event? In: Doniach D, Bottazzo GF, eds. *Endocrine and Other Organ Orientated Autoimmune Disorders. Clin Immunol Allergy* 1987; **1**: 1−27. London: Baillière Tindall.

9 10th Forum in Immunology. Is the immune system a functional idiotypic network? *Ann Inst Pasteur/Immunol* 1986; **137C**: 5−48.

10 Stoolman LM. Adhesion molecules controlling lymphocyte migration. *Cell* 1989; **56**: 907−10.

11 Eisenbarth GS. Type 1 diabetes mellitus: a chronic autoimmune disease. *N Engl J Med* 1986; **314**: 1360−8.

12 Bottazzo GF, Pujol-Borrell R, Gale EAM. Autoimmunity and Type 1 diabetes: bringing the story up to date. In: Alberti KGMM, Krall LP, eds. *The Diabetes Annual*. Vol 3. Amsterdam: Elsevier Science Publications, 1987: 15−38.

13 Bottazzo GF. Death of a beta cell: homicide or suicide? *Diabetic Med* 1986; **3**: 119−30.

14 Bottazzo GF, Floriu-Christensen A, Doniach D. Islet cell antibodies in diabetes mellitus with autoimmune polyendocrine deficiency. *Lancet* 1974; ii: 1279−83.

15 Lendrum R, Walker IG, Gamble DR. Islet cell antibodies in juvenile diabetes mellitus of recent onset. *Lancet* 1975; i: 880−2.

16 Lendrum R, Walker IG, Cudworth AG, Theophanides C, Pyke DA, Bloom A, Gamble DR. Islet cell antibodies in diabetes mellitus. *Lancet* 1976; ii: 1273−6.

17 Bottazzo GF, Doniach D. Autoimmunity in diabetes mellitus. In: Podolsky S, Viswanathan M, eds. *Secondary Diabetes: The Spectrum of the Diabetes Syndrome*. New York: Raven Press, 391−408.

18 Bottazzo GF, Dean BM, Gorsuch AN, Cudworth AG, Doniach D. Complement-fixing islet-cell antibodies in Type 1 diabetes: possible monitors of active beta-cell damage. *Lancet*: 1980; i: 668−72.

19 Lernmark Å, Freedman ZR, Hofman C, Rubenstein A, Steiner DF, Jackson RL, Winter RJ, Traisman HS. Islet cell surface antibodies in juvenile diabetes mellitus. *N Engl J Med* 1978; **299**: 375−80.

20 Pujol-Borrell R, Khoury EL, Bottazzo GF. Islet cell surface antibodies in Type 1 (insulin-dependent) diabetes mellitus: use of human fetal pancreas cultures as substrate. *Diabetologia* 1982; **22**: 85−89.

21 Van de Winkel M, Smets G, Gepts W, Pipeleers DG. Islet cell surface antibodies from insulin-dependent diabetics bind specifically to pancreatic B cells. *J Clin Invest* 1982; **70**: 41−9.

22 Papadopoulos GK, Lernmark Å. The spectrum of islet cell antibodies, In: Davies TF, ed. *Autoimmune Endocrine Disease*. New York: Wiley, 1983: 176−80.

23 Boitard C, Sai P, Debray-Sachs M, Assan R, Hamburger J. Anti-pancreatic immunity. *In vitro* studies of cellular and humoral immune reactions directed towards pancreatic islets. *Clin Exp Immunol* 1984; **55**: 571−80.

24 Baekkeskov S, Landin M, Kristensen JK, Srikanta S, Bruining GJ, Mandrup-Poulsen T, De Beaufort C, Soeldner JS, Eisenbarth G, Lindgren F, Sundquist G, Lernmark Å. Antibodies to a 64000 Mr human islet cell protein precede the clinical onset of insulin-dependent diabetes. *J Clin Invest* 1987; **79**: 926−34.

25 Colman PG, Eisenbarth GS. Immunology of Type 1 diabetes − 1987. In: Alberti KGMM, Krall LP, eds. *The Diabetes Annual*. Vol. 4. Amsterdam: Elsevier Scientific Publications, 1988: 17−45.

26 Palmer JP, Asplin CM, Clemons P, Lyen K, Tatpati O, Raghu PK Paquette TL. Insulin antibodies in insulin-dependent diabetics before insulin treatment. *Science* 1983; **222**: 1337−9.

27 Srikanta S, Ricker AT, McCulloch DK, Soeldner JS, Eisenbarth GS, Palmer SP. Autoimmunity to insulin, beta cell dysfunction and development of insulin-dependent diabetes mellitus. *Diabetes* 1986; **39**: 139−42.

28 Dean BM, Becker F, McNally JM, Tarn AC, Schwarz G, Gale EAM, Bottazzo GF. Insulin autoantibodies in the pre-diabetic period: correlation with islet cell antibodies and the development of diabetes. *Diabetologia* 1986; **29**: 339−42.

29 Wilkin T, Palmer J, Kurtz A, Bonifacio E, Diaz JL. The second international workshop on the standardization of insulin autoantibody (IAA) measurement. *Diabetologia* 1988; **31**: 449−50.

30 Palmer JP. Insulin autoantibodies: their role in the pathogenesis of IDDM. *Diabetes Metab Rev* 1987; **3**: 1005−15.

31 Bottazzo GF, Lendrum R. Separate autoantibodies to human pancreatic glucagon and somatostatin cells. *Lancet* 1976; ii: 873−6.

32 Bottazzo GF. Beta-cell damage in diabetic insulitis: are we approaching the solution? *Diabetologia* 1984; **26**: 241−50.

33 Buschard K. The thymus-dependent immune system in the pathogenesis of Type 1 (insulin-dependent) diabetes mellitus. *Dan Med Bull* 1985; **32**: 139−51.

34 Nerup J, Andersen O, Bendixen G, Egeberg J, Gunnarsson R, Kromann G, Poulsen JE. Cell mediated immunity in diabetes mellitus. *Proc R Soc Med* 1974; **67**: 506−13.

35 Irvine WJ. Immunological aspects of diabetes mellitus: a review. In: Irvine WJ, ed. *Immunology of Diabetes*. Edinburgh: Teviot Science Publications, 1980: 1−53.

36 Selam JL, Clot S, Andary M, Mirouze J. Circulating lymphocyte subpopulations in juvenile insulin-dependent diabetes: correction of abnormalities by adequate blood glucose control. *Diabetologia* 1979; **16**: 35−40.

37 Bottazzo GF, Pujol-Borrell R, Gale EAM. Etiology of diabetes: the role of autoimmune mechanisms. In: Alberti KGMM, Krall LP, eds. *The Diabetes Annual*. Vol. 1. Amsterdam: Elsevier Science Publications, 1985: 16−52.

38 Pozzilli P, Sensi M, Dean B, Gorsuch AN, Cudworth AG. Evidence for raised K cell levels in Type 1 diabetes. *Lancet* 1979; ii: 173−5.

39 Alviggi L, Johnston C, Hoskins DJ, Tee DEH, Pyke D, Leslie RDG, Vergani D. Pathogenesis of insulin-dependent diabetes: a role for activated T lymphocytes. *Lancet* 1984; ii: 4−6.

40 Bach JF. Mechanisms of autoimmunity in insulin-dependent diabetes mellitus. *Clin Exp Immunol* 1988; **72**: 1−8.

41 De Berardinis P, Londei M, James RFL, Lake SP, Wise PH,

Feldmann M. Do CD4-positive cytotoxic T cells damage islet B cells in Type 1 diabetes? *Lancet* 1988; ii: 823–4.

42 Shafrir E, Renold AE, (eds.) *Frontiers in Diabetes Research. Lesson from Animal Diabetes II.* London: J. Libby & Co., 1988.

43 Gepts W. Pathologic anatomy of the pancreas in juvenile diabetes mellitus. *Diabetes* 1965; **14**: 619–33.

44 Bottazzo GF, Dean BM, McNally JM, Mackay EH, Swift PGF, Gamble DR. *In situ* characterisation of autoimmune phenomena and expression of HLA molecules in the pancreas in diabetic insulitis. *N Engl J Med* 1985; **313**: 353–60.

45 Trowsdale J, Campbell RD. Physical map of the human HLA region. *Immunol Today* 1981; **9**: 34–5.

46 Rotter JI, Vanheim CM, Raffel LJ, Rimoin DL, Riley WJ, Maclaren NK. Genetic etiologies of diabetes. *Pediatr Adolesc Endocrin* 1986; **15**: 1–8.

47 McCluskey J, McCann VJ, Kay PH, Zilko PJ, Christiansen FT, O'Neill GJ, Dawkins RL. HLA and complement allotypes in Type 1 (insulin-dependent) diabetes. *Diabetologia* 1983; **24**: 162–5.

48 Owerbach D, Rich C, Carnegie S, Tanga K. Molecular biology of the HLA system in insulin-dependent diabetes mellitus. *Diabetes Metab Rev* 1987; **3**: 819–34.

49 Todd JA, Acha-Orbea H, Bell GI, Chao N, Frorek Z, Jacob CO, McDermott M, Sinha AA, Timmerman B, Steinman L, McDevitt HO. A molecular basic for MHC Class II-associated autoimmunity. *Science* 1988; **240**: 1003–9.

50 Hitman GA. The major histocompatibility complex and insulin-dependent (Type 1) diabetes. *Autoimmunity* 1989; **4**: 119–30.

51 Bottazzo GF, Pujol-Borrell R, Gale EAM. Autoimmunity and diabetes: progress, consolidation and controversy. In: Alberti KGMM, Krall LP, eds. *The Diabetes Annual.* Vol. 2. Amsterdam: Elsevier Science Publications, 1986: 13–29.

52 Andreani D, Kolb H, Pozzilli P, eds. In: *Immunotherapy of Type 1 Diabetes.* Chichester: J. Wiley & Sons, 1989.

53 Bingley PJ, Gale EAM. The incidence of insulin-dependent diabetes in England: a study in the Oxford region 1985–1986. *Br Med J* 1989; **289**: 558–60.

54 Wolf E, Spencer KM, Cudworth AG. The genetic susceptibility to Type 1 (insulin-dependent) diabetes: analysis of the HLA-DR association. *Diabetologia* 1984; **24**: 224–30.

55 Gorsuch AN, Spencer KM, Lister J, McNally JM, Dean BM, Bottazzo GF, Cudworth AG. The natural history of Type 1 (insulin-dependent) diabetes mellitus: evidence for a long prediabetic period. *Lancet* 1981; ii: 363–5.

56 Tarn AC, Thomas JM, Dean BM, Ingram D, Schwarz G, Bottazzo GF, Gale EAM. Predicting insulin-dependent diabetes. *Lancet* 1988; i: 845–50.

57 Srikanta S, Ganda OP, Jackson RA, Gleason RE, Kaldany A, Garovoy MR, Milford EL, Carpenter GB, Soeldner JS, Eisenbarth GS. Type I diabetes mellitus in monozygotic twins: chronic progressive beta cell dysfunction. *Ann Intern Med* 1983; **99**: 320–6.

58 Bruining GJ, Molenaar JL, Grobee DE, Hofman A, Scheffer GJ, Bruining HA, DeBrujn AM, Valkenburg NA. Ten year follow up study of islet cell antibodies and childhood diabetes mellitus. *Lancet* 1989; i: 1100–3.

59 Betterle C, Presotto F, Pedini B, Moro L, Slack RS, Zanette F, Zanchetta R. Islet cell and insulin autoantibodies in organ-specific autoimmune patients. Their behaviour and predictive value for the development of Type 1 (insulin-dependent) diabetes mellitus. A 10 year follow-up study. *Diabetologia* 1987; **30**: 292–7.

60 Gleichmann H, Bottazzo GF. Islet-cell and insulin autoantibodies in diabetes. *Immunol Today* 1987; **8**: 167–8.

61 Vardi P, Dib SA, Tuttleman M, Connelly JE, Grinbergs M,

Radizabeh A, Riley WJ, Maclaren NK, Eisenbarth GS, Soeldner JS. Competitive insulin autoantibody assay. Prospective evaluation of subjects at high risk for development of Type I diabetes mellitus. *Diabetes* 1987; **36**: 1286–91.

62 Dean BM, McNally JM, Bonifacio E, Jennings AM, Dunger DB, Gale EAM, Bottazzo GF. Insulin autoantibodies in diabetes-related and normal populations: comparative evaluation using a precise displacement ELISA. *Diabetes* (in press).

63 Al-Sakkaf L, Pozzilli P, Tarn AC, Schwarz G, Gale EAM, Bottazzo GF. Persistent reduction of CD4/CD8 lymphocyte ratio and cell activation before the onset of Type 1 (insulin-dependent) diabetes. *Diabetologia* 1989; **32**: 322–5.

64 Bosi E, Todd I, Pujol-Borrell R, Bottazzo GF. Mechanisms of autoimmunity: relevance to the pathogenesis of Type 1 (insulin-dependent) diabetes mellitus. *Diabetes/Metab Rev* 1987; **3**: 893–924.

65 Foulis AK, Bottazzo GF. Insulitis in the human pancreas. In: Lefèbvre PJ, Pipeleers DG, eds. *The Pathology of the Endocrine Pancreas in Diabetes.* Berlin: Springer-Verlag, 1988: 41–52.

66 Bottazzo GF, Pujol-Borrell R, Hanafusa T, Feldmann M. Role of aberrant HLA-DR expression and antigen presentation in the induction of endocrine autoimmunity. *Lancet* 1983; ii: 1115–19.

67 Volpe R. The immunoregulatory disturbance in autoimmune thyroid disease. *Autoimmunity* 1988; **2**: 55–72.

68 Pujol-Borrell R, Todd I, Doshi M, Bottazzo GF, Sutton R, Gray D, Adolf G, Feldmann M. HLA Class II induction in human islet cells by interferon-gamma plus tumor necrosis factor or lymphotoxin. *Nature* 1987; **326**: 304–6.

69 Jacob CO, McDevitt HO. Tumour necrosis factor-alpha in murine autoimmune "lupus" nephritis. *Nature* 1988; **331**: 356–8.

70 Badenhoop K, Schwarz G, Trowsdale J, Lewis V, Usadel KH, Gale EAM, Bottazzo GF. TNF-α gene polymorphisms in Type 1 (insulin-dependent) diabetes mellitus. *Diabetologia* 1989; **32**: 445–8.

71 Bendtzen K. Immune hormones (cytokines): pathogenic role in autoimmune rheumatic and endocrine diseases. *Autoimmunity* 1989; **2**: 177–89.

72 Nerup J, Mandrup-Paulsen T, Molvig J, Helqvist S, Wogensen DLD. On the pathogenesis of insulin-dependent diabetes mellitus — a discussion of three recently proposed models. In: Creutzfeldt W, Lefèbvre PJ, eds. *Diabetes Mellitus: Pathophysiology and Therapy.* Berlin: Springer-Verlag, 1989; 39–50.

73 Bottazzo GF, Foulis AK, Bosi E, Todd I, Pujol-Borrell R. Pancreatic B cell damage: in search of novel pathogenetic factors. *Diabetes Care* 1988; **11** (suppl 1): 24–8.

74 Campbell IL, Cutri A, Wilson D, Harrison LC. Evidence of interleukin-6 production by and effects on the pancreatic beta cells. *J Immunol* (in press).

75 Foulis AK, Farquharson MA, Meager A. Immunoreactive α-interferon in insulin-secreting β cells in Type 1 diabetes mellitus. *Lancet* 1987; ii: 1423–7.

76 Foulis AK, Farquharson A, Hardman R. Aberrant expression of Class II major histocompatibility complex molecules by B cells and hyperexpression of Class I major histocompatibility complex molecules by insulin containing islets in Type I (insulin-dependent) diabetes mellitus. *Diabetologia* 1987; **30**: 333–43.

77 Sibley RK, Sutherland DER. Pancreas transplantation: an immunohistologic and histopathologic examination of 100 grafts. *Am J Pathol* 1987; **128**: 151–70.

78 Foulis AK, Farquharson MA. Aberrant expression of HLA-

DR antigens by insulin containing Beta cells in recent onset Type 1 (insulin-dependent) diabetes mellitus. *Diabetes* 1986; **35**: 1215–24.

79 Streeter PR, Berg EL, Rouse BTN, Bargatze RL, Butcher EC. A tissue-specific endothelial cell molecule involved in lymphocyte homing. *Nature* 1988; **331**: 41–6.

80 Altmann DM, Hogg N, Trowsdale J, Wilkinson D. Contrasfection of ICAM-1 and HLA-DR reconstitutes human antigen-presenting cell function in mouse L cells. *Nature* 1989; **338**: 512–14.

81 Campbell IL, Cutri A, Wilkinson D, Boyd AW, Harrison LC. Intercellular adhesion molecule-1 is induced on isolated endocrine islet cells by cytokines but not by reovirus infection. *Proc Natl Acad Sci USA* 1989; **86**: 4282–6.

82 Pujol-Borrell R, Vives M, Badenas J, Foz M, Buscema M, Soldevilla G, Bottazzo GF. Modulation of intercellular adhesion molecule-1 (ICAM-1) in human islet cells. *Diabetes* 1989; **38** (suppl 22): 733A.

83 La Porte RE, Dorman JS, Orchard TJ. Preventing insulin dependent diabetes mellitus: the environmental challenge. *Br Med J* 1987; **295**: 479–81.

84 Pak CY, Eun H-M, McArthur RG, Yoon JW. Association of cytomegalovirus infection with autoimmune Type 1 diabetes. *Lancet* 1988; i: 1–4.

85 Leiter EH, Wilson GL. Viral interactions with pancreatic B cells. In: Lefèbvre PJ, Pipeleers DH, eds. *The Pathology of the Endocrine Pancreas in Diabetes*. Berlin: Springer-Verlag, 1988: 86–105.

86 Ciampolillo A, Marini V, Mirakian R, Buscema M, Schulz T, Pujol-Borrell R, Bottazzo GF. Retrovirus-like sequences in Graves' Disease: implications for human autoimmunity. *Lancet* 1989; i: 1096–100.

87 Bottazzo GF, Todd I, Mirakian R, Belfiore A, Pujol-Borrell R. Organ-specific autoimmunity: a 1986 overview. *Immunol Rev* 1986; **94**: 137–69.

16 Viruses in the Pathogenesis of Insulin-Dependent Diabetes Mellitus

Summary

- Involvement of viruses in causing human IDDM is suggested by epidemiological evidence, by the isolation of viruses from the pancreas and other tissues of a few recently diagnosed IDDM patients, and by the ability of certain viruses to induce diabetes in animals.
- Viruses may damage B cells by direct invasion or by triggering an autoimmune response; they may also persist within B cells, causing long-term interference with their metabolic and secretory functions.
- Mumps virus can cause acute pancreatitis, sometimes with hyperglycaemia, but serological and epidemiological evidence implicating mumps infection in IDDM patients is equivocal.
- *Intrauterine* rubella infection is definitely associated with subsequent development of IDDM; the virus may persist within T cells and predispose to autoimmune disease. *Postnatal* rubella can stimulate islet cell and insulin autoantibody formation but does not apparently lead to IDDM.
- Coxsackie B viruses (especially B4) can cause acute pancreatitis and B-cell destruction in man; although usually tropic for pancreatic exocrine tissue, certain strains become able to invade B cells. Some (but not all) serological studies suggest exposure to the virus in newly diagnosed IDDM patients. Coxsackie B viruses have been isolated from acute cases of IDDM and some of these are diabetogenic in animals.
- Other viruses implicated in human IDDM include echoviruses, cytomegalovirus and herpes viruses.
- Viruses which can induce IDDM-like conditions in experimental animals include encephalomyocarditis virus, Coxsackie B and rubella.

Viruses have long been implicated in the development of IDDM and are generally assumed to be the most likely environmental agents triggering the disease in at least a proportion of cases. The age and seasonal incidence of IDDM in many countries in both northern and southern hemispheres (Chapter 7) show peaks which coincide with the age of maximum exposure to infectious diseases and with the time of year when infections in the general population are most common [1–3]. Recently, a rising incidence of IDDM has been observed in several northern European countries, which is more likely to be due to altered exposure to environmental agents (such as viruses) than to other factors such as improved diagnosis or shifting population age-structures [4]. These epidemiological findings provide circumstantial evidence for an association between viruses and IDDM in man, and the onset of the disease has, in a few cases, been directly attributed to infection with specific viruses [5, 6].

Table 16.1 shows the extensive list of viruses suggested to play a role in the pathogenesis of IDDM in man and, experimentally, in other mammals. The most convincing evidence is for those viruses which have been isolated from IDDM patients, including the Coxsackie B viruses which have induced insulitis and a condition resembling IDDM when injected into mice [5, 6]. Other virus antigens have occasionally been demonstrated by immunostaining within the B cells of IDDM patients. Islet cell antibodies and insulin auto-

Table 16.1. Viruses implicated in the development of insulin-dependent diabetes.

Virus	Family	Nucleic acid	*In vivo* evidence	*In vitro* islet cell damage
Coxsackie B1	Picornaviridae	RNA	Man, mouse	
Coxsackie B2	Picornaviridae	RNA	Man, mouse	
Coxsackie B3	Picornaviridae	RNA	Mouse, monkey	Human B cells
Coxsackie B4	Picornaviridae	RNA	Man[‡], mouse, monkey	Human B cells, human islets
Coxsackie B5	Picornaviridae	RNA	Man[†], mouse	
Coxsackie B6	Picornaviridae	RNA	Man, mouse	
Echovirus 4	Picornaviridae	RNA	Man	
Encephalomyocarditis	Picornaviridae	RNA	Mouse	Mouse islets, mouse B cells
Foot-and-mouth disease	Picornaviridae	RNA	Pig, cow	
Poliovirus	Picornaviridae	RNA	Man	
Mengovirus	Picornaviridae	RNA	Mouse	
Mumps	Paramyxoviridae	RNA	Man	Human B cells, monkey B cells
Rubella	Togaviridae	RNA	Man[*+], hamster, rabbit	
Tick-borne encephalitis	Togaviridae	RNA	Man	
Venezuelan equine encephalitis	Togaviridae	RNA	Monkey, hamster, mouse	
Infectious hepatitis	Pararetroviridae	RNA	Man	
Reovirus	Reoviridae	RNA	Mouse	Human B cells
Influenza	Orthomyxoviridae	RNA	Man	
Cytomegalovirus	Herpesviridae	DNA	Man[*†]	Human islets
Herpes virus 6	Herpesviridae	DNA	Man	
Epstein–Barr virus	Herpesviridae	DNA	Man	
Varicella zoster	Herpesviridae	DNA	Man	
Scrapie agent	?	?	Hamster	
Lymphocytic choriomeningitic virus	Arenaviridae	DNA	Mouse	

* Intrauterine infection. † Virus isolated from tissues. ‡ Virus isolated from pancreas.

antibodies, both thought to be markers of the 'prediabetic' phase of IDDM (Chapter 15), are sometimes associated with postnatal rubella and also with other viral infections such as Echo 4, Coxsackie B6 and herpes virus 6, although IDDM only rarely follows these latter infections.

This section will discuss the evidence that individual viruses may be involved in causing human IDDM and describe the experimental models of the disease which have helped to clarify the mechanisms through which viruses may be diabetogenic.

Viral infections and human IDDM

Mumps

Anecdotal evidence suggesting an association between mumps infection and diabetes dates back to the 19th century [7]. Although mumps can cause pancreatitis, this is rare and pancreatitis severe enough to cause hyperglycaemia is rarer still. A recent survey has shown that fewer than 1% of IDDM children had serological evidence of recent mumps infection [8]. However, the serological

methods in general use may have underestimated the prevalence of mumps: Hyöty *et al.*, using an enzyme-linked immunosorbent assay (ELISA), have demonstrated abnormally high IgA-class antibody titres against mumps virus antigen in IDDM patients [9], suggesting that the IgA response may be a better indicator of exposure to the virus. There is marked geographical variation in the strength of the association between mumps and IDDM, which may be related to strain differences in the virus [8]. Mumps infection is sometimes associated with islet cell antibodies in the absence of diabetes [10].

Rubella

An aetiological connection between intrauterine rubella infection and the subsequent development of IDDM, which affects 10–20% of cases, was first established by Menser *et al.* [11] and later confirmed in a North American study [12]. The mechanism by which the rubella virus is pathogenic *in utero* and the reason for the delayed appearance of IDDM are of great interest but largely unexplained. Circulating T lymphocytes in children with congenital rubella are functionally abnormal and it has been suggested that rubella infection persisting in T cells could predispose to autoimmune disease [13]. Islet-cell antibodies occur in children with congenital rubella, but are not necessarily associated with IDDM [14]. A link between *postnatal* rubella infection and IDDM is less clear. Both islet-cell antibodies and insulin autoantibodies may be found after postnatal rubella infection [15] but serological studies of IDDM patients do not suggest exposure to the virus [16].

Coxsackie viruses

The Coxsackie viruses are picornaviruses of the enterovirus class. Coxsackie B viruses, which can cause diarrhoeal illnesses and various extra-intestinal syndromes including myopericarditis and myalgia, are subdivided into serotypes B1–B6. Like the mumps virus, certain Coxsackie B viruses (especially B4) can occasionally cause acute pancreatitis in man, sometimes with inflammatory destruction of the B cells [17].

It was these viruses which revived interest some years ago in the possible viral aetiology of IDDM, with the demonstration of high titres of neutralizing antibodies against Coxsackie B4 (and also B1, B2 and B5) in the serum of newly diagnosed IDDM patients [18]. However, this finding has not been confirmed by certain other studies [19]; indeed, some IDDM cases have shown consistently lower Coxsackie B antibody titres than non-diabetic controls. This discrepancy may be partly explained by major differences between studies in the selection of controls and by the small size of certain survey populations. Interpretation of Coxsackie B antibody levels in IDDM patients may also be difficult because their antibody responses to these viruses may be weaker than in non-diabetic subjects [20], and titres may fall to lower levels than in non-diabetic controls some years after diabetes is diagnosed [21]; timing of samples is therefore critical. Further complications are the very high mutation rate of Coxsackie B4 viruses and the fact that only certain uncommon strains are diabetogenic [22]. This latter finding may explain why random Coxsackie B4 outbreaks are not usually associated with IDDM.

As mentioned above, Coxsackie B4 and B5 have been isolated from tissues of a few patients with recently diagnosed IDDM, Coxsackie B4 from the pancreas [5, 6] (Fig. 16.1). Moreover, injection of these isolates into mice causes insulitis and B-cell damage, together with hyperglycaemia or abnormal glucose tolerance [5, 6]. Coxsackie B6 infection has been associated in one case with islet-cell antibody formation and temporary hyperglycaemia and glycosuria [23].

Coxsackie B viruses may therefore be diabetogenic in man, but their overall aetiological importance in IDDM is not clear.

Echovirus

In a recent Cuban epidemic of Echovirus 4 (another enterovirus), 36% of patients' sera were found to contain islet-cell antibodies [24], which persisted for up to 6 months and were accompanied in some cases by minor glucose intolerance. This potentially important virus deserves further study.

Cytomegalovirus

Cytomegalovirus (CMV) is tropic for B cells in both infants and adults and several cases with histological islet-cell damage following CMV infection have been reported; one patient with disseminated CMV infection and diabetes showed B cells which were degranulated and contained CMV inclusion bodies [17].

Viruses and exocrine pancreatic damage

Some putative diabetogenic viruses (e.g. mumps, Coxsackie B) may cause generalized pancreatitis, as is also seen with many of the viruses causing experimental IDDM in animals. Viral infection of the exocrine pancreas could theoretically be associated with IDDM, perhaps by lysing acinar cells and releasing proteolytic and other enzymes which could damage the B cells. Alternatively, a virus persisting in acinar tissue could change its tropism and become able to invade B cells directly, a mechanism observed in animal models (see below).

Many cases of IDDM have been associated with clinically apparent acute pancreatitis. *Postmortem* studies have shown that the pancreas (of which over 95% is composed of exocrine tissue) is significantly smaller in IDDM patients than in non-diabetic subjects and that exocrine tissue shows histological features of atrophy. Moreover, IDDM patients have subnormal serum levels of trypsin and other pancreas-derived enzymes [25]. Sub-

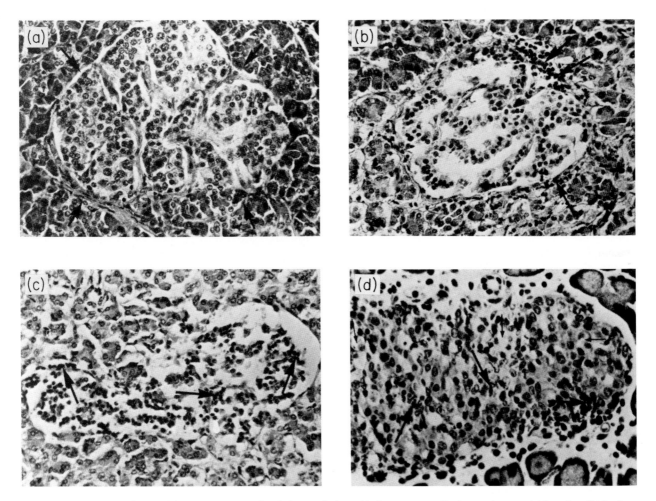

Fig. 16.1. (a) Section of normal human pancreas. (b, c) Accumulation of inflammatory cells (arrows) around islets (insulitis) of a patient with newly diagnosed IDDM. Coxsackie B4 virus isolated from this patient's pancreas induced a similar reaction when injected into mice (d). (Reproduced with permission from Yoon *et al.* 1979 [5].)

clinical viral infection persisting in pancreatic exocrine tissue may therefore be commoner than suspected in IDDM, and could be associated with or precede B-cell damage.

Diabetogenic mechanisms of viral infection

Viruses might cause B-cell damage through a direct cytopathic action and/or indirectly by activating autoimmune mechanisms. They could also be diabetogenic through effects not specifically involving the B cell, such as by causing a deterioration in glucose tolerance which might expose pre-existing B-cell dysfunction. These various possibilities are illustrated by the animal models of virus-induced, insulin-deficient diabetes described below.

Experimental studies of virus-induced IDDM

The myocardial (M) variant of the encephalomyocarditis (EMC) virus, a picornavirus closely related to Coxsackie B4, induces B-cell damage and hyperglycaemia in certain inbred strains of mice [26]. This model of IDDM has been intensively studied. EMC-M comprises two antigenically similar variants, the non-diabetogenic EMC-B and the diabetogenic EMC-D, which itself consists of several mutants of varying pathogenicity [27, 28]. The recent elucidation of the complete nucleotide sequences of EMC-B (7825 bases) and EMC-D (7830 bases) has shown that diabetogenicity is determined by differences in only 13 nucleotides [29] (Fig. 16.2). The nature and effects of the diabetogenic gene products are unknown, but animal experiments have shown that EMC-D induces

Fig. 16.2. Differences in nucleotide sequence and in deduced amino acid residues between diabetogenic (EMC-D) and non-diabetogenic (EMC-B) strains of the encephalomyocarditis virus. Deletion or insertion are denoted for the EMC-B sequence as compared with the EMC-D sequence. Three Cs are deleted from the poly (C) tract of EMC-B. ND: no difference. (Redrawn with permission from Bae *et al.* 1989 [29].)

	Sequence position based on EMC-D	Nucleotide difference		Deduced amino acid difference		Genomic position
		EMC-D	EMC-B	EMC-D	EMC-B	
Point mutation	874	U̲UU	C̲UU	Phe	Leu	L
	1929	ACU̲	ACC̲	ND	ND	1B
	2839	G̲CU	A̲CU	Ala	Thr	1D
	2872	G̲CC	A̲CC	Ala	Thr	1D
	2887	G̲AA	C̲AA	Glu	Gln	1D
	3154	G̲CC	A̲CC	Ala	Thr	1D
	3241	U̲CG	A̲CG	Ser	Thr	1D
	4395	UCA̲	UCG̲	ND	ND	2B
Insertion	765		U			5′-Noncoding
Deletion	149–278	CCC				5′-Noncoding
	7828	A				3′-Noncoding
	7829	G				3′-Noncoding

interferon production less effectively than EMC-B. The development of diabetes in EMC-infected mice also depends on the genetic background of the host: extensive viral replication occurs in the B cells of susceptible strains, whereas only 10% of B cells are infected in resistant strains.

The EMC-induced model of IDDM shows evidence of both direct viral destruction of islets [30–2] and of immune-mediated damage [33–6]. Gould *et al.* [37] have demonstrated that both mechanisms can operate, whereas others conclude that diabetes results from direct viral damage alone but, in certain strains of mice, may be compounded by immune mechanisms [38, 39]. EMC-M may also induce biochemical changes in isolated islets — such as impaired insulin synthesis [40] and cellular metabolism [41] — in the absence of cell lysis. Certain biochemical abnormalities induced by EMC viruses can persist for many months after the acute infection. For example, Hellqvist *et al.* [42] found transient hyperglycaemia 60 days after inoculation, associated with abnormal insulin production: basal insulin secretion was increased but glucose-stimulated synthesis and release of insulin were both reduced. Moreover, mice infected 1 year previously still showed abnormal glucose tolerance even though islet ultrastructure was normal [43].

Coxsackie B viruses

Coxsackie B viruses are pathogenic in mice and have been used in murine models of IDDM. Coxsackie B4 generally invades acinar tissue of the pancreas but its tropism can be redirected against B cells by passage through B-cell cultures, which presumably selects specific variants (Fig. 16.3). The very rapid spontaneous mutation of Coxsackie viruses may similarly encourage the emergence of B-cell-tropic, diabetogenic variants *in vivo*, which could precipitate IDDM in susceptible individuals. Susceptibility could be conferred, for example, by structural abnormalities of B-cell surface receptors to which pathogenic strains of virus might attach more readily. Hyperglycaemic syndromes have been induced in mice using unadapted human isolates of Coxsackie B4 [5, 44] or B-cell-passaged Coxsackie viruses of B1–B6 serotypes [45]; pretreatment with subdiabetogenic doses of the B-cell toxin, streptozotocin, enhances the diabetogenic effect of Coxsackie viruses [46]. Recently, transient diabetes has been induced in monkeys inoculated with a Coxsackie B4 virus previously passaged through monkey B cells [47].

As with the EMC-induced model, it is not clear whether Coxsackie virus-induced diabetes is due to direct viral destruction of the islets or to

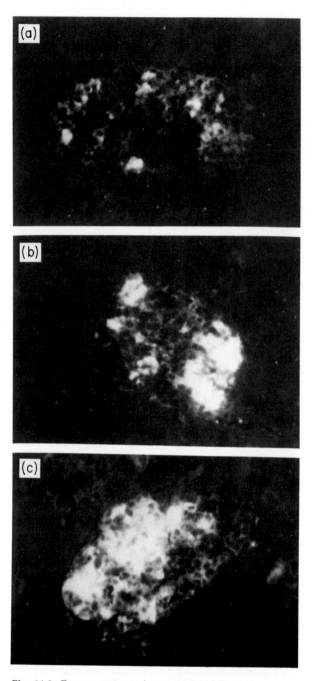

Fig. 16.3. Frozen sections of mouse islets following experimental infection with Coxsackie B4 virus stained with fluorescein-labelled antibody to Coxsackie virus B4 and showing features of structural damage and the presence of intracellular viral particles. (a−c) Islets with increasing areas of infection. (Reprinted with permission from Yoon JW *et al. J Exp Med* 1978; **148**: 1068−80.)

immune attack activated by the viral infection. Biochemical defects in the absence of B-cell lysis (increased basal secretion but impaired glucose-stimulated release of insulin) have been observed *in vitro* following acute Coxsackie B4 infection

[48], and impaired islet metabolism (without abnormalities of blood glucose concentration or of pancreatic histology) [49] and reduced insulin synthesis [50] may remain for several months after inoculation (Fig. 16.4). These long-term effects may relate to the ability of cytolytic viruses such as the picornaviruses to persist chronically in various tissues [51, 52]. Coxsackie B4 RNA remains detectable in mouse B cells for at least 8 weeks after inoculation, when infective virus particles are no longer present; at this stage, insulin mRNA levels are reduced, indicating inhibition of insulin synthesis [53]. Other ways in which viruses cause cell damage, which may be relevant to the effects of Coxsackie viruses on the B cells, include altering cell-membrane permeability [54, 55] or the cytoskeleton [56].

The diabetogenic effects of unadapted human isolates of Coxsackie B4 viruses have been investigated in mice [57, 58], which show relatively minor glycaemic disturbances. The basis of diabetogenicity is unexplained, although one diabetogenic strain is known to lack a specific protein, kinase [59]. The nucleotide sequence of a prototype Coxsackie B4 virus has now been determined [60] and, as with the EMC virus, it should soon be possible to identify the part of the genome responsible for diabetogenicity.

Rubella

Rubella-induced diabetes has been studied in various rodent models. Menser *et al.* [11] found that the offspring of rubella virus-infected rabbits had lower blood glucose and serum insulin levels than uninfected controls and showed degranulation and other ultrastructural changes in the B cells. Hamster pups infected with vaccine or wild-type strains of rubella develop hyperglycaemia and hyperinsulinaemia approximately 4−5 weeks after inoculation. Rayfield *et al.* [61] have recently described a model for rubella virus-induced diabetes in neonatal golden Syrian hamsters. Rubella virus (passaged five times in B cells) inoculated into hamsters produced hyperglycaemia and hypoinsulinaemia persisting for 15 weeks. Insulitis occurred, virus was isolated from the pancreas and viral antigen demonstrated in the B cells, and islet-cell antibodies were found in 40% of infected animals [61]. Although the precise mechanisms by which rubella virus induces diabetes are yet to be determined, this study supports the hypothesis that the virus triggers an autoimmune response.

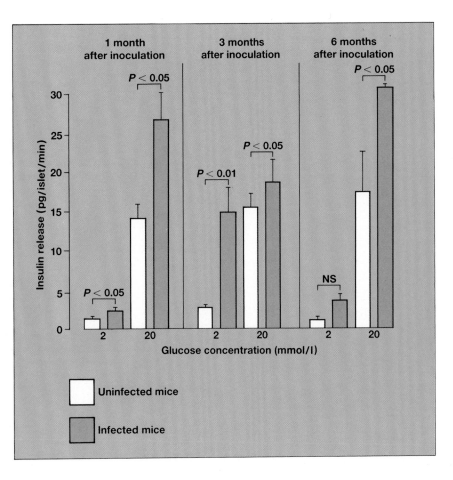

Fig. 16.4. Insulin release from islets isolated from mice at 1, 3 and 6 months after inoculation with Coxsackie B4 virus passaged through B-cell cultures. Insulin release is greater from infected than from control uninfected islets at all three time-points, both in the basal state (ambient glucose concentration, 2 mmol/l) and when stimulated by 20 mmol/l glucose. (Redrawn from Szopa *et al.* 1985 [49].)

The virus may also have more subtle functional effects: studies in rat insulinoma (RINm5F) cells have suggested that the rubella virus persists within B cells and specifically alters their secretory function [62].

Virus infection of human islets and B cells in vitro

Several groups have studied the effects of putative diabetogenic viruses on human islets or B cells *in vitro*. Human B-cell monolayers have been infected with Coxsackie B3 virus [63], mumps virus [64], reovirus type 3 [65], and in some cases, viral antigen has been demonstrated in B cells by immunostaining. As in animal studies, infection was limited with unpassaged virus but more extensive with passaged strains. Human islets have been infected with an unadapted Coxsackie B4 strain [66] and in short-term *in vitro* culture showed abnormally high release of insulin at nonstimulatory glucose levels (Fig. 16.5).

Conclusions

It is increasingly clear that the disease process leading to IDDM develops over many months or years. The precise sequence of events resulting in near-total insulin deficiency is unknown and probably varies from patient to patient, but it seems that the number of functional B cells becomes reduced following each unspecified insult. At a certain point, the reserve falls below the critical level required to maintain normal glucose homeostasis, resulting in clinical IDDM and insulin dependency.

Is the process triggered by a viral attack? The only firm evidence in man relates to rubella and to the rare cases shown in Table 16.1, but many would argue that viruses (especially certain picornaviruses) remain the most likely of the possible environmental agent(s) involved. The initial viral attack may not itself be diabetogenic but could induce subtle metabolic or immune changes in the islets, perhaps predisposing the

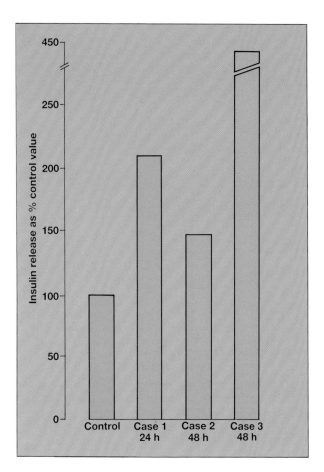

Fig. 16.5. Insulin release from human pancreatic islets cultured *in vitro* at non-stimulatory (2 mmol/l) glucose concentration, 24 or 48 h after inoculation with a tissue-culture passaged Coxsackie B4 isolate. Islets were isolated from three separate donors (cases 1–3). Insulin release in infected islets was significantly higher than in uninfected control islets in each case (TM Szopa and KW Taylor, unpublished observations).

islets to later destruction by other mechanisms such as autoimmune responses, additional viruses or other unknown environmental factors. The primary attack may take place early in an individual's life, a suggestion supported by the observation of islet-cell antibodies induced by an outbreak of Echo 4 virus infection in children [24]. The prolonged evolution of IDDM may in some way reflect persisting viral infection, which has been shown to cause long-term metabolic abnormalities in animals.

Study of the possible diabetogenic role of viruses is important. Not only is it likely to elucidate the pathogenesis of the disease, but specific environmental triggers of IDDM may be identified, raising the possibility that immunization against key viruses may ultimately be exploited in the primary prevention of the disease.

TERESA M. SZOPA

KEITH W. TAYLOR

References

1 Gamble DR. Epidemiological and virological observations on juvenile diabetes. *Postgrad Med J* 1974; **50** (suppl 3): 538–43.

2 Gamble DR, Taylor KW. Seasonal incidence of diabetes mellitus. *Br Med J* 1969; **3**: 631–63.

3 Durruty P, Ruiz F, Garcia de Los Rios M. Age at diagnosis and seasonal variation in the onset of insulin-dependent diabetes in Chile (Southern Hemisphere). *Diabetologia* 1979; **17**: 357–60.

4 Królewski AS, Warram JH, Rand LI, Kahn CR. Epidemiologic approach to the etiology of Type 1 diabetes mellitus and its complications. *N Engl J Med* 1987; **317**: 1390–9.

5 Yoon JW, Austin M, Onodera T, Notkins AL. Virus-induced diabetes mellitus. Isolation of a virus from the pancreas of a child with diabetic ketoacidosis. *New Engl J Med* 1979; **300**: 1173–9.

6 Champsaur H, Dussaix E, Samolyk D, Fabre M, Bach CH, Assan R. Diabetes and Coxsackie virus B5 infection. *Lancet* 1980; i: 251.

7 Gundersen E. Is diabetes of infectious origin? *J Infect Dis* 1927; **41**: 197–202.

8 Gamble DR. Relation of antecedent illness to development of diabetes in children. *Br Med J* 1980; **281**: 99–101.

9 Hyöty H, Huupponen T, Kotola L, Leinikki P. Humoral immunity against viral antigens in type 1 diabetes: altered IgA class immune response against Coxsackie B4 virus. *Acta Path Microbiol Immunol Scand, Sect C* 1986; **94**: 83–8.

10 Helmke K, Otten A, Willenis W. Islet cell antibodies in children with mumps infection. *Lancet* 1980; ii: 211–12.

11 Menser MA, Forrest JM, Bransby RD. Rubella infection and diabetes mellitus. *Lancet* 1978; i: 57–60.

12 Ginsberg-Fellner F, Klein E, Dobersen M, Jenson AB, Rayfield E, Notkins AL, Rubenstein P, Cooper LZ. The interrelationship of congenital rubella (CR) and insulin-dependent diabetes mellitus (IDDM). *Pediatr Res* 1980; **14**: 572.

13 Rabinowe SL, George KL, Laughlin R, Soeldner JS, Eisenbarth GS. Congenital rubella: monoclonal antibody defined T-cell abnormalities in young children. *Am J Med* 1986; **81**: 779–82.

14 Ginsberg-Fellner F, Witt ME, Yagihashi S, Dobersen MJ, Davies TF, Cooper LZ, Rubinstein P, Notkins AL. Congenital rubella syndrome as a model for Type 1 (insulin-dependent) diabetes mellitus: increased prevalence of islet cell surface antibodies. *Diabetologia* 1984; **27**: 87–9.

15 Bodansky HJ, Grant PJ, Dean BM, McNally J, Bottazzo GF, Hambling MH, Wales JK. Islet cell antibodies and insulin autoantibodies in association with common viral infections. *Lancet* 1986; ii: 1351–3.

16 Banatvala JE, Bryant J, Borkenstein M, Schernthaner G, Schober E, De Silva M, Brown D, Menser MA. Coxsackie B, mumps, rubella and cytomegalovirus-specific IgM responses in patients with juvenile-onset insulin-dependent diabetes mellitus in Britain, Austria and Australia. *Lancet* 1985; i: 1409–12.

17 Jenson AB, Rosenberg HS, Notkins AL. Virus-induced

diabetes mellitus XVII. Pancreatic islet cell damage in children with fatal viral infections. *Lancet* 1980; ii: 354–8.

18 Drash A, Cavender D, Atchison R, Becker D, Eberhardt M, LaPorte R, Kuller L, Orchard T, Rabin B, Wagener D. Pittsburgh Diabetes Mellitus Study: studies on the etiology of insulin-dependent diabetes mellitus with special reference to viral infections. *Behring Inst Mitt* 1984; **75**: 58–72.

19 Dippe SE, Bennett PH, Miller M, Maynard JE, Berquist KR. Lack of causal association between Coxsackie B4 virus infection and diabetes. *Lancet* 1975; i: 1314–17.

20 Palmer JP, Cooney MK, Ward RH, Hansen JA, Brodsky JB, Ray CG, Crossley JR, Asplin CM, Williams RH. Reduced Coxsackie antibody titres in Type 1 (insulin dependent) diabetic patients during an outbreak of Coxsackie B3 and B4 infection. *Diabetologia* 1982; **22**: 426–9.

21 Buschard K, Madsbad S. A longitudinal study of virus antibodies in patients with newly diagnosed type 1 (insulin dependent) diabetes mellitus. *J Clin Lab Immunol* 1984; **10**: 127–31.

22 Prabhakar BS, Menegus MA, Notkins AL. Detection of conserved and non-conserved epitopes on Coxsackievirus B4: frequency of antigenic change. *Virology* 1985; **146**: 302–6.

23 Nigro G, Pacella ME, Patanè E, Midulla M. Multi-system Coxsackievirus B-6 infection with findings suggestive of diabetes mellitus. *Eur J Paediatr* 1986; **145**: 557–9.

24 Uriarte A, Cabrera E, Ventura R, Vargas J. Islet cell antibodies and Echo-4 virus infection. *Diabetologia* 1987; **30**: 590A.

25 Gamble DR, Moffatt A, Marks V. Serum immunoreactive trypsin concentrations in infectious and non-infectious illnesses and in juvenile diabetes. *J Clin Path* 1979; **32**: 897–901.

26 Craighead JE, McLane MF. Diabetes mellitus induction in mice by encephalomyocarditis virus. *Science* 1968; **162**: 913–14.

27 Yoon JW, McClintock PR, Onodera T, Notkins AL. Virus-induced diabetes mellitus. XVIII. Inhibition by a non-diabetogenic variant of encephalomyocarditis virus. *J Exp Med* 1980; **152**: 878–92.

28 Kruppenbacher JP, Mertens T, Müntefering H, Eggers HJ. Encephalomyocarditis virus and diabetes mellitus: studies on virus mutants in susceptible and non-susceptible mice. *J Gen Virol* 1985; **66**: 727–32.

29 Bae YS, Eun HM, Yoon JW. Molecular identification of diabetogenic viral gene. *Diabetes* 1989; **38**: 316–20.

30 Chairez R, Yoon JW, Notkins AL. Virus induced diabetes mellitus. X. Attachment of encephalomyocarditis virus and permissiveness of cultured pancreatic cells to infection. *Virology* 1978; **85**: 606–11.

31 Vialettes B, Baume D, Charpin C, De Maeyer-Guinard J, Vague P. Assessment of viral and immune factors in EMC virus-induced diabetes: effects of cyclosporin A and interferon. *J Clin Lab Immunol* 1983; **10**: 35–40.

32 Yoon JW, McClintock PR, Bachurski CJ, Longstreth JD, Notkins AL. Virus-induced diabetes. No evidence for immune mechanisms in the destruction of B-cells by the D-variant of encephalomyocarditis virus. *Diabetes* 1985; **34**: 922–5.

33 Buschard K, Rygaard J, Ropke C, Lund E. Circulating islet cell surface antibodies in virus-induced diabetes antecede clinical disease. *Diabetes* 1986; **35**: 185A.

34 Jansen FK, Thurneyssen O, Müntefering H. Virus induced diabetes and the immune system. II. Evidence for immune pathogenesis in the acute phase of diabetes. *Biomedicine* 1979; **31**: 1–2.

35 Dafoe DC, Naji A, Barker CF. Susceptibility to murine viral diabetes: host versus intrinsic pancreatic factors. *Transplant Proc* 1981; **13**: 829–31.

36 Dafoe DC, Moore CL, Plotkin SA, Naji A, Barker CF. The importance of immunological factors in the pathogenesis of encephalomyocarditis virus-induced diabetes in mice. *Behring Inst Mitt* 1984; **75**: 17–25.

37 Gould CT, McMannama KG, Bigley NJ, Giron DJ. Virus induced murine diabetes. Enhancement by immunosuppression. *Diabetes* 1985; **34**: 1217–21.

38 Huber SA, Babu PG, Craighead JE. Genetic influences on the immunologic pathogenesis of encephalomyocarditis (EMC) virus-induced diabetes mellitus. *Diabetes* 1985; **34**: 1186–90.

39 Haynes MK, Huber SA, Craighead JE. Helper–inducer T-lymphocytes mediate diabetes in EMC infected BALB/c ByJ mice. *Diabetes* 1987; **36**: 877–81.

40 Petersen KG, Heilmeyer P, Kerp L. Synthesis of proinsulin and large glucagon immunoreactivity in isolated Langerhans islets from EMC-virus infected mice. *Diabetologia* 1975; **11**: 21–5.

41 Hellqvist L, Taylor KW, Zaluzny S. Selective disorganization of biochemical function in B cells of islets of Langerhans infected by EMC-M virus in tissue culture. *FEBS Lett* 1981; **132**: 215–18.

42 Hellqvist LNB, Rhodes CJ, Taylor KW. Long-term biochemical changes in the islets of Langerhans in mice following infection with encephalomyocarditis virus. *Diabetologia* 1984; **26**: 370–4.

43 Wellmann KF, Amsterdam D, Volk BW. Glucose tolerance and pancreatic ultrastructure in mice with long-term diabetes induced by EMC virus. *Proc Soc Exp Biol Med* 1975; **148**: 261–2.

44 Coleman TJ, Gamble DR, Taylor KW. Diabetes in mice after Coxsackie B4 virus infection. *Br Med J* 1973; **3**: 25–7.

45 Toniolo A, Onodera T, Jordan G, Yoon JW, Notkins AL. Virus induced diabetes mellitus: glucose abnormalities produced in mice by six members of the Coxsackie B virus group. *Diabetes* 1982; **31**: 496–9.

46 Toniolo A, Onodera T, Yoon JW, Notkins AL. Induction of diabetes by cumulative environmental insults from viruses and chemicals. *Nature* 1980; **288**: 383–5.

47 Yoon JW, London NT, Curfman BL, Brown RL, Notkins AL. Coxsackie virus B4 produces transient diabetes in non-human primates. *Diabetes* 1986; **35**: 712–16.

48 Szopa TM, Gamble DR, Taylor KW. Coxsackie B4 virus induces short-term changes in the metabolic functions of mouse pancreatic islets *in vitro*. *Cell Biochem Function* 1986; **4**: 181–7.

49 Szopa TM, Gamble DR, Taylor KW. Long-term disturbances of the metabolic functions of pancreatic islets from mice infected with Coxsackie B4 virus. *Diabetes Res Clin Prac* 1985; (suppl 1): S542 A.

50 Chatterjee NK, Haley TM, Nejman C. Functional alterations in pancreatic cells as a factor in virus-induced hyperglycaemia. *J Biol Chem* 1985; **260**: 12 786–91.

51 Frank JA, Schmidt EV, Smith RE, Wilfert CM. Persistent infection of rat insulinoma cells with Coxsackie B4 virus. *Arch Virol* 1986; **87**: 143–50.

52 Matteuci D, Paglianti M, Giangregorio AM, Capobianchi MR, Dianzani F, Bendinelli M. Group B Coxsackie viruses readily establish persistent infections in human lymphoid cell lines. *J Virol* 1985; **56**: 651–4.

53 Chatterjee NK, Nejman C. Insulin mRNA content in pancreatic beta cells of Coxsackievirus B4-induced diabetic mice. *Mol Cell Endocrinol* 1988; **55**: 193–202.

54 Impraim CC, Foster KA, Micklem KJ, Pasternak CA. Nature of virally mediated changes in membrane permeability to small molecules. *Biochem J* 1980; **186**: 847–60.

55 Pasternak CA, Micklem KJ. Virally induced alterations in cellular permeability: a basis of cellular and physiological damage. *Bioscience Rept* 1981; **1**: 431–48.

56 Sharpe AH, Fields BN. Pathogenesis of viral infections. Basic concepts derived from the reovirus model. *N Engl J Med* 1985; **312**: 486–97.

57 Jordan GW, Bolton V, Schmidt NJ. Diabetogenic potential of Coxsackie B viruses in nature. *Arch Virol* 1985; **86**: 213–21.

58 Kuno S, Itagaki A, Yamazaki I, Katsumoto T, Kurimura T. Pathogenicity of newly isolated Coxsackie viruses B4 for mouse pancreas. *Acta Virol* 1984; **28**: 433–6.

59 Chatterjee NK, Nejman C. Protein kinase in non-diabetogenic Coxsackievirus B4. *J Med Virol* 1986; **19**: 353–65.

60 Jenkins O, Booth JD, Minor PD, Almond JW. The complete nucleotide sequence of Coxsackievirus B4 and its comparison to other members of the picornaviridae. *J Gen Virol* 1987; **68**: 1835–48.

61 Rayfield EJ, Kelly KJ, Yoon JW. Rubella virus-induced diabetes in the hamster. *Diabetes* 1986; **35**: 1278–81.

62 Rayfield EJ, Kelly KJ. A direct mechanism by which rubella virus impairs insulin secretion. *Diabetes* 1985; **34** (suppl 1): 68A.

63 Yoon JW, Onodera T, Jenson AB, Notkins AL. Virus-induced diabetes mellitus XI. Replication of Coxsackie B3 virus in human pancreatic beta cell cultures. *Diabetes* 1978; **27**: 778–81.

64 Prince G, Jenson AB, Billups LC, Notkins AL. Infection of human pancreatic beta cell cultures with mumps virus. *Nature* 1978; **271**: 159–60.

65 Yoon JW, Selvaggio S, Onodera T, Wheeler T, Jenson AB. Infection of cultured human pancreatic B cells with reovirus type 3. *Diabetologia* 1981; **20**: 462–7.

66 Szopa TM, Ward T, Taylor KW. Impaired metabolic function in human pancreatic islets following infection with Coxsackie B4 virus *in vitro*. *Diabetologia* 1987; **30**: 587A.

17 Animal Models of Insulin-Dependent Diabetes Mellitus

Summary

• Insulin-deficient diabetes can be induced in animals by administration of a number of chemicals, principally alloxan, streptozotocin and zinc chelators.

• Alloxan may act at several sites in the B cell, such as on glucose transporters on the cell surface, and intracellularly on the sulphydryl groups of glucokinase, on the mitochondria, by inducing free radical formation, and by inducing DNA strand breaks. DNA damage stimulates DNA repair by poly(ADP-ribose) synthetase and leads to cellular NAD depletion.

• Streptozotocin in a single large dose probably has similar effects to alloxan, including DNA damage and free radical generation. It also causes diabetes after repeated injection of sub-diabetogenic doses into genetically susceptible mice, where there is pancreatic insulitis and an immune mechanism is implicated.

• Vacor is a rodenticide which has caused IDDM following ingestion by man and is B-cytotoxic. Dietary nitrosamines (present in some smoked meats) may also be diabetogenic in man and animals.

• Spontaneous diabetes occurs in the BB rat and the NOD mouse which are the best models of human IDDM.

• The BB rat is characterized by a genetic predisposition to IDDM which occurs after a long prediabetic period and is associated with hypoinsulinaemia, ketoacidosis and a mononuclear cell infiltrate of the islets which precedes the overt hyperglycaemia.

• Defects in cellular and humoral immunity are involved in diabetes in the BB rat, e.g. the presence of islet-cell-surface antibodies in diabetes-prone and newly diabetic animals and destruction of normal rat islets by splenic lymphoid cells from BB rats. Diabetes may be prevented by many immunomodulatory procedures such as cyclosporin-A or anti-lymphocyte serum treatment and neonatal thymectomy.

• Diabetes in the NOD mouse is similar to that in the BB rat (e.g. insulitis preceding the hyperglycaemia) but only 80% of females and 20% of males are affected.

• Spontaneous IDDM occurs in other animals — *Macaca nigra*, Keeshond dog, Chinese hamster, colonies of guinea pigs and the New Zealand white rabbit — but these are less well studied and/or less closely related to human IDDM.

It is one hundred years since Minkowski and Von Mering removed the pancreas from a dog and produced a condition indistinguishable from diabetes mellitus. The use of the same animal model of diabetes some 30 years later was instrumental in the discovery of insulin by Frederick Banting and Charles Best (see Chapter 2 and Fig. 17.1). Apart from pancreatectomy, several other approaches, including the use of chemical toxins and viral infection, have been subsequently adopted to induce experimental insulin-dependent diabetes in different animal species (Table 17.1). More recently, however, interest has focused on strains of spontaneously diabetic animals in which the disease is genetically transmitted rather than experimentally produced (Table 17.2). Of the many known animal models of experimental and spontaneous diabetes [1], those listed in Tables 17.1 and 17.2 are most relevant to

Fig. 17.1. Charles Best and Frederick Banting pictured in 1922, together with perhaps the most famous animal model of IDDM, anecdotally known as Marjorie.

the study of the aetiology and pathogenesis of human IDDM.

It is now generally accepted that IDDM results from interactions between various environmental factors and immune mechanisms in genetically susceptible individuals. Animal models have contributed much to our understanding of the mechanisms of pancreatic B-cell destruction by experimental cytotoxic agents such as chemicals and viruses. However, the discovery of animals with spontaneous diabetes has allowed investi-

Table 17.2. Animal models with spontaneous IDDM.

Species	Reference
Large	
Monkey (*Macaca nigra*)	Howard 1972 [104]
Keeshond dog	Kramer *et al.* 1980 [106]
Small	
Chinese hamster	Meier & Yerganian 1959 [115]
Guinea pig	Munger & Lang 1973 [108]
BB rat	Nakhooda *et al.* 1976 [56]
NOD mouse	Makino *et al.* 1980 [91]
New Zealand white rabbit	Conaway *et al.* 1980 [110]

gation of the altered immunity and autoimmune phenomena observed in individuals genetically predisposed to the disease, particularly since these models are not complicated by possible direct effects of exogenous B-cell cytotoxic agents on the immune system. The roles of toxic chemicals and viruses as diabetogenic agents and of possible environmental triggers of IDDM will be discussed first, followed by a more detailed analysis of the immunological and genetic components of the disease, illustrated by the various spontaneously diabetic animal models.

Insulin-dependent diabetes and chemical toxins

Several diabetogenic chemicals, including zinc chelators, alloxan and streptozotocin, have been used to induce permanent diabetes in animals (see Table 17.3). Another toxin, the rodenticide Vacor, has been shown to cause IDDM in man following attempted suicidal or accidental ingestion [2].

Zinc chelators

As long ago as 1942, Okamoto [3] used histochemical techniques to demonstrate that pancreatic B cells contained large amounts of zinc, and suggested that compounds capable of modifying circulating zinc levels might also

Agent	Species	Reference
Chemical		
Alloxan	Rats	Dunn & McLetchie 1943 [6]
Zinc chelators	Rabbits/mice	Kadota 1950 [4]
Streptozotocin	Dogs/rats	Rakieten *et al.* 1963 [31]
Viral		
EMC	Mice	Craighead & McLane 1968 [114]

Table 17.1. Animal models of experimentally induced IDDM. (See Chapter 16.)

Table 17.3. Chemical diabetogenic agents.

	Zinc chelator (8-hydroxyquinoline)	Alloxan	Streptozotocin
Name	8-hydroxybenzopyridine	2,4,5,6-tetraoxohexa-hydropyrimidine	2-deoxy-2-[((methyl-nitrosoamino) carbonyl)-amino]-D-glucopyranose
Structure	OH / N	H, N, O, O, NH, O	CH₂OH / H, H, O, H, OH, HO, OH, H, HNCONCH₃, NO
Therapeutic use	Fungistatic Disinfectant	Antineoplastic agent	Antineoplastic agent Antibiotic
Diabetogenic effects	Permanent diabetes No B-cell lysis No insulitis	Permanent diabetes Direct B-cell cytotoxicity Necrosis but no insulitis	Permanent diabetes Direct B-cell cytotoxicity Insulitis at low doses

produce profound functional changes in the islets. This hypothesis was confirmed in 1950, when the zinc chelating compounds, dithizone and 8-hydroxyquinoline, were found to induce permanent diabetes in mice and rabbits [4]. Dithizone injection caused rapid deposition of zinc dithizonate granules within the islets, followed by progressive hyperglycaemia. Although links between diabetes and disordered zinc metabolism have been reported in both man and animals [5], the relevance of these findings to the pathogenesis of IDDM remains unclear.

Alloxan

Alloxan became the first known diabetogenic chemical agent when, in 1943, Dunn and co-workers [6] accidentally produced islet-cell necrosis in rabbits while investigating the nephrotoxicity of uric acid derivatives. Interestingly, some six years earlier, Jacobs [7] had reported a profound *hypoglycaemic* effect of alloxan (due to acute insulin release from necrotic B cells), but did not follow up these observations.

There are several practical problems inherent in the induction of diabetes by *in vivo* administration of alloxan, including: (1) its instability at physiological pH [8]; (2) the possible protective effects of dietary sugars [9]; (3) dosage variation with age and species [10]; and (4) the toxicity of high doses on other organs [11]. When islets are exposed to alloxan *in vitro*, however, the drug exhibits exceptional B-cell specificity, the other islet cells remaining largely unaffected by both its inhibitory and cytotoxic effects.

The cellular site of action of alloxan and the chemical mechanisms underlying its cytotoxicity have been partly elucidated. Several studies have shown that alloxan alters the properties of the B-cell plasma membrane: for example, rodent islets treated *in vitro* with alloxan display abnormal membrane morphology [12] and altered ion flux [13], both effects being prevented by high glucose concentrations. The precise location at which alloxan interacts with the B-cell membrane is unclear, but involvement of the glucose transport system is suggested by the observations that alloxan inhibits D-glucose-stimulated insulin release [14] and that its diabetogenic effects are blocked by both metabolizable (D-glucose) and non-metabolizable (3-O-methyl-D-glucose) sugars [14, 15], which share a common transport mechanism in the membrane.

Although alloxan has an effect at the plasma membrane, these changes may be secondary to actions of the drug on the cellular and molecular components of the B cell. Following its uptake by the B cell [16], alloxan has been shown to interact with sulphydryl-containing cellular components, particularly sulphydryl enzymes known to be essential for B-cell function [11]. Glucokinase, which has a signal-recognition function in coupling glucose concentration to insulin release [17] is particularly sensitive to inhibition by alloxan [18]. These and other findings (reviewed in reference [19]) have led to the hypothesis that the sulphydryl groups of glucokinase may be the primary intracellular target for alloxan and responsible ultimately for its B cytotoxicity. Other enzymes, including hexokinase [20] and protein kinase [21] are also inhibited by alloxan, albeit at higher concentrations.

Other proposed mechanisms for alloxan cyto-toxicity include direct induction of mitochondrial abnormalities [22]; extreme sensitivity of B cells to the cytotoxic effects of free radicals generated during the reduction/re-oxidation cycle of alloxan [23–5] and damage to DNA within the B-cell nucleus. Alloxan induces fragmentation of DNA both *in vivo* [26] and *in vitro* [27], which stimulates DNA repair by nuclear poly(ADP-ribose) syn-thetase, leading to a depletion of cellular NAD [27] and impaired B-cell function [28]. This possible sequence of events may be prevented by administration of poly(ADP-ribose) synthetase inhibitors [29].

In summary, alloxan may exert its effects at several sites including the plasma membrane, mitochondria and nucleus of the B cell.

Streptozotocin

Streptozotocin, a metabolite of the soil fungus *Streptomyces achromogenes*, was originally dis-covered in 1960 during a search for new anti-microbial agents [30] and subsequent investigation of its antibiotic and anti-tumour properties revealed its diabetogenic effect in 1963 [31]. Diabetes can be induced by streptozotocin when it is given either as a single large dose (as with alloxan), or as multiple subdiabetogenic injec-tions; with the latter, hyperglycaemia and symptoms develop gradually [32].

SINGLE-DOSE STREPTOZOTOCIN DIABETES

Streptozotocin may share several common B cytotoxic mechanisms with alloxan, although some of these effects of streptozotocin are less well documented. Streptozotocin may damage the B-cell membrane, producing changes similar to those induced by alloxan [33], although it is not clear whether D-glucose exerts the protective effect which it does against alloxan [34]: reported findings range from complete protection [35] to lack of effect [36] to exacerbation of diabetes [37]. Streptozotocin is also thought to act intra-cellularly, where it may deplete the islet content of NAD [38]; consistent with this is the obser-vation that treatment of islets with nicotinamide prevented NAD depletion and blocked the dia-betogenic effects of streptozotocin [39, 40]. Al-though there is considerable evidence that free

radicals may be important in the diabetogenic action of alloxan, there is less information avail-able on such a role in streptozotocin diabetes, although the free-radical scavenger, superoxide dismutase, has been shown to alleviate strepto-zotocin diabetes *in vivo* [41] and to reduce the inhibitory effects of streptozotocin on insulin release [42]. Streptozotocin shares with alloxan the ability to induce strand breaks in B-cell DNA [29]. Moreover, the induction of these lesions by streptozotocin is followed by a cascade of intra-cellular events similar to those provoked by ex-posure to alloxan, i.e. stimulation of DNA repair (via poly-ADP-ribose synthetase) [27], reduction of islet NAD content [43] and subsequent inhi-bition of islet functions [28]. Moreover, the poly-ADP-ribose synthetase inhibitor, nicotinamide, has been shown to protect the B cell against these detrimental effects of streptozotocin [44].

Despite some evidence that streptozotocin and alloxan exert their B-cytotoxic effects via a common mechanism, other work suggests that this may not be the case. Sandler and his co-workers have shown that alloxan fails to induce DNA repair synthesis in islets *in vitro* [45] and also that nic-otinamide does not protect B-cell metabolism against alloxan toxicity [46].

MULTIPLE LOW-DOSE STREPTOZOTOCIN DIABETES

In 1976, Like and Rossini [32] showed that dia-betes could be induced in mice by repeated injec-tions of subdiabetogenic doses of streptozotocin. Signs of diabetes appeared 5–6 days after the last injection of streptozotocin and were associated with marked pancreatic insulitis, which suggested the pathogenic involvement of cell-mediated im-munity and a similarity to human IDDM. This hypothesis was supported by observations that diabetes could be ameliorated by various immunosuppressive treatment regimens, includ-ing: (1) treatment with anti-lymphocyte serum [47]; (2) total-body irradiation [48]; and (3) administration of immune-response gene anti-bodies [49]. Moreover, passive transfer exper-iments have also indicated a role for cell-mediated immune reactions [50]. A further similarity of this model to human IDDM is that the susceptibility to develop diabetes is influenced by genetic factors, as the disease occurs only in certain inbred strains of mice [32]. Low-dose streptozotocin-induced diabetes is a useful tool to study the ways in which immune processes may augment the effects of a B-cytotoxic agent but not the spontaneous development of IDDM. Models more appropriate to IDDM are described below.

Vacor-induced diabetes in man

Ingestion of the rodenticide, Vacor, which has as its active ingredient N-3-pyridylmethyl-N-p-nitrophenyl urea, has caused over 30 cases of insulin-deficient diabetes mellitus in man since 1976 [2]. The syndrome consists of severe diabetes with ketoacidosis with subsequent neuropathy affecting both autonomic and peripheral nerves [51]. The extreme neurotoxicity of Vacor (which is lethal to laboratory rodents) has hampered animal studies of its diabetogenic action. Investigation of a series of some 200 Korean patients accidentally exposed to Vacor has led to the suggestion that diabetes may be due to peripheral insulin resistance [52, 53], although clinical and autopsy data, together with *in vitro* studies using isolated islets, have confirmed a direct toxic effect of Vacor on the B cell [2]. The inhibitory effects on the islets may be prevented by nicotinamide [2], suggesting a mechanism of action similar to that of streptozotocin.

Dietary N-nitroso compounds and diabetes in man

Attention was first drawn to the possible diabetogenic effects of environmental nitrosamines in 1974 [54]. Some 8 years later, an association between IDDM in young Icelandic males and the consumption of smoked cured mutton (containing N-nitroso compounds) by their parents at about the time of conception was reported by Helgason and co-workers [55]. This relationship was further examined in mice fed smoked mutton before mating, during pregnancy and after weaning. Diabetes was never observed in the parents but was recorded in more than 16% of male and 5% of female offspring. These studies provide direct evidence that environmental nitrosamines may induce B cell damage leading ultimately to diabetes.

Environmental agents as triggers of IDDM

The role of viruses in the pathogenesis of IDDM is discussed in detail in Chapter 16. However, it is appropriate to include viruses in the schematic summary of the ways in which various environmental agents may interact with each other and/or the B cell to trigger IDDM (Fig. 17.2). Although IDDM may be a result of viral infection, there is little evidence for viruses exerting a direct B-cytotoxic effect. It seems more likely that they may in some way modify the B cell, thus triggering immune or autoimmune reactions directed against the latter. The possible mechanisms of B-cell destruction by possible environmental toxins are also unclear and will depend on the nature of the agent. By analogy with alloxan and streptozotocin, sites of action may be located both at the plasma membrane and inside the B cell. Generation of free radicals which may exert toxic effects on both the mitochondria and cellular DNA is one possible mechanism of cytotoxicity, with B-cell specificity being conferred by selective uptake of the toxin. Nitrosamines and certain other toxins could directly attack the DNA strand, so inducing the repair mechanisms and leading to depletion of cellular NAD.

In summary, therefore, although certain environmental agents can destroy B cells on their own, it is more likely that IDDM results from a combination of factors which may be triggered by various infectious and/or chemical agents.

Animal models with spontaneous IDDM

It is now generally accepted that two main contributory factors are involved in the pathogenesis of IDDM, namely the immune system and a genetically determined predisposition to the disease. Clearly, therefore, only those animals which develop diabetes spontaneously can serve as models to assess rigorously the roles of these two complementary factors. Two spontaneously diabetic rodents, the BB rat and the non-obese diabetic (NOD) mouse, have emerged as the models of choice as they develop diabetic syndromes which most closely resemble human IDDM.

The BB rat

The BB rat was discovered in 1974 by Drs Reginald and Clifford Chappel in a commercial rodent breeding company (BioBreeding Laboratories Ltd) in Ottawa. The diabetic syndrome of the BB rat shares many characteristics with human IDDM (Table 17.4). There is a genetic predisposition to develop the disease and a long prediabetic period followed by an apparently abrupt onset of symptoms at around 3 months of age, often co-

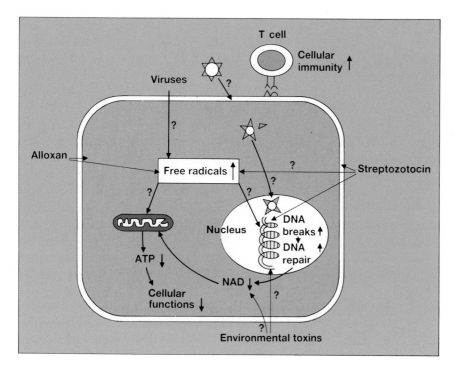

Fig. 17.2. Effects of environmental factors on the pancreatic B cell. (Redrawn from the original with kind permission of the author, Dr Stella Sandler — *Abstracts of Uppsala Dissertations from the Faculty of Medicine*, University of Uppsala, Sweden, 1983.)

inciding with puberty. Features include weight loss, glycosuria, hyperglycaemia and hypo-insulinaemia, with subsequent ketoacidosis which often proves fatal unless exogenous insulin is given [56]. The onset of disease is invariably accompanied by a pancreatic mononuclear cell infiltrate (insulitis) [56], whose degree varies between animals but which always precedes overt hyperglycaemia [57] and is related to the severity of the syndrome. The insulitis is similar to that described in human IDDM [58], with T cells (including both helper and cytotoxic/suppressor subsets), macrophages, natural killer cells and B lymphocytes being

present at the onset of diabetes [59].

Although it is not known how BB rats inherit diabetes, disease susceptibility appears to be associated with the major histocompatibility complex (MHC), as it is in man. Cross-breeding experiments have shown that the RT1^u MHC haplotype is necessary for the development of diabetes [60], which may require the presence of one MHC gene and at least two further genes not linked to the MHC [61].

Many studies have indicated direct involvement of both cellular and humoral immunity in the pathogenesis of diabetes in the BB rat. These have

Characteristic	Man	BB rat	NOD mouse
MHC association	Yes	Yes	Yes
Long prediabetic period	Yes	Yes	Yes
Insulitis	Yes	Yes	Yes
Insulin-dependent/ketosis-prone	Yes	Yes	Yes
Obese	No	No	No
Sex difference	No	No	♀ > ♂
ICA/ICSA	Yes/yes	No/yes	Yes/yes
64kDa islet-cell protein antibodies	Yes	Yes	Yes
Other autoantibodies (thyroid, etc.)	Yes	Yes	Yes
Lymphopenia	No	Yes*	Yes
Functional T-cell defects	No	Yes*	Yes
Thyroiditis	Yes	Yes	Yes
Probable role of environmental agents	Yes	Yes	Yes

Table 17.4. Characteristics of IDDM in man, BB rats and NOD mice.

* Not in all BB rat colonies.
MHC = major histocompatibility complex.
ICA/ICSA = islet-cell/islet-cell-surface antibodies.

included passive transfer experiments, immune intervention studies, *in vitro* investigations of islet-cell cytotoxicity and estimations of islet-cell antibodies.

PASSIVE TRANSFER EXPERIMENTS

The transfer of insulitis to athymic nude mice using lymphocytes from newly diabetic BB rats has been achieved by some workers [62] but not by others [63]. Concanavalin-A-stimulated lymphocytes previously isolated from diabetic rats have been shown to provoke an early onset of diabetes in BB rats [64]. These studies suggest that activated lymphocytes may cause diabetes by a direct or indirect effect upon the B cells.

INTERVENTION STUDIES

Various treatment regimens have been reported to prevent diabetes in BB rats, including neonatal thymectomy [65], total lymphoid irradiation [66], treatment with anti-lymphocyte serum [67], treatment with cyclosporin-A [68] and transfusion with either whole blood [69] or lymphocytes [70] from diabetes-resistant BB rats. Other treatments, including injection of monoclonal antibodies to T cells [71] or to class II MHC antigens [72] and the administration of silica [73] (a non-specific inhibitor of the immune system) have also been shown to prevent diabetes in BB rats. These experiments all provide evidence that the immune system of the BB rat is directly involved in the pathogenesis of IDDM.

IN VITRO ISLET-CELL CYTOTOXICITY

More direct evidence for an immune reaction directed against islet cells was provided by the demonstration that splenic lymphoid cells from diabetic and diabetes-prone BB rats were able to lyse normal rat islet cells in monolayer culture [74]. Further studies showed that these B-cytotoxic cells had the properties of natural killer (NK) cells [75] and were responsive to both concanavalin-A and interleukin-2 [76].

ISLET-CELL AND OTHER AUTOANTIBODIES

Although islet-cell *cytoplasmic* antibodies (ICA) are prevalent in human IDDM, they have never been detected in the BB rat [77, 78]. However, a high incidence of islet-cell *surface* antibodies

(ICSA) has been reported in diabetes-prone and newly diabetic BB rats [79, 80]. The occurrence of ICSA together with lymphocyte antibodies [78] has been proposed as a potentially useful marker for the development of diabetes in BB rats [81]. Insulin autoantibodies (IAA) [80] and antibodies against parietal, thyroid and smooth muscle cells [77, 82] have all been demonstrated in BB rats, but none appears to correlate with the development of diabetes [80]. By contrast, autoantibodies to a 64 kDa islet-cell plasma membrane protein are associated with diabetes in the BB rat [83]. A similar 64 kDa autoantibody has been reported in newly diagnosed human IDDM [84]. Moreover, these autoantibodies have also been detected prior to the onset of diabetic symptoms in both man and the BB rat, fuelling speculation that the 64 kDa islet protein may be a major target antigen in the immune destruction of the B cells [83].

Several research groups have reported that lymphopenia occurs in all diabetic and diabetes-prone BB rats [85–7], with the decrease being mainly due to T-cell deficiency [86]. It was previously stated that diabetes could not develop in the absence of lymphopenia, although lymphopenia without diabetes could occur [61]. At this time, other immunological deficiencies, predominantly depression of T-cell function [87, 88], were reported in diabetic and diabetes-prone BB rats. These early reports of lymphopenia and abnormal T-cell responses in diabetic rats (which do not occur in IDDM in man) provoked criticism of the BB rat as a model for the human disease, which is not associated with T-cell abnormality. More recently, however, it has been reported that BB rats can develop diabetes in the absence of lymphopenia and/or depressed T-cell responses [89, 90], suggesting that neither abnormality is essential to the development of diabetes in this model.

The NOD (non-obese diabetic) mouse

The NOD mouse was discovered in 1974 at the Shionogi Research Laboratories in Osaka, having been derived from a subline of outbred Jc1-ICR mice which developed spontaneous cataracts [91]. The diabetic syndrome of the NOD mouse is remarkably similar to that of the BB rat, with onset of glycosuria, hyperglycaemia and hypo-insulinaemia and insulin-dependence occurring at approximately 14 weeks of age [91]. Insulitis (with both helper and cytotoxic T cells and NK cells in the infiltrate, as in the BB rat [92] is observed in virtually all diabetes-prone NOD mice from about 5 weeks of age [93] but overt diabetes subsequently develops in only 80% of female and 20% of male mice [91]. The apparent failure of a proportion of NOD mice to develop diabetes following pancreatic infiltration and the marked sex difference in predilection are two of the major differences between the NOD mouse and the BB rat.

The NOD mouse is strikingly similar to the BB rat regarding the roles of cellular and humoral immunity in the pathogenesis of diabetes. The NOD mouse exhibits abnormalities of cellular immunity, including decreased numbers of T lymphocytes [94] and decreased NK cell and antibody-dependent cell-mediated cytotoxicity activities [95]. As with the BB rat, many studies (mostly performed in Japan) have aimed to induce or prevent insulitis and overt diabetes in the NOD mouse [96]. Transfer of splenocytes and thymocytes from euthymic NOD×nude cross mice induced insulitis in athymic nude mice, suggesting an obligatory role of T cells in the development of insulitis [96]. It was possible to prevent insulitis and overt diabetes in the NOD mouse by various immunomodulatory procedures including neonatal thymectomy, bone marrow transplantation, irradiation and whole-blood transfusion. Moreover, treatment of susceptible animals with agents such as anti-lymphocyte serum, cyclosporin, steroids, nicotinamide and free-radical scavengers, similarly prevented the onset of disease [96]. Altogether, these studies provide evidence for a pathogenic role of cell-mediated immunity in B-cell destruction in the NOD mouse. Humoral immunity is also implicated, as ICA, ICSA and IAA have all been reported in the sera of prediabetic NOD mice [97, 98]. Although it is not clear whether these autoantibodies predict the development of diabetes in the NOD mouse, the disease appears only in those animals which previously showed the antibodies [98].

The genetic characteristics of the NOD mouse differ from those of the BB rat. Morphological, biochemical and immunological markers [96] indicate that NOD mice have high genetic uniformity, whereas BB rats are often non-uniform within the MHC and as such are not so well suited for genetic studies.

The validity of extrapolating animal data to human disease must always be open to question. Nevertheless, the BB rat and NOD mouse have contributed much to our knowledge of the pathogenesis of IDDM, with regard to several issues:

1 The exact nature of the genetic control of diabetes susceptibility remains unclear although an association with the MHC genes is well recognized.

2 The agent or agents responsible for triggering the cascade of events culminating in B-cell destruction are also unknown but environmental toxins and/or viruses have been implicated.

3 The immune effector cells leading to the development of insulitis still have to be positively identified but involvement of macrophages, T cells and NK cells has been suggested.

4 The precise mechanisms resulting in B-cell death are still uncertain although direct B-cytotoxic effects of cytokines such as interleukin-1 are a possibility.

Based on our own longitudinal studies performed using the BB rat [59, 99], the following sequence of events leading ultimately to destruction of the B-cell mass could be proposed (Fig. 17.3). An as yet undefined intra-islet disturbance results in the increased expression of MHC class I molecules on islet cells. Subsequent infiltration of these islets by macrophages may release cytokines which may be directly cytotoxic to islet B cells [100], and/or by local release of interleukin-1 and tumour necrosis factor, which activate endothelial cells of pancreatic venules and ducts to bind increased numbers of lymphocytes [101]. The infiltrating lymphocytes would then be attracted to the already macrophage-infiltrated islets by a chemotactic gradient of interleukin-1 [102]. Within the infiltrated islets, presentation of B-cell-specific antigens by activated macrophages to MHC class II-restricted T-helper cells may then initiate further immune mechanisms leading to the specific destruction of the B cells. The involvement of the early hyperexpression of MHC class I molecules on the islet cells in this proposed sequence of events is unclear. However, viral infection is known to be a common stimulus for the release of interferons from epithelial cells. Thus, this proposed sequence of events does not support an earlier hypothesis that early aberrant expression of MHC class II antigens on the B cell may allow the presentation of specific autoantigens to potentially autoreactive T-helper lymphocytes, thereby leading to an autoimmune destruction of the B-cell mass [103]. For a discussion of immune mechanisms in human IDDM, see Chapters 13 and 15.

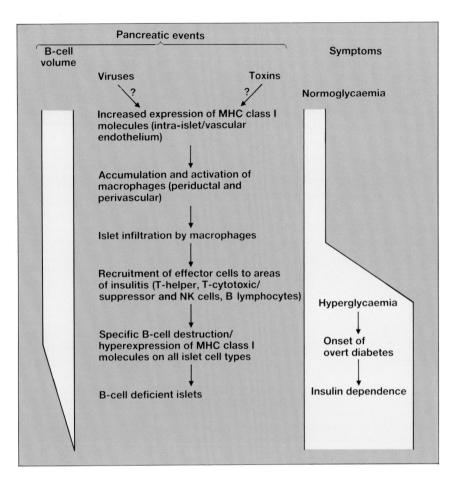

Fig. 17.3. Schematic outline of proposed sequence of pancreatic events culminating in overt IDDM in BB rats.

Other animal models with spontaneous IDDM

A closed breeding colony of *Macaca nigra* (Celebes black ape) shows an incidence of IDDM of approximately 20% [104]. The aetiology and pathogenesis of diabetes in these animals is uncertain, but their evolutionary closeness to man may make this a useful model for the study of long-term diabetic complications, particularly atherosclerosis [105].

A familial form of insulin-requiring diabetes has been reported in non-obese Keeshond dogs [106]. The pathogenesis of the B-cell destruction is not known but no insulitis has ever been reported in these animals.

Diabetes occurs in Chinese hamsters with variable and unpredictable severity; some animals become heavily ketotic and die without insulin treatment (reviewed by Grodsky and Frankel [107]). The mechanisms resulting in diabetes in the Chinese hamster have not been identified. However, pancreatic pathology has revealed a gradual loss of B cells associated with an increased functional demand for insulin.

IDDM develops in approximately 50% of a breeding colony of guinea pigs [108]. The aetiology and pathogenesis of the disease are not known, although a viral infection has been implicated [109]. Diabetic guinea pigs are perhaps most potentially useful for the study of specific diabetic complications, including retinopathy and nephropathy [109].

The New Zealand white rabbit shows an incidence of spontaneous diabetes of approximately 18% in one colony [110]. The cause of the disease is uncertain but a defect in insulin secretion has been suggested in the absence of insulitis [111].

It is perhaps appropriate to conclude this review of the contribution of animal models to our understanding of the pathogenesis of IDDM with a look to the future. The role of aberrant expression of class II MHC molecules in IDDM has recently been studied in transgenic mice, i.e. those which have foreign DNA integrated experimentally into both their somatic and germ cells (see also Chapter 14). Use of these animals has made it possible to study the molecular basis not only of tissue-specific gene expression during normal development but also the effects of abnormal gene expression. Sarvetnic and coworkers [112] produced transgenic mouse strains harbouring class II MHC or interferon-gamma (IFN-gamma) genes linked to the human insulin promoter. Transgenic mice expressing class II genes showed progressive atrophy of the islets whilst mice expressing IFN-gamma suffered inflammatory destruction of the islets. In a second recent study [113], transgenic mice which expressed class II MHC molecules on B cells were generated. Diabetes was detected in the transgenic mice but without any evidence of lymphocytic infiltration, suggesting that aberrant MHC expression is by itself insufficient to initiate autoimmune responses against tissue-specific antigens.

ADRIAN J. BONE

References

1 Herberg L. The specific pathophysiology in spontaneously diabetic animals. *J Obesity* 1982; **6** (suppl 1): 1–7.

2 Karam JH, Lewitt PA, Young CW, Nowlain RE, Frankel BJ, Fujiya H, Freedman ZR, Grodsky GM. Insulinopenic diabetes after rodenticide (Vacor) ingestion. *Diabetes* 1980; **29**: 971–8.

3 Okamoto K. Biologische Intersuchungen der Metalle. Histochemischer Nachweis einiger Metalle in den Geweben, Besonders in den Nieren, und deren Veranderunge. *Trans Soc Pathol Japan* 1942; **32**: 99–105.

4 Kadota I. Studies on experimental diabetes produced by organic reagents. *J Lab Clin Med* 1950; **35**: 568–91.

5 Tarui S. Studies on zinc metabolism. II. Effect of the diabetic state on zinc metabolism: An experimental aspect. *Endocrinol Japan* 1963; **10**: 1–8.

6 Dunn JS, McLetchie NGB. Experimental alloxan diabetes in the rat. *Lancet* 1943; ii: 384–7.

7 Jacobs HR. Hypoglycaemic action of alloxan. *Proc Soc Exp Biol Med* 1937; **37**: 407–9.

8 Patterson JW, Lazarow A, Levey S. Alloxan and dialuric acid: their stabilities and ultraviolet absorption spectra. *J Biol Chem* 1949; **177**: 187–96.

9 Sen PB, Bhattacharya G. Protection against alloxan diabetes by glucose. *Indian J Physiol* 1952; **6**: 112–14.

10 Webb JL. Alloxan. In: Webb JL, ed. *Enzyme and Metabolic Inhibitors*. New York: Academic Press, 1966: 367–419.

11 Rerup CA. Drugs producing diabetes through damage of the insulin secreting cells. *Pharmacol Rev* 1970; **22**: 485–518.

12 Orci L, Amhardt M, Malaisse-Lagae F, Ravazzola M, Malaisse WJ, Perrelet A, Renold AE. Islet cell membrane alterations by diabetogenic drugs. *Lab Invest* 1976; **34**: 451–9.

13 Idahl L-A, Lernmark Å, Sehlin J, Taljedal I-B. Alloxan cytotoxicity *in vitro*. Inhibition of rubidium ion pumping in pancreatic beta-cells. *Biochem J* 1977; **162**: 9–18.

14 Tomita T, Lacy PE, Matschinsky FM, McDaniel ML. Effect of alloxan on insulin secretion in isolated rat islets perfused *in vitro*. *Diabetes* 1974; **23**: 517–24.

15 Rossini AA, Cahill GF, Jeanloz DA, Jeanloz RW. Anomeric specificity of 3-O-methyl-D-glucopyranose against alloxan diabetes. *Science* 1975; **187**: 70–1.

16 Weaver DC, McDaniel ML, Lacey PE. Alloxan uptake by isolated rat islets of Langerhans. *Endocrinology* 1978; **102**: 1847–55.

17 Lenzen S, Panten U. Signal recognition by pancreatic B-cells. *Biochem Pharmacol* 1988; **37**: 371–8.

18 Lenzen S, Tiedge M, Panten U. Glucokinase in pancreatic B-cells and its inhibition by alloxan. *Acta Endocrinol* 1987; **115**:21–9.

19 Lenzen S, Panten U. Alloxan: history and mechanism of action. *Diabetologia* 1988; **31**: 337–42.

20 Villar-Palasi C, Carballido A, Sols A, Arteta JL. Sensitivity of pancreas hexokinase toward alloxan and its modification by glucose. *Nature* 1957; **180**: 387–8.

21 Colca JR, Kotagal N, Brooks CL, Lacy PE, Landt M, McDaniel ML. Alloxan inhibition of Ca^{2+}- and calmodulin-dependent protein kinase activity in pancreatic islets. *J Biol Chem* 1983; **258**: 7260–3.

22 Boquist L. A new hypothesis for alloxan diabetes. *Acta Pathol Microbiol Scand* 1980; **88**: 201–9.

23 Cohen G, Heikkila RE. The generation of hydrogen peroxide, superoxide radical and hydroxyl radical by 6-hydroxydopamine, dialuric acid, and related cytotoxic agents. *J Biol Chem* 1974; **249**: 2447–52.

24 Malaisse WJ. Alloxan toxicity to the pancreatic B-cell. *Biochem Pharmacol* 1982; **31**: 3527–34.

25 Fischer LJ, Hamburger SA. Inhibition of alloxan action in isolated pancreatic islets by superoxide dismutase, catalase and a metal chelator. *Diabetes* 1980; **29**: 213–16.

26 Yamamoto H, Uchigata Y, Okamoto H. DNA strand breaks in pancreatic islets by *in vivo* administration of alloxan or streptozotocin. *Biochem Biophys Res Commun* 1981; **103**: 1014–20.

27 Yamamoto H, Uchigata Y, Okamoto H. Streptozotocin and alloxan induce DNA strand breaks and poly(ADP-ribose) synthetase in pancreatic islets. *Nature* 1981; **294**: 284–6.

28 Okamoto H. Regulation of proinsulin synthesis in pancreatic islets and a new aspect to insulin dependent diabetes. *Molec Cell Biochem* 1981; **37**: 43–61.

29 Uchigata Y, Yamamoto H, Kawamura A, Okamoto H. Protection by superoxide dismutase, catalase and poly(ADP-ribose) synthetase inhibitors against alloxan and streptozotocin induced DNA strand breaks and against the inhibition of proinsulin biosynthesis. *J Biol Chem* 1982; **257**: 6084–8.

30 Vaura JJ, Deboer C, Dietz A, Hanka LJ, Sokolski WT. Streptozotocin, a new antibacterial antibiotic. In: Marti-Ibanez F, ed. *Antibiotic Annual 1959–1960*. New York: Antibiotica Inc., 1960; 230–5.

31 Rakieten N, Rakieten ML, Nadkarni MV. Studies on the diabetogenic actions of streptozotocin (NSC 37919). *Cancer Chemother Rep* 1963; **29**: 91–8.

32 Like AA, Rossini AA. Streptozotocin-induced pancreatic insulitis: A new model of diabetes mellitus. *Science* 1976; **193**: 415–17.

33 Cooperstein SJ, Watkins D. Action of toxic drugs on islet cells. In: Cooperstein SJ, Watkins D, eds. *The islets of Langerhans*. New York: Academic Press, 1981: 387–425.

34 Bhattacharya G. On the protection against alloxan diabetes by hexoses. *Science* 1954; **120**: 841–3.

35 Rossini AA, Like AA, Dulin WE, Cahill GE Jr. Pancreatic B-cell toxicity by streptozotocin anomers. *Diabetes* 1977; **26**: 1120–4.

36 Dulin WE, Wyse BM. Studies on the ability of compounds to block the diabetogenic activity of streptozotocin. *Diabetes* 1969; **18:** 459–66.

37 Brodsky G, Logothetopoulos J. Streptozotocin diabetes in the mouse and guinea pig. *Diabetes* 1969; **18:** 606–11.

38 Schein PS, Cooney DA, McMenamin MG, Anderson T. Streptozotocin diabetes — further studies on the mechanism of depression of nicotinamide adenine dinucleotide concentrations in mouse pancreatic islets and liver. *Biochem Pharmacol* 1973; **22:** 2625–31.

39 Ho CK, Hashim SA. Pyridine nucleotide depletion in pancreatic islets associated with streptozotocin-induced diabetes. *Diabetes* 1972; **21:** 789–93.

40 Gunnarsson R, Berne C, Hellerström C. Cytotoxic effects of streptozotocin and N-nitrosomethylurea on the pancreatic B cells with special regard to the role of nicotinamide–adenine dinucleotide. *Biochem J* 1974; **140:** 487–94.

41 Robbins MJ, Sharp AR, Slonim AE, Burr IM. Protection against streptozotocin-induced diabetes by superoxide dismutase. *Diabetologia* 1980; **18:** 55–8.

42 Gandy SM, Buse MG, Crouch RK. Protective role of superoxide dismutase against diabetogenic drugs. *J Clin Invest* 1982; **70:** 650–8.

43 Yamamoto H, Okamoto H. Protection by picolinamide, a novel inhibitor of poly(ADP-ribose) synthetase, against both streptozotocin-induced depression of proinsulin synthesis and reduction of NAD content in pancreatic islets. *Biochem Biophys Res Commun* 1980; **95:** 474–81.

44 Uchigata Y, Yamamoto H, Nagai H, Okamoto H. Effect of poly(ADP-ribose) synthetase inhibitor administration to rats before and after injection of alloxan and streptozotocin on islet proinsulin synthesis. *Diabetes* 1983; **32:** 316–18.

45 Sandler S, Swenne I. Streptozotocin, but not alloxan, induces DNA repair synthesis in mouse pancreatic islets *in vitro*. *Diabetologia* 1983; **25:** 444–7.

46 Sandler S, Welsh M, Andersson A. Nicotinamide does not protect the islet B-cell metabolism against alloxan toxicity. *Diabetes* 1984; **33:** 937–43.

47 Rossini AA, Williams RM, Appel MC, Like AA. Complete protection from low-dose streptozotocin-induced diabetes in mice. *Nature* 1978; **276:** 182–4.

48 Nedergaard M, Egeberg J, Kroman H. Irradiation protects against pancreatic islet degeneration and hyperglycaemia following streptozotocin treatment of mice. *Diabetologia* 1983; **24:** 382–6.

49 Kiesel U, Kolb H. Suppressive effect of antibodies to immune response gene products on the development of low-dose streptozotocin-induced diabetes. *Diabetes* 1983; **32:** 869–71.

50 Kiesel U, Freytag G, Biener J, Kolb H. Transfer of experimental autoimmune insulitis by spleen cells in mice. *Diabetologia* 1980; **19:** 516–20.

51 Johnson D, Kubic P, Levitt C. Accidental ingestion of Vacor rodenticide: the symptoms and sequelae in a 25 month old child. *Am J Dis Child* 1980; **134:** 161–4.

52 Lee TH, Kang JC, Han MD, Kim JS, Roh JW, Chung MY, Choi BJ. A clinical analysis of rodenticide RH-787 intoxication in Korea. *J Korean Diabetes Assoc* 1977; **4:** 43–51.

53 Lee TH. Immunoreactive insulin and C-peptide responses to oral glucose loads in the patients with RH-787 intoxication. *Korean J Intern Med* 1978; **21:** 507–11.

54 Berne C, Gunnarsson R, Hellerström C, Wilander E. Diabetogenic nitrosamines? *Lancet* 1974; 173–4.

55 Helgason T, Ewen SWB, Ross IS, Stowers JM. Diabetes produced in mice by smoked/cured mutton. *Lancet* 1982;

i: 1017–22.

56 Nakhooda AF, Like AA, Chappel CI, Murray FT, Marliss EB. The spontaneously diabetic Wistar rat. Metabolic and morphologic studies. *Diabetes* 1976; **26:** 100–12.

57 Seemayer TA, Tannenbaum GS, Goldman H, Colle E. Dynamic time course studies of the spontaneously diabetic BB Wistar rat. III Light microscopic and ultrastructural observations of pancreatic islets of Langerhans. *Am J Pathol* 1982; **106:** 237–49.

58 Foulis AK, Liddle CN, Farquharson MA, Richmond JA, Weir RA. The histopathology of the pancreas in Type 1 (insulin-dependent) diabetes mellitus: a 25 year review of deaths in patients under 20 years of age in the United Kingdom. *Diabetologia* 1986; **29:** 267–74.

59 Walker R, Bone AJ, Cooke A, Baird JD. Distinct macrophage subpopulations in the pancreas of pre-diabetic BB/E rats: A possible role for macrophages in the pathogenesis of insulin-dependent diabetes. *Diabetes* 1988; **37:** 1301–4.

60 Colle E, Guttmann RD, Seemayer T. Spontaneous diabetes mellitus in the rat. I. Association with the major histocompatibility complex. *J Exp Med* 1981; **154:** 1237–42.

61 Guttmann RD, Colle E, Michel F, Seemayer T. Spontaneous diabetes mellitus syndrome in the rat. II. T lymphopenia and its association with clinical disease and pancreatic lymphocytic infiltration. *J Immunol* 1983; **130:** 1732–5.

62 Nakhooda AF, Sima AA, Poussier P, Marliss EB. Passive transfer of insulitis from the BB rat to the nude mouse. *Endocrinology* 1981; **109:** 2264–6.

63 Rossini AA, Mordes JP, Williams RM, Pelletier AM, Like AA. Failure to transfer insulitis to athymic recipients using BB/W rat lymphoid tissue transplants. *Metabolism* 1983; **32** (suppl 1): 80–3.

64 Koevary S, Rossini AA, Stoller W, Chick WL, Williams RM. Passive transfer of diabetes in the BB/W rat. *Science* 1983; **220:** 727–8.

65 Like AA, Kislauskis E, Williams RM, Rossini AA. Neonatal thymectomy prevents spontaneous diabetes mellitus in the BB/W rat. *Science* 1982; **216:** 644–6.

66 Rossini AA, Slavin S, Woda BA, Geisberg M, Like AA, Mordes JP. Total lymphoid irradiation prevents diabetes mellitus in the Bio-Breeding/Worcester (BB/W) rat. *Diabetes* 1984; **33:** 543–7.

67 Like AA, Rossini AA, Appel MC, Guberski DL, Williams RM. Spontaneous diabetes mellitus: reversal and prevention in the BB/W rat with antiserum to rat lymphocytes. *Science* 1979; **206:** 1421–3.

68 Laupacis A, Gardell C, Dupre J, Stiller CR, Keown P, Wallace AC, Thibert P. Cyclosporin prevents diabetes in BB Wistar rats. *Lancet* 1983; i: 10–11.

69 Rossini AA, Mordes JP, Pelletier AM, Like AA. Transfusions of whole blood prevent spontaneous diabetes mellitus in the BB/W rat. *Science* 1983; **219:** 975–7.

70 Rossini AA, Faustman D, Woda BA, Like AA, Szymanski I, Mordes JP. Lymphocyte transfusions prevent diabetes in the Bio-Breeding/Worcester rat. *J Clin Invest* 1984; **74:** 39–46.

71 Like AA, Biron CA, Weringer EJ, Byman K, Sroczynski E, Guberski DL. Prevention of diabetes in Bio-Breeding Worcester rats with monoclonal antibodies that recognise T lymphocytes or natural killer cells. *J Exp Med* 1986; **164:** 1145–59.

72 Boitard C, Michie S, Surrurier P, Butcher GW, Larkins AP, McDevitt HO. *In vivo* prevention of thyroid and pancreatic autoimmunity in the BB rat by antibody to class II major histocompatibility complex gene products. *Proc Natl Acad Sci USA* 1985; **82:** 6627–31.

73 Oschilewski U, Kiesel U, Kolb H. Administration of silica prevents diabetes in BB rats. *Diabetes* 1985; **34**: 197–9.

74 MacKay P, Boulton A, Rabinovitch A. Lymphoid cells of BB/W diabetic rats are cytotoxic to islet beta cells *in vitro*. *Diabetes* 1985; **34**: 706–9.

75 MacKay P, Jacobson J, Rabinovitch A. Spontaneous diabetes mellitus in the Bio-Breeding/Worcester rat. Evidence *in vitro* for natural killer cell lysis of islet cells. *J Clin Invest* 1986; **77**: 916–24.

76 Pukel C, Baquerizo H, Rabinovitch A. Interleukin 2 activates BB/W diabetic rat lymphoid cells cytotoxic to islet cells. *Diabetes* 1987; **36**: 1217–22.

77 Like AA, Appel MC, Rossini AA. Autoantibodies in the BB/W rat. *Diabetes* 1982; **31**: 816–20.

78 Dyrberg T, Nakhooda AF, Baekkeskov S, Lernmark Å, Poussier P, Marliss EB. Islet cell surface antibodies and lymphocyte antibodies in the spontaneously diabetic BB Wistar rat. *Diabetes* 1982; **31**: 278–81.

79 Dyrberg T, Poussier P, Nakhooda AF, Marliss EB, Lernmark Å. Islet cell surface and lymphocyte antibodies often precede the spontaneous diabetes in the BB rat. *Diabetologia* 1984; **26**: 159–65.

80 Dean BM, Bone AJ, Varey AM, Walker R, Baird JD, Cook A. Insulin autoantibodies, islet cell surface antibodies and the development of spontaneous diabetes in the BB/Edinburgh rat. *Clin Exp Immunol* 1987; **69**: 308–13.

81 Bone AJ, Walker R, Dean BM, Baird JD, Cooke A. Prediabetes in the spontaneously diabetic BB/E rat: pancreatic infiltration and islet cell proliferation. *Acta Endocrinol* 1987; **115**: 447–54.

82 Elder M, Maclaren N, Riley W, McConnell T. Gastric parietal cell and other autoantibodies in the BB rat. *Diabetes* 1982; **31**: 313–18.

83 Baekkeskov S, Dyrberg T, Lernmark Å. Autoantibodies to a 64-kilodalton islet cell protein precede the onset of spontaneous diabetes in the BB rat. *Science* 1984; **224**: 1348–50.

84 Gerling I, Baekkeskov S, Lernmark Å. Islet cell and 64K autoantibodies are associated with plasma IgG in newly diagnosed insulin-dependent diabetic children. *J Immunol* 1986; **137**: 3782–5.

85 Poussier P, Nakhooda AF, Falk JA, Lee C, Marliss EB. Lymphopenia and abnormal lymphocyte subsets in the BB rat: relationship to the diabetic syndrome. *Endocrinology* 1982; **110**: 1825–7.

86 Jackson R, Rassi N, Crump T, Haynes B, Eisenbarth GS. The BB diabetic rat: profound T cell lymphopenia. *Diabetes* 1981; **30**: 887–9.

87 Elder ME, Maclaren N. Identification of profound peripheral T lymphocyte immunodeficiencies in the spontaneously diabetic BB rat. *J Immunol* 1983; **130**: 1723–31.

88 Bellgrau D, Naji A, Silvers WK, Markmann JK, Barker CF. Spontaneous diabetes in BB rats — evidence for a T cell dependent immune response defect. *Diabetologia* 1982; **23**: 359–64.

89 Like AA, Guberski DL, Butler L. Diabetic BioBreeding/Worcester (BB/Wor) rats need not be lymphopenic. *J Immunol* 1986; **136**: 3254–8.

90 Varey AM, Dean BM, Walker R, Bone AJ, Baird JD, Cooke A. Immunological responses of the BB rat colony in Edinburgh. *Immunology* 1987; **60**: 131–4.

91 Makino S, Kunimoto K, Muraoka Y, Mizushima Y, Katagiri K, Tochino Y. Breeding of a non-obese, diabetic strain of mice. *Exp Anim* 1980; **29**: 1–13.

92 Kawazawa Y, Komeda K, Sato S, Mori S, Akanuma K, Takaku F. Non-obese diabetic mice: immune mechanisms of pancreatic B-cell destruction. *Diabetologia* 1984; **27**: 113–15.

93 Fujita T, Yui R, Kusumoto Y, Serizawa Y, Makino S, Tochino Y. Lymphocytic insulitis in a non-obese diabetic (NOD) strain of mice: an immunohistochemical and electron microscope investigation. *Biomed Res* 1982; **3**: 429–43.

94 Kataoka S, Satoh J, Fujiya H, Toyota T, Suzuki R, Itoh K, Kumagai K. Immunologic aspects of the non-obese diabetic (NOD) mouse: abnormalities of cellular immunity. *Diabetes* 1983; **32**: 247–53.

95 Maruyama T, Takei I, Taniyama M, Kataoka K, Matsuki S. Immunological aspect of non-obese diabetic mice: immune islet cell killing mechanism and cell-mediated immunity. *Diabetologia* 1984; **27**: 121–3.

96 Tochino Y. The NOD mouse as a model of Type 1 diabetes. *CRC Critical Rev Immunol* 1987; **8**: 49–81.

97 Toyota T, Kataoka S, Sato J, Fujiya H, Hayashida Y, Goto Y, Kumagai K. Islet cell antibody and immunologic aspects of NOD mice. In: Mimura G, Baba S, Goto Y, Kobberling J, eds. *Clinico-genetic genesis of diabetes mellitus. Excerpta Med* 1982; **597**: 185–92.

98 Reddy S, Bibby NJ, Elliott RB. Ontogeny of islet cell antibodies, insulin autoantibodies and insulitis in the non-obese diabetic mouse. *Diabetologia* 1988; **31**: 322–38.

99 Dean BM, Walker R, Bone AJ, Baird JD, Cooke A. Prediabetes in the spontaneously diabetic BB/E rat: lymphocyte subpopulations in the pancreatic infiltrate and expression of rat MHC class II molecules in endocrine cells. *Diabetologia* 1985; **28**: 464–6.

100 Mandrup-Poulsen T, Bendtzen K, Nerup J, Dinarello CA, Svenson M, Nielsen JH. Affinity purified human interleukin 1 is cytotoxic to isolated islets of Langerhans. *Diabetologia* 1986; **29**: 63–7.

101 Cavender D, Saegusa Y, Ziff M. Stimulation of endothelial cell binding of lymphocytes by tumor necrosis factor. *J Immunol* 1987; **139**: 1855–60.

102 Miossec P, Yu CL, Ziff M. Lymphocyte chemotactic activity of human interleukin 1. *J Immunol* 1984; **133**: 2007–11.

103 Bottazzo GF, Pujol-Borrell R, Hanafusa T, Feldmann L. Hypothesis: role of aberrant HLA-DR expression and antigen presentation in the induction of endocrine autoimmunity. *Lancet* 1983; ii: 1115–19.

104 Howard CF Jr. Diabetes in *Macaca nigra*. *Diabetes* 1972; **21**: 1077–90.

105 Howard CF Jr. Aortic atherosclerosis in normal and spontaneously diabetic *Macaca nigra*. *Atherosclerosis* 1979; **33**: 479–93.

106 Kramer JW, Nottingham S, Robinette J, Lenz G, Sylvester S, Dessouky MI. Inherited, early onset, insulin-requiring diabetes mellitus of Keeshond dogs. *Diabetes* 1980; **29**: 558–65.

107 Grodsky GM, Frankel BJ. Diabetes mellitus in the Chinese hamster. In: Martin JM, Ehrlich RM, Holland FJ, eds. *Etiology and pathogenesis of insulin-dependent diabetes mellitus*. New York: Raven Press, 1981: 239–49.

108 Munger BL, Lang CM. Spontaneous diabetes mellitus in guinea pigs. The acute cytopathology of the islets of Langerhans. *Lab Invest* 1973; **29**: 685–702.

109 Lang CM, Munger BL, Rapp F. The guinea pig as an animal model of diabetes mellitus. *Lab Anim Sci* 1977; **27**: 789–805.

110 Conaway HH, Brown CJ, Sanders LL, Cernosek SF, Farris HE, Roth SI. Spontaneous diabetes mellitus in the New Zealand white rabbit. History, classification and genetic analysis. *J Heredity* 1980; **71**: 179–86.

111 Roth SI, Conaway HH, Sanders LL, Casali RE, Boyd AE. Spontaneous diabetes mellitus in the New Zealand white rabbit. Preliminary morphological characterisation. *Lab Invest* 1980; **42**: 572−9.

112 Sarvetnic N, Liggitt D, Pitts SL, Hansen SE, Stewart TA. Insulin-dependent diabetes mellitus induced in transgenic mice by ectopic expression of class II MHC and interferon-gamma. *Cell* 1988; **52**: 773−82.

113 Lo D, Burkly LC, Widera G, Cowling C, Flavell RA, Palmiter RD, Brinster RL. Diabetes and tolerance in transgenic mice expressing class II MHC molecules in pancreatic beta cells. *Cell* 1988; **53**: 159−68.

114 Craighead JE, McLane MF. Diabetes mellitus: Induction in mice by encephalomyocarditis virus. *Science* 1968; **162**: 913−14.

115 Meier H, Yerganian GA. Spontaneous hereditary diabetes mellitus in the Chinese hamster. I. Pathological findings. *Proc Soc Exp Biol Med* 1959; **100**: 810−15.

SECTION 7
PATHOGENESIS OF NON-INSULIN-DEPENDENT DIABETES MELLITUS

18   The Pathology of the Pancreas in Non-Insulin-Dependent Diabetes Mellitus

Summary

- Total islet and B-cell mass is reduced to 50–60% of normal in NIDDM.
- A cell mass is increased.
- The most important morphological feature is amyloid deposition in the islets. These deposits consist of islet amyloid polypeptide (IAPP or amylin).
- IAPP has 50% homology with the regulatory peptide, calcitonin-gene-related peptide (CGRP) and there is evidence that it originates in the B-cell secretory granules.

The pathological changes in both the endocrine and exocrine tissue of the pancreas in non-insulin-dependent diabetes mellitus (NIDDM) are more subtle than in insulin-dependent diabetes mellitus (IDDM). It has even been claimed that the morphology of the islets is normal in NIDDM, whereas in fact, both quantitative and qualitative alterations typical of NIDDM are demonstrable in most (but not all) cases.

Alterations in endocrine pancreatic tissue in NIDDM

Quantitative changes

TOTAL ISLET-CELL VOLUME

The mean total islet volume is moderately diminished (50–60% of the mean normal value) in NIDDM, which is reflected in a lower percentage of islet tissue in the whole pancreas [1–4]. However, all studies show a considerable overlap between diabetic and non-diabetic individuals.

VOLUMES OF THE DIFFERENT ISLET CELLS

Most studies have shown that the volume of B cells in NIDDM is reduced to about 50% of the normal value [1–3]; only one study has claimed a normal B cell mass [5]. The observed decrease is not sufficient to explain the diabetic condition, and is much less than that seen in IDDM. The increased proportion of A cells in islets of persons with NIDDM has generally been assumed to be a consequence of the decreased B-cell mass, although two studies [3, 5] have indicated a true increase in A cell mass in this form of diabetes which may contribute to the hyperglucagonaemia in NIDDM [6]. There are no significant changes in the volumes of D or PP cells.

Morphological changes

ISLET AMYLOID DEPOSITION

The most characteristic islet alteration in NIDDM is deposition of amyloid [7–9]. The amyloid, formerly called 'hyalin', forms unstructured masses between the basement membranes of the epithelial cells and the capillaries. Amyloid deposition is strictly limited to the islets (Fig. 18.1). Like all other amyloids, it is composed of fine (about 10-nm thick) 'rigid' fibrils (Fig. 18.2) and has certain typical staining properties, notably affinity for Congo red and green birefringence after such staining [10].

Islet amyloid is seen in most patients with NIDDM. The frequency varies in different studies but careful examination reveals that it occurs in more than 90% of the patients at death (unpublished observations) and that about two-thirds of

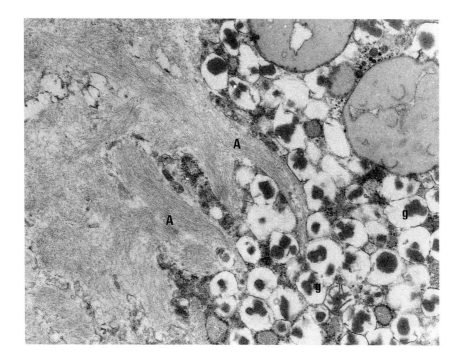

Fig. 18.4. Electron micrograph of islet amyloid adjacent to a B cell which contains many secretory, insulin-containing granules (g). The amyloid fibrils (A) are arranged in bundles running into deep pockets in the cell membrane. This appearance is not seen when the amyloid occurs close to other islet cells and is interpreted as a sign of fibril production by the B cells. (Reproduced with permission from Marrink J, von Rijswijk MH, eds. *Amyloidosis.* Amsterdam: Martinus Nijhoff, 1986.)

as amyloid. This must mean that in NIDDM, B-cell granules are depleted of IAPP while their insulin content is more or less unaltered. These granules are therefore probably abnormal, although they appear morphologically normal. The functional significance of this finding is not known at present.

Alterations in exocrine pancreatic tissue

The total volume of the pancreas in NIDDM is not significantly altered [4, 5] but fatty infiltration [4] and diffuse fibrosis [22] are commonly found. It is unclear, however, whether fatty infiltration is directly connected to the diabetes and diffuse fibrosis is most probably one of the sequelae of atherosclerosis.

PER WESTERMARK

References

1 Klöppel G, Drenck, CR. Immunozytochemische Morphometrie beim Typ-I- und Typ-II-Diabetes mellitus. *Dtsch Med Wschr* 1983; **108**: 188–9.

2 Saito K, Yaginuma N, Takahashi T. Differential volumetry of A, B and D cells in the pancreatic islets of diabetic and nondiabetic subjects. *Tohoku J Exp Med* 1979; **129**: 273–83.

3 Stefan Y, Orci L, Malaisse-Lagae F, Perrelet A, Patel Y, Unger RH. Quantitation of endocrine cell content in the pancreas of nondiabetic and diabetic humans. *Diabetes* 1982; **31**: 694–700.

4 Westermark P, Wilander E. The influence of amyloid deposits on the islet volume in maturity onset diabetes mellitus. *Diabetologia* 1978; **15**: 417–21.

5 Rahier J, Goebbels RM, Henquin JC. Cellular composition of the human diabetic pancreas. *Diabetologia* 1983; **24**: 366–71.

6 Unger RH, Orci L. Role of glucagon in diabetes. *Arch Int Med* 1977; **137**: 482–91.

7 Opie EL. On relation of chronic interstitial pancreatitis to the islets of Langerhans and to diabetes mellitus. *J Exp Med* 1900; **5**: 397–428.

8 Gellerstedt N. Die elektive, insuläre (Para-)Amyloidose der Bauchspeicheldrüse. *Beitr Path Anat* 1938; **101**: 1–13.

9 Bell ET. Hyalinization of the islets of Langerhans in diabetes mellitus. *Diabetes* 1952; **1**: 341–4.

10 Ehrlich JC, Ratner IM. Amyloidosis of the islets of Langerhans. A restudy of islet hyalin in diabetic and nondiabetic individuals. *Am J Path* 1961; **38**: 49–59.

11 Westermark P. Quantitative studies of amyloid in the islets of Langerhans. *Uppsala J Med Sci* 1972; **77**: 91–4.

12 Clark A, Holman RR, Matthews DR, Hockaday TDR, Turner RC. Non-uniform distribution of amyloid in the pancreas of "maturity-onset" diabetic patients. *Diabetologia* 1984; **27**: 527–8.

13 Melato M, Antonutto G, Ferronato E. Amyloidosis of the islets of Langerhans in relation to diabetes mellitus and ageing. *Beitr Path* 1977; **160**: 73–81.

14 Westermark P. Fine structure of islets of Langerhans in insular amyloidosis. *Virchows Arch Path Anat* 1973; **359**: 1–18.

15 Westermark P, Grimelius L, Polak JM, Larsson L-I, van Noorden S, Wilander E, Pearse AGE. Amyloid in polypeptide hormone-producing tumors. *Lab Invest* 1977; **37**: 212–15.

16 Westermark P, Wernstedt C, Wilander E, Sletten K. A novel peptide in the calcitonin gene related peptide family as an amyloid fibril protein in the endocrine pancreas. *Biochem Biophys Res Commun* 1986; **140**: 827–31.

17 Westermark P, Wernstedt C, Wilander E, Hayden DW, O'Brien TD, Johnson KH. Amyloid fibrils in human in-

sulinoma and islets of Langerhans of the diabetic cat are derived from a novel neuropeptide-like protein also present in normal islet cells. *Proc Natl Acad Sci USA* 1987; **84**: 3881–5.

18 Westermark P, Wernstedt C, O'Brien TD, Hayden DW, Johnson KH. Islet amyloid in type 2 human diabetes mellitus and adult diabetic cats contains a novel putative polypeptide hormone. *Am J Path* 1987; **127**: 414–17.

19 Cooper GJS, Willis AC, Clark A, Turner RC, Sim RB, Reid KBM. Purification and characterization of a peptide from amyloid-rich pancreases of type 2 diabetic patients. *Proc Natl Acad Sci USA* 1987; **84**: 8628–32.

20 Westermark P, Wilander E, Westermark GT, Johnson KH. Islet amyloid polypeptide (IAPP)-like immunoreactivity in the islet B-cells of type 2-diabetic and non-diabetic individuals. *Diabetologia* 1987; **30**: 887–92.

21 Johnson KH, O'Brien TD, Hayden DW, Jordan K, Ghobrial HKG, Mahoney WC, Westermark P. Immunolocalization of islet amyloid polypeptide (IAPP) in pancreatic beta cells by means of peroxidase antiperoxidase (PAP) and protein A–gold techniques. *Am J Path* 1988; **130**: 1–8.

22 Warren S, LeCompte PM, Legg MA. *The Pathology of Diabetes Mellitus*, 4th edn. Philadelphia: Lea & Febiger, 1966.

23 Molina JM, Cooper GJS, Leighton B, Olefsky JM. Induction of insulin resistance *in vivo* by amylin and calcitonin gene-related peptide. *Diabetes* 1990; **39**: 260–5.

19 Genetics of Non-Insulin-Dependent Diabetes Mellitus

Summary

• NIDDM is one of the commoner diseases with a strong genetic component, affecting 1–2% of Caucasian races.

• An important genetic contribution to NIDDM is suggested by the very high concordance rates of the disease in monozygotic, genetically identical twins. Many of the apparently unaffected co-twins of the diabetic twins have subclinical defects in insulin secretion, sometimes with mild hyperglycaemia. Dizygotic, nonidentical twins show much lower concordance rates.

• The inheritance of NIDDM is apparently polygenic in most pedigrees. However, maturity-onset diabetes of the young (MODY) is transmitted as an autosomal dominant gene and various rare syndromes which include glucose intolerance and/or NIDDM are inherited by classical Mendelian patterns.

• Molecular biological techniques have identified the molecular lesions in certain cases of insulinopathy and of inherited insulin receptor abnormalities which cause rare NIDDM-like syndromes.

• As defects in the control of insulin secretion and in insulin sensitivity are known to occur in NIDDM, the region of the insulin gene thought to regulate insulin gene expression (in the 5' flanking region adjacent to the insulin coding sequence) and the insulin receptor gene have both been studied in NIDDM. So far, however, no link has been discovered between NIDDM and polymorphism of either the insulin or insulin receptor gene.

• In contrast to IDDM, there are no strong associations between NIDDM and HLA types in Caucasian populations. However, certain associations with HLA status have been discovered in other races, notably the complement component, C4B (an HLA class III antigen), in South Indian subjects and Bw61 in South African Indians.

It has been known for many years that diabetes runs in families but the precise genetic factors involved have remained elusive. Non-insulin-dependent diabetes mellitus (NIDDM) is one of the more common genetic diseases and affects all parts of the world, with an estimated prevalence from 1–2% in most Caucasian races to as much as 5% in some Third World countries, e.g. India. It is an important cause of morbidity and mortality in these countries. In some populations where a founder effect can be demonstrated, the prevalence of IDDM is even higher — for instance, in the inhabitants of the South Pacific island of Nauru, 83% of individuals above the age of 60 years have NIDDM compared with 17% in whom foreign gene admixture can be demonstrated by HLA-typing [1]. It is also interesting to note that in populations with a very high prevalence of NIDDM, there is a bimodal distribution of glucose tolerance (Nauru and Pima Indians), which is suggestive of a single gene defect (reviewed in [2]).

Twin studies

Twin studies have been important in proving a genetic contribution to diabetes. Early twin studies demonstrated a higher rate of concordance of diabetes presenting above the age of 40

172

years (presumably NIDDM) in monozygotic (genetically identical) twin pairs as compared with dizygotic twins (not necessarily genetically identical) [3, 4]. These studies were greatly extended by Pyke and colleagues at King's College Hospital, London [5]. In their series of 53 monozygotic twins ascertained by one twin already having NIDDM, 91% of the co-twins also had NIDDM. In many of the discordant co-twins, abnormalities of insulin secretory response can be demonstrated [6]. Thus, almost 100% of monozygotic NIDDM twins show evidence of abnormalities.

One criticism of the King's series is ascertainment bias, thereby favouring concordance of disease. A study by Newman et al. [7] overcomes this latter problem, although differences in diagnostic criteria for diabetes limit possible comparison with the King's group studies. Newman et al. screened 'white' Americans recruited to the army between 1917 and 1927 and identified 250 monozygotic and 264 dizygotic twins [7]. Diabetes in these twins was defined as a glycaemic value exceeding 13.9 mmol/l 1 h after a 50-g oral glucose challenge, or by the previous diagnosis of diabetes presenting after the age of 40; IDDM was excluded. Of both monozygotic and dizygotic twins, 28% (mean age 47 years) were concordant for diabetes at initial testing. After 10 years, 58% of 176 monozygotic, as compared with 17% of 186 dizygotic co-twins of diabetic twins, had diabetes; the expected general population prevalence of diabetes in this age-group was 10%, thus demonstrating the difference between the monozygotic and dizygotic twins and the importance of age in expression of NIDDM. In agreement with the King's group data, only one out of 15 monozygotic twins originally discordant for diabetes remained so after 10 years. Furthermore, at 10 years, 65% of the non-diabetic monozygotic co-twins of diabetic twins had mild hyperglycaemia, but not sufficient to diagnose diabetes. Lastly, in 19 out of 20 monozygotic twin pairs who were newly discordant at 10 years compared with the unaffected twins, the only predictor 10 years previously for future diabetes, was a higher 1-h glycaemic value in the former group. The only factor found to be different in the non-diabetic co-twin of the newly diagnosed diabetic twin compared to the non-diabetic monozygotic twins was a tendency to gain weight in adult life.

This highlights another dilemma in the genetics of NIDDM: could one of the genes determining NIDDM susceptibility also influence weight gain, or is obesity entirely environmentally determined?

Family studies

Many groups have demonstrated that NIDDM subjects have an increased frequency of diabetes amongst relatives when compared with the non-diabetic population. Pincus and White in 1933 examined 523 diabetic probands and found the prevalence of the disease in close relatives to be 23%, compared with 10% in comparable relatives of 153 non-diabetic probands [8]. If both parents have NIDDM, there is an increased prevalence of NIDDM in their offspring — in 164 such families in South India, 50% of offspring had diabetes and 12% impaired glucose tolerance [9]. Family studies in Caucasian subjects are beset by the possible problems of heterogeneity of the disease and its relationship to age of onset and obesity. Kobberling demonstrated that lean, as compared with obese, diabetic patients seem to have an increased familial aggregation of diabetes [10]. O'Rahilly has focused attention on the importance of early age of onset of NIDDM by studying families ascertained by identifying islet-cell antibody negative probands in whom NIDDM had been diagnosed before the age of 40 [11]. In two separate studies, 9/10 and 8/9 of the parents had either abnormal glucose tolerance or NIDDM [11]. These families may also exhibit a gene dosage effect, as the parents (presumed heterozygotes) showed a later onset of disease compared with the 69% of offspring (presumed homozygotes) who had either impaired glucose tolerance or NIDDM. The effect of gene dosage leading to earlier expression of disease could also explain the younger age of onset of NIDDM (compared to Caucasians) in ethnic groups in whom there is a high background prevalence of NIDDM.

Maturity-onset diabetes of the young (MODY)

This term defines an apparently specific subgroup of NIDDM patients presenting before the age of 25 years, in which non-insulin-requiring diabetes is transmitted vertically in affected families, consistent with autosomal dominant inheritance. MODY is apparently heterogeneous, for example with regard to the extent of complications, which were originally said to be absent [12]. The clinical features are described in detail in Chapter 25 and reference [2].

Depending on ethnic origin, the clinical presentation varies. In Caucasians, the onset is insidious and many individuals within a pedigree are only diagnosed after screening. In South Indians and Indians in South Africa, however, patients are symptomatic at diagnosis and are often treated without insulin [9]. American Black subjects present acutely and initially require insulin for glycaemic control but subsequently run a non-insulin-dependent course [13]. There is also considerable heterogeneity in insulin secretion, some families showing hyperinsulinaemia and others hypoinsulinaemia. Some rare hyperinsulinaemic families secrete a mutant insulin, with a single amino-acid substitution within the B chain (typically position 25 or 26) or the A chain (position 2), or defective cleavage of C peptide from either the A or B chain (reviewed in [14] and Chapter 30).

Thus, although MODY appears to be compatible with a single gene defect, it is likely that in different families and different ethnic groups, different genes may lead to the same diabetic syndrome. The features of MODY outlined above highlight the problems of searching for genetic markers in anything other than a single pedigree which is large enough for independent analysis. This may be why progress in identifying genetic factors in NIDDM has been so slow.

Rare genetic syndromes associated with IGT and NIDDM

NIDDM and impaired glucose tolerance (IGT) are associated with a number of rare genetic syndromes [15] (Chapter 31). They display all possible modes of inheritance (autosomal dominant, autosomal recessive, sex linked, sporadic), various degrees and progression of abnormal glucose tolerance, and a variable extent of insulin resistance. A list adapted from Rotter *et al.* [15] of genetic syndromes associated with abnormal glucose tolerance is presented in Table 19.

Table 19.1. Genetic syndromes associated with abnormal glucose tolerance. (Adapted from Rotter *et al.* [15].)

	Autosomal dominant	Autosomal recessive	X-linked	Sporadic

IGT	Phaeochromocytoma
	Multiple endocrine
	  neoplasia
	Acute intermittent
	  porphyria
	Steroid-induced
	  ocular hypertension
		Alpha$_1$−antitrypsin
		  deficiency
		Achondroplastic
		  dwarfism
		Von Gierke's disease
				Down's syndrome

IGT → NIDDM	Myotonic dystrophy Muscular dystrophies Huntington's chorea Hyperlipidaemias	Ataxia telangectasia Thalassaemia Muscular dystrophy	Muscular dystrophy	Klinefelter's syndrome Turner's syndrome Down's syndrome

NIDDM	Lipoatropic diabetes
	  syndromes
	Acanthosis nigricans
	Haemochromatosis
	Isolated growth
	  hormone deficiency
	Machado disease
	Hermann's syndrome
	Friedreich's syndrome
	Pseudo-Refsum's
	  disease
	Prader−Willi syndrome
		Lipoatropic diabetes
		  syndromes
		Leprechaunism
		Fanconi's syndrome
		  hypophosphataemia
		Isolated growth
		  hormone deficiency
		Hereditary
		  panhypopituitary
		  dwarfism
		Laron dwarfism
		Alström syndrome
		Laurence−Moon−
		  Biedl syndrome
		Werner's syndrome
			Hereditary
			  panhypopituitary
			  dwarfism	

Key: IGT, impaired glucose tolerance; NIDDM, non-insulin-dependent diabetes; IGT → NIDDM, IGT progressing to NIDDM.

Markers for NIDDM

Molecular genetic studies in NIDDM have so far been disappointing in elucidating the factors involved in its pathogenesis. The most widely studied genes have been those for insulin and the insulin receptor.

The insulin gene

The insulin gene is located on the short arm of chromosome 11, situated between the insulin-like growth factor 2 (IGF-2) gene and the Harvey ras oncogene (Fig. 19) [16]. The insulin gene is 1355 base pairs in length, comprising three coding regions (exons) specifying the mRNA transcript: a ribosomal binding sequence (exon 1), the start codon (exon 2), B chain (exon 2), C peptide (exons 2 and 3), the A chain (exon 3), the stop codon (exon 3) and the polyadenylation site (3' flanking region) [17]. In the 5' flanking region, up to 258 base pairs (−258) from the first codon are sequences shown to be important for gene regulation, in particular at −25 the Grunstein–Hogress box (TATAA box) and at −50 the CAAT sequence [17, 18]. At −363, is the hypervariable (polymorphic) region adjacent to the insulin gene. It is comprised of a 14-base-pair consensus sequence of ACAGGGTCTGGGG, tandemly repeated [19].

The number of repeats determines the length of the region which in black populations has a trimodal distribution, on average possessing 40 (class 1 allele), 80 (class 2 allele) or 160 (class 3) repeated sequences [19, 20]. The frequency of alleles at this locus differs in various parts of the world, with the class 2 allele hardly ever found in Caucasian, Asian and Oriental populations [21–5], whereas the class 3 allele is more commonly found in Caucasian populations [21].

Studies so far have identified the molecular basis of mutant insulins and have examined the possible associations of the polymorphic 5' flanking region with NIDDM.

MUTATIONS WITHIN THE INSULIN CODING REGION (INSULINOPATHIES)

As described in Chapter 30, a number of point mutations have been described within the coding regions of the insulin gene which are associated with hyperinsulinaemia and either IGT or NIDDM [14].

STUDIES USING THE HYPERVARIABLE REGION AS A GENETIC MARKER

These have examined possible associations in populations and in family pedigrees.

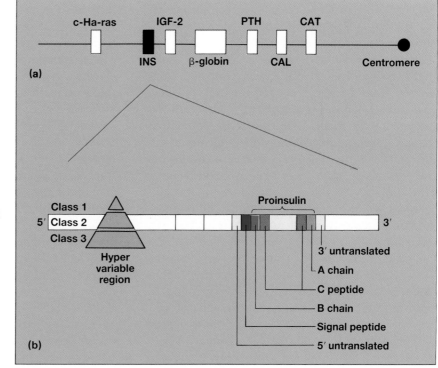

Fig. 19.1. Chromosomal location and details of the insulin gene. Key: (a) Short arm of chromosome 11. INS = insulin gene; IGF-2 = insulin-like growth factor 2; β-globin = β-globin gene cluster; PTH = parathyroid hormone gene; CAL = calcitonin/calcitonin-gene-related protein gene; CAT = catalase gene. (b) Insulin gene and 5' flanking region. Coloured areas represent coding regions.

Population studies. The hypervariable region can be studied using Southern blot hybridization techniques and the use of a radioactive probe complementary to the hypervariable region itself or the insulin gene, in conjunction with restriction enzymes which cut on either side of the hypervariable region.

A possible association of the class 3 allele with NIDDM has proved highly controversial. Studies showing such an association include those of Danish Caucasians [21], British Caucasians [26], Japanese subjects [24, 25], American Caucasians in San Francisco [27] and Dravidians in South India [23]. However, no association has been found in Pima Indians [28], Punjabi Sikhs [22], Nauruan Indians [1] or Black Americans [20]. Finally, one study of American Caucasians in Los Angeles revealed a weak association with the class 1 allele [29]. These divergences could have several explanations, which are not necessarily mutually exclusive:

1 The various studies represent random variations of the marker between the populations studied and thus there is no association of the hypervariable region with NIDDM.

2 NIDDM differs in aetiology between the populations studied.

3 The hypervariable region is not associated primarily with NIDDM, but with a complication or associated disorder of the disease. For instance, the various studies might differ by the number of NIDDM subjects who have diabetic complications. Jowett *et al.* [30] proposed that the primary association was with the combination of diabetes and hypertriglyceridaemia, on the basis that a much higher proportion of individuals with both conditions were homozygous for the class 3 allele than other subject groups [30]. Although an interesting observation, it should be noted that insulin genotype distribution does not differ significantly within diabetic subjects according to the presence or absence of hypertriglyceridaemia. Furthermore, no other groups have found differences within diabetic populations, although all studies suffer with small number biases [24, 31]. An alternate proposal by Mandrup-Poulsen and colleagues was that the primary association was with atherosclerosis, as significantly higher frequencies of the class 3 allele were found in both NIDDM [31] and non-diabetic subjects [31, 32] who had clinical evidence of atherosclerosis [31] or angiographically proven coronary artery disease [32], as compared with controls without

atherosclerosis. However, in a similar coronary angiographically based study by Rees *et al.* [33], these observations were not confirmed.

4 The hypervariable region is linked to a diabetes susceptibility gene only in certain ethnic groups. This might be similar to a 3'-flanking region Hpa I beta-globin polymorphism which is in linkage with the sickle mutation in the beta-globin gene in West but not East Africans [34]. The aetiology of disease in East and West Africa is the same — a single nucleotide substitution (valine for glutamine at position 6) in the beta-globin molecule. It cannot be concluded that, simply because the 3' Hpa I polymorphism is not associated with sickle-cell anaemia in East Africans, the beta-globin gene has nothing to do with the sickle mutation, or that the cause of sickle-cell anaemia differs between East and West Africans. A similar situation with respect to the hypervariable region on chromosome 11 might apply to a gene predisposing to NIDDM. The 'linked' gene in NIDDM might be the insulin gene locus (mutations within the gene regulatory or coding regions) or another gene (as yet unidentified but in close proximity to the insulin gene) which might be involved in some aspect of B-cell metabolism or insulin secretion. Thus, in the population groups not showing an association of NIDDM with the hypervariable gene, the same diabetes susceptibility gene may be located on chromosome 11.

5 The insulin gene association is one of many factors in a multifactorial disease. This can be partly investigated by seeking associations of the hypervariable region with diabetes secondary to a well-defined environmental factor, such as the elevated growth hormone levels of acromegaly or the pancreatic disease leading to fibrocalculous pancreatic diabetes (FCPD) (Chapter 26). Recent studies in these two conditions suggest that abnormal glucose tolerance was associated with homozygosity for the class 1 allele in British Caucasian acromegalic patients [35] and possession of the class 3 allele in South Indian (Dravidian) subjects with FCPD. Although relatively small-scale, these findings suggest that individuals with a genetic predisposition related to the insulin gene will develop abnormal glucose handling in these two causes of secondary diabetes.

Pedigree studies. Many large MODY families have been studied, and all agree that there is no linkage of the hypervariable region with this type of diabetes [36–8]. In families more typical of NIDDM, similar negative results have been obtained [26, 39]. Successful linkage analysis requires three-generation families in which diabetes segregates in all generations. As this condition is not commonly met in NIDDM, there must be doubt as to how representative the families so far studied are of NIDDM. Moreover, most family studies have assumed a single-gene, autosomal dominant mode of inheritance; the increasing likelihood that NIDDM is a polygenic disease would further limit the general applicability of the conclusions from pedigree analysis.

The insulin receptor gene

The insulin receptor gene, located on chromosome 19 [40−42], encodes a protein of 1370 amino acids, corresponding to the alpha-subunit and the beta-subunit (including the transmembrane domain and the tyrosine kinase domain) (Fig. 19.2 and

Chapter 11). The insulin receptor promoter region does not possess the TATAA and CAAT boxes but instead shares a promoter region in common with other 'housekeeping' and 'growth control' genes such as those for the epidermal growth factor receptor and hydroxymethylglutaryl co-enzyme A reductase.

MUTATIONS AFFECTING THE INSULIN RECEPTOR GENE

At the time of writing, three insulin receptor mutations have been described, all associated with diabetes and Type A insulin resistance (see Chapter 29). In one family described by Yoshimasa and colleagues [43], the propositus had severe insulin resistance, NIDDM, acanthosis nigricans, hirsutism, virilization, mental retardation, short stature and dental dysplasia. The patient was able to synthesize a normal insulin

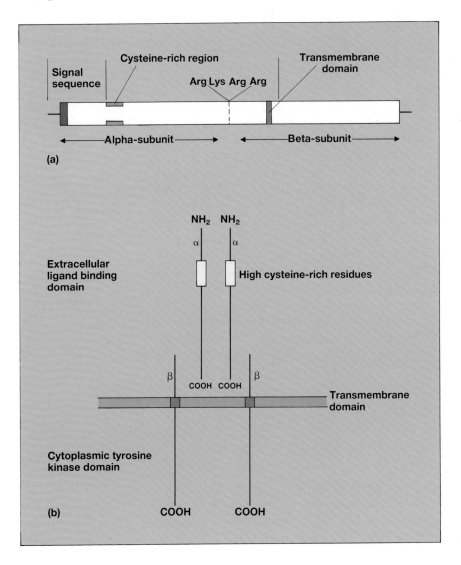

Fig. 19.2. The insulin receptor. (a) Insulin receptor gene (cDNA). (b) Schematic diagram of insulin receptor protein. (Redrawn with permission from Ebina *et al.* [41].)

receptor which was inserted into the plasma membrane, but failed to cleave the alpha and beta subunits because of a single nucleotide substitution (codon 735: AGG to AG*T*) causing a single amino-acid substitution (from Arg-Lys-Arg-*Arg* to Arg-Lys-Arg-*Ser*), which blocked the proteolytic cleavage site.

In a second subject with leprechaunism, extreme insulin resistance and NIDDM, Kadowaki *et al.* [44] identified eight mutations in the insulin receptor gene sequence. Six of these would not alter the amino-acid sequence, but one nonsense mutation would prematurely terminate transcription of the alpha-subunit and delete both the transmembrane and tyrosine kinase domains of the beta-subunit. The subject's father was heterozygous for the truncation mutation and had impaired glucose tolerance and moderate insulin resistance comparable with that in NIDDM or obesity. The authors postulated that heterozygosity for this mutation might account for a subgroup of insulin-resistant NIDDM subjects.

ASSOCIATION AND LINKAGE STUDIES

Population studies in British Caucasians [22], Punjabi Sikhs [22], Dravidian [23] and Japanese subjects [45], have not yet shown an association of insulin receptor polymorphisms with NIDDM. In a study of four NIDDM families by Elbein *et al.* [46] no linkage was demonstrated between insulin receptor polymorphisms and NIDDM. However, in two specific families (which because of their small size did not significantly influence the overall linkage analysis), an Sst I (isoschizomer of Sac I) polymorphism segregated with the diabetic subjects. Analysis of this polymorphism revealed it to be a 500-base-pair insertion in the B chain. If linkage of the insulin receptor Sst polymorphism is substantiated in larger pedigrees or population studies, it would support the contention of genetic heterogeneity in the aetiology of NIDDM.

Other genes

ERYTHROCYTE GLUCOSE TRANSPORTER GENE

An association of polymorphism of the erythrocyte glucose transporter gene with NIDDM is controversial [47, 48]. Studies using the insulin-sensitive glucose transporter are in progress.

HLA GENES

In contrast to the strong HLA associations in IDDM, there are only weak links with NIDDM in some ethnic groups, and none have yet been identified in Caucasian races. In Dravidian (South Indian) subjects, an association of NIDDM was found with the fourth component of complement (a decrease of C4B1 and an increase of C4B2) [49]. In South African Indians, HLA-Bw61 was significantly more frequent in NIDDM than in non-diabetic subjects [50]. A similar Bw61 association has also been seen in Indian NIDDM subjects living in Fiji [51].

Conclusions

Given the clear demonstration that NIDDM is a genetic disease, it is disappointing that the search for genetic markers has not so far been as successful as in IDDM. The various associations described with genes for insulin, insulin receptor, glucose transporter and the HLA antigens point to heterogeneity within NIDDM and also highlight the difficulty of performing satisfactory population-based studies; in the words of Professor Jerome Rotter 'the genetics of diabetes is no longer a nightmare but still a headache' [52].

GRAHAM A. HITMAN

References

1 Serjeantson SW, Owerbach D, Zimmet P, Nerup J, Thomas K. Genetics of diabetes in Nauru: effects of foreign admixture, HLA antigens and the insulin gene linked polymorphism. *Diabetologia* 1983; **25**: 13−17.

2 Fajans SS. MODY — a model for understanding the pathogenesis and natural history of Type II diabetes. In: *Hormone Metabol Res.* 1987; **19**: 591−9.

3 Then Berg H. The genetic aspect of diabetes mellitus. *JAMA.* 1939; **112**: 1091.

4 Gottlieb MS, Root HF. Diabetes mellitus in twins. *Diabetes* 1968; **17**: 693−704.

5 Barnett AH, Eff C, Leslie RDG, Pyke DA. Diabetes in identical twins. *Diabetologia* 1981; **20**: 87−93.

6 Heaton DA, Millward BA, Gray P *et al.* Evidence of β-cell dysfunction which does not lead on to diabetes: a study of identical twins with insulin dependent diabetes. *Br Med J* 1987; **294**: 145−6.

7 Newman B, Selby JV, King MC, Slemenda C, Fabsitz R, Friedman GD. Concordance for Type 2 (non-insulin-dependent) diabetes mellitus in male twins. *Diabetologia* 1987; **30**: 763−8.

8 Pincus G, White P. On the inheritance of diabetes mellitus. *Am J Med Sci* 1933; **186**: 1−14.

9 Viswanathan M, Mohan V, Snehalatha C, Ramachandran

A. High prevalence of Type 2 (non-insulin-dependent) diabetes among the offspring of conjugal type 2 diabetic parents in India. *Diabetologia* 1985; **28**: 907–10.

10 Kobberling J. Studies on the genetic heterogeneity of diabetes mellitus. *Diabetologia* 1971; **7**: 46–9.

11 O'Rahilly S, Spivey RS, Holman RR, Nugent Z, Clark A, Turner RC. Type II diabetes of early onset: a distinct clinical and genetic syndrome. *Br Med J* 1987; **294**: 923–8.

12 Tattersall RB. Mild familial diabetes with dominant inheritance. *Q J Med* 1974; **70**: 339–57.

13 Winter WE, Maclaren NK, Riley W, Clarke DW, Kappy MS, Spillar RP. Maturity-onset diabetes of youth in Black Americans. *N Engl J Med* 1987; **316**: 285–91.

14 Gabay KH. The insulinopathies. *N Engl J Med* 1980; **302**: 165–7.

15 Rotter JI, Anderson CE, Rimoin DL. Genetics of diabetes mellitus. In: Ellenberg M, Rifkin H, eds. *Diabetes Mellitus; Theory and Practice*, 3rd edn. New York: Medical Examination Publishing Co., 1983.

16 Bell GI, Gerhard DS, Fong NF, Sanchez-Pescador R, Rall LB. Isolation of the human insulin-like growth factor genes: insulin-like growth factor II and insulin genes are contiguous. *Proc Natl Acad Sci USA* 1985; **82**: 6450–54.

17 Bell GI, Pictet RL, Rutter WJ, Cordell B, Tischer E, Goodman HM. Sequence of the human insulin gene. *Nature* 1980; **284**: 26–32.

18 Walker MD, Edlund T, Boulet AM, Rutter WJ. Cell specific expression controlled by the 5'-flanking region of insulin and chymotrypsin genes. *Nature* 1983; **306**: 557–61.

19 Bell GI, Karam JH, Rotter WJ. Polymorphic DNA region adjacent to the 5' end of the human insulin gene. *Proc Natl Acad Sci USA* 1981; **78**: 5759–63.

20 Elbein S, Rotwein P, Permutt MA, Bell GI, Sanz N, Karam JH. Lack of association of the polymorphic locus in the 5' flanking region of the human insulin gene and diabetes in American blacks. *Diabetes* 1985; **5**: 433–9.

21 Owerbach D, Nerup J. Restriction fragment length polymorphism of the insulin gene in diabetes mellitus. *Diabetes* 1982; **31**: 275–7.

22 Hitman GA, Karir PK, Mohan V *et al*. A genetic analysis of Type 2 (non-insulin-dependent) diabetes mellitus in Punjabi Sikhs and British Caucasoid patients. *Diabetic Med* 1987; **4**: 526–30.

23 Kambo PK, Hitman GA, Mohan V *et al*. The genetic predisposition to fibrocalculous pancreatic diabetes. *Diabetologia* 1989; **32**: 45–51.

24 Nomura M, Iwama N, Mukai M *et al*. High frequency of Class 3 allele in the human insulin gene in Japanese Type 2 (non-insulin-dependent) diabetic patients with a family history of diabetes. *Diabetologia* 1986; **29**: 402–4.

25 Awata T, Shibasaki Y, Hirai H, Okabe T, Kanazawa Y, Takaku F. Restriction fragment length polymorphism of the insulin gene in Japanese diabetic and non-diabetic subjects. *Diabetologia* 1986; **28**: 911–13.

26 Hitman GA, Jowett NI, Williams LG, Humphries S, Winter RM, Galton DJ. Polymorphisms in the 5' flanking region of the insulin gene and non-insulin-dependent diabetes. *Clin Sci* 1984; **66**: 383–8.

27 Rotwein PS, Chirgwin J, Province M *et al*. Polymorphism in the 5' flanking region of the human insulin gene: a genetic marker for non-insulin-dependent diabetes mellitus. *N Engl J Med* 1983; **308**: 65–71.

28 Knowler WC, Pettitt DJ, Vasquez B, Rotwein P, Andreone TL, Permutt MA. Polymorphism in the 5' flanking region of the human insulin gene. Relationships with non-insulin-dependent diabetes mellitus, glucose and insulin concentrations and diabetes in Pima Indians. *J Clin Invest* 1984; **74**: 2129–35.

29 Bell GI, Horita S, Karam JH. A highly polymorphic locus near the human insulin gene is associated with insulin-dependent diabetes mellitus. *Diabetes* 1984; **33**: 176–83.

30 Jowett NI, Williams LG, Hitman GA, Galton DJ. Diabetic hypertriglyceridaemia and related 5' flanking polymorphism of the human insulin gene. *Br Med J* 1984; **288**: 96–9.

31 Mandrup-Poulsen T, Owerbach D, Nerup J *et al*. Insulin gene flanking sequences, diabetes mellitus and atherosclerosis: a review. *Diabetologia* 1985; **28**: 556–64.

32 Mandrup-Poulsen T, Owerbach D, Mortensen SA, Johansen K, Meinertz-Sorensen H, Nerup J. DNA sequences flanking the insulin gene on chromosome 11 confer risk of atherosclerosis. *Lancet* 1984; i: 253–5.

33 Rees A, Stocks J, Williams LG *et al*. DNA polymorphisms of the Apo CIII and insulin genes and atherosclerosis. *Atherosclerosis* 1985; **58**: 266–75.

34 Kan YW, Dozy AM. Evolution of the haemoglobin S and C genes in world populations. *Science* 1980; **209**: 388–91.

35 Hitman GA, Katz J, Lytras N *et al*. Are there genetic determinants for the glucose intolerance of acromegaly? *Clin Endocrinol* 1985; **23**: 817–22.

36 Bell JI, Wainscoat JS, Old JM *et al*. Maturity onset diabetes of the young is not linked to the insulin gene. *Br Med J* 1983: **286**: 590–2.

37 Andreone T, Fajan S, Rotwein P, Skolnick M, Permutt MA. Insulin gene analysis in a family with maturity-onset diabetes of the young. *Diabetes* 1985; **34**: 108–14.

38 Owerbach D, Thomsen B, Johansen K, Lamm LU, Nerup J. DNA insertion sequences near the insulin gene are not associated with maturity-onset diabetes of young people. *Diabetologia* 1983; **25**: 18–20.

39 Elbein SC, Corsetti L, Goldgar D, Skolnick M, Permutt MA. Insulin gene in familial NIDDM: lack of linkage in Utah Mormon pedigrees. *Diabetes* 1988; **37**: 569–76.

40 Ullrich A, Bell JR, Chen EY *et al*. Human insulin receptor and its relationship to the tyrosine kinase family of oncogenes. *Nature* 1985; **313**: 756–61.

41 Ebina Y, Ellis C, Jarnagin K *et al*. The human insulin-receptor cDNA: the structural basis for hormone-activated transmembrane signalling. *Cell* 1985; **40**: 747–58.

42 Straus DS, Pang KJ, Dull FC, Jacobs S, Mohandas T. Human insulin receptor gene: data supporting assignment to chromosome 19. *Diabetes* 1985; **34**: 816–20.

43 Yoshimasa Y, Seino S, Whittaker J *et al*. Insulin-resistant diabetes due to a point mutation prevents insulin pro-receptor processing. *Science* 1980; **240**: 784–7.

44 Kadowaki T, Bevins CL, Cama A *et al*. Two mutant alleles of the insulin receptor gene in a patient with extreme insulin resistance. *Science* 1988; **240**: 787–90.

45 Takeda J, Seino Y, Yoshimasa Y *et al*. Restriction fragment length polymorphism (RFLP) of the human insulin receptor gene in Japanese: its possible usefulness as a genetic marker. *Diabetologia* 1986; **29**: 667–9.

46 Elbein SC, Borecki I, Corsetti L *et al*. Linkage analysis of the human insulin receptor gene and maturity onset diabetes of the young. *Diabetologia* 1987; **30**: 641–7.

47 Li SR, Baroni MG, Oelbgum RS *et al*. Association of genetic variant of the glucose transporter with non-insulin dependent diabetes. *Lancet* 1988; ii: 368–70.

48 Cox NJ, Xiang K, Bell GI. Glucose transporter gene and non-insulin dependent diabetes. *Lancet* 1988; ii: 793–4.

49 Kirk RL, Ranford IR, Serjeantson SW *et al*. HLA complement C2, C4, properdin factor B and glyoxalase types in

South Indian diabetics. *Diabetes Res Clin Pract* 1985; **1**: 41−7.

50 Omar MAK, Hanmon MG, Motala AA, Seedaf MA. HLA Class I and II antigens in South African Indians with NIDDM. *Diabetes* 1988; **37**: 796−9.

51 Serjeantson SW, Ryan DP, Ram P, Zimmet P. HLA and non-insulin dependent diabetes in Fiji Indians. *Med J Austral* 1981; **1**: 462−3.

52 Keen H. The genetics of diabetes: from nightmare to head-ache. *Br Med J* 1987; **294**: 917−18.

20 Obesity, Body Fat Distribution and Diet in the Aetiology of Non-Insulin-Dependent Diabetes Mellitus

Summary

• NIDDM is primarily a disease of excessive nutrient storage, compounded by insulin deficiency.

• NIDDM is strongly associated with obesity; the risks of developing NIDDM increase progressively with rising body-mass index, with an added risk from high waist/hip ratio indicating central fat deposition. Insulin resistance associated with obesity may demand excessive insulin secretion and contribute to B-cell exhaustion.

• The tendency to obesity is partly inherited but its development depends on environmental factors such as food availability and cultural influences.

• Total energy expenditure is increased in overweight people although diet-induced thermogenesis may be relatively reduced in some individuals.

• A central body fat distribution, with a high waist/hip ratio and an 'android' or 'apple-shaped' habitus, is associated with insulin resistance, NIDDM, hyperlipidaemia and premature mortality. A peripheral ('gynoid' or 'pear-shaped') distribution with a lower waist/hip ratio is found in individuals who exercise and does not carry these disease associations.

• A Western-style, high-fat, low-carbohydrate, low-fibre diet predisposes to obesity and is associated with NIDDM; the dietary factors responsible have complex interactions.

• Dietary sugar does not uniquely cause obesity or NIDDM but in large amounts can aggravate hyperglycaemia in decompensated diabetes.

• Soluble dietary fibre (e.g. pectin and guar) and insoluble fibre (e.g. bran) both tend to lower blood glucose concentrations. Soluble fibre is partially fermented and absorbed and may delay nutrient absorption; insoluble fibre is less absorbed and increases stool bulk.

• Exercise may protect against NIDDM as well as increasing energy expenditure and so opposing weight gain.

• Deficiencies of chromium or copper have been postulated to cause NIDDM but are likely to account for only a very small proportion of cases.

The syndrome of NIDDM probably encompasses several heterogeneous conditions caused by variable interactions between genetic and environmental factors. The major association between NIDDM and obesity has been recognized for centuries, but its specific basis is still incompletely understood. There are also strong epidemiological links between NIDDM and obesity and a 'Westernized' lifestyle, which includes a diet generally lower in fibre-rich complex carbohydrate and higher in fat than traditional diets. However, not all those who are obese or who have diets suspected to be 'diabetogenic' will develop NIDDM and, conversely, it remains possible that for some people a genetic susceptibility alone is sufficient to lead to NIDDM, irrespective of their diet.

The contribution of genetic components to NIDDM is described in Chapter 19. This chapter discusses some of the dietary factors which are thought to be important in the pathogenesis of NIDDM, and the relationship of generalized obesity and a central (abdominal) pattern of body fat distribution to the condition.

Overweight and obesity

Overweight and obesity are lay terms which denote increased body fat content above a defined normal, ideal or standard range. These terms do not apply to an elevation of muscle bulk, for example in manual workers or in athletes. There is no specific definition or diagnostic criterion for 'obesity', a word whose etymology implies over-eating. Two measurements of body weight and fat content are commonly used in clinical practice:

Body-mass index (BMI), or 'Quetelet index'

BMI is derived from body weight in kilograms divided by the square of height in metres (kg/m^2). A desirable BMI for the general population lies between 19–25 [1] but the lower part of this range may be preferable for diabetic subjects (Table 20.1).

Body fat content

The simplest estimation is by measuring skinfold thicknesses at four sites (biceps, triceps, sub-scapular and suprailiac) using a spring-loaded caliper and then applying the published equations derived from underwater densitometric measurements (Table 20.1) as standards [2]. Normal body fat content is 10–20% of body weight for men and 20–30% for women (Table 20.1). In diabetic subjects, centralized fat distribution (see below) will lead to some underestimation of total body fat content from subcutaneous skinfold measurements and severe obesity can also invalidate these calculations; separate equations may be required in these populations.

Energy balance and the metabolic aetiology of obesity

Energy stores — largely in the form of body fat — must represent the difference which has accrued over a period of time between energy intake and energy expenditure. The fact that the overweight constantly deny that they overeat has stimulated many searches for metabolic defects, particularly reduced metabolic rate, as a cause for obesity. Becoming and maintaining overweight involves complex psychological and social adaptations;

Table 20.1. Acceptable values for BMI (kg/m^2), composition and waist/hip ratio in the general population.

	Men	Women
BMI (kg/m^2)	20–25	19–24
% Body fat*	10–20%	20–30%
Waist/hip ratio†	0.8–1.0	0.7–0.85

Notes:
Desirable figures for diabetic subjects may be in the lower part of these ranges.
* Body fat content may be estimated from four skinfold thicknesses (biceps, triceps, subscapular, suprailiac) using the equations of Durnin and Womersley 1974 [2].
% Fat = (4.95/density − 4.50) × 100.
Density = $c − m ×$ log(sum of four skinfolds, in cm).

	Age (years)			
	20–9	30–9	40–9	>50
Men:				
c	1.1631	1.1422	1.1620	1.1715
m	0.0632	0.0544	0.0700	0.0779
Women:				
c	1.1599	1.1423	1.1333	1.1339
m	0.0678	0.0717	0.0612	0.0645

† See text for method of measurement.

there are also clear indications of genetic factors and these can only become manifest by altering metabolic processes. The general considerations regarding the aetiology of simple obesity described in this section probably also apply to the overweight NIDDM subject, and there may be aetiological links between the metabolic and genetic bases for NIDDM and overweight.

Is a genetic defect responsible for metabolic obesity?

Studies of populations, families, twins and adopted siblings indicate a high 'heritability' of overweight, of about 0.8 [3]. This figure should be compared with a heritability of about 0.5 for ischaemic heart disease, which is commonly considered to have an important genetic component. Clearly, the genetic basis for obesity is complex, being polygenic rather than a single gene defect, and ultimately is dependent on food availability. A simple conceptual model has been proposed for the genetic and environmental factors which determine continuously distributed variables in populations [4]:

$$V_P = V_G + V_E + V_{G×E} + e,$$

where variance (V) in the phenotype (P, in this case fatness) is determined by purely genetic (G) variance, purely environmental (E) variance and also by an interaction term (G×E). (The error variance (e) is assumed to be zero.) This analysis emphasizes that different individuals can respond differently to environmental conditions, and the possible links between specific environmental (or dietary) factors which are responsible for weight gain in people genetically predisposed to obesity.

The genetic defects underlying simple obesity and overweight with NIDDM in man are complex and have only been elucidated in a few rare inherited syndromes (see Chapter 31). An interesting model for overweight with NIDDM is the Prader–Willi syndrome, in which both metabolic abnormalities are apparently due to a defect of chromosome 15, commonly a translocation [5]. The mechanisms through which such genetic defects — and those of the animal models of obesity and NIDDM (see Chapter 24) — influence the regulation of energy expenditure or food intake are still unknown but may ultimately shed some light on the biochemical basis of the more common forms of these conditions.

Altered energy balance in obesity

From first principles of energy balance (Fig. 20.1), increased fat stores in the overweight can only have derived from excess energy intake above energy expenditure at some time. Energy is stored mainly as fat, and the total body energy stores can be estimated simply by assuming that adipose tissue contains 75% lipid. Overweight subjects have therefore stored approximately 7000 kcal per kg excess weight; for example, a man of 1.75 m who weighs 87 kg (20 kg overweight) has accumulated an excess of about 140 000 kcal.

A search for metabolic defects causing overweight is obviously justifiable, but much effort has been wasted in studying overweight subjects, in whom any abnormalities are more likely to be secondary to obesity rather than its cause. Negative findings may also be misleading. To elucidate the metabolic factors which underlie weight gain, it is therefore necessary to study subjects known to be prone to overweight, i.e. either before they gain weight or after slimming ('post-obese').

When weight is steady at any level, energy intake must equal energy expenditure (or metabolic rate). The latter can be measured accurately by indirect calorimetry. As BMR accounts for

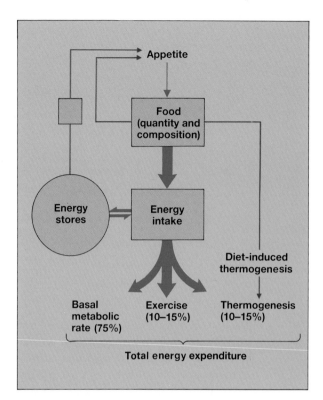

Fig. 20.1. A schematic flow-chart of energy balance. At stable weight, total energy intake must equal total energy expenditure. Appetite is altered by food intake and may be modulated by changes in body weight or energy stores so as to maintain a 'set-point' weight. Food composition as well as quantity may modify energy expenditure through diet-induced thermogenesis.

about 70–75% of total energy expenditure, it seems reasonable to consider this component first for variations in metabolism which could lead to weight gain; there is less scope to improve efficiency (i.e. increase storage) in other aspects of energy expenditure, such as physical activity, or the thermogenic responses to feeding and other stimuli, but it must be remembered that weight gain leading to obesity is generally slow and sometimes barely perceptible. Weight gain of 2 kg/ year, totalling 40 kg in 20 years, represents an imbalance of only 2% in energy balance. Defects of this order are extremely difficult to detect even with sophisticated modern equipment.

The conclusion of many energy balance studies is that individuals prone to weight gain do not have detectably reduced metabolic rates overall. Indeed, the obese have considerably *increased* energy expenditure, in direct proportion to their greater body weight [6–9] (Fig. 20.2). Since their metabolic rate is increased, the overweight must consume more energy than thin people, if their

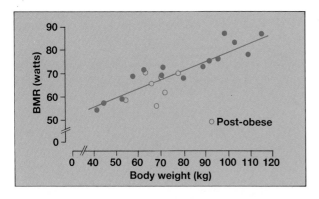

Fig. 20.2. Energy expenditure is greater in the overweight. The correlation between energy expenditure and body weight also applies to 'post-obese' subjects (open circles) who have slimmed from BMI>30 to <25 kg/m². Data from Lean & James 1988 [8].

body weight is to remain steady. Whether or not the primary genetic and metabolic defect acts to produce overeating (primary hyperphagia), there *must* be increased appetite at least as a secondary mechanism to maintain overweight and prevent weight loss. It has been postulated from twin studies that appetite and food selection are under direct genetic control [10] but this is unlikely to be a major factor.

Are BMR or diet-induced thermogenesis reduced in obesity?

Although obesity is not attributable to reduced metabolism in absolute terms, it has been suggested from adult twin studies that BMR may still be under genetic influence to a degree, and related to the long-term risks of weight gain [11]. This work is open to criticism in that BMR may have been initially suppressed in obesity-prone individuals if they were in fact 'restrained eaters', although a small-scale study in infants reached the similar conclusion that babies with lower energy expenditures tended to gain more weight subsequently [12]. This issue is unresolved.

At least certain subgroups of overweight subjects have reduced 'thermogenesis' (metabolic heat production) in response to feeding and other stimuli. One group of obese women, studied using whole-body indirect calorimetry, showed diet-induced thermogenesis (from eating three meals) amounting to 9% of total daily energy expenditure, compared with 15% in lean controls, even though BMR and total 24-h energy expenditure were substantially greater in the obese [7]. The importance

of this finding is that, if diet-induced thermogenesis were reduced in obesity-prone subjects before weight gain, then total daily energy expenditure would also be subnormal. Weight gain would therefore occur if the obesity-prone ate the same diet as controls. Other indirect calorimetry data using glucose loads [13], formula feeds [14] and mixed meals [8, 15] all suggest reduced diet-induced thermogenesis in groups of 'post-obese' (slimmed) subjects, perhaps particularly in response to dietary carbohydrates.

The association between high-fat, low-carbohydrate diets and overweight has been established from epidemiological studies, both between and more recently within populations [16]. A current hypothesis is that this may reflect a propensity, inherited by a proportion of the population, for a low carbohydrate intake to cause exaggerated suppression of metabolic rate (a gene−nutrient interaction) and thus weight gain [15].

Is thermogenesis impaired in NIDDM?

In addition to alterations in diet-induced thermogenesis, some overweight NIDDM subjects appear to have an impaired thermogenic response during exposure to mild cold, showing a highly abnormal fall in metabolic rate instead of the normal physiological increase [17]. The normal increases in circulating TSH and T_3 concentrations evoked by mild cold were also absent in these patients, possibly reflecting a generalized defect in the sympathetic regulation of metabolic rate. This situation is strikingly similar to the thermogenic defect of congenitally obese and diabetic rodents, in which the main site of thermogenesis is brown adipose tissue. Humans possess brown adipose tissue with identical functional potential [18]. Its role in overall energy balance in adults is probably small under most conditions, but subtle alterations in its activity could contribute to the small percentage changes in energy expenditure which could ultimately produce obesity. Another theoretical possibility for increasing energetic efficiency, as yet untested, is that metabolic rate may be suppressed further during periods of relative energy deficiency or starvation. Such energy-saving mechanisms may contribute to weight gain, but will have to be demonstrated in subjects before weight gain or after slimming.

Once diabetes has developed, metabolic rate is actually increased until hyperglycaemia has been corrected, irrespective of any weight change [19, 20]. This phenomenon explains to some degree the weight gain of diabetic patients when treatment is established, which is not entirely attributable to reduced glycosuria.

Estimating energy requirements

Changes in body weight and metabolic rate can be serious confounding factors in metabolic research, and energy balance is difficult to evaluate in clinical practice. Regardless of the underlying aetiology of weight gain, and for reasons which are still obscure, the overweight tend consistently to underestimate their food intake [6] and dietary recall is inadequate even in lean and highly intelligent young subjects [9]. The true dietary composition cannot therefore be reliably calculated by any current dietetic technique. The daily energy requirement of individuals is best estimated using standard formulae derived from metabolic rate measurements [21] (Table 20.2). These predictions have coefficients of variation of about 8%, which make them the most accurate practical approach for diet prescription, particularly for use in clinical research [9] (see Chapter 47).

Overweight as a cause of NIDDM

Epidemiological evidence

In Britain, about 75% of NIDDM patients are overweight (BMI >25 kg/m^2) [22] compared with a prevalence of 40−50% in the general population of comparable age [23]. The proportion of the population who will ultimately develop NIDDM has been estimated at 10−30% in different populations. There may be a contribution from ageing

itself (see Chapter 89), but much of the risk of NIDDM is attributed to Western-style acculturation and overweight [24−6]. Under 'primitive' conditions in many parts of the world, diabetes is rare but its prevalence rises to about 25% in some Asian groups and reaches 40% in Nauruans [27] and Pima Indians [25, 28]. In other obesity-prone populations such as Polynesians, there appears to be some protection from NIDDM until Western acculturation occurs [29].

There has been debate as to whether NIDDM is associated only with gross obesity or whether its frequency rises in proportion to the degree of overweight. The early but somewhat incomplete data of Joslin [30] from 1000 cases of diabetes suggest an increasing likelihood of diabetes with quite moderate overweight, a conclusion also reached in a male Norwegian population [31]. These studies could have been biased by under-reporting of diabetes in thinner people, but they are supported by the epidemiological studies of West [26] who found that the prevalence of NIDDM was closely associated with average body weight in different populations. More systematic screening studies have shown the same relationship in the Pima Indians [28]. In Israelis, on the other hand, little increase in the prevalence of NIDDM was found until BMI exceeded 31 kg/m^2, although in the same population impaired glucose tolerance (IGT) increased steadily with rising BMI [32]. These results are summarized in Fig. 20.3. Some apparent conflict in the relationship between overweight and NIDDM may reflect a difference between the sexes. Modan et al. [32] found a stepwise increase in the prevalence of IGT with weight in men, whereas in women, prevalence rose only in the highest BMI category (>27 kg/m^2).

Table 20.2. Formulae to calculate the energy expenditure (metabolic rate) of individuals [21].

BMR (MJ/24 h): Age	Men	Women
18−30	(0.063 × weight) + 2.896	(0.062 × weight) + 2.036
31−60	(0.048 × weight) + 3.653	(0.034 × weight) + 3.538
>60	(0.049 × weight) + 2.459	(0.038 × weight) + 2.755
24 h energy expenditure*: BMR ×	1.55 (light activity)	1.56 (light activity)
	1.79 (moderate activity)	1.64 (moderate activity)
	2.10 (very heavy activity)	1.82 (very heavy activity)

* The figures for 24 h energy expenditure are intended as prescriptions for health, and assume that at least light activity will be undertaken [21]. A reduction of 15% must be made for subjects who remain essentially sedentary. Weight is in kg.

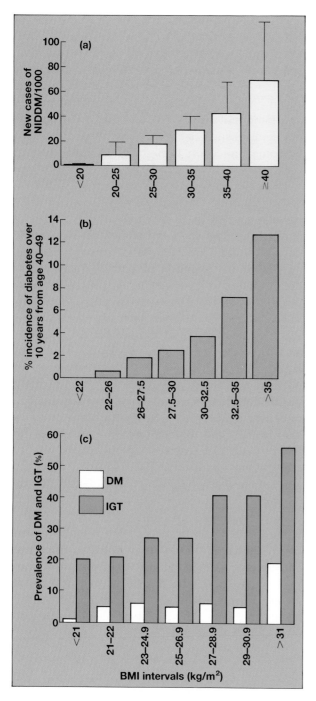

Fig. 20.3. Likelihood of developing NIDDM increases with degree of obesity (BMI). Data from (a) Pima Indians [28] (error bars represent 95% confidence intervals); (b) Norwegian men [31]; (c) Israelis with steady body weight over 10 years [32].

Physical exercise may be an independent protective factor against NIDDM, but it is difficult to distinguish this from the opposite effect of overweight [33, 34]. A further possible confounding factor is the inclusion in some study populations of significant numbers of markedly underweight individuals. The literature is consistent in that being underweight protects against NIDDM. Whether this results from undernutrition or physical exertion is uncertain, but the diabetogenic effect of being overweight appears to override the protective effect of exercise [26].

Overweight seems particularly intractable in these NIDDM-prone groups, suggesting a special metabolic origin. This possibility is supported by the evidence discussed above for a specific defect of thermogenesis in response to mild cold in overweight NIDDM women [17] and by the fact that increased risk of NIDDM remains even after obese subjects have lost weight [32].

Aetiological links between overweight and NIDDM

How overweight promotes NIDDM has been the subject of intensive, but still inconclusive, research.

During an oral glucose tolerance test, overweight subjects have consistently elevated blood insulin concentrations compared with thin controls, but without marked hyperglycaemia. This indicates insulin resistance which has been further characterized using hyperglycaemic and euglycaemic insulin clamp techniques. Insulin-mediated glucose metabolism is reduced by almost 50% in the obese, with impairments of both oxidative and non-oxidative glucose utilization in peripheral tissues. Furthermore, hepatic glucose production is normal in the basal state but fails to suppress under the influence of insulin [35]. Fatty acid metabolism is enhanced in obesity and NIDDM, and this may interfere with glucose utilization [35]. These defects (which do not seem to correlate with the degree of overweight) are accompanied by insulin resistance, elevated triglyceride and total cholesterol concentrations and often by hypertension in a constellation of metabolic abnormalities which may progress to NIDDM in susceptible subjects. Those at risk of NIDDM, with insulin resistance presumably being genetically determined, probably constitute a large subgroup of most populations. Individuals may be identified from a history of gestational diabetes [36], by developing diabetes transiently while under stress (e.g. myocardial infarction) or during corticosteroid treatment, or by displaying a central fat distribution (see below). Overweight is a superimposed factor which, perhaps by demanding excessive insulin secretion to overcome insulin resistance, contributes to B-cell 'exhaustion' and a final decline into NIDDM. This is supported by the recent demonstration that insulin secretion is impaired in all subjects with NIDDM (see Chapter 22).

Fat distribution and NIDDM

NIDDM patients characteristically have a central fat distribution similar to that in Cushing's syndrome, with a high proportion of body fat stored around, and particularly within, the abdomen, rather than in peripheral and subcutaneous sites [18]. This is particularly noticeable in women with NIDDM, since females normally have a predominantly peripheral ('pear-shaped') fat distribution when compared with a more central ('apple-shaped') distribution in men (Fig. 20.4).

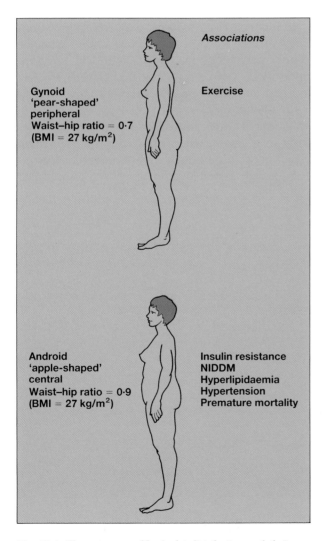

Fig. 20.4. The extremes of body fat distribution and their main metabolic associations.

Fat distribution can be assessed simply from the waist/hip ratio (WHR), i.e. the ratio of circumferential measurement at the waist (midway between the iliac crest and lowest rib) to that around the hips (at the level of the trochanters). Skeletal landmarks are used to reduce inter-observer error, and the measurements should be made with the subject standing. In most populations, WHR is continuously distributed within the range 0.7–1.0 (Table 20.1), and is partly genetically determined [4]. Body fat distribution does not appear to relate to dietary macronutrient composition, at least in studies between populations, but a more central fat distribution is associated with obesity and with increasing age, and may be inversely related to physical exercise [37].

WHR is weakly correlated with BMI, but the two have different distributions within the population and independent disease associations [37, 38] (Fig. 20.6). A central fat distribution in young women or in middle-aged men and women, has been identified as an important predictor of NIDDM in later life and has an additive effect with generalized obesity (Fig. 20.5) [39]. Central fat distribution is also associated with other

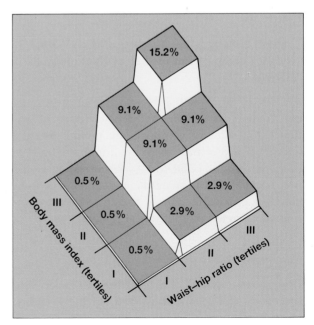

Fig. 20.5. Predictive values of BMI and WHR for the development of NIDDM. BMI and WHR were classified into tertiles (I = lowest, III = greatest) in a population of middle-aged Swedish men. The risk of developing diabetes during the 13-year study period is shown on top of each bar. Adapted from Larsson 1985 [39] and reproduced with permission from Elsevier Science.

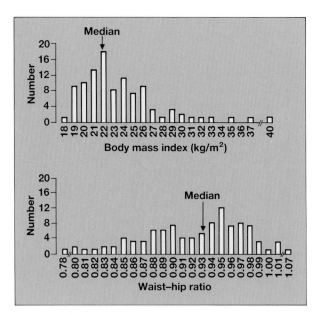

Fig. 20.6. Distributions of WHR and BMI in 101 young women. Adapted from Lean *et al.* 1989 [38].

Table 20.3. Energy content of nutrients and body tissues.

	kcal/g
Fat/lipid	9
Alcohol	7
Protein	4
Carbohydrate	3.75
Dietary fibre	2–3
Adipose tissue	7
Muscle	1.3

cardiovascular risk factors, namely hypercholesterolaemia, hypertriglyceridaemia, hypertension and smoking and there is an inverse relationship between WHR and level of exercise. How central fat distribution is related to NIDDM is uncertain but insulin resistance is an early feature.

Nutrient composition of diet and aetiology of NIDDM

NIDDM is principally a disease of energy storage, exacerbated by insulin deficiency. There is evidence that dietary composition, as well as total energy intake, may also be important in the pathogenesis of NIDDM. As discussed in detail in Chapter 26, the quantity and quality of food are also crucial factors in causing malnutrition-related diabetes in subtropical regions.

Macronutrients: fat, carbohydrate, protein

Dietary energy is derived from fat (9 kcal/g), protein (4 kcal/g) and carbohydrate (3.75 kcal/g). Dietary fibre, particularly of the soluble type, is variably fermented in the large bowel to provide up to 3 kcal/g (Table 20.3). The contribution of alcohol (7 kcal/g) can easily be overlooked. It is essentially impossible to consider the role of one energetic macronutrient individually since a change in one necessitates changes in the others

unless the total energy content of the diet changes. Furthermore, few foods are pure sources of individual nutrients. It has therefore become customary to consider the percentage contribution of macronutrients to total energy in the diet. In general, protein intakes vary relatively little, so that changes in fat and carbohydrate tend to mirror one another.

Epidemiological studies between populations suggest that NIDDM may be associated with the higher percentage fat intakes found in Western-style diets. Conversely, the higher carbohydrate content of many traditional diets is associated with a lower incidence of diabetes [26] (Fig. 20.7). Data from a Greek study based on dietary histories indicate the same association within a population [40]. For geographical, economic and other reasons this broad generalization may be complicated

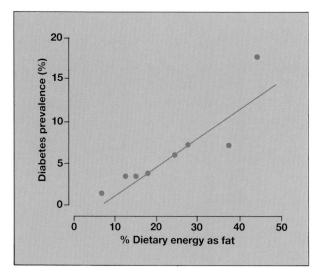

Fig. 20.7. Prevalence of diabetes in different populations is associated with the fat content of the diet. Protein is assumed to account for 12% of total energy intake. Adapted from West 1978 [26].

by differences in intakes of sugar, dietary fibre, protein quality and other dietary components. There are also obvious exceptions, such as the low frequency of NIDDM in Eskimos despite their traditional high-fat diet [41]. A key confounding factor is probably the protective effect of exercise against NIDDM [26, 34]: high exercise levels require high energy intakes and the extra energy is likely to come from the cheapest food sources, which in most countries are rich in carbohydrate.

The epidemiological evidence is supported by experimental data from the 1930s [42] showing that a tendency to (what is now called) IGT or NIDDM is aggravated by a high fat and low carbohydrate intake. Glucose tolerance is improved by a preceding high carbohydrate intake [43]. At present, however, the published data are strong enough only to suggest that high-fat, low-carbohydrate diets may be 'diabetogenic'.

Dietary fibre

The term 'dietary fibre' has become confusing because of changing definitions based on either physical, chemical or functional characteristics. Initially, it described the coarse plant cell-wall material which is not digested in the small bowel. This became equated with non-starch (i.e. acid-resistant) polysaccharide. However, it is now clear that some starch, chemically altered by food preparation and cooking, also passes through the small bowel undigested. This 'resistant starch' is also refractory to in vitro enzyme digestion and was therefore measured by older assays as dietary fibre.

Dietary fibre may be subdivided into soluble (gel-forming) fibres such as pectin (from fruits) and guar gum (a virtually pure galactomannan extracted from the cluster bean) and insoluble fibres such as cellulose and bran; none of the soluble fibres appear 'fibrous' in the lay sense.

Resistant starch and some of the non-starch polysaccharides are fairly completely fermented by bacteria in the large bowel and absorbed as short-chain fatty acids (acetate, butyrate, propionate). Up to 5−10% of total carbohydrate may be absorbed in this way, mainly as acetate [44, 45]. Gel-forming dietary fibre and that in legumes are therefore absorbed and can have metabolic effects. These are the nutrients associated with improved insulin sensitivity and less atherogenic blood lipid profiles, whereas insoluble cereal fibre exerts its main effect on stool bulking [44, 46].

Both the soluble and insoluble types of dietary fibre can improve blood glucose control [47]. The mechanisms through which dietary fibres produce their metabolic effects are complicated. In addition to the possible actions of acetate and other fermentation products, there are obvious effects on bowel motility: insoluble fibre accelerates gut transit whereas soluble fibre slows it down and probably delays absorption [46].

The epidemiological evidence linking NIDDM with high-fat, low-carbohydrate diets can also be interpreted as incriminating a lack of naturally occurring dietary fibre, particularly of the soluble and leguminous types [48, 49]. This theory is strengthened by studies which show beneficial effects from soluble dietary fibre in conjunction with high complex carbohydrate intake in the diets of NIDDM patients [50, 51, 47].

Sugar intake and NIDDM

In common parlance, 'sugar' usually refers to the glucose−fructose disaccharide, sucrose, but a variety of other sugars occur in the diet. Only a small proportion of blood glucose in diabetic or normal subjects is derived directly from dietary glucose, most coming from starches, other complex carbohydrates and sucrose in fruits. Very little fructose is converted into glucose. Dietary sugars contribute specific nutrients, which may have particular metabolic actions, as well as energy which exerts separate metabolic effects.

A distinction must be drawn between acute effects of dietary sugar and any possible chronic effect from long-term ingestion which could provoke diabetes. High glucose intake undoubtedly exaggerates hyperglycaemia and dehydration in decompensated NIDDM, and many newly presenting NIDDM patients will admit to drinking large volumes of glucose-containing drinks because of severe thirst. The fructose moiety of sucrose may also be detrimental in this situation (see below). The long-term diabetogenic potential of dietary sugar is more controversial. A recent extensive review of the epidemiological literature concluded that there is no direct causal link between dietary sugar and NIDDM [52]. Similarly, sugars do not seem especially important in causing weight gain [51, 53]. However, a high intake of sugar is often associated with high fat intake and other more important lifestyle factors. Sugar is a valuable source of energy and tends to be consumed in large amounts as a supplement by those who need high energy intakes where (as in the UK) it is cheaply available [54].

It has been proposed that some individuals display exaggerated insulinaemic and triglyceridaemic responses to fructose [55]. Normally, ingestion of glucose suppresses plasma triglyceride concentrations. It seems that some people — who may be those at risk of NIDDM and vascular disease — respond to oral carbohydrate (fructose in particular) with increased triglyceride synthesis and elevated plasma concentrations [56–57]. This ill-understood syndrome has more recently been related to subclinical copper deficiency, perhaps through regional down-regulation of insulin receptors [58]. A direct role of fructose in causing NIDDM has not, however, been suggested.

Micronutrient deficiencies and NIDDM: chromium and copper

The diet of some groups, particularly the elderly, may be marginal for chromium and some individuals are demonstrably chromium-deficient. Foods high in chromium include certain strains of yeast and cereals. Incomplete data have suggested that pentavalent organic chromium supplementation may improve glucose tolerance [26]. Even if this is confirmed, chromium deficiency is likely to be important as a cause of NIDDM in only a small proportion of cases.

As mentioned above, copper deficiency may aggravate a tendency to insulin resistance and hypertriglyceridaemia in certain susceptible individuals [58]. Copper is present in barely adequate amounts in some Western diets. The possible role of copper deficiency deserves further research.

Alcohol

Chronic pancreatic damage in alcoholics can lead to diabetes which is usually ketosis-resistant although it often requires insulin therapy. Lower but regular intakes of alcohol make an important contribution to energy intake [53] (Table 20.3) and to non-compliance with slimming diets.

Conclusions

Dietary factors are of undoubted importance in causing NIDDM. Large-scale attempts to modify the diet and lifestyle of the population at large, which are broadly similar to those already covered by coronary heart disease prevention programmes,

may help to reduce the enormous costs which NIDDM imposes on the community and health resources. This general approach is particularly important as it is not yet possible to screen for individuals with a genetic susceptibility to the disease.

MIKE E. J. LEAN
JIM I. MANN

References

1 Royal College of Physicians. *Report of a Working Party on Obesity*. London: Royal College of Physicians, 1983.
2 Durnin JVGA, Womersley J. Body fat assessed from total body density and its estimation from skinfold thickness: measurements on 481 men and women aged from 16 to 72 years. *Br J Nutr* 1974; **32**: 77–97.
3 Stunkard AJ, Foch TT, Hrubeck Z. A twin study of human obesity. *JAMA* 1986; **256**: 51–4.
4 Bouchard C. Inheritance of fat distribution and adipose tissue metabolism. In: Vague J, Björntorp P, Guy-Grand B, Rebuffe-Scrive M, Vague P, eds. *Metabolic Complications of the Human Obesities*. Amsterdam: Elsevier, 1985: 87–96.
5 Butler MG, Meaney FJ, Palmer CG. Clinical and cytogenetic survey of 39 individuals with Prader–Labhart–Willi syndrome. *Am J Med Genet* 1986; **23**: 793–809.
6 Prentice AM, Black AE, Coward WA, Davies HL, Goldberg GR, Murgatroyd PR, Ashford H, Sawyer M, Whitehead RG. High levels of energy expenditure in obesity. *Br Med J* 1986; **292**: 983–7.
7 Schutz Y, Bessard T, Jéquier E. Diet-induced thermogenesis measured over a whole day in obese and nonobese women. *Am J Clin Nutr* 1984; **40**: 542–52.
8 Lean MEJ, James WPT. Metabolic effects of isoenergetic nutrient exchange over 24 hours in relation to obesity in women. *Int J Obesity* 1988; **12**: 15–28.
9 Lean MEJ. Achieving energy balance in clinical studies. *Proc Nutr Soc* 1988; **47**: 65A.
10 Wade J, Milner J, Krondl M. Evidence for a physiological regulation of food selection and nutrient intake in twins. *Am J Clin Nutr* 1981; **34**: 143–7.
11 Ravussin E, Lillioja S, Knowler WC *et al*. Reduced rate of energy expenditure as a risk factor for body-weight gain. *N Engl J Med* 1988; **318**: 467–72.
12 Roberts SB, Savage J, Coward WA *et al*. Energy expenditure and intake in infants born to lean and overweight mothers. *N Engl J Med* 1988; **318**: 461–6.
13 Schutz Y, Golay A, Felber JP, Jéquier E. Decreased glucose-induced thermogenesis after weight loss in obese subjects: a predisposing factor for relapse of obesity. *Am J Clin Nutr* 1984; **39**: 380–7.
14 Jung RT, Shetty PS, James WPT, Barrand B, Callingham BA. Reduced thermogenesis in obesity. *Nature* 1979; **279**: 322–3.
15 Lean MEJ, James WPT, Garthwaite PH. Obesity without overeating? Reduced diet-induced thermogenesis in post-obese women, dependent on carbohydrate and not fat intake. In: Björntorp P, Rossner S, eds. *Obesity in Europe 88*. London: J. Libbey, 1989; 281–6.
16 Tremblay A, Plourde G, Despres J-P, Bouchard C. Impact of dietary fat intake and fat oxidation on energy intake in humans. *Am J Clin Nutr* 1989; **49**: 799–805.

17 Lean MEJ, Murgatroyd PR, Rothnie I, Reid IW, Harvey R. Metabolic and thyroidal responses to mild cold are abnormal in obese diabetic women. *Clin Endocrinol* 1988; **28**: 665–73.

18 Lean MEJ. Brown adipose tissue in humans. *Proc Nutr Soc* 1989; **48**: 243–56.

19 Leslie P, Jung RT, Isles TE, Baty J, Newton RW, Illingworth P. Effect of optimal glycaemic control with continuous subcutaneous insulin infusion on energy expenditure in Type I diabetes mellitus. *Br Med J* 1986; **293**: 1121–6.

20 de Leeuw I, van Gaal L, van Acker K, Vansant G, Noe M. Why do insulin dependent diabetic patients (IDDM) gain weight during an intensified conventional insulin treatment (ICIT) programme? *Proceedings of 6th International Symposium on Diabetic Nutrition, Diabetes and Nutrition Study Group of the EASD*, 1988.

21 FAO/WHO/UNU. *Energy and protein requirements.* Technical Report Series Vol 724. Geneva: WHO, 1985.

22 Lean MEJ, Powrie JK, Anderson AS, Garthwaite PH. Obesity, weight loss and prognosis in NIDDM. *Diabetic Med* 1990; **7**: 3228–33.

23 Knight I. *The heights and weights of adults in Great Britain.* London: OPCS-HMSO, 1984.

24 Falconer DS, Duncan LJP, Smith C. A statistical and genetic study of diabetes. *Ann Hum Genet* 1971; **34**: 347–61.

25 Bennett PH, Rushforth NB, Miller M, LeCompte PM. Epidemiologic studies in diabetes in the Pima Indians. *Recent Prog Horm Res* 1976; **32**: 333–76.

26 West KM. *Epidemiology of Diabetes and its Vascular Lesions.* New York: Elsevier, 1978.

27 Zimmet P, Guinea A, Taft P, Guthrie W, Thoma K. The high prevalence of diabetes mellitus on a Pacific island (abstract). *Diabetologia* 1976; **12**: 428.

28 Knowler WC, Pettit DJ, Savage PJ, Bennett PH. Diabetes incidence in Pima Indians: contributions of obesity and parental diabetes. *Am J Epidemiol* 1981; **113**: 144–56.

29 Zimmet P, Whitehouse S. Bimodality in glucose tolerance — the phenomenon and its significance. *Diabetologia* (abstract) 1977; **13**: 441.

30 Joslin EP. The prevention of diabetes mellitus. *JAMA* 1921; **76**: 79–84.

31 Westlund K, Nicolaysen R. Ten year mortality and morbidity related to serum cholesterol. *Scand J Clin Lab Invest* 1972; **30**: (suppl 127): 1–24.

32 Modan M, Karasik A, Halkin H *et al.* Effect of past and present body mass index on prevalence of glucose intolerance and Type 2 (non-insulin-dependent) diabetes and on insulin response. *Diabetologia* 1986; **29**: 82–9.

33 King H, Taylor R, Zimmet P *et al.* Non-insulin-dependent diabetes (NIDDM) in a newly independent nation: the Republic of Kirbati. *Diabetes Care* 1984; **7**: 409–15.

34 Modan M, Lubin F, Lusky A, Chetrit A, Fuchs Z, Halkin H. Interrelationships of obesity, habitual diet, physical activity and glucose tolerance in the four main Jewish ethnic groups. In: Berry EM, Blondheim SH, Eliahou HE, Shafrir E, eds. *Recent Advances in Obesity Research.* Vol V. London: J. Libbey, 1987: 46–53.

35 DeFronzo RA, Golay A, Felber JP. Glucose and lipid metabolism in diabetes mellitus. In: Garrow JS, Halliday D, eds. *Substrate and Energy Metabolism.* London: J.Libbey, 1985: 70–81.

36 Harris MI. Gestational diabetes may represent discovery of preexisting glucose intolerance. *Diabetes Care* 1988; **11**: 402–11.

37 Björntorp P, Smith U, Lonroth P, eds. Health implications of regional obesity. Stockholm: Almquist & Wiksell Int. *Acta Med Scand* 1988; Suppl 723: 1–237.

38 Lean MEJ, Sutherland HW, Sutherland F, Bruce P, Garthwaite P. Body mass index, waist/hip ratio and carbohydrate tolerance in pregnancy. *Diabetes Nutr Metab* 1989 **2**: 291–7.

39 Larsson B. Obesity and prospective risk for associated diseases. In: Vague J, Björntorp P, Guy-Grand B, Rebuffe-Scrive M, Vague P, eds. *Metabolic Complications of the Human Obesities.* Amsterdam: Elsevier, 1985: 21–9.

40 Karamanos B, Toundas C, Karamanos G, Roussi-Penessi D, Kofinis A. The composition of the diet and its relation with glucose intolerance. *Proceedings of the 6th International Symposium on Diabetic Nutrition, Diabetes and Nutrition Study Group of the EASD*, 1988.

41 Sagild U, Littauer J, Jesepersen CS, Andersen S. Epidemiological studies in Greenland. 1962–1964. *Acta Med Scand* 1966; **179**: 29–39.

42 Himsworth HP. Diet and the incidence of diabetes mellitus. *Clin Sci Molec Med* 1935–6; **2**: 67, 117–48.

43 Grey N, Kipnis DM. Effect of diet composition on the hyperinsulinemia of obesity. *N Engl J Med*, 1971; **285**: 827–31.

44 Cummings JH. Short chain fatty acids in the human colon. *Gut* 1983; **22**: 763–79.

45 Cummings JH. Fermentation in the large intestine: evidence and implications for health. *Lancet* 1981; i: 1206–9.

46 Vinik AI, Jenkins DJA. Dietary fibre in the management of diabetes. *Diabetes Care* 1988; **11**: 160–73.

47 Karlström B. Dietary treatment of type 2 diabetes mellitus. *Acta Univ Uppsaliensis* 1988; **153**: 1–50.

48 Trowell HC. Dietary fibre hypothesis of the etiology of diabetes mellitus. *Diabetes* 1975; **24**: 762–5.

49 Mann JI. Diabetes mellitus: some aspects of aetiology and management of non-insulin-dependent diabetes. In: Trowell H, ed. *Fibre-depleted Foods and Disease.* London: Academic Press, 1985: 263–87.

50 Simpson HCR, Simpson RW, Lousley S, Carter RD, Geekie M, Hockaday TDR, Mann JI. A high leguminous fibre diet improves all aspects of diabetic control. *Lancet* 1981; i: 1–5.

51 Reiser S. Effects of dietary sugars on metabolic risk factors associated with heart disease. *Nutr Health* 1985; **3**: 203–16.

52 Mann JI. Simple sugars and diabetes. *Diabetic Med* 1987; **4**: 135–9.

53 Kromhout D. Energy and macronutrient intake in lean and obese middle-aged men (the Zutphen study). *Am J Clin Nutr* 1983; **37**: 295–9.

54 Gibney MJ, Lee P. Patterns of food and nutrient intake in the chronically unemployed consuming high and low levels of table sugar. *Proc Nutr Soc* 1989; **48**: 132A: 190.

55 Ahrens EH, Hirsch S, Oette K, Farquar JW, Stein Y. Carbohydrate-induced and fat-induced lipemia. *Trans Ass Am Phys* 1961; **74**: 134–46.

56 Maruhama Y. Conversion of ingested carbohydrate ^{14}C into glycerol and fatty acids of serum triglycerides in patients with myocardial infarction. *Metabolism* 1970; **19**: 1085–91.

57 McDonald IA. Effect on serum lipids of dietary sucrose and fructose. *Acta Med Scand* 1972; Suppl 542: 215–20.

58 Bhathena SJ, Reiser S, Smith JC, Revett K, Kennedy BW, Powell AS, Voyles NR, Recant L. Increased insulin receptors in carbohydrate-sensitive subjects: a mechanism for hyperlipaemia in these subjects? *Eur J Clin Nutr* 1988; **42**: 465–72.

21 The Pathogenesis of Non-Insulin-Dependent Diabetes Mellitus: the Role of Insulin Resistance

Summary

• The biological response to insulin is reduced by about 40% in NIDDM, the evidence including the normal or high circulating insulin levels, and studies with the euglycaemic clamp, insulin tolerance tests and mathematical modelling of i.v. glucose tolerance tests.

• Insulin resistance in NIDDM involves effects on both hepatic glucose output and peripheral glucose uptake.

• Hyperglycaemia itself causes insulin resistance and impaired insulin secretion ('glucose toxicity') but many factors also contribute to the insensitivity, including obesity, age, lack of exercise, diet and genetic components.

• The mechanisms of insulin resistance in NIDDM are unclear but may involve reduced insulin receptor numbers (secondary to hyperinsulinaemia and hyperglycaemia), reduced tyrosine kinase activity of the insulin receptor and abnormalities distal to the receptor.

In the 1930s, Himsworth [1] first provided evidence of reduced insulin sensitivity in older, non-ketotic diabetic patients, by assessing the reduction of the glycaemic response to oral glucose during administration of intravenous insulin. In 1951, Bornstein [2], using a bioassay for insulin, showed that non-insulin-dependent diabetic (NIDDM) subjects do not lack insulin, although it was not until the development of the radioimmunoassay for insulin by Yalow and Berson (Chapter 35), that they and others proved conclusively that absolute insulin levels in NIDDM are often elevated or normal rather than depressed [3, 4]. However, insulin secretion is not normal in NIDDM. There is a sluggish early insulin rise in response to a meal [5] and the diurnal insulin levels are inappropriately low when related to the prevailing blood glucose level.

Evidence for a reduced biological response to insulin in NIDDM has subsequently been supported by a variety of different techniques. Using the insulin tolerance test, it was demonstrated that an intravenous dose of insulin in NIDDM subjects produced a relatively small fall in blood glucose [6]. The glycaemic response to a fixed-rate insulin and glucose infusion during endogenous B-cell suppression (achieved either by adrenaline plus propranolol [7], or by somatostatin [8]) results in greater hyperglycaemia in NIDDM than in matched non-diabetic controls. More detailed data have been provided by the glucose clamp technique, where a fixed-rate insulin infusion is combined with a variable-rate glucose infusion adjusted to maintain precise euglycaemia; the glucose delivery required is used to derive an index of whole-body insulin sensitivity. In absolute terms, this index is reduced by 35–40% in NIDDM [4], but as the increase in glucose disposal induced by insulin in NIDDM is also subnormal, the relative impairment of insulin action is even greater [9].

Most recently, Bergmann and colleagues have used 'minimal' mathematical modelling of the insulin and glucose responses to an intravenous glucose tolerance test to derive estimates of insulin secretion, insulin sensitivity and non-insulin-mediated glucose uptake. This approach has also demonstrated significant insulin resistance in NIDDM [10].

Where is the insulin resistance?

Insulin lowers blood glucose through two separate mechanisms, namely by suppressing glucose release from the liver and by promoting uptake of glucose into peripheral tissues, especially muscle. Using a constant infusion of radioactively labelled (usually tritiated) glucose in the fasted state or during glucose clamping, it is possible to quantitate hepatic glucose output. When insulin levels are raised during the clamp, the relative contributions of suppression of hepatic glucose output and increased peripheral glucose uptake to net glucose disposal can be determined. This technique has clearly demonstrated that in NIDDM the responsiveness of peripheral tissues to insulin is substantially impaired [4]. As muscle accounts for the majority of insulin-mediated glucose disposal during hyperinsulaemia [11], it is reasonable to conclude that insulin resistance must be present in muscle, a view supported by measurements of arteriovenous glucose differences in the leg [4] where muscle is the dominant tissue (Fig. 21.1). On the other hand, there are also some data suggesting that hepatic glucose output is less easily suppressed by insulin in NIDDM [12], implying that the liver shares in the insulin resistance. In particular, it is noteworthy that hepatic glucose output in NIDDM is normal or elevated in the basal state and less suppressible by a glucose load [4] despite hyperglycaemia and insulin levels which are often normal or elevated in absolute terms. Moreover, there is a strong positive correlation between hepatic glucose output and the fasting blood glucose level [4, 13]. Although NIDDM is characterized by insulin resistance of peripheral tissues and reduced glucose clearance, the mass action effect of hyperglycaemia itself results in an absolute increase in glucose assimilation into peripheral tissues in the postabsorptive (overnight fasting) state [4]. As glucose oxidation and glycogen synthesis tend to be reduced, a higher than usual percentage of the glucose is returned to the circulation as three-carbon units; these in turn provide a substrate for enhanced hepatic gluconeogenesis which sustains the increased hepatic glucose output (accelerated Cori cycle) [4]. It is not easy to determine whether this cycle is driven by the liver itself or whether the liver is simply responding to substrate supply and other influences such as elevated fatty acid levels [4]. In any case, whatever the primary mechanism, both peripheral tissues and the liver appear to respond poorly to insulin in NIDDM.

Is the defect in glucose metabolism related purely to an impaired response to insulin?

The evidence mentioned above clearly indicates an impaired response to insulin in NIDDM, although it is possible that the defect(s) is not purely associated with insulin action and might involve processes that would impair glucose metabolism independently of the effect of insulin. In addition to insulin-stimulated transport in insulin-sensitive tissues, glucose may enter any tissue by facilitated diffusion, a process termed 'non-insulin-mediated glucose uptake'. Present evidence [14] does not support a defect of non-insulin-mediated glucose transport — which could affect both insulin-mediated and non-insulin-mediated glucose utilization — in NIDDM. However, in the case of the liver, it is important to note that hepatic glucose output in NIDDM is resistant to the normal suppressive effect of hyperglycaemia as well as to insulin. Thus, the excessive hepatic glucose output in NIDDM could possibly be related to an abnormal driving force (perhaps neural [15]) rather than primary insensitivity of the liver to insulin.

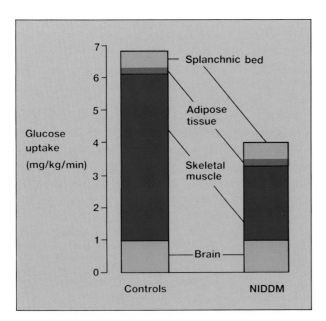

Fig. 21.1. Glucose assimilation in various tissues with elevated insulin levels (euglycaemic clamp) in non-diabetic and NIDDM subjects. These results highlight the major contribution of muscle to insulin resistance in NIDDM. (From De Fronzo 1988, [4].)

Is insulin resistance a primary or secondary event in NIDDM?

There is now considerable evidence that hyper-glycaemia itself may both generate insulin resist-ance and impair insulin secretion [4, 16]. These effects are sufficiently prominent that the term 'glucose toxicity' has been coined. At the bio-chemical level, the reduction in insulin sensitivity may be explained, at least partially, by the ability of hyperglycaemia to down-regulate the glucose transport system [4]. In view of this evidence, it is not surprising that correction of hyperglycaemia in NIDDM whether by diet, sulphonylurea or in-sulin therapy significantly improves insulin sen-sitivity [4, 17, 18]. This enhanced insulin sensitivity seems to outweigh completely any tendency of high insulin levels to down-regulate the insulin receptor. Indeed, insulin sensitivity may improve markedly even when normoglycaemia has been achieved by administering over 100 units of in-sulin per day [18]. However, correction of the hyperglycaemia does not completely normalize insulin sensitivity, suggesting that the insulin resistance of NIDDM cannot be fully explained by the effects of hyperglycaemia alone.

The contribution of obesity, age, diet and exercise to insulin resistance

Obesity *per se* is clearly associated with reduced insulin sensitivity (Chapter 20) which may be of similar magnitude to that seen in NIDDM. However, in the obese diabetic patient, the added contribution of obesity to the insulin resistance of NIDDM is probably only moderate [4]. In-creased age is associated with a reduced respon-siveness to insulin (Chapter 89), although this may be corrected by a high carbohydrate diet [10]. Regular physical activity improves insulin sensitivity [19] (Chapter 78).

The dietary contribution to insulin resistance is of considerable interest. Evidence suggests that low fat and high fibre contents of the diet improve insulin sensitivity [20]. Such diets are usually rich in complex carbohydrates which themselves are recognized to improve insulin sensitivity. How-ever, there is evidence that substitution of protein for carbohydrate in a low-fat, high-fibre diet pro-duces an equivalent benefit (K. O'Dea, personal communication). Specific dietary fats and car-bohydrates may also have an influence. In animal experiments [21], sucrose or fructose, but not glucose, have an equally adverse effect on insulin sensitivity. The adverse effect of fructose may be at least partially mediated by an elevation of tri-glyceride levels. Also in animals, saturated fats adversely affect insulin sensitivity to a greater extent than unsaturated (safflower) oil and the ω-3 fatty acids of fish oils actually protect against development of insulin resistance [22]. However, fish oils do not improve glycaemic control or in-sulin sensitivity in human NIDDM [23]. The reason for the disparity between animal and human studies is not clear at the present time.

These various lifestyle factors, ranging from physical activity to diet, clearly modulate the in-sulin resistance of NIDDM. However, insulin re-sistance has a genetic component [24] and this is clearly still present in NIDDM compared to non-diabetic subjects, even when carefully matched for known environmental factors [4].

The role of fatty acids and lipid oxidation

In NIDDM, free fatty acid levels are elevated in obese and some non-obese patients and lipid oxidation is increased [4]. According to the Randle hypothesis, increased fatty acid supply to muscle can reduce glucose metabolism through mechan-isms related to increased acetyl CoA production. There is some human evidence [4] to support a contribution of elevated fatty acid levels to insulin resistance. However, in a recent animal study, an acute elevation of fatty acids increased rather than decreased insulin-induced glucose uptake and glycogen synthesis in skeletal muscle although the anticipated reduction occurred in cardiac muscle [26]. Thus, there may be a time delay and in-creased glycogen storage may be a part of the mechanism by which increased fatty acid avail-ability causes a reduction in skeletal muscle insulin response. Fatty acids can also increase gluconeogenesis [27] and hepatic glucose output and so may also contribute to the hyperglycaemia of NIDDM via hepatic mechanisms [4].

What is the biochemical defect causing insulin resistance?

When insulin receptors were first measured in NIDDM, the finding that receptor numbers were reduced provoked considerable excitement. How-ever, subsequent studies have indicated that the reduction in receptors may be a secondary conse-quence of hyperglycaemia and hyperinsulinaemia and does not relate well to the impairment of insulin action [4, 28]. It therefore seems unlikely that a defect in the number or affinity of insulin receptors is a primary abnormality in NIDDM. On the other hand, it is possible that an abnormality of the portion of the insulin receptor projecting into the cell (β-subunit, Chapters 11, 12) could contribute to insulin resistance. Tyrosine kinase activity of the β-subunit appears to be intimately involved in mediating insulin action; this tyrosine kinase activity is reduced in some animal models of diabetes and there is some evidence that the same is true in human NIDDM [29, 30]. Further study will be required to determine whether this abnormality is secondary to the diabetic state or could be a primary defect in at least some patients with NIDDM.

Alternatively, it is quite possible that the primary cause of insulin resistance in NIDDM is located distal to the insulin receptor in the chain of events mediating insulin action. As these post-receptor mechanisms are still not well defined (Chapter 12), it is not surprising that the defect(s) in NIDDM remain uncertain. Considerable current research activity is centred on clarifying the intracellular mediators of insulin action and the structure and function of the glucose transporter proteins [31, 32] in the hope of identifying an abnormality which could explain the insulin resistance of NIDDM.

Which defect is primary? Are there multiple defects?

There is good physiological evidence of heterogeneity in NIDDM, which may therefore comprise various discrete subgroups, each with their own genetically determined abnormality (see Chapters 19, 25). There is certainly marked insulin resistance in the majority of patients with NIDDM, even though a defect in insulin secretion may be an important or dominant lesion in some cases. The insulin resistance may be in part secondary to obesity or to hyperglycaemia and hyperinsulinaemia. However, a substantial component of the insulin resistance appears to be unexplained by these factors and may well represent a manifestation of the primary defect(s) in NIDDM.

It must be remembered that many obese people, who may have marked insulin resistance, do not develop NIDDM. Thus, it would seem that a metabolic defect causing insulin resistance must be associated with some other abnormality of hepatic glucose output or insulin secretion in order to cause diabetes. Hypothetically, an abnormality of a single regulator or mediator which influences both insulin secretion and action could provide a unifying mechanism. Such defects could involve, *inter alia*, the glucose transporter proteins, guanine regulatory proteins, phosphoinositides or enzymes of glycogen synthesis or glucose metabolism.

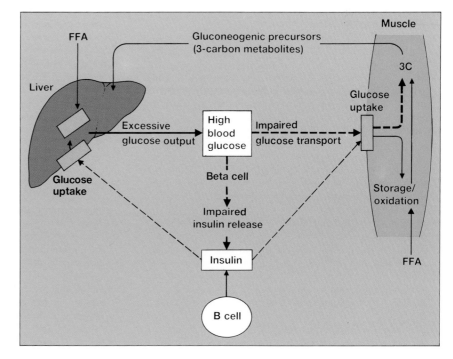

Fig. 21.2. A scheme for the disturbance of glucose metabolism in NIDDM. The hyperglycaemia is driven by excessive hepatic glucose output, fuelled by availability of three-carbon substrates for gluconeogenesis. Insulin resistance in muscle reduces the clearance of glucose but the mass-action effect of hyperglycaemia causes an absolute increase in muscle glucose uptake. As glucose storage and oxidation are reduced, three-carbon units are rechannelled via the circulation to the liver. Hyperglycaemia compounds the problem by impairing both B-cell insulin release and peripheral insulin action (glucose transport). Elevated free fatty acids (FFA) contribute to the excessive hepatic gluconeogenesis and impaired peripheral glucose metabolism.

It is possible to choose one of the several metabolic abnormalities of NIDDM and to construct a hypothesis as to how the other defects could follow (Fig. 21.2). The possibility of a primary defect of insulin secretion will be discussed subsequently (Chapter 22). A second possibility would be a primary defect in hepatic glucose output leading to oversupply of glucose to the peripheral tissues, resulting in insulin resistance and hyperglycaemia which in turn, could impair B-cell function. Finally, a primary defect in insulin sensitivity (especially if it affected both liver and periphery) could explain hyperglycaemia with, once again, secondary impairment of B-cell function.

Until the pathogenesis of NIDDM is more fully explained, it remains important therapeutically to recognize the secondary impairments of insulin secretion and insulin action which can result from hyperglycaemia. Thus, the attainment of normoglycaemia, by whatever means, is likely in itself to reverse partially the metabolic derangements of the disease.

DONALD J. CHISHOLM

EDWARD W. KRAEGEN

References

1 Himsworth HP, Kerr RB. Insulin-sensitive and insulin insensitive types of diabetes mellitus *Clin Sci* 1942; **4**: 120−52.

2 Bornstein J, Lawrence RD. Plasma insulin in human diabetes mellitus. *Br Med J* 1951; **2**: 1541−4.

3 Yalow RS, Berson SA. Immunoassay of endogenous plasma insulin in man. *J Clin Invest* 1960; **39**: 1157−65.

4 DeFronzo R. The triumvirate: β-cell, muscle, liver. A collusion responsible for NIDDM. Lilly Lecture 1987. *Diabetes* 1988; **37**: 667−875.

5 Bruce DG, Chisholm DJ, Storlien LH, Kraegen EW. The physiological importance of the deficiency in early prandial insulin secretion in noninsulin dependent diabetes. *Diabetes* 1988; **37**: 736−44.

6 Alford FP, Martin FI, Pearson MF. The significance and interpretation of mildly abnormal oral glucose tolerance. *Diabetologia* 1971; **7**: 173−80.

7 Ginsberg H, Kimmerlin G, Olefsky JM, Reaven GM. Demonstration of insulin resistance in untreated adult-onset diabetic subjects with fasting hyperglycemia. *J Clin Invest* 1975; **55**: 454−61.

8 Harano Y, Ohgaku S, Hidaka H, Haneda K, Kikkawa R, Shigeta Y, Abe H. Glucose, insulin and somatostatin infusion for the determination of insulin sensitivity. *J Clin Endocrinol Metab* 1977; **45**: 1124−7.

9 Donner CC, Fraze E, Chen Y-DI, Reaven GM. Quantification of insulin-stimulated glucose disposal in patients with non-insulin dependent diabetes mellitus. *Diabetes* 1985; **34**: 831−5.

10 Bergman RN, Finegood D, Ader M. Assessment of insulin sensitivity *in vivo*. *Endocrine Rev* 1985; **6** (suppl 1): 45−86.

11 Kraegen EW, James DE, Jenkins AB, Chisholm DJ. Dose response curves for *in vivo* insulin sensitivity in individual tissues in rats. *Am J Physiol* 1985; **248**: E353−62.

12 Olefsky JM, Kolterman OG. Mechanism of insulin resistance in obesity and non-insulin dependent (Type II) diabetes. *Am J Med* 1981; **70**: 151−68.

13 Bogardus C, Lillioja S, Howard BV, Reaven G, Mott D. Relationships between insulin secretion, insulin action and fasting plasma glucose concentration in non-diabetic and non-insulin dependent diabetic subjects. *J Clin Invest* 1984; **74**: 1238−46.

14 Baron DA, Kolterman OG, Bell J, Mandarino LJ, Olefsky JM. Rates of noninsulin-mediated glucose uptake are elevated in Type II diabetic patients. *J Clin Invest* 1985; **76**: 1782−8.

15 Storlien LH, Grunstein HS, Smythe GA. Guanethidine blocks the 2 deoxy-D glucose induced hypothalamic noradrenergic drive to hyperglycaemia. *Brain Res* 1985; **335**: 144−7.

16 Unger RH, Grundy S. Hyperglycaemia as an inducer as well as a consequence of impaired islet cell function and insulin resistance: implication for the management of diabetes. *Diabetologia* 1985; **28**: 119−21.

17 Kosaka K, Kuzuya T, Akanuma Y, Hagura R. Increase in insulin response after treatment of overt maturity onset diabetes mellitus is independent of the mode of treatment. *Diabetologia* 1980; **18**: 23−8.

18 Garvey WT, Olefsky JM, Griffin J, Hamman RF, Kolterman OG. The effect of insulin treatment on insulin secretion and insulin action in type II diabetes mellitus. *Diabetes* 1985; **34**: 222−34.

19 James DE, Kraegen EW, Chisholm DJ. Effects of exercise training on *in vivo* insulin action in individual tissues in rats. *J Clin Invest* 1985; **76**: 657−66.

20 Riccardi G, Rivellese A, Paioni D, Genovese S, Mastranzo P, Mancino N. Separate influence of dietary carbohydrate and fibre on the metabolic control in diabetes. *Diabetologia* 1984; **27**: 116−21.

21 Thorburn AW, Storlien LH, Jenkins AB, Khouris S, Kraegen EW. Association between fructose-induced *in vivo* insulin resistance and elevated plasma triglyceride levels in rats. *Am J Clin Nutr* 1989; **49**: 1155−1163.

22 Storlien LH, Kraegen EW, Chisholm DJ, Ford GL, Bruce DG, Pascoe WS. Fish oil prevents insulin resistance induced by high fat feeding. *Science* 1987; **237**: 885−8.

23 Borkman M, Chisholm DJ, Furler SM, Storlien LH, Kraegen EW, Simons LA, Chesterman CN. Effects of fish oil supplementation on glucose and lipid metabolism in non-insulin-dependent diabetes. *Diabetes* 1989; **38**: 1314−1319.

24 Lillioja S, Mott DM, Zawadzki JK, Young AA, Abbott WGH, Knolwer WC, Bennett PH, Moll P, Bogardus C. *In vivo* insulin action is familial characteristic in nondiabetic Pima Indians. *Diabetes* 1987; **36**: 1329−35.

25 Randle PLJ, Hales CN, Garland PB, Newsholme EA. The glucose-fatty acid cycle. Its role in insulin sensitivity and the metabolic disturbances of diabetes mellitus. *Lancet* 1963; i: 785−789.

26 Jenkins AB, Storlien LH, Chisholm DJ, Kraegen WE. Effects of nonesterified fatty acid availability on tissue specific glucose utilisation in rats *in vivo*. *J Clin Invest* 1988; **82**: 293−9.

27 Blumenthal SA. Stimulation of gluconeogenesis by palmitic acid in rat hepatocytes: evidence that this effect can be dissociated from provision of reducing equivalents. *Metabolism* 1983; **32**: 971−6.

28 Seltzer H. Are insulin receptors clinically significant? *J Lab*

Clin Med 1982; **100**: 815–21.

29 Comi RJ, Grunberger G, Gorden P. Relationship of insulin binding and insulin-stimulated tyrosine kinase activity is altered in type II diabetes. *J Clin Invest* 1987; **79**: 453–62.

30 Caro J, Sinha MK, Raju SM, Ittoop O, Pories WJ, Flickinger EG, Meelheim D, Dohm GL. Insulin receptor kinase in human skeletal muscle from obese subjects with and without noninsulin dependent diabetes. *J Clin Invest* 1987; **79**: 1330–7.

31 James DE, Brown R, Navarro J, Pilch PF. Insulin-regulatable tissues express a unique insulin-sensitive glucose transport protein. *Nature* 1988; **333**: 183–5.

32 Mueckler M. Family of glucose-transporter genes: implications for glucose homeostasis and diabetes. *Diabetes* 1990; **39**: 6–11.

22 Pancreatic Abnormalities in Non-Insulin-Dependent Diabetes Mellitus

Summary

• In early NIDDM, the absolute basal insulin levels are normal or elevated, but inappropriately low in comparison with the raised blood glucose concentrations. The pulsatility of basal insulin secretion is abnormal in NIDDM, possibly making the insulin less biologically effective.

• The first phase of insulin secretion in response to glucose is deficient in NIDDM, causing postprandial hyperglycaemia through insulin deficiency and the lack of the priming effect of the first-phase insulin on the target organs. The response to non-glucose stimuli is normal, suggesting a specific glucoreceptor abnormality.

• With persistent hyperglycaemia, the second phase of insulin release in response to glucose becomes attenuated in NIDDM.

• There is a 'horseshoe-shaped' relationship between the insulin response and the plasma glucose level in NIDDM. Insulin secretion increases progressively as the glucose level increases to about 7 mmol/l, after which further increases cause a decline in insulin secretion. This may indicate a toxic effect of hyperglycaemia on the B cells.

• There are three major defects in A-cell responses in NIDDM: an absolute or relative hyperglucagonaemia, an exaggerated glucagon response to amino acids and impaired suppression of glucagon secretion by hyperglycaemia.

• The D-cell mass is reduced in NIDDM, and there is reduced somatostatin secretion in response to insulin-induced hypoglycaemia, glucose and mixed meals.

In the lean, non-diabetic subject, glucose levels are maintained by a balance between insulin secretion from the B cells of the pancreas and insulin action in the splanchnic (liver and gut) and peripheral (muscle and adipose) tissues. Ultimately, non-insulin-dependent diabetes (NIDDM) occurs when this balance is upset and either impaired B-cell function (reduced insulin secretion) or abnormal insulin action (insulin resistance) or both are present.

Although it has been suggested for several decades that insulin action is impaired in many diabetic subjects, it was not until plasma insulin concentrations could be reliably measured that insulin resistance was confirmed as a characteristic feature of NIDDM [1]. The role of insulin resistance in the pathogenesis of NIDDM has been reviewed in Chapter 21. However, there is considerable evidence that both insulin resistance and islet-cell abnormalities contribute to the pathogenesis of NIDDM. This section outlines the relevant defects in the B, A and D cells of the islets and discusses the notion that high glucose levels *per se* may be toxic to the B cells in NIDDM.

The B cell and insulin secretion in NIDDM

Absolute or relative insulin deficiency is present in all types of diabetes and is an integral part of the diabetic syndrome. In IDDM, an immunological process is involved in the destruction of the B cells [2] (Chapter 15). The islets are shrunken and devoid of B cells and consist primarily of glucagon-secreting A cells, with some somatostatin-secreting D cells [3]. In patients with NIDDM, there are different anatomical (Chapter 18) and physiological alterations in the B cell, with four major defects in insulin secretion (Table 22.1): a decrease in basal insulin secretion relative to the ambient plasma glucose level [4], deficient first- and second-phase insulin secretory responses [5], and a selective glucoreceptor dysfunction [6]. The latter is suggested by the subnormal glucose-stimulated insulin secretion in the presence of normal responsiveness to secretagogues other than glucose (e.g. amino acids) [6].

The basal plasma insulin concentration in NIDDM is generally thought to be normal or elevated compared with non-diabetic subjects [7]. However, there is in fact a relative insulin deficiency: when the raised plasma glucose concentration is taken into account, the insulin level is inappropriately low in NIDDM [4, 8]. It should also be noted that recent studies [9] using a highly specific two-site immunoradiometric assay for insulin, which does not cross-react with proinsulin-like molecules, also show normal basal levels of

plasma insulin in NIDDM, although post-glucose-load levels are significantly reduced (see below).

During periods of fasting, insulin is secreted in a pulsatile fashion [10], and indeed insulin is more bio-effective when delivered in pulses rather than continuously [11]. The basal pulsatility of insulin secretion is abnormal in NIDDM, with irregular oscillations of small amplitude, compared with those of non-diabetic subjects [12, 13].

The pathophysiological and clinical consequences of the abnormalities in basal insulin secretion are still a matter of continuing research and debate. Insulin resistance is comparable in both non-diabetic obese subjects [14] and in NIDDM patients, but only the latter develop glucose intolerance. Insulin resistance alone therefore seems insufficient to cause overt glucose intolerance, implying that for NIDDM to develop, there must be a defect in insulin secretion in addition to insulin resistance. The question of whether defective insulin secretion or impaired insulin sensitivity is the primary defect in NIDDM is still unresolved. Evidence of insulin resistance in patients with impaired glucose tolerance who have quantitatively normal insulin secretion has suggested that the primary defect in NIDDM might be insulin resistance, but recent reports of B-cell dysfunction rather than insulin insensitivity and of impaired pulsatile secretion in the non-diabetic, first-degree relatives of NIDDM patients [15, 16] challenge this assumption. It is possible that irregular pulsatile insulin secretion might eventually cause down-regulation of the insulin receptor, resulting in insulin resistance.

The relationship between the fasting and post-glucose-load insulin levels, and the fasting plasma glucose concentrations in subjects with NIDDM shows a so-called 'horseshoe-shaped' curve [17]: the plasma insulin response is initially greater with mild hyperglycaemia but insulin secretion diminishes as the magnitude of hyperglycaemia increases (Fig. 22.1). One interpretation of this effect is that hyperglycaemia occurs because of decreasing insulin secretion. The alternative view is that hyperglycaemia itself causes a reduction in insulin secretion.

The latter possibility — that hyperglycaemia *per se* has a toxic effect and may be an inducer as well as a consequence of impaired islet cell function and insulin resistance [18] — deserves discussion. Chronic hyperglycaemia, in the presence of a reduced B-cell mass, results in a defect in insulin secretion [19, 20], and insulin treatment has been

Table 22.1. Abnormalities of the islet secretory cells in NIDDM.

Cell type	Hormone	Abnormality
B	Insulin	• Relative decrease in basal secretion • Decreased first-phase insulin response • Decreased second-phase insulin response • Selective glucoreceptor dysfunction
A	Glucagon	• Absolute or relative increase in basal glucagon secretion • Increased glucagon response to aminogenic stimuli • Hyposuppressibility of glucagon by hyperglycaemia
D	Somatostatin	• Decreased stimulated somatostatin secretion in response to hypoglycaemic and glucose-load stimuli

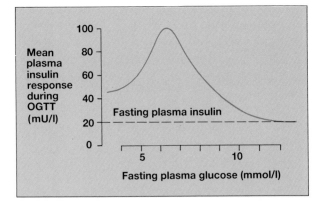

Fig. 22.1. 'Starling's curve' of the pancreas. In normal-weight patients with impaired glucose tolerance or mild diabetes mellitus, plasma insulin response to ingested glucose increases progressively until the fasting glucose concentration reaches 120 mg/dl (6.7 mmol/l). Thereafter, further increases in fasting glucose level are associated with progressive decline in insulin secretion. The same curve depicts the relationship between fasting plasma insulin and glucose concentration (DeFronzo 1988 [28]).

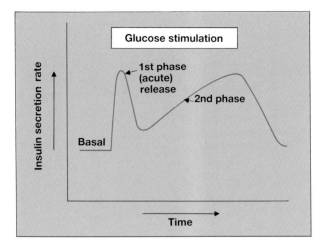

Fig. 22.2. The biphasic insulin response to a constant glucose stimulus. A theoretical response to a square-wave (constant) change in glucose level is shown. The peak of the first phase in man is between 3 and 5 min and lasts 10 min. The second phase begins at 2 min but is not evident until after 10 min. It continues to increase slowly for at least 60 min or until the stimulus stops. (Ward *et al.* 1984 [4].)

shown to improve glucose-induced insulin release in experimental models of NIDDM [21]. On the other hand, experimental evidence shows that hyperglycaemia also affects insulin-mediated glucose disposal in subjects with NIDDM [22]. This evidence of glucose toxicity in the bipolar pathogenesis of NIDDM may have important therapeutic implications.

When the B cell is stimulated, insulin is secreted in a biphasic response [23]. The *first phase* of the insulin response (Fig. 22.2) consists of a rapid rise in the insulin level occurring 1–3 min after the glucose level is increased, followed by a return toward baseline 6–10 min after the stimulus. The *second-phase* insulin response, which increases gradually according to the degree of hyperglycaemia, begins about 2 min after the intravenous glucose challenge and persists for the duration of the stimulus [24].

The first-phase insulin response to the intravenous administration of glucose is characteristically lacking in NIDDM [5]. By contrast, the first-phase insulin response to secretagogues other than glucose is of normal magnitude in most NIDDM patients (Fig. 22.3). This selective abnormality, suggesting glucoreceptor dysfunction, has been demonstrated by several experimental studies [6, 25, 26]. Abnormalities in the first-phase insulin response may play an important role in the pathogenesis of NIDDM as it appears to have a priming effect on the ability of the target tissues of insulin, primarily the liver, to maintain glucose

homeostasis [27]. A reduced first-phase insulin response may therefore result in postprandial hyperglycaemia due to both insulin deficiency and decreased insulin sensitivity.

The second-phase insulin response is determined by the plasma glucose concentration. In the early stages of glucose intolerance, the B cell responds to this persistent stimulus with increased insulin secretion [28] and hyperinsulinaemia ensues. Prolonged hyperinsulinaemia can lead to a down-regulation of insulin action [29, 30], causing or worsening insulin resistance. Increased insulin resistance will impose a heavier burden on an already overstimulated and partially deficient B cell. Eventually, plasma insulin concentrations become insufficient to prevent fasting and postprandial hyperglycaemia. At this stage, when fasting plasma glucose levels are elevated, NIDDM subjects have a decreased second-phase insulin response [5], in addition to the defective first-phase response.

The relationship between IDDM and HLA antigens DR3/DR4 has been well documented (see Chapter 14). Recently, it has been reported that the presence of HLA antigens DR3/DR4 correlates with impaired B-cell function in patients with NIDDM [31, 32], perhaps suggesting a specific susceptible subset of NIDDM patients.

The appearance of the islets in NIDDM differs from that in IDDM and in normal individuals (see Chapter 18). In NIDDM subjects, the number

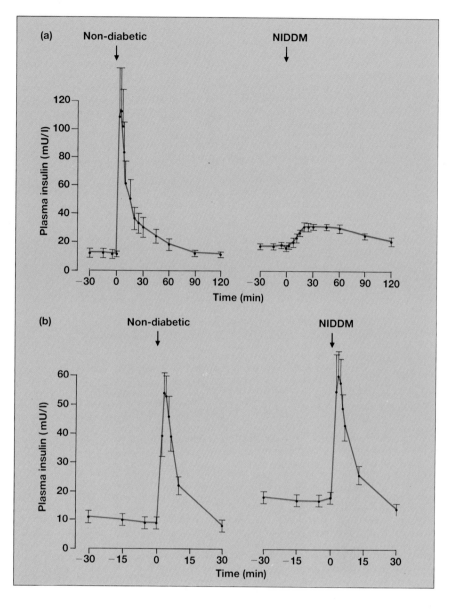

Fig. 22.3. (a) Mean ± SEM plasma insulin in non-diabetic subjects and NIDDM patients after 20 g glucose given intravenously (arrow). Note lack of first-phase insulin response and relatively well-preserved second-phase response in NIDDM. (b) Mean ± SEM plasma insulin in non-diabetic subjects and NIDDM patients in response to intravenous arginine (arrow). Note normal response in NIDDM to this non-glucose stimulant, indicating a glucoreceptor abnormality. (From Ward *et al.* 1984 [4].)

of B cells and the volume and calculated weight of islet tissue are significantly lower than in the non-diabetic controls [32, 33]. In addition, a significant increase is found in the A:B cell ratio in NIDDM subjects compared with controls, suggesting a specific decrease of the B-cell mass [33], as the A-cell mass is apparently unchanged in NIDDM subjects. Some of the microscopic changes reported in subjects with NIDDM include a variable degree of hyalinization of the islets [34], interacinar and perilobular fibrosis [35] and, rarely, focal infiltration with inflammatory cells [35]. Fatty atrophy has also been described associated with interacinar fibrosis [36]. Amyloid deposits rich in the recently characterized peptide, amylin, are also found in the pancreas of subjects with NIDDM [37, 38]. Amylin is apparently synthesized

by B cells but its pathophysiological significance remains unknown (see Chapters 8 and 18).

The A cell and glucagon secretion in NIDDM

There are three major defects in the A cells and glucagon secretion in subjects with NIDDM (Table 22.1), namely basal hyperglucagonaemia, either absolute or relative in relation to the ambient plasma glucose levels; an exaggerated glucagon response to amino-acid stimulation; and finally, impaired suppressibility of glucagon secretion by hyperglycaemia.

Glucagon secretion by A cells is primarily regulated by the plasma glucose concentration. Subjects with NIDDM exhibit hyperglucagonaemia in the fasting state and throughout the day, despite elevated plasma glucose levels [39] which, if induced in normal subjects, would suppress the circulating glucagon level to approximately 50% of its initial value.

In addition to basal hyperglucagonaemia, diabetic patients have an abnormal glucagon response to carbohydrate ingestion [40]. In non-diabetic subjects, plasma glucagon levels are suppressed after eating carbohydrate meals, whereas NIDDM patients fail to show this suppression and, in some cases, may even show a paradoxical rise in plasma glucagon levels (Fig. 22.4). In non-diabetic subjects, hyperglycaemia produced by any means — be it a glucose or carbohydrate meal or intravenous administration of glucose — results in an immediate suppression of glucagon. All diabetic patients fail to show glucagon suppression in response to oral glucose, although there are differences in the abnormal A-cell responses, depending on whether or not the diabetes is insulin-dependent. Patients with hypoinsulinaemic diabetes display a paradoxical increase in circulating glucagon levels following oral glucose administration, whereas NIDDM subjects show a biphasic plasma glucagon response, with an initial increase in glucagon levels followed by a late decline to levels below baseline [40].

The other major aspect of disordered A-cell function in NIDDM is glucagon hypersecretion in response to various aminogenic stimuli. In non-diabetic subjects, glucagon levels rise following intravenous administration of arginine or alanine or the ingestion of a protein meal; in NIDDM patients, these responses are exaggerated [41].

Several theories have been advanced to explain the above-mentioned abnormalities. The predominant hypothesis, that the hyperglucagonaemia of human diabetes is merely a consequence of insulin deficiency, seems appropriate in insulin-deficient diabetic patients, but may not explain A-cell dysfunction in NIDDM patients who often have normal or even elevated levels of circulating insulin. The abnormality in A-cell function in untreated IDDM is generally considerably more severe than in NIDDM. Hyperglucagonaemia in IDDM can be modified and, in some cases even normalized, by the administration of exogenous insulin, albeit in supraphysiological amounts which raise plasma insulin levels to values well above those seen in non-diabetic subjects under similar circumstances. The 'bihormonal abnormality' in IDDM can therefore be corrected by insulin treatment.

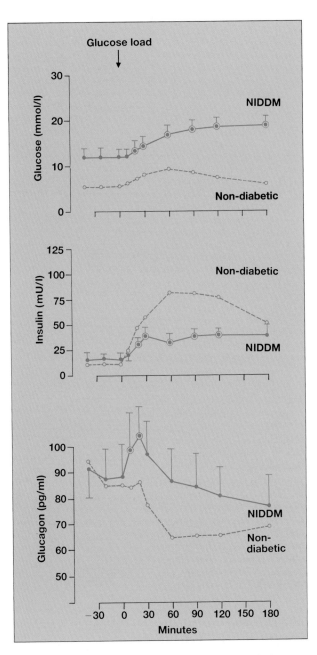

Fig. 22.4. Mean ± SEM plasma glucose, insulin and glucagon in normal subjects (○) and NIDDM patients (●) in response to a 100 g oral glucose load. Note failure to suppress glucagon in NIDDM patients. (From Aydin *et al.* 1977 [40] with permission from Springer-Verlag.)

The situation differs in NIDDM. A-cell abnormalities (such as the defective responses to oral glucose and protein and to intravenous arginine) are unaffected by even pharmacological doses of exogenous insulin. In NIDDM, therefore, A-cell dysfunction is apparently unrelated to insulin deficiency. It is possible that the A cells of these patients are resistant to the glucagon-suppressive effects of insulin in much the same way as the fat cells are resistant to the glucose-transporting effects of insulin. This hypothesis remains to be proven.

The D cell and somatostatin secretion in NIDDM

Somatostatin is a hormone with many physiological actions (see Chapter 33), including inhibition of release of several pituitary and pancreatic hormones (including both insulin and glucagon) [42] and reduction of intestinal nutrient absorption which may be relevant to the regulation of fuel homeostasis [43].

Two major abnormalities have been described in the D cells and somatostatin secretion in NIDDM (Table 22.1). The first is a reduction of the D-cell mass and D-cell numbers in experimental models of NIDDM, in contrast with the increased numbers found in IDDM [44]. Secondly, there is a nonselective reduction in stimulated somatostatin secretion in response to insulin-induced hypoglycaemia or ingestion of a mixed meal. Similarly, although nutrients such as glucose and amino acids stimulate somatostatin secretion in non-diabetic subjects [46], the response to glucose ingestion is absent in NIDDM patients [47].

No morphological data are available concerning D cells in human subjects with NIDDM. The relevance of these abnormalities in somatostatin to the pathophysiology of NIDDM is at present unknown.

Conclusion

Current knowledge of the pathogenesis of NIDDM suggests that the hyperglycaemia of the classical condition is attributable to both defective islet cells (mainly B cells) and insulin resistance. Insulin resistance may play a significant role in states such as obesity where there is known impairment of insulin action. However, defective islet-cell function is the primary defect producing hyperglycaemia in NIDDM subjects. Insulin resistance alone is insufficient to cause overt glucose intolerance. The concept that hyperglycaemia itself may have a detrimental effect on the islets (and insulin action) and thus a role in the pathogenesis of NIDDM may have relevant clinical implications and merits further research.

LUIS C. RAMIREZ
PHILIP RASKIN

References

1 Reaven GM. Insulin resistance in non-insulin dependent diabetes mellitus: does it exist and can it be measured? *Am J Med* 1983; **74** (suppl 1A): 3–17.

2 Eisenbarth GS. Type I diabetes mellitus: A chronic autoimmune disease. *N Engl J Med* 1986; **314**: 1360–8.

3 Orci L. Morphological aspects of the islets of Langerhans. *Metabolism* 1976; **25** (suppl 1): 1303–13.

4 Ward WK, Beard JC, Halter JB, Pfeiffer MA, Porte D. Pathophysiology of insulin secretion in non-insulin-dependent diabetes mellitus. *Diabetes Care* 1984; **7**: 491–502.

5 Pfeifer MA, Halter JB, Porte D Jr. Insulin secretion in diabetes mellitus. *Am J Med* 1981; **70**: 579–88.

6 Hermansen K, Ørskov H, Christensen SE. Streptozotocin diabetes: a glucoreceptor dysfunction affecting D cells as well as B and A cells. *Diabetologia* 1979; **17**: 385–9.

7 DeFronzo RA, Ferrannini E, Koivisto V. New concepts in the pathogenesis and treatment of non-insulin-dependent diabetes mellitus. *Am J Med* 1983; **75**: 52–81.

8 Ward WK, Bolgiano DC, McKnight B, Halter J, Porte D. Diminished beta cell secretory capacity in patients with non-insulin-dependent diabetes mellitus. *J Clin Invest* 1984; **74**: 1318–28.

9 Temple RC, Carrington CA, Luzio SD, Owens DR, Schneider AE, Sobey WJ, Hales CN. Insulin deficiency in non-insulin-dependent diabetes. *Lancet* 1989; i: 293–5.

10 Lang DA, Matthews DR, Peto J, Turner RC. Cyclic oscillations of basal plasma glucose and insulin concentrations in human beings. *N Engl J Med* 1979; **301**: 1023–7.

11 Matthews DR, Naylor BA, Jones RG, Ward GM, Turner RC. Pulsatile insulin has greater hypoglycemic effect than continuous delivery: *Diabetes* 1983; **32**: 617–21.

12 Lang DA, Matthews DR, Burnett M, Turner RC. Brief, irregular oscillation of basal plasma insulin and glucose concentration in diabetic man. *Diabetes* 1981; **30**: 435–9.

13 Polonsky KS, Given BD, Hirsch LJ, Tillil H, Shapiro ET, Beebe C, Frank BH, Gallaway JA, Van Cauter E. Abnormal patterns of insulin secretion in non-insulin dependent diabetes mellitus. *N Engl J Med* 1988; **318**: 1231–9.

14 Karam JM, Grodsky GM, Forsham PM. Excessive insulin response to glucose in obese subjects as measured by immuno chemical assay. *Diabetes* 1963; **12**: 197–204.

15 O'Rahilly SP, Rudenski AS, Burnett MA, Nugent Z, Hosker JP, Darling P. Beta-cell dysfunction, rather than insulin insensitivity, is the primary defect in familial type 2 diabetes. *Lancet* 1986; ii: 360–4.

16 O'Rahilly S, Turner RC, Matthews DR. Impaired pulsatile secretion of insulin in relatives of patients with non-insulin-dependent diabetes. *N Engl J Med* 1988; **318**: 1225–30.

17 Bogardus C, Lillioja S, Howard BV, Reaven G, Mott D. Relationship between insulin secretion, insulin action, and fasting plasma glucose concentration in non-diabetic and non-insulin dependent diabetic subjects. *J Clin Invest* 1984; **74**: 1238–46.

18 Unger RH, Grundy S. Hyperglycemia as an inducer as well as a consequence of impaired islet cell function and insulin resistance: Implication for the management of diabetes. *Diabetologia* 1985; **28**: 119–21.

19 Bonner-Weir S, Trent DF, Weir GC. Partial pancreatectomy in the rat and subsequent defect in glucose-induced insulin release. *J Clin Invest* 1983; **71**: 1544–53.

20 Imamura T, Koffler M, Helderman JM, Prince D, Thirlby R, Inman L, Unger RH. Severe diabetes induced in subtotally

depancreatized dogs by sustained hyperglycemia. *Diabetes* 1988; **37**: 600–9.

21 Kergoat M, Bailbe D, Portha B. Insulin treatment improves glucose-induced insulin release in rats with NIDDM induced by streptozocin. *Diabetes* 1987; **36**: 971–7.

22 Rossetti L, Smith D, Shulman GI, Papachristou D, De Fronzo RA. Correction of hyperglycemia with phlorizin normalizes tissue sensitivity to insulin in diabetic rats. *J Clin Invest* 1987; **79**: 1510–15.

23 Porte D Jr, Pupo AA. Insulin responses to glucose: evidence for a two-pool system in man. *J Clin Invest* 1969; **48**: 2309–19.

24 Karam JM, Grodsky GM, Ching KN, Schmid F, Burril K, Forsham PH. Staircase glucose stimulation of insulin secretion in obesity. *Diabetes* 1974; **23**: 763–70.

25 Weir GC, Clore ET, Zmachinski CJ, Bonner Weir S. Islet secretion in a new experimental model for non insulin-dependent diabetes. *Diabetes* 1981; **30**: 590–5.

26 Giroix MH, Portha B, Kergoat M, Bailbe D, Picon L. Glucose insensitivity and amino-acid hypersensitivity of insulin release in rats with non-insulin dependent diabetes. A study with the perfused pancreas. *Diabetes* 1983; **32**: 445–51.

27 Luzi L. Effect of the loss of first phase insulin secretion on glucose production and disposal in man. *Diabetes* 1987; **36** (suppl 1): 10a, (abstract).

28 De Fronzo R. The triumvirate: B cell, muscle, liver. A collusion responsible for NIDDM. *Diabetes* 1988; **34**: 667–87.

29 Rizza RA, Mandarino LJ, Genest J, Baker BA, Gerich JE. Production of insulin resistance by hyperinsulinaemia in man. I. *Diabetologia* 1985; **28**: 70–5.

30 Sheehan P, Leonetti F, Rosenthal N. Effect of prolonged hyperinsulinemia on glucose metabolism. *Diabetes* 1986; **35** (suppl 1): 16A: 63.

31 Groop L, Groop PH, Koskimies S. Relationship between B-cell function and HLA antigens in patients with type 2 (non-insulin-dependent) diabetes. *Diabetologia* 1986; **29**: 757–60.

32 Groop L, Miettinen A, Groop PH, Meri S, Koskimies S, Bottazzo GF. Organ-specific autoimmunity and HLA-DR antigens as markers for B-cell destruction in patients with Type II diabetes. *Diabetes* 1988; **37**: 99–103.

33 Gepts W. Contribution a l'étude morphologique des îlots de Langerhans au cours du diabète. *Ann Soc R Sci Med Nat Bruxelles* 1957; **10**: 5–108.

34 Ehrlich JC, Ratner IM. Amyloidosis of the islets of Langerhans. A restudy of islet hyalin in diabetic and non

diabetic subjects. *Am J Pathol* 1961; **38**: 49–59.

35 Volk BW, Wellman KF. In: Volk BW, Wellman KF, eds. *The Diabetic Pancreas*. New York: Plenum, 1977: 239.

36 Lazarus SS, Volk BN. *The Pancreas in Human and Experimental Diabetes*. New York: Grune and Stratton, 1962: 204.

37 Cooper GJS, Willis AC, Clark A, Turner RC, Sim RB, Reid KBM. Purification and characterization of a peptide from amyloid-rich pancreases of type 2 diabetic patients. *Proc Natl Acad Sci USA* 1987; **84**: 8628–32.

38 Clark A, Lewis CE, Willis AC, Cooper GJS, Morris JF, Reid KBM. Islet amyloid formed from diabetes-associated peptide may be pathogenic in type 2 diabetes. *Lancet* 1987; i: 231–4.

39 Raskin P, Unger RH. Hyperglucagonemia and its suppression. *N Engl J Med* 1978; **299**: 433–6.

40 Aydin I, Raskin P, Unger RH. The effect of short-term intravenous insulin administration on the glucagon response to a carbohydrate meal in adult-onset and juvenile-type diabetes. *Diabetologia* 1977; **13**: 629–36.

41 Raskin P, Aydin I, Unger RH. Effect of insulin on the exaggerated glucagon response to arginine stimulation in diabetes mellitus. *Diabetes* 1976; **25**: 227–9.

42 Mortimer CH, Carr D, Lind T, Bloom SR, Mallinson CN, Schally AV, Tunbridge WMG, Yeomans L, Coy D, Kastin A, Besser GM, Hall R. Effects of growth hormone release-inhibiting hormone on circulating glucagon, insulin and growth hormone in normal, diabetic, acromegalic and hypopituitary patients. *Lancet* 1974; i: 697–701.

43 Wahren J, Felig P. Influence of somatostatin on carbohydrate disposal and absorption in diabetes mellitus. *Lancet* 1976; i: 1213–16.

44 Baetens D, Coleman DL, Orci L. Islet cell population in ob/ob and db/db mice. *Diabetes* 1976; **25** (suppl 1): 344.

45 Vinik AI, Levitt NS, Pimstone BL, Wagner L. Peripheral plasma somatostatin-like immunoreactive response to insulin, hyperglycemia, and a mixed meal in healthy subjects and in noninsulin-dependent maturity-onset diabetics. *J Clin Endocrinol Metab* 1981; **52**: 330–7.

46 Schusdziarra V, Raviller D, Harris V, Conlon JM, Unger RH. The response of plasma somatostatin-like immunoreactivity to nutrients in normal and alloxan diabetic dogs. *Endocrinology* 1978; **103**: 2264–73.

47 Grill IV, Gutniak KM, Roovete A, Efendic S. A stimulating effect of glucose on somatostatin release is impaired in noninsulin-dependent diabetes mellitus. *J Clin Endocrinol Metab* 1986; **59**: 293–7.

23   Neuroendocrine Factors in the Pathogenesis of Non-Insulin-Dependent Diabetes Mellitus

Summary

• The key metabolic abnormalities of NIDDM — hyperglycaemia, impaired insulin secretion, insulin insensitivity, increased glucagon secretion and obesity — can all be reproduced by neuroendocrine manipulation.

• The hypothalamus regulates energy balance, insulin and counter-regulatory hormone secretion and blood glucose homeostasis largely through its output into the autonomic nervous system. Other brain areas and extracerebral systems are also important.

• Hypothalamic regulation of food intake involves the ventromedial (VMH) and paraventricular (PVN) nuclei and the lateral hypothalamic area (LHA). Damage to the VMH (or adjacent fibre tracts) and PVN produces hyperphagia, hyperinsulinaemia and obesity whereas LHA lesions produce hypophagia and weight loss.

• Neurotransmitters implicated in appetite regulation include the monoamines and several peptides. Possible 'satiety' factors include serotonin, cholecystokinin (CCK), corticotrophin releasing factor (CRF) and insulin, whereas noradrenaline, dynorphin and neuropeptide Y are powerful central appetite stimulants.

• Non-shivering and diet-induced thermogenesis are mainly mediated by brown adipose tissue (BAT) in rodents and by other tissues including skeletal muscle in man. These adaptive components of energy expenditure can be partly varied according to need.

• BAT is regulated by several brain regions including the VMH and LHA which respectively stimulate and inhibit its sympathetically mediated thermogenic activity. Neurotransmitters which may act centrally to activate BAT include CRF and insulin.

• Acute hyperglycaemia can be produced by stimulation of several brain areas, including the VMH and the upper ventral medulla. Many peptides and other substances also cause acute hyperglycaemia when injected centrally, through sympathetic activation leading to increased hepatic glycogenolysis and glucose production. LHA stimulation enhances glycogen synthesis and insulin secretion through increased vagal activity, tending to lower glycaemia.

• The key abnormalities in rodent models of obesity or NIDDM are reduced energy expenditure (attributable to impaired BAT-mediated thermogenesis) and increased insulin secretion. An autonomic disturbance leading to reduced sympathetic and increased parasympathetic activity could be responsible.

• Disturbances in brain and pancreas neurotransmitters — e.g. CCK, insulin and opioid peptides — have been identified in rodents with obesity/NIDDM syndromes but their significance is uncertain.

• In human NIDDM, obesity is probably an important contributory factor in most cases. Thermogenic responses to various stimuli may be impaired in certain patients. Insulin secretion is defective, and glucagon secretion is increased. The neuroendocrine basis for these abnormalities is unknown, although opioid peptides have been postulated to play a role.

The cause of NIDDM remains elusive but its metabolic abnormalities include hyperglycaemia, impaired insulin secretion, insulin insensitivity, increased glucagon secretion and obesity. The fact that each of these abnormalities can be reproduced by neural or endocrine manipulation of the nervous system or pancreas has stimulated research into possible neuroendocrine causes of the condition.

This chapter describes the neuroendocrine regulation of metabolism, the defects identified in animal models of obesity and NIDDM, and their possible relevance to human NIDDM.

Anatomical and functional background

The neuroendocrine control of energy balance, secretion of insulin and counter-regulatory hormones and blood glucose homeostasis is centred in the hypothalamus, with the participation of other areas within and outside the CNS. The major hypothalamic areas in the rat (Fig. 23.1) are the ventromedial nucleus (VMH) occupying most of the middle third of the ventrobasal hypothalamus, the paraventricular nucleus (PVN) projecting laterally from the apex of the third ventricle, and the lateral hypothalamic area (LHA). The dorsomedial nucleus (DMH) lies above the VMH, and the suprachiasmatic nucleus (SCN) immediately above the optic chiasm, from which it receives neural inputs. The preoptic area (POA) lies an-

teriorly between the optic chiasm and the anterior commissure, a transverse fibre bundle at the rostral boundary of the hypothalamus. The organization of the human hypothalamus (Fig. 23.2) is broadly similar [1–3].

The hypothalamus has many complex afferent, efferent and intrinsic neural pathways involved in metabolic regulation. Major inputs include the ventral noradrenergic bundle, ascending from cell bodies in the upper medulla to supply the PVN, DMH and POA; serotonergic fibres originating in the raphe and other midbrain nuclei; and a dopaminergic innervation derived partly from the nigrostriatal pathway projecting from the substantia nigra to the cortex [4].

The hypothalamus largely controls metabolism through its output into the autonomic nervous system (Figs 23.3 and 23.4). Stimulation of the VMH, and also of the PVN and SCN, activates the sympathetic system through polysynaptic pathways descending through the sympathetic centres in the medulla to cell bodies in the intermediolateral column of the spinal cord. These are the source of the sympathetic splanchnic nerves supplying the liver, pancreatic islets, adrenal medulla and brown adipose tissue (Fig. 23.3). By contrast, stimulation of the ventral LHA activates the dorsal motor nucleus of the vagus and the parasympathetic innervation to the viscera (Fig. 23.4) [5].

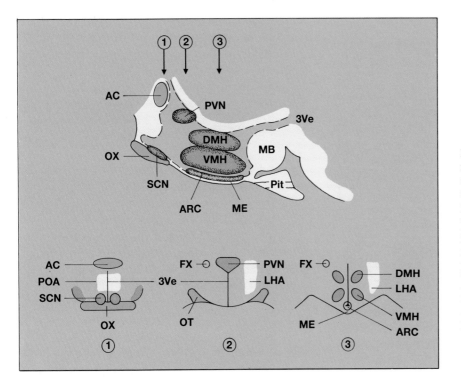

Fig. 23.1. Schematic diagram of the rat hypothalamus in longitudinal section (top) and in transverse section at three levels, showing principal areas implicated in metabolic regulation.
Key: VMH = ventromedial nucleus; DMH = dorsomedial nucleus; PVN = paraventricular nucleus; SCN = suprachiasmatic nucleus; ARC = arcuate nucleus; LHA = lateral hypothalamic area. AC = anterior commissure; FX = fornix; MB = mammillary body; ME = median eminence; OX = optic chiasm; Pit = pituitary; 3Ve = outline of third ventricle.

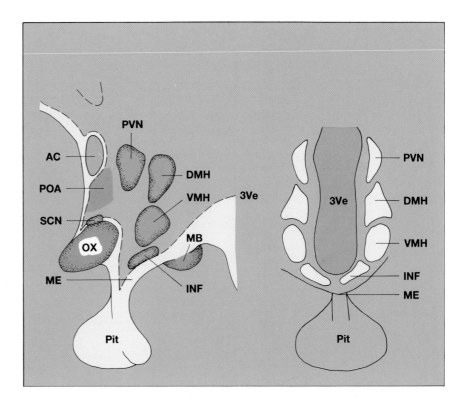

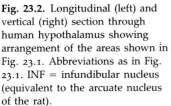

Fig. 23.2. Longitudinal (left) and vertical (right) section through human hypothalamus showing arrangement of the areas shown in Fig. 23.1. Abbreviations as in Fig. 23.1. INF = infundibular nucleus (equivalent to the arcuate nucleus of the rat).

The hypothalamus is extremely rich in proven and putative neurotransmitters, including over 30 known regulatory peptides. As well as neural inputs, the VMH and other hypothalamic regions where the blood–brain barrier is weak [6] are probably accessible to circulating substances including insulin and peptides.

The autonomic regulation of energy balance (i.e. energy intake and expenditure), insulin and counter-regulatory hormone secretion and glucose homeostasis is considered in the following sections.

Regulation of energy intake

Disturbances in energy balance are particularly relevant to NIDDM, in which obesity is probably a major aetiological factor (see Chapter 20).

Eating behaviour is largely controlled by the hypothalamus, interacting with other brain areas (including the olfactory cortex, amygdala and nucleus accumbens), various extracerebral sites and environmental cues. The VMH has been regarded as a 'satiety' centre, as its electrical stimulation terminates feeding whereas physical or chemical damage produces hyperphagia and obesity [7]. The LHA was postulated to contain a 'feeding' centre, whose stimulation causes feeding and whose destruction leads to aphagia and weight loss [8]. However, feeding is not controlled simply by the VMH inhibiting the LHA, as was originally proposed [9]. Despite their proximity, the two areas are not apparently directly interconnected but may instead receive inputs from the DMH [2]. Moreover, other areas are undoubtedly involved, including the SCN which may function as a circadian pacemaker regulating diurnal feeding rhythms [10] and the PVN, another putative satiety centre where damage induces a VMH-lesion-like syndrome [11, 12]. Finally, the syndromes classically attributed to VMH and LHA lesions may be due instead to damage to fibre tracts passing nearby, notably ascending noradrenergic (VMH) and dopaminergic (LHA) projections [5, 13].

The mechanisms which adjust food intake so as to maintain body weight and fat content are poorly understood but may include stretch receptors in the gut, changes in availability of glucose and other nutrients, and circulating mediators (e.g. insulin and gut peptides) whose levels rise after eating or are related to body composition. Glucose may affect glucose-sensitive neurones in the VMH and elsewhere [14] and peptides may act on various hypothalamic and related regions [15].

Many putative neurotransmitters have experimental effects — often of dubious significance —

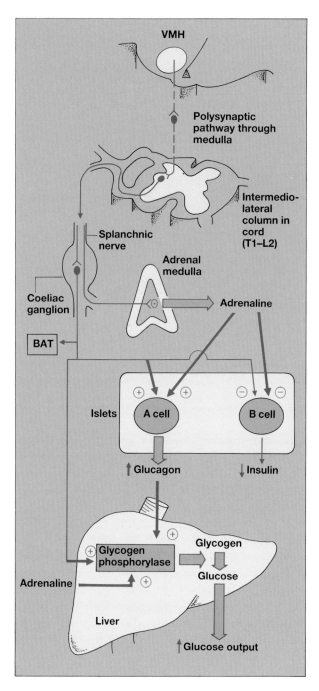

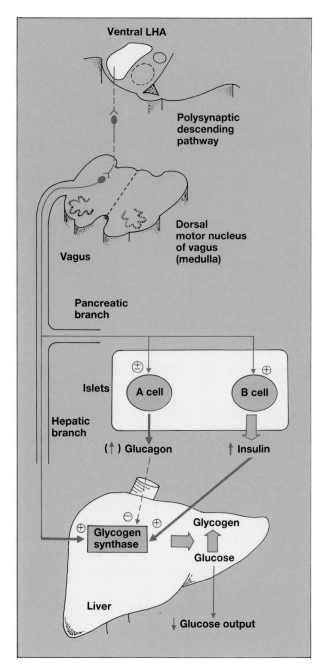

Fig. 23.3. Scheme of sympathetic activation following stimulation of the VMH region. BAT = brown adipose tissue.

Fig. 23.4. Scheme of parasympathetic activation following stimulation of the ventral LHA. Vagal stimulation increases glucagon secretion in some species (including man), but to a lesser extent than insulin secretion.

on feeding behaviour in various species, including man (Table 23.1) [16, 17]. Some of the more convincing examples are discussed below.

Non-peptide ('classical') neurotransmitters and feeding behaviour

Monoamines, possibly released by the afferent pathways described above [4], exert various site-

and receptor-specific effects on feeding [18]. Noradrenaline acts on α2-adrenoceptors in the PVN to stimulate eating, preferentially of carbohydrate, perhaps by inhibiting neurones which suppress feeding [18−20]. By contrast, adrenaline injected into the LHA inhibits feeding, apparently via β2-adrenoceptors [18]. Serotonin may signal satiety, as its injection into the PVN and other hypothalamic areas inhibits feeding in hungry rats; serotonergic drugs such as fenfluramine, which stimulates serotonin release from nerve-endings, and fluoxetine, which blocks serotonin reuptake into endings, have the same effect [16, 18]. The hypothalamus contains several subtypes of serotonergic receptors whose specificity and distribution vary considerably between species. Dopamine injected into the LHA stimulates feeding at low dosages but is inhibitory at higher dosages. Eating is increased by GABA injected into the VMH and by GABA antagonists injected into the LHA [16].

Peptides and feeding behaviour

Most peptides tested inhibit feeding, generally at grossly supraphysiological dosages and often in a behaviourally non-specific fashion. Only a few inhibitory peptides — notably cholecystokinin (CCK), corticotrophin-releasing factor (CRF), insulin and bombesin-like peptides seem likely mediators of satiety.

CCK, which exists in several molecular forms in gut and brain, terminates feeding when injected either peripherally or centrally in several species [17, 21–23]. It may mediate satiety through an integrated, multi-stage CCK-ergic pathway. After eating, CCK is released from the gut into the circulation and apparently interacts with specific peripheral (CCK-A) receptors on vagal afferents. These project ultimately to the PVN and other brain areas where they may trigger release of CCK which, functioning as a neurotransmitter, activates central (CCK-B) receptors. In the PVN, CCK apparently opposes the appetite-stimulating action of noradrenaline [24–27]. CCK released postprandially may also constrict the pylorus (which is rich in CCK-A receptors), causing gastric distension which may signal satiety [28]. Specific CCK-B receptor antagonists prolong eating, suggesting that central CCK-ergic pathways are particularly important in signalling satiety in rats [29]; the relative importance of peripheral and central mechanisms may vary in different species.

CRF is found at high concentrations in the PVN, stimulation of which activates the pituitary–adrenocortical axis. CRF has very potent central appetite-suppressant actions and blocks the feeding induced by central injection of noradrenaline, dynorphin and neuropeptide Y (NPY). CRF apparently acts on the PVN and may underlie its 'satiety centre' functions [17, 30–32]. Increased

hypothalamic CRF-ergic activity resulting from reduced negative feedback by glucocorticoids could contribute to the hypophagia induced by adrenalectomy in certain obese rodents [13]. CRF may also mediate the anorectic effect of interleukin-1β, a cytokine which may be responsible for hypophagia during infection [33].

Insulin may be an important satiety- and weight-regulating peptide. Its circulating levels are generally proportional to body fat content and increase postprandially [34]. Circulating insulin apparently enters the CSF and hypothalamic areas with a weak blood–brain barrier; the hypothalamus and other brain areas contain both insulin and insulin receptors [34–36]. Insulin administered centrally, or peripherally at sub-hypoglycaemic dosages, inhibits feeding in several species [34, 37, 38] and insulin antibodies injected specifically into the VMH increase feeding in rats [39]. Insulin could act as a satiety signal regulating body weight, as increasing adiposity would cause a parallel rise in circulating insulin levels and so inhibit feeding [34]. This hypothesis may explain the hunger and hyperphagia of hypoinsulinaemic states such as starvation and insulin-deficient diabetes; the apparent paradox of hyperphagia in certain hyperinsulinaemic, obese rodents may be due to insensitivity of the brain to the appetite-suppressant action of insulin [40]. Large insulin doses causing hypoglycaemia or neuroglycopenia stimulate eating [14, 17].

Few peptides induce feeding. The opioid peptides, dynorphin and β-endorphin, apparently acting on κ- and ε-receptors respectively, stimulate eating in several species when injected into the PVN and other hypothalamic sites and preferentially increase fat and protein intake [17, 41–44]. Conversely, opioid antagonists (e.g. naloxone) reduce food intake in various species including rodents, tigers, slugs and man [17, 45].

NPY, a major brain peptide structurally related to pancreatic polypeptide, is densely concentrated in the PVN and other hypothalamic areas [46–48]. NPY is one of the most potent central appetite stimulants known when injected into the PVN, VMH, DMH or LHA [17, 49–52]. Repeated injection causes sustained hyperphagia and ultimately obesity, NPY being the only peptide with this action [50]. NPY-stimulated hyperphagia overcomes CCK-induced anorexia and normal postprandial satiety but is attenuated by centrally injected CRF or bombesin [17, 52, 59]. NPY

Table 23.1. Examples of putative or proven neurotransmitters with experimental effects on feeding.

	Agent	Species	Likely site(s) of action	Comments	References
	Adrenaline	Rat	LHA	• Act on β_2-adrenoceptors	18
	Serotonin	Rat, mouse	PVN, VMH; other hypothalamic sites	• Various receptors implicated • Selectively reduces carbohydrate intake	16, 18
	Dopamine	Rat	LHA	• Lower dosages may stimulate feeding	16, 18
	Cholecystokinin (CCK)	Rat, mouse, cat, dog, monkey, man	PVN, LHA; other hypothalamic and medullary sites; peripheral sites	• Peripheral action via CCK-A receptors (vagus, etc.) • Central action via CCK-B receptors • Antagonizes noradrenaline action in PVN • May also cause satiety through gastric distension	21–29
	Corticotrophin-releasing factor (CRF)	Rat, mouse	PVN	• Very potent • Inhibits noradrenaline-, NPY- and dynorphin-induced feeding • May mediate anorexic effects of interleukin-Iβ and adrenalectomy	30–33
Inhibit feeding	Insulin	Rat, cat, dog, monkey	?Hypothalamus or other brain sites	• Given into CSF, or peripherally at subhypoglycaemic dosages • Circulating insulin may enter CSF and brain	34–38
	Bombesin	Rat, mouse, dog	LHA, medial hypothalamus, amygdala	• Peripheral administration or central injection • Chronic peripheral injection may cause weight loss	58, 59
	Growth hormone releasing-factor (GRF)	Rat	Third ventricle	• High dosages (low dosages stimulate feeding)	57
	Neurotensin	Rat	PVN; peripheral sites		60
	Somatostatin	Rat, monkey	Third ventricle; peripheral sites		46

		ICV			
No effect	Somatostatin	Man	Third ventricle	• By i.v. infusion in non-obese, obese and bulimic subjects	46
	Cholecystokinin		?		17
	Noradrenaline	Rat	PVN	• Acts on α₂-adrenoceptors • Selectively increases carbohydrate intake • Chronic central administration causes obesity • Dependent on adequate corticosterone levels	16, 18
	Dynorphin	Rat	PVN, DMH; peripheral sites	• Acts on κ-receptors • Selectively increases fat and protein intake; may act on ε-receptors	42, 43
	β-endorphin	Rat	VMH; peripheral sites		41, 43
Stimulate feeding	Neuropeptide Y (NPY)	Rat, mouse, dog	PVN, VMH, DMH, LHA; Fourth ventricle	• Most potent central appetite-stimulant known (together with closely related peptide YY) • Selectively increases carbohydrate intake • Hyperphagia overcomes normal satiety and CCK • Chronic administration causes obesity • Also stimulates drinking	47, 49–53
	Galanin	Rat	PVN	• Selectively increases fat intake	55
	Growth hormone releasing-factor (GRF)	Rat	Third ventricle	• Low dosages (higher dosages inhibit feeding)	56
	Somatostatin	Rat	Third ventricle		46

Notes:
1 For abbreviations, see p. 206.
2 Note conflicting data obtained for somatostatin by different workers and the divergent effects of high- and low-dose GRF and dopamine.
3 Effects of peptides are comprehensively reviewed by Morley [17].

selectively increases carbohydrate intake [49]. Adrenaline and NPY are co-stored in fibres supplying the PVN but apparently have independent appetite-stimulating effects [17, 51]. NPY-immunoreactive terminals closely surround CRF-containing cell bodies in the PVN [53], suggesting that the two peptides may interact: they have opposite effects on feeding but both activate the pituitary—adrenocortical axis [54].

Feeding is also stimulated by galanin [55] and low doses of growth-hormone releasing factor [56, 57] (Table 23.1).

Fact or artefact?

Even the most subtle stereotactic studies are grossly unphysiological, and a substance's exper-imental effects on feeding may have little relevance to its true role (if any) in regulating appetite. However, dynamic changes in the activity of some neurotransmitters have been identified under conditions which alter feeding behaviour, such as the onset of darkness (the main cue for eating in rodents), starvation, and insulin-deficient diabetes which causes carbohydrate-selective hyperphagia (Table 23.2). These observations hint, for example, at involvement of noradrenaline [61, 62], β-endorphin [73] and NPY [77] in initiating dark-phase eating; of CCK in terminating feeding [69]; and of opioids [72, 75], insulin [71] and NPY [78—81] in regulating food intake so as to maintain body weight. The many other neuroendocrine changes accompanying starvation and diabetes undoubtedly confuse the issue and, for example,

Table 23.2. Examples of changes in putative appetite-modulating neurotransmitters under conditions of altered feeding.

Agent	Species	Observation	References
Noradrenaline	Rat	• Released in discrete hypothalamic regions during feeding	61
		• Increased α_2-adrenoceptor binding in PVN after darkness	62
		• Decreased α_2-adrenoceptor binding in PVN during starvation	18
		• Reduced hypothalamic levels in STZ-DM	63
		• Increased hypothalamic levels (some areas) in STZ-DM	64
Serotonin	Rat	• Increased synthesis in hypothalamus during starvation	65
GABA	Rat	• Increased hypothalamic content after eating	66
Cholecystokinin (CCK)	Rat	• Increased hypothalamic levels after eating (in lean and obese Zucker rats)	67
		• No change in hypothalamic levels after eating or over-feeding	68
	Monkey, cat	• Released in discrete hypothalamic areas after eating	69
Corticotrophin-releasing factor (CRF)	Rat	• Decreased hypothalamic levels during starvation	70
Insulin	Rat	• Increased insulin binding in PVN during starvation	71
Dynorphin	Rat	• Increased hypothalamic levels after darkness • Increased hypothalamic levels in daytime during starvation	72
β-endorphin	Rat	• Increased levels in DMH after darkness	73
		• Hypothalamic levels increased [72], unchanged [74] or decreased [75] during starvation	72, 74, 75
		• Increased pituitary and circulating levels during starvation	74
		• Reduced hypothalamic and pituitary levels in STZ-DM rats	76
Neuropeptide Y (NPY)	Rat	• Increased levels in LHA after darkness	77
		• Increased levels in PVN and other areas during starvation; increase in PVN reversed by refeeding	78
		• Increased hypothalamic levels (especially in PVN, DMH, VMH and LHA) in STZ-DM and BB/E diabetic rats	79—81
Neurotensin	Rat	• Hypothalamic levels decreased [82] or unchanged [83] in STZ-DM rats	82, 83

Notes:

1 For abbreviations, see p. 206. STZ-DM = streptozotocin-induced diabetes.

2 Note conflicting findings for noradrenaline, CCK, β-endorphin and neurotensin.

may explain the apparent inconsistency of reportedly increased activity of the 'satiety factors', serotonin [65] and CRF [70], in starvation.

Regulation of energy expenditure

In rodents, energy expended other than through the basal metabolic rate and muscular activity may be partly varied according to need. These 'adaptive' components of energy expenditure, non-shivering thermogenesis and diet-induced thermogenesis, are stimulated by cold exposure and ingested nutrients respectively, and both are largely dissipated by brown adipose tissue (BAT) [84–86]. BAT adipocytes are activated by their dense sympathetic innervation and circulating catecholamines, acting through a specific, atypical β_3 adrenoceptor [87]. This stimulates an 'uncoupling protein' (thermogenin) unique to BAT, which short-circuits proton conductance through the inner mitochondrial membrane, uncoupling oxidative phosphorylation and generating heat instead of ATP. BAT is extremely rich in active mitochondria (which contain the cytochrome pigments responsible for its brown colour) and its great vascularity — with the capacity to increase its blood flow by up to 50-fold [88] — rapidly distributes heat and raises body temperature [86].

BAT activity is regulated centrally by the VMH and LHA, which have reciprocal actions, together with the PVN, preoptic area and other regions [89]. VMH stimulation, either electrically or by injection of thermogenic agents, activates the sympathetic outflow to BAT, increasing heat production and blood flow [90, 91]. Conversely, LHA stimulation reduces BAT activity [89]. The central pathways mediating non-shivering thermogenesis and diet-induced thermogenesis differ. Non-shivering thermogenesis is activated by cooling, possibly sensed by the preoptic area and peripheral receptors [89]. The signals for diet-induced thermogenesis are unknown but insulin, which can enter the hypothalamus and which activates sympathetic outflow and stimulates BAT activity when injected into the VMH, is one candidate [92]. Chronic cold exposure or overeating (e.g. induced by a varied 'junk-food' or 'cafeteria' diet which rats apparently enjoy) induce adaptive increases in BAT mass and uncoupling protein content; the resulting rise in energy expenditure prevents hypothermia during cold exposure and limits weight gain during overeating. Conversely, starvation reduces diet-induced thermogenesis [85, 86].

Many substances affect BAT activity when injected centrally [89]. Virtually all increase thermogenesis to some extent (Table 23.3) and most of these also reduce food intake (cf. Table 23.1). This

Table 23.3. Examples of substances reported to affect thermogenesis when injected centrally.

Effect	Substance	Comments
Large increase	Serotonin	—
	GABA	• GABA$_A$-agonists; cf. reduced thermogenesis caused by GABA$_B$-agonists
	CRF	• Probably acts on PVN
		• May mediate thermogenic effect of interleukin-lβ
	TRH	• May activate thermogenesis at end of hibernation
	Insulin	• Injected into VMH
	CCK-4	• CCK-8 has no effect
Slight Increase	Bombesin	• Cause hypothermia on central injection as increased body heat losses overcome small thermogenic effect
	Neurotensin	
	Neuropeptide Y	
	Somatostatin	
Decrease	Noradrenaline	• Infused into the VMH; reduced thermogenesis inferred as weight gain was disproportionate to hyperphagia
	GABA	• GABA$_B$-agonists
	2-deoxyglucose	• Causes neuroglycopenia
		• May act on ventral premammillary nucleus

Notes:
1 Adapted from Rothwell [89].
2 These data relate to intracerebroventricular injections in the rat, except where indicated.

hints at an integrated mechanism to reduce body weight, although the physiological relevance of many of these observations is uncertain.

One of the most potent thermogenic agents is CRF which causes general sympathetic activation, including that of BAT, when injected centrally [31, 93]. Altered CRF-induced thermogenesis may partly explain the striking effects of glucocorticoid status on energy expenditure in obese rodents (see below). CRF may also mediate the thermogenic effect of interleukin-1β, implicated in the pyrexia of infection [33].

The above observations apply to rodents. As discussed below, the magnitude of adaptive thermogenesis and the importance of BAT in man remain controversial [94].

Neuroendocrine regulation of glucose homeostasis

The ability of the CNS to influence blood glucose concentration was first demonstrated experimentally in the 1850s by the 'piqûre diabetes' induced by Claude Bernard [95]. Transfixing the medulla of a rabbit with a metal probe caused acute hyperglycaemia and glycosuria, lasting several hours (Fig. 23.5). Attention was subsequently diverted from the medullary 'diabetic centre of Bernard' by evidence implicating pancreatic damage as the cause of diabetes. However, the model was used in 1924 [96] to test the therapeutic effect of insulin and its possible relevance to NIDDM is still keenly debated [97]. The region mediating piqûre diabetes, and possibly the hyperglycaemia provoked by central injection of morphine and certain peptides, is apparently the ventral surface of the upper medulla [97].

Glucoregulation also involves the hypothalamus [5]. Glucose-sensitive neurones are found in the VMH, LHA and SCN, those in the VMH and LHA showing reciprocal responses to neuroglycopenia [98, 99]. The VMH and LHA exert mutually antagonistic glycaemic effects through the autonomic nervous system. VMH stimulation or induction of neuroglycopenia increases the sympathetic outflow to the viscera and causes hyperglycaemia (Fig. 23.6), whereas LHA activation increases vagal activity and tends to lower glycaemia [100, 101]. Stimulation of the SCN also causes hyperglycaemia [10]. The glucoreceptors sensing hypoglycaemia may lie in extrahypothalamic sites, perhaps including the hindbrain, spinal cord or even the liver [102–104].

The autonomic mechanisms regulating glucose homeostasis are shown in Figs. 23.3 and 23.4. The autonomic innervation of the liver directly modulates the activity of enzymes controlling glycogen and glucose metabolism and can rapidly alter hep-

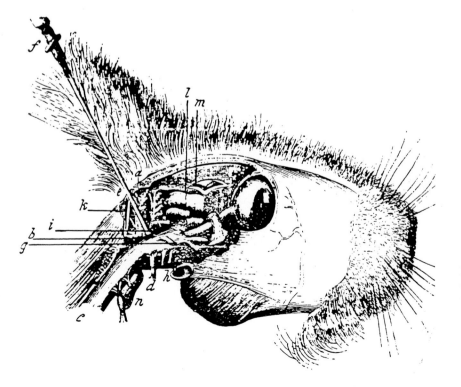

Fig. 23.5. Experimental induction of 'piqûre' diabetes. The area mediating piqûre hyperglycaemia is thought, by analogy with morphine-induced hyperglycaemia [97], to be the ventral surface of the upper medulla. (From Bernard C, Leçons de physiologie [95].)

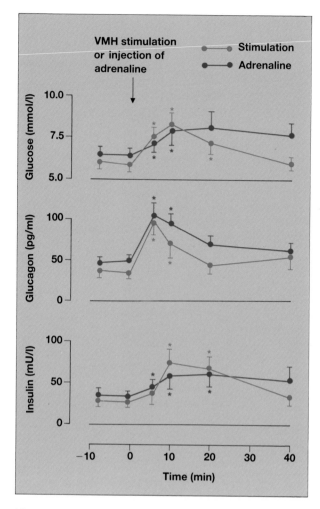

Fig. 23.6. Effects of electrical stimulation of VMH and injection of adrenaline into the VMH in rabbits, showing significant rises (*) in plasma glucose, glucagon and insulin levels. (Redrawn from Shimazu R *et al.* 1981 [122].)

atic glucose output, the main source of basal hyperglycaemia in NIDDM. Sympathetic stimulation activates glycogenolysis and therefore increases hepatic glucose output, whereas increased vagal activity stimulates glycogen synthesis and so reduces glucose production [5, 105].

The autonomic supply of the pancreatic islets profoundly affects insulin and glucagon secretion [106]. VMH stimulation reduces insulin release, mainly through the inhibitory effects of released catecholamines [107]. Vagal stimulation increases insulin secretion [106]. Under resting conditions, sympathetic tone to the B cell predominates over parasympathetic and insulin secretion is restrained [108]. Glucagon secretion is rapidly and markedly increased by sympathetic activation

and, to a lesser degree in some species, by vagal stimulation [5, 106, 107].

The third major glucoregulatory organ is the adrenal medulla. Adrenaline released during generalized sympathetic activation acts on the islets to increase glucagon and suppress insulin secretion, and on the liver to increase glucose production [5]. This mechanism is responsible for acute hyperglycaemic responses to various central stimuli [97].

Growth hormone and cortisol (corticosterone in rodents) are also released and contribute to hyperglycaemia during sympathetic activation by antagonizing insulin action; glucocorticoids also inhibit insulin release.

Neurotransmitters and glucoregulation

Various substances affect islet-cell secretion and/or glycaemia when injected into the hypothalamus or third ventricle (Table 23.4) [97, 109, 110]. The central pathways influencing insulin and glucagon release are generally unknown but presumably terminate at the autonomic innervation of the islets.

Most of the compounds reported to alter blood glucose levels cause hyperglycaemia, an action shared by so many dissimilar substances (including anaesthetics, carbachol and magnesium salts [97]) that its specificity and relevance are questionable. Several peptides including β-endorphin [111], CRF [112], glucagon [113], and bombesin [114] (as well as morphine [97]) apparently trigger adrenomedullary discharge of adrenaline, which stimulates hepatic glycogenolysis and glucose output; their site of action when injected intracerebroventricularly may be the upper ventral medulla, VMH or PVN [97]. Somatostatin injected into the third ventricle blocks hyperglycaemia induced by stress, neuroglycopenia and centrally injected peptides [109, 110], and itself causes mild hypoglycaemia when injected into the VMH or LHA [115].

The significance of these experimental actions is unknown. Relatively small doses injected into discrete areas [115] may elicit more relevant responses than large intraventricular doses. The striking influence of the light–dark cycle on the effects of insulin injected into the SCN [116] may indicate a true physiological action. Increased glucagon-like immunoreactivity in the brains of dogs rendered hypoglycaemic [117] may suggest a role for glucagon or related peptides in central glucoregulation.

Table 23.4. Examples of substances reported to affect glycaemia or insulin or glucagon secretion when injected centrally.

Effect	Substance	Species	Likely site(s) of action	Mechanism and comments	References
Hyperglycaemia	Bombesin	Rat	ICV; VMH; LHA		114
	β-endorphin	Rat	ICV		111
	CRF	Rat	ICV	• Increased adrenaline secretion	112
	Glucagon	Rat, mouse	ICV		113
	TRH	Rat	ICV		109, 110
	Somatostatin	Rat	ICV		46
	CCK	Rat	ICV	• ?Sympathetic activation	118
	Insulin	Rat	SCN (dark-phase)	• ?Sympathetic activation	116
	Neurotensin	Rat	ICV	• Large dosages (effect disputed)	109, 110
	Morphine	Rat, cat	ICV		97
	2-Deoxyglucose	Rat	ICV	• Sympathetic activation	119
	Cyclic AMP	Rat	ICV	• Increased adrenaline secretion	120
Hypoglycaemia	Insulin	Rat	VMH; ICV	• Decreased hepatic glycogenolysis and glucose output	121
		Rat	SCN (light-phase)		116
	Somatostatin	Rat	VMH, LHA	• Decreased hepatic venous glucose	46
Increased insulin secretion	Adrenaline, Noradrenaline	Rabbit	VMH		122
	Neuropeptide Y	Rat	ICV		123
	Noradrenaline	Rat	VMH, LHA		123
	Bombesin	Rat	VMH, LHA		115
	Neurotensin	Rat	VMH, LHA		115
Decreased insulin secretion	Insulin	Dog	ICV		125
Increased glucagon secretion	Adrenaline, Noradrenaline	Rabbit	VMH		122
	Bombesin	Rat	VMH, LHA		115
	TRH	Rat	ICV		109, 126
	Acetylcholine	Rabbit	VMH		122
	Noradrenaline	Rat	VMH, LHA		123

Notes:

1 Some peptides and drugs causing hyperglycaemia when injected intracerebroventricularly (ICV) may act on the upper central medulla.

2 Conflicting data may be related to site, dosage and species differences.

3 The effects of peptides are reviewed by Brown [109] and Frohman [110].

Neuroendocrine defects in animal models of NIDDM

No animal model accurately simulates human NIDDM (see Chapter 24). Four commonly considered models (Table 23.5) are obese, hyperphagic, hyperinsulinaemic and insulin-insensitive at various stages of development. *ob/ob* and *db/db* mice are hyperglycaemic; the latter tend to develop progressive insulin deficiency and so resemble human NIDDM more closely, although severe insulinopenia and ketosis may ultimately supervene. Fatty (*fa/fa*) Zucker and VMH-lesioned rats are only mildly glucose-intolerant rather than diabetic but are of interest because they display obesity, an important feature of human NIDDM. These models display various neuroendocrine defects.

Role of hyperphagia

All four models are hyperphagic but still become obese if food intake is restricted to that of lean animals [13]. This indicates that obesity is due to reduced energy expenditure rather than increased consumption. By contrast, hyperphagia appears to be aetiologically important in the Chinese hamster, as food restriction prevents obesity (which is relatively mild) and ultimately ameliorates diabetes [127].

Role of reduced energy expenditure

The reduced energy expenditure in these syndromes is apparently due to decreased adaptive thermogenesis, mediated by BAT. In *ob/ob* mice, both non-shivering and diet-induced thermogenesis are impaired, both in adults and in pups before hyperphagia and obesity develop [128–131]. BAT mitochondria are structurally abnormal and have a reduced uncoupling protein content [132]. This may suggest a primary BAT abnormality but, given the remarkable plasticity of BAT (e.g. following dietary manipulation), a primary hypothalamic defect is not excluded. Both diet-induced and non-shivering thermogenesis are also reduced in *db/db* mice, whereas fatty Zucker and VMH-lesioned rats have decreased diet-induced but normal non-shivering thermogenesis (133–138). These different thermogenic defects reflect the divergence of central pathways regulating BAT activity [89].

Role of abnormal insulin and counter-regulatory hormone secretion

Hyperinsulinaemia is an early feature of all the syndromes, appearing within 30 minutes of acute bilateral VMH lesions [13, 139–142]. It is due primarily to increased insulin secretion, which is

Table 23.5. Metabolic features of obesity and NIDDM syndromes in man and rodents.

	Man		Rodents			
	NIDDM	Obesity	*db/db* mouse	*ob/ob* mouse	*fa/fa* rat	VMH-lesioned rat
Body weight	N, +, ++	+, ++	++	++	++	++
Food intake	+(?)	+(?)	++	++	++	++
Energy expenditure:						
Total	+	+	− −	− −	− −	− −
DIT	−(?)	−(?)	− −	− −	− −	− −
NST	−(?)	−(?)	− −	− −	N	N
Insulinaemia	−	+, ++	++ (early) − (late)	++	++	++
Insulin sensitivity	−, − −	−, − −	− −	− −	− −	− −
Glucagonaemia	+	N	N, +	N, +	N, +	N, +
Glycaemia	+, ++	N	++	++	N	N
Ketosis	o	o	− (early) ++ (late)	o	o	o

Notes:
1 DIT, NST = diet-induced and non-shivering thermogenesis.
2 N = normal; +, ++ = moderately, greatly increased; −, − − = moderately, greatly decreased; o = absent.
3 Reports of glucagon levels in the rodent models vary considerably [13].

vagally mediated as it is abolished by vagotomy at various levels or atropine treatment [141, 143–145]; reduced hepatic extraction of insulin may also contribute to peripheral hyperinsulinaemia. Hyperinsulinaemia is considered a key pathogenic factor in these syndromes [13]. Firstly, it correlates with and may induce insulin insensitivity in the liver, resulting in unrestrained glucose output despite hyperinsulinaemia and therefore hyperglycaemia [146]. Secondly, it promotes fat deposition in adipocytes (which, unlike the liver, remain sensitive to insulin's lipogenic action) and therefore causes obesity [147]. The failure of high insulin levels either to suppress eating or to stimulate thermogenesis in these animals, according to the hypotheses discussed above, could be due to induction of insulin insensitivity in the brain, analogous to that affecting the liver.

Nutrient-stimulated glucagon secretion may be increased in some models, although reports vary [13, 148–150]. Hyperglucagonaemia, also attributed to increased vagal stimulation of the islets [149], may exacerbate insulin insensitivity of the liver and therefore increase hepatic glucose output.

Glucocorticoid status critically affects the expression of the rodent obesity syndromes [13, 151]. Circulating corticosterone levels are increased in obese animals, and *ob/ob* mice in particular display marked adrenocortical hypertrophy. Adrenalectomy reverses or prevents most of the syndromes' features — hyperphagia, reduced thermogenesis, obesity, hyperinsulinaemia and insulin insensitivity — and accurate corticosterone replacement will restore these abnormalities [152, 153]. These effects may be explained by corticosterone inhibiting the potent anorectic, thermogenic and sympathetic-activating effects of hypothalamic CRF [31, 93] through negative feedback. Corticosterone is also necessary for noradenaline to exert its appetite-stimulating action in the PVN [154].

Overall, much evidence favours disturbed neuroendocrine regulation, probably at hypothalamic level, as the primary cause of the rodent obesity/NIDDM syndromes (see Chapter 24). Bray and York have attributed the key abnormalities — reduced energy expenditure and increased insulin secretion — to autonomic imbalance, with a loss of sympathetic and a predominance of parasympathetic activity [13]. Many observations support this 'autonomic hypothesis'. Evidence of sympathetic under-activity includes reduced electrical activity in the sympathetic nerves supplying interscapular BAT soon after acute VMH lesioning [13,

89] and subnormal noradrenaline turnover in peripheral organs of obese Zucker rats [155]. Parasympathetic over-activity is confirmed by the fact that vagotomy reverses or prevents hyperphagia, hyperinsulinaemia and obesity [141, 143–145]. Autonomic dysfunction in the hereditary models and its relationship to hypothalamo–pituitary–adrenocortical and other defects is unexplained.

Neurotransmitter abnormalities in animal models

Various abnormalities in brain neurotransmitters have been reported in animal models (Table 23.6) but their significance remains uncertain, for several reasons. Firstly, alterations in transmitter activity in localized brain regions have not yet been fully characterized; altered peptide levels in whole brain or hypothalamus are particularly difficult to interpret. Secondly, the physiological effects of these changes is unknown; changes in CCK, for example, are generally linked with appetite disturbances but could affect other metabolic functions. Thirdly, it is not known whether these changes represent primary defects, secondary responses to hyperphagia or other features of the syndromes, or merely epiphenomena.

Of the brain peptides, CCK and insulin have been intensively studied. Initial reports of reduced whole brain and hypothalamic CCK levels in *ob/ob* and *db/db* mice [158] were not confirmed and indeed, no changes in CCK concentrations were found in other obese rodents or following major dietary manipulation [68]. However, subtle disturbances in brain CCK — increased receptor numbers (but not in the hypothalamus) [161, 162] and increased *in vitro* release from hypothalamic tissue [163] — have been demonstrated in fatty Zucker rats. The satiety action of CCK is also blunted in weanling fatty Zucker rats [164]. These animals also show abnormalities of brain insulin. CSF insulin levels are low in relation to the degree of hyperinsulinaemia [166], brain insulin content is abnormally low [167] and insulin receptor numbers are reduced in the olfactory bulb and hypothalamus [168]; heterozygous lean (Fa/*fa*) rats also show reduced insulin receptor numbers, indicating a gene-dosage effect rather than a consequence of obesity. Fatty Zucker rats have an additional, specific defect in central insulin action, perhaps analogous to their hepatic insulin insensitivity: insulin infused intracerebroventricularly inhibits eating and causes weight loss in lean, but not in obese animals [40].

Table 23.6. Examples of disturbances in brain neurotransmitters reported in animal models of obesity or NIDDM.

Agent	Model	Observation	References
Noradrenaline	ob/ob mouse	• Increased hypothalamic levels	156
	db/db mouse	• Increased hypothalamic levels	156
	fa/fa Zucker rat	• Decreased levels in PVN	157
Cholecystokinin (CCK)	ob/ob mouse	• Reduced brain and hypothalamic levels	158
		• Unchanged brain and hypothalamic levels	68
		• Increased CCK binding in cortex (not in hypothalamus)	159
	fa/fa rat	• Unchanged hypothalamic levels	68, 160
		• Increased CCK receptor binding in cortex, hippocampus and midbrain (not in hypothalamus)	161, 162
		• Increased in vitro release from hypothalamic tissue	163
		• Impaired satiety response to CCK (in weanlings)	164
CCK/gastrin	Sand rat	• Reduced numbers of neurones immunoreactive for CCK/gastrin in various brain regions	165
Insulin	fa/fa rat	• Reduced brain insulin content, notably in hypothalamus	167
		• Reduced brain insulin-binding capacity (also in lean Fa/fa heterozygotes)	168
		• Impaired satiety response to ICV insulin	40
β-endorphin	ob/ob mouse	• Increased pituitary and circulating levels	169
	fa/fa rat	• Increased pituitary levels	169
Dynorphin	ob/ob mouse	• Increased posterior pituitary levels	170
		• Exaggerated hyperphagia induced by κ-agonists	170
Leu-enkephalin	ob/ob mouse	• Increased posterior pituitary levels, preceding obesity	170
Neuropeptide Y	Chinese hamster	• Reduced hypothalamic concentrations	171
Somatostatin	Chinese hamster	• Reduced hypothalamic concentrations	171, 172
Bombesin	fa/fa rat	• Unchanged hypothalamic levels	160
Neurotensin	fa/fa rat	• Unchanged hypothalamic levels	160

Notes:
1 ICV = intracerebroventricular.
2 Note conflicting data for CCK and β-endorphin.

Pituitary β-endorphin levels are increased in both *ob/ob* mice and *fa/fa* rats compared with lean controls [169]. An opioid peptide abnormality in these models is further suggested, as low-dose naloxone selectively reduces feeding in obese but not lean animals [169]. Another opioid antagonist, naltrexone, prevents *ob/ob* mice from becoming obese but has no effect on weight gain in lean animals [173]. Furthermore, posterior pituitary dynorphin and Leu-enkephalin levels are increased in *ob/ob* mice and κ-agonists stimulate feeding more in *ob/ob* than in lean mice [170].

Many neurotransmitter changes have been identified in the pancreas and could contribute to disturbed insulin and/or glucagon secretion. However, the marked changes in somatostatin seem to be the result of altered insulin availability rather than its cause (see Chapter 33) [46]. Pancreatic opioid peptides, which affect islet-cell secretion in various ways, display complex and often conflicting changes which as yet have no clear aetiological significance [174, 175].

Possible neuroendocrine defects in human NIDDM

The relative roles of obesity, impaired insulin secretion and insulin insensitivity in human NIDDM remain controversial. Theoretically, each could have a neuroendocrine basis, although there is no firm evidence of this.

Disturbances in energy balance

Obesity is common in NIDDM and probably aetiologically important in most cases, although it is now clear that insulin secretion must also be defective (Chapters 20 and 22). Even those subjects who are not 'obese' by population definitions may have a body fat content which outstrips the capacity of their B cells to maintain normoglycaemia.

It is uncertain whether human obesity is due to reduced energy expenditure and/or increased intake, but thermogenic defects are undoubtedly less important than in rodent models. Functional BAT is prominent in neonates but has a small bulk and limited calculated thermogenic capacity in normal adults, whose main thermogenic tissue is probably skeletal muscle [176]. Unlike obese rodents, total energy expenditure in overweight people is not reduced and indeed rises in proportion to the increase in lean body mass which accompanies obesity. As discussed in Chapter 20, certain subgroups of obese people may show specific reductions in thermogenesis induced by stimuli such as eating or oral glucose [177–180], infusion of glucose [181] and infusion of noradrenaline [182]. Some of these defects persist after weight loss, suggesting that they are not simply due to obesity [94, 183]. In susceptible people who overeat, such defects could theoretically exacerbate energy storage during the dynamic phase of weight gain which leads to obesity. However, many other studies have failed to demonstrate convincing thermogenic defects [94]. In obese people with NIDDM, blunted thermogenic responses to cold exposure [184] and glucose with insulin infusion [181, 185] have been documented. The thermogenic defect to glucose infusion is abolished if insulin resistance is overcome by increased insulin infusion rates [186]. This suggests that reduced thermogenesis may be another manifestation of insulin resistance in NIDDM, and may also support the possible role of insulin as a thermogenic signal [92].

Hyperphagia in excess of energy requirements is probably the main cause of energy accumulation in obesity. Careful measurements under 'free-range' conditions suggest that obesity-prone individuals consume about 20% more energy than lean people [187]. Human obesity is therefore probably due to overeating, perhaps exacerbated by reduced energy expenditure in some cases. Whether this is due to failure of satiety mechanisms, defective sensing of a body weight 'set-

point', over-riding social or cultural pressures to overeat, or the ready availability of varied and palatable food in Westernized societies is a matter for speculation. The possibilities of disturbances in neurotransmitters influencing taste (which can also affect insulin secretion as well as the palatability of food [188]) and the fact that certain foods contain 'exorphins' with opioid-like activity [189] which could affect satiety, mood and glucoregulation, are intriguing and unexplored.

Insulin and counter-regulatory hormone secretion

Simple obesity is accompanied by and probably causes hyperinsulinaemia and insulin insensitivity. NIDDM differs fundamentally in that insulin secretion is impaired, as is demonstrated by impaired spontaneous pulsatility of insulin secretion and the recent finding that 'true' circulating insulin levels are reduced in probably all NIDDM patients (see Chapters 22 and 35). This even includes subjects with 'hyperinsulinaemia' as measured by conventional radioimmunoassays which also detect biologically inert split products of proinsulin; comparisons with hyperinsulinaemic rodents (e.g. *ob/ob* mice) are therefore invalid. Insulin deficiency is presumably due to a separate defect in B-cell function which is unmasked when insulin secretion is stretched beyond its normal limits by conditions such as obesity, pregnancy, steroid treatment or perhaps an inherited tendency to insulin insensitivity.

Such defects could be intrinsic to the B cell itself or due to abnormal neuroendocrine regulation of insulin secretion. This latter possibility is supported by the observation that *in vitro* insulin release from pancreatic islets removed from NIDDM patients at operation is normal [190] suggesting that their environment, rather than the B cells themselves, is responsible for reduced insulin secretion. However, very few patients have been studied in this way and the improvement may simply have been due to removal of hyperglycaemia which itself can impair insulin secretion.

Glucagon secretion is increased in NIDDM, as in some rodent models, and by exacerbating hepatic insulin insensitivity and increasing hepatic glucose production, contributes to basal hyperglycaemia [191] (see Chapter 33). Its mechanism is unknown. A recent report [192] has indicated reduced plasma noradrenaline turnover in response to eating in obese subjects, which could be analogous to the reduced sympathetic activity of the 'autonomic hypothesis' [13]. Cortisol secretion is increased in some obese people and growth hormone levels may be increased, but less than in IDDM (see Chapter 28).

The CNS, obesity and NIDDM

Obesity is a well-known complication of hypothalamic disease, analogous to VMH-lesioned rodents, but is only rarely linked with identifiable brain lesions (Fig. 23.7). Most people with hypothalamic obesity are hyperphagic and hyperinsulinaemic, but glucose intolerance is absent or trivial, even if obesity is gross [193]; this presumably reflects the necessity for a coexistent B-cell defect. An interesting case, which recalls the 'autonomic hypothesis' is that of a patient with hypothalamic obesity in whom truncal vagotomy reduced hyperinsulinaemia and apparently enhanced diet-induced weight loss [194]. There is little evidence for a hypothalamic defect in most obese people. A subgroup of patients who developed massive obesity during childhood show blunted growth hormone and prolactin responses to hypoglycaemia; the prolactin defect persisted after weight loss, suggesting primary hypothalamic dysfunction [195, 196]. The unknown neurotransmitter disturbance(s) responsible could, in theory, also cause obesity; a recent report has

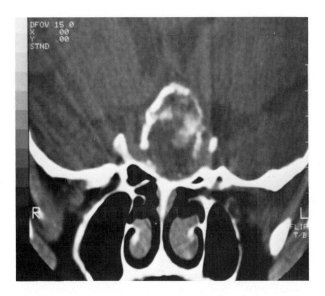

Fig. 23.7. CT scan showing a large craniopharyngioma which has destroyed the pituitary fossa and is distorting the ventro—basal hypothalamus. This patient became severely obese after starting adrenal and thyroid replacement therapy.

suggested that underactivity of the serotonergic system may account for both defects [197].

Temporary hyperglycaemia may follow head injuries, strokes, subarachnoid haemorrhage or meningitis and, like the stress hyperglycaemia complicating serious illness such as myocardial infarction, may be due to excessive counter-regulatory hormone (especially catecholamines) secretion. However, chronic hyperglycaemia classifiable as NIDDM is extremely rare. Occasional cases of diabetes, including those reported by Osler [198], have been associated with irritative lesions such as tumours and cysticercus in the region of the fourth ventricle. Hyperglycaemia is a common feature of the Prader—Willi syndrome, characterized by hyperphagia, obesity and various hypothalamo—pituitary disturbances (see Chapter 31). Its metabolic basis is unknown, although endogenous opioid peptides may be involved in some of the neuroendocrine abnormalities (see below).

Stress, with its potential to induce acute hyperglycaemia, has attracted attention as a possible cause of NIDDM. However, anecdotal and retrospective descriptions of NIDDM following stressful life-events have not been substantiated (Chapter 77) and the fall in incidence of NIDDM during both World Wars [199] suggests that over-availability of food, rather than stress, is aetiologically important. The reports that ECT improved or 'cured' NIDDM in depressed patients [200, 201] are not detailed enough to exclude possible causes such as major alterations in compliance with treatment.

Neurotransmitters in human NIDDM and obesity

Hypothalamic or brain neurotransmitter levels have not been systematically investigated in obesity or NIDDM, although disturbances in CSF levels of putative appetite-regulating neurotransmitters have been reported in bulimic and anorexic patients; at least some of these, such as a rise in CRF-like immunoreactivity in anorexia, are reversed when normal weight is restored and are therefore probably the result rather than the cause of altered food intake [202].

The opioid peptides have received much attention in human NIDDM since abnormalities were first demonstrated in the rodent syndromes. Some metabolic effects of β-endorphin are enhanced in obese people, raising the hypothesis that increased sensitivity to its hyperphagic and other actions may be a cause of obesity [174, 203]. Met-enkephalin inhibits nutrient-stimulated insulin secretion, and to a greater degree in NIDDM than in normal subjects [204]. Circulating enkephalin-like immunoreactivity is reportedly greater in some NIDDM patients treated with chlorpropamide than in normal people [174]. Exaggerated sensitivity to the insulin-inhibiting activity of certain opioids is postulated to contributed to the defective insulin secretion of NIDDM [174], although this could be secondary to hyperglycaemia which is known to modulate the insulin-secretory action of β-endorphin. Opiate addicts, like NIDDM patients, display both selective impairment of insulin secretion to glucose together with hyperglucagonaemia, but differ in that they have *hyper*insulinaemia and only mild glucose intolerance [174, 205]; the relevance of these suprapharmacological doses of opiates to NIDDM is dubious. Short-term naloxone administration to two patients with Prader–Willi syndrome reduced food intake but had no effect in a third; hyperphagia and other hypothalamo–pituitary disturbances were attributed to excessive β-endorphin activity [206]. The picture remains confused because of the multiplicity of opioid peptides, the several levels at which they might affect glucose regulation and their non-linear dose-response curves.

Conclusions

The neuroendocrine defects of the rodent models of obesity and NIDDM are now well characterized, but evidence that similar abnormalities operate in man remains equivocal. Nonetheless, further research in this challenging area may be rewarded by the identification of the systems which play a crucial role in regulating metabolism and, with this, the possibility of a rational treatment for obesity and NIDDM.

GARETH WILLIAMS

References

1 Morgane PJ, Panksepp J, eds. *The Handbook of the Hypothalamus*, vol 1. Anatomy of the hypothalamus. New York: Dekker, 1979.

2 Bleier R, Byne W. In: Paxinos G, ed. *The Rat Nervous System*, vol 1. Forebrain and midbrain. Sydney: Academic Press, 1985, 87–118.

3 Paxinos G, Watson C. *The Rat Brain in Stereotaxic Coordinates*. Sydney: Academic Press, 1982.

4 Palkovits M, Zaborsky L. Neural connections of the hypothalamus. In: Morgane PJ, Panksepp J, eds. *Handbook of the Hypothalamus*, vol 2. Physiology of the hypothalamus. New York: Dekker, 1979: 379–510.

5 Benzo CA. The hypothalamus and blood glucose regulation. *Life Sci* 1983; **32**: 2509–15.

6 Hashimoto PH, Hama K. An electron microscope study on protein uptake into brain regions devoid of the blood-brain barrier. *Med J Osaka Univ* 1967; **18**: 331–46.

7 Hetherington AW, Ranson SW. The spontaneous activity and food intake of rats with hypothalamic lesions. *Am J Physiol* 1942; **136**: 609–17.

8 Anand BK, Brobeck JR. Localisation of a feeding center in the hypothalamus of the rat. *Proc Soc Exp Biol Med* 1951; **77**: 323–4.

9 Grossman SP. Role of the hypothalamus in the regulation of food and water intake. *Psychol Rev* 1975; **82**: 200–24.

10 Nagai K, Fujii T, Inoue S, Takamura Y, Nakagawa H. Electrical stimulation of the suprachiasmatic nucleus of the hypothalamus causes hyperglycaemia. *Horm Metab Res* 1988; **20**: 37–9.

11 Gold RM, Jones AP, Sawchenko PE, Kapatos G. Paraventricular area: Critical focus of a longitudinal neurocircuitry mediating food intake. *Physiol Behav* 1977; **18**: 1111–19.

12 Leibowitz SF, Hammer NJ, Chang K. Hypothalamic paraventricular nucleus lesions produce overeating and obesity in the rat. *Physiol Behav* 1981; **27**: 1031–40.

13 Bray GA, York DA. Hypothalamic and genetic obesity in experimental animals: an autonomic and endocrine hypothesis. *Physiol Rev* 1979; **59**: 719–809.

14 Grossman SP. The role of glucose, insulin and glucagon in the regulation of food intake and body weight. *Neurosci Behav Rev* 1986; **10**: 295–302.

15 Willis GL, Hansky J, Smith GC. Ventricular, paraventricular and circumventricular structures involved in peptide-induced satiety. *Regul Pept* 1984; **9**: 87–99.

16 Sugrue MF. Neuropharmacology of drugs affecting food intake. *Pharmac Ther* 1987; **32**: 145–82.

17 Morley JE. Neuropeptide regulation of appetite and weight. *Endocr Rev* 1987; **8**: 256–87.

18 Leibowitz SF. Brain monoamines and peptides: role in the control of eating. *Fed Proc* 1986; **45**: 1396–403.

19 Leibowitz SF. Paraventricular nucleus: a primary site mediating adrenergic stimulation of feeding and drinking. *Pharmacol Biochem Behav* 1987; **8**: 163–75.

20 Goldman CK, Marino L, Leibowitz SF. Postsynaptic alpha$_2$-noradrenergic receptors mediate feeding induced by paraventricular nucleus injection of norepinephrine and clonidine. *Eur J Pharmacol* 1985; **115**: 11–19.

21 Gibbs J, Smith GP. Cholecystokinin and satiety in rats and rhesus monkeys. *Am J Nutr* 1977; **30**: 758–61.

22 Silver AJ, Flood JF, Song AM, Morley JE. Evidence for a physiological role for CCK in the regulation of food intake in mice. *Am J Physiol* 1989; **256**: R646–51.

23 Kissilef HR, Pi-Sunyer FX, Thornton J. C-terminal octapeptide of cholecystokinin decreases food intake in man. *Am J Clin Nutr* 1981; **34**: 154–60.

24 Smith GP, Jerome C, Cushin BJ, Eterno E, Simansky KJ. Abdominal vagotomy blocks the satiety effect of cholecystokinin in rat. *Science* 1981; **213**: 1036–7.

25 Tsai SH, Passaro E, Lin MT. Cholecystokinin acts through catecholaminergic mechanisms in the hypothalamus to influence ingestive behaviour in the rat. *Neuropharmacology* 1984; **23**: 1351–6.

26 Crawley JH, Kiss JZ. Paraventricular nucleus lesions abolish the inhibition of feeding induced by systemic cholecystokinin. *Peptides* 1985; **6**: 927–35.

27 Innis RB, Snyder SH. Distinct cholecystokinin receptors in brain and pancreas. *Proc Natl Acad Sci USA* 1980; **77**: 6917–21.

28 McHugh PR, Moran TH. The stomach, cholecystokinin, and satiety. *Fed Proc* 1986; **45**: 1384–90.

29 Dourish CT, Rycroft W, Ivesen SD. Postponement of satiety by blockade of brain cholecystokinin (CCK-B) receptors. *Science* 1989; **245**: 1509–11.

30 Morley JE, Levine AS. Corticosteroid releasing factor, grooming and ingestive behaviour. *Life Sci* 1982; **31**: 1459–64.

31 Arase K, York DA, Shimizu H, Shargill N, Bray GA. Effects of corticotropin releasing factor on food intake and brown adipose tissue thermogenesis in rats. *Am J Physiol* 1988; **255**: E255–E259.

32 Krahn DD, Gosnell BA, Levine AS, Morley JE. Localisation of the effects of corticotropin-releasing factor on feeding. *Proc Soc Neurosci Abstr* 1984; **10**: 302.

33 Rothwell NJ. CRF is involved in the pyrogenic and thermogenic effects of interleukin 1β in the rat. *Am J Physiol* 1989; **256**: E111–15.

34 Baskin DG, Figlewicz DP, Woods SC, Porte D, Dorsa DM. Insulin in the brain. *Ann Rev Physiol* 1987; **49**: 335–47.

35 Baskin DG, Woods SC, Best DB, Van Houten M, Posner BI, Dorsa MD, Porte D. Immunological detection of insulin in rat hypothalamus and its possible uptake from cerebrospinal fluid. *Endocrin Immunol* 1983; **113**: 1818–25.

36 Corp ES, Woods SC, Porte D, Dorsa DM, Figlewicz DP, Baskin DG. Localization of insulin binding sites in the rat hypothalamus by quantitative autoradiography. *Neurosci Lett* 1986; **70**: 17–22.

37 Woods SC, Lotter EC, McKay D, Porte D. Chronic intracerebroventricular insulin infusion reduces food intake and body weight in baboons. *Nature* 1979; **282**: 502–4.

38 Van der Weele DA, Pi-Sunyer FX, Novin D, Bush MJ. Chronic insulin infusion suppresses food ingestion and body weight gain in rats. *Brain Res Bull* 1980; **5**: 7–12.

39 Strubbe JH, Mein CG. Increased feeding in response to bilateral injection of insulin antibodies in the VMH. *Physiol Behav* 1977; **19**: 309–13.

40 Ikeda H, West DB, Pustek JJ, Figlewicz DP, Greenwood MRC, Porte D, Woods SC. Intraventricular insulin reduces food intake and body weight of lean but not obese Zucker rats. *Appetite* 1986; **1**: 381–6.

41 McKay LD, Kenney NJ, Edens NK, Williams RH, Woods SC. Intracerebroventricular beta-endorphin increases food intake of rats. *Life Sci* 1981; **29**: 1429–34.

42 Morley JE, Levine AS. Dynorphin-(1–13) induces spontaneous feeding in rats. *Life Sci* 1981; **29**: 1901–3.

43 Morley JE, Levine AS, Gosnell BA, Billington CJ. Which opioid receptor mechanism modulates feeding? *Appetite* 1984; **5**: 61–8.

44 Gosnell BA, Morley JE, Levine AS. Opioid-induced feeding: localisation of sensitive brain sites. *Brain Res* 1986; **369**: 177–184.

45 Cohen MR, Cohen RM, Pickar D *et al*. Naloxone reduces food intake in humans. *Psychosom Med* 1985; **7**: 132–8.

46 Williams G, Bloom SR. Regulatory peptides, the hypothalamus and diabetes. *Diabetic Med* 1989; **6**: 472–85.

47 Williams G, Steel JM, Polak JM, Bloom SR. Neuropeptide Y in the hypothalamus. In: Mutt V, Fuxe K, Hökfelt T, Lundberg JM, eds. *Neuropeptide Y* (Karolinska Institute Nobel Conference Series). New York: Raven Press, 1989: 243–51.

48 Chronwall BM, DiMaggio DA, Massari VJ, Pickel VM, Ruggiero D, O'Donohue TL. The anatomy of neuropeptide Y containing neurons in rat brain. *Neuroscience* 1985; **15**: 1159–81.

49 Stanley BG, Daniel DR, Chin AS, Leibowitz SF. Paraventricular nucleus injections of peptide YY and neuropeptide Y preferentially enhance carbohydrate ingestion. *Peptides* 1985; **6**: 1205–11.

50 Stanley BG, Kyrkouli SE, Lampert S, Leibowitz SF. Neuropeptide Y chronically injected into the hypothalamus: a powerful neurochemical inducer of hyperphagia and obesity. *Peptides* 1986; **7**: 1189–92.

51 Morley JE, Levine AS, Gosnell BA, Kneip J, Grace M. Effect of neuropeptide Y on ingestive behaviours in the rat. *Am J Physiol* 1987; **252**: R599–609.

52 Rowland NE. Peripheral and central satiety factors in neuropeptide Y-induced feeding in rats. *Peptides* 1988; **9**: 989–94.

53 Liposits Z, Sievers L, Paull WK. Neuropeptide-Y and ACTH-immunoreactive innervation of corticotrophin-releasing factor (CRF)-synthesising neurones in the hypothalamus of the rat. *Histochemistry* 1988; **88**: 227–34.

54 Wahlestedt C, Skagerberg G, Ekman R, Heilig M, Sundler F, Håkanson R. Neuropeptide Y (NPY) in the area of the hypothalamic paraventricular nucleus activates the pituitary-adrenocortical axis in the rat. *Brain Res* 1987; **417**: 33–8.

55 Tempel DL, Leibowitz KJ, Smith D, Leibowitz SF. Galanin in the paraventricular nucleus preferentially enhances fat intake. *Proc Soc Neurosci* 1986; **12**: 594–99.

56 Vaccarino FJ, Bloom FE, Rivier J, Vale W, Koob GF. Stimulation of food intake in rats by centrally-administered hypothalamic growth hormone-releasing hormone. *Nature* 1985; **314**: 167–8.

57 Maki T, Shibasaki T, Hotta M, Masuda A, Demura H, Shizuma K, Ling N. The satiety effect of growth hormone-releasing factor in rats. *Brain Res* 1985; **340**: 186–91.

58 Stein LJ, Woods SC. Gastrin-releasing peptide reduces meal size in rats. *Peptides* 1982; **3**: 833–5.

59 West DB, Williams RH, Braget DJ, West SC. Bombesin reduces food intake of normal and hypothalamically obese rats and lowers body weight when given chronically. *Peptides* 1982; **3**: 61–7.

60 Stanley BG. Suppression of norepinephrine-elicited feeding by neurotensin: evidence for behavioural, anatomical and pharmacological specificity. *Brain Res* 1985; **343**: 297–304.

61 Van der Gugten J, Slangen JL. Release of endogenous catecholamines from rat hypothalamus *in vivo* related to feeding and other behaviours. *Pharmacol Biochem Behav* 1977; **7**: 211–19.

62 Jhanwar-Uniyal M, Roland CR, Leibowitz SF. Diurnal rhythm of alpha$_2$-noradrenergic receptors in the paraventricular nucleus and other brain areas: relation to circulating corticosterone and feeding behaviour. *Life Sci* 1986; **38**: 473–82.

63 Chu PC, Lin MT, Shian LR, Leu SY. Alterations in physiologic functions and in brain monoamine content in streptozotocin-diabetic rats. *Diabetes* 1986; **35**: 481–85.

64 Bitar M, Koulu M, Linnoila M. Diabetes-induced changes in monoamine concentrations of rat hypothalamus nuclei. *Brain Res* 1987; **409**: 236–42.

65 Perez-Cruet J, Tagliamonte A, Tagliamonte P, Gessa GL. Changes in brain serotonin metabolism associated with fasting and satiation in rats. *Life Sci* 1972; **11**: 31–9.

66 Cattabeni F, Maggi A, Monduzzi M, De Angelis L, Racagni G. GABA: circadian fluctuations in rat hypothalamus. *J Neurochem* 1978; **31**: 565–7.

67 McLaughlin CL, Baile CA, Della-Fera MA, Kasser TG. Meal-stimulated increased concentrations of CCK in the hypothalamus of Zucker obese and lean rats. *Physiol Behav* 1985; **35**: 215–20.

68 Schneider BS, Monahan JW, Hirsch J. Brain cholecystokinin and nutritional status in rats and mice. *J Clin Inv* 1979; **64**: 1348–56.

69 Schick RR, Reilly WM, Roddy DR, Yaksh TL, Go VLW. Neuronal cholecystokinin-like immunoreactivity is postprandially released from primate hypothalamus. *Brain Res* 1987; **418**: 20–6.

70 Suemaru S, Hashimoto K, Hattori T, Inoue H, Kageyama J, Ota Z. Starvation-induced changes in rat brain corticotropin-releasing factor (CRF) and pituitary-adrenocortical response. *Life Sci* 1986; **39**: 1161–4.

71 Corp ES, Bohannon NJ, Wilcox BJ, Woods SC, Dorsa DM, Porte D, Baskin DG. Increased insulin binding in the paraventricular nucleus of rats after chronic caloric restriction: *in vitro* quantitative autoradiography. *Soc Neurosci Abstr* 1986; **12**: 612.

72 Reid LD, Konecka AM, Przewlocki R, Millan MH, Millan MJ, Herz A. Endogenous opioids, circadian rhythms, nutrient deprivation, eating and drinking. *Life Sci* 1982; **31**: 1829–32.

73 Kerdelhue B, Karteszi M, Pasqualini C, Reinberg A, Mezey E, Palkovits M. Circadian variations in beta-endorphin concentrations in pituitary and some brain nuclei of the adult male rat. *Brain Res* 1983; **261**: 243–8.

74 Majeed NH, Lason PV, Przewlocka B, Przewlocki R. Brain and peripheral opioid peptides after changes in ingestive behaviour. *Neuroendocrinology* 1986; **42**: 267–72.

75 Gambert SR, Garthwaite TL, Pontzer CH, Hagen TC. Fasting associated with decrease in hypothalamic beta-endorphin. *Science* 1980; **210**: 1271–2.

76 Forman LJ, Marquis DE, Stevens R, Adler R, Vasilenko P. Diabetes induced by streptozotocin results in a decrease in immunoreactive beta-endorphin levels in the pituitary and hypothalamus of female rats. *Diabetes* 1985; **34**: 1104–7.

77 McKibbin PE, Rodgers P, Williams G. Increased neuropeptide Y in the lateral hypothalamic area: the trigger for dark-phase eating? *Diabetic Med* 1989; 6 Suppl. 2: 164.

78 Sahu A, Kalra PS, Kalra SP. Food deprivation and ingestion induce reciprocal changes in neuropeptide Y concentrations in the paraventricular nucleus. *Peptides* 1988; **9**: 83–6.

79 Williams G, Cardoso HM, Ghatei MA, Lee YC, Gill JS, Burrin JM, Bloom SR. Increased hypothalamic neuropeptide Y (NPY) concentrations in diabetic rat. *Diabetes* 1988; **37**: 763–72.

80 Williams G, Gill JS, Lee YC, Cardoso HM, Okpere BE, Bloom SR. Increased neuropeptide Y in specific hypothalamic regions of streptozotocin-induced diabetic rats. *Diabetes* 1989; **38**: 321–7.

81 Williams G, Lee YC, Ghatei MA *et al.* Elevated neuropeptide Y concentrations in the central hypothalamus of the spontaneously diabetic BB/E Wistar rat. *Diabetic Med* 1989; **6**: 601–7.

82 Fernstrom MH, Mirski MAZ, Carraway RE, Leeman SE. Immunoreactive neurotensin levels in pancreas: elevation in diabetic rats and mice. *Metabolism* 1981; **30**: 853–5.

83 Berelowitz M, Frohman LA. The role of neurotensin in the regulation of carbohydrate metabolism and in diabetes. *Ann NY Acad Sci* 1982; **386**: 150–9.

84 Rothwell NJ, Stock MJ. A role for brown adipose tissue in diet-induced thermogenesis. *Nature* 1979; **281**: 31–3.

85 Stock MJ. The role of brown adipose tissue in diet-induced thermogenesis. *Proc Nutr Soc* 1989; **48**: 189–96.

86 Nicholls DG, Locke RM. Thermogenic mechanisms in brown fat. *Physiol Rev* 1984; **64**: 1–45.

87 Arch JRS. The brown adipocyte β-adrenoceptor. *Proc Nutr Soc* 1989; **48**: 215–23.

88 Foster DO, Frydman ML. Non-shivering thermogenesis in the rat. II. Measurements of blood flow with microspheres point to brown adipose tissue as the dominant site of calorigenesis induced by noradrenaline. *Can J Physiol Pharmacol* 1978; **56**: 110–15.

89 Rothwell NJ. Central control of brown adipose tissue. *Proc Nutr Soc* 1989; **48**: 197–206.

90 Perkins MN, Rothwell NJ, Stock MJ, Stone TW. Activation of brown adipose tissue thermogenesis by the ventromedial hypothalamus. *Nature* 1981; **289**: 401–2.

91 Niijima A, Rohner-Jeanrenaud F, Jeanrenaud B. Electrophysiological studies on the role of the ventromedial hypothalamus on the sympathetic efferent nerve activity of brown adipose tissue in the rat. *Am J Physiol* 1984; **247**: R650–4.

92 Rothwell NJ, Stock MJ. Insulin and thermogenesis. *Int J Obes* 1988; **12**: 93–102.

93 Le Feuvre RA, Rothwell NJ, Stock MJ. Activation of brown fat thermogenesis in response to central injection of corticotropin releasing hormone in the rat. *Neuropharmacology* 1987; **26**: 1217–21.

94 Sims EAH, Danforth E. Expenditure and storage of energy in man. *J Clin Inv* 1987; **79**: 1019–25.

95 Bernard C. *Leçons de Physiologie Expérimentale Appliquée à la Médecine*, vol 1. Paris: Baillière, 1855: 296–313.

96 Banting FC, Best CH, Collip JB, MacLeod JJR, Noble EC. The effects of insulin on experimental hyperglycaemia in rabbits. *Am J Physiol* 1922; **42**: 559–80.

97 Feldberg W, Pyke DA, Stubbs WA. On the origin of non-insulin-dependent diabetes. *Lancet* 1985; i: 1263–4.

98 Oomura Y, Ono T, Ooyama H, Wayner MJ. Glucose and osmosensitive neurones of the rat hypothalamus. *Nature* 1969; **222**: 282–4.

99 Minami T, Oomura Y, Sugimori M. Electrophysiological properties and glucose responsiveness of guinea-pig ventromedial hypothalamic neurones *in vitro*. *J Physiol* 1986; **380**: 127–43.

100 Shizamu T, Fukuda A, Ban T. Reciprocal influences of the ventromedial and lateral hypothalamic nuclei on blood glucose level and liver glycogen content. *Nature* 1960; **210**: 1178–9.

101 Frohman LA, Bernardis LL. Effect of hypothalamic stimulation on plasma glucose, insulin, and glucagon levels. *Am J Physiol* 1971; **221**: 1596–603.

102 Cane P, Artal R, Bergman RN. Putative hypothalamic glucoreceptors play no essential role in the response to moderate hypoglycemia. *Diabetes* 1986; **35**: 268–77.

103 Ritter RC, Slusser PG, Stone S. Glucoreceptors controlling feeding and blood glucose: location in the hindbrain. *Science* 1981; **213**: 451–3.

104 Friedmann MI, Granneman J. Food intake and peripheral factors after recovery from insulin-induced hypoglycemia. *Am J Physiol* 1983; **244**: R374–9.

105 Shimazu T, Ogasawara S. Effect of hypothalamic stimulation on gluconeogenesis and glucolysis in rat liver. *Am J Physiol* 1975; **228**: 1787–93.

106 Woods SC, Porte D. Neural control of the endocrine pancreas. *Physiol Rev* 1974; **54**: 596–619.

107 Shimazu T, Ishikawa K. Modulation by the hypothalamus of glucagon and insulin secretion in rabbits: studies with

electrical and chemical stimulations. *Endocrinology* 1981; **108**: 605–11.

108 Curry DL. Direct tonic inhibition of insulin secretion by central nervous system. *Am J Physiol* 1983; **244**: E425–9.

109 Brown M. Neuropeptides: central nervous system effects on nutrient metabolism. *Diabetologia* 1981; **20**: 299–304.

110 Frohman LA. CNS peptides and glucoregulation. *Ann Rev Physiol* 1983; **45**: 95–107.

111 Van Loon GR, Appel NM. β-endorphin-induced hyperglycaemia is mediated by increased central sympathetic outflow to adrenal medulla. *Brain Res* 1981; **204**: 236–41.

112 Brown MR, Fisher LA, Spiess J, Rivier C, Rivier J, Vale W. Corticotropin-releasing factor: actions on the sympathetic system and metabolism. *Endocrinology* 1982; **111**: 928–31.

113 Amir S. Central glucagon-induced hyperglycemia is mediated by combined activation of the adrenal medulla and sympathetic nerve endings. *Physiol Behav* 1986; **37**: 563–6.

114 Brown M, Taché Y, Fisher D. Central nervous system action of bombesin: mechanism to induce hyperglycemia. *Endocrinology* 1979; **105**: 660–5.

115 Iguchi A, Matsunaga H, Nomura T, Gotoh M, Sakamoto N. Glucoregulatory effects of intrahypothalamic injections of bombesin and other peptides. *Endocrinology* 1984; **114**: 2242–6.

116 Mori T, Nagai K, Hara M, Nakagawa H. Time-dependent effect of insulin in suprachiasmatic nucleus on blood glucose. *Am J Physiol* 1985; **249**: R23–30.

117 Kaneda H, Tominaga H, Marubashi S, Kamimura T, Katagiri T, Sasaki H. Effect of insulin-induced hypoglycemia and glucose-insulin infusion on brain glucagon-like materials in dog. *Biomed Res* 1984; **5**: 61–6.

118 Morley JE, Levine AS. Intraventricular cholecystokinin-octapeptide produces hyperglycemia in rats. *Life Sci* 1981; **28**: 2187–97.

119 Novin D, Vanderweele DA, Rezek M. Infusion of 2-deoxy-D-glucose into the hepatic portal system causes eating: evidence for peripheral glucoreceptors. *Science* 1973; **181**: 858–60.

120 Iguchi A, Gotoh M, Matsunaga H, Ohuchi M, Nomura T, Sakamoto N. Increase in plasma glucose concentration after intracerebroventricular injection of N,O′-dibutyryl cyclic adenosine 3′, 5′-monophosphate. *Endocrinology* 1986; **119**: 125–9.

121 Iguchi A, Burleson PD, Szabo AJ. Decrease in plasma glucose concentration after microinjection of insulin into ventromedial nucleus. *Am J Physiol* 1981; **240**: E95–9.

122 Shimazu R, Ishikawa K. Modulation by the hypothalamus of glucagon and insulin secretion in rabbits: studies with electrical and chemical stimulation. *Endocrinology* 1981; **108**: 605–11.

123 De Jong A, Strubbe JH, Steffans AB. Hypothalamic influence on insulin and glucogen release in the rat. *Am J Physiol* 1977; **233**: E380–7.

124 Moltz JH, McDonald JK. Neuropeptide Y: direct and indirect action on insulin secretion in the rat. *Peptides* 1985; **6**: 1155–9.

125 Woods SC, Porte D. Effect of intracisternal insulin on plasma glucose and insulin in the dog. *Diabetes* 1975; **24**: 905–9.

126 Brown M. Thyrotropin releasing hormone: A putative cell regulator of the autonomic nervous system. *Life Sci* 1981; **28**: 1789–95.

127 Gerritsen GC, Blanks MC, Miller RL, Dulin WE. Effect of diet limitation on the development of diabetes in prediabetic Chinese hamsters. *Diabetologia* 1974; **10**: 559–65.

128 Trayhurn P, Thurlby PL, James WPT. Thermogenic defect in pre-obese *ob/ob* mice. *Nature* 1977; **266**: 60–2.

129 Trayhurn P, James WPT. Thermoregulation and non-shivering thermogenesis in the genetically obese (*ob/ob*) mouse. *Pflügers Archiv* 1978; **373**: 189–93.

130 Thurlby PL, Trayhurn P. The role of thermoregulatory thermogenesis in the elevated energy gain of obese (*ob/ob*) mice pair-fed with lean siblings. *Br J Nutr* 1979; **42**: 377–82.

131 Hogan A, Himms-Hagen J. Abnormal brown adipose tissue in obese mice (*ob/ob*): response to acclimation to cold. *Am J Physiol* 1980; **239**: 301–9.

132 Ashwell M, Jennings G, Trayhurn P. Evidence from radioimmunoassay for a decreased concentration of mitochondrial 'uncoupling' protein from brown adipose tissue of genetically obese (*ob/ob*) mice. *Biochem Soc Trans* 1983; **11**: 727–34.

133 Seydoux J, Rohner-Jeanrenaud F, Assimacopoulos-Jeannet F, Jeanrenaud B, Girardier L. Functional disconnection of brown adipose tissue in hypothalamic obesity in rats. *Pflügers Arch* 1981; **390**: 1–4.

134 Hogan S, Coscina DV, Himms-Hagen J. Brown adipose tissue of rats with obesity-inducing ventromedial hypothalamic lesions. *Am J Physiol* 1982; **243**: E334–8.

135 Godbole VY, York DA, Bloxham DP. Developmental changes in the fatty (*fa/fa*) rat: evidence for defective thermogenesis preceding the hyperlipogenesis and hyperinsulinaemia. *Diabetologia* 1978; **15**: 41–4.

136 Planche E, Joliff M, De Gasquet P, Le Liepvre X. Evidence of a defect in energy expenditure in 7 day old Zucker rats (*fa/fa*). *Am J Physiol* 1983; **245**: E107–113.

137 Triandafillou J, Himms-Hagen J. Normal cold but defective diet-induced activation of brown adipose tissue mitochondria in genetically obese (*fa/fa*) rats. *Am J Physiol* 1983; **244**: E145–1.

138 Himms-Hagen J. Brown adipose tissue thermogenesis in obese animals. *Nutr Rev* 1983; **41**: 261–7.

139 Flatt PR, Bailey CJ. Dietary components and plasma insulin responses to fasting and refeeding in genetically obese hyperglycaemic (*ob/ob*) mice. *Br J Nutr* 1984; **51**: 403–13.

140 Bryce GF, Johnson PR, Sullivan AC, Stern JS. Insulin and glucagon: plasma levels and pancreatic release in the genetically obese Zucker rat. *Horm Metab Res* 1977; **9**: 360–70.

141 Berthoud HR, Jeanrenaud B. Acute hyperinsulinaemia and its reversal by vagotomy after lesions of the ventromedial hypothalamus in anesthetized rats. *Endocrinology* 1979; **105**: 146–51.

142 Rohner-Jeanrenaud R, Jeanrenaud B. Consequences of ventromedial hypothalamic lesions upon insulin and glucagon secretion by subsequently isolated perfused pancreases in the rat. *J Clin Invest* 1980; **65**: 902–10.

143 Lee HC, Curry DL, Stern JC. Direct effect of CNS on insulin hypersecretion in obese Zucker rats: involvement of vagus nerve. *Am J Physiol* 1989; **256**: E439–44.

144 Powley TL, Opsahl CA. Ventromedial hypothalamic obesity abolished by subdiaphragmatic vagotomy. *Am J Physiol* 1974; **226**: 25–32.

145 Courtney ND, Woods SC. Vagotomy reduces weight of genetically obese (Zucker) female rats and their lean littermates. *Nutr Behav* 1984; **2**: 1–7.

146 Terrettaz J, Assimacopoulos-Jeannet F, Jeanrenaud B. Severe hepatic and peripheral insulin resistance as evidenced by euglycemic clamps in genetically obese *fa/fa* rats. *Endocrinology* 1986; **118**: 674–8.

147 Pénicaud L, Ferre P, Terretaz J, Kineban-Yan M-F, Leturque

A, Dore E *et al.* Development of obesity in Zucker rats. Early insulin resistance in muscles but normal sensitivity in white adipose tissue. *Diabetes* 1987; **36**: 626–31.

148 Seino Y, Seino S, Takemura J, Tsuda K, Nishi S, Ishida H *et al.* Changes in insulin, somatostatin and glucagon secretion during the development of obesity in ventromedial hypothalamic-lesioned rats. *Endocrinology* 1984; **114** (2): 457–61.

149 Rohner-Jeanrenaud F, Jeanrenaud B. Involvement of the cholinergic system in insulin and glucagon oversecretion of genetic pre-obesity. *Endocrinology* 1985; **116**: 830–4.

150 Penicaud L, Rohner-Jeanrenaud F, Jeanrenaud B. *In vivo* metabolic changes as studied longitudinally after ventromedial hypothalamic lesions. *Am J Physiol* 1986; **250**: E662–8.

151 York DA, Bray GA. Dependence of hypothalamic obesity on insulin, the pituitary and the adrenal gland. *Endocrinology* 1972; **90**: 885–94.

152 King BM. Hypothalamic obesity after hypophysectomy or adrenalectomy: dependence on corticosterone. *Am J Physiol* 1985; **249**: R522–6.

153 York DA. Corticosteroid inhibition of thermogenesis in obese animals. *Proc Nutr Soc* 1989; **48**: 231–5.

154 Leibowitz SF, Roland CR, Hor L, Squillari V. Noradrenergic feeding elicited via the paraventricular nucleus is dependent upon circulating corticosterone. *Physiol Behav* 1984; **32**: 857–64.

155 Levin BE, Triscari J, Sullivan AC. Defective catecholamine metabolism in peripheral organs of genetically obese Zucker rats. *Brain Res* 1981; **224**: 353–66.

156 Lorden JF, Olimans GA, Margules DL. Central catecholamine levels in genetically obese mice (*ob/ob* and *db/db*). *Brain Res* 1975; **96**: 390–4.

157 Cruce JAF, Thoa NB, Jacobowitz DM. Catecholamines in the brains of genetically obese rats. *Brain Res* 1976; **101**: 165–70.

158 Straus E, Yalow RS. Cholecystokinin in the brains of obese and nonobese mice. *Science* (Washington) 1979; **203**: 68–9.

159 Saito A, Williams JA, Goldfine ID. Alteration of brain cerebral cortex CCK receptors in the *ob/ob* mouse. *Endocrinology* 1981; **109**: 984–6.

160 Oku J, Inoue S, Glick Z, Bray GA, Walsh JH. Cholecystokinin, bombesin and neurotensin in brain tissue from obese animals. *Int J Obes* 1984; **8** (2): 171–82.

161 Hays SE, Goodwin FK, Paul SM. Cholecystokinin receptors in brain: effects of obesity, during treatment and lesions. *Peptides* 1981; **2** (suppl 2): 21–6.

162 Finkelstein JA, Steggles AW, Martinez PA, Praissman M. Cholecystokinin receptor binding levels in the genetically obese rat brain. *Peptides* 1984; **5**: 11–14.

163 Micevych PE, Go VLW, Yaksh TL, Finkelstein J. *In vitro* release of cholecystokinin from hypothalamus and frontal cortex of Sprague–Dawley, Zucker lean (Fa/-) and obese (*fa/fa*) rats. *Peptides* 1984; **5**: 73–80.

164 McLaughlin CL, Baile CA. Feeding response of weanling Zucker obese rats to cholecystokinin and bombesin. *Physiol Behav* 1980; **25**: 341–6.

165 Dorn A, Bernstein HG, Schmidt K, Schmidt W, Hahn HJ, Rinne A. Brain gastrin/CCK immunoreactivity in sand rat (*Psammomys obesus*): decrease of number of positive neurons in diabetic animals. *Endocrinol Exp* 1984; **18**: 131–5.

166 Stein LJ, Dorsa DM, Baskin DG, Figlewicz DP, Ikeda H, Frankmann SP *et al.* Immunoreactive insulin levels are elevated in the cerebrospinal fluid of genetically obese Zucker rats. *Endocrinology* 1983; **113**: 2299–301.

167 Baskin DG, Porte D, Guest K, Dorsa DM. Genetically obese Zucker rats have abnormally low brain insulin content. *Life Sci* 1985; **36**: 627–33.

168 Figlewicz DP, Dorsa DM, Stein LJ, Baskin DG, Paquette T, Greenwood MRC *et al.* Brain and liver insulin binding is decreased in Zucker rats carrying the '*fa*' gene. *Endocrinology* 1985; **117**: 1537–43.

169 Margules DL, Moisset B, Lewis MJ, Shibuya H, Pert CB. β-endorphin is associated with over-eating in genetically obese mice (*ob/ob*) and rats (*fa/fa*). *Science* 1978; **202**: 988–91.

170 Ferguson-Segall M, Flynn JJ, Walker J, Margules DL. Increased immunoreactive dynorphin and leu-enkephalin in posterior pituitary of obese mice (*ob/ob*) and supersensitivity to drugs that act at kappa-receptors. *Life Sci* 1982; **31**: 2233–6.

171 Williams G, Ghatei MA, Diani AR, Gerritsen GC, Bloom SR. Reduced hypothalamic somatostatin and neuropeptide Y concentrations in the spontaneously diabetic Chinese hamster. *Horm Metab Res* 1988; **20**: 668–70.

172 Petersson B, Elde R, Efendic S. Somatostatin in the pancreas, stomach and hypothalamus of the diabetic Chinese hamster. *Diabetologia* 1977; **13**: 463–6.

173 Recant L, Voyles NR, Luciano M, Pert CB. Naltrexone reduces weight gain, alters 'β-endorphin', and reduces insulin output from pancreatic islets of genetically obese mice. *Peptides* 1980; **1**: 309–13.

174 Giugliano D, Torella R, Lefèbvre PJ, D'Onofrio F. Opioid peptides and metabolic regulation. *Diabetologia* 1988; **31**: 3–15.

175 Timmers K, Voyles NR, Zalenski C, Wilkins S, Recant L. Altered β-endorphin, Met- and Leu-enkephalins, and enkephalin-containing peptides in pancreas and pituitary of genetically obese diabetic (*db/db*) mice during development of diabetic syndrome. *Diabetes* 1986; **35**: 1143–51.

176 Lean MEJ. Brown adipose tissue in humans. *Proc Nutr Soc* 1989; **48**: 243–56.

177 Schutz Y, Golay A, Felber J-P, Jequier E. Decreased glucose-induced thermogenesis after weight loss in obese subjects: a predisposing factor for relapse of obesity. *Am J Clin Nutr* 1984; **39**: 380–6.

178 Shetty PS, Jung RT, James WPT, Barrand MA, Collingham BA. Postprandial thermogenesis in obesity. *Clin Sci* 1981; **60**: 519–25.

179 Schwartz RS, Halter JB, Bierman E. Reduced thermic effect of feeding in obesity: role of norepinephrine. *Metabolism* 1983; **32**: 114–19.

180 Lean MEJ, James WPT, Garthwaite PH. Obesity without overeating? Reduced diet-induced thermogenesis in post-obese women, dependent on carbohydrate and not fat intake. In: Björntorp P, Rossner S, eds. *Obesity in Europe* 88. London: J. Libbey, 1989: 281–6.

181 Ravussin E, Bogardus C, Schwartz RS, Robbins DC, Wolfe RR, Horton ES, Danforth E, Sims EAH. Thermic effects of infused insulin and glucose in man. Decreased response with increased insulin resistance in obesity and non-insulin-dependent diabetes mellitus. *J Clin Invest* 1983; **72**: 893–902.

182 Jung RT, Shetty PS, James WPT, Barrand MA, Callingham BA. Reduced thermogenesis in obesity. *Nature* 1979; **279**: 322–3.

183 Sims EAH. Energy balance in human beings; problems of plenitude. In: Auerbach GD, McCormick DB, eds. *Vitamins and Hormones*, vol 43. New York: Academic Press, 1987: 1–101.

184 Lean MEJ, Murgatroyd PR, Rothnie I, Reid IW, Harvey R. Metabolic and thyroidal responses to mild cold are abnormal in obese diabetic women. *Clin Endocrinol* 1988; **28**: 665–73

185 Golay A, Schutz Y, Felber J-P, DeFronzo RA, Jequier E. Lack of thermogenic response to glucose/insulin infusion in diabetic obese subjects. *Int J Obes* 1986; **10**: 107–16.

186 Ravussin E, Acheson KJ, Vernet O, Danforth E, Jequier E. Evidence that insulin resistance is responsible for the decreased thermic effect of glucose in human obesity. *J Clin Invest* 1985; **76**: 1268–73.

187 Porikos KP, Pi-Sunyer FX. Regulation of food intake in human obesity: studies with calorie dilution and exercise. In: James WPT, ed. *Obesity; Clin Endocrinol Metab*, vol 13. London: WB Saunders, 1984: 547.

188 Ionescu E, Rohner-Jeanrenaud F. Proietto J, Rivest R, Jeanrenaud B. Taste-induced changes in plasma insulin and glucose turnover in lean and genetically obese rats. *Diabetes* 1988; **37**: 773–9.

189 Schusdziarra V, Holland A, Schick R, De La Fuente A, Klier M, Maier V, Brantl V, Preiffer EF. Modulation of post-prandial insulin release by ingested opiate-like substances in dogs. *Diabetologia* 1983; **24**: 113.

190 Lohmann D, Jahr H, Verlohren H-J. Insulin secretion in maturity-onset diabetes: Function of isolated islets. *Horm Metab Res* 1980; **12**: 349–53.

191 Reaven GM, Chen Y-DI, Golay A, Swislocki ALM, Jaspan JB. Documentation of hyperglucagonemia throughout the day in non-obese and obese patients with non-insulin-dependent diabetes mellitus. *J Clin Endocr Metab* 1987; **64**: 106–10.

192 Bazelmans J, Nestel PJ, O'Dea K, Esler MD. Blunted norepinephrine responsiveness to changing energy states in obese subjects. *Metabolism* 1985; **34**: 154–60.

193 Bray GA, Gallagher TF. Manifestations of hypothalamic obesity in man: a comprehensive investigation of eight patients and a review of the literature. *Medicine* 1975; **54**: 301–30.

194 Smith DK, Sarfeh J, Howard L. Truncal vagotomy in hypothalamic obesity. *Lancet* 1983; **i**: 1330–1.

195 Kopelman PG, Pilkington TRE, White N, Jeffcoate SL. Evidence for existence of two types of massive obesity. *Br Med J* 1980; **280**: 82–3.

196 Kopelman PG, Pilkington TRE, Jeffcoate SL. Persistence of defective hypothalamic control of prolactin secretion in some obese women after weight reduction. *Br Med J* 1980; **281**: 358–9.

197 Bernini GP, Argenio GF, Vivaldi MS, Del Corso C, Sgro M, Franchi F, Luisi M. Effects of fenfluramine and ritanserin on prolactin response to insulin-induced hypoglycaemia in obese patients. *Horm Res* 1989; **31**: 133–7.

198 Osler W. *The Principles and Practice of Medicine*. New York: D. Appleton, 1892: 295–6.

199 West KM. *Epidemiology of Diabetes and its Vascular Lesions*. New York: Elsevier, 1978: 280–1.

200 Fakhri O, Fadhli AA, El Kawi RM. Effect of electroconvulsive therapy on diabetes mellitus. *Lancet* 1980; **ii**: 775–7.

201 Thomas A, Goldney R, Phillips P. Depression, electroconvulsive therapy and diabetes mellitus. *Aust NZ J Psychiatr* 1983; **17**: 289–91.

202 Fava M, Copeland PM, Schweiger U, Herzog DB. Neurochemical abnormalities of anorexia nervosa and bulimia nervosa. *Am J Psychiatr* 1989; **146**: 963–71.

203 Giugliano D, Salvatore T, Cozzolino D, Ceriello A, Torella R, D'Onofrio F. Sensitivity to beta-endorphin as a cause of human obesity. *Metabolism* 1987; **36**: 974–8.

204 Giugliano D, Quatraro A, Consoli G, Ceriello A, Torella R, D'Onofrio F. Inhibitory effect of enkephalin on insulin secretion in healthy subjects and in non-insulin-dependent diabetic subjects. *Metabolism* 1987; **36**: 286–9.

205 Passariello N, Giugliano D, Quatraro A, Consoli G, Sgambato S, Torella R, D'Onofrio F. Glucose tolerance and hormone responses in heroin addicts. A possible role for endogenous opiates in the pathogenesis of non-insulin-dependent diabetes. *Metabolism* 1983; **23**: 1163–7.

206 Kyriakides M, Silverstone T, Jeffcoate W, Laurance B. Effect of naloxone on hyperphagia in Prader–Willi syndrome. *Lancet* 1980; **i**: 876–7.

24 Animal Models of Non-Insulin-Dependent Diabetes Mellitus

Summary

• No single animal model accurately represents NIDDM in man but individual syndromes closely resemble aspects of the human disease.
• Spontaneously occurring NIDDM-like syndromes may be inherited as autosomal recessive (e.g. *ob/ob* and *db/db* syndromes in mice), autosomal dominant (e.g. A^y — yellow obese mice) or polygenic traits (e.g. the NZO mouse). Phenotypic expression of these syndromes is greatly influenced by the animal's background genome (strain), age and environmental factors, notably food availability and dietary composition.
• Most spontaneously occurring syndromes comprise moderate hyperglycaemia without ketosis, accompanied by hyperphagia, obesity, hyperinsulinaemia, insulin resistance and B cell hyperplasia; insulin replacement is not needed for survival. These non-ketotic NIDDM-like syndromes are typified by the obese (*ob/ob*) mouse.
• *ob/ob* mice show an early increase in metabolic efficiency (i.e. reduced energy expenditure) which, together with hyperinsulinaemia and increased food intake, promotes fat deposition and obesity. Insulin hypersecretion is stimulated by hyperphagia and other factors, possibly including hypothalamic dysfunction. Hyperglycaemia only supervenes when progressive insulin resistance develops, apparently through defects at both receptor and post-receptor levels.
• Some syndromes (e.g. the *db/db* mouse) deteriorate from a state of mild non-ketotic hyperglycaemia, hyperinsulinaemia and obesity into severe insulin deficiency, with progressive hyperglycaemia and weight loss, sometimes with ketosis and eventual death without insulin replacement. The cause is apparently B-cell degeneration, which may be partly genetically determined.
• The primary defects in spontaneous syndromes are unknown; reduced activity of a thyroid-dependent $Na^+-K^+-ATPase$ with potentially widespread metabolic and neural regulatory effects has been implicated in the *ob/ob* mouse.
• NIDDM-like states may be induced experimentally by subtotal pancreatectomy or by administering low dosages of B-cell toxins (streptozotocin or alloxan) to neonatal or adult rodents.
• As in human NIDDM, animal syndromes display both defective insulin secretion in response to glucose stimulation (although other secretagogues remain effective) and tissue resistance to insulin action.
• Only a few animal models of NIDDM develop macro- or microvascular complications analogous to those of the human disease.

Non-insulin dependent forms of diabetes mellitus have been recognized in many mammalian species including domestic pets, livestock and animals maintained in captivity [1, 2]. The most extensively studied have been the diabetic syndromes of laboratory rodents, in which diabetes is often preceded and accompanied by obesity (see reviews [3−8]). This chapter summarizes the general features of spontaneous and experimentally induced NIDDM syndromes in laboratory animals, and examines recent studies concerning their aetiology and natural history.

Animal versus human NIDDM

NIDDM is a highly heterogeneous disorder both in man and in animals [8, 9] (Fig. 24.1). This presumably reflects the diverse and multiple aetiologies of the disease and emphasizes that no single animal model is entirely typical of NIDDM in man. It is therefore valuable to consider the lessons learned from a wide range of animal models which closely resemble various aspects of the human disease [8].

Animal models of NIDDM are conveniently divided into those occurring spontaneously and those induced experimentally. Most spontaneous syndromes do not exhibit ketosis, but some may eventually develop extensive B-cell degeneration with severe hyperglycaemia and occasionally ketosis. In human diabetes, ketosis is generally synonymous with IDDM; none the less, animal syndromes which occasionally develop ketosis also exhibit features of the more severe forms of NIDDM.

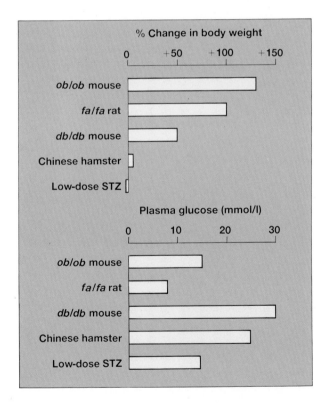

Fig. 24.1. Indication of percentage change in body weight and extent of hyperglycaemia in some models of NIDDM. The *db/db* mouse and Chinese hamster can develop marked hyperglycaemia and islet B-cell degeneration with advancing age, leading to weight loss and sometimes ketosis. The *ob/ob* mouse and low-dose streptozotocin (STZ) rat exhibit a more modest hyperglycaemia, and the *fa/fa* rat shows only a very small increase in basal glycaemia.

Spontaneous NIDDM-like syndromes without ketosis

Spontaneous syndromes of NIDDM without ketosis are listed in Table 24.1. The extent of hyperglycaemia is variable although typically does not-exceed 20 mmol/l, but the commonly associated features of obesity, hyperphagia, B-cell hyperplasia, hyperinsulinaemia and insulin resistance may be very pronounced. The fatty (*fa/fa*) Zucker rat is not sufficiently glucose-intolerant to fulfil the criteria for true diabetes, but it is included here because it is widely used as a model of insulin resistance.

The inheritance of the different syndromes varies considerably. Single autosomal recessive mutant genes are responsible for the syndromes of the obese (*ob/ob*) mouse and fatty (*fa/fa*) Zucker rat, whereas the A^y gene in yellow obese mice behaves as an autosomal dominant (homozygosity being lethal) and inheritance of diabetes in the New Zealand Obese (NZO) mouse is polygenic. Multiple genetic defects are suspected in several other syndromes, such as the KK mouse.

The evolution and possible cause−effect relationships of the different metabolic abnormalities in these syndromes have stimulated much research. Although not entirely representative of all these syndromes, the *ob/ob* mouse has been intensively studied and serves as a general model which will be described in detail.

The obesity diabetes syndrome in the ob/ob *mouse*

The obese (*ob*) gene has been transferred to several strains of mice (Fig. 24.2). Phenotypic expression of the homozygous *ob/ob* syndrome depends on the background strain, nutritional state and age of the animals, but always includes hyperphagia, obesity, insulin resistance and hyperinsulinaemia. A schematic time-course of these features is illustrated in Fig. 24.3.

ONSET OF SYNDROME

The earliest metabolic defect observed in *ob/ob* mice is increased metabolic efficiency, manifested by decreased cold-induced thermogenesis and an increased proportion of body fat in the second week of life [10, 11]. Circulating insulin concentrations are raised by the end of the second week,

Table 24.1. Spontaneous syndromes of NIDDM without ketosis.

Animal	Inheritance	Environmental influence	Body weight	Food intake	Glycaemia	Insulinaemia	Insulin action	B-cell population
Obese mouse (*ob*), C57BL/6J, V Stock, Aston	AR	?	++[e]	++[b,e]	+[e]	++[e]	--[e]	++
New Zealand Obese mouse (NZO)	P	?	++	++[b]	N/+	+[e]	-	++
Yellow Obese mouse (A^y, A^{vy}, A^{iy})	AD	?	+[e]	+[e]	+[e]	+	-[e]	+
Japanese KK mouse	P?	HED	++	+[e]	+[e]	+	-?	+?
Paul Bailey Black mouse (PBB/Ld)	P?	?	+	+	+	++	--	++
Wellesley Hybrid mouse	P?	?	++	+	+	+	-	+
Fatty Zucker rat (*fa*)	AR	?	++	+	N[f]	+	-	+
Selectively Inbred Cohen Diabetic rat	?	HCD	N	N?	+	+[b]/N/-[c]	-	?
Goto–Kakizaki rat (GK)	?	?	N	?	+	N/-	?	N/-
Mongolian gerbil, *Meriones unguiculatus*	?	HED/RE	+?	+?	N[f]	?	?	+
Yucatan miniature swine	?	?	?	?	N[f]/+	N/-	N/-	N
Celebes Black ape, *Macaca nigra*	?	?	N	?	+	-[a,d]	-?	-?
Rhesus monkey, *Macaca malatta*	?	?	+	?	+	+/-[a,c,d]	-?	?
Squirrel monkey, *Saimiri sciureus*	?	?	N	N?	N[f]/+	N/-	?	?
Spontaneous hypertensive/NIH corpulent rat (SHR/N-cp)	AR	?	++	+	+	++	-	N/+
Male Wistar fatty rat	?	HCD	+	?	+	+	-	?
Non-obese non-insulin-dependent diabetic mouse (NON)	?	?	N	?	+	-	?	?
Ageing laboratory rats and mice	?	?	N/+	N	N[f]	N/+	-	N/+

Abbreviations: ++ severe increase; + moderate increase; N normal; - moderate decrease; -- severe decrease. ?, Uncertain or not reported; AR, autosomal recessive; AD, autosomal dominant; P, polygenic; HED, high-energy diet; RE, reduced exercise; HCD, high-carbohydrate diet.

Superscript letters denote: [a] insulin-requiring; [b] during early development; [c] in ageing animals; [d] in severely diabetic animals; [e] regresses towards normal in ageing animals; [f] impaired glucose tolerance.

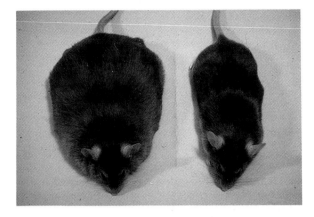

Fig. 24.2. An obese (*ob/ob*) Aston mouse with a lean (+/+) littermate.

favouring fat deposition even though milk intake at this stage is normal [12, 13]. Hyperinsulinaemia precedes the development of insulin resistance and hyperglycaemia and mild, transient hypo-

glycaemia may occur before weaning [14, 15]. After weaning, if solid food is available *ad libitum*, hyperphagia becomes manifest.

HYPERPHAGIA AND HYPERINSULINAEMIA

Hyperphagia presumably indicates a defect in either the hypothalamic or peripheral satiety mechanisms (see Chapter 23). Hyperphagia is essential for the full expression of the *ob/ob* syndrome, especially by promoting hyperinsulinaemia (Fig. 24.4) which in turn may contribute to many of the metabolic disturbances in obesity–diabetes syndromes, particularly enhanced lipogenesis in adipose tissue and liver [16].

Early in the syndrome, the B cells are responsive to glucose and the extra intake of carbohydrate-rich foods directly stimulates insulin hypersecretion. Excessive nutrient absorption also

Fig. 24.3. Age-related pattern of metabolic abnormalities in the Aston strain of *ob/ob* mouse, an example of a spontaneous NIDDM-like syndrome without ketosis. Hyperinsulinaemia and increased adiposity are apparent by 2 weeks, and hyperphagia occurs by 4 weeks (after weaning at 3 weeks). Hyperglycaemia develops with increasing insulin resistance at 6–8 weeks. Transient hypoglycaemia may precede weaning. In old *ob/ob* mice, the syndrome ameliorates.

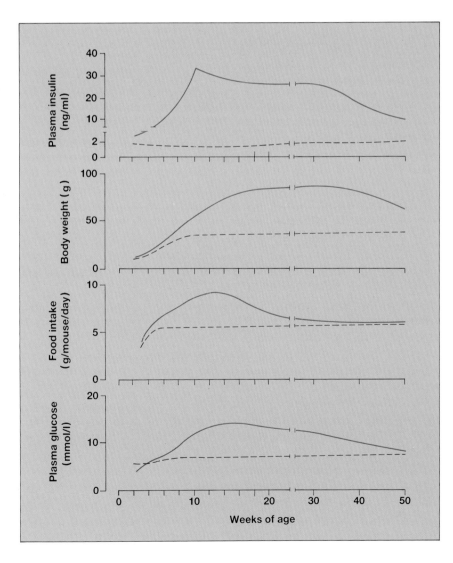

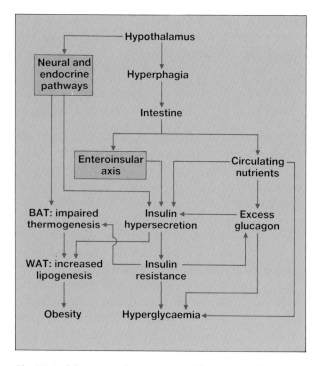

Fig. 24.4. Schematic representation of factors contributing to the development of NIDDM after weaning in the obese (*ob/ob*) mouse, an example of a syndrome without ketosis. BAT, brown adipose tissue; WAT, white adipose tissue.

increases activity of endocrine and neural components of the enteroinsular axis [17], causing hyperplasia and hyperfunction of enteroendocrine cells secreting insulinotropic hormones such as gastric inhibitory polypeptide (GIP), enteroglucagon and glucagon-like peptides (see Chapter 33). Increased insulinotropic activity of the enteroinsular axis in *ob/ob* mice is demonstrated by their enhanced insulin response to conditioned feeding [18]. If food is withheld, circulating insulin levels rapidly decline, confirming that hyperphagia makes a major contribution to hyperinsulinaemia. However, food restriction does not entirely normalize insulin concentrations which, as noted above, are raised during suckling when nutrient intake is normal; factors other than hyperphagia are therefore implicated in the hypersecretion of insulin.

Hypothalamic dysfunction itself has been shown to promote hyperinsulinaemia in obesity—diabetes syndromes, through neural and humoral effects on the pancreatic islets [16] (see Chapter 23). Overactivity of the hypothalamic—pituitary—adrenal axis resulting in hyperplasia and hyperfunction of the adrenal cortex may contribute to hyperphagia, hyperinsulinaemia and insulin resistance as these abnormalities are ameliorated

by adrenalectomy [4, 19]. ACTH and B-cell tropin (ACTH 22−39) might also promote hypersecretion of insulin [20, 21].

Increased insulin secretion is accompanied by islet hypertrophy, B-cell hyperplasia and reduced pancreatic insulin content [22]. Depending upon their background genome, age and nutritional status, *ob/ob* mice may show progressive impairment of the insulin response to parenterally administered glucose, although responses to various other nutrients, hormones and neural insulin secretagogues remain essentially intact [17, 23]. In *ob/ob* mice derived from the V stock background, the insulin response to glucose is well preserved, whereas animals from C57BL/KsJ or Aston backgrounds show a severely compromised insulin response to glucose in the fed state; this secretory response is most impaired when basal hyperinsulinaemia is greatest and is partially restored by fasting.

HYPERGLYCAEMIA AND INSULIN RESISTANCE

Hyperglycaemia only develops after hyperinsulinaemia is well established, when insulin resistance becomes detectable. Increased nutrient intake increases hyperglycaemia both directly from absorbed glucose and indirectly through glucagon secretion stimulated by amino acids. Glucagon release is not appropriately suppressed by hyperglycaemia [24], a defect also found in human NIDDM (Chapters 22 and 33). Glucagon is an important contributor to hyperglycaemia, as glucose concentrations fall after administration of glucagon antiserum [25].

Insulin resistance in *ob/ob* mice includes impaired insulin action at both submaximally stimulating and maximally stimulating insulin concentrations [26]. Defects at both receptor and postreceptor levels may be involved. The number of insulin receptors is reduced in tissues of *ob/ob* mice but receptor affinity is normal. Insulin-stimulated receptor autophosphorylation and receptor kinase activity are also reduced, independently of decreased insulin−receptor binding [27]. This suggests a fault in coupling between the α-subunit of the receptor (which binds insulin) and the β-subunit, which exhibits kinase activity. A further signalling defect has been suggested between the β-subunit and postreceptor pathways activated by the kinase activity. Reduced insulin receptor numbers may be explained by down-regulation in response to chronic hyperinsulinaemia. Fasting, which markedly reduces circulating insulin levels and increases the number of insulin receptors, greatly improves insulin action. This indicates that other cellular defects of insulin resistance may be largely due to chronic hyperinsulinaemia. In *ob/ob* mice, postreceptor defects may appear *before* reduced insulin-receptor binding [28], in contrast to human NIDDM in which reduced insulin-receptor binding apparently precedes any detectable postreceptor defect [29].

Resistance to insulin action varies between tissues, which may explain the coexistence of obesity and diabetes. In young *ob/ob* mice, lipogenesis in adipose tissue is less severely impaired than glycogenesis in skeletal muscle [30]. Hepatic insulin resistance appears to develop later than resistance in peripheral tissues; the failure of insulin to suppress hepatic glucose production is an important determinant of hyperglycaemia [31].

POSSIBLE NATURE OF THE PRIMARY LESION

The primary lesion and the biochemical basis of increased metabolic efficiency and increased insulin secretion have not been established in any of these syndromes. In animals with a single-gene defect, a single primary causative lesion presumably exists but must somehow account for several metabolic abnormalities. Studies in *ob/ob* mice have implicated reduced activity of a $Na^+-K^+-ATPase$ enzyme which is normally thyroid-dependent but in these animals is unresponsive to changes in thyroid hormone concentrations [4]. Such a lesion could explain the diversity of early metabolic disturbances, notably increased metabolic efficiency due to reduced energy expenditure; in addition, insulin secretion could be enhanced by alterations of the B-cell membrane potential and, as the cycling of synaptic neurotransmitters is a $Na^+-K^+-ATPase$ dependent process, neural function could be disturbed, perhaps leading to defective hypothalamic satiety regulation. Hypothalamic dysfunction may indicate a generalized defect in the autonomic nervous system, consistent with evidence that parasympathetic activity may predominate over sympathetic in obese rodents [4]. In *ob/ob* mice, impaired sympathetic stimulation of thermogenesis by brown adipose tissue (BAT) and in-

sensitivity of BAT to insulin appear to make a major contribution to increased metabolic efficiency. Analogous defects in one or more widely distributed enzymes with multiple metabolic effects could theoretically underlie obesity and diabetes in certain other models.

Despite their often striking experimental effects on feeding, there is no convincing evidence that primary disturbances of hypothalamic neurotransmitters cause these syndromes (see Chapter 23).

Spontaneous NIDDM-like syndromes with occasional ketosis

Table 24.2 shows spontaneous syndromes of diabetes in which B-cell degeneration supervenes, leading to weight loss and sometimes ketosis. Several of these models pass through an initial non-insulin-dependent phase of obesity, B-cell hyperplasia, hyperinsulinaemia and insulin resistance, lasting much of the animal's lifespan. Hyperglycaemia usually becomes severe (> 20 mmol/l) in later life, when some animals may require insulin to sustain life. Inheritance is autosomal recessive in the diabetes (*db/db*) mouse and the Keeshond dog, and polygenic in the Chinese hamster and several other models.

The primary lesions are unknown, but the background genome and environmental factors undoubtedly strongly influence the progression of these syndromes. The *db/db* syndrome in C57BL/KsJ mice results in more severe diabetes than that expressed on the C57BL/6J background [32]. Dietary composition can further modify the syndrome: foods rich in refined sugars accelerate the onset and increase the severity of islet lesions and aggravate hyperglycaemia [33]. The sand rat (*Psammomys obesus*) and spiny mouse (*Acomys catirinus*) illustrate well the influence of energy intake and exercise. In the wild state, these animals are slim, active, non-diabetic foragers accustomed to a meagre diet. When constrained under laboratory conditions with free access to an energy-rich diet, they overeat and develop hyperinsulinaemia, obesity, insulin resistance and hyperglycaemia [34]. It has been suggested that their metabolic efficiency is due to selection of 'thrifty genes' which ensure survival under their natural conditions of food scarcity [6, 7].

Insulin resistance contributes to worsening hyperglycaemia in these syndromes but B-cell degeneration, which may be preceded by a

Table 24.2. Spontaneous syndromes of NIDDM with possible ketosis.

Animal	Inheritance	Environmental influence	Body weight	Food intake	Glycaemia	Insulinaemia	Insulin action	B-cell population
Chinese hamster, *Cricetulus griseus*	P	?	+[b]/N	+[b]	+/++	+[b]/N/−[ac]	N/−	+[b]/−
South African hamster, *Mystromys albicaudatus*	P	?	N	+	+/++	?	?	−
Djungarian hamster, *Phodopus sungorus*	P	HED/RE	N/+	N/+	+/++	+/++	−	+
Diabetes mouse *(db)* C57BL/KsJ	AR	?	++	++	++	++[b]/N	−−	+/−[c]
Egyptian Sand rat, *Psammomys obesus*	?	HED/RE	+	+	+/++	+/N/−[d]	−	N/+
Tuco-tuco, *Ctenomys talarum*	?	HED/RE	+	+	+	+	−	+
Keeshond dog	AR	?	N	N/−	++	−−[ac]	?	−−
Spiny mouse, *Acomys cahirinus*	?	HED/RE	+	+	N/+/++	+[b]/N/−[c]	−	+
New Zealand White rabbit (NZW)	?	?	N	N/+	++	−/−−	?	N

Abbreviations: ++ severe increase; + moderate increase; N normal; − moderate decrease; −− severe decrease.
?, Uncertain or not reported; AR, autosomal recessive; AD, autosomal dominant; P, polygenic; HED, high-energy diet; RE, reduced exercise.
Superscript letters denote: [a] insulin-requiring; [b] during early development; [c] in ageing animals; [d] in severely diabetic animals.

phase of B-cell hyperplasia, appears to be more important. A stage usually appears at which the insulin response to glucose becomes impaired, although responses to other insulin secretagogues may be preserved. An inherited defect in B-cell proliferation is likely to exist, its expression being modified by the background genome and the environment. For example, B cells cultured from C57BL/KsJ *db/db* mice show a reduced capacity for proliferation, and transfer of the *db/db* mutation onto a different background genome alters the rate of B-cell proliferation [35]. Sustained exposure to hyperglycaemia may itself lead to loss of the insulin response to glucose [36, 37]. B-cell loss and impaired insulin responses to glucose may eventually combine to produce insulin deficiency and possibly ketosis (Fig. 24.5).

Experimentally induced NIDDM

Various models of experimentally induced hyperglycaemia which are not insulin-dependent are listed in Table 24.3.

Partial pancreatectomy can induce hypoinsulinaemic diabetes but it is difficult to achieve reproducible results and to avoid fatal insulinopenia. About 90% of the gland must be removed

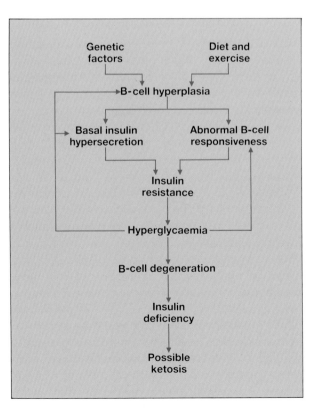

Fig. 24.5 Schematic representation of factors contributing to the development of NIDDM in syndromes showing a progression from hyperinsulinaemia to insulin deficiency with B-cell degeneration and possible ketosis.

Table 24.3. Experimentally induced NIDDM.

Method	Body weight	Food intake	Glycaemia	Insulinaemia	Insulin action	B-cell population
Surgical						
Partial pancreatectomy	N/−	N/+	+	N/−	−	−−
Chemical						
Low-dose alloxan	N/−	N/+	+	N/− .	−	−−
Low-dose streptozotocin	N/−	N/+	+	N/−	−	−−
Neonatal streptozotocin	N/−	?	+	N/−	N/−	−−
Hormonal						
Anti-insulin antibodies	−	+?	++	−− ··	?	−
Catecholamines	N	+[c]	+	−	−	N?
Glucagon	N	−	+	+	−	+
Glucocorticoids	+	+	+	−[a]/+	−	+
Growth hormone	N/+	N	−[a]/+	−[a]/+	+[a]/−	+
Somatostatin	N	−	+	−	?	?
Thyroid hormones	N/−	+	N[b]/+	N/+	+/−?	N/−

Abbreviations: ++ severe increase; + moderate increase; N normal; − moderate decrease; −− severe decrease.
?, Uncertain or not reported.
Superscript letters denote: [a] initial transient effect; [b] IGT; [c] blocked at very high doses.

to induce a stable increase in glycaemia of 1–2 mmol/l [37]; basal plasma insulin concentrations usually remain normal and although the insulin response to glucose is impaired, that to arginine is preserved [37]. Tissue sensitivity to insulin is reduced [38].

The use of *insulin antisera* also yields erratic results. Excessive administration of *counter-regulatory hormones* such as glucagon and cortisol can produce hyperglycaemic states analogous to those of the equivalent endocrinopathies (Chapter 28).

Low-dose alloxan or streptozotocin

As discussed in Chapter 17, alloxan and strep-tozotocin are B-cell toxins which can induce insulin-deficient diabetes if given at high dosage. Low dosages of either agent can produce non-insulin-dependent diabetes, although the prognosis is variable and often leads to either gradual recovery or deterioration into an insulin-dependent state [39]. Streptozotocin (2-deoxymethyl-nitroso-urea-glucopyranose) has a more specific B-cell cytotoxic action but it is difficult to select a low dosage to create a stable NIDDM-like condition. Moreover, sensitivity to streptozotocin varies with species, strain, sex, age and nutritional state, and there are batch differences in activity. In freely fed adult male Sprague–Dawley rats, a single in-travenous injection of streptozotocin (40–45 mg/kg) has been reported to produce a model of NIDDM, and in older rats lower doses (20–30 mg/kg) have been used [40, 41]; by contrast, 65 mg/kg given to adult rats (200 mg/kg to mice) will produce severe insulin-dependent diabetes. Relatively stable mild hyperglycaemia of 12–15 mmol/l glucose is achieved when the pancreatic insulin content falls to 3–5% of normal. Basal plasma insulin concentrations are unchanged or marginally reduced and body weight gain is slightly reduced despite a tendency to hyper-phagia. Mild insulin resistance is demonstrable: for example, glucose clearance by a perfused hind-limb preparation at insulin levels of 200 mU/l is reduced by 35%.

Neonatal streptozotocin

An alternative approach is to inject streptozotocin intraperitoneally or intravenously into neonatal rats, within two days of birth [37, 42, 43]. This results in NIDDM in later life; the earlier the drug is injected, the later is the onset and the less severe the subsequent hyperglycaemia. Neonatal injection of streptozotocin quickly destroys most of the B-cell mass, to be followed by gradual regeneration to about half the normal population. Plasma glucose concentrations rise by 2–5 mmol/l within 1–3 months and the insulin response to glucose is almost completely lost, although responses to other secretagogues are preserved. Insulin resistance is demonstrable in the more hyperglycaemic animals.

Specific biochemical abnormalities in models of NIDDM

As in human NIDDM (see Chapters 21 and 22), relative insulin deficiency and insulin resistance contribute to the metabolic disturbance in these syndromes but it is not yet clear which is the prime mover.

Defective glucose-induced stimulation of insulin secretion

Spontaneous and experimentally induced models of NIDDM invariably exhibit qualitative and/or quantitative disturbances in glucose-induced insulin release which depend on age, sex, genetic background and dietary quantity and composition. By adulthood, many syndromes display complete loss of secretory responsiveness to glucose, although the insulin secretagogue activities of hormones (e.g. glucagon, GIP), neurotransmitters (e.g. acetylcholine) and amino acids are retained or even enhanced. This suggests a selective defect in the chain of metabolic and ionic events through which glucose triggers insulin secretion, while the stimulus—secretion coupling pathways mediated by adenylate cyclase and phospholipase C apparently remain largely intact (Fig. 24.6).

Although the exact lesion may differ between the various models, studies of islets from C57BL/KsJ *db/db* rats, Chinese hamsters or neonatal-streptozotocin rats do not indicate an important role for disturbances in islet glucose metabolism leading to altered redox state or cellular ATP levels [43, 44]. Thus, the activities of glucokinase, hexokinase and phosphofructokinase are not compromised in diabetic Chinese hamster islets and the glucose-induced increase of glycolytic flux is unchanged in islets of C57BL/KsJ *db/db* mice and neonatal-streptozotocin rats, although changes in the rate of islet glucose oxidation have been noted in the latter model [43, 45, 46]. However, the capacity of glucose to regulate the B-cell membrane potential, K^+ permeability and Ca^{2+} fluxes is demonstrably abnormal in spontaneous models (e.g. *db/db* and *ob/ob* mice and Chinese hamsters) and in neonatal-

streptozotocin mice [43—48]. *ob/ob* mice are unresponsive to glibenclamide and quinine, agents known to close ATP-sensitive K^+ channels in the B-cell membrane [44]. K^+ permeability is considered the major determinant of membrane potential and controls Ca^{2+} influx by opening voltage-dependent Ca^{2+} channels; these observations therefore point to a key role of K^+ channels and their regulation in the secretion defect.

Defective insulin secretion versus impaired insulin action

Impaired insulin responses to glucose accompany the reductions in B-cell mass in streptozotocin-treated and partially pancreatectomized rats, and in ageing *db/db* mice. In these models, remaining B cells presumably suffer increased demands on their capacities to release insulin and to regenerate. *ob/ob* mice of certain genetic backgrounds display extensive B-cell hyperplasia and excessive basal insulin secretion associated with blunted insulin responses to glucose. Rats receiving chronic infusions of glucose show insulin hypersecretion, yet their ability to produce an acute insulin response to raised glucose concentrations is diminished. All these studies suggest that increased demand on the B cells, due either to a reduced B-cell mass or to excessive stimulation, is associated with an impaired acute insulin response to glucose.

It is often difficult to separate the onset of hyperinsulinaemia and insulin resistance in the NIDDM syndromes but in some models, such as *ob/ob* mice and *fa/fa* rats, insulin hypersecretion precedes any measurable impairment of insulin action. Insulin resistance might develop subsequent to chronic hyperinsulinaemia, as raised insulin concentrations are known to reduce the number of insulin receptors and to impede postreceptor events. However, insulin resistance associated with a postreceptor lesion also occurs in insulin-*deficient* models [38]. The extent to which this is due to insulin deprivation or to persistent mild hyperglycaemia or other factors remains to be established.

Complications of NIDDM

Macrovascular and microvascular complications are well recognized in models of insulin-dependent diabetes [5]. However, complications

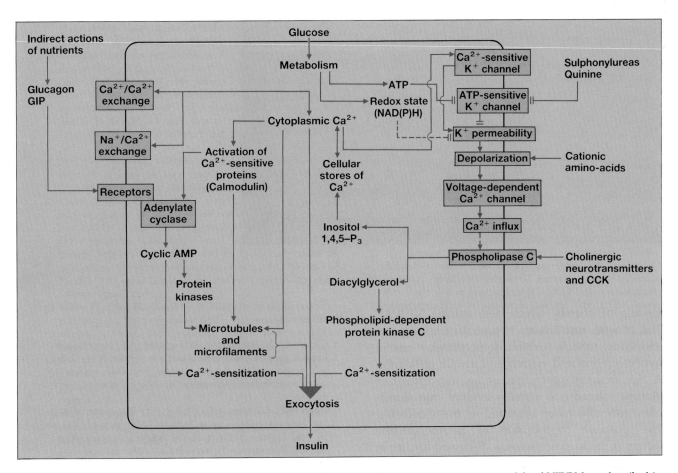

Fig. 24.6 Events controlling insulin secretion by the B cell. Sites at which lesions can occur in models of NIDDM are described in the text. ⟶ Stimulate; ⊣⊢ inhibit; – – – pathway controversial. ATP, adenosine triphosphate; cyclic AMP, cyclic adenosine monophosphate; NAD(P)H, nicotinamide adenine dinucleotide (phosphate); GIP, gastric inhibitory polypeptide; CCK, cholecystokinin.

similar to those in human NIDDM have been detected in only a few laboratory models of NIDDM; they are generally mild and so far have contributed little to the understanding of human diabetic complications [5].

Models of NIDDM commonly display raised plasma concentrations of total cholesterol, triglycerides, and very low density and low-density lipoproteins. Atheromatous macrovascular disease develops spontaneously in Celebes Black apes and in the corpulent (LA/N-*cp*) and corpulent spontaneously hypertensive (SHR-*cp*) rats [49], and can be induced in some models of NIDDM (e.g. spiny mice) by feeding with high-cholesterol diets. Capillary basement membrane thickening is evident in old, severely diabetic Chinese hamsters and spiny mice, and thickening of glomerular basement membranes and the mesangial matrix develops in *db/db* and KK mice and SHR/N-*cp* rats. Decreases in the number, diameter, extent of myelination and conduction velocity of peripheral nerves occurs in Chinese hamsters, *db/db* mice, GK rats and modestly hyperglycaemic alloxan- and streptozotocin-diabetic rats. Ocular complications reported in models of NIDDM comprise cataracts in desert rodents, retinal microangiopathy in old *fa/fa* rats and calcium deposition in the cornea of KK mice.

Several models show endocrine disturbances, but it is not clear whether these are the result of a primary hypothalamic or other defect, or a consequence of the metabolic disturbance. Spontaneously diabetic rodents which are homozygous for a single gene are typically subfertile or infertile.

Models of obesity

Animal models of obesity are listed in Table 24.4 [4]; Tables 24.1 and 24.2 include spontaneous

SECTION 8
OTHER TYPES OF
DIABETES MELLITUS

25   Maturity-Onset Diabetes of the Young (MODY)

Summary

• MODY is currently best defined as hyperglycaemia diagnosed before 25 years of age and treatable for at least 5 years without insulin in patients without immune or HLA markers of IDDM.

• MODY is rare in Caucasians, but commoner in Black races.

• MODY is generally inherited as an autosomal dominant gene.

• Many MODY families have low susceptibility to microvascular and/or macrovascular disease, but the syndrome shows considerable heterogeneity.

• Most newly diagnosed young diabetic patients, even if of normal weight, will prove to have IDDM; all such patients should therefore be treated initially with insulin unless a strong family history suggests MODY.

The existence of maturity-onset type diabetes of the young (MODY) was first suggested in 1973 by three atypical subjects from a group of 92 patients who had started insulin treatment before 1930 [1]. They were women who had developed symptomatic diabetes in their teens or early twenties and had been treated with insulin for 20 or more years, but were eventually found to be easily controlled by sulphonylureas (Table 25.1). None had ever been ketoacidotic and, after 40 years of diabetes, only one had any chronic diabetic complication (retinopathy). Each had a strong family history of diabetes and their 20 living diabetic relatives showed a similar clinical picture with early age at onset, no insulin dependence, surprisingly minor microvascular complications and no greater degree of obesity than would be expected by chance (Table 25.2). Their family trees showed a pattern highly suggestive of autosomal dominant inheritance (Fig. 25.1). In two of the three families, diabetes was associated with a low renal threshold for glucose. Since the original report, at least 15 similar families have been described, but it has also become clear that NIDDM in the young is heterogeneous.

Table 25.1. Propositi of the three original MODY families. (After Tattersall 1974 [1].)

Family	Age at diagnosis (years)	Duration of insulin treatment (maximum dose per day)	Status in 1973		
			Duration of diabetes (years)	Complications	Treatment
M	12	1943–70 (36 U)	30	None	Chlorpropamide, 375 mg
H	14	1926–70 (30 U)	48	1 Microaneurysm	Acetohexamide, 250 mg
R	22	1928–70 (30 U)	45	Absent ankle reflexes	Glibenclamide, 10 mg

Table 25.2. Clinical features of 20 living diabetic patients in three MODY families.

Mean age (years) at diagnosis (range)	22 (9–42)
Presentation: Routine urine test	11
Symptoms	9
Mean duration (years) of diabetes (range)	22 (2–54)
Ketoacidosis	0
Number remaining on insulin	1
Retinopathy	2/20
Proteinuria	0
Neuropathy	0

Definitions

MODY was originally defined as diabetes diagnosed under the age of 25 years, in which fasting hyperglycaemia could be normalized without using insulin for more than 2 years. This definition is no longer satisfactory, since we now know that IDDM may have a long asymptomatic prodrome during which the disease can be detected by chance or by deliberate screening of high-risk groups (see Chapter 15). This was clearly shown in the Barts–Windsor study in which 13 of 700 first-degree relatives of diabetic children had persistent islet-cell antibodies (ICA); seven of these developed symptomatic diabetes within a follow-up period of 5.5 years [2]. We should, therefore, redefine MODY as 'hyperglycaemia diagnosed before the age of 25 years and treatable for more than 5 years without insulin, in patients who do not have ICA and are not HLA DR3/DR4 heterozygotes'.

Prevalence

There have been no systematic surveys but the available data are summarized in Table 25.3. In Europeans, MODY appears to be rare. Only 69 (4%) of 1690 diabetic children in France could be treated satisfactorily without insulin for more than 2 years and of these, 49 eventually became insulin-dependent, mostly within 4 years [3]. The remaining 20 (1%) were managed indefinitely without insulin and 16 had a three-generation family history of a similar condition. Of 41 000 registered diabetic patients in East Germany, only 61 (0.15%) were diagnosed before age 25 years and treated for more than 2 years without insulin. One-third showed three-generation inheritance and 75% had a diabetic parent [4]. In contrast, NIDDM in the young seems relatively common in Black races. In southern India, 18.5% of consecutive patients with NIDDM were diagnosed before age 35 [5], the equivalent figure in South Africa being 10% [6]. Of young American Blacks who present with symptomatic diabetes, 10% have an atypical clinical course in that they can discontinue insulin after some months or years, do not possess HLA DR3 and/or DR4 haplotypes and do not have ICA [8].

Heterogeneity of the syndrome

The striking feature of the original families was the virtual absence of retinopathy and nephropathy after up to 40 years of diabetes. This appears typical of certain individual families but is not a constant feature of larger series. In the patients described by Fajans [9], there has been a relatively high frequency of micro- and macrovascular complications while in southern India, microvascular complications are common but macrovascular disease is rare [5]. It was once suggested that the relative resistance of MODY families to complications was genetically determined by a factor associated with chlorpropamide

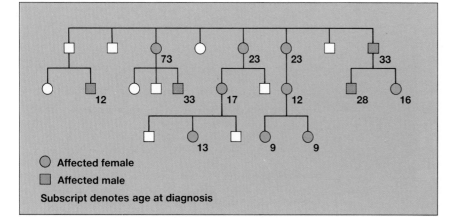

○ **Affected female**

□ **Affected male**

Subscript denotes age at diagnosis

Fig. 25.1. Family tree of MODY family showing autosomal dominant inheritance.

Table 25.3. Prevalence of MODY.

Authors	Reference	Country	Reference population	Cut-off age at diagnosis (years)	Prevalence (%)
Pinelli and Lestradet (1980)	3	France	1690 diabetic children	25	1
Panzram and Adolph (1983)	4	East Germany	41 000 registered diabetic patients	25	0.15
Mohan et al. (1985)	5	Southern India	4560 consecutive referrals	25	4.8
Asmal et al. (1981)	6	South Africa	Indian diabetic patients	35	10
Vague et al. (1987)	7	France	240 NIDDM under 60 years at diagnosis	30	17.5
Winter et al. (1987)	8	Florida	129 Black Americans with youth-onset diabetes	?	10

alcohol flushing. This notion has now been discredited but it remains possible that the low susceptibility to complications of some families is genetically determined, further highlighting the heterogeneity of MODY. An alternative explanation is that MODY is simply classical NIDDM with the young age at diagnosis being an artefact because awareness of diabetes in these families is so strong that it is diagnosed early by routine urine tests. According to this hypothesis, the freedom from complications would be explained by extremely good control over many years from the 'unnecessary' use of insulin. This explanation is strongly supported by Vague [7] in a study of NIDDM patients diagnosed before age 60 years in the South of France. Seventeen per cent of these subjects had been diagnosed before 40 years, of whom half were overweight and 72% had a diabetic parent (Table 25.4). In these French patients with younger onset NIDDM, macro- and micro-

Table 25.4. Features of early-onset NIDDM. (After Vague et al. 1987 [7] and reproduced with permission from the publishers.)

	Age at diagnosis (years)		
	< 30	30–45	46–60
Number	42	48	150
Obese	57%	50%	86%
With diabetic parent	72%	62%	36%
Retinopathy	21%	29%	33%
Cardiovascular disease	26%	27%	33%

vascular complications were as common as in older onset NIDDM.

There are other patients who would have been classified as having MODY, in whom the course of the disease was anything but benign. For example, two women diagnosed under age 25 years and never treated with insulin became blind in their 20s and 30s from proliferative retinopathy [10].

Pathophysiology of MODY

Little is known as yet. No associations have been found with any HLA type or with the insulin gene. No pancreatic pathology has been reported. Insulin secretion is usually subnormal but is greatly stimulated by sulphonylureas.

Conclusions and suggested management

Giving a condition a name tends to suggest that it is a definite entity. At present the terminology relating to MODY is in disarray, as illustrated by Table 25.5. There is a danger that the use of the term MODY will lead to the unwarranted assumption that all cases of NIDDM in the young have the same aetiology and prognosis. Indeed, there are many types of NIDDM in the young which are associated with specific genetic diseases ([11] and Table 25.6). We shall only be able to define the syndrome and the extent of its heterogeneity when we have better genetic markers.

Without an unequivocal test to identify MODY,

Table 25.5. Synonyms for NIDDM in young people.

- Diabetes Innocens in Jugenalter
- Asymptomatic diabetes in young people
- Mild familial diabetes with dominant inheritance
- Maturity-onset type diabetes of young people (MODY)
- Maturity-onset type of hyperglycaemia in young people (MOHY)
- Non-insulin-dependent diabetes in the young (NIDDY)
- Mason-type diabetes

Table 25.6. Genetic disorders which may be associated with NIDDM at an early age (see also Chapter 31).

Syndrome	Clinical features
Alström	Retinitis pigmentosa, deafness, obesity
Laurence—Moon—Biedl	Retinitis pigmentosa, obesity, polydactyly, hypogonadism
Pseudo—Refsum	Retinitis pigmentosa, ataxia, muscle wasting
Werner's	Premature senility, cataracts
Prader—Willi	Obesity, short stature, mental retardation, micropenis
Progressive cone dystrophy	Colour blindness, liver disease, deafness, mental retardation
Turner's	45,XO karyotype; short stature, gonadal dysgenesis, and other somatic abnormalities
Thalassaemia	Iron overload
Isolated growth hormone deficiency	Short stature
Laron dwarfism	Short stature

the clinician is in a dilemma when faced with a newly diagnosed, normal-weight, young diabetic patient without any of the conventional indications for immediate insulin treatment [12]. Statistically, most will have IDDM and treatment with insulin should be started unless there is a three-generation history of MODY. If patients with MODY are treated with insulin they are easily controlled by small doses and little is lost.

ROBERT B. TATTERSALL

References

1 Tattersall RB. Mild familial diabetes with dominant inheritance. *Q J Med* 1974; **43**: 339–57.
2 Tarn AC, Smith CP, Spencer KM, Bottazzo GF, Gale EAM. Type 1 (insulin dependent) diabetes: a disease of slow clinical onset? *Br Med J* 1987; **294**: 342–5.
3 Pinelli L, Lestradet H. Personal communication.
4 Panzram G, Adolph W. Ergebnisse einer Populationsstudie über den nichtinsulinabgangingem Diabetes mellitus in Kindes und Jugenalter. *Schweiz Med Wschr* 1983; **113**: 779–84.
5 Mohan V, Ramachandran A, Snehalatha C, Mohan R, Bharini G, Vishwanathan M. High prevalence of maturity-onset diabetes of the young (MODY) among Indians. *Diabetes Care* 1985; **8**: 371–4.
6 Asmal AC, Dayal B, Jialal I, Learly WP, Omar MAK, Pillay NL, Thandroyen FT. Non-insulin dependent diabetes mellitus with early onset in Blacks and Indians. *S Afr Med J* 1981; **60**: 93–6.
7 Vague P, Lassmann V, Grosset C, Vialettes B. Type 2 diabetes in young subjects: a study of 92 unrelated cases. *Diabète Métab* 1987; **13**: 92–8.
8 Winter WE, MacLaren NK, Riley WJ, Clarke DW, Kappy MS, Spillar RP. Maturity onset diabetes of youth in black Americans. *N Engl J Med* 1987; **316**: 285–91.
9 Fajans SS, Cloutier MC, Crowther RL. Clinical and etiologic heterogeneity of idiopathic diabetes mellitus. *Diabetes* 1978; **27**: 1112–15.
10 Tattersall R. Maturity onset diabetes in young people. *Pediatr Adolesc Endocrinol* 1979; **7**: 339–46.
11 Rotter JI, Anderson CE, Rimoin DL. Genetics of diabetes mellitus. In: Ellenberg M, Rifkin H, eds. *Diabetes Mellitus*: *Theory and Practice*, 3rd edn. New York: Medical Examination Publishing Co., 1983: Ch 23.
12 Wilson PM, Clarke P, Barkes H, Heller SR, Tattersall RB. Starting insulin treatment as an outpatient: report of 100 consecutive patients followed for 1 year. *J Am Med Ass* 1986; **256**: 877–80.

26   Malnutrition-Related Diabetes Mellitus

Summary

• Malnutrition-related diabetes mellitus (MRDM) is a major form of secondary diabetes, restricted to tropical developing countries, which comprises two subgroups, fibrocalculous pancreatic diabetes (FCPD) and protein-deficient pancreatic diabetes (PDPD).

• FCPD accounts for about 1% of diabetes in southern India and typically affects malnourished young adults. Possible aetiological factors include malnutrition, dietary toxins and genetic susceptibility.

• The diagnostic triad of classical FCPD comprises diabetes, pancreatic calculi and recurrent abdominal pain (usually starting in childhood), but clinical features are highly variable. Pancreatic calculi affect 90% of cases and are often large, lying within dilated ducts in a fibrotic gland.

• Diabetes in FCPD varies in severity but ketosis is usually absent. Microvascular complications develop as in primary diabetes.

• FCPD is diagnosed by demonstrating calculi and signs of chronic pancreatitis by radiographic or ultrasound imaging, together with evidence of pancreatic exocrine insufficiency.

• Most FCPD patients require insulin, at conventional dosages; pain may be severe and refractory to medical or surgical treatment.

• PDPD, also known as 'J-type' diabetes, is a less clearly defined entity affecting young patients with evidence of protein-calorie malnutrition, characterized by high insulin requirements and resistance to ketosis.

Malnutrition-related diabetes mellitus (MRDM) is a form of diabetes peculiar to developing countries within the tropical belt. Descriptions of MRDM first appeared at the beginning of this century [1] but the disease was generally neglected by Western medicine until its recognition as a major form of diabetes by the 1985 WHO Study Group [2] (see Chapter 6). The WHO report has brought MRDM considerable international attention, but 'automatically legitimizes what may yet prove to be a child or children of indeterminate origin'.

The WHO Study Group classified MRDM into two subgroups: fibrocalculous pancreatic diabetes (FCPD) and protein-deficient pancreatic diabetes (PDPD).

Fibrocalculous pancreatic diabetes (FCPD)

FCPD is a form of diabetes secondary to chronic, calcific pancreatitis, which is not due to alcohol consumption and tends to affect younger people.

Geographical distribution

The world-wide distribution of FCPD (Fig. 26.1) demonstrates its striking restriction to tropical countries. Even within India, FCPD is more common in southern India (situated within the tropics) than in the subtropical north (Fig. 26.2) The reasons for this tropical distribution of the disease are still far from clear.

Prevalence

Population–prevalence data for FCPD are not available and most data are clinic-based. Even within the tropical belt, FCPD is an uncommon form of diabetes. At our unit in Madras, NIDDM constitutes about 96% of all diabetic patients,

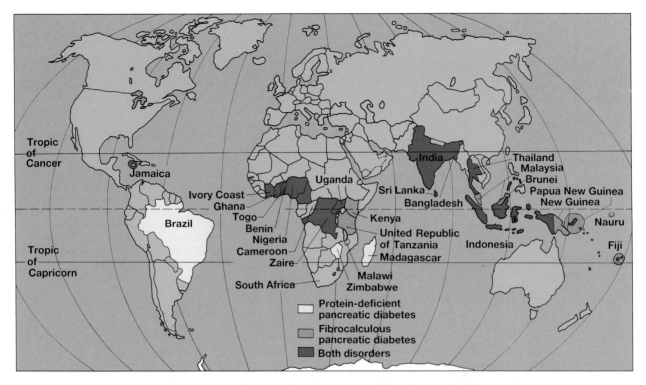

Fig. 26.1. World-wide distribution of the two forms of MRDM. Note the strict limitation of the disease to the tropical regions of the world. (Reproduced from WHO Study Group report 1985 [2] with kind permission of Office of Publications, WHO, Geneva.)

IDDM about 2% and FCPD only 1%. FCPD constitutes about 4% of diabetic patients diagnosed before 30 years of age.

Aetiopathogenesis

Figure 26.3 summarizes current views concerning the aetiopathogenesis of FCPD, which is largely unexplained. Genetic factors have generally been thought to be unimportant, although familial clustering of FCPD cases and recent preliminary studies of DNA markers may suggest an inherited contribution. (See p. 176.)

Of the possible environmental agents, protein-calorie malnutrition and cassava (tapioca) ingestion are the two main factors implicated. Malnutrition alone is unlikely to cause FCPD but a secondary role cannot be excluded. The role of undernutrition in the causation of diabetes has been extensively reviewed by Rao [4].

Certain varieties of cassava (tapioca, manihot) contain cyanogenic glycosides which in the presence of protein-calorie malnutrition (particularly deficiency of sulphur-containing amino acids) are believed to lead to toxic pancreatitis and diabetes. Studies in rats have shown that cyanide adminis-

tration can lead to transient hyperglycaemia but not to permanent diabetes [5]. Although there is some geographical overlap between the areas of cassava consumption and the distribution of FCPD, the occurrence of the disease in non-cassava areas suggests that other factors may also be involved. The cassava hypothesis, although theoretically attractive, needs to be evaluated more closely, especially as a recent study from Central Africa has suggested that cyanide intake from dietary cassava is too low to be diabetogenic [6].

Pathology of the pancreas

The pathological findings in FCPD are striking [7]. The pancreas is small, atrophic and fibrosed. The pancreatic duct is dilated and usually contains multiple calculi in the major duct or its tributaries (Fig. 26.4). The calculi are composed mainly of calcium carbonate around a nidus containing iron, chromium and nickel [8]. Microscopic examination of the pancreas reveals extensive atrophy of the acini with their replacement by sheets of fibrous tissue (Fig. 26.5). Periductal fibrosis is characteristic.

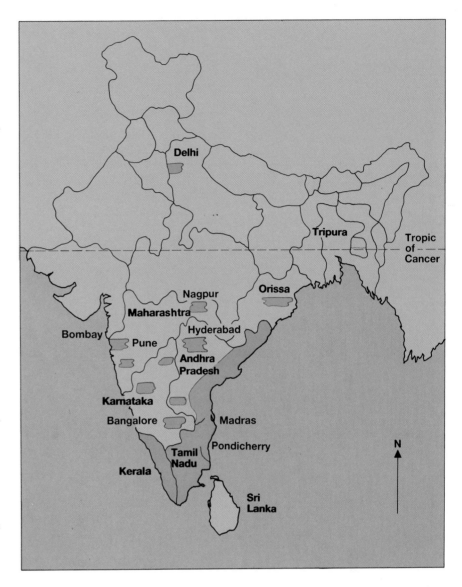

Fig. 26.2. Occurrence of FCPD in India (tinted orange here). Southern India, situated within the tropical belt, has a higher frequency of FCPD than northern India.

Clinical features of FCPD

The following clinical description is compiled from over 300 subjects with FPCD seen at our unit. In its classical form, FCPD is seen in patients from the poorest strata of society. There is 2:1 male:female predominance. FCPD is also a disease of youth: 61% of our patients were diagnosed below 30 years and 93% below 40 years of age (Table 26.1).

Patients with classical FCPD (Fig. 26.6) usually present with extreme degrees of protein-calorie malnutrition, generalized wasting and decreased muscle mass, sunken eyes, painless bilateral parotid gland enlargement and a protruberant abdomen [9, 10]. There may be evidence of multiple vitamin deficiencies and skin infections are common. In recent times, however, the clinical picture has changed considerably. Overt protein-calorie malnutrition is less common, although most patients are still lean. Many patients now come from the middle or even the upper strata of society.

The classical clinical triad of FCPD consists of abdominal pain, pancreatic calculi and diabetes, but the occurrence of these is variable. The disease usually starts with recurrent abdominal pain in childhood. The diagnosis is often missed at this stage and the pain wrongly attributed to peptic ulceration, appendicitis, amoebiasis, or even hysteria. In most cases the pain is severe but may be mild or, occasionally, totally absent. After several years, pancreatic calculi develop and are usually detected during adolescence by radiographic or ultrasound imaging of the abdomen.

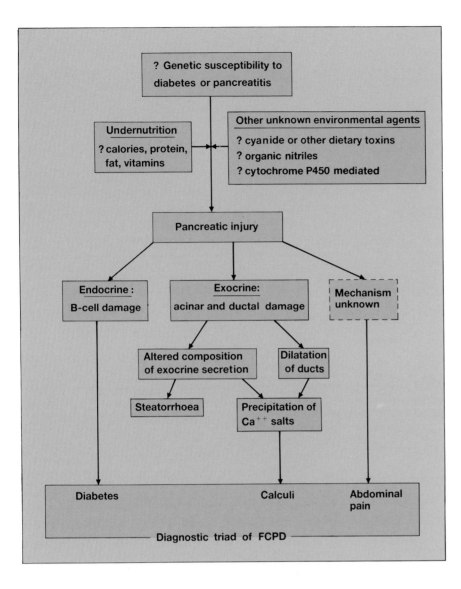

Fig. 26.3. Factors implicated in the pathogenesis of FCPD.

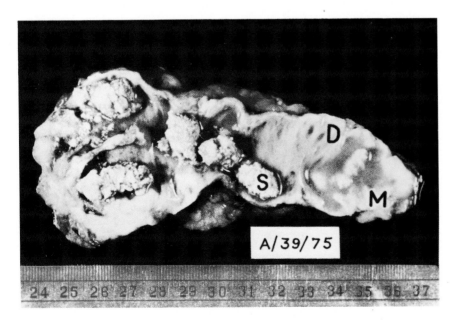

Fig. 26.4. Pancreas in FCPD cut longitudinally to show a greatly dilated, thick-walled main duct containing large stones (S) submerged in tenacious mucin (M). The openings of the tributary ducts are also dilated (D). (Reprinted from Nagalotimath 1980 [7] with kind permission of the author and the publishers.)

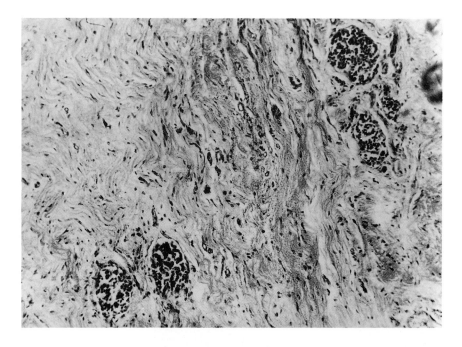

Fig. 26.5. Histopathology of pancreas in FCPD demonstrating dense fibrosis entirely replacing exocrine tissue. The islets appear undisturbed. Haematoxylin and eosin; original magnification, ×100. (Reproduced from Nagalotimath 1980 [7] with permission of the author and the publishers.)

Table 26.1. Age at diagnosis of diabetes in FCPD.

Age group (years)	Number	%
<10	0	0
11−20	24	14.7
21−30	77	46.6
31−40	52	31.5
41−50	9	5.4
51−60	2	1.2
>60	1	0.6
Total	165	100%

PANCREATIC CALCULI

Pancreatic calculi are the hallmark of FCPD, and affect up to 90% of patients. These are usually seen to the right of the first or second lumbar vertebrae; they may be solitary or multiple and occasionally occupy the whole pancreas (Fig. 26.7). Ultrasonography will confirm the location of the calculi (which are almost always intraductal) and may identify other characteristic features, such as ductal dilatation, irregularity of the gland margins and increased echogenicity of the parenchyma [11] (Fig. 26.8). Similar appearances may be seen on computerized tomographic scanning. Endoscopic retrograde cholangiopancreatography (ERCP) helps to delineate pancreatic ductal pathology [12] (Fig. 26.9).

DIABETES

Hyperglycaemia is usually severe, with fasting plasma glucose levels in the range 15−20 mmol/l,

but may be mild and occasionally falls within the category of impaired glucose tolerance. Despite marked hyperglycaemia, most patients do not develop ketoacidosis. It has been suggested that ketosis resistance is due to the small adipose tissue mass in patients with FCPD, or to delayed mobilization of free fatty acids [13]. However, subjects with FCPD have higher C-peptide levels than those with IDDM [14], indicating that relatively preserved endogenous insulin reserve may be a factor protecting FCPD patients against ketosis. Greater suppressibility of postprandial glucagon levels, which has also been implicated in PDPD (see below), may be another mechanism [15].

Contrary to earlier belief, insulin requirements in FCPD are not unusually high. The average insulin dosage in our series was 40 U/day and true resistance (>200 U/day) is rare. Moreover, insulin tolerance tests have shown that the degree of insulin resistance in FCPD is similar to that in NIDDM [16].

Specific diabetic microvascular complications were previously believed to be rare and mild in FCPD, as in many other secondary forms of diabetes. Recent studies, however, have shown that their prevalences are similar to those seen in primary diabetes [8]. Both the sight-threatening forms of retinopathy, namely proliferative retinopathy and maculopathy, occur in FCPD patients [17] (Fig. 26.10), as do neuropathy and advanced nephropathy [18]. The frequency of macrovascular complications may be lower than in primary forms of diabetes, perhaps because the patients tend to

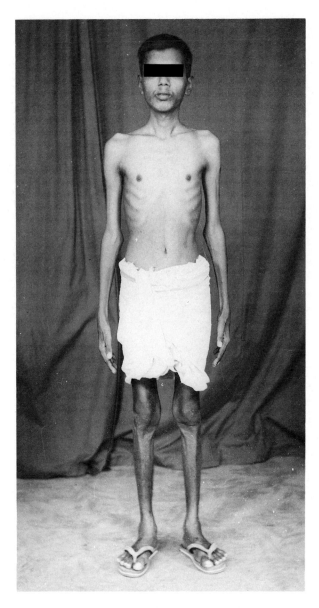

Fig. 26.6. Classical form of FCPD in a young man with extreme emaciation and loss of muscle bulk.

be young and lean and have low cholesterol levels [18].

STEATORRHOEA

Steatorrhoea is not a prominent feature in FCPD, affecting less than one-third of patients, largely because of their low dietary fat intake. Specialized investigations such as the secretin–pancreozymin, Lundh meal, PABA or faecal chymotrypsin tests help to document the presence of exocrine pancreatic insufficiency [19] (see Chapter 27).

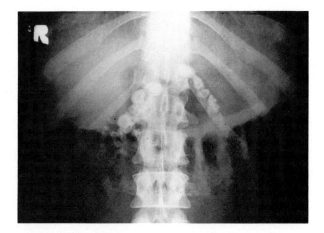

Fig. 26.7. Plain abdominal radiograph showing multiple pancreatic calculi extending across the whole region of the pancreas. These smooth, round calculi are typical of intraductal stones.

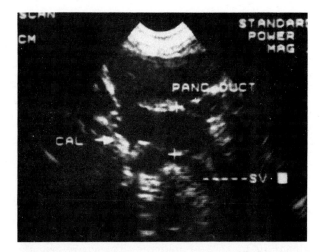

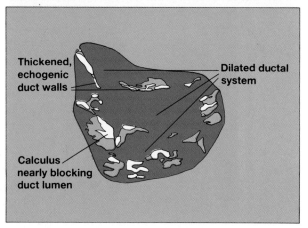

Fig. 26.8. Ultrasonography of the pancreas of a patient with FCPD showing grossly dilated pancreatic ducts and intraductal calculi. Note highly echogenic gland parenchyma and thickened duct walls. (Reproduced courtesy of Dr S. Suresh.)

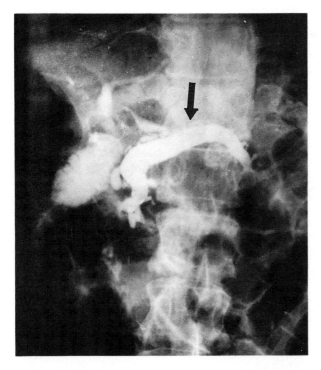

Fig. 26.9. ERCP of a patient with FCPD. Note markedly dilated and irregular pancreatic duct. (Reproduced courtesy of Dr N. Madanagopal and Dr Suresh Chari.)

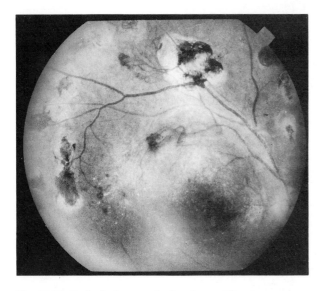

Fig. 26.10. Retinal photograph showing proliferative retinopathy and multiple haemorrhages in a patient with FCPD. (Reprinted from Mohan *et al*. 1985 [17] with kind permission of the publishers.)

Diagnosis of FCPD

The diagnostic triad of FCPD in its classical form — diabetes, pancreatic calculi and abdominal pain — has been described above. However, there

is considerable heterogeneity within the disease. Individual carbohydrate tolerance ranges from severe hyperglycaemia to mild impairment only; some patients develop ketosis; C-peptide status is variable; and some patients require insulin whereas others respond satisfactorily to diet alone. Calculi may be absent in up to 10% of cases, and the extent of ductal changes ranges from mild to marked. Symptoms of abdominal pain and steatorrhoea also vary widely, being virtually absent in some cases. Table 26.2 indicates clinical clues which should raise the suspicion of FCPD in a diabetic patient.

Figure 26.11 represents a flow chart for the diagnosis of FCPD. Where present, pancreatic calculi are easily visualized by plain radiography and diagnosis is straightforward. When calculi are absent, ERCP evidence of ductal pathology is a reliable marker of chronic pancreatitis. Ultrasonography or CT scanning also help to identify the ductal changes characteristic of the disease. Occasionally, the only feature of chronic pancreatitis seen on ultrasound or CT scan is increased echogenicity of the pancreas; as this appearance is non-specific, an additional marker, such as the demonstration of exocrine pancreatic insufficiency, is required to confirm the diagnosis.

Management of FCPD

About 80% of patients require insulin to control hyperglycaemia, the remainder responding to sulphonylureas or, rarely, to diet alone. The response appears to be related to the patient's C-peptide status [18]. As already mentioned, insulin resistance is rare.

Pain, if severe and intractable, often leads to surgical intervention, and a wide variety of procedures have been attempted; pancreatic duct sphincterotomy is of limited benefit.

Table 26.2. Clinical clues for suspecting FCPD. Diagnostic triad: diabetes + pancreatic calculi + abdominal pain.

- Occurrence in tropics
- Young patient
- Poor socio-economic background
- Leanness or overt protein-calorie malnutrition
- Requirement for insulin within 5 years of diagnosis
- Severe hyperglycaemia
- Past or present history of recurrent abdominal pain
- History of passing greasy or oily stools

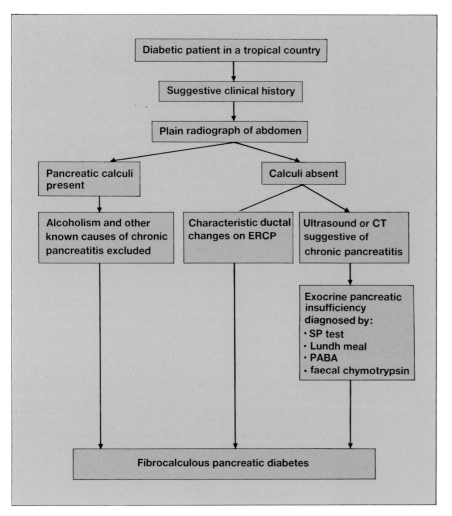

Fig. 26.11. Flow chart for diagnosis of FCPD. SP test: secretin–pancreozymin test.

Steatorrhoea can be reduced by oral administration of pancreatic enzyme preparations (see Chapter 27).

Protein-deficient pancreatic diabetes (PDPD)

In 1955, Hugh-Jones [20] described 13 patients with an atypical form of diabetes which was designated 'J-type diabetes' as the report originated from Jamaica. The special features of this form of diabetes were the following: onset at young age; requirement of large doses of insulin to control glycaemia (i.e. insulin resistance); ketosis resistance even if insulin is withdrawn; and evidence of protein-calorie malnutrition. Cases of 'J-type diabetes' (later redesignated 'PDPD' by the WHO Study Group) soon appeared from several tropical countries [2].

One of the major problems with PDPD is that it is difficult to define accurately, as none of the above clinical characteristics is highly specific. High insulin requirements are certainly not restricted to PDPD, especially in developing countries where most insulins in use are still conventional, impure preparations which can induce immune insulin resistance. 'Ketosis resistance', perhaps the most challenging aspect of MRDM, also defies accurate description. In Ethiopia, for example, certain patients initially diagnosed as PDPD became ketotic on follow-up, indicating a slowly progressive form of IDDM [21], perhaps with an extended 'prediabetic' phase (see Chapter 15). Furthermore, clinical evidence of protein-calorie malnutrition is an unhelpful clinical sign in societies where poverty is common and where many patients with classical NIDDM or IDDM are also grossly undernourished; indeed, body-mass indices in Indian IDDM patients were indistinguishable from those in MRDM patients [21].

Unfortunately, PDPD lacks a reliable diagnostic

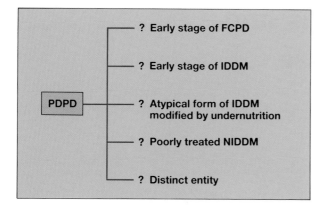

Fig. 26.12. Current theories regarding the possible nature of PDPD.

marker. HLA studies are not contributory and islet-cell antibody studies have produced conflicting reports [23]. Until such a marker is found, it will be impossible to determine whether PDPD is a separate entity or an atypical form of IDDM. Figure 26.12 outlines the several theories regarding the entity recognized today as PDPD.

Conclusions

Malnutrition-related diabetes mellitus is now recognized as a major form of the disease. Of the two subgroups, PDPD is more difficult to diagnose because of its non-specific clinical features, whereas FCPD is often readily identified by the presence of pancreatic calculi. Recent evidence suggests that there is considerable heterogeneity in the clinical and biochemical profile of FCPD. MRDM deserves further study, not only because of its importance in developing countries, but also because it may improve our understanding of other forms of diabetes.

V. MOHAN
A. RAMACHANDRAN
M. VISWANATHAN

References

1 West KM. *Epidemiology of Diabetes and its Vascular Lesions*. New York: Elsevier, 1978.
2 WHO study group report on diabetes mellitus. *WHO Technical Report Series, No. 727*. Geneva: WHO, 1985.
3 Abu-Bakare A, Taylor R, Gill GV, Alberti KGMM. Tropical or malnutrition related diabetes: a real syndrome? *Lancet* 1986; i: 1135−8.
4 Rao RH. Diabetes in the undernourished: coincidence or consequence? *Endocrine Rev* 1988; **9**: 67−87.
5 McMillan DE, Geevarghese PJ. Dietary cyanide and tropical malnutrition diabetes. *Diabetes Care* 1979: **2**: 202.
6 Teuscher T, Baillod P, Rosman JB et al. Absence of diabetes in a small west African population with a high carbohydrate/cassava diet. *Lancet* 1987; i: 765−8.
7 Nagalotimath SJ. Pancreatic pathology in pancreatic calcification with diabetes. In: Podolsky S, Viswanathan M, eds. *Secondary Diabetes: The Spectrum of the Diabetic Syndromes*. New York: Raven Press, 1980: 117−45.
8 Pitchumoni CS, Viswanathan KV, Geevarghese PJ, Banks PA. Ultrastructure and elemental composition of human pancreatic calculi. *Pancreas* 1987; **2**: 152−8.
9 Geevarghese PJ. *Pancreatic Diabetes*. Bombay: Popular Prakashan, 1968.
10 Viswanathan M. Pancreatic diabetes in India: an overview. In: Podolsky S, Viswanathan M, eds. *Secondary Diabetes: The Spectrum of the Diabetic Syndromes*. New York: Raven Press, 1980: 105−16.
11 Mohan V, Sreeram D, Ramachandran A, Viswanathan M, Doraiswamy KR. Ultrasonography of the pancreas in tropical pancreatic diabetes. *Acta Diabetol Lat* 1985; **22**: 143−5.
12 Balakrishnan V, Hariharan M, Rao VRK, Anand BS. Endoscopic pancreatography in chronic pancreatitis of the tropics. *Digestion* 1985; **32**: 128−31.
13 Ahuja MMS. Profile of young Indian diabetics: biochemical studies. *Acta Diabetol Lat* 1973; **10**: 439−53.
14 Mohan V, Snehalatha C, Jayashree R, Ramachandran A, Viswanathan M. Pancreatic beta cell function in tropical pancreatic diabetes. *Metabolism* 1983; **32**: 1091−2.
15 Rao RH, Vigg BL, Rao KSJ. Suppressible glucagon secretion in young ketosis resistant, type 'J' diabetic patients in India. *Diabetes* 1983; **32**: 1168−71.
16 Mohan V, Ramachandran A, Vijay Kumar G, Snehalatha C, Viswanathan M. Insulin resistance in fibrocalculous (tropical) pancreatic diabetes. *Horm Metab Res* 1988; **20**: 146−8.
17 Mohan R, Rajendran B, Mohan V, Ramachandran A, Viswanathan M. Retinopathy in tropical pancreatic diabetes. *Arch Ophthal* 1985; **103**: 1487−9.
18 Mohan V, Mohan R, Susheela L et al. Tropical pancreatic diabetes in South India: heterogeneity in clinical and biochemical profile. *Diabetologia* 1985; **28**: 229−32.
19 Balakrishnan V. Chronic calcifying pancreatitis in the tropics. *Ind J Gastroenterol* 1984; **3**: 65−7.
20 Hugh-Jones P. Diabetes in Jamaica. *Lancet* 1955; ii: 891−7.
21 Lester FT. A search for malnutrition related diabetes in an Ethiopian diabetic clinic. *Bull Int Diabetes Fed* 1984; **29**: 14−16.
22 Ramachandran A, Mohan V, Snehalatha C et al. Clinical features of diabetes in the young as seen at a diabetes centre in South India. *Diabetes Res Clin Pract* 1988; **4**: 117−25.
23 Mohan V, Ramachandran A, Viswanathan M. Malnutrition related diabetes mellitus. In: Alberti KGMM, Krall LP, eds. *World Book of Diabetes in Practice*, vol 3. Amsterdam: Excerpta Medica, 1988; 31−6.

27   Diabetes Mellitus and Pancreatic Disease

Summary

• Pancreatic disease, especially the forms associated with malnutrition in tropical countries, is an important cause of secondary diabetes.

• Acute pancreatitis is often accompanied by transient, mild hyperglycaemia but true diabetes develops in under 2% of cases. Acute pancreatitis is twice as common in diabetic as in non-diabetic subjects.

• Chronic pancreatitis, due especially to alcohol abuse in Western countries, is complicated by diabetes in about 30% of cases with non-calcific and 70% of those with calcific disease. Ketoacidosis is rare but one-third of cases require insulin; insulin-related hypoglycaemia may be severe. Abstention from alcohol is crucial and pancreatic enzyme supplements should be prescribed.

• Glucose intolerance occurs in 30% of patients with cystic fibrosis; overt diabetes develops in 1–2% of affected children and in up to 13% of patients surviving beyond the age of 25 years.

• Diabetes with variable insulin resistance and sometimes accompanied by microvascular complications develops in 50–60% of patients with haemochromatosis. Effective reduction of the iron overload may improve glucose tolerance and lower insulin requirements.

• Diabetes is weakly associated with carcinoma of the pancreas and is usually a consequence rather than the cause of the tumour. Carcinoma of the pancreas should be suspected in older diabetic patients with weight loss, anorexia, abdominal pain or obstructive jaundice.

• Totally pancreatectomized subjects develop IDDM and are susceptible to ketoacidosis and to microvascular complications. Because of the lack of pancreatic glucagon counter-regulation, insulin replacement frequently causes severe and prolonged hypoglycaemia.

'Secondary' diabetes due to pancreatic disease has long been recognized [1] and remains an important category of diabetes, especially in tropical countries where malnutrition is associated with fibrocalculous pancreatic diabetes and protein-deficient pancreatic diabetes. Tropical malnutrition-related diabetes is described in detail in Chapter 26; this section will discuss diabetes resulting from other pancreatic disorders and also the ways in which diabetes itself may predispose to pancreatic disease.

Diabetes as a cause of pancreatic disease

In many patients with IDDM, the pancreas is smaller than expected and sometimes markedly atrophic. As the B cells occupy only a small proportion of the total volume of the gland, exocrine tissue must also be damaged and this has been confirmed histologically in patients with newly diagnosed IDDM [2]. Involution of exocrine tissue may be due to lack of insulin, which is postulated to exert an essential trophic action and may be carried from the islets to the acinar tissue in a local portal system (the 'insulin–pancreatic acinar axis' [3]). Impaired pancreatic exocrine function is observed in both experimental [4] and human IDDM [5, 6] and the response to secretin is likely to be reduced after 5 years of IDDM [5]. Pancreatic exocrine failure may also result from damage to secretomotor nerves in patients with autonomic neuropathy [6]. Overall, however, the functional reserve of the exocrine pancreas is considerable and clinical pancreatic insufficiency is very rarely due to diabetes *per se*. Furthermore, diabetes does not seem to be a risk factor for the development of chronic pancreatitis.

The incidence of pre-existing diabetes in patients with acute pancreatitis is about 7% [7] and acute pancreatitis is probably about twice as common in diabetic as in non-diabetic subjects. Diabetes is, however, only a minor aetiological factor when compared with alcohol, gallstones, hyper-lipidaemia, drugs and hypercalcaemia. Abnormal gall-bladder function may contribute by predisposing to gallstone formation. When acute pancreatitis does occur in a diabetic patient, ketoacidosis is likely to be severe and mortality is high [8].

Diabetes as a consequence of pancreatic disease

Acute pancreatitis

Considering the extensive damage to the gland which occurs in acute pancreatitis, clinical diabetes is a surprisingly uncommon complication. Mild hyperglycaemia occurs in about 50% of cases and glycosuria in about 25% but are nearly always transient. Insulin may be required for short-term therapy in about 5% of patients but persisting insulin dependency affects fewer than 2% [9]. Acute pancreatitis may also rarely be complicated by transient hypoglycaemia.

Chronic pancreatitis

The central role of malnutrition in causing chronic pancreatitis and diabetes in tropical countries is described in Chapter 26. In Western countries, alcohol accounts for about 85% of cases of chronic pancreatitis, the majority of the remaining cases being idiopathic. Gallstones, although a common cause of acute pancreatitis, have not been convincingly linked with chronic pancreatitis.

Insulin release in response to a glucose load is reduced early in the course of chronic pancreatitis and is followed later by asymptomatic glucose intolerance. Clinical diabetes develops in about 45% of all cases, representing 30% of those with non-calcific and 70% of those with calcific pancreatitis [10]. The cause of the chronic pancreatitis seems to have little influence on the eventual risk of diabetes but there is evidence from a Mayo Clinic survey that diabetes occurs relatively early in the evolution of alcoholic chronic pancreatitis [11].

Pancreatitic diabetes is usually mild. Keto-acidosis is rare but insulin therapy is eventually required to maintain adequate glycaemic control in approximately one-third of patients. Vascular complications are infrequent although it has been reported that retinopathy may be as common as in primary diabetes if correction is made for the duration of the diabetes [12]. Neuropathy is common but probably reflects alcohol-related damage rather than diabetes itself.

Approximately 50% of cases of chronic pancreatitis are diagnosed after an attack of acute pancreatitis; 35% present with insidious onset of abdominal pain and the remaining 15% are diagnosed after they have developed diabetes, malabsorption or jaundice. Pain is variable but may be very severe with a high risk of analgesic addiction. Owing to the large secretory reserve of the exocrine pancreas, malabsorption of fat, carbohydrate and protein is rare and only occurs after a greater than 90% reduction in enzyme secretion. Biliary obstruction may occur and must be diagnosed promptly because biliary bypass surgery may be necessary to prevent the development of secondary biliary cirrhosis.

Convincing pancreatic calcification on plain abdominal X-ray (Fig. 27.1) is diagnostic but in its absence, the diagnosis can usually be made by ultrasound or computerized tomographic scanning. Endoscopic cholangiopancreatography (Fig. 27.2) should be used if the results of scanning are equivocal or if there is any suspicion of malignancy or biliary obstruction. Function tests such as the secretin test or the more recent 'tube-less' tests such as the pancreolauryl or NBT−PABA tests [13] are less reliable and cannot be used to distinguish benign from malignant disease. Serum amylase is normal except in an acute attack.

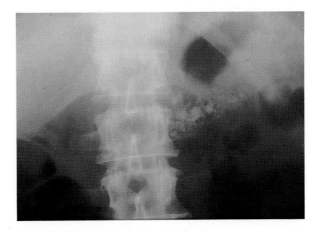

Fig. 27.1. Plain abdominal radiograph showing pancreatic calcification due to chronic pancreatitis.

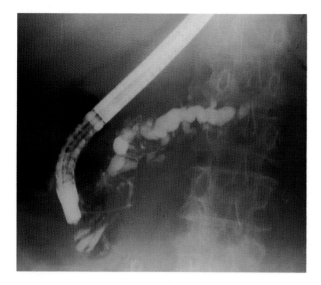

Fig. 27.2. Endoscopic retrograde cholangiopancreatogram showing irregularity and dilatation of the ductal system due to chronic pancreatitis.

PROGNOSIS AND TREATMENT

The prognosis depends above all else on the patient's ability to abstain from alcohol. Destructive surgery (subtotal or total pancreatectomy) usually results in diabetes (see below) and should only be contemplated if the patient still suffers severe pain after a full year of abstinence from alcohol. Pancreatic enzyme supplements should be prescribed and can be very effective at reducing fat malabsorption; they should either be taken in combination with histamine H_2 antagonists (to prevent deactivation by gastric acid) or in the form of granules with a pH-dependent coating. The diet should be high in protein and starch but low in sugar and fat. Medium-chain triglyceride supplements may occasionally be necessary if there has been marked weight loss. If insulin is required, care should be taken to avoid hypoglycaemia, as this is often unpredictable and severe in chronic pancreatitis.

Cystic fibrosis

Cystic fibrosis is the commonest lethal genetic defect in Caucasians, occurring in about 1 in 2000 live births. It shows an autosomal recessive pattern of inheritance and is linked with a genetic defect on chromosome 7. The exact biochemical abnormality has still not been determined but elevated concentrations of sodium and chloride in sweat are a universal feature. Although chronic respiratory infection is the main cause of morbidity and mortality, fat malabsorption due to pancreatic exocrine failure occurs in about 90% of cases. The pancreatic ductules are blocked by inspissated secretions, with subsequent cyst formation and fibrosis and fatty replacement of the acinar tissue (Fig. 27.3). The islets of Langerhans are spared from damage until late in the disease.

Glucose intolerance occurs in about 30% of cases, with clinically significant diabetes in only 1–2% although the incidence rises to 13% in patients over 25 years old [14]; approximately 80% of patients now live past their twentieth birthday.

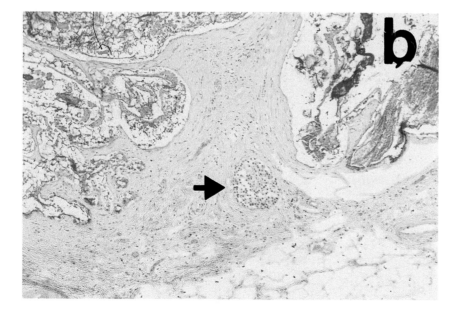

Fig. 27.3. Section of pancreas from a patient with cystic fibrosis, showing extensive damage of acinar tissue and blockage of the ducts (b) with relative preservation of the islets of Langerhans (arrow). Stained with haematoxylin and eosin. Magnification × 375 (Reproduced by kind permission of Dr A.H. Cruickshank, Royal Liverpool Hospital.)

Haemochromatosis

Idiopathic haemochromatosis is an inherited metabolic disorder characterized by excessive absorption of dietary iron, with a prevalence of about 3 per 1000 [15]. Its inheritance, as an autosomal recessive condition, is closely linked to the presence of the HLA-A3 allele on the short arm of chromosome 6 [16]. The disease is ten times as common in men as in women and is very rare in premenopausal women.

The mechanism for the iron overload is still not fully understood. It has been reported that hepatocytes have increased iron uptake [17] and that Kuppfer cells have reduced iron uptake [18] but most evidence favours enhanced uptake of iron by the gut mucosa with increased transport into the plasma as the major defects [19, 20]. The mechanism of tissue damage by iron is also unclear but iron is known to catalyse the generation of the highly active hydroxyl free radical which is a potent cause of lipid peroxidation.

Diabetes mellitus develops in 50–60% of cases and is probably due mainly to the heavy iron infiltration and fibrosis of the pancreas although the histological appearance of the islets tends to be relatively well preserved [21] (Fig. 27.4). Insulin resistance is also a contributory factor and there is reduced hepatic clearance of insulin even in precirrhotic patients [22]. Some earlier reports emphasized the occurrence of extreme insulin resistance (up to several thousand units per day) in some patients with haemochromatosis [23]; the

cause of this is unknown, although the possibility of coincidental immune insulin resistance cannot be excluded at the time these studies were performed. The diabetes varies considerably in its ease of control and frequently requires insulin treatment. The disease may be complicated by nephropathy, neuropathy, retinopathy and peripheral vascular disease [24]. Effective therapy of the iron overload leads to reduced insulin dosages in one-third of insulin-dependent diabetic patients and improved carbohydrate tolerance in one-half of those not requiring insulin [25].

The diagnostic clinical triad of haemochromatosis is diabetes, hepatomegaly and skin pigmentation ('bronzed diabetes', Fig. 27.5). Pigmentation is due mainly to increased melanin in the basal layers of the skin but in many cases, iron is also deposited in deeper connective tissues. Anterior pituitary gland function is impaired in about two-thirds of patients due to iron deposition, and commonly results in secondary gonadal failure. Other features include calcium pyrophosphate crystal arthropathy ('pseudogout') associated with chondrocalcinosis (Fig. 27.6), splenomegaly and cardiomyopathy. In the late stages of the disease, cirrhosis, liver failure and problems associated with portal hypertension are common and hepatocellular carcinoma develops in about 14% of cases [25].

The diagnosis is likely if the serum transferrin is more than 80% saturated but can only be made with certainty by liver biopsy. Histochemical evidence of excessive iron deposition is highly suggestive but may be difficult to distinguish from

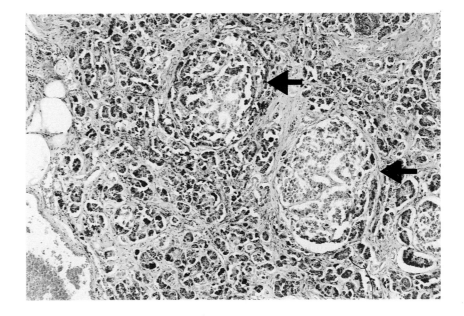

Fig. 27.4. Section of pancreas from a patient with haemochromatosis, showing heavy deposition of iron (stained blue) in acinar tissue and islets (arrows). Perl's stain. Magnification × 375. (Reproduced by kind permission of Dr Alastair Clark, Arrowe Park Hospital, Wirral.)

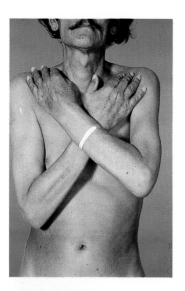

Fig. 27.5. Bronze pigmentation of skin in a patient with haemochromatosis. (Reproduced by kind permission of Guy's Hospital, London.)

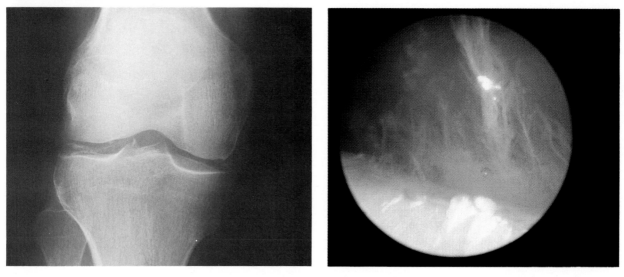

Fig. 27.6. Chondrocalcinosis in a patient with haemochromatosis, showing calcification of the articular cartilages and meniscus, on plain radiography (left). Arthroscopy (right) shows flakes of calcium pyrophosphate both on the surface of the articular cartilage and in strands of synovial tissue. (Reproduced by kind permission of Dr Tom Kennedy, Arrowe Park Hospital, Wirral.)

other causes of cirrhosis. Direct measurement of the iron content of the biopsy is preferable; a liver iron content of more than 1% of the dry weight supports the diagnosis. Non-invasive tests such as computerized tomography of the liver and magnetic resonance imaging are promising and may eventually obviate the need for liver biopsy [26].

Venesection is the mainstay of treatment and in an early trial was shown to increase average survival from 4.9 to 8.2 years [27]. Early detection and screening has improved survival still further and a 50% 20-year survival has been reported [25]. Cirrhosis can occasionally be reversed [28] but there is no convincing reduction in the risk of

hepatocellular carcinoma [29] which is a major cause of death in venesected patients. Hyperglycaemia and insulin requirements may fall with effective removal of the iron overload. Hypogonadism and cardiomyopathy, however, respond poorly if at all to venesection. Many patients with haemochromatosis have an above-average consumption of alcohol which considerably enhances not only the liver damage but also the excessive intestinal absorption of iron. Abstinence from alcohol is therefore a very important component of the therapy.

First-degree relatives should be screened for the disease from the age of 10 years. HLA typing is increasingly used and relatives with the same

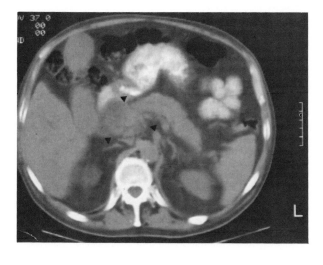 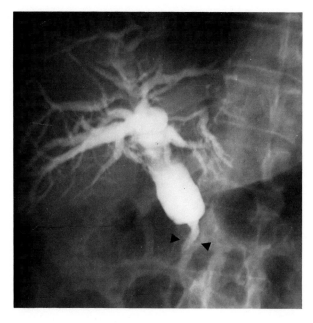

Fig. 27.7. Carcinoma of the pancreas in a 65 year old man who presented with obstructive jaundice and abdominal pain and was found to be diabetic. The CT scan (left) shows a large mass arising from the head of the pancreas (arrows) and the percutaneous transhepatic cholangiogram (right) shows greatly-dilated bile ducts with compression of the common bile duct (arrows).

HLA haplotype as the propositus are likely to be homozygous for the disease. Serum transferrin saturation and serum ferritin should also be estimated at 2-year intervals and followed up by liver biopsy if persistently elevated.

Diabetes in other metabolic pancreatic disorders

Non-ketotic diabetes may sometimes complicate pancreatic damage due to iron overload in thalassaemia, and may rarely develop in cystinosis.

Diabetes and carcinoma of the pancreas

Diabetes has long been associated with various malignancies, including leukaemia, lymphoma and endometrial carcinoma [30]. A possible link with carcinoma of the pancreas has received much attention. About 20% of patients with pancreatic cancer have impaired glucose tolerance (IGT) at the time of presentation [31, 32] but in 80% of these cases, IGT predates the presentation with cancer by less than a year, implying that the diabetes is the result of the cancer rather than its cause. Patients with carcinoma of the pancreas may show a blunted insulin response to glucagon injection, even though the hyperglycaemia elicited may be normal and clinical diabetes absent [33]. A follow-up survey of 21 447 diabetic patients in Boston showed that when short-term diabetes was

eliminated from analysis, the relative risk for pancreatic cancer was 1.27 in male diabetic and 1.82 in female diabetic subjects [34]. The association is strong enough for it to be essential to exclude carcinoma of the pancreas in older diabetic patients with unexplained problems such as weight loss, anorexia, or abdominal pain (Fig. 27.7) [35].

Diabetes following pancreatectomy

Pancreatectomy removes not only the B-cell mass but also the A cells which are the principal source of glucagon, a major counter-regulatory hormone (see Chapter 33). Totally pancreatectomized patients are truly insulin-dependent and may suffer ketoacidosis although, presumably because of the absence of pancreatic glucagon, their daily insulin requirements are often lower than in primary IDDM [36, 37]. Loss of glucagon counter-regulation also accounts for their tendency to frequent, profound and prolonged hypoglycaemia, which can be fatal. With improved survival, it is now apparent that these patients are ultimately susceptible to diabetic microvascular complications such as retinopathy [38] and advanced nephropathy [39].

CHI KONG CHING
JONATHAN M. RHODES

References

1 Labbé M. The pancreas in diabetes. In: *A Clinical Treatise on Diabetes Mellitus*. London: William Heinemann, 1922: Ch XVIII, 186–94.

2 Foulis AK, Stewart JA. The pancreas in recent-onset Type 1 (insulin-dependent) diabetes mellitus: insulin content of islets, insulitis and associated changes in the exocrine acinar tissue. *Diabetologia* 1983; **26**: 456–61.

3 Williams JA, Goldfine ID. The insulin–pancreatic acinar axis. *Diabetes* 1985; **34**: 980–6.

4 Okabayashi Y, Otsuki M, Ohki A, Suehiro I, Baba S. Effect of diabetes mellitus on pancreatic exocrine secretion from isolated perfused pancreas in rats. *Digest Dis Sci* 1988; **33**: 712–17.

5 Frier BM, Saunders JBH, Wormsley KG, Bouchier IAD. Exocrine pancreatic function in juvenile-onset diabetes mellitus. *Gut* 1976; **17**: 685–891.

6 El Ne Wihi H, Dooley CP, Saad C et al. Impaired exocrine pancreatic function in diabetics with diarrhoea and peripheral neuropathy. *Digest Dis Sci* 1988; **33**: 705–10.

7 Durr GHK. Acute pancreatitis. In: Howat HT, Sarles H, eds. *The Exocrine Pancreas*. London: WB Saunders, 1979: 352–401.

8 Goyal RK, Spiro HM. Gastrointestinal manifestations of diabetes mellitus. *Med Clin North Am* 1971; **55**: 1031–44.

9 Strohmeyer G, Gottesburen H, Behr C. Diabetes mellitus bei akuter und chronischer Pankreatitis. *Deutsche Med Wochenschr* 1974; **99**: 1481–8.

10 Stasiewicz J, Adler M, Delcourt A. Pancreatic and gastro-intestinal hormones in chronic pancreatitis. *Hepatogastroenterology* 1980; **27**: 152–60.

11 Kalthoff L, Layer P, Clain JE, DiMagno EP. The course of alcoholic and non-alcoholic chronic pancreatitis. *Digest Dis Sci* 1984; **29**: 953.

12 Covet C, Genton P, Pointel JP, Gross P, Saudax E, DeBry G, Drovin P. The prevalence of retinopathy is similar in diabetes mellitus secondary to chronic pancreatitis with or without pancreatectomy and in idiopathic diabetes mellitus. *Diabetes Care* 1985; **8**: 323–8.

13 Lankisch PD, Brauneis J, Otto J, Goke B. Pancreolauryl and NBT–PABA tests. Are serum tests more practicable alternatives to urine tests in the diagnosis of exocrine pancreatic insufficiency? *Gastroenterology* 1986; **90**: 350–4.

14 Shwachman H. Cystic fibrosis. *Curr Prob Pediatr* 1978; **8**: 1–16.

15 Edwards CQ, Griffin LM, Goldgar D, Drummond C, Sholnick MH, Kushner JP. Prevalence of hemochromatosis among 11, 065 presumably healthy blood donors. *N Engl J Med* 1988; **318**: 1355–62.

16 Simon M, Le Mignon L, Fauchet R, Yaouang J, David V, Edan G, Bourel M. A study of 609 HLA haplotypes marking for the hemochromatosis gene: (1) Mapping of the gene near the HLA-A locus and characters required to define a heterozygous population and (2) hypothesis concerning the underlying cause of hemochromatosis-HLA association. *Am J Hum Genet* 1987; **41**: 89–105.

17 Batey RG, Pettit JE, Nicholas AW et al. Hepatic iron clearance from serum in treated hemochromatosis. *Gastroenterology* 1978; **75**: 856–9.

18 Fillet G, Marsaglia P. Idiopathic haemochromatosis. Abnormality in RBC transport of iron by the reticulo-endothelial system. *Blood* 1976; (abstract) **46**: 1007.

19 Cox TM, Peters TJ. Uptake of iron by duodenal biopsy specimens from patients with iron deficiency anaemia and primary haemochromatosis. *Lancet* 1978; i: 123–4.

20 McLaren GD, Nathanson MH, Trevitt D, Jacobs A. Mucosal iron kinetics in normal subjects and patients with haemochromatosis. In: *Hemochromatosis*. Proceedings of the First International Conference. *Ann NY Acad Sci* 1988; **526**: 185–98.

21 Rahier J, Loozen S, Goebbels RM, Abrahem M. The haemochromatotic human pancreas: a quantitative immuno-histochemical and ultrastructural study. *Diabetologia* 1987; **30**: 5–12.

22 Niederau C, Berger M, Stremmel W et al. Hyperinsu-linaemia in non-cirrhotic hemochromatosis: impaired hepatic insulin degradation? *Diabetologia* 1984; **26**: 441–4.

23 Buchanan J, Young EJ. Insulin resistance in haemochromatosis. *Postgrad Med J* 1966; **42**: 551–9.

24 Dymock IW, Cassar J, Pyke DA et al. Observations on the pathogenesis, complications and treatment of diabetes in 115 cases of haemochromatosis. *Am J Med* 1972; **52**: 203.

25 Strohmeyer G, Niederau C, Stremmel W. Survival and causes of death in hemochromatosis. Observations in 163 patients. *Ann NY Acad Sci* 1988; **526**: 245–57.

26 Brittenham GM. Noninvasive methods for the early detection of hereditary haemochromatosis. *Ann NY Acad Sci* 1988; **526**: 199–208.

27 Williams R, Smith PM, Spicer EJF, Barry M, Sherlock S. Venesection therapy in idiopathic haemochromatosis. *Q J Med* 1969; **38**; 1–16.

28 Powell LW, Kerr JFR. Reversal of 'cirrhosis' in idiopathic haemochromatosis following long-term intensive vene-section therapy. *Aust Ann Med* 1970; **19**: 54.

29 Bomford A, Williams R. Long term results of venesection therapy in idiopathic haemochromatosis. *Q J Med* 1976; **45**: 611–23.

30 O'Mara BA, Byers T, Schoenfeld E. Diabetes mellitus and cancer risk: a multisite case-control study. *J Chron Dis* 1985; **38**: 435–41.

31 Berk JE. Diagnosis of carcinoma of the pancreas. *Arch Intern Med* 1941; **68**: 525–59.

32 Karmody AJ, Kyle J. The association between carcinoma of the pancreas and diabetes mellitus. *Br J Surg* 1969; **56**: 362–4.

33 Fox JN, Frier BM, Armitage M, Ashby JP. Abnormal insulin secretion in carcinoma of the pancreas: response to glucagon stimulation. *Diabetic Med* 1985; **2**: 113–16.

34 Kessler II. Cancer mortality among diabetics. *J Nat Cancer Inst* 1970; **44**: 673–86.

35 Rosa JA, Van Linda BM, Abourizk NN. New-onset diabetes mellitus as a harbinger of pancreatic carcinoma. A case report and literature review. *J Clin Gastroenterol* 1989; **11**: 211–15.

36 McCullagh EP, Cook JR, Shirley EK. Diabetes following total pancreatectomy; clinical observations of ten cases. *Diabetes* 1958; **7**: 298–307.

37 Barnes AJ, Bloom SR, Mashiter K, Alberti KGMM, Smythe P, Turnell D. Persistent metabolic abnormalities in diabetes in the absence of glucagon. *Diabetologia* 1977; **13**: 71–5.

38 Burton TY, Kearns TP, Rynearson EH. Diabetic retinopathy following total pancreatectomy. *Proc Staff Meet Mayo Clin* 1957; **32**: 735–9.

39 Doyle AP, Balgerzak SP, Jeffrey WL. Fatal diabetic glomerulosclerosis after total pancreatectomy. *N Engl J Med* 1964; **270**: 623–4.

28 Diabetes Mellitus and Endocrine Diseases

Summary

• Diabetes may disturb endocrine function through its metabolic effects, autonomic neuropathy or vascular disease. IDDM is associated with other autoimmune endocrinopathies.

• Growth hormone secretory spikes are increased in both IDDM and NIDDM, especially in peripubertal, poorly controlled IDDM patients. Growth hormone excess may worsen glycaemic control and may contribute to the 'dawn phenomenon'; increased growth hormone and insulin-like growth factor 1 production in diabetes may also be involved in the pathogenesis of diabetic retinopathy.

• Impaired glucose tolerance (IGT) and overt diabetes each affect up to 30% of acromegalic patients, and improve with effective treatment of the acromegaly. The development of growth hormone deficiency in insulin-treated diabetic patients can lead to severe hypoglycaemia.

• In poorly controlled IDDM and NIDDM, impaired peripheral metabolism of thyroid hormones causes the 'low T_3' syndrome (reduced serum T_3 and increased reverse T_3 levels).

• Hyperthyroidism causes mild glucose intolerance (reversible with anti-thyroid treatment) and can worsen metabolic control in diabetic patients.

• Autoimmune hypothyroidism is commoner in both IDDM and NIDDM than in the general population; onset of hypothyroidism will reduce insulin requirements in diabetic patients.

• IDDM affects about 10% of patients with Addison's disease; diabetic patients who develop Addison's disease become increasingly insulin-sensitive and suffer frequent hypoglycaemia.

• Diabetes (usually non-ketotic) affects about 25% of patients with Cushing's syndrome and resolves with effective treatment. Glucocorticoids stimulate hepatic gluconeogenesis and inhibit glucose uptake into peripheral tissues.

• About 50% patients with Conn's syndrome have glucose intolerance and a few have NIDDM; potassium depletion apparently impairs insulin secretion.

• Up to 75% of phaeochromocytoma patients have glucose intolerance, attributed to catecholamine-mediated increases in hepatic glycogen breakdown and to inhibition of insulin secretion.

• Mild, non-ketotic diabetes is a feature of the very rare glucagonoma, somatostatinoma and VIPoma syndromes.

• Diabetes has many effects on the hypothalamic–pituitary–gonadal axis but the endocrine mechanisms of menstrual disturbance and ovulatory failure in women and of impotence in men require clarification.

Diabetes mellitus frequently coexists with altered function of the pituitary, adrenal and thyroid glands and gonads. Diabetes can interfere with hormone secretion by these glands through factors such as metabolic disturbance, autonomic neuropathy and vascular disease. Conversely, specific endocrine disorders can have a major influence on metabolic control in patients with diabetes and on glucose metabolism in non-diabetic subjects. In addition, there is an increased prevalence of certain primary endocrine disorders in diabetic patients.

Diabetes and growth hormone

Growth hormone is an important counter-regulatory hormone, implicated not only in the

263

neuroendocrine response to hypoglycaemia (Chapter 50) but also in the hour-to-hour regulation of glycaemic control in diabetes, including the 'dawn phenomenon' (Chapter 51). It may also be directly or indirectly involved in the pathogenesis of certain microvascular complications of diabetes.

Growth hormone secretion in diabetes

The growth hormone–insulin-like growth factor 1 (IGF-1) axis in diabetes has received considerable attention [1]. Subjects with either IDDM or NIDDM, and particularly young IDDM patients in the active phase of growth, show large and frequent spontaneous growth hormone peaks throughout the day and night (Fig. 28.1). High circulating growth hormone levels are most obvious during periods of poor diabetic control and return towards normal with improved control [2, 3]. As the metabolic clearance rate of growth hormone in diabetes is normal, high levels must reflect

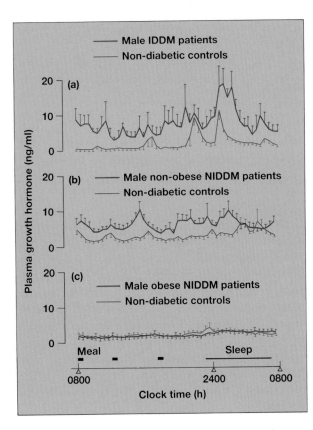

Fig. 28.1. Diurnal plasma growth hormone concentrations (mean+SEM) in IDDM subjects (a), non-obese NIDDM patients (b) and obese NIDDM patients (c), each compared with age- and sex-matched controls. (Reprinted with permission from Hansen *et al.* 1981 [2].)

increased pituitary secretion [4]. The cause of this is unknown. Diabetic patients show inappropriate or exaggerated growth hormone responses to a wide range of physiological stimuli such as sleep and exercise, and to various agents acting on the hypothalamus or pituitary, including dopamine, arginine, clonidine, LHRH and TRH [1]. Responses to growth-hormone-releasing hormone (GHRH) may also be inappropriately high [5]. Insulin deficiency is probably the main cause of growth hormone hypersecretion in uncontrolled diabetes, as this impairs the production of IGF-1 which normally exerts negative-feedback inhibition on growth hormone release [1, 6, 7].

Growth hormone hypersecretion in diabetes has two important consequences. First, growth hormone excess worsens metabolic control by accentuating insulin resistance [8]; nocturnal growth hormone secretion may contribute to the 'dawn phenomenon' (Chapter 51). Secondly, growth hormone and IGF-1 may play a role in the development of diabetic retinopathy, particularly proliferative changes. The association of growth hormone with retinopathy stems from the observations that diabetic patients with life-long growth hormone deficiency rarely develop retinopathy [9]; that pituitary ablation can lead to an improvement in retinopathy [10]; and that patients with retinopathy have higher circulating growth hormone and IGF-1 levels than those without [11]. Moreover, growth hormone secreted by some diabetic patients may have increased biological activity as judged by enhanced binding in a radioreceptor assay [12]. IGF-1 might act by stimulating retinal vessel growth (see Chapter 57).

For these reasons, pharmacological agents capable of selectively suppressing growth hormone secretion could theoretically be useful in diabetic patients. One potential agent is somatostatin (Chapter 33 and 104), but the available somatostatin analogues are non-specific and have many endocrine and other side-effects [13]. Cholinergic muscarinic blockade is an alternative approach which is under investigation [14].

Diabetes and acromegaly

Acromegaly (Fig. 28.2) is due to growth hormone hypersecretion, almost always from a pituitary adenoma but very rarely due to GHRH secreted by a gastroentero-pancreatic tumour. Elevated IGF-1 levels mediate the growth-promoting and certain metabolic effects of growth hormone.

Impaired glucose tolerance (IGT) and diabetes occur frequently in patients with acromegaly. Although the reported prevalence of glucose intolerance varies, recent studies indicate that overt diabetes affects 15–30% of patients and IGT a similar proportion [15, 16]. When diabetes is diagnosed, acromegaly has usually been present for 5–10 years. Diabetes is most often non-insulin-dependent and its clinical course is similar to that in non-acromegalic subjects. Microvascular diabetic complications — notably severe retinopathy — can occur.

Growth hormone levels are higher in acromegalic patients with abnormal glucose tolerance than in those who are normoglycaemic [16]. Diabetes arises in acromegaly because growth hormone excess is associated with insulin resistance, which is indicated by fasting hyperinsulinaemia. Acromegalic patients with borderline glucose intolerance have an exaggerated insulin response to intravenous glucose, whereas in those with established diabetes, insulin secretion is nearly maximal in the fasting state and glucose-stimulated release is impaired. In most patients with acromegaly, glucose tolerance improves and plasma insulin levels fall towards normal after reduction of growth hormone secretion by pituitary surgery, irradiation or treatment with bromocriptine or somatostatin [17–19]. Diabetes should otherwise be treated along conventional lines.

It must be remembered that acromegaly may be falsely diagnosed by biochemical criteria in certain diabetic patients because of their high circulating growth hormone levels which fail to suppress during an oral glucose tolerance test.

Growth hormone deficiency and glycaemic regulation

Loss of the counter-regulatory action of growth hormone, together with cortisol deficiency, is the basis for the tendency to severe hypoglycaemia in insulin-treated diabetic patients who develop hypopituitarism. It has been suggested that ischaemic necrosis of the pituitary occurs more frequently in diabetic than in non-diabetic subjects, presumably due to vascular disease [20].

Diabetes and the thyroid gland

Thyroid function in diabetes

It is well recognized that stress, illness and star-

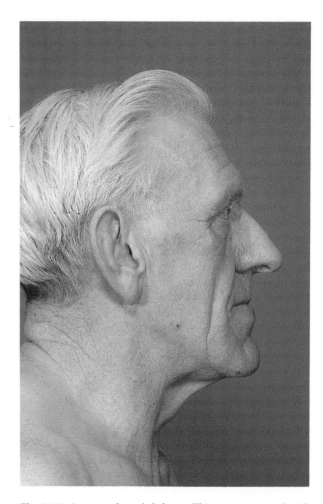

Fig. 28.2. Acromegaly and diabetes. This man presented with thirst and polyuria and was found to have a fasting blood glucose concentration of 11 mmol/l. Further questioning revealed a 15-year history of acral enlargement, sweating and headache. Growth hormone levels were moderately high (30–40 mU/l) during hyperglycaemia. Computerized tomography (CT) scanning demonstrated a large pituitary adenoma which was successfully removed by the transphenoidal route. Postoperatively, he has remained normoglycaemic.

vation are accompanied by alterations in the peripheral metabolism of thyroid hormones. Circulating triiodothyronine (T_3) levels are low, whereas reverse T_3 (rT_3) levels are increased and thyroxine (T_4) levels usually remain within normal limits. These changes, which constitute the 'low T_3 syndrome', have also been described in uncontrolled diabetes, both IDDM and NIDDM [21–5]. The changes are attributable to impaired 5'-monodeiodination of T_4 and rT_3 in peripheral tissues (see Fig. 28.3). The abnormal thyroid hormone concentrations revert towards normal when effective diabetic treatment achieves good metabolic control (Fig. 28.4).

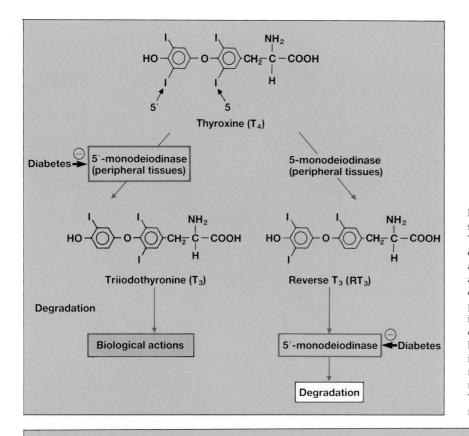

Fig. 28.3. Basis of the 'low T_3 syndrome' in uncontrolled diabetes. Thyroxine (T_4) is normally converted by loss of the iodine atom at its 5' position into T_3, the active thyroid hormone. Alternative cleavage of iodine from the 5 position yields the biologically inactive reverse T_3, which is degraded by 5' monodeiodination. Diabetes, like starvation and intercurrent illness, apparently reduces the activity of the 5' monodeiodinases, causing a fall in T_3 and a rise in rT_3 levels. T_4 levels remain essentially normal.

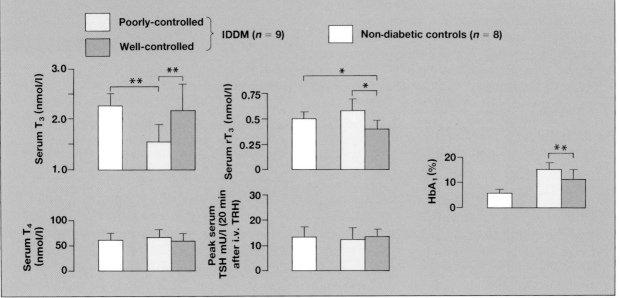

Fig. 28.4. Effects of metabolic control on indices of thyroid function in IDDM patients. Poorly controlled IDDM patients display the 'low T_3' syndrome. This is reversed, with a significant rise in serum T_3 levels and a fall in reverse T_3 (rT_3), after 8 weeks of intensified insulin treatment which produced a significant fall in HbA_1 levels. Serum T_4 and peak TRH-stimulated TSH concentrations remained within the normal range throughout. *: $P<0.05$; **: $P<0.01$. (Redrawn from MacFarlane *et al.* 1984 [23] with permission from the publisher.)

Investigation of the hypothalamic–pituitary–thyroid axis in diabetes has shown that basal thyroid-stimulating hormone (TSH) concentrations are usually normal. TSH release after intravenous thyrotrophin-releasing hormone (TRH) is also normal in metabolically stable IDDM and NIDDM patients [23, 24]. However, impaired TSH responses to TRH have been reported in patients recovering from ketoacidosis and in patients with uncontrolled NIDDM at the time of diagnosis of diabetes [22, 24].

Diabetes and hyperthyroidism

Glucose tolerance may be reduced in hyperthyroid patients, but only mildly so in most cases. Glycosuria and elevated peak blood glucose and insulin levels may occur during oral glucose tolerance testing [26]. The several factors implicated in the glucose intolerance of hyperthyroidism include: increased glucose absorption from the gut; increased sympathetic activity leading to reduced insulin secretion; enhanced hepatic glucose production; and impaired tissue glucose uptake and abnormal glucagon suppression in response to glucose ingestion [26–28]. Glucose tolerance is normalized following treatment of the thyrotoxicosis [26].

There is no clear evidence that hyperthyroidism occurs more frequently in diabetic than in nondiabetic subjects. When hyperthyroidism supervenes in a diabetic patient, metabolic control can deteriorate, with weight loss, an apparently unexplained increase in insulin requirements and sometimes ketosis. Tachycardia, and especially the onset of atrial fibrillation, in the older patient should arouse the suspicion of thyrotoxicosis. Effective treatment of hyperthyroidism with carbimazole, surgery or radio-iodine, will lead to stabilization of diabetic control [28, 29].

Diabetes and hypothyroidism

On oral glucose tolerance testing, hypothyroid patients have slightly reduced blood glucose concentrations which return to normal with thyroxine replacement therapy [26], but clinical hypoglycaemia does not occur. Autoimmune thyroid disease, with subclinical or overt hypothyroidism and elevated serum TSH levels, coexists with diabetes more often than predicted by their individual frequencies [30, 31]. The prevalence of hypothyroidism is increased in both IDDM and NIDDM, females being particularly affected. Thyroid autoantibodies are most commonly found in patients with long-standing IDDM, sometimes associated with Addison's disease, pernicious anaemia and other features of autoimmune polyglandular failure [32–35].

With the development of hypothyroidism in a diabetic patient, insulin requirements may fall but will rise again with adequate thyroxine replacement [28].

The adrenal gland and diabetes

Cortisol and the catecholamines are major counter-regulatory hormones. Clinical disorders of either the adrenal cortex (Addison's disease, Cushing's and Conn's syndromes) or the adrenal medulla (phaeochromocytoma) are rare but have important metabolic consequences.

Addison's disease (adrenocortical insufficiency)

Addison's disease is due to autoimmune destruction of the adrenal cortex in about 80% of cases, when it is commonly associated with other organ-specific autoimmune endocrine disorders. Most remaining cases are secondary to tuberculosis. Autoimmune Addison's disease predominantly affects females and generally presents between the third and fifth decades. One or more of the following disorders are present in 40–50% of patients with Addison's disease: gonadal failure, hyperthyroidism, hypothyroidism, Hashimoto's thyroiditis, diabetes mellitus, vitiligo, hypoparathyroidism and pernicious anaemia (Table 28.1). Circulating autoantibodies against the affected glands or tissues are usually present. The association of Addison's disease with these conditions is termed Schmidt's syndrome [33, 35] (Fig. 28.5). Autoimmune endocrinopathies, usually only thyroiditis or IDDM without Addison's disease, are found in the close relatives of some 50% of patients with Schmidt's syndrome.

Diabetes mellitus is present in about 10% of patients with autoimmune Addison's disease and, consistent with its presumed autoimmune basis, is typically IDDM. In patients with both conditions, the sex distribution is equal and islet-cell autoantibodies are common. A striking clinical feature in diabetic patients who develop Addison's disease is their increased sensitivity to insulin, with falling insulin requirements and frequent hypoglycaemic reactions. With glucocorticoid replacement, insulin requirements increase and the tendency to hypoglycaemia diminishes. The main cause of increased insulin sensitivity is a reduction in gluconeogenesis secondary to glucocorticoid deficiency.

	Associated conditions	Other features
Endocrinopathies	Addison's disease*	Autosomal dominant inheritance
	IDDM	Linked to inheritance of chromosome 6
	Primary hypothyroidism	Associated with HLA-B8 and DR3
	Graves' disease	Multiple generations affected
	Primary gonadal failure	Peak incidence at 20−60 years
	Pernicious anaemia	
	Vitiligo	
	Alopecia	
	Myasthenia gravis	
	Coeliac disease	

Table 28.1. Type II autoimmune polyglandular syndrome.

* Addison's disease associated with one or more other autoimmune endocrinopathies is defined as Schmidt's syndrome.
Note that the Type II syndrome does not include hypoparathyroidism or muco-cutaneous candidiasis; these conditions, together with Addison's disease, constitute the Type I syndrome (see Eisenbarth 1985 [33]).

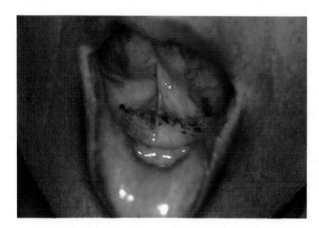

Fig. 28.5. Increased oral pigmentation in a 40-year-old woman with Schmidt's syndrome including IDDM. She presented with an acute hypoadrenal crisis and following saline repletion and hydrocortisone replacement, was found to be hyperglycaemic and ketotic. Anti-adrenal and islet-cell-surface antibodies were present.

Cushing's syndrome (adrenocortical hyperfunction)

Cushing's syndrome encompasses all causes of glucocorticoid excess, whether of cortisol or synthetic steroids; drug-induced Cushing's syndrome is discussed in Chapter 79. Glucose tolerance is impaired in most patients with Cushing's syndrome and overt diabetes affects approximately 25% [36]. In patients with pre-existing diabetes, metabolic control worsens if Cushing's syndrome develops. Glucocorticoids stimulate gluconeogenesis both by increasing the availability of precursors (through their catabolic action on muscle

and fat) and by inducing hepatic gluconeogenic enzymes. In addition, glucocorticoids reduce tissue glucose uptake by decreasing the binding affinity of the insulin receptor; the resulting insulin resistance is reflected by hyperinsulinaemia [37]. The diabetes associated with Cushing's syndrome is generally non-ketotic and non-insulin-dependent. Successful treatment of the raised glucocorticoid levels cures the diabetes in most patients (Fig. 28.6).

Primary aldosteronism (Conn's syndrome)

Increased secretion of aldosterone by abnormal *zona glomerulosa* tissue, either an adenoma (Conn's syndrome; Fig. 28.7) or bilateral hyperplasia, causes primary aldosteronism. This is characterized by sodium retention, hypertension and potassium depletion [38, 39]; the latter may cause muscular weakness and tetany (Fig. 28.8). Some 50% of patients with Conn's syndrome have minor degrees of glucose intolerance and occasionally overt diabetes, usually NIDDM; moderate potassium depletion is thought to impair endogenous insulin secretion (see Chapter 9). Potassium repletion and successful treatment of hyperaldosteronism can normalize carbohydrate tolerance.

Phaeochromocytoma

Phaeochromocytomas are tumours arising from chromaffin cells of the sympathetic nervous system, which secrete adrenaline and/or noradrena-

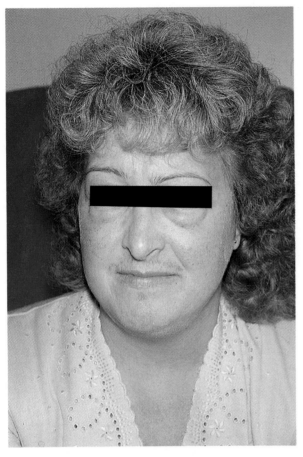

(a)

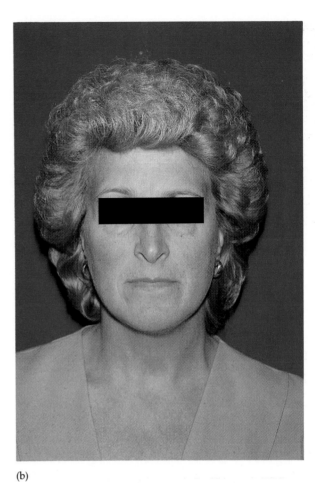

(b)

Fig. 28.6. This 43-year-old woman was referred to the diabetic clinic with glycosuria. Oral glucose tolerance testing revealed IGT. Cushing's syndrome, suggested by her rounded, plethoric face and facial hirsutes (a) and truncal obesity, was diagnosed and successfully treated by transphenoidal removal of a pituitary microadenoma. Postoperatively, her Cushingoid features resolved (b) and a repeat glucose tolerance test was normal.

line and occasionally dopamine (Fig. 28.9). The prevalence of IGT in patients with phaeo-chromocytoma may be as high as 75%, and is probably due to catecholamine-mediated increases in hepatic glycogen breakdown and inhibition of insulin secretion via α_2-adrenergic receptors [40, 41].

Gastroentero-pancreatic tumours

These rare syndromes (affecting about 1 in 100 000 of the population) are due to the effects of peptides synthesized and released by tumours derived from neuroendocrine cells associated with the fetal gut and its derivatives (including the pancreas and lungs). The general features of the tumours, their peptide products and clinical consequences have been reviewed by Polak and Bloom [42].

The glucagonoma syndrome

The metabolic effects of glucagon (Chapter 33) predict some of the features of this syndrome (Table 28.2), which is due to glucagon hypersecretion by a pancreatic A-cell tumour [43, 44]. Glucagonomas are slow-growing but most are malignant and have metastasized to the liver before presentation (Fig. 28.10). Most patients are middle-aged or elderly, and women predominate.

The syndrome's most striking clinical feature is the characteristic rash, *necrolytic migratory erythema* (Fig. 28.11) which commonly affects the trunk and perineum and is associated with angular stomatitis and glossitis (see Chapter 72). Loss of weight and muscle bulk due to excessive catabolism, non-specific anaemia and diabetes also occur. The diabetes is presumably secondary to increased gluconeogenesis caused by hyperglucagonaemia; plasma insulin levels may be

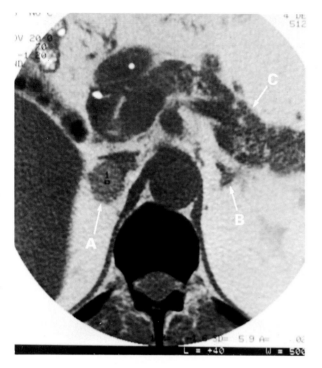

Fig. 28.7. Conn's syndrome. Aldosterone-producing adenoma of the right adrenal gland demonstrated by CT scanning in a 55-year-old man with hypertension, hypokalaemia and IGT. A = tumour in the right adrenal; B = left adrenal; and C = pancreas. (Reproduced by kind permission of Dr Austin Carty, Royal Liverpool Hospital.)

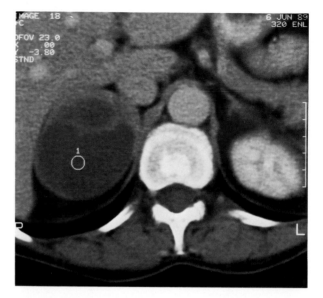

Fig. 28.9. Large phaeochromocytoma arising from the right adrenal gland (targeted) in a 49-year-old woman. Glucose tolerance was impaired. (Reproduced by kind permission of Dr Austin Carty, Royal Liverpool Hospital.)

Table 28.2. Clinical features of the glucagonoma syndrome.

Necrolytic migratory erythematous rash (Fig. 28.11)
Angular stomatis and glossitis
Mild diabetes mellitus, usually without ketosis
Weight loss and muscle wasting
Normochromic normocytic anaemia
Hypoaminoacidaemia
Thromboembolism
Neuropsychiatric disturbances

Fig. 28.8. Tetany with carpo-pedal spasm due to hypokalaemia in a young woman with Conn's syndrome. Serum calcium and magnesium concentrations were normal. She had mild IGT which resolved after removal of an aldosterone-secreting adrenal adenoma.

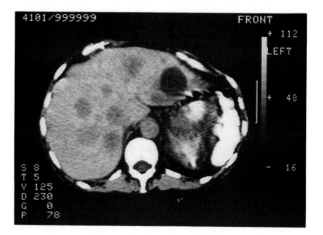

Fig. 28.10. CT scan of the abdomen of a patient with the glucagonoma syndrome, showing multiple hepatic metastases.

normal or elevated, hyperglycaemia is generally mild and ketosis is rare. Perhaps because of the relatively short duration of the disease, microvascular complications are unknown. Glucagon stimulates hepatic uptake of amino acids for gluconeogenesis and significantly reduces their

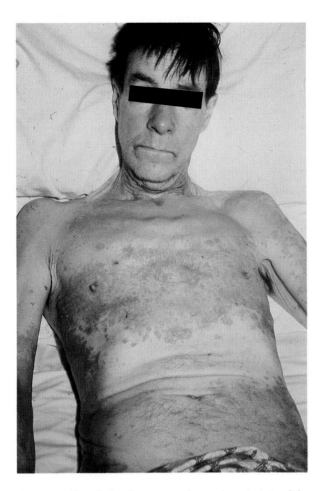

Fig. 28.11. Necrolytic migratory erythema characteristic of the glucagonoma syndrome. This patient had recurrent episodes of the rash together with non-ketotic diabetes which was easily controlled with low dosages of insulin. Despite his increasingly cachectic appearance and several large hepatic metastases, he survived for over 5 years before dying of massive pulmonary embolism. (Photograph reproduced by kind permission of Professor Stephen Bloom, Royal Postgraduate Medical School, London.)

The somatostatinoma and VIPoma syndromes

The extremely rare somatostatinoma syndrome, first described in 1979 [47], includes diabetes, gallstone formation, steatorrhoea, indigestion, hypochlorhydria and anaemia. The pancreatic D-cell tumour responsible is often found incidentally during cholecystectomy for gallstones. Plasma somatostatin concentrations are markedly raised and plasma insulin and glucagon levels are suppressed; the diabetes presumably results from inhibition of insulin secretion and is mild and non-ketotic. The tumour is usually single but liver metastases are common. When benign, successful surgical excision of the tumour is curative.

IGT may also accompany the VIPoma (Verner–Morrison, watery diarrhoea/hypokalaemia/achlorhydria, or pancreatic cholera) syndrome but is usually minor in comparison with its other features [48].

Hypothalamic–pituitary–gonadal function and diabetes

Systematic data on menstrual disturbance and anovulation in diabetic women are surprisingly lacking, although it is believed that diabetes may interfere with the hypothalamic–pituitary–gonadal feedback system [49, 50]. Hypogonadism may in some cases contribute to the impotence which is common in diabetic men (Chapter 76), but psychological factors, autonomic neuropathy and vascular disease are mainly responsible.

Gonadotrophin secretion

In female streptozotocin-diabetic rats, diabetes causes reproductive failure through irregularity of the oestrous cycle and loss of ovulation. Gonadotrophin release is impaired because of increased negative and reduced positive feedback responses to gonadal steroids [51]. Insulin therapy can prevent most of the effects of diabetes on the rat hypothalamic–pituitary–gonadal axis [52].

Most diabetic women with amenorrhoea or oligomenorrhoea have anovulation with low or normal basal gonadotrophin levels despite low oestrogen levels, and may show a decreased luteinizing hormone (LH) response to LHRH [49, 50]. Serum follicle-stimulating hormone (FSH) levels are usually normal. Improving metabolic control in a group of IDDM women with hypogonadotrophic secondary amenorrhoea neither restored

circulating levels. Thromboembolic disease is common and pulmonary embolism a frequent cause of death. Patients often survive for up to several years after presentation.

The diagnosis is made by confirming grossly elevated glucagon levels (>50 pmol/l), which may be associated with high gastrin and/or pancreatic polypeptide concentrations. Treatment is by reducing the tumour burden by surgical excision, chemotherapy or arterial embolization. The rash tends to remit and relapse cyclically but may improve with oral zinc supplementation or administration of somatostatin or its analogues; the mechanism of action of the latter is unknown and is apparently not due solely to suppression of glucagon release [45, 46].

normal menstruation nor improved basal or LHRH-stimulated LH levels [50]. In male IDDM patients, short-term alterations in diabetic control do not affect basal or LHRH-stimulated gonadotrophin secretion [53]. Studies of gonadotrophin secretion in diabetic men with impotence have produced divergent results [54].

Prolactin secretion

Basal circulating prolactin (PRL) levels and PRL responses to TRH are normal in children and adolescents with IDDM [25]. In adult male diabetic patients, basal serum PRL levels are normal or slightly raised, but a relationship between serum PRL and impotence has not been established [54, 55]. TRH-stimulated PRL release in diabetic men appears normal [56]. Female diabetic patients with regular menstruation have normal basal and TRH- or metoclopramide-stimulated PRL levels [49]. Diabetic women with amenorrhoea, however, may have low basal and metoclopramide-stimulated PRL levels, perhaps suggesting that increased central dopaminergic activity is partly responsible for the menstrual disturbance [49]. There is no evidence that PRL secretion is involved in the pathogenesis of diabetic retinopathy [25, 55].

Primary gonadal dysfunction

One study has suggested that primary testicular hypofunction — manifested by increased urinary LH and reduced serum free testosterone levels — may occur in some diabetic men with impotence [54]. Optimizing diabetic control in these patients did not alter pituitary—testicular function. However, their potency improved and urinary LH levels fell after parenteral testosterone administration, perhaps indicating initial testosterone deficiency. Further studies are required to clarify these observations.

Patients with gonadal dysgenesis (Turner's or Klinefelter's syndromes) may have an increased prevalence of diabetes [57] (see Chapter 31), which is unexplained.

Hypothalamic—pituitary dysfunction in response to hypoglycaemia

The secretion of the major counter-regulatory hormones in response to hypoglycaemia becomes impaired in patients with long-standing IDDM. This topic is discussed in detail in Chapter 50.

Vasopressin secretion and thirst in diabetes

A number of abnormalities of vasopressin secretion have been reported in diabetes. Poorly controlled IDDM, especially with ketoacidosis, is associated with increased vasopressin levels, possibly related to nausea (a potent stimulus to vasopressin release) and fluid depletion. During moderate hyperglycaemia, osmoregulation in IDDM patients is apparently normal, although the threshold plasma sodium level triggering vasopressin release and perception of thirst is lowered through an unknown mechanism [58]. IDDM patients also display exaggerated vasopressin release in response to hypoglycaemia [59]. Experimental vasopressin administration causes hyperglycaemia; it has been speculated that elevated vasopressin levels may contribute to poor metabolic control as well as being a consequence of this.

Alterations of bone and mineral metabolism in diabetes

Diabetic osteopenia and other abnormalities of mineral metabolism in the disease are discussed in Chapter 74.

Miscellaneous endocrine syndromes

Diabetes insipidus, diabetes mellitus, optic atrophy and deafness (DIDMOAD syndrome)

This rare autosomal recessively inherited condition is usually diagnosed when IDDM presents in childhood; diabetes insipidus later develops insidiously [60]. Optic atrophy and nerve deafness are also present (Fig. 28.12). Dilatation of the urinary tract often occurs, apparently as a result of high urine flow-rates, and improves with vasopressin therapy.

Non-autoimmune endocrine failure

The POEMS syndrome (polyneuropathy, organomegaly, endocrinopathy, M (myeloma) protein and skin changes) has recently been described in patients with plasma cell dyscrasias [61]. Primary gonadal failure and diabetes occur in most patients and there is associated severe sensori-motor polyneuropathy, hepatosplenomegaly and lymphadenopathy. The syndrome is assumed to be secondary to circulating immunoglobulins,

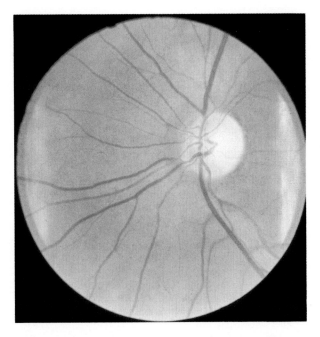

Fig. 28.12. Optic atrophy in a 55-year-old woman with diabetes insipidus, non-insulin-dependent diabetes and bilateral nerve deafness (DIDMOAD syndrome). (Reproduced by kind permission of Dr Michael White, Royal Liverpool Hospital.)

although tissue-specific autoantibodies are absent. Temporary resolution of the disease, including normalization of blood glucose levels, may follow radiotherapy to localized plasma cell lesions of bone.

Conclusions

Diabetes is frequently associated with various endocrine diseases. Although those conditions accompanying IDDM have received the most attention, NIDDM patients may also develop most of these disorders. Endocrine disturbances may be related to poor metabolic control, a fact which must be recognized in order to avoid the mistaken diagnosis of primary endocrine disease. On the other hand, unexpected alterations in metabolic control may alert the clinician to the development of disorders such as Addison's disease and hyperthyroidism in diabetic patients.

Finally, it must be emphasized that although endocrine causes of glucose intolerance such as Cushing's disease and acromegaly are rare, these conditions are rewarding to diagnose and treat.

IAN A. MACFARLANE

References

1 Holly JMP, Amiel SA, Sandhu RR, Rees LH, Wass JAH. The role of growth hormone in diabetes mellitus. *J Endocrinol* 1988; **118**: 353−64.

2 Hansen AP, Ledet T, Lundbaek K. Growth hormone and diabetes. In: Brown M, ed. *Handbook of Diabetes Mellitus, Biochemical Pathology*, vol 4. Chichester: Wiley and Sons, 1981: 231−75.

3 Hayford JT, Danney MM, Hendrix JA, Thompson RG. Integrated concentrations of growth hormone in juvenile onset diabetes. *Diabetes* 1980; **29**: 391−8.

4 Navalesi R, Pilo A, Vigneri R. Growth hormone kinetics in diabetic patients. *Diabetes* 1975; **24**: 317−27.

5 Press M, Tamborlane WV, Thorner MO, Vale W, Rivier J, Gertner JM, Sherwin RS. Pituitary response to growth hormone releasing factor in diabetes. Failure of glucose mediated suppression. *Diabetes* 1984; **33**: 804−6.

6 Tamborlane WV, Hintz RL, Bergman M, Genel M, Felig P, Sherwin RS. Insulin infusion pump treatment of diabetics. Influence of improved metabolic control on plasma somatomedin levels. *N Engl J Med* 1981; **305**: 303−7.

7 Amiel SA, Sherwin RS, Hintz RL, Gertner JM, Press M, Tamborlane WV. Effect of diabetes and its control on insulin like growth factors in the young subject with type 1 diabetes. *Diabetes* 1984; **33**: 1175−9.

8 Press M, Tamborlane WV, Sherwin RS. Importance of raised growth hormone levels in mediating the metabolic derangements of diabetes. *N Engl J Med* 1984; **310**: 810−15.

9 Merimee TJ. A follow-up study of vascular disease in growth hormone deficient dwarfs with diabetes. *N Engl J Med* 1978; **298**: 1217−22.

10 Sharp PS, Fallon TJ, Brazier OJ, Sandler, L, Joplin GF, Kohner EM. Long term follow-up of patients who underwent yttrium-90 pituitary implantation for treatment of proliferative diabetic retinopathy. *Diabetologia* 1987; **30**: 199−207.

11 Merimee TJ, Zapf J, Froesch ER. Insulin like growth factors. Studies in diabetics with and without retinopathy. *N Engl J Med* 1983; **309**: 526−30.

12 MacFarlane IA, Stafford S, Wright AD. Increased circulating radioreceptor-active growth hormone in insulin dependent diabetics. *Clin Endocrinol* 1986; **25**: 607−16.

13 Davies RR, Turner SJ, Alberti KGMM, Johnston DG. Somatostatin analogues in diabetes mellitus. *Diabetic Med* 1989; **6**: 103−11.

14 Arends J, Wagner ML, Willms BL. Cholinergic muscarinic receptor blockade suppresses arginine and exercise induced growth hormone secretion in type 1 diabetic subjects. *J Clin Endocrinol Metab* 1988; **66**: 389−94.

15 Gordon DA, Hill FM, Ezrin C. Acromegaly: a review of 100 cases. *Canad Med Ass J* 1962; **87**: 1106−9.

16 Jadresic A, Banks LM, Child DF, Diamant L, Doyle FH, Fraser TR, Joplin GF. The acromegaly syndrome. Relation between clinical features, growth hormone values and radiological characteristics of the pituitary tumours. *Q J Med* 1982; **202**: 189−204.

17 Sönksen PH, Greenwood FC, Ellis JP, Lowy C, Rutherford A, Nabarro JDN. Changes of carbohydrate tolerance in acromegaly with progress of the disease and in response to treatment. *J Clin Endocrinol* 1967; **27**: 1418−30.

18 Eastman RC, Gorden P, Roth J. Conventional supervoltage irradiation is an effective treatment for acromegaly. *J Clin Endocrinol Metab* 1979; **48**: 931−40.

19 Wass JAH, Cudworth AG, Bottazzo GF, Woodrow JC, Besser

GM. An assessment of glucose intolerance in acromegaly and its response to medical treatment. *Clin Endocrinol* 1980; **12**: 53–9.

20 Olson LD, Winternitz WW. Hypopituitarism: a complication of diabetes. *Southern Med J* 1977; **70**: 411–13.

21 Utiger RD. Decreased extra thyroidal triiodothyronine production in non-thyroidal illness: benefit or harm? *Am J Med* 1980; **69**: 807–10.

22 Naeije R, Goldstein J, Clumeck N, Meinhold H, Wenzel K, Van Haelst L. A low T3 syndrome in diabetic ketoacidosis. *Clin Endocrinol* 1978; **8**: 467–72.

23 MacFarlane IA, Sheppard MC, Black EG, Gilbey S, Wright AD. The hypothalamic–pituitary–thyroid axis in Type 1 diabetes: influence of diabetic metabolic control. *Acta Endocrinol* 1984; **106**: 92–8.

24 Kabadi UM. Impaired pituitary thyrotroph function in uncontrolled type II diabetes mellitus: normalisation on recovery. *J Clin Endocrinol Metab* 1984; **59**: 521–5.

25 Salardi S, Fava A, Cassio A, Cicognani A, Tassoni P, Pirazzoli P, Frejaville E, Balsamo A, Cozzuti E, Cacciari E. Thyroid function and prolactin levels in insulin-dependent diabetic children and adolescents. *Diabetes* 1984; **33**: 522–6.

26 Holdsworth CD, Besser GM. Influence of gastric emptying rate and of insulin response on oral glucose tolerance in thyroid disease. *Lancet* 1968; ii: 700–3.

27 Karlander SG, Khan A, Wajngot A, Torring O, Vranic M, Efendic S. Glucose turnover in hyperthyroid patients with normal glucose tolerance. *J Clin Endocrinol Metab* 1989; **68**: 780–6.

28 Kozak GP, Cooppan R. Diabetes and other endocrinology disorders. In: Marble A, ed. *Joslin's Diabetes Mellitus*, 12th edn. Philadelphia: Lea and Febinger, 1985: 785–816.

29 Cooppan R, Kozak GP. Hyperthyroidism and diabetes mellitus. *Arch Intern Med* 1980; **140**: 370–3.

30 Feely J, Isles TE. Screening for thyroid dysfunction in diabetics. *Br Med J* 1979; **1**: 1678.

31 Gray RS, Borsey DQ, Seth J, Herd R, Brown NS, Clarke BF. Prevalence of subclinical thyroid failure in insulin dependent diabetes. *J Clin Endocrinol Metab* 1980; **50**: 1034–7.

32 Ganz K, Kozak GP. Diabetes mellitus and primary hypothyroidism. *Arch Intern Med* 1974; **134**: 430–2.

33 Eisenbarth GS. The immunoendocrinopathy syndromes. In: Wilson JD, Foster DW, eds. *Williams' Textbook of Endocrinology*, 7th edn. Philadelphia: ·W.B. Saunders and Co., 1985: 1290–9.

34 Whittingham S, Mathews JD, Mackay IR, Stocks AE, Ungar B, Martin FIR. Diabetes mellitus, autoimmunity and ageing. *Lancet* 1971; i: 763–6.

35 Soloman N, Carpenter CCJ, Bennett IL, Harvey AM. Schmidt's syndrome (thyroid and adrenal insufficiency) and coexistent diabetes mellitus. *Diabetes* 1965; **14**: 300–4.

36 Soffer LJ, Iannaccone A, Gabrilove JL. Cushing's syndrome: a study of fifty patients. *Am J Med* 1961 30: 129–46.

37 Rizza RA, Mandarino LJ, Gerich JE. Cortisol induced insulin resistance in man: impaired suppression of glucose production and stimulation of glucose utilisation due to a postreceptor deficit of insulinisation. *J Clin Endocrinol Metab* 1982; **54**: 131–9.

38 Conn JW, Knopf RF, Nesbit RM. Clinical characteristics of primary aldosteronism from analysis of 145 cases. *Am J Surg* 1964; **107**: 159.

39 Conn JW. Hypertension, the potassium ion and impaired carbohydrate tolerance. *N Engl J Med* 1965; **273**: 1135–43.

40 Wilber JF, Turtle JR, Crane NA. Inhibition of insulin secretion by a phaeochromocytoma. *Lancet* 1966; ii: 733.

41 Isles CG, Johnson JK. Phaeochromocytoma and diabetes mellitus: further evidence that α 2 receptors inhibit insulin release in man. *Clin Endocrinol* 1983; **18**: 37–41.

42 Polak JM, Bloom SR, eds. *Endocrine Tumours. The Pathobiology of Regulatory Peptide-Producing Tumours*. Edinburgh: Churchill Livingstone, 1985.

43 Mallinson CN, Bloom SR, Warin AP, Salmon PR, Cox B. A glucagonoma syndrome. *Lancet* 1974; ii: 1–5.

44 Bloom SR, Polak JM. Glucagonoma syndrome. *Am J Med* 1987; **82**: 25–36.

45 Sohier J, Jeanmougin M, Lombrail P, Passa P. Rapid improvement of skin lesions in glucagonomas with intravenous somatostatin infusions. *Lancet* 1980; i: 40.

46 Williams G, Anderson JV, Bloom SR. Treatment of gut-associated neuroendocrine tumors with the long-acting somatostatin analog, SMS 201–995. In: Reichlin S, ed. *Somatostatin. Basic and Clinical Status*. New York: Plenum Press, 1987: 343–56.

47 Krejs GJ, Orci L, Conlon M, Ravazzola M, Davis GR, Raskin P, Collins SM, McCarthy DM, Baetens D, Rubenstein A, Aldor TAM, Unger RH. Somatostatinoma syndrome. *N Engl J Med* 1979; **301**: 285–92.

48 Said SI, ed. *Vasoactive Intestinal Peptide*. Advances in Peptide Hormone Research series. New York: Raven Press, 1982.

49 Djursing H, Hagen C, Nyholm HC, Carstensen L, Andersen AN. Gonadotropin responses to gonadotropin releasing hormone and prolactin responses to thyrotropin releasing hormone and metoclopramide in women with amenorrhea and insulin-treated diabetes mellitus. *J Clin Endocrinol Metab* 1983; **38**: 471–6.

50 O'Hare JA, Eichold BH, Vignati L. Hypogonadotropic secondary amenorrhea in diabetes: effects of central opiate blockade and improved metabolic control. *Am J Med* 1987; **83**: 1080–4.

51 Spindler-Vomachka M, Johnson DC. Altered hypothalamic–pituitary function in the adult female rat with streptozotocin-induced diabetes. *Diabetologia* 1985; **28**: 38–44.

52 Bestetti GE, Junker U, Locatelli V, Rossi GL. Continuous subtherapeutic insulin counteracts hypothalamo–pituitary–gonadal alterations in diabetic rats. *Diabetes* 1987; **36**: 1315–19.

53 Vierhapper H, Grubeck-Loebenstein B, Bratusch-Marrain P, Panzer S, Waldhaüsl W. The impact of euglycemia and hyperglycemia on stimulated pituitary hormone release in insulin-dependent diabetics. *J Clin Endocrinol Metab* 1981; **52**: 1230–4.

54 Murray FT, Wyss HU, Thomas RG, Spevack M, Glaros AG. Gonadal dysfunction in diabetic men with organic impotence. *J Clin Endocrinol Metab* 1987; **65**: 127–35.

55 Mooradian AD, Morley JE, Billington CJ, Slag MF, Elson MK, Shafer RB. Hyperprolactinaemia in male diabetes. *Postgrad Med J* 1985; **61**: 11–14.

56 Harrower ADB. Growth hormone, prolactin and thyrotrophin responses to thyrotrophin-releasing hormone in diabetic patients. *Postgrad Med J* 1980; **56**: 481–4.

57 Forbes AP, Engel E. The high incidence of diabetes mellitus in 41 patients with gonadal dysgenesis and their close relatives. *Metabolism* 1963; **12**: 428–39.

58 Thompson CJ, Thow J, Jones IR, Baylis PH. Vasopressin secretion during insulin-induced hypoglycaemia: exaggerated response in people with type 1 diabetes. *Diabetic Med* 1989; **6**: 158–63.

59 Thompson CJ, Davis SN, Baylis PH. Effect of blood glucose

concentration on osmoregulation in diabetes mellitus. *Am J Physiol* 1989; **256**: R597−R604.

60 Page MMJ, Asmal AC, Edwards CRW. Recessive inheritance of diabetes: the syndrome of diabetes insipidus, diabetes mellitus, optic atrophy and deafness. *Q J Med* 1976; **45**: 505−20.

61 Bardwick PA, Zvaifler NJ, Gill GN, Newman D, Greenway GD, Resnick DL. Plasma cell dyscrasias with polyneuropathy, organomegaly, endocrinopathy, M protein and skin changes: the POEMS syndrome. *Medicine* (Baltimore) 1980; **59**: 311−22.

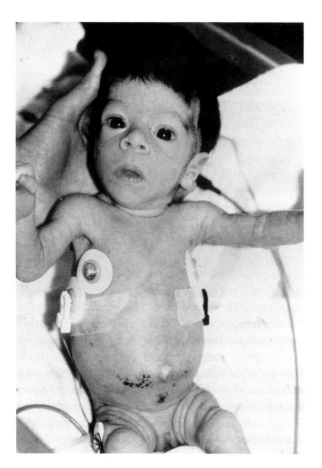

Fig. 29.2. Leprechaunism in a neonate. Note the characteristic elfin-like facies, lipoatrophy in the proximal extremities and hirsutism.

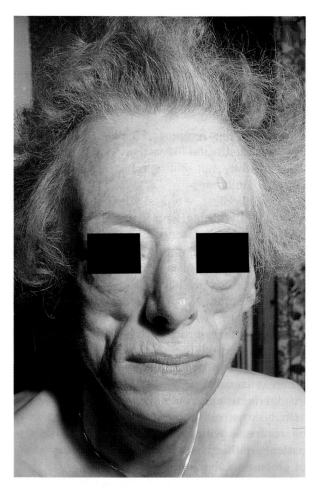

Fig. 29.3. Loss of subcutaneous adipose tissue from the face gives a characteristically gaunt appearance in partial lipodystrophy. (Reproduced by kind permission of Dr Joe Silas, Clatterbridge Hospital, Wirral.)

syndrome without these features. There is some evidence that patients with leprechaunism may be resistant to several growth factors, such as IGF-1 and epidermal growth factor, as well as insulin [21]. This generalized multi-hormone resistance, whose biochemical basis is unknown, may well contribute to the phenotypic defects and severity of the disease.

Lipoatrophic diabetes

Lipoatrophic diabetes encompasses a heterogeneous group of rare syndromes characterized by insulin-resistant diabetes mellitus and an absence of subcutaneous adipose tissue (Figs 29.3 and 29.4). Several different forms are distinguished by their mode of inheritance and the extent of lipoatrophy. These include two congenital types of generalized (total) lipoatrophy, one with dominant inheritance (Dunnigan syndrome) and one with recessive inheritance (Seip–Berardinelli syndrome). In addition, syndromes of acquired total lipoatrophy (Lawrence syndrome) and various types of partial lipoatrophy have been described.

THE DUNNIGAN SYNDROME

Dominantly inherited, congenital generalized lipoatrophy was described by Dunnigan in two Scottish families [22]. Lipoatrophy affected the trunk and limbs symmetrically but spared the face. Other clinical features included acanthosis nigricans, insulin-resistant diabetes and tubero-eruptive xanthomata.

THE SEIP–BERARDINELLI SYNDROME

This autosomal recessive form of congenital generalized lipoatrophy [23, 24] is commoner. Parental consanguinity is frequent. Males and females are

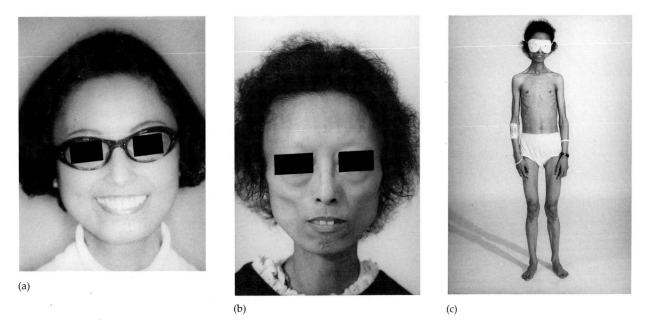

(a)

(b)

(c)

Fig. 29.4. Acquired, generalized (total) lipoatrophy. (a) Appearance of patient before onset of lipoatrophy. (b) Facial features of patient showing dramatic loss of subcutaneous adipose tissue. (c) Generalized loss of body fat in frontal view.

equally affected. The lack of subcutaneous fat is noted in early infancy; perirenal, retroperitoneal and epicardial fat and, unlike the Dunnigan syndrome, buccal fat are also absent. Loss of subcutaneous fat causes the thyroid, peripheral veins and skeletal muscles to appear more prominent. Mammary fat tissue may be spared. Acanthosis nigricans is frequent and more severe than in the acquired form of the disease.

Mental retardation, malformations in the region of the third ventricle and psychiatric disturbances are associated with congenital lipoatrophy. Other features include accelerated growth and advanced bone age, muscular hypertrophy (causing so-called 'Herculean' features) and acromegaloid facies with thick skin and large hands and feet (circulating growth hormone levels are normal). Hepatomegaly, due to increased lipid and glycogen storage, is frequent and can be massive. Gross hypertriglyceridaemia (usually >17 mmol/l), apparently due to decreased clearance as well as increased synthesis of lipoproteins, may cause eruptive xanthomas and lipaemia retinalis. Polycystic ovaries and menstrual irregularity are common in affected females.

The basal metabolic rate (BMR) is strikingly increased, with normal thyroid function. Pancreatic B-cell function has reportedly been normal. No circulating insulin inhibitors or antibodies directed against insulin or the insulin receptor have been found to account for the insulin resistance.

Diabetes appears at an average age of 12 years and is associated with the long-term complications of nephropathy, peripheral neuropathy and retinopathy. Hepatomegaly may lead to cirrhosis with portal hypertension, often fatal.

THE LAWRENCE SYNDROME

Acquired, generalized lipoatrophy was first described by Lawrence in 1946 [25]. These patients exhibit a generalized absence of body fat, insulin-resistant diabetes mellitus without ketosis, an elevated BMR, and hyperlipidaemia with hepatomegaly (Fig. 29.4). This condition occurs sporadically, without familial inheritance, and although often preceded by a viral illness, a direct viral aetiology has not been demonstrated.

There is a 2:1 female preponderance. Onset is usually in childhood or shortly after puberty and clinical diabetes typically follows after an average of 4 years. As in congenital lipoatrophic diabetes, hepatomegaly can lead to fatal cirrhosis. Accelerated atherosclerosis may cause premature coronary artery disease.

SYNDROMES OF PARTIAL LIPOATROPHY [26]

In *progressive partial lipoatrophy*, fat is most commonly lost from the face and trunk (Fig. 29.3); fat deposition below the waist is often normal or even increased, although occasionally loss may affect only the lower half of the body or specific segments (perhaps suggesting a dermatomal dysfunction). Females are predominantly affected. This syndrome may represent a less severe variant of the generalized type, and rarely, may develop into the latter. Families have been described in which both forms of the disease occur. As with acquired generalized lipoatrophy, the partial form usually develops in childhood and is sometimes preceded by an infectious illness; familial clustering (not clearly Mendelian) may occur. Some patients with partial lipoatrophy have an associated hypocomplementaemic glomerulonephritis and some clinical features of systemic lupus erythematosus [27]. This is unlike congenital lipoatrophy, where no immune disorders have been described.

AETIOLOGY OF THE LIPOATROPHIC SYNDROMES

Many theories on the aetiology of lipoatrophic diabetes have appeared over the years. In congenital lipoatrophy, fat cells are not absent but appear to be immature and contain little lipid. Insulin receptor number has been shown to be decreased in some kindreds with the congenital form, but other studies have shown normal or even increased insulin binding [28]. Studies with fibroblasts cultured from lipoatrophic patients have suggested that their severe insulin resistance may be due to a postreceptor defect in insulin action affecting primarily glucose uptake and/or metabolism [29]. Increased insulin clearance has also been described as a cause of insulin resistance in a single case [30]. A circulating lipid-mobilizing factor was previously implicated in the disease, but remains poorly characterized. This factor was initially isolated from the urine of lipoatrophic patients and, when injected into animals, produced insulin resistance and lipolysis of fat stores [31]. However, the factor is not specific to this syndrome as it is also found in the urine of diabetic patients with proteinuria. A hypothalamic aetiology has also been considered because of the association of lipoatrophic diabetes with lesions in this area in some patients. The elevated BMR, hyperlipidaemia and insulin resistance suggest hyperactivity of the sympathetic nervous system, but catecholamine levels have been normal.

Management of syndromes of insulin resistance

The primary causes of these syndromes, be they genetic or a poorly understood form of autoimmunity, are not currently amenable to treatment. The problems of insulin resistance and the dermatological and other features will be considered separately.

Dermatological complications

Although the skin complications are often only cosmetic, some patients seek medical advice primarily for acanthosis nigricans or hirsutism. Acanthosis may be controlled locally by careful application of tretinoin cream or gel. The elevated ovarian androgens causing hirsutism can be managed with oral contraceptive oestrogen preparations, and spironolactone or ketoconazole have also been used with good results [32]. Patients with marked virilization may occasionally benefit from ovarian wedge resection.

Insulin resistance

TYPE A SYNDROME AND LIPOATROPHIC DIABETES

In patients with the Type A syndrome or the congenital form of lipoatrophic diabetes, no remissions of the insulin resistance have been observed. Treatment goals are therefore dictated by the individual's level of glucose intolerance. Titration of insulin dosage against the glucose level may be attempted, but due to the intrinsic receptor and/or postreceptor abnormalities in these patients, hyperglycaemia may fail to respond. For unknown reasons, U-500 insulin may be more effective than equivalent doses of U-100 [33]. The neuroleptic agent, pimozide, was reported to produce dramatic clinical improvement in peripubertal lipoatrophic patients, perhaps through a central mechanism affecting hypothalamic function [34], although the therapeutic value of this drug has been disputed [35, 36].

TYPE B SYNDROME

In many patients with the Type B syndrome and other autoimmune features, glucose intolerance is only a minor component of their disease. Management should be planned accordingly, but careful follow-up of the diabetes is mandatory, as several patients have progressed from severe insulin resistance to profound hypoglycaemia, in some cases fatal [15]. Assessment of the efficacy of any treatment of the Type B syndrome is confounded by the cyclical remissions and relapses of autoimmune disease. Many immunosuppressive drugs, such as glucocorticoids, cyclophosphamide and anti-metabolites [37] have been tried, and combination therapy has been successful in two patients. Plasmapheresis temporarily lowers antibody levels and is a useful adjunct to other immuno-suppressive therapy.

LEPRECHAUNISM

As its exact pathophysiology is unknown, man-agement of leprechaunism can only be symp-tomatic. The most important aspect is close surveillance of blood sugars, the judicious use of insulin, and frequent small feeds to avoid fast-ing hypoglycaemia. Despite this, most patients survive for only 1−2 years.

Clinical approach to the insulin-resistant patient

The pathogenesis of the above states of severe insulin resistance is summarized in Fig. 29.5. The Type A syndrome and its variants have either genetic defects in insulin action or defects in the insulin receptor. The Type B syndrome and its variants are associated with circulating anti-insulin-receptor antibodies. Congenital lipo-dystrophy and leprechaunism with acanthosis nigricans affect receptor and/or postreceptor pathways and may actually represent different ends of a single disease spectrum.

A careful history and physical examination will usually distinguish these disorders from each other and from immune-mediated insulin resistance in IDDM patients, which nowadays is generally less severe and is associated with elevated levels of anti-insulin antibodies.

The most frequent diagnostic problem in this area is that of a diabetic patient requiring in-creasing doses of insulin. Patients taking more than 1.5−2.0 U/kg/day probably require further investigation. A complete dietary and drug history, the patient's understanding of insulin therapy and his compliance, and possible clinical signs of in-sulin resistance syndromes should all be evaluated.

If insulin resistance is still present during a supervised hospital admission (to exclude the common problem of factitious insulin resistance — see Chapter 88), further investigation is war-ranted. Peripheral insulin resistance can be confirmed by graded intravenous insulin tolerance tests or euglycaemic clamp studies. A normal re-sponse to 0.1 U/kg of short-acting insulin injected i.v. is a 50% decrement in fasting blood glucose.

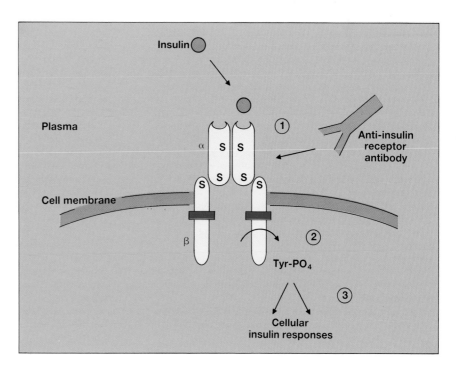

Fig. 29.5. Pathogenesis of insulin resistance syndromes. Specific steps in the cellular signalling response by insulin include insulin receptor binding to the α subunit, tyrosine autophosphorylation of the receptor β subunit and the transmission of several intracellular responses. These events may be affected in syndromes of severe insulin resistance as follows: (1) insulin–receptor interaction: inhibited by anti-insulin-receptor antibody in Type B syndrome; (2) insulin receptor binding and kinase function: affected by genetic defects in receptor structure in some patients with Type A syndrome or leprechaunism; (3) postreceptor signalling pathway: affected in patients with a variant Type A syndrome (biochemically normal insulin receptors) and in some patients with lipoatrophic diabetes.

Proven insulin resistance should be further investigated by assays for circulating antagonists, anti-insulin-receptor antibodies and insulin receptor function, which can be performed at specialized research centres. This logical approach should avoid unnecessary and costly investigations.

C. RONALD KAHN
BARRY J. GOLDSTEIN
S. SETHU K. REDDY

References

1 Kahn CR. Insulin resistance: a common feature of diabetes mellitus. *N Engl J Med* 1986; **315**: 252–4.

2 Flier JS. Insulin receptors and insulin resistance. *Ann Rev Med* 1983; **34**: 145–60.

3 Kahn CR, Flier JS, Bar RS *et al*. The syndromes of insulin resistance and acanthosis nigricans: insulin-receptor disorders in man. *N Engl J Med* 1976; **294**: 739–45.

4 Bar RS, Muggeo M, Roth J *et al*. Insulin resistance, acanthosis nigricans, and normal insulin receptors in a young woman: evidence of a postreceptor defect. *J Clin Endocrinol Metab* 1978; **47**: 620–5.

5 Flier JS, Young JB, Landsberg L. Familial insulin resistance with acanthosis nigricans, acral hypertrophy and muscle cramps. *N Engl J Med* 1980; **303**: 970–3.

6 Poretsky L, Kalin MF. The gonadotropic function of insulin. *Endocrine Rev* 1987; **8**: 132–41.

7 Taylor SI. Receptor defects in patients with extreme insulin resistance. *Diabetes/Metab Rev* 1985; **1**: 171–202.

8 Grigorescu F, Herzberg V, King G *et al*. Defects in insulin binding and autophosphorylation of erythrocyte insulin receptors in patients with syndromes of severe insulin resistance and their parents. *J Clin Endocrinol Metab* 1987; **64**: 549–56.

9 Yoshimasa Y, Seino S, Whittaker J *et al*. Insulin-resistant diabetes due to a point mutation that prevents insulin proreceptor processing. *Science* 1988; **240**: 784–7.

10 West RJ, Leonard JV. Familial insulin resistance with pineal hyperplasia: metabolic studies and effects of hypophysectomy. *Arch Dis Child* 1980; **55**: 619–21.

11 Flier JS, Eastman RC, Minaker KL *et al*. Acanthosis nigricans in obese women with hyperandrogenism. Characterization of an insulin-resistant state distinct from the Type A and B syndromes. *Diabetes* 1985; **34**: 101–7.

12 Peters EJ, Stuart CA, Prince MJ. Acanthosis nigricans and obesity: acquired and intrinsic defects in insulin action. *Metabolism* 1986; **35**: 807–13.

13 Kahn CR, Flier JS, Muggeo M *et al*. Autoantibodies to the insulin receptor in insulin resistant diabetes. In: Irvine WJ, ed. *Immunology of Diabetes*. Edinburgh: Teviot Scientific Publications Ltd, 1980: 205–18.

14 Tsokos GC, Gorden P, Antonovych T *et al*. Lupus nephritis and other autoimmune features in patients with diabetes mellitus due to autoantibody to insulin receptors. *Ann Intern Med* 1985; **102**: 176–81.

15 Taylor SI, Grunberger G, Marcus-Samuels B *et al*. Hypoglycemia associated with antibodies to the insulin receptor. *N Engl J Med* 1982; **307**: 1422–6.

16 Bar RS, Levis WR, Rechler MM *et al*. Extreme insulin resistance in ataxia telangiectasia. Defect in affinity of insulin receptors. *N Engl J Med* 1978; **298**: 1164–71.

17 Donahue WL, Uchida I. Leprechaunism: euphemism for a rare familial disorder. *J Pediatr* 1954; **45**: 505–19.

18 Kobayashi M, Olefsky JM, Elders J *et al*. Insulin resistance due to a defect distal to the insulin receptor: demonstration in a patient with leprechaunism. *Proc Natl Acad Sci USA* 1978; **75**: 3469–73.

19 Reddy SS, Lauris V, Kahn CR. Insulin receptor function in fibroblasts from patients with leprechaunism: differential alterations in binding, autophosphorylation, kinase activity and receptor mediated internalization. *J Clin Invest* 1988; **82**: 1359–65.

20 Kadowaki T, Bevins CL, Cama A *et al*. Two mutant alleles of the insulin receptor gene in a patient with extreme insulin resistance. *Science* 1988; **240**: 787–90.

21 Reddy SSK, Kahn CR. EGF receptor defects in leprechaunism: a multiple growth factor-resistant syndrome. *J Clin Invest* 1989; **84**: 1569–76.

22 Dunnigan MG, Cochrane MA, Kelly A *et al*. Familial lipoatrophic diabetes with dominant transmission: A new syndrome. *Q J Med* 1974; **43**: 33–48.

23 Seip M. Generalized lipodystrophy. *Ergeb Inn Med Kinderheilk* 1971; **31**: 59–95.

24 Berardinelli W. An undiagnosed endocrinometabolic syndrome: report of two cases. *J Clin Endocrinol* 1954; **14**: 193–204.

25 Lawrence RD. Lipodystrophy and hepatomegaly with diabetes, lipaemia, and other metabolic disturbances. A case throwing new light on the action of insulin. *Lancet* 1946; i: 724–31.

26 Senior B, Gellis SS. The syndromes of total lipodystrophy and of partial lipodystrophy. *Pediatrics* 1964; **33**: 593–612.

27 Ipp MM, Minta JO, Gelfand SW. Disorders of the complement system in lipodystrophy. *Clin Immunol Immunopathol* 1977; **7**: 281–7.

28 Wachslicht-Rodbard H, Muggeo M, Kahn CR *et al*. Heterogeneity of the insulin–receptor interaction in lipoatrophic diabetes. *J Clin Endocrinol Metab* 1981; **52**: 416–25.

29 Magré J, Reynet C, Capeau J *et al*. *In vitro* studies of insulin resistance in patients with lipoatrophic diabetes. Evidence for heterogeneous postbinding defects. *Diabetes* 1988; **37**: 421–8.

30 Golden MP, Charles MA, Arquilla ER *et al*. Insulin resistance in total lipodystrophy. Evidence for a pre-receptor defect in insulin action. *Metabolism* 1985; **34**: 330–5.

31 Foss I, Trygstad D. Lipoatrophy produced in mice and rabbits by a fraction prepared from the urine from patients with congenital generalized lipodystrophy. *Acta Endocrinol* 1975; **80**: 398–416.

32 Pepper GM, Poretsky L, Gabrilove JL *et al*. Ketoconazole reverses hyperandrogenism in a patient with insulin resistance and acanthosis nigricans. *J Clin Endocrinol Metab* 1987; **65**: 1047–52.

33 Nathan DM, Axelrod L, Flier JS *et al*. U-500 insulin in the treatment of antibody-mediated insulin resistance. *Ann Intern Med* 1981; **94**: 653–6.

34 Corbin A, Upton GV, Mabry CC *et al*. Diencephalic involvement in generalized lipodystrophy: rationale and treatment with the neurolytic agent, pimozide. *Acta Endocrinol* 1974; **77**: 209–20.

35 Rossini AA, Self J, Aoki TT *et al*. Metabolic and endocrine studies in a case of lipoatrophic diabetes. *Metabolism* 1977; **26**: 637–50.

36 Hager A, Hedrig LG, Larsson Y *et al*. Pancreatic β-cell function and abnormal urinary peptides in a boy with lipoatrophic diabetes and stenosis of the aqueduct of Sylvius. *Acta Paediatr Scand* 1980; **69**: 537−45.

37 Kawaniski K, Kawamura K, Nishina Y *et al*. Successful immunosuppressive therapy in insulin resistant diabetes caused by anti-insulin receptor autoantibodies. *J Clin Endocrinol Metab* 1977; **44**: 15−21.

30   Insulinopathies

Summary

• Insulinopathies arise from rare mutations in the human insulin gene which lead to the synthesis and secretion of abnormal gene products.

• Such patients usually display hyperinsulinaemia, varying degrees of glucose intolerance (sometimes normal) and a normal response to exogenous insulin administration. The defect is inherited in an autosomal fashion with all subjects to date being heterozygous for the normal and mutant alleles.

• Sophisticated techniques of peptide chemistry and DNA analysis have shown single nucleotide changes resulting in an amino-acid replacement and either an abnormal insulin of similar molecular weight to native insulin or interference with the processing of proinsulin to insulin (e.g. C peptide remaining joined at the insulin A chain).

• Subjects with insulinopathy and diabetes may have additional abnormalities in, for example, the insulin secretion process or at the receptor site.

Clinical aspects

Insulinopathies arise from mutations in the human insulin gene which result in the biosynthesis, storage and secretion of abnormal gene products. The matter of insulin gene mutations and potential clinical disease has been considered for at least 20 years [1, 2], and the subject has been studied intensively during the past decade [3–6]. Our current knowledge of clinical findings associated with expression of abnormal insulin genes is summarized in Table 30.1. Patients later found to

secrete abnormal insulin gene products resulting from mutation usually exhibit hyperinsulinaemia and varying degrees of glucose intolerance, but with no evidence of insulin resistance [3–5]. Affected patients seem not to respond as expected to their own high levels of serum insulin (typically about 100 mU/l, as measured by radioimmunoassay), but apparently respond normally to administration of insulin [3–5], which leads inescapably to the conclusion that the patients' insulin must somehow be different from normal human insulin. Detailed studies have indeed confirmed that, in cases of insulinopathy, the patient's insulin is structurally abnormal and that the abnormality arises from mutation within the insulin gene. Moreover, the mutant gene and the expression of an abnormal insulin is inherited in an autosomal fashion (often through several generations), and all affected individuals studied to date have been found to be heterozygous for normal and mutant insulin alleles [3–8]. Evidence documenting the co-dominant expression of normal and abnormal insulin alleles (and the storage of the two gene products in equimolar amounts in the pancreatic islet) has now been obtained in two affected subjects [7, 11]. Since the abnormal gene products invariably have low receptor binding and biological potencies, they are cleared from the circulation at greatly decreased rates [9, 10]. The rapid clearance of normal insulin, however, results in a ratio of normal to abnormal gene products corresponding to 1:9 (or less) in the peripheral blood [6, 7, 9]. The hyperinsulinaemia that characterizes the syndrome therefore arises exclusively from the high levels of the mutant insulin gene product in the circulation [9]. In most cases, the abnormal hormone would be expected to contribute only marginally (or not at all) to glucose homeostasis.

Although most identified cases of insulinopathy

Table 30.1. Clinical findings in insulinopathies associated with diabetes.

Abnormal findings	Normal findings
Elevated level of serum immunoreactive insulin[*]	Normal levels of monocyte insulin receptors[§]
Elevated serum insulin: C peptide molar ratio[†]	Normal levels of contrainsulin hormones
Mild to severe glucose intolerance[‡]	Normal response to administered insulin[¶]

[*] Immunoreactive insulin is determined by the application of radioimmunoassay directly to serum. The hyperinsulinaemia may result from either 5000 Da molecular weight abnormal insulin-like material or 9000 Da molecular weight abnormal proinsulin-like material.

[†] Whereas C-peptide levels may themselves be slightly elevated, the ratio is elevated by the high levels of immunoreactive insulin appearing in serum.

[‡] The degrees of fasting hyperglycaemia and glucose intolerance are variable. They can be severe (where a compounding perturbation of the insulin system is present), but are usually mild to moderate. Many subjects secreting abnormal products of a mutant insulin gene exhibit normal glucose tolerance.

[§] Normal receptor number is frequently observed, but receptor number may be at the lower limits of normal.

[¶] Normal responses during insulin tolerance tests (in the presence of endogenous hyperinsulinaemia) are key findings in the insulinopathies. Nevertheless, compounding defects which lead to mild, apparent insulin resistance could be present.

exhibit mild fasting hyperglycaemia (~8.3 mmol/l) and varying degrees of glucose intolerance, others do not show detectable abnormalities of glucose metabolism [3–5, 8, 9]. In one kindred with six affected subjects spanning three generations, only two exhibited marked glucose intolerance or diabetes [9]. The autosomal pattern of inheritance of abnormal insulin alleles does not, therefore, necessarily imply that any associated clinical features are also dominantly inherited. As the 50% deficit in the secretion of normal insulin (in individuals codominantly expressing both normal and abnormal alleles) would not necessarily be expected to result in clinical symptoms, it becomes clear that a separate perturbation of the insulin system must coexist in those subjects with diabetes. In at least one example, the secondary perturbation represents a defect in insulin secretion: one diabetic subject within the kindred expressing Insulin Los Angeles (see later) exhibits a very poor secretory response to oral glucose, whereas two genetically affected, but asymptomatic, siblings respond to oral glucose with increased secretion of equimolar amounts of normal and abnormal insulins [4, 9]. It is technically difficult to test insulin sensitivity, even in apparently normal subjects, but an alternative secondary perturbing factor in some diabetic subjects expressing abnormal insulin genes may eventually be found to be varying degrees of peripheral insulin resistance.

It is evident that insulin gene mutations and the clinical abnormalities associated with abnormal insulin gene expression appear to be rare in man and that, in many cases, the clinical findings alone will not be conclusive. Proof for the existence of insulin gene mutations, the secretion of abnormal insulin gene products, and therefore the presence of insulinopathy must ultimately rely on structural analysis of the secreted product or of the mutant insulin allele.

Methods of analysis

Characterization of abnormal products of the human insulin gene is made difficult by their low levels in serum (usually less than 1 pmol/ml) and by the scarcity of pancreatic biopsies from which larger amounts of peptides might be isolated [7, 11]. Most methods of analysis require relatively sophisticated techniques. Gel filtration [12] and immunochemical methods [13, 14] can be applied to advantage, but are generally useful only when the abnormal product is a proinsulin variant or a variant intermediate of proinsulin processing. Radioreceptor assays (which test the ability of serum-derived insulin to compete for the binding of ^{125}I-labelled insulin to insulin receptors on isolated membranes) have recently been applied to the detection of low-activity, abnormal human insulins [15]. As radioreceptor analysis tests the biological potency of an insulin preparation, it

Table 30.2. Known examples of mutant human insulin genes and associated abnormal insulins.

Name	Amino-acid replacement	Designation	Normal codon	Mutant codon	Abnormal secreted product
Insulin Chicago	Phe^{B25} by Leu	Human insulin B25 (Phe → Leu)	TTC	TTG	[Leu^{B25}] insulin*
Insulin Los Angeles	Phe^{B24} by Ser	Human insulin B24 (Phe → Ser)	TTC	TCC	[Ser^{B24}] insulin*
Insulin Wakayama	Val^{A3} by Leu	Human insulin A3 (Val → Leu)	GTG	TTG	[Leu^{A3}] insulin*
Proinsulin Tokyo	Arg^{65} by His	Human proinsulin 65 (Arg → His)	CGC	CAC	des-Arg^{31}, Arg^{32}-[His^{65}] proinsulin†
Proinsulin Boston	Arg^{65} by ?‡	Human proinsulin 65 (Arg →?)‡	?‡	?‡	des-Arg^{31}, Arg^{32}-[Xxx] proinsulin†‡
Proinsulin Providence	His^{B10} by Asp	Human proinsulin 10 (His → Asp)	CAC	GAC	?§

* The secreted product is an abnormal insulin which contains a single amino-acid replacement.
† The secreted product is an abnormal intermediate of proinsulin processing in which the C peptide remains joined to the insulin A chain due to an amino-acid replacement at the processing site.
‡ The gene for Proinsulin Boston has not yet been subjected to sequence analysis. The nature of the secreted product is the same as that for Proinsulin Tokyo, but the amino-acid replacement is not yet known.
§ The exact structures of the secreted products are not known. They appear, for the most part, to represent intact proinsulin (rather than insulin or a processing intermediate), but they have not yet been analysed in detail.

represents an important aspect of any investigation involving the identification of an abnormal human insulin [3–5, 17, 15]. Analysis of immunoaffinity-purified serum insulin by high-performance liquid chromatography, followed by detection of separated components using radioimmunoassay, allows determination of whether or not a suspected abnormal insulin has physical attributes and structure different from normal insulin. Reverse-phase chromatography permits the separation of insulins differing from one another by only single amino-acid residues, and therefore the detection of abnormal insulins arising from insulin gene mutations [6, 16]. It should be noted, however, that analysis by high-pressure liquid chromatography can determine only whether an insulin structure is abnormal; it does not provide information on the site or identity of the amino-acid replacement.

The identification of abnormal insulin gene structure provides the ultimate proof of insulin gene mutation in any potential example of insulinopathy. The methods of molecular cloning, recombinant DNA analysis and DNA sequence determination can identify both the site of mutation and the amino-acid replacement that would occur in the expressed and secreted insulin gene product. Although these and related methods do not necessarily identify the entire character of the resulting abnormal product (because of potential complexities arising from precursor segregation and processing in the islet B cell), they provide very critical information [5, 17–20]. In two

examples, they alone have provided the basis for our understanding of abnormal insulin structures [5, 20]. Single nucleotide replacements in the human insulin gene which affect restriction enzyme cleavage sites can often be detected by Southern analysis of leucocyte DNA [6, 16, 21, 22]. Not all insulin gene mutations can be detected by such methods, as the number of specific restriction enzyme cleavage systems is limited; however, the technique has been used to screen diabetic populations for insulin gene mutations [22].

Examples of abnormal insulin gene products

Table 30.2 describes the known examples of insulin gene mutation which lead to the synthesis and secretion of abnormal insulin gene products in man. In most cases, the structural information has accumulated from a combination of techniques involving peptide chemistry and recombinant-DNA analysis [5–8, 11, 13, 14, 16–21] and in many, the abnormal peptide products have been prepared by synthetic methods [6, 8, 10, 16, 23–26].

Insulin gene mutations fall into two groups, those leading to the secretion of abnormal insulins with molecular weights close to that of normal insulin (~ 5000 Da) and those which interfere with the processing of proinsulin to insulin. Insulins Chicago, Los Angeles and Wakayama result from mutations in the first group. In each case, a single nucleotide change in the insulin gene has resulted in the synthesis of an abnormal insulin bearing an amino-acid replacement at a site known to be important for insulin−receptor interactions [3−10, 16−18, 20, 21, 23−30]. Proinsulins Tokyo, Boston and Providence result from mutations in the second group, where single nucleotide substitutions lead to the secretion of abnormal hormone precursors bearing single amino-acid replacements [8, 13, 14, 19, 20, 31]. The mutations leading to Proinsulins Tokyo and Boston (mutations causing amino-acid replacements in a sequence important for conversion of the precursor to product) give rise to the secretion of intermediates of proinsulin processing in which the C peptide remains joined to the insulin A chain [13, 14, 19]. Interestingly, these products contain the normal structure of insulin, but this remains cryptic since complete conversion of the precursor to insulin is not possible. For reasons not yet fully understood, the mutation leading to Proinsulin Providence apparently yields a hormone precursor which is not even converted to an intermediate of proinsulin processing [20, 31].

The clinical and biochemical implications of insulin gene mutations in the insulinopathies represent critical matters for further study. They may well represent only a portion of related genetic defects which apply more broadly to many aspects of endocrine disease.

HOWARD S. TAGER

References

1 Elliott RB, O'Brien D, Roy CC. An abnormal insulin in juvenile diabetes mellitus. *Diabetes* 1966; **14**: 780−7.

2 Kimmel JR, Pollack HG. Studies of human insulin from nondiabetic and diabetic pancreas. *Diabetes* 1967; **16**: 687−94.

3 Given BD, Mako ME, Tager HS, Baldwin D, Markese J, Rubenstein AH, Olefsky J, Kobayashi M, Kolterman O, Poucher R. Diabetes due to secretion of an abnormal insulin. *N Engl J Med* 1980; **302**: 129−35.

4 Haneda M, Polonsky KS, Bergenstal RM, Jaspan JB, Shoelson SE, Blix PM, Chan SJ, Kwok SCM, Wishner WB, Zeidler A, Olefsky JM, Friedenberg G, Tager HS, Steiner DF, Rubenstein AH. Familial hyperinsulinemia due to a structurally abnormal insulin: definition of an emerging new clinical syndrome. *N Engl J Med* 1984; **310**: 1288−94.

5 Nanjo K, Sanke T, Miyano M, Okai K, Sowa R, Kondo M, Nishimura S, Iwo K, Miyamura K, Given BD, Chan SJ, Tager HS, Steiner DF, Rubenstein AH. Diabetes due to secretion of a structurally abnormal insulin (Insulin Wakayama). *J Clin Invest* 1986; **77**: 514−19.

6 Shoelson S, Haneda M, Blix P, Nanjo K, Sanke T, Inouye K, Steiner D, Rubenstein A, Tager HS. Three mutant insulins in man. *Nature* 1983; **302**: 540−3.

7 Tager H, Given B, Baldwin D, Mako M, Markese J, Rubenstein AH, Olefsky J, Kobayashi M, Kolterman O, Poucher P. A structurally abnormal insulin causing human diabetes. *Nature* 1979; **281**: 122−5.

8 Tager H. Insulin gene mutations and abnormal products of the human insulin gene. In: Cohen PC, Foa PP, eds. *Hormone Resistance and Other Endocrine Paradoxes.* New York: Springer-Verlag, 1987: 35−61.

9 Shoelson SE, Polonsky KS, Zeidler A, Rubenstein AH, Tager HS. Human insulin (Phe → Ser): Secretion and metabolic clearance of the abnormal insulin in man and in a dog model. *J Clin Invest* 1984; **73**: 1351−8.

10 Haneda M, Kobayashi M, Maegawa H, Watanabe N, Takata Y, Ishibashi O, Shigeta Y, Inouye K. Decreased biological activity and degradation of human [Ser^{B24}]-insulin, a second mutant insulin. *Diabetes* 1985; **34**: 568−73.

11 Iwamoto Y, Sakura H, Yui R, Fukita T, Sakamoto Y, Matsuda A, Kuzuya T. Identification and characterization of a mutant insulin isolated from the pancreas of a patient with abnormal insulinemia. *Diabetes* 1986; **35** (suppl 1): 77A.

12 Gabbay KH, DeLuca K, Fisher NJ Jr, Mako ME, Rubenstein AH. Familial hyperproinsulinemia: An autosomal dominant defect. *N Engl J Med* 1976; **249**: 911−15.

13 Robbins DC, Blix PM, Rubenstein AH, Kanazawa Y, Kosaka K, Tager HS. A human proinsulin variant at arginine 65. *Nature* 1981; **291**: 679−81.

14 Robbins DC, Shoelson SE, Rubenstein AH, Tager HS. Familial hyperproinsulinemia: two cohorts secreting indistinguishable type II intermediates of proinsulin conversion. *J Clin Invest* 1984; **73**: 714−19.

15 Iwamoto Y, Sakura H, Ishii Y, Yamamoto R, Kumakura S, Sakamoto Y, Masuda A, Kuzuya T. Radioreceptor assay for serum insulin as a useful method for detection of abnormal insulin with a description of a new family of abnormal insulinemia. *Diabetes* 1986; **35**: 1237−42.

16 Shoelson S, Fickova M, Haneda M, Nahum A, Musso G, Kaiser ET, Rubenstein AH, Tager HS. Identification of a mutant insulin predicted to contain a serine-for-phenlalanine substitution. *Proc Natl Acad Sci USA* 1983; **80**: 7390−4.

17 Kwok SCM, Steiner DF, Rubenstein AH, Tager HS. Identification of the mutation giving rise to Insulin Chicago. *Diabetes* 1983; **32**: 872−5.

18 Haneda M, Chan SJ, Kwok SCM, Rubenstein AH, Steiner DF. Studies on mutant insulin genes: Identification and sequence analysis of a gene encoding [Ser^{B24}] insulin. *Proc Natl Acad Sci USA* 1983; **80**: 6366−70.

19 Shibasaki Y, Kawakami T, Kanazawa Y, Akamura Y, Takaku T. Posttranslational cleavage of proinsulin is blocked by a point mutation in familial hyperproinsulinaemia. *J Clin Invest* 1985; **76**: 378−80.

20 Chan SJ, Seino SU, Gruppuso PA, Schwartz R, Steiner DF. A mutation in the B chain coding region is associated with impaired proinsulin conversion in a family with hyperproinsulinemia. *Proc Natl Acad Sci USA* 1987; **84**: 2194−7.

21 Kwok SCM, Chan SJ, Rubenstein AH, Poucher R, Steiner DF. Loss of restriction endonuclease cleavage site in the gene of a structurally abnormal insulin. *Biochem Biophys Res Commun* 1981; **98**: 844−9.

22 Sanz N, Karam JH, Horita S, Bell GI. DNA screening for insulin gene mutations in non-insulin-dependent diabetes mellitus (NIDDM). *Diabetes* 1985; **34** (suppl 1): 85A (abstract).

23 Tager H, Thomas N, Assoian R, Rubenstein A, Saekow M, Olefsky J, Kaiser ET. Semisynthesis and biological activity of porcine [Leu^{B24}] insulin and [Leu^{B25}] insulin. *Proc Natl Acad Sci USA* 1980; **77**: 3181−5.

24 Inouye K, Watanabe K, Tochino Y, Kobayashi M, Shigeta Y. Semisynthesis and properties of some insulin analogs. *Biopolymers* 1981; **20**: 1845—58.

25 Kobayashi M, Ohgaku S, Iwasaki M, Maegawa H, Shigeta Y, Inouye K. Characterization of [Leu^B24]- and [Leu^B25]-insulin analogs. *Biochem J* 1982; **206**: 597—603.

26 Kobayashi M, Takata Y, Ishibashi O, Sasoka T, Iwasaki M, Shigeta Y, Inouye K. Receptor binding and negative cooperativity of a mutant insulin [Leu^A3]-insulin. *Biochem Biophys Res Commun* 1986; **137**: 250—7.

27 Peavy DE, Brunner MR, Duckworth WC, Hooker CS, Frank BH. Receptor binding and biological potency of several split forms (conversion intermediates) of human proinsulin. *J Biol Chem* 1985; **26**: 13989—94.

28 Blundell T, Dodson G, Hodgkin D, Mercola D. Insulin: the structure in the crystal and its reflection in chemistry and biology. *Adv Protein Chem* 1972; **26**: 279—402.

29 DeMeyts P, Van Obberghen E, Roth J, Wollmer A, Brandenburg D. Mapping of the residues responsible for the negative cooperativity of the receptor-binding region of insulin. *Nature* 1978; **273**: 504—9.

30 Dodson EJ, Dodson GG, Hubbard RE, Reynolds CD. Insulin's structural behavior and its relationship to activity. *Biopolymers* 1983; **22**: 281—91.

31 Gruppuso PA, Gorden P, Kahn CR, Cornblath M, Zeller WP, Schwartz R. Familial hyperproinsulinemia due to a proposed defect in conversion of proinsulin to insulin. *N Engl J Med* 1984; **311**: 629—34.

31   Genetic and Other Disorders Associated with Diabetes Mellitus

Summary

● Diabetes, often insulin-requiring, affects up to 2% of children with Down's syndrome.

● Two-thirds of women with Turner's syndrome have a diabetic oral glucose tolerance curve although symptomatic diabetes is rare.

● One-quarter of men with Klinefelter's syndrome have mild insulin resistance and a diabetic oral glucose tolerance curve; overt diabetes affects fewer than 10%.

● Impaired glucose tolerance (IGT) and occasionally diabetes may complicate acute intermittent porphyria, in which attacks may be provoked by chlorpropamide, tolbutamide and tolazamide. Biguanides, glipizide and insulin can be used safely in acute intermittent porphyria.

● Group I inherited insulin resistance syndromes, a heterogeneous group of conditions characterized by moderate insulin resistance and hypogonadism, include Alström's, Laurence—Moon—Biedl and Prader—Willi syndromes (all with autosomal recessive inheritance) and dystrophia myotonica (autosomal dominant). Diabetes is usually mild.

● Group II inherited insulin resistance syndromes, displaying severe insulin resistance together with sexual precocity, various somatic defects and acanthosis nigricans, include the Rabson—Mendenhall syndrome, leprechaunism and the lipodystrophic syndromes. Hyperglycaemia may be severe and may fail to respond even to massive doses of insulin.

● The Type II polyglandular autoimmune syndrome (Schmidt's syndrome), often inherited as an autosomal recessive condition, includes IDDM together with autoimmune thyroiditis and adrenal failure.

● The prevalence of diabetes in adults with coeliac disease is 4%, some 2—3 times higher than in the general population. Hypoglycaemia may be troublesome, especially during exacerbations of diarrhoea. A gluten-free diet may increase insulin requirements.

In addition to the endocrine and pancreatic diseases described in Chapters 27 and 28, diabetes or glucose intolerance may accompany many genetic syndromes and other conditions. These disorders are rare: taken together, they account for fewer than 10% of all cases of diabetes. This chapter will describe the diabetic syndromes occurring in some of the commoner genetic syndromes and in coeliac disease.

Genetic disorders associated with diabetes

A classification of genetic disorders in which diabetes or glucose intolerance may occur is shown in Table 31.1. Most are either associated with numerical or structural chromosomal abnormalities or with an inheritance pattern suggesting a single-gene defect. Chromosomal abnormalities are relatively common, and affect 1 in 200 live births. One in 700 newborns has a trisomy, usually affecting chromosome 21 (Down's syndrome). Diabetes is commoner in people with Down's syndrome than in the general population, as is also true of the other common chromosomal defects, Turner's and Klinefelter's syndromes. Autoantibodies and autoimmune endocrine disorders, such as thyroiditis, are comparatively common in patients with chromosomal abnormalities and in their relatives [1—3]. However, there is no proof that the diabetes in patients

Table 31.1. Classification of genetic disorders associated with increased prevalence of diabetes mellitus.

CHROMOSOMAL DEFECTS
Down's syndrome (trisomy or translocation 21)
Turner's syndrome (45,XO or variants)
Klinefelter's syndrome (47,XXY)

SINGLE-GENE DEFECTS
Pancreatic disorders (Chapter 27)
Cystic fibrosis (autosomal recessive)
Haemochromatosis (autosomal recessive)

Inborn errors of metabolism
Acute intermittent porphyria

Inherited insulin resistance syndromes
Group I (with hypogonadism):
  Alström's syndrome (autosomal recessive)
  Laurence−Moon−Biedl syndrome (autosomal recessive)
  Prader−Willi syndrome (deletion/translocation chromosome 15)
  Werner's syndrome (autosomal recessive)
  Cockayne's syndrome (autosomal recessive)
  Ataxia telangiectasia (autosomal recessive)
  Dystrophia myotonica (autosomal dominant)
Group II (with sexual precocity):
  Rabson−Mendenhall syndrome (autosomal recessive)
  Leprechaunism (various inheritance patterns)
  Lipodystrophic syndromes (various inheritance patterns)

Miscellaneous endocrine and other syndromes
Type II polyglandular autoimmune syndrome
  (Schmidt's syndrome) (autosomal dominant or recessive in some pedigrees)
DIDMOAD (Wolfram's syndrome) (autosomal recessive)
Friedreich's ataxia (autosomal recessive)
Huntington's chorea (autosomal dominant)

with chromosomal disorders is caused by an auto-immune process. The single-gene defects include diseases which damage the pancreatic parenchyma (described in detail in Chapter 27), certain inborn errors of metabolism and a heterogeneous group of inherited disorders which are associated with insulin resistance.

Chromosomal disorders

DOWN'S SYNDROME

Down's syndrome is due to trisomy of chromosome 21 or translocations of parts of this chromosome. The frequency of trisomy 21 rises with maternal age, from less than 0.5 per 1000 live births at age 20 to over 33 per 1000 at age 40.

Characteristic physical stigmata include short stature; a large, fissured protruding tongue; muscular hypotonia; brachycephaly; short neck; typical facies; short broad hands with incurving fifth fingers (clinodactyly); abnormal dermatographic patterns; Brushfield spots in the iris; and cardiac septal defects. The degree of mental retardation is variable and an Alzheimer-type cerebral degeneration may also develop in middle-aged patients with Down's syndrome.

The prevalence of diabetes among children with Down's syndrome aged up to 14 years has been estimated to be 21 per 1000, which is considerably higher than the expected figure of 0.6−1.3 per 1000 in an age-matched normal population [4]. In a series of 88 patients with Down's syndrome and diabetes, over one-half were under the age of 20 years; 74% were insulin treated, 12% were taking oral hypoglycaemic agents, and 14% could be controlled on diet alone [5]. A triad of Down's syndrome, primary hypothyroidism and IDDM (including a tendency to ketoacidosis) has been reported by several groups [6−11]. The presence or absence of diabetic microvascular complications has not been documented in the above studies.

TURNER'S SYNDROME

Turner's syndrome affects approximately 1 in 2500 newborn females. Most patients are sex-chromatin negative and have a 45,XO karyotype but 40% are mosaics usually with a 46,XX/45,XO pattern. There are bilateral 'streak' ovaries, largely replaced by fibrous tissue. The external genitalia are unambiguously female but normal puberty does not occur, with failure of sexual development and primary amenorrhoea. Physical stigmata include lymphoedema of hands and feet at birth; webbed neck; low hairline; a broad shield-like chest; epicanthic folds; low-set or deformed ears; fish-like mouth or micrognathia; ptosis; short fourth metacarpals and hypoplastic nails; coarctation of the aorta; and pigmented naevi (Fig. 31.1). These features are extremely variable and, especially in people with Turner's mosaicism, may be absent.

Some 15% of prepubertal subjects with Turner's syndrome have impaired glucose tolerance [12] and 60% of young adults have frankly diabetic oral glucose tolerance tests [13], although symptomatic diabetes seems less common and is usually non-insulin-dependent. The insulin response to an oral glucose load is delayed and diminished,

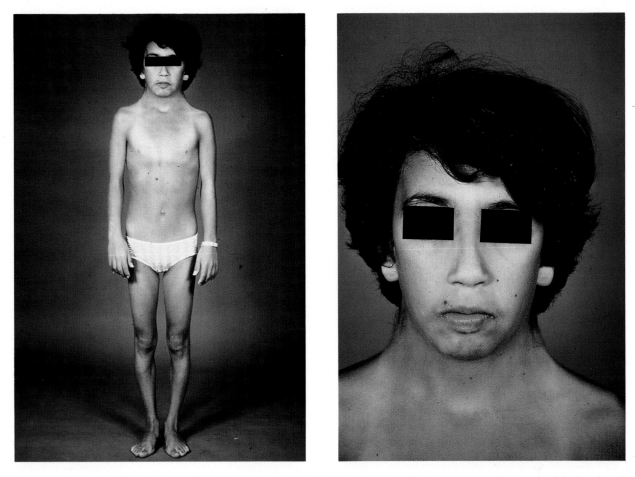

Fig. 31.1. A 15-year-old patient with Turner's syndrome, showing short stature, lack of pubertal development, webbed neck and broad chest with widely spaced nipples. These patients often have mild hypertension and may develop diabetes, both of which may be exacerbated by oestrogen replacement. (Reproduced by kind permission of Professor G.F. Joplin, Royal Postgraduate Medical School, London.)

suggesting B-cell hyporesponsiveness to glucose [14]. A paradoxical rise in growth hormone in response to oral glucose [13] is more common in patients taking oestrogen treatment [15] and may partly account for the impaired glucose tolerance (IGT) in Turner's syndrome. Exogenous growth hormone treatment apparently does not produce significant changes in fasting glucose or insulin concentrations [12]. Autoimmune thyroiditis is also common [3].

KLINEFELTER'S SYNDROME

Individuals with Klinefelter's syndrome are phenotypically male. Most have a 47,XXY karyotype but 10% are mosaics, with a 46,XY/47,XXY pattern. Clinical features include increased height with eunuchoid proportions; gynaecomastia (55% of cases); and small, soft testes and azoospermia, due to hyalinization of seminiferous tubules (Fig.

31.2). In patients with Klinefelter's syndrome, there is an increased incidence of diabetic oral glucose tolerance tests (26%), but overt symptomatic diabetes is less common (7%) and is usually non-insulin-dependent [16]. There is a rapid and prolonged insulin response to oral glucose among patients with Klinefelter's syndrome [16], suggesting some degree of insulin resistance, and abnormal insulin receptor binding has also been demonstrated [17]. The presence of autoantibodies to insulin has been reported [1], but was not confirmed in a subsequent study [16].

Single-gene defects

INBORN ERRORS OF METABOLISM

Acute intermittent porphyria. This is an autosomal dominant disorder which is expressed more frequently and more severely in females. Porphyrin

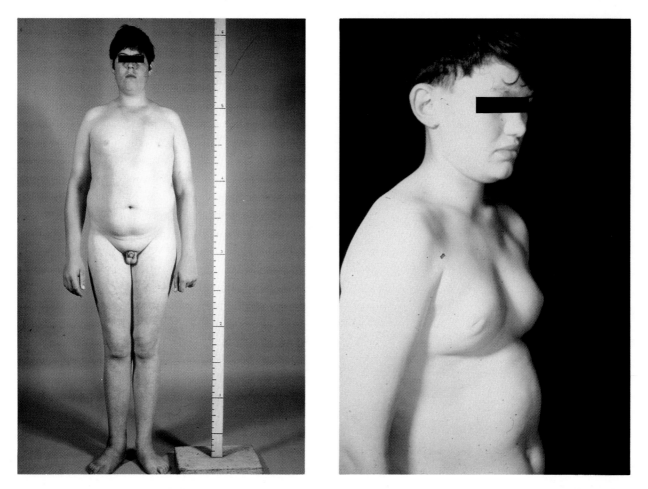

Fig. 31.2. Two patients with Klinefelter's syndrome, showing increased height with eunuchoid build, gynaecomastia and underdeveloped external genitalia. Glucose tolerance may be impaired in this syndrome. (Reproduced by kind permission of Professor G.F. Joplin, Royal Postgraduate Medical School, London.)

metabolism in the haem biosynthetic pathway is interrupted by a defect in porphobilinogen (PBG) deaminase. The frequency of the abnormal gene is estimated to be between 1 in 10000 and 1 in 50000 persons. Reduced negative feedback inhibition by haem causes increased activity of delta-aminolaevulinic acid (ALA) synthetase, which leads to excessive accumulation and excretion of ALA and PBG.

Acute attacks of porphyria may be precipitated by infection, pregnancy or exposure to drugs including barbiturates, sulphonamides, oral contraceptives and certain sulphonylureas. During these episodes, patients may suffer gastrointestinal symptoms (colicky pain and constipation), neuropsychiatric disorders (psychosis, acute peripheral neuropathy with pain or wrist or foot drop, paraplegia, convulsions), or cardiovascular manifestations (tachycardia, with either hypotension or hypertension). Endocrine abnormalities include

inappropriate secretion of growth hormone and ADH, isolated ACTH deficiency, and impaired glucose tolerance [18, 19].

The extensive list of drugs thought to precipitate acute porphyria [20] means that treatment of these patients is fraught with potential disaster. Fortunately, diabetes only occasionally requires drug treatment; the biguanides and glipizide are said to be safe for use in AIP, whereas chlorpropamide, tolbutamide and tolazamide must be avoided. Even dietary measures alone may be hazardous, as acute calorie restriction may provoke an acute attack. Insulin is safe, other than the general caution regarding hypoglycaemia in patients predisposed to epilepsy.

Inherited insulin resistance syndromes

These can be divided into two groups [21]. *Group I* is characterized by insulin resistance and hyperinsulinaemia, which except for the severe syndrome found in ataxia telangiectasia, are usually relatively mild. These conditions are accompanied by hypogonadism. *Group II* disorders display severe insulin resistance together with precocious sexual development and acanthosis nigricans. Some of these syndromes, particularly leprechaunism and the lipodystrophies, are now known to be due to defects of the insulin receptor or postreceptor pathways (see Chapter 29).

GROUP I INHERITED INSULIN RESISTANCE SYNDROMES

Alström's syndrome. Alström's syndrome is an autosomal recessive disorder first described in 1959 in Sweden [22]. The principal features of this condition are blindness in childhood due to retinitis pigmentosa; severe nerve deafness; obesity; diabetes mellitus; and diabetes insipidus. The absence of mental retardation and polydactyly help to distinguish Alström from the Laurence−Moon−Biedl syndrome (see below). Diabetes insipidus, diabetes mellitus and hypogonadism may partly be explained by tissue resistance to vasopressin, insulin and gonadotrophins. Other metabolic abnormalities include hypertriglyceridaemia and hyperuricaemia.

IGT or diabetes mellitus develop in the second decade of life in approximately 90% of patients [23]. The diabetes mellitus clinically resembles NIDDM and is associated with hyperinsulinaemia and acanthosis nigricans. Treatment with sulphonylureas and insulin may be needed to control hyperglycaemic symptoms.

Laurence−Moon−Biedl syndrome. This is an autosomal recessive condition, but the basic genetic defect is not known. There are no diagnostic tests for this disorder and the clinical diagnosis is therefore based on the typical spectrum of somatic abnormalities. These include obesity; mental retardation (only 10% have a normal IQ); abnormal digits (polydactyly, syndactyly, brachydactyly); hypogonadotrophic hypogonadism or primary gonadal failure; retinal degeneration due to retinitis pigmentosa; and renal disease (glomerular sclerosis). Diabetes is rare, occurring in 6% of cases in one series [23].

Prader−Willi syndrome. Prader−Willi syndrome is characterized by obesity; hypogonadotrophic

hypogonadism due to deficiency of hypothalamic releasing factors; muscular hypotonia; and mental retardation (Fig. 31.3). A deletion or translocation of chromosome 15 has been found in 50% of patients with the syndrome [24, 25]. In a review of the first 46 patients with Prader−Willi syndrome to be reported, diabetes was present in 10%, but the prevalence seems lower in more recent large series [26]. Diabetes is generally non-insulin dependent, with mild insulin resistance and little tendency to ketoacidosis [26]. A reduction in insulin receptor numbers has been described [27]. Diabetic retinopathy may occur [28]. Hyperglycaemia is easily controlled by dietary restriction alone, and weight reduction may improve tissue insulin resistance.

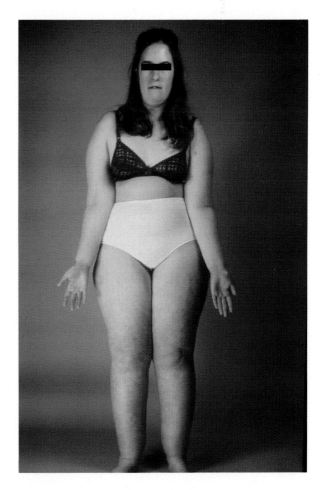

Fig. 31.3. An 18-year-old girl with Prader−Willi syndrome. She was below the 3rd centile for height, above the 75th centile for weight and had delayed puberty. Her IQ was 52. At this time, glucose tolerance was normal; impaired glucose tolerance or diabetes ultimately develop in up to 10% of cases. (Reproduced by kind permission of Professor G.F. Joplin, Royal Postgraduate Medical School, London.)

Werner's syndrome. This autosomal recessive condition is characterized by signs of premature senility; growth retardation; alopecia; premature greying of the hair; cataracts; hypogonadism; atrophy of muscle and subcutaneous fat; and soft-tissue calcification. There is a tendency to develop tumours, mainly sarcomas and meningiomas. Diabetes mellitus affects 20–45% of patients [29–31] and is usually associated with mild hyperinsulinaemia and insulin resistance. Some cases show severe insulin resistance but even in these patients, ketoacidosis is notably absent. Hyperglycaemia may be adequately controlled by dietary measures alone. Diabetic complications are unusual but both retinopathy and nephropathy have been reported [31].

Cockayne's syndrome. This is an autosomal recessive syndrome affecting children, which consists of cachetic dwarfism; kyphosis; retinal degeneration; deafness; microcephaly and mental retardation; and glomerulonephritis leading to renal failure. Photosensitivity and atrophy of the skin give these patients a markedly senile appearance. Abnormal glucose tolerance and hyperinsulinaemia, but not overt diabetes, have been reported [32, 33]. (See p. 279.)

Ataxia telangiectasia. Ataxia telangiectasia is an autosomal recessive syndrome characterized by cerebellar ataxia and apraxia of ocular movements; choreoathetosis; telangiectasia affecting the conjunctivae, facial skin and flexor creases and disorders of the immune system (deficiency of IgA, impaired cellular responses and thymic dysplasia). Diabetes mellitus, sometimes with severe hyperglycaemia but without ketosis, may occur together with the presence of moderate hyperinsulinaemia and acanthosis nigricans [34]. The insulin resistance in ataxia telangiectasia appears to be due to circulating antibody which interferes with binding of insulin to its receptor [35].

Dystrophia myotonica. Dystrophia myotonica is an autosomal dominant disorder carried on chromosome 19. Physical stigmata of this condition include frontal baldness; cataracts; cardiomyopathy; muscle wasting and myotonia (Fig. 31.4). Testicular fibrosis or atrophy, gynaecomastia and elevated gonadotrophin levels occur in males and ovarian deficiency affects some females. IGT is common, affecting about 20–30% of patients.

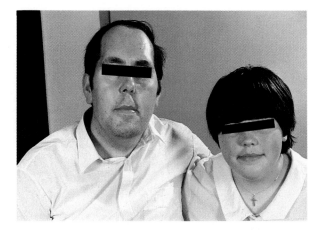

Fig. 31.4. Dystrophia myotonica in a 42-year-old man and his daughter. The father shows the characteristic facies, with frontal balding and a smooth forehead. Diabetes affects up to 20–30% of cases. (Reproduced by kind permission of Professor Richard Edwards, Department of Medicine, University of Liverpool.)

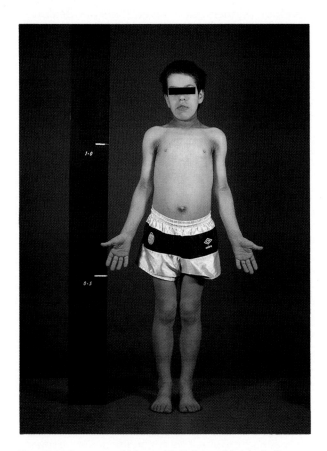

Fig. 31.5. A 13-year-old boy with Rabson–Mendenhall syndrome, showing stunted growth, prominent acanthosis nigricans affecting the neck, axillae and antecubital fossae, and typical facies. He had moderate hyperglycaemia associated with grossly elevated plasma insulin levels (300–400 mU/l). Insulin resistance was confirmed by the failure of up to 150 U insulin per day to restore normoglycaemia. (Reproduced by kind permission of Drs A.C. McCuish and J.D. Quin, Glasgow Royal Infirmary.)

Overt diabetes mellitus is rare and is associated with mild insulin resistance and hyper-insulin-aemia [21].

Abnormal glucose tolerance has also been reported in facio-scapulo-humeral and Duchenne muscular dystrophies [36].

GROUP II INHERITED INSULIN RESISTANCE SYNDROMES

Rabson–Mendenhall syndrome. Mendenhall first described three siblings with deformed early dentition; dry skin; thick nails; hirsutism; precocious puberty with enlarged external genitalia; pineal hyperplasia; and diabetes [37] (Fig. 31.5). The severe insulin resistance in this autosomal recessive condition is due to decreased insulin receptor numbers [38] and affinity [39]. Affected individuals generally die in ketoacidosis at puberty. Insulin resistance is so severe that administration of even several thousands of units of insulin per day may fail to lower blood glucose and ketone concentrations [40]. Insulin-like growth factor 1, which resembles proinsulin and exerts some insulin-like metabolic effects including hypoglycaemia in normal subjects, has been shown to lower blood glucose levels in one case [41].

Leprechaunism and lipodystrophic syndromes. These conditions are described in detail in Chapter 29.

Miscellaneous endocrine and other syndromes

POLYGLANDULAR AUTOIMMUNE SYNDROMES

Most patients with these conditions, characterized by endocrine and other tissue damage due to autoimmune disease, fall into one of two broad categories [42] (see Chapter 28). The type II syndrome (Schmidt's syndrome) frequently includes IDDM together with adrenal and thyroid failure. By contrast, IDDM and autoimmune thyroid disease are rare in the type I syndrome, in which adrenal failure, hypoparathyroidism and mucocutaneous candidiasis are prominent. Associated autoimmune disorders include alopecia, vitiligo, juvenile-onset pernicious anaemia, chronic active hepatitis and gonadal failure. Both types may be inherited as autosomal recessive conditions in some families, although many cases are sporadic.

DIDMOAD SYNDROME

This condition is described in Chapter 28.

FRIEDREICH'S ATAXIA

This is an autosomal recessive form of spino-cerebellar degeneration characterized by ataxia; dysarthria; nystagmus; posterior column sensory loss; scoliosis; and pes cavus. The prevalence of diabetes is 8–18%, and is usually insulin-dependent [43, 44]. Diabetic retinopathy and nephropathy have been reported [45].

HUNTINGTON'S CHOREA

Of a series of ten patients with Huntington's chorea, six had a diabetic response to an oral glucose tolerance test but none had symptoms of diabetes [46]. Hypersecretion of insulin occurs in response to oral glucose and intravenous arginine.

Diabetes associated with non-genetic diseases

Coeliac disease

The incidence of diabetes may be higher than expected in patients with coeliac disease. In a series of 317 adult patients with coeliac disease, diabetes was present in 14 individuals (4.3%) [47]. Diabetic treatment was by diet alone in two cases, oral hypoglycaemic drugs in another two and insulin in the remaining ten individuals. In these 14 patients, the diagnosis of diabetes predated that of coeliac disease by an average of 15 years. Diarrhoea in such patients may be wrongly attributed to diabetic autonomic neuropathy but the absence of neuropathy and the presence of significant weight loss both suggest coeliac disease rather than diabetic diarrhoea. Hypoglycaemia may be more frequent during episodes of diarrhoea, and a gluten-free diet may increase insulin requirements [48, 49]. Ketoacidosis and long-term microvascular and macrovascular complications have been reported [47].

Conclusions

Although mostly very rare, these conditions must be diagnosed early and accurately as their prognosis, treatment and complications often differ markedly from those of the primary forms of diabetes. They also present an important scientific challenge in that these 'experiments of nature' have helped to guide research into broader aspects of insulin action and metabolism in health and in the commoner types of diabetes.

AH WAH CHAN

References

1 Engelberth O, Charvat J, Jezkova Z, Rabouch J. Autoantibodies in chromatin-positive men. *Lancet* 1966; ii: 1194.

2 Vallotton MB, Forbes AP. Autoimmunity in gonadal dysgenesis and Klinefelter's syndrome. *Lancet* 1967; i: 648–51.

3 Williams ED, Engel E, Forbes AP. Thyroiditis and gonadal dysgenesis. *N Engl J Med* 1964; 270: 805–10.

4 Jeremiah DE, Leyshon GE, Rose T, Francis HWS, Elliot RW. Down's syndrome and diabetes. *Psychol Med* 1973; 3: 455–7.

5 Milunsky A, Neurath PW. Diabetes in Down's syndrome. *Arch Environ Health* 1968; 17: 372–6.

6 Daniels DM, Simon JL. Down's syndrome, hypothyroidism and diabetes. *J Pediatr* 1968; 72: 697–9.

7 Litman NN. Down's syndrome, hypothyroidism and diabetes mellitus. *J Pediatr* 1968; 73: 798.

8 Shaheed WA, Rosenbloom L. Down's syndrome with diabetes mellitus and hypothyroidism. *Arch Dis Child* 1973; 48: 917–18.

9 Parkin JM. Down's syndrome, hypothyroidism, and diabetes mellitus. *Br Med J* 1974; ii: 384.

10 Ong EA, Schneider G. Down's syndrome, hypothyroidism, and diabetes mellitus. *Am J Dis Child* 1976; 130: 335–6.

11 Stein GR, Jewell RC. Down's syndrome, hypothyroidism and diabetes mellitus in an adult. *Med J Austral* 1979; 2: 9–10.

12 Wilson DM, Frane JW, Sherman B, Johanson AJ, Hintz RL, Rosenfeld RG. Carbohydrate and lipid metabolism in Turner's syndrome: effect of therapy with growth hormone, oxandrolone, and a combination of both. *J Pediatr* 1987; 112: 210–17.

13 Nielson J, Johansen K, Yde H. The frequency of diabetes mellitus in patients with Turner's syndrome and pure gonadal dysgenesis. *Acta Endocrinol* 1969; 62: 251–69.

14 van Campenhout J, Antaki A, Rasio E. Diabetes mellitus and thyroid autoimmunity in gonadal dysgenesis. *Fertil Steril* 1973; 24: 1–9.

15 Polychronakos C, Letarte J, Collu R, Ducharme JR. Carbohydrate intolerance in children and adolescents with Turner's syndrome. *J Pediatr* 1980; 96: 1009–14.

16 Nielson J, Johansen K, Yde H. Frequency of diabetes mellitus in patients with Klinefelter's syndrome of different chromosomal constitutions and the XYY syndrome. Plasma insulin and growth hormone level after a glucose load. *J Clin Endocrinol* 1969; 29: 1062–73.

17 Breyer D, Cvitkovic P, Zdenko S, Pedersen O, Rocic B. Decreased insulin binding to erythrocytes in subjects with Klinefelter's syndrome. *J Clin Endocrinol Metab* 1981; 53: 654–5.

18 Waxman AD, Schalch DS, Odell WD, Tschudy DP. Abnormalities of carbohydrate metabolism in acute intermittent porphyria. *J Clin Invest* 1967; 46 (suppl 1): 1129.

19 Waxman AD, Berk PD, Schalch D, Tschudy DP. Isolated adrenocorticotrophic hormone deficiency in acute intermittent porphyria. *Ann Intern Med* 1969; 70: 317–23.

20 Goldberg A, Moore MR, eds. The porphyrias. In: *Clinics in Haematology*, vol 9. London: Saunders, 1980: 225–457.

21 Hudson AJ, Huff MW, Wright CG, Silver MM, Lo TCY, Banerjee D. The role of insulin resistance in the pathogenesis of myotonic muscular dystrophy. *Brain* 1987; 110: 469–88.

22 Alström CH, Hallgren B, Nilsson LB, Asander H. Retinal degeneration combined with obesity, diabetes, and neurogenous deafness: a specific syndrome (not hitherto described) distinct from Laurence–Moon–Bardet–Biedl syndrome. *Acta Psychiatr Neurol Scand* 1959; 129 (suppl): 1–35.

23 Goldstein JL, Fialkow PJ. Alström syndrome. *Medicine* 1973; 52: 53–71.

24 Hawkey CJ, Smithies A. The Prader–Willi syndrome with a 15/15 translocation. *J Med Genet* 1976; 13: 152–63.

25 Ledbetter DH, Riccardi VM, Airhart SD, Strobel RJ, Keenan BS, Crawford JD. Deletions of chromosome 15 as a cause of the Prader–Willi syndrome. *N Engl J Med* 1981; 304: 325–9.

26 Bray GA, Dahms WT, Swerdloff RS, Fiser RH, Atkinson RL, and Carrell RE. The Prader–Willi Syndrome: a study of 40 patients and review of the literature. *Medicine* 1983; 63: 59–80.

27 Kousholt AM, Beck-Neilson H, Lund HT. A reduced number of insulin receptors in patients with Prader–Willi syndrome. *Acta Endocrinol* 1983; 104: 345–51.

28 Savir A, Dickerman Z, Zarp M, Laron Z. Diabetic retinopathy in an adolescent with Prader–Labhardt–Willi syndrome. *Arch Dis Child* 1974; 49: 963–4.

29 Irwin GW, Ward PB. Werner's syndrome – with a report of two cases. *Am J Med* 1953; 15: 266–71.

30 Field JB, Loube SD. Observations concerning the diabetes mellitus associated with Werner's syndrome. *Metabolism* 1960; 9: 118–24.

31 Epstein CJ, Martin GM, Schultz AL, Motulsky AG. Werner's syndrome. *Medicine* 1966; 45: 177–218.

32 Neil CA, Dingwall MM. A syndrome resembling progeria: a review of two cases. *Arch Dis Child* 1950; 25: 213–21.

33 Fujimoto WY, Greene ML, Seegmiller JE. Cockayne's syndrome: report of a case with hyperlipoproteinemia, hyperinsulinemia, renal disease, and normal growth hormone. *J Pediatr* 1969; 75: 881–4.

34 Schalch DS, McFarlin DE, Barlow ML. An unusual form of diabetes mellitus in ataxia telangiectasia. *N Engl J Med* 1970; 282: 1396–402.

35 Bar RS, Levis WR, Rechler MM, Harrison LC, Siebert C, Podskalny J, Roth J, Muggeo M. Extreme insulin resistance in ataxia telangiectasia. *N Engl J Med* 1978; 298: 1164–71.

36 Ionasecu V, Luca N. Investigations on carbohydrate metabolism in progressive muscular dystrophy. *Psychiatr Neurol* 1963; 146: 309–25.

37 Rabson SM, Mendenhall EN. Familial hypertrophy of pineal body, hyperplasia of adrenal cortex, and diabetes mellitus. *Am J Clin Pathol* 1956; 26: 283–90.

38 West RJ, Leonard JV. Familial insulin resistance with pineal hyperplasia: metabolic studies and effect of hypophysectomy. *Arch Dis Child* 1980; 55: 619–21.

39 Taylor SI, Underhill LH, Hedo JA, Roth J, Rios MS, Blizzard RM. Decreased insulin binding to cultured cells from a patient with the Rabson–Mendenhall syndrome: dichotomy between studies with cultured lymphocytes and cultured fibroblasts. *J Clin Endocrinol Metab* 1983; 56: 856–61.

40 West RJ, Lloyd JK, Turner WML. Familial insulin-resistant diabetes, multiple somatic anomalies, and pineal hyper-

plasia. *Arch Dis Child* 1975; **50**: 703−8.

41 Quin JD, Fisher BM, Paterson KR, Beastall GH, MacCuish AC. Preliminary studies with subcutaneous and intravenous insulin-like growth factor-1 in Mendenhall's syndrome. *Diabetic Med* 1989; **6** Suppl. 2: 5A.

42 Neufield M, Maclaren NK, Blizzard RM. Two types of autoimmune Addison's disease with different Polyglandular Autoimmune (PGA) Syndromes. *Medicine* 1981; **60**: 355−62.

43 Hewer RL, Robinson N. Diabetes mellitus in Friedreich's ataxia. *J Neurol Neurosurg Psychiatr* 1968; **31**: 226−31.

44 Thoren C. Diabetes in Friedreich's ataxia. *Acta Paediatr* 1962; (suppl 135): 239−47.

45 Podolsky S, Sheremata WA. Insulin-dependent diabetes mellitus and Friedreich's ataxia in siblings. *Metabolism* 1970; **19**: 555−61.

46 Podolsky S, Leopold NA, Sax DS. Increased frequency of diabetes mellitus in patients with Huntington's chorea. *Lancet* 1972; i: 1356−9.

47 Walsh CH, Cooper BT, Wright AD, Malins JM, Cooke WT. Diabetes mellitus and coeliac disease: a clinical study. *Q J Med* 1978; **47**: 89−100.

48 Komrower GM. Coeliac disease in a diabetic child. *Lancet* 1969; i: 1215.

49 Thain ME, Hamilton JR, Ehrlich RM. Co-existence of diabetes mellitus and celiac disease. *J Pediatr* 1974; **48**: 527−9.

SECTION 9
BIOCHEMICAL ABNORMALITIES IN DIABETES MELLITUS

32 Mechanisms of Hyperglycaemia and Disorders of Intermediary Metabolism

Summary

- Glucose is produced by the liver through gluconeogenesis and glycogenolysis.
- The main substrates for gluconeogenesis are alanine and glutamine (derived from muscle protein), glycerol (derived from triglyceride in adipose tissue) and lactate and pyruvate.
- Gluconeogenesis is controlled by both substrate supply (influenced by hormones and ambient blood glucose levels) and at the level of the liver, where a low insulin:glucagon ratio, catecholamines and the sympathetic nervous system, and fatty acid oxidation stimulate gluconeogenesis.
- Glycogenolysis is controlled by integration of synthesis and degradation of glycogen; glucagon and catecholamines stimulate and insulin inhibits glycogenolysis, whilst insulin stimulates glycogen synthesis.
- In IDDM, hepatic glucose production is, therefore, increased because the decreased insulin:glucagon ratio stimulates liver glycogenolysis and gluconeogenesis directly and because gluconeogenic substrate supply increases. Elevated non-esterified fatty acid (NEFA) levels also stimulate gluconeogenesis in the liver.
- In NIDDM, hepatic glucose production is increased when the fasting blood glucose level is greater than about 8 mmol/l.
- Glucose utilization in the normal fasting state is mainly by non-muscle tissue such as brain, intestine, and kidneys; the principal muscle fuel is NEFA whose oxidation inhibits glucose uptake and metabolism via the glucose–fatty acid cycle. In prolonged starvation, ketone bodies are utilized by non-muscle tissue and, like NEFA, also inhibit glucose uptake and use.
- In IDDM, NEFA and ketone levels are increased and inhibit glucose utilization. In NIDDM, NEFA concentrations are elevated but ketones are near-normal.
- Ketone bodies are synthesized in the liver from NEFA. Production is partly regulated by NEFA release from adipose tissue (increased lipolysis or decreased re-esterification). The major stimuli to lipolysis are catecholamine activity and insulin deficiency.
- Hepatic ketogenesis is regulated by transfer of fatty acyl CoA into mitochondria by the carnitine shuttle via alterations in carnitine palmitoyl transferase-1 activity. A low insulin:glucagon ratio in IDDM stimulates the enzyme by increasing malonyl CoA levels. There are no major ketone body disturbances in NIDDM.

Glucose production in the non-diabetic subject

The liver makes glucose by both gluconeogenesis and glycogenolysis.

Gluconeogenesis

The principal substrates for gluconeogenesis are illustrated in Fig. 32.1.

1 *Amino acids — alanine and glutamine.* Amino acids derived from muscle protein are the major source of glucose synthesis *de novo*. Muscle protein amino acids are converted to glucogenic amino acids, of which alanine and glutamine are quantitatively the most important. A proportion of the alanine taken up by the liver is derived originally

303

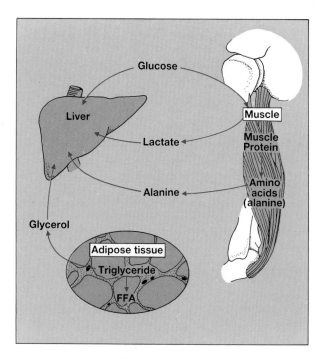

Fig. 32.1. Principal substrates for gluconeogenesis.

from glucose, following its metabolism to pyruvate and subsequent conversion to alanine. The activity of this cycle (the glucose–alanine cycle) does not contribute to glucose synthesis *de novo*.

2 *Glycerol*. Glycerol is derived from the hydrolysis of triglyceride. In man, adipose tissue does not contain sufficient glycerol kinase, the enzyme necessary for the subsequent metabolism of glycerol, and glycerol is released into the circulation for uptake by the liver and conversion to glucose.

3 *Lactate and pyruvate*. Much of the carbon skeleton of lactate and pyruvate derives initially from glucose (the Cori cycle).

Gluconeogenesis is controlled both by the supply of these substrates, and by intrahepatic mechanisms.

CONTROL OF GLUCONEOGENESIS THROUGH SUBSTRATE SUPPLY

The control of muscle protein synthesis and degradation is not well understood, but endocrine influences are important. Growth hormone has anabolic effects and muscle protein degradation is also inhibited by insulin. Insulin thereby limits the supply of amino acids for gluconeogenesis.

Lipolysis (and therefore glycerol supply) is inhibited by insulin, and stimulated by the sympathetic nervous system and circulating catecholamines. Glucagon has important lipolytic

effects in other species, but has minor importance in man. The control of peripheral lactate release is complex, and is dictated by the ambient blood glucose concentration.

CONTROL OF GLUCONEOGENESIS WITHIN THE LIVER

Uptake of amino acids across the liver cell membrane is stimulated by glucagon. Within the liver, the intrahepatic sites at which gluconeogenesis is controlled are illustrated in Table 32.1. The minute-to-minute control is exerted by insulin and glucagon [1, 2]. Glucagon stimulates gluconeogenesis at several sites, and these effects are inhibited by insulin. Most evidence suggests that the ratio of insulin to glucagon is more important than the absolute concentration of either alone (Fig. 32.2). The catecholamines and the sympathetic nervous system stimulate gluconeogenesis, through both α- and β-adrenergic actions. Cortisol has a delayed stimulatory effect, through an increase in the synthesis of certain gluconeogenic enzymes.

These hormonal influences on gluconeogenesis are superimposed on other intrahepatic mechanisms. Notable amongst these is the stimulatory effect of fatty acid oxidation, perhaps through an increase in intrahepatic citrate and acetyl-CoA concentrations. Whatever the mechanism, gluconeogenesis tends to be stimulated under certain conditions in which fatty acid oxidation is high.

Glycogenolysis

Liver glycogen is the major body store of carbohydrate, for rapid release as glucose [3]. The control of glycogen synthesis and degradation is integrated by now classical phosphorylation/dephosphorylation mechanisms involving cyclic AMP (cAMP) (Fig. 32.3). As with gluconeogenesis,

Table 32.1. Sites for the intrahepatic control of gluconeogenesis.

1 Glucose $\rightleftharpoons$ glucose 6-phosphate (glucokinase; glucose-6-phosphatase)

2 Fructose 6-phosphate $\rightleftharpoons$ fructose 1,6-bisphosphate (6-phosphofructo-1-kinase; fructose-1,6-bisphosphatase)

3 Phosphoenolpyruvate $\rightleftharpoons$ pyruvate (pyruvate kinase; pyruvate carboxylase; phosphoenolpyruvate carboxykinase)

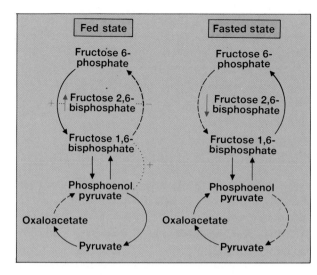

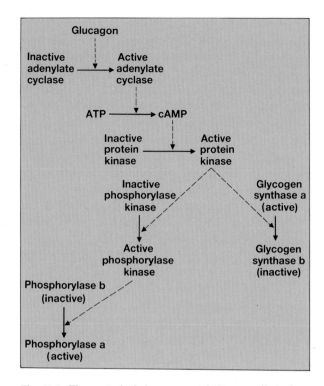

Fig. 32.2. Intrahepatic regulation of gluconeogenesis by insulin and glucagon acting through fructose 2,6-bisphosphate. In the fed state, high insulin and glucose and relatively low glucagon concentrations lead to low hepatic cAMP levels and increased production of the intermediate, fructose 2,6-bisphosphate. This regulatory intermediate activates 6-phosphofructo-1-kinase and inhibits fructose-1,6-bisphosphatase. The resultant increased production of fructose 1,6-bisphosphate causes activation of pyruvate kinase. Pyruvate kinase is also activated by dephosphorylation under these nutritional conditions, and the activity of phosphoenolpyruvate carboxykinase is low. In fasting, the decrease in insulin and increase in glucagon result in increased hepatic cAMP production and a decrease in fructose 2,6-bisphosphate. The sequence described above reverses. Changes in enzyme activities in the other substrate cycle (glucose:glucose 6-phosphate, not illustrated) also favour gluconeogenesis.

Fig. 32.3. The control of glycogen metabolism — effect of glucagon.

insulin and glucagon have antagonistic actions on glycogenolysis. Glucagon stimulates glycogenolysis and inhibits glycogen synthesis, with insulin having the opposite actions. Catecholamines and the sympathetic nervous system have stimulatory effects on glycogen degradation, with the β-adrenergic actions mediated by cAMP and the α-adrenergic actions operating through another intracellular messenger system. Superimposed on these hormonal influences on glycogen degradation are the effects of certain metabolic substrates. The most notable is glucose, which has a suppressive effect on glycogenolysis, which is direct and does not require an increase in insulin release for its expression.

Glucose production in diabetes

Insulin-dependent diabetes

Insulin deficiency leads to an early increase in hepatic glucose output, which is evident within 1 h of insulin withdrawal. Under controlled conditions, this results in a mean twofold rise in hepatic glucose output 12 h after the cessation of insulin treatment. In the presence of normal glucagon levels, the decrease in the insulin:glucagon ratio [4] leads to an increase of both glycogenolysis and gluconeogenesis. The insulin deficiency also results in an increase in the supply of certain gluconeogenic substrates from the peripheral tissues to the liver. Muscle amino acid release is increased, and with the hydrolysis of triglyceride, glycerol supply rises. The increase in fatty acid oxidation favours hepatic gluconeogenesis further.

During more prolonged insulin deficiency, there is increased secretion of the stress hormones [5]. In clinical practice, a coexisting illness frequently precipitates diabetic ketoacidosis (Chapter 49), and under these circumstances there may be a considerable early stress hormone response. Glucagon secretion is increased over basal levels, leading to a further decline in the insulin:glucagon ratio. An increase in cortisol release may increase gluconeogenesis through a direct hepatic action of cortisol. Glucocorticoids also increase amino acid release from muscle and increase lipolysis to add to the glycerol supply. Growth hormone is released in stress, and the levels of growth hormone are elevated in 50% of patients with established diabetic ketoacidosis. The lipolytic effect of growth hormone will increase glycerol supply for glucose formation. Finally, activity of the sympathetic nervous system is increased, particularly if myocardial infarction or a cerebrovascular accident has precipitated the episode of ketoacidosis. The increased sympathetic nervous activity and high circulating catecholamine levels will increase both glycogenolysis and gluconeogenesis through their direct hepatic actions, and the supply of glycerol will be increased from adipose tissue.

In established diabetic ketoacidosis, the production of glucose by splanchnic tissues has been estimated using catheterization techniques. Glucose production is increased, but there is great inter-individual variation. In one series, splanchnic glucose production ranged from 0 to 2.44 mmol/min, with a mean level of 1.57 mmol/min. This compared with a mean value for non-diabetic subjects of 1.49 mmol/min. It is evident that even though the mean glucose production rate is not greatly increased, glucose production rates are inappropriate for the blood glucose levels observed in diabetic ketoacidosis. These values must be viewed in the context of the situation in non-diabetic subjects in whom a rise in blood glucose of 1 mmol/l leads to an 80–85% decrease in glucose production rate by the liver.

Non-insulin-dependent diabetes

Hepatic glucose output in NIDDM has been reported as lower than, higher than, and similar to that observed in non-diabetic subjects [6, 7]. As with insulin-deficient IDDM, the values for hepatic glucose output are always inappropriately high in the light of the elevated blood glucose concentration. Hepatic glucose output is most elevated in patients with the most severe NIDDM, as reflected in a positive correlation between hepatic glucose output and fasting plasma glucose. Resistance to the action of insulin in suppressing hepatic glucose output is observed in NIDDM when the patients are hyperglycaemic. The hepatic sensitivity to insulin returns to normal with good diabetic control, suggesting that the initial insulin resistance may not be a primary abnormality (see Chapter 21, 22).

The increased hepatic glucose output is the main cause of fasting hyperglycaemia in NIDDM. In patients with less severe NIDDM (fasting blood glucose less than 8 mmol/l), hepatic glucose output may be normal and the mild increase in blood glucose levels reflects impairment of glucose utilization alone.

Glucose utilization in the non-diabetic subject

After an overnight fast, most of the glucose produced by the liver is utilized by tissues with an obligatory requirement for glucose metabolism. At this stage, tissues such as skeletal muscle are utilizing primarily non-esterified fatty acids (NEFA) for fuel. Muscle NEFA oxidation causes a decrease in glucose uptake and subsequent glucose metabolism through operation of the glucose–fatty acid (Randle) cycle [8], i.e. the decrease in glucose utilization and oxidation in skeletal and heart muscle caused by increased availability of fatty acids. At a biochemical level (Fig. 32.4), NEFA metabolism generates citrate which inhibits 6-phosphofructo-1-kinase, and acetyl CoA, which decreases the activation of pyruvate dehydrogenase. In addition, glucose transport across the muscle membrane is decreased.

The glucose–fatty acid cycle operates in man, as evidenced by the decrease in glucose utilization and oxidation observed when NEFA levels in the circulation are elevated artificially. Administration of an anti-lipolytic agent such as nicotinic acid causes a decrease in circulating NEFA, and is associated with an increase in glucose utilization and oxidation.

The metabolism of glucose in tissues other than muscle, e.g. brain, intestine, kidney and lactating breast, is considerable following an overnight fast. With more prolonged starvation, glucose utilization by these tissues decreases as ketone-body utilization rises. The intracellular mechanisms are similar to those which operate in the glucose–fatty acid cycle, with the generation of citrate and acetyl CoA, as ketone bodies are utilized for fuel (Fig. 32.5). Ketone bodies are utilized progressively during prolonged starvation, so that 70% of the fuel for brain metabolism is supplied by the ketone bodies after 5–6 weeks of starvation. The operation of this glucose–fatty acid–ketone body cycle is an important mechanism in the conservation of glucose (and thus protein) in starvation.

On refeeding with a carbohydrate-containing meal, the absorption of glucose stimulates insulin

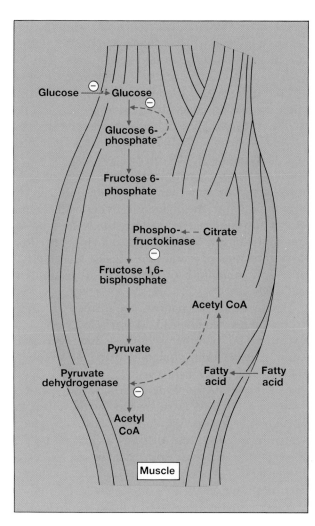

Fig. 32.4. The glucose–fatty acid cycle in muscle. The oxidation of fatty acid in muscle inhibits the transport of glucose into the muscle cell and its subsequent intracellular metabolism at several sites (shown as ⊖).

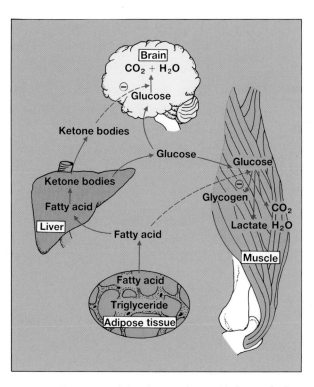

Fig. 32.5. Operation of the glucose–fatty acid–ketone body cycle in starvation. Fatty acid metabolism in muscle and ketone-body metabolism in brain are high when circulating NEFA and ketone-body concentrations rise in starvation. In consequence, glucose utilization and oxidation are decreased in these tissues.

release. A small rise in circulating insulin concentration (by 5–10 mU/l) has no direct effect on glucose transport across muscle-cell membranes, but does suppress fatty acid mobilization from adipose tissue. The resulting decrease in circulating NEFA will lead to an increase in glucose utilization by muscle. This may be the major mechanism by which glucose utilization is modulated in man. With a greater elevation in serum insulin to circulating levels of 30–40 mU/l or more, glucose transport into insulin-sensitive tissues is stimulated directly. Muscle is the major insulin-sensitive tissue. The most frequently employed methods by which insulin sensitivity is assessed in man create circulating insulin concentrations at or above these values. During the hyper-insulinaemic, euglycaemic clamp, for example,

circulating insulin values are frequently between 50 and 1000 mU/l. The defects of insulin sensitivity which have been demonstrated using these techniques predominantly reflect impaired stimulation of glucose transport across muscle-cell membranes. It is important to remember that under normal physiological circumstances in normal weight subjects, circulating insulin levels fluctuate between 5 and 40 mU/l, and never reach these high values (Fig. 32.6). The results from the standard methods for assessment of insulin sensitivity must, therefore, be viewed with caution as the glucose utilization in the different protocols may be unphysiological.

Glucose utilization in diabetes

Insulin-dependent diabetes

In insulin-deficient patients with IDDM, fatty acid mobilization and ketogenesis increase. The result-ant decrease in glucose uptake which occurs secondary to the glucose–fatty acid–ketone body cycle contributes to the hyperglycaemia. The more

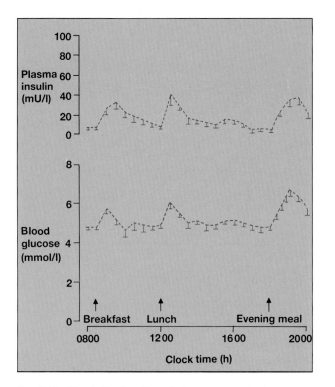

Fig. 32.6. Circulating insulin and glucose concentrations over a 12-h period with breakfast, lunch and evening meal, in ten normal weight (<120% ideal body weight) subjects. Values are mean ± SEM. Meal times are indicated by arrows.

direct effects of insulin deficiency, with loss of insulin-stimulated glucose uptake, are also deficient in this situation. Loss of glucose in the urine is a significant means for glucose disposal in these circumstances. As diabetic ketoacidosis develops, the salt and water depletion which occurs induces a decrease in renal perfusion and the impairment of glucose clearance in the urine contributes to the development of hyperglycaemia.

In treated IDDM, peripheral insulin concentrations are two- to threefold higher than those observed in the non-diabetic subject (there is, however, portal hypoinsulinaemia relative to the non-diabetic state, in which the liver is exposed to five- to tenfold higher insulin levels than are peripheral tissues). Some resistance to the hypoglycaemic action of insulin has been demonstrated in IDDM, probably reflecting a decrease in insulin-stimulated glucose uptake into muscle.

Non-insulin-dependent diabetes

Plasma NEFA are increased, and ketone body concentrations are normal or near-normal in NIDDM. The increase in circulating NEFA levels, despite high peripheral insulin levels, suggests

resistance at the adipocyte to the anti-lipolytic action of insulin. This conclusion assumes that the high circulating insulin levels measured by radioimmunoassay reflect biologically active insulin. The recent demonstration in NIDDM of high circulating concentrations of proinsulin and split proinsulin, both of which are detected by standard insulin radioimmunoassays (Chapter 22), casts some doubt on the conclusions about insulin resistance at the adipocyte. Resistance to exogenous insulin has not been extensively examined, and the standard hyperinsulinaemic clamp techniques are poor methods for assessment of this process. Studies utilizing very low dose infusions of insulin do suggest some resistance of inhibition of lipolysis of insulin in NIDDM.

Whatever the mechanism, the increase in circulating NEFA would lead to increased fatty acid oxidation by peripheral tissues, and decreased basal glucose utilization and oxidation through the glucose−fatty acid cycle [9, 10]. That high circulating NEFA levels do contribute to hyperglycaemia in NIDDM is suggested by the effect of anti-lipolytic agents, e.g. nicotinic acid analogues, which increase glucose disposal as plasma NEFA levels fall. Basal rates of lipid oxidation are increased in obese NIDDM, but not in the non-obese subject. The importance of this mechanism of hyperglycaemia in the non-obese subject is, therefore, uncertain at present.

Resistance to the hypoglycaemic actions of insulin has been demonstrated in NIDDM, as previously mentioned, by techniques which achieve serum insulin levels of greater than 50−60 mU/l. Direct stimulation of glucose uptake into tissues such as muscle is the major process under these experimental conditions. The liver itself is an important organ in the fed state for glucose disposal. Following an oral glucose load, catheterization studies have suggested that 60% of 100-g oral glucose load is taken up by the splanchnic bed (Fig. 32.7). In NIDDM, the escape of glucose from the splanchnic bed is 100% greater than in the non-diabetic state. These calculations assume that hepatic glucose production is unchanged following oral glucose ingestion, and this is extremely unlikely. Further studies utilizing a double isotope method and forearm catheterization have also demonstrated some failure of splanchnic glucose uptake. By this technique, however, the major defect was a failure of suppression of endogenous hepatic glucose production following oral glucose.

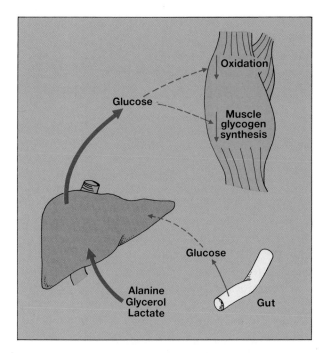

Fig. 32.7. Glucose metabolism in non-insulin-dependent diabetes. In NIDDM, where the fasting blood glucose is >8 mmol/l, hepatic production of glucose is increased. Uptake of glucose by the liver (following an oral glucose load) is decreased. The utilization of glucose by muscle is impaired.

In the hyperinsulinaemic, euglycaemic clamp techniques, the defect in muscle glucose uptake reflects both impaired glucose storage as glycogen and decreased glucose oxidation. The site of this insulin resistance is unknown, but it occurs distal to the level of membrane transport, because storage and oxidation defects can vary independently under different experimental conditions.

Although insulin resistance, as demonstrated by the clamp techniques, undoubtedly occurs, it should be remembered that the direct effects of insulin on glucose disposal may not be the major effects of insulin under normal physiological conditions. Further work is required on the suppression of fatty acid mobilization by insulin in NIDDM.

Ketone-body metabolism in the non-diabetic subject

Ketone bodies are synthesized in the liver from fatty acids. Most of the fatty acid in the circulation has been released from the adipose tissue stores of triglyceride. There are two major sites for the regulation of ketone-body synthesis:
1 Fatty acid release from adipose tissue.
2 Ketone-body synthesis in the liver.

Fatty acid mobilization in the non-diabetic subject

Adipose tissue triglyceride stores constitute 10–30% of the total body weight; if adipose tissue were the sole fuel available during starvation, there would be sufficient for survival for 30 days in a normal-weight subject. A substrate cycle exists between triglyceride and fatty acid (Fig. 32.8). Triglyceride is constantly degraded to fatty acids and glycerol, and some of the fatty acid is re-esterified back to triglyceride if glycerol-3-phosphate is available. The activity of this cycle means that fatty acids may be mobilized from adipose tissue either through an increase in lipolysis, or through a decrease in fatty acid re-esterification [11].

Triacylglycerol lipase is the regulatory enzyme in the control of lipolysis. It is activated by phosphorylation using cAMP-dependent protein kinase. The major stimulus for activation of triacylglycerol lipase activity in man is from the catecholamines, either noradrenaline at sympathetic nerve endings, or from adrenaline and noradrenaline in the circulation. The stimulatory effects are β-adrenergic, while in man, α-adrenergic activity is anti-lipolytic.

Other hormones have lipolytic actions. Glucagon is an important lipolytic agent in several species, but in man assumes importance only in absolute insulin deficiency. Growth hormone has delayed lipolytic actions, which are independent of cAMP. Glucocorticoids and the thyroid hormones also have delayed stimulatory effects on lipolysis. In addition, glucocorticoids potentiate the lipolytic effects of adrenaline.

Insulin is the only major agent in man which inhibits lipolysis. Both basal and stimulated lipolysis are affected. The actions of insulin may arise through its effect to decrease cAMP concentrations in adipose tissue, at least when a stimulus to cAMP formation is present. It is probable that insulin has additional effects which are independent of cAMP.

Control of fatty acid esterification is much less completely understood. Many of the enzymes involved in this process are membrane-bound, and less readily studied. Glycerol phosphate acyl transferase is phosphorylated and inactivated by cAMP under certain experimental conditions, although the importance of this as a regulatory mechanism for triglyceride synthesis has been questioned. Insulin increases fatty acid esterification, possibly

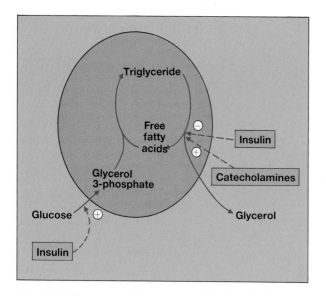

Fig. 32.8. The control of fatty acid mobilization. In the adipocyte, triglyceride is hydrolysed to fatty acid and glycerol. Some of the fatty acid is re-esterified back to triglyceride. Insulin inhibits lipolysis and stimulates re-esterification. β-adrenergic activity provides the major stimulus to lipolysis.

through increasing glucose transport into adipocyte membranes and thereby increasing the availability of glycerol-3-phosphate.

Fatty acid mobilization in diabetes

INSULIN-DEPENDENT DIABETES

In insulin-deficient IDDM, plasma NEFA levels are elevated at 1–3 mmol/l (compared with values in the non-diabetic subject of 0.3–1.5 mmol/l. Fatty acid production rates are increased up to threefold. The increased production of fatty acids reflects the deficiency of insulin, in the presence of normal sympathetic nervous system activity and normal levels of circulating catecholamines. Lipolysis is increased and fatty acid esterification is decreased. As patients become more ill, the stress response contributes to the increased fatty acid mobilization. Circulating catecholamines and sympathetic nervous system activity are increased, as are levels of cortisol and growth hormone. With insulin therapy in IDDM, fatty acid production rates decrease to non-diabetic values.

NON-INSULIN-DEPENDENT DIABETES

Fatty acid mobilization is increased in NIDDM, and fatty acid oxidation is increased. This reflects

either insulin deficiency, or if radioimmunoassayable insulin levels are high and all the immunoreactive insulin is biologically active, there must also be resistance to the anti-lipolytic effects of insulin.

Ketone-body metabolism in the non-diabetic subject

The ketone bodies, acetoacetate and 3-hydroxybutyrate, are synthesized in the liver. Fatty acid uptake by the liver is concentration-dependent within the physiological range. Once inside the hepatocyte, fatty acids may be synthesized in the cell cytosol to triglyceride, or alternatively they may enter the mitochondria as fatty acyl CoA. Inside mitochondria, fatty acyl CoA undergoes β oxidation to acetyl CoA, which is then either totally oxidized in the Krebs' cycle or converted to acetoacetate. Activity of the Krebs' cycle is relatively fixed, whereas mitochondrial generation of ketone bodies is variable. Transfer of acyl CoA into mitochondria via the carnitine shuttle is the regulatory step in ketogenesis, acting through alterations in activity of the enzyme carnitine palmitoyl transferase-1 (Fig. 32.9).

Insulin and glucagon have opposite effects on carnitine palmitoyl transferase-1 activity. Insulin decreases activity of the enzyme, through increased production of malonyl CoA which is an inhibitor of carnitine palmitoyl transferase-1. By contrast, glucagon decreases malonyl CoA production and increases activity of the enzyme. When the glucagon effect is dominant, transfer of acyl CoA into mitochondria is therefore increased. As with glucose metabolism in the liver, ketogenesis is dictated by the relative amounts of insulin and glucagon present. Although other hormones may have minor effects, it is insulin and glucagon which exert the major influence on hepatic ketone-body synthesis.

Ketone bodies are utilized as fuel by oxidation in extrahepatic tissues. Uptake is concentration-dependent in tissues such as brain which utilize increasing amounts of ketone bodies as fuel during prolonged starvation.

Ketone-body metabolism in diabetes

Ketone-body synthesis increases more than threefold as patients with IDDM are deprived of insulin for 12 h (from 5.4±1.4 to 18.3±3.9 μmol/kg/min) (Fig. 32.10). This increase in synthesis

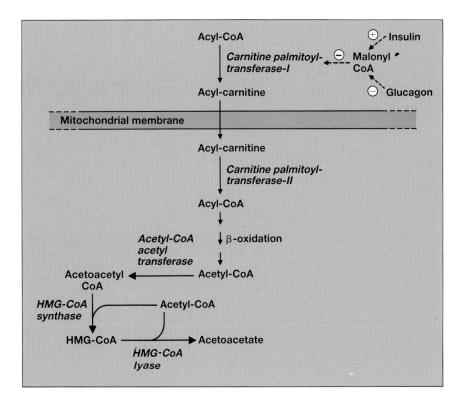

Fig. 32.9. Synthesis of ketone bodies in hepatic mitochondria.

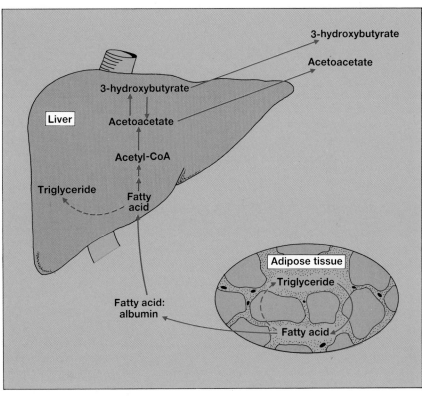

Fig. 32.10. Ketone-body production in insulin deficiency. Lipolysis is increased and fatty acid esterification decreased, resulting in increased fatty acid mobilization from adipose tissue. In the liver, ketogenesis is increased.

reflects an increase in NEFA supply to the liver, and the prevailing hormonal milieu with low insulin and high glucagon concentrations favours ketone-body production. Insulin normally stimulates the uptake of ketone bodies by extrahepatic tissues and this effect is lacking in insulin-deprived patients with IDDM.

In NIDDM, ketone-body levels in the circulation are either mildly increased or normal. Ketone-body synthesis is also increased or normal. No major disturbance of ketone-body metabolism is obvious, and this reflects the fact that sufficient insulin is available to restrain hepatic ketone-body production and to stimulate peripheral ketone-body utilization.

PATRICK SHARP

DESMOND G. JOHNSTON

References

1 Hue L. Gluconeogenesis and its regulation. *Diabetes/Metab Rev* 1987; **3**: 111–26.

2 Pilkis SJ, El-Maghrabi MR, Claus TH. Hormonal regulation of hepatic gluconeogenesis and glycolysis. *Ann Rev Biochem* 1988; **57**: 755–83.

3 Hems DA, Whitton PD. Control of hepatic glycogenolysis. *Physiol Rev* 1980; **60**: 1–50.

4 Cherrington AD, Stevenson RW, Steiner KE, Davis MA, Myers SR, Adkins BA, Abumrad NN, Williams PE. Insulin, glucagon and glucose as regulators of hepatic glucose uptake and production *in vivo*. *Diabetes/Metab Rev* 1987; **3**: 307–32.

5 Johnston DG, Alberti KGMM. Hormonal control of ketone body metabolism in the normal and diabetic state. *Clin Endocrinol Metab* 1982; **11**: 329–61.

6 Alford FP, Best JD. The aetiology of type 2 diabetes. In: Nattrass M, ed. *Recent Advances in Diabetes*, Vol. 2. Edinburgh: Churchill Livingstone, 1986: 1–22.

7 DeFronzo RA. The triumvirate: beta cell, muscle, liver. A collusion responsible for NIDDM. *Diabetes* 1988; **37**: 667–86.

8 Randle PLJ, Hales CN, Garland PB, Newsholme EA. The glucose fatty-acid cycle. Its role in insulin sensitivity and the metabolic disturbances of diabetes mellitus. *Lancet* 1963; i: 785–9.

9 Felber J-P, Ferrannini E, Golay A, Meyer HU, Thiebaud D, Curchod B, Maeder E, Jequier E, DeFronzo RA. Role of lipid oxidation in pathogenesis of insulin resistance of obesity and type II diabetes. *Diabetes* 1987; **36**: 1341–50.

10 Golay A, Swislocki ALM, Chen YDI, Reaven GM. Relationships between plasma free fatty acid concentration, endogenous glucose production, and fasting hyperglycemia in normal and non-insulin dependent diabetic individuals. *Metabolism* 1987; **36**: 92–6.

11 Johnston DG, Pernet A, Nattrass M. Hormonal regulation of fatty acid mobilization in normal and diabetic man. In: Nattrass M, Santiago JV, eds. *Recent Advances in Diabetes*, Vol. 1. Edinburgh: Churchill Livingstone, 1984: 91–106.

33　Glucagon and the Gut Hormones in Diabetes Mellitus

Summary

• Glucagon is a 29-amino acid peptide synthesized in the islet A cells. Its precursor, preproglucagon, is cleaved differently in the gut to yield glicentin and oxyntomodulin (together comprising enteroglucagon) and glucagon-like peptide-1 7−36 amide (GLP-1 7−36 amide).

• Glucagon secretion is stimulated by hypoglycaemia, amino acids and free fatty acids; gastric inhibitory peptide, growth hormone and catecholamines; and both sympathetic and parasympathetic stimulation. Glucagon release is inhibited by glucose, insulin and somatostatin.

• Glucagon is a major catabolic hormone, acting primarily on the liver to stimulate glycogenolysis and gluconeogenesis and inhibit glycogenesis and glycolysis, overall increasing hepatic glucose output. Inhibition of fatty acid and triglyceride synthesis, together with increased fatty acid oxidation, leads to increased ketone body formation.

• Circulating glucagon concentrations are increased in NIDDM and IDDM, probably because of insulin deficiency and the failure of the diabetic A cell to be suppressed by glucose. Hyperglucagonaemia contributes to the insulin resistance and hyperglycaemia of diabetes.

• Somatostatin (SRIF) is synthesized in D cells of the islets and gut and in specific neurones. It exists as two molecular forms, SRIF-14 and SRIF-28. SRIF release from the pancreas and gut is stimulated by glucose and amino acids and by insulin deficiency, and apparently inhibits its own secretion.

• SRIF has many inhibitory endocrine and exocrine actions, including inhibition of secretion of growth hormone, insulin, glucagon and gut peptides; suppression of pancreatic and gastric exocrine secretions; and impairment of gastrointestinal absorption of nutrients.

• SRIF levels in pancreas, gut and circulation are increased in diabetes, apparently as a consequence of insulin deficiency.

• Pancreatic polypeptide (PP), produced by PP cells in the pancreatic islets and exocrine tissue, is released into the circulation after meals as a result of vagal stimulation. PP has no known effects on insulin or glucagon secretion and its physiological function is unknown.

• An 'entero-insular axis', through which hypothetical 'incretin' hormones secreted into the bloodstream after eating stimulate insulin release, has been postulated to explain the greater insulin secretory response when glucose or amino acids are given orally rather than intravenously. Candidate incretins include GLP-1 7−36 amide (the most potent insulinotropic gut peptide yet identified) and gastric inhibitory peptide.

Many peptides are now known to be produced by the gut and pancreas and some have experimental actions which suggest that they are involved in regulating insulin secretion or other aspects of metabolism. Of these peptides, glucagon and somatostatin have been the subject of much research because of their possible contributions to the metabolic syndrome of diabetes. The 'entero-insular axis', through which gut hormones released into the circulation are postulated to influence insulin secretion, has also attracted much attention. Indeed, consideration of this possible mechanism led Moore [1], soon after the turn of the twentieth century and some 15 years before the discovery of insulin, to speculate that acid extracts of the gut might be used to treat diabetes.

This chapter will first describe the basic biochemistry and physiology of the major gut and pancreatic peptides and hormones, and will then outline their abnormalities and possible roles in diabetes.

Glucagon

Source, synthesis and structure

Glucagon is a 29-amino acid peptide found in the A cells of the islets of Langerhans (see Chapter 8). Peptides structurally related to glucagon are also found in the gut, particularly the ileum; the term 'enteroglucagon' embraces two of these peptides, glicentin and oxyntomodulin, which cross-react with antibodies directed against the N-terminus of glucagon itself. Glucagon and these related peptides are derived by enzymatic cleavage from a large precursor molecule, proglucagon [2], which was deduced by cDNA analysis to contain several other peptides in addition to glucagon itself [3]. As shown in Fig. 33.1, the post-translational

processing of proglucagon differs markedly between the A cell and the gut [4]. In the A cell, glucagon and a larger peptide, the major proglucagon fragment, are produced, whereas the main products in the ileum are glicentin and oxyntomodulin (i.e. enteroglucagon) and a C-terminal fragment of glucagon-like peptide-1 (GLP-1). This latter carries an amide group at its C-terminus, a feature of many biologically active peptides, and has been given the rather clumsy title of 'GLP-1 7−36 amide'. The physiological role of glucagon and the possible functions of GLP-1 7−36 amide are described below. A wide range of possible actions including promotion of mucosal growth, inhibition of gastric acid secretion and regulation of endocrine and exocrine pancreatic function − have been proposed for the other proglucagon-derived peptides [5].

Secretion of glucagon

Glucagon secretion is regulated by three main factors, namely nutrients, circulating peptide hormones and the autonomic innervation surrounding the A cell (Table 33.1). Glucose rapidly

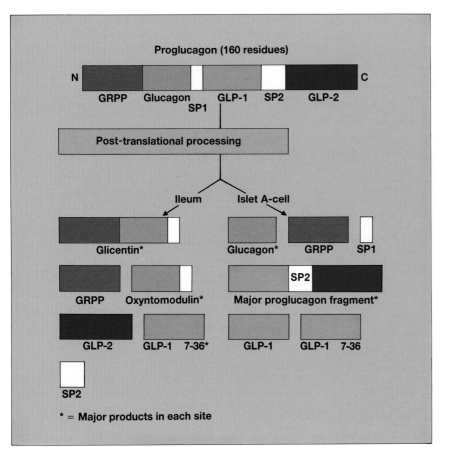

Fig. 33.1. Tissue-specific processing of proglucagon. The main products in ileum are glicentin and oxyntomodulin (together comprising enteroglucagon) and glucagon-like peptide-1 7−36 amide (GLP-1 7−36) linked by spacer peptide 2 (SP2). Other cleavage fragments include glicentin-related pancreatic peptide (GRPP) and the glucagon-like peptides −1 and −2 (GLP-1 and GLP-2).

Table 33.1. Factors affecting glucagon secretion.

Factors	Stimulators	Inhibitors
Nutrients	Amino acids Free fatty acids Glucopenia	Glucose
Gut peptides and hormones	GIP CCK Secretin	Insulin Somatostatin GLP-1 7−36 amide
Counter-regulatory hormones	Growth hormone Adrenaline Cortisol	
Autonomic innervation	Cholinergic Adrenergic Peptidergic?	

suppresses glucagon secretion in a reciprocal fashion to its stimulation of insulin release; this is now thought to be a direct effect rather than mediated by insulin (Fig. 33.2) [6]. Conversely, hypoglycaemia is a potent stimulus to glucagon release. Free fatty acids and amino acids stimulate glucagon secretion [7], which would tend to prevent hypoglycaemia following food-induced release of insulin, whose secretion is stimulated by all three classes of nutrient. Of the circulating gut- and pancreas-derived peptides, glucagon release is stimulated by gastric inhibitory peptide, cholecystokinin and secretin, and is inhibited by insulin and somatostatin (perhaps acting through a local paracrine mechanism) and by GLP-1 7−36 amide (8−10). As these peptides are released in response to food, many interrelated factors may act to modulate changes in glucagon secretion after eating. Glucagon secretion is also stimulated by the other counter-regulatory hormones released during stress and hypoglycaemia — growth hormone, adrenaline and cortisol — and by β-endorphin [11−13].

The A cell is innervated by cholinergic, adrenergic and peptidergic components of the autonomic nervous system [14]. Stimulation of the sympathetic pancreatic nerves elicits glucagon release; combined α- and β-adrenergic blockade does not inhibit this response [15], suggesting that it may be mediated by neuropeptides co-stored in sympathetic endings (see Chapter 8) [14]. Vagal stimulation also causes glucagon secretion which is inhibited by atropine in some species but not in others, implying that receptors other than muscarinic cholinergic (perhaps VIP-ergic) may be involved [14, 16, 17].

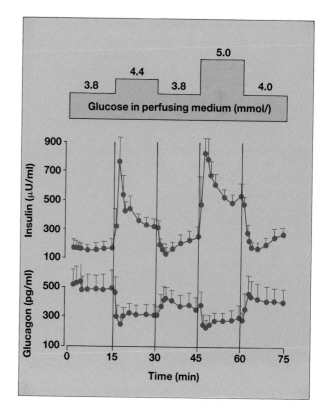

Fig. 33.2. Changes in release of insulin (upper panel) and glucagon (lower panel) from the isolated, perfused dog pancreas, showing reciprocal changes following alterations in the glucose concentration in the perfusion medium. Adapted from ref. 6.

The actions of glucagon

Glucagon is a major catabolic, counter-regulatory hormone which opposes the metabolic effects of insulin. Its actions are described in detail in Chapter 32. Glucagon acts primarily on the liver, where it affects the metabolism of all three types of nutrient (Fig. 33.3). Glycogen synthesis is inhibited and glycogenolysis stimulated [18]; the latter effect is short-lived as hepatic glycogen stores are rapidly depleted, which explains why repeated glucagon injections may finally fail to reverse hypoglycaemia. Increased glucose production is further enhanced because glucagon also inhibits glycolysis and stimulates gluconeogenesis which is fuelled by increased hepatic uptake of alanine and other amino acid gluconeogenic precursors [19]. The net result on carbohydrate metabolism is to increase glucose output from the liver. Glucagon also acts on the liver to inhibit fatty acid synthesis and triglyceride formation and to increase fatty acid oxidation, leading to ketone body formation [20].

The other major metabolic effect of glucagon is exerted on adipose tissue where, if insulin levels are deficient (as in IDDM), it stimulates lipolysis. Glucagon also directly stimulates insulin secretion from the B cell, which is the basis of its diagnostic use to elicit a maximal C peptide response.

Glucagonoma syndrome

This rare tumour of A cells [21], which illustrates many of the metabolic actions of glucagon, is described in Chapter 28.

Glucagon in diabetes

Because glucagon and insulin have mutually antagonistic actions, the relative proportions of the two hormones are thought to be an important determinant of the balance between anabolism and catabolism [7]. Indeed, glucagon excess has been suggested by Unger and others to be almost as significant as insulin deficiency in mediating the metabolic disturbance of diabetes — the so-called 'bihormonal abnormality' hypothesis [6, 22, 23]. There is no doubt that both IDDM and NIDDM, and particularly uncontrolled IDDM, are accompanied by glucagon excess which may be partly due to insulin deficiency and partly to failure of the diabetic A cell to be suppressed by hyperglycaemia [24]. NIDDM is also characterized by a marked increase in A-cell numbers in the islets [25, 26]. Patients with either IDDM or NIDDM have absolute or relative hyperglucagonaemia [22, 23, 27] which in NIDDM is related to hyperglycaemia and may contribute to this by increasing hepatic glucose output [27, 28]. Hyperglucagonaemia may be a cause of insulin resistance in diabetes as prolonged glucagon infusion significantly impairs glucose disposal [29].

On the other hand, several lines of evidence argue against the importance of glucagon excess in diabetes. Massive hyperglucagonaemia in the

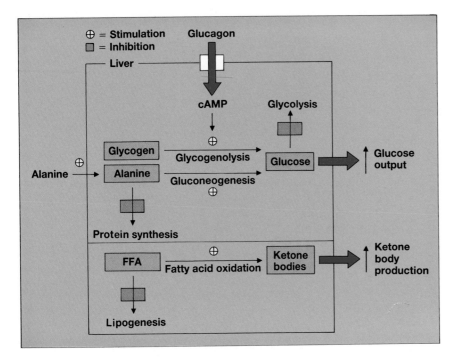

Fig. 33.3. Scheme of major metabolic actions of glucagon on the liver.

glucagonoma syndrome (Chapter 28) which may cause severe wasting and loss of muscle bulk is accompanied only by relatively mild, usually non-ketotic diabetes [21]. Moreover, total pancreatectomy produces truly insulin-dependent diabetes despite undetectable plasma glucagon levels [30]. The balance of evidence therefore suggests that hyperglucagonaemia is not essential in causing the metabolic disturbance of diabetes but is nonetheless an important contributory factor, particularly in NIDDM.

Somatostatin

Somatostatin (somatotrophin-release inhibiting factor, or SRIF) was first isolated from the sheep hypothalamus and named for its ability to inhibit growth hormone release from the pituitary [31]. It has many more actions than this name implies, including various effects on glucoregulation which are relevant to diabetes.

Source, synthesis and structure

SRIF is synthesized in specialized endocrine cells (D cells) of the pancreatic islets and gut (especially in the gastric fundus and antrum) and in specific neurones [32]. D cells carry long cytoplasmic processes along which SRIF is transported distally to bulbous terminations ending on other endocrine or exocrine cells, capillaries or the gut lumen (Fig. 33.4) [32, 33]. SRIF may be released to affect adjacent cells (a 'paracrine' action) or into capillaries, perhaps to exert an endocrine effect on distant target tissues. SRIF-immunoreactive neurones occur in the hypothalamus (especially the anterior and periventricular regions), hippocampus and cortex and in the peripheral nervous system [34].

The product of the somatostatin gene (Fig. 33.5) is preprosomatostatin, consisting of prosomatostatin carrying an N-terminal 'signal' sequence [35]. Prosomatostatin may be cleaved by alternate pathways into SRIF-14, which predominates in the pancreas and gut nerves, or its N-terminally extended form (SRIF-28) which is the major product in the gut mucosa and retina; both forms are found in the brain. Biological activity is conferred by four residues of the cyclic portion of SRIF-14.

Secretion of somatostatin

SRIF release is influenced by various nutrients, peptides and neurotransmitters acting through cAMP- or phosphokinase C-dependent mechanisms. SRIF release from pancreatic D cells is powerfully stimulated by glucose secretagogues such as glucose, free fatty acids and 3-hydroxybutyrate. Other secretagogues include amino acids, secretin, cholecystokinin, opioid peptides and acetylcholine [36–38]; SRIF apparently inhibits its own secretion [39]. Gastric SRIF secretion is stimulated by glucose, secretin

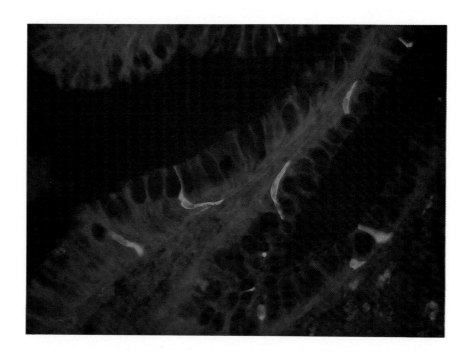

Fig. 33.4. D cells in the gut, showing cytoplasmic processes along which SRIF is actively transported to be released at their terminations.

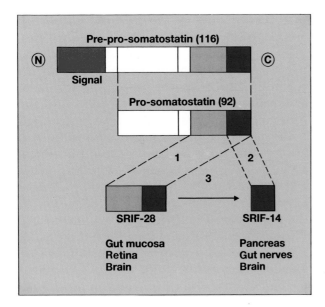

Fig. 33.5. Principal processing pathways of preprosomatostatin to yield SRIF-14 (pathway 1) and SRIF-28 (pathway 2). The 'signal' or 'leader' peptide at the N-terminus of preprosomatostatin may facilitate transport and processing of the nascent peptide. A convertase enzyme in certain tissues may cleave SRIF-14 from SRIF-28 (pathway 3). Numbers in parentheses refer to the numbers of amino acid residues in precursor peptides.

and cholecystokinin and also by gastrin and H^+ ions, and is inhibited by SRIF itself, insulin, acetylcholine and HCO_3^- ions.

Plasma SRIF apparently derives mainly from the stomach, as circulating levels fall after gastrectomy but are less affected by pancreatectomy [40]. SRIF release increases after eating a mixed meal (fat and protein are the main secretagogues), hypoglycaemia or exercise [41, 42].

Actions of somatostatin

SRIF has an extremely wide range of actions, mostly inhibitory, on endocrine, exocrine and other functions (Table 33.2). The principal actions relevant to diabetes are its inhibition of insulin secretion [43, 44] and of the counter-regulatory hormones, glucagon and growth hormone [44–46] (Fig. 33.6). It also suppresses the release of various gut peptides including gastrin and gastric inhibitory peptide [46], and impairs gastrointestinal absorption of glucose and other nutrients [44, 47]. SRIF also has various neuroendocrine effects and may influence food intake (see Chapter 23).

Table 33.2. Experimental actions of somatostatin.

Endocrine actions (inhibits secretion of the listed hormones and regulatory peptides)	**Pancreas:**	Insulin Glucagon Somatostatin Pancreatic polypeptide
	Pituitary:	Growth hormone TSH ACTH
	Gut:	Gastrin Gastric inhibitory peptide Enteroglucagon Cholecystokinin Secretin Motilin Vasoactive intestinal peptide
Exocrine actions (inhibits secretion)		Salivary glands Stomach: acid, pepsin, intrinsic factor Pancreas: bicarbonate, enzymes Colonic fluid
Other gastrointestinal actions		Reduces motility of stomach, intestine, gall bladder Reduces splanchnic blood flow Reduces intestinal nutrient absorption
Central nervous system actions		Inhibits (or stimulates) eating Inhibits centrally mediated hyperglycaemia Analgesia
Miscellaneous actions		Inhibits growth of some tumours Cytoprotection (gastric mucosa)

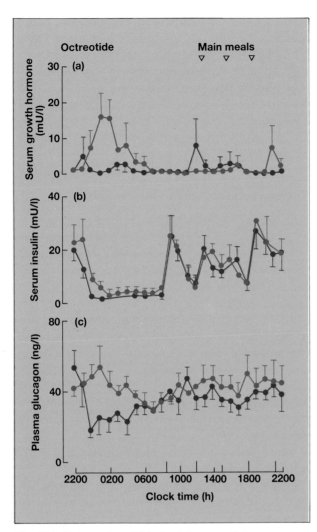

Fig. 33.6. Suppression of (a) circulating growth hormone, (b) insulin, and (c) glucagon levels in normal subjects after subcutaneous injection of a somatostatin analogue (octreotide) at 2200 hours. Values after octreotide injection are shown in blue and after control saline injection in red. Error bars are SEM. The prolonged action profile of this analogue is apparent. (Adapted from RR Davies *et al.*, *Clin Endocrinol* 1986; **24**: 665.)

Because of these various antidiabetic actions, selective analogues of SRIF could in theory find a place in the treatment of diabetes; so far, however, their therapeutic performance has been disappointing (see Chapter 104).

Somatostatin and diabetes

Diabetic animals and man show disturbances of SRIF in the pancreas, other tissues and circulation, which have fuelled speculation that SRIF abnormalities might contribute to the metabolic disorders of diabetes. Animal studies, for example, have shown that insulin-deficient diabetes in arti-ficially induced or spontaneous syndromes in rodents is accompanied by an increase in pancreatic and circulating (gut-derived) SRIF levels [48–52], together with defective pancreatic SRIF release: basal secretion is increased but glucose elicits no additional response [53]. *In vitro* release of SRIF from hypothalamic cells may also be abnormal [54]. It now seems likely that many of these alterations in somatostatin are secondary to insulin deficiency, and do not play an active role in causing the diabetic syndrome [52].

There is no evidence to implicate SRIF disturbances in the pathogenesis of human diabetes. In both IDDM and NIDDM, relative alterations in D-cell numbers are simply the consequence of B-cell fallout in IDDM and of A-cell hyperplasia in NIDDM [25, 26]. Circulating SRIF concentrations are increased both in IDDM – especially in keto-acidosis – and in NIDDM, presumably because SRIF release from the gut or pancreas is stimulated by absolute or relative insulin deficiency [55–57]. As in diabetic animals, the responsiveness of SRIF to normal secretagogues such as oral glucose or a mixed meal is impaired in human diabetes, both IDDM and NIDDM [55, 57]; in the latter, the elevated basal SRIF levels and the blunted response to oral glucose are normalized by a period of euglycaemia [57].

Somatostatinoma syndrome

A somatostatinoma syndrome, due to a D-cell tumour, has been described in a few cases. The features include weight loss, malabsorption, gallstones (due to the inhibitory effects of SRIF on gall-bladder emptying), hypochlorhydria and diabetes. These tumours tend to present late and large, and may metastasize to the liver [59]. Diabetes is normally mild, presumably because counter-regulatory hormones are suppressed as well as insulin, although ketosis may occur. In one case, hypoglycaemia was the presenting complaint [60], evidently because the antidiabetic effects of SRIF outweighed its inhibition of insulin release.

Pancreatic polypeptide

This straight-chain, 36-amino acid peptide appears to be almost entirely restricted to the PP(D₁) cells of the pancreas, as its circulating levels are undetectable after pancreatectomy [61, 62]. PP cells occur at the periphery of the islets of Langerhans and also between the acinar cells in the duct walls of the exocrine pancreas. Throughout most of the gland, PP cells are scattered sparsely in the islets but they dominate the islets in the 'PP-rich' dorsal part of the head of the pancreas [63]. PP is a major contaminant of insulin extracted from animal pancreases [64].

PP release is mainly under vagal control, which mediates the dramatic rise in plasma concentrations after a meal, especially if rich in protein, and during hypoglycaemia [65–67]. Other causes of increased circulating PP levels are shown in Table 33.3. PP secretion by gastroenteropancreatic tumours — for which it is useful marker — is autonomous and may be distinguished from most other causes by its failure to suppress after atropine administration [68].

Despite its marked postprandial rise, there is little evidence for an important physiological role of PP. Its suggested actions, based on infusion of supraphysiological quantities, include gall-bladder relaxation [69], inhibition of pancreatic exocrine secretion [69], and possibly a trophic effect on pancreatic exocrine tissue [70]. PP does not seem to affect either insulin or glucagon secretion. PP injected peripherally or centrally terminates feeding in rodents [71] and is a candidate 'anorectic' or 'satiety' factor (see Chapter 23).

Pancreatic polypeptide and diabetes

Pancreatic and circulating PP levels are increased in diabetic rodents and in the plasma of some diabetic patients [72, 73]. Prolonged PP infusion apparently improves glucose tolerance in dogs with surgically induced pancreatitis which is associated with reduced plasma PP concentrations [74]. The relevance of these observations is not clear but PP is unlikely to be important in the diabetic syndrome.

Table 33.3. Causes of increased pancreatic polypeptide levels in blood.

- Postprandial } Vagally mediated
- Hypoglycaemia }
- Acute pancreatitis } Pancreatic damage
- Ethanol abuse }
- Pancreatic endocrine tumours (gastrinoma, glucagonoma, VIPoma)
- Renal failure (reduced clearance)
- Miscellaneous — Acute diarrhoea
  — Bowel resection

In diabetic patients with autonomic neuropathy, PP responses to hypoglycaemia and eating are blunted, presumably because of vagal denervation of the pancreas [75–77]. A blunted PP rise after hypoglycaemia may be an early sign to identify IDDM patients who will later develop symptomatic autonomic neuropathy, including defective counter-regulation which may delay recovery from hypoglycaemia [77].

Incretins and the entero-insular axis

The plasma insulin response to a given rise in plasma glucose is much greater when glucose has been taken orally rather than injected intravenously [78]. A similar effect is found with amino acids [79]. The enhanced insulin levels after ingestion are attributed to the *entero-insular axis*, through which a postulated hormonal factor, now termed an 'incretin', is released into the bloodstream from the gut in response to food and stimulates insulin secretion [80]. It now seems likely that the greater plasma insulin levels are due to reduced hepatic extraction of insulin from the bloodstream as well as to increased release [81].

The relevance of the entero-insular axis to the physiological regulation of insulin secretion, and the ways in which abnormalities of this mechanism could contribute to diabetes, are unknown. However, the incretin response to oral glucose has been found to be diminished in NIDDM subjects [82].

The identity of the incretin(s) is also unknown. Several gut hormones are released into the bloodstream after a meal and some stimulate insulin secretion. The major peptides with these potential incretin properties are gastric inhibitory peptide, GLP-1 7–36 amide, cholecystokinin and secretin.

Gastric inhibitory polypeptide (GIP)

The N-terminal amino acid sequence of this 42-amino acid peptide, also named 'glucose-dependent insulinotropic polypeptide', bears considerable similarities to those of secretin, glucagon and GLP-1 7–36 [83]. GIP is found in mucosal endocrine cells of the upper small intestine [84]. Plasma GIP concentrations rise rapidly after a meal; glucose, fat and amino acids have all been shown to cause GIP release [10, 85, 86].

Some NIDDM patients show exaggerated GIP release during a high-calorie test meal but no correlation was observed between GIP concentrations and insulin release [82]. A similar increased response in obese subjects was reversed by food restriction [87]. Experimental infusions of GIP significantly increase insulin secretion in non-diabetic and NIDDM subjects [10, 88]. However, the insulinotropic properties of GIP seem to be less potent than those of GLP-1 7−36 amide, and GIP also enhances glucagon secretion (see Fig. 33.7) [10]. Moreover, GIP did not alter glucose clearance in NIDDM subjects despite its stimulation of insulin secretion [88]. Although long considered a likely incretin, the contribution of GIP to the entero-insular axis is still not convincing.

Glucagon-like peptide-1 7−36 amide

GLP-1 7−36 amide is 30 amino acid residues long and is a flanking peptide of glucagon (Fig. 33.1) [2]. Its highest concentrations are found in the terminal ileum but it is also present in other parts of the gut [10]. It is released into the circulation after a normal breakfast or oral glucose [10]. Infusion of GLP-1 7−36 amide into man at a dose which achieved the same plasma concentration as after an oral glucose load resulted in greater enhancement of insulin release and reduction of hyperglycaemia after intravenous glucose when compared with the effects of GIP or saline infusions (Fig. 33.7) [10]. Indeed, GLP-1 7−36 amide is the most potent insulin-releasing hormone of the gastrointestinal tract so far identified. It also suppresses glucagon levels in the fasting state (Fig. 33.7).

In patients with post-gastrectomy dumping syndrome, plasma GLP-1 7−36 amide concentrations are greatly increased, suggesting that it may mediate the hyperinsulinaemia and reactive hypoglycaemia of this disorder [10]. The possible role of GLP-1 7−36 amide in diabetes mellitus has still to be elucidated.

Cholecystokinin (CCK)

CCK occurs in multiple molecular forms but its biological activity resides in the last eight C-terminal amino acid residues [89]. CCK-8 is thought to circulate free in the plasma, where other forms (including 22-, 33-, 39- and 58-amino acid moieties) have also been characterized [90]. In the gut, the highest tissue concentrations of CCK are in the upper small intestine but it can

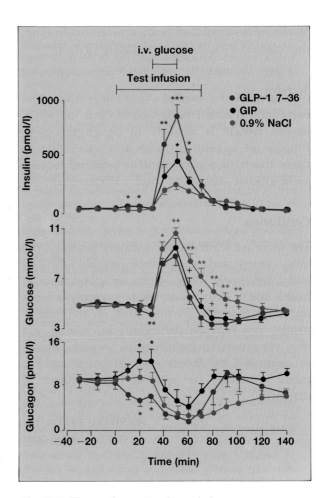

Fig. 33.7. Plasma glucose, insulin and glucagon concentrations and their responses to intravenous (i.v.) glucose administration, during infusion of GLP-1 7−36 amide, GIP or saline. Both peptides enhanced the insulin secretory response and the subsequent rate of glycaemic fall but the effects of GLP-1 7−36 amide were significantly greater than those of GIP. Adapted from [10].

also be detected in the ileum [91]; it is present in the mucosa and the muscle layer of the intestine. CCK is also widespread in the brain where it probably acts as neurotransmitter. CCK-8 and other larger forms are released into the circulation after eating [89, 90]. Meal-stimulated CCK release is greatly enhanced in NIDDM patients but the pathophysiological significance of this effect is unknown [92]. In addition to its well-known action in stimulating gall-bladder contraction, CCK may also function as a satiety factor in regulating food intake [71] (see Chapter 23).

Although postprandial rises in CCK are spectacular, evidence that it exerts a physiological insulinotropic effect is less convincing. In man, infusion of CCK to postprandial levels enhanced

endocrine tumours. *New Engl J Med* 1986; **315**: 287–91.

69 Greenberg GR, McCloy RF, Adrian TE, Chadwick VS, Baron JH, Bloom SR. Inhibition of pancreatic and gall bladder functions by pancreatic polypeptide in man. *Lancet* 1978; ii: 1280–3.

70 Greenberg GR, Mitznegg P, Bloom SR. Effect of pancreatic polypeptide on DNA synthesis in the pancreas. *Experientia* 1977; **33**: 1332–3.

71 Morley JE. Neuropeptide regulation of appetite and weight. *Endocrinol Rev* 1987; **8**: 256–287.

72 Gingerich RV, Gersell DJ, Greider MH, Finke EH, Lacy PE. Elevated levels of pancreatic polypeptide in obese hyperglycemic mice. *Metabolism* 1978; **27**: 1526–32.

73 Service FJ, Koch MB, Jay JM, Rizza RA, Go VLW. Pancreatic polypeptide: a marker for lean non-insulin dependent diabetes mellitus? *Diabetes Care* 1985; **8**: 349–53.

74 Sun YS, Brunicardi FC, Druck P, Walfisch S, Berlin SA, Chance RE, Gingerich RL, Elahi D, Andersen DK. Reversal of abnormal glucose metabolism in chronic pancreatitis by administration of pancreatic polypeptide. *Am J Surg* 1986; **151**: 130–9.

75 Lugari R, Gnudi A, Dall'Argine A. Diabetic autonomic neuropathy and impaired pancreatic polypeptide secretion in response to food. *J Clin Endocrinol Metab* 1987; **64**: 279–82.

76 Buysschaert M, Donckier J, Dive A, Ketelslegers J-M, Lambert AA. Gastric acid and pancreatic polypeptide responses to sham feeding are impaired in diabetic subjects with autonomic neuropathy. *Diabetes* 1985; **34**: 1181–5.

77 White NH, Gingerich RL, Levandoski LA, Cryer PE, Santiago JV. Plasma pancreatic polypeptide response to insulin induced hypoglycemia as a marker for defective glucose counter-regulation in insulin-dependent diabetes mellitus. *Diabetes* 1985; **34**: 870–5.

78 Perley MJ, Kipnis DM. Plasma insulin responses to oral and intravenous glucose: studies in normal and diabetic subjects. *J Clin Invest* 1967; **46**: 1954–62.

79 Raptis S, Dollinger HC, Schroder KE *et al.* Differences in insulin, growth hormone and pancreatic enzyme secretion after intravenous and intraduodenal administration of mixed amino acids in man. *N Engl J Med* 1973; **288**: 1199–202.

80 Zunz E, La Barre J. Contributions a l'étude des variations physiologiques de la sécrétion interne du pancréas. *Arch Int Physiol Biochem* 1929; **31**: 22–44.

81 Shapiro T, Tilil H, Miller AM *et al.* Insulin secretion and clearance. *Diabetes* 1987; **36**: 1365–71.

82 Creutzfeld W, Ebert R, Nauck M, Stockmann F. Disturb-ances of the entero-insular axis. *Scand J Gastroenterol* 1983; **18** (Suppl 82): 111–19.

83 Schmidt M, Siegel EG, Creutzfeldt W. Glucagon-like peptide-1 but not glucagon-like peptide-2 stimulates insulin release from isolated rat pancreatic islets. *Diabetologia* 1985; **28**: 704–7.

84 Krarup T, Holst JJ. The heterogeneity of gastric inhibitory polypeptide in porcine and human gastrointestinal mucosa evaluated with five different antisera. *Regul Pept* 1984; **9**: 35–46.

85 Falko J, Crockett S, Cataland S, Mazzaferri E. Gastric inhibitory polypeptide (GIP) stimulated by fat ingestion in man. *J Clin Endocrinol Metab* 1975; **41**: 260–5.

86 Thomas F, Mazzaferri E, Crockett S *et al.* Stimulation of secretion of gastric inhibitory polypeptide and insulin by intraduodenal amino acid perfusion. *Gastroenterology* 1976; **70**: 523–7.

87 Willms B, Ebert W, Creutzfeldt W. Gastric inhibitory polypeptide (GIP) and insulin in obesity: II. Reversal of increased response to stimulation by starvation or food restriction. *Diabetologia* 1978; **14**: 379–87.

88 Jones IR, Owens DR, Moody AJ *et al.* The effects of glucose-dependent insulinotropic polypeptide infused at physiological concentrations in normal subjects and type 2 (non-insulin-dependent) diabetic patients on glucose tolerance and B-cell secretion. *Diabetologia* 1987; **30**: 707–12.

89 Jorpes JE, Mutt V. Secretin, cholecystokinin (CCK). In: Jorpes JE, Mutt V, eds. *Secretin, Cholecystokinin, Pancreozymin, and Gastrin*. Berlin: Springer-Verlag, 1976: 1–144.

90 Eberlein GA, Eysselein VE, Hesse WH *et al.* Detection of cholecystokinin-58 in human blood by inhibition of degradation. *Am J Physiol* 1987; **253**; G: 477–82.

91 Rehfeld JF. Immunochemical studies on cholecystokinin. Distribution and molecular heterogeneity in the central nervous system and small intestine of man and dog. *J Biol Chem* 1978; **253**: 4122–30.

92 Nakano I, Funakoshi A, Shinozki H *et al.* High plasma cholecystokinin response following ingestion of test meal by patients with non insulin-dependent diabetes mellitus. *Regul Pept* 1986; **14**: 229–36.

93 Rushakoff RJ, Goldfine ID, Carter JD, Liddle RA. Physiological concentrations of cholecystokinin stimulate amino acid-induced insulin release in humans. *J Clin Endocrinol Metab* 1987; **65**: 395–401.

94 Fahrenkrug J, Schaffalitzky de Muckadell O, Kühl C. Effect of secretin on basal and glucose-stimulated insulin secretion in man. *Diabetologia* 1978; **14**: 229–34.

34   The Concept and Measurement of 'Control'

Summary

- The presence or absence of glycosuria may be highly misleading even in diabetic patients with a normal threshold for glucose reabsorption, and urinary glucose measurements do not warn of hypoglycaemia. Testing for glycosuria is therefore a very unsatisfactory means of assessing glycaemic control.

- Single blood glucose measurements are a poor guide to overall glycaemic control in IDDM patients, but fasting or postprandial levels correlate significantly with HbA_1 levels in NIDDM and may therefore be used to monitor control in these patients.

- The lability of glycaemic control, i.e. the degree of variation about the mean, is not necessarily related to the average blood glucose concentration or to HbA_1. Indices of lability include the *M value* (mathematically weighted to emphasize hypoglycaemia), the *mean amplitude of glycaemic excursion* (MAGE — a measure of major glycaemic swings) and the *mean of daily differences* (MODD).

- Glycated (or glycosylated) haemoglobin (HbA_1) comprises a series of minor haemoglobin components (HbA_{1a}, HbA_{1b} and HbA_{1c}) formed by the non-enzymatic adduction of glucose and glucose-derived products to normal adult haemoglobin (HbA_o).

- The level of HbA_1 (expressed as a percentage of total HbA) reflects the integrated glycaemic level and therefore the mean blood glucose concentration over the preceding 6−8 weeks (i.e. the half-life of the red cell).

- HbA_1 can be measured by several methods; affinity chromatography is widely used and is not affected by the presence of the labile component of HbA_1 (which is unrelated to long-term glycaemic levels) or by haemoglobinopathy.

- Target ranges for HbA_1 depend on the assay and the laboratory; the non-diabetic range is usually about 5−9%. Nearly normal HbA_1 values are more easily obtained in NIDDM or C-peptide-positive IDDM patients early in the course of their disease.

- HbA_1 values may be spuriously lowered by reduced red cell survival (e.g. bleeding or haemolysis) and by slowly migrating haemoglobins (HbS and/or HbC), and falsely raised by rapidly migrating haemoglobins (HbF, or the carbamylated HbA occurring in uraemia).

- Glycated serum proteins (notably albumin, measured by the 'fructosamine' reaction) turn over more rapidly than haemoglobin and provide a measure of short-term (7−14 days) integrated glycaemic control.

- Fructosamine assays are cheap and simple to perform but levels fluctuate widely in diabetic patients due to variations in serum protein concentrations and are also affected by uraemia and other conditions. Fructosamine measurements are not a substitute for the more expensive HbA_1 estimations and their place in routine diabetic management remains controversial.

The verb 'to control' (derived from medieval Latin *contrarotulus*, a check-list) is defined as 'to exercise restraining or directing influence over, to regulate or curb' [1]. Although opinions may differ over the finer points of what constitutes tight control [2], few would disagree that the pursuit of blood glucose control in the diabetic patient seeks to emulate both the pattern and the level of glycaemia in the non-diabetic individual.

Measurements of glucose control were first devised several decades ago to determine the effectiveness of newly developed modified insulin preparations [3–9]. Many of these techniques relied on periodic blood glucose measurements or determinations of urinary glucose excretion, and are adequate for the symptomatic management of diabetes. However, the suggestion that the chronic complications of the disease are in some way related to the quality of 'control', and the development in recent years of new approaches to insulin delivery which can practically achieve near-normoglycaemia, have made the precise measurement of glycaemic control a scientific and clinical priority. It is not known whether diabetic tissue damage results from a chronically elevated blood glucose concentration, or glycaemic fluctuations, or both. It is therefore essential to be able to quantify both the following factors reliably and practicably, as they do not necessarily go hand in hand: (1) overall glycaemic control, i.e. the average degree of glycaemia over a period of time; and (2) lability of control, i.e. the degree to which the blood glucose level fluctuates about the mean.

The approach to measuring glucose control may necessarily vary between clinical and research settings, between the in-patient and the out-patient clinic, and conceivably also between patients with IDDM and NIDDM.

Glycosuria

The traditional semi-quantitative tests of urine glucose concentration in second-void urine specimens, although cheap and commonly performed, are at best crude reflections of prevailing blood glucose and in some instances may be misleading [10–12]. Glycosuria is the net result of two distinct processes, glomerular filtration and tubular reabsorption of glucose, both of which may differ among patients [13]. The renal threshold for glucose varies more widely in diabetic patients than is generally recognized. A negative urine test, even when performed on a double-void specimen may be found with a blood glucose level between 2 and 22 mmol/l, and a 2% result may occur with normoglycaemia [14, 15]. Negative urine tests do not warn the 'well-controlled' patient of impending hypoglycaemia, a complication which patients may fear most. As a result, many patients feel safer when they have some glucose in their urine, to the detriment of good control [16]. Urine tests may be highly misleading even in those patients

with a normal renal threshold and the fact that they do not make sense may seriously demoralize the patient (and the physician) and jeopardize compliance [16] (see Chapter 95). Percentage scores derived from testing four urine samples per day and quantitative estimation of mean 24-h urinary glucose excretion are beyond the scope of routine out-patient monitoring [17, 19].

Overall, urine testing is a poor tool with which to assess long-term control, or upon which to base anything more than the most rudimentary management decisions.

Single blood glucose measurement

Single or random blood glucose estimations are performed in most diabetic clinics, but are difficult to interpret because the conditions and timing of the samples are not standardized [20].

In IDDM, isolated glucose readings yield little information about overall control [21] because they tend to be performed at the same time of day and may not be representative of blood glucose levels at other times of the day. Random blood glucose levels in IDDM bear little relationship to HbA_1 concentrations (see below), but the average of random glucose readings, is significantly but weakly correlated with HbA_1 [22, 23], as illustrated by Fig. 34.1.

In NIDDM the situation is rather different, in that 24-h glycaemic profiles exhibit a similar pattern to those in non-diabetic individuals, albeit at a higher level and with wider postprandial excursions [24] (Fig. 34.2). This is presumably because NIDDM patients retain a greater capacity to secrete insulin than in IDDM. As a result, a single blood glucose estimation — either fasting or postprandial — may be expected to give a reasonable reflection of overall glycaemic control in NIDDM [23–5] (see Fig. 34.3). Theoretically, fasting plasma glucose measurements could be spuriously lowered into the 'good control' range by patients dieting just before a clinic visit. However, the excellent correlation between fasting plasma glucose and HbA_1 levels obtained over a wide range of glycaemia [23] suggests that such attempted deception is relatively rare.

Indices of glycaemic lability

Mean blood glucose provides no information about the glycaemic lability which is an inevitable consequence of insulin injection and eating. Frequent

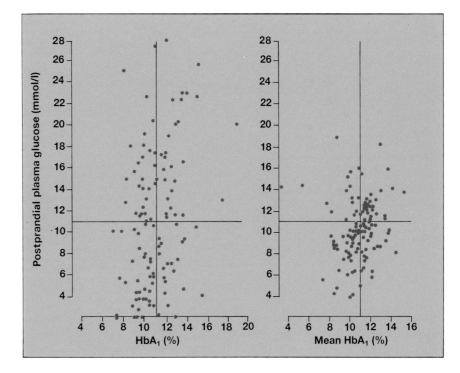

Fig. 34.1. Postprandial plasma glucose (PPG) versus HbA₁ in 114 patients with IDDM. Left, values for each patient at most recent out-patient review, $r=0.24$; right, mean values for each patient over previous 5 years, $r=0.26$. Defining poor control arbitrarily as $HbA_1 > 11.0$ mmol/l, only 58% of the patents had concordant HbA_1 and postprandial blood glucose values. Single blood glucose estimations are therefore a poor index of glycaemic control in IDDM. (Reproduced from McCance *et al.* 1988 [23], with kind permission of the American Diabetes Association.)

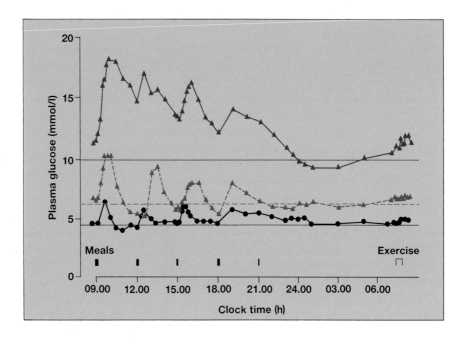

Fig. 34.2. Mean 24-h plasma glucose profiles for eight normal subjects, five mildly and six moderately hyperglycaemic normal-weight NIDDM patients. The overnight glucose concentration (mean 1, 3, 5 and 7 h values) for each mean profile is shown as a horizontal line. ●———●, normal subjects; ▲--------▲, NIDDM patients, basal glucose <8 mmol/l; ▲———▲, NIDDM subjects, basal glucose >8 mmol/l. (Reproduced from Holman & Turner 1981 [25], with permission of the publishers.)

episodes of hypoglycaemia or ketoacidosis are obviously evidence of excessive glycaemic lability but do not indicate blood glucose behaviour during the long asymptomatic periods.

The *M value* of Schlichtkrull [7] as modified by Mirouze is a quantitative index of the deviations of several blood glucose determinations (during a 24-h period) from an arbitrarily selected mean standard [26]. The mathematical formula

$$M = \sum |10 \log_{10} \frac{BG}{\text{ref.}}|^3 \div n,$$

where BG = blood glucose value; ref. = reference glucose value (e.g. 5 mmol/l); n = number of

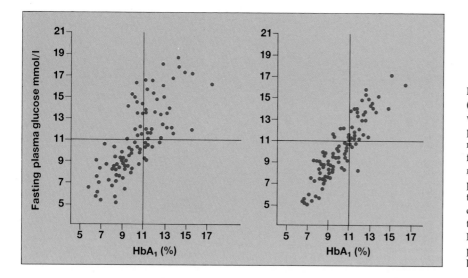

Fig. 34.3. Fasting plasma glucose (FPG) versus HbA$_1$ in 96 patients with NIDDM. Left, values for each patient at most recent out-patient review, $r=0.68$; right, mean values for each patient over 5 years, $r=0.86$. Single fasting (or post-prandial) blood glucose estimations therefore reflect overall glycaemic control more accurately in NIDDM than in IDDM. (Reproduced from McCance *et al.* 1988 [23], with kind permission of the American Diabetes Association.)

samples, is weighted mathematically to give proportionately greater emphasis to hypoglycaemia than to hyperglycaemia and the reference value may be altered accordingly [24, 27, 28]. The M value is therefore a single numerical expression, which describes a combination of general glycaemic control and stability.

A measure of within-day glycaemic instability is the *mean amplitude of glycaemic excursions (MAGE)* [28]. This was proposed in an effort to improve the measurement of glucose swings by taking account of major excursions and excluding minor ones. Only swings whose amplitude exceeds 1 standard deviation of the mean glycaemic values obtained during the study period are included in the calculation, a criterion selected because only meal-related glucose swings in non-diabetic subjects exceed this limit. Unlike the M value, MAGE is independent of mean glycaemia [12]. An 80-min post-breakfast value is reported to correlate with MAGE, as is that calculated from a limited number of carefully timed plasma glucose estimations on successive days [1, 29].

The *mean of daily differences (MODD)* is calculated by comparing plasma glucose values obtained at the same time on two successive days, using the formula:

$$MODD = (PG_{1a} - PG_{2a})/n,$$

where PG_{1a} and PG_{2a} are paired plasma glucose values and n is the number of such paired observations [27]. More recently, attention has been drawn to the influence of meal size on postprandial glycaemic behaviour: *MIME* [1, 27, 30, 31] is the *mean indices of meal excursion. FAGE (fasting as-*

cending glycaemic excursion) describes the difference between the prebreakfast plasma glucose concentration and the nocturnal nadir occurring between midnight and 06.00, and is a putative measure of the 'dawn phenomenon' [32] (see Chapter 51).

These measures of glycaemic variability are probably best suited to reducing detailed data to a few more manageable numbers, particularly in research applications. Simple inspection of home blood glucose records (see Chapter 39) is probably more useful in the routine management of individual patients.

Glycated (glycosylated) haemoglobin

The generic term 'glycated' is now preferred by many to 'glycosylated', and refers to a series of minor haemoglobin components formed by the adduction of glucose, or glucose-derived products, to normal adult haemoglobin (HbA$_o$). These minor components — HbA$_{1a}$, HbA$_{1b}$ and HbA$_{1c}$, collectively referred to as HbA$_{1(a+b+c)}$ or HbA$_1$ — were first isolated by cation-exchange chromatography in 1958 [33]. The differences in ionic charge between these minor components and unmodified HbA$_o$ are due to the adduction of a glucose molecule to the N-terminal valine residue of the B chain via an aldimine linkage, which then undergoes an Amadori rearrangement to form a more stable, indeed virtually irreversible, ketoamine product (Fig. 34.4) [34, 35]. Several studies during the 1960s showed that these fractions were considerably increased in diabetic patients, and in 1975, Flückiger and Winterhalter were able to synthesize HbA$_{1c}$

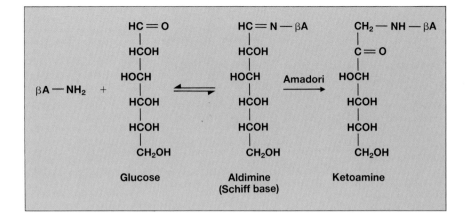

Fig. 34.4. Schematic representation of the adduction of glucose to the N-terminal valine of the B chain of HbA to form HbA$_{1c}$.

by incubating whole blood or purified haemoglobin with glucose at 37°C [36].

It was therefore suggested that in diabetes the level of glycated haemoglobin (either HbA$_{1c}$ or HbA$_1$) would reflect the integrated blood glucose concentration over a period approximating to the half-life of the red blood cell, i.e. 6–8 weeks. Convincing confirmatory evidence was provided by Koenig *et al.* who demonstrated a significant decrease in glycated haemoglobin levels approximately 4 weeks after improving glycaemic control in five poorly controlled patients [37] (Fig. 34.5). Numerous workers have subsequently confirmed that glycated haemoglobin measurement provides an objective and retrospective index of integrated glycaemia. There was temporary concern that the presence of a labile component (corresponding to the unstable aldimine Schiff base) might invalidate the measurement as an index of *long-term* integrated glycaemia [38], but this labile fraction does not interfere in some assays (such as weak acid hydrolysis and affinity chromatography) and is easily eliminated from other commonly used methods such as ion-exchange chromatography and agar-gel electrophoresis [39].

The role of glycated haemoglobin measurement in the routine out-patient management of diabetes is now firmly established. As mentioned earlier, measurement of fasting or postprandial blood glucose may be satisfactory in NIDDM; glycated haemoglobin measurement, which is more costly in both reagents and labour, need only be performed once or twice per year in NIDDM patients. In IDDM or insulin-treated patients, however, glycated haemoglobin should probably be measured every 2–3 months, and is likely to provide more useful information than fasting or postprandial blood glucose measurements [40–2].

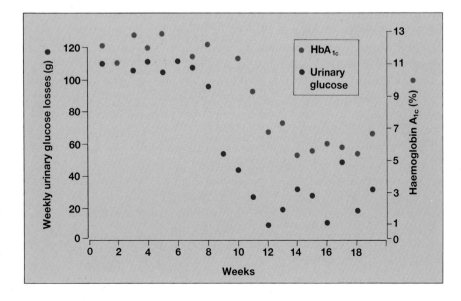

Fig. 34.5. Response of HbA$_{1c}$ and urinary glucose in a diabetic patient when glycaemic control was improved from week 7 onwards. (Reproduced from Koenig *et al.* 1976 [37], with kind permission of the *New England Journal of Medicine.*)

Table 34.1. Factors affecting glycated haemoglobin assays.

Spuriously low HbA$_1$	Spuriously high HbA$_1$
Reduced red-cell survival (blood loss, haemolysis)	Carbamylated HbA$_o$ (in uraemia)
Haemoglobinopathy: HbS and/or HbC	Haemoglobinopathy (HbF)

Note: affinity chromatography is not affected by abnormal haemoglobins.

Persistence of endogenous insulin secretion, which may remain for a variable period of time after the clinical onset of IDDM, would be expected to improve glycaemic control (see Chapter 36) and lower levels of glycated haemoglobin are more easily achieved in the first few years of IDDM than later. Some studies have demonstrated a correlation between detectable levels of C peptide and the maintenance of near-normal glycated haemoglobin levels [43, 44]. However, even C-peptide-negative patients show a tendency for glycated haemoglobin levels to rise with increasing duration of diabetes, suggesting that other factors, perhaps including dietary and drug compliance, emotional and physical stress and the degree of physical activity, may be of importance.

Effect of other medical conditions on glycated haemoglobin assay (Table 34.1)

Both acute and chronic blood loss will decrease red-cell survival, and therefore tend to lower glycated haemoglobin levels [45, 46]. Results must therefore be interpreted with caution in patients with iron-deficiency anaemia or a recent history of haematemesis or melaena. In the rare diabetic patients with haemochromatosis, glycated haemoglobin measurements are invalidated by therapeutic venesection. Erythrocyte life-span is also decreased considerably in haemolytic anaemias, resulting in much lower than normal glycated haemoglobin levels [47].

Haemoglobin F, which is increased in β-thalassaemia or may persist in adults as a familial trait, coelutes with HbA$_1$ in separation methods dependent on haemoglobin charge, and will give rise to misleadingly high results in both diabetic and non-diabetic subjects. Conversely, the presence of HbS or HbC leads to underestimation of HbA$_1$ because they coelute with HbA$_o$ [48]. In populations with a known high prevalence of haemoglobinopathy, an assay which is free from interference from haemoglobin variants (e.g. affinity chromatography) should be employed.

In uraemic patients, glycated haemoglobin levels may be influenced in various ways. Glucose tolerance itself may be impaired in uraemia, tending to raise levels of glycated haemoglobin. Cyanate derived from urea leads to carbamylation of haemoglobin (a process analagous to glycation), and carbamylation of the N-terminal valine residue of the B chain causes an increase in HbA$_{1(a+b)}$, and hence the HbA$_1$ peak [49], although this interference is relatively unimportant when serum urea levels are less than 30 mmol/l [50]. Chronic renal failure may also be associated with increased haemolysis, gastrointestinal blood loss and decreased erythropoiesis, all of which may affect glycated haemoglobin levels as described above.

Assay methods for glycated haemoglobin

Any laboratory measurement should be accurate, reproducible and easily standardized, and especially in clinical practice, ideally rapid and relatively inexpensive. The most commonly used methods fall into two broad groups — those which depend on charge to separate HbA$_1$ or HbA$_{1c}$ from HbA$_o$, and those which depend on some other property of the glycated product and measure 'total' glycated haemoglobin.

Ion-exchange chromatography is the prototype charge separation method. Mini-column systems, which measure HbA$_1$, have now largely replaced the original macro-column technique [51, 52]. As well as being sensitive to small changes in pH, the separation is influenced by the temperature of the column, which must therefore be kept constant between assays [53]. In most assays, the range of HbA$_1$ in non-diabetic subjects is approximately 5–9%, with levels in poorly controlled diabetic patients ranging up to approximately 20%. The coefficient of variation is approximately 2–3% for same-day estimations, while interassay variation is 4–5%.

High-performance liquid chromatography, with the use of finely divided resins and high flow pressures, permits faster and more precise separation of HbA$_{1c}$ or HbA$_1$, but is expensive to establish.

Agar-gel electrophoresis is now widely used to separate HbA$_1$ [54, 55]. The gel is cast on to flexible polyester films and fixed by drying after electrophoresis, when the HbA$_1$ fraction can be quantified by scanning densitometry. Reported intra-assay variation is 2−7% and inter-assay variation 3−7% [40, 53−5].

In the technique of isoelectric focusing, haemolysate is applied to a thin layer of polyacrylamide gel containing ampholyte [56, 57] and the various haemoglobin components (which migrate to their isoelectric points when a voltage is applied) are quantified by high-resolution microdensitometry. This technique is quite expensive to set up and maintain.

Of the methods which rely on some other property of the glycoadduct, affinity chromatography is now the most widely used. The theoretical basis for this assay lies in the known affinity of boronic acid for *cis*-diol groups. Aminophenol boronate immobilized on cross-linked agarose provides a suitable matrix for the affinity chromatography columns [58, 59]. Glycated haemoglobin adsorbs to the affinity gel, while non-glycated haemoglobin passes through the system. The adsorbed fraction is then removed by elution with high concentrations of a competing ligand and the percentage of total glycated haemoglobin is calculated. Perhaps because this method detects haemoglobin glycated at sites other than the N-terminal valine, results are slightly higher than percentage HbA$_1$ [53]. The method is precise, with the interassay coefficient of variation for replicate samples being reported as 2−2.6% [53, 60]. There is no interference from variant haemoglobins, but the method is sensitive to temperature change and labile HbA$_1$ should probably be removed before measurement.

Weak acid hydrolysis of glycated haemoglobin releases 5-hydroxymethylfurfural, which can be measured colorimetrically after reaction with thiobarbituric acid [36, 61]. Although cheap and previously popular, this is a cumbersome method which has gone out of fashion. A number of other methods can detect and quantify glycoadducts, but are unsuitable for routine use. These include fluorometric detection of formaldehyde released by periodate oxidation [62], acid hydrolysis to form furosine [63], and amino-acid hydrolysis [64].

Reasonable goals

The variety of glycated haemoglobin assays available means that different laboratories will continue to report their own normal and diabetic ranges [65]. Specific recommendations will therefore be modified according to the local assay characteristics.

Most patients quickly grasp the concept of non-enzymatic glycation, and their interest in glycated haemoglobin levels can be a useful motivating force towards achieving better self-care [66]. The ideal of achieving normal glycated haemoglobin levels (in our laboratory, <7.6%) is certainly possible early in the course of IDDM, particularly if remission occurs, but potentially at the cost of increasingly frequent or severe hypoglycaemia [66]. This is particularly true when endogenous insulin secretion is exhausted. We aim to achieve levels of <8.5% for about the first 2 years of IDDM and <9% for up to 5 years' duration. After that, few patients will have endogenous insulin secretion and 10% seems a more realistic upper limit. Maintaining the HbA$_1$ constantly below 10% in the long term can be quite difficult in some long-standing IDDM patients and, particularly if long-term complications have already developed, it may be easy for the physician (and unfortunately also the patient) to tolerate higher levels of HbA$_1$. With few exceptions, however, we regard levels of greater than 12% as an indication that management needs to be improved.

Many NIDDM patients can maintain HbA$_1$ levels of less than 10% through simple dietary therapy, although few achieve completely normal levels. As with IDDM patients, we feel that an HbA$_1$ level >12% suggests the need for some therapeutic adjustment.

A problem arises when there is a large discrepancy between other measures of glycaemic control (including the patient's self-monitored results) and the glycated haemoglobin result. Provided that assay errors and the confounding medical conditions mentioned above have been ruled out, the glycated haemoglobin usually proves to be the more valid index.

Glycated albumin and serum proteins

Like haemoglobin, albumin and other serum proteins have amino-acid residues susceptible to glycation. It has been shown that *in vivo* glycation of albumin accounts for approximately 90% of total serum protein glycation [67]. Because of the shorter half-lives of serum proteins in comparison to haemoglobin, measurement of glycated albumin or glycated serum proteins reflects integrated glycaemia over a much shorter time period, approximately 7−14 days [67, 68] (Fig. 34.6). This offers the theoretical advantage of being able to detect significant changes in overall glycaemia in

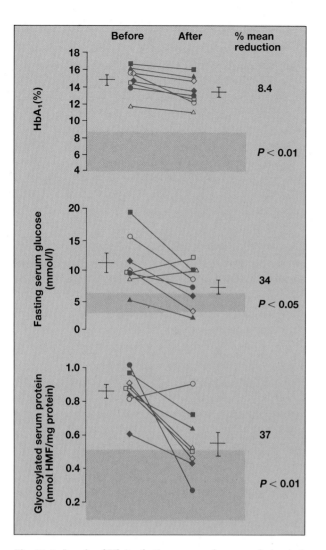

Fig. 34.6. Levels of HbA₁, fasting serum glucose and glycated serum protein in eight diabetic patients before and after a week of intensive therapy. Shaded areas represent normal ranges. Mean ± SEM represented by bars. (Reproduced from Kennedy *et al.* 1981 [68], with kind permission of *Diabetologia*.)

containing nitroblue tetrazolium, which is reduced to its formasan form in proportion to the concentration of glycated proteins in the serum. This surprisingly simple assay is easily automated, rapid, cheap and highly reproducible, with a between-assay coefficient of variation of around 2–3% [70, 71].

However, there is concern about the specificity of the fructosamine assay. Mean glycated haemoglobin or glycated serum albumin levels are generally 2–2.5 times higher in diabetic subjects than in non-diabetic subjects, whereas with fructosamine the diabetic level is only approximately 1.5 times greater, suggesting that factors other than glycated protein also contribute to the reaction. Another problem is short-term fluctuations in serum protein levels in diabetic patients, which can lead to variations in the measured serum fructosamine of as much 10–12% in an individual patient in a matter of hours. This undermines the value of fructosamine assays as a measure of average glycaemia, unless correction is made for protein levels [72, 73]. Fructosamine levels are also abnormal in uraemic patients and in a variety of pathological conditions in which serum protein disturbances occur [74].

We would argue against the notion that measurement of glycated serum protein by the fructosamine assay may be an adequate clinical substitute for the more expensive assay of glycated haemoglobin [75]. The two assays yield different information, and the observation in some prospective studies that changes in glycated serum proteins tend to follow very closely short-term changes in plasma glucose levels suggests that glycated protein assays may be superfluous [76].

DAVID R. MCCANCE

LAURENCE KENNEDY

response to some therapeutic manoeuvre earlier than would be possible with glycated haemoglobin. This has led to the suggestion that glycated albumin or serum protein measurements may be particularly useful in the management of diabetic pregnancy.

Glycated albumin or serum proteins may be measured by affinity chromatography, as described above. This gives reproducible results with between-assay coefficients of variation of approximately 4–6% [69]. A different method, known as the fructosamine assay, uses the ability of keto-amines to act as reducing agents in alkaline solution [70]. Serum is added to carbonate buffer

References

1 Service FJ, O'Brien PC, Rizza RA. Measurements of glucose control. *Diabetes Care* 1987; **10**: 225–37.
2 Service FJ. What is 'tight control' of diabetes? Goals, limitations and evaluation of therapy. *Mayo Clin Proc* 1986; **61**: 792–5.
3 Izzo JL, Crump SL. A clinical comparison of modified insulins. *J Clin Invest* 1950; **29**: 1514–27.
4 Hallas-Møller K, Jersild M, Peterson K, Schlichtkrull J. The centre insulins: insulin–zinc suspensions. *Dan Med Bull* 1954; **1**: 132–42.
5 Gurling KJ, Robertson JA, Whittaker H, Oakley W, Lawrence RD. Treatment of diabetes mellitus with insulin zinc suspension: a clinical study based on 479 cases. *Br Med J* 1955; **1**: 71–4.

6 Jersild M. Insulin zinc suspension: four year's experience. *Lancet* 1956; ii: 1009–13.

7 Schlichtkrull J, Munch O, Jersild M. The M-value, an index of blood sugar control in diabetics. *Acta Med Scand* 1965; **177**: 95–102.

8 Molnar GD, Gastineau CF, Rosevear JW, Moxness KE. Quantitative aspects of labile diabetes. *Diabetes* 1965; **14**: 279–88.

9 Hedner LP, Norden A. Analysis of variance applied to blood glucose values for assessing insulin preparations and state of lability in diabetes. *Diabetologia* 1969; **5**: 108–15.

10 Danowski TS, Ohlsen P, Fisher FR *et al.* Parameters of good control in diabetes mellitus. *Diabetes Care* 1980; **3**: 88–93.

11 Ohlsen P, Danowski TS, Rosenblum DH, Mreiden T, Fisher ER, Sunder JH. Discrepancies between glycosuria and home estimates of blood glucose in insulin-treated diabetes mellitus. *Diabetes Care* 1980; **3**: 178–83.

12 Service FJ, Molnar GD, Taylor WF. Urine glucose analyses during continuous blood glucose monitoring. *J Am Med Assoc* 1972; **222**: 294–8.

13 Walford S, Page MM, Allison SP. The influence of renal threshold on the interpretation of urine tests for glucose in diabetic patients. *Diabetes Care* 1980; **6**: 72–4.

14 Malone JI, Rosenbloom AL, Grgic A, Weber FT. The role of urine sugar in diabetic management. *Am J Dis Child* 1976; **130**: 1324–7.

15 Scobie IN, Sönksen PH. Methods of achieving better diabetic control. In: Nattrass M, Santiago JV, eds. *Recent Advances in Diabetes*. Edinburgh: Churchill Livingstone, 1984: 107.

16 Tattersall R, Walford S, Peacock I, Gale E, Allison S. A critical evaluation of methods of monitoring diabetic control. *Diabetes Care* 1980; **3**: 150–4.

17 Blanc MH, Barnett DM, Gleason RE *et al.* Hemoglobin A$_{1c}$ compared with three conventional measures of diabetes control. *Diabetes Care* 1981; **4**: 349–53.

18 Gabbay KH, Hasty K, Brteslow JL *et al.* Glycosylated hemoglobins and long term blood glucose control in diabetes mellitus. *J Clin Endocrinol Metab* 1977; **44**: 859–64.

19 Hayford JT, Weydert JA, Thompson RG. Validity of urine glucose measurements for estimating plasma glucose concentration. *Diabetes Care* 1983; **6**: 40–4.

20 Molnar GD. Clinical evaluation of metabolic control in diabetes. *Diabetes* 1978; 27(suppl 1): 216–25.

21 Gonen B, Rochman H, Rubenstein AH. Metabolic control in diabetic patients: assessment by haemoglobin A$_1$ values. *Metabolism* 1979; **28**: 448–52.

22 Tchobroutsky G, Charitanski D, Blouquit Y *et al.* Diabetic control in 102 insulin treated patients. *Diabetologia* 1980; **18**: 447–52.

23 McCance DR, Ritchie CM, Kennedy L. Is HbA$_1$ measurement superfluous in NIDDM? *Diabetes Care* 1988; **11**: 512–14.

24 Holman RR, Turner RC. Maintenance of basal plasma glucose and insulin concentrations in maturity onset diabetes. *Diabetes* 1979; **28**: 227–30.

25 Holman RR, Turner RC. The basal plasma glucose: a simple relevant index of maturity onset diabetes. *Clin Endocrinol* 1981; **14**: 279–86.

26 Mirouze J, Satingher A, Sany C, Jaffiol C. Coéfficient d'efficacité insulinique: coéfficient M de Schlichtkrull carriagé et simplifié par la technique de l'enregistrement glycémique continu. *Diabetes* 1963; **11**: 267–73.

27 Service FJ, Nelson RL. Characteristics of glycemic stability. *Diabetes Care* 1980; **3**: 58–62.

28 Service FJ, Molnar GD, Rosevear JW, Ackerman E, Gatewood LC, Taylor WF. Mean amplitude of glycaemic excursions, a measure of diabetic instability. *Diabetes* 1970; **19**: 644–55.

29 Molnar GD, Taylor WF, Langworthy A. On measuring the adequacy of diabetes regulation: comparison of continuously monitored blood glucose patterns with values at selected time points. *Diabetologia* 1974; **10**: 139–43.

30 Service FJ. Parameters for the assessment of glycaemic control. In: Irsigler K, Kunz KN, Owens DR, Regal H, eds. *New Approaches to Insulin Therapy*. Vienna: MTP, 1980: 237–44.

31 Service FJ. Normalization of plasma glucose of unstable diabetes: studies under ambulatory fed conditions with pumped intravenous insulin. *J Lab Clin Med* 1978; **91**: 480–9.

32 Bending JJ, Pickup JC, Collins AGG, Keen H. Rarity of a marked dawn phenomenon in diabetic subjects treated by continuous subcutaneous insulin infusion. *Diabetes Care* 1985; **8**: 28–33.

33 Allen DW, Schroeder WA, Balog J. Observations on the chromatographic heterogeneity of normal adult and fetal haemoglobin. *J Am Chem Soc* 1958; **80**: 1628–34.

34 Bookchin RM, Gallop PM. Structure of hemoglobin A$_{1c}$: nature of the N-terminal chain blocking group. *Biochem Biophys Res Commun* 1968; **32**: 86–93.

35 Bunn HF, Haney DN, Gabbay KH *et al.* Further identification of the nature of linkage of the carbohydrate in hemoglobin A$_{1c}$. *Biochem Biophys Res Commun* 1975; **67**: 103–9.

36 Flückiger R, Winterhalter KH. *In vitro* synthesis of haemoglobin A$_{1c}$. *FEBS Lett* 1976; **71**: 356–60.

37 Koenig RJ, Peterson CM, Jones RL, Saudek C, Lehrman M, Cerami A. Correlation of glucose regulation and hemoglobin A$_{1c}$ in diabetes mellitus. *N Engl J Med* 1976; **295**: 417–20.

38 Goldstein DE, Peth SB, England JD, Hess RL, DaCosta J. Effects of acute changes in blood glucose on HbA$_{1c}$. *Diabetes* 1980; **29**: 623–8.

39 Kennedy L. Labile glycosylated haemoglobin — is it clinically important? *Diabetic Med* 1985; **2**: 86–7.

40 Kennedy L, Byrne E, Savage G, Merrett JD. Routine measurement of haemoglobin A$_1$ at the diabetic outpatient clinic. *Ulster Med J* 1984; **53**: 51–7.

41 Schleicher ED, Gerbitz KD, Dolhofer R *et al.* Clinical utility of nonenzymatically glycosylated blood proteins as an index of glucose control. *Diabetes Care* 1984; **7**: 548–56.

42 Pecoraro RE, Koepsell TD, Chen MS, Lipsky BA, Belcher DW, Inui TS. Comparative clinical reliability of fasting plasma glucose and glycosylated hemoglobin in non-insulin-dependent diabetes mellitus. *Diabetes Care* 1986; **9**: 35–7.

43 Goldstein DE, Walker B, Rawlings SS *et al.* Hemoglobin A$_{1c}$ levels in children and adolescents with diabetes mellitus. *Diabetes Care* 1980; **3**: 503–7.

44 Dahlqvist G, Blom L, Bolme P *et al.* Metabolic control in 131 juvenile-onset diabetic patients as measured by HbA$_{1c}$: relation to age, duration, C-peptide, insulin dose, and one or two insulin injections. *Diabetes Care* 1982; **5**: 399–403.

45 Bernstein RE. Glycosylated hemoglobins: hematologic considerations determine which assay for glycohemoglobin is advisable. *Clin Chem* 1980; **26**: 174–5.

46 Starkman HS, Wacks M, Soeldner S, Kim A. Effect of acute blood loss on glycosylated hemoglobin determinations in normal subjects. *Diabetes Care* 1983; **6**: 291–4.

47 Horton BF, Huisman THJ. Studies on the heterogeneity of haemoglobin: VII. Minor haemoglobin components in haematological diseases. *Br J Haematol* 1965; **11**: 296–304.

48 Eberentz-Lhomme C, Ducrocq R, Intrator S, Elion J, Nunez E, Assan R. Haemoglobinopathies: a pitfall in assessment of glycosylated haemoglobin HbA₁. *Diabetologia* 1984; **27**: 596–8.

49 Flückiger R, Marmon W, Meier W, Loo S, Gabbay KH. Hemoglobin carbamylation in uremia. *N Engl J Med* 1981; **304**: 823–7.

50 Paisey R, Banks R, Holton R, Young K, Hopton M, White D, Hartog M. Glycosylated haemoglobin in uraemia. *Diabetic Med* 1986; **3**: 445–8.

51 Trivelli LA, Ranney HM, Lai H-T. Hemoglobin components in patients with diabetes mellitus. *N Engl J Med* 1971; **284**: 353–7.

52 Welch SG, Boucher BJ. A rapid micro-scale method for the measurement of haemoglobin A$_{1(a+b+c)}$. *Diabetologia* 1978; **14**: 209–11.

53 Kortlandt W, Van Rijn HJM, Hocke JOO, Thissen JHH. Comparison of three different assay procedures for the determination of HbA₁ with special attention to the influence of pre-HbA$_{1c}$, temperature and haemoglobin concentration. *Ann Clin Biochem* 1985; **22**: 261–8.

54 Menard L, Dempsey ME, Blankstein LA, Aleyassine H, Wacks M, Soeldner JS. Quantitative determination of glycosylated hemoglobin A₁ by agar gel electrophoresis. *Clin Chem* 1980; **26**: 1598–602.

55 Thornton WE, Schellekens APM, Sanders GTB. Assay of glycosylated haemoglobin using agar electrophoresis. *Ann Clin Biochem* 1981; **18**: 182–4.

56 Spicer KM, Allen RC, Buse MG. A simplified assay of hemoglobin A$_{1c}$ in diabetic patients by use of isoelectric focusing and quantitative microdensitometry. *Diabetes* 1978; **27**: 384–8.

57 Simon M, Cuan J. Hemoglobin A$_{1c}$ by isoelectric focusing. *Clin Chem* 1982; **28**: 9–12.

58 Mallia AK, Hermanson GT, Krohn RI, Fujimoto EK, Smith PK. Preparation and use of a boronic acid affinity support for separation and quantitation of glycosylated hemoglobins. *Analyt Lett* 1981; **14**: 649–61.

59 Bouriotis V, Stott J, Galloway A, Bellingham AJ, Dean PDG. Measurement of glycosylated haemoglobins using affinity chromatography. *Diabetologia* 1981; **21**: 577–80.

60 Hall PM, Cook JGH, Gould BJ. An inexpensive, rapid and precise affinity chromatography method for the measurement of glycosylated haemoglobins. *Ann Clin Biochem* 1983; **20**: 129–35.

61 Parker KM, England JD, Da Costa J, Hess RL, Goldstein DE. Improved colorimetric assay for glycosylated hemoglobin. *Clin Chem* 1981; **27**: 669–72.

62 Gallop PM, Flückiger R, Hanneken A *et al.* Chemical quantitation of hemoglobin glycosylation: fluorometric detection of formaldehyde released upon periodate oxi-dation of glycoglobin. *Ann Biochem* 1981; **117**: 427–32.

63 Schleicher E, Wieland OH. Specific quantification by HPLC of protein (lysine) bound glucose in human serum albumin and other glycosylated proteins. *J Clin Chem Clin Biochem* 1981; **19**: 81–7.

64 Trueb B, Hughes GJ, Winterhalter KH. Synthesis and quantitation of glucitollysine, a glycosylated amino acid elevated in proteins from diabetics. *Ann Biochem* 1982; **119**: 330–4.

65 Boucher BJ, Burrin JM, Gould BJ *et al.* A collaborative study of the measurement of glycosylated haemoglobin by several methods in seven laboratories in the United Kingdom. *Diabetologia* 1983; **24**: 265–71.

66 Goldstein DE, Parker KM, England JD *et al.* Clinical application of glycosylated hemoglobin measurements. *Diabetes* 1982; **31**(suppl 3): 70–8.

67 Dolhofer R, Wieland OH. Glycosylation of serum albumin: elevated glycosylalbumin in diabetic patients. *FEBS Lett* 1979; **103**: 282–6.

68 Kennedy L, Mehl TD, Riley WJ, Merimee TJ. Nonenzymatically glycosylated serum protein in diabetes mellitus: an index of short-term glycaemia. *Diabetologia* 1981; **21**: 94–8.

69 Gould BJ, Hall PM, Cooke JGH. A sensitive method for the measurement of glycosylated plasma proteins using affinity chromatography. *Ann Clin Biochem* 1984; **21**: 16–21.

70 Johnson RN, Metcalf PA, Baker JR. Fructosamine: a new approach to the estimation of serum glycosylprotein. An index of diabetic control. *Clin Chim Acta* 1982; **127**: 87–95.

71 Lloyd DR, Nott M, Marples J. Comparison of serum fructosamine with glycosylated serum protein (determined by affinity chromatography) for the assessment of diabetic control. *Diabetic Med* 1985; **2**: 474–8.

72 McCance DR, Coulter D, Smye M, Kennedy L. Effect of fluctuations in albumin on serum fructosamine. *Diabetic Med* 1987; **4**: 434–6.

73 Flückiger R, Woodtli T, Berger W. Evaluation of the fructosamine test for the measurement of plasma protein glycation. *Diabetologia* 1987; **30**: 648–52.

74 McCance DR, Clarke KC, Kennedy L. Serum fructosamine in uraemia, myeloma and acute inflammatory disorders — relationship to serum glucose and albumin levels. *Ann Clin Biochem* 1989; **26**: 63–8.

75 Hindle EJ, Rostron GM, Gatt JA. The estimation of serum fructosamine: an alternative measurement to glycated haemoglobin. *Ann Clin Biochem* 1985; **22**: 84–9.

76 Baker JR, Johnson RN, Scott DJ. Serum fructosamine concentrations in patients with Type II (non-insulin-dependent) diabetes mellitus during changes in management. *Br Med J* 1984; **288**: 1484–6.

35   Assay of Insulin

Summary

• Bioassays for insulin have the advantage of measuring biologically active rather than immunoreactive moieties, but the techniques are lengthy, relatively imprecise and insensitive, and are also affected by insulin agonists (e.g. insulin-like growth factors) and antagonists (e.g. counter-regulatory hormones).

• Immunologically based insulin assays are of two main types: 'immunoassays', where there is limited anti-insulin antibody concentration and labelled insulin, and 'immunometric assays' with excess and labelled antibody.

• The advent of monoclonal antibodies to insulin has considerably reduced the technical difficulties of immunometric assays.

• The main difficulties with insulin assays are the cross-reaction of proinsulin and its intermediates and the presence of endogenous insulin antibodies which interfere with the assay.

• Several methods exist for separating free and antibody-bound insulin in blood samples; the most commonly used is precipitation of bound insulin by polyethylene glycol solution.

• Recent advances in assay technology include the use of monoclonal antibodies for two-site immunometric methods, and various non-isotopic labels, such as europium chelates, for time-resolved fluorescence measurement.

• Though there are many research uses for insulin assays in diabetes, the main clinical application is in the investigation of hypoglycaemia and the diagnosis of insulinoma.

History of insulin assays

The use of insulin to treat diabetes mellitus led to the development in the 1920s of *in vivo* bioassays and chemical assays for the measurement of the hormone in pharmaceutical preparations [1]. These assays were relatively insensitive and *in vitro* bioassays were found to be more suitable for the determination of insulin concentrations in blood. It was, however, the introduction of the radioimmunoassay by Yalow and Berson in 1959 [2, 3] which revolutionized the analysis of insulin and the study of its clinical endocrinology. Immunometric assays [4–7] were later developed as a means of enhancing the sensitivity and specificity of antibody-based assays. Their widespread use was made possible by methods for producing large quantities of monoclonal antibodies, first described by Kohler and Milstein [8, 9]. The recent production of biosynthetic proinsulin has had a profound effect on the development of specific and sensitive assays for insulin and related hormones [10–12].

Bioassays for insulin

Various animal systems have been used for the bioassay of insulin (Table 35.1). The theoretical advantage of bioassay over immunoassay is that immunoreactivity does not necessarily equate with biological activity, and it is the latter which is of greater physiological relevance. Although insulin bioassays measure net insulin-like activity, they may be affected by insulin antagonists (e.g. growth hormone and catecholamines) and insulin-like substances (e.g. proinsulin and insulin-like growth factors). All bioassay systems require skill in animal preparation and are lengthy, relatively imprecise and insensitive. In recent years, the main use of these assays has been in the commercial standardization of therapeutic insulins (Chapter 37), currently against the Fourth International Standard [13]. *Radioreceptor assays* (which measure

Table 35.1. Some bio- and radioreceptor assays for insulin.

Animal/tissue used	Principle	Comment
In vivo assays		
Rabbit [13, 123]	Reduction in blood glucose to less than 2.5 mmol/l	Insensitive. Variation in animal sensitivity. Twin-crossover studies needed
Mouse [13, 123]	Induction of convulsions or death	Environmental factors critical
In vitro assays		
Rat [1, 13, 124–8]	Increase in glycogen of isolated diaphragm in glucose medium	Many variations of this method described
Rat [13, 129–31]	Glucose uptake by rat epididymal fat pad	Isolated adipocytes also used
Radioreceptor assays [14, 123, 132–4]		
Human placental membranes		
Rat liver membrane	Competition between radiolabelled and unlabelled hormone for binding to specific receptor	Less sensitive than immunoassays
Rat fat cells		
Rat erythrocyte membrane		

Table 35.2. Nomenclature of immunoassay methods.

Assay component labelled	Limited antibody concentration	Excess antibody concentration
	Antigen	Antibody
Label		
Radioisotope e.g. ^{125}I	Radioimmunoassay (RIA)	Immunoradiometric assay (IRMA)
Enzyme e.g. alkaline phosphatase, peroxidase	Enzyme immunoassay (EIA)	Immunoenzymometric assay (IEMA)
Fluorophor e.g. europium chelate	Fluoroimmunoassay (FIA)	Immunofluorometric assay (IFMA)
Luminescence e.g. acridinium ester	Luminescent immunoassay (LIA)	Immunoluminometric assay (ILMA)

the interaction of hormone ligands with specific receptor sites on larger cells or cellular components) share the theoretical advantages of bioassays and obviate the need to use live animals, although animal tissue preparations are still required. Radioreceptor assays are reported to be more sensitive than immunoassays to degradation of the insulin molecule [14].

General principles of immunoassays

An immunoassay involves the measurement of an antigen such as insulin using its specific reaction with an antibody. Assays can be divided into two basic types depending on whether the antibody is used at a limited concentration ('immunoassays') or in excess ('immunometric assays'). Further classification defines the label used to follow the reaction and the system used to separate antibody-bound and free fractions of antigen (Table 35.2). Radioactive isotopes (especially ^{125}I) have been most widely used as labels. However, alternative non-isotopic labels have recently been developed and offer advantages with regard to safety, longer shelf-life and possibly sensitivity [15−20].

Immunoassays: limited antibody concentration and labelled antigen

In this type of assay (Fig. 35.1) the antibody is present in limited amounts, such that the total number of binding sites for antigen is less than the total number of antigen molecules (i.e. labelled antigen reagent plus unlabelled antigen in sample or standard). A variable amount of unlabelled antigen (either unknown samples, or known standards) is incubated with constant amounts of labelled antigen and antibody. After reaction, the antibody-bound and the free antigen fractions are separated by one of several methods, and the amount of labelled antigen bound to antibody is measured. Over the working range of the assay, the percentage of label bound to antibody is *inversely* proportional to the amount of unlabelled antigen present in the sample. Antigen concentrations in unknown samples are calculated by comparing their percentage of label bound with a curve derived from a series of standards containing known antigen concentrations (Fig. 35.2) [21−3].

Immunometric assays: excess antibody concentrations and labelled antibody

In immunometric assays, varying concentrations of antigen react with a constant and excess amount of antibody and the bound antigen:antibody complex is measured. Within the assay's working range, the percentage of label bound is *directly* proportional to the antigen concentration in the sample (Fig. 35.2). There are three possible

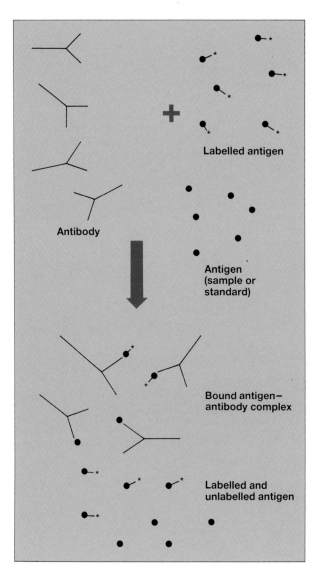

Fig. 35.1. Principle of limited antibody assays.

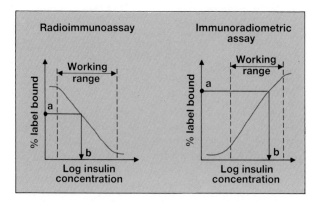

Fig. 35.2. Standard curves for immunoassays and immunometric assays. In each case, the linear (working range) portion of the standard curve is shown. The percentage label bound in an unknown sample (a) is read off the standard curve to give the unknown antigen concentration (b).

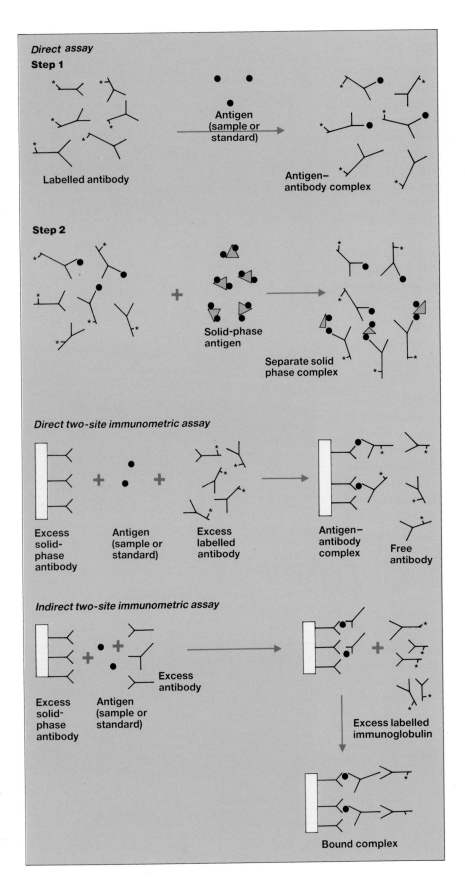

Fig. 35.3. Configuration of immunometric assays.

configurations of this type of assay, namely the direct assay, the indirect assay and the two-site assay [4, 5, 24] (Fig. 35.3). As mentioned above, the development of monoclonal antibody production techniques [8, 9] has considerably reduced the technical difficulty of immunometric assays (Table 35.3) [25, 26].

Monoclonal antibody production

Lymphocytes from immunized animals may be immortalized by fusion with myeloma cell lines (Fig. 35.4). The resulting hybridoma cells are cloned and may then be grown indefinitely *in vitro* or *in*

Table 35.3. Features of immunometric assays.

Factors influencing performance of assays
Concentration and affinity of antibodies
Specificity of antibodies
Nature and specific activity of label
Background signal
Precision of measurement of signal
Precision of sample/reagent handling

Advantages of immunometric assays
Improved sensitivity
Increased specificity particularly with use of two
    monoclonal antibodies
Standardized, easier labelling techniques
Wider working range
Faster assays

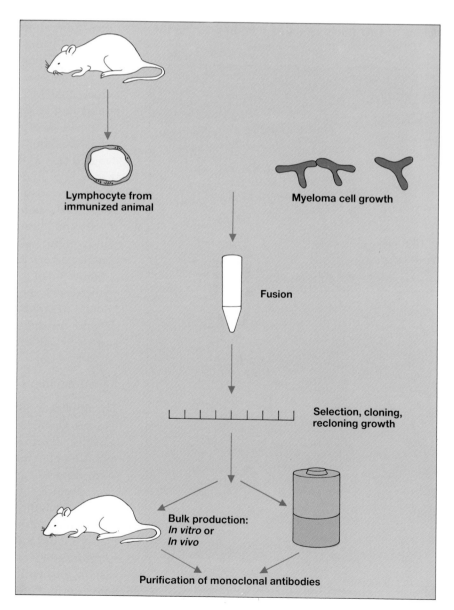

Fig. 35.4. Production of monoclonal antibodies.

vivo as tumour cells which retain the ability to secrete the antibody characteristic of the lymphocyte. The techniques involved require considerable skill, time and money [27]. Further developments in hybridoma technology (e.g. the use of bispecific hybridomas [28–31]) may further improve immunometric assays.

Insulin assays

Insulin assays face a number of specific difficulties. First, there is a need to measure the insulin molecule specifically in the presence of compounds of similar structure, such as proinsulin and its intermediates (Fig. 35.5). This problem mostly affects immunoassays which use polyclonal antisera and can be overcome by two-site immunometric assays, which exploit the binding specificities of two (monoclonal) antibodies. Secondly,

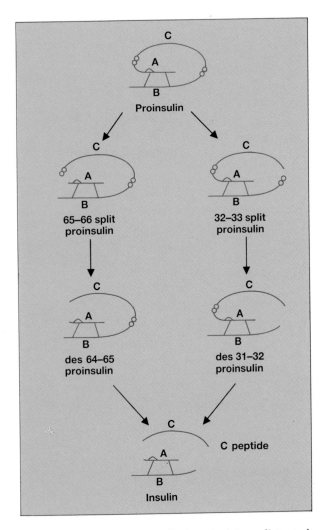

Fig. 35.5. Processing of proinsulin to major intermediates and to insulin.

endogenous antibodies to insulin may interfere with the assay. Such antibodies may occur spontaneously in newly diagnosed and 'prediabetic' IDDM patients [32–4], healthy subjects [34] and patients with thyroid disease [35], and in response to exogenous insulin treatment (see Chapter 40). Endogenous insulin antibodies may cause an elevation *in vivo* of total immunoreactive insulin, whereas the biologically active, non-antibody-bound or 'free' fraction may be within normal limits.

Autoantibodies against proinsulin have also been described [36]. These antibodies may also interfere directly in immunoassay systems by binding labelled antigen; this causes either falsely high or low results, depending on the separation system and antibody used. Some assays measure total immunoreactive insulin [37–9], whereas others have attempted to separate antibody-bound and free insulin using methods such as precipitation with polyethylene glycol or ethanol, or steady-state gel filtration [40, 41]. It has been argued that the equilibrium established between bound and free fractions *in vivo* may be rapidly altered *in vitro*, and separation of the sample immediately after venepuncture has been recommended [42–4]. However, it remains to be proven that such procedures allow an accurate estimation of the free insulin concentrations which exist *in vivo*. Steady-state gel filtration yields reproducible results and is probably the method of choice with which other separation techniques should be compared [41].

Many insulin immunoassays have been described since the early 1960s. Some of the factors known to affect their performance (which will depend on the exact assay conditions used) are shown in Table 35.4.

Recent advances in insulin immunoassays

The application of monoclonal antibodies to two-site insulin assays has represented a significant advance. A number of groups have now produced monoclonal antibodies to insulin and described immunometric assays with improved sensitivity and specificity [6, 24, 45–9].

Both isotopic and non-isotopic labels, e.g. horseradish peroxidase [50–3] and β-galactosidase [54, 55], have been used for both competitive immunoassays and immunometric assays for insulin, but with little significant improvement in assay performance. The use of a europium chelate

Table 35.4. Factors affecting immunoassays for insulin.

Standard
Source of standard [135]
Enzymatic degradation of standard insulin [1]
Aggregation of insulin [136]
Adsorption of insulin on to glass and plastic surfaces [136, 137]

Sample
Serum vs plasma
Stability of insulin [138]
Haemolysis [139, 140]
Dimerization of insulin [141]
Heterophilic antibodies, rheumatoid factor, etc. [142]

Sample matrix/separation system
Serum 'factors' and protein concentrations [1, 143]
Non-linearity on dilution [144]

as label, detected by time-resolved fluorescence (Fig. 35.6), and of monoclonal antibodies in an immunometric assay has led to a tenfold improvement in sensitivity. The detection limit (defined as mean plus two standard deviations of the zero signal) of this assay is 0.24 mU/l compared to 2.8 mU/l for competitive immunoassays [56].

Although the use of monoclonal antibodies in two-site immunometric assays has increased sensitivity and specificity, endogenous antibodies can still lead to analytical problems with such techniques. A number of different types of antibody have been shown to cause falsely elevated results in immunometric assays [57–61], namely anti-mouse antibodies (if mouse monoclonal antibodies are used), autoantibodies (such as rheumatoid factor or anti-mitochondrial antibody), anti-carbohydrate matrix and anti-label

antibodies. The addition of non-immune mouse serum to reagent buffers and the use of Fab' conjugates should avert these problems.

Assays for proinsulin and proinsulin-like intermediates

In 1967, Steiner and colleagues [62, 63] showed that the formation of insulin (see Chapter 9) was preceded by the biosynthesis of proinsulin, which was subsequently demonstrated in human plasma [64, 65]. The conversion of proinsulin to insulin is thought to occur by a potentially branched pathway which may generate a number of intermediates (Fig. 35.5). The details of these conversion processes and the biological activity and physiological significance of the intermediates have yet to be firmly established [66, 67].

The major analytical problems to be addressed are those of specificity and sensitivity. Proinsulin and its intermediates contain the sequences of both C peptide and insulin and may therefore cross-react in immunoassays for either of these. Conversely, C peptide and insulin can interfere in proinsulin assays. These problems of specificity may be accentuated by the fact that insulin concentrations may be much higher than those of proinsulin and its intermediates.

Early assays for proinsulin employed physical separation of proinsulin from insulin and C peptide (e.g. by gel-filtration chromatography) followed by insulin or C-peptide immunoassays of each separated fraction [68, 69]. Such methods are laborious, imprecise and insensitive and require large sample volumes. An alternative method first removed insulin from serum using an insulin-

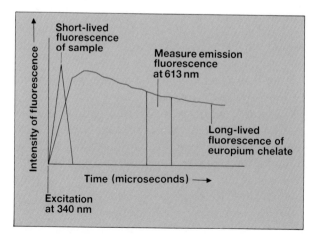

Fig. 35.6. Principles of time-resolved fluorescence of europium chelates.

specific protease before immunoassay for proinsulin-like material, but was shown to be unreliable [70]. Subsequently, immunoassays for proinsulin have been developed which use two antibodies, one directed against insulin and one against C peptide. With appropriate washing and incubation steps, only proinsulin will bind both antibodies and so can be measured [71−4].

Human proinsulin produced by recombinant-DNA technology [10−12] has now become available in quantity for use as standard, labelled antigen and immunogen. It now seems that established proinsulin assays may measure proinsulin fragments (65−66 and 32−33 split proinsulins), rather than the intact hormone [75]. Subsequently, biosynthetic proinsulin has been used as an immunogen for the production of both polyclonal and monoclonal antibodies for use in both radio-immunoassays [76−8] and immunoradiometric assays [79]. With the appropriate choice of pairs of monoclonal antibodies, immunometric assays for the various proinsulin intermediates should become widely available. Use of these more specific assays should improve understanding of the possible changes in insulin and proinsulin turnover in diabetes.

Physiological considerations

Distribution of insulin and proinsulin in body fluids

It must be appreciated that peripheral venous concentrations of insulin and proinsulin do not necessarily reflect their relative rates of secretion [80]. This is mainly because of the different proportions of each hormone extracted by the liver from the portal vein before they enter the general circulation (Chapter 36). Although the liver is the most important organ in insulin metabolism, the kidney is also a major site of insulin degradation. Insulin is filtered through the glomerulus, then reabsorbed and degraded in the proximal tubule, less than 1% of the filtered load normally being excreted in the urine [81, 82]. Proinsulin has also been identified in urine [83, 84]. Valid measurements of insulin in urine demand collection conditions which minimize hormone degradation, and correction for body size and creatinine clearance may be necessary. Insulin has also been identified in saliva [85−8] and cerebrospinal fluid (CSF) [89] derived from the circulation. Recovery of insulin from saliva may be low, probably

because of enzymatic degradation. Immunoassay of insulin in urine, saliva or CSF usually requires preliminary sample preparation and concentration, using acid/alcohol extraction, chromatography or lyophilization.

Physiological and pathological variations

Plasma concentrations of insulin and proinsulin are determined by their rates of secretion and their clearance rates. The secretion of insulin is pulsatile, with a periodicity of approximately 13 min (Chapter 9). Disease states may alter either insulin secretion [90] or clearance [91]. Plasma insulin concentrations vary with age, [92, 93] exercise [94] and body weight [95]. Increased concentrations have been reported in liver disease [96], renal disease and hyperthyroidism [97]. A rare cause of greatly elevated plasma concentrations of insulin (and of proinsulin) is a point mutation affecting the structures of the molecules, which reduces clearance [97, 98] (Chapter 30).

Clinical uses of insulin and proinsulin assays

Insulin and proinsulin assays have wide research applications and are also used to assess residual B-cell function. However, their main clinical use is in the investigation of hypoglycaemia and the diagnosis of insulinoma. These rare tumours may be difficult to identify, as symptoms are often non-specific and intermittent. Clinical features — such as a family history of multiple endocrine neoplasia type 1 (MEN1) — are only rarely helpful. Having established that symptoms are associated with hypoglycaemia and relieved by glucose administration, the diagnosis of insulinoma rests on the demonstration of inappropriately raised plasma insulin levels during fasting hypoglycaemia. Insulin or sulphonylurea treatment must be positively excluded.

There are several protocols for the investigation of hypoglycaemia [99−101] (Table 35.5) most exploiting the failure of neoplastic endocrine cells to respond normally to events such as starvation and exercise, stimulation with glucagon, tolbutamide or leucine, or suppression by diazoxide, hypoglycaemia or hyperinsulinaemia. These procedures should always be carried out under close medical supervision, especially in patients at special risk of hypoglycaemia (ischaemic heart disease, epilepsy) and there must be immediate access to resuscitation equipment, intravenous

Table 35.5. Biochemical investigation of insulinomas.

Conditions	Demonstration of inappropriate insulin response	
	Measure in plasma	Interpretation and comments
1 Fasting [99–105, 145]		
• Overnight on several occasions	Glucose	Blood glucose <2.2 mmol/l, insulin >10 mU/l (60 pmol/l), proinsulin >15 pmol/l,
• After 72-h fast	Insulin C peptide Proinsulin	C peptide >1.5 µg/l (500 pmol/l), suggest insulinoma in a lean individual
• With exercise		
2 Suppression tests [111–16]		
• Insulin	Glucose C peptide Proinsulin	If blood glucose <2.2 mmol/l, then normally plasma C peptide <1.2 µg/l (400 pmol/l)
• Fish insulin	Human insulin	No longer used
3 Stimulation tests [117]		
• Glucagon	Glucose	No longer recommended
• Leucine		
• Tolbutamide	Insulin	Exaggerated insulin response in 70% of insulinomas
4 Euglycaemic insulin clamp techniques [118–22]		
• Insulin infused to produce hyperinsulinaemia	Insulin Glucose	Specialist technique. In insulinoma, C peptide and proinsulin fail to suppress during hyperinsulinaemia
• Glucose infused to maintain euglycaemia	C peptide Proinsulin	
Localization of tumour		
Selective venous catheterization with matched peripheral samples	Glucose Insulin	Specialist technique

glucose and hydrocortisone. Diseases and drug treatments known to influence plasma insulin or pro-insulin concentrations should be considered. As the assays used vary widely, clinicians are strongly recommended to contact their local laboratory to establish the detailed sample requirements, protocols and reference ranges. All samples taken for insulin or proinsulin determinations should be accompanied by plasma glucose measurements.

Most cases of insulinoma show an unequivocal elevation of plasma insulin concentrations and of the insulin:glucose ratio [102, 103] when hypoglycaema is induced by fasting with or without exercise. Insulin secretion in these patients may be irregular so that plasma insulin and glucose may need to be measured frequently; false negative results have been reported [104, 105]. The quoted diagnostic criteria depend partly on the sensitivity and specificity of the assay system used. In healthy subjects, proinsulin comprises less than 20% of the total immunoreactive insulin [105–9] with levels of less than approximately 8 pmol/l [97, 103, 110]. In patients with insulinoma, this proportion may be as high as 80% and proinsulin levels may reach 400 pmol/l. The role of specific assays for proinsulin-like intermediates in diagnosis of insulinoma is yet to be established.

Measurements of insulin and proinsulin in the pancreatic veins using selective venous catheterization may also be useful in localizing insulinomas before or during surgery. Many insulinomas are small and may escape detection by even advanced imaging methods, including CT scanning, angiography and endoscopic or per-operative ultrasound.

Dynamic suppression or stimulation tests have now largely been abandoned because they are hazardous and often unhelpful. In the suppression tests [111–16], plasma C peptide or proinsulin is assayed following administration of insulin to induce hypoglycaemia. C peptide and proinsulin levels are generally suppressed unless an insulinoma is present. However, the tests are un-reliable, and negative results are of no diagnostic value [117]. A safer but complicated alternative is the euglycaemic clamp technique. This exploits the principle that insulin itself normally inhibits its own release. Insulin is infused intravenously to produce hyperinsulinaemia, with enough glu-cose to maintain normoglycaemia. Hyperinsulin-aemia suppresses plasma C peptide and proinsulin in normal subjects, but in insulinoma patients sup-pression fails to occur [118–22]. The technique is technically demanding and can be lengthy; glucose delivery must be maintained for some time after the insulin infusion. At present, it remains the preserve of the specialist centre.

PENELOPE M. S. CLARK

C. NICK HALES

References

1 Stewart GA. Methods of insulin assay. *Br Med Bull* 1960; **16**: 196–201.

2 Yalow RS, Berson SA. Assay of plasma insulin in human subjects by immunological methods. *Nature* 1959; **184**: 1648–9.

3 Yalow RS, Berson SA. Immunoassay of endogenous plasma insulin in man. *J Clin Invest* 1960; **39**: 1157–75.

4 Miles LEM, Hales CN. Labelled antibodies and immuno-logical assay systems. *Nature* 1968; **219**: 186–9.

5 Miles LEM, Hales CN. The preparation and properties of purified ^{125}I-labelled antibodies to insulin. *Biochem J* 1968; **108**: 611–18.

6 Woodhead JS, Addison GM, Hales CN. The immunoradio-metric assay and related techniques. *Br Med Bull* 1974; **30**: 44–9.

7 Addison GM, Hales CN. Two-site assay of human growth hormone. *Horm Metab Res*; 1971; **3**: 59–60.

8 Kohler G, Milstein C. Continuous cultures of fused cells secreting antibody of predefined specificity. *Nature* 1975; **256**: 495–7.

9 Kohler G, Milstein C. Derivation of specific antibody-producing tissue culture and tumour lines by cell fusion. *Eur J Immunol* 1976; **6**: 511–19.

10 Frank BH, Pettee JM, Zimmerman RE, Burck PJ. The pro-duction of human proinsulin and its transformation to human insulin and C-peptide. In: Rich DH, Gross E, eds. *Peptides: Synthesis — Structure — Function*. Proceedings of the Seventh American Peptide Symposium, Madison WI. Pierce Chemical Company, 1987: 729–38.

11 Keefer LM, Piron MA, De Meyts P. Human insulin prepared by recombinant DNA techniques and native human insulin interact identically with insulin receptors. *Proc Natl Acad Sci USA* 1981; **78**: 1391–5.

12 Chan SJ, Weiss J, Konrad M *et al*. Biosynthesis and peri-plasmic segregation of human proinsulin in *Escherichia coli*. *Proc Natl Acad Sci USA* 1981; **78**: 5401–5.

13 Bangham DR, Mussett MV. The Fourth International Standard for Insulin. *Bull WHO* 1959; **20**: 1209–20.

14 Freychet P, Kahn R, Roth J, Neville M. Insulin interactions with liver plasma membranes. *J Biol Chem* 1972; **247**: 3953–61.

15 Tijssen P. Practice and theory of enzyme immunoassays. In: Burdon RH, Van Knippinberg PM, eds. *Laboratory Techniques in Biochemistry and Molecular Biology*, vol 15. Amsterdam: Elsevier, 1985.

16 Stanley CJ, Johannsson A, Self CH. Enzyme amplification can enhance both the speed and the sensitivity of immuno-assays. *J Immunol Methods* 1985; **83**: 89–95.

17 Weeks I, Woodhead JS. Chemiluminescence immunoassay. *J Clin Immunoassay* 1984; **7**: 82–9.

18 Kricka LJ, Carter TJN. Luminescent immunoassays. In: Kricka LJ, Carter TJN, eds. *Clinical and Biochemical Lumi-nescence*. New York: Marcel Dekker, 1982: 153–78.

19 Smith DS, Al-Hakiem MHH, Landon J. A review of fluoro-immunoassay and immunofluorometric assay. *Ann Clin Biochem* 1981; **18**: 253–74.

20 Hemmilä I, Dakubu S, Mukkala V-M, Siitari H, Lövgren T. Europium as a label in time-resolved immunofluoro-metric assays. *Anal Biochem* 1984; **137**: 335–43.

21 Ekins R. Towards immunoassays of greater sensitivity, specificity and speed: An overview. In: Albertini A, Ekins RP, eds. *Monoclonal Antibodies and Developments in Immuno-assay*. Amsterdam: Elsevier, 1981: 3–21.

22 Raggatt PR, Hales CN. Immunoassays using labelled anti-gens or antibodies. In: Lachmann PJ, Peters DK, eds. *Clinical Aspects of Immunology*, 4th edn. Oxford: Blackwell Scientific Publications, 1982: 309–42.

23 Edwards R. *Immunoassay: An introduction*. London: W Heinemann Medical Books, 1985.

24 Hales CN, Woodhead JS. Labelled antibodies and their use in immunoradiometric assay. *Methods Enzymol* 1980; **70**: 334–55.

25 Hunter WM, Budd PS. Immunoradiometric versus radio-immunoassay: a comparison using alpha-fetoprotein as the model analyte. *J Immunol Methods* 1981; **45**: 255–73.

26 Siddle K, Gard TG, Soos MA, Gray IP, Hales CN. Immuno-radiometric assay of polypeptide hormones using mono-clonal antibodies. In: Forti G, Serio M, Lipsett MB, eds. *Monoclonal Antibodies: Basic Principles, Experimental and Clinical Applications in Endocrinology*. Vol. 30. New York: Serono Symposium Publications from Raven Press, 1986: 49–57.

27 Siddle K. Monoclonal antibodies in clinical biochemistry. In: Price CP, Alberti KGMM, eds. *Recent Advances in Clinical Biochemistry*. Edinburgh: Churchill Livingstone, 1985: 63–102.

28 French D, Fischberg E, Buhl S, Scharff MD. The production of more useful monoclonal antibodies. I. Modifications of the basic technology. *Immunol Today* 1986; **7**: 344–6.

29 Aguila HL, Pollack RR, Spira G, Scharff MD. The production of more useful monoclonal antibodies. II. The use of somatic-cell genetic and recombinant DNA technology to tailor-make monoclonal antibodies. *Immunol Today* 1986; **7**: 380–3.

30 Suresh MR, Cuello AC, Milstein C. Advantages of bispecific hybridomas in one-step immunocytochemistry and immunoassays. *Proc Natl Acad Sci USA* 1986; **83**: 7989–93.

31 Samoilovich SR, Dugan CB, Macario AJL. Hybridoma technology: new developments of practical interest. *J Immunol Methods* 1987; **101**: 153–70.

32 Palmer JP, Asplin CM, Clemons P *et al*. Insulin antibodies in insulin-dependent diabetics before insulin treatment. *Science* 1983; **222**: 1337–9.

33 Eisenbarth GS. Type I diabetes mellitus: a chronic autoimmune disease. *N Engl J Med* 1986; **314**: 1360–8.

34 Wilkin T, Hoskins PJ, Armitage M *et al*. Value of insulin autoantibodies as serum markers for insulin-dependent diabetes mellitus. *Lancet* 1985; i: 480–1.

35 Nuovo JA, Baker JR, Wartofsky L, Lukes YG, Burman KD. Autoantibodies to insulin are present in sera of patients with autoimmune thyroid disease. *Diabetes* 1988; **37**: 317–20.

36 Kuglin G, Gries FA, Kolb H. Evidence of IgG autoantibodies against human proinsulin in patients with IDDM before insulin treatment. *Diabetes* 1988; **37**: 130–2.

37 Heding LG. Determination of total serum insulin (IRI) in insulin-treated diabetic patients. *Diabetologia* 1972; **8**: 260–6.

38 Kuzuya M, Blix PM, Horwitz DL, Steiner DF, Rubenstein AH. Determination of free and total insulin and C-peptide in insulin-treated diabetics. *Diabetes* 1977; **36**: 22–9.

39 Kohno T, Ishikawa E, Sugiyama S *et al*. Enzyme immunoassay of total insulin in human serum containing anti-insulin antibodies. *Clin Chim Acta* 1987; **163**: 105–12.

40 Nakagawa S, Nakayama H, Sasaki T *et al*. A simple method for the determination of serum free insulin levels in insulin-treated patients. *Diabetes* 1973; **22**: 590–600.

41 Asplin CM, Goldie DJ, Hartog M. The measurement of serum free insulin by steady-state gel filtration. *Clin Chim Acta* 1977; **75**: 393–9.

42 Collins ACG, Pickup JC. Sample preparation and radioimmunoassay for circulating free and antibody-bound insulin concentrations in insulin-treated diabetics: a re-evaluation of methods. *Diabetic Med* 1985; **2**: 456–60.

43 Hanning I, Home PD, Alberti KGMM. Measurement of free insulin concentrations: the influence of the timing of extraction of insulin antibodies. *Diabetologia* 1985; **28**: 831–5.

44 Arnqvist J, Olsson PO, von Schenck H. Free and total insulin as determined after precipitation with polyethylene glycol: analytical characteristics and effects of sample handling and storage. *Clin Chem* 1987; **33**: 93–6.

45 Schroer JA. Hybridoma antibody recognition of the insulin molecule. In: Fellows R, Eisenbarth G, eds. *Monoclonal Antibodies in Endocrine Research*. New York: Raven Press, 1981: 167–79.

46 Comitti R, Racchetti G, Gnocchi P, Morandi E, Galente YM. A monoclonal-based, two-site enzyme immunoassay for human insulin. *J Immunol Methods* 1987; **99**: 25–37.

47 Bender TP, Schroer JA. Site specific monoclonal antibodies to insulin. *Methods Enzymol* 1985; **109**: 704–21.

48 Storch MJ, Licht T, Petersen KG, Obermeier R, Kerp L. Specificity of monoclonal anti-human insulin antibodies. *Diabetes* 1987; **36**: 1005–9.

49 Sobey WJ, Beer SF, Carrington CA *et al*. Sensitive and specific two-site immunoradiometric assays for human insulin, proinsulin, 65–66 and 32–33 split proinsulins. *Biochem J* 1989; **260**: 535–41.

50 Matsuoka K, Maeda M, Tsuji A. Fluorescence enzyme immunoassay for insulin using peroxidase–tyramine–hydrogen peroxide. *Chem Pharm Bull* 1979; **27**: 2345–50.

51 Albert WHW, Kleinhammer G, Linke R, Staehler F. Quantitative determination of proteins at the pMol/l-level by enzyme immunoassay (EIA) in antibody coated polystyrene tubes. In: Pal SB, ed. *Enzyme Labelled Immunoassay of Hormones and Drugs*. Berlin: Walter de Gruyter, 1978: 3–14:

52 Kekow J, Ulrichs K, Muller-Ruchhaltz W, Gross WL. Enzyme-linked immunosorbent assay with increased sensitivity, high accuracy and greater practicability than established radioimmunoassay. *Diabetes* 1988; **37**: 321–6.

53 Hinsberg WD, Milby KH, Zare RN. Determination of insulin in serum by enzyme immunoassay with fluorimetric detection. *Anal Chem* 1981; **53**: 1509–12.

54 Kato K, Umeda Y, Suzuki F, Hayashi D, Kosaka A. Evaluation of a solid-phase enzyme immunoassay for insulin in human serum. *Clin Chem* 1979; **25**: 1306–8.

55 Umeda Y, Suzuki F, Kosaka A, Kato K. Enzyme immunoassay for insulin with a novel separation method using activated thiol-sepharose. *Clin Chim Acta* 1980; **107**: 267–72.

56 Tolvonen E, Hemmilä I, Marnlemi J, Jorgensen PN, Zeuthen J, Lovgren T. Two-site time-resolved immunofluorometric assay of human insulin. *Clin Chem* 1986; **32**: 637–40.

57 Boscato LM, Stuart MC. Incidence and specificity of interference in two-site immunoassays. *Clin Chem* 1986; **32**: 1491–5.

58 Barlett WA, Browning MCK, Jung RT. Artefactual increase in serum thyrotropin concentration caused by heterophilic antibodies with specificity for IgG of the family *Bovidea*. *Clin Chem* 1986; **32**: 2214–19.

59 Clark PMS, Price CP, Ellis DH. Removal of interference by immunoglobulins in an enzyme-amplified immunoassay for thyrotropin in serum. *Clin Chem* 1987; **33**: 414.

60 Ericsson UB, Larsson I. Interference of endogenous lactoperoxidase antibodies in a solid-phase immunosorbent radioassay for antibodies to protein hormones. *Clin Chem* 1984; **30**: 1836–8.

61 Hamilton RG, Adkinson NF. Naturally occurring carbohydrate antibodies: Interference in solid-phase immunoassays. *J Immunol Methods* 1985; **77**: 95–108.

62 Steiner DF, Oyer PE. The biosynthesis of insulin and a probable precursor of insulin by a human islet cell adenoma. *Proc Natl Acad Sci USA* 1967; **57**: 473–80.

63 Steiner DF, Cunningham D, Spigelman L, Aten B. Insulin biosynthesis: evidence for a precursor. *Science* 1967; **157**: 697–700.

64 Rubenstein AH, Cho S, Steiner DF. Evidence for proinsulin in human urine and serum. *Lancet* 1968; i: 1353–5.

65 Roth J, Gorden P, Pastan I. 'Big insulin': a new component of plasma insulin detected by immunoassay. *Proc Natl Acad Sci USA* 1968; **61**: 138–45.

66 Robbins DC, Tager HS, Rubenstein AH. Biologic and clinical importance of proinsulin. *N Engl J Med* 1984; **310**: 1165–75.

67 Given BD, Cohen RM, Shoelson SE, Frank BH, Rubenstein AH, Tager HS. Biochemical and clinical implications of proinsulin conversion intermediates. *J Clin Invest* 1985; **76**: 1398–1405.

68 Gordon P, Roth J. Plasma insulin: fluctuations in the 'big' insulin component in man after glucose and other stimuli. *J Clin Invest* 1969; **48**: 2225–34.

69 Melani F, Rubenstein AH, Oyer PE, Steiner DF. Identification of proinsulin and C-peptide in human serum by a specific immunoassay. *Proc Natl Acad Sci USA* 1970; **67**: 148–55.

70 Starr JI, Juhn DD, Rubenstein AH, Kitabchi AE. Degradation in serum by insulin specific protease. *J Lab Clin Med* 1975; **86**: 631–7.

71 Heding LG. Specific and direct radioimmunoassay for human proinsulin in serum. *Diabetologia* 1977; **13**: 467–74.

72 Rainbow SJ, Woodhead JS, Yue DK, Luzio SD, Hales CN. Measurement of human proinsulin by an indirect two-site immunoradiometric assay. *Diabetologia* 1979; **17**: 229–34.

73 Naylor BA, Matthews DR, Turner RC. A soluble-phase proinsulin radioimmunoassay and its use in diagnosis of hypoglycaemia. *Ann Clin Biochem* 1987; **24**: 352–63.

74 Hartling SG, Dinesen B, Kappelgård AM, Faber OK, Binder C. ELISA for proinsulin. *Clin Chim Acta* 1986; **156**: 289–98.

75 Gray IP, Siddle K, Docherty K, Frank BH, Hales CN. Proinsulin in human serum: problems in measurement and interpretation. *Clin Endocrinol* 1984; **21**: 43–7.

76 Deacon CF, Conlon JM. Measurement of circulating human proinsulin concentrations using a proinsulin-specific antiserum. *Diabetes* 1985; **34**: 491–7.

77 Cohen RM, Nakabayashi T, Blix PM *et al*. A radioimmunoassay for circulating proinsulin. *Diabetes* 1985; **34**: 84–91.

78 Cohen RM, Given BD, Licinio-Paixao J *et al*. Proinsulin radioimmunoassay in the evaluation of insulinomas and familial hyperproinsulinemia. *Metabolism* 1986; **35**: 1137–46.

79 Gray IP, Siddle K, Frank BH, Hales CN. Characterization and use in immunoradiometric assay of monoclonal antibodies directed against human proinsulin. *Diabetes* 1987; **36**: 684–8.

80 Horwitz DL, Starr JI, Mako ME, Blackard WG, Rubenstein AH. Proinsulin, insulin and C-peptide concentrations in human portal and peripheral blood. *J Clin Invest* 1975; **55**: 1278–83.

81 Chamberlain MJ, Stimmler L. The renal handling of insulin. *J Clin Invest* 1967; **46**: 911–19.

82 Von Gerbitz K-D. Pancreatic cell peptides: Kinetic behaviour and concentrations of proinsulin, insulin and C-peptide in plasma and urine, problems of assay methods, clinical significance and literature review. *J Clin Chem Clin Biochem* 1980; **18**: 313–26.

83 Rubenstein AH, Cho S, Steiner DF. Evidence for proinsulin in human urine and serum. *Lancet* 1968; i: 1353–5.

84 Constan L, Mako M, Juhn D, Rubenstein AH. The excretion of proinsulin and insulin in urine. *Diabetologia* 1975; **11**: 119–23.

85 Sweeney EA, Antoniades HN. The presence of immunologically reactive insulin in parotid saliva and its relation to changes in serum insulin concentration. *Vox Sang* 1967; **13**: 54–6.

86 Pasic J, Pickup JC. Salivary insulin in normal and type I diabetic subjects. *Diabetes Care* 1988; **11**: 489–94.

87 Simionescu L, Aman E, Museteanu P, Dinulescu E, Giureaneanu M. Peptide hormones in saliva. I. Insulin in saliva during the oral glucose tolerance test in female patients. *Endocrinologie* 1985; **23**: 179–87.

88 Vallejo G, Mead PM, Gayner DH, Devlin JT, Robbins DC. Characterization of immunoreactive insulin in human saliva: evidence against production *in situ*. *Diabetologia* 1984; **27**: 441–6.

89 Wood SC, Porte D, Bobbioni E *et al*. Insulin: its relationship to the central nervous system and to the control of food intake and body weight. *Am J Clin Nutr* 1985; **42**: 1063–71.

90 Lefèbvre PJ, Paolisso G, Scheen AJ, Henquin JC. Pulsatility of insulin and glucagon release: physiological significance and pharmacological implications. *Diabetologia* 1987; **30**: 443–52.

91 Cohen P, Barzilai N, Barzilai D, Karnieli E. Correlation between insulin clearance and insulin responsiveness: studies in normal, obese, hyperthyroid, and Cushing's syndrome patients. *Metabolism* 1986; **35**: 744–9.

92 Knip M, Åkerblom HK. Plasma C-peptide and insulin in neonates, infants and children. *J Pediatr* 1981; **99**: 103–5.

93 Andronikou S, Hanning I. Parental nutrition effect on serum insulin in the preterm infant. *Paediatrics* 1987; **80**: 693–7.

94 Franckson JRM, Vanroux R, Leclerq R, Brunengraber H, Ooms HA. Labelled insulin catabolism and pancreatic responsiveness during long-term exercise in man. *Horm Metab Res* 1971; **3**: 366–73.

95 Kreisberg RA, Boshell BR, di Placido J, Roddam RF. Insulin secretion in obesity. *N Engl J Med* 1967; **276**: 314–19.

96 Ballmann M, Hartmann H, Deacon CF, Schmidt WE, Conlon JM, Creutzfeldt W. Hypersecretion of proinsulin does not explain the hyperinsulinaemia of patients with liver cirrhosis. *Clin Endocrinol* 1986; **25**: 351–61.

97 Cohen RM, Given BD, Licinio-Paixao J *et al*. Proinsulin radioimmunoassay in the evaluation of insulinomas and familial hyperproinsulinemia. *Metabolism* 1986; **35**: 1137–46.

98 Yamamoto R, Iwamoto Y, Sakura H *et al*. Reduced urinary insulin clearance in patient with abnormal insulinemia. *Diabetes* 1987; **36**: 602–6.

99 Fajans SF, Floyd JC. Diagnosis and medical management of insulinomas. *Ann Rev Med* 1979; **30**: 313–29.

100 Marks V. The investigation of hypoglycaemia. In: Marks V, Rose FC, eds. *Hypoglycaemia*. Oxford: Blackwell Scientific Publications, 1981: 411–63.

101 Cohen RM, Camus F. Update on insulinomas or the case of the missing (pro) insulinoma. *Diabetes Care* 1988; **11**: 506–8.

102 Beastall GH, Auld CD, Gray CE, Carter DC. Insulinoma in the West of Scotland: the role of biochemistry in diagnosis. *Ann Clin Biochem* 1987; **24** (suppl): 211–12.

103 Teale JD, Pearse AG, Hampton S, Marks V. The significance of insulin, proinsulin, C-peptide and β-hydroxybutyrate measurement in spontaneous hypoglycaemia. *Ann Clin Biochem* 1987; **24**: 212–14.

104 Dons RF, Hodge J, Ginsberg BH, Brennan MF, Cryer PE, Kourides IA, Gorden P. Anomalous glucose and insulin responses in patients with insulinoma. *Arch Intern Med* 1985; **145**: 1861–3.

105 Alsever RN, Roberts P, Gerber JG, Mako ME, Rubenstein AH. Insulinoma with low circulating insulin levels: the diagnostic value of proinsulin measurements. *Ann Int Med* 1975; **82**: 347–50.

106 Gorden P, Sherman B, Roth J. Proinsulin-like component of circulating insulin in the basal state and in patients and hamsters with islet cell tumors. *J Clin Invest* 1971; **50**: 2113–22.

107 Sherman BM, Pek S, Fajans SS, Floyd JC, Conn JW. Plasma proinsulin in patients with functioning islet cell tumors. *J Clin Endocrinol Metab* 1972; **35**: 271–80.

108 Gutman RA, Fink G, Shapiro JR, Selawry H, Recant L. Proinsulin and insulin release with a human insulinoma and adjacent nonadenomatous pancreas. *J Clin Endocrinol Metab* 1973; **36**: 978–87.

109 Melani F, Ryan WG, Rubenstein AH, Steiner DF. Proinsulin secretion by a pancreatic beta-cell adenoma. *N Engl J Med*

1970; **283**: 713−19.

110 Heding LG, Kruse V. Usefulness of fasting proinsulin in the diagnosis of insulinoma. *Diabetes* 1984; **33**: 148A (Suppl 1).

111 Turner RC, Johnson PC. Suppression of insulin release by fish-insulin-induced hypoglycaemia with reference to the diagnosis of insulinoma. *Lancet* 1973; i: 1483−5.

112 Turner RC, Harris E. Diagnosis of insulinomas by suppression tests. *Lancet* 1974; ii: 188−90.

113 Horwitz DL, Rubenstein AH. Insulin suppression. *Lancet* 1974; ii: 1021.

114 Horwitz DL, Rubenstein AH, Reynolds C, Molnar GD, Yanaithara N. Prolonged suppression of insulin release by insulin-induced hypoglycaemia demonstration by C-peptide assay. *Horm Metab Res* 1975; **7**: 449−52.

115 Turner RC, Heding LG. Plasma proinsulin, C-peptide and insulin in diagnostic suppression tests for insulinomas. *Diabetologia* 1977; **13**: 571−7.

116 Cryer P. Glucose homeostasis and hypoglycaemia. In: Wilson JD, Foster DW, eds. *Williams' Textbook of Endocrinology*. Philadelphia: WB Saunders. 1985: 989−1017.

117 Schein PS, De Lellis RA, Kahn CR, Gorden P, Kraft AR. Islet cell tumors: current concepts and management. *Ann Intern Med* 1973; **79**: 239−57.

118 Reynolds JH, Kaminsky N, Schode S *et al*. Use of a computerized glucose clamp technique to diagnose an insulinoma. *Ann Intern Med* 1984; **101**: 648−9.

119 Yki-Järvinen H, Pelkonen R, Koivisto VA. Failure to suppress C-peptide secretion by euglycaemic hyperinsulinaemia: a new diagnostic test for insulinoma? *Clin Endocrinol* 1985; **23**: 461−6.

120 Koivisto VA, Yki-Järvinen H, Hartling SG, Pelkonen R. The effect of exogenous hyperinsulinemia on proinsulin secretion in normal man, obese subjects, and patients with insulinoma. *J Clin Endocrinol Metab* 1986; **63**: 1117−20.

121 Cohen P, Barzilai N, Bar-Ilan R, Yassin K, Karnieli E. Lack of suppression of insulin secretion by hyperinsulinemia in a patient with an insulinoma. *J Clin Endocrinol Metab* 1986; **63**: 1411−13.

122 Gin H, Brottier E, Dupuy B, Guillaume D, Ponzo J, Aubertin J. Use of the glucose clamp technique for confirmation of insulinoma autonomous hyperinsulinism. *Arch Intern Med* 1987; **147**: 985−7.

123 Jakob A, Hauri CH, Froesch ER. Non suppressible insulin-like activity in human serum. *J Clin Invest* 1968; **47**: 2678−88.

124 Antoniades HN. Assay of insulin activity in blood using isolated rat diaphragm. In: Antoniades HN, ed. *Hormones in Human Blood*. Cambridge, Mass: Harvard University Press, 1976: 280−5.

125 Vallance-Owen J, Hurlock B. Estimation of plasma-insulin by the rat diaphragm method. *Lancet* 1954; i: 68−70.

126 Wright PH. Plasma-insulin estimation by the rat diaphragm method *Lancet* 1957; ii: 621−4.

127 Groen J, Kamminga CE, Willebrands AF, Blickman JR. Evidence for the presence of insulin in blood serum. A method for an approximate determination of the insulin content of blood. *J Clin Invest* 1952; **31**: 97−106.

128 Cunningham NF. The insulin activity of bovine and ovine blood plasma. I. Biological assay of insulin using the isolated rat diaphragm. *J Endocrinol* 1962; **25**: 35−42.

129 Martin DB, Renold AE, Dagenais YM. An assay for insulin-like activity using rat adipose tissue. *Lancet* 1958; ii: 76−7.

130 Samaan NA, Dempster WJ, Fraser R, Please NW, Stillman D. Further immunological studies on the form of circulating insulin. *J Endocrinol* 1962; **24**: 263−77.

131 Simon JD. Assay of insulin using isolated adipocytes. In: Antoniades HN, ed. *Hormones in Human Blood*. Cambridge, Mass: Harvard University Press, 1976: 270−9.

132 Nakao K, Takeda A, Kagawa S, Shimizu S, Matsuoka A. A radioreceptor assay for insulin: direct measurement of human serum insulin. *Horm Metabol Res* 1982; **14**: 339−42.

133 Posner BI, Guyda HJ. A human placental radioreceptor assay for insulin and insulin-like substances. In: Antoniades HN, ed. *Hormones in Blood*. Cambridge, Mass: Harvard University Press, 1976: 247−53.

134 Ozaki S, Kalant N. A radioreceptor assay for serum insulin. *J Lab Clin Med* 1977; **90**: 686−99.

135 Shishiba Y, Takino H, Takagi A, Sato S, Irie M. The large 'kit-to-kit' variation in insulin radioimmunoassay is mainly due to difference in standard concentration. *Clin Chem* 1982; **28**: 2443−4.

136 Chawla AS, Hinberg I, Blais P, Johnson D. Aggregation of insulin, containing surfactants, in contact with different materials. *Diabetes* 1985; **34**: 420−4.

137 Livesey JH, Donald RA. Prevention of adsorption losses during radioimmunoassay of polypeptide hormones: effectiveness of albumins, gelatin, caseins, Tween 20 and plasma. *Clin Chim Acta* 1982; **123**: 193−8.

138 Livesey JH, Hodgkinson SC, Roud HR, Donald RA. Effect of time, temperature and freezing on the stability of immunoreactive LH, FSH, TSH, growth hormone, prolactin and insulin in plasma. *Clin Biochem* 1980; **13**: 151−5.

139 Brodal BP. Evidence of an enzymatic degradation of insulin in blood *in vitro*. *Eur J Biochem* 1971; **18**: 201−6.

140 O'Rahilly S, Burnett MA, Smith RF, Darley JH, Turner RC. Haemolysis affects insulin but not C-peptide immunoassay. *Diabetologia* 1987; **30**: 394−6.

141 Csorba TR, Cannon MM, Ungar M, Track NS. Incubation of insulin in hyperglycaemic blood generates insulin dimers. In: Brandenberg D, ed. *Insulin, Chemistry, Structure and Function of Insulin and Related Hormones*. Berlin: Walter de Gruyter, 1980: 539−47.

142 Kato K, Umeda U, Suzuki F, Hayashi D, Kosaka A. Use of antibody Fab' fragments to remove interference by rheumatoid factors with the enzyme-linked sandwich immunoassay. *FEBS Lett* 1979; **102**: 253−6.

143 Kato Y, Umeda Y, Suzuki F, Hayashi D, Kosaki A. Use of gelatin to remove interference by serum with the solid phase enzyme-linked sandwich immunoassay for insulin. *FEBS Lett* 1979; **99**: 172−4.

144 Sankaran H, Harrington MG. Attempts to prepare 'insulin-free plasma' from human subjects: effects of serial dilution and insulin recovery studies on immunoreactive insulin activity of partially insulin-free plasma. *Acta Diabetol Lat* 1978; **15**: 133−42.

145 Järhult J, Ericsson M, Holst J, Ingemansson J. Lack of suppression of insulin secretion by exercise in patients with insulinoma. *Clin Endocrinol* 1981; **15**: 391−4.

36   C-Peptide and B-Cell Function in Diabetes Mellitus

Summary

• Peripheral insulin levels cannot be used to assess B-cell function because of large and variable uptake from the portal circulation into the liver, and because insulin assays cannot distinguish endogenous from exogenous insulin.

• C peptide is a marker for B-cell function because it is secreted in equimolar amounts to insulin and is minimally extracted by the liver.

• Urinary C-peptide excretion is correlated with integrated plasma C-peptide levels but the excretion is highly variable between and within individuals and is, therefore, an imprecise measure of B-cell function.

• The best established measures of B-cell function are the plasma C-peptide responses to a standard meal (e.g. 'Sustacal') or the intravenous injection of glucagon.

• Even minimally preserved B-cell function is metabolically beneficial, being associated with lower insulin dosages, lower HbA$_{1c}$ levels and lesser metabolic decompensation after insulin withdrawal.

Qualitative and quantitative evaluation of B-cell function is not only of use in the pre- and post-diagnostic study of the natural history of diabetes mellitus, but is also relevant in clinical practice as a guide to the correct choice of treatment.

Insulin is produced in the B cells of the islets of Langerhans by cleavage of its precursor, proinsulin, into insulin, C peptide, and two pairs of basic amino acids. The cleavage of proinsulin comprises several intermediate steps as illustrated in Fig. 36.1 (see also Chapter 35). Insulin and C peptide are subsequently secreted into the portal circulation in near-equimolar quantities, together with small amounts of proinsulin and minimal amounts of split products — less than 1% of total proinsulin immunoreactivity.

Insulin secretion rates cannot be calculated directly from the peripheral insulin concentration because insulin secreted into the portal vein by the pancreas is taken up to a large and variable degree by the liver before it enters the general circulation. Measurements of plasma insulin concentration are further complicated in insulin-treated patients because of the presence of circulating insulin antibodies, and because most insulin immunoassays cannot distinguish endogenous from exogenous insulin (Chapter 35).

In contrast to insulin, C peptide is only minimally extracted by the liver. Peripheral C peptide concentrations therefore reflect the secretion of the B cells more accurately than insulin. Moreover, C-peptide antibodies are species-specific: an antibody raised against human C peptide reacts only with human C peptide or (to a variable degree) with the C-peptide part of human proinsulin and its split products.

For these reasons, measurements of C peptide in plasma, and to a lesser extent in urine, have entered general use as a measure of B-cell function.

Diagnostic significance of C peptide in diabetes

In clinical research, there is a need for quantitative measurement of insulin secretion. It has recently been shown that C peptide fulfils the requirements of a peripheral marker [1].

It is important to realize that neither fasting C-peptide values nor a series of values obtained in response to a stimulus, give more than a semi-

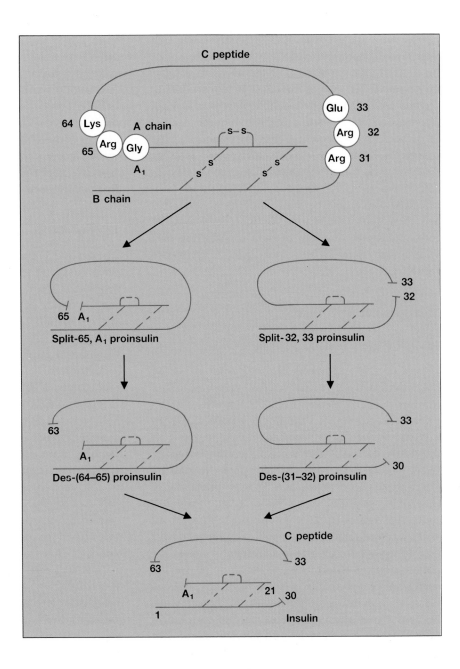

Fig. 36.1. Processing of human proinsulin.

quantitative measure of B-cell function [2]. Such measurements, however, have proved diagnostically useful, not only in discriminating between IDDM and NIDDM, but also in identifying remission or relapses in the course of IDDM.

As described above, C peptide is secreted in equimolar amounts with insulin from the B cells and its hepatic extraction is negligible under a wide variety of conditions. The metabolic clearance rate of C peptide is constant from low to supraphysiological plasma concentrations and unaffected by changes in glucose concentration or the ingestion of a mixed meal [3]. Its peripheral distribution and metabolism can be adequately

described by a two-compartment mathematical model. Model parameters can be determined for individual subjects by administering exogenous biosynthetic human C peptide [4], or indirectly by the 'minimal modelling' method based upon the time-courses of plasma C peptide and insulin changes in response to a defined stimulus [5, 6]. The use of *a priori* mean population values of model parameters will give less precise, but still useful, estimates in individual studies. The mean metabolic clearance rate of C peptide in normal subjects is about 4 ml/kg/min, with a coefficient of variation of about 5%.

Quantitative studies are of course cumbersome.

The incremental areas under the plasma C-peptide time curve after a defined stimulus provide a useful quantitative expression of the amount of insulin secreted, but only if the curve is followed until plasma levels return to baseline. This is of special importance when estimating the hepatic uptake of insulin by comparing the incremental area under the C-peptide curve with that of insulin. Assumptions based on the molar ratios of the B-cell hormones, (C peptide, insulin, and proinsulin) should also be made cautiously. Not only are their half-lives different, but there may be fundamental differences in their distribution and equilibrium time which can totally invalidate these methods.

Measurement of C peptide

Plasma C-peptide determination

C-peptide concentrations are measured either by radioimmunoassay (RIA) or by enzyme linked immunosorbent assay (ELISA). Because the C-peptide sequence is contained within the proinsulin molecule, antibodies raised against C peptide will cross-react with proinsulin, whether they are poly- or monoclonal. Normally, the plasma concentration of proinsulin is less than 5% of that of C peptide, on a molar basis. Provided that cross-reactivity is low, the error introduced will therefore generally be small. However, under conditions where circulating proinsulin levels are abnormally elevated, either because of hypersecretion of proinsulin relative to C peptide or because of binding of proinsulin to insulin antibodies, the contribution of proinsulin to total C-peptide immunoreactivity can become significant and the results misleading. Proinsulin can be removed from serum by immunoabsorption using high-affinity insulin antibodies or by high-pressure liquid chromatography. If insulin antibodies are present, a preliminary step to precipitate these should first be introduced to remove antibody-bound proinsulin.

There is still no international reference assay or recognized international standard for C peptide. Highly purified biosynthetic C peptide is the most commonly used assay standard. Despite this, there is still significant inter-laboratory variation in normal and pathological values. The differences seem to be due to assay conditions and particularly in labelling quality. Care should, therefore, be taken when considering data from the literature. Direct comparisons can only be carried out when the assays are identical or at least adjusted using appropriate quality controls.

C-peptide immunoreactivity in biological fluids is heterogeneous, but this seems unimportant for most assays. Some assays are sensitive to inadequate sample storage. This can be circumvented by separating serum within 2 h of sampling and freezing immediately to below −25°C until assay (for review, see Bouser & Garcia-Webb 1984 [7]).

Fasting plasma C-peptide concentration

The fasting C-peptide level is generally correlated with the blood glucose concentration, but this correlation is weak in diabetic patients [8]. The fasting C-peptide concentration is inversely correlated with creatinine clearance, calling for caution in interpreting C-peptide values when kidney function is impaired.

Subnormal fasting C-peptide values (<0.4 nmol/l) have been widely used to distinguish IDDM subjects from others who are insulin treated but not truly insulin-dependent. The sensitivity, i.e. = (number of subjects requiring insulin, with subnormal fasting plasma C peptide)/(total number of subjects requiring insulin) × 100, has been found to be more than 90% [9]. The specificity, i.e. = (number of subjects not requiring insulin, with normal fasting C peptide)/(total number of subjects not requiring insulin) × 100, was 80% [9]. Undetectable fasting values will falsely classify only 7% as having no B-cell function, while the presence of measurable amounts of C peptide always correctly indicates residual B-cell function [10].

Urinary C-peptide determination

As urine collection is non-invasive, C-peptide measurements in timed urine collections have some appeal in evaluating endogenous insulin secretion. Normally, about 50% of total daily C-peptide secretion will be extracted by the kidneys, but only a few per cent can be found in a 24 h urine collection [11, 12].

Determination of C peptide in the urine follows the same principles as for plasma. Some assays do not show linear dilution, which always seems a problem when the solute concentration is very low. Dilution with isotonic buffers seems to be of importance.

Urinary C-peptide clearance varies substantially

within an individual [13]. It increases post-prandially [14] and decreases during prolonged fasting, at least in obese subjects [15]. Clearance is higher in diabetic patients than in control subjects, and IDDM patients show larger variability than normals and patients with NIDDM [16]. Total daily C-peptide excretion is also highly variable, with a coefficient of variation of day-to-day excretion of the order of 40% [17−19]. Patients with NIDDM show a larger variability than normal subjects [13]. The urinary excretion of C peptide not only correlates with the total energy intake, but also with the composition of food [13, 20, 21]. Excretion is higher on high-carbohydrate or high-protein intake and correlates with the dietary content of carbohydrate and protein, but not with that of fat.

The 24-h urinary excretion of C peptide is closely correlated with body weight [18] and the inter-patient variation seems lower in lean normal subjects than in obese normal and obese diabetic subjects [22]. Even though the excretion of C peptide over short periods correlates well with 24-h excretion, the intra-patient variability increases when shorter collection periods are used [21].

Although urinary C-peptide excretion is closely correlated with C-peptide secretion as determined by integrated plasma measurements [22], the substantial multifactoral intra- and inter-patient variability makes urinary C-peptide determinations a less precise measure of B-cell function than those based upon plasma determinations. However, it has provided useful information in group comparisons, confirmatory to that obtained by plasma measurements. Urinary levels generally parallel the plasma C-peptide responses to various stimuli including glucagon, but with greater variability [9].

The 24-h excretion of C peptide in normal adults lies between 11.5 and 21.4 nmol [13, 19, 23−6]. In children of either sex, median excretion is about 0.25 nmol/kg/day [27−9]. Excretion is positively correlated with age, weight, height, body surface area and 24-h urinary creatinine. Children at puberty show a significantly higher excretion than younger children [27].

Dynamic tests of B-cell function

The response of plasma C peptide to specified stimuli has been used to identify insulin dependency. These stimuli include a standard meal, oral or intravenous glucose, intravenous arginine, a combination of intravenous glucose and glibenclamide, intravenous glucagon, intravenous secretin or a combination of these.

The available data suggest no need for tests other than intravenous glucagon or a standard test meal for clinical evaluation of B-cell function. However, other tests may have specific clinical research applications.

Standard meal test

Various standard meal tests have been used. Of these, the administration of a mixed liquid meal (Sustacal; Mead Johnson, Belleville, Ontario, Canada) has been employed especially in children. 7 ml/kg is given after fasting overnight and C peptide measured in blood collected through an in-dwelling catheter at 0, 60, 90 and 120 min. The response is usually expressed as the increment from basal to peak level, which usually occurs between 60 and 120 min after ingesting the meal. The reproducibility of the Sustacal test seems to be very high in children when carried out within a 2-week period. The response seems to be independent of prevailing blood-glucose concentration [30].

Intravenous glucagon test

Only the response to the intravenous injection of glucagon has been systematically evaluated and compared with the response to a meal consistent with the ordinary diabetic diet. After an overnight fast, blood is sampled for baseline C-peptide determination and 1 mg of glucagon is given as an intravenous bolus. The maximal C-peptide concentration is reached after about 6 min in diabetic patients and after about 3 min in normal healthy subjects, returning to basal levels after 15−20 min. The peak value after glucagon stimulation is strongly correlated with that obtained after a standard breakfast (which occurs after about 90 min). Whereas the response to a standard breakfast is independent of the fasting blood-glucose concentration, the response to glucagon is suppressed if the fasting blood glucose is below 7 mmol/l, when the correlation is lost with the meal response [31]. The outcome of the test seems fairly reproducible, with coefficients of variation of about 10% in normal subjects and 15% in NIDDM but up to 30% in IDDM patients [32].

By 1981, it had been shown that the result of a

glucagon test was highly predictive of insulin dependency, as has subsequently been amply confirmed [9, 33, 50] (Fig. 36.2). When samples are measured with the M1230 C-peptide antibody, a fasting value below 0.20 nmol/l confirms the necessity of insulin treatment, whereas fasting values exceeding 0.60 nmol/l indicate that insulin requirement is not obligatory. Subjects with values between these two limits can be divided by their response to glucagon: stimulated values below 0.60 nmol/l indicate the need for supplementary exogenous insulin treatment.

Corresponding discriminatory values have been defined for other assay systems [34].

Metabolic consequences of residual B-cell function

Most data are in favour of a beneficial metabolic effect of even minimal B-cell function [35]. It is also established beyond reasonable doubt that severe metabolic derangement, as in diabetic ketoacidosis, can suppress B-cell function [36, 37].

The improvement of glycaemic control with intensified insulin therapy seems to enhance B-cell function in insulin-treated, normal-weight, ketosis-prone subjects [38], but only temporarily [39, 40], and not in patients with previously absent B-cell function [41].

Even minimal B-cell function inhibits the development of ketosis in insulin-dependent diabetic patients [42] (Fig. 36.3). After 12 h of insulin deprivation, patients with no B-cell function develop more pronounced metabolic derangement, with higher levels of glucose, 3-hydroxybutyrate, glycerol and non-esterified fatty acids, despite similar peripheral insulin concentrations. Individual mean C-peptide concentrations show a significant inverse correlation with the final blood-glucose values. Lesser metabolic decompensation was seen even where fasting C-peptide values were barely detectable.

Insulin-dependent patients without residual B-cell function show exaggerated lipolysis and ketogenesis in response to insulin-induced hypoglycaemia, compared with that in patients with B-cell function [43]. It has also been found

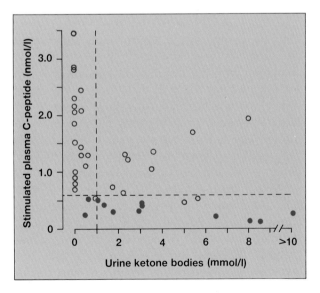

Fig. 36.2. The relationship between urinary ketone body levels and glucagon-stimulated plasma C-peptide concentrations during the first 3 days after diagnosis in patients who were insulin-requiring (●) or non-insulin-requiring (○) 12 months later. All subjects with a stimulated C-peptide value > 0.6 nmol/l were subsequently non-insulin-requiring. Also, urinary ketone levels are a poor predictor of classification into insulin or non-insulin-requiring. (Redrawn from Hother-Nielson et al. 1988 [50].)

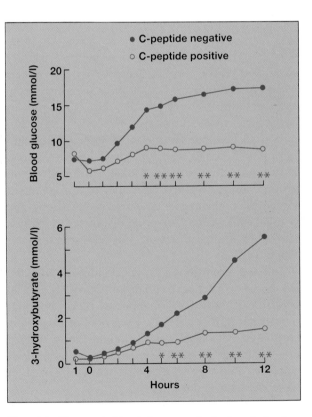

Fig. 36.3. Changes in blood glucose and 3-hydroxybutyrate concentrations in response to insulin withdrawal in IDDM patients with B-cell function (detectable C peptide) or without B-cell function (undetectable C peptide). (Redrawn from Madsbad et al. 1979 [42] and reproduced with permission from the Editor of the British Medical Journal.)

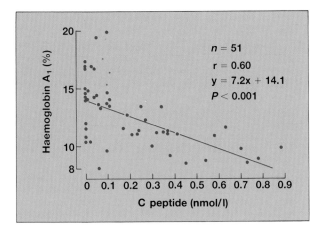

Fig. 36.4. Correlation in insulin-treated diabetic patients between B-cell function, plasma C-peptide concentration and glycaemic control (measured by glycosylated haemoglobin, HbA₁). (Redrawn from Gonen *et al.* 1979 [46].)

that the glucagon response to hypoglycaemia is significantly smaller compared with the patients with preserved B-cell function, who show an almost normal response.

The importance of preserved B-cell function for day-to-day metabolic control is difficult to evaluate, because of the mutual relationship between B-cell function, food composition, physical activity, insulin sensitivity, insulin dosage, insulin pharmacokinetics and the degree of metabolic control. However, in a 36-month prospective study of 215 insulin-dependent patients followed from the time of diagnosis, those patients with initially undetectable B-cell function showed consistently lower fasting C-peptide levels during follow-up as compared with patients having significant initial B-cell function. Despite having identical levels of HbA$_{1c}$, the average doses of insulin were significantly higher at all time-points in the group with no initial B-cell function [44]. In other studies, HbA$_{1c}$ levels have been found to be inversely correlated with both C-peptide secretory capacity and the average daily dose of insulin [45, 46] (Fig. 36.4).

IDDM patients who subsequently enter remission show significantly higher C-peptide levels than those who do not go into remission, and remission occurs more often in patients with high initial basal C-peptide levels. Sex, age, and initial HbA$_{1c}$ levels are unrelated to the frequency of remission [44].

There has been much speculation that preserved B-cell function might reduce or delay the development of late diabetic complications. However, this view is entirely based on cross-sectional studies [47–49] and remains controversial.

CHRISTIAN BINDER

References

1 Polonsky KS, Rubenstein AH. Current approaches to measurement of insulin secretion. *Diabetes Metab Rev* 1986; **2**: 315–29.
2 Faber OK, Binder C. C peptide: an index of insulin secretion. *Diabetes Metab Rev* 1986; **2**: 331–45.
3 Polonsky KS, Given BD, Van Cauter E. Twenty-four-hour profiles and pulsatile patterns of insulin secretion in normal and obese subjects. *J Clin Invest* 1988; **81**: 442–8.
4 Polonsky KS, Rubenstein AH. C-Peptide as a measure of the secretion and hepatic extraction of insulin. Pitfalls and Limitations. *Diabetes* 1984; **33**: 486–94.
5 Cobelli C, Pacini G. Insulin secretion and hepatic extraction in humans by minimal modeling of C-peptide and insulin kinetics. *Diabetes* 1988; **37**: 223–31.
6 Vølund AA, Polonsky KS, Bergman RN. Calculated pattern of intraportal insulin appearance without independent assessment of C peptide kinetics. *Diabetes* 1987; **36**: 1195–1202.
7 Bonser AM, Garcia-Webb P. C-peptide measurement: methods and clinical utility. *CRC Critical Rev Clin Lab Sci* 1984; **19**: 297–352.
8 Faber OK, Binder C. Plasma C-peptide during the first year of insulin-dependent diabetes mellitus. In: *Diabetes. Proceedings of the IX Congress of the International Diabetes Federation*, New Delhi, 1976. Excerpta Medica, International Congress Series No. 413.
9 Koskinen P, Viikari J, Irjala K et al. Plasma and urinary C-peptide in the classification of adult diabetics. *Scand J Clin Lab Invest* 1986; **46**: 655–63.
10 Faber OK, Regeur L, Lauritzen T et al. The glucagon/C peptide test in the evaluation of beta-cell function. In: *Proceedings of the Symposium on Proinsulin, Insulin and C-Peptide*, Tokushima, 1978. Excerpta Medica, International Congress Series No. 468.
11 Brodows RG. Use of urinary C-peptide to estimate insulin secretion during starvation. *J Clin Endocrinol Metab* 1985; **61**: 654–7.
12 Kruszynska YT, Home PD, Hanning I et al. Basal and 24-h C-peptide and insulin secretion rate in normal man. *Diabetologia* 1987; **30**: 16–21.
13 Takai K, Nonaka K, Ichihara K et al. Food constituents as a cause of variation of C-peptide excretion in the urine. *Endocrinol Japan* 1984; **31**: 291–9.
14 Blix PM, Boddie-Willis C, Landau L et al. Urinary C-peptide: An indicator of β-cell secretion under different metabolic conditions. *J Clin Endocrinol Metab* 1982; **54**: 574–7.
15 Pasquali R, Buratti P, Casimirri F et al. Urine excretion rate of C-peptide in fed and fasted obese humans. *Acta Endocr (Copenhagen)* 1988; **118**: 38–44.
16 Fernandez-Castañer M, Rosel P, Ricart W et al. Evaluation of B-cell function in diabetics by C-peptide determination in basal and postprandial urine. *Diabète Métab* 1987; **13**: 538–42.
17 Gjessing HJ, Damsgaard EM, Matzen LE et al. Reproducibility of β-cell function estimates in non-insulin-dependent diabetes mellitus. *Diabetes* 1987; **10**: 558–62.
18 Meistas MT, Zadik Z, Margolis S et al. Correlation of urinary excretion of C-peptide with the integrated concentration and secretion rate of insulin. *Diabetes* 1981; **30**: 639.

19 Horwitz DL, Rubenstein AH, Katz AI. Quantitation of human pancreatic beta-cell function by immunoassay of C-peptide in urine. *Diabetes* 1977; **26**: 30–4.

20 Hoogwerf BJ, Laine DC, Greene E. Urine C-peptide and creatinine (Jaffe method) excretion in healthy young adults on varied diets: Sustained effects of varied carbohydrate, protein, and meat content. *Am J Clin Nutr* 1986; **43**: 350–60.

21 Hoogwerf BJ, Goetz FC. Urinary C-peptide: A simple measure of integrated insulin production with emphasis on the effects of body size, diet, and corticosteroids. *J Clin Endocrinol Metab* 1983; **56**: 60–7.

22 Meistas MT, Rendell M, Margolis S *et al*. Estimation of the secretion rate of insulin from the urinary excretion rate of C-peptide. Study in obese and diabetic subjects. *Diabetes* 1982; **31**: 449–57.

23 Osei K. Clinical evaluation of determinants of glycemic control. A new approach using serum glucose, C-peptide, and body mass indexes in Type II diabetic patients. *Arch Intern Med* 1986; **146**: 281–5.

24 Pasquali R, Buratti P, Biso P *et al*. Interrelationships between body weight, insulin secretion from B-cell and metabolic control in type 2 (non-insulin-dependent) diabetics with fasting hyperglycemia. *Pan Med* 1987; **29**: 181–8.

25 Kuzuya T, Matsuda A, Sakamoto Y *et al*. C peptide immunoreactivity (CPR) in urine. *Diabetes* 1978; **27** (suppl 1): 210–12.

26 Kajinuma H, Tanabashi S, Ishiwata K *et al*. Urinary excretion of C-peptide in relation to renal function. In: Baba, A, Koneko A, Yanaihara H, eds. *Proinsulin, Insulin, C-peptide*. Excerpta Medica, Amsterdam 1979: 183–9.

27 Wallensteen M, Persson B, Dahlqvist G. The urinary C-peptide excretion in normal healthy children. *Acta Paediatr Scand* 1987; **76**: 82–6.

28 Zick R, Hürter P, Lange P *et al*. Die C-Peptidausscheidung im 24 Std-Urin als Indikator der B-Zell-Residualfunktion bei Kindern und Jugendlichen mit Typ-I-Diabetes. *Monatsschr Kinderheilkd* 1982; **130**: 209–13.

29 Gäcs G, Jakabfi P, Zubovich L. The effect of age and body size on the urinary excretion of C-peptide from birth to 14 years of age. *Eur J Pediatr* 1985; **143**: 183–6.

30 Clarson C, Daneman D, Drash AL *et al*. Residual beta-cell function in children with IDDM: Reproducibility of testing and factors influencing insulin secretory reserve. *Diabetes Care* 1987; **10**: 33–8.

31 Madsbad S, Sauerbrey N, Møller-Jensen B *et al*. Outcome of the glucagon test depends upon the prevailing blood glucose concentration in Type I (insulin-dependent) diabetic patients. *Acta Med Scand* 1987; **222**: 71–4.

32 Arnold-Larsen S, Madsbad S, Kühl C. Reproducibility of the glucagon test. *Diabetic Med* 1987; **4**: 299–303.

33 Hoekstra JBL, Van Rijn HJM, Thijssen JHH *et al*. C-peptide reactivity as a measure of insulin dependency in obese diabetic patients treated with insulin. *Diabetes Care* 1982; **5**: 585–91.

34 Matsuda S, Kamata I, Iwamoto Y *et al*. A comparison of serum C-peptide response to intravenous glucagon, and urine C-peptide, as indexes of insulin dependence. *Diabetes Res Clin Pract* 1985; **1**: 161–7.

35 Binder C, Faber OK. C-peptide and proinsulin. In: Alberti KGMM, Krall LP, eds. *The Diabetes Annual*, Vol. 1. Amsterdam: Elsevier Science Publishers BV, 1985: 406–17.

36 Block MB, Mako ME, Steiner DF *et al*. Diabetic ketoacidosis: evidence for C-peptide and proinsulin secretion following recovery. *J Clin Endocrinol Metab* 1972; **35**: 402–7.

37 Glaser B, Leibovich, G, Nesher R *et al*. Improved beta-cell function after intensive insulin treatment in severe non-insulin-dependent diabetes. *Acta Endocrinol* (Copenhag) 1988; **118**: 365–73.

38 Mirouze J, Selam JL, Pham TC *et al*. Sustained insulin-induced remissions of juvenile diabetes by means of an external artificial pancreas. *Diabetologia* 1978; **14**: 223–7.

39 Madsbad S, Krarup T, Regeur L *et al*. Effect of strict blood glucose control on residual B-cell function in insulin-dependent diabetics. *Diabetologia* 1981; **20**: 530–4.

40 Madsbad S, Krarup T, Faber OK *et al*. The transient effect of strict glycaemic control on B cell function in newly diagnosed Type 1 (insulin-dependent) diabetic patients. *Diabetologia* 1982; **22**: 16–21.

41 Seigler DE, Reeves ML, Skyler JS. Lack of effect of improved glycaemic control on C-peptide secretion in patients without residual B-cell function. *Diabetes Care* 1982; **5**: 334–40.

42 Madsbad S, Alberti KGMM, Binder C *et al*. Role of residual insulin secretion in protecting against ketoacidosis in insulin-dependent diabetes. *Br Med J* 1979; **2**: 1257–61.

43 Madsbad S, Hilsted J, Krarup T *et al*. Hormonal, metabolic and cardiovascular responses to hypoglycaemia in Type 1 (insulin-dependent) diabetes with and without residual B-cell function. *Diabetologia* 1982; **23**: 499–507.

44 Agner T, Damm P, Binder C. Remission in IDDM: prospective study of basal C-peptide and insulin dose in 268 consecutive patients. *Diabetes Care* 1987; **10**: 164–9.

45 Dahlqvist G, Blom L, Bolme P *et al*. Metabolic control in 131 juvenile-onset diabetic patients as measured by HbA$_{1c}$: relation to age, duration, C-peptide, insulin dose, and one or two insulin injections. *Diabetes Care* 1982; **5**: 399–403.

46 Gonen B, Goldman J, Baldwin D *et al*. Metabolic control in diabetic patients. Effects of insulin-secretory reserve (measured by plasma C-peptide levels) and circulating insulin antibodies. *Diabetes* 1979; **28**: 749–53.

47 Madsbad S. Prevalence of residual B-cell function and its metabolic consequences of *Type* 1 (insulin-dependent diabetes. Academic Dissertation, University of Copenhagen, 1986.

48 Madsbad S, Lauritzen E, Faber OK *et al*. The effect of residual beta-cell function on the development of diabetic retinopathy. *Diabetic Med* 1986; **3**: 42–5.

49 Mosier MA. Circulating C-peptide and diabetic retinopathy. *Diabetes Res* 1984; **1**: 151–4.

50 Hother-Nielsen O, Faber O, Schwarz-Sorensen N, Beck-Nielsen H. Classification of newly-diagnosed diabetic patients as insulin-requiring or non-insulin requiring based on clinical and biochemical variables. *Diabetes Care* 1988; **11**: 531–7.

SECTION 10
MANAGEMENT OF INSULIN-DEPENDENT DIABETES MELLITUS

37 Insulin Manufacture and Formulation

Summary

- Insulin in pharmaceutical preparations is mostly in the form of self-associated hexamers.
- Insulin is least soluble at its isoelectric point of pH 5.4 and the addition of zinc ions and high salt concentrations broadens the pH range of precipitation.
- The manufacture of pancreas-derived bovine and porcine insulin involves long-established acid–ethanol extraction and salting-out procedures. The large-scale production of human insulin is by enzymatic conversion of porcine insulin (semisynthesis) or biosynthesis.
- 'emp' (enzymatically modified porcine) insulin is made by the trypsin-catalyzed replacement of the B30 alanine residue of porcine insulin with a threonine ester.
- Biosynthetic insulin is made by recombinant-DNA technology with either separate A- and B-chain fermentation in *Escherichia coli* (crb — chain recombinant, bacterial), proinsulin gene insertion into a single organism (prb — proinsulin recombinant, bacterial) or biosynthesis of a single-chain precursor in the yeast, *Saccharomyces cerevisiae*.
- Purification to a high degree involves crystallization, gel filtration and ion-exchange chromatography, and a final HPLC step in some human insulin preparations.
- Over 300 insulin preparations exist but they can be classified simply into short-acting preparations (insulin in solution); prolonged-acting (neutral suspensions with added protamine (isophane) or zinc ions (the lente series), or acid solutions with cationic substances (surfen or globin insulins)); and premixed formulations.
- Protein engineering and recombinant DNA technology now allow new shorter-acting and soluble prolonged-acting insulin analogues to be produced.

The history of the galenic pharmacy* of insulin represents a remarkable and unique chapter in the history of therapeutics. Shortly after the discovery of insulin by Banting and Best in 1921 (Chapter 2), several manufacturers were licensed to produce bovine and porcine insulins (Table 37.1). The early preparations, although very impure and of variable quality, instantly and dramatically improved the prospect for life of thousands of diabetic people. The intervening seven decades have witnessed a stream of developments in insulin production, purification and formulation, aimed at improving metabolic control, safety and convenience of use. The advent of recombinant DNA technology, improved knowledge of structure–function relationships and molecular modelling has recently fuelled a new phase in this developmental process.

Properties of insulin relevant to its galenic pharmacy

A grasp of some of the physico-chemical characteristics of the insulin molecule significantly helps with understanding many of the processes underlying the commercial production, purification, formulation and storage requirements of insulin preparations.

* *Galenic pharmacy* is the discipline dealing with the production of drugs from raw materials and their formulation into pharmaceutical preparations with the desired quality, efficacy, safety and stability during storage.

357

Table 37.1. Insulin manufacturers.

Name	Started production
Connaught Laboratories, Canada	1922
Eli Lilly, USA	1922
Allen and Hanbury, UK	1923
Boots Pure Drug Company, UK	1923
British Drug House, UK	1923
Burroughs-Wellcome, UK	1923
Commonwealth Serum Laboratories, Australia	1923
Farbwerke Hoechst, FRG	1923
Nordisk Insulinlaboratorium, Denmark	1923
NV Organon, The Netherlands	1923
E.R. Squibb & Sons, USA	1924
Novo Industri A/S, Denmark	1925
Swiss Serum and Vaccine Institute, Switzerland	1938
Hormon-Chemie, Munich, FRG	1945
Weddel Pharmaceuticals, UK	1950s

Within a few years of its isolation, it was established that insulin is a protein [1]. The primary structure of bovine insulin was elucidated in 1955 by Sanger [2] and the sequences of insulins from several species were soon determined, culminating in 1960 with that of man (Fig. 37.1; see also Chapter 10). Human insulin has a molecular weight of 5807 Da, contains 51 amino-acid residues, and differs structurally from bovine and porcine insulins as shown in Table 37.2. Insulin contains several ionizable residues, with six capable of attaining positive charge and ten capable of attaining negative charge. Fig. 37.2 shows the calculated net charge of the insulin molecule as a function of pH. At the isoelectric point, electrostatic repulsion between molecules and therefore solubility is at a minimum, whereas insulin is relatively soluble at a pH below 4 or above 7; the addition of Zn^{2+} (see below) or high salt concentrations will broaden the pH range in which precipitation occurs. Solubility also shows species variation: of the three insulins used therapeutically, bovine precipitates most readily, and human least.

In aqueous solutions, insulin monomers self-associate by *non-covalent* bonding to form equi-

Table 37.2. Differences in amino-acid sequence for bovine, porcine and human insulins.

	Positions		
	A chain		B chain
	8	10	30
Bovine	Alanine	Valine	Alanine
Porcine	Threonine	Isoleucine	Alanine
Human	Threonine	Isoleucine	Threonine

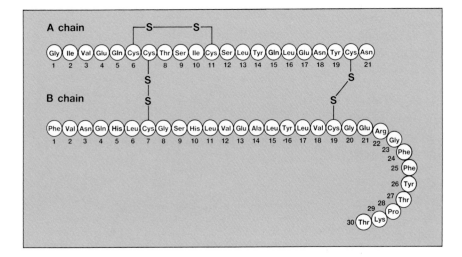

Fig. 37.1. The primary structure of human insulin.

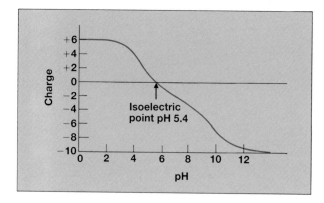

Fig. 37.2. Calculated net charge of insulin monomer as a function of pH.

librium mixtures of dimers, tetramers, hexamers and possibly even higher association states (see Fig. 37.3). Monomeric insulin only occurs in very dilute solutions or at the extremes of pH. In most pharmaceutical preparations (at neutral pH and in the presence of Zn^{2+}), the predominant form (75% or more) of the total insulin is hexamers containing two Zn^{2+} ions [4].

Insulin can aggregate to form crystals. Of the several crystalline forms described, the most important is the rhombohedron composed of multiple units of hexamers of insulin with two or four structural zinc atoms (see Figs 37.3 and 37.4).

Like other proteins, insulin is not a stable entity but is susceptible to chemical degradation and to inter- and intramolecular transformations. Hydrolysis, particularly in acid solutions, may lead to

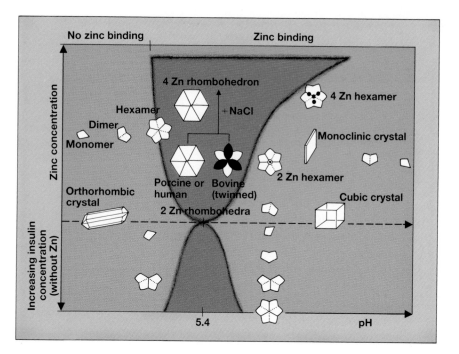

Fig. 37.3. Schematic diagram of association and crystallization behaviour of insulin; the shaded area represents the insulin precipitation zone. (Reproduced with permission from Springer-Verlag [5]).

Table 37.3. Biological potency of some de-amidation and transformation products of insulin. (Adapted from Brange 1987 [5].)

Compound	Formulation	Species	Assay method*	Potency relative to insulin
Mono-desamido (A-21) insulin	Acid soluble	Pork	MBG + MCA	92%
		Beef	MBG + MCA	85%
Mono-desamido (B-3) insulin	Neutral soluble	Pork	MCA	97%
Covalent insulin dimer	Ultralente	Pork	MBG	15%
Covalent polymer	Semilente	Pork	MBG	<2%

*MBG: Mouse blood glucose assay.
MCA: Mouse convulsion assay (see Table 35.1).

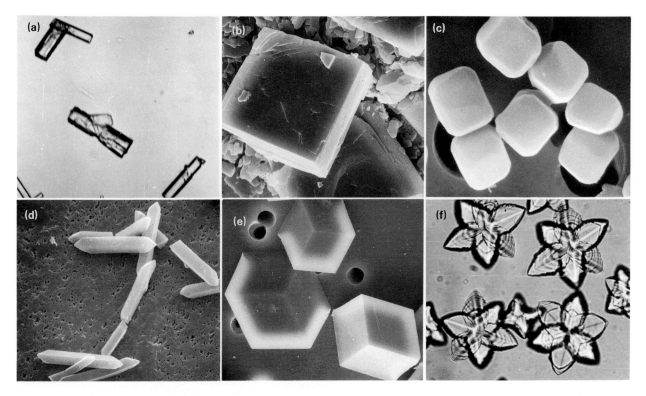

Fig. 37.4. (a) Orthorhombic insulin crystals (×500). (b) Monoclinic insulin crystals (×2400; scanning electron micrograph). (c) Cubic insulin crystals (×6000; scanning electron microscopy). (d) Tetragonal protamine zinc insulin (NPH) crystals (×3000; scanning electron micrograph). (e) Rhombohedral zinc insulin crystals (×1400; scanning electron micrograph). (f) Twinned, distorted rhombohedral beef insulin crystals ('stars') (×500). (Reproduced with permission from Springer-Verlag [5].)

the loss of one or more of the amide groups in the insulin molecule (deamidation). The rate of de-amidation varies with formulation, being greatest with soluble and least with isophane. Deamidated insulin has essentially normal biological potency (see Table 37.3). However, alkaline solutions (pH >10) degrade insulin, primarily by oxidising cysteine residues, and reduce its potency.

Under unusual circumstances (e.g. storage at very high temperatures), insulin molecules dimerize *covalently*. Further covalent bonding can lead to polymer formation. These products, which form most readily in isophane preparations, have low biological potency (see Table 37.3). Exposure of insulin preparations to direct sunlight affects histidyl residues, leading to discolouration and significantly reduced biological activity after only a few days or weeks.

Insulin can also polymerize *non-covalently* to form insoluble, biologically inactive fibrils. This process is favoured at temperatures exceeding 30°C, movement and contact with hydrophobic surfaces. Its considerable importance in insulin infusion devices is discussed in Chapter 45.

Production of insulin

Pancreas-derived bovine and porcine insulins

Until recently, virtually all insulin for therapeutic use was produced from porcine and bovine pancreas using long-established acid-ethanol extraction and 'salting-out' methods. Scott's demonstration [6] that insulin crystallizes in the presence of zinc ions led to the introduction of crystallization as an important step in purification. The production of non-chromatographed crude (amorphous) insulin is illustrated in Fig. 37.5.

Human insulin

As early as the second decade of insulin therapy, several clinicians postulated that there might be benefits to diabetic patients of treatment with human insulin [7, 8]. Early reports [9] of factors in serum capable of neutralizing beef or pork but not human insulin were later substantiated by Yalow and Berson [10], who demonstrated that certain insulin antibodies had less affinity for human than porcine insulin.

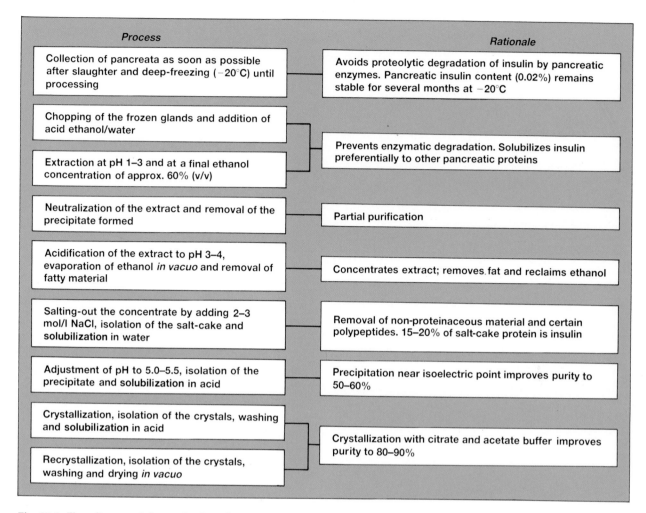

Process	Rationale
Collection of pancreata as soon as possible after slaughter and deep-freezing (−20°C) until processing	Avoids proteolytic degradation of insulin by pancreatic enzymes. Pancreatic insulin content (0.02%) remains stable for several months at −20°C
Chopping of the frozen glands and addition of acid ethanol/water	Prevents enzymatic degradation. Solubilizes insulin preferentially to other pancreatic proteins
Extraction at pH 1–3 and at a final ethanol concentration of approx. 60% (v/v)	
Neutralization of the extract and removal of the precipitate formed	Partial purification
Acidification of the extract to pH 3–4, evaporation of ethanol *in vacuo* and removal of fatty material	Concentrates extract; removes fat and reclaims ethanol
Salting-out the concentrate by adding 2–3 mol/l NaCl, isolation of the salt-cake and solubilization in water	Removal of non-proteinaceous material and certain polypeptides. 15–20% of salt-cake protein is insulin
Adjustment of pH to 5.0–5.5, isolation of the precipitate and solubilization in acid	Precipitation near isoelectric point improves purity to 50–60%
Crystallization, isolation of the crystals, washing and solubilization in acid	Crystallization with citrate and acetate buffer improves purity to 80–90%
Recrystallization, isolation of the crystals, washing and drying *in vacuo*	

Fig. 37.5. Flow-diagram of the production of porcine and bovine insulin from pancreas.

Human insulin was originally prepared by extraction from human cadaveric pancreas [3] and later by end-to-end synthesis from amino acids, which involved 200 separate reaction steps [11, 12]. Neither method was therapeutically or commercially viable. Human insulin is now manufactured on a large scale by two fundamentally different processes, enzymatic conversion of porcine insulin and biosynthesis.

ENZYMATIC CONVERSION OF PORCINE TO HUMAN INSULIN (SEMI-SYNTHESIS)

The first commercially available human insulin preparations were produced by enzymatically converting pancreas-derived porcine insulin to human insulin. Porcine and human insulins differ only in a single residue at the C terminus of the B chain (position B30). Markussen [13–15] perfected a transpeptidation technique which converted porcine insulin to an ester of human insulin by replacing the B30 alanine residue by a threonine ester. The reaction is catalysed by porcine trypsin in a mixture of water and organic solvents in the presence of a large excess of the threonine ester (Fig. 37.6).

The yield of human insulin ester in the transpeptidation reaction is about 97%. Proinsulin and certain derivatives present in crude porcine insulin likewise undergo transpeptidation to human insulin ester, contributing about 3% to the yield. The further processing to human monocomponent insulin is shown in Fig. 37.7. Semi-synthetic insulin manufactured in this way is designated 'emp' ('enzymatically modified porcine').

BIOSYNTHESIS

Three basic strategies have been adopted for the production of human insulin by biosynthesis in micro-organisms, such as the bacterium, *Escherichia coli*, and the yeast, *Saccharomyces*

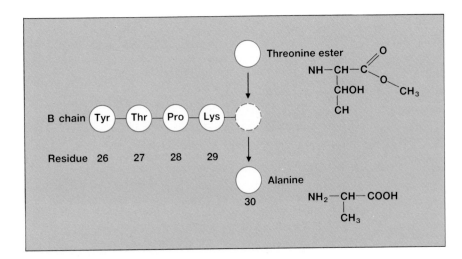

Fig. 37.6. Transpeptidation of porcine insulin to human insulin ester.

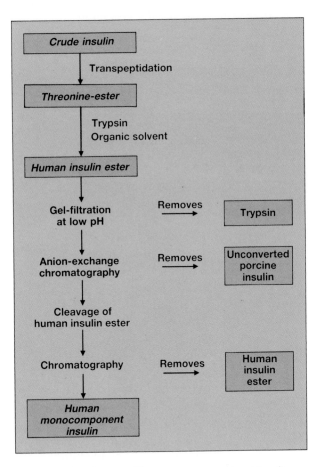

Fig. 37.7. Manufacture of human monocomponent insulin from crude porcine insulin.

cerevisiae. Certain underlying principles concerning biosynthesis will first be discussed.

Biosynthesis employs an organism with known fermentation characteristics, into which a synthetic gene sequence of DNA coding for the de-

sired protein is inserted using an extra-nuclear vector such as a plasmid. In addition to the protein 'gene', others are included to enhance the protein transcription rate (see below) and to promote selective propagation of the encoded organism, for example a specific antibiotic resistance gene may be transferred to the organism, allowing the addition of the antibiotic to the fermentation broth to suppress growth of contaminants.

The organism containing this recombinant DNA is then cultured and synthesizes the desired protein, which is harvested by lysing the bacteria, purified and converted chemically as appropriate to produce the biosynthetic protein. This superficially simple process represents a remarkable *tour de force* combining modern molecular genetics, fermentation technology and purification techniques.

Separate fermentation of A- and B-chain proteins. The strategy first adopted to produce biosynthetic human insulin [16–19] is shown in Fig. 37.8. The DNA sequences coding for the A and B chains of insulin were synthesized chemically. The A-chain gene was then linked to that of a larger protein (tryptophane synthetase) by a codon for methionine, which prevented the intracellular destruction of the susceptible A chain. The B-chain gene was treated similarly. Separate cultures of *E. coli* were then transformed with these artificial genes. Fermentation produced chimeric proteins consisting of a tryptophane synthetase fragment followed by methionine and either the A or B chain. After fermentation, the cells are harvested, disrupted and the chimeric protein isolated from the cell. The insulin chains are released from the trypto-

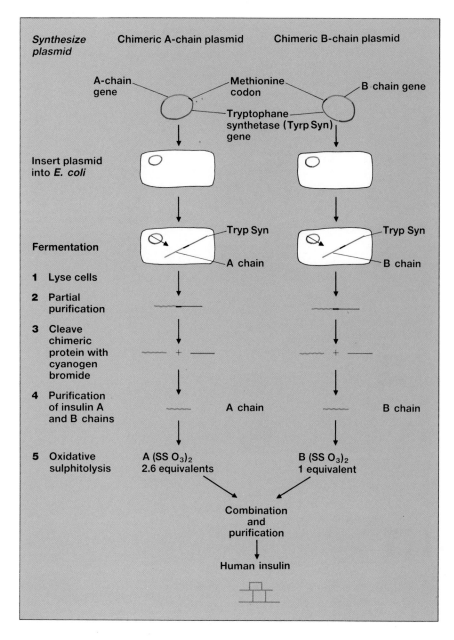

Fig. 37.8. The production of human insulin by *E. coli*. Separate A- and B-chain route.

phane synthetase molecule by treatment with cyanogen bromide, which cleaves specifically at methionine residues.

Separate A and B chains then have to be combined. Insulin is only one of 12 possible isomeric compounds which may result and specific reaction conditions were determined to optimize the yield of insulin [19]. After removal of isomers and polymers, human insulin with a purity of about 97% [18] is obtained. Insulin synthesized by this method is referred to as 'crb' ('chain recombinant, bacterial').

Proinsulin route. This involves inserting the entire proinsulin gene in a single organism rather than separate A and B chains (Fig. 37.9) [20]. The fermentation steps of this method are broadly similar to those for A- and B-chain biosynthesis but the postfermentation processing is considerably simpler. After purification, proinsulin is cleaved enzymatically using a mixture of trypsin and carboxypeptidase B to yield human insulin, which is then purified, and C peptide. This type of insulin is described as 'prb' ('proinsulin recombinant, bacterial').

Biosynthesis in Saccharomyces cerevisiae. Human insulin has recently been biosynthesized by a continuous culture of *Saccharomyces cerevisiae* (brewers' yeast) [21, 22]. Insulin is derived from a

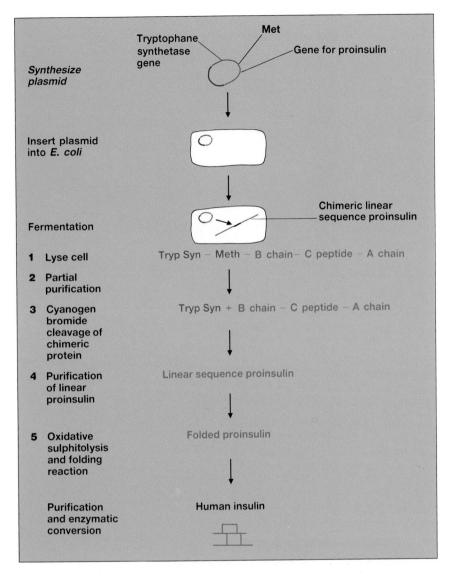

Met

Tryptophane
synthetase
gene

Gene for proinsulin

Synthesize plasmid

Insert plasmid into *E. coli*

Fermentation

Chimeric linear
sequence proinsulin

1 Lyse cell

Tryp Syn — Meth — B chain — C peptide — A chain

2 Partial purification

3 Cyanogen bromide cleavage of chimeric protein

Tryp Syn + B chain — C peptide — A chain

4 Purification of linear proinsulin

Linear sequence proinsulin

5 Oxidative sulphitolysis and folding reaction

Folded proinsulin

Purification and enzymatic conversion

Human insulin

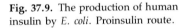

Fig. 37.9. The production of human insulin by *E. coli*. Proinsulin route.

single-chain precursor containing a modified C-peptide region which ensures correct folding. This precursor is exported by the yeast into the culture medium and so may be isolated without lysing the cells. It is converted to insulin by a tryptic transpeptidation process similar to that used to convert porcine into human insulin.

It is perhaps worth emphasizing that synthetic human insulin, irrespective of the method of production, has identical primary (sequence), secondary (helices), tertiary (overall spatial configuration) and quaternary (association behaviour) structure to the native hormone.

Purification

As much as 10−20% of the twice-crystallized insulin preparations used early in the insulin era consisted of contaminating pancreatic proteins,

including pancreatic polypeptide and glucagon. These contaminants have been largely held responsible for the immune-mediated complications (local and systemic allergic reactions, immune insulin resistance and injection-site lipodystrophy [23−6]) which were common at that time (Chapter 40). Repeated crystallization considerably increased purity, but more refined analytical methods in the 1950s demonstrated that various impurities were still present (see Fig. 37.10). Vigorous efforts have since been made to produce insulin devoid of contaminating peptides, using methods based on separation according to molecular size (gel filtration) or charge (ion-exchange chromatography) [27].

Porcine and bovine insulins currently used therapeutically fall into three main categories of purification:

1 Crystallized but non-chromatographed insulin.

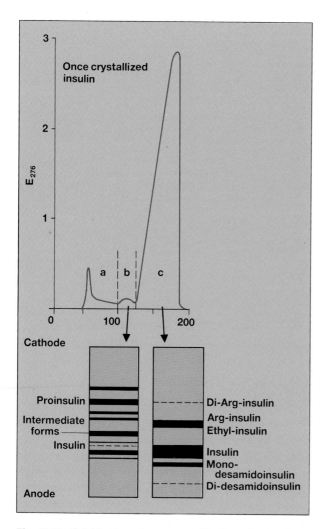

Fig. 37.10. Gel filtration of once-crystallized porcine insulin on Bio-gel P-30 and disc electrophoresis of b and c components with approximate positions of protein contents.

2 Crystallized insulin purified by gel filtration, e.g. 'single peak' (SP) insulin.

3 Crystallized insulin purified by both gel filtration and ion-exchange chromatography, e.g. 'monocomponent' (MC) insulin (Novo), 'single component' (SC) insulin (Lilly) and 'rarely immunogenic' (RI) insulin (Nordisk).

All human insulin preparations conform to category (3), some achieving extremely high degrees of purity through the use of preparative high-performance liquid chromatography (HPLC).

Standardization of insulin preparations

Bioassay methods

Several *in vitro* and *in vivo* bioassay methods have been developed (Chapter 35). Only the *in vivo*

assays based on the hypoglycaemic effect of insulin injected into experimental animals are recognized by Health Authorities for specification control of biological potency. Current assays depend on comparing the fall in blood glucose in either rabbits [28] or mice [29–31] or the percentage of mice developing hypoglycaemic convulsions caused by the unknown with the effects of an international standard. Several studies have confirmed that these three assays give essentially similar results [32].

Chemical methods

Major improvements in insulin purification have now made it possible to calculate the potency of insulin preparations using accurate chemical methods such as Kjeldahl nitrogen determination [33] or HPLC [34].

Insulin preparations

The first preparations contained very impure insulin dissolved in an acid (pH 3.5) medium which was required to solubilize foreign proteins and prevent degradation of insulin by contaminating pancreatic proteases. These acid insulin solutions had a short duration of action and needed to be injected three to six times daily.

At present, given the differences in species, strength, purity and formulation and the number of manufacturers, over 300 different insulin preparations exist world-wide. They may, however, be simply classified according to their duration of action, as short, intermediate, long-acting or pre-mixed preparations (Table 37.4). However, it must be appreciated that subcutaneous insulin absorption is extremely variable and subject to many influences (Chapter 38), including individual patient responses, site of injection, dose size, temperature, exercise [35] and species of insulin [36]. The coefficient of variation of absorption is up to 25% in a given subject, and may exceed 50% between subjects. Quoted action profiles therefore provide only a rough guide (see Chapter 38).

Short-acting preparations

These contain insulin in solution, and are described by various synonyms (Table 37.5). Initially, as described above, insulin could only be dissolved in acid media (which made injection painful) and over 40 years elapsed before the purity

Table 37.4. A classification of insulin preparations.

	Approximate timing of action (h)			Physical state	'Usual' pattern of use
	Onset	Peak	'Maximum' duration		
Short-acting					
Neutral or acid soluble	0.25–1	2–4	5–8	Clear solution	With meals. Twice daily or more
Intermediate-acting					
Semilente	0.5–1	4–6	8–12	Cloudy suspension	Twice daily
Lente	2–4	6–10	12–24	Cloudy suspension	Twice (or once) daily
Isophane	2–4	6–10	12–24	Cloudy suspension	Twice (or once) daily
Long-acting					
Ultralente	3–4	14–20	24–36	Cloudy suspension	Once (or twice) daily
Protamine zinc	3–4	14–20	24–36	Cloudy suspension	Once daily
Biphasic/premixed					
Rapitard™	0.25–1	2–10	12–24	Cloudy suspension	Twice (or once) daily
or soluble/isophane					
mixtures	N.B. reflects constituent parts				

N.B. Values are approximate only. Timings vary with dose, site of injection, species of insulin and individual patients.

Table 37.5. Synonyms for short-acting insulin.

Clear insulin	Quick-acting insulin
Crystalline insulin	Rapid-acting insulin
Crystalline zinc insulin	Regular insulin
Insulin injection	Soluble insulin
Normal insulin	Toronto insulin
Ordinary insulin	Unmodified insulin
Plain insulin	

was improved sufficiently to allow the use of neutral solutions.

Of the three species of insulin used therapeutically, human soluble insulins are absorbed slightly more rapidly than their porcine and bovine counterparts [36–38]. However, in view of the great variability of absorption, these differences are probably clinically unimportant. Preservatives and other additives (see below) do not significantly alter the absorption of soluble insulins, but may influence that of mixtures with longer-acting insulins.

Soluble insulins have also been obtained from other species, notably sheep and fish. These have occasionally been used to treat patients allergic to conventional insulins, and fish insulin was previously used in a provocative test to diagnose insulinoma.

Stable neutral solutions can be made in concentrations of up to 500 IU/ml which have been used for treatment of patients with insulin resistance [39].

Longer-acting preparations

Shortly after the introduction of insulin, the search started for longer-acting preparations to avoid the need for multiple injection therapy. The first long-acting preparations (in the mid-1920s) used insulin in combination with substances such as gum arabic, lecithin and cholesterol or in oil suspensions, but were abandoned because of poor stability, pain upon injection or unreliable absorption.

The basic principle now used to prolong the action profile of insulin after subcutaneous injection involves reducing its solubility at physiological pH. Several different approaches have been adopted.

1 Neutral suspensions of insulin combined with basic proteins, e.g. protamine insulins (isophane and protamine zinc).
2 Neutral suspensions of insulin complexes with small amounts of zinc ions, e.g. lente insulins.
3 Cationic organic compounds added to acid solutions of insulin, e.g. globin and surfen insulins.

PROTAMINE INSULINS

'Protamine' is the generic name of a group of strongly basic proteins present in cell nuclei in combination with the nucleic acids. Protamines used with insulin are normally obtained from the sperm of salmon (salmine) or trout (iridine).

Salmine and iridine are not discrete proteins but comprise heterogeneous families of peptides, each having about 30 amino-acid residues and an average molecular weight of approximately 4300 Da. Basic residues constitute about two-thirds of all the amino acids, resulting in an isoelectric point about pH 12.

Protamine zinc insulin. The first effective protamine insulin preparation was produced in 1936 by Hagedorn and his colleagues at the Nordisk Insulin Laboratorium in Denmark. This neutral protamine insulin suspension was unstable and was superseded in the same year when Scott and Fischer [40] discovered that the addition of zinc to protamine insulin ('protamine zinc insulin', or PZI) further prolonged its duration of activity and enhanced its stability.

Isophane insulin. In 1946 at the Hagedorn laboratories, Krayenbuhl and Rosenberg [41] produced a specific crystalline variant of PZI, by combining insulin and protamine in near-stoichiometric proportions at neutral pH, in the obligatory presence of a small amount of zinc and phenolic preservative. An amorphous insulin precipitate forms initially and is gradually transformed into oblong tetragonal crystals with pyramidal terminations (Fig. 37.4), leaving behind no free insulin or protamine. Hagedorn coined the term 'isophane' (Greek: *iso* = equal; *phane* = appearance) for this reaction. The isophane ratio is empirically derived for each batch of protamine and insulin used. Isophane insulin is also known as NPH ('neutral protamine Hagedorn').

The action profiles of different brands of isophane differ markedly, due largely to variations in crystal size and shape rather than to differences in insulin species [42].

INSULIN ZINC SUSPENSIONS: LENTE AND ULTRALENTE PREPARATIONS

In 1951, Hallas-Møller and co-workers at the Novo Research Institute in Denmark demonstrated that long-acting insulin preparations could be obtained by causing insulin to crystallize in the presence of zinc ions, without the need for a modifying protein. These preparations were termed 'lente' ('slow-acting') [43]. Two physical forms of lente insulins may be produced by careful adjustment of the pH. A crystalline form which contained larger particles and was much less soluble and

therefore very long-acting was named 'ultralente'. An amorphous (microcrystalline) form containing smaller particles was more quickly absorbed and was named 'semilente'. Clinical studies determined that an intermediate duration of activity, similar to that of isophane, could be produced by a mixture of approximately 70% ultralente and 30% semilente. This preparation became known as lente insulin. Originally, bovine crystalline and porcine amorphous insulins were used. Later preparations used only bovine, porcine or human insulin for both components.

For a detailed survey of the physical chemistry of the lente insulins, see Schlichtkrull [44].

PREMIXED PREPARATIONS

Many people require a more pronounced initial insulin effect to cover meals than is offered by the lente or isophane preparations alone. The need for a stronger initial effect led to the search for stable mixtures of short-acting and intermediate- or long-acting insulins, and resulted in the development of Rapitard™ (biphasic insulin injection). Rapitard contains 75% crystalline bovine insulin suspended in a solution of 25% mainly porcine insulin, exploiting the different solubilities of the two molecules.

More recently, a series of so-called biphasic preparations (more accurately termed premixed preparations) have been introduced which are based on mixtures of neutral short-acting and isophane insulin (human or porcine). A wide range of pre-mixed insulin preparations has now evolved, in many cases removing the need to mix insulins before injection.

GLOBIN AND SURFEN INSULINS

Intermediate- and long-acting preparations may also be obtained by complexing insulin with bovine or human globin (the protein moiety of haemoglobin) in acid solutions, or with 'surfen' (1, 3-bis 4-amino-2-methyl-6-quinolyl urea) in neutral solutions [45]. Both preparations were previously widely used in Europe but have now become obsolete.

Additives

Apart from insulin itself and any absorption-retarding substances, insulin formulations contain preservative (e.g. phenol, *m*-cresol, para-amino-benzoate) to prevent growth of micro-organisms in multidose containers. The diluent is buffered with acetates or phosphates and rendered isotonic with glycerol or sodium chloride. The discomfort of injection is greatly reduced by using isotonic diluents and by buffering at physiological pH.

Insulin strength

The strength of insulin preparations is expressed in international units per ml or IU/ml. The first insulin preparations contained only 1 IU/ml, necessitating large injection volumes. As isolation and purification procedures improved, progressively higher concentrations (20, 40 and 80 IU/ml) became available. For many years, preparations containing 40 or 80 IU/ml were in standard use. Medication errors caused by confusing the 40-IU/ml and the 80-IU/ml preparations [46] led the American Diabetes Association to decide that a single insulin concentration should be available. In 1973, 100 IU/ml insulin was introduced in the USA, followed by Canada (1975), Australia and New Zealand (1980), the UK (1983) and Scandinavia. All other strengths have been largely withdrawn in these countries.

Storage requirements

The stated 'shelf life' for most insulin preparations is 30 months at a recommended storage temperature of 2–8°C and out of direct sunlight. Freezing must be avoided [47]. If maintained under these conditions, insulin retains its potency for longer, the 30-month limit allowing for possible exposure to higher temperatures during transportation and so on. Patients going on holiday can store their insulin at room temperature (maximum 25°C) for 1 month without significant loss of potency (see also Chapter 94).

Insulin for infusion devices (see Chapters 44 and 45)

Proinsulin

During the mid-1980s, interest focused on the possible use of biosynthetic human proinsulin to treat diabetes [48]. Initial work suggested that proinsulin acted mainly to suppress hepatic glucose output and had a prolonged intermediate duration of action [49, 50]. Unfortunately, a failure to demonstrate any major therapeutic benefits, coupled with concerns about adverse side-effects, has halted further clinical investigation.

Insulin preparations of the future

Although insulin treatment represents one of the outstanding successes of modern therapeutics, the available preparations have several disadvantages. It is still not possible to mimic the normal physiological pattern of insulin release, in part because of the site of delivery (systemic rather than portal) and in part because of the time-action characteristics of injected insulins. Both the prandial and the background insulin requirements are difficult to meet.

Compared with physiological insulin secretion at mealtimes, short-acting insulins have a comparatively slow onset and prolonged duration. Patients therefore have to inject insulin 30–45 min before meals and are at risk of postprandial hypoglycaemia.

Two approaches to accelerate the absorption of short-acting insulin have met with some degree of success. Nasal absorption of insulin, which has the added advantage of avoiding injections, has been demonstrated in animals and humans (Chapter 46). Even with a surfactant (e.g. bile-salt derivatives) to enhance absorption, only 10% or so of the dose administered enters the circulation [51, 52]. Patients have been treated for several months using this approach but it remains to be seen whether the problems of poor bioavailability can be overcome and whether a well-tolerated stable formulation can be produced.

A second approach has involved the development of analogues of insulin with amino-acid substitutions at the monomer–monomer interface, which prevent non-covalent linkage into dimers and hexamers [53]. These monomeric insulins are absorbed two to three times faster after subcutaneous injection than neutral soluble human insulin while maintaining near-normal biological activity [54].

Constant basal insulin concentrations — essential to reduce hepatic glucose output in diabetes — cannot be achieved with available long-actions insulins because of their variable absorption. In an attempt to produce a better long-acting preparation, Markussen [55] has produced various derivatives of insulin with amino-acid substitutions which shift the isoelectric point from pH 5.4 towards neutrality and maintain solubility in slightly acid solutions. Upon subcutaneous injection, the ambient pH rises to 7, and insulin comes out of solution as small crystals. Animal experiments have demonstrated that these analogues have essentially normal potency and a prolonged duration of action, with smaller intra-individual day-to-day variation of absorption than with currently available long-acting insulins. Recent preliminary studies in IDDM patients have confirmed these potentially useful characteristics [56]. Both the rapid-acting and prolonged-acting derivatives of insulin are currently under investigation to assess their suitability for routine therapeutic use.

Improved understanding of the fundamental relationships of insulin structure and function coupled with the ability to produce 'designer' molecules in quantity using recombinant-DNA technology, has brought us to the threshold of a new era in therapeutics. It remains to be seen whether these exciting possibilities will produce tangible benefits for our patients.

TERENCE CHADWICK

References

1 Wintersteiner O, du Vigneaud V, Jensen H. Studies on crystalline insulin. V. The distribution of nitrogen in crystalline insulin. *J Pharmacol Exp Ther* 1928; **32**: 397–411.

2 Sanger F. Chemistry of insulin. *Science* 1959; **129**: 1340–4.

3 Nicol DS, Smith LF. Amino-acid sequence of human insulin. *Nature* 1960; **187**: 483–5.

4 Milthorpe BK, Nichol LW, Jeffery PD. The polymerization pattern of zinc(II)-insulin at pH 7.0. *Biochim Biophys Acta* 1977; **495**: 195–202.

5 Brange J. *Galenics of Insulin*. Berlin: Springer-Verlag, 1987: Table 17, p. 60.

6 Scott DA. Crystalline insulin. *Biochem J* 1934; **28**: 1592–602.

7 Karr WG, Kreidler WA, Scull CW, Petty OH. Certain immunologic studies in insulin sensitivity. *Am J Med Sci* 1931; **181**: 293–6.

8 Lewis JH. The antigenic properties of insulin. *J Am Med Assoc* 1937; **108**: 1336–8.

9 Lowell FC. Immunologic studies in insulin resistance: the presence of a neutralising factor in the blood exhibiting some characteristics of an antibody. *J Clin Invest* 1944; **23**: 225–40.

10 Yalow RS, Berson SA. Immunological specificity of human insulin: Application of immunoassay to insulin. *J Clin Invest* 1961; **40**: 2190–8.

11 Sieber R, Kamber B, Hartmann A, Johl A, Riniker B, Rittel W. Totalsynthese von Humaninsulin unter gezielter Bildung der Disulfidbindungen. *Helv Chim Acta* 1974; **57**: 2617–21.

12 Sieber R, Kamber B, Hartmann A, Johl A, Riniker B, Rittel W. Totalsynthese von Humaninsulin IV.

Beschreibung der Endstufen. *Helv Chim Acta* 1977; **60**: 27–37.

13 Markussen J. US Patent 4343898. 1980.

14 Markussen J. Human-Monocomponent aus Schweinerohinsulin. In: Petersen K-G, Schluter KJ, Kerp L, eds. *Neue Insuline*. Freiburg: Freiburger Graphische Betriebe, 1982: 38–44.

15 Markussen J, Schaumburg K. Reaction mechanism in trypsin catalyzed synthesis of human insulin studies by NMR spectroscopy. In: Blaha K, Malon P, eds. *Peptides 1982*. Proceedings 17th European Peptide Symposium, Prague. Berlin, New York: Walter de Gruyter, 1983: 387–94.

16 Goeddel DV, Kleid DG, Bolivar F et al. Expression in *Escherichia coli* of chemically synthesized genes for human insulin. *Proc Natl Acad Sci USA* 1979; **76**: 106–10.

17 Chance RE, Hoffman JA, Kroeff EP et al. The production of human insulin using recombinant-DNA technology and a new chain combination procedure. In: Rich DH, Gross E, eds. *Peptides: Synthesis–Structure–Function*. Proceedings of the Seventh American Peptide Symposium. Rockford IL: Pierce Chemical Co, 1981: 721–8.

18 Chance RE, Kroeff EP, Hoffman JA, Frank BH. Chemical, physical and biologic properties of biosynthetic human insulin. *Diabetes Care* 1981; **4**: 147–54.

19 Chance RE, Kroeff EP, Hoffman JA. Chemical, physical and biological properties of recombinant human insulin. In: Gueriguian JL, ed. *Insulins, Growth Hormone and Recombinant DNA technology*. New York: Raven Press, 1981: 71–86.

20 Frank BH, Pettee JM, Zimmermann RE, Burck PJ. The production of human proinsulin and its transformation to human insulin and C-peptide. In: Rich DH, Gross E, eds. *Peptides: Synthesis–Structure–Function*. Proceedings of the Seventh American Peptide Symposium. Rockford IL: Pierce Chemical Co, 1981: 729–38.

21 Markussen J, Damgaard U, Diers I et al. Biosynthesis of human insulin in yeast via single-chain precursors. In: Theodoropoulos, ed. *Peptides*. Berlin: Walter de Gruyter, 1987: 189–94.

22 Thim L, Hansen MT, Norris K et al. Secretion and processing of insulin precursors in yeast. *Proc Natl Acad Sci USA* 1986; **83**: 6766–70.

23 Joslin EP. *The Treatment of Diabetes Mellitus*, 8th edn. Philadelphia: Lea & Febiger, 1946.

24 Schlichtkrull J, Brange J, Ege H et al. Proinsulin and related proteins. *Diabetologia* 1970; **6**: 80–1.

25 Schlichtkrull J, Brange J, Christiansen AH, Hallund O, Heding LG, Jørgensen KH. Clinical aspects of insulin-antigenicity. *Diabetes* 1972; **21**(suppl 2): 649–56.

26 Schlichtkrull J, Brange J, Christiansen AH et al. Monocomponent insulin and its clinical implications. *Horm Metab Res* 1974; **5**(suppl 1): 134–43.

27 Jørgensen KH, Brange J, Hallund O, Pingel M. A method for the preparation of essentially pure insulin. In: Rodriguez RR, Eblin FJG, Henderson I, Assan R, eds. *VII Congress of the International Diabetes Federation*. Amsterdam: Excerpta Medica Int. Congress Series 1970; **209**: 149 (Abstract 334).

28 Smith KL. Insulin. In: Dorfmann RI, ed. *Methods in Hormone Research. Bioassay*. New York: Academic Press, 1969; **IIA**: 365–414.

29 Eneroth G, Aahlund K. Biological assay of insulin by blood sugar determination in mice. *Acta Pharm Suec* 1968; **5**: 591–4.

30 Eneroth G, Aahlund K. A twin cross-over method for bioassay of insulin using blood glucose levels in mice — a comparison with a rabbit method. *Acta Pharm Suec* 1970; **7**: 457–62.

31 Eneroth G, Aahlund K. Exogenous insulin and blood glucose levels in mice, *Acta Pharm* 1970; **7**: 491–500.

32 Bangham DR, de Jonge H, van Noordwijk J. The collaborative assay of the European pharmacopoeia biological reference preparations for insulin. *J Biol Stand* 1978; **6**: 301–4.

33 Pingel M, Vølund Aa, Sørensen E, Sørensen AR. Assessment of insulin potency by chemical and biological methods. In: Gueriguian JL, Bransome ED, Outschoorn AS, eds. *Hormone Drugs*. United States Pharmacopeial Convention, Rockville, MD, 1982: 200–7.

34 Kroeff EP, Chance RE. Applications of high performance liquid chromatography for the analysis of insulins. In: Gueriguian JL, Bransome ED, Outschoorn AS, eds. *Hormone Drugs*. United States Pharmacopeial Convention, Rockville, MD, 1982: 148–62.

35 Berger M, Cüppers HJ, Hegner H, Jörgens V, Berchtold P. Absorption kinetics and biologic effects of subcutaneously-injected insulin preparations. *Diabetes Care* 1982; **5**: 77–91.

36 Federlin K, Laube H, Velcovsky HG. Biologic and immunologic *in vivo* and *in vitro* studies with biosynthetic human insulin. *Diabetes Care* 1981; **4**: 170–4.

37 Cüppers HJ, Franzke D, Esken P, Jörgens V, Berger M. Pharmakokinetik und biologische Aktivität von semisynthetischen und biologischen Humaninsulin-präparaten. *Aktuel Endokrinol Stoffwechsel* 1982; **3**: 102.

38 Owens DR. *Human Insulin: Clinical Pharmacological Studies in Normal Man*. Thesis. Lancaster, Boston, The Hague, Dirdrecht: MTP Press Limited, 1986.

39 Baumann G, Drobny EC. Enhanced efficacy of U-500 insulin in the treatment of insulin resistance caused by target tissue insensitivity. *Am J Med* 1984; **76**: 529–32.

40 Scott DA, Fischer AM. Studies on insulin with protamine. *J Pharmacol Exp Ther* 1936; **58**: 78–92.

41 Krayenbuhl C, Rosenberg T. Crystalline protamine insulin. *Rep Steno Mem Hosp Nord Insulinlab* 1946; **1**: 60–73.

42 Schlichtkrull J, Ege H, Jørgensen KH, Markussen J, Sundby F. Die Chemie des Insulins. In: Oberdisse K, ed. *Diabetes Mellitus A* (*Handbuch der Inneren Medizin*, Bd 7/2A). Berlin, Heidelberg, New York: Springer, 1975: 77–127.

43 Hallas-Møller K, Petersen K, Schlichtkrull J. Crystalline and amorphous insulin–zinc compounds with prolonged action (in Danish). *Ugeskr Laeger* 1951; **113**: 1761–7.

44 Schlichtkrull J. New insulin crystal suspensions with various timings of action and containing no added zinc. In:

Oberdisse K, Jahnje K, eds. *Diabetes Mellitus III*. Kongress der International Diabetes Federation, Düsseldorf. Stuttgart: Georg Thieme, 1959: 773–7.

45 Lautenschlager KL, Dorzbach E, Schaumann O. Verfähren zur Herstellung von Präparaten aus dem blutzuckersenkenden Hormon der Bauchspeicheldruse. D.R. Patent 727888. 1937.

46 Watkins JD, Roberts DE, Williams TF, Martin DA, Coyle C. Observation of medication errors made by diabetic patients in the home. *Diabetes* 1967; **16**: 882–5.

47 Graham DT, Pomeroy AR. The effects of freezing in commercial insulin suspensions. *Int J Pharm* 1978; **1**: 315–22.

48 Galloway JA. Highlights of clinical experiences with recombinant human insulin (rDNA) and human proinsulin (rDNA). *Neth J Med* 1985; **28**(suppl 1): 37–42.

49 Cohen RM, Licino J, Polonsky KS *et al.* The effect of biosynthetic human proinsulin on the hepatic response to glucagon in insulin-deficient diabetes. *J Clin Endocrinol Metab* 1987; **64**: 476–81.

50 Glauber HS, Henry RR, Wallace P *et al.* The effects of biosynthetic human proinsulin on carbohydrate metabolism in non-insulin-dependent diabetes mellitus. *N Engl J Med* 1987; **316**: 443–9.

51 Moses AC, Gordon GS, Carey MC, Flier JS. Insulin administered intranasally as an insulin–bile salt aerosol. Effectiveness and reproducibility in normal and diabetic subjects. *Diabetes* 1983; **32**: 1040–7.

52 Salzman R, Manzon JE, Griffing GT *et al.* Intranasal aerosolized insulin. Mixed-meal studies and long-term use in type I diabetes. *N Engl J Med* 1985; **312**: 1078–84.

53 Brange J, Ribel U, Hansen JF *et al.* Monomeric insulins obtained by protein engineering and their medical implications. *Nature* 1988; **333**: 679–82.

54 Vora JP, Owens DR, Dolbien J, Atiea JA, Dean JD, Kang S, Burch A, Brange J. Recombinant DNA derived monomeric insulin analogue: comparison with soluble human insulin in normal subjects. *Br Med J* 1988; **297**: 1236–9.

55 Markussen J, Hougaard P, Tibel U, Sørensen AR, Sørensen E. Soluble, prolonged-acting insulin derivatives. I. Degree of protraction and crystallizability of insulins substituted in the termini of the B-chain. *Protein Eng* 1987; **1**: 205–13.

56 Jørgensen S, Vaag A, Jangkjaer L, Hougaard P, Markussen J. NovoSol Basal: pharmacokinetics of a novel soluble long acting insulin analogue. *Br Med J* 1989; **299**: 415–19.

38   The Pharmacokinetics of Insulin

Summary

• Insulin absorption can be studied by measuring the disappearance of radioactivity from a depot of radiolabelled insulin, the appearance of unlabelled insulin in the circulation, or the hypoglycaemic effect of the injected insulin.

• Insulin absorption depends critically on the physical state of the insulin, short-acting insulin being absorbed much more rapidly than protamine or zinc insulins which are particulate or crystalline and must first dissolve.

• The association state of insulin also determines its absorption; hexameric insulin at injection sites must dissociate into monomers or dimers before absorption can occur. Synthetic insulin analogues which remain predominantly in the monomeric state are very rapidly absorbed.

• Human insulin preparations are generally absorbed slightly faster than porcine or bovine equivalents and human long-acting insulins have a relatively short action profile.

• Mixing short-acting with lente zinc insulin may reduce the availability of the former through interaction with excess zinc but this effect seems unimportant clinically.

• The subcutaneous absorption rate of insulin falls with increasing volume or increasing concentration of the injected preparation.

• Insulin is absorbed directly into the capillaries by diffusion which is generally limited by the capillary barrier rather than capillary blood flow. Changes in absorption due to heating, cooling, exercise, or massage are apparently due to alteration in capillary recruitment and/ or dissociation of insulin hexamers.

• Subcutaneous insulin absorption is too slow and prolonged to achieve physiological insulinaemic profiles and is also extremely variable both between and within individuals.

• Subcutaneous absorption is faster from the abdomen than the leg and may be accelerated by exercising the injected limb, by heating or massaging the injection site, by using a 'sprinkler' needle or jet injector, or by mixing the injected insulin with a local vasodilator. Absorption is also accelerated in ketoacidosis.

• Subcutaneous absorption may be delayed by cooling, hypoglycaemia and injection into lipohypertrophic areas.

• Insulin given intranasally or intraperitoneally is absorbed faster than that injected subcutaneously or intramuscularly. In the limbs, intramuscular absorption is faster than subcutaneous but comparable with subcutaneous absorption in the abdomen. Perpendicular injection with a standard 13-mm needle will frequently deliver insulin intramuscularly rather than subcutaneously.

• Plasma levels of free insulin, the biologically active fraction, depend predominantly on the insulin entering the circulation but are also affected by its binding to insulin antibodies and by its clearance from the bloodstream.

• Insulin clearance occurs mainly in the liver (60–80%) and kidneys (10–20%); circulating insulin levels may be elevated in renal failure and in cirrhosis due to impaired clearance.

Insulin substitution therapy for IDDM patients poses several intriguing problems. In health, insulin is secreted by the pancreas into the portal vein in a precise, feedback-controlled fashion which produces a physiological plasma insulin profile consisting of acute, high peaks after meals and stable low levels in between. This complicated pattern has to be mimicked by the administration of exogenous insulin in various pharmaceutical preparations, adjusted on the basis of relatively infrequent blood or urine glucose measurements and the experience of the patient and his advisors. A further complication is the narrow safety margin for insulin and, therefore, the high risk of hypoglycaemia when aiming for near-normoglycaemia.

Many biopharmaceutical, pharmacokinetic and pharmacodynamic factors are now known to affect insulin absorption, the availability of insulin to its target tissues and insulin action. As discussed in this chapter, an understanding of these factors will help to optimize glycaemic control and improve the quality and expectancy of life for people with IDDM.

The fate of exogenous insulin

After exogenous administration, insulin forms a depot in which the drug is transformed to an absorbable state via dissociation and dissolution (Fig. 38.1). In very rare cases, insulin may be partly degraded at the site of administration. Insulin is absorbed from the depot into the circulation by diffusion and like endogenous insulin, is distributed within the plasma phase as 'free' (unbound) insulin. However, in most insulin-treated subjects part of the circulating insulin is reversibly bound to insulin antibodies, forming a circulating depot of insulin which may change the free insulin levels unpredictably (see Chapter 40). The biologically active free insulin is distributed by diffusion into the extravascular compartment to reach insulin receptors on target cells, after which it is eliminated, mainly by degradation. Only a small proportion (about 1% of the filtered load) is excreted in the urine. As the clearance of insulin from plasma is normally rapid, circulating insulin levels and ultimately insulin delivery to its target tissues depend primarily on the entry of insulin to the circulation and therefore on the factors affecting its absorption. Apart from the amounts of insulin reaching its receptors, insulin action is also influenced by many factors such as insulin sensitivity, the action of the counter-regulatory hormones, physical exercise and diet.

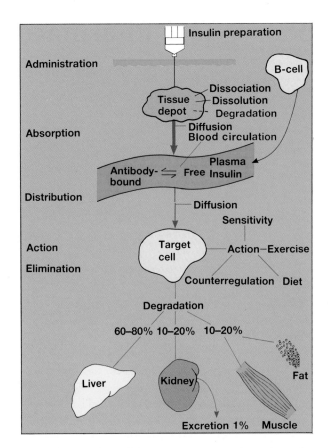

Fig. 38.1. Flow chart of the various processes determining the absorption of insulin its distribution in the circulation its delivery to and action in as well as its elimination from its target tissues.

The following sections will describe the pharmacology and pharmacokinetics of insulin; these topics have been reviewed in detail in recent years [1–7].

Measurements of insulin kinetics

The absorption of insulin can be studied in man in three main ways: by measuring the disappearance of radioactive (e.g. ^{125}I-labelled) insulin from the injection-site using a gamma counter mounted over the site [8]; by calculating increases in the plasma free insulin level after injection; and by measuring the fall in plasma glucose concentrations induced by the injection. Combining these three methods provides the most complete picture of absorption.

The radioactively labelled insulin technique (Fig. 38.2) is theoretically the most attractive in that it reflects the actual rate of absorption and is the method of choice for examining absorption mechanisms. Reservations have been expressed that iodinated insulin may not behave similarly

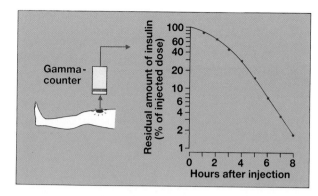

Fig. 38.2. Measuring insulin absorption as the disappearance of radiolabelled (e.g. ^{125}I-) insulin from an injection site. After an initially slow decline lasting a few hours, radioactivity remaining at the site decreases in a mono-exponential fashion and therefore shows a linear fall when plotted logarithmically against time. The slope of the line is proportional to the absorption rate (from [8]).

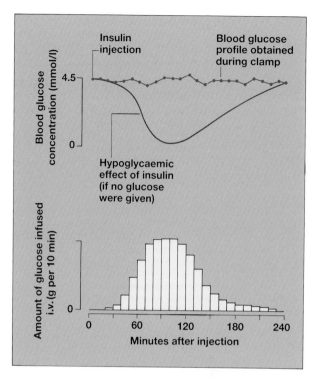

Fig. 38.3. Principle of the euglycaemic clamp. Blood glucose concentration is measured frequently and the rate of a continuous intravenous glucose infusion is adjusted so as to maintain the blood glucose level at a constant normal value (e.g. 4.5 mmol/l). The profile of glucose administration is a quantitative measure of the time-course of insulin action.

to native insulin, or that slight changes in the geometrical relationship between the isotope depot and the detector might vitiate the technique. For subcutaneous administration, however, this method has now been thoroughly validated using ^{125}I-labelled insulin [2].

Measuring absorption as the appearance of insulin in the circulation poses different problems. Absorption is the major determinant of plasma insulin levels but these are also altered by any residual endogenous insulin secretion, as well as by the clearance of insulin and its binding to circulating insulin antibodies, thus rendering this method less sensitive as a measure of absorption. Moreover, a high-quality radioimmunoassay is essential for this technique.

Measurement of the hypoglycaemic effect has long been used to study absorption kinetics but is even less reliable than the previous technique, being influenced by factors such as insulin sensitivity, the action of counter-regulatory hormones (especially if hypoglycaemia supervenes) and eating. By using the euglycaemic clamp technique, the effects of hypoglycaemia and counter-regulation can be avoided; the glucose, infusion rates needed to maintain a steady plasma glucose level can be used as a measure of insulin action (see Fig. 38.3).

The post-absorptive processes of insulin distribution and clearance can be elucidated independently of absorption by studying the concentration–time curves of radiolabelled or unlabelled insulin injected or infused intravenously.

Insulin preparations

A major determinant of the absorption rate is the physical state of the injected insulin (Table 38.1). Manipulation of the solubility characteristics of insulin at physiological pH can therefore be used to change the absorption rate.

Insulin administered in solution is rapidly absorbed, yielding short-acting preparations, whereas suspensions of soluble insulin particles of different sizes give intermediate-acting and long-acting preparations with more sustained action profiles. Two main principles are used to prolong the action profile, namely the addition of either the basic protein protamine to neutral insulin suspensions, giving isophane (NPH) or protamine zinc insulins, or of small amounts of zinc ions without protamine, yielding lente insulins. Mixtures of short- and intermediate-acting preparations produce biphasic responses (see Chapter 37).

Fig. 38.4 illustrates typical plasma glucose profiles after subcutaneous injection of insulin preparations with short, intermediate and long

Table 38.1. Factors influencing insulin absorption.

The insulin preparation	Mode of administration	Site of administration	
		Differences between sites	Changes within site
Physical state (soluble or particulate)	Injection Needle Jet 'Sprinkler' needle Number of depots Infusion	Route Subcutaneous Intramuscular Depth Anatomical region Presence of lipohypertrophy	Heat, + Cold, − Exercise, + Massage, + Adrenaline (circulating), − Hypoglycaemia, − Ketoacidosis, + Smoking, − Addition of local hyperaemic agents (PGE₁, phentolamine, aprotinin), + Local insulin degradation, −
Dose Concentration Volume Species			

+, enhancing effect; −, reducing effect.

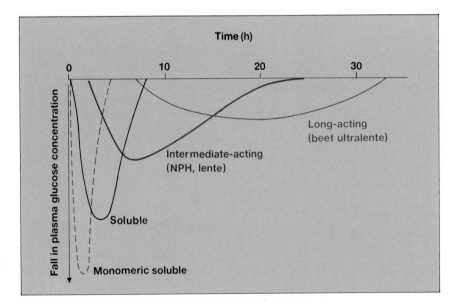

Fig. 38.4. Action profiles of the commonly used insulin preparations, injected subcutaneously. The very rapid and short-lived profile of a monomeric insulin analogue, not yet in clinical use, is also shown (broken red line).

durations. The profile of an extremely short-acting monomeric insulin analogue (not yet in clinical use; see Chapter 37) is also indicated.

Absorption mechanisms

Biopharmaceutical aspects

ABSORPTION KINETICS OF SHORT-ACTING INSULIN

When injected, soluble (short-acting) insulin consists of an equilibrium mixture of monomers and their non-covalently associated dimers, tetramers, hexamers and possibly higher states of association [9] (see Fig. 38.5). The predominant form at physiological pH and under the conditions prevailing at injection sites appears to be hexamers containing two Zn²⁺ ions. In blood, insulin occurs as a monomer. Calculations based on absorption rates in human skeletal muscle suggest that the association state of insulin undergoing absorption is no more than dimeric [10]; experimental studies in pigs also indicate that insulin hexamers dissociate before absorption [11]. A recent mathematical model of the absorption kinetics of short-acting insulin proposes insulin in a subcutaneous depot to be present in a low molecular weight form, a

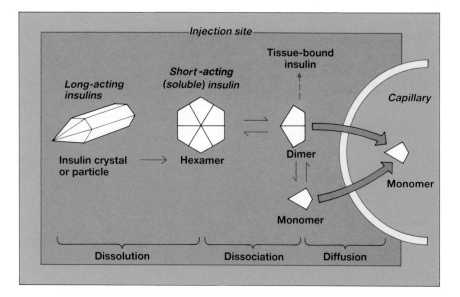

Fig. 38.5. Events occurring at the insulin injection site.

high molecular weight form and an immobile, tissue-bound fraction [12]. This model can account for the experimentally observed decreases in absorption rate with increasing concentration or volume of the injected solution, and for the typical non-linear course of subcutaneous absorption of short-acting insulin. The latter shows an initially low but continuously rising absorption rate with time [8]. The low rate was previously attributed to local depression of the microcirculation; however, direct measurements of blood flow close to subcutaneous injection sites have indicated that injected insulin causes local hyperaemia [13].

The importance of the association state of insulin in determining its absorption has been highlighted by the recent development of insulin analogues whose structure favours specific states [14]. A monomeric analogue which resists dimerization at physiological pH is absorbed 2−3 times faster and without the initial delay typical of conventional short-acting preparations [15] (see Fig. 38.4). Alteration in the association state of insulin may partly explain the changes in insulin absorption induced by mechanical factors such as massage and exercise [28].

ABSORPTION KINETICS OF LONG-ACTING PREPARATIONS

Zinc insulins are probably dissolved *in situ* and protamine insulins cleaved before absorption takes place. The rate-limiting step for the absorption of insulin in suspension is held to be the rate of dissolution of the particles. This is primarily determined by the particle size, but may also be influenced by changes occurring at the injection site [16].

MIXING SHORT- AND INTERMEDIATE-ACTING INSULINS

The consequences for absorption of mixing NPH or lente insulin with short-acting preparations in the same syringe has been a matter of debate (see Chapter 39). Admixture of short-acting insulin to NPH insulin does not significantly alter the absorption characteristics of the former, and pre-mixed preparations containing these insulins are available. However, similar mixtures with lente insulin reduce the availability of the short-acting insulin, probably due to interaction of the surplus zinc in the lente insulin with part of the soluble insulin, giving a less steep rise in the plasma insulin profiles. However, this effect of the zinc insulins seems to be small and a recent double-blind cross-over comparison of metabolic control in IDDM patients showed no clinically important differences between mixtures of short-acting with lente or NPH insulins, given twice-daily [17].

EFFECTS OF DOSE, CONCENTRATION AND SPECIES

A higher insulin dosage reduces the absorption rate due to the volume effect mentioned above but the plasma insulin peak may still be higher and the duration is always more prolonged, in accordance with general pharmacokinetic principles. When the same dose of insulin is given at a higher concentration, the reduced volume essentially counter-balances the depressive effect of the higher concentration. Although a significantly lower absorption rate has been reported with insulin at 100 U/ml compared to 40 U/ml [18, 19], the clinical relevance is probably slight.

Short-acting human insulin is absorbed somewhat faster than its porcine equivalent, possibly due to higher water solubility or a lesser tendency to associate into hexamers [9], but the clinical consequences of this difference seem to be negligible. A similar tendency has been seen with NPH insulin. Zinc-insulin suspensions of long duration containing human insulin appear to be absorbed considerably faster than the bovine preparation, but similarly to the porcine. The implications of species differences have been reviewed recently [3].

Physiological aspects

After the subcutaneous injection of short-acting insulin, the absorption rate is initially low and dominated by the biopharmaceutical factors mentioned above (see Figs 38.4 and 5). Later after injection, local haemodynamic factors become increasingly important.

The main route of insulin absorption from subcutaneous tissue is probably directly into the bloodstream, as lymphatic uptake seems to be unimportant [8]. Insulin transport within the interstitial space and across the capillary membrane is considered to occur mainly by diffusion. The size of the water-soluble insulin molecule (molecular weight of monomeric insulin ~5800 Da) implies that its diffusion across the continuous capillaries in subcutaneous tissue and skeletal muscle is predominantly barrier-limited, rather than flow-limited, at basal or higher blood flow rates [10, 20]. Accordingly, the properties of the barrier, i.e. its surface area and permeability characteristics (capillary diffusion capacity), in combination with the intercapillary distances, are more important determinants of the absorption rate than the blood flow rate *per se*. Differences in insulin absorption between injection sites predominantly reflect differences in the diffusion capacity for insulin. Changes in insulin absorption from a given site, induced by exposure to heat, cold and other factors altering blood flow, are probably mainly

due to changes in capillary recruitment and the secondary effects on intercapillary distance accompanying the blood flow alterations [21, 22]. The distribution of blood flow also seems to be important, since insulin absorption may decrease despite unaltered or even increased total blood flow, e.g. as during i.v. infusion of adrenaline [23].

Once dissolved, the insulin of long-acting preparations will be subject to the same forces as the short-acting insulins.

Routes of administration

Apart from the nature of the preparation itself, the route of administration is the single most important factor determining the absorption kinetics of insulin and illustrates the major significance of differences in vascularity (Table 38.1). Figure 38.6 shows typical plasma insulin profiles after intranasal, intraperitoneal, intramuscular and subcutaneous administration of short-acting insulin; the profile after intravenous injection is included as a reference. Following intranasal and intraperitoneal administration, insulin appearance in the circulation is much more rapid and the duration shorter than by either the intramuscular or subcutaneous routes [24, 25]. Intraperitoneal and intravenous administration have occasionally been used therapeutically, for example in diabetic patients with high subcutaneous insulin requirements (see Chapter 88), and can achieve more

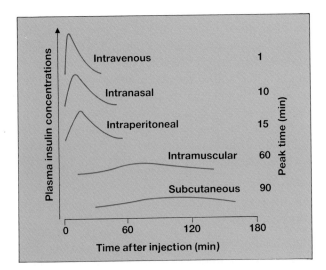

Fig. 38.6. Plasma insulin profiles following administration of short-acting soluble insulin by different routes.

physiological plasma insulin profiles but are not practically feasible in most patients. Intranasal administration has a promisingly rapid action suitable for covering meals but is still in the experimental stage. Alternative routes of administration are discussed further in Chapter 46.

Subcutaneous administration

Subcutaneous administration has been the common route for insulin delivery for almost seven decades and will probably remain so for most diabetic patients for many years to come. Besides the drawback of systemic rather than intraportal delivery, subcutaneous administration also produces unphysiological plasma insulin profiles: after injection of short-acting insulins, insulin levels rise too slowly to peak levels that are too low and then decay too slowly. Another major problem is the marked variability in subcutaneous absorption, which is known to have adverse effects on glucose homeostasis. The intra-individual coefficient of variation for the amount absorbed of insulin injected on separate days is approximately 25% and between patients it may amount to 50%. However, the inappropriate plasma insulin profiles and their great variability can to some extent

be improved through several logical strategies (Table 38.2).

THE PLASMA INSULIN PROFILE

Physiological plasma insulin and glucose profiles depend on injecting the most appropriate insulin preparation into the best site at the correct time.

The most physiological plasma insulin profiles are obtained by treating mealtime and basal insulin requirements as separate entities (Chapter 39). *Mealtime insulin* needs to be absorbed as soon as possible; a short-acting insulin should therefore be injected into a region where absorption is rapid, such as the abdomen or arm (see below). The need for insulin levels to be as high as possible when food is ingested makes the timing of the injection important [26], and postprandial glycaemic excursions are reduced if insulin is given 30–60 min before eating.

Various means have been attempted to accelerate the absorption of short-acting insulin. Massage over the injection site is known to be highly effective and if performed regularly, even for only a few minutes, can significantly improve long-term glycaemic control in IDDM patients [27]. Massage may act by encouraging dissociation of insulin

Table 38.2. Major pharmacokinetic problems during subcutaneous insulin therapy. Some possible causes and suggestions for measures to be taken.

Problems	Causes	Measures
Unphysiological insulinaemic profile	Mealtime and basal insulins combined	Treat mealtime and basal needs separately
	Preparations too slow-acting for meals and too short-acting for basal needs	Use short-acting insulin (possibly with massage or a sprinkler needle) for meals and long-acting (or CSII) for the basal supply
	Wrong timing of injections to cover meals	Give mealtime doses 30–60 min before meals
	Unsuitable injection site	Inject short-acting into 'fast' region (abdomen, arm). Inject long-acting into 'slow' region (leg, buttock)
	Ignorance about factors of importance	Education about action profiles of insulin and injection strategies
Great variability in absorption	Wrong type and/or dose of preparation	Use short-acting at small doses for meals (multiple injections or CSII) and long-acting (or CSII) for the basal supply
	Perpendicular injection with possible accidental intramuscular injection	Inject into lifted skinfold
	Random rotation between regions	Change region on purpose only
	Presence of lipohypertrophy	Avoid palpably abnormal sites
	Ignorance about factors of importance	Avoid marked changes in temperature and exercise soon after injection

hexamers and does not appear to depend on increased local blood flow [28]. Absorption may also be enhanced by injection using a jet injector or a sprinkler needle, which both increase dispersion of the insulin, as well as by a division of the dose into several smaller depots [2, 29], but none of these methods are in general use. The addition to short-acting insulin of prostaglandin E_1 [30] or phentolamine, both local vasodilatating agents, accelerates absorption but these agents have not yet been used clinically. The protease inhibitor, aprotinin, also increases absorption when added to injected insulin [1], probably through vasodilatation rather than by inhibiting local insulin degradation [31]. The new monomeric insulins of very short duration, which may be available soon, afford another possibility of making mealtime insulin profiles more physiological [15].

The *basal insulin* should have as long a duration as possible. Insulin analogues which are soluble but precipitate after injection have recently been synthesized by recombinant-DNA technology [32] and have even longer durations than existing long-acting preparations. It will, however, be some years before these are available for clinical use. The basal insulin should generally be injected into a region where absorption is slow, i.e. the leg or gluteal region. With continuous subcutaneous insulin infusion (CSII), the basal insulin supply is given as a slow infusion of short-acting insulin, usually into the abdomen.

VARIABILITY IN ABSORPTION

The variability in insulin absorption can be partly reduced by a number of simple manoeuvres and by considering its various causes (Tables 38.1 and 38.2).

Dose and properties of the preparation. Variability in absorption will have greater consequences with increasing intervals between insulin doses. One way of reducing this variability is to use short-acting insulin in small doses, as in multiple insulin injection therapy or CSII. Unpredictable dissociation of the hexamers in the currently used short-acting insulins may also increase the variability in absorption, as monomeric insulin analogues seem to have more consistent action profiles [33].

Mode of administration. Perpendicular injections with needles 12–13 mm long are quite likely to enter muscle rather than, or as well as, subcu-

taneous tissue. Computerized tomography (CT) scanning has recently demonstrated that the subcutaneous fat layer in regions generally used for insulin injection is considerably thinner than generally assumed [34] (Fig. 38.7). In the limbs, where insulin absorption from muscle is faster than from the overlying subcutaneous tissue, accidental intramuscular injection will add to the variability in absorption. Perpendicular injections are therefore unsatisfactory and should be replaced by injection into a lifted skinfold (Chapter 39). The depth of the injection appears to be unimportant as long as it lies within subcutaneous tissue.

CSII carries the pharmacokinetic benefits of small insulin depots and the sole use of short-acting insulin, factors which both favour rapid absorption and low variability. The pharmacokinetics of CSII have recently been reviewed [5].

Differences between injection sites. Insulin absorption differs considerably between body regions, being most rapid from the abdominal area, intermediate from the arm and slowest from the thigh and gluteal regions [4, 8] (Fig. 38.8). Random rotation between regions should therefore be avoided because it increases the variation in absorption. Absorption rates may also vary within a particular region, and is considerably faster from the upper than the lower abdomen [35].

Absorption has also been found to be slower from lipohypertrophic areas, which should therefore be avoided for injection [36].

Changes at a given site. Careful choice of an anatomical site for insulin injection may help to improve diabetes control. However, insulin absorption from a given injection site may also vary as a result of exogenous and endogenous influences (Table 38.1). Knowledge of such factors can further improve treatment and patients should be instructed accordingly.

A higher ambient temperature (e.g. a sauna) and local heating of an injected site (e.g. a hot bath) both accelerate insulin absorption, whereas cooling causes slowing [1, 4]. Physical exercise increases absorption, especially when the depot is located near the exercising muscles, suggesting a massage-like effect (Fig. 38.9). Accordingly, the effects of exercise are less marked when insulin is injected into the abdomen, another reason for this to be the region of choice for the injection of short-acting insulin. The effects of physical exer-

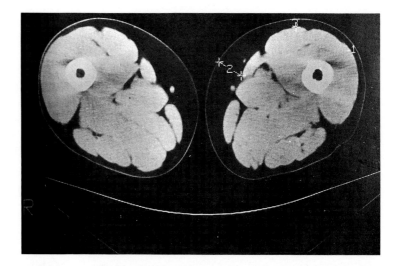

Fig. 38.7. CT scan of the thighs showing typical asymmetrical fat distribution in a normal weight patient. (Copyright 1988 by the American Diabetes Association. Reproduced with permission from [42].)

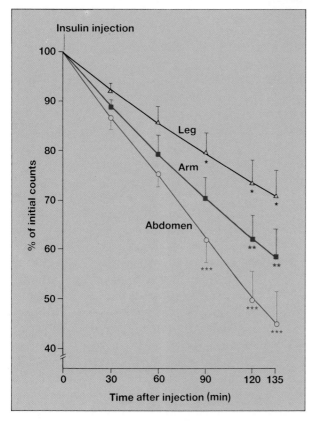

Fig. 38.8. Insulin absorption (measured as the disappearance of ^{125}I-insulin) is fastest in the abdomen, slowest in the leg, and intermediate in the arm. (From Koivisto VA, Felig P. *Ann Intern Med* 1980; **92**: 59–61.)

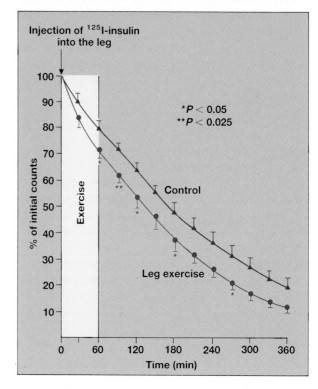

Fig. 38.9. Effect of exercise on the absorption of insulin injected into the leg. Disappearance of ^{125}I-insulin is significantly accelerated. (From Koivisto VA, Felig P. *N Engl J Med* 1978; **298**: 79–83.)

cise and environmental heat seem to be additive [37] and appear to affect short- and long-acting insulin preparations [1, 16]. To reduce the variability in absorption, patients should therefore be instructed to avoid marked changes in temperature as well as physical exercise soon after injection (when the insulin depot is large), and especially to avoid leg exercise soon after a thigh injection.

Adrenaline infused intravenously to levels typical of moderate physical stress has been found to depress insulin absorption [23]. This effect may be relevant to glycaemic control during physical stress. Mental stress, on the other hand, does not seem to change insulin absorption [38].

Ketoacidosis and hypoglycaemia also affect absorption, ketoacidosis apparently accelerating absorption [36], whereas hypoglycaemia has the opposite effect [39]. Smoking, in addition to its many other adverse effects in diabetic patients (see Chapter 92), probably tends to reduce insulin absorption [8], although this is not a consistent finding [40].

A further factor which could variably alter the bioavailability of insulin would be significant insulin degradation at its injection site. This possibility, suggested mainly by animal studies, is probably only very rarely of clinical importance in humans. Patients with this defect may need daily insulin doses of a thousand units or more and their requirements may change unpredictably (see Chapter 88). Insulin degradation can be inhibited by mixing insulin with protease inhibitors such as aprotinin, but due to their serious adverse effects, it is preferable to bypass the subcutaneous route with intramuscular, intraperitoneal or intravenous insulin administration in these patients.

Intramuscular administration

Intramuscular administration achieves better absorption of insulin than subcutaneous injection in both the leg and arm [2, 41] but not the abdomen [42]. The faster absorption from muscle has been exploited clinically in treating ketoacidosis and patients with high subcutaneous insulin requirements, but has not been used in routine insulin therapy. In view of the exaggerated hypoglycaemic effect during exercise after intramuscular injection [43], the inconvenience and discomfort of the injection, and the fact that absorption from leg muscle is no faster than from abdominal subcutaneous tissue, the intramuscular route seems unsuitable for everyday treatment.

Kinetics of circulating insulin

Effects of insulin antibodies

The presence of insulin-binding antibodies alters the distribution of insulin in the plasma phase, as part of the administered insulin binds reversibly to the antibodies which act as a circulating depot of insulin. Antibody binding reduces the elimination rate of insulin from plasma and the availability of free insulin to its target tissues. The biological activity of insulin may therefore be blunted and prolonged in the presence of insulin-binding antibodies [44] but the absorption rate of insulin is not influenced [45]. The reservoir of bound insulin could theoretically act as a buffer under conditions of insulin deficiency and could also evoke unpredictable hypoglycaemia, but in the vast majority of patients insulin-binding antibodies appear to have little or no clinical effect (see Chapter 40) [46].

Degradation and excretion

Insulin elimination does not regulate plasma insulin levels under physiological conditions. However, the circulating levels may change during serious failure of the main organs mediating insulin degradation, notably the liver, which is responsible for approximately 60–80% of the body's total insulin disposal, and the kidneys, which account for approximately 10–20%. The remaining degrading activity is located in peripheral tissues, mainly skeletal muscle and adipose tissue, with a minor contribution from blood cells, fibroblasts, endothelial cells, the pituitary and the islet B cells.

Elimination of insulin in the liver seems to occur mainly through receptor-mediated degradation, whereas that in the kidney follows two routes [47]. Approximately two-thirds is eliminated through passive filtration in the glomeruli and subsequent reabsorption in proximal tubular cells, where filtered insulin is degraded; less than 1% of the amount filtered is finally excreted in the urine. One-third of the renal clearance of insulin takes place in postglomerular, peritubular vessels, probably by a receptor-mediated process.

In renal failure with impaired tubular reabsorption, urinary losses are markedly enhanced. However, as the reabsorbed insulin is normally degraded, the increased urinary losses do not significantly change the plasma insulin levels. In untreated uraemia, on the other hand, plasma insulin levels may be elevated, due both to the absence of degradation in the kidney and to toxic effects on other insulin-degrading sites. Accordingly, the insulin dosage may have to be adjusted.

Insulin disappearance from plasma

Various compartmental and non-compartmental approaches have been used to analyse the course of insulin elimination from plasma [7, 48]. Insulin disappearance undoubtedly describes a multiexponential curve but the number of exponents and the identification of their corresponding compartments have been controversial. The frequently cited model of Sherwin identifies three compartments, one corresponding to the plasma space and two extravascular compartments, one equilibrating rapidly and the other slowly with plasma [49]. The time-course of the latter compartment correlates well with that of the glucose-lowering effect of insulin, suggesting that it corresponds to the site of insulin action (Fig. 38.10).

The half-life of insulin in plasma is approximately 3–5 min in healthy subjects, corresponding to an average metabolic clearance rate of 800–900 ml/min with an inter-individual variability of approximately 20%. Under physiological conditions, the elimination of insulin from plasma seems to follow first-order kinetics. In fact, at insulin levels below approximately 500 mU/l, the removal rate appears to be proportional to its plasma concentration. Various pathological states may alter the elimination rate (Table 38.3). Clearance is considerably reduced in undialysed uraemic

Table 38.3. Clearance of insulin in various pathological states.

IDDM	=
Ketoacidosis	–
NIDDM	=
Obesity	=
Uraemia, undialysed	–
Uraemia, dialysed	=
Liver cirrhosis	–
Acromegaly	+

= normal; – reduced; + increased.

patients and in cirrhosis of the liver, for the reasons discussed above, and is also impaired in ketoacidosis.

Conclusions

Subcutaneous administration of insulin will remain the major route for treating IDDM patients and is unlikely ever to become a precision tool. However, consideration of the basic pharmacokinetic principles outlined in this chapter will help to optimize the insulin therapy available today

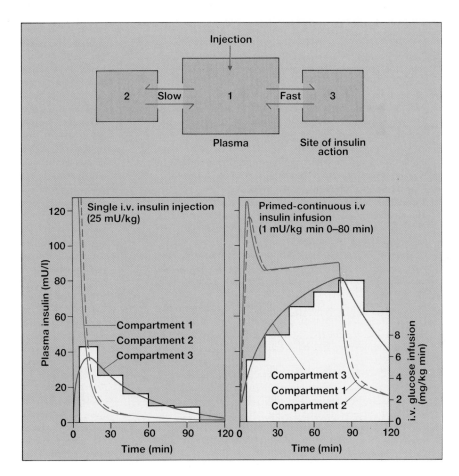

Fig. 38.10. The three-compartment model proposed by Sherwin *et al.* [49] to explain the kinetics of circulating insulin. The model has been used to predict the plasma insulin concentrations in each compartment following a single intravenous injection (lower panel, left) and a bolus followed by an 80-min continuous intravenous infusion. The action profile of each protocol was found using the euglycaemic clamp technique (see Fig. 38.3) and is shown as the shaded area. This corresponds closely to compartment 3 of the model, suggesting that this represents the site of insulin action.

and considerable refinements and improvements are to be expected in the near future. A substantial research effort has already been rewarded by the development of insulin analogues which may be able to overcome the major pharmacokinetic problems of conventional short- and long-acting preparations and which may make a considerable impact on the treatment of IDDM.

BIRGITTA LINDE

References

1 Berger M, Cüppers HJ, Hegner H, Jörgens V, Berchtold P. Absorption kinetics and biologic effects of subcutaneously injected insulin preparations. *Diabetes Care* 1982; **5**: 77–91.

2 Binder C, Lauritzen T, Faber O, Pramming S. Insulin pharmacokinetics. *Diabetes Care* 1984; **7**: 188–99.

3 Brogden R, Heel R. Human insulin. A review of its biological activity, pharmacokinetics and therapeutic use. *Drugs* 1987; **34**: 350–71.

4 Koivisto VA. Various influences on insulin absorption. *Neth J Med* 1985; **28** (suppl 1): 25–8.

5 Kraegen EW, Chisholm DJ. Pharmacokinetics of insulin. Implications for continuous subcutaneous insulin infusion therapy. *Clin Pharmacokinet* 1985; **10**: 303–14.

6 Skyler J. Insulin pharmacology. *Med Clin North Am* 1988; **72**: 1337–53.

7 Turnheim K, Waldhäusl WK. Essentials of insulin pharmacokinetics. *Wiener Klin Wochenschr* 1988; **100**: 65–72.

8 Binder C. Absorption of injected insulin: A clinical–pharmacological study. *Acta Pharmacol Toxicol* 1969; **27** (suppl 2): 1–84.

9 Brange J. Galenics of insulin. *The Physico-chemical and Pharmaceutical Aspects of Insulin and Insulin Preparations*. Berlin: Springer-Verlag, 1987.

10 Binder C. A theoretical model for the absorption of soluble insulin. In: Brunetti P, Alberti KGMM, Albisser AM, Hepp KP, Massi-Benedetti M, eds. *Artificial Systems for Insulin Delivery*. New York: Raven Press, 1983: 53–7.

11 Ribel U, Jørgensen K, Brange J, Henriksen U. The pig as a model for subcutaneous insulin absorption in man. In: Serrano-Rios M, Lefèbvre PJ, eds. *Diabetes 1985*. Amsterdam: Elsevier Science Publications BV, 1986: 891–6.

12 Mosekilde E, Skovbo Jensen K, Binder C, Pramming S, Thorsteinsson B. Modeling absorption kinetics of subcutaneous injected soluble insulin. *J Pharmacokinet Biopharmaceut* 1989; **17**: 67–87.

13 Williams G, Pickup J, Clark A, Bowcock S, Cooke E, Keen H. Changes in blood flow close to subcutaneous insulin injection sites in stable and brittle diabetics. *Diabetes* 1983; **32**: 466–73.

14 Brange J, Ribel U, Hansen JF, Dodson G, Hansen MT, Havelund S, Melberg SG, Norris F, Norris K, Snel L, Sørensen AR, Voight HO. Monomeric insulins obtained by protein engineering and their medical implications. *Nature* 1988; **333**: 679–82.

15 Vora JP, Owens DR, Dolbien J, Atiea JA, Dean JD, Kang S, Burch A, Brange J. Recombinant DNA derived monomeric insulin analogue: comparison with soluble human insulin in normal subjects. *Br Med J* 1988; **297**: 1236–9.

16 Thow JC, Johnson AB, Antsiferov M, Home PD. Exercise augments the absorption of isophane (NPH) insulin. *Diabetic Med* 1989; **6**: 342–5.

17 Tunbridge FKE, Owens A, Home PD, Davis SN, Murphy M, Burrin JM, Alberti KGMM, Jensen I. Double-blind crossover trial of isophane (NPH)- and Lente-based insulin regimens. *Diabetes Care* 1989; **12**: 115–19.

18 Hildebrandt P, Sestoft L, Nielsen SL. The absorption of subcutaneously injected short-acting soluble insulin: Influence of injection technique and concentration. *Diabetes Care* 1983; **6**: 459–62.

19 Owens DR. *Human Insulin: Clinical Pharmacological Studies in Normal Man*. Thesis. Boston, The Hague, Dirdrecht. Lancaster: MTP Press Limited, 1986.

20 Pappenheimer JR. Passage of molecules through capillary walls. *Physiol Rev* 1953; **33**: 387–423.

21 Hildebrandt P, Sejrsen P, Nielsen SL, Birch K, Sestoft L. Diffusion and polymerization determines the insulin absorption from subcutaneous tissue in diabetic patients. *Scand J Clin Invest* 1985; **45**: 685–90.

22 Hildebrandt P, Mehlsen J, Birch K, Kühl C. Relationship between subcutaneous blood flow and absorption of lente type insulin. *Diabetes Res* 1987; **4**: 179–81.

23 Fernqvist E, Gunnarsson R, Linde B. Influence of circulating epinephrine on absorption of subcutaneously injected insulin. *Diabetes* 1988; **37**: 694–701.

24 Moses AC, Gordon GS, Carey MC, Flier JS. Insulin administered intranasally as an insulin bile salt aerosol. Effectiveness and reproducibility in normal and diabetic subjects. *Diabetes* 1983; **32**: 1040–7.

25 Micossi P, Cristallo M, Librenti C et al. Free insulin profiles after intraperitoneal, intramuscular and subcutaneous insulin administration. *Diabetes Care* 1986; **9**: 575–8.

26 Kinmonth AL, Baum JD. Timing of pre-breakfast insulin injection and postprandial metabolic control in diabetic children. *Br Med J* 1980; **280**: 604–6.

27 Dillon R. Improved serum insulin profiles in diabetic individuals who massaged their insulin injection sites. *Diabetes Care* 1983; **6**: 399–401.

28 Linde B. Dissociation of insulin absorption and blood flow during massage of a subcutaneous injection site. *Diabetes Care* 1986; **9**: 570–4.

29 Edsberg B, Herly D, Hildebrandt P, Kühl C. Insulin bolus given by sprinkler needle: effect on absorption and glycaemic response to a meal. *Br Med J* 1987; **294**: 1373–6.

30 Williams G, Pickup JC, Collins CG, Keen H. Prostaglandin E₁ accelerates subcutaneous insulin absorption in insulin-dependent diabetic patients. *Diabetic Med* 1984; **1**: 109–13.

31 Williams G, Pickup JC, Bowcock S, Cooke E, Keen H. Subcutaneous aprotinin causes local hyperaemia. A possible mechanism by which aprotinin improves control in some diabetic patients. *Diabetologia* 1983; **24**: 91–4.

32 Markussen J, Diers I, Hougaard P, Langkjær L, Norris K, Snel L, Sørensen AR, Sørensen E, Voigt HO. Soluble, prolonged-acting insulin derivatives. III. Degree of protraction, crystallizability and chemical stability of insulins substituted in positions A21, B13, B23, B27 and B30. *Protein Eng* 1988; **2**: 157–66.

33 Owens DR. Data presented at IDF Conference, Sydney, Australia, 1988.

34 Frid A, Lindén B. Where do lean diabetics inject their insulin? A study using computed tomography. *Br Med J* 1986; **292**: 1638.

35 Frid A, Linde B. Clinically important differences in insulin absorption rates within the abdomen in IDDM. *Diabetes* 1989; **38** (suppl 2): 144A.

36 Kølendorf K, Bojsen J, Deckert T. Clinical factors influencing the absorption of ^{125}I-NPH insulin in diabetic patients. *Horm Metab Res* 1983; **15**: 274–8.

37 Rönnemaa T, Koivisto VA. Combined effect of exercise and ambient temperature on insulin absorption and postprandial glycemia in type I patients. *Diabetes Care* 1988; **11**: 769−73.

38 Fernqvist E, Linde B. Potent mental stress and insulin absorption in normal subjects. *Diabetes Care* 1988; **11**: 650−5.

39 Fernqvist-Forbes E, Linde B, Gunnarsson R. Insulin absorption and subcutaneous blood flow in normal subjects during insulin-induced hypoglycemia. *J Clin Endocrinol Metab* 1988; **67**: 619−23.

40 Mühlhauser I, Cüppers HJ, Berger M. Smoking and insulin absorption from subcutaneous tissue. *Br Med J* 1984; **288**: 1875−6.

41 Spraul M, Chantelau E, Koumoulidou J, Berger M. Subcutaneous or nonsubcutaneous injection of insulin. *Diabetes Care* 1988; **11**: 733−6.

42 Frid A, Gunnarsson R, Güntner P, Linde B. Effects of accidental intramuscular injection on insulin absorption in IDDM. *Diabetes Care* 1988; **11**: 41−5.

43 Frid A, Östman J, Linde B. Hypoglycemia risk during exercise after intramuscular thigh injection of insulin in IDDM. *Diabetes Care* 1990; **13**: 473−77.

44 Francis AJ, Hanning I, Alberti KGMM. The influence of insulin antibody levels on the plasma profiles and action of subcutaneously injected human and bovine short acting insulins. *Diabetologia* 1985; **28**: 330−4.

45 De Meijer PHEM, Lutterman JA, van't Laar A. Insulin antibodies do not influence the absorption rate of subcutaneously injected insulin. *Diabetic Med* 1988; **5**: 776−81.

46 Kurtz AB, Nabarro JDN. Circulating insulin-binding antibodies. *Diabetologia* 1980; **19**: 329−34.

47 Rabkin R, Ryan MP, Duckworth WC. The renal metabolism of insulin. *Diabetologia* 1984; **27**: 351−7.

48 Ferrannini E, Cobelli C. The kinetics of insulin in man. I. General aspects. *Diabetes Metab Rev* 1987; **3**: 335−63.

49 Sherwin RS, Kramer KJ, Tobin JD, Insel PA, Liljenquist JE, Berman M, Andres R. A model of the kinetics of insulin in man. *J Clin Invest* 1974; **53**: 1481−92.

39 Insulin Injection Treatment for Insulin-Dependent Diabetic Patients

Summary

• The development of 'intensified' insulin regimens which mimic physiological insulin profiles has been facilitated by the advent of blood glucose self-monitoring and improved diabetes education for patients.

• Many types of insulin injection regimen are available. Intermediate- or long-acting insulins injected once or twice daily provide the basal requirement and short-acting insulin injected 30–40 min before meals covers the additional prandial needs.

• A common problem with twice-daily intermediate- and short-acting insulins is the relatively short-action profile of the intermediate insulin, which when injected in the early evening, tends to run out in the few hours before breakfast and so exacerbates fasting hyperglycaemia. This may be overcome by injecting the intermediate-acting insulin before bedtime.

• The action profiles of lente and isophane insulins are indistinguishable in everyday use. However, excess zinc ions in lente (and ultralente) insulins may combine with soluble insulin when the two are mixed, significantly retarding the action profile of the short-acting component. This problem which does not occur with isophane insulins, is not clinically important.

• Ultralente formulations using human insulin have a significantly shorter action profile than the original bovine preparation which was often effective when injected once daily. Human ultralente insulin may require two injections per day.

• Premixed (biphasic) combinations of short- with intermediate-acting insulin may achieve good glycaemic control in patients with residual endogenous insulin secretion but are often not flexible enough for C-peptide deficient IDDM patients.

• 'Pen devices' containing prefilled cartridges of soluble or isophane insulin are convenient to use and popular with patients, but their use does not apparently improve glycaemic control.

• Indwelling cannulae, with a self-sealing rubber diaphragm through which several insulin injections can be made, can be implanted subcutaneously for 1–2 days in patients who find multiple injections unacceptable.

• Insulin should be injected into the abdomen, outer thigh, buttock or upper arm, ideally in a fixed rotation to reduce variability in insulin absorption. Because of the possibility of vertical injections entering muscle in thin patients, injections should probably be given at an angle into a pinched-up skin-fold. There is no need to clean the skin.

• Disposable syringes can safely be re-used for at least 7 days, and needles until they become blunt. Infections at insulin injection sites are very rare.

• Reagent strips for blood glucose measurement contain glucose oxidase immobilized together with peroxidase and a chromogen whose colour changes on exposure to the hydrogen peroxide generated by glucose oxidation.

• Reagent strips can be compared visually against a standard colour chart, or read using a reflectance meter. Meters are useful for patients with colour vision defects due to retinopathy or other causes.

• Blood for glucose monitoring should be obtained by pricking the sides of the fingertips, rather than the sensitive pulps. The blood drop must be applied correctly to the strip and the reaction timed precisely in order to achieve accurate results.

● Algorithms (sequences of rules) for adjusting insulin dosages and food intake according to blood glucose values can be drawn up for individual patients.

● Patients who are not acutely ill (i.e. vomiting) may begin insulin treatment outside hospital if under the close supervision of a diabetes specialist nurse. Initial insulin dosages should be low (e.g. 6−10 U intermediate-acting insulin twice-daily) to avoid hypoglycaemia.

Until the mid-1970s it was widely thought by physicians that obtaining and maintaining near-normoglycaemia throughout the day in most patients with IDDM was, for all intents and purposes, impossible. Increasing the frequency of insulin injections, for example, might lower the mean blood glucose level, but only at the expense of inducing wide glycaemic fluctuations and unacceptable hypoglycaemia [1].

However, in the last decade or so there has been renewed interest and much success in achieving strict long-term control in IDDM patients using insulin injections. Several factors have contributed:

1 The increasing evidence that the microvascular complications of diabetes are related to both the duration and the degree of metabolic disorder (see Chapter 52) led several organizations to call for new efforts in improving diabetic control, particularly using strategies which mimic the physiological insulin profile. This consists of a continuous basal supply throughout the 24 hours, with superimposed boosts at mealtimes [2].

2 The introduction of continuous subcutaneous insulin infusion (CSII) set new standards of glycaemic and intermediary metabolite control in IDDM (Chapter 42) and undoubtedly encouraged many to try to match this success both by devising new insulin injection regimens and by optimizing existing treatment schedules.

3 The use of capillary blood glucose self-monitoring with reagent strips, with or without a reflectance meter, became popular from the late 1970s onwards [3−5]. This first enabled patients and doctors to see how badly conventional treatment schedules performed and also allowed them to adjust insulin doses according to the prevailing blood glucose values. It therefore became realistic

to aim to achieve near-normoglycaemia (so-called 'closing the loop' of blood glucose homeostasis).

4 The recent rediscovery of the importance of diabetes education (Chapter 97) emphasized the crucial role of the patient in determining the success or failure of treatment and the need for him to learn about his own management and to share responsibility for the maintenance of good control.

Many modern insulin injection (and infusion) treatments are described as 'intensified'. This term encompasses a package of aspects of treatment: 'physiological' insulin injection regimens or CSII; blood glucose self-monitoring; the understanding and use of algorithms for adjusting insulin delivery according to the self-monitored blood glucose values or anticipated exercise or diet; diabetes education; and adherence to an appropriate diabetic diet (Table 39.1).

Insulin injection regimens in current use

These may be divided into three types: combinations of short- and intermediate-acting insulins, short and long-acting insulin (ultralente), and pre-mixed insulins (short-acting combined with isophane insulin in various proportions).

Short- and intermediate-acting insulin regimens

Fig. 39.1 shows in diagrammatic form the use of regimens in which the basal insulin requirement is supplied by lente- or isophane-type insulin and the mealtime supplements by short-acting insulin injections. Most experience has been obtained with option 1, in which there are twice-daily injections of each of the two insulin formulations, given before breakfast and before the evening meal. No short-acting insulin is given for lunch with this option, both for convenience and because, in practice, blood insulin levels remain

Table 39.1. The components of 'intensified' insulin regimens.

Physiological insulin delivery (basal plus bolus)

Blood glucose self-monitoring

Insulin dosage adjustment based on:
● blood glucose levels
● anticipated exercise
● anticipated food intake

Diabetes education

Diet

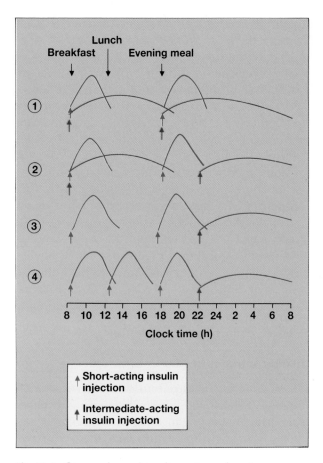

Fig. 39.1. Commonly used insulin regimens based on subcutaneous injections of short- and intermediate-acting (isophane or lente) insulins.

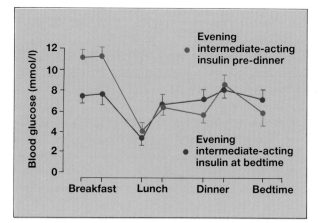

Fig. 39.2. Effect of delaying the evening injection of intermediate-acting insulin until bedtime. Mean ± SEM blood glucose values in six IDDM patients treated by twice-daily short- and intermediate-acting insulin injections. Samples were collected at home and analysed later in the laboratory. (Redrawn from ref. 6.)

sufficiently high after the morning short- and intermediate-acting insulin injection to cover (at least in part) any midday meal-related glycaemic excursions. For optimal postprandial control, short-acting insulin should be injected about 30–40 min before eating.

The main disadvantage of option 1 is that when lente or isophane insulins are given at approximately 1800–1900 h, insulin action in many patients does not last through the entire night, and blood glucose values begin to rise in the few hours before breakfast (see Chapter 51). To counter this effect, injection of the evening intermediate-acting insulin can be delayed until shortly before bedtime, perhaps 2200 h (option 2) [6]. Pre-supper short-acting insulin is given at the usual time. Pre-breakfast blood glucose values may be significantly reduced in this way (Fig. 39.2), while avoiding the risks of early-morning hypoglycaemia which might be induced by simply increasing the dosage of intermediate-acting insulin given in the early evening (see Chapter 52).

In selected patients who do not miss meals, the morning lente or isophane insulin may be omitted, and the between-meals basal insulin supplied by two or three preprandial injections of short-acting insulin (options 3 and 4). The introduction of insulin 'pens' with a prefilled cartridge of short-acting (and recently isophane) insulin has greatly encouraged the use of these regimens using multiple daily insulin injections (see below).

LENTE VERSUS ISOPHANE INSULIN

Charts produced by the insulin manufacturers which show the theoretical duration of action of isophane and lente-type insulins suggest slight differences in the pharmacodynamics between the two preparations. In practice, however, glycaemic control is reported to be exactly the same in randomized, cross-over trials comparing short-acting insulin plus human lente versus short-acting plus human isophane insulin (Fig. 39.3) [7]. Most diabetologists would also attest that porcine lente and isophane insulins are indistinguishable in everyday use.

Many patients routinely mix short- and intermediate-acting insulin within the syringe shortly before injection. There is general agreement that isophane insulin does not modify the absorption or time-action characteristics of added short-acting insulin [8, 9], but several studies show that when lente (or ultralente) is mixed with short-acting insulin, there is a delayed rise in plasma free

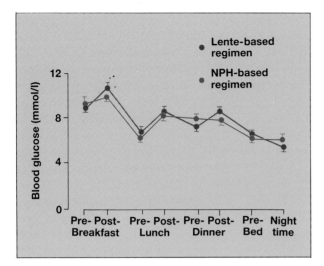

Fig. 39.3. The glycaemic equivalence of regimens based on isophane insulin or lente insulin. Mean ± SEM blood glucose values from samples collected by patients on filter paper and analysed in the laboratory. (Redrawn from ref. 7.)

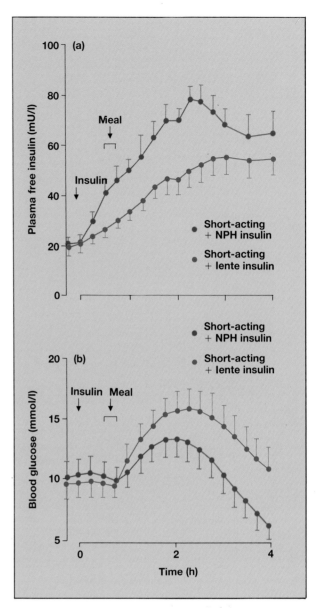

Fig. 39.4. The effect of mixing short-acting insulin with isophane or lente insulins. (a) plasma free insulin levels after injection of isophane or lente; (b) equivalent blood glucose concentrations. (Redrawn from ref. 10.)

insulin levels and higher postprandial blood glucose values as compared with a mixture of isophane and short-acting insulin [8, 10–12] (Fig. 39.4). Presumably this is because a proportion of the short-acting insulin interacts with excess zinc ions in the lente and is effectively converted into lente insulin. It has been suggested that there is no loss of the rapid biological action of short-acting insulin if porcine lente is mixed with porcine short-acting insulin and injected almost immediately afterwards, but with human insulin formulations the interaction seems to occur more quickly and a delayed action profile may be unavoidable [12]. Nevertheless, outpatient trials [7] have shown that glycaemic control is not significantly different in patients injecting mixtures of either human isophane with short-acting or human lente with short-acting insulins. Miscibility effects may be less apparent for U100 insulin than for the U40 strength.

Short- and long-acting insulin regimens

The strategy of this type of regimen is to provide the basal insulin requirement with one or two daily injections of the long-acting, ultralente insulin [13, 14]. Short-acting insulin is given before main meals, two or three times daily, by syringe or pen injector (Fig. 39.5). Originally, ultralente was given as a single injection before breakfast (option 5), or, in a few patients, before the evening meal (option 6). However, the beef ultra-

lente available previously has now been largely replaced by the manufacturers with human ultralente, which has a significantly shorter duration of action [15]. Because of this, many patients may need twice-daily injections of human ultralente in order to maintain adequate blood levels of free insulin throughout the day (option 7) [16].

A number of other regimens based on ultralente and short-acting insulin may also be used (options 8–10, Fig. 39.5), depending on the number of mealtime injections of short-acting insulin. The morning dose of ultralente may be omitted (option

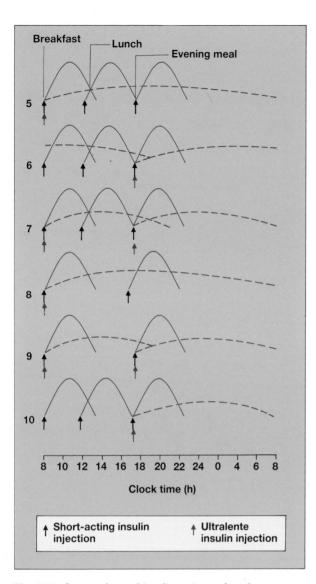

Fig. 39.5. Commonly used insulin regimens based on subcutaneous injections of short-acting and ultralente-type insulins.

isophane insulin. They are, of course, especially intended for the elderly, mostly NIDDM, diabetic patient who is receiving insulin (see Chapter 48) [18]. In NIDDM patients who have significant endogenous insulin production, a single daily injection of insulin often restores near-normoglycaemia. In the elderly subject, whether IDDM or NIDDM, multiple daily injections may not be possible and indeed, in this group, treatment may not aim to achieve as strict glycaemic control as in younger patients (Chapter 89).

The use of premixed insulins in young and middle-aged IDDM subjects is less popular and less thoroughly studied. Although it has been claimed that a group of patients were as well controlled by biphasic insulin as by their usual short- and intermediate-acting insulins [19], many subjects in this report probably had remaining endogenous insulin and were studied for such a short time that the effects on insulin dosage of intercurrent illness, varying exercise patterns, dietary changes and so on were not apparent. Most physicians still prefer the flexibility of the patient being able to mix short- and intermediate-acting insulins according to need.

Insulin 'pens'

The first fountain pen-like device for facilitating multiple insulin injections was described by the late Dr John Ireland and colleagues [20], and consisted of a conventional syringe inside a holder. A number of similar devices are now available commercially [21–26], which contain a prefilled cartridge of short-acting or, most recently, isophane insulin (Fig. 39.6).

10; cf. option 4 using intermediate-acting insulin). With human ultralente insulin, there is probably no difference in glycaemic control with regimens based on once-daily injection in the morning versus injection in the evening [17].

Premixed insulin formulations

Premixed or 'biphasic' formulations consist of combinations of short-acting and isophane insulin prepared by the manufacture in a fixed proportion. In the UK there are currently several such mixtures, marketed by a number of manufacturers, and available as 10/90%, 20/80%, 30/70% and 50/50% combinations of short-acting and

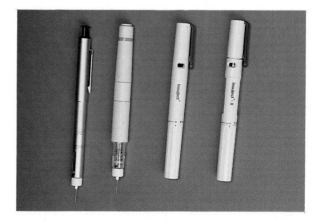

Fig. 39.6. Insulin 'pens' (left to right: NovoPen I, NovoPen II, Insuject, Insuject X; Novo–Nordisk).

The NovoPen I injection device (Novo—Nordisk) was one of the first to be marketed on a large scale and consists of a pen case which holds a 1.5 ml cartridge of human short-acting insulin, delivered through a detachable 27-gauge disposable needle. Metered insulin doses are delivered by pressing a button on the pen cap, each press injecting 2 U of insulin. A side window allows the quantity of insulin remaining in the pen to be checked. In later model (NovoPen II), the insulin dose can be selected before injection by rotating a ring on the pen barrel and then delivered with a single push of the button. This has clear advantages when large doses are necessary. Insulin pen cartridges are also becoming available which are filled with human isophane insulin (Protaphane Penfill for the Insuject-X; Novo—Nordisk) [25] and a number of other pens are now being marketed (e.g. Autopen, Owen Mumford).

The main advantages of insulin pens relate to the convenience, speed and ease of injection with the device, all of which encourage multiple-injection regimens (Table 39.2). Patient acceptance of pens has been good [27, 28] and many subjects have opted to use pen-based schedules rather than conventional regimens such as twice-daily injections of short- and intermediate-acting insulin [28]. As expected, there is no evidence that glycaemic control is improved by the mere substitution of injecting short-acting insulin with a pen device rather than a syringe [26].

Other devices for facilitating multiple insulin injections

For some patients, multiple injections are unacceptable even when a pen is available. The frequency of needle insertion in these cases can be reduced by using an indwelling subcutaneous cannula [29–31]. A recently described device [31] employs a flexible Teflon 24-gauge cannula with low dead-space (<0.01 ml); insulin is injected through a self-sealing rubber diaphragm (Fig. 39.7). These devices should be inserted

Table 39.2. Advantages of insulin 'pens'.

- *Convenience* — not necessary to carry syringe, needle and insulin vial
- *Patient acceptance* — encourages use of multiple insulin injection regimens
- *Speed* — quicker than conventional injection techniques
- *Ease* — possible to inject with one-handed technique

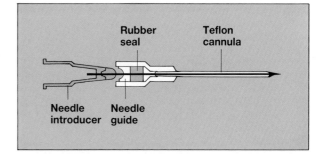

Fig. 39.7. Diagram of an implantable Teflon cannula suitable for multiple subcutaneous insulin injections (H.G. Wallace Ltd, Colchester, UK). (Redrawn from ref. 31.)

using the same precautions as for the indwelling delivery cannulae of CSII (Chapter 42) — i.e. 'no-touch' technique, re-implantation at a new site every 1–2 days, adequate skin preparation and protecting the cannula insertion site with a sterile cover.

Subcutaneous insulin injection: sites, techniques and complications

The best sites for subcutaneous insulin injection are the abdomen, outer thighs, buttocks and upper arms (Fig. 39.8). Injections should be either rotated within one of these anatomical areas for a few weeks, taking care to avoid repeated injection into the same spot, or given into one area each morning and another area each evening, or at other regular times of injection. The rationale for this advice is that absorption of insulin varies from one site to another, being fastest in the abdomen, followed by the arm and leg [32], and the inevitable large differences in biological effect from injection to injection can be reduced to some extent by confining insulin administration to one area at a time. Injection into exactly the same subcutaneous area, however, may cause lipohypertrophy, which may hinder insulin absorption [33] as well as being unsightly. Rotation of injection sites can also help to avoid this problem.

With modern needles which are usually about 12 mm long, it has become common practice to stretch an area of skin between the thumb and forefinger and to push the needle vertically into the tissue up to the hub of the needle. However, in some patients at some sites, the subcutaneous tissue is relatively thin and insulin is probably injected intramuscularly quite often [34] (see Chapter 38). Since absorption is likely to be faster from muscle than from the subcutaneous

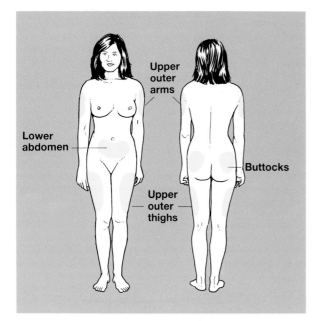

Fig. 39.8. Suitable sites for subcutaneous insulin injection.

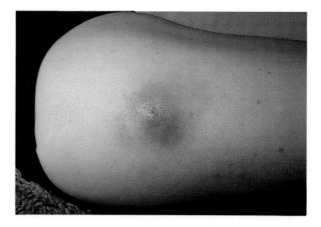

Fig. 39.9. An injection site abscess. Reproduced courtesy of Dr G.V. Gill, Arrowe Park Hospital, Wirral.

tissue (at least in the leg), inadvertent intramuscular injection is another possible cause of unpredictable control. It may therefore be preferable to suggest pinching up a fold of skin and injecting vertically or at a slight angle into the skin mound.

Swabbing the skin with alcohol, or withdrawal of the syringe plunger to check that a vein has not been entered, are both now thought to be unnecessary.

There is ample evidence that disposable plastic syringes can be safely reused for a period of at least 7 days, and that needles need not be changed until they become blunt [35, 36]. After replacing the needle guard, the syringe may be kept in a domestic refrigerator between injections, without washing or sterilization. The local infection rate using this method is no greater than with the traditional glass syringe and metal needle, which were cleaned in spirit or boiled in water. It has been estimated that in the UK there was a cost saving of more than two-thirds by adopting the use of disposable syringes used for 7 days.

Injection-site abscesses (Fig. 39.9) are very rare in diabetic patients [37], the main discouragement to infection being the insulin preservatives, m-cresol, phenol or methylhydroxybenzoate. Some patients reuse disposable plastic syringes for several months until the markings wear off; as long as the syringes are kept under dry conditions, they remain bacteriologically safe. Abscesses have in fact been attributed to the

'surgical' spirit which was used to sterilize glass syringes [38]. This contains additives such as castor oil, methyl salicylate and diethylphthalate which cause local irritation and leave an oily residue when the alcohol has evaporated. Similarly, an injection site infection caused by an atypical Mycobacterium chelonei var abscessus was attributed to the hypochlorite solution used to 'sterilize' the syringe [39].

Blood glucose self-monitoring (BGSM)

Glucose oxidase dry-reagent strips for the measurement of capillary blood glucose were first used by medical personnel in the 1960s and reflectance meters for reading the result became available from 1970. However, it was not until 1978 that several groups reported that many diabetic patients could be taught to measure their own capillary blood glucose concentrations several times during the day. Good glycaemic control was achieved in a reasonable number of cases, presumably as a result of the monitoring [3–5]. At about the same time, BGSM was being used in the first outpatient studies of continuous subcutaneous insulin infusion (Chapter 42) so as to document the control achieved, to warn against metabolic deterioration and to adjust the insulin infusion rates in order to maintain near-normoglycaemia [40].

BGSM has now become an essential part of modern insulin therapy. The many benefits are summarized in Table 39.3.

Techniques and technology of BGSM

Most reagent strips for BGSM consist of glucose

oxidase immobilized together with peroxidase and a chromogen:

$$\text{Glucose} + O_2 \xrightarrow{\text{Glucose oxidase}} \text{Hydrogen peroxide} + \text{gluconic acid}$$

$$H_2O_2 + \underset{\text{chromogen}}{\underset{\text{(colourless)}}{\text{reduced}}} \xrightarrow{\text{Peroxidase}} \underset{\text{chromogen}}{\underset{\text{(colour)}}{\text{Oxidized}}} + H_2O$$

The colour developed is proportional to the glucose concentration and may be compared visually with the standard colour charts on the side of the strip container or read in a reflectance meter (Fig. 39.10). Many of the strips are suitable for both visual and meter assessment. In the UK, strips are currently prescribable as a National Health Service expense, but meters are not.

The best sites for obtaining capillary blood samples are the sides of the distal phalanges on both hands. Although many patients use the finger pulp, this is a sensitive area and is not to be recommended. Hands should be socially clean;

Table 39.3. Some benefits of blood glucose self-monitoring.

More accurate and patient-acceptable than urine tests for glucose

Provides information for feedback-control of insulin delivery
- on a day-to-day basis, by the patient
- in the long-term, by the physician

Defines the level of glycaemic control achieved
- for research
- for routine clinical assessment

Identifies hypoglycaemia
- impossible with urine testing
- particularly valuable in patients with loss of hypoglycaemic awareness

Acts as an educational aid

Increases patient participation, motivation and interest

Reinforces the patient's feeling of being 'in control', thus offering independence, shared responsibility and self-confidence

Allows the patient to relate level of control to feeling of well-being

Improves quality of life

Reduces hospital admission (?)

Fig. 39.10. Glucose oxidase reagent strips and reflectance metres (left to right: Glucostix and Glucometer II (Ames); Reflolux II and BM Test 1—44 Strips (Boehringer Mannheim).

washing is not usually necessary and swabbing with alcohol definitely contraindicated. A number of automatic spring-loaded lancet devices are available for obtaining blood samples (Fig. 39.11). It is important that the drop of blood is large enough to cover the test zone(s). After applying the drop of blood to the strip, testing should be according to the manufacture's instructions with the blood left on the testing pad for the required time (usually 1 min), the blood wiped, blotted or washed away (as defined for the particular strip) and the reading made at the specified time.

In the UK, several reflectance meters made by various companies, e.g. Medistron (Glucochek meters), Ames (Glucometer meters), Hypoguard (Hypo-Count meters) and BCL (Boehringer Mannheim; Reflolux meters). Similar meters are available in other countries. They are particularly

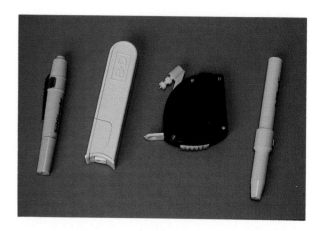

Fig. 39.11. Devices for automatic finger pricking (left to right): Glucolet (Ames), Autolance (Becton Dickinson), Autolet II (Owen Mumford); and Soft Touch (Boehringer Mannheim)).

indicated for patients with diabetic retinopathy who may have defects of colour vision, patients with other colour vision difficulties and those who prefer an objective reading for the blood glucose value. A recently introduced pen-sized meter (Exactech, Medisense, Oxford, UK) is unusual in that the strip is a biosensor, based on the electrochemical detection of the oxidation of glucose, the pen measuring the current produced rather than the colour developed, as in a conventional meter (see Chapter 105).

There is no general agreement about the frequency of BGSM and clearly this depends on factors such as the ability of control, the compliance, motivation and age of the patient, and the level of control sought. During pregnancy, for example, obtaining very good control carries a high priority and the patients are usually highly-motivated. One pattern of routine testing frequently recommended is a 7-point day-profile once every 2 weeks (before and 90 min after each main meal and at bedtime), together with a single test at a different time each day (fasting first day, 90 min after breakfast next day, etc.).

Accuracy and precision of BGSM: the need for training

There is general agreement that the accuracy (correlation with a laboratory test method) and precision (repeatability) of BGSM by patients, using either visual comparison or a reflectance meter,

Table 39.4. Some reasons for poor results with blood glucose self-monitoring.

Poor training in technique of BGSM
Reflectance meter fault
Poor eyesight (e.g. because of age, retinopathy, colour vision defects)
Poor timing of tests
Insufficiently large blood sample
Incorrect removal of blood sample from strip
Out-of-date or improperly stored test strips
Altered haemotocrit
Overt misinterpretation of readings
Deliberate mis-recording of results (e.g. omission of very high and low results)

can be very good under optimal conditions [41, 42]. However, the system is highly 'user-dependent' and there are many reasons for unreliable results (Table 39.4). In practice, it is recognized that if the system is used properly, the results are sufficiently accurate and precise for routine clinical purposes but that everyday performance is probably inadequate in many patients. It has been estimated, for example, that up to 50% of results may differ by more than 20% from the reference value [41].

There are several ways in which the results of BGSM could be improved, including checks on meter functioning, regular use of calibration standards to assess accuracy of meters and strips, and frequent review and evaluation of the patient's

Table 39.5. Simple algorithm for adjusting insulin dosage by BGSM, for patients receiving twice-daily short- and intermediate-acting insulin.

• *Target blood glucose levels:*
Before meals: 4–6 mmol/l
After meals: less than 10 mmol/l

• *If blood glucose result is too high for 2 days or more:*

Before breakfast	Before lunch	Before evening meal	At bedtime
Increase evening long-acting insulin	Increase morning short-acting insulin	Increase morning long-acting insulin	Increase evening short-acting insulin

• *If blood glucose result is too low for 2 days or more:*

Before breakfast	Before lunch	Before evening meal	At bedtime
Reduce evening long-acting insulin	Reduce morning short-acting insulin	Reduce morning long-acting insulin	Reduce evening short-acting insulin

Note: Increase or decrease insulin by 2 U at a time.

technique together with correction by trained personnel of any deficiencies. Indeed, training in the use of BGSM is a central requirement for its effective application, and there is a case for standardization of programmes and for qualification schemes to ensure that the trainers themselves are proficient at the technique.

How is BGSM used in patient management?

Rules (algorithms) for adjusting insulin dosage and dietary intake according to the BGSM results can be made reasonably simple. For example, the patient can be given individualized target blood glucose levels before and after meals. It is essential that patients are taught the duration of action of the insulins used (e.g. the evening long- or intermediate-acting insulin lasts all night, so the blood glucose value at the end of the night — before breakfast — tells us whether there is too much or too little of this insulin being injected). Table 39.5 shows an algorithm for a patient receiving twice-daily short- and intermediate-acting insulins.

As with the accuracy of BGSM, there is a widespread feeling that the practical performance of patients and doctors in using BGSM data falls far short of the theoretical possibilities.

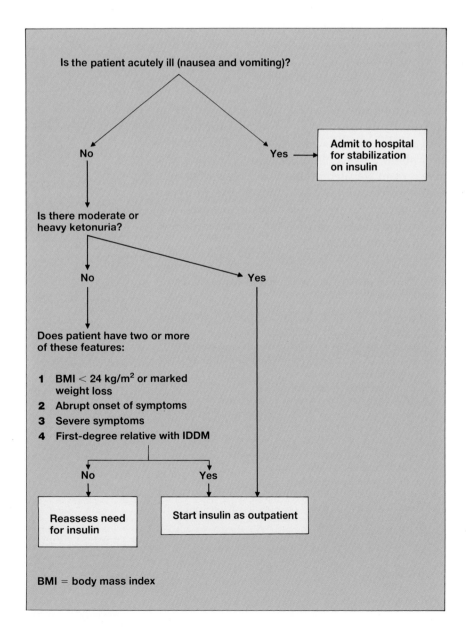

Fig. 39.12. An algorithm for the decision to start outpatient insulin treatment. (Redrawn from ref. 44.)

Starting the newly diagnosed IDDM patient on insulin treatment

It is not known whether it is better to start IDDM subjects on insulin treatment as outpatients or during a hospital admission. Although outpatient stabilization has traditionally been uncommon, it has been used at a few centres for many years [43] and is now becoming increasingly popular in the UK [44] and the USA [45] for those patients who are not acutely ill. A diabetes specialist nurse is essential for starting treatment out of hospital, as it is she who instructs the patient in insulin injection techniques, provides basic information and maintains contact in the first few weeks.

An algorithm for deciding which patients are suitable for starting insulin as outpatients is given in Fig. 39.12 and a programme for the first weeks is shown in Table 39.6. Both are based on the work of Wilson *et al.* [44], and aim to teach the patient to give his own insulin injections as soon as possible. The modest starting insulin dosage of 6–10 U intermediate-acting insulin twice-daily is specifically designed to avoid hypoglycaemia.

In most patients, symptoms generally improve after about 4 days, although blood glucose levels may remain elevated at this time. Insulin dosages are adjusted after introducing BGSM into the programme and about one-third of patients will require the addition of short-acting insulin during the first 6 months or so.

Table 39.6. Programme for starting insulin treatment as an outpatient (adapted from ref. 44).

1st session
Short talk with physician (~ 30 min)
One-to-one instruction by diabetes nurse specialist
Nurse demonstrates drawing up of insulin dose and injection technique
Patient injects himself with insulin
Patient learns to draw up insulin
Starting insulin dosage: 6–10 U intermediate-acting insulin twice-daily
'Survival' information
• recognition and treatment of hypoglycaemia
• reassurance about specific anxieties
• advice on driving and work
• contact telephone number of nurse and doctor
• advice to eat regular meals (no specific diet instruction)

After 1 week
Review above

After 2 weeks
Teach BGSM
Full dietary instruction

Table 39.7. Some variations and problems in the life of diabetic patients which may influence the choice of insulin regimen.

Employment	• Shift-workers • Long working day (early breakfast, late evening meal) • Missed midday meal or frequent business lunches • International travel
Eating	• National variations (e.g. traditional large breakfast in UK, main meal at midday in some countries, dietary composition country to country, etc.). • Individual variations (fads, availability, affordability, preferences, eating out at restaurants).
Travel	• Long-haul air travel • Travel to work, e.g. long walk
Exercise	• Sportsmen and women • Sedentary office workers • Labourers
Leisure	• Strenuous hobbies, e.g. gardening, sport, etc.
Age and disability	• Elderly • Children • Handicapped (visual impairment, arthritis, etc.).
Diabetic complications	• Nephropathy (hypoglycaemia-prone) • Retinopathy (inability to perform BGSM) • Autonomic neuropathy (hypoglycaemia prone)
Intercurrent illness and events	• Other chronic illnesses • Pregnancy
Injection preferences	• Dislike of multiple injections
Insulin absorption	• Individual variations in absorption and its predictability • 'Brittle diabetes' and 'subcutaneous insulin resistance syndrome'
Stability of diabetes	• Long duration of diabetes (no endogenous insulin) • Multiple hospital admissions for ketoacidosis and/or hypoglycaemia
Psychological state of patient	• Poor compliance
Intelligence and education	• Poor education about diabetes • Reduced ability to adjust insulin dosages
Medical facilities	• Poorly trained staff • Lack of diabetes education facilities

Choosing an insulin regimen for each patient

It is not yet possible to predict which insulin regimen will best suit which patient. Many individual characteristics of patients and their lifestyles may influence the level of control which is achievable with insulin and perhaps, therefore, the choice of regimen (Table 39.7).

Conclusions

Given the immense variability in the process of insulin absorption and the unpredictability of daily life for many people, finding an insulin regimen to suit the particular needs of an individual patient may seem a difficult task. However, the development of novel treatment schedules, supported by self-monitoring of blood glucose levels and the education necessary for the patient to know how to react to these, has meant that most patients can now achieve satisfactory control of their diabetes.

JOHN C. PICKUP
GARETH WILLIAMS

References

1 Service FJ, Molnar GD, Rosevear JW, Ackerman E, Gatewood LC, Taylor WT. Mean amplitude of glycemic excursions, a measure of diabetic instability. *Diabetes* 1970; **19**: 644–55.

2 Cahill GF, Etzweiler DD, Freinkel N. Blood glucose control and diabetes. *Diabetes* 1976; **25**: 237–40.

3 Sönksen PH, Judd SL, Lowy C. Home monitoring of blood glucose. *Lancet* 1978; i: 729–32.

4 Walford S, Gale EAM, Allision SP, Tattersall RB. Self-monitoring of blood glucose. *Lancet* 1978; i: 732–5.

5 Danowski TS, Sunder JH. Jet injection of insulin during self-monitoring of blood glucose. *Diabetes Care* 1978; **1**: 27–33.

6 Francis AJ, Home PD, Hanning I, Alberti KGMM, Tunbridge WMG. Intermediate acting insulin given at bedtime: effect on blood glucose concentrations before and after breakfast. *Br Med J* 1983; **286**: 1173–6.

7 Tunbridge FKE, Newens A, Home PD *et al*. Double-blind crossover trial of isophane (NPH) and lente-based insulin regimens. *Diabetes Care* 1989; **12**: 115–19.

8 Berger M, Cüppers HJ, Hegner H, Jörgens V, Berchtold P. Absorption kinetics and biologic effects of subcutaneously injected insulin preparations. *Diabetes Care* 1982; **5**: 77–91.

9 Kølendorf K, Bojsen J, Deckert T. Absorption and miscibility of regular porcine insulin after subcutaneous injection in insulin-treated diabetic patients. *Diabetes Care* 1983; **6**: 6–9.

10 Heine RJ, Bilo HJG, Sikkenk AC, van der Veen EA. Mixing short and intermediate acting insulins in the syringe: effect on postprandial blood glucose concentrations in type 1 diabetics. *Br Med J* 1985; **290**: 204–5.

11 Owens DR, Vora JP, Jones IR *et al*. Soluble and lente human insulin mixtures in normal man. *Diabetes Res* 1988; **7**: 35–40.

12 Berger M. Insulin therapy: conventional. In: Alberti KGMM, Krall LP, eds. *Diabetes Annual*. Amsterdam: Elsevier, 1985; **1**: 111–28.

13 Philips M, Simpson RW, Holman RR, Turner RC. A simple and rational twice daily insulin regime. Distinction between basal and meal insulin requirements. *Q J Med* 1979; **191**: 493–506.

14 Turner RC, Philips MA, Ward EA. Ultralente based insulin regimens — clinical applications, advantages and disadvantages. *Acta Med Scand* 1983; (suppl 671): 75–86.

15 Hildebrandt P, Berger A, Volund A, Kühl C. The subcutaneous absorption of human and bovine ultralente insulin formulations. *Diabetic Med* 1985; **2**: 355–9.

16 Francis AJ, Hanning I, Alberti KGMM. Human ultralente: a comparison with porcine lente insulin as a twice daily insulin in insulin-dependent diabetic patients with fasting hyperglycaemia. *Diabetes Res* 1986; **3**: 263–8.

17 Edsberg B, Dejgaard A, Kühl C. Comparison of glycaemic control in diabetic patients treated with morning or evening human ultratard insulin. *Diabetic Med* 1987; **4**: 53–5.

18 Roland JM, Leush IG, O'Brien IAD *et al*. A comparative study of once daily insulin injection regimes in the treatment of elderly diabetics. *Diabetes Res* 1987; **4**: 131–4.

19 Roland JM. Need stable diabetics mix their insulin? *Diabetic Med* 1984; **1**: 37–53.

20 Paton JS, Wilson M, Ireland JT, Reith SBM. Convenient pocket insulin syringe. *Lancet* 1981; i: 189–90.

21 Berger AS, Saubrey N, Kühl C, Villumsen J. Clinical experience with a new device that will simplify insulin injections. *Diabetes Care* 1985; **8**: 73–6.

22 Walters DP, Smith PA, Marteau TM, Brimble A, Borthwick LJ. Experience with NovoPen, an injection device using cartridged insulin, for diabetic patients. *Diabetic Med* 1985; **2**: 496–8.

23 Jefferson IG, Marteau TM, Smith MA, Baum JD. A multiple injection regimen using an insulin injection pen and pre-filled cartridged soluble human insulin in adolescents with diabetes. *Diabetic Med* 1985; **2**: 493–7.

24 Kølendorf K, Beck-Nielsen H, Øxenboll B. Clinical experience with NovoPen II and insulin Protaphane HM Penfill. *Postgrad Med J* 1988; **64** (suppl 3): 14–16.

25 Jørgensen JOL, Flyvbjerg A, Jørgensen JT, Holmegaard H, Rose Johansen B, Christiansen JS. NPH insulin administration by means of a pen injector. *Diabetic Med* 1988; **5**: 574–6.

26 Anonymous Insulin pen: mightier than the syringe? *Lancet* 1989; i: 307–8.

27 Murray DP, Keenan P, Gayer E *et al*. A randomised trial of the efficacy and acceptability of a pen injector. *Diabetic Med* 1988; **5**: 750–4.

28 Houtzagers CMGJ, Berntzen PA, van der Stap H *et al*. Efficacy and acceptance of two intensified conventional insulin therapy regimens: a long-term cross-over comparison. *Diabetic Med* 1989; **6**: 416–21.

29 Schiffrin A, Belmonte MM. Comparison between continuous subcutaneous insulin infusion and multiple injections of insulin: a one year prospective study. *Diabetes* 1982; **31**: 255–64.

30 Alexander WD, Wells M. The Button Infuser: an assessment. *Pract Diabetes* 1987; **2**: 66–7.

31 Rayman G, Wise PH. An indwelling subcutaneous FEP cannula for intermittent insulin injection: patient experience and effect on diabetic control. *Diabetic Med* 1988; **5**: 592–5.

32 Koivisto V, Felig P. Alterations in insulin absorption and in blood glucose control associated with varying injection sites in diabetic patients. *Ann Int Med* 1980; **92**: 59−61.

33 Henry DA, Lowe JM, Manderson WG. Defective absorption of injected insulin. *Lancet* 1978; ii: 741.

34 Frid A, Gunnarsson R, Gunter P, Linde B. Effects of accidental intra-muscular injection on insulin absorption in IDDM. *Diabetes Care* 1988; **11**: 41−5.

35 Anonymous Re-use of disposable insulin syringes. *Lancet* 1983; i: 570.

36 Collins BJ, Richardson SG, Spence BK, Hunter J, Nelson JK. Safety of reusing disposable plastic insulin syringes. *Lancet* 1983; i: 559−61.

37 Anonymous Insulin injections and infections. *Br Med J* 1981; **282**: 340.

38 Leigh DA, Hough GW. Dangers of storing glass syringes in surgical spirit. *Br Med J* 1980; **281**: 541−2.

39 Jackson PG, Keen H, Noble CJ, Simmons NA. Injection abscesses in a diabetic due to *Mycobacterium chelonei var abscessus. Br Med J* 1980; **281**: 1105−6.

40 Pickup JC, White MC, Keen H, Parsons JA, Alberti KGMM. Long-term continuous subcutaneous insulin infusion in diabetics at home. *Lancet* 1979; ii: 870−3.

41 American Diabetes Association. Consensus statement on self-monitoring of blood glucose. *Diabetes Care* 1987; **10**: 95−9.

42 Tattersall RB. Self-monitoring of blood glucose 1978−1984. In: Alberti KGMM, Krall LP, eds. *Diabetes Annual*. Amsterdam: Elsevier, 1985; **1**: 162−76.

43 Walker JD. Fieldwork of a diabetic clinic *Lancet* 1953; ii: 445−7.

44 Wilson RM, Clarke P, Barkes H, Heller S, Tattersall RB. Starting insulin treatment as an outpatient. *J Am Med Assoc* 1986; **256**: 877−80.

45 Whitehouse FW, McGrath Z, Whitehouse IJ. Ambulatory insulin regulation. *Diabetes Spectrum* 1988; **1**: 257−60.

40 Insulin Antibodies

Summary

● Insulin, together with its polymers and other chemical derivatives, is immunogenic. Bovine insulin is more immunogenic than porcine; human-sequence insulin is the least immunogenic but can nonetheless provoke antibody formation. Highly purified insulins have low immunogenicity.

● Insulin-binding antibodies (mostly polyclonal) are detectable in most insulin-treated patients but in most cases are clinically irrelevant.

● The binding of insulin to antibody is governed by the law of mass action; only free (or unbound) insulin is thought to be biologically active.

● Insulin antibodies may 'buffer' against sudden fluctuations in free insulin levels under experimental conditions, but generally do not seem to influence clinical insulin requirements or metabolic stability.

● The clinical manifestations of insulin antibodies, now rare, include:

1 local allergic reactions (either immediate, IgE-mediated, or delayed Arthus-type reactions due to IgG immune complexes) and lipoatrophy at injection sites;

2 anaphylaxis, due to IgE antibody formation;

3 insulin resistance, due to rapid clearance of injected insulin which forms large immune complexes with polyclonal antibodies.

● Treatment of these problems is by substituting another insulin species which does not cross-react with the antibodies, by desensitization, or by local or systemic administration of glucocorticoids.

● Insulin autoantibodies can develop without previous exposure to exogenous insulin in some patients receiving methimazole or other drugs, and may cause a syndrome of postprandial glucose intolerance combined with fasting hypoglycaemia.

● Insulin autoantibodies also occur in 30–40% of IDDM children at presentation and in their high-risk siblings, and may be a marker for the 'prediabetic' stage of IDDM.

Insulin is a large polypeptide (MW~6 kDa) and so would be expected to be immunogenic, either alone or acting as a hapten. This is particularly likely when patients are treated with exogenous insulin which is derived from different species and whose structure differs from that of the human hormone. Insulin-binding antibodies can indeed be detected in the serum of many insulin-treated diabetic patients — especially those who have received relatively impure bovine insulins — but, in most cases, these are of little or no clinical significance. With the introduction in the last decade of highly purified porcine insulins (which are essentially free from contaminating pancreatic proteins) and more recently, of synthetic insulin of human sequence, immune problems due to insulin antibody formation have become extremely uncommon.

As well as being raised against *exogenous* insulin, antibodies may occasionally develop against *endogenous* insulin as part of an autoimmune response. The factors determining the formation of insulin antibodies and their clinical consequences will be discussed in this chapter.

Antibodies to exogenous insulin

Historical background

Allergic reactions, including urticaria and anaphylaxis, occurred with early insulin preparations [1] but as these were very impure, the antigen responsible may not necessarily have been insulin. The first clear demonstration of a clinically significant immune response to insulin itself resulted from the practice, widespread in the 1930s, of inducing hypoglycaemic convulsions with insulin to treat various psychiatric disorders. With repeated treatment, increasing doses of insulin were often required to produce hypoglycaemia and some patients ultimately became completely resistant to the action of insulin. Banting [2] showed that the gamma-globulin fraction of serum from an insulin-resistant patient neutralized the hypoglycaemic effect of insulin injected into mice. During the next 20 years, occasional cases of resistance to continued insulin therapy were reported, insulin antibodies being demonstrated either by their neutralization of insulin in bioassays, or by passive cutaneous anaphylaxis in guinea-pigs [3].

In the 1950s, Berson and Yalow and their colleagues [4] used ^{131}I-insulin to identify and characterize insulin antibodies *in vitro*, and were able to detect antibodies in virtually all insulin-treated subjects. These antibodies did not fix complement or form precipitates with insulin, and in most cases had no apparent clinical effect. Berson and Yalow described the kinetics of the interaction between ^{131}I-insulin and antibody and were able to exploit these observations to measure insulin concentrations over a wide range — the birth of radioimmunoassay (see Chapter 35). Most subsequent studies have used radioimmunoassay to detect insulin antibodies.

Determinants of antibody formation

The immune response to exogenous insulin is determined by both the insulin administered and the individual receiving it (Fig. 40.1).

The immunogenicity of an insulin preparation depends on both the structure of the insulin molecule and on other compounds present, which may themselves be immunogenic or act as an adjuvant. Bovine insulin, which differs in three amino-acid residues from the human hormone, is more immunogenic than porcine insulin, which differs from the human in only a single residue (see Chapter 37). Insulin of human sequence is less immunogenic than porcine insulin but, probably because of the presence of chemical derivatives of insulin and the adjuvant properties of the formulation, can still provoke an immune

response in a few individuals; rare clinical manifestations have included both local allergic reactions and anaphylaxis [5, 6].

Insulin preparations contain various derivatives of insulin, which may be generated during chemical extraction or form spontaneously on standing. Although preparations are generally stable for several years, deamidation and polymerization occur to a limited extent under normal conditions and at an increased rate at higher temperatures or with shaking. It is likely that the immunogenicity of currently available highly purified insulin preparations is due to the presence of minute quantities of insulin polymers [7].

In the early 1970s, improved chromatographic separation methods showed that insulin prepared by recrystallization was far from pure. When separated by molecular weight, 'insulin' was found to consist of three separate components: 'a', with the highest molecular weight, contained polymerized insulin; 'b' had a molecular weight approximately twice that of insulin and comprised both insulin dimers and proinsulin; and the 'c' peak contained monomeric insulin, together with arginine insulin (a cleavage product) and the deamidated derivatives which form during storage (Fig. 40.2) [8]. In addition to these products, insulin extracted from animal pancreases is inevitably contaminated by other pancreatic proteins, notably the islet-cell peptides, proinsulin, pancreatic polypeptide, glucagon and somatostatin. Antibodies to all these antigens have been identified in insulin-treated patients, although those to somatostatin are rare [9]. All insulin preparations contain diluent and preservative and isophane insulins also contain the basic polypeptide, protamine, derived from fish sperm. The highly purified porcine and bovine insulins in current use are purified by chromatography (according to both molecular weight and charge) following recrystallization and have very low immunogenicity. With the increasing use of highly purified insulin, and especially of human-sequence insulin, clinically significant immune problems are becoming exceedingly rare.

The immune response to insulin is also dependent on the individual and may be genetically determined. This has been clearly demonstrated in animal studies using different species and fragments of insulins [10]. In man, a similar but less well-defined genetic link is suggested by the finding of lower antibody titres in subjects with the HLA B8/DR3 phenotype than in those with

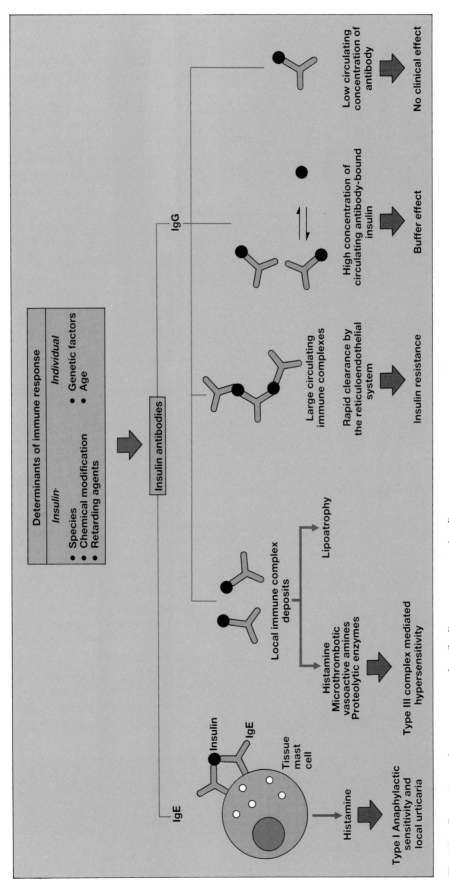

Fig. 40.1. Formation and consequences of antibodies to exogenous insulin.

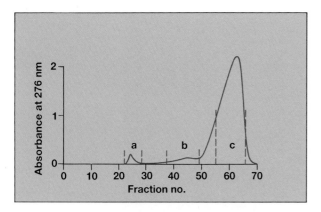

Fig. 40.2. Elution pattern following gel filtration (Sephadex G-50) of once-crystallized bovine insulin in 1 M acetic acid. Monomeric insulin largely accounts for the 'c' peak, whereas the 'a' peak consists of high molecular-weight insulin polymers and the 'b' peak of insulin dimers and proinsulin. (Adapted from ref. 8.)

B15/DR4 [11]; furthermore, the IgG heavy-chain haplotype Gm xag is also associated with higher antibody titres [12].

Autoantibodies to insulin

Insulin autoantibodies are antibodies which develop spontaneously without prior administration of exogenous insulin (Table 40.1). These have been reported in various groups of patients, including some with Graves' disease treated with methimazole [13] and others treated with hydralazine or procaineamide [14], penicillamine [15] or alpha-mercaptopropionylglycine [16]. In certain cases, no precipitating factor has been identified [17] and low-titre insulin autoantibodies may rarely occur in apparently normal subjects. These antibodies may or may not have clinically apparent consequences; a syndrome of carbohydrate intolerance with fasting hypoglycaemia (see below)

Table 40.1. Characteristics of insulin autoantibodies.

1 Form spontaneously (without exogenous insulin administration) in association with:
  • drugs (methimazole, hydralazine, procaineamide)
  • prediabetic phase of IDDM (?marker)
  • normal subjects (very rare)

2 Best measured by ELISA (low affinity)

3 Clinical manifestations
  • silent
  • glucose intolerance postprandially, with fasting hypoglycaemia

has been reported in association with high titres of high-affinity autoantibodies in some of the drug-induced cases described above.

Insulin autoantibodies also occur in some IDDM patients, at or before clinical presentation of the disease. These evidently arise as part of the auto-immune process during the 'prediabetic' phase (see Chapter 15) and are associated with islet-cell antibodies [18]. Their titres usually fall rapidly within a few months of presentation.

Certain insulin autoantibodies have such low affinity that they are not reliably detected by radioimmunoassay, which is better suited to measuring high-affinity antibodies such as those induced by insulin therapy. Enzyme-linked immunosorbent assays (ELISA) are much less dependent on antibody affinity and are considerably more sensitive to low-avidity antibodies.

Kinetics of insulin–antibody interactions

The binding of insulin to IgG immunoglobulin is described by the law of mass action, which defines the association constant, K, as:

$$K = [Ab.Ag]/[Ab][Ag]$$

where Ab, Ag and Ab.Ag represent the concentrations at equilibrium of free antibody, free antigen and antibody–antigen complex respectively. This equation can, with modification, be used to calculate the free and bound fractions of both antibody and ligand (antigen). For a monoclonal serum, the values for K and the binding-site concentration can be determined by Scatchard analysis, in which the ratio of antibody-bound insulin divided by the free insulin concentration is plotted against the bound insulin concentration, when increasing amounts of unlabelled insulin are added to fixed amounts of antibody and labelled insulin [19, 20]. However, most sera contain a mixture of polyclonal antibodies of differing affinity, directed against various epitopes (i.e. those regions of the antigen molecule which interact with the antibody's binding site) [21]; for polyclonal sera, the Scatchard plot is curvilinear and the analysis imprecise. Dynamic analyses of the rates of association and dissociation *in vitro* can also be made: insulin dissociates from high-affinity antibodies much more slowly than from those of low-affinity [22]. Insulin-treated patients generally produce both high- and low-affinity antibodies, the latter predominating.

The situation in the circulation of an insulin-treated diabetic patient with polyclonal antibodies is far more complicated than is suggested by the law of mass action, in that insulin will be increasingly bound by high-affinity antibody with time. Nevertheless, with one exception, a simple equilibrium exists between antibody-bound and free insulin and bound insulin only becomes biologically available when it dissociates, a situation analogous to the binding of thyroxine by thyroxine-binding globulin. The exception occurs in the presence of high titres of two or more antibodies directed against widely separated epitopes on the insulin molecule. The resulting multimolecular complexes are of sufficiently high molecular weight to be cleared from the circulation by the reticulo-endothelial system. The insulin is therefore destroyed and the clinical result is insulin resistance.

In vivo *effects of insulin antibodies*

The kinetics of short-acting insulin injected subcutaneously in diabetic patients with insulin-binding antibodies were studied by Kruse [23]. A multicompartment model was used to examine the effect of variations in insulin antibody concentration and affinity on the circulating free insulin concentration. The presence of antibodies generally delayed and reduced the peak concentration of free insulin after each injection and increased its trough levels. The effect of very high affinity antibodies ($K = 10^{-11}$ l/mol and $t_{1/2} \sim$ 4 h) was minimal. By contrast, antibodies of intermediate affinity ($K = 10^{-9}$ l/mol and $t_{1/2} \sim$ 5−7 min) had a more marked effect, reducing the peak free insulin level by more than 50% and increasing its trough concentration to 50% of the peak (Fig. 40.3). Such antibodies thus damp down the fluctuations in circulating free insulin levels. Low-affinity antibodies ($K = 10^{-7}$ l/mol and $t_{1/2} \sim$ 5 s) were not studied but would be expected to have virtually no physiological effect.

The concept that only free insulin can interact with the insulin receptor seems sound and is supported by the finding that metabolically stable diabetic patients invariably show *free* insulin concentrations which are close to the physiological range (5−50 mU/l), despite immense individual variations in insulin antibody titre and in total insulin concentrations, which can be as high as 200 U/l [24]. Moreover, there is no relationship between the presence or absence of antibodies and insulin requirement [25].

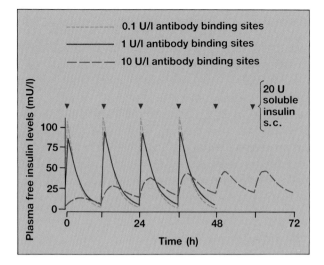

Fig. 40.3. Computer simulation of plasma free insulin levels in diabetic patients with low (0.1 U/l), medium (1 U/l) and high (10 U/l) titres of insulin-binding antibodies with intermediate affinity, following subcutaneous injection of 20 U soluble insulin every 12 h (▼). High antibody titres exert a 'buffering' effect, both reducing the peak insulin concentration by over 50% and maintaining levels for several hours. (Data derived by multi-compartment kinetic modelling; redrawn from ref. 23.)

Insulin-binding antibodies can, however, affect the pharmacokinetics of injected insulin. Antibody-bound insulin may act as a reservoir or buffer, from which free insulin can be released over a prolonged period (Fig. 40.3) [26]. In the early 1960s, it was reported that, in patients taking only short-acting insulin, the daily number of injections was correlated with the disappearance rate of labelled insulin from the circulation [27]. Insulin antibody levels were generally high in insulin-treated diabetic patients at this time and those subjects with slow insulin clearance (some of whom required only a single daily injection of soluble insulin) presumably had high levels of 'buffering' antibody. More recently, this effect was confirmed by the demonstration that C-peptide-negative IDDM subjects with high levels of antibody-bound insulin showed a significant delay in developing metabolic decompensation after temporary withdrawal of insulin [24]. A similar stabilizing effect of high-titre antibodies has also been found after interrupting continuous subcutaneous insulin infusion [28]. Release of free insulin from an antibody-bound reservoir may also cause episodic falls in insulin requirement or hypoglycaemia: one case with exceptionally high insulin-binding antibody titres (over 100 U/l) was able to omit insulin for several days at a time [29].

Clinical manifestations of insulin antibodies

Insulin-binding antibodies can be demonstrated in most diabetic patients who were treated with insulin before the introduction of the highly purified preparations. In the vast majority of cases, however, these antibodies are clinically irrelevant [30] and very few now develop the clinical problems previously encountered in a minority of patients who received 'impure' insulins. The various possible consequences of insulin antibody formation are illustrated in Fig. 40.1.

Allergic reactions to insulin

Urticarial reactions and anaphylaxis were previously rare complications of insulin therapy [1] and have virtually disappeared since the introduction of highly purified insulins. In affected subjects, insulin-specific IgE can be detected in serum and the allergen can be identified by skin-prick testing of insulin preparations; occasionally, the insulin diluent is responsible. Treatment depends on the specificity of the IgE antibody. If it does not cross-react substantially with another species of insulin, a change to that species will reduce the allergic response [31] but desensitization is required if cross-reactivity is complete. This is easier in NIDDM subjects who can be maintained without exogenous insulin. In IDDM patients, subcutaneous insulin administration is stopped and insulin is given by continuous intravenous infusion, initially with extreme caution. After one or two days, any residual insulin at subcutaneous injection sites will have been absorbed and desensitization can then proceed. Under close supervision, a very small initial dose of insulin (10^{-5}U) is given subcutaneously, with gradually increasing amounts given at intervals until a full therapeutic dose is reached. If an allergic response occurs during the process, the dose is reduced (to one-tenth) and then gradually increased again.

Another manifestation of insulin allergy, which is also now rare, is a delayed local reaction to injected insulin. This presents as a tender subcutaneous lump developing at the injection site half an hour or so after injection and lasting for 12–24 h. This is a local Arthus-type reaction, mediated by IgG rather than IgE, due to complement activation by insulin–IgG immune complexes. It often responds to addition of hydrocortisone to the injected insulin.

The closely related phenomenon of lipoatrophy (Fig. 40.4) was previously quite common, being reported in 10–55% of insulin-treated patients [32]. An immune basis for this condition has been suggested by the immunohistochemical demonstration by Reeves et al. [32] of deposits of both insulin and IgG in subcutaneous tissue biopsied from lipoatrophic areas (Fig. 40.5). Patients with lipoatrophy usually have moderately high circulating insulin antibody titres [32].

Insulin resistance

Antibody-mediated resistance to insulin may be defined as an insulin requirement of more than 2 U/kg/day, with no apparent endocrine or other explanation and accompanied by high titres of high-avidity insulin antibody. Affected patients with insulin dosages of several thousand U/day have been reported [33] but this syndrome is now rare. As described above, insulin resistance is due to polyclonal antibodies directed against

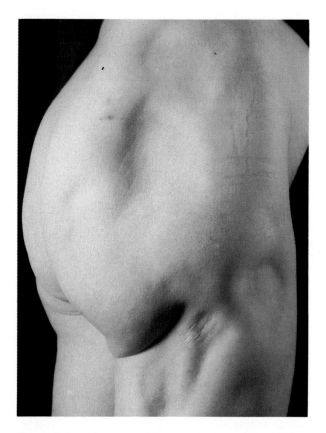

Fig. 40.4. Extensive areas of lipoatrophy in a 39-year-old woman treated for over 20 years with various 'impure' insulin preparations, including protamine–zinc. (Reproduced with permission of the Editor of the *British Medical Journal* from ref. 32.)

(a)

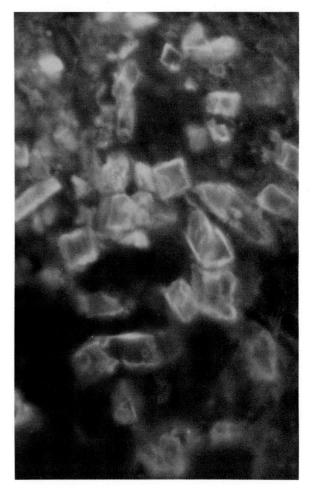

(b)

Fig. 40.5. Skin biopsies from areas of lipoatrophy, immunostained for complement component C3 (a), which is deposited in epidermal vessel walls, and for insulin (b), which is found as crystals in the dermis. (Reproduced with permission of the Editor of the *British Medical Journal* from ref. 32.)

separate epitopes on the insulin molecule, with the formation of stable, high-molecular-weight complexes of insulin with two or more IgG molecules. Insulin dissociates extremely slowly from such complexes and is effectively destroyed as the complexes are cleared from the circulation by the reticulo-endothelial system [34]. Even large insulin dosages are unable to achieve adequate free insulin concentrations [35].

The presence of high-avidity antibody complexes can be suspected in the laboratory from an unexpected binding pattern of labelled insulin when the patient's serum is used as the antibody in a radioimmunoassay for insulin [35]. The large size of the complexes can be demonstrated chromatographically and their clearance by the reticulo-endothelial system has been shown under experimental conditions, using ^{123}I-labelled insulin and gamma-camera imaging [34].

The management of insulin resistance depends on the extent to which the antibodies cross-react with other species of insulin. The degree of cross-reactivity can be determined in the laboratory by radioimmunoassay. If cross-reactivity is limited, a different insulin species may not form complexes and so may retain its biological activity: many patients resistant to bovine insulin remain sensitive to porcine or human insulins. Sensitivity is also often maintained to insulins from unusual species (e.g. sheep and bonito) or to chemically modified insulins (e.g. sulphated insulin) but long-term treatment with these expensive and scarce preparations is not practicable. In cases where complexes form with all available insulins, a short course of steroid treatment (e.g. prednisolone 40 mg/day for 14 days) is usually effective [3]; the antibody titre falls, complexes are no longer formed and insulin sensitivity returns [35].

The insulin–autoantibody hypoglycaemia syndrome

Quite different clinical manifestations are seen in certain non-diabetic patients who have high titres of insulin autoantibodies [36]. High titres of relatively high avidity antibody lead to the formation of *monovalent* insulin–antibody complexes which are of relatively low molecular weight and are not cleared by the reticulo-endothelial system. The antibody instead buffers the effect of insulin. During a meal (or glucose tolerance test), insulin release is stimulated but the free insulin concentration rises only slowly, as much of the secreted insulin is bound by antibody. Subsequently, there is prolonged release of insulin by dissociation from the antibody-bound fraction, and free insulin levels fall only slowly. The clinical result is the apparently paradoxical association of postprandial carbohydrate intolerance with hypoglycaemia during periods of fasting [16]. In one patient with this syndrome, the epitope was found to be a single amino-acid residue (threonine at position B30); the antibody bound human insulin, with no cross-reactivity against either bovine or porcine insulins, which carry an alanine residue at this site [20].

In this syndrome, antibody titres usually fall spontaneously, but no specific treatment is available; steroids are ineffective. Any drugs likely to be responsible (typically those containing a sulphydryl group) should be withdrawn if possible.

A similar syndrome of glucose intolerance/hypoglycaemia in a neonate was due to transplacental transfer of maternal insulin autoantibodies [37]. IgG insulin antibodies transferred across the placenta from an insulin-treated mother can also rarely cause neonatal hypoglycaemia [38]. As discussed in Chapter 83, neonatal hypoglycaemia in the babies of diabetic mothers is more usually due to fetal hyperinsulinaemia, stimulated by maternal hyperglycaemia.

Clinical pharmacokinetic effects

Although several studies have demonstrated that circulating insulin antibodies act to smooth and delay fluctuations in the free insulin concentration [24, 28, 39], the significance of this effect in the day-to-day clinical setting remains controversial [40–42]. It has been argued that the presence of insulin-binding antibodies could be beneficial in 'buffering' against sudden changes in circulating insulin levels. However, there is no firm evidence that either insulin requirements or stability of metabolic control are influenced by antibody levels [43], although this may be because of the confounding effects of other variables (diet, exercise, etc.) which also affect diabetic treatment. Moreover, the individual's immune response is unpredictable and the effects of insulin antibodies are extremely variable. It therefore seems more logical to aim to modulate the time-course of injected insulin through pharmacological means rather than by having to rely on immunological serendipity.

Microvascular diabetic complications

The presence of insulin antibodies has been suggested by some workers [44] to contribute to the development of microvascular complications. Initial animal studies, using an impure insulin preparation, showed that immunization with insulin caused histological lesions in the kidney, but subsequent investigations with pure insulin have not confirmed this finding [45]. Moreover, the prevalence of antibodies does not differ between groups of patients with and without retinopathy [46].

Insulin autoantibodies as a marker of the prediabetic state

As many as 30–40% of IDDM children have been reported to have circulating insulin autoantibodies at presentation, and those of their siblings who have islet-cell antibodies and insulin autoantibodies appear to be particularly likely to develop the disease [47]. Insulin autoantibodies may therefore find application as markers of the early autoimmune process which leads ultimately to IDDM, and could potentially be exploited to identify subjects at high risk of developing IDDM and who might ultimately benefit from immunosuppressive treatment (see Chapter 15). However, these autoantibodies are usually of low avidity and present at low titre, and it is essential that they can be detected with confidence before this application can be seriously considered.

Modified insulins

The development of insulin analogues and of new formulations and additives (e.g. to promote insulin absorption by the intranasal route) may have important immunological consequences. It is possible that some of these preparations will be immunogenic, and that antibody formation will interfere with their desired effect, e.g. the rapid action profile of the monomeric insulin analogues could be blunted (see Chapter 38). Monitoring the immunogenicity of these compounds will be an important part of their clinical evaluation.

ANTONY KURTZ

References

1 Williams JR. A clinical study of the effects of insulin in severe diabetes. *J Metab Res* 1922; **2**: 729–51.

2 Banting FG, Franks WR, Cairns S. Anti-insulin activity of serum of insulin treated patients. *Am J Psychiatr* 1938; **95**: 562–5.

3 Oakley WG, Jones VE, Cunliffe AC. Insulin resistance. *Br Med J* 1967; **2**: 134–8.

4 Berson SA, Yalow RS, Bauman A, Rothschild MA, Newerly K. Insulin I¹³¹ metabolism in human subjects. Demonstrations of insulin binding globulin in circulation of insulin treated subjects. *J Clin Invest* 1956; **35**: 170–90.

5 Grammer LC, Metzger BE, Patterson R. Cutaneous allergy to human (recombinant DNA) insulin. *J Am Med Assoc* 1984; **251**: 1459–60.

6 Gossain VV, Rovner DR, Mohan K. Systemic allergy to human (recombinant DNA) insulin. *Ann Allergy* 1985; **55**: 116–18.

7 Hansen B, Hoiriis Nielsen J, Welinder B. Immunogenicity of insulin in relation to its physicochemical properties. In: Keck K, Erb P, eds. *Basic and Clinical Aspects of Immunity to Insulin*. Berlin, New York: Walter de Gruyter, 1985: 335–52.

8 Schlichtkrull J, Brange J, Christiansen AaH, Hallund O, Heding LG, Jørgensen KH. Clinical aspects of insulin-antigenicity. *Diabetes* 1972; **21** (suppl 2): 649–56.

9 Kurtz AB, Matthews JA, Mustaffa BE, Daggett PR, Nabarro JDN. Decrease of antibodies to insulin, proinsulin and contaminating hormones after changing treatment from conventional beef to purified pork insulin. *Diabetologia* 1980; **18**: 147–50.

10 Rosenthal AS, Lin CS, Hansen T. Genetic control of the immune response to insulin. In: Keck K, Erb P, eds. *Basic and Clinical Aspects of Immunity to Insulin*. Berlin, New York: Walter de Gruyter, 1981: 17–27.

11 Reeves WG. Immunological aspects of therapy. *The Diabetes Annual 1*. Amsterdam: Elsevier, 1985: 67–81.

12 Nakao Y, Matsumoto H, Miyazaki T, Mizuno N, Arima N, Wakisaka A. IgG heavy chain (Gm) allotypes and immune response to insulin in insulin-requiring diabetes mellitus. *New Engl J Med* 1981; **304**: 407–9.

13 Hirata Y, Tominaga M, Ito JI, Noguchi A. Spontaneous hypoglycemia with insulin autoimmunity in Graves' disease. *Ann Int Med* 1974; **81**: 214–18.

14 Blackshear PJ, Rofner HE, Kriauciunas KAM, Kahn CR. Reactive hypoglycemia and insulin autoantibodies in drug induced lupus erythematosus. *Ann Int Med* 1983; **99**: 182–4.

15 Benson EA, Healy LA, Barron EJ. Insulin antibodies in patients receiving penicillamine. *Am J Med* 1985; **78**: 857–60.

16 Ichihara K, Shima K, Saito Y, Noraka K, Tarui S, Nishikawa M. Mechanism of hypoglycemia observed in a patient with insulin autoimmune syndrome. *Diabetes* 1977; **26**: 500–6.

17 Folling I, Norman N. Hyperglycemia, hypoglycemia attacks and production of anti-insulin antibodies without previous known immunization. *Diabetes* 1972; **21**: 814–26.

18 Palmer JP, Asplin CM, Clemons P, Lyen K, Tatpati O, Raghu PK, Paquette TL. Insulin antibodies in insulin-dependent diabetics before treatment. *Science* 1983; **222**: 1337–9.

19 Scatchard G. The attraction of proteins for small molecules and ions. *Ann NY Acad Sci* 1949; **51**: 660–73.

20 Diaz J-L, Wilkin T. Differences in epitope restriction of autoantibodies to native human insulin (IAA) and antibodies to heterologous insulin (IA). *Diabetes* 1988; **37**: 66–72.

21 Keck K. Ir gene control of carrier recognition: III Cooperative recognition of two or more carrier determinants on insulins of different species. *Eur J Immunol* 1977; **7**: 811–16.

22 Berson SA, Yalow RS. Quantitative aspects of the reaction between insulin and insulin-binding antibody. *J Clin Invest* 1959; **38**: 1996–2016.

23 Kruse V. Effect of insulin-binding antibodies on free insulin in plasma and tissue after subcutaneous injection, a model study. In: Keck K, Erb P, eds. *Basic and Clinical Aspects of Immunity to Insulin*. Berlin, New York: Walter de Gruyter, 1981; 319–34.

24 Vaughan NJA, Matthews JA, Kurtz AB, Nabarro JDN. The bioavailability of circulating antibody-bound insulin following insulin withdrawal in Type I (insulin-dependent) diabetes. *Diabetologia* 1983: **24**: 206–12.

25 Walford S, Allison S, Reeves W. The effects of insulin-antibodies on insulin dose and diabetic control. *Diabetologia* 1982; **22**: 106–10.

26 Dixon K, Exon PD, Malins JM. Insulin antibodies and the control of diabetes. *Q J Med* 1975; **44**: 543–55.

27 Bolinger RE, Morris JH, McKnight FG, Diederich DA. Disappearance of ¹³¹I labelled insulin from plasma as a guide to management of diabetes. *N Engl J Med* 1964; **270**: 767–70.

28 Scheen AJ, Henrivaux P, Jaudrain B, Lefèbvre PJ. Anti-insulin antibodies and metabolic deterioration after interruption of continuous subcutaneous insulin infusion. *Diabetes Care* 1986; **9**: 673–4.

29 Harwood R. Insulin-binding antibodies and spontaneous hypoglycemia. *New Engl J Med* 1960; **262**: 978–9.

30 Kurtz AB, Nabarro JDN. Circulating insulin-binding antibodies. *Diabetologia* 1980; **19**: 329–34.

31 Carini C, Brostoff J, Kurtz AB. An anaphylactic reaction to highly purified pork insulin. Confirmation by RAST and RAST inhibition. *Diabetologia* 1982; **22**: 324–6.

32 Reeves WG, Allen BR, Tattersall RB. Insulin-induced lipoatrophy: evidence for an immune pathogenesis. *Br Med J* 1980; **280**: 1500–3.

33 Field JB. Insulin allergy and resistance. In: De Groot LJ et al. eds. *Endocrinology*, vol. 7. New York: Grune & Stratton, 1979: 1069–74.

34 Sodoyez JC, Sodoyez-Goffaux F. Effects of insulin antibodies on bioavailability of insulin: preliminary studies using 123-I-insulin in patients with insulin-dependent diabetes. *Diabetologia* 1984; **27**: 143–5.

35 Kurtz A. Intérêt clinique de la résistance à l'insuline et des anticorps anti-insuline. *Journ Annu Diabétol Hotel Dieu* 1986; 145–54.

36 Goldman J, Baldwin D, Rubenstein AH et al. Characterization of circulating insulin and proinsulin-binding antibodies in autoimmune hypoglycemia. *J Clin Invest* 1979; **63**: 1050–9.

37 Nakagawa S, Suda N, Kudo M, Kawasaki M. A new type of hypoglycaemia in a newborn infant. *Diabetologia* 1973; **9**: 367−75.

38 Martin FI, Dahlenburg GW, Russell J, Jeffrey P. Neonatal hypoglycaemia in infants of insulin-dependent mothers. *Arch Dis Child* 1975; **50**: 472−6.

39 Nabarro JDN, Mustaffa BE, Morris DV, Walport MJ, Kurtz AB. Insulin deficient diabetes. *Diabetologia* 1979; **16**: 5−12.

40 Yue D, Baxter R, Turtle J. C-peptide secretion and insulin antibodies as determinants of stability in diabetes mellitus. *Metabolism* 1978; **27**: 35−44.

41 Francis A, Hanning I, Alberti KGMM. The influence of insulin antibody levels on the plasma profiles and action of subcutaneously injected human and bovine short acting insulins. *Diabetologia* 1985; **28**: 330−4.

42 Van Haeften TW, Heiling VJ, Gerich JE. Adverse effects of insulin antibodies on postprandial plasma glucose and insulin profiles in diabetic patients without immune insulin resistance. Implications for intensive insulin regimens.

Diabetes 1987; **36**: 305−9.

43 Asplin CM, Hartog M, Goldie DJ, Alberti KGMM, Smythe P, Binder C, Faber O. A comparison between diabetics receiving a high or low daily insulin dosage. *Horm Metab Res* 1978; **10**: 365−9.

44 Andersen OO. Clinical significance of anti-insulin antibodies. *Acta Endocrinol (Kbh)* 1976; **83** (suppl 205): 231−8.

45 Deckert T, Egeberg J, Frimodt-Moller C, Sander E, Svejgaard A. Basement membrane thickness, insulin antibodies and HLA-antigens in longstanding insulin dependent diabetes with and without severe retinopathy. *Diabetologia* 1979; **17**: 91−6.

46 Bodansky HJ, Wolf E, Cudworth AG *et al*. Genetic and immunologic factors in microvascular disease in type 1 insulin-dependent diabetes. *Diabetes* 1982; **31**: 70−4.

47 Srikanta S, Ricker AT, McCulloch DK, Soeldner JS, Eisenbarth GS, Palmer JP. Autoimmunity to insulin, beta cell dysfunction and development of insulin-dependent diabetes mellitus. *Diabetes* 1986; **35**: 139−42.

41 Diet in the Management of Insulin-Dependent Diabetes Mellitus

Summary

- The nutritional requirements of people with IDDM are similar to those of non-diabetic subjects. Dietary management in IDDM should aim in the short term to prevent hypoglycaemia and in the long term to reduce the risks of chronic diabetic complications.
- Previous 'diabetic diets' emphasizing carbohydrate restriction may have encouraged excessive fat intake to make up energy requirements and may have contributed to the increased tendency of diabetic people to develop atheromatous disease.
- Fat is the macronutrient richest in energy, providing 9 kcal/g; carbohydrate and protein each provide 4 kcal/g.
- The 'glycaemic index' of a foodstuff is the area under the glycaemic curve up to 3 h after eating 50 g of it, expressed as a percentage of that following 50 g of glucose taken orally.
- As a starting point for diet prescription nomograms are available to calculate a person's daily energy requirements on the basis of sex, age, height and level of physical activity.
- Fat should provide ≤30% of total energy intake for a person with IDDM. Saturated fat should account for ≤10%, the remainder from monounsaturated fats (e.g. olive oil) and polyunsaturated fats (e.g. other vegetable and fish oils) which may improve the lipaemic profile, reducing LDL cholesterol and increasing HDL cholesterol levels. Fat intake up to 35% of total energy is acceptable when the extra comes mainly from monounsaturated fats.
- Carbohydrate should provide >55% of total energy intake. Complex carbohydrates (starch-rich foods) should predominate but moderate amounts of simple sugars (up to 25 g per day) are acceptable. High-carbohydrate diets only improve blood glucose and lipid levels if accompanied by at least 30 g/day of dietary fibre (concentrating on 'soluble fibre', found in vegetables, pulses, fruits and some whole grain cereals); this is nearly twice as high as the average British intake.
- Protein should contribute about 10–15% to total energy intake with emphasis on vegetable sources. High-protein diets may accelerate the progression of diabetic nephropathy.
- Dietary recommendations must be carefully adapted to each patient's individual needs; children and people from ethnic minorities require special consideration.
- Food exchange systems help to keep the diet varied while maintaining the daily pattern of food intake. Exchanges based on whole meals may be preferable to those concentrating on the carbohydrate content of different foods.
- Sodium intake should not exceed 6 g/day; a reduction to <3 g/day may usefully reduce blood pressure.
- Alcohol intake, as in the general population, should not exceed 3 units per day. 'Diabetic' beverages have low sugar but high alcohol contents, increasing the risks of hypoglycaemia, and should therefore be avoided.
- 'Diabetic' foods and sweets are often expensive, unpalatable, and associated with gastrointestinal side-effects. They have no nutritional or metabolic benefits and should be avoided. Low-energy sweeteners such as saccharine or aspartame are safe and useful in obese patients.
- Regular daily exercise (20 min of moderate exertion) is recommended for diabetic as for non-diabetic people. Hypoglycaemia during or after exercise can be minimized by carefully timing exercise and eating, by reducing pre-exercise insulin dosages and by taking 'slow-release' carbohydrate in foods before exertion.

Insulin-dependent diabetes is a disease of insulin deficiency and its logical treatment is therefore insulin treatment. However, entirely physiological insulin replacement cannot be obtained in practice. This failure leads to the short-term complications of hypoglycaemia and hyperglycaemia and ultimately, perhaps indirectly, to the long-term vascular complications. The role of diet in the treatment of IDDM is first to minimize the short-term fluctuations in blood glucose, particularly hypoglycaemia, and secondly to reduce the risks of long-term complications, perhaps by mechanisms other than those which follow improved glycaemic control. This second point is vitally important. Previous dietary recommendations in diabetes have concentrated on eating less carbohydrate, so encouraging excessive fat intake to make up energy requirements. This high-fat, low-carbohydrate diet may have contributed significantly to the accelerated atheromatous disease common in diabetic patients in Western societies during the last 50 years. By contrast, the 'poorer' diets lower in fat and total calories and higher in carbohydrate and fibre found in developing countries are associated with much lower rates of macrovascular disease. Considerations such as these have led in recent years to a completely different approach to the dietary treatment of IDDM, a change which has sometimes confused patients and doctors alike.

The general nutritional requirements of diabetic patients are now considered to be no different from those of non-diabetic people, and the dietary recommendations are now essentially identical to those for the general population [1] (Table 41.1). The same principles apply in NIDDM, although the emphasis and practical approaches may be different (see Chapter 47).

Dietary fat intake

As fat is the most energy-rich of all the macronutrients (9 kcal/g), fat restriction is fundamental to achieving weight loss. Fat restriction, particularly of saturated fatty acids, also leads to a lowering of total cholesterol and an improvement (increase) in the HDL:LDL ratio. This action is particularly valuable for diabetic subjects because of their high risk of premature vascular disease.

It is therefore recommended that *saturated fats* should generally provide 10% or less of total energy intake; further restriction is indicated if serum lipids, especially LDL, remain elevated. The remaining fats in the diet, namely the poly- and mono-unsaturated fats, may have beneficial effects on serum lipids but the *total fat* intake should not exceed 30% of total energy. Mono-unsaturated fatty acids, such as oleic acid which forms a large component of olive oil, specifically lower LDL without reducing HDL-cholesterol [2]. Diets with

	Recommendations for diabetes mellitus	Approximate content of usual UK diet
Energy intake:	To approach BMI 22	Maintains BMI 24–25
Carbohydrate:	>55% of energy	45% of energy
Fat:	<30–35% of energy* (saturated fat ≤10%)	40% of energy (saturated fat 17%)
Protein:	10–15% of energy	12–15% of energy
Salt:	<6 g daily (<3 g if hypertensive)	10 g daily
Sucrose (added):	<25 g daily	50–100 g daily
Dietary fibre:	>30 g daily	20 g daily
Special so-called 'diabetic' foods:	None (avoid)	None

Table 41.1. General principles of diet for diabetic patients, as compared with the current average diet in Britain.

BMI: body-mass index (weight in kg) (height in m)^2.
* A higher total fat content is permissible when monounsaturated fatty acids form a major component, as from olive oil in Mediterranean diets.

a higher total fat content (35–40% energy) may therefore be acceptable provided that monounsaturated fatty acids make up the extra lipid.

The overall diet most consistent with these suggestions is one based on vegetable or fish dishes, rather than meat or eggs, as the main meals. Long-chain polyunsaturated fatty acids (omega-3) derived from fish oils may have beneficial lipid-lowering effects, notably by reducing VLDL and triglycerides [3] and high fish intakes have been related to reduced rates of ischaemic heart disease in non-diabetic subjects [4, 5, 6]. Fish, including oily sea fish, can reasonably be encouraged in the diets of diabetic patients but the evidence does not at present justify extreme dietary advice or marine fatty acid supplementation. The place of fish oils and plant oils rich in gamma-linoleic acid in the treatment of diabetes is discussed further in Chapter 104.

In a diet which derives 10% or less of total energy from saturated fats, the dietary cholesterol intake is almost invariably low. There is no special indication in diabetic populations for restriction of dietary cholesterol below the 300 mg or less per day which is recommended for the general population, although hypercholesterolaemic patients might benefit from further restriction.

Dietary carbohydrate fibre and glycaemic index

A total carbohydrate intake in the range 50–60% of overall energy intake is associated with a reduced tendency to atheromatous disease among diabetic patients in developing countries (see Chapter 20). As discussed above, this may be because an increased carbohydrate intake generally permits a reciprocal fall in fat intake.

There is a wide range in the degree and duration of acute hyperglycaemia caused by eating different foods which contain the same amount of carbohydrate. This has led to the concept of the *glycaemic index*, defined as the area under the blood glucose curve up to 3 h after eating a standard carbohydrate load (usually 50 g), expressed as a percentage of the area following ingestion of the same amount of glucose, i.e.

$$\text{Glycaemic index}(\%) = \frac{\text{3-h glycaemic area after carbohydrate}}{\text{3-h glycaemic area after glucose}} \times 100.$$

(Confusingly, some authorities use 50 g white bread as the standard.)

It is important for patients treated with insulin to take food which contains carbohydrate regularly to prevent hypoglycaemia. The optimum amount in each meal is best gauged from blood glucose profiles. An understanding of the carbohydrate content of foods remains necessary but the glycaemic response to food is governed by many factors other than simply the carbohydrate content, including the content of fat, protein, dietary fibre, the presence of resistant starch, the physical form of the food (even the shape of different varieties of pasta), water content, temperature and how much it is chewed [6]. For these reasons, detailed and apparently accurate carbohydrate exchange lists can be misleading. The composition of foods in standard tables is in any case likely to be accurate only to within 10 or 20% [7]. Tables based on the glycaemic indices of foods have been proposed as an alternative basis for diabetic diet. In principle this is attractive, but the theory is probably too complicated and there are still too many uncertain elements before this approach can be used directly with patients. In a simpler form, the concept of low, glycaemic, index staple foods forming the basic and major component of each meal may offer advantages. Thus an approximately equivalent amount of cereal, bread, pasta, rice, or potato may be suggested as a basis for a meal-planning approach to diabetic diets together with appropriate guidance about cooking, the use of vegetables and the limits they place on the high fat component of the meal. Eggs, cheese, fish, poultry, and meat should thus form a small part of each meal in the form of a garnish to the staple component.

Low-glycaemic-index foods (e.g. pulses, oats, barley) are associated with longer-term benefits in terms of glycaemic and blood lipid control, arguing that these foods should be the principal carbohydrate sources in the diet of IDDM patients [8]. For some foods, e.g. potatoes, there are widely varying glycaemic indices because of variations in composition and food preparation. It has therefore been difficult to design standard food lists on the basis of the glycaemic index and local research is often necessary.

The amount of carbohydrate to be prescribed per day will vary with the energy requirement of the patient (see Fig. 41.1). In physiological terms, as it is not possible to synthesize carbohydrate from fatty acids, a total of 180 g glucose is necessary each day to allow complete fat oxidation. A daily dietary intake of 50 g is probably essential. Up to 130 g of glucose can become available each day from endogenous protein sources during starvation, but an intake of approximately 100 g/day

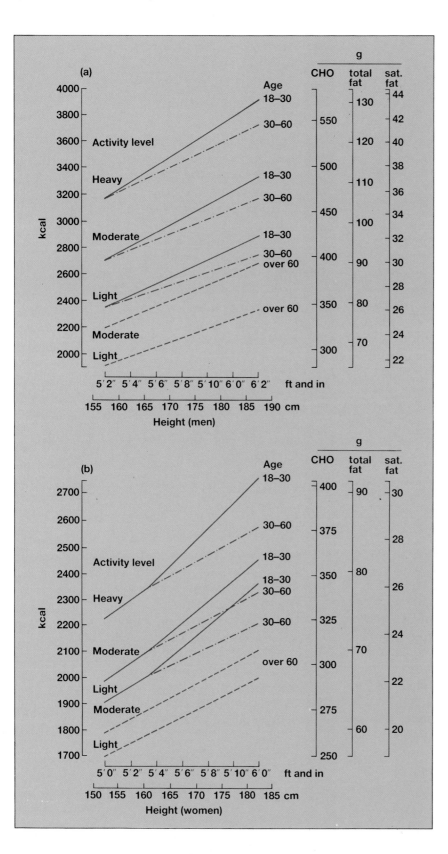

Fig. 41.1. Detailed energy and nutrient prescription guidelines for (a) men and (b) women, assuming a diet which provides 55% of energy as carbohydrate. From the patient's height, age and level of physical activity, total daily energy requirement (left *y*-axis) and carbohydrate, total fat and saturated fat (right *y*-axes) can be estimated. *Notes*:

1 Activity levels are defined as: light — active on feet for 2 h/day; moderate — active on feet for 6 h/day; heavy — serious athletes in training and heavy labouring only.

2 Overweight people have increased metabolic rates and therefore increased energy requirements; they will therefore lose weight if they eat the amounts indicated by the charts (which are based on the ideal body weight). For sustained weight loss, daily energy intake should be 500 kcal (1.2 MJ) below that required to maintain body weight.

3 These estimates assume that the subject will undertake at least light exercise. If sedentary, the energy requirement should be reduced by 15%. (Adapted from ref. 21.)

(i.e. 400 kcal from carbohydrate) is usually necessary to avoid dietary ketosis [9]. This latter should not be confused with ketoacidosis from insulin deficiency. In practice, most diets other than strict slimming regimens contain carbohydrate well above these lower limits.

Despite uncertainties in the past about the role of complex carbohydrate, the evidence is now consistent that if a higher carbohydrate intake is to be taken, then it must be accompanied by a high soluble fibre intake for glycaemic and lipaemic control to benefit. Conversely, it has been difficult to prove any useful effect of dietary fibre in the absence of a high carbohydrate intake [1, 9]. The exact mechanisms of dietary fibre are uncertain, but delayed food absorption (possibly by increasing the viscosity of the 'unstirred' layer of gut contents in contact with the mucosa) is considered to play at least a part (see Chapter 104).

It is recommended that the intake of dietary fibre should be increased to about 20 g per 1000 kcal, i.e. roughly double the present average intake in most Western countries. This should be derived principally from soluble-type dietary fibre rather than insoluble fibre such as bran and cellulose. Carbohydrate-containing foods rich in natural soluble fibre include legumes, lentils, fruits, oats and barley, roots and green-leafy vegetables, as well as grain cereals.

The basis and largest component for all meals and snacks should be the staple cereal, bread, pasta or potato, all of which provide good sources of filling, but relatively low-energy, complex carbohydrate. Certain foods such as pasta are not particularly high in dietary fibre yet appear to have a similar beneficial effect on glycaemic control and are also recommended. By the same token, high intakes of fibre-depleted starchy foods should be avoided.

Dietary sugars in IDDM

Over the years, dietary advice on simple sugars in diabetic diets has become confused, dogmatic and unnecessarily emotive.

Simple sugars (including sucrose), naturally present in milk and fruits and often in large amounts, have always been an integral part of a balanced diabetic diet. Sucrose used as a sweetener is not chemically different from that found naturally in other foods and, in moderation, is acceptable in the diabetic diet as it is for anybody else. As well as containing 50% fructose, which does not contribute significantly to blood glucose, dietary sucrose depends for hydrolysis on mucosal disaccharidase action, and is relatively slowly absorbed from the gut, as compared with the rapid absorption of glucose itself or the glucose hydrolysed from starch in foods such as

bread or potatoes. Sucrose has a relatively low glycaemic index, about 60% of that of glucose or 80% that of bread [11].

There are anxieties about the long-term effects of large amounts of fructose (70−80 g/day) on blood lipids, particularly triglycerides, in diabetic subjects [12−14]. A limit of 25 g fructose per day as an added sweetener and in sweets and snacks has been suggested [15]. This is equivalent to the fructose content of 50 g (ten teaspoons) of sucrose per day, which is the recommended allowance for the general population [16]; the current average intake in the general UK population is about twice this limit (Table 41.1). The current recommendation from the Nutritional Subcommittee of the British Diabetic Association is that where 25 g of fructose is used as a sweetener, it is quite acceptable to use 25 g of sucrose (i.e. the same energy load) instead. This figure is similar to the 30 g/day (10 kg/year) of sucrose in confectionery, soft drinks and snacks suggested (mainly because of dental considerations) as a long-term goal for the general population [16]. An extra 10 kg per year is considered acceptable for sucrose (or an equivalent amount of its inverted monosaccharides) provided that this is contained within fruit and other foods.

This is no longer considered a rigid rule of prescription: people with high-energy requirements may perhaps take more, whereas small children should probably aim for less; certainly, no diabetic patient should totally exclude foods which contain a moderate amount of sugar. It makes nutritional sense for sugars to be consumed as part of complete meals and snacks. Sweets or sugar-sweetened drinks should therefore not be taken alone.

When hypoglycaemia occurs, glucose is required for treatment, as either glucose tablets or a solution. Sucrose can be equally effective in emergencies but tends to be unpalatable. Glucose gel and other foods are less effective [17]. 10−15 g of glucose is usually an appropriate amount of treatment and this should be taken in addition to the normal foods at the next snack or meal.

Protein

The recommended daily amount of protein for the general population is 10% of total energy, which represents about 50−60 g daily [18]. Most people eat more than this (around 12%), which is probably permissible if a high proportion of protein comes from vegetable sources. There is some evidence to suggest that much higher protein intakes (about 100 g/day), particularly if derived from animal sources, may be related to accelerated renal damage in diabetic patients [19, 20]. Once renal failure has developed, negative nitrogen balance may compound the problem by increasing tissue loss; at this late stage, therefore, unnecessary protein restriction should be avoided.

Designing a diet for a patient with IDDM

Dietary advice for a patient with IDDM must take into account many factors, including his actual and ideal body weight, timing and pattern of insulin injections and periods of exercise, and the presence of other conditions such as hyperlipidaemia, macrovascular disease or diabetic nephropathy.

Calculating energy requirements

Unlike patients with NIDDM, many IDDM patients will be close to their ideal body weight and may even be substantially below this, requiring an increased total energy intake. As discussed in Chapter 47 dietary histories are notoriously unreliable and the patient's energy requirement is better calculated according to sex, age, height and level of physical activity (see Fig. 41.1) [21]. As circumstances change, energy requirements and the dietary prescription must be kept under review.

Food exchange systems

It may be best *not* to describe the patient's diet in terms of carbohydrate content. This practice dates from before the discovery of insulin, when starvation diets were the only form of treatment available, and has the unfortunate consequence of convincing the patient that carbohydrate-rich foods are harmful and, therefore, that other foods are less damaging. Eating to appetite with 'non-forbidden' high-fat foods may have been an important contributory cause of macrovascular disease in diabetic patients.

Food requirements and eating patterns throughout the day in an IDDM patient will largely be determined by his insulin regimen and the degree and timing of physical exercise which he undertakes. To maintain good glycaemic control, the size and timing of individual meals and snacks, and also the total energy and fat intake must be carefully regulated. Formal *carbohydrate exchange systems* are still widely recommended in the UK for IDDM patients as a means of allowing variety while regulating food intake at different times of day, in attempts to balance the usually more rigid insulin administration and provide regular carbohydrate as a precaution against hypoglycaemia. For the reasons outlined above, this approach is unsatisfactory and many other countries now employ *meal planning systems* in which entire meals or snacks are designed, rather than just considering the carbohydrate content of individual foodstuffs (which may be of little relevance, as is emphasized by the variability in the glycaemic index) [22]. It is argued that the accuracy of diet prescription using meal exchanges is more consistent with the imprecise nature of everyday eating and that inappropriate carbohydrate exchanging is less likely. Formal studies of the different approaches in clinical practice are awaited.

Improved insulin regimens may have reduced the need for rigid mealtimes but regular main meals are probably still helpful as a basis for stable control of IDDM. Most IDDM patients also still require regular snacks between main meals if large glycaemic swings and hypoglycaemia are to be avoided. As a general rule, food is required every 2–3 h and some patients find it can be helpful to eat two snacks between breakfast and lunch, or an extra snack between the main evening meal and the bedtime snack. More frequent snacks can reduce the problem of having to eat very high volume meals, which is encountered by those patients prescribed a high-carbohydrate diet.

Other dietary advice

Sodium

A trial of sodium restriction should probably be included as a first-line general measure in hypertensive diabetic patients, in whom controlled trials of a low-sodium, low-fat, high-fibre diet have produced clinically significant falls in blood pressure [23]. The current recommendation [1] is that sodium intake should not exceed 6 g/day and that <3 g/day is a reasonable starting-point for subjects with or at risk of hypertension.

Micronutrients

It has been suggested that the anti-oxidant, beta-carotene and vitamins E and C may exert a protective influence against free-radical-mediated tissue damage [24]. These substances may reasonably be encouraged as normal food components, although the role of free radicals in mediating long-term diabetic complications remains unclear (Chapter 54).

Alcohol

Alcohol presents a particular problem for IDDM patients because it may both mask the early symptoms of hypoglycaemia and also block the hepatic glucose production which is necessary to recover from hypoglycaemia. So-called 'diabetic' beers often contain larger than normal amounts of alcohol as well as a low sugar content and are particularly likely to cause severe hypoglycaemia; normally brewed beers and lagers are preferable. In line with general recommendations, alcohol intake should not exceed 3 units daily, preferably not taken at one sitting nor every day of the week. In diabetic patients, food intake should not be reduced to compensate for alcohol consumed [25] or hypoglycaemia may result.

'Diabetic' foods and sweeteners

The widely advertised so-called 'diabetic foods' are not recommended. Many are expensive, most are unpalatable, and none has any proven long-term therapeutic benefit. These products often contain sorbitol which causes diarrhoea and other gastrointestinal side-effects, or fructose which may increase blood lipid levels. Many are high in energy and therefore unsuitable for the overweight.

Low-calorie, sugar-free drinks containing essentially non-nutritive (very low energy) sweeteners such as saccharine and aspartame may be useful for some overweight patients. These products seem to have no undesirable metabolic or other side-effects, although aspartame (which contains a phenylalanine residue) is contraindicated in patients with phenylketonuria. The long-term effects of sugars such as fructose or maltose, or of sugar alcohols like sorbitol, when ingested in large amounts as sweeteners are not known. It is recommended that fructose intake should be kept below 25 g/day, but the same amount of sucrose seems a preferable alternative.

Advice and compliance

The psychological and social importance of food and eating must not be underestimated; the diet prescribed to a patient with IDDM often demands major changes in lifestyle. Physicians are rarely competent to be the sole providers of appropriate and balanced advice, and an experienced dietitian or dietetically trained nurse specialist is essential to provide individual guidance. Simply giving advice, even if this is accurately assimilated by patients with IDDM, may be insufficient to produce significant changes in eating habits unless the patients' underlying attitudes and beliefs can also be modified [26]. Poor dietary compliance may be an important cause of unsatisfactory metabolic control in some IDDM patients [27]. On the other hand, the high within-individual day-to-day variability of food intake in IDDM patients may not always be 'non-compliance' but may represent conscious efforts to correct erratic self-monitored blood glucose measurements [28]. It is certainly all too easy to blame dietary indiscretions for high blood glucose at clinic visits: in a controlled study, a large piece of cake containing 500 kcal and 90 g of carbohydrate taken in addition to the usual evening meal was found to produce a mean increase in fasting plasma glucose of only 2 mmol/l in IDDM patients [29].

The diet must be tailored to suit the individual and his family food, culture, economic and cooking conditions, and reviewed regularly to accommodate any necessary changes. New techniques for food preparation may need to be taught; providing recipes and cookery demonstrations is often helpful. The British Diabetic Association have a wide range of publications on aspects of diet for IDDM patients, including special leaflets for Asian and Caribbean patients.

Special considerations are necessary when advising children with diabetes and, more importantly, their parents (see Chapter 87) [31]. It seems reasonable to try to institute a cardioprotective diet at an early stage, but any interference with the family's eating patterns or with the potent and sensitive psychosocial associations of food and eating for children can lead to disaster. In the past, the punishing and ill-founded sugar-avoidance dogma has led to much unhappiness and has ultimately been unsuccessful. A gradual modification of eating habits is now recommended. It is particularly important not to present 'don'ts' at the first interview with a newly diagnosed patient, as this can create an enduring negative impression. Examples of simple positive advice, which are adequate for initial dietary advice in IDDM, are shown in Table 41.2.

Table 41.2. Initial dietary advice for a newly diagnosed diabetic patient.

1 Drink *water* to quench thirst
2 Eat to appetite with *normal foods*, and take regular meals
3 Make the *main part of each meal* the cereal, bread, pasta or potatoes
4 Make meat and cheese a *small* part of meals

Exercise and diet

The current FAO/WHO/UNU recommendation [32] to maintain cardiovascular health in the general population is to exercise moderately vigorously for 20 min per day, in addition to any exercise undertaken at work. There is no reason why this should not apply to most fit IDDM patients, and for social integration as well as health, it is particularly valuable for children with IDDM to take regular exercise. The perceived problem, that exercise may provoke hypoglycaemia, requires careful consideration and discussion with the patient (Chapter 78).

During exercise, IDDM patients cannot reduce their blood insulin concentrations physiologically by decreasing insulin secretion. This predisposes to hypoglycaemia, although severe episodes occur relatively infrequently during exercise itself, perhaps because the secretion of catecholamines and other counter-regulatory hormones is already increased. However, hypoglycaemia is a common problem in the hours after exercise and particularly in the morning following strenuous exercise the previous evening (see Chapter 78).

In the case of strenuous and sustained exercise, reducing the insulin dose is clearly important. A modest snack containing 'slow-release' carbohydrate may be effective although some patients find that this impairs athletic performance. For more modest exercise, a snack of glucose-releasing foods (either glucose itself or a high-starch food) beforehand is appropriate. Late hypoglycaemia following exercise can be reduced by additional carbohydrate loading after exercise to replenish glycogen stores; a modest reduction in insulin dosage is also helpful. Athletes should keep detailed records of insulin and diet adjustments in order to plan for exercise. In training, it is best to exercise at the same time of day, as this is particularly helpful in planning insulin dosage reductions.

Conclusions

Dietary advice for patients with IDDM has changed radically within the last few years. The salient points of the new recommendations for the composition of diet and the reasons for abandoning the concepts of carbohydrate restriction and carbohydrate exchanges will require careful explanation to many patients. It is to be hoped that these new dietary measures will be rewarded by less stigmatization of diabetic patients through any need for an unusual diet, better day-to-day metabolic control and, more importantly, by a reduced risk of the long-term complications of diabetes.

MIKE E.J. LEAN
JIM I. MANN

References

1 Nutrition and Diabetes Study Group of the European Association for the Study of Diabetes. Nutritional recommendations and principles for individuals with diabetes mellitus. *Diabetic Nutr Metab* 1988; **1**: 145–9.

2 Garg A, Bonanome A, Grundy SM, Zhang Z-J, Unger RH. Comparison of a high-carbohydrate diet with a high-monounsaturated-fat diet in patients with diabetes mellitus. *N Engl J Med* 1988; **319**: 829–34.

3 Phillipson BE, Rothrock DW, Connor WE, Harris WS, Illingworth DR. Reduction of plasma lipids, lipoproteins, and apolipoproteins by dietary fish oils in patients with hypertriglyceridemia. *N Engl J Med* 1985; **312**: 1210–16.

4 Kromhout D, Bosschieter EB, Coulander C de L. The inverse relation between fish consumption and 20-year mortality from coronary heart disease. *N Engl J Med* 1985; **312**: 1205–9.

5 Burr ML, Fehily AM, Gilbert JF et al. Effects of changes in fat, fish and fibre intakes on death and myocardial reinfarction: diet and reinfarction trial (DART). *Lancet* 1989; ii: 757–61.

6 Wolever TMS, Jenkins DJA, Kalmusky J et al. Glycemic response to pasta: effect of surface area, degree of cooking, and protein enrichment. *Diabetes Care* 1986; **9**: 401–4.

7 Stockley L. Food composition tables in the calculation of the nutrient content of mixed diets. *J Hum Nutr Dietet* 1988: **1**: 187–95.

8 Jenkins DJA, Jenkins AL. The glycemic index, fiber and the dietary treatment of hypertryglyceridemia and diabetes. *J Am Coll Nutr* 1987; **61**: 11–17.

9 McDonald I. Metabolic requirements for dietary carbohydrate. *Am J Clin Nutr* 1987; **45**: 1193–6.

10 Mann JI. Diabetes mellitus: some aspects of aetiology and management of non-insulin-dependent diabetes. In: Trowell H, ed. *Fibre depleted foods and disease*. London: Academic Press, 1985: 263–87.

11 Jenkins DJA, Wolever TMS, Jenkins AL, Josse RG, Wong GS. The glycaemic response to carbohydrate foods. *Lancet* 1984; ii: 388–91.

12 Pelkonen R, Aro A, Nikkilä EA. Metabolic effects of dietary fructose in insulin dependent diabetes of adults. *Acta Med Scand* 1972; suppl 542: 187–93.

13 Reiser S. Effects of dietary sugars on metabolic risk factors associated with heart disease. *Nutr Health* 1985; **3**: 203–16.

14 McAteer EJ, O'Reilly G, Hadden DR. The effects of one month high fructose intake on plasma glucose and lipid levels on plasma glucose and lipid levels in non-insulin-dependent diabetes. *Diabetic Med* 1987; **4**: 62–4.

15 MAFF (Ministry of Agriculture, Fisheries and Food). The food labelling regulations 1984. *Statutory Instr* 1984: 1305.

16 NACNE (National Advisory Committee on Nutrition Education). *Proposals for Nutritional Guidelines for Health Education in Britain*. London: Health Education Council, 1983.

17 Slama G, Traynard P, Desplanque N *et al*. The search for an optimized treatment of hypoglycemia. *Arch Intern Med* 1990; **150**: 589–93.

18 DHSS (Department of Health and Social Services). *Recommended Food Allowances*. London: HMSO, 1979.

19 Ciavarella A, di Mizio G, Stefoni S *et al*. Reduced albuminuria after dietary protein restriction in insulin dependent diabetic patients with clinical nephropathy. *Diabetes Care* 1987; **10**: 407–13.

20 Cohen D, Dodds R, Viberti GC. Effect of protein restriction in insulin dependent diabetics at risk of nephropathy. *Br Med J* 1987; **294**: 795–8.

21 Lean MEJ, James WPT. Prescription of diabetic diets in the 1980s. *Lancet* 1986; i: 723–5.

22 Swedish Diabetic Association. *Food for Diabetes, Good Food for All*. Alvsjo: Svenska Diabetes Forbundet, 1987: 1–27.

23 Pacy PJ, Dodson PM, Fletcher RF. Effect of high carbohydrate, low sodium, low fat diet in Type 2 diabetics with moderate hypertension. *Int J Obesity* 1986; **10**: 43–52.

24 Slater TF, Cheeseman KH, Davies MJ, Proudfoot K, Xin W. Free radical mechanisms in relation to tissue injury. *Proc Nutr Soc* 1987; **46**: 1–12.

25 Connor H, Marks V. Alcohol and diabetes. *Hum Nutr Appl Nutr* 1985; **39A**: 393–9.

26 Lean MEJ, Anderson AS. Clinic strategies for obesity management. *Diabetic Med* 1988; **5**: 515–18.

27 McCulloch DK, Young RJ, Steel JM, Wilson EM, Prescott RJ, Duncan LJP. Effect of dietary compliance on metabolic control in insulin-dependent diabetics. *Hum Nutr Appl Nutr* 1983; **37A**: 287–92.

28 Anderson AS, Lean MEJ, Pearson DWM, Sutherland HW. Comparison between the diets of pregnant diabetic women and pregnant non-diabetic women. *Diabetic Med* 1990; **7**: 452–6.

29 Belkhadir J, Rosset T, Elgrably F *et al*. Effect of an extra intake of carbohydrate at dinner on morning after fasting plasma glucose values in Types I and II diabetes. *Br Med J* 1985; **291**: 1608.

30 McCulloch DK, Mitchell RD, Ambler J, Tattersall RB. Influence of imaginative teaching of diet on compliance and metabolic control in insulin-dependent diabetes. *Br Med J* 1983; **287**: 1858–62.

31 British Diabetic Association Nutrition Subcommittee. Dietary recommendations for children and adolescents with diabetes mellitus. *Diabetic Med* 1989; **6**: 537–47.

32 FAO/WHO/UNU. Energy and protein requirements. *Technical Report Series*. Vol 724. Geneva: WHO, 1985.

42 Continuous Subcutaneous Insulin Infusion (CSII)

Summary

- Continuous subcutaneous insulin infusion (CSII) mimics non-diabetic insulin delivery by infusing insulin from a portable pump at an adjustable basal rate with patient-activated boosts before meals.
- Patients started on CSII must receive comprehensive education, including details of pump operation, home blood glucose monitoring, insulin dosage adjustments and corrective action in case of illness, hypoglycaemia, hyperglycaemia or pump breakdown.
- CSII should only be undertaken by centres which can provide supervision by experienced staff and a 24-h telephone service for immediate advice about management problems.
- Long-term strict control of blood glucose, intermediary metabolite and hormone levels can be obtained with CSII, although (as with insulin injection treatment) at the expense of higher blood insulin levels than in non-diabetic subjects.
- Infusion site infections during CSII, commonly due to *Staphylococcus aureus* or *S. epidermidis*, occur more frequently than injection site abscesses. The risk of infection can probably be reduced by measures such as changing the delivery cannula and its site every day or so, washing the hands and cleaning the implantation site before insertion.
- CSII-treated patients are at increased risk of developing ketoacidosis because the subcutaneous insulin depot is smaller than with injection therapy. However, at experienced centres with careful attention to patient and physician education, ketoacidosis rates are usually no greater than for injection therapy.
- Hypoglycaemic coma is also not usually increased during CSII as compared with injection therapy, but improved control by CSII and other regimens may decrease the warning symptoms of hypoglycaemia.
- CSII is an alternative form of intensified insulin therapy for IDDM patients and may be used for experimental studies, e.g. investigating the links between control and diabetic complications. Routine treatment by CSII is suitable for a relatively small number of selected patients.

The origins of CSII

Treatment of IDDM by continuous infusion of insulin from a portable pump is based on the assumption that optimal metabolic control can only be achieved when insulin is administered in a way which mimics the nondiabetic insulin secretion pattern, i.e. low 'basal' delivery maintained throughout the entire day with boosts at mealtimes (Fig. 42.1). When the insulin delivery is pre-set or adjusted by the patient, the infusion system is known as 'open-loop', as opposed to the 'closed-loop' circuit when there is automatic feedback control of the infusion rate from a glucose sensor in the blood or tissues. The latter system is popularly known as an 'artificial endocrine pancreas' — see Chapter 43.

In the mid-1970s, several groups demonstrated that open-loop *intravenous* insulin infusion from a portable pump, at a basal rate with prandial boosts, could produce near-normoglycaemia in IDDM patients for several days [1–3]. Similar intravenous infusion systems have subsequently been maintained for some months under ambulatory conditions [4] but even short-term

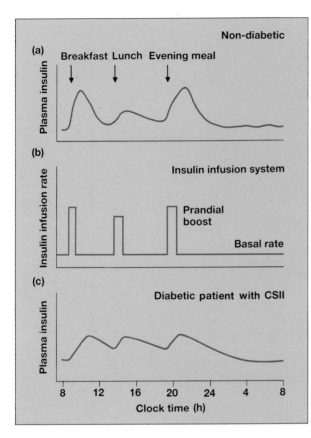

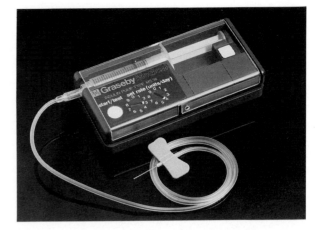

Fig. 42.2. An insulin infusion pump used for CSII.

Fig. 42.1. The simulation of non-diabetic insulin secretory profiles by open-loop insulin infusion, e.g. CSII; (a) plasma insulin levels in a non-diabetic subject; (b) basal infusion and prandial boost of CSII mimicking non-diabetic insulin secretion; (c) resultant plasma free insulin levels in diabetic subjects treated by CSII.

intravenous insulin infusion carries the risks of septicaemia and thrombosis. Continuous subcutaneous insulin infusion (CSII) was developed [5, 6] to avoid these potential complications. Although originally introduced [5] as a research tool to explore the links between quality of metabolic control and the progression of diabetic microvascular disease, CSII is able to provide long-term strict control in selected patients and has become a routine treatment option in certain indications.

Technology of CSII

The first pump used for CSII (the Mill Hill Infuser) was a specially adapted battery-driven syringe pump [5] which was developed initially for experimental infusion of hormones into animals. Several improved pumps for CSII have become available commercially in the last decade (Fig. 42.2). The basal rate may be set by switches or

keys and the prandial boost is usually activated by the patient pressing a button on the pump. Some models have the facility for pre-programming one or more changes in infusion rate at set times during the day (e.g. a pre-breakfast increase) and many have alarms for events such as blockage of the cannula or an empty reservoir or low battery. All pumps use a neutral short-acting insulin; the insulin reservoir is either a disposable syringe or, for example in the Nordisk Infuser, a pre-filled glass cartridge.

The plastic delivery cannula ends in a fine-gauge metal needle with 'butterfly' wings. The needle is inserted subcutaneously by the patient, usually in the anterior abdomen, and is secured to the skin by taping over the wings. The needle is inserted most easily with the patient sitting and must not be placed too superficially, as this impairs insulin absorption and results in more erratic control. The implantation site should be changed every day or two, or immediately if local inflammation develops.

How to start patients on CSII

Patients are usually admitted to hospital for a few days to start CSII, both to enable frequent blood-glucose measurements and titration of insulin delivery, and to provide sufficient time to educate the patient about pump therapy.

A typical initial infusion strategy (Fig. 42.3) is to administer half of the patient's usual daily insulin dosage during injection therapy as the basal infusion (an average of about 1.1 U/h in adults or 15 mU/kg/h), and to divide the remaining half equally amongst the three main

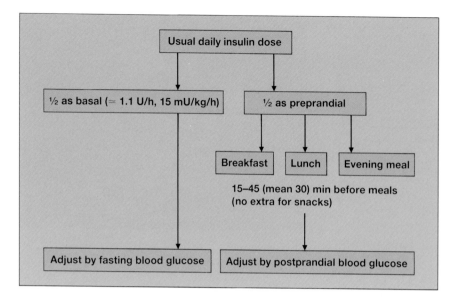

Fig. 42.3. The infusion strategy used for starting patients on CSII.

meals; these prandial boosts are given 15–45 min before eating. There is usually no need for extra insulin before snacks. The basal rate can be adjusted for an individual patient by using the fasting blood glucose concentration as a measure of the adequacy of insulinization, and the blood glucose value about 90 min after meals may similarly be used to adjust the prandial supplements. The final proportions of prandial and basal insulin are usually about 45:55% respectively.

A comprehensive education programme must be followed during the hospital stay and should include instruction about the principles and day-to-day operation of CSII, home blood glucose monitoring (see Chapter 39), dosage adjustments, and what to do in the event of illness, hypoglycaemia, hyperglycaemia, or pump breakdown (see Tables 42.1 and 42.2).

Target blood glucose values on CSII should be about 4–6 mmol/l in the fasting state and <10 mmol/l postprandially. Various algorithms have been published for dosage adjustments with CSII, based on self-monitored blood glucose values [9]. The frequency and timing of blood glucose monitoring will clearly vary with factors such as the level of control desired and the ease of achieving this, the motivation of the patient and his employment and lifestyle. Testing 1–3 times daily, particularly with a fasting, postprandial and bed-time blood glucose value, and a seven-point day profile about every 2 weeks (alternating between working days and weekends) is a reasonable goal for many patients. The frequency should

Table 42.1. Education and information about CSII.

- Explain the principles of CSII, why CSII is being undertaken, how to operate the pump and what to do in emergencies (see below) to both the patient and relatives or partners who will be with the patient at home.
- Demonstrate the pump and how it works, the alarms, battery insertion and expected lifetime, adjustment of basal rate, activation of mealtime boost, the cannula insertion and its securing to skin, and cannula changes.
- Re-educate about blood glucose self-monitoring and urinary ketone monitoring and teach simple rules for basal and preprandial dosage adjustments.
- Provide general and CSII-related dietary advice, noting possible weight gain but opportunities for more flexibility at mealtimes.
- Give instructions on CSII and exercise, sports, bathing and sexual intercourse.
- Give instructions for action in case of hypo- and hyperglycaemia, intercurrent illness, ketonuria, infusion site problems and pump breakdown.
- Give information about 24-h on-call telephone service for contacting hospital.
- Supply insulin and syringes for emergency reversion to injection therapy.
- Supply with identification card (e.g. 'I am a diabetic receiving insulin via an infusion pump. In the event of an emergency please telephone Dr X at Y Hospital').

be increased during illness. Urine glucose testing is obviously inappropriate for monitoring CSII treatment, as the target glycaemic range is below the renal threshold in most cases.

The role of the hospital

CSII is a specialist procedure, still regarded by many as experimental, and should only be under-

Table 42.2. Patient guidelines if blood glucose during CSII > 20 mmol/l and/or the patient feels ill.

- Measure blood glucose and test urine for ketones
- Check pump operation:
  Infuser working
  Battery working
  Sufficient insulin in reservoir
  Cannula connected to pump, implanted s.c.
  Infusion site not red or tender
  No kinks or blockages in cannula
- If in doubt, insert new battery and delivery cannula, at a new site
- Give 10 U short-acting insulin by syringe or, if pump clearly working, by mealtime boost on pump
- Remeasure blood glucose 2 h later and repeat insulin injection if blood glucose > 10 mmol/l
- If after 4 h blood glucose is still > 15 mmol/l, contact hospital via telephone

taken by centres which can provide experienced staff for the instruction and close supervision of patients. A 24-h telephone service is essential so that all pump patients can obtain immediate advice if management problems arise or the pump breaks down.

Life on the pump

Once established on CSII, patients need out-patient review only about every 2–3 months. Patients should be instructed to record home-monitored blood glucose values together with any untoward events in a log book.

Everyday activities are hindered relatively little by the pump. The cannula and infuser should be removed for bathing; the blood glucose concentration remains fairly constant during the first

hour after disconnection [21]. During mild to moderate exercise the pump can be kept in place without a change of infusion rate. It should be removed for sports in which it may be damaged, such as football or swimming.

Metabolic effects of CSII

Most patients achieve excellent glycaemic control throughout the day during CSII treatment (Fig. 42.4) and this has been extended to periods of many years in some subjects. The results of several randomized clinical trials, such as the Kroc study which involved six centres in the UK and North America [10], and those at the Steno Hospital in Copenhagen [11] and Aker Hospital, Oslo [12] where conventional (non-optimized) insulin injection treatment has been compared with CSII, clearly demonstrate superior glycaemic control during CSII (Fig. 42.5).

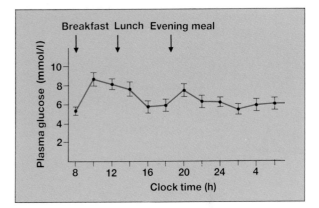

Fig. 42.4. Plasma glucose concentrations throughout the day (mean ± SEM) in 30 IDDM subjects treated by CSII.

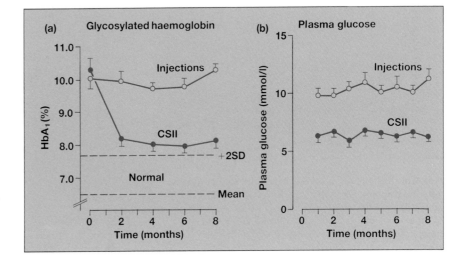

Fig. 42.5. Glycaemic control in patients randomly assigned to continued conventional insulin injection therapy (○) or CSII (●); (a) changes in glycosylated haemoglobin (HbA₁); (b) changes in plasma glucose levels calculated from home-collected samples taken throughout the day (mean ± SEM). (Data from Kroc Collaborative Study 1984 [10] with permission from *The New England Journal of Medicine*.)

Early studies with CSII confirmed that the disordered blood metabolite and hormonal concentrations of conventionally treated IDDM are mainly due to sub-optimal insulin replacement [6, 13]. After 1−14 days of CSII, disturbances in pyruvate, lactate, branched-chain amino acids, cholesterol, triglyceride, 3-hydroxybutyrate and free fatty acids were improved or normalized (Fig. 42.6). Plasma lipoproteins may take longer to change: one 26-week study has found gradual decreases in VLDL-cholesterol and LDL-cholesterol and an increase in HDL-cholesterol during CSII as compared with conventional injection treatment [14].

CSII only achieves metabolic near-normalization at the expense of plasma free insulin concen-

trations which exceed the normal range in the basal and pre-meal states [15, 16] (Fig. 42.7). Comparable hyperinsulinaemia also occurs during conventional insulin injection treatment. Fears have been expressed (but without definite proof) that hyperinsulinaemia may contribute to the accelerated development of atherosclerosis in diabetes [17].

Pharmacological aspects of CSII

In most infusion pumps, the apparently constant basal rate is achieved by frequent, small pulses of insulin which because of the sluggish absorption of insulin, simulate true continuous infusion; in fact, plasma free insulin and glucose concentrations remain at about the same level at pulse frequencies of up to 2 h [18]. This strategy greatly prolongs battery life. Volumetric insulin delivery can be altered by changing the frequency of pulses.

It has been demonstrated that the steady-state free plasma insulin levels achieved by either subcutaneous or intravenous insulin infused at the same constant rate are comparable [19]. This suggests that local degradation of subcutaneously infused insulin is very limited but the long delay (6−8 h) in achieving the plateau after the start of basal-rate CSII implies a considerable accumulation of insulin at the subcutaneous infusion site — probably about 5 U, depending on the blood flow at the site of subcutaneous infusion [20]. This depot allows a 'safe period' after deliberate or accidental interruption of CSII, e.g. for bathing, when glycaemic values should remain

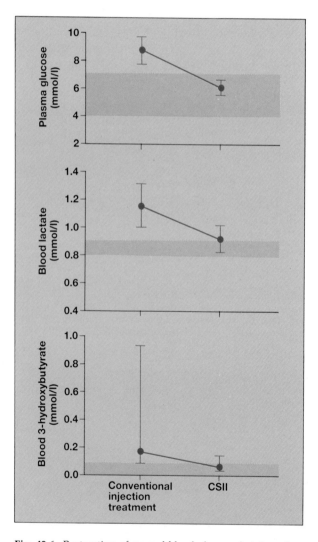

Fig. 42.6. Restoration of normal blood glucose, lactate and 3-hydroxybutyrate concentrations in seven IDDM subjects after 1 day of CSII (mean ± SEM for glucose and lactate, mean ± range for 3-hydroxybutyrate). Shaded area represents normal range. (Data from Pickup et al. 1979 [6] with permission from The Lancet.)

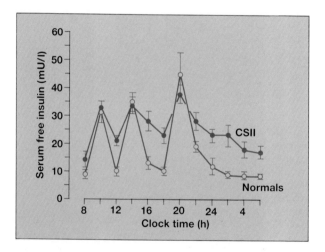

Fig. 42.7. Hyperinsulinaemia during CSII. Mean ± SEM serum free insulin levels in IDDM subjects treated by CSII and in non-diabetic subjects.

fairly stable for an hour or two [21]. A further consequence of the slow absorption of insulin at the basal rate is that acute adjustments in insulin delivery during CSII are best made by altering the boosts rather than the basal rate. Furthermore, with programmable pumps, the best tactic to counteract the pre-breakfast glycaemic rise ('dawn phenomenon' — see Chapter 51) which occurs in some patients, is to give extra insulin either by increasing the basal rate shortly after midnight or by administering a bolus at a time nearer to dawn.

The absorption of the mealtime supplements during CSII follows the pattern of subcutaneous injections of short-acting insulin [22]: plasma free insulin levels peak at about 75 min after administration, compared with a peak endogenous insulin level at about 45 min after eating in normal subjects. Thus, giving the bolus at about 30 min before a main meal will approximately match the circulating insulin peak to maximal nutrient absorption.

Complications of CSII

Malfunctions

In one study [23] of a large number of patients undergoing CSII with a variety of pumps in a clinical setting, 86% of subjects reported a system problem of some kind during 1 year of treatment. Ninety-six per cent of these failures involved the insulin syringe, cannula, needle or infusion site and only 4% were connected with the pump. Most of the infusion system failures were due to obstruction or leakage of the cannula, which other series have not identified as a common cause of malfunction [24]. Such problems may partly explain the high frequency of ketoacidosis found in some studies of CSII [25] (see below). There is evidence that buffered, purified porcine insulin is much less likely to cause occlusion of delivery cannulae than unbuffered, beef—pork combined preparations [26, 27].

Skin complications

The complications of CSII at the infusion site are lipohypertrophy, infection and abscesses, local insulin allergy and allergic reactions to the securing tape.

Subcutaneous infections (Fig. 42.8) are more common during CSII than injection therapy

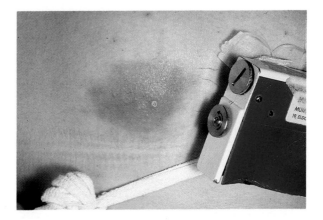

Fig. 42.8. An infusion site abscess which developed during CSII.

(about one episode per 27 patient-months), the organisms most often involved being *Staphylococcus aureus* and *S. epidermidis* [28, 29]. The carriage rate of *S. aureus* has been reported to be either increased [25] or unaltered [29] in CSII patients with pyogenic infections at the infusion site, but the infection rate may be more common when the insulin preservative is *m*-cresol rather than methylhydroxybenzoate [29]. The risk of infections can probably be reduced by changing the needle at no more than 48-h intervals, not re-using catheters, washing the hands, cleaning the implantation site with antiseptic before implantation, and covering the needle with a sterile dressing. Some plastic CSII catheters adsorb up to 88% of bacteriostatic agents from insulin solutions [30], but it remains to be seen if this loss of preservative predisposes to cutaneous infection.

Ketoacidosis and hypoglycaemia

The patient undergoing CSII is clearly at increased risk of developing ketoacidosis because the subcutaneous insulin depot is smaller than with conventional insulin injection regimens and because of the possibility of technical problems such as pump breakdown and cannula detachment. Deliberate cessation of pump therapy under hospital conditions causes a rapid rise in blood ketone levels [21], and the infected, exercising or otherwise stressed patient may be particularly susceptible to insulin deficiency. At experienced centres, however, the actual frequency of ketoacidosis is no greater than in matched groups of IDDM subjects treated by conventional injection therapy

[31]. Several centres have reported that keto-acidosis is relatively common during CSII [10, 25, 32], but these high rates may have been partly increased by remediable factors (see Table 42.3) including cannula occlusion occurring with certain unbuffered insulin formulations [26, 27], leaking of infusion sets [25] and inexperience of both patients and doctors during the early months of setting up a CSII programme. Fig. 42.9 shows the decrease in the frequency of ketoacidosis on CSII at our own centre as experience was gained with the technique.

Hypoglycaemic coma is not increased and indeed is probably less frequent during CSII than during conventional injection treatment [31]. This is, at first sight, in conflict with the suggestion that improved metabolic control by methods such as CSII reduces the threshold for the release of adrenaline during hypoglycaemia and diminishes the awareness of hypoglycaemia [33, 34]. Other studies, however, found no changes in the frequency of biochemical hypoglycaemia, or alterations in the symptoms of the counter-regulatory hormone response to hypoglycaemia during CSII as compared with injection treatment [35]. An explanation for this discrepancy may be that awareness of hypoglycaemia is determined by the frequency of hypoglycaemic events rather than the average glycaemic level [36]; correct selection of infusion rates may therefore be important.

Other potential complications of CSII

Contrary to early reports, there is no evidence for the development of reactive systemic amyloidosis during CSII: no significant differences in the serum levels of the acute phase proteins, serum amyloid-A or C-reactive protein, can be found between patients receiving injection therapy or CSII [37].

Like multiple-injection therapy, CSII slightly increases circulating levels of anti-insulin anti-bodies [38] but this does not seem to be a hindrance to achieving strict control.

Pumps versus multiple insulin injection regimens

Various studies show that the level of control achievable by CSII is broadly comparable with that of modern intensified multiple insulin injection regimens such as once-daily ultralente plus short-acting insulin given before meals [15], or with prandial short-acting insulin given by a pen device [39] (see Chapter 39). In some cases, however, CSII may confer some glycaemic advantages [40, 41] and good control may be

Table 42.3. Factors likely to increase the frequency of diabetic ketoacidosis during CSII.

- Patient and doctor inexperience (first few months after starting CSII)
- Insulin formulation (cannula blockage)
- Pump breakdown
- Cannula dislodgement
- Infusion site infection
- Reduced or inadequate education programme (perhaps outpatient initiation of CSII)
- Poor access to hospital and advice, e.g. patient lives far away
- Wrong technique (e.g. choice of infusion rates, failure to test for urinary ketones)
- Brittle diabetes (see Chapter 88)
- Patient does not meet prerequisites of motivation, compliance, ability to perform blood glucose self-monitoring and knowledge of CSII

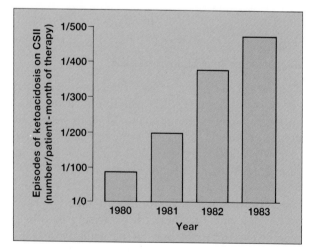

Fig. 42.9. The decreasing frequency of ketoacidosis in IDDM subjects treated by CSII at Guy's Hospital 1980–83. (Data from Bending *et al.* 1985 [31] with permission from *The American Journal of Medicine*.)

Table 42.4. When to consider CSII.

- When optimized conventional insulin injection treatment has failed (e.g. in some hypoglycaemia-prone diabetic subjects)
- When the centre has special expertise and experience of CSII
- When the patient prefers CSII (e.g. dislikes multiple injections)
- When the patient has an erratic lifestyle (more flexibility to omit or delay mealtimes)

achieved more quickly with a pump. CSII should, therefore, be regarded as an alternative, optimized form of insulin therapy. The decision to use CSII for a particular patient will depend on the skill and experience of the physician with this method, the available facilities and resources and the patient's own preference. Some specific indications for CSII are given in Table 42.4.

CSII and microvascular disease

The *raison d'être* for CSII was as an experimental tool for testing the hypothesis that long periods of strict metabolic control will retard the progression of diabetic microvascular disease [5]. Several controlled trials using CSII have been conducted and to date have reported results over periods of 6 months to approximately 3.5 years, all in relatively few patients. The Diabetes Control and Complications Trial (DCCT), comparing CSII with multiple insulin injection regimens as the means of achieving good control, is currently in progress in North America [42].

The detailed results of these and other trials relating CSII to the development of diabetic microangiopathy are described elsewhere (see Section 13) but their conclusions can be summarized as follows.

Retinopathy

In patients with *background* retinopathy, there is, unexpectedly, a transient deterioration in the retinopathy during the first 3−12 months of CSII therapy [10−12], with the appearance of cotton-wool spots and intra-retinal microvascular abnormalities, and increased numbers of micro-aneurysms and haemorrhages. This deterioration is not sustained and during the second year of CSII, the 'mean retinopathy level' improves so that retinopathy then becomes indistinguishable between the CSII and injection-treated groups [43] (see Fig. 42.10). In one study with 41 months of follow-up [44], there was no evidence that the progression of background retinopathy from baseline differed during CSII as compared with conventional injection treatment; studies with larger numbers of patients are awaited.

There is no consistent evidence that *proliferative* or *pre-proliferative* retinopathy is retarded by a period of good control [45] and these lesions may even be worsened by a sudden return to near-normoglycaemia [46].

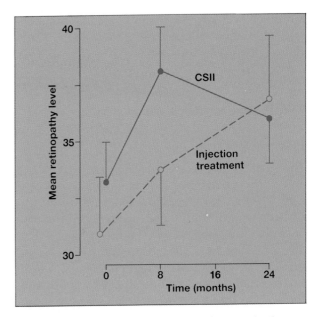

Fig. 42.10. Mean retinopathy level in patients randomly assigned to CSII or continued conventional injection therapy. (Data from Kroc Collaborative Study 1988 [43] with permission from the publishers and The American Medical Association.)

Diabetic nephropathy

In at least some patients, only a few days of CSII-induced strict control can reduce *microalbuminuria* [47], the subclinical proteinuria which predicts the later development of severe nephropathy [48] (Chapters 53, 64 and 65). During several months of CSII, there is a progressive decline in urinary albumin excretion rates which is not seen during injection treatment [10]. A 4-year study of CSII also showed lower urinary albumin levels than at baseline in CSII-treated patients but not during conventional therapy [49], and fewer patients may progress to clinical proteinuria during CSII as compared with injection treatment [50].

In patients with *established diabetic nephropathy* and clinical proteinuria, however, CSII fails to influence either the rate of decline of GFR or the increase in plasma creatinine levels [51].

Diabetic neuropathy

Nerve conduction velocities, especially in motor rather than sensory nerves, are improved by a period of CSII [52], and uncontrolled studies have shown symptomatic relief of painful diabetic neuropathy during CSII treatment [53, 54]. Information on autonomic neuropathy is much less evident, particularly for the major clinical problems of impotence, diarrhoea and postural hypotension, although some preliminary data suggest subclinical improvements in cardiovascular reflexes during CSII [55].

CSII in special groups of patients

Pregnancy

The need for impeccable glycaemic control before and during pregnancy is now generally accepted (see Chapter 83). In highly-motivated pregnant diabetic women [56], there seems to be no difference in the quality of control achievable in any trimester by CSII as opposed to intensified injection therapy. Not enough patients have been investigated to assess the relative effects of pump therapy on the outcome of pregnancy but small-scale studies have found no evidence of differences in gestational age at delivery, mode of delivery, birth weight, congenital anomalies or the occurrence of neonatal hypoglycaemia compared with intensified injection treatment.

There is thus no special advantage to using CSII in pregnancy, although occasional patients who fail to achieve adequate control with injections may benefit from a trial of pump therapy. The increased risk of developing ketoacidosis during CSII should, of course, be borne in mind. A case of intra-uterine death during CSII has been recorded, probably due to accidental cessation of the infusion [57].

CSII in children and adolescents

The success of CSII in teenagers is variable. In motivated and intensively supervised patients, the results are comparable with treatment in adults (58), but for less highly selected subjects in a routine clinical setting, the level of control on CSII is often not good [59–61] and the discontinuation rate is high (30–80%). The cosmetic appearance of the pump, the demands of therapy (e.g. frequent blood glucose monitoring) and certain restrictions on vigorous exercise are, for many adolescents, important impediments.

In young children, the acceptance of CSII is much greater, perhaps because parental influence is stronger [62].

Conclusions

CSII has an established place as a routine treatment for a relatively small number of selected patients and is currently limited by its cost and the need for a high level of commitment by the diabetes care team, who must be fully trained in the technique and able to provide an immediately available, constant advisory service. The importance of CSII lies more in its use as a research procedure and the quest for new standards in glucose, metabolite and hormone control in diabetes.

JOHN C. PICKUP

References

1 Slama G, Hautecouverture M, Assan R, Tchobroutsky G. One to five days of continuous intravenous insulin infusion in seven diabetic patients. *Diabetes* 1974; **23**: 732–8.
2 Deckert T, Lorup B. Regulation of brittle diabetes by a preplanned infusion programme. *Diabetologia* 1976; **12**: 573–9.
3 Hepp KD, Renner R, Funcke HJ, Mehnert H, Haerten R, Kresse H. Glucose homeostasis under continuous intravenous insulin therapy in diabetics. *Horm Metab Res* 1977; Suppl. **7**. 72–6.
4 Irsigler K, Kritz H. Long-term continuous intravenous insulin therapy with a portable insulin dosage regulating apparatus. *Diabetes* 1979; **28**: 196–203.
5 Pickup JC, Keen H, Parsons JA, Alberti KGMM. Continuous subcutaneous insulin infusion: an approach to achieving normoglycaemia. *Br Med J* 1978; **1**: 204–7.
6 Pickup JC, Keen H, Parsons JA, Alberti KGMM, Rowe AS. Continuous subcutaneous insulin infusion: improved blood glucose and intermediary metabolite control in diabetes. *Lancet* 1979; i: 1255–8.
7 American Diabetes Association. Policy statement: continuous subcutaneous insulin infusion. *Diabetes* 1985; **34**: 946–7.
8 Pickup JC. Continuous subcutaneous insulin infusion as a treatment option: a perspective after seven years of research applications. *Diabetic Med* 1984; **1**: 27–32.
9 Skyler JS, Seigler DE, Reeves ML. Optimizing pumped insulin delivery. *Diabetes Care* 1982; **5**: 135–47.
10 Kroc Collaborative Study Group. Blood glucose control and the evolution of diabetic retinopathy and albuminuria. *N Engl J Med* 1984; **311**: 365–72.
11 Lauritzen T, Frost-Larsen K, Larsen HW, Deckert T. Effect of 1 year of near-normal blood glucose levels on retinopathy in insulin-dependent diabetes. *Lancet* 1983; i: 200–4.
12 Dahl-Jørgensen K, Brinchman-Hansen O, Hanssen KF et al. Effect of near normoglycaemia for two years on progression of early diabetic retinopathy, nephropathy, and neuropathy: the Oslo study. *Br Med J* 1986; **293**: 1195–9.
13 Tamborlane WV, Sherwin RS, Genel M, Felig P. Restoration of normal lipid and amino acid metabolism in diabetic patients treated with a portable insulin-infusion pump. *Lancet* 1979; i: 1258–61.
14 Dunn FL, Pictri A, Raskin P. Plasma lipid and lipoprotein levels with continuous subcutaneous insulin infusion in type 1 diabetes mellitus. *Ann Int Med* 1981; **95**: 426–31.
15 Rizza RA, Gerich JE, Haymond MW, Westland RE, Hall LD, Clemens AH, Service FJ. Control of blood sugar in insulin-dependent diabetes: comparison of an artificial

endocrine pancreas, continuous subcutaneous insulin infusion, and intensified conventional insulin therapy. *N Engl J Med* 1980; **303**: 1313–18.

16 Pickup JC, Collins ACG, Walker JD, Viberti GC, Pasic J. Patterns of hyperinsulinaemia in insulin-dependent diabetes with and without nephropathy. *Diabetic Med* 1989; **6**: 685–91.

17 Stout RW. Insulin and atheroma — an update. *Lancet* 1987; i: 1077–8.

18 Levy-Marchal C, Albisser AM, Zinman B. Overnight metabolic control with intermittent versus continuous subcutaneous insulin infusion therapy. *Diabetes Care* 1983; **6**: 356–60.

19 Kraegen EW, Chisholm DJ. Pharmacokinetics of insulin: implications for continuous subcutaneous insulin infusion therapy. *Clin Pharmacokinetics* 1985; **10**: 303–14.

20 Hildebrandt P, Birch K. Basal rate subcutaneous insulin infusion: absorption kinetics and relation to local blood flow. *Diabetic Med* 1988; **5**: 434–40.

21 Pickup JC, Viberti GC, Bilous RW *et al*. Safety of continuous subcutaneous insulin infusion: metabolic deterioration and glycaemic autoregulation after deliberate cessation of infusion. *Diabetologia* 1982; **22**: 175–9.

22 Home PD, Pickup JC, Keen H, Alberti KGMM, Parsons JA, Binder C. Continuous subcutaneous insulin infusion: comparison of plasma insulin profiles after infusion or bolus injection of the mealtime dose. *Metabolism* 1981; **30**: 439–42.

23 Mecklenburg RS, Guinn TS, Sannar CA, Blumenstein BA. Malfunction of continuous subcutaneous insulin infusion systems: a one-year prospective study of 127 patients. *Diabetes Care* 1986; **9**: 351–5.

24 Pickup JC, Sherwin RS, Tamborlane WV *et al*. The pump life: patient responses and clinical and technological problems. *Diabetes* 1985; **34** (suppl 3): 37–41.

25 Mecklenburg RS, Benson EA, Benson JW *et al*. Acute complications associated with insulin infusion pump therapy. Report of experience with 161 patients. *J Am Med Assoc* 1984; **252**: 3265–9.

26 Mecklenburg RS, Guinn TS. Complications of insulin pump therapy: the effect of insulin preparation. *Diabetes Care* 1985; **8**: 367–70.

27 Eichner HL, Selam J-L, Woertz LL, Cornblath M, Charles MA. Improved metabolic control of diabetes with reduction of occlusions during continuous subcutaneous insulin infusion. *Diabetic Nutr Metab* 1988; **1**: 283–7.

28 Chantelau E, Lange G, Sonnenberg GE, Berger M. Acute cutaneous complications and catheter needle colonization during insulin-pump treatment. *Diabetes Care* 1987; **10**: 478–82.

29 Van Faassen I, Razenberg PPA, Simoons-Smit AM, van der Veen EA. Carriage of *Staphylococcus aureus* and inflamed infusion sites with insulin pump therapy. *Diabetes Care* 1989; **12**: 153–5.

30 Chantelau E, Lange G, Gasthaus M, Boxberger M, Berger M. Interaction between plastic catheter tubings and regular insulin preparations used for continuous insulin infusion therapy. *Diabetes Care* 1987; **10**: 348–51.

31 Bending JJ, Pickup JC, Keen H. Frequency of diabetic keto-acidosis and hypoglycemic coma during treatment with continuous subcutaneous insulin infusion *Am J Med* 1985; **79**: 685–91.

32 Knight G, Jennings AM, Boulton AJM, Tomlinson S, Ward JD. Severe hyperglycaemia and ketoacidosis during routine treatment with an insulin pump. *Br Med J* 1985; **91**: 371–2.

33 Amiel SA, Sherwin RS, Simonson DC, Tamborlane WV.

Effect of intensive insulin therapy on glycemic thresholds for counterregulatory hormone release. *Diabetes* 1988; **37**: 901–7.

34 Lager I, Attvall S, Blöhme G, Smith U. Altered recognition of hypoglycaemic symptoms in type 1 diabetes during intensified control with continuous subcutaneous insulin infusion. *Diabetic Med* 1986; **3**: 322–5.

35 Ng Tang Fui S, Pickup JC, Bending JJ, Collins ACG, Keen H, Dalton N. Hypoglycemia and counterregulation in insulin-dependent diabetic patients: a comparison of continuous subcutaneous insulin infusion and conventional insulin injection therapy. *Diabetes Care* 1986; **9**: 221–7.

36 Gulan M, Perlman K, Sole M, Albisser AM, Zinman B. Counterregulatory hormone reponses preserved after long-term intravenous insulin infusion compared to continuous subcutaneous insulin infusion. *Diabetes* 1988; **37**: 526–31.

37 Bending JJ, Pickup JC, Rowe IF, Gallimore R, Tennent G, Keen H, Pepys M. Continuous subcutaneous insulin infusion does not induce a significant acute phase response of serum amyloid A protein. *Diabetologia* 1985; **28**: 113–15.

38 Dahl-Jørgensen K, Torjesen P, Hanssen KF, Sandvik L, Aagenaes O. Increase in insulin antibodies during continuous subcutaneous insulin infusion and multiple-injection therapy in contrast to conventional treatment. *Diabetes* 1987; **36**: 1–5.

39 Saurbrey N, Arnold-Larsen S, Moller-Jensen B, Kühl C. Comparison of continuous subcutaneous insulin infusion with multiple insulin injections using the NovoPen. *Diabetic Med* 1988; **5**: 150–3.

40 Nathan D, Lou P, Avruch J. Intensive conventional and insulin pump therapies in adult type 1 diabetes. A crossover study. *Ann Int Med* 1982; **97**: 31–6.

41 Home PD, Capaldo B, Burrin JM, Worth R, Alberti KGMM. A comparison of continuous subcutaneous insulin infusion (CSII) against multiple insulin injections in insulin-dependent diabetes subjects: improved control with CSII. *Diabetes Care* 1982; **5**: 466–71.

42 DCCT Research Group. Diabetes control and complications trial (DCCT): results of feasibility study. *Diabetes Care* 1987; **10**: 1–19.

43 Kroc Collaborative Study Group. Diabetic retinopathy after two years of intensified insulin treatment. Follow-up of the Kroc Collaborative Study. *J Am Med Assoc* 1988; **260**: 37–41.

44 Brinchman-Hansen O, Dahl-Jørgensen K, Hanssen KF, Sandvik L. The response of diabetic retinopathy to 41 months of multiple insulin injections, insulin pumps, and conventional insulin therapy. *Arch Ophthalmol* 1988; **106**: 1242–6.

45 Lawson PM, Champion MC, Canny C, Kingsley R, White MC, Dupre J, Kohner EM. Continuous subcutaneous insulin infusion (CSII) does not prevent progression of proliferative and preproliferative retinopathy. *Br J Ophthalmol* 1982; **66**: 762–6.

46 Van Ballegooie E, Hooymans JMM, Timmerman Z *et al*. Rapid deterioration of diabetic retinopathy during treatment with continuous subcutaneous insulin infusion. *Diabetes Care* 1984; **7**: 236–42.

47 Viberti GC, Pickup JC, Jarrett RJ, Keen H. Effect of control of blood glucose on urinary excretion of albumin and β2-microglobulin in insulin-dependent diabetes. *N Engl J Med* 1979; **300**: 638–41.

48 Viberti GC, Hill RD, Jarrett RJ, Argyropoulos A, Mahmud U, Keen H. Microalbuminuria as a predictor of clinical nephropathy in insulin-dependent diabetes mellitus. *Lancet* 1982; i: 1430–2.

49 Dahl-Jørgensen K, Hanssen KF, Kierulf P, Bioro T, Sandvik L, Aagenaes O. Reduction of urinary albumin excretion after 4 years of continuous subcutaneous insulin infusion in insulin-dependent diabetes mellitus. *Acta Endocrinol* 1988; **117**: 19–25.

50 Feldt-Rasmussen B, Mathiesen ER, Deckert T. Effect of two years of strict metabolic control on progression of incipient nephropathy in insulin-dependent diabetes. *Lancet* 1986; ii: 1300–4.

51 Viberti GC, Bilous RW, Mackintosh D, Bending JJ, Keen H. Long term correction of hypoglycaemia and progression of renal failure in insulin dependent diabetes. *Br Med J* 1983; **286**: 598–602.

52 Pietri A, Ehle AL, Raskin P. Changes in nerve conduction velocity after 6 weeks of glucoregulation with portable insulin infusion pump. *Diabetes* 1980; **29**: 668–71.

53 Boulton AJM, Drury J, Clarke B, Ward JD. Continuous subcutaneous insulin infusion in the management of diabetic neuropathy. *Diabetes Care* 1982; **5**: 386–90.

54 Bertelsmann FW, Heimans JJ, Van Rooy JCGM, Dankmeijer HF, Visser SL, Van der Veen EA. Peripheral nerve function in patients with painful diabetic neuropathy treated with continuous subcutaneous insulin infusion. *J Neurol Neurosurg Psychiatr* 1987; **50**: 1337–41.

55 Sachse G, Nenzner J, Federlin K. Long-term effect of continuous subcutaneous insulin infusion therapy on autonomic diabetic neuropathy of the cardiovascular system. *Diabetologia* 1983; **25**: 191–6.

56 Coustan DR, Reece A, Sherwin RS *et al*. A randomised clinical trial of the insulin pump vs intensive conventional therapy in diabetic pregnancies. *J Am Med Assoc* 1986; **255**: 631–6.

57 Steel JM, West CP. Intrauterine death during continuous subcutaneous infusion of insulin. *Br Med J* 1985; **290**: 1787.

58 Schiffrin AD, Desrosiers M, Aleyassine H *et al*. Intensified insulin therapy in type 1 diabetic adolescents: a controlled trial. *Diabetes Care* 1984; **7**: 107–19.

59 Greene SA, Smith MA, Baum JD. Clinical application of insulin pumps in the management of insulin dependent diabetes. *Arch Dis Child* 1983; **58**: 578–81.

60 Brink SJ, Stewart C. Insulin pump treatment in insulin-dependent diabetes mellitus. Children, adolescents and young adults. *J Am Med Assoc* 1986; **255**: 617–21.

61 Knight G, Boulton AJM, Ward JD. Experience of continuous subcutaneous insulin infusion in the outpatient management of diabetic teenagers. *Diabetic Med* 1986; **3**: 82–4.

62 De Beaufort CE, Bruining GJ. Continuous subcutaneous insulin infusion in children. *Diabetic Med* 1987; **4**: 103–8.

43 The Artificial Pancreas and Related Devices

Summary

• The 'artificial endocrine pancreas' is a closed-loop insulin delivery system where blood is withdrawn from the patient, glucose measured and insulin or dextrose infused according to computer algorithms so as to maintain normoglycaemia.

• Its use is presently limited to a few days at a time by reason of size, complexity and the use of peripheral veins for sampling and delivery.

• Glycaemic control with open-loop insulin delivery systems, such as CSII and conventional insulin injection regimens, can be optimized by blood glucose self-monitoring and insulin dosage adjustments (i.e. the patient 'closing the loop').

• Microcomputers are one approach to enable patients to adjust insulin doses more easily. Such computers can be programmed with information such as the individual's current insulin dosage, maximum insulin to be given and glycaemic targets, and subsequent self-monitored blood glucose values can be entered into the computer and dosage advice given based on preset algorithms.

The 'artificial endocrine pancreas' (AEP) was man's first attempt at imitating the function of an endocrine gland using automatic techniques. It involved an engineering approach known as 'closed-loop' or 'feedback-controlled' because blood glucose measurements are used to increase or decrease insulin delivery so as to maintain normoglycaemia. Open-loop systems such as continuous subcutaneous insulin infusion (CSII), where there is no glucose sensing or automatic feedback control, are described in Chapter 42.

Diabetes control: the closed-loop approach

A bench-top artificial pancreas was described by Kadish as long ago as 1964 [1] and consisted of an autoanalyser to measure blood glucose and simple servo-mechanisms to control insulin- and glucose-delivering pumps. Ten years later [2, 3] two groups reported a more sophisticated type of device which became the basis for a commercially available AEP, the Biostator®. Fig. 43.1 shows the principle of operation of the machine described by Albisser's group at Toronto. Venous blood is withdrawn continuously from a peripheral vein in the patient using the inner lumen of a dual-lumen catheter. A glucose analyser is used to measure blood glucose concentrations averaged over 1 min and a computer calculates the rates of dextrose, or insulin infusion, needed to be given intravenously according to preset algorithms which take account of both actual blood glucose levels and their rate of change. Fig. 43.2 shows the Biostator in use.

The AEP has mostly been used as a short-term research tool, mainly because it is a fairly large, complex and expensive piece of apparatus, blood is gradually withdrawn from the patient and access to the intravenous compartment risks thrombosis and infection. Nevertheless, normoglycaemia is quickly attained, maintained or restored following a wide variety of challenges in the IDDM subject, including caloric intake, stress and physical exercise [4—9]. Research studies have included the effect of glycaemic normalization on hormones and intermediary metabolites other than glucose [10—12] and the assessment of the potency of insulin preparations, using the AEP to clamp the blood glucose concentration and the amount of insulin infused as a measure of the biological action of the preparation [13]. Therapeutic applications include the management of diabetes

427

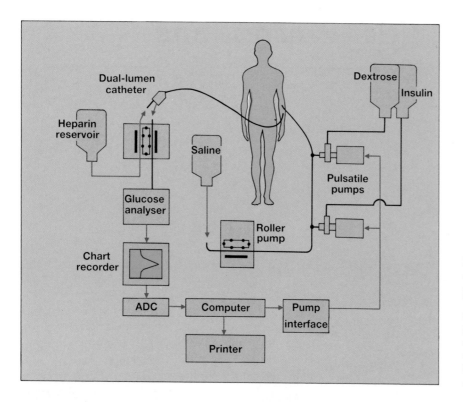

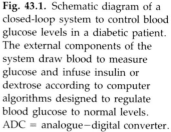

Fig. 43.1. Schematic diagram of a closed-loop system to control blood glucose levels in a diabetic patient. The external components of the system draw blood to measure glucose and infuse insulin or dextrose according to computer algorithms designed to regulate blood glucose to normal levels. ADC = analogue−digital converter.

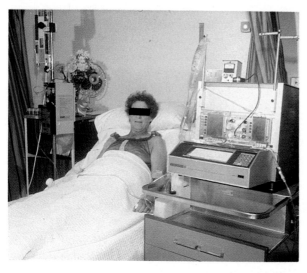

Fig. 43.2. The Biostator®, a commercial version of the artificial endocrine pancreas.

during surgery [14], childbirth [15] and ketoacidosis [16].

Clearly, the ultimate technological development of the AEP would be to miniaturize and implant it. The difficulties in doing this chiefly relate to instability of glucose sensors, a problem discussed in Chapter 105. Progress with open-loop implantable insulin pumps is described in Chapter 44.

Diabetes control with and without computers

Several groups [17, 18] have recognized the technological limitations to achieving a closed-loop system and sought to exploit the demonstrated beneficial effects of a constant background or basal insulin rate by continuous *subcutaneous* insulin infusion and to handle the detailed insulin requirements for caloric intake with pre-meal boluses simply added to the basal rate (Chapter 42). As a guide to achieving such open-loop control, dosage adjustment is coupled to frequent capillary blood glucose self-monitoring [19] (up to nine times per day). As expected, major improvements in glucose control occur compared with conventional therapy. It is not so much the frequency of blood glucose measurements but the judicious use of this information to alter insulin delivery that contributes to the success of the open-loop method [20−22].

In the past, clinical practice has generally been to fix insulin dosages at set times and to adjust the daily schedule and meals around these. The tendency now is for insulin dosages to be variable and adjusted at each injection time to meet the lifestyle requirements of the individual. In addition, only minor adjustments ('fine tuning') of the composition and timing of meals and snacks should be made and then only if necessary. This approach requires much better understanding of

Fig. 43.3. This hand-held computer is used by the patient, and removes the guesswork from insulin dosage determination.

the principles of glycaemic control by the patient, but will free him from a rigid timetable. The major difficulty in such an approach is the high level of expertise demanded of the patient in order to optimize control.

Several strategies have been suggested to enable IDDM patients on a large scale to adjust their insulin dosages in a rational manner. One is to educate the patient intensively [23] and to provide 'algorithms' (mathematical flow-charts) [22, 24−8] to determine insulin dosage in terms of factors such as current blood glucose value, size of an impending meal and exercise about to be undertaken. Algorithms are derived from clinical studies on the time-course of insulin action and can also take account of the individual's previous patterns of glycaemic behaviour under similar circumstances. However, this approach demands mathematical skill as well as a considerable investment of time (by both diabetic care team and patient) if it is to be successful. It is not, therefore, widely applicable.

Another approach is for the patient to calculate dosage adjustments with a 'user-friendly' microcomputer, which has two functions. The first is to store data, namely previous blood glucose results and corresponding insulin dosages and the timing of these; records can be held for up to several days. The second is to calculate dosage changes on the basis of the variables described above and using the stored records and algorithms incorporated within the microprocessor [29−32]. The devices are about the size of a pocket calculator (Fig. 43.3) and many patients find them easy to use. Information such as the patient's current insulin dosage, maximum insulin to be given and glycaemic targets are programmed into the device. Self-monitored blood glucose values are entered a number of times a day and a recommended insulin dosage displayed according to the present algorithms. Some microprocessors can receive data on urine testing, and achieve equivalent results [30] using algorithms uniquely designed for this purpose.

A. MICHAEL ALBISSER

References

1 Kadish A. Automation control of blood sugar. A servo mechanism for glucose monitoring and control. *Am J Med Electron* 1964; **3**: 82−6.
2 Albisser AM, Leibel BS, Ewart TG, Davidovac Z, Botz CK, Zingg W. An artificial endocrine pancreas. *Diabetes* 1974; **23**: 389−96.
3 Pfeiffer EF, Thum CH, Clemens AH. The artificial beta cell — continuous control of blood sugar by external regulation of insulin infusion (glucose controlled insulin infusion system). *Horm Metab Res* 1974; **487**: 339−42.
4 Albisser AM, Leibel BS, Ewart TG *et al.* Clinical control of diabetes by the artificial pancreas. *Diabetes* 1974; **23**: 397−404.
5 Kraegen EW, Campbell LV, Chia YO, Meler H, Lazarus L. Control of blood glucose in diabetics using an artificial pancreas. *Aust NZ J Med* 1977; **7**: 280−6.
6 Mirouze J, Selam J-L, Pham T-C. Le pancréas artificiel extra-corporel. Applications en clinique et en recherche diabétologique. *Nouv Presse Méd* 1977; **6**: 1837−41.
7 Slama G, Klein J-C, Tardieu M-C, Tchobroutsky G. Normalisation de la glycémie par pancréas artificiel non-miniaturisé. *Nouv Presse Méd* 1977; **6**: 2309−13.
8 Fischer U, Jutzi E, Freyse E-J, Salzsieder E. Derivation and experimental proof of a new algorithm for the artificial B-cell based on the individual analysis of the physiological insulin−glucose relationship. *Endokrinologie* 1978; **71**: 65−75.
9 Albisser AM. The artificial pancreas: Open- and closed-loop systems for the management of diabetes mellitus. In: Isselbacher KJ, Adams RD, Braunwald E, Martin JB, Petersdort RG, Wilson JS, eds. *Updates I. Harrison's Principles of Internal Medicine*, 9th edn. New York: McGraw-Hill, 1981: 43−56.
10 Horwitz DL, Gonen B, Jaspan JB, Langer BG, Rodman D, Seidler A. An artificial beta cell for control of diabetes

Subcutaneous injection ports

These devices are simply modified needles or cannulae, implanted subcutaneously for some days, through which insulin is injected intermittently. The rationale is to make multiple insulin injections more acceptable, or to help patients with needle phobia or shyness. The first ports were standard 'butterfly' needles or plastic cannulae, fitted with a self-sealing access stopper. Purpose-designed injection ports, which have recently become available, are small and have a minimal dead space.

Experience with injection ports is limited, but the metabolic control obtained seems satisfactory, despite the theoretical problems of variable mixing and 'hangover' when different insulin preparations are injected through devices with significant dead space. Ports with softer injection chambers and flexible plastic (PTFE) cannulae, rather than hard plastic or metal needles, appear to be more acceptable to the patient [3].

Experience with continuous subcutaneous insulin infusion (CSII) catheters suggests that significant scarring might occur in some patients if implanted ports are left in place for more than 3–5 days and that there is a risk of insulin precipitation and blocking after 7–10 days (Chapter 45). Injection-site infections may also be a hazard in certain susceptible individuals.

Pen injectors (see Chapter 39)

Invention of the pen injector is credited to Dr John Ireland, whose first commercial model (Penject) carried the barrel of a standard disposable insulin syringe within a casing which delivered a dose on pressing a button [4]. Subsequent devices using special insulin cartridges have been smaller, and some are now truly pocket-sized (see Fig. 46.2). The simple 'second-generation' pen injector (containing an insulin cartridge, but with no variable metering function) has proved very popular and fairly robust. The production of 'third-generation' devices capable of injecting variable dosages has been delayed by the difficulties in engineering an inexpensive metering mechanism capable of delivering precise dosages at unit intervals over a wide range. These more sophisticated devices are less easy to use and their acceptability will take some years to evaluate. The precision and accuracy of all these instru-

Fig. 46.2. The original Penject (left) incorporating parts of a standard insulin syringe, compared with a second-generation pen injector without variable dose delivery function (NovoPen I, centre), and a third-generation device with dose delivery function (NovoPen II, right).

ments are very good, particularly when compared with the use of syringes [5].

Initially, only short-acting insulin was used in pen injectors, mainly because long-acting, complexed insulin preparations (especially crystalline zinc-insulin) were difficult to keep in suspension, causing concern over the precision of the dosages administered. Clinical trials have, however, demonstrated that isophane (NPH) insulin preparations in pen-injector cartridges can easily be resuspended by patients and maintain a stable concentration for prolonged periods [6].

Disposable insulin injection pens may offer a further advance in portability and convenience, provided that sufficiently precise metering mechanisms can be manufactured at little extra cost.

Implantable insulin pellets

Implanted pelleted insulin preparations are designed to release insulin steadily over a period of days or longer. In principle, these could be placed in any tissue, although in practice only subcutaneous tissue is suitable for repeated implantation. Langer and colleagues incorporated powdered sodium insulin into polymerized ethylene-vinyl acetate and were able to obtain controlled insulin release, dependent on the geometry of the pellet [7], capable of achieving good blood glucose control in diabetic rats.

Theoretically, a 12-month supply of basal insulin requirement for a diabetic patient could be contained in a pellet of volume 0.3 ml. Residual polymer could be removed, or could be slowly biodegradable; one pellet matrix material under investigation is compressed cholesterol, which is cleared from the implantation site. Although the delivery rate could not be changed after implantation, a fixed rate might be adequate in many stable insulin-treated patients. It remains to be seen whether insulin absorption from the rather fatty subcutaneous tissue of man would be excessively variable.

Alternative routes of insulin delivery

Physiological insulin delivery is a continuously regulated process which responds in a matter of seconds to changes in substrate concentration. There is some evidence that insulin secretion is synchronized in pulses lasting around 3 min in every 14, but the regulation and significance of this process are not clear [8]. After its secretion by the pancreas, insulin passes first to the portal vein and thus to the liver, where around two-thirds is extracted in the basal state (around one-half at higher secretion rates). Owing to the efficiency of hepatic extraction and the short plasma half-life of insulin, the hormone shows a marked concentration gradient between portal and peripheral veins.

By contrast, all routes of therapeutic insulin delivery lead into peripheral veins, with the exception of a proportion of intraperitoneally infused insulin (see below). In the basal state, peripheral insulin concentrations in insulin-treated diabetic patients are at least twice those in normal subjects, although this may not be due solely to the route of insulin delivery. The biochemical consequences of peripheral insulin delivery have proved difficult to disentangle from those of diabetes itself, as it is currently impossible to maintain normoglycaemia for more than about 24 h. Although it has been suggested that peripheral hyperinsulinaemia may cause atherosclerosis and other forms of tissue damage, the available evidence is purely associative [9]. Moreover, animal experiments using transplanted islets suggest that any differences between portal and peripheral insulin administration are unimportant [10].

Only with intravenous insulin delivery would it be possible to mimic pulsatile secretion. So far, this has only been attempted clinically in very short-term experiments, in which insulin sensitivity may have been somewhat improved [11].

When considering other routes of insulin delivery, their specific pharmacokinetic characteristics must be considered as these may have important clinical consequences. For each route, it is essential to define the shape and duration of the insulin absorption profile, the variability of insulin absorption from that site, and the bioavailability of insulin (i.e. the proportion of insulin delivered to the site which is actually absorbed into the circulation). A summary of alternative routes of insulin delivery is given in Table 46.2.

Intramuscular insulin delivery

Intramuscular insulin delivery has not been intentionally used in clinical practice, except in the treatment of ketoacidosis. However, the frequently recommended perpendicular subcutaneous injection technique using a 12.5-mm needle will deliver insulin into muscle in many men and some women.

It has been recognized for many years that intramuscularly injected insulin is absorbed more rapidly than subcutaneous insulin, presumably because of the higher capillary density in muscle [12] (see Fig. 46.3). Faster absorption of soluble insulin would be of advantage at mealtimes to

Table 46.2. Alternative routes of insulin delivery.

Intravenous	
Peripheral	Limb vein or
Portal	central vein
Subcutaneous and transcutaneous	
Injection	Needle
	Pressure injection
	Sprinkler needle
Infusion	
Transcutaneous	Adjuvant-enhanced iontophoresis
Intramuscular	
Injection	
Intraperitoneal	
Injection	
Infusion	
Transmucosal	
Intranasal	Adjuvant-enhanced
Intrapulmonary	
Intrarectal	Adjuvant-enhanced
Intravaginal	
Buccal	
Intestinal	Adjuvant-enhanced
	Polymer-protected
	Liposome-enhanced

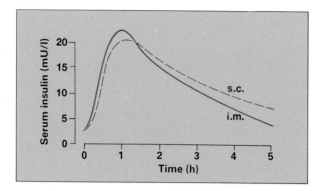

Fig. 46.3. Plasma insulin concentrations after s.c. or i.m. injection of 6 U soluble insulin. Kinetic analysis shows the steady-state tissue depot clearance rate of insulin to be approximately double when the insulin is placed i.m. (After Owens DR *et al. Lancet* 1981; ii: 118–22.)

produce a sharper, more physiological insulin profile. Absorption could perhaps be further accelerated by exercise (which increases effective capillary density) or massage, but unlike subcutaneous absorption (see Chapter 38) these possibilities have not been formally studied. Neither is it clear whether the unpredictable day-to-day differences in subcutaneous insulin absorption [12] occur to the same extent with the intramuscular route.

Intravenous insulin delivery

Intravenous insulin delivery requires access to central veins for all but short-term use. Central venous catheters commonly provoke thrombosis, usually complicated by catheter obstruction rather than embolism. Percutaneous catheters, even if tunnelled subcutaneously, also carry a significant risk of septicaemia. With the rare exception of patients with special problems such as extremely brittle diabetes (see Chapter 88), or those using subcutaneously implanted pumps (see Chapter 44), intravenous insulin delivery is therefore suitable only for short-term clinical use at present.

As with CSII, carefully regulated intravenous insulin infusion under experimental conditions can achieve very good blood glucose control. With its short plasma half-life and the absence of any absorption barrier, plasma insulin concentrations will follow the infusion rate faithfully with a delay of around 20 min, and bioavailability is 100%. Because access is instantaneous, delivery must be tailored to produce suitable mealtime insulin profiles; in practice, a square-wave increase in

infusion rate lasting around 60 min generally provides reasonable blood glucose control. Overnight basal insulin delivery rates may need to be decreased, and then increased by around 25% after 0400 h to overcome the hyperglycaemic tendency of the 'dawn phenomenon' (see Chapter 51).

Intraperitoneal insulin administration

The peritoneum has attracted interest as a possible site of insulin delivery for various reasons:
1 The visceral peritoneal membrane has the same blood supply as the small and large bowel, draining via the portal vein to the liver and therefore following the route of physiological insulin delivery.
2 The large surface area of the peritoneum would be expected to encourage rapid dispersal and absorption of insulin.
3 The peritoneum might be suitable for long-term implantation of an infusion cannula, without the thrombotic risks of intravenous infusion.

Animal studies have confirmed directly that a proportion of intraperitoneally delivered insulin is absorbed into the portal vein, and in man the relatively lower peripheral levels during intraperitoneal insulin delivery suggest prior extraction by the liver [13]. Nevertheless, some insulin is probably absorbed through the parietal peritoneum into the peripheral venous circulation, to an extent which is likely to vary with the position of the catheter tip and with changes in mesenteric blood flow. Insulin delivered above the transverse mesocolon may be absorbed to a greater extent into the portal vein than if given below it, and virtually all insulin administered into the lesser sac might be expected to be absorbed portally.

As discussed previously, it is not clear whether intraportal insulin administration is physiologically superior to peripheral routes. Studies using feedback-controlled insulin delivery failed to find significant metabolic differences at mealtimes with intraportal or intraperitoneal as compared with intravenous insulin delivery in animals [14], although the algorithms developed for intravenous insulin delivery may be inappropriate to the portal route. Other studies in animals have suggested differences in glucoregulation between portal and peripheral administration, but none are conclusive. Moreover, extensive comparisons of insulin delivery from transplanted islets placed either peripherally or intrasplenically (draining portally) in rats have demonstrated no metabolic differences between the two sites [10].

The second potential advantage of peritoneal insulin delivery is the large surface area available for absorption. Insulin should disperse rapidly in the peritoneum and, with concentrations falling below 10^{-6} mol/l, insulin hexamers should dissociate to the more rapidly absorbed dimeric and monomeric forms. Furthermore, the peritoneum is relatively vascular and the diffusion pathway to the capillary lumen should therefore be short. Indeed, human studies suggest that insulin administered intraperitoneally is absorbed faster than that injected subcutaneously or intramuscularly (see Fig. 38.6); the peripheral plasma insulin profile after an intraperitoneal bolus injection rises and falls with a time-course very similar to that of physiological prandial insulin secretion [15]. One consequence of these absorption characteristics is that intraperitoneal insulin has to be given prospectively in a single dose at mealtimes and so would be difficult to control by feedback from a glucose sensor.

Initial difficulties with intraperitoneal precipitation of insulin have largely been overcome with surface-active additives. However, around 25% of cannulae become occluded within the first year after insertion. These difficulties apparently relate to various forms of omental reaction to the cannula itself or to some component of the infusate. Laparoscopy can reveal whether occlusion is due to a local fibrous reaction, a more general omental response, or to material within the cannula lumen, but even if the cannula is resited or shortened, the problem is likely to recur [16]. Novel catheter materials and changes in cannula tip design are now under investigation.

Transmucosal absorption of insulin

Most drugs administered to man are designed for absorption across the intestinal mucosa, a route denied to native insulin because of its relatively large size and its susceptibility to digestion by proteases. Other mucosal surfaces in different parts of the gastrointestinal, respiratory and genital tracts have been investigated as potential routes for insulin absorption.

As early as 1924, Fisher investigated the absorption of insulin from the vagina, and found it to be minimal [17]. This site — in common with the buccal mucosa and skin — is lined by a compound squamous epithelium which constitutes a very effective barrier to the uptake of such a large and fat-insoluble molecule such as insulin. Under certain circumstances, however, it is possible to promote absorption across such epithelia, including the skin, which is particularly impermeable to high- and low-molecular-weight molecules. An electrochemical gradient has been used to drive insulin by iontophoresis from a high-concentration depot across the skin in rabbits [18]. As absorption only occurred when the rabbits' skin (which is relatively thin) had been gently abraded to reduce the transport distance, therapeutic prospects in man seem very poor. Other techniques to enhance transcutaneous absorption (e.g. applying the drug in an oily base under an occlusive dressing) are not usefully applicable to the insulin molecule.

Even a simple columnar epithelium (e.g. in the nose, lungs or rectum) presents a significant barrier to insulin absorption, unless appropriate adjuvants are added to promote the passage of insulin across the mucosa to the capillaries. However, any effective adjuvant inevitably disrupts epithelial integrity to some extent, and concern must be expressed about possible long-term damage due to repeated exposure to the adjuvant itself.

INTRANASAL INSULIN

Intranasal insulin delivery was attempted soon after the hormone became available, and interest in this route has been rekindled recently with the effective administration of smaller peptides and glycopeptides. In order to cross the nasal mucosal barrier in significant amounts, insulin must be mixed with absorption-enhancers, which have included bile acids and their derivatives, polyoxyethylene ethers and fusidic acid; the long-term consequences of chronic administration of any of these agents are unknown.

Insulin delivered to the nasal mucosa with an adjuvant is rapidly but partially absorbed into the circulation, producing an early peak in concentration and a rapid return to basal levels within 1 h [19] (see Fig. 46.4). Unfortunately, large amounts of insulin need to be given to obtain effective plasma insulin concentrations, bioavailability being some 10–30%. Much of the non-absorbed insulin and adjuvant is presumably cleared with normal epithelial secretions (eventually to the gut) by ciliary action, as with any foreign material entering the nose. Bioavailability may be further reduced by local degradation of

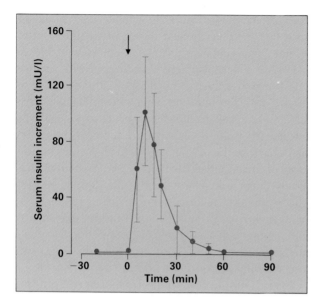

Fig. 46.4. The serum insulin increment (mean ± SD) after intranasal administration of insulin 0.5 U/kg in 1% desoxycholate at time 0, indicated by the arrow. (After Moses AC *et al. Diabetes* 1983; **32**: 1040−7.)

insulin by the peptidases which are present at high activity in many mucosae.

Nasal insulin absorption is erratic, depending on the condition of the nasal mucosa at the time of administration and the exact site of delivery, and its hypoglycaemic effect is correspondingly highly variable. Although the rapidity of intranasal absorption seems suitable for mealtime insulin delivery, the clinical usefulness of this route is severely limited by its variability (including the unknown effects of upper respiratory tract infection) and the potential hazards of adjuvant-induced tissue damage.

INTRAPULMONARY INSULIN

The alveolar membrane is much more permeable to large peptides than the nasal or intestinal mucosae, but is much less accessible. The distance over which nebulized drugs are carried into the respiratory tree depends on the size of the particles and the rate and pattern of inhalation, but with most conventional aerosols, only a small proportion of the drug is deposited beyond the larger bronchioles. The optimal conditions for dispersal of a molecule as large as insulin would probably damage the peptide itself.

Relatively large amounts of nebulized insulin can produce a detectable hypoglycaemic effect in man, with a rapid time-course best suited to

mealtime dosages. Most of the inhaled insulin is probably deposited on bronchial walls and a small percentage is probably absorbed by this route, the rest presumably being cleared or degraded as in the nose. As expected with such poor bioavailability, absorption is highly variable.

INTRARECTAL INSULIN

Despite its poor social acceptability, the rectal mucosa has also been investigated as a potential route of insulin administration. Although many smaller molecules are freely absorbed from the rectum, adjuvants are again essential for significant absorption of insulin to occur. Few studies have been performed in man, but the hypoglycaemic effect of a 100 U insulin suppository (with polyoxyethylene lauryl ether as adjuvant) in normal and diabetic subjects was less than would be found with 10 U of subcutaneously-injected insulin [20]. Variable faecal loading would probably further exaggerate the variability likely to accompany this poor bioavailability. Moreover, the potential problems of adjuvant-induced mucosal damage are as significant as with the other routes.

INTESTINAL INSULIN ABSORPTION

Oral insulin administration has the theoretical advantages of convenience, absorption simultaneously with food and portal delivery to the liver. Unfortunately, the prospects of achieving reliable intestinal absorption appear very remote at present, because of the susceptibility of insulin to digestion by proteases and its very limited capacity for transport intact across the gut mucosa.

Few studies have been reported in man, although attempts have been made to prepare insulin enclosed in protective membranes (e.g. lipoprotein, to form 'liposomes') which might be absorbed across the small or large bowel. Insulin in the form of liposomes might be expected to cross the intestinal mucosa intact into the lymphatics, and ultimately, after some time in the circulation, might be taken up by the liver. However, this aim has not been realized experimentally. In limited animal studies, attempts to coat insulin particles with other agents have been rewarded only with slow and variable colonic absorption.

PHILIP D. HOME

References

1 Taylor R, Home PD, Alberti KGMM. Plasma free insulin profiles after administration of insulin by jet and conventional syringe injection. *Diabetes Care* 1981; **4**: 377−9.

2 Worth R, Anderson J, Taylor R, Alberti KGMM. Jet injection of insulin: comparison with conventional injection by syringe and needle. *Br Med J* 1980; **281**: 713−14.

3 Rayman G, Wise PH. An indwelling subcutaneous FEP canula for intermittent insulin injection: patient experience and effect on diabetic control. *Diabetic Med* 1988; **6**: 592−5.

4 Paton JS, Wilson M, Ireland JT, Reith SBM. Convenient pocket insulin syringe. *Lancet* 1981; i: 189−90.

5 Kesson CM, Baillie GR. Do diabetic patients inject accurate doses of insulin? *Diabetes Care* 1981; **4**: 333.

6 Jørgensen JOL, Flyvbjerg A, Jorgensen JT *et al.* NPH insulin administration by means of a pen injector. *Diabetic Med* 1988; **5**: 574−6.

7 Brown L, Siemer L, Munoz C *et al.* Controlled release of insulin from polymer matrices: control of diabetes in rats. *Diabetes* 1985; **35**: 692−7.

8 Bratusch-Marrain PR, Komjati M, Waldhäusl W. Pulsatile insulin delivery: physiology and clinical implications. *Diabetic Med* 1987; **4**: 197−200.

9 Stout RW. The role of insulin in atherosclerosis in diabetic and non-diabetics. A review. *Diabetes* 1981; **30** (Suppl 2): 54−7.

10 Kruszynska YT, Home PD, Alberti KGMM. Comparison of portal and peripheral insulin delivery on carbohydrate metabolism in streptozotocin diabetic rats. *Diabetologia* 1985; **28**: 167−71.

11 Matthews DR, Naylor BAA, Jones RG, Ward GM, Turner RC. Pulsatile insulin has a greater hypoglycemic effect than continuous delivery. *Diabetes* 1983; **32**: 617−21.

12 Binder C. Absorption of injected insulin: a clinical−pharmacological study. *Acta Pharmacol Toxicol* 1969; **27** (Suppl 2): 1−84.

13 Schade DS, Eaton RP, Davis T *et al.* The kinetics of peritoneal insulin absorption. *Metabolism* 1981; **30**: 149−55.

14 Botz CK, Leibel BS, Zingg W, Gander RE, Albisser AM. Comparison of peripheral and portal routes of insulin infusion by a computer controlled insulin infusion system (artificial endocrine pancreas). *Diabetes* 1976; **25**: 691−700.

15 Jimenez JT, Walford S, Home PD, Alberti KGMM. Free-insulin levels and metabolic effects of meal-time bolus and square-wave intraperitoneal insulin infusion on insulin dependent diabetic patients. *Diabetologia* 1985; **28**: 728−33.

16 Selam J-L. Development of implantable insulin pumps: long is the road. *Diabetic Med* 1988; **5**: 724−33.

17 Fisher NF. The absorption of insulin from the intestine, vagina, and scrotal sac. *Am J Physiol* 1923; **67**: 65−71.

18 Kari B. Control of blood glucose levels in alloxan-diabetic rabbits by iontophoresis of insulin. *Diabetes* 1986; **35**: 217−21.

19 Salzman R, Manson JE, Griffing GT *et al.* Intranasal aerosolized insulin: mixed-meal studies and long-term use in Type 1 diabetes. *N Engl J Med* 1985; **312**: 1078−84.

20 Yamasaki Y, Shichiri M, Kawamori R *et al.* The effectiveness of rectal administration of insulin suppository on normal and diabetic subjects. *Diabetes Care* 1981; **4**: 454−8.

SECTION 11
MANAGEMENT OF
NON-INSULIN-DEPENDENT
DIABETES MELLITUS

47 Dietary Management of Non-Insulin-Dependent Diabetes Mellitus

Summary

• The energy-dense 'Westernized' diet, rich in fats and relatively low in carbohydrate and fibre, is a major cause of obesity and a contributor to NIDDM. Dietary modification, concentrating on fat restriction, to reduce energy intake and body weight should be the starting point and mainstay of long-term treatment of NIDDM.

• Reducing energy intake acutely reduces glycaemia and diabetic symptoms, even before significant weight loss occurs, but achieving full glycaemic and metabolic normalization requires considerable weight loss.

• Weight loss reduces cardiovascular risk factors, lowering blood pressure and the atherogenicity of blood lipid profiles, and extends the life expectancy of NIDDM patients.

• The current energy intake of an individual patient, the necessary energy restriction for slimming and the expected rate of weight loss during a given diet, are all best estimated from standard formulae; overweight patients greatly underestimate their food intake.

• Changing to a high-carbohydrate, high-fibre, low-fat diet sometimes increases body water and weight initially, but will often lead to weight loss even without formal energy restriction. Such diets stimulate energy expenditure, reduce hyperinsulinaemia and the tendency to fat deposition, and improve atherogenic lipaemic profiles.

• Most NIDDM patients cannot comply with slimming diets and fail to reach their ideal weight. Advice must take account of individual dietary preferences, attitudes and lifestyle as well as the degree of overweight. A 'target' weight and the time taken to achieve it should be based on realistic predictions of weight loss.

• Slimming diets should aim for an energy deficit of 500 kcal/day, leading to weight loss of about 0.5 kg/week. Weight loss should not exceed 2–3 kg/week, as this suggests excessive loss of muscle rather than fat.

• Diets containing less than 700 kcal/day (very low calorie diets), even with adequate vitamin and mineral supplements, have not been shown to produce better long-term results than conventional slimming diets and are probably contraindicated in NIDDM because of the uncertain risks of subclinical heart disease.

• Dietary supplementation with soluble fibre can improve glycaemic and lipaemic profiles in NIDDM. Fish oil and vegetable preparations rich in essential fatty acids also improve blood lipids but the former may worsen hyperglycaemia in NIDDM patients.

• Regular exercise taken in conjunction with energy restriction will enhance weight loss in NIDDM patients and maximize loss of fat while preserving muscle. Advice regarding exercise must be appropriate to the patient's lifestyle, physical condition and capability.

• Smoking poses much greater cardiovascular risks than overweight, and should be actively discouraged in all diabetic patients. About one-half of patients who become non-smokers gain some weight initially but generally lose this within a few months under standard dietetic guidance.

The value of reducing food intake in NIDDM patients has long been recognized and dietary measures remain the mainstay for the current management of NIDDM. This chapter will discuss the benefits of weight loss in obese NIDDM patients and suggest rational guidelines for the prescription of diets suitable for NIDDM.

Benefits of reduced energy intake and weight loss in NIDDM

Moderate energy restriction will reduce blood glucose concentrations and so lead to symptomatic improvement within days or weeks in most cases, often before there is any detectable fall in body weight. Diet should therefore always be the first consideration in treating NIDDM. Much more prolonged dietary restriction with considerable weight loss is required to normalize glycaemia completely (e.g. to reduce fasting blood glucose levels to below 6 mmol/l) [1, 2]. However, improving blood glucose concentrations has not been shown to affect the prognosis of NIDDM; long-term dieting cannot, therefore, be justified on this basis alone.

Weight loss carries other long-term benefits for NIDDM patients (Table 47.1), notably by reducing risk factors for macrovascular and particularly ischaemic heart disease, the main causes of death in NIDDM. Weight loss lowers blood pressure, often as effectively as anti-hypertensive drugs and without the risk of side-effects (see Chapter 69), and improves blood lipid concentrations, especially triglycerides and VLDL cholesterol. These specific lipid-lowering actions, which are not shared by oral hypoglycaemic agents, are of particular value in NIDDM, where VLDL cholesterol and triglycerides (rather than LDL cholesterol in the general population) appear to be the main adverse determinants of ischaemic heart disease [3, 4]. HDL cholesterol still has a protective role in NIDDM, and its concentrations can be maintained if regular exercise is taken together with the dietary prescription.

There is now evidence that these theoretical

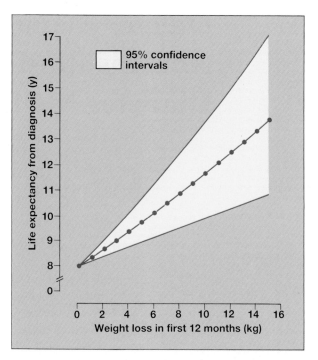

Fig. 47.1. Weight loss in the first year of treatment improves the prognosis of NIDDM. Expected survival time without weight loss would be 8 years from a median age of presentation of 64 years. Each kilogram of weight lost during the first year is associated with 3–4 months prolongation of survival on average. (Reproduced with permission from ref. 6.)

benefits of weight loss in NIDDM are translated into an extended life-span. The average life expectancy of newly diagnosed NIDDM patients is reduced by about 35% compared with the general population [5, 6], but this prognosis can be improved by weight loss. Each kilogram of weight lost during the first year of treatment (under dietetic supervision) is associated on average with 3–4 months' prolonged survival which does not appear to depend on improved glycaemia (Fig. 47.1) [6]. It is therefore justifiable to encourage further weight loss in overweight NIDDM patients even after they have become asymptomatic.

Although weight loss is crucial, other lifestyle factors which affect energy balance or cardiovascular risks must not be neglected. The importance of diet composition, exercise and not smoking is discussed below.

Designing a diet for a patient with NIDDM

The mathematics of energy balance and treatment of overweight

It is usually stated that dietary prescription should

Table 47.1. Benefits of reduced energy intake and weight loss in NIDDM.

Acute energy restriction before detectable weight loss
Marked fall in blood glucose concentrations
Symptomatic improvement

Long-term energy restriction, with significant weight loss
Gradual fall (possibly normalization) of blood glucose
    concentrations
Improved insulin sensitivity
Reduced atherogenicity of blood lipid profiles
Fall in blood pressure
Increased life expectancy

be based on the previous diet and lifestyle of an individual patient, taking into account other factors such as age, sex, occupation, and the presence of hyperlipidaemia, hypertension or other medical conditions. This general principle is sound but it must be recognized that whatever metabolic defect may underlie the development of overweight (Chapter 20), dietary patterns cannot be reliably estimated in the overweight as they consistently record significant underestimates of their food intakes [7]. The daily energy intake of individuals with steady weight is best estimated using standard formulae derived from metabolic rate measurements [8] (Chapter 20). These predictions have low coefficients of variation, which makes them the most accurate and convenient approach for dietary prescription, particularly for use in clinical studies where minor energy imbalance is often a major confounding factor, even when body weight seems constant [9]. For most overweight NIDDM patients, sedentary or light activity can be assumed in these formulae (see Fig. 41.1).

Ideal body weight

'Ideal' body weight is usually defined as that associated with the longest life expectancy and is derived from actuarial tables according to age and sex, prepared by life assurance companies [10, 11]. These ideal weights were derived some decades ago for non-diabetic Americans who obtained life assurance. Actuarial data are not available for diabetic populations, but the standard tables are generally considered an acceptable guide. It can be argued that lower weights might be desirable for diabetic patients, in order to optimize their metabolic state. The standard 'ideal' weights may also be excessive for some Asian immigrant groups. Conversely, sufficient weight loss to abolish symptoms could be considered 'ideal' for very elderly patients.

Target weight

Most obese diabetic patients find it very difficult to lose weight under routine clinic management, perceiving dieting as presenting a greater threat to quality of life than obesity and its often asymptomatic complications. Discussing ideal body weight may be instructive for some patients but is too daunting for others. A short-term 'target' weight, which must not be confused with ideal

weight by patients or health professionals, is a useful form of contract between the patient and doctor or dietitian, over a clearly stated time period. It is critically important for the therapeutic relationship that targets are based on realistic predictions of the rate of weight loss.

Predicting the rate of weight loss

Inappropriate expectations of slimming diets, and disappointment at a slow rate of progress, are perhaps the main reasons for poor dietary compliance in diabetic clinics.

Long-term weight loss is seldom maintained at rates greater than 2 kg per month (1 lb per week). As adipose tissue contains about 7000 kcal/kg, this rate of weight loss is obtained by an energy deficit of about 500 kcal each day, representing a reduction of about 20% in the normal energy intake of overweight patients. It must therefore be understood, and explained clearly to patients, that even with this marked dietary restriction, weight loss will be slow in relation to the total excess weight. Faster rates of weight loss imply disproportionate losses of lean tissue, mostly muscle, which contains less energy and more water per unit weight.

The rate of weight loss for an individual patient following a particular diet can be predicted quite accurately from estimates of energy expenditure for his or her weight, allowing for the suppression of BMR which occurs after prolonged slimming [8, 12, 13] (Table 47.2). For example, the commonly prescribed 1000 kcal reducing diet would lead to an energy deficit of 1000–1500 kcal/day, and thereby to weight loss of 4–6 kg/month. In practice, however, patients rarely comply with such strict energy restriction for more than a few weeks.

Nutrient composition of the diet for NIDDM

Evidence is mounting to incriminate high-fat, relatively low-carbohydrate, low-fibre diets typical of Western societies, in the aetiology of overweight in susceptible individuals (see Chapter 20). Several factors may contribute. First, if overeaten, dietary fat is more efficiently converted to adipose tissue lipid stores than carbohydrate [14]. Second, dietary fat provokes less diet-induced thermogenesis than carbohydrate or protein, so that metabolic rate is relatively suppressed by high-fat diets [15, 16]. Thirdly, high fat intakes are associated with hyperinsulinaemia [17], perhaps mediated by gastric inhibitory peptide (GIP) or

Weight (kg)		Mean (range) weight loss (kg/month)		
		1000 kcal/day	1500 kcal/day	2000 kcal/day
70–80	Male	5.0 (3.1–6.8)	2.8 (1.0–4.7)	0.7 (0–2.5)
	Female	3.5 (1.9–5.0)	1.4 (0–2.9)	0 (0–0.7)
80–90	Male	5.6 (3.6–7.6)	3.4 (1.5–5.4)	1.3 (0–3.3)
	Female	3.9 (2.3–5.6)	1.8 (0.2–3.5)	0 (0–1.3)
90–100	Male	6.2 (4.1–8.2)	4.1 (2.0–6.1)	2.0 (0–4.0)
	Female	4.4 (2.6–6.1)	2.3 (0.5–4.0)	0.2 (0–1.8)
100–110	Male	6.8 (4.6–9.0)	4.7 (2.5–6.9)	2.6 (0.4–4.9)
	Female	4.8 (3.0–6.6)	2.7 (0.9–4.5)	0.6 (0–2.3)
110–120	Male	7.4 (5.1–9.8)	5.3 (3.2–7.7)	3.2 (0.8–5.5)
	Female	5.2 (3.3–7.1)	3.1 (2.2–5.0)	0.9 (0–2.8)

Table 47.2. Predicting weight loss during different diets in subjects aged 30–60 years.

These predictions assume that total daily energy expenditure = 1.25 × BMR and that expenditure will be suppressed by 15% following weight loss (adapted from Flatt 1985 [13]). The ranges are calculated for BMR ±20% of average.
Notes:
1 Initial weight loss will be more rapid.
2 Regular exercise will accelerate weight loss.
3 Subjects aged over 60 years will lose weight more slowly: subtract 1.4 kg/month for men and 0.6 kg/month for women.

other components of the enteroinsular axis (see Chapter 33). Hyperinsulinaemia which accompanies and may aggravate insulin resistance in NIDDM may favour fat deposition and is also a possible risk factor for atheroma [18]. A further practical problem with such diets is that, as their energy densities are high and their fibre contents are low, food is less satisfying and tends to encourage overeating.

Current evidence is sufficient to recommend a high-carbohydrate diet to maintain weight loss in NIDDM patients (Table 47.3). Changing to a high-carbohydrate, low-fat diet is often enough to produce significant weight loss, even without formal energy restriction. Indeed, many overweight patients have such high energy requirements (which they usually deny vehemently) that their overweight can probably only be maintained

by an energy-dense, high-fat, low-carbohydrate Western-style diet. Specific dietary recommendations for NIDDM are essentially identical to those for the general population [19, 20] and patients with IDDM (Chapter 41). Overweight NIDDM patients need considerable reassurance that, despite cultural opposition, larger intakes of bread and other sources of complex carbohydrate are beneficial and will in fact help weight loss.

Initial dietary prescription

The initial dietary prescription for an overweight NIDDM patient is critically important, especially as this is often the only advice which is remembered. In the past, when sugar restriction was stressed at the outset, this was often the only dietary change to be made in the long-term. If only one nutrient is specified in a diet, then this is inevitably viewed as the most important restriction. In the past for diabetes this was usually carbohydrate, and when patients finally reject their initial prescription (as most do) they are likely to satisfy their appetite with extra fats, resulting in a potentially harmful atherogenic diet which will be continued indefinitely. It is therefore important to stress the importance of *fat restriction* at the outset, as it is preferable for failed dieters to make up their energy needs with high carbohydrate foods.

Simple guidelines for initial dietary advice, suit-

Table 47.3. Advantages of high-carbohydrate, low-fat diets for slimming and maintenance of weight loss in NIDDM subjects.

Lower energy density of carbohydrate ⎫ Increased bulk,
Higher dietary fibre content ⎬ more satisfying
Improved insulin sensitivity
Reduced hyperinsulinaemia (? reduced GIP-mediated stimulation of insulin secretion)
Increased diet-induced thermogenesis, therefore increased energy expenditure
If overeaten, less tendency to fat deposition (more energy expended in converting carbohydrate to fat for storage)

Table 47.4. Initial dietary advice for a newly diagnosed diabetic patient (IDDM or NIDDM).

- Drink *water* to quench thirst
- Eat to appetite with *normal foods*; take regular meals
- Make the *main part of each meal* cereal, bread or pasta
- Make meat or cheese a *small* part of each meal

able for the general practitioner or practice nurse to provide at the time of diagnosis, or for use on a hospital ward until the dietitian can give more detailed advice, are shown in Table 47.4.

Dietary prescriptions are best described in terms of meal and snack exchanges, as these are more easily understood than nutrient prescriptions and more likely to improve compliance. Converting nutrient recommendations into acceptable day-to-day eating advice is a specialized challenge for clinic dietitians.

The energy intake for the initial dietary prescription is best calculated from standard equations [21] (Fig. 41.1) and subsequently modified according to progress (or the lack of it). Once weight has re-stabilized, even if it is still too high, the dietary prescription should be revised, again based on realistic estimates of energy requirement at the new weight [8, 21]. This may mean increasing the original carbohydrate prescription if the patient is to avoid overeating with fats.

Dietary failures

As discussed above, NIDDM patients seldom reach their ideal body weight and most will stop slimming while still severely overweight, hyperglycaemic and hyperlipidaemic. Most clinics can boast an average weight loss of only 3–5 kg, representing adherence to a 1000 kcal/day diet for 3–4 weeks [13]. For some patients, the rate of weight loss even with this rather strict regimen is disheartening and is often cited as a reason for discontinuing the diet. Faster weight loss could theoretically be achieved for short periods, but more extreme dietary restriction may be unsuccessful in the long term.

Dietary non-compliance ultimately signifies that the diet is perceived as less tolerable than continuing overweight; as discussed above, unrealistic expectations of the rate of weight loss are probably an important contributing factor. The theory of compliance and the management of non-compliance with diet as with all areas of diabetic care is complex (see Chapter 95). Consistent en-couragement about the planned diet is worthwhile, but advice should probably be simplified, rather than made more detailed, once a patient has 'failed to comply'. A clear discussion of the risks of over-weight can be helpful, but is often viewed by some patients as a value judgement. It is usually more helpful to concentrate on the steps a patient has taken, rather than those not taken, with a view to encouraging further action. A radical attempt to change many different aspects of diet and lifestyle is sometimes a welcome relief to the patient who has been demoralized by repeated castigations or unsuccessful attempts to tackle single problems.

Direct accusations of 'cheating' are usually un-helpful, but the non-complying patient may lose confidence in an advisor who blandly accepts assertions that slimming instructions are being followed rigidly. It may help to explain that, although there is undoubtedly a metabolic component to the weight problem which makes it particularly hard for the individual to lose weight (see Chapter 20), there is no doubt at all that weight loss can be achieved. As the lowest 24-hour metabolic rate ever measured in an adult was 1400 kcal/day (in a 6-stone woman), an energy intake lower than this will produce weight loss.

A large number of behavioural approaches are available to the dietitian, of which 'contract' systems or 'cash payment and reward' schemes are perhaps the most successful [22]. There is a consistent and strong placebo effect which produces weight loss when patients are included in clinical trials; diabetic clinics should perhaps consider conducting and evaluating long-term clinical trials with the aim of optimizing a sequence of locally available strategies for weight reduction.

Finally, although rare, endocrine causes of refractory obesity such as Cushing's syndrome or hypothyroidism, must always be considered.

Very low calorie diets (VLCDs)

Conventional meal-based diets containing as few as 700 kcal, which are nutritionally adequate from the point of view of vitamins and minerals, can be designed by dietitians. Below this level, supplementation with vitamin C, iron, potassium, magnesium and zinc become necessary if the diet is to be followed for more than a few days. A variety of synthetic and food-based formula diets are now available which provide energy intakes as low as 300–400 kcal/day, complete with sufficient vitamin and mineral supplements. These modern very low calorie diets (VLCDs) are probably safe, at least in the short-to-medium term, in the general population, although minor side-effects including lethargy, dry skin, constipation, brittle nails, hair loss and cold intolerance are common [23].

There are still uncertainties about how VLCDs should be used [24]. Most people find that they can only adhere to the diet for a week or two at a time (as evidenced by their weight changes outside study conditions). Although serious adverse effects do not appear inside 3 weeks, anxieties are expressed about the possible cumulative effects on body composition of continued cyclical VLCD/refeeding regimes of 3 weeks of VLCD alternating with 1 week off the regimen. Episodic dieting with more than 10% swings in body weight has been associated with increased risk of vascular disease [25]. An alternative approach is to use VLCD products instead of other low-energy substitutes for one or two meals per day [26]. This seems nutritionally acceptable — and indeed does not amount to a VLCD as such — but other low-energy snacks may be more palatable and much cheaper.

SAFETY AND EFFICACY OF VLCDs IN NON-DIABETIC PEOPLE

Modern VLCDs must be distinguished from the earlier fasting or modified fasting regimens which caused cardiac arrhythmias and some deaths, probably through electrolyte disturbances and elevation of fatty acids in subjects with early heart disease [27]. The disproportionate loss of body protein, mainly muscle and perhaps including cardiac muscle, during strict diets has been another source of concern. Most commercial VLCDs have high protein contents in an attempt to minimize negative nitrogen balance. This issue has been confused as it was not appreciated until recently that lean body mass is increased by up to 35% in severely obese subjects [28], and this extra tissue (mainly extra muscle, vascular and supporting tissue) will be lost when patients slim [26].

Some VLCDs have achieved notoriety because of high-pressure marketing and misleading advertising tactics. The energy deficit produced by a VLCD, even if regular exercise is employed, cannot exceed 2000–3000 kcal/day. If this were lost entirely as adipose tissue, then weight would fall at 2–3 kg/week. Faster weight loss can only result from loss of other, denser, tissue — usually muscle — and

should be a warning to modify the diet. During the first week of a strict diet, there is additional loss of liver glycogen with its associated water (about 4 g water to each 1 g of glycogen). Thus weight loss of 5 kg may occur in the first week, but this will not continue. The rate of weight loss during a fixed low energy intake will also decline by about 15% as metabolic rate adapts [29], and subsequently falls further in proportion to body weight unless regular exercise is also taken (see Fig. 20.2). Incorporating an exercise programme with a VLCD is the best way to promote loss of excess adipose tissue while maintaining muscle mass and thus metabolic rate [30], but this could be hazardous in some NIDDM subjects (see below).

SAFETY AND EFFICACY OF VLCDs IN NIDDM SUBJECTS

Specific complications of VLCD use in NIDDM patients have not yet been reported, but the possible presence of subclinical ischaemic heart disease in these patients, coupled with the disturbances of fatty acid metabolism which may be aggravated by these diets, urges caution.

The justification for using VLCDs in NIDDM will depend finally on their long-term effects on body weight and metabolic variables. Short-term VLCDs improve plasma glucose, insulin and lipid concentrations, and also lower blood pressure in NIDDM patients [23], but a Swedish study [31] suggests that a conventional 800 kcal/day reducing diet achieves better results after 12 months.

Exercise

Exercise and physical training confer particular metabolic advantages in NIDDM in terms of improved insulin sensitivity and glucose disposal [32]. Moreover, regular exercise helps to maintain muscle mass and promotes the preferential loss of adipose tissue [30]; the lean body mass of obese subjects can therefore be maintained so that metabolic rate tends to fall less during weight loss. For this reason, more rapid weight loss may be expected if an exercise regimen is combined with slimming programmes. Exercise also increases energy expenditure acutely and so further favours weight loss but in practice, in the ageing overweight population of NIDDM subjects, the level of exercise necessary can seldom be maintained on a regular daily basis.

Exercise regimens for NIDDM patients should

be suited to the individual's capabilities; guidelines are suggested in Chapter 78. Simple advice should be offered to every patient, for example to walk for an *extra* 30–60 min *daily*, or to use stairs rather than lifts. More strenuous exercise, such as jogging, should be avoided if there is any possibility of ischaemic heart disease, and undertaken only with careful training. An exercising ECG is a wise precaution.

As little as 25 min brisk walking daily for 12 months has a beneficial effect on plasma lipids without producing weight loss [33], but even this programme requires considerable reorganization of lifestyle. Patients often suggest that they might take up swimming (forgetting the critical gaze of others) or exercise bicycles, but these activities are rarely sustained on a daily basis.

Smoking and body weight

The pathogenic role of smoking in diabetic patients is likely to have similar importance as a cardiovascular risk factor to that in the non-diabetic populations. Its causative role in leg gangrene is beyond dispute. In non-diabetic subjects, the risks from moderate smoking are only matched by overweight when body weight is doubled (Fig. 47.2). It may therefore even be questioned whether pursuit of weight loss is appropriate at all, until patients have become non-smokers.

Advising smokers, diabetic or non-diabetic, to give up the habit is often unsuccessful (see Chapter 92). It may help to emphasize the positive health and social benefits of becoming a non-smoker. Fear of weight gain is a reservation often expressed by smokers when advised to become non-smokers and this is obviously very relevant to NIDDM patients. As smoking elevates the metabolic rate and depresses appetite there are some theoretical grounds for this anxiety. However, although smokers tend to be about 10% below average weight, they have a 10% elevation of metabolic rate and so eat 10% more energy than non-smoking subjects of the same weight in order to maintain body weight [34–36]. Non-diabetic people who stop smoking tend to gain about 5–8 kg in the first year, after which weight falls again [37; J Friend, personal communication]. In practice, as long as standard diabetic clinic dietetic advice is followed, weight gain after stopping smoking is not a problem. Roughly one-half of diabetic patients will gain some weight after becoming non-smokers but will tend to lose it again over the subsequent year or so and many actually lose weight when they stop smoking permanently (Fig. 47.3). The important step is for the patient to make a decision to become a non-smoker; confident dietetic guidance will be reassuring and help to minimize any transient weight gain.

Supplementary dietary products: fibre and oils

Both cereal fibre and viscous (soluble) dietary fibre have a small hypoglycaemic effect. Soluble fibre also improves blood lipid profiles, reducing LDL and VLDL cholesterol while maintaining HDL cholesterol [38]. These benefits for NIDDM patients are seen when dietary fibre is incorporated in

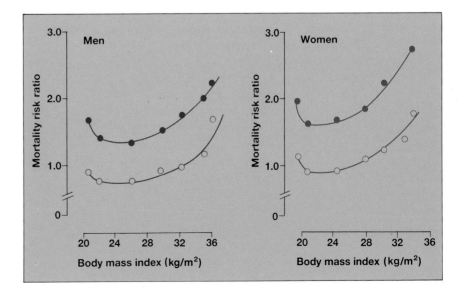

Fig. 47.2. Relationship between BMI and mortality in smokers (filled circles) and non-smokers (open circles) in the general population. The added risk from smoking would be equivalent to that from at least a further 50% overweight. (Adapted from James 1984 [11].)

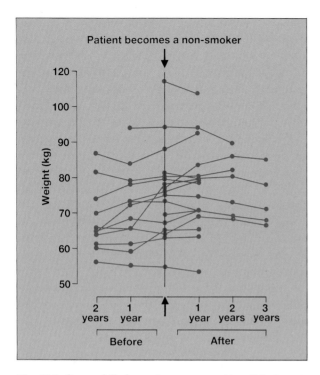

Fig. 47.3. Successfully becoming a non-smoking diabetic patient does not consistently increase body weight.

high-carbohydrate diets, and indeed the dietary fibre component is essential to the efficacy of such diets [39]. Dietary fibre also increases satiety and thereby can assist weight loss. Given the widespread lack of success in implementing modern dietary advice effectively, supplements of soluble fibre, particularly guar gum (which is essentially pure galactomannan) have been recommended for diabetic patients. The nutritional objection to this approach is that it tends to divert attention away from other, possibly more important aspects of diet composition. Fears about interference with mineral and micronutrient absorption appear to be unfounded. If guar supplements are to be used, then they are best administered mixed with meals, rather than taken as a separate drink [40]. For the average NIDDM patient, addition of 15 g guar per day can achieve 10% falls in fasting plasma glucose, glycosylated haemoglobin, total and LDL cholesterol.

Marine fatty acids of the ω-3 series have recently been shown to have beneficial pharmacological effects on blood lipids, particularly in lowering the serum triglycerides which are often elevated in NIDDM [41]. They also increase the HLD:LDL ratio and are being promoted to reduce cardiovascular risks in the general population. Recent reports have suggested that eating fish regularly is associated with lower risks of ischaemic heart disease in non-diabetic subjects [42]. However, the amount of fish that can reasonably be eaten does not include sufficient ω-3 fatty acid for this to be the mechanism reducing heart disease, implying that some other component or associated lifestyle factor must also operate. Unfortunately, marine oil supplements also tend to aggravate hyperglycaemia in NIDDM patients [41]. At present, caution must therefore be advised over the use of fish oil supplements in diabetic subjects: it may be reasonable to suggest eating fatty fish to replace red meat for 2 or 3 meals per week.

Supplements of other oils containing essential fatty acids, particularly γ-linolenic acid in evening primrose oil, have also been vigorously promoted for a wide variety of medical conditions including diabetes and its complications. They have various pharmacological effects, but results of controlled studies are as yet scanty and variable. At present, there seem no secure grounds for their general use in NIDDM, and it must be remembered that, as fats, their energy content is 9 kcal/g. These compounds are discussed further in Chapter 104.

Conclusions

Dietary modification remains the key to the treatment of NIDDM, and recent research has stimulated new approaches to the rationale, prescription and monitoring of dietary regimens. Dietary non-compliance remains the greatest obstacle to the successful management of NIDDM. Further research is required to identify the optimal strategies, perhaps combining dietary measures with refined behavioural methods and appetite suppressant or thermogenic drugs.

MIKE E.J. LEAN
JIM I. MANN

References

1 Bitzen PO, Melander A, Schersten B, Svensson M. Efficacy of dietary regulation in primary health care patients with hyperglycaemia detected by screening. *Diabetic Med* 1988; **5**: 640−8.

2 Hadden DR, Howard-Williams J, Nugent Z, Turner RC. For the UK Prospective Diabetes Study Group. Response of fasting plasma glucose to diet therapy in newly presenting type 2 diabetic patients. *Diabetic Med* (in press).

3 Pyöräalä K. Diabetes and coronary heart disease. *Acta Endocrinol* 1985; **110** (suppl 272): 11−19.

4 Nikkilä EA. Are plasma lipoproteins responsible for the

excess atherosclerosis in diabetes? *Acta Endocrinol* 1985; **110** (suppl 272): 27−30.

5 Jarrett RJ, Shipley MJ. Mortality and associated risk factors. *Acta Endocrinol* 1985; **110** (suppl 272): 21−6.

6 Lean MEJ, Powrie JK, Anderson AS, Garthwaite PH. Obesity, weight loss and prognosis in NIDDM. *Diabetic Med* 1989; **7**: 228−33.

7 Prentice AM, Black AE, Coward WA *et al*. High levels of energy expenditure in obesity. *Br Med J* 1986; **292**: 983−7.

8 FAO/WHO/UNU. *Energy and Protein Requirements. Technical Report Series*, Vol 724. Geneva: WHO, 1985.

9 Lean MEJ. Achieving energy balance in clinical studies. *Proc Nutr Soc* 1988; **47**: 67A.

10 Metropolitan Life Insurance Company. Mortality amongst overweight men and women. *Stat Bull Metropol Life Ins Co* 1960; **41**: 6.

11 Royal College of Physicians. Obesity. *J Roy Coll Physicians Lond* 1983; **17**: 1−58.

12 James WPT. Treatment of obesity: the constraints on success. *Clin Endocrinol Metab* 1984; **13**: 635−59.

13 Lean MEJ, Anderson AS. Clinic strategies for obesity management. *Diabetic Med* 1988; **5**: 515−20.

14 Flatt JP. Energetics of intermediary metabolism. In: Garrow JS, Halliday D, eds. *Substrate and Energy Metabolism*. London: J. Libbey, 1985: 58−69.

15 Lean MEJ, James WPT. Metabolic effects of isoenergetic nutrient exchange over 24 hours in relation to obesity in women. *Int J Obes* 1988; **12**: 15−28.

16 Lean MEJ, James WPT, Garthwaite PH. Obesity without overeating? In: Björntorp P, Rössner S, eds. *Obesity in Europe 88*. London: J. Libbey, 1989: 281−6.

17 Grey N, Kipnis DM. Effect of diet composition on the hyperinsulinemia of obesity. *N Engl J Med* 1971; **285**: 827−31.

18 Stout RW. Insulin and atheroma — an update. *Lancet* 1987; i: 1077−9.

19 Nutrition and Diabetes Study Group of the European Association for the Study of Diabetes. Nutritional recommendations and principles for individuals with diabetes mellitus. *Diabet Nutr Metab* 1988; **1**: 145−9.

20 DHSS−COMA. *Diet and Cardiovascular Disease. Report on Health and Social Subjects* Vol 28. London: HMSO, 1984.

21 Lean MEJ, James WPT. Prescription of diabetic diets in the 1980s. *Lancet* 1986; i: 723−5.

22 Dunbar JM, Marshall GD, Hovel MF. Behavioural strategies for improving compliance. In: Hayes RB, Taylor DW, Sackett DL, eds. *Compliance in Health Care*. Baltimore: Johns Hopkins University Press, 1979: 174−90.

23 Hanefeld M, Weck M. Very low calorie diet therapy in obese non-insulin dependent diabetes patients. *Int J Obes* 1989; **13** (suppl 2): 33−7.

24 Lean MEJ, Stordy J, James WPT, Garrow JS. Discussion. In: James WPT, ed. *Current Approaches: Obesity*. Southampton, UK: Duphar Medical Relations, 1988: 60.

25 Hamm P, Shekelle RB, Stamler J. Large fluctuations in body weight during young adulthood and 25-year risk of coronary death in men. *Am J Epidemiol* 1989; **129**: 312−18.

26 Howard AN. Safety and efficacy of the Cambridge diet. In: Berry EM, Blondheim SH, Eliahou HE, Shafrir E, eds. *Recent Advances in Obesity Research*. Vol V. London: J. Libbey, 1987: 332−7.

27 Sours HE, Frattali VP, Brand CD, Feldman RA, Forbes AL, Swanson RC, Paris AL. Sudden death associated with very low calorie weight regimens. *Am J Clin Nutr* 1981; **34**: 453−61.

28 James WPT, Bailes J, Davies HL, Dauncey MJ. Elevated metabolic rates in obesity. *Lancet* 1978; i: 1122−5.

29 Bray GA. Effect of caloric restriction on energy expenditure in obese patients. *Lancet* 1969; ii: 397−8.

30 Stern JS, Titchenal CA, Johnson PR. Obesity: does exercise make a difference? In: Berry EM, Blondheim SH, Eliahou HE, Shafrir E, eds. *Recent Advances in Obesity Research*. Vol V. London: J. Libbey, 1987: 352−64.

31 Vessby B. A one year follow up of a weight reduction programme in obese type 2 diabetic patients. In: *Proceedings of the 6th EASD International Symposium on Diabetes and Nutrition*, Helsinki, 1988.

32 Devlin JT, Horton ES. Glucose metabolism and thermogenesis in lean, obese and noninsulin-dependent diabetic men following exercise. In: Berry EM, Blondheim SH, Eliahou HE, Shafrir E, eds. *Recent Advances in Obesity Research*. Vol V. London: J. Libbey, 1987: 365−72.

33 Hudson A, Hardman AE, Jones PRM, Morgan NG. Brisk walking influences plasma cholesterol in sedentary women in the absence of a change in fatness. *Proc Nutr Soc* (in press).

34 Dallosso HM, James WPT. The role of smoking in the regulation of energy balance. *Int J Obes* 1984; **8**: 365−75.

35 Hofstetter A, Schutz Y, Jéquier E, Wahren J. Increased 24-hour energy expenditure in cigarette smokers. *N Engl J Med* 1986; **314**: 79−82.

36 Stamford BA, Matter S, Fell RD, Papanek P. Effects of smoking cessation on weight gain, metabolic rate, caloric consumption and blood lipids. *Am J Clin Nutr* 1986; **43**: 486−94.

37 Wack JT, Rodin J. Smoking and its effects on body weight and the systems of caloric regulation. *Am J Clin Nutr* 1982; **35**: 366−80.

38 Vinik AI, Jenkins DJA. Dietary fiber in management of diabetes. *Diabetes Care* 1988; **11**: 160−73.

39 Riccardi G, Rivellese A, Pacioni D, Genovese S, Mastranzo P, Mancini M. Separate influence of dietary carbohydrate and fibre on the metabolic control in diabetes. *Diabetologia* 1984; **26**: 116−21.

40 Füessl HS, Williams G, Adrian TE, Bloom SR. Guar sprinkled on food: effect on glycaemic control, plasma lipids and gut hormones in non-insulin dependent diabetic patients. *Diabetic Med* 1986; **4**: 463−8.

41 Axelrod L. Omega-3 fatty acids in diabetes mellitus: gift from the sea? *Diabetes* 1989; **38**: 539−43.

42 Kromhout D, Bosschieter EB, Coulander C de L. The inverse relation between fish consumption and 20-year mortality from coronary heart disease. *N Engl J Med* 1985; **312**: 1205−9.

General principles when aiming for near-normoglycaemia

Defining treatment targets

Although it is not yet known whether very tight glycaemic control can prevent chronic diabetic complications, it is reasonable at present to aim for near-normoglycaemia in most NIDDM patients, as in IDDM. A European consensus working party has recommended that the FBG should be reduced below 7.8 mmol/l [6]. We suggest that a target of <6 mmol/l is both feasible and preferable, in view of the epidemiological evidence that even minimal hyperglycaemia is associated with an increased risk of major cardio-vascular complications [7, 8]. This target may be achieved by following a structured hierarchy of treatment, beginning with dietary restriction alone and adding oral agents and then insulin if needed.

Adjusting dietary intake, composition and distribution remains the mainstay of therapy in NIDDM. However, only about 15% of patients are able to attain an FBG <6 mmol/l with diet therapy alone and of these, only one-half can maintain fasting normoglycaemia for more than one year [9]. Most patients will therefore need additional treatment, which can be adjusted on the basis of their FBG [10]. Such a scheme is described briefly below.

For relatively mild hyperglycaemia (FBG <10 mmol/l) after diet treatment, the target FBG levels of <6 mmol/l can be reached in about 50% of patients by adding a sulphonylurea [11]. Metformin is sometimes recommended as an alternative in obese subjects because, unlike sulphonylureas and insulin, it does not tend to cause weight gain [12]. If fasting normogly-caemia cannot be achieved despite maximal sulphonylurea doses, metformin can be added.

If this combination is ineffective, insulin is required. This can be given most easily as a single daily long-acting basal insulin supplement, and the dose should be adjusted to reduce the FBG to <6 mmol/l. The metformin can then be stopped and the patient treated with either a sulphonyl-urea/insulin combination or with insulin alone. At this stage patients have little B-cell reserve and are close to requiring full insulin replacement therapy. When short-acting insulin becomes necessary to cover meals, sulphonylureas have no additional benefit and should be discontinued [13, 14].

Monitoring glycaemic control

BLOOD GLUCOSE CONCENTRATIONS

Attempts to achieve near-normoglycaemia require detailed information about prevailing glycaemic levels. This has recently become possible, with the wide availability of capillary blood glucose test strips and portable blood glucose meters [15] which allow blood glucose levels to be measured easily, including by the patient. Various indices of glycaemic behaviour can be used to assess and adjust treatment.

As mentioned above, the *fasting blood glucose concentration* is a useful index. Values should be in the range 4–6 mmol/l in patients in whom 'good control' is being attempted [16]. When the FBG during diet or basal insulin therapy remains stable at below 6 mmol/l, FBG need only be measured 3-monthly, but more frequent measure-ments are needed when adjusting therapy. It should be remembered that a whole blood glucose concentration of 6 mmol/l corresponds to a plasma glucose of 7 mmol/l.

'Random' blood glucose values are often measured after meals and their interpretation can be difficult. Blood glucose concentrations in a patient receiving oral therapy can rise from a normal fasting value of 5.5 mmol/l to 12 mmol/l by 1 hour after breakfast; this might be thought to represent poor control, yet values may return to 3 mmol/l within 4 hours after a meal. Random blood glucose values can be more informative if the size and timing of the preceding meal are known [3], but are usually too variable to allow precise adjustment of glycaemic control. Never-theless, a random blood glucose value exceeding 12 mmol/l almost certainly implies a raised FBG and poor glycaemic control.

In more severely hyperglycaemic patients who need basal insulin supplements, occasional 4-point *blood glucose profiles* (before breakfast, lunch, dinner and bed in one day) can be helpful in assessing the need for short-acting insulin to cover meals. Preprandial glucose profiles should be performed regularly in patients receiving short-acting insulin.

HAEMOGLOBIN A_{1c} OR FRUCTOSAMINE CONCENTRATIONS

In NIDDM, the value of these measurements of overall glucose control taken in isolation is limited by their wide normal ranges, the imprecision of many assays and the difficulty of interpreting high values. As the measurements reflect integrated blood glucose values over an extended period (Chapter 34), the distinction between overall poor control, a short period of hyperglycaemia from an intercurrent illness or basal normoglycaemia with exaggerated postprandial excursions may be difficult. When the FBG has fallen to within the range 4−6 mmol/l with diet or oral therapy, HbA_{1c} is usually near the upper end of the normal range [11] and provides little additional information. Routine measurements of HbA_{1c} or fructosamine are therefore most useful in the more severely hyperglycaemic patients, particularly if treated with insulin.

URINARY GLUCOSE MEASUREMENTS

Urinalysis for glucose gives little information about blood glucose levels within and up to about twice the normal range. It should therefore only be used in elderly patients in whom the sole aim is to avoid symptoms associated with heavy glycosuria.

Sulphonylureas

The hypoglycaemic effect of antibacterial sulphonamide compounds was noted by Loubatières and others in the early 1940s and led to the development of the sulphonylurea agents, carbutamide, chlorpropamide, tolbutamide, and acetohexamide in the early 1950s. Subsequently, more potent sulphonylureas such as glibenclamide, glipizide, gliclazide and glibornuride were synthesized and termed 'second-generation' agents. All these agents have become widely accepted and remain the first-line therapy for patients with NIDDM who cannot maintain acceptable blood glucose levels by dietary means alone.

The clinical effect of sulphonylurea compounds is similar in normal-weight and obese subjects. Although obese NIDDM subjects have considerable obesity-associated insulin resistance and usually relatively less impaired B-cell function than those with normal weight, the FBG in each is dependent on the combination of the degree of B-cell dysfunction and the magnitude of insulin resistance [17]. A two-fold greater stimulation of B-cell function (or a two-fold reduction in insulin resistance) has a similar hypoglycaemic effect in both normal weight and obese subjects.

Mechanisms of action

B-CELL STIMULATION

Sulphonylureas stimulate the B cell to secrete insulin. This acute response is easily demonstrated by oral or intravenous administration, which increases plasma insulin concentrations and decreases glucose levels in normal subjects or patients with NIDDM; sulphonylureas are ineffective in C-peptide deficient IDDM patients. Direct B-cell stimulation can be shown *in vitro* using a perfused pancreas preparation [18].

The sulphonylureas bind to surface receptors on the B-cell membrane and inhibit the ATP-sensitive potassium channel, preventing the egress of potassium and thereby depolarizing the cell membrane (Fig. 48.3) [19, 20]; glibenclamide is now routinely used by physiologists to demonstrate this particular channel in cell membrane transport experiments. Depolarization opens voltage-dependent calcium channels, allowing extracellular calcium to flood into the cell, and the resulting increase in cytosolic calcium stimulates insulin secretion (see Chapter 9).

Other mechanisms have been suggested, including inhibition of phosphodiesterase leading to increased cyclic AMP levels which are postulated to mobilize intracellular bound calcium and so increase cytosolic free calcium concentrations. As well as their direct stimulatory effect, sulphonylurea agents sensitize the B cell to various other insulin secretagogues and in particular increase insulin release in response to prevailing glucose levels [21, 22]. Sulphonylureas therefore act primarily by stimulating insulin release. They do not appear to increase insulin biosynthesis.

The overall effect is to maintain similar basal and postprandial insulin levels at lower plasma glucose levels than when treated by diet alone [2, 23]. This readjustment of insulin and glucose levels has often been misinterpreted as indicating that chronic sulphonylurea therapy fails to continue to stimulate the B cells. However, when long-term sulphonylurea therapy is stopped, blood glucose levels rise and the insulin secretory responses decline [24]. When identical glucose levels are imposed in patients on and off sulphonylurea therapy by means of a glucose clamp, it is apparent that sulphonylureas stimulate insulin release approximately two-fold [25]. Sulphonylurea drugs are moderately weak in relation to the degree of hyperglycaemia which may occur in NIDDM.

Accordingly, it is not surprising that, whereas an FBG of 8 mmol/l may be reduced to 5 or 6 mmol/l, it is unusual for an FBG of over 10 mmol/l to fall to below 6 mmol/l with the addition of sulphonylurea therapy.

IMPROVED INSULIN SENSITIVITY

The suggestion that sulphonylureas have an additional major effect on peripheral tissues has repeatedly been raised [26–28]. This possibility originated in part from the finding of similar insulin levels at lower glucose levels in sulphonylurea-treated diabetic patients, which was misinterpreted as indicating enhanced insulin action rather than B-cell stimulation. Any method of reducing the blood glucose level will diminish the insulin resistance which occurs secondarily to hyperglycaemia, so that some decrease in insulin resistance and increased insulin receptor binding might be expected [29, 30]. In fact, insulin sensitivity is not increased during sulphonylurea treatment *per se*, as has been demonstrated by clamping blood glucose concentrations at similar levels in treated and untreated patients [25]. *In vitro* studies at high sulphonylurea concentrations show increased insulin-mediated glucose uptake into tissues [31, 32] or increased insulin receptor numbers [33]. However, the concentrations used may not be relevant to the therapeutic levels obtained in diabetic patients. These possible 'extra-pancreatic' actions of sulphonylureas continue to stimulate debate [20, 28].

Primary and secondary failure

The term 'sulphonylurea failure', as originally used, denotes that symptoms from glycosuria persist after starting treatment; this dates from the period when the main treatment aim was simply to abolish symptoms rather than to achieve near-normoglycaemia. *Primary failure* occurs when sulphonylurea therapy does not improve symptoms from the outset of treatment, whereas *secondary failure* is when symptoms recur months or years after initial therapeutic success.

Primary failure, which occurs in about 5% of newly presenting NIDDM patients, signifies that the sulphonylurea does not stimulate the B cells sufficiently to reduce the blood glucose concentration to below the renal threshold. This depends both on the degree of hyperglycaemia and on the level of the renal threshold. Variation in the latter implies that symptoms can occur with an FBG in the range 8–20 mmol/l, although this generally happens with an FBG of 11–12 mmol/l. In this range, sulphonylurea therapy decreases FBG by approximately 4 mmol/l, so that a reduction from 14 to 10 mmol/l will usually result in clinical success. Primary failure is likely when the patient has an average renal glucose threshold and the FBG is much above 14 mmol/l, or when marked B-cell deficiency is apparent from ketonuria (++ with Ketostix). Sulphonylureas are of course contraindicated in heavily ketotic patients, who will require insulin treatment.

Secondary failure has been taken to imply that

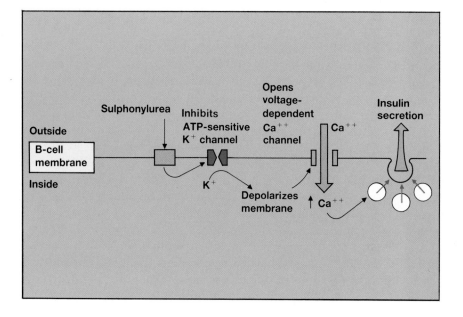

Fig. 48.3. Sequence of events through which sulphonylureas stimulate insulin secretion.

the sulphonylurea is no longer effective and hence the blood glucose has increased [34, 35]. This hypothesis in part arose from the observation, discussed above, of similar insulin levels at lower glucose levels during treatment. Rather than representing a loss of B-cell stimulation, it is more likely that secondary sulphonylurea failure arises from a progressive deterioration in B-cell function, perhaps compounded by any increase in insulin resistance secondary to weight gain in the interim [36]. As symptoms can arise from a small increase in FBG which exceeds the renal threshold (e.g. from 11 to 13 mmol/l), it does not require a great deterioration in either to produce secondary failure. The alternative hypotheses of a true, progressive loss of efficacy of the sulphonylurea or of sulphonylurea induced 'exhaustion' of the B-cell reserve cannot be excluded, but equally are unsupported by data.

The terms 'primary' and 'secondary' are probably no longer appropriate; the statement that maximal doses of sulphonylurea are ineffective is all that is required. 'Sulphonylurea inadequacy' [37] is a term recently introduced to describe patients whose FBG is not reduced below a desired target level, e.g. 6 mmol/l. A value below 6 mmol/l is only obtained in about 50% of patients who have an FBG less than 10 mmol/l after diet therapy and rarely in those whose FBG exceeds 10 mmol/l.

Pharmacokinetics of sulphonylureas

Chlorpropamide is largely excreted unchanged in the urine, whereas most other sulphonylureas are metabolized primarily in the liver. Sulphonylurea metabolites may be biologically active, such as the L-hydroxyhexamide derivative of acetohexamide which is excreted by the kidneys. The biological effect of sulphonylureas often lasts longer than is indicated by pharmacokinetic studies of the plasma pool, probably because active metabolites are produced or because a peripheral pool remains bound to the B-cell membrane potassium channels.

Plasma sulphonylurea concentrations in different patients often show a poor correlation with the dose given [38]. The wide intra- and inter-individual variation is unexplained but may relate to differences in protein-bound or B-cell-bound components rather than the 'free' plasma fraction of sulphonylurea. Measurement of plasma sulphonylurea levels has no place in the management of NIDDM other than to detect non-compliance.

Pharmacokinetic and prescribing data for the commonly used sulphonylurea agents are shown in Table 48.1 (see [39, 40]).

Side-effects

Profound hypoglycaemia may occur as the result of accidental (or intentional) overdosage or through the accumulation of those drugs with a long half-life, particularly if their elimination is impaired. An important culprit has been chlorpropamide in patients with renal failure. Chlorpropamide is not recommended for use in the elderly who have renal damage and who are at particular risk of hypoglycaemia. This problem was prominent in the past when sulphonylurea therapy was adjusted only by urine glucose monitoring. The risks of hypoglycaemia can be reduced with careful and frequent measurements of the FBG as the clinical response criterion. The UK Prospective Diabetes Study found mild hypoglycaemia to be commoner with glibenclamide than with chlorpropamide therapy [9]. Glibenclamide therapy in mildly hyperglycaemic patients (e.g. those with FBG 6–10 mmol/l) tends to produce reactive hypoglycaemia after breakfast, possibly because it elicits a delayed B-cell response [41]. By contrast, chlorpropamide tends to produce nocturnal hypoglycaemia.

Hypoglycaemia can occur with any sulphonylurea, and occasionally causes death. Population studies in Sweden [42], Switzerland [43] and Britain [44] have indicated that patients treated with glibenclamide are particularly prone to hypoglycaemia. Melander [40] has suggested that both glibenclamide and chlorpropamide should be used with 'particular caution' in the elderly and perhaps avoided altogether in those aged over 75 years.

Adequate monitoring of the blood glucose response to therapy is essential to minimize the risk of hypoglycaemia. Sulphonylurea therapy can induce chronic hypoglycaemia which reduces adrenergic counter-regulatory responses so that neuroglycopenic symptoms predominate; patients may be found without warning in deep coma, or fitting or having apparently suffered a stroke. Non-selective β-adrenergic blocking agents given concurrently may mask the warning signs of hypoglycaemia. Sulphonylurea agents are lipid-soluble and are transported bound to albumin so that displacement by other protein-bound drugs such as aspirin, warfarin and monoamine oxidase inhibitors occasionally induces hypoglycaemic

First generation	Dose range	Dose distribution	Half-life
Tolbutamide (1956)	1.0–3.0 g	Divided	3–8 h
Chlorpropamide (1957)	100–500 mg	Single daily	35 h
Acetohexamide (1962)	0.25–1.5 g	Single or divided	6–8 h
Tolazamide (1962)	100–750 mg	Single or divided	7 h
Second generation			
Glymidine (1964)	0.5–2.0 g	Single or divided	4 h
Glibenclamide (1969)	2.5–20 mg	Single or divided	5 h
Glibornuride (1970)	12.5–75 mg	Single or divided	8 h
Glipizide (1971)	2.5–20 mg	Single or divided	4 h
Gliclazide (1979)	80–320 mg	Single or divided	12 h
Gliquidone (1975)	60–180 mg	Single or divided	4 h

Table 48.1. Sulphonylureas: pharmacokinetic and prescribing information. The year in which each drug was introduced is shown in parentheses.

episodes (see Table 79.3) [20]. Alcohol, by inhibiting hepatic gluconeogenesis, can exacerbate hypoglycaemia.

Weight gain can occur with sulphonylurea therapy, but in a 3-year prospective study it has amounted on average to 2 kg, which is little more than in patients treated with diet alone [9]. The weight gain may in part be due to patients being less strict with their diet when tablet therapy is introduced.

Sensitivity reactions, notably skin rashes including erythema multiforme (Fig. 72.9) and cholestatic jaundice can occur with any sulphonylurea, but are uncommon. Such reactions are usually specific to a given sulphonylurea and do not recur if another sulphonylurea is substituted. Bone marrow dyscrasias are very rare. Chlorpropamide and tolbutamide in particular may precipitate acute intermittent porphyria.

Chlorpropamide sensitizes the kidney tubules to antidiuretic hormone action and occasionally causes water retention and hyponatraemia, particularly in elderly patients; hyponatraemia may be exacerbated by concomitant administration of a thiazide diuretic. A few reports have suggested that water retention can induce heart failure but the contribution of sulphonylureas is likely to be minor and exacerbation of heart failure is not a clinical problem. Chlorpropamide-alcohol flushing ('Antabuse' effect) occurs in about 10% of patients receiving the drug [45]. Flushing may be very pronounced and is occasionally associated with bronchospasm. It may be precipitated by less than one unit of any alcoholic drink. Patients with troublesome symptoms should be transferred to a different sulphonylurea, although similar

(but milder) flushing can occur with any of these agents.

Choice of sulphonylurea

The pharmaceutical companies have implied that second-generation sulphonylureas carry specific advantages but in clinical practice there is little difference between any of the agents [46]. The reports that second-generation sulphonylureas were effective in patients with 'sulphonylurea failure' during treatment with a first-generation drug may simply have been a regression to mean phenomenon, partly due to more attentive care of the patients and partly to previously inadequate medication. Parallel studies of NIDDM treated with different therapies have revealed no systematic differences between first- and second-generation drugs [9, 47].

The choice of sulphonylurea thus depends on factors such as convenience and cost. The large tablet size of tolbutamide and acetohexamide and their customary thrice-daily administration has discouraged their use. Most patients prefer once-daily medication and for this reason and because of its low cost, the long-acting chlorpropamide can be used (with the provisos that subjects who develop ethanol-induced flushing may need to be switched to a different drug and that great care is taken in monitoring glycaemia in elderly patients).

Other agents which are routinely prescribed twice daily can probably be given once per day. In patients with mild hyperglycaemia, glibenclamide may be associated with hypoglycaemic episodes before lunch, in which case the first dose of the day should be given at lunch time.

Chlorpropamide should be avoided in renal impairment as it accumulates and can cause severe and prolonged hypoglycaemia. Suitable alternatives include gliclazide and gliquidone, but patients with a serum creatinine level exceeding 250 μmol/l are best transferred to insulin.

Biguanides

Metformin (dimethyl biguanide) is the only biguanide used in the UK since phenformin (phenethyl biguanide) was withdrawn because of its considerably higher risk of provoking fatal lactic acidosis. Metformin reduces the FBG level to a degree similar to that with the sulphonylureas [9, 48]. The slight weight gain seen with sulphonylurea agents is not a feature of metformin therapy, and it is sometimes preferred in obese subjects. Metformin is commonly thought to have a mild anorectic action, possibly related to its gastrointestinal side-effects. Very high dosages in animal studies significantly reduce food intake [49].

Mechanisms of action

Biguanides appear to act by enhancing peripheral glucose uptake [50] and may also reduce gluconeogenesis in the liver and therefore lower hepatic glucose output [51]. These actions combine to produce slightly raised blood lactate levels in all subjects [52]. A suggested cellular mechanism may be via a G protein which overcomes the failure of insulin to inhibit adenylate cyclase activity [51]. Metformin reduces raised glucose levels but does not normally cause hypoglycaemia, possibly because it is acting on a mechanism through which hyperglycaemia itself impairs insulin sensitivity. Metformin is not metabolized and is eliminated through the kidneys. Its use must therefore be avoided in patients with renal impairment.

Side-effects

Gastrointestinal side-effects from metformin are relatively common (up to 20% of patients) but can be minimized by starting therapy at a low dose (500 or 850 mg daily) and increasing slowly as tolerance develops. Recognized problems include dyspepsia, anorexia, diarrhoea and occasionally an unpleasant metallic taste. Patients may also complain of general malaise. These side-effects often limit the dose which a patient can tolerate.

Lactic acidosis is the major and potentially dangerous side-effect. It can occur in any metformin-treated patient, although most cases have proved to have had contraindications to metformin treatment, particularly renal or hepatic impairment. Predisposing factors include severe intercurrent illness such as myocardial infarction or pneumonia, especially if associated with hypotension which causes tissue anoxia, and particularly if occurring in older people. Ingestion of ethanol is another precipitant.

Lactic acidosis is diagnosed by an arterial pH of less than 7.25 together with a raised blood lactate level (>5 mmol/l). The presence of the latter may be suspected by finding a large 'anion gap' ($[Na^+ + K^+] - (Cl^- + HCO_3^-] > 20$ mmol/l).

The mortality of lactic acidosis remains high and its treatment controversial. The use of intravenous bicarbonate may paradoxically exacerbate intracellular acidosis (see p. 487) and aggravate both hepatic lactate metabolism and cardiac output [53, 54]. Haemodialysis may be helpful, by removing both lactate and metformin [55].

It must be stressed that metformin should be avoided in patients with cirrhosis, alcoholism or heart failure because these can contribute to fatal lactic acidosis.

Basal insulin supplement

Patients who fail to achieve their target FBG with a combination of diet and oral agents require insulin. The purpose of insulin treatment is to normalize the major defect in NIDDM, namely the raised basal blood glucose concentration. The basal insulin supplement acts predominantly on the liver, reducing hepatic glucose output; any peripheral effects in improving glucose uptake into the tissues are due mostly to increased insulin sensitivity following the reduction in hyperglycaemia. The patient's own B-cell reserve should provide the extra insulin needed at mealtimes but if there is marked insulin deficiency, additional short-acting insulin will have to be injected to cover meals.

The need for a continuous basal supply of insulin implies that a long-acting insulin is the most appropriate. The only long-acting preparation available at present is human ultralente. This has an absorption half-life of 18—24 hours

[56] but in practice, its action profile is shorter than that of the bovine ultralente preparation which it replaced (see Chapters 38 and 39). Nonetheless, a single daily injection is satisfactory in many patients, producing a glycaemic effect similar to that of the sulphonylureas (Fig. 48.4). Because of the declining action profile after 18 hours or so, the injection should be given before the evening meal or at bedtime. Most patients can continue their normal lifestyle without restrictions on everyday levels of exercise or the size of individual meals; the risks of hypoglycaemia are relatively low but the FBG must be monitored carefully. An alternative insulin is isophane injected in the evening [57]. This is shorter-acting than ultralente, gives less constant glycaemic control overnight [58] and hence is more likely to cause hypoglycaemia. An insulin infusion from an external or implanted pump might give better control but such complex technology seems superfluous. The advent of long-acting biosynthetic insulin analogues (see Chapters 37 and 38) may provide another means of supplying a basal insulin supplement. Preliminary evidence indicates that such compounds have a very prolonged and reproducible action [59], but they have not yet been tested in clinical practice.

Indications and strategy for use of insulin

When to start insulin treatment, how to give it and who should receive it are all contentious subjects [60]. The strategy which we employ is outlined in Table 48.2.

Insulin regimens

The initial dose required can be judged from the FBG when treated with diet alone, with more obese subjects requiring larger doses in line with their obesity-associated insulin resistance (Table 48.2). If a prompt effect is needed, the initial dose should be increased by 50% to provide a loading dose. This should achieve the steady-state plasma insulin levels which would otherwise be attained only after 3–5 days. In most patients who begin therapy out of hospital, this loading dose is not required.

Insulin dosage should then be titrated to reduce the FBG to 4–6 mmol/l. If the FBG falls to below 4 mmol/l, the insulin dose should be reduced. If it remains above 6 mmol/l in the absence of an intercurrent illness, a general guide is that in normal weight subjects, the dose needs to be increased by 1.5 U for each 1 mmol/l that the FBG exceeds 6 mmol/l. Greater increases are needed in obese subjects in proportion to their weight (× 2 for 40% overweight, × 3 for 80% overweight), as shown in Table 48.2. The indications for adding short-acting insulin to cover meals are discussed below.

Table 48.2. Guide to doses required for a basal insulin supplement for an average 5' 10" person. Dosages are suggested according to the fasting blood glucose level and degree of obesity. It is assumed that the patient will maintain the same diet and oral therapy and remains in good health. The doses are those suitable for starting as an outpatient and will need to be altered according to the glycaemic control achieved. Patients should be warned about the possibility of hypoglycaemia although this is rarely a problem with these doses. Most patients will eventually need 20–30% more than these doses to obtain a fasting blood glucose below 6 mmol/l.

	Fasting blood glucose (mmol/l)	Patients with ideal body weight	% over ideal body weight				
			+20	+40	+60	+80	+100
Males	6	6	9	12	15	18	21
	8	10	15	20	25	30	35
	10	14	21	28	35	42	49
	12	18	27	36	45	54	63
	>14	22	33	44	55	66	77
Females	6	5	7	9	11	14	16
	8	8	11	15	19	23	26
	10	11	16	21	26	32	37
	12	14	20	27	34	41	47
	>14	17	25	33	41	50	58

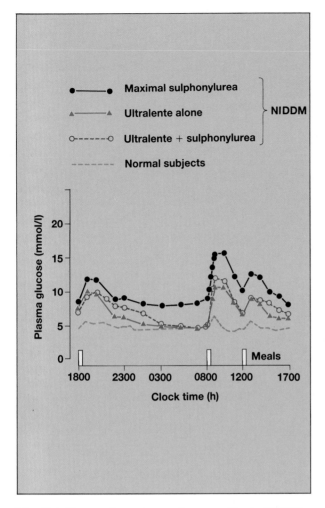

Fig. 48.4. Mean 24-hour plasma glucose profiles in NIDDM patients with fasting hyperglycaemia despite maximal sulphonylurea treatment. Addition of once-daily ultralente insulin, and treatment with ultralente alone lowered the fasting blood glucose towards normal.

Side-effects

Hypoglycaemia due to treatment is the only major side-effect. Hypoglycaemic episodes usually occur during the night or on waking. Chronic hypo-glycaemia in some patients presents as vague headaches and depression, sometimes with influenza-like malaise. Daytime hypoglycaemia is unusual except after prolonged exercise without food, such as during shopping or gardening.

Combined insulin and sulphonylurea therapy

Where a combination of a sulphonylurea and metformin do not achieve near-normal FBG levels, glycaemic control can often be improved by combining a long-acting insulin preparation such as human ultralente [61, 62] (Fig. 48.4).

At this stage, we prefer to stop metformin and to use either insulin alone or a combination of a sulphonylurea and insulin, for which Tables 48.3 and 48.4 give guidelines. The advantages of combined therapy are that, as endogenous insulin secretion is enhanced by the sulphonylurea, less exogenous insulin is needed, and slightly better glucose control may be obtained, particularly when intercurrent infections cause insulin resistance [62]. On the other hand, the addition of a sulphon-ylurea could be said to be of little additional benefit and may be criticized as the patient is given another potentially harmful drug. Inter-mittent insulin therapy in sulphonylurea-treated patients has been advocated to 'rest' the B cells and improve their insulin secretory response [63]. This strategem has not been rigorously investi-gated but appears to have no long-term benefit.

The possibility of giving isophane at night as a basal supplement together with a 'short-acting' sulphonylurea to stimulate insulin secretion at meals has also been suggested [57]. This schedule fails to take into account the prolonged biological action of even 'short half-life' sulphonylureas and the fact that sulphonylureas in effect provide 24-hour B-cell stimulation. Addition of a sulphon-ylurea to insulin therapy does not therefore have a markedly greater effect on the prandial as opposed to basal insulin supply.

The combination of a sulphonylurea and a basal insulin supplement can be monitored by the FBG level as for a basal insulin supplement alone. The major question of whether additional short-acting insulin is required to cover meals is addressed below.

An alternative combination is metformin with insulin. This has not been formally investigated but as metformin therapy has little effect at normal glucose levels, it is unlikely that metformin will be very effective when additional insulin is being given to maintain normoglycaemia. Metformin is known to add little if any benefit to insulin-treated IDDM patients.

Full (basal plus prandial) insulin treatment

The indications for adding short-acting insulin to the long-acting basal supplement are shown in Table 48.5. Patients with persistent symptoms or hyperglycaemia while treated with a basal insulin supplement (with or without a sulphonylurea) should perform home blood glucose monitoring 4 times per day (before meals and before bed) in

Current therapy	Fasting blood glucose (mmol/l)	Suggested action
Diet only	6–8	Add chlorpropamide 100 mg/day
	8–10	Add chlorpropamide 250 mg/day
	10–12	Add chlorpropamide 500 mg/day
	12–18	Add chlorpropamide 500 mg/day but will almost certainly require an additional therapeutic agent
	> 18	Add basal and prandial insulin
Maximum chlorpropamide	6–8	Add metformin 500 mg b.d.
	8–12	Add once-daily ultralente insulin
	>12	Stop chlorpropamide. Start basal and prandial insulin
Maximum chlorpropamide + maximum metformin	6–10	Stop metformin Add once-daily ultralente insulin Stop chlorpropamide and metformin
	>10	Start basal and prandial insulin
Maximum chlorpropamide + ultralente insulin	Preprandial blood glucose >7	Stop chlorpropamide Add prandial insulin

Table 48.3. Guide to therapy when aiming for basal normoglycaemia (FBG < 6 mmol/l).

Note: Chlorpropamide is shown as an example. Other sulphonylureas may be substituted.

Current therapy	Fasting blood glucose (mmol/l)	Suggested action
Diet only	6–8	Add chlorpropamide 100 mg/day
	8–10	Add chlorpropamide 250 mg/day
	10–18	Add chlorpropamide 500 mg/day
	18–25	Add chlorpropamide 500 mg/day but will almost certainly require an additional therapeutic agent
	>25	Add once-daily insulin, e.g. lente ± soluble mixture
Maximum chlorpropamide	6–10	Continue maximum chlorpropamide
	10–14	Add metformin 500 mg b.d.
	14–20	Add once-daily ultralente insulin
	>20	Stop chlorpropamide. Start once-daily insulin, e.g. lente ± soluble mixture
Maximum chlorpropamide + maximum metformin	6–10	Continue maximum chlorpropamide and metformin
	10–20	Stop metformin Add once-daily ultralente insulin
	>20	Stop chlorpropamide and metformin Start once-daily insulin, e.g. lente ± soluble mixture
Maximum chlorpropamide + ultralente insulin	>20 or symptoms	Stop chlorpropamide and ultralente Start insulin, e.g. once-daily lente ± soluble insulin or twice-daily soluble/ premixed formulation isophane

Table 48.4. Guide to therapy when aiming to abolish symptoms and to reduce the fasting blood glucose to below 10 mmol/l.

Table 48.5. Features suggesting the need for full (basal and prandial) insulin treatment in NIDDM patients.

- FBG with diet alone >12 mmol/l
- FBG with diet plus maximal oral agents >10 mmol/l
- Blood glucose remains >7 mmol/l before meals when treated with ultralente alone
- Raised HbA$_{1c}$ but normal FBG when treated with ultralente alone
- Basal insulin requirement >14 U/day in lean patients (>0.2 U/kg/day in obese)

order to detect when blood glucose levels do not return to <6−7 mmol/l before the next meal. A raised HbA$_{1c}$ in the presence of a normal FBG also suggests this, and an FBG exceeding 12 mmol/l in diet-treated patients or 10 mmol/l in those receiving full-dose sulphonylureas further indicates severe insulinopenia and the likely need for full insulin therapy. As in IDDM, it is logical to try to simulate the physiological pattern of insulin secretion, using a basal and prandial regimen [10, 64], even though these patients are not necessarily insulin-dependent.

With the introduction of soluble insulin before main meals, it becomes important to control dietary distribution, meal and snack sizes, and to encourage home blood glucose monitoring together with regular HbA$_{1c}$ measurements. By this stage, there is little endogenous insulin production and attempting to increase this with a sulphonylurea has little additional effect. As soluble insulin is introduced, sulphonylurea treatment can therefore be stopped [13].

In non-diabetic subjects, roughly one-half of daily insulin secretion is the basal component (which restrains hepatic glucose output and permits normal metabolic function) and one-half is released in response to meals. In NIDDM patients whose basal insulin supplementation is satisfactory, preprandial short-acting insulin can be given in proportion to the meal size and planned exercise. Unfortunately, even short-acting insulin lasts for 6 hours or more with a peak at 2 hours, and a snack is usually required 2−3 hours after a main meal in order to prevent hypoglycaemia. It is this mis-match of timing of the action profile of insulin which makes it difficult to add soluble insulin effectively to the basal insulin supplement described above. If a non-obese person is taking a basal insulin supplement of less than 14 U, the blood glucose level usually returns to <6 mmol/l before the next meal, and the addition of only 1 or 2 U soluble insulin can induce marked hypo-

glycaemic reactions before the next meal. The advent of shorter-acting insulins whose action profile approaches the normal prandial insulin response (e.g. monomeric insulins (Chapters 37 and 38), and the use of alternative methods of administration such as intranasal insulin (Chapter 46)), may improve the prandial glycaemic profile in more NIDDM patients.

Depending on their degree of insulin deficiency, patients will require varying amounts of basal and prandial insulin. As previously discussed, obese patients need larger doses. Table 48.6 gives a guide to the range of prandial insulin doses needed in these patients, taking into account the insulin resistance associated with obesity. Appropriate dosages can also be calculated using a slide rule obtainable from Owen Mumford Ltd, Woodstock, Oxford, UK.

Regular home blood glucose monitoring is essential in these patients. Four preprandial blood glucose estimations on one or two days each week generally suffice to maintain reasonable overall control, but patients with variable control or intercurrent infections need to test more frequently. It may then be necessary to measure

Table 48.6. Guide to prandial insulin doses. This table assumes that the patient is receiving a basal dose which maintains the fasting blood glucose at 4−6 mmol/l. Determine the patient's percentage of ideal body weight and read off the prandial dose which corresponds to the empirical basal requirement.

This is the *total* daily prandial requirement and will need to be subdivided according to meal-size and exercise. Final adjustments must be on the basis of glycaemic monitoring.

	Ideal weight	% over ideal body weight				
		+20	+40	+60	+80	+100
Basal	16	24	32	40	48	56
Prandial	2	3	4	5	6	7
Basal	20	30	40	50	60	70
Prandial	6	9	12	15	18	21
Basal	24	36	48	60	72	84
Prandial	10	15	20	25	30	35
Basal	28	42	56	70	84	98
Prandial	18	27	36	45	54	63
Basal	32	48	64	80	96	112
Prandial	28	42	56	70	84	98
Basal	36	54	72	90	108	126
Prandial	42	63	84	105	126	147

the glucose concentration before every meal and to adjust the insulin dose accordingly.

The elderly diabetic patient

In the elderly, the treatment goals need to be modified, aiming for the least demanding regimen which avoids both hyperglycaemic symptoms and unacceptable side-effects. Concomitant treatment such as thiazide diuretics and corticosteroids which exacerbate diabetes needs to be critically reviewed. Using this less intensive approach (Table 48.4), sulphonylurea and/or metformin therapy can be given only when the patient is symptomatic, although it is best to aim to reduce FBG to below 10 mmol/l to allow some margin for intercurrent infections. A basal insulin supplement can be introduced if the FBG during sulphonylurea and metformin treatment exceeds 10 mmol/l, although many would only add insulin in response to significant symptoms. This regimen can be continued even if there is considerable post-prandial hyperglycaemia; the addition of short-acting insulin will not only demand a more regimented lifestyle but will also increase the risks of hypoglycaemia if meals and snacks are missed. Should basal and prandial insulin replacement be required, it is often easier to give this as once-daily lente insulin with a short-acting insulin injected once-daily before the main meal, or as a twice-daily mixture of soluble and isophane insulins.

Which regimen?

It is assumed that long-term near-normoglycaemia will benefit middle-aged diabetic patients, but there is no reliable evidence to support this view. To date, only two studies have been established to determine whether any particular treatment schedule is better than the others in preventing long-term complications.

The *University Group Diabetes Program* (UGDP) was an American study set up in 1961 in 12 centres with the aim of determining whether or not improved control of blood glucose would help to prevent or delay vascular disease. Over 1000 patients were randomly assigned to placebo, tolbutamide, phenformin, or fixed or variable doses of insulin. The study was discontinued prematurely as interim data appeared to show excess cardiovascular mortality in those groups allocated to phenformin or tolbutamide therapy. Sub-sequent re-analysis of the data [65] suggested that the cardiovascular events during sulphonylurea treatment occurred mainly in the more severely hyperglycaemic patients. However, such *post hoc* analyses are unreliable and the UGDP study was intrinsically too small to provide a definitive answer. Other criticisms have included apparent bias in the allocation of patients to the placebo group and the fact that many patients during the trial were continued on treatment regimens which in usual practice would have been modified. Other observational studies of large numbers of patients receiving sulphonylureas did not find an obviously high rate of cardiovascular death but could have failed to detect the size of increase noted in the UGDP study.

The *UK Prospective Diabetes Study* (UKPDS) has randomized over 3500 patients to treatment with diet alone, a sulphonylurea, metformin or insulin. The aim is to determine whether improved glycaemic control will reduce diabetic morbidity and mortality and whether it is better to lower the blood glucose with oral agents or insulin. The study is due to report in 1994, by which time over 5000 patients will have been followed for a minimum of 3 years.

Conclusions

Near-normoglycaemia can be achieved in most NIDDM patients who fail to respond to diet alone, through the use of oral agents and/or insulin. The outcome of large-scale studies such as the UKPDS is awaited with interest, as it might then become feasible to make recommendations on treatments which are based on firm data. At present, it is perfectly reasonable for a physician to justify any specific therapy, as none has been shown to be advantageous.

RURY R. HOLMAN
ROBERT C. TURNER

References

1 Turner RC, Holman RR. Insulin rather than glucose home-ostasis in the patho-physiology of diabetes. *Lancet* 1976; i: 1272–4.
2 Holman RR, Turner RC. Maintenance of basal plasma glucose and insulin concentrations in maturity-onset diabetes. *Diabetes* 1979; **28**: 227–30.
3 Holman RR, Turner RC. The basal plasma glucose: A simple relevant index of diabetes. *Clin Endocr* 1981; **14**: 279–86.
4 Holman RR, Turner RC. Diabetes: The quest for basal normoglycaemia. *Lancet* 1977; i: 469–74.

5 Holman RR, Steemson J, Darling P, Turner RC. No glycemic benefit from guar administration in NIDDM. *Diabetes Care* 1987; **10**: 68–71.

6 Alberti KGMM, Gries FA. Management of non-insulin dependent diabetes mellitus in Europe: a consensus view. *Diabetic Med* 1988; **5**: 275–81.

7 Fuller JH, Shipley MJ, Rose G et al. Coronary-heart-disease risk and impaired glucose tolerance. The Whitehall study. *Lancet* 1980; i: 1373–6.

8 Ducimetière P, Eschwège E, Richard J et al. Clinical complications of coronary heart disease according to plasma insulin and glucose levels. A further analysis of the Paris Prospective Study. In: Eschwège E, ed. *Advances in Diabetes Epidemiology*. New York: Elsevier Biomedical, 1987: 149.

9 UK Prospective Study of Therapies of Maturity-onset Diabetes: I. Effect of diet, sulphonylurea, insulin or biguanide therapy on fasting plasma glucose and body weight over one year. Multi-centre study. *Diabetologia* 1983; **24**: 404–11.

10 Holman RR, Turner RC. Optimizing blood glucose control in type 2 diabetes: an approach based on fasting blood glucose measurements. *Diabetic Med* 1988; **5**: 582–8.

11 UK Prospective Study of Therapies of Maturity-onset Diabetes: II. Reduction in HbAlc with basal insulin supplement, sulfonylurea or biguanide therapy. Multi-centre study. *Diabetes* 1985; **34**: 793–8.

12 Bailey CJ, Nattrass M. Treatment – metformin. In: Nattrass M, Hale PJ, eds. *Non-insulin-dependent diabetes mellitus, Clin Endocrinol Metab*, vol. 2. London: Baillière, 1988: 455–76.

13 Ward EA, Ward GM, Turner RC. Effect of sulphonylurea therapy on insulin secretion and glucose control of insulin-treated diabetics. *Br Med J* 1981; **283**: 278–80.

14 Castillo M, Scheen A, Paolisso G, Lefèbvre P. The addition of glipizide to insulin therapy in Type II diabetic patients with secondary failure to sulphonylureas is useful only in the presence of a significant residual insulin secretion. *Acta Endocrinol* 1987; **116**: 364.

15 Matthews DR, Bown E, Watson A, Holman RR, Steemson J, Hughes S, Scott D. Pen-sized digital 30-second blood glucose meter. *Lancet* 1987; i: 778–9.

16 Howe-Davies S, Holman RR, Phillips M, Turner RC. Home blood sampling for plasma glucose assay in control of diabetes. *Br Med J* 1978; **2**: 596–8.

17 Turner RC, Holman RR, Matthews DR, Peto J, Hockaday TDR. Insulin deficiency and insulin resistance interaction in diabetes: estimation of their relative contributions by feedback analysis from basal plasma insulin and glucose concentrations. *Metabolism* 1979; **28**: 11: 1086–96.

18 Efendic S, Enzmann, Nylen A, Uvnas-Wallensten, Luft R. Effect of glucose/sulfonylurea interaction on release of insulin, glucagon, and somatostatin from isolated perfused rat pancreas. *Proc Natl Acad Sci USA* 1979; **76**: 5901–4.

19 Sturgess NC, Ashford ML, Cook DL, Hales CN. The sulphonylurea receptor may be an ATP-sensitive potassium channel. *Lancet* 1985; ii: 474–5.

20 Bailey CJ, Flatt PR, Marks V. Drugs inducing hypoglycaemia. *Pharmac Ther* 1989; **42**: 361–84.

21 Judzewitsch RG, Pfeifer MA, Best JD, Beard JC, Halter JB, Porte D Jr. Chronic chlorpropamide therapy of noninsulin-dependent diabetics augments basal and stimulated insulin secretion by increasing islet sensitivity to glucose. *J Clin Endocrinol Metab* 1982; **55**: 321–8.

22 Pfeifer MA, Halter JB, Graf R, Porte D Jr. Potentiation of insulin secretion to nonglucose stimuli in normal man by tolbutamide. *Diabetes* 1980; **29**: 335–40.

23 Greenfield MS, Doberne L, Rosenthal M, Schulz B, Widstrom A, Reaven GM. Effect of sulphonylurea treatment on *in vivo* insulin secretion and action in patients with non-insulin dependent diabetes mellitus. *Diabetes* 1982; **31**: 307.

24 Kosaka K. Clinical studies of diabetes mellitus. *J Jpn Soc Int Med* 1977; **66**: 1343–9.

25 Hosker JP, Burnett MA, Davies EG, Turner RC. Sulphonylurea therapy doubles beta-cell response to glucose in Type 2 diabetic patients. *Diabetologia* 1985; **28**: 809–14.

26 Feldman JM, Lebovitz HE. Endocrine and metabolic effects of glibenclamide. Evidence for an extrapancreatic mechanism of action. *Diabetes* 1971; **20**: 745.

27 Feinglos MN, Lebovitz HE. Sulphonylureas increase the number of insulin receptors. *Nature* 1978; **275**: 184–5.

28 Lockwood DH, Gerich JE, Goldfine I. Symposium on effects of oral hypoglycaemic agents on receptor and postreceptor actions of insulin. *Diabetes Care* 1984; **7** (suppl 1): 1–129.

29 Beck-Nielsen H, Hjøllund E, Pedersen O, Richelsen B, Sorensen NS. Sulfonylureas improve insulin binding and insulin action in non-insulin-dependent diabetes mellitus. *Diabetes Care* 1984; **7** (suppl 1): 100–5.

30 Olefsky MD, Reaven GM. Effects of sulfonylurea therapy on insulin binding to mononuclear leukocytes of diabetic patients. *Am J Med* 1976; **60**: 89–95.

31 Maloff BL, Lockwood DH. *In vitro* effects of a sulfonylurea on insulin action in adipocytes. *J Clin Invest* 1981; **68**: 85–90.

32 DeFronzo RA, Ferrannini E, Koivisto Y. New concepts in the pathogenesis and treatment of non-insulin dependent diabetes mellitus. *Am J Med* 1983; **74** (suppl 1A): 52–81.

33 Prince M, Olefsky J. Direct *in vitro* effects of a sulfonylurea to increase human fibroblast insulin receptors. *J Clin Invest* 1980; **66**: 608–12.

34 Camerini-Davalos R, Marble A. Incidence and causes of secondary failure in treatment with tolbutamide. *J Am Med Ass* 1962; **181**: 89–94.

35 Kolterman O, Gray R, Shapiro G et al. The acute and chronic effects of sulfonylurea therapy in type II diabetic subjects. *Diabetes* 1984; **33**: 346–54.

36 Groop L, Schalin C, Franssila-Kallunki A, Widén E, Ekstrand A, Eriksson J. Characteristics of non-insulin-dependent diabetic patients with secondary failure to oral antidiabetic therapy. *Am J Med* 1989; **87**: 183–90.

37 Turner RC, Holman RR, Matthews DR. Sulphonylureas and inadequacy. In: Cameron D, Colagiuri S, Heding L, Kühl C, Ma A, Mortimer R, eds. *Non-insulin-dependent Diabetes Mellitus*. Satellite Symposium of 13th IDFF 1988; pp. 52–6. Amsterdam: Excerpta Medica.

38 Melander A, Sartor G, Wåhlin E, Scherstén B, Bitzén P-O. Serum tolbutamide and chlorpropamide concentrations in patients with diabetes mellitus. *Br Med J* 1978; **1**: 142–4.

39 Ferner RE, Chaplin S. The relationship between the pharmacokinetics and pharmacodynamic effects of oral hypoglycaemic drugs. *Clin Pharmacokinet* 1987; **12**: 379–401.

40 Melander A. Sulphonylureas in the treatment of non-insulin-dependent diabetes. In: Nattrass M, Hale PJ, eds. *Non-insulin-dependent Diabetes. Clin Endocrinol Metab*, vol. 2. London: Baillière, 1988: 443–53.

41 Raptis S, Rau RM, Schroder KE, Faulhaber JD, Pfeiffer EF. Comparative study of insulin secretion following repeated administration of glucose, tolbutamide and glibenclamide (HB 419) in diabetic and non-diabetic human subjects. *Horm Metab Res* 1969; **1** (suppl): 65–76.

42 Asplund K, Wilholm B, Lithner F. Glibenclamide associated hypoglycaemia: a report on 57 cases. *Diabetologia* 1983; **24**: 412–17.

43 Berger W, Cardiff F, Pasquel M, Rump A. Die relative Haüfigkeit der schweren Sulfonylharnstoff-Hypoglykämie in den letzen 25 Jahren in der Schweiz. *Schweiz Med Wochenschr* 1986; **116**: 145–51.

44 Campbell IW. Metformin and the sulphonylureas: the comparative risks. *Horm Metab Res Suppl* 1985; **15**: 105–11.

45 Wiles PG, Pyke DA. The chlorpropamide alcohol flush. *Clin Sci* 1984; **67**: 375–81.

46 Lev J, Zeidler A, Kumar D. Glyburide and glipizide in treatment of diabetic patients with secondary failure to tolazamide or chlorpropamide. *Diabetes Care* 1987; **10**: 679.

47 Clarke BF, Campbell IW. Long-term comparative trial of glibenclamide and chlorpropamide in diet-failed, maturity-onset diabetics. *Lancet* 1975; i: 246–8.

48 Clarke BF, Campbell IW. Comparison of metformin and chlorpropamide in non-obese, maturity-onset diabetics uncontrolled by diet. *Br Med J* 1977; **2**: 1576–8.

49 Bailey CJ. Metformin revisited: its actions and indications for use. *Diabetic Med* 1988; **5**: 315–20.

50 Prager R, Schernthaser G, Graf H. Effect of metformin on peripheral insulin sensitivity in non-insulin dependent diabetes mellitus. *Diabète Métab* 1986; **12**: 346–50.

51 Gawler DJ, Milligan G, Houslay MD. Treatment of streptozotocin diabetic rats with metformin restores the ability of insulin to inhibit adenylate cyclase activity. *Biochem J* 1988; **249**: 537–42.

52 Nattrass M, Todd PG, Hinks L, Lloyd B, Alberti KGMM. Comparative effects of phenformin, metformin and glibenclamide on metabolic rhythms in maturity-onset diabetes. *Diabetologia* 1977; **13**: 145–52.

53 Graf H, Leach W, Arieff AI. Effects of dichloroacetate in the treatment of hypoxic lactic acidosis in dogs. *J Clin Invest* 1985; **76**: 919–23.

54 Ryder RE. Lactic acidosis: high-dose or low-dose bicarbonate therapy. *Diabetes Care* 1984; **7**: 99–102.

55 Lalau JD, Andrejak M, Morinière P *et al*. Hemodialysis in the treatment of lactic acidosis in diabetics treated by metformin: a study of metformin elimination. *Int J Clin Pharmacol Therap Toxicol* 1989; **27**: 285–8.

56 Owens DR. *Human Insulin: Clinical Pharmacological Studies in Normal Men*. Lancaster: MTP Press, 1986.

57 Riddle MC. New tactics for type 2 diabetes: regimens based on intermediate-acting insulin taken at bedtime. *Lancet* 1985; i: 192–4.

58 Ward GM, Simpson RW, Ward EA, Turner RC. Comparison of two twice-daily insulin regimens: ultralente/soluble and soluble/isophane. *Diabetologia* 1981; **21**: 383–6.

59 Jørgensen S, Vaag A, Langkjær L, Hougaard P, Markussen J. NovoSol Basal: pharmacokinetics of a novel soluble long acting insulin analogue. *Br Med J* 1989; **299**: 415–19.

60 Peacock I, Tattersall RB. The difficult choice of treatment for poorly controlled maturity onset diabetes: tablets or insulin? *Br Med J* 1984; **288**: 1956–9.

61 Gutniak M, Karlander S, Efendic S. Glyburide decreases insulin requirement, increases B cell response to mixed meal and does not affect insulin sensitivity: effects of short- and long-term combined treatment in secondary failure of sulphonylureas. *Diabetes Care* 1987; **10**: 545.

62 Holman RR, Steemson J, Turner RC. Sulphonylurea failure in type 2 diabetes: Treatment with a basal insulin supplement. *Diabetic Med* 1987; **4**: 457–62.

63 Yki-Järvinen H, Esko N, Eero H, Marja-Ritta T. Clinical benefits and mechanisms of a sustained response to intermittent insulin therapy in Type 2 diabetic patients with secondary failure. *Am J Med* 1988; **84**: 185.

64 Phillips M, Simpson RW, Holman RR, Turner RC. A simple and rational twice daily insulin regime. *Q J Med* 1979; **191**: 493–506.

65 Kilo C, Miller JP, Williamson JR. The crux of the UGDP: spurious results and biologically inappropriate data analysis. *Diabetologia* 1980; **18**: 179–85.

SECTION 12
ACUTE METABOLIC COMPLICATIONS

49 Diabetic Ketoacidosis, Non-Ketotic Hyperosmolar Coma and Lactic Acidosis

Diabetic ketoacidosis

Summary

- Diabetic ketoacidosis is the largest single cause of death in diabetic patients under the age of 20 years in the UK, with an average mortality of about 7% of episodes. Mortality is particularly high in the elderly.
- The common precipitating causes are infection, management errors and new cases of diabetes, but there is no obvious cause in about 40% of episodes.
- Ketoacidosis is initiated by an absolute or relative insulin deficiency and an increase in catabolic hormones, leading to hepatic overproduction of glucose and ketone bodies.
- Symptoms include increasing polyuria and polydipsia, weight loss, weakness, drowsiness and eventual coma (10% of cases); abdominal pain may be present, particularly in the young.
- Signs include dehydration, hypotension, tachycardia, hyperventilation and hypothermia.
- Immediate investigations should include bedside blood glucose and ketone estimations by reagent strips, followed by laboratory measurements of blood glucose, urea, Na^+, K^+, full blood count, arterial blood pH (and gases in shocked patients), and blood and urine culture in all subjects.
- Treatment involves:

  rehydration with isotonic saline (e.g. 1 l/h for first 3 h, 6–10 l for first 24 h);

  short-acting insulin, ideally by low-dose intravenous infusion (e.g. 5–10 U/h until blood glucose level reaches 14 mmol/l, then 2–4 U/h), or by intramuscular injection (e.g. 20 U initially followed by 5–10 U/h until blood glucose reaches 14 mmol/l);

  potassium replacement (generally 20 mmol K^+ per litre of saline, adjusted by careful monitoring).
- Small doses of sodium bicarbonate (100 mmol, given as isotonic (1.4%) solution) may be given if the blood pH is <7.0 or cardio-respiratory collapse seems imminent.
- Complications of ketoacidosis include cerebral oedema (especially in the young), adult respiratory distress syndrome and thromboembolism.

Ketoacidosis is the largest single cause of death in diabetic patients under the age of 20 years in the UK and accounted for 15% of deaths in diabetic patients under the age of 50 years in a recent survey [1]. Although it principally affects younger IDDM patients, ketoacidosis may be precipitated in patients of any age during severe intercurrent illness. Although many ketoacidosis-related deaths are inevitable consequences of associated medical conditions such as overwhelming infection or myocardial infarction, others are still potentially preventable, and due to delays in presentation or diagnosis or to errors in management [1]. Despite improvements in general medical care, the incidence of diabetic ketoacidosis in Western countries has not fallen substantially in recent years [2].

Definition

The cardinal biochemical features of diabetic ketoacidosis are hyperglycaemia, hyperketonaemia and metabolic acidosis. The working definition of Alberti [3] continues to be useful: 'severe

479

uncontrolled diabetes requiring emergency treatment with insulin and intravenous fluids and with a blood ketone body (acetoacetate and 3-hydroxybutyrate) concentration of greater than 5 mmol/l. Few centres routinely measure ketone body concentrations and biochemical confirmation of the diagnosis is usually based on semi-quantitative methods such as Acetest or Ketostix applied to plasma.

Mortality

Before the introduction of insulin in 1923, diabetic ketoacidosis was invariably fatal. The current average mortality rate for ketoacidosis is approximately 7% although reported rates vary from 0 to 19% [4]. Although differences in defining ketoacidosis and selecting patients partly account for variation, mortality is generally higher in less specialized centres and in certain groups of patients such as the elderly [5].

In our own centre, 746 episodes of ketoacidosis were observed over a 15-year period (1971–85) in 506 patients, followed by a second episode in 47% of these patients. As in previous reports, female patients predominated, with a female to male ratio of nearly 2:1. The age distribution of the 746 episodes is given in Fig. 49.1a.

In our series, 32 patients died, producing a mortality rate of 4.3% per episode (6.3% of cases). All hospital deaths occurring in patients admitted with ketoacidosis are included in this series. Increasing age was associated with higher mortality rates (Fig. 49.1b). The principal causes of death are given in Table 49.1.

Precipitating factors

In our series, infection was the commonest identifiable cause of ketoacidosis, accounting for 207 (28%) episodes (Fig. 49.2). New cases of diabetes accounted for 10% of episodes and management errors (including inappropriate changes in insulin treatment, initiated either by patient or doctor) contributed to a further 13%. Myocardial infarction was responsible for only 1% of episodes, and miscellaneous conditions for the remaining 5%.

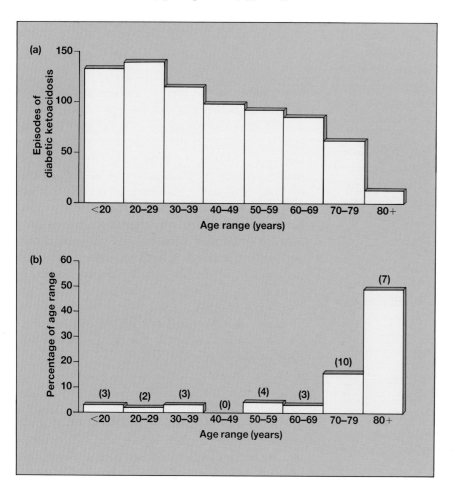

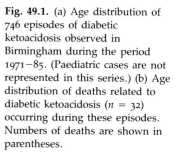

Fig. 49.1. (a) Age distribution of 746 episodes of diabetic ketoacidosis observed in Birmingham during the period 1971–85. (Paediatric cases are not represented in this series.) (b) Age distribution of deaths related to diabetic ketoacidosis (n = 32) occurring during these episodes. Numbers of deaths are shown in parentheses.

Table 49.1. Principal causes of mortality occurring in 746 episodes of diabetic ketoacidosis.

Cause of death	Number of deaths
Primary metabolic causes	10
Myocardial infarction/ congestive cardiac failure	9
Pneumonia	7
Pulmonary embolism	3
Other conditions	3
Total	32

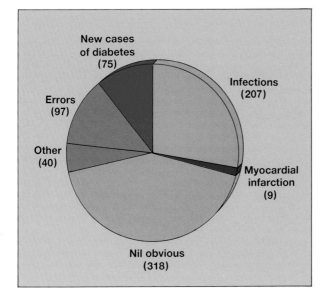

Fig. 49.2. Precipitating causes of 746 episodes of diabetic ketoacidosis observed in Birmingham during the period 1971−85.

No precipitating cause was identified in 43% of episodes.

In other centres, increased rates of ketoacidosis have been observed following initiation of continuous subcutaneous insulin infusion (CSII) [6, 7] (see Chapter 42) but ketoacidosis apparently becomes rarer as patients and clinicians become more experienced with the technique [8, 9]. Intercurrent illness, mechanical pump failure, and inadequate monitoring appear to be important factors; the small subcutaneous depot of insulin with CSII may fail to impede the development of ketoacidosis.

Pathogenesis

Diabetic ketoacidosis is characterized by increased counter-regulatory (catabolic) hormone concen-trations (glucagon, catecholamines, cortisol and growth hormone), in the presence of an absolute or, more commonly, a relative deficiency of insulin [10, 11]. Although residual endogenous insulin secretion may protect against ketoacidosis in some patients [12] (Chapter 32), suppression of B-cell secretion by catecholamines during intercurrent illness may precipitate ketoacidosis in patients with NIDDM.

Withdrawal of insulin from IDDM patients leads to a rapid rise in plasma glucagon levels [13, 14] (Fig. 49.3). Dehydration and acidosis stimulate the release of catecholamines [15] and cortisol [16], producing a vicious circle in which worsening metabolic decompensation further stimulates catabolic hormone secretion.

Glucose and ketone body kinetics

Diabetic ketoacidosis is initiated primarily by hepatic overproduction of glucose and ketone bodies [17], while impaired disposal of these substrates by peripheral tissues such as muscle and brain acts to maintain the metabolic disturbance [18]. Following withdrawal of insulin from

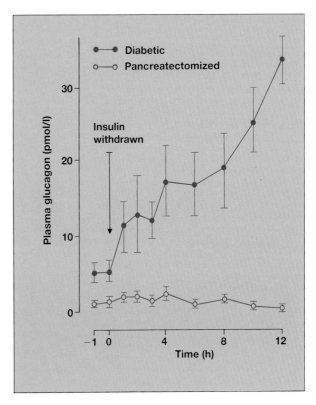

Fig. 49.3. Plasma concentrations (mean ± SEM) of glucagon in six IDDM patients and four pancreatectomized subjects after withdrawal of insulin. (Reproduced with permission from Barnes *et al.* 1977 [14].)

IDDM patients, hepatic production of glucose and ketone bodies rapidly increases (Fig. 49.4). The rate of glucose production decreases towards normal after 4 hours but hyperglycaemia is maintained because the rates of production and utilization become equal. Insulin withdrawal results in a progressive increase in both production and utilization of ketone bodies (Fig. 49.4); however, as the former always exceeds the latter, plasma ketone body concentrations rise progressively.

HYPERGLYCAEMIA

Insulin deficiency and elevated plasma levels of catabolic hormones (particularly glucagon and catecholamines) cause increased rates of hepatic glycogenolysis and gluconeogenesis. Renal gluconeogenesis is also enhanced in the presence of acidosis.

Glucose disposal by peripheral tissues such as muscle and adipose tissue is reduced by insulin deficiency while elevated plasma levels of catabolic hormones and fatty acids induce relative insulin resistance [19]. Thus, the blood glucose concentration falls more slowly during insulin treatment of patients with higher levels of catabolic hormones due to infection [20], although this degree of insulin resistance is readily overcome by 'low-dose' intravenous insulin regimens.

HYPERKETONAEMIA

Plasma ketone body concentrations are often raised to 200–300 times the normal fasting values. Ketone bodies are strong organic acids which dissociate fully at physiological pH to generate

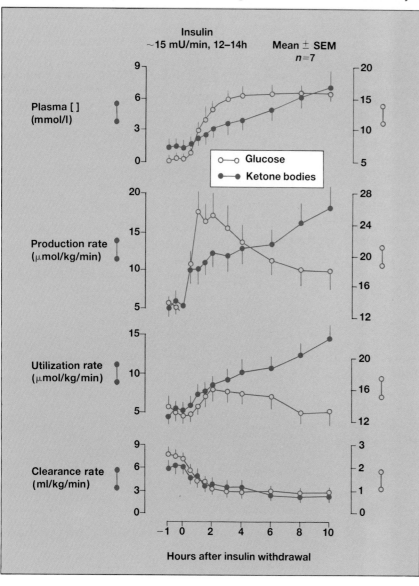

Fig. 49.4. Changes in plasma concentrations and in the rates of production, utilization and clearance of glucose and ketone bodies following withdrawal of insulin from seven IDDM patients. (Reproduced from Miles *et al.* 1980 [17] with permission of the authors and the American Diabetes Association Inc.)

equimolar amounts of hydrogen ions. Rapid rises in plasma hydrogen ion concentration in keto-acidosis outstrip the buffering capacity of the body fluids and tissues, causing metabolic acidosis which has several serious detrimental physio-logical effects accounting for many of the cardinal clinical features of ketoacidosis. Acidosis has a negative inotropic effect on cardiac muscle [21] and exacerbates systemic hypotension by inducing peripheral vasodilatation. The risk of ventricular arrhythmias may be increased [22] and severe acidosis (pH < 7.0) may cause respiratory de-pression [23]. Both ketogenesis and ketone body disposal are disturbed in ketoacidosis.

Ketogenesis. In diabetic ketoacidosis, insulin deficiency and catabolic hormone excess (particu-larly the catecholamines) promote excessive break-down of adipose tissue triglyceride (lipolysis), while re-esterification is impaired, resulting in the release of large quantities of long-chain, non-esterified fatty acids. These effects are mediated via the activity of hormone-sensitive lipase, an enzyme exquisitely sensitive to inhibition by insulin.

Long-chain, non-esterified fatty acids are the principal substrate for hepatic ketogenesis, keto-genesis being directly enhanced by the increased portal delivery of fatty acids.

In diabetic ketoacidosis, concurrent with the impaired hepatic re-esterification, fatty acids are preferentially partially oxidized to ketone bodies [24]. Fatty acids are converted to coenzyme A (CoA) derivatives before transportation into the mitochondria by an active transport system (the 'carnitine shuttle'). Within the mitochondria, fatty acyl CoA undergoes β-oxidation to produce acetyl CoA which is then either completely oxi-dized in the tricarboxylic acid cycle, utilized in lipid synthesis, or partially oxidized to ketone bodies (acetoacetate and 3-hydroxybutyrate). The combination of insulin deficiency with elevated levels of catabolic hormones in uncontrolled dia-betes strongly favours entry of fatty acids into the mitochondria and the preferential formation of ketone bodies.

Acetoacetate is in equilibrium with 3-hydroxy-butyrate, according to the redox state of the liver:

acetoacetate $\rightleftharpoons$ 3-hydroxybutyrate
+ NADH *3-hydroxybutyrate* + NAD
+ H$^+$ *dehydrogenase*

In ketoacidosis, the plasma 3-hydroxybutyrate:

acetoacetate ratio is elevated, reflecting hepatic intramitochondrial acidosis. Acetone is formed by the spontaneous decarboxylation of acetoacetate:

$$acetoacetate \longrightarrow acetone + CO_2$$

Ketone body disposal. Most extrahepatic tissues have the capacity to utilize ketone bodies, but this is impaired in uncontrolled diabetes. Oxidation of ketone anions during treatment neutralizes the acidosis by generating bicarbonate ions. In ad-dition, increased excretion of ketone bodies through the kidneys and lungs is important in eliminating ketone bodies in ketoacidosis.

Fluid and electrolyte depletion

Hyperglycaemia causes an osmotic diuresis when the renal threshold for glucose is exceeded, leading to dehydration and secondary losses of electrolytes [25, 26] (Table 49.2). Insulin deficiency and glu-cagon excess exacerbate the renal sodium de-pletion by impairing tubular sodium reabsorption [27]. Metabolic acidosis displaces intracellular potassium ions into extracellular fluid, which may subsequently be lost in vomit or urine. Hyper-ventilation, fever and sweating due to infection may further exacerbate fluid and electrolyte depletion.

In adults, average losses of body water are ap-proximately 5 l [28]. By reducing renal blood flow, dehydration impairs a major route of elimination of glucose and ketone bodies; early in treatment, fluid replacement is therefore as important as insulin administration.

Despite a considerable total body potassium deficit (often 300–700 mmol) plasma potassium levels may be low, normal or high, although hypo-kalaemia at presentation signifies severe depletion of total body potassium [29].

Phosphate deficiency in ketoacidosis is associ-ated with reduced red-cell 2, 3-diphosphoglycerate

Table 49.2. Average adult deficits of electrolytes in diabetic ketoacidosis.

Sodium	500 mmol
Chloride	350 mmol
Potassium	300–1000 mmol
Calcium	50–100 mmol
Phosphate	50–100 mmol
Magnesium	25–50 mmol

levels, which would tend to reduce oxygen delivery to the tissues [30]. However, the acidaemia of ketoacidosis partially offsets the adverse effects on the oxyhaemoglobin dissociation curve and the benefits of phosphate supplements have not been substantiated in clinical trials [31].

Clinical features

The cardinal symptoms of ketoacidosis are increasing polyuria and polydipsia, weight loss and generalized weakness, followed by drowsiness and eventually coma (Table 49.3). Symptoms usually develop over several days and all too often it is the onset of vomiting which finally precipitates emergency hospital admission.

Dehydration, hypotension and tachycardia are prominent in severe diabetic ketoacidosis. Metabolic acidosis stimulates the medullary respiratory centre, causing rapid and deep respiration (Kussmaul breathing). The odour of acetone (like 'pear drops' or nail-varnish remover) may be detectable on the patient's breath, although many people are anosmic for acetone.

Some impairment of conscious level is common, although frank coma occurs in only 10% of patients. The mechanism of ketoacidosis-induced coma remains obscure; blunting of consciousness correlates with plasma osmolarity but not with the degree of acidosis [32]. Coma at presentation is associated with a worse prognosis [33]. The possibility of coexisting causes of coma such as stroke, head injury or drug overdose should always be considered and excluded if appropriate (see Table 49.7). Acidosis causes peripheral vasodilatation which, as well as exacerbating hypotension, may lead to hypothermia, thereby masking a valuable sign of infection [34]. Rectal temperature should be checked with a low-reading thermometer if hypothermia is suspected. A non-specific leukocytosis is common in ketoacidosis and does not necessarily indicate the presence of infection.

Table 49.3. Clinical features of diabetic ketoacidosis.

Polyuria, nocturia; thirst
Weight loss
Weakness
Visual disturbance
Abdominal pain
Leg cramps
Nausea, vomiting
Confusion, drowsiness, coma

A succussion splash due to gastric stasis may be evident on abdominal examination. Generalized abdominal pain may occur in younger patients with severe acidosis [35]. If pain does not resolve within a few hours of treatment, a separate cause should be suspected; measurement of plasma amylase is unhelpful, as levels are often non-specifically raised in ketoacidosis [36].

Diagnosis and possible pitfalls

Diabetic ketoacidosis is a medical emergency. The diagnosis should be considered in any unconscious or hyperventilating patient [37] and can often be made in the casualty department following a rapid clinical examination and bedside blood and urine tests. If suspected, treatment must be started *without delay*: patients have died while waiting for laboratory confirmation of the diagnosis.

Hyperglycaemia may be rapidly determined using a glucose–oxidase reagent test strip, and urine (if available) should be tested for the presence of glucose and, most importantly, for ketones (using Acetest tablets or Ketostix dip sticks).

Venous blood is taken for laboratory measurement of glucose, urea, sodium and potassium concentrations, and a full blood count. Plasma ketone body concentrations should be measured (semi-quantitatively) using a nitroprusside-based reaction such as Ketostix or Acetest. These tests are essentially specific for acetoacetate and do not react with 3-hydroxybutyrate.

Euglycaemic diabetic ketoacidosis is recognized but is relatively uncommon [38]. Severe metabolic acidosis in the absence of hyperglycaemia (or other obvious cause of acidosis such as renal failure) raises the possibility of lactic acidosis (see later) or alcoholic ketoacidosis [39]. The latter occurs in alcoholics following a binge and reduced carbohydrate intake (often due to abdominal pain). As the metabolism of alcohol induces a more reduced hepatic mitochondrial redox state, the ratio of blood 3-hydroxybutyrate:acetoacetate is elevated, sometimes resulting in a false-negative or 'trace' Ketostix reaction despite significant ketonaemia. The same diagnostic caveat applies to lactic acidosis coexisting with ketoacidosis [40].

Despite a proportionally greater loss of body water, plasma sodium concentrations are usually normal or low, although plasma electrolyte concentrations may be falsely depressed by grossly elevated plasma glucose and lipid concentrations in diabetic ketoacidosis [41]; conversely, plasma sodium levels may appear to rise as hyperglycaemia and hyperlipidaemia are corrected by insulin treatment. Plasma should therefore be inspected for turbidity. Eruptive xanthomata and lipaemia retinalis are rare but recognized complications of ketoacidosis, which respond to its treatment. Plasma creatinine concentration is often falsely elevated in ketoacidosis due to assay interference and may lead to an erroneous diagnosis of renal failure [42].

Acidosis is quantified by measuring capillary blood pH, Pco_2 and bicarbonate concentration. Arterial Po_2 should be measured in severely shocked patients in order to determine the degree of hypoxia [43]. Tests for sickle cell disease and G-6-PD deficiency may be indicated in selected patients.

Bacteriological culture of urine and blood (collected before antibiotics are given) is mandatory in all cases and broad-spectrum antibiotics should be given if infection is suspected. An underlying cause should be diligently sought in all patients, but investigations should not delay essential treatment or management decisions such as transfer to an intensive care unit.

Some of the potential pitfalls in the diagnosis and management of diabetic ketoacidosis are summarized in Table 49.4.

Treatment of diabetic ketoacidosis in adults

Specific treatment comprises rehydration with intravenous fluids, the administration of insulin and replacement of electrolytes. The treatment of ketoacidosis in children is considered in Chapter 87.

The importance of general medical care and close supervision of the ketoacidotic patient by trained medical and nursing staff cannot be over-emphasized. A treatment flow-chart should always be employed and updated meticulously. Accurate recording of fluid balance is crucial; a urinary catheter should be inserted if no urine is passed in the first 4 hours. An initial treatment plan for diabetic ketoacidosis in adults is shown in Table 49.5.

FLUID AND ELECTROLYTE REPLACEMENT

Rehydration. Patients show considerable variation in fluid and electrolyte disturbances and the following recommendations are only a guide to therapy.

Rehydration is started with isotonic saline (150 mmol/l) containing appropriate potassium supplements (see below). Isotonic saline is used in preference to hypotonic saline (unless plasma osmolarity is significantly raised), to minimize the rapid movement of extracellular water into cells as blood glucose and osmolarity fall with treatment; such shifts have been implicated in the serious complication of cerebral oedema, discussed below.

Rehydration of the patient must take account of continuing polyuria and 6–10 l of fluid are commonly required during the first 24 h. In an average adult, 1 l of saline is infused every hour for the first 3 h. The rate of infusion is then adjusted according to the patient's clinical state. Considerable care is required in elderly patients or those with cardiac disease, in whom monitoring of central venous or pulmonary wedge pressure is strongly recommended. Occasionally, patients with relatively low plasma glucose concentrations on admission may require a simultaneous infusion of glucose.

Severe hypernatraemia (plasma sodium concentration exceeding 150 mmol/l) may necessitate

Table 49.4. Potential pitfalls in the diagnosis and management of diabetic ketoacidosis.

- *Smell of 'ketones' (acetone) on the breath*: may be absent (many people are anosmic for acetone)
- *Fever*: may be absent (peripheral vasodilation causes cooling)
- *Leukocytosis*: neutrophil count may be non-specifically raised
- *Plasma sodium concentration*: may be artificially lowered initially by high lipid and glucose levels and may appear to rise suddenly after insulin treatment lowers plasma glucose and lipid levels
- *Plasma potassium concentration*: may be temporarily raised (by acidosis) despite severe total body potassium depletion
- *Plasma creatinine concentration*: may be falsely elevated (assay interference)
- *'Ketostix' testing*: may show negative or trace result when diabetic ketoacidosis and either lactic acidosis or alcoholic ketoacidosis coexist (predominance of 3-hydroxybutyrate)

Fluids and electrolytes
Volumes
- 1 l/h × 3, thereafter according to need

Fluids
- Isotonic ('normal') saline (150 mmol/l) generally
- Hypotonic ('half-normal') saline (75 mmol/l) if plasma sodium exceeds 150 mmol/l (1 l)
- 5% glucose when blood glucose falls below 14 mmol/l
- Sodium bicarbonate (600 ml of 1.4%; or 100 ml of 8.4% if large vein cannulated) if pH < 7.0

Potassium
- Add dosages below to each 1 l of infused fluid:
  if plasma K <3.5 mmol/l, add 40 mmol KCl
            3.5−5.5 mmol/l, add 20 mmol KCl
            >5.5 mmol/ l, add no KCl

Insulin
Continuous i.v. infusion
- 5−10 U/h initially; maintenance (until able to eat), 2−4 U/h titrated against blood glucose levels

Intramuscular injections
- 20 U immediately, then 5−10 U/h, titrated against blood glucose levels

Other measures
- Treat precipitating cause (e.g., infection, myocardial infarction)
- Hypotension should respond to adequate fluid replacement
- Pass nasogastric tube if conscious level impaired
- Adult respiratory distress syndrome — ventilation (100% O_2, IPPV)
- Cerebral oedema — consider i.v. dexamethasone, mannitol
- Treat specific thromboembolic complications if they occur

Table 49.5. Initial treatment plan for diabetic ketoacidosis in adults.

the temporary replacement of isotonic saline with hypotonic saline (75 mmol/l) or 5% glucose (with an appropriate increase in the dose of insulin).

When the plasma glucose level has fallen to about 14 mmol/l, 5% dextrose solution is administered at a rate of around 250 ml/h until the patient is eating again, in order to avoid hypoglycaemia. The use of hypertonic (10%) glucose at this stage of treatment appears to confer no clinical advantage over 5% glucose [44].

Potassium replacement. Cardiac arrhythmias induced by iatrogenic hypokalaemia represent a major and avoidable cause of death. Insulin treatment and rising pH cause extracellular potassium to enter cells and, on average, 20 mmol of potassium (administered as 1.5 g potassium chloride) will be required in each litre of fluid following the start of insulin therapy. Continuous ECG monitoring may indicate signs of hypo- or hyperkalaemia, but the serum potassium concentration must be checked regularly (2-hourly at first) and potassium supplements adjusted appropriately. Particular care must be exercised in patients with

renal failure, anuria or oliguria (urine output less than 40 ml/h). If hypokalaemia is present (plasma potassium <3.5 mmol/l), potassium supplements should be doubled to 40 mmol per litre of infused fluid; if hyperkalaemia develops, potassium should be temporarily withheld.

INSULIN THERAPY

The aims of insulin treatment in ketoacidosis are to inhibit lipolysis (and thus ketogenesis) and hepatic glucose production and to enhance the disposal of glucose and ketone bodies by peripheral tissues.

As short-acting insulin has a plasma half-life of only about 5 min [45], intermittent injections produce unpredictable and fluctuating plasma insulin concentrations. Maximal stimulation of potassium transport into cells occurs at pharmacological plasma insulin concentrations [46] and large doses of insulin therefore increase the risk of hypokalaemia. With current 'low-dose' insulin regimens, complications of treatment such as hypokalaemia and late hypoglycaemia are less common than with the obsolete 'high-dose' regimens [47].

Short-acting insulin (e.g. Human Actrapid (Novo), Human Velosulin (Nordisk) or Humulin S (Lilly)) is best administered as a continuous intravenous infusion at a rate of 5–10 U/h. This produces steady plasma insulin concentrations in the high physiological range which adequately suppress lipolysis, ketogenesis and hepatic glucose production, even in the presence of elevated levels of catabolic hormones. Insulin is diluted to a convenient concentration (usually 1 U/ml) with isotonic saline in a large syringe and delivered by a syringe-driver infusion pump connected via a Y-connector. The infusion apparatus should be flushed through before connection to the patient in order to prevent insulin from adsorbing on to the plastics. Alternatively, insulin may be diluted in a 500-ml bag of isotonic saline; the insulin must be injected using a needle long enough to clear the injection port of the bag, and a few millilitres of the patient's plasma or whole blood can be added to discourage insulin adsorption (see Figs 81.1 and 81.2).

With intravenous regimens, blood glucose is checked at the bedside at hourly intervals and the infusion rate is reduced to 2–4 U/h when glucose has fallen to 14 mmol/l or below. The blood glucose concentration should then be maintained at between 5–10 mmol/l until the patient is eating and subcutaneous insulin is recommenced.

If intravenous insulin administration is impracticable, an intramuscular regimen can be used. This begins with a bolus of 20 U short-acting insulin, followed by 5–10 U each hour until blood glucose (checked hourly at the bedside) has reached 14 mmol/l. Subcutaneous insulin is commenced at this time, with the start of a 5% dextrose infusion, at a dosage of 10 U 4-hourly and continued for about 24 hours, when the patient's usual insulin regimen is reintroduced.

Both intravenous and intramuscular regimens should produce a steady and predictable fall in plasma glucose concentrations, averaging 4–6 mmol/h [48]. The commonest causes of failure to respond to intravenous insulin are the pump being inadvertently switched off or set at the wrong rate, and blockage of the delivery line. Insufficient rehydration has been said to cause erratic absorption of intramuscular injections, resulting in apparent insulin resistance. If the plasma glucose concentration has not fallen after 2 hours of intramuscular treatment, the patient's fluid balance should be reappraised and intravenous insulin started.

BICARBONATE

The place of bicarbonate in the management of diabetic ketoacidosis remains controversial [49]. Blood pH levels below 7.0 may lead to life-threatening respiratory depression and small doses of bicarbonate (approximately 100 mmol) may be beneficial if the patient is severely acidotic or if cardiorespiratory collapse appears imminent. However, it is possible that administration of bicarbonate to the *extracellular* space may actually aggravate *intracellular* acidosis. Bicarbonate ions (which cannot diffuse across cell membranes) combine with H^+ ions extracellularly, producing carbonic acid which dissociates into water and CO_2. The latter readily enters cells, where the reverse reaction occurs, generating H^+ (and bicarbonate) ions intracellularly.

Bicarbonate should be infused as 100 ml of 8.4% solution or 600 ml of 1.4% solution over 30 min and repeated if necessary to raise the pH above 7.0. Complete correction of the acidosis should not be attempted as concurrent metabolism of ketone anions may lead to over-alkalinization.

Administration of alkali is associated with a number of potentially serious adverse effects including hypokalaemia, paradoxical acidosis of cerebrospinal fluid [50], adverse effects on the oxyhaemoglobin dissociation curve [51], overshoot alkalosis [52] and a delayed fall in lactate and ketone body concentrations [53]. Extra potassium (20 mmol potassium per 100 mmol bicarbonate) must always be administered when bicarbonate is infused. A solution of 8.4% sodium bicarbonate is extremely irritant and because of its tendency to cause thrombosis should only be infused into a large (ideally central) vein; extravasated solution often causes extensive local tissue necrosis (see Fig. 49.5).

OTHER MEASURES

The stomach of a patient with diabetic ketoacidosis may contain 1–2 l of fluid which can be vomited and inhaled if consciousness is blunted, occasionally with fatal results. Although attempts to pass a nasogastric tube may precipitate vomiting in uncooperative patients, this should be done (by an experienced person) if there is

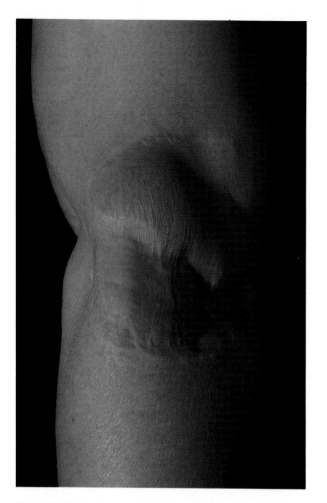

Fig. 49.5. Extensive necrosis of superficial tissues, which required skin grafting, following extravasation of 8.4% sodium bicarbonate solution.

any nausea or vomiting in a patient who is not fully awake.

It is generally suggested that persistent hypotension (<80 mm Hg systolic) should be treated with plasma expanders, but we have not required this in our last 746 episodes of ketoacidosis and consider it unnecessary, as long as general rehydration is adequate.

Complications of diabetic ketoacidosis

CEREBRAL OEDEMA

Cerebral oedema is a rare and poorly understood cause of death in diabetic ketoacidosis which appears to have a predilection for younger patients [54]. Characteristically, the patient initially responds well to treatment but then develops neurological signs and deepening coma.

Subclinical elevations in cerebrospinal fluid pressure are common during the treatment of ketoacidosis, due to alterations in cerebral osmolarity [55]. Cerebral swelling has been demonstrated in children using computerized tomography [56] (see Fig. 87.7). Animal experiments suggest that rapid reductions of plasma glucose concentration to below 14 mmol/l may contribute to cerebral oedema [57], although it is difficult to find support for this view in case reports. The use of hypotonic fluids during treatment has also been implicated [58, 59] but the evidence is again inconclusive. No fatalities attributable to cerebral oedema occurred in the 746 episodes of ketoacidosis treated in our centre between 1971 and 1985, although paediatric cases are not represented in this series. Dexamethasone and/or mannitol are often suggested in the treatment of cerebral oedema, but there is no firm evidence that either is beneficial.

ADULT RESPIRATORY DISTRESS SYNDROME

The adult respiratory distress syndrome (ARDS) has recently been reported as a major cause of death in younger patients with ketoacidosis. Clinical features include dyspnoea, tachypnoea, central cyanosis and non-specific chest signs. Arterial hypoxia is characteristic and chest radiography reveals bilateral pulmonary infiltrates. Management involves respiratory support with intermittent positive pressure ventilation (IPPV) and avoidance of fluid overload. Corticosteroids do not seem to have a useful place in the treatment of ARDS.

THROMBOEMBOLISM

Thromboembolic complications, due to dehydration and increased blood viscosity and coagulability, are an important cause of mortality in diabetic ketoacidosis [61]. Disseminated intravascular coagulation has also been reported as a rare complication of diabetic ketoacidosis [62].

The role of prophylactic anticoagulation has not been clearly established in diabetic ketoacidosis but does not improve survival in hyperosmolar coma where thromboembolic complications are common; routine anticoagulation is therefore not recommended, although proven thromboembolic disease should be treated in the usual way.

Diabetic non-ketotic hyperosmolar coma

Summary

- Non-ketotic hyperosmolar coma is characterized by the insidious development of marked hyperglycaemia (usually >50 mmol/l) and dehydration and pre-renal uraemia; significant hyperketonaemia does not develop.
- The absence of ketosis is unexplained but may be related to suppression of lipolysis by hyperosmolarity, or a reduced catabolic hormone response.
- Two-thirds of cases are in previously undiagnosed cases of diabetes. Infection, diuretic treatment, and drinking glucose-rich beverages may all be precipitating factors.
- The condition usually affects middle-aged or elderly patients and carries a mortality of over 30%.
- Treatment involves rehydration, insulin therapy and electrolyte replacement in a manner similar to that used for diabetic ketoacidosis.

Pathophysiology

Diabetic hyperosmolar non-ketotic coma is characterized by marked hyperglycaemia (plasma glucose usually in excess of 50 mmol/l), with profound dehydration, pre-renal uraemia and depressed consciousness [63]. Gross hyperketonaemia and ketonuria are absent.

Insulin concentrations in peripheral blood are similar to those in patients with ketoacidosis [64, 65] and the absence of significant ketosis is unexplained. Suppression of lipolysis by the hyperosmolar state is one suggested mechanism [66]; the catabolic hormone response may also be less marked than in patients with ketoacidosis [64, 67].

Incidence and mortality

In our own centre, 95 cases of hyperosmolar non-ketotic decompensation occurred in 89 patients between 1971–85, accounting for about 11% of hyperglycaemic emergencies. The mortality rate for our patients was 31% per 100 episodes (33% per 100 patients). The condition's high mortality reflects the high incidence of serious associated disorders and complications [68].

Clinical features

Patients with hyperosmolar non-ketotic decompensation are usually middle-aged or elderly [60, 69]. Patients of Afro-Carribean origin accounted for 26% of episodes of hyperosmolar non-ketotic decompensation in our series, compared with only 3% of episodes of ketoacidosis. Up to two-thirds of cases occur in patients with previously undiagnosed diabetes [68]. Hypertension and treatment with diuretics are well-recognized features.

Symptoms of polyuria, intense thirst and gradual clouding of consciousness are characteristic. Many patients drink carbonated glucose drinks, which only exacerbate thirst and hyperglycaemia. The symptoms may develop over several weeks. Coma and severe dehydration with arterial hypotension are common and reversible focal neurological signs or motor seizures may occur [70]. Kussmaul respiration is not a feature of the hyperosmolar non-ketotic state as significant acidosis is absent. Many patients are moribund when admitted to hospital.

Precipitating factors

Hyperosmolar non-ketotic coma has many precipitating causes, which often coexist in one patient [71]. Infections are frequent and hyperosmolar coma may follow treatment with antihypertensive drugs such as diuretics and β-blockers [72, 73]. Steroids, phenytoin and cimetidine have also been associated with hyperosmolar coma. The possible contribution of glucose-rich drinks has already been mentioned.

Diagnosis

The insidious nature of the condition often leads to delays in diagnosis; an erroneous diagnosis of stroke is commonly made. Hyperosmolar non-ketotic coma must therefore enter the differential diagnosis of any patient presenting with otherwise unexplained impairment of consciousness, focal neurological signs, dehydration or shock [74].

Urinalysis reveals glycosuria and a negative or 'trace' reaction with Ketostix. The diagnosis is confirmed by a markedly raised plasma glucose concentration. Pre-renal uraemia and a raised haematocrit are common. Depression of consciousness generally occurs when plasma osmolarity exceeds about 340 mosmol/l [75], although there is considerable inter-individual variation [76]. Plasma osmolarity can be measured formally (e.g. by freezing-point depression) in the laboratory, and can be estimated approximately as:

$$\begin{aligned} \text{plasma osmolarity} &= 2 \times (\text{plasma Na} + \text{plasma K}) \\ (\text{mosmol/l}) \quad &+ \text{plasma glucose} \\ &+ \text{plasma urea} \end{aligned}$$

(Na, K, glucose and urea concentrations are in mmol/l).

Treatment

Successful management of hyperosmolar non-ketotic coma depends on good general care of the unconscious patient and prompt recognition and treatment of underlying causes.

Fluid, electrolyte and insulin replacement are similar to those recommended for the treatment of diabetic ketoacidosis [77]. Isotonic saline is used in preference to hypotonic saline for rehydration unless plasma sodium exceeds 150 mmol/l. A rise in sodium is frequently observed as blood glucose falls with treatment. This observation may be partially explained by the reciprocal relationship that exists between plasma glucose and sodium concentrations [78].

Despite the high frequency of thromboembolic complications in patients with hyperosmolar non-ketotic coma, the role of routine anticoagulation remains unclear [79], and it is probably best to treat thromboembolic disease only if it occurs. Neurological signs usually reverse when hyperglycaemia is controlled; epilepsy also responds to insulin and fluid replacement, but often not to specific anti-epileptic drugs [80].

Although insulin treatment is usually recommended for the first few months, these patients generally secrete significant quantities of endogenous insulin, allowing successful long-term treatment with oral hypoglycaemic agents [81]. Possible precipitating factors (thiazides, glucose drinks) must be carefully avoided in the future.

Lactic acidosis

Summary

• Severe lactic acidosis in diabetic patients (type B) occurs as a feature of ketoacidosis (in about 15% of cases) and as a rare complication of metformin therapy.
• When associated with ketoacidosis, lactic acidosis resolves with standard treatment of the ketoacidosis; that due to other causes may be treated by intravenous sodium bicarbonate.
• Sodium dichloroacetate, which lowers lactate levels by stimulating pyruvate dehydrogenase, is a potential new treatment for lactic acidosis, but clinical experience with this agent is limited to date.

The principal organs producing lactic acid are skeletal muscle, brain, erythrocytes and the renal medulla. The liver, kidneys and heart normally *extract* lactate but may become net producers of lactic acid under conditions of severe ischaemia [82]. Lactate produced by glycolysis is either oxidized to CO_2 and water or utilized in the gluconeogenic pathway in the liver and kidney (the Cori cycle).

Pathological degrees of lactic acidosis may arise from overproduction of lactate and hydrogen ions, a decrease in their clearance or a combination of

Table 49.6. Classification and causes of lactic acidosis. (Modified from Cohen and Woods 1976 [85]).

Type A (Primarily associated with tissue hypoxia)
Shock:
   Cardiogenic
   Endotoxic
   Hypovolaemic
Cardiac failure
Asphyxia
Carbon monoxide poisoning

Type B
1 Systemic disorders:
   Diabetes mellitus
   Neoplasia
   Liver disease
   Convulsions
2 Drugs and toxins:
   Biguanides
   Ethanol
   Methanol
   Salicylates
   Fructose/sorbitol/xylitol (in parenteral nutrition)
3 Inborn errors of metabolism

these two processes. Normal fasting blood lactate concentrations range from 0.4–1.19 mmol/l [83]. Severe lactic acidosis (defined as a metabolic acidosis with a blood lactate concentration of greater than 5 mmol/l) is encountered in two main clinical settings [84] (Table 49.6):

Type A lactic acidosis is primarily associated with states of tissue hypoxia such as shock or cardiac failure.

Type B lactic acidosis is considerably less common and is associated with several systemic diseases including diabetes, drugs, toxins and inborn errors of metabolism (e.g. Type 1 glycogen storage disease). Tissue hypoxia is not an obvious feature of type B lactic acidosis, although hypotension and hypoxia may supervene as preterminal events. The clinical features of lactic acidosis are similar to those of a severe metabolic acidosis of any cause.

Lactic acidosis associated with diabetes

Despite the frequent macrovascular and microvascular complications which favour tissue hypoxia, severe lactic acidosis is only rarely associated with diabetes [85]. Type B lactic acidosis is a well-recognized complication of biguanide therapy (Chapter 48) and a significant degree of hyperlactataemia is relatively common in diabetic ketoacidosis.

BIGUANIDE THERAPY

The incidence of lactic acidosis in diabetic patients has declined dramatically since the withdrawal of the biguanide, phenformin, in 1977 [86]. Lactic acidosis associated with phenformin treatment carried a 50% mortality rate [87]; lactic acidosis complicating metformin therapy is now rare and occurs almost exclusively in patients in whom biguanide therapy is contraindicated [88].

Many diabetic patients treated with insulin or biguanides show daily fluctuations in blood lactate concentration of up to 3 mmol/l [89].

DIABETIC KETOACIDOSIS

Significant hyperlactataemia is found in 15% of cases of diabetic ketoacidosis and usually responds to routine treatment of the ketoacidosis [89]. It is difficult to know whether this is a true mixed picture of lactic and ketoacidosis or simply an effect upon redox potential of the hydrogen ions generated in ketoacidosis. Resolution with treatment of ketoacidosis favours the latter explanation as insulin–glucose infusions are ineffective in the treatment of lactic acidosis.

It is not surprising that rises in blood lactate concentration occur when treatment of ketoacidosis is instituted. Insulin suppresses gluconeogenesis, thus reducing hepatic extraction of lactate from the blood, while facilitating peripheral glucose uptake and metabolism and therefore promoting lactate generation. This rise in lactate is generally transient and insignificant but massive rises in lactate were seen during the treatment of ketoacidosis treatment with the now-obsolete high-dose insulin regimens [90]. Hyperlactataemia also follows primary hypoxia, when it represents a preterminal event. Treatment is directed at the underlying cause of the hypoxia.

Treatment and prognosis

The generally poor prognosis associated with lactic acidosis is largely determined by the severity of the underlying condition. Despite considerable controversy surrounding the theoretical and clinical benefits of alkali therapy, intravenous bicarbonate remains the mainstay of supportive treatment for cases of severe lactic acidosis [91]. Massive quantities of bicarbonate may be required to elevate arterial pH, and simultaneous dialysis has been recommended to avoid sodium overload [92].

Sodium dichloroacetate has recently received attention as a potential adjunct in the management of lactic acidosis [93]. By stimulating the activity of pyruvate dehydrogenase, dichloroacetate lowers blood lactate levels in patients with lactic acidosis associated with a variety of conditions [94]. To date, clinical experience with this compound remains limited and there is no evidence that the overall prognosis is improved.

Finally, hyperglycaemia may induce generalized epileptic convulsions in susceptible patients causing a severe but self-limiting lactic acidosis. In such cases, bicarbonate therapy is both unnecessary and potentially hazardous [95].

Differential diagnosis of coma in a diabetic patient

The commonest causes of impaired consciousness in diabetic patients presenting to hospital casualty departments in the UK are ketoacidosis, hypoglycaemia and hyperosmolar, non-ketotic coma.

Table 49.7. Causes of coma or impaired consciousness in diabetic patients.

- Diabetic ketoacidosis
- Non-ketotic hyperosmolar coma
- Hypoglycaemia
- Lactic acidosis
- Other causes (sometimes related to diabetes):
  stroke
  postictal (including hypoglycaemia)
  trauma
  drug overdose, ethanol intoxication

However, it is essential to remember that diabetic people, like anyone else, may suffer other causes of coma, some of which may be associated with diabetes or its treatment (see Table 49.7).

Immediate measurement of the blood glucose concentration (using a glucose–oxidase reagent strip rather than waiting for a formal laboratory result) is mandatory and will usually determine the initial course of treatment, which can often be started while awaiting more detailed laboratory results. The diagnostic criteria for the metabolic causes of coma in diabetes are described in the relevant sections above. It must be appreciated that lactic acidosis or a hyperosmolar state may each complicate diabetic ketoacidosis, and that (for example) unconsciousness may follow a generalized epileptic seizure provoked by hypoglycaemia or a head injury sustained during a hypoglycaemic attack.

A.J. KRENTZ

MALCOLM NATTRASS

References

1 Tunbridge WMG. Factors contributing to deaths of diabetics under fifty years of age. *Lancet* 1981; i: 569–72.

2 Keller U. Diabetic ketoacidosis: current views on pathogenesis and treatment. *Diabetologia* 1986; **29**: 71–7.

3 Alberti KGMM. Diabetic ketoacidosis — aspects of management. In: Ledingham JG, ed. *Tenth Advanced Medicine Symposium*. Tunbridge Wells: Pitman Medical Press, 1974: pp. 68–82.

4 Schade DS, Eaton RP, Alberti KGMM, Johnston DG. *Diabetic coma, ketoacidotic and hyperosmolar*. Albuquerque: University of New Mexico Press, 1981: pp. 6–9.

5 Gale EAM, Dornan TL, Tattersall RB. Severely uncontrolled diabetes in the over-fifties. *Diabetologia* 1981; **21**: 25–8.

6 Mecklenburg RS, Benson EA, Benson JW Jr *et al*. Acute complications associated with insulin infusion pump therapy. *J Am Med Assoc* 1984; **252**: 3265–9.

7 Teutsch SM, Herman WH, Dwyer DM, Lane JM. Mortality among diabetic patients using continuous subcutaneous insulin infusion pumps. *N Engl J Med* 1984; **310**: 361–8.

8 Knight G, Jennings AM, Boulton AJM, Tomlinson S, Ward JD. Severe hyperkalaemia and ketoacidosis during routine treatment with an insulin pump. *Br Med J* 1985; **291**: 371–2.

9 Mecklenburg RS, Guinn TS, Sannar CA, Blumenstein BA. Malfunction of continuous subcutaneous insulin infusion systems: a one-year prospective study of 127 patients. *Diabetes Care* 1986; **9**: 351–5.

10 Chernick SS, Clark CM, Gardiner RJ, Scow RO. Role of lipolytic and glucocorticoid hormones in the development of diabetic ketoacidosis. *Diabetes* 1972; **21**: 946–54.

11 Schade DS, Eaton RP. The role of insulin deficiency in the pathogenesis of diabetic ketoacidosis: A reappraisal. *Diabetes Care* 1979; **2**: 296–306.

12 Madsbad S, Alberti KGMM, Binder C *et al*. Role of residual insulin secretion in protection against diabetic ketoacidosis in insulin-dependent diabetes. *Br Med J* 1979; **2**: 1257–9.

13 Alberti KGMM, Christensen NJ, Iversen J, Ørskov H. Role of glucagon and other hormones in development of diabetic ketoacidosis. *Lancet* 1975; i: 1307–11.

14 Barnes AJ, Bloom SR, Alberti KGMM, Smythe P, Alford FP, Chisholm DJ. Ketoacidosis in pancreatectomised man. *N Engl J Med* 1977; **296**: 1250–3.

15 Christensen NJ. Plasma norepinephrine and epinephrine in untreated diabetics during fasting and after insulin administration. *Diabetes* 1974; **23**: 1–8.

16 Jacobs JS, Nabarro JDN. Plasma 11-hydroxycorticosteroid and growth hormone levels in acute medical illnesses. *Br Med J* 1969; **2**: 595–8.

17 Miles JM, Rizza RA, Haymond MW, Gerich JE. Effects of acute insulin deficiency on glucose and ketone body turnover in man. *Diabetes* 1980; **29**: 296–30.

18 Owen OE, Block B, Patel Y *et al*. Human splanchnic metabolism during diabetic ketoacidosis. *Metabolism* 1977; **26**: 381–9.

19 Ginsberg HN. Investigation of insulin resistance during diabetic ketoacidosis: role of counterregulatory substances and effect of insulin therapy. *Metabolism* 1977; **26**: 1135–46.

20 Page M McB, Alberti KGMM, Greenwood R *et al*. Treatment of diabetic coma with continuous low-dose infusion of insulin. *Br Med J* 1974; **2**: 687–90.

21 Ng ML, Levy MN, Zieslle HA. Effects of changes in pH and of carbon dioxide tension on left ventricular performance. *Am J Physiol* 1967; **213**: 115–20.

22 Gerst PH, Fleming WH, Malm JR. A quantitative evaluation of the effects of acidosis and alkalosis upon the ventricular fibrillation threshold. *Surgery* 1966; **59**: 1050–60.

23 Alberti KGMM, Hockaday TDR. Diabetic coma: a reappraisal after five years. *Clin Endocrinol Metab* 1977; **6**: 421–55.

24 McGarry JD, Foster DW. Regulation of hepatic fatty acid oxiation and ketone body production. *Ann Rev Biochem* 1980; **49**: 395–420.

25 Nabarro JDN, Spencer AG, Stowers JM. Metabolic studies in severe diabetic ketoacidosis. *Q J Med* 1952; **21**: 225–48.

26 Podolsky S, Emerson K Jr. Potassium depletion in diabetic ketoacidosis. *Diabetes* 1973; **22**: 299.

27 Saudek CD, Boulier PR, Knopp RH, Arky RA. Sodium retention accompanying insulin treatment of diabetes mellitus. *Diabetes* 1974; **23**: 240–6.

28 Waldhäusl W, Kleinberger G, Korn A, Dudczak R, Bratusch-Marrain P, Nowotny P. Severe hyperglycemia: effects of rehydration on endocrine derangements and blood glucose concentration. *Diabetes* 1979; **28**: 577–84.

29 Beigelman PM. Potassium in severe diabetic ketoacidosis. *Am J Med* 1973; **54**: 419–20.

30 Alberti KGMM, Darley JH, Emerson PM, Hockaday TDR. 2, 3-diphosphoglycerate and tissue oxygenation in uncon-

trolled diabetes mellitus. *Lancet* 1972; ii: 391–5.

31 Nattrass M, Hale PJ. Clinical aspects of diabetic ketoacidosis. In: Nattrass M, Santiago JV, eds. *Recent Advances in Diabetes*. 1st edn. Edinburgh: Churchill Livingstone, 1984: 231–8.

32 Fulop M, Tannenbaum H, Dreyer N. Ketotic hyperosmolar coma. *Lancet* 1973; ii: 635–9.

33 Soler NG, Bennett MA, FitzGerald MG, Malins JM. Intensive care in the management of diabetic ketoacidosis. *Lancet* 1973; i: 951–4.

34 Gale EAM, Tattersall RB. Hypothermia: a complication of diabetic ketoacidosis. *Br Med J* 1978; **2**: 1387–9.

35 Campbell IW, Duncan LJP, Innes JA, McCuish AC, Munro JF. Abdominal pain in diabetic metabolic decompensation. Clinical significance. *J Am Med Assoc* 1975; **233**: 166–8.

36 Warshaw AL, Feller ER, Lee KH. On the cause of raised serum amylase in diabetic ketoacidosis. *Lancet* 1977; i: 929–31.

37 Treasure RAR, Fowler PBS, Millington HT, Wise PH. Misdiagnosis of diabetic ketoacidosis as hyperventilation syndrome. *Br Med J* 1987; **294**: 630.

38 Munro JF, Campbell IW, McCuish AC, Duncan LJP. Euglycaemic diabetic ketoacidosis. *Br Med J* 1973; **2**: 578–80.

39 Thompson CJ, Johnston DG, Baylis PH, Anderson J. Alcoholic ketoacidosis: an underdiagnosed condition? *Br Med J* 1986; **292**: 463–5.

40 Marliss EB, Ohman JL Jr, Aoki TT, Kozak GP. Altered redox state obscuring ketoacidosis in diabetic patients with lactic acidosis. *N Engl J Med* 1970; **283**: 978–80.

41 Bell JA, Hilton PJ, Walker G. Severe hyponatraemia in hyperlipidaemic diabetic ketosis. *Br Med J* 1972; **4**: 709–10.

42 Watkins PJ. The effect of ketone bodies in the determination of creatinine. *Clin Chim Acta* 1967; **18**: 191–6.

43 Hale PJ, Nattrass M. A comparison of arterial and non-arterialized capillary blood gases in diabetic ketoacidosis. *Diabetic Med* 1988; **5**: 76–8.

44 Krentz AJ, Hale PJ, Singh BM, Nattrass M. The effect of glucose and insulin infusion on the fall of ketone bodies during treatment of diabetic ketoacidosis. *Diabetic Med* 1989; **6**: 31–6.

45 Turner RC, Grayburn JA, Newman GB, Nabarro JDN. Measurement of the insulin delivery rate in man. *J Clin Endocrinol Metab* 1971; **33**: 279–86.

46 Schade DS, Eaton RP. Dose response to insulin in man: differential effects on glucose and ketone body regulation. *J Clin Endocrinol Metab* 1977; **44**: 1038–53.

47 Kitabchi AE, Fisher JN. Insulin therapy of diabetic ketoacidosis: physiological versus pharmacological doses of insulin and their routes of administration. In: Brownlee M, ed. *Diabetes Mellitus*. Chichester: John Wiley and Sons, 1981: 95–149.

48 Alberti KGMM. Low-dose insulin in the treatment of diabetic ketoacidosis. *Arch Intern Med* 1977; **137**: 1367–76.

49 Lever E, Jaspan JB. Sodium bicarbonate therapy in severe diabetic ketoacidosis. *Am J Med* 1983; **75**: 263–8.

50 Posner JB, Plum F. Spinal fluid pH and neurological symptoms in systemic acidosis. *N Engl J Med* 1967; **277**: 605–13.

51 Ditzel J, Standl E. The oxygen transport system of red blood cells during diabetic ketoacidosis and recovery. *Diabetologia* 1975; **11**: 255–60.

52 Addis GJ, Thomson WST, Welch JD. Bicarbonate therapy in diabetic acidosis. *Lancet* 1964; ii: 223–5.

53 Hale PJ, Crase J, Nattrass M. Metabolic effects of bicarbonate in the treatment of diabetic ketoacidosis. *Br Med J* 1984; **289**: 1035–8.

54 FitzGerald MG, O'Sullivan DJ, Malins JM. Fatal diabetic ketoacidosis. *Br Med J* 1961; **1**: 247–50.

55 Clements RS, Blumenthal SA, Morrison AD, Winegrad AI. Increased cerebrospinal fluid pressure during treatment of diabetic ketosis. *Lancet* 1971; ii: 671–5.

56 Krane EJ, Rockoff MA, Wallman JK, Wolfsdorf JI. Subclinical brain swelling in children during treatment of diabetic ketoacidosis. *N Engl J Med* 1985; **312**: 1147–51.

57 Arieff AI, Kleeman CR. Studies of mechanisms of cerebral edema in diabetic comas. *J Clin Invest* 1973; **52**: 571–83.

58 Rosenbloom AL, Riley WJ, Weber FT, Malone JI, Donnelley WH. Cerebral edema complicating diabetic ketoacidosis in childhood. *J Pediatr* 1980; **96**: 357–61.

59 Fein IA, Rackow EC, Sprung CL, Grodman R. Relation of colloid osmotic pressure to arterial hypoxaemia and cerebral edema during crystalloid volume loading in patients with diabetic ketoacidosis *Ann Intern Med* 1982; **96**: 570–5.

60 Carroll P, Matz R. Uncontrolled diabetes in adults: experience in treating diabetic ketoacidosis and hyperosmolar non-ketotic coma with low-dose insulin and a uniform treatment regimen. *Diabetes Care* 1983; **6**: 579–85.

61 Paton RC. Haemostatic changes in diabetes coma. *Diabetologia* 1981; **21**: 172–7.

62 Timperley WR, Preston FE, Ward JD. Cerebral intravascular coagulation in diabetic ketoacidosis. *Lancet* 1974; ii: 952–6.

63 Arieff AI, Carroll HJ. Non-ketotic hyperosmolar coma with hyperglycaemia: clinical features, pathophysiology, renal function, acid-base balance, plasma-cerebrospinal fluid equilibria and the effects of therapy in 37 cases. *Medicine* 1972; **51**: 73–94.

64 Gerich JE, Martin MM, Recant L. Clinical and metabolic characteristics of hyperosmolar non-ketotic coma. *Diabetes* 1971; **20**: 228–38.

65 Watkins PJ, Hill DM, FitzGerald MG, Malins M. Ketonaemia in uncontrolled diabetes mellitus. *Br Med J* 1970; **4**: 522–5.

66 Gerich JE, Penhos JC, Gutman RA, Recant L. Effect of dehydration and hyperosmolarity on glucose, free fatty acid and glucose metabolism in the rat. *Diabetes* 1973; **22**: 264–71.

67 Lindsay CA, Faloona CR, Unger R. Plasma glucagon in non-ketotic hyperosmolar coma. *J Am Med Assoc* 1974; **229**: 1771–3.

68 McCurdy DK. Hyperosmolar hyperglycaemic nonketotic diabetic coma. *Med Clin North Am* 1970; **54**: 683–99.

69 Pyke DA. Diabetic ketosis and coma. *J Clin Pathol* 1969; **22** (suppl 2): 57–65.

70 Grant C, Warlow C. Focal epilepsy in diabetic non-ketotic hyperglycaemia. *Br Med J* 1985; **290**: 1204–5.

71 Schade DS, Eaton RP, Alberti KGMM, Johnston DG. *Diabetic Coma, Ketoacidotic and Hyperosmolar*. Albuquerque: University of New Mexico Press, 1981: 201–9.

72 Podolsky S, Pattavina CG. Hyperosmolar non-ketotic diabetic coma. A complication of propranolol therapy. *Metabolism* 1973; **22**: 685–93.

73 Fonesca V, Phear DN. Hyperosmolar non-ketotic diabetic syndrome precipitated by treatment with diuretics. *Br Med J* 1982; **284**: 36–7.

74 Mather H. Management of hyperosmolar coma. *J Roy Soc Med* 1980; **73**: 134–8.

75 Fulop M, Rosenblatt A, Kreitzer SM, Gerstenhaber B. Hyperosmolar nature of diabetic coma. *Diabetes* 1975; **24**: 594–9.

76 Small M, Alzaid A, MacCuish AC. Diabetic hyperosmolar non-ketotic decompensation. *Q J Med* 1988; **66**: 251–7.

77 Wright AD, FitzGerald MG, Walsh CH, Malins JM. Low-dose insulin treatment of hyperosmolar diabetic coma. *Postgrad Med J* 1981; **57**: 556–9.

78 Katz MA. Hyperglycemia-induced hyponatremia — calculation of expected sodium depression. *N Engl J Med* 1973; **289**: 843−4.

79 Keller U, Berger W, Ritz R, Truog P. Course and prognosis of 86 episodes of diabetic coma. A five year experience with a uniform schedule of treatment. *Diabetologia* 1975; **11**: 93−100.

80 Podolsky S. Hyperosmolar non-ketotic coma in the elderly diabetic. *Med Clin North Am* 1978; **62**: 815−28.

81 Grant C, Warlow C. Focal epilepsy in diabetic non-ketotic hyperglycaemia. *Br Med J* 1985; **290**: 1204−5.

82 Cohen RD, Iles RA. Lactic acidosis: Diagnosis and treatment. *Clin Endocrinol Metab* 1980; **9**: 513−27.

83 Foster KJ, Alberti KGMM, Hinks L *et al*. Blood intermediary metabolite and insulin concentrations after an overnight fast: reference ranges for adults, and interrelations. *Clin Chem* 1978; **24**: 1568−72.

84 Cohen RD, Woods HF. *Clinical and Biochemical Aspects of Lactic Acidosis*. Oxford: Blackwell Scientific Publications, 1976: pp. 276.

85 Kreisberg RA. Pathogenesis and management of lactic acidosis. *Annu Rev Med* 1984; **35**: 181−93.

86 Kreisberg RA. Lactate homeostasis and lactic acidosis. *Ann Intern Med* 1980; **92**: 227−37.

87 Luft D, Schmulling RM, Eggstein M. Lactic acidosis in biguanide-treated diabetics. *Diabetologia* 1978; **14**: 75−87.

88 Nattrass M, Alberti KGMM. Biguanides. *Diabetologia* 1978; **14**: 71−4.

89 Nattrass M, Alberti KGMM. Lactate metabolism in diabetes. In: Bossart H, Perret C, eds. *Lactate in Acute Conditions*. Basel: Karger, 1979: 83−101.

90 Watkins PJ, Smith JS, FitzGerald MG, Malins JM. Lactic acidosis in diabetes. *Br Med J* 1969; **1**: 744−7.

91 Mizock BA. Controversies in lactic acidosis. *J Am Med Assoc* 1987; **258**: 497−501.

92 Frommer JP. Lactic acidosis. *Med Clin North Am* 1983; **67**: 815−29.

93 Relman AS. Lactic acidosis and a possible new treatment. *N Engl J Med* 1978; **298**: 564−6.

94 Stacpoole PW, Harman EM, Curry SH, Baumgartner TG, Misbin RI. Treatment of lactic acidosis with dichloroacetate. *N Engl J Med* 1983; **309**: 390−6.

95 Krentz AJ. Post-convulsive lactic acidosis in diabetic patients. *Ann Clin Biochem* 1988; **25**: 327−9.

50 Hypoglycaemia and Diabetes Mellitus

Summary

- Over 30% of insulin-treated diabetic patients experience hypoglycaemic coma at least once, about 10% suffer coma in any one year, and about 3% are incapacitated by frequent and severe episodes.
- Hypoglycaemia kills at least 3–4% of insulin-treated diabetic patients.
- Hypoglycaemia in diabetic patients is due to mismatching of hypoglycaemic medication, food and exercise.
- Intensification of insulin treatment alone does not itself cause more frequent or severe hypoglycaemia, but may blunt symptomatic awareness of it.
- Reduced insulin requirements during the 'honeymoon period', after delivery, or following weight loss or the onset of adrenal or pituitary failure, may predispose to hypoglycaemia.
- Mild neuroglycopenia (blood glucose ≤3.0 mmol/l) produces subtle intellectual and psychomotor impairment; severe neuroglycopenia (blood glucose ≤1.0 mmol/l) causes confusion, disturbed behaviour, fits and ultimately unconsciousness. Permanent brain damage is unusual after hypoglycaemic coma, but more likely in people with excessive alcohol intake.
- Generalized autonomic activation (triggered by blood glucose ≤2.0 mmol/l) causes tremor, tachycardia, sweating, altered salivation and hunger.
- Awareness of hypoglycaemia may be reduced or lost in IDDM patients, especially those with long-standing disease; autonomic neuropathy or the effect of intensified insulin treatment may be partly responsible.
- Reduced hypoglycaemia awareness in a few patients following transfer to human insulin is probably due to differences in pharmacokinetics and prescription practice.
- Recovery from hypoglycaemia depends on glucose counter-regulation, mediated largely by hormones opposing insulin's action, namely glucagon, adrenaline, growth hormone, cortisol and vasopressin. Recovery may be delayed by deficiencies of these counter-regulatory hormones (common in long-standing IDDM) and by non-selective β-adrenergic blockade.
- Sulphonylurea-induced hypoglycaemia affects 20 in 1000 patients per year; it is commoner with long-acting agents such as chlorpropamide and glibenclamide, which should therefore be avoided in the elderly.
- Glycaemic control may have to be relaxed in patients at high risk of hypoglycaemia.
- First-aid treatment of hypoglycaemia in conscious patients is by oral administration of 15–20 g glucose. Unconscious patients should be given glucose gel or jam smeared inside the cheeks, intravenous glucose (30 ml of 20% solution) or glucagon (1 mg subcutaneously or intramuscularly). Hypoglycaemia due to long-acting sulphonylureas may require prolonged intravenous glucose infusion.

Hypoglycaemia has many causes but in the diabetic population it is almost invariably a side-effect of therapy. It occurs most commonly during treatment with insulin but is sometimes caused by sulphonylurea drugs, particularly the long-acting agents. Despite refinements in insulin delivery and formulation, insulin replacement is still far removed from endogenous insulin secretion and devoid of the complex homeostatic mechanisms which normally maintain blood glucose within its narrow physiological range. Blood glucose concentrations can fluctuate widely in the diabetic patient and unexpected hypoglycaemia is a common problem. The presentation of hypoglycaemia may be both dramatic and potentially dangerous; hypoglycaemia remains the therapeutic hazard most feared by patients with insulin-treated diabetes.

Frequency of hypoglycaemia

The inherent risk of hypoglycaemia has increased with the modern aim of pursuing optimal glycaemic control in the hope of preventing the long-term development of diabetic complications. The frequency of hypoglycaemia is difficult to estimate accurately and probably varies according to local treatment policies. Most clinical surveys underestimate the number of hypoglycaemic events, because minor episodes are not reported and nocturnal hypoglycaemia is often unrecognized. Sulphonylurea-induced hypoglycaemia is relatively uncommon, causing an estimated 19 episodes of symptomatic hypoglycaemia per 1000 patients per year [1] with only few requiring hospital treatment [2]. This contrasts with insulin-induced hypoglycaemia, for which conservative estimates suggest that approximately 100/1000 patients/year require hospital treatment [3−5].

The use of differing definitions of 'severe hypoglycaemia' in various surveys prevents comparative assessment of the frequency of hypoglycaemia. Coma can be used as a clear end-point, although profound hypoglycaemia without loss of consciousness can also be very damaging. At least one-third of all insulin-treated patients experience an episode of hypoglycaemic coma at some time, 10% have a hypoglycaemic coma in any single year, and 3% suffer frequent, recurrent episodes of hypoglycaemic coma which are incapacitating.

The presumption that intensification of insulin regimens provokes more frequent and severe hypoglycaemia is not supported by many studies comparing conventional insulin regimens with continuous subcutaneous insulin infusion (CSII), although intensive therapy may aggravate the effects of hypoglycaemia by diminishing symptomatic awareness [6−9]. One exception is the North American Diabetes Control and Complications Trial (DCCT) in which the frequency of severe hypoglycaemia was three times greater in the intensively treated group [10]. Diabetic patients with good glycaemic control are more prone to hypoglycaemia: the lower the median blood glucose concentration, the higher is the frequency of biochemical (not always symptomatic) hypoglycaemia [11] and children with lower glycosylated haemoglobin concentrations are more susceptible to hypoglycaemia [12].

Causal factors

Hypoglycaemia may be an early manifestation of undiagnosed diabetes, and diabetic patients are subject to any of the many causes of spontaneous hypoglycaemia unrelated to diabetic treatment, such as advanced liver disease or insulin-producing tumours. However, in the context of clinical diabetes, these causes are rare and the principal factors implicated in hypoglycaemia in the diabetic patient are:
1 Excessive doses of insulin or sulphonylureas.
2 Inadequate or delayed ingestion of food.
3 Sudden or sustained exercise.

One or more of these factors may be involved and a definite cause can usually be identified. Many episodes result from patients' errors in measuring or administering insulin, failing to follow a sensible diet, or ignoring the usual precautions when the risk of hypoglycaemia is increased. Most errors are attributable to simple carelessness and lack of attention to the basic principles of self-management. When attempting to identify the likely cause of a hypoglycaemic episode, it may be necessary to examine the patient's activities during the preceding 24 hours, as late-onset hypoglycaemia can occur several hours after physical exercise [13].

A number of specific clinical situations associated with hypoglycaemia require active modification of treatment. The problem of nocturnal hypoglycaemia is covered separately in Chapter 51.

Decreased insulin requirement

Insulin requirements often decline during the 'honeymoon' remission of IDDM after treatment is commenced in the newly diagnosed patient, and during progressive renal impairment. Failure to reduce the dose of insulin increases the risk of hypoglycaemia. Some women experience a temporary reduction in insulin requirement during menstruation, when hypoglycaemia may be troublesome. During diabetic pregnancy, a sudden fall in insulin requirement in the third trimester may signal intrauterine fetal death, and insulin requirement usually falls dramatically following delivery, when insulin may have to be discontinued for several hours to avoid hypoglycaemia.

Increased insulin bioavailability or sensitivity

Changing insulin species or formulation may induce hypoglycaemia by altering the pharmacokinetic properties of insulin and enhancing its efficacy. Transfer from animal to human insulin is associated with reduced titres of insulin antibodies and therefore increased bioavailability of insulin; the total insulin dosage may need to be reduced to prevent hypoglycaemia. Insulin absorption may be enhanced by changing the injection site, by avoiding areas of lipohypertrophy, or by increased temperature (hypoglycaemia sometimes occurs after a hot bath or sauna [14]). Significant weight loss or the development of disorders associated with increased insulin sensitivity such as Addison's disease, hypopituitarism or hypothyroidism may provoke frequent hypoglycaemia in previously stable patients.

Inadequate diet

Dietary factors commonly predisposing to hypoglycaemia include failure to eat additional carbohydrate during strenuous domestic or sporting activities, miscalculating time intervals between insulin injections and meals, and drinking alcohol without food. Athletic training, or a change from a sedentary to an active occupation, necessitates an increase in carbohydrate intake. Breast feeding by a diabetic mother usually requires an extra 30–50 g of carbohydrate to avoid hypoglycaemia during lactation. Travel may disrupt normal food intake, and airline meals are notoriously deficient in carbohydrate content. Carbohydrate absorption may be delayed by gastroparesis (see Chapter 71) or reduced in malabsorptive states. The popularity of weight-reducing diets for slimming, particularly in young women, may precipitate hypoglycaemia; the extreme situation of anorexia nervosa in the diabetic patient may cause hypoglycaemia and starvation ketosis to occur simultaneously and can cause major management problems (see Chapter 82).

Factitious hypoglycaemia

A few patients deliberately induce hypoglycaemia by manipulating their insulin dose or diet (Chapter 88). This surreptitious behaviour is often difficult to detect even when strongly suspected, and is usually a manifestation of an underlying psychological disorder.

Symptoms

The symptoms of hypoglycaemia may be very varied and depend on whether hypoglycaemia is acute or chronic. The latter generally manifests with mental deterioration, personality change and disordered behaviour, and is more typical of spontaneous hypoglycaemia. Diabetic individuals are usually exposed to acute hypoglycaemia, the symptoms of which can be subdivided into those of neuroglycopenia and autonomic activation.

Neuroglycopenia

The brain is vitally dependent on glucose as its source of energy, and acute deprivation of glucose rapidly interferes with cerebral function. Mild or moderate neuroglycopenia is characterized by impairment of intellectual activity and cognitive function, with difficulty in concentrating, diminished psychomotor skills, incoordination and a sensation of drowsiness. Cognitive dysfunction has been shown to develop when the blood glucose concentration falls to 3.0 mmol/l (Fig. 50.1), a level above the threshold for the activation of autonomic symptoms. A 'twilight zone' of subclinical hypoglycaemia can occur, in which higher

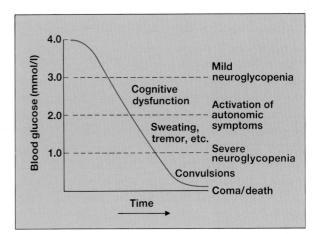

Fig. 50.1. Glycaemic thresholds for onset of symptoms of acute hypoglycaemia in non-diabetic subjects.

cerebral executive functions and decision making are seriously impaired, while simpler repetitive psychomotor activity is spared [15]. In the early stages, neuroglycopenia is often recognized by relatives or colleagues rather than by the affected individual; the main danger of the insidious onset of neuroglycopenia is that it may itself reduce perception of impending hypoglycaemia. Irrational or aggressive behaviour with automatism, amnesia and progressive confusion — sometimes resembling inebriation — may develop as blood glucose concentration declines further. Convulsions and loss of consciousness may supervene when neuroglycopenia becomes profound.

Autonomic activation

When blood glucose concentration falls below a threshold of about 2.0 mmol/l (Fig. 50.1), activation of hypothalamic autonomic centres triggers a generalized autonomic discharge involving both sympathetic and parasympathetic divisions. Autonomic manifestations include sweating, tremor, palpitations, blurring of vision, hunger and altered salivation. Other non-specific symptoms include headache, dizziness, generalized weakness and paraesthesia, and these, combined with the autonomic symptoms, alert the patient to the development of hypoglycaemia and usually permit appropriate action to be taken to abort the episode. The sympathetic manifestations are amplified by the concomitant secretion of catecholamines, which may heighten the perception of hypoglycaemic symptoms and produce a classical 'fight or flight' reaction. The hypoglycaemic individual often looks pale and tired with visible sweating and has a tachycardia with widening of the pulse pressure.

Symptoms of hypoglycaemia are diverse and do not always conform to the classical description. Although some symptoms are common, considerable variation occurs between individuals and it is important that the newly diagnosed, insulin-dependent patient is familiar with his or her own personal constellation of symptoms. Many diabetic centres deliberately expose young patients to an episode of moderate hypoglycaemia under controlled conditions as part of their education about its recognition and management. This should be avoided in older patients who may have vascular disease, and in any patient with epilepsy or ischaemic heart disease. The manifestations of hypoglycaemia may also differ considerably between age groups. Hypoglycaemia in children may be mistaken for antisocial behaviour with irritability or temper tantrums, while in the elderly it may resemble vertebrobasilar insufficiency.

Hypoglycaemic symptoms during normoglycaemia

Some diabetic patients experience overt symptoms of hypoglycaemia when their blood glucose concentrations lie within the normal range. This discrepancy is well-recognized clinically, and is more common in diabetic patients with poor glycaemic control [16]. In some diabetic patients, a rapid fall from high to normal blood glucose values may provoke the release of counter-regulatory hormones including adrenaline, without true hypoglycaemia being produced [17]. However, this effect has not been demonstrated by others [18] and even when it does occur, may have no symptomatic effect. The altered threshold for perception of symptoms may be related to a reduced rate of transport of glucose across the blood–brain barrier during chronic hyperglycaemia, permitting the development of neuroglycopenia within a normoglycaemic range.

Hypoglycaemia unawareness

The symptoms of hypoglycaemia often change with increasing duration of diabetes. Many autonomic symptoms become attenuated or are even lost altogether, so that patients become unaware of the onset of hypoglycaemia and may suffer severe and prolonged neuroglycopenia as they are unable to take early corrective action [19, 20]. In some cases, hypoglycaemia unawareness may be a consequence of autonomic neuropathy preventing the normal autonomic discharge and increased catecholamine secretion. It may also occur, however, in diabetic patients who have no evidence of autonomic dysfunction [21].

Two types of hypoglycaemia awareness can be identified:

1 *Acute.* Loss of symptomatic awareness is associated with very tight glycaemic control and is often observed in young insulin-treated patients with diabetes of relatively short duration, or during the first trimester of pregnancy. The perception of hypoglycaemic symptoms occurs at a much lower blood glucose level than normal [22, 23], and the glycaemic threshold for the adrenaline secretion is also lower [24]. Strict glycaemic control also reduces the magnitude of counter-

regulatory hormone secretion [24–26]. These patients usually have glycosylated haemoglobin values within the normal range and are taking too much insulin. This is a reversible state and symptomatic awareness is restored when glycaemic control is relaxed.

2 *Chronic.* This develops in insulin-treated patients with long-standing diabetes and is sometimes associated with autonomic neuropathy [27]. These patients experience recurrent and unpredictable hypoglycaemia, often with loss of consciousness. This can be very disabling and should be regarded as a major diabetic complication, as it is irreversible and has no effective treatment. In patients without autonomic dysfunction, severe neuroglycopenia developed before the autonomic response to hypoglycaemia, the glycaemic threshold for which was lower than normal [28]. Although the autonomic reaction was preserved in these patients, it occurred too late for them to perceive the warning symptoms of hypoglycaemia. This might represent adaptation of central glucose receptors to glucopenia, resetting the glycaemic threshold for autonomic activation, or alternatively peripheral adrenergic sensitivity may be diminished [29]; the mechanism is unclear.

Hypoglycaemia unawareness may initially be intermittent or partial, with retention of some symptoms, but usually progresses to the full syndrome of total symptomatic unawareness. A survey of 302 insulin-dependent diabetic patients in Edinburgh revealed that 7% had total loss of awareness and 16% had partial unawareness. Some of these patients had coexisting autonomic neuropathy, but this was not invariably related to hypoglycaemia unawareness [21].

Glycaemic control has to be relaxed in these vulnerable patients to allow generally higher blood glucose values than are usually desirable. A flexible basal/bolus insulin regimen, adjusted according to frequent blood glucose monitoring, may be helpful.

Human insulins and hypoglycaemia unawareness

An uncontrolled Swiss survey reported that more than one-third of insulin-treated diabetic patients experienced a significant reduction of autonomic hypoglycaemic symptoms following transfer from animal to human insulins [30]. There is no obvious physiological basis for this phenomenon, which is most probably due to pharmacokinetic differences between human and animal insulins, together with the general tendency of physicians to try to tighten control whenever insulin treatment is changed [30]. This problem seems to be generally rare, and was reported by only 6% of randomly selected diabetic patients transfered to human insulin in our recent survey in Edinburgh [31]. It would seem prudent for the few patients affected to use highly purified porcine rather than human insulin. This topic has been reviewed recently [32] and remains an area of considerable controversy.

Effects of β-adrenergic blockade

Non-selective β-adrenergic blocking drugs have been blamed for masking certain symptoms of hypoglycaemia, although sweating (which is cholinergically mediated) is preserved and even accentuated. This potential hazard is well recognized [33] but probably of limited clinical importance, although these drugs should be avoided in patients with autonomic neuropathy.

Metabolic recovery processes

Insulin administration promotes glucose uptake to peripheral tissues (muscle and fat), and suppresses glucose outflow from the liver. Insulin inhibits hepatic glycogenolysis and gluconeogenesis, while also preventing lipolysis and proteolysis, the products of which are required for the synthesis of glucose. As a result, blood glucose falls rapidly. To maintain homeostasis and to protect the brain from prolonged glucose deprivation, hypoglycaemia activates several neural and hormonal mechanisms which reverse the metabolic effects of insulin. This process, known as glucose counter-regulation, is mediated principally by glucagon and adrenaline, which both stimulate hepatic glycogenolysis and gluconeogenesis. Adrenaline also promotes muscle glycogenolysis, proteolysis and lipolysis, thus providing three-carbon substrates (lactate, alanine and glycerol) for the synthesis of glucose; the energy required for this process is provided by the hepatic oxidation of free fatty acids (Fig. 50.2). Other counter-regulatory hormones include cortisol, growth hormone and vasopressin, which have synergistic actions, but are less important for rapid counter-regulation. The magnitude of the counter-regulatory hormonal response is not influenced by the rate of fall of blood glucose [34].

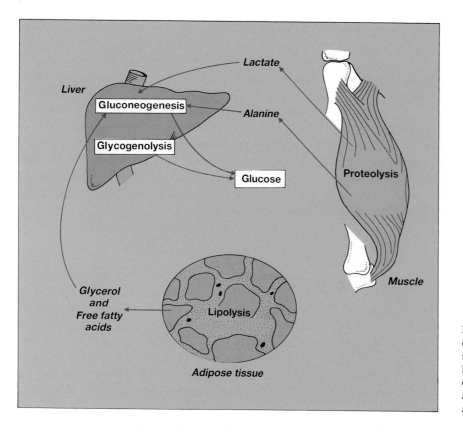

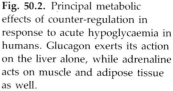

Fig. 50.2. Principal metabolic effects of counter-regulation in response to acute hypoglycaemia in humans. Glucagon exerts its action on the liver alone, while adrenaline acts on muscle and adipose tissue as well.

Counter-regulatory failure in diabetes

Isolated deficiencies of counter-regulatory hormones develop in many patients, particularly those with insulin-dependent diabetes of long duration. Individual hormonal deficiencies do not compromise blood glucose recovery from hypoglycaemia unless the secretion of glucagon and adrenaline are both diminished. This dual hormonal deficiency seriously threatens blood glucose recovery, exposing the patient to severe and prolonged hypoglycaemia [35], and increases the risk of developing severe hypoglycaemia during intensive insulin therapy [25].

Glucagon deficiency

In many diabetic patients, the glucagon response to hypoglycaemia declines within 5 years of the development of diabetes [36], and the magnitude of the deficit increases with time (see Fig. 50.5, p. 503). This acquired secretory deficit is permanent and cannot be restored by improving glycaemic control [37, 38]. It may represent reduced sensitivity of pancreatic A cells to glucopenia [39]; a possible local paracrine effect of insulin defic-

iency has now been discounted [40]. It is unlikely to be associated with autonomic neuropathy, as the glucagon response to hypoglycaemia in humans occurs independently of autonomic innervation [41].

Adrenaline deficiency

Increased secretion of catecholamines following hypoglycaemia is mediated via central autonomic activation within the hypothalamus (see Chapter 23). In diabetes, impaired secretion of adrenaline following hypoglycaemia develops later than the diminished glucagon response, and is associated both with long duration of diabetes and with autonomic neuropathy [27, 36, 42]. In the absence of demonstrable autonomic neuropathy, reduced secretion of adrenaline in long-standing diabetes may result from diminished sympatho-adrenal activation, possibly caused by altered glycaemic thresholds for the hypothalamic activation of counter-regulation. Multiple deficiencies of pituitary hormone secretion following hypoglycaemia have been demonstrated in a few diabetic patients [43, 44], and the rises in growth hormone and

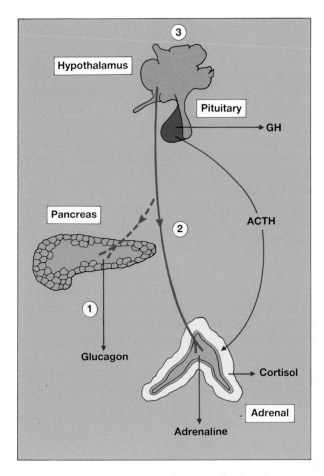

Fig. 50.3. Principal counter-regulatory mechanisms in humans, releasing glucagon, adrenaline, cortisol and growth hormone (GH). In diabetes, deficiencies can occur at different sites: (1) intrinsic pancreatic A-cell secretion; (2) autonomic neuropathy; (3) diminished central activation of glucose counter-regulation.

cortisol are often inappropriately low for the prevailing degree of hypoglycaemia [45]. This suggests that some patients develop an intrinsic defect in the central initiation of glucose counter-regulation. The principal sites of potential hormonal counter-regulatory failure are shown in Fig. 50.3.

Insulin antibodies

High titres of antibodies to exogenous insulin may be associated with severe impairment of blood glucose recovery following hypoglycaemia [45]. These patients have increased circulating reserve of antibody-bound insulin which effectively prolongs the half-life of insulin and predisposes to more severe and protracted hypoglycaemia. Intensive insulin therapy is hazardous in these individuals.

Pharmacological blockade

Factors which interfere with adrenergic mechanisms of glucose counter-regulation assume greater importance in patients with established glucagon deficiency. Non-selective β-blockade with drugs such as propranolol delays blood glucose recovery in IDDM patients [46] but recovery is unaffected by β₁-selective blocking agents such as atenolol or metoprolol [47]. Although autonomic neuropathy may reduce the symptomatic warning of hypoglycaemia, there is no evidence that blood glucose recovery is impaired more frequently [42], or that the frequency of hypoglycaemia is increased [48].

Several mechanisms may be responsible for counter-regulatory failure in patients with long-standing diabetes, and may be aggravated further by concurrent development of hypoglycaemic unawareness. The recommendation that routine investigation of counter-regulatory responses to controlled hypoglycaemia should be performed in all IDDM patients to identify those at risk [25] is not practical in a large diabetic clinic with limited resources. However, possible counter-regulatory deficiencies should be considered in all patients treated with insulin for more than 10 years before attempting to intensify insulin therapy in order to improve glycaemic control.

Sulphonylureas and hypoglycaemia

Hypoglycaemia may occur with any sulphonylurea drug, but is more common with the longer-acting preparations such as chlorpropamide. Although glibenclamide has a shorter average half-life than chlorpropamide, it is slowly metabolized by certain individuals and can also cause prolonged hypoglycaemia. Sulphonylureas are more commonly prescribed in older patients, in whom the presentation of hypoglycaemia may be insidious, with subtle alterations in cerebral function and behaviour or focal neurological signs, rather than acute autonomic symptomatology. Hypoglycaemia is more likely in patients with hepatic or renal impairment, which may reduce clearance of sulphonylureas. Although mortality is relatively low, the risks of hypoglycaemia increase with age. Clinicians must remain alert to this potential side-effect of sulphonylurea therapy in the elderly, in whom hypoglycaemic symptoms may be readily attributed to cerebrovascular disease, and chlorpropamide and glibenclamide should be avoided in this group. The hypoglycaemic effect of sulphonylureas may be potentiated by various drugs, including aspirin, β-blockers and sulphonamides [49, 50] (see Table 79.3).

Profound hypoglycaemia requires treatment in hospital, and when induced by sulphonylureas, may need the infusion of intravenous dextrose to be continued for several days. In severe cases, steroid therapy may be a useful adjunct and diazoxide has also been recommended [2]. Glucagon is contraindicated as it stimulates the release of endogenous insulin.

Morbidity and mortality

Hypoglycaemic coma is relatively common but fortunately permanent brain damage appears to be rare unless there is associated excessive alcohol consumption which suppresses gluconeogenesis. There is some evidence that recurrent hypoglycaemia may produce cumulative damage to cerebral function and impair intellectual capacity [51].

Acute hypoglycaemia provokes major haemodynamic and haemostatic changes in humans, primarily related to sympatho-adrenal activation and the secretion of catecholamines. When the stress of acute hypoglycaemia is inflicted upon a diseased vascular system, it may exacerbate localized ischaemia. Transient ischaemic attacks, strokes, cardiac arrythmias, angina and myocardial infarction are all associated with hypoglycaemia. This metabolic insult can also provoke generalized or focal convulsions, which may cause serious musculo-skeletal injury (including fractures and joint dislocations) and other trauma [52]. It may be difficult to differentiate convulsions induced by hypoglycaemia from idiopathic epilepsy, which is less common in the diabetic population. Anti-convulsant therapy appears to have no prophylactic benefit in preventing convulsions caused by hypoglycaemia. Acute hypoglycaemia causes persistent electroencephalographic disturbances; EEG should therefore be deferred for several days following a convulsion. Moreover, blood glucose concentration should be measured in any diabetic patient having an EEG to detect concurrent hypoglycaemia, which could confuse its interpretation. Misdiagnosis of hypoglycaemia-induced convulsions as idiopathic epilepsy is common and may have serious consequences for the patient, such as revocation of his or her driving licence [53].

The pathophysiological effects of acute hypoglycaemia include increases in haematocrit, blood viscosity, and platelet activation and aggregation, which may have deleterious effects on capillary blood flow and might promote localized intravascular coagulation (Fig. 50.4). These acute changes, which are primarily catecholamine induced, could theoretically precipitate capillary closure in patients with pre-existing microvascular disease, and may account for the deterioration in diabetic retinopathy observed with tight glycaemic control [54]. Anecdotal reports of vitreous haemorrhage following hypoglycaemia may be related to an acute fall in intra-ocular pressure [55].

The mortality from profound hypoglycaemia in insulin-treated patients is 3–4% in most series [41]. This may be an underestimate, as hypoglycaemia may precipitate fatal accidents, hypothermia, or major vascular events which are then designated as the cause of death. Hypoglycaemia is therefore a dangerous side-effect of treatment with insulin or oral hypoglycaemic therapy and should never be regarded lightly.

Treatment

Although the diagnosis of hypoglycaemic coma in the insulin-treated diabetic patient may seem obvious, coma can occur from diverse causes, and the blood glucose level must always be estimated in the unconscious diabetic patient before treatment is initiated. This has been simplified by the availability of strips to measure capillary blood

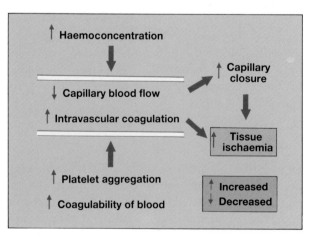

Fig. 50.4. Potential effects of the acute changes of haemoconcentration and haemostasis induced by hypoglycaemia on capillary blood flow. These changes may accelerate closure of diseased capillaries in microangiopathy, causing ischaemia of affected tissues.

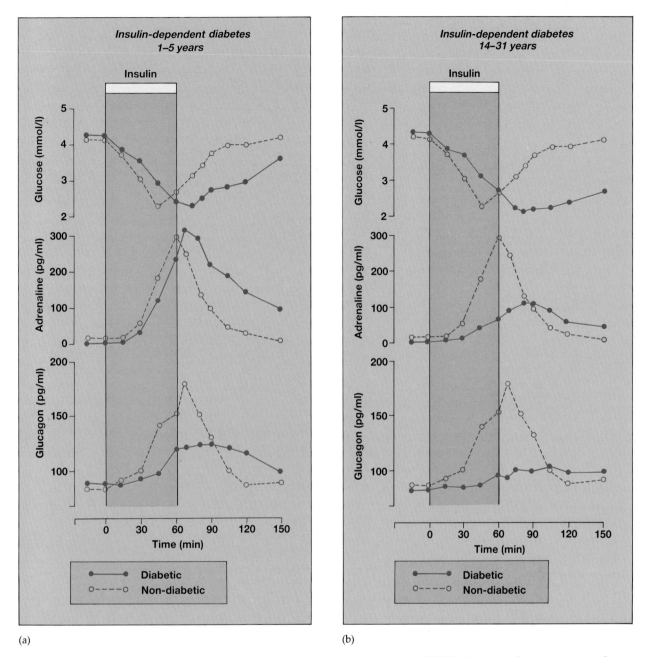

(a)

(b)

Fig. 50.5. Impairment of counter-regulatory responses in IDDM. (a) After 1–5 years of IDDM, the mean glucagon response (lower panel) is blunted but the rise in adrenaline secretion is preserved (middle panel); glycaemic recovery is delayed (upper panel). (b) With long-standing IDDM, both glucagon and adrenaline responses are severely impaired and glycaemic recovery is markedly delayed and slowed.

glucose, and hospital and general practitioners should carry a supply for emergency use. Blood glucose is usually below 2.0 mmol/l in the hypoglycaemic patient, but may be higher if counter-regulation has commenced.

The acute episode is most effectively treated with glucose (15–20 g), the route of administration depending upon the patient's level of consciousness and ability to co-operate. Glucose, whether

in the form of tablets, or a drink, generally acts within minutes, as does sucrose [56]. Giving food or a glucose drink (15–20 g) may not be practical if the patient is semi-conscious and cannot swallow, or is aggressive and difficult to control. Intravenous dextrose (30 ml of a 20% solution) is by far the most effective therapeutic measure because glucose reaches the central nervous system rapidly by this route, and the restorative effect is often dramatic. Once the patient has regained consciousness, oral glucose should be given as hypoglycaemia may recur. Glucagon (1 mg) given subcutaneously or intramuscularly can be administered in an emergency by a friend or relative previously instructed in the technique. Glucagon acts primarily by stimulating hepatic glycogenolysis and occasionally may be ineffective if hypoglycaemia has been protracted and the hepatic glycogen stores are exhausted. An alternative means of delivering glucose to the semiconscious patient is to smear jam inside the cheeks or to squeeze a 40% glucose gel ('Hypostop®') between the teeth and gums. Local massage over the cheek promotes mucosal absorption of glucose and may allow consciousness to return to the point where it is safe for the patient to swallow glucose drinks or food. A recent study has, however, suggested that glucose gel administered in this way is ineffective [56]. After recovery, the blood glucose concentration should be rechecked to ensure that it has risen satisfactorily.

Failure to recover consciousness after intravenous dextrose may be associated with cerebral oedema, which often has a poor prognosis but may respond to treatment with parenteral steroids (hydrocortisone or dexamethasone) or an osmotic diuretic such as mannitol. In this situation a CT scan is advisable to exclude an alternative cause of depressed consciousness such as intracerebral haemorrhage.

Prophylactic measures

Adequate education of diabetic patients and their relatives is necessary so that hypoglycaemia can be avoided or treated effectively at an early stage. Patients should carry a card stating that they have diabetes and are treated with insulin or oral hypoglycaemic agents. Relatives, friends or colleagues at work or at school should be familiar with the signs of hypoglycaemia and its emergency treatment. The importance of regular meals and snacks must be emphasized, and treatment should be adjusted appropriately for sporting activities or for special situations such as fasting before radiological procedures or minor surgery. If β-blocking drugs are needed, cardio-selective agents should be prescribed. The widespread use of highly purified human insulins should reduce the problem of hypoglycaemia associated with high titres of insulin antibodies.

The therapeutic goal has to be modified in diabetic patients with autonomic neuropathy, hypoglycaemia unawareness or severe diabetic complications. Very strict glycaemic control should be avoided where the risks of hypoglycaemia outweigh any potential benefit, such as in long-standing, IDDM patients who have impaired glucose counter-regulation, or in elderly or mentally subnormal patients. Intensive insulin therapy may also be impractical in treating infants or very young children. Moderate hyperglycaemia may have to be accepted in these individuals to avoid the greater risks of low blood glucose concentrations. Although there is no evidence in humans that hypoglycaemia causes fetal damage in early pregnancy, very tight glycaemic control reduces the ability to perceive hypoglycaemic symptoms and increases the risk of coma and convulsions, which are clearly undesirable for fetal development. Rapid tightening of glycaemic control is now considered to have an initial potentially adverse effect on established microangiopathy (see Chapter 42), and also increases vulnerability to hypoglycaemia.

Social implications

Because of the potential risk of hypoglycaemia, IDDM individuals are usually advised not to participate in high-risk sporting activities such as hang-gliding, parachute-jumping or scuba-diving. They may also be excluded from certain types of employment, e.g. steeplejacks, deep-sea divers and airline pilots (see Chapter 92). They are usually debarred from driving public-service vehicles and may not be permitted to operate some forms of machinery. Problematical hypoglycaemia is a frequent reason for a patient's driving licence to be revoked, which may have medico-legal implications and repercussions on employment. The potential problems of hypoglycaemia and driving are discussed in a separate section (Chapter 93). The relationship of hypoglycaemia to criminal responsibility has recently been reviewed [57].

BRIAN M. FRIER

References

1 Clarke BF, Campbell IW. Long-term comparative trial of glibenclamide and chlorpropamide in diet-failed maturity-onset diabetes. *Lancet* 1974; i: 246–8.
2 Ferner RE, Neil HAW. Sulphonylureas and hypoglycaemia. *Br Med J* 1988; **296**: 949–50.

3 Potter J, Clarke P, Gale EAM, Dave SH, Tattersall RB. Insulin-induced hypoglycaemia in an accident and emergency department: the tip of an iceberg? *Br Med J* 1982; **285**: 1180–2.

4 Goldgewicht C, Slama G, Papoz L, Tchobroutsky G. Hypoglycaemic reactions in 172 Type 1 (insulin-dependent) diabetic patients. *Diabetologia* 1983; **24**: 95–9.

5 Casparie AF, Elving LD. Severe hypoglycemia in diabetic patients: frequency, causes, prevention. *Diabetes Care* 1985; **8**: 141–5.

6 Chisholm DJ, Kraegen EW, Hewett MJ. Hypoglycemic episodes during continuous subcutaneous insulin infusion: decreased frequency but increased susceptibility. *Aust NZ J Med* 1984; **14**: 255–9.

7 Mühlhauser I, Berger M, Sonnenberg G, Koch J, Jörgens V, Scherthaner G, Scholz V. Incidence and management of severe hypoglycemia in 434 adults with insulin-dependent diabetes mellitus. *Diabetes Care* 1985; **8**: 268–73.

8 Arias P, Kerner W, Zier H, Navascues I, Pfeiffer EF. Incidence of hypoglycemic episodes in diabetic patients under continuous subcutaneous insulin infusion and intensified conventional insulin treatment: assessment by means of semiambulatory 24-hour continuous blood glucose monitoring. *Diabetes Care* 1985; **8**: 134–40.

9 Ng Tang Fui S, Pickup JC, Bending JJ, Collins ACG, Keen H, Dalton N. Hypoglycemia and counterregulation in insulin-dependent diabetic patients: a comparison of continuous subcutaneous insulin infusion and conventional insulin injection therapy. *Diabetes Care* 1986; **9**: 221–7.

10 DCCT Research Group. Diabetes control and complications trial (DCCT): results of feasibility study. *Diabetes Care* 1987; **10**: 1–19.

11 Thorsteinsson B, Pramming S, Lauritzen T, Binder C. Frequency of daytime biochemical hypoglycaemia in insulin-treated diabetic patients: relation to daily median blood glucose concentrations. *Diabetic Med* 1986; **3**: 147–51.

12 Macfarlane PI, Walters M, Stitchfield P, Smith CS. A prospective study of symptomatic hypoglycaemia in childhood diabetes. *Diabetic Med* 1989; **6**: 627–30.

13 Macdonald MJ. Postexercise late-onset hypoglycemia in insulin-dependent diabetic patients. *Diabetes Care* 1987; **10**: 584–8.

14 Koivisto VA, Fortney S, Hendler R, Felig P. A rise in ambient temperature augments insulin absorption in diabetic patients. *Metabolism* 1981; **30**: 402–5.

15 Pramming S, Thorsteinsson B, Theilgaard A, Pinner EM, Binder C. Cognitive function during hypoglycaemia in type 1 diabetes mellitus. *Br Med J* 1986; **292**: 647–50.

16 Boyle PJ, Schwartz NS, Shah SD, Clutter WE, Cryer PE. Plasma glucose concentrations at the onset of hypoglycemic symptoms in patients with poorly controlled diabetes and in non-diabetics. *N Engl J Med* 1988; **318**: 1487–92.

17 DeFronzo RA, Hendler R, Christensen N. Stimulation of counter-regulatory hormonal responses in diabetic man by a fall in glucose concentration. *Diabetes* 1980; **29**: 125–31.

18 Lilavivathana U, Brodows RG, Woolf PD, Campbell RG. Counter-regulatory hormonal responses to rapid glucose lowering in diabetic man. *Diabetes* 1979; **28**: 873–7.

19 Balodimos C, Root HF. Hypoglycemic insulin reactions without warning symptoms. *J Am Med Assoc* 1959; **171**: 261–6.

20 Sussman KE, Crout JR, Marble A. Failure of warning in insulin-induced hypoglycemic reactions. *Diabetes* 1963; **12**: 38–45.

21 Hepburn DA, Patrick AW, Eadington DW, Ewing DJ, Frier BM. Unawareness of hypoglycaemia in insulin-treated diabetic patients: prevalence and relationship to autonomic neuropathy. *Diabetic Med* (in press).

22 Lager I, Attvall S, Blöhme G, Smith U. Altered recognition of hypoglycaemic symptoms in type 1 diabetes during intensified control with continuous subcutaneous insulin infusion. *Diabetic Med* 1986; **3**: 322–5.

23 Amiel SA, Tamborlane WV, Simonson DC, Sherwin RS. Defective glucose counter-regulation after strict glycemic control of insulin-dependent diabetes mellitus. *N Engl J Med* 1987; **316**: 1376–83.

24 Amiel SA, Sherwin RS, Simonson DC, Tamborlane WV. Effect of intensive insulin therapy on glycemic thresholds for counter-regulatory hormone release. *Diabetes* 1988; **37**: 901–7.

25 White NH, Skor DA, Cryer PE, Levandoski LA, Bier DM, Santiago JV. Identification of type 1 diabetic patients at increased risk for hypoglycemia during intensive therapy. *N Engl J Med* 1983; **308**: 485–91.

26 Simonson DC, Tamborlane WV, DeFronzo RA, Sherwin RS. Intensive insulin therapy reduces counter-regulatory hormone responses to hypoglycemia in patients with type 1 diabetes. *Ann Intern Med* 1985; **103**: 184–90.

27 Hoeldtke RD, Boden G, Shuman CR, Owen OE. Reduced epinephrine secretion and hypoglycemic unawareness in diabetic autonomic neuropathy. *Ann Intern Med* 1982; **96**: 459–62.

28 Hepburn DA, Patrick AW, Frier BM. Severe neuroglycopenia precedes autonomic activation during acute hypoglycemia in insulin-dependent diabetic patients with hypoglycemia unawareness. *Diabetes* 1989; **38** (suppl 2): 76A.

29 Berlin I, Grimaldi A, Landault C, Zoghbi F, Thervet F, Puech AJ, Legrand JC. Lack of hypoglycemic symptoms and decreased β-adrenergic sensitivity in insulin-dependent diabetic patients. *J Clin Endocrinol Metab* 1988; **66**: 273–8.

30 Teuscher A, Berger WG. Hypoglycemia unawareness in diabetics transferred from beef/porcine insulin to human insulin. *Lancet* 1987; ii: 382–5.

31 Hepburn DA, Eadington DW, Patrick AW, Colledge NR, Frier BM. Symptomatic awareness of hypoglycaemia: does it change on transfer from animal to human insulin? *Diabetic Med* 1989; **6**: 586–90.

32 Pickup J. Human insulin. *Br Med J* 1989; **299**: 991–3.

33 Smith U, Blöhme G, Lager I, Lonroth P. Can insulin-treated diabetics be given beta-adrenergic blocking drugs? *Br Med J* 1980; **281**: 1143–4.

34 Amiel SA, Simonson DC, Tamborlane WV, DeFronzo RA, Sherwin RS. Rate of glucose fall does not affect counter-regulatory hormone responses to hypoglycemia in normal and diabetic humans. *Diabetes* 1987; **36**: 518–22.

35 Cryer PE, Gerich JE. Glucose counter-regulation, hypoglycemia and intensive insulin therapy in diabetes mellitus. *N Engl J Med* 1985; **313**: 232–41.

36 Bolli G, De Feo P, Compagnucci P *et al.* Abnormal glucose counter-regulation in insulin-dependent diabetes mellitus. Interaction of anti-insulin antibodies and impaired glucagon and epinephrine secretion. *Diabetes* 1983; **32**: 134–41.

37 Bergenstal RM, Polonsky KS, Pons G, Jaspan JB, Rubenstein AH. Lack of glucagon response to hypoglycemia in type 1 diabetics after long-term optimal therapy with a continuous subcutaneous insulin infusion pump. *Diabetes* 1983; **32**: 398–402.

38 Bolli G, De Feo P, De Cosmo S, Perriello G, Angeletti G, Ventura MR, Santeusanio F, Brunetti P, Gerich JE. Effects of long-term optimization and short-term deterioration of

glycemic control on glucose counter-regulation in type 1 diabetes mellitus. *Diabetes* 1984; **33**: 394−400.

39 Gerich JE, Langlois M, Noacco C, Karam JH, Forsham PH. Lack of glucagon response to hypoglycemia in diabetes: evidence for an intrinsic pancreatic alpha cell defect. *Science* 1973; **182**: 171−3.

40 Bolli G, De Feo P, Perriello G, De Cosmo S, Campagnucci P, Santeusanio F, Brunetti P, Unger RH. Mechanisms of glucagon secretion during insulin-induced hypoglycemia in man. Role of the beta cell and arterial hyperinsulinemia. *J Clin Invest* 1984; **73**: 917−22.

41 Frier BM. Hypoglycaemia and diabetes. *Diabetic Med* 1986; **3**: 513−25.

42 Hilsted J, Madsbad J, Krarup T, Sestoft L, Christensen NJ, Tronier B, Galbo H. Hormonal, metabolic and cardiovascular responses to hypoglycemia in diabetic autonomic neuropathy. *Diabetes* 1981; **30**: 626−33.

43 Boden G, Reichard GA, Hoeldtke RD, Rezvani I, Owen OE. Severe insulin-induced hypoglycemia associated with deficiencies in the release of counter-regulatory hormones. *N Engl J Med* 1981; **305**: 1200−5.

44 Frier BM, Fisher BM, Gray CE, Beastall GH. Counter-regulatory hormonal responses to hypoglycaemia in Type 1 (insulin-dependent) diabetes: evidence for diminished hypothalamic-pituitary hormonal secretion. *Diabetologia* 1988; **31**: 421−9.

45 Bolli GB, Dimitriadis GD, Pehling GB, Baker BA, Haymond MW, Cryer PE, Gerich JE. Abnormal glucose counter-regulation after subcutaneous insulin in insulin-dependent diabetes mellitus. *N Engl J Med* 1984; **310**: 1706−11.

46 Popp DA, Shah SD, Cryer PE. The role of epinephrine-mediated β-adrenergic mechanisms in hypoglycemic glucose counter-regulation and posthypoglycemic hyperglycemia in insulin-dependent diabetes mellitus. *J Clin Invest* 1982; **69**: 315−26.

47 Lager I, Blöhme G, Smith U. Effect of cardio-selective and non-selective β-blockade on the hypoglycaemic response in insulin-dependent diabetics. *Lancet* 1979; i: 458−62.

48 Polonsky K, Bergenstal R, Pons G, Schneider M, Jaspan J, Rubenstein A. Relation of counter-regulatory responses to hypoglycemia in type 1 diabetes. *N Engl J Med* 1982; **307**: 1106−12.

49 Asplund K, Wiholm B-E, Lithner F. Glibenclamide-associated hypoglycaemia: a report on 57 cases. *Diabetologia* 1983; **24**: 412−17.

50 Selzer HS. Drug-induced hypoglycemia: a review based on 473 cases. *Diabetes* 1972; **21**: 955−66.

51 Langan SJ, Hepburn DA, Deary IJ, Frier BM. Recurrent hypoglycaemia causes cumulative cognitive impairment in patients with Type 1 (insulin dependent) diabetes (abstract). *Diabetic Med* 1989; 6 (suppl 2): 7A.

52 Hepburn DA, Steel JM, Frier BM. Hypoglycemic convulsions cause serious musculoskeletal injuries in patients with IDDM. *Diabetes Care* 1989; **12**: 32−4.

53 Fisher BM, Frier BM. Nocturnal convulsions and insulin-induced hypoglycaemia in diabetic patients. *Postgrad Med J* 1987; **63**: 673−6.

54 Frier BM, Hilsted J. Does hypoglycaemia aggravate the complications of diabetes? *Lancet* 1985; ii: 1175−7.

55 Frier BM, Hepburn DA, Fisher BM, Barrie T. Fall in intra-ocular pressure during acute hypoglycaemia in patients with insulin dependent diabetes. *Br Med J* 1987; **294**: 610−11.

56 Sloma G, Traynard PY, Desplanque N *et al*. The search for an optimized treatment of hypoglycaemia. Carbohydrates in tablets, solution, or gel for the correction of insulin reactions. *Arch Int Med* 1990; **150**: 589−93.

57 Frier BM, Maher G. Diabetes and hypoglycaemia: medico-legal aspects of criminal responsibility. *Diabetic Med* 1988; **5**: 521−6.

51 Problems with Overnight Glycaemic Control in Insulin-Treated Diabetic Patients

Summary

- In normal subjects, overnight blood glucose levels are tightly regulated because the pancreas delivers insulin continuously to the liver at a variable rate which follows changes in insulin resistance.
- Excessive fasting hyperglycaemia in insulin-treated IDDM patients is due mainly to waning of the circulating insulin levels from intermediate-acting insulin injected the previous evening. This may be exaggerated by the 'dawn phenomenon' and the 'Somogyi effect'.
- The *dawn phenomenon* is the increase in insulin resistance (and therefore in insulin requirements) which occurs between 05.00 and 08.00 hours. It is seen in normal, NIDDM and IDDM subjects and is particularly marked in IDDM, apparently because of excessive growth hormone secretion soon after the onset of sleep.
- The *Somogyi effect* is 'rebound' hyperglycaemia following hypoglycaemia, attributed to increased insulin resistance following secretion of counter-regulatory hormones (cortisol, catecholamines, growth hormone) during hypoglycaemia.
- Nocturnal hypoglycaemia occurs in at least one-third of IDDM patients, especially if treated with intensified regimens. Most episodes are asymptomatic but may be manifested by night sweats, nightmares and morning headache and depression.
- Fasting hyperglycaemia may be reduced by injecting intermediate-acting insulin later in the evening rather than by increasing the dose, which will only worsen early nocturnal hypoglycaemia; by using variable-rate CSII to deliver higher rates after 05.00 hours; and by suppressing early nocturnal growth hormone secretion with somatostatin or atropinic drugs.

A major problem in replacing insulin in IDDM patients who have lost virtually all their pancreatic B-cell mass is the lack of a depot preparation capable of mimicking the relatively constant background secretion of insulin by the healthy pancreas. The currently available intermediate- or long-acting insulin preparations all have a 'peaked' action profile, with excessively high blood insulin levels 3–5 h after injection followed by rapidly worsening insulin deficiency after 6–8 h. This time-course poses particular difficulties during the night and contributes to the common clinical problem of excessive fasting hyperglycaemia in IDDM patients. An intermediate-acting insulin given at suppertime will tend to cause hypoglycaemia in the early night followed by hyperglycaemia at dawn, as the insulin levels wane.

This tendency to fasting hyperglycaemia is accentuated by two other factors. The first is termed the 'dawn phenomenon', and refers to a physiological increase in insulin resistance during the 'dawn hours' (05.00–08.00), which is particularly marked in IDDM patients [1–4]. The second is the 'Somogyi effect' which, as originally described [5], was the sequence of nocturnal hypoglycaemia followed by 'rebound' hyperglycaemia attributed to the release of counter-regulatory hormones during hypoglycaemia [6]. Although this effect may be less significant than previously thought, a period of insulin resistance undoubtedly follows hypoglycaemia and probably increases fasting hyperglycaemia [6–8].

The dawn phenomenon

Non-diabetic subjects maintain perfect blood glucose homeostasis overnight because the normal pancreas delivers insulin to the liver continuously at a carefully modulated rate (Fig. 51.1) [9]. Normally, insulin secretion initially decreases between midnight and 05.00 hours and later increases to a peak at 07.00 hours which is approximately 30% greater than the nadir value at around 05.30. In the early night, there is a decrease in the rate of glucose output by the liver (synchronous with the fall in insulin secretion) and then an increase after 06.00 hours. Hepatic insulin sensitivity must therefore be greater in the early part of the night than in the dawn hours.

Nocturnal insulin requirements in IDDM patients have been studied under 'closed-loop' conditions (i.e. insulin is infused intravenously at a rate which is continuously adjusted to maintain near-normoglycaemia). Overnight insulin requirements of IDDM patients are similar to those of non-diabetic subjects [2] (Fig. 51.2), i.e. approximately 30% greater at dawn than in the early night. Indeed, the exogenous insulin delivery rate required to maintain overnight euglycaemia in IDDM patients has a very similar profile to that of the endogenous insulin secretory rate of non-diabetic subjects (Fig. 51.3). This study confirms that nearly perfect nocturnal glycaemic profiles can be obtained in IDDM patients, provided that insulin is delivered in a physiological way.

The increase in insulin requirements which occurs between 05.00 and 08.00 hours in the absence of either nocturnal hypoglycaemia or inadequate blood insulin levels is defined as the 'dawn phenomenon'. The dawn phenomenon occurs in normal non-diabetic subjects [9], in subjects with IDDM [2], and in NIDDM patients whose fasting plasma glucose concentrations are either less than 8 mmol/l or over 8 mmol/l [4]. The need for more insulin at dawn is not due to an increase in plasma insulin clearance [2, 10], but to a decrease in insulin sensitivity which affects both the liver and extrahepatic tissues [11]. Among the factors which could reduce insulin sensitivity in the early morning are the counter-regulatory hormones. It has been shown that nocturnal secretion of catecholamines [12, 13], cortisol [14] and glucagon [15] are apparently unimportant, whereas growth hormone appears to play a key role [11, 13, 16]. Large and frequent growth hormone surges occurring soon after the onset of sleep account for much of the total daily growth hormone secretion and reduce insulin sensitivity some hours later through the late insulin-antagonistic action of

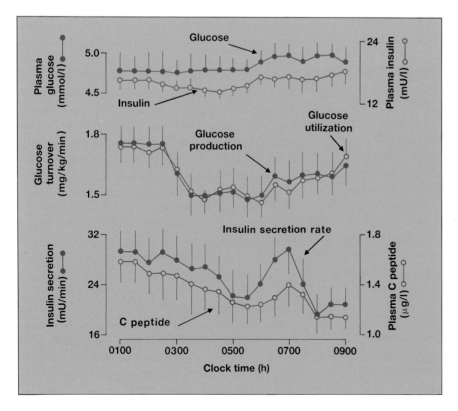

Fig. 51.1. Plasma glucose concentration, glucose turnover rates (utilization and production), plasma insulin and C-peptide concentration, and calculated rates of endogenous insulin secretion in normal subjects studied overnight during physiological sleep. Mean ± SEM (*n* = 8). (From Bolli *et al.* 1984 [9], reproduced with permission.)

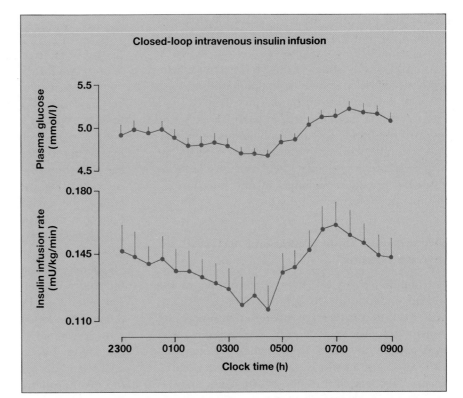

Fig. 51.2. Plasma glucose concentration and intravenous insulin infusion rates required to maintain euglycaemia overnight in IDDM patients. Mean ± SEM (*n* = 11). Insulin was infused by a syringe pump. (From De Feo *et al.* 1986 [2], reproduced with permission from Springer-Verlag.)

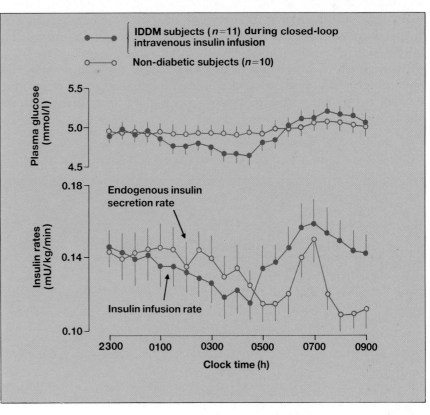

Fig. 51.3. The overnight insulin requirements in IDDM patients closely resemble the physiological pattern of endogenous insulin secretion in non-diabetic subjects. (Perriello *et al.*, unpublished observations.)

growth hormone [17]. The dawn phenomenon can be reduced or abolished by suppressing early-night growth hormone secretion with either somatostatin [13] or anti-cholinergic agents [16],

and can be reproduced by giving hourly 'spikes' of growth hormone to somatostatin-suppressed IDDM patients [11, 13].

The dawn phenomenon is present in virtually

all diabetic patients, and is reproducible from day to day [15]. An interesting question is the extent to which the dawn phenomenon contributes to fasting hyperglycaemia. If the need for more insulin between 05.00 and 08.00 hours is not satisfied, plasma glucose concentration increases by 1–2 mmol/l in the dawn hours [3, 5, 10, 18–21]. The net contribution of the dawn phenomenon to fasting hyperglycaemia is therefore rather modest, but will be greatly increased if circulating insulin levels from the previous evening's insulin injection are waning at the same time [22].

Depot insulin action profiles and nocturnal glycaemic control

As mentioned above, the action profile of the available depot insulin preparations (Fig. 51.4) will lead to progressive insulin deficiency and hyperglycaemia some 6–8 h after injection, i.e. after about 02.00–03.00 hours, when intermediate- or long-acting insulin is given before the evening meal. This early-morning insulin deficiency is the major cause of fasting hyperglycaemia in IDDM patients. Attempts to overcome this by simply increasing the evening dosage of intermediate-acting insulin are likely to result in hypoglycaemia between midnight and 02.00 hours, because the peak circulating insulin levels coincide with the period of greatest nocturnal insulin sensitivity [11].

Nocturnal hypoglycaemia and the Somogyi effect

Because of the pharmacokinetics of intermediate-acting insulin preparations (Fig. 51.4) and the enhanced insulin sensitivity in the early night [11], nocturnal hypoglycaemia (usually asymptomatic) occurs frequently in insulin-treated diabetic patients between midnight and 03.00 hours [23]. After nocturnal hypoglycaemia, a hyperglycaemic rebound (Somogyi effect [24]) may or may not occur (Fig. 51.5), depending on the balance between the prevailing plasma insulin concentrations and those of the counter-regulatory hormones [7]. Adrenaline, growth hormone and cortisol are apparently most important, the secretion of glucagon in response to hypoglycaemia being blunted or absent in many IDDM patients [25]. The extent of the increase in fasting glycaemia depends on factors such as the timing of nocturnal hypoglycaemia (the later it occurs, the less likely is fasting hyperglycaemia [26, 27]); the time-course and dosage of the insulin preparation given the evening before; the residual ability to secrete counter-regulatory hormones [28]; and the amount of glucose ingested to correct hypoglycaemia [15].

Overall, it has been estimated that fasting hyperglycaemia develops after one-quarter of asymptomatic nocturnal hypoglycaemic episodes [6]. However, even when fasting glycaemia is only modestly increased, postbreakfast plasma glucose levels may be considerably raised following noc-

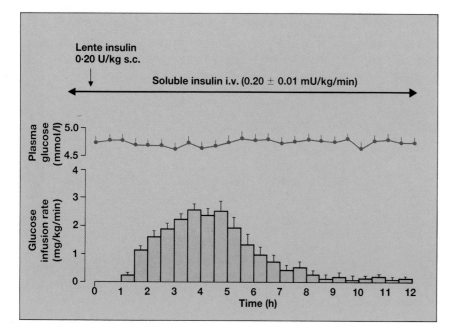

Fig. 51.4. Action profile of lente insulin injected subcutaneously in IDDM patients, as assessed by the euglycaemic clamp technique. Subjects with IDDM ($n = 6$); mean ± SEM. (Perriello et al., unpublished observations.)

Fig. 51.5. Plasma glucose may or may not rebound after an episode of hypoglycaemia induced by a subcutaneous injection of insulin in IDDM patients (filled symbols). In this example, the limiting factor for lack of posthypoglycaemic rebound in Group A (filled circles) was the excessive hyperinsulinaemia late after the insulin injection, due to a high titre of insulin antibodies. On the contrary, in diabetic subjects with low titres of insulin antibodies and normal insulin pharmacokinetics Group B (filled squares), posthypoglycaemic hyperglycaemia (Somogyi effect) developed as a result of activated counter-regulation and insulin deficiency. Normal non-diabetic subjects (open circles) do not exhibit posthypoglycaemic rebound because their pancreatic B cells secrete insulin in response to glucose recovery from hypoglycaemia. (From Bolli *et al.* 1984 [7], reproduced with permission from *The New England Journal of Medicine*.)

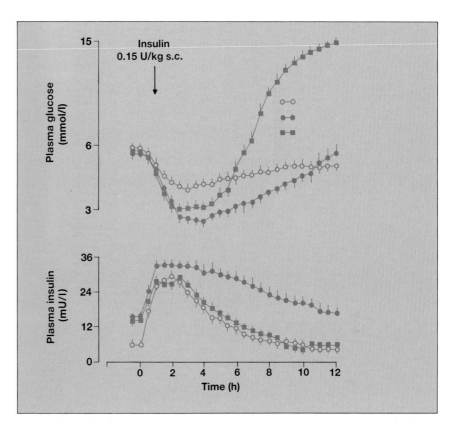

Fig. 51.6. Nocturnal and early morning plasma glucose concentrations in 12 IDDM patients treated with continuous subcutaneous insulin infusion at either fixed rate (open circles), or variable rate (increased insulin infusion rate after midnight; filled triangles). Normal non-diabetic subjects are shown as controls (open squares). Mean ± SEM. (From Koivisto *et al.* 1986 [19], reproduced with permission.)

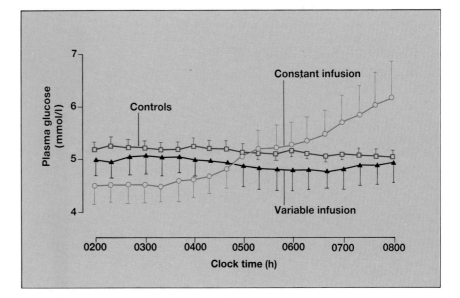

turnal hypoglycaemia [6, 29]. This is because posthypoglycaemic insulin resistance is prolonged for several hours [30] and affects both the liver and the extrahepatic tissues (primarily muscle), the key sites for disposal of ingested glucose [31].

Hazards of nocturnal hypoglycaemia

Nocturnal hypoglycaemia occurs at least in one-third of insulin-treated diabetic patients [23]. As mentioned above, this is usually asymptomatic, as the perception of hypoglycaemia is greatly reduced during sleep. Patients may wake or suffer convulsions if hypoglycaemia is profound. Nocturnal hypoglycaemia should be suspected clinically by complaints of night sweats, disturbed sleep and restlessness (often reported by the patient's spouse), vivid dreams or nightmares, and symptoms of headache, feeling 'hung-over', depressed or fatigued on the following morning. The suspicion of nocturnal hypoglycaemia should be followed up by checking the blood glucose level between 02.00 and 04.00 hours.

Severe, prolonged hypoglycaemia is known to be dangerous for the brain, but even brief and asymptomatic episodes of mild hypoglycaemia can impair cortical brain function in non-diabetic subjects [32] and, especially if repeated, could cause brain damage in insulin-treated diabetic patients. In addition, nocturnal hypoglycaemia may cause excessive hyperglycaemia the following day and so initiate a vicious circle of 'hypoglycaemia–hyperglycaemia' [6]. Thus, in planning for overnight diabetic control, the strategy of insulin therapy and meal plan should aim primarily to prevent nocturnal hypoglycaemia by maintaining the blood glucose concentration at over 4 mmol/l.

Methods to improve overnight glycaemic control

In general, the lower the target glycaemic range in a given therapeutic regimen, the greater is the risk of hypoglycaemia [33]; certain 'intensified' injection or CSII regimens may increase the frequency of severe nocturnal hypoglycaemia by up to three-fold [34]. The blood glucose level at bedtime is a significant predictor of nocturnal hypoglycaemia, with an 80% risk if below 6 mmol/l [23]. In patients in whom suboptimal glycaemic control is acceptable (such as the elderly, to whom hypoglycaemia is particularly hazardous), nocturnal hypoglycaemia should be prevented by maintaining the blood glucose values at bedtime and at 03.00 hours consistently above 8 mmol/l. To prevent nocturnal hypoglycaemia during more intensified regimens, insulin should ideally be delivered according to the physiological profile shown in Fig. 51.2, i.e. less in the early night and then more during the dawn hours. Such a profile can be achieved using CSII delivered by programmable, variable-rate infusion pumps (Fig. 51.6), but is expensive and therefore currently limited to a minority of diabetic subjects (see Chapter 42). With CSII given at a fixed rate which meets the insulin requirements at dawn, excessive

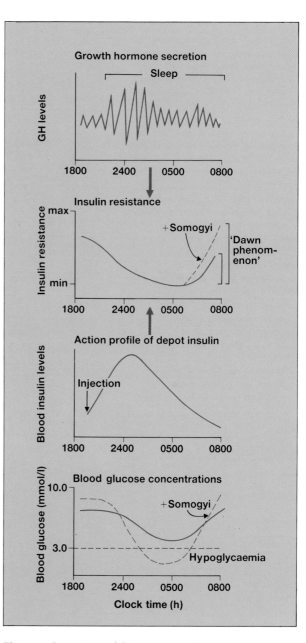

Fig. 51.7. Interaction of factors causing fasting hyperglycaemia in insulin-treated IDDM patients. Exaggerated growth-hormone spikes early in the night increase insulin resistance between 05.00 and 08.00. This 'dawn phenomenon' is exaggerated by the waning insulin levels from depot insulin given early the previous evening and possibly by hypoglycaemia in the early night, which increases insulin resistance further through counter-regulatory hormone release (the Somogyi effect).

hyperinsulinaemia will occur during the early night, resulting in frequent hypoglycaemia between midnight and 03.00 hours [35]. Therefore, in order to prevent nocturnal hypoglycaemia during CSII, the insulin infusion rate should be titrated to meet the lower insulin requirements between midnight and 03.00 hours, regardless of the greater insulin requirements at dawn; fortunately, the resultant fasting hyperglycaemia is usually modest [35] (see Fig. 51.6).

With injections of intermediate-acting insulin at night, it is much more difficult to prevent nocturnal hypoglycaemia while obtaining satisfactory fasting glycaemia. The non-physiological peaked action profile of these preparations is compounded by the highly erratic subcutaneous absorption of both isophane and lente insulins; the coefficient of variation of absorption is as high as 40% [36, 37], much greater than that of soluble insulin infused subcutaneously by a pump [36]. Excessive fasting hyperglycaemia may often be avoided by injecting the intermediate-acting insulin preparation at bedtime, rather than before supper [38]. This requires an additional insulin injection, but will provide high blood insulin levels to coincide with the predawn increase in insulin resistance. As discussed above, giving a higher dosage before supper will only tend to cause hypoglycaemia between midnight and 03.00 hours which, through the Somogyi effect, may aggravate fasting hyperglycaemia.

A light snack of 'lente' carbohydrate at bedtime will help to prevent nocturnal hypoglycaemia and should be taken if the blood glucose concentration is less than 6 mmol/l [23]. Blood glucose concentrations may rise relatively high between midnight and 03.00 hours, but will decrease thereafter to acceptable values, provided that a sufficient dose of intermediate-acting insulin is given at bedtime.

Finally, it may be possible to attenuate or abolish the dawn phenomenon by suppressing growth hormone secretion early in the night. This may be achieved with either somatostatin analogues [13, 39], which may be effective when given by intranasal spray [39], or atropinic drugs such as pirenzepine [16]. However, the efficacy of both these agents seems variable [40, 41], suggesting that dosage and/or timing of administration are critical.

GEREMIA B. BOLLI

References

1 Perriello G, De Feo P, Bolli GB. The dawn phenomenon: nocturnal blood glucose homeostasis in insulin-dependent diabetes mellitus. *Diabetic Med* 1988; **5**: 13−21.

2 De Feo P, Perriello G, Ventura MM *et al*. Studies on overnight insulin requirements and metabolic clearance rate of insulin in normal and diabetic man: relevance to the pathogenesis of the dawn phenomenon. *Diabetologia* 1986; **29**: 475−80.

3 Ateia JA, Ryder RRJ, Vora J, Owens DR, Luzio SD, Williams S, Hayes TM. Dawn phenomenon: its frequency in non-insulin-dependent diabetic patients on conventional therapy. *Diabetes Care* 1987; **10**: 461−5.

4 Yki-Järvinen H, Helve E, Sane T, Nurjhan N, Taskinen MR. Mechanism for insulin inhibition of overnight glucose production and gluconeogenesis from lactate in NIDDM. *Am J Physiol* 1989; **256**: E732−9.

5 Somogyi M. Exacerbation of diabetes by excess insulin action. *Am J Med* 1959; **26**: 169−91.

6 Perriello G, De Feo P, Torlone E, Calcinaro F, Ventura MM, Basta G *et al*. Asymptomatic nocturnal hypoglycemia: a cause for deterioration of glycemic control in diabetes mellitus. *N Engl J Med* 1988; **319**: 1233−9.

7 Bolli GB, Dimitriadis GD, Pehling GB, Baker BA, Haymond NW, Cryer PE, Gerich JE. Abnormal glucose counter-regulation after subcutaneous insulin in insulin-dependent diabetes mellitus. *N Engl J Med* 1984; **310**: 1706−11.

8 Attvall S, Fowelin J, Von Schenck H, Lager I, Smith U. Insulin resistance in Type 1 diabetes following hypoglycaemia. Evidence for the importance of β-adrenergic stimulation. *Diabetologia* 1987; **130**: 691−7.

9 Bolli GB, De Feo P, De Cosmo S, Perriello G, Ventura MM, Calcinaro F, Lolli C *et al*. Demonstration of a dawn phenomenon in normal human volunteers. *Diabetes* 1984; **33**: 1150−3.

10 Campbell P, Gerich J. Occurrence of the dawn phenomenon without a change in insulin clearance in patients with insulin-dependent diabetes mellitus. *Diabetes* 1986; **35**: 749−52.

11 Perriello G, De Feo P, Torlone E, Fanelli C, Santeusanio F, Brunetti P, Bolli GB. Nocturnal spikes of growth hormone secretion cause the dawn phenomenon in Type 1 diabetes mellitus by decreasing hepatic (and extrahepatic) sensitivity to insulin in the absence of insulin waning. *Diabetologia* 1990; **33**: 52−9.

12 Clutter W, Bier DM, Shah SD, Cryer PE. Epinephrine plasma metabolic clearance rates and physiologic thresholds for metabolic and hemodynamic actions in man. *J Clin Invest* 1980; **66**: 94−101.

13 Campbell PJ, Bolli GB, Cryer PE, Gerich JE. Pathogenesis of the dawn phenomenon in patients with insulin-dependent diabetes mellitus: accelerated glucose production and impaired glucose utilization due to nocturnal surges in growth hormone. *N Engl J Med* 1985; **312**: 1473−9.

14 Bright GM, Melton TW, Rogal AD, Clarke WL. Failure of cortisol blockade to inhibit early morning increases in basal insulin requirements in fasting insulin-dependent diabetics. *Diabetes* 1980; **29**: 662−4.

15 Bolli GB. The dawn phenomenon: its origin and contribution to early morning hyperglycaemia in diabetes mellitus. *Diabètes Métab* 1988; **14**: 675−86.

16 Davidson MB, Harris MD, Ziel FH, Rosenberg CS. Suppression of sleep-induced growth hormone secretion by anticholinergic agents abolishes dawn phenomenon. *Diabetes* 1988; **37**: 166−71.

17 McGorman L, Rizza R, Gerich J. Physiologic concentrations of growth hormone exert insulin-like and insulin antagonistic effects on both hepatic and extrahepatic tissues in man. *J Clin Endocrinol Metab* 1981; **53**: 556−9.

18 Deckert T, Lorup B. Regulation of brittle diabetes by a preplanned insulin infusion programme. *Diabetologia* 1976; **12**: 573−9.

19 Koivisto VA, Yki-Järvinen H, Helve E, Karonen S-L,

Pelkonen R. Pathogenesis and prevention of the dawn phenomenon in diabetic patients treated with CSII. *Diabetes* 1986; **35**: 78–82.

20 Kerner W, Navascués I, Torres AA, Pfeiffer EF. Studies on the pathogenesis of the dawn phenomenon in insulin-dependent diabetic patients. *Metabolism* 1984; **33**: 458–64.

21 Beaufrère B, Beylot M, Metz C, Ruitton A, François R, Riou JP, Mornex R. Dawn phenomenon in Type 1 (insulin-dependent) diabetic adolescents: influence of the nocturnal growth hormone secretion. *Diabetologia* 1988; **31**: 607–11.

22 Schmidt MI, Hadji-Georgopoulos A, Rendell M, Margolis M, Kowarski A. The dawn phenomenon, an early morning glucose rise: implications for diabetic intraday blood glucose variation. *Diabetes Care* 1981; **4**: 579–85.

23 Pramming S, Thorsteinsson B, Bendtson I, Ronn B, Binder C. Nocturnal hypoglycaemia in patients receiving conventional treatment with insulin. *Br Med J* 1985; **291**: 376–9.

24 Bolli GB, Gottesman IS, Campbell PJ, Haymond MW, Cryer PE, Gerich JE. Glucose counter-regulation and waning of insulin in the Somogyi phenomenon (post-hypoglycemic hyperglycaemia). *N Engl J Med* 1984; **311**: 1214–19.

25 Bolli G, Calabrese G, De Feo P, Compagnucci MG, Zega G, Angeletti G, Cartechini MG, Santeusanio F, Brunetti P. Lack of glucagon response in glucose counter-regulation in type 1 (insulin-dependent) diabetics: absence of recovery after prolonged optimal insulin therapy. *Diabetologia* 1982; **22**: 100–5.

26 Havlin CE, Cryer PE. Nocturnal hypoglycemia does not result commonly in major hyperglycemia in patients with diabetes mellitus. *Diabetes Care* 1987; **10**: 141–7.

27 Tordjman KM, Havlin CE, Levandoski LA, White NH, Santiago JV, Cryer PE. Failure of nocturnal hypoglycemia to cause fasting hyperglycemia in patients with insulin-dependent diabetes mellitus. *N Engl J Med* 1987; **317**: 1552–9.

28 Bolli G, De Feo P, Compagnucci P, Cartechini MG, Angeletti G, Santeusanio F, Brunetti P, Gerich JE. Abnormal glucose counter-regulation in insulin-dependent diabetes mellitus. Interaction of anti-insulin antibodies and impaired glucagon and epinephrine secretion. *Diabetes* 1983; **32**: 134–41.

29 Hirsch IB, Smith LJ, Havlin CE, Shah SD, Clutter WE, Cryer PE. Failure of nocturnal hypoglycemia to cause daytime hyperglycemia in patients with IDDM. *Diabetes Care* 1990; **13**: 133–42.

30 Køllind M, Adamson U, Lins PE. Insulin resistance following nocturnal hypoglycemia in insulin-dependent diabetes mellitus. *Acta Endocrinol* (Copenhagen) 1987; **116**: 314-20.

31 Kelley D, Mitrakou A, Marsh H, Schwenk F, Benn J, Sonnenberg G et al. Skeletal muscle glycolysis, oxidation, and storage of an oral glucose load. *J Clin Invest* 1988; **81**: 1563–71.

32 De Feo P, Gallai V, Mazzotta G, Crispino G, Torlone E, Perriello G et al. Modest decrements in plasma glucose concentration cause early impairment in cognitive function and later activation of glucose counter-regulation in the absence of hypoglycemic symptoms in normal man. *J Clin Invest* 1988; **82**: 436–44.

33 Thorsteinsson B, Pramming S, Lauritzen T, Binder C. Frequency of daytime biochemical hypoglycaemia in insulin-treated diabetic patients: relation to daily median blood glucose concentration. *Diabetic Med* 1986; **3**: 147–51.

34 DCCT research group. Diabetes control and complications trial (DCCT): results of feasibility study. *Diabetes Care* 1987; **10**: 1–19.

35 Bending JJ, Pickup JC, Collins ACG, Keen H. Rarity of a marked "dawn phenomenon" in diabetic subjects treated by continuous subcutaneous insulin infusion. *Diabetes Care* 1985; **8**: 28–33.

36 Binder C, Lauritzen T, Faber O, Pramming S. Insulin pharmacokinetics. *Diabetes Care* 1984; **3**: 188–99.

37 Kennedy F, Mitrakou M, Gerich J. Comparison of variability, potency, and kinetics of subcutaneous human proinsulin and human NPH insulin. *Diabetologia* 1987; **30** (abstract): 538A.

38 Francis AJ, Home PD, Hanning I, Alberti KGMM, Tunbridge WMG. Intermediate acting insulin given at bedtime: effect on blood glucose concentrations before and after breakfast. *Br Med J* 1983; **286**: 1173–6.

39 Campbell PJ, Bolli GB, Gerich JE. Prevention of the dawn phenomenon (early morning hyperglycemia) in insulin-dependent diabetes mellitus by bedtime administration of a long-acting somatostatin analogue. *Metabolism* 1988; **37**: 34–7.

40 Aarsen RSR, Bruining GJ, Goose WFA, van Strik R, Lambert SWJ, Harris AG. Long-acting somatostatin analogue (Sandostatin) reduces late-night insulinopenic ketogenesis in diabetic teenagers. *Acta Endocrinol* 1987; **116** (suppl. 286): 45–53.

41 Page MD, Koppeschaar HPF, Dieguez C et al. Cholinergic muscarinic receptor blockade with pirenzepine abolishes slow wave sleep-related growth hormone release in young patients with insulin-dependent diabetes mellitus. *Clin Endocrinol* 1987; **26**: 355–9.

Index

A- and B-chain proteins of insulin, separate fermentation 362–3
A cells
  embryology 58
  glucagon secretion in NIDDM 201–3
  islets of Langerhans 63–4
  volume in NIDDM 167
Abscesses
  CSII 421
  injection site 390
  perinephric 817
Acanthosis nigricans 757–8
  management 282
  syndromes of insulin resistance 277–82
Acarbose 979–80
Acetoacetate, synthesis 310
Acetone 483
Acetyl-CoA carboxylase activation 101–2
Acipimox 987
Acromegaly and diabetes 264–5
Actin, B cells 75
Adaptation to diabetes 784–5
Addison's disease 267
Additives, insulin preparation 367–8
Adenosine triphosphate (ATP), regulation of insulin secretion 78
'Adhesion' molecules 125, 127
Adhesive capsulitis 765
  treatment 768
Adolescence 881–2
  clinics 944
  CSII in 424
  insulin regimens 872
Adrenal gland and diabetes 267–9
Adrenal medulla, and glucoregulation 215
Adrenaline 208
  deficiency, hypoglycaemia 500–1
Adrenocortical hyperfunction 268
Adrenocortical insufficiency 267
Adult respiratory distress syndrome,

ketoacidosis 488
Advanced glycosylated end products (AGE) see Glycosylation
Affinity chromatography
  glycated albumin and serum protein assay 332
  glycated haemoglobin assay 331
Agar-gel electrophoresis, glycated haemoglobin assay 330–1
AGE (advanced glycosylated end products) see Glycosylation
  as determination of microvascular complications 520
  insulin resistance 194
  renal replacement therapy 688
Air travel 924–5
Alanine, gluconeogenesis 303–4
Albumin see Microalbuminuria, Proteinuria
Alcohol 916–17
  and chlorpropamide 468
  chronic pancreatitis 257–8
  hypertension 724
  IDDM 413
  NIDDM 190
Alcoholic ketoacidosis 484
Aldose reductase 528
  cataract 571
  inhibitors 984–7
    and advanced glycosylation end products (AGE)
    and complications 985–7
    neuropathy 632
    retinopathy 566
Aldosteronism, primary 268
Algorithms, adjusting insulin dosage and dietary intake 392–3
Alloxan
  animal models of IDDM 153–4
  low-dose, animal models of NIDDM 235
Alpha-glucosidase inhibitors 979–80
Alpha-methyldopa 729

Alström's syndrome 295
American Diabetes Association 966
Amino acids
  gluconeogenesis 303–4
  regulation of glucagon secretion 314–15
  regulation of insulin secretion 79
Aminoguanidine 542–4, 987
Amputation 703
  renal replacement therapy 693
Amylin 67, 168
Amyloid, deposition in islet 167–8
  nature and origin 168
  in NIDDM 201
Amyotrophy, diabetic 624, 626, 627
Analgesics, neuropathy 632
Anaphylaxis, and insulin antibodies 402
Anencephaly 852
Angina pectoris 713
Angiography, fluorescein, in retinopathy 596
Angioplasty 713–14
  neuro-ischaemic foot 742
  percutaneous transluminal balloon 715
Angiotensin-converting enzyme (ACE) inhibitors 666, 686
  heart failure 711
  hypertension 729
  nephropathy 677, 686
Animal models
  IDDM 113–16
    spontaneous 155–60
  NIDDM 228–38
    neuroendocrine defects 217–19
Anionic proteoglycans 540
Ankle-brachial pressure index 743
Ankylosing hyperostosis of spine 765
Ankylosing spondylitis 765
Anorectal dysfunction 749
Anorexia nervosa 827
  see also Eating disorders
Antenatal clinics 945

Antibiotics, neuropathic ulcer 737
Antibodies
  exogenous insulin 397—405
    clinical manifestations 402—5
    clinical pharmacokinetic effects
      404
    determinants of formation
      398—400
    historical background 397—8
    insulin receptor 276—9
    in vivo effects 401
  islet cell 126—7, 132, 157
    see also Autoantibodies
Antidepressant drugs 789
Antigen-presenting cells 123—4
Antihypertensive drugs 725—9
  effects on glucose tolerance 721
Antihypertensive treatment 665—6,
  685—6
Antilipolytic agents 980
Anti-obesity agents 981
Aretaeus of Cappadocia 3—4
Arterial abnormalities, in
  retinopathy 582
Arthropathy
  crystal 767—8
  neuropathic (Charcot) 739—40
  pyrophosphate 767—8
Artificial endocrine pancreas *see*
  Pancreas, artificial
Ascending cholangitis 818
Aspirin 987
Ataxia telangiectasia 279, 296
Atenolol
  hypertension 729
  insulin sensitivity 805
Atherosclerosis
  haemostatic function 704—5
  and smoking 916
  see Macrovascular disease,
    Cardiovascular disease
    Coronary heart disease,
Athletes, insulin and diet
  adjustment 414
Atrophic gastritis 751
Autoantibodies, insulin 128, 400
  as marker of prediabetic state 404
Autoimmunity
  IDDM 126—33
  in prediabetic period 131—3
Autonomic activation during
  hypoglycaemia 498
Autonomic dysfunction, articular
  and periarticular disease
  related to 765—7
Axonal transport, diabetic
  neuropathy 619
Azathioprine 972

7B2 66—7
B cells 19—20
  alterations in islets with amyloid
    168—70

autoimmune attack 133
autoimmune destruction 128
cytoskeleton, role 74—5
effects of alloxan 153
function
  cyclosporin 972
  dynamic tests 351—2
  residual, metabolic
    consequences 352—3
granules, translocation 74—5
IDDM 107—8
insulin secretion in NIDDM
  198—201
islets of Langerhans 61—3
microfilaments 75
microtubules 74—5
NIDDM 167
secretory granules 62—3
stimulation, sulphonylureas
  465—6
ultrastructure 62—3
virus infection 147
volume in NIDDM 167
Banting, Frederick Grant 10—13
Barium meal, gastroparesis 747
Basal metabolic rate (BMR), in
  obesity 184
Benfluorex 980
Bernard, Claude 7
Best, Charles H. 11, 12—13
β_2-adrenergic agonists, inducing
  hyperglycaemia 805
β-adrenergic blockade, and
  hypoglycaemia 499
β_1-adrenoceptor blockers 686
Beta-blockers
  angina pectoris 713
  hypertension 728—9
  hypoglycaemia 806—7
Beta cell *see* B cell
Beta-glucuronidase 852
Bezafibrate 708, 987
Bicarbonate
  ketoacidosis 487
    children 877
  lactic acidosis 491
Biguanides 469
  lactic acidosis 491
Bile acid absorption 749
Bioassays for insulin 335—6
Biosensors, mode of action 994, 995
Biostator 427—8
Bladder
  dysfunction, autonomic
    neuropathy 639—40
  function tests, autonomic
    neuropathy 644—5
Blindness
  diabetic maculopathy 584—5
  pathogenesis 601
  practical management of diabetes
    606—9
  psychological aspects 605—6

registration 609—10
social aspects 605—6
social services 609—10
statistics 606
sudden 595
Third World 905
Blood
  flow, increased in
    microangiopathy 529
  glucose, single measurement 326
  insulin absorption 371, 375—6
  supply, islets of Langerhans 67—8
Blood glucose
  cardiovascular disease 705
  concentrations, NIDDM 464
  meters 960
  monitoring
    children 872—3
    computers 960—1
    see Blood glucose self-
      monitoring
  myocardial infarction 712
  profiles 464
  random values 646
  self-monitoring (BGSM) 390—3
    accuracy and precision 392—3
    benefits 391
    blind and partially sighted
      607—9
    NIDDM 473
    reasons for poor results 392
    techniques 390—2
    use 393
Blood pressure
  measurement 723, 724
  microalbuminuria 661
  nephropathy 679, 680
    control 667
  response to standing up 643
  response to sustained handgrip
    643
Body fat
  content, estimation 182
  distribution, and NIDDM 181—96
Body fluids, insulin and proinsulin
  342
Body-mass index 182
Bone
  density 771
  loss
    clinical implications 772—3
    mechanisms 772
  metabolism 771—3
Bovine insulin, structure 84, 85
Brain damage, nocturnal
  hypoglycaemia 512
British Afro-Caribbeans, diabetes
  911
British Asians, diabetes 909—11
  complications 910
  management 910—11
  prevalence 909—10
    factors contributing to 910

British Diabetic Association 965−6
'Brittle' diabetes 884−94
  causes 886−91
  definition 884−6
  idiopathic 891
  investigations 892−3
  psychosocial influences 890−1
  psychotherapy and counselling
    894
  treatment approaches 893−4
Bronzed diabetes 259
Brown adipose tissue (BAT),
    regulation of activity 213−14
Bulimia 827
  multiple impulsive 828
  see also Eating disorders
Bullae, diabetic 758
Bullosis diabeticorum 758

Caesarean section 825, 847
Calcium
  balance, effects of diabetes 773
  and insulin secretion 80−1
Calcium channel antagonists, angina
    pectoris 713
Calcium channel blockers 686
Calcium entry blockers,
    hypertension 729
Calculi, pancreatic, FCPD 251
cAMP
  lowering of intracellular levels
    99−100
  regulation of insulin secretion 79
Calmodulin and insulin secretion
    80−1
Camps, diabetic 881
Candidiasis 776
Cannula, indwelling subcutaneous
    389
CAPD (chronic ambulatory
    peritoneal dialysis) 691−2
Capillary basement membrane 528
  biochemical changes 528−9
  functional changes 529−31
  normal, structure and function
    527
Capillary blood samples 391
Capillary dilatation 576
  and leakage, retinopathy 567−8
Capillary occlusion 576
Capillary wall, structure 565−6
Carbohydrate
  exchange systems 412
  IDDM 409−11
  metabolism, effect of age on
    898−900
  NIDDM 188−9
Cardiovascular autonomic function,
    practical assessment 643−4
Cardiovascular disease
  complications 901
  epidemiology 702−3

nephropathy 679
renal replacement therapy 688−9
  causes of death 693
  progression 692−3
  risk factors 703−9
Cardiovascular tests, autonomic
    neuropathy 641−4
Carpal tunnel syndrome 627, 764−5
Cassava and FCPD 248
Cataract
  formation and polyol pathway 570
  lens protein glycation 571−2
  pathogenesis 564−72
Cation-exchange pumps, cell
    membranes 661−3
Caudal regression syndrome 852,
    853
Cawley, Thomas 6
Celebes black ape, models of IDDM
    159
Cell movement during infection 813
Cell-mediated immune
    abnormalities, IDDM 128
Cellular defects during infection
    813−14
Cellular receptors, effects of AGE
    540−1
Cerebral oedema
  children 878
  ketoacidosis 488
Cerebrovascular disease,
    epidemiology 703
Charcot (neuropathic) arthropathy
    739−40, 766
  autonomic neuropathy 639
Cheiroarthropathy see Limited joint
    mobility
Chemical toxins and IDDM 152−5
Childhood diabetes
  aetiology 868
  assessment of control 872−3
  complications 875−81
  clinics 944
  CSII 424
  diagnosis 44, 869−90
  diagnostic criteria and tests
    869−70
  diet 413−14, 872
  exercise 873−4
  initial diabetes education 870−1
  insulin therapy 871−2
  intercurrent illness 874
  living with 874−5
  management 870−4
    immediately after diagnosis 870
  organization of care 881
  presentation 869−70
  prevalence and geographical
    variations 868
  surgery 874
Chiropody services 945
Chlorpropamide
  during surgery 821

side-effects 467−8
  see also Sulphonylureas
Chlorpropamide-alcohol flush 759
Cholecystitis 751
  emphysematous 818
Cholecystokinin 321−2
  abnormalities in animal models
    218
  and feeding behaviour 209
Cholecystopathy, diabetic 748
Cholesterol
  guar 978
  measurement 706
  see also Hypercholesterolaemia,
    Hyperlipidaemia
Cholestyramine 709, 987
Chromatography
  affinity 331, 332
  high-performance liquid 330
  ion-exchange 330
Chromium deficiency and
    NIDDM 190
Chromogranins 67
Chromosomal disorders 292−3
Cisapride 987
  gastroparesis 750
Clinics
  adolescents 944
  antenatal 945
  children's 881, 944
  evening 946
  foot 945
  general practice 949
  hospital
    disadvantages 942
    facilities 942
  paediatric diabetic 881, 944
  patient's view 930
Clonidine 987
  diabetic diarrhoea 987
  hypertension 729
Closed-loop infusion 427−8
Cockayne's syndrome 296
Coeliac disease 297, 748
Colestipol 709
Collagen deposition 762−5
  pathophysiology 768
Collip, James B. 11, 12−13
Colonic dysfunction 749
Coma
  differential diagnosis 491−2
  hypoglycaemia 506−8
  ketoacidosis 484
  lactic acidosis 492
  non-ketotic hyperosmolar 489−90
Combined oral contraceptive
    pill 857−8
  gestational diabetes 858
Computers 946, 958−63
  adjustment of insulin dosages 961
  blood glucose monitoring 960−1
  diabetes control 428−9
  education 961−3

Computers (con't)
  knowledge assessment 963
  management systems 958—60
  registers 958—60
Connective tissue
  changes in diabetes,
    pathophysiology 768
  disease 762—9
Conn's syndrome 268
Constipation 749
  treatment 750
Continuous ambulatory peritoneal
    dialysis (CAPD) 691—2
Continuous intramuscular insulin
    infusion 893
Continuous intravenous insulin
    infusion 893
Continuous subcutaneous insulin
    infusion (CSII) 416—24
  brittle diabetes 893
  complications 421—2
  education and information
    about 418
  indications for 422—3
  malfunctions 421
  metabolic effects 419—20
  microvascular disease 422—4
  nocturnal hypoglycaemia 512
  origins 416—17
  pharmacological aspects 420—1
  role of hospital 418—19
  special groups of patients 424
  starting patients on 417—18
  technology 417
Contraception 856—60
  methods 857—60
  reliability 857
Control
  concept and measurement 325—32
  monitoring, during travel 924
Convulsions, hypoglycaemia 502
Copper deficiencies and
    NIDDM 190
Cori cycle 304
Coronary angiography 687
Coronary artery disease
  see Coronary heart disease
Coronary artery surgery 713—14
Coronary heart disease
  epidemiology 703
  risk factors and reduction 704
Coronary occlusive disease,
    nephropathy 680
Corticosteroids and
    hyperglycaemia 803—4
Corticotrophin-releasing factor
  feeding behaviour 209
  thermogenesis 213
Cotton-wool spots,
    retinopathy 580—1
Counselling, diabetes specialist
    nurses 956—7
  see also Genetic counselling
Counter-regulatory hormones

abnormalities, brittle diabetes 889
  failure in diabetes 500
Coxsackie viruses and IDDM 143
  experimental studies 145—6, 147
C-peptide
  diagnostic significance 348—50
  fasting plasma concentration 350
  measurement in plasma and
    urine 350—1
crb insulin 363
Creatinine, measurement 683
Crinophagy 74
Crystal arthropathy 767—8
Crystallin glycation 571
CSII see Continuous subcutaneous
    insulin infusion
Cushing's syndrome 268
Cyclosporin 972—3
  adverse effects 973
  pancreatic transplantation 1004
  treatment of IDDM 20
Cystic fibrosis 258
Cystitis 817
Cytokines 125
  in pathogenesis of IDDM 134
Cytomegalovirus and IDDM 143
Cytotoxic T lymphocytes 123
  destruction of B cells 135

D cells
  islets of Langerhans 64—6
  somatostatin secretion in
    NIDDM 203
Danazol, causing
    hyperglycaemia 805
Dawn phenomenon 507, 508—10
  CSII 421
Death, autonomic neuropathy 639
De Meyer, Jean 8
Depression 785
  general measures to treat 788—9
Dermopathy, diabetic 755—6
Diabetes care systems,
    organizing 944—6
Diabetes centres 942—4
  appointment and waiting,
    timing 946
  planning, running and
    staffing 934—4
  purpose 943
  record-keeping and
    computers 946
  secretarial support 946
  setting up 943
Diabetes mellitus
  adjustment to life with 926—8
  British Afro-Caribbeans 911
  British Asians 909—11
  'brittle' see 'Brittle' diabetes
  causes of death 702
  childhood see Childhood diabetes
  classification 37—41
    historical background 38—9

WHO 39—40
  cutaneous conditions as markers
    of 754—8
  definitions 17
  diagnosis 41—4
    casual and fasting criteria 41—2
    special groups 43—4
  drug-induced, treatment 805—6
  endocrine diseases and 263—73
  epidemiology 47—52
  fibrocalculous 247—54
  genetic disorders associated
    with 291—7
  gestational see Gestational
    diabetes
  history 3—9
    ancient period 3—5
    diagnostic period 5—7
    experimental period 7—9
  insulin-dependent see Insulin-
    dependent diabetes mellitus
  J-type 254
  malnutrition-related see
    Malnutrition-related diabetes
    mellitus
  misconceptions about 927
  mortality rates 52
  non-insulin-dependent see Non-
    insulin-dependent diabetes
    mellitus
  in old age 897—903
  other types 40
  and pancreatic disease 256—61
  patient's view 929—30
  protein-deficient pancreatic
    254—5
  relationship to ageing 900
  Third World 905—8
Diabetic associations
  history 965—8
    early development 965—6
  and medical and scientific
    community 967
  and patient 966—7
Diabetic control and eating
    disorders 828
Diabetic foods, IDDM 413
Diabetic gastroparesis 746—8
Diabetic thick skin 756—7
Diabetic treatment, cutaneous
    complications 758—60
Dialysis, peritoneal (CAPD) 691—2
Diarrhoea, diabetic 748—9
  treatment 750
Diazoxide, causing
    hyperglycaemia 805
DIDMOAD syndrome 272
Diet
  adjustment during exercise 801
  British Asians 911
  childhood diabetes 872
  designing for NIDDM 454—8
  and exercise 414
  hyperlipidaemia 708—9

hypertension 724
IDDM
  advice and compliance 413−14
  children 413−14
  management 407−14
  inadequate, and
    hypoglycaemia 497
  insulin resistance 194
  low-protein, in nephropathy
    667−8, 686−7
  NIDDM 181−96
    nutrient composition 188−90
  old age 901−2
  pregnancy 844
  travel 922
  very low calorie 457−8
    safety and efficacy 458
Dietary fibre 978−9
  adverse effects 978
  clinical effects 978
  indications and dosage 979
  metabolic effects 978
  NIDDM 189
Dietitians, patient's view 929
Diffuse motor neuropathy 626, 627
Dimethylsulphoxide 987
Diuretics
  heart failure 711
  hypertension 726−8
  inducing hyperglycaemia 804
  nephropathy 685, 686
DNA synthesis, effects of
  insulin 102
Dobson, Matthew 5−6
Domperidone, gastroparesis 750
Down's syndrome 292
Drinks, travel 922−3
Drivers, problems with
  diabetes 920−1
Driving 919−21
  licence 919−20
    vocational 920
Drugs in diabetes 803−12
  inducing hyperglycaemia 803−5,
    809−10
    mechanisms 804
  inducing hypoglycaemia 811
  interactions with oral
    hypoglycaemic agents 806
  new 977−89
  requiring caution in specific
    complications 812
Dunnigan syndrome 280
Duodenal ulceration 751
Dupuytren's contractures 756, 764
Dynamic suppression tests 343, 344
Dyslipoproteinaemia, and AGE 542
Dystrophia myotonica 296−7

Eating behaviour, control 207
Eating disorders 827−30
  association with diabetes 828
  brittle diabetes 891

clinical problem 828−9
  relationship to diabetic
    complications 829
  treatment 829−30
Ebers papyrus 3, 5
Echovirus and IDDM 143
Economics of diabetes
  importance of analysis 33
  studies 32−3
Education, diabetes 933−8
  British Asians 910
  'brittle' diabetes 889
  children 870
  computers 961−3
  curriculum planning 936
  diabetes specialist nurse 953−6
  general practice 950−1
  hypertension 724
  IDDM 954, 955
  NIDDM 955
  record keeping 950
  reinforcing and maintaining 937
Educational programmes
  audiovisual materials 935−6
  evaluation 936−7
  group teaching 935
  individual assessment 936−7
  learning methods 934−5
  objectives 934
  principles 933−4
  structure 934−6
Ejaculation, normal, physiology 779,
  780
Elderly patient, NIDDM 474
Electrolytes, ketoacidosis 483−4
  replacement 485−6
Electron microscopy
  B cells 62−3
  islets of Langerhans 60−1
Embryogenesis 852−4
Emergency surgery 824−5
emp insulin 361
Emphysematous cholecystitis 817,
  818
Emphysematous cystitis 816, 817
Emphysematous pyelonephritis 816,
  817
Employment and diabetes 915−16
Enalapril 666
Encephalomyocarditis virus and
  IDDM 144−5
Encephalopathy, diabetic 641
Endothelial cells, capillaries 565−6
  metabolic causes of damage
    566−7
Endothelial-derived relaxing
  factor 530, 531
Endothelin 565
Energy balance
  aetiology of obesity 182−5
  altered in obesity 183−4
  disturbances in human
    NIDDM 220
Energy expenditure

reduced, role in NIDDM 217
  regulating 213−14
Energy intake
  reduced, benefits in NIDDM 454
  regulation 207−13
Energy requirements
  estimating 185
  IDDM, calculating 412
Enterococcal meningitis 816
Enteroglucagon 314
Entero-insular axis
  incretins 320
  regulation of insulin
    secretion 78−9
Enzyme electrodes, for glucose
  sensors 996
Epidermal growth factor (EGF),
  receptor for 96
Erectile dysfunction, autonomic
  neuropathy 639−40
Erections
  autonomic neuropathy 639−40
  factors necessary for 781
  failure in diabetes, causes 781
  nocturnal 782
  normal, physiology 779, 780
Erythema multiforme major 758−9
Erythrocyte glucose transporter
  gene, NIDDM 178
Essential fatty acids 988−9
Ethnic communities, diabetes
  909−11
Euglycaemic insulin clamp,
  techniques 343, 344
Excess antibody assays 337−9
Exercise 795−801
  adjustment of diet and
    treatment 801
  atherosclerosis 704
  children 873−4
  and diet 414
  hormonal effects in diabetes
    797−81
  and insulin absorption 378−9
  insulin resistance 194
  metabolic effects
    diabetics 797−801
    healthy individuals 795−7
  NIDDM 458−9
  prevention of diabetes 800
  protection against NIDDM 186
  recommendations for 800−1
Extracellular protein cross-
  linking 539−40
Exudative maculopathy 585
Eye disease, diabetic 557−610
  advanced 592−4
    natural history 587
    surgical management 589−603

Factitious disease 889−90
Faecal incontinence 749
  treatment 750−1

Family studies
  IDDM 116–17
  NIDDM 173
Fasting ascending glycaemic
    excursion (FAGE) 328
Fasting blood glucose concentration,
    NIDDM 464
Fat
  intake, IDDM 408–9
  NIDDM 188–9
    distribution 187–8
Fatty acid mobilization
  in diabetes 310
  in non-diabetic subjects 309–10
Fatty acids
  essential 988–9
  non-esterified (NEFA) 306–7
    myocardial infarction 712
    in NIDDM 308
  role in insulin resistance 194
FCPD see Fibrocalculous pancreatic
    diabetes
Feeding behaviour
  and non-peptide
      neurotransmitters 208–9
  peptides and 209–12
Fenfluramine 981
Fenofibrate 987
Ferrocene 997
Fertility, diabetic women 776
Fetal development 854
Fetus
  effects of GDM 847
  growth 840–1
  later development 841
  macrosomia 840–1
  malformations 838–40
    genetic counselling 862–3
    incidence 838, 839
  risks 837–41
    mortality 837–8
Fibrates 987
Fibre
  IDDM 409–11
  NIDDM 459–60, 978–9
Fibre optic probe systems, glucose
    sensors 997–8
Fibroblast growth factor, retinal
    neovascularization 569
Fibrocalculous pancreatic diabetes
    (FCPD) 247–54
  aetiopathogenesis 248
  clinical features 249–52
  diagnosis 253, 254
  geographical distribution 247
  management 253–4
  prevalence 247–8
Fibrous retinitis proliferans 582–4
Finger-pricking devices 391
Fish, diet
  IDDM 409
  NIDDM 460
Fish oils 460, 988–9

Fludrocortisone 645
Fluid
  balance, ketoacidosis, children
      877–8
  depletion, ketoacidosis 483
  replacement 485–6
Fluorescein angiography 596
Fluorescein leakage, retinal
    capillaries 530
Fluphenazine 987
Focal vascular neuropathies 627
Food
  Exchange systems 412
  travel 922
Foot, diabetic 735–44
  assessment 742–3
  care, organization 743–4
  clinics 945
  danger signs 744
  integrated examination 742–3
  nephropathy 687
  neuro-ischaemic 741–2
  neuropathic (Charcot arthropathy)
      739–40
  neuropathic ulcer 736–8
  ulcers 816–17
Forefoot osteolysis 767
Forestier's disease 765
Fournier's gangrene 816
Friedreich's ataxia 297
Frozen shoulder 765
Fructosamine
  assay 332
  concentrations, NIDDM 464–5
Fructose, IDDM 411
Frusemide and hyperglycaemia 804
Fundus photography, retinopathy
    596

Galactosaemia 566
Galen 4
Galenic pharmacy 357
Gall-bladder dysfunction 748
Gallstones 751
Gamma-linolenic acid 989
  neuropathy 632
Ganglion blockers 729
Gangliosides 987
  neuropathy 632
Gangrene
  digital 681, 682
  Fournier's 816
  neuro-ischaemic foot 741
  progressive synergistic 816
Garrod's knuckle pads 756, 757
Gastric inhibitory polypeptide
    320–1
Gastric ulceration 751
Gastritis, atrophic 751
Gastroentero-pancreatic tumours
    269–71
Gastrointestinal problems 745–51

  clinical features 746–9
  pathophysiology 745–6
  treatment 749–51
Gastrointestinal tests, autonomic
    neuropathy 644
Gastroparesis, diabetic 746–8
  treatment 750
Gastropathy, diabetic 746–8
GAWK 67
Gemfibrozil 708, 987, 988
General practice 948–51
  clinical care 949–50
  computers 959
  education 950–1
  organizational aspects 948–51
  requirements for clinic 949, 950
  shared care 949
  team members 948–9
Genetic counselling 861–4
  IDDM 861–3
  NIDDM 863–4
Genetic disorders
  associated with diabetes 291–7
  classification 292
Genito-urinary infections, diabetic
    women 776
Gestational diabetes 846–9
  combined pill 858
  effects
    fetus 874
    long-term 847–8
    neonate 847
  secreening and diagnosis 848
  treatment 848–9
  WHO classification 39
Gingivitis 818
GKI glucose–potassium–insulin
    infusion system 822–3, 824,
    825
Glaucoma
  neovascular 594
  thrombotic 587
Glibenclamide, side-effects 467
Glicentin 64
Globin insulins 367
Glomerular filtration rate (GFR)
  evolution of changes in
      nephropathy 654
  and glomerular structure 674–5
  measurement 683
  microvascular complications 529
Glomerular hyperfiltration 663–5
  factors leading to 663–4
  metabolic and endocrine
      determinants 664–5
Glomerulosclerosis, diabetic 652
GLP-1 7–36 amide see Glucagon-like
    peptide-1 7–36 amide
Glucagon 316–17
  actions 315–16
  deficiency, hypoglycaemia 500
  hypoglycaemia, children 879–90
  production by A cells 63–4

release in *ob/ob* mouse 232
secretion 314—15
  A cells in NIDDM 201—3
  in human NIDDM 220—1
source, synthesis and structure
  314
test, intravenous, β-cell function
  351—2
treatment, hypoglycaemia 503
Glucagon-like peptide-1 7—36 amide
  321
Glucagonoma syndrome 268—71
skin complications 760
Glucocheck meter 608
Glucokinase, effects of alloxan 153
Gluconeogenesis 303—4
control through substrate supply
  304
control within liver 304, 305
inhibitors 980
Glucoregulation, neuroendocrine
  regulation of 215—16
Glucose
concentrations in blood, NIDDM
  464
control, concept and measurement
  325—32
dietary, IDDM 411
homeostasis, neuroendocrine
  regulation 214—16
intolerance, old age 898—900
metabolism 984
  disturbance in NIDDM 195, 196
  during acute exercise 796
  during physical training 797
production
  in IDDM 305—6
  in ketoacidosis 481—2
  in NIDDM 306
  in non-diabetic subjects 303—5
regulation of insulin secretion
  76—7
sensors 994—9
  difficulty 997
  drift 999
  implantable 998—9
  implantable, configurations for
    995
  technology 996—8
  uses 995
single blood measurement 326
stimulation of uptake 100—1
tolerance
  effect of pregnancy 836—7
  impaired, WHO classification
    39—40
  potential abnormality 40
  in pregnancy 43—4
  previous abnormality 40
  test, oral 42—3
  test, oral, procedure 43
toxicity 194
transporters 100—1

treatment, hypoglycaemia 503—4
utilization
  in IDDM 307—8
  in NIDDM 308—9
  in non-diabetic subjects 306—7
Glucose oxidase reagent strips
  390—3
Glucose-alanine cycle 304
Glucose-fatty acid cycle 306—7
Glucose-fatty acid-ketone body cycle
  306, 307
Glucose—potassium—insulin (GKI)
  system 822—3, 824, 825
Glutamine, gluconeogenesis 303—4
Glycaemia *see* Blood glucose
Glycaemic control
children 873
diabetic neuropathy 617—18
glomerular hyperfiltration 664—5
and haemodynamic abnormalities
  548—9
microvascular complications
  523—4
nephropathy
  improvement 665
  management 686
overnight 507—13
  methods to improve 512—13
pregnancy 844—5
Glycaemic index 409
Glycaemic lability, indices 326—8
Glycaemic re-entry phenomenon
  549
Glycated albumin, measurement
  331—2
Glycated (glycosylated) haemoglobin
  (HbA$_1$) 328—31
assay
  effect of medical conditions on
    330
  goals 331
  methods 330—1
Glycerol
gluconeogenesis 304
stabilized insulin preparations
  440
Glycogen synthesis, stimulation by
  insulin 101
Glycogenolysis 304, 305
Glycosuria 326
Glycosylated haemoglobin 328
  see also Glycated haemoglobin
Glycosylated inositol phosphate
  (GIP), insulin second
  messenger 102—3
Glycosylation
advanced glycosylation end-
  products (AGE) 539
  cardiovascular disease 705
  pathological consequences of
    formation 539—41
  relationship to other
    pathogenetic factors 542

advanced glycosylation reactions,
  pharmacological modulation
  542—4
excessive formation of early
  products 538—9
non-enzymatic
  microvascular disease 528—9
  nerve proteins 619
Gonadal dysfunction, primary 272
Gonadotrophin secretion in diabetes
  271—2
Gout 767—8
Granuloma annulare 755
Growth, children 873
Growth hormone 263—5
dawn phenomenon 508—9
deficiency and glycaemic
  regulation 265
retinal neovascularization 569—70
secretion
  in diabetes 264
  suppression 573, 982
Guar 978
Guar gum supplements 460
Guinea pigs, IDDM 159
Gut
glucagon 64
infections 817—18
motility disturbance 745

Haemochromatosis 259—61
Haemodialysis 690—1
problems 691
Haemodynamic abnormalities
acceleration with passage through
  puberty 548
diabetic retinopathy 567
early expression 547—8
microvascular complications,
  implications for therapy
  550—2
relationship to disease duration
  548
relationship to glycaemic control
  548—9
relationship to microangiopathy
  547—9
Haemodynamic hypothesis,
  development of diabetic
  microangiopathy 549—50
Haemoglobin, glycated 328—31
  see also Glycosylated haemoglobin
Haemorrhages
retinopathy 578—9
vitreous 587, 592, 594
Haemostatic function, cardiovascular
  disease 704—5
Hamsters, Chinese, IDDM 159
Hand, diabetic 762—5
limited joint mobility 763—4
Hard exudates, retinopathy 579—80
HbA$_1$ *see* Haemoglobin, glycated

Health care, studies 32–3
Health services 30–1
Heart
  disease, management in diabetes
    709–14
  failure 709–11
    assessment and management
      711
    pathophysiology 709–11
  rate
    autonomic neuropathy 640
    response to deep breathing
      642–3
    response to standing up 642
    response to Valsalva manoeuvre
      641–2
Heavy Goods Vehicle Licence 920
High-performance liquid
    chromatography, glycated
    haemoglobin assay 330
Hip
  capsulitis 765
  transient osteoporosis 766
Hirsutism, management 282
HLA class II expression,
    inappropriate 133
HLA genes, NIDDM 178
HLA (MHC) restriction
    phenomenon 125, 126
HLA-Dr, risks associated with in
    IDDM 117–18
Hoechst 21 PH insulin formulation
    439–40
Home visiting 953
'Homing' molecules 125
Hormonal responses during exercise
    797
Hormones, lipolysis 309
Hospital
  admissions 30–1
  bed occupancy 30–1
  diabetes care
    communication, morale and
      staff education 947
    evening clinics 946
    facilities and equipment 942–4
    minimal staffing requirements
      941–2
    organization 940–7
    organization, responsibility
      940–1
    team 941–2
  services for in-patients 946–7
Human capital estimates, costs of
    diabetes 32
Huntington's chorea 297
Hydralazine 729
3-hydroxybutyrate (Beta-
    hydroxybutyrate)
  ketoacidosis 483
  measurement 484
  synthesis 310
Hypercalciuria 773

Hypercholesterolaemia, drug
    therapy 709
Hypercoagulability and AGE 542
Hyperglucagonaemia 316
  in NIDDM 201–2, 218
Hyperglycaemia
  acute reversible metabolic
    changes 536–9
  and autonomic neuropathy 636
  biochemical consequences 536
  children 869
  chronic irreversible changes
    539–41
  drugs inducing 803–5, 809–10
  and hypertension 720
  insulin resistance 194, 199–200
  ketoacidosis 482
  in NIDDM, treatment 463
  ob/ob mouse 232–3
  protein kinase C activity,
    microvascular disease 528
  temporary 221
  teratogenesis 838, 853
  tissue damage 535
  vulnerability to effects of 549
Hyperinsulinaemia 93
  CSII 420
  exercise during 798
  ob/ob mouse 231–2
  role in NIDDM 217–18
Hyperketonaemia, ketoacidosis
    482–3
Hyperlactataemia 491
  see also Lactic acidosis
Hyperlipidaemia
  combined, drug therapy 708
  hypertension 725
  management 708, 709, 710
  secondary, causes 708, 709
  see also Hypercholesterolaemia
Hyperphagia
  in human NIDDM 217, 220
  ob/ob mouse 231–2
Hypertension 719–31
  aetiology 720–1
  and AGE 542
  associations 720, 721
  control 685–6
  diagnosis 722–3
  epidemiology 719–20
  genetic predisposition 661
  haemodialysis 691
  investigations 723, 726
  management 723–31
  microvascular complications
    222–3
  morbidity and mortality 721–2
  progression, in nephropathy 654
  screening 722–3
  Third World 906
  treatment
    strategy 730–1
    targets 723

Hyperthyroidism and diabetes 267
Hypertriglyceridaemia 705–6
  drug therapy 708
  fish oils 988
  see also Hyperlipidaemia
Hypocalcaemia, neonatal 841
Hypocount meters 607–8
Hypoglycaemia 495–504
  alarm 995–6
  alcohol 916
  awareness of, see Hypoglycaemia,
    symptoms and Hypoglycaemic
    unawareness
  beta-blockers and 806–7
  biochemical investigations 342–4
  causal factors 496–7
  children 878–80
    long-term sequelae 880
    treatment 879–80
  CSII 421–2
  drivers 920–1
  drugs causing 811
  and exercise 414
  factitious 497
  fetal malformations 838–9
  frequency 496
  metabolic recovery processes
    499–501
  morbidity and mortality 502
  neonatal 841
  nocturnal
    hazards 511–12
    and Somogyi effect 510–11
  patient's view 929
  pregnancy 845
  prophylactic measures 504
  social implications 504
  sulphonylureas 467–8, 501–2
  symptoms 497–8
    during normoglycaemia 498
  teratogenesis 853
  treatment 502–4
Hypoglycaemia unawareness 498–9
  autonomic neuropathy 639
  drivers 920–1
  and human insulins 499
Hypoglycaemic agents
  drug interactions with 806, 812
  nephropathy 686
  new 980–1
  oral
    cardiovascular disease 705
    old age 902
  see also Biguanides,
    Sulphonylureas
Hypoinsulinaemia, exercise during
    798–9
Hypothalamic dysfunction, ob/ob
    mouse 232, 233
Hypothalamic obesity 221
Hypothalamic-pituitary dysfunction
    in response to hypoglycaemia
    272

Hypothalamic-pituitary-gonadal
function and diabetes 271–2
Hypothalamus 206–7
glucoregulation 214
Hypothyroidism and diabetes 267

IDDM see Insulin-dependent
diabetes mellitus
Immune response, normal,
mechanism 125–6
Immune system 123–6
cells 123–4
Immunization 924
Immunoassay methods,
nomenclature 336
Immunoassays, general principles
337–40
Immunocytochemistry, islets of
Langerhans 59–61
Immunometric assays 337–9
features 339
Immunosuppression
adverse effects 973
drugs 981
in IDDM 20, 971–3
pancreatic transplantation 1004
predictability of response to 973
renal transplantation 690
Immunosuppressive drugs 981
Immunotherapy, IDDM 20, 971–3
Impotence
causes 780–1
investigation 781–2
management 782–3
Incretins and entero-insular axis 320
Infection 813–18
brittle diabetes 889
CSII 421
Injection guns 443
Injection ports, subcutaneous 444
Injection regimens 385–9
factors influencing choice 394, 395
premixed insulin 388
short- and intermediate-acting
insulin 385–6
short- and long-acting insulin
387–8
Injection sites, differences 378
Injections
children 871–2
multiple, devices for facilitating
388–9
subcutaneous
complications 390
sites 389, 390
techniques 389–90
Inositol polyphosphates 537
Insulin
A chain 84–6
absorption, subcutaneous
enhancement 377–8
factors influencing 374

absorption mechanisms 374–6
biopharmaceutical aspects
374–6
physiological aspects 376
activation
glycogen synthesis 101
lipogenesis 101–2
adjustment during exercise 801
allergic reactions to 402
skin 759–60
alternative devices for
administration 443–5
alternative routes of delivery
445–8
analogues 95, 368–9
antibodies 397–405
hypoglycaemia 501
assays 335–44
clinical uses 342–4
difficulties 340
factors affecting 341
history 335
recent advances 340–1
autoantibodies 128, 400
as marker of prediabetic state
404
B cells 61–3
B chain 85
basal supplement, NIDDM
469–71
binding sites 92–3
binding to cells 90–2
biosynthesis 72–4
bovine 84, 85
CAPD 691–2
changes in treatment around
puberty 872
Chicago 288
childhood therapy 871–2
circulating, kinetics 380–1
clearance from plasma 380–1
abnormal 888
combined with sulphonylurea
therapy 471
crystallization behaviour 359–60
cutaneous complications of
treatment 759–60
decreased requirement,
hypoglycaemia 496–7
defective subcutaneous absorption
887–8
degradation 380
denaturation 438–9
disappearance from plasma 380–1
discovery 8–9, 11–14
distribution in body fluids 342
dosages, computers 961
drawing up, blind patients 606–7
effects on RNA and DNA
synthesis 102
enzymatic conversion of porcine
to human 361
excretion 380

exogenous, fate 372
extremes of temperature 924
and feeding behaviour 209
formulation 357–69
full treatment, NIDDM 471–4
gene, IDDM 119
gene, NIDDM 175–7
mutations 175
studies using hypervariable
region 175–7
gene mutations 286–8
examples 288–9
methods of analysis 287–8
gestational diabetes 848–9
glucose
production in 305–6
utilization 307–8
hypertrophy 760
impaired action, animal models
236
impaired response in NIDDM 193
inappropriate regimens 887
increased bioavailability and
sensitivity 497
injection treatment, IDDM 384–95
ketone body metabolism 310–11
kinetics, measurements 372–3
Los Angeles
lowering of cAMP 99–100
manufacture 357–69
manufacturers 358
nasal absorption 368
old age 902
withdrawal 902
pharmacokinetics 371–82
phosphorylation of intracellular
protein 102
phylogeny 88
porcine 84, 86
prb 363
precipitation
irreversible 438–9
reversible 437, 438
preparations 365–8
absorption 373–4
absorption, effects of dose,
concentration and species
375–6
additives 367–8
future 368–9
immunogenicity 398
intramuscular administration
380
long-acting, absorption
kinetics 375
menstrual cycle, altered
requirements during 775
modified 404–5
and nocturnal glycaemic
control 510
premixed 367
premixed, injection regimens
388

Insulin (*con't*)
protracted 366
regular *see* Insulin, short-acting
routes of administration 376—80
short-acting 365—6
short-acting, absorption kinetics
374—5
short- and intermediate-acting,
mixing 375
soluble *see* Insulin, short-acting
stabilized 439—40
standardization 364—5
storage requirements 368
strength 368
subcutaneous administration
377—80
subcutaneous administration,
plasma insulin profile 377—8
subcutaneous administration,
variability in absorption
378—80
with improved action profiles
981—2
primary structure 358
production
by biosynthesis 361—4
bovine and porcine 360, 361
human 360—4
relevant to galenic pharmacy
357—60
puberty, changes in treatment at
872
pumps *see* CSII
purification 364—5
receptor gene, NIDDM 177—8
association and linkage studies
178
mutations affecting 177—8
receptor-binding region 86—8
receptors
and insulin resistance 194—5
internalization 93—5
numbers, down-regulation 93
recycling 93—5
sites 92—3
structure 95—7
renal transplantation 690
resistance
animal models 236
biochemical defect causing
194—5
brittle diabetes 888
classification 276
clinical approach 283—4
haemochromatosis 259
hereditary and acquired
syndromes 276—84
immune 402—3
and insulin antibodies 402—3
ob/ob mouse 232—3
old age 899
role in NIDDM 192—6
site 193

subcutaneous, implantable
pumps 434
resistance syndromes
inherited 294—7
management 282—3
pathogenesis 283
Type A 277—8
Type A, management 282
Type A, variant syndromes 278
Type B 278—9
Type B, management 282—3
Type B, variant syndromes 279
role of abnormal secretion in
NIDDM 217—18
second messenger 102—3
secretagogues 980
secretion 74—82
defective, animal models 236
defective glucose-induced
stimulation, animal models
236
endogenous, absence 888
impaired in old age 899
neurotransmitter disturbances
in human NIDDM 220—1
regulation 76
self-association 437
semi-synthesis 361
sensitivity
improved by drugs 980
improved by sulphonylureas
466
see also Insulin resistance
stimulation of glucose uptake
100—1
structure 84—8
teratogenesis 853
travel 923
treatment
British Asians 911
in pregnancy 844—5
Wakayama 288
zinc suspensions 367
Insulin-antibody interactions,
kinetics 400—1
Insulin-autoantibody hypoglycaemia
syndrome 404
Insulin-binding antibodies, effect of
380
Insulin-dependent diabetes mellitus
(IDDM) 17—23
abnormalities of MHC expression
109—11
age of onset 47
animal models 113—16, 151—60
autoantibody response 126—8
autoimmune pathogenesis 133—6
autoimmunity 126—33
'brittle' 434, 884—94
causes 18—20
chemical toxins 152—5
clinical features 18, 19
definition 17

diet, designing 412
and dietary N-nitroso compounds
155
effects of exercise 797—9
employment 915
environmental agents as triggers
155
epidemiology 18, 47—9
evolution, possible sequence of
events 108, 112
exercise, effects of 797—9
family studies 116—17
fatty acid mobilization 310
genetic counselling 861—3
epidemiological and aetiological
background 861—2
genetics 113—20
histology of islet 107—12
honeymoon period 19—20
immune factors in pathogenesis
122—37
immunogenetic associations
130—1
immunosuppressive treatments
971—3
incidence 48—9
insulin injection treatment *see*
Insulin, injection treatment,
IDDM
long-standing 22
management, diet in 407—14
mortality rates 20—1, 52
natural history 18—20
nocturnal insulin requirements
508, 509
non-MHC associations 119—20
outcome 20—2
pathogenesis, viruses 141—8
physical training, effects 799—800
population studies 117—18
pre-diabetic period 974—5, 131—3
predictability 973—5
prevalence 18
prevention 971—5
prognosis 20—2
risks
to children of patients 862—3
for developing 131—3
to siblings of patients 863
to twins of patients 863
seasonal variation of incidence
47—8
spontaneous, animal models
155—60
stages 974
studies in man 116—18
surgery 822—3
survival advantage 120
twin studies 116
unstable *see* IDDM, 'brittle'
vacor-induced in man 155
viruses 141—8
virus-induced, experimental

studies 144–7
WHO classification 39, 41
Insulin-like growth factor 1
    (IGF-1) 88, 264
    receptor for 96
    retinal neovascularization 569, 570
Insulin-like growth factor 2 88
Insulinomas, biochemical
    investigation 342–4
Insulinopathies 175, 286–9
    clinical aspects 286–7
Insulin-resistant patient, clinical
    approach to 283–4
Insulin-resistant states, classification
    276
Insulins, Chicago, Los Angeles and
    Wakayama 288
    see also Insulinopathies
Insulitis 107–9
    BB rat 156–7
    dilated islet capillary cells 135, 137
    immune factors 128–30
Insurance
    life 916
    motor 920
    travel 923–4
Integrins 540
Interferon-alpha
    IDDM 134
    islets 111
Interleukin-1 in IDDM 134
Intermittent claudication 714
International Diabetes Federation
    967
Intestinal insulin absorption 448
Intramuscular insulin delivery
    445–6
Intranasal insulin 447–8
Intraperitoneal insulin
    administration 446–7
Intrapulmonary insulin 448
Intrarectal insulin 448
Intraretinal microvascular
    abnormalities (IRMA) 582
Intra-uterine contraceptive device
    859
Intravenous insulin delivery 446
Ion-exchange chromatography,
    glycated haemoglobin assay
    330
Iron, haemochromatosis 259
Ischaemia, diabetic neuropathy
    619–20
Ischaemic heart disease see Coronary
    heart disease
Ischaemic maculopathy 585–6
Islet amyloid polypeptide 67, 168
    see also Amylin
Islet cells see Islets of Langerhans
Islet secretory cells, abnormalities in
    NIDDM 199
Islet-cell antibodies 126–7
    in pre-diabetic period 132

Islet-cell-surface antibodies 127
    BB rat 157
Islets of Langerhans 7, 57–69
    amyloid deposition 167–8
        nature and origin 168
    blood supply 67–8
    cell types 61–6
    cells, morphological characteristics
        61
    cellular composition 59
    embryology 58–9
    histological and histochemical
        characteristics 59
    IDDM
        histology 107–12
        lobular distribution of types
            108–9
    immunocytochemistry 59–61
    innervation 68–9
    insulin-deficient 107–9
    integration of secretory activity
        67–9
    morphological features 59–66
    NIDDM
        histology 167–70
        secretory abnormalities 199
    recently discovered peptides 66–7
    virus infection 147, 148
    volumes 167
        alterations in NIDDM 167
Isoelectric focusing, glycated
    haemoglobin assay 331
Isophane insulin 367
    injection regimens 386–7

Jaundice, neonatal 841
Joint disease 762–9
J-type diabetes 254

Keeshond dogs, IDDM 159
Ketoacidosis, alcoholic 484
Ketoacidosis, diabetic 479–88
    children 875–8
        biochemical monitoring 876
        complications 878
        fluid balance 877–8
        insulin therapy 878
        investigation of causes 878
        management 876
    clinical features 484
    complications 488
    CSII 421–2
    definition 479–80
    diagnosis 484–5
    fluid and electrolyte depletion
        483–4
    glucose and ketone body kinetics
        481–3
    lactic acidosis 491
    mortality 480, 481
    precipitating factors 480–1

treatment in adults 485–8
Ketogenesis, ketoacidosis 483
Ketone bodies
    disposal, ketoacidosis 483
    production in ketoacidosis 481–3
    teratogenesis 839–40, 853
Ketone body metabolism
    in diabetes 310–12
    in non-diabetic subjects 309, 310
Ketonuria, pregnancy 840
Kidneys
    basement membrane, thickening
        672
    biopsy, indications for 675
    elimination of insulin 380
    glomerular structure
        and albuminuria 675
        and GFR 674–5
    hyaline lesions 673
    mesangium, enlargement 672–3
    monitoring function 683–5
    normal glomerular histology 671
    pathology in diabetes 671–4
    transplantation see Renal
        replacement therapy
    tubular and interstitial change
        673–4
Killer cells 123
Kleiner, Israel 10
Klinefelter's syndrome 293
Körner minimum dataset 958, 959
Küssmaul, Professor A. 7

Labbé, Professor M. 9
Labetolol, hypertension 729
Lactate, gluconeogenesis 304
Lactic acidosis 490–1
    biguanides 469
Laguesse, Edouard 7
Langerhans, Paul 7, 8, 57
    see also Islets of Langerhans
Laser photocoagulation 596–8
Laurence-Moon-Biedl syndrome 295
Lawrence R.D. 965–6
Lawrence syndrome 281
Leg, diabetic, diagnostic approach
    630–1
    see also Foot, diabetic
Lens
    metabolism 570–1
    polyol pathway 570
    proteins, non-enzymatic glycation
        571–2
Lente insulins 367
    injection regimens 386–7
Leprechaunism 279–80
    management 283
Licences, driving 919–20
    vocational 920
Life insurance 916
Light microscopy, islets of
    Langerhans 59

Lignocaine, use in neuropathy 632, 987
Limited antibody assays 337
Limited joint mobility 763–4
  treatment 768
Lipid metabolism, during physical training 797
Lipid oxidation, role in insulin resistance 194
Lipid-lowering drugs 987–8
  see also Hypercholesterolaemia, Hyperlipidaemia, Hypertriglyceridaemia
Lipoatrophic diabetes 280–2
  aetiology 282
  management 282
Lipoatrophy
  acquired generalized 281
  and insulin antibodies 402, 403
  insulin injection sites 760
  partial, syndromes 281–2
  progressive partial 281–2
Lipodystrophy, insulin injection 760
  see also Lipoatrophy, Lipohypertrophy
Lipogenesis, activation by insulin 101–2
Lipohypertrophy, insulin injection 760
Lipolysis 304
Lipoprotein abnormalities 705–9
  assessment 706
  drug therapy 708–9
  management 706–8
  see also Hyperlipidaemia
Lipoproteins
  classification 706
  effects of diabetes 705–6
  high-density 706, 708
  low-density 706, 707
  very low-density 706, 707
Liver
  control of gluconeogenesis 304, 305
  elimination of insulin 380
  insulin
    receptors 95
    resistance 193
Locus of control 926
Lovastatin 987, 988
Low T_3 syndrome 265, 266
Lung infections 817–18
Lymphocytes 123
  B lymphocytes 123–5
  T helper 109–10, 123
  T suppressor 123
Lymphokines 125
  IDDM 133–4
Lymphopenia, BB rat 157

M value 327
Macleod, J.J.R. 11–13

Macroalbuminuria 658
  see also Albuminuria, Proteinuria
Macronutrients, NIDDM 188–9
Macroproteinuria 658
  see also Macroalbuminuria
Macrosomia 840–1
Macrovascular disease, Third World 906
Macular distortion 592, 594
Macular oedema
  classification 590–1
  clinically significant 590–1, 592
  frequency 560
  treatment 600
    photocoagulation 598
Maculopathy, diabetic 584–6
Magnesium balance, effects of diabetes 773
Major histocompatibility complex (MHC)
  abnormalities of product exoression 109–11
  Class I molecules 124
  Class II molecules 124–5
  relevance of molecules 124–5
Maladaptation 785
  management 785–6
Malingering 889–90
Malnutrition-related diabetes mellitus 247–55
  WHO classification 39
Manometry, gastrointestinal problems 746
Maturity-onset diabetes of the young (MODY) 173–4, 243–6
  definitions 244
  heterogeneity 244–5
  management 245–6
  pathophysiology 245
  prevalence 244, 245
Mauriac syndrome 873
  'brittle' diabetes 887
Meal planning systems 412
Mean amplititude of glycaemic excursions (MAGE) 328
Mean of daily differences (MODD) 328
Mean indices of meal excursion (MIME) 328
Meningitis, enterococcal 816
Menstrual irregularity, progestogen-only pill 859
Menstruation 775–6
Mental imagery, blindness 606
Mental mapping 606
Metabolic instability, brittle diabetes 885–6
Metabolic recovery processes, hypoglycaemia 499–501
Metabolism, inborn errors 293–4
Metformin 469, 472
  drug interactions with 806, 812
  and lactic acidosis 490

old age 902
  with insulin therapy 471
Metoclopramide 987
  gastroparesis 750
Metoprolol, insulin sensitivity 805
Mexiletine 987
Mice
  db/db 233, 234
  non-obese diabetic (NOD), IDDM 113–14, 157–8
    spontaneous 157–8
  ob/ob, obesity diabetes syndrome 229–33
  transgenic, IDDM 114–16
Microalbuminuria 652, 658–63
  concomitants 660–1, 662
  CSII 423
  definition 658–9
  and glomerular structure 675
  measurement 658–9
  nephropathy, relationship to 523, 659–60
  prognostic significance 659–60
  screening for 666–7
Microaneurysms 576–8
Microcomputers, diabetes control 429
Micrognathia 852
Micronutrient deficiencies and NIDDM 190
Micronutrients and IDDM 412–13
Microvascular complications
  biochemical basis 534–44
  children 880–1
  CSII 422–4
  determinants 519–24
  duration of diabetes 520–2
  exacerbation during diabetes 549
  genetic factors 522
  glycaemic control 523–4
  health care 524
  and insulin antibodies 404
  pathogenesis 535–6, 551
  pathophysiology 526–31
  rheological factors 530–1
  structural factors 527–8
Microvascular control systems 546–7
  extrinsic 546–7
  intrinsic 547
Microvascular function, regulation 546–52
Midaglizole 980
MIDMED syndrome 829
Miglitol 980
Mineral metabolism 771–3
Mini-pill 858
Mini-pump, infusion of glucose and insulin 822
Minkowski, Oskar 7, 8, 10, 11
MODY see Maturity-onset diabetes of the young
Monoamines 208

Monoclonal antibodies to insulin 340–1
Monoclonal antibody production 339–40
Monokines 125
Motilin 748
Mucor (Mucormycosis) 814, 815
Mumps virus and IDDM 142
Muscle
  glucose-fatty acid cycle 306, 307
  insulin resistance 193
Myocardial infarction 712–13
  management 712–13
Myoinositol depletion in diabetes 536–7
Myoinositol metabolism and diabetic neuropathy 618–19
Myopathy, proximal motor 624, 626
Myosin, B cells 75

N-3 essential fatty acids 988–9
N-6 essential fatty acids 989
Natural killer cells 123
Necrobiosis lipoidica diabeticorum 754, 755
Necrolytic migratory erythema 269, 271, 760
Necrotizing cellulitis 816
NEFA *see* Fatty acids, non-esterified
Negative co-operativity 91
Neonatal problems 841
Neonate, effects of GDM 847
Neovascular glaucoma 594
Nephropathy, diabetic
  assessment and management of other complications 687
  cardiovascular risk factors, reducing 668
  causes of death 678
  clinical features 679–82
  CSII 423
  definition 652
  diagnosis 682–3
  genetic factors 521, 661–3
  and hypertension 721
  incidence 522, 652–3
  incipient 652
    see Microalbuminuria
  management 684, 685–7
  natural history 653–4
  pregnancy 837, 856
  prevalence 652–3
  renal abnormalities, correction 665–6
  renal replacement therapy 687–93
  screening for 666–8
  structural and functional abnormalities 671–5
  Third World 906
Nerve function, assessment 628–30
Nerve proteins, non-enzymatic glycosylation 619

Nerves
  conduction velocity measurement 628
  electrophysiological measurements 628
Neural tube defects 852
Neuroarthropathy, lower limb 766
Neuroendocrine factors in NIDDM 205–22
Neuroendocrine tests, autonomic neuropathy 645
Neuroglycopenia, hypoglycaemia 497–8
Neuro-ischaemic foot 741–2
Neuron-specific enolase (NSE) 60
Neuropathic (Charcot) arthropathy 739–40, 766
Neuropathic cachexia 624
Neuropathic oedema 740–1
Neuropathic ulcer, foot 736–8
  management 736–8
  presentation 736
  see also Foot, diabetic
Neuropathies
  focal vascular 627
  pressure 627
Neuropathy, diabetic
  acute painful 624, 626
  alcohol consumption 917
  aldose reductase inhibitors 618, 632, 985–6
  autonomic 635–46
    aetiology 636–7
    articular and periarticular disease 765–7
    asymptomatic abnormalities 640
    central neuropathic damage 641
    clinical features 638–41
    curative measures 646
    diabetic diarrhoea 749
    diagnosis 641–5
    epidemiology 636
    gastrointestinal problems 745–6
    impotence 781
    management 645–6
    natural history 637–8
    and nephropathy 681–2
    neuroendocrine changes 640
    pregnancy 857
    relationship to other complications 637
    sexual responsiveness, diabetic women 776–7
    sweating abnormalities 638–9
    sudden death and 639
  chronic insidious sensory 624
  classification 613
  clinical presentation 623–7
  cranial nerve palsies 627
  CSII 423–4
  diffuse motor 626, 627

  epidemiology 613–15
  implantable pumps 434–5
  management 631–2
  natural history 620–1
  and nephropathy 680–1
  neurophysiological changes 616–17
  new drugs 987
  pathogenesis 617–20
  pathological changes 615–16
  pregnancy 837
  prevalence 614
  prevention 632–3
  prognosis 621
  sex differences 614
  staging 630
  Third World 906
Neuropeptide Y and feeding behaviour 209, 212
Neurotransmitters
  abnormalities in animal models 218–19
  appetite-modulating changes in 212
  effect on feeding 210–11
  and glucoregulation 215–16
  non-peptide, and feeding behaviour 208–9
  regulation of insulin secretion 78
New Zealand white rabbit, IDDM 159
Nicotinic acid 708, 987
NIDDM *see* Non-insulin-dependent diabetes mellitus
Nitrates, angina pectoris 713
N-nitroso compounds, dietary, and IDDM 155
Non-autoimmune endocrine failure 272–3
Non-insulin-dependent diabetes mellitus (NIDDM) 24–8
  aetiological links with obesity 186–7
  aetiology, obesity, body fat distribution and diet 181–96
  animal models 228–38
    specific biochemical abnormalities 236
  basal insulin supplement 469–71
  choice of regimen 474
  clinical features 25
  complications 27
    animal models 236–7
  defining treatment targets 464
  definition 24
  dietary management
    designing diet 454–8
    failures 456–7
    initial prescription 456–7
    nutrient composition 455–6
  early-onset 245
  effects of exercise 799
  elderly 474

Non-insulin-dependent (con't)
  epidemiology 49–52
  experimentally induced 234–6
  family studies 173
  fatty acid mobilization 310
  full insulin treatment 471–4
  genetic counselling 863–4
    epidemiological and aetiological
      background 863
  genetic disorders associated with
    174, 246
  genetics 172–8
  glucose
    production 306
    utilization 308–9
  glucose transporters and 178
  glycaemic abnormalities requiring
    treatment 463
  hypertension 721
  implantable insulin pumps 435
  insulin
    indications and strategy for
      use 470
    regimens 470
    regimens, side-effects 471
    resistance 95
  ketone body metabolism 310–11
  management 451
    dietary 453–60
  markers for 175–8
  monitoring glycaemic
    control 464–5
  mortality 27
    rates 52
  natural history 26–7
  neuroendocrine defects
    animal models 217–19
    human 219–22
  neurotransmitters 221–2
  outcome 27–8
  overweight as cause 185–7
  pancreatic abnormalities 198–203
  pathogenesis 192–6
    neuroendocrine factors 205–22
  pathology of pancreas 167–70
  physical training, effects 800
  prevalence 24–5, 49–52
    comparisons between
      populations 50–1
    comparisons within populations
      51–2
  prognosis 27–8
  risks
    to children of patients 864
    to siblings of patients 864
    to twins of patients 864
  surgery 821–2
  synonyms, in young people 246
  WHO classification 39
NIDDM-like syndromes
  with occasional ketosis,
    spontaneous in animals
    233–4

without ketosis, spontaneous in
    mice 229–33
Non-insulin-mediated glucose
    uptake 193
Non-ketotic hyperosmolar coma
    489–90
  treatment 490
Non-peptide neurotransmitters and
    feeding behaviour 208–9
Noradrenaline 208
Nortriptyline 987
NovoPen I and II injection devices
    389
Noyes, H.D. 7
NPH insulin 367
Nucleic acid cross-linking,
    intracellular 541–2
Nurse, diabetes specialist 952–7
  advice 956
  co-ordinating care 953
  counselling 956–7
  education 953–6
  functions 953–7
  organization of care 953
  training 952–3

Obesity 182
  altered energy balance 183–4
  animal models 237–8
  BMR in 184
  cardiovascular disease 703–4
  diet-induced thermogenesis 184
  energy balance and 182–5
  hypothalamic 221
  insulin resistance 194
  metabolic, possible genetic defect
    182–3
  neurotransmitters 221–2
  NIDDM 25, 181–96, 217
  treatment 454–5
Obesity diabetes syndrome, ob/ob
    mouse 229–33
Octreotide 982–4
Oedema
  autonomic neuropathy 639
  neuropathic 740–1
Oedematous maculopathy 585, 586
Oesophageal dysfunction 746
  treatment 750
Oils, supplements in NIDDM 460
  see also Fish oils
Old age, diabetes 897–903
  carbohydrate metabolism
    898–900
  clinical features 900
  community and social support
    902–3
  complications 900–1
  diagnosis 900
  frequency 897–8
  management 901–2

monitoring treatment 902
  social impact 897–8
Oncotic pressure, glomerular
    hyperfiltration 663–4
Open-heart surgery 825
Open-loop insulin infusion 416, 417
Ophthalmological care 560–2
Ophthalmological referral,
    indications for 602
Ophthalmoscopes 596
Opioid peptides
  abnormalities in animal models
    219
  and feeding behaviour 209
  in human NIDDM 221–2
Optical paedabarograph 736, 738
Oral contraceptives 857–8
  inducing hyperglycaemia 804–5
Oral hypoglycaemic agents see
    Hypoglycaemic agents
Oral infections 751
Osteoarthritis 767
Osteolysis, forefoot 767
Osteomyelitis 739, 818
Osteopenia, diabetic 771–3
  prevalence 771–2
Otitis, malignant external 815
Out-patient services 31
Over-insulinization 887
  see also 'Brittle' diabetes, Mauriac
    syndrome
Overweight 182
  aetiological links with diabetes
    186–7
  as cause of NIDDM 185–7
    epidemiological evidence
      185–6
  treatment 454–5
Oxymetholone, insulin action and
    850

P cells, islets of Langerhans 66
Paediatric diabetic clinic 881
  see also Childhood diabetes,
    clinics
Pain
  neuro-ischaemic 741
  neuropathy 631–2
Pancreas
  abnormalities in NIDDM 198–203
  artificial 427–9
  carcinoma and diabetes 261
  embryology 58
  innervation 68–9
  neuroendocrine elements 60
  NIDDM
    alterations in endocrine tissue
      167–70
    alterations in exocrine tissue
      170
  pathology

in FCPD 248
in NIDDM 167–70
studies, history 6, 7
transplantation 1001–11
development 1002
fetal 1010–11
graft rejection 1004
immunosuppression 1004
morbidity and mortality 1005
recurrence of disease 1004
results 1004–5
surgical techniques 1002–4
Pancreastatin 67
Pancreatectomy
diabetes following 261
experimentally induced NIDDM
234–5
Pancreatic calculi, FCPD 251
Pancreatic damage, and viruses
143–4
Pancreatic disease
diabetes as cause of 256–7
diabetes as consequence of
257–61
Pancreatic islet transplantation
1005–10
allogeneic transplantation and
rejection 1007–8
development 1005
human 1010
reversal of diabetes 1006–7
sites of implantation 1005–66
spontaneous diabetes of rodent
1009–10
Pancreatic polypeptide 319–20
causes of increased levels 326
and diabetes 320
production in islets 65–6
Pancreatitis
acute 257
chronic 257–8
prognosis and treatment 258
Pan-retinal photocoagulation 597
Papillary necrosis 816, 817
Paronychia 815, 816
Partially sighted, practical
management of diabetes
606–9
Paulesco N.C. 10
Pellets, implantable insulin 444–5
Pen injectors 444
blind and partially sighted 607
'Pens', insulin 388–9
Pentamidine, causing
hyperglycaemia 805
Peptides
and feeding behaviour 209–12
gut, regulation of insulin secretion
78–9
Pericytes
metabolic causes of damage
566–7
microaneurysms 576–8

in retinal capillaries 565–6
Perinephric abscess 817
Periodontal disease 818
Peripheral artery disease 714–16
Peritoneal dialysis 691–2
Peritoneum, insulin administration
446–7
Peritonitis, CAPD 692
Phaeochromocytoma 268–9
Phagocytes
function, abnormalities 813–14
killing 814
Phagocytosis 813–14
Phenformin 469
Phenytoin 987
Phosphate
balance, effects of diabetes 773
deficiency, ketoacidosis 483–4
Phosphatidyl inositol 537
Phosphoinositides and insulin
secretion 81–2
Photocoagulation see Laser
photocoagulation and Pan-
retinal photocoagulation
Physical training, effects in
diabetes 799–800
Pigmented pretibial patches 755–6
Piqûre diabetes 214
Pirenzepine 980
Placental development 851–2
Plant medicines 980–1
Plasma, insulin elimination from
380–1
Platelet abnormalities, retinopathy
568–9
Platelet aggregation
and AGE 542
inhibitors 987
Platelets
atherosclerosis 704
diabetes 530
retinopathy 568–9
POEMS syndrome 272
Polyglandular autoimmune
syndromes 297
Polyol metabolism and diabetic
neuropathy 618–19
Polyol pathway 984
cataract formation 571
and diabetic lens 571
microvascular disease 528
pericyte damage 566
Polyol production, hyperglycaemia
536
Ponalrestat 985
Population studies, IDDM 117–18
Porcine insulin, structure 84, 86
Porphyria, acute intermittent 293–4
Portugese Association for the
Protection of Poor Diabetics
965
Postural hypotension 638–9
treatment 645

Potassium
ketoacidosis 483
replacement
PP cells, islets 65–6
pancreatic polypeptide 319–20
Prader–Willi syndrome 183, 221,
295
hyperglycaemia 221
Pravastatin 987
'Prayer sign' 763, 764
see also Limited joint mobility
Prazosin, hypertension 729
prb insulin 363
Preconception counselling 842–3,
945
Pre-embryonic development 851–2
Pregnancy 835–49
contraindications to 856–7
CSII 424
delivery
mode 846
timing 845–6
effect of diabetes 837–41
glucose tolerance 43–4, 846–7
glycaemic control 844–5
historical perspective 836
labour
management 845–6
metabolic control 846
management 841–5
microvascular complications 549
monitoring metabolic control 845
prepregnancy counselling 842–3,
945
risks to fetus 837–41
risks to mother 837
routine antenatal assessments
843–4
Prepregnancy counselling 842–3
Preproinsulin 73
Preprosomatostatin 317, 318
Preretinal haemorrhages,
retinopathy 579
Pressure neuropathy 627
Primary care 31
see also General practice
Progestogen-only pill 858–9
Progestogens, injectable 859
Proglucagon 314
Proinsulin 73–4
assays for 341–2
clinical uses 342–4
autoantibodies 340
biosynthesis 363, 368
distribution in body fluids 342
mutations 288–9
Proinsulin-like intermediates, assays
for 341–2
Proinsulins Tokyo, Boston, and
Providence 288, 289
Prolactin secretion in diabetes 272
Prosomatostatin 317
Prostaglandin E, analogues 987

Prostaglandins, glomerular
   hyperfiltration 664
Protamine insulins 366–7
Protamine zinc insulin 367
Protein
   denaturation 438
   dietary restriction, nephropathy
      666, 667–8
   IDDM 411–12
   intake, control in nephropathy
      686–7
   intracellular, insulin-stimulated
      phosphorylation 102
   NIDDM 188–9
   serum, measurement 331–2
Protein gene product 9.5 60
Protein kinase C
   and insulin secretion 81
   microvascular disease 528
Protein-deficient pancreatic diabetes
   254–5
Proteinuria 679
   clinical 658
   definition 652
   evolution 660
   mortality 678
   see also Microalbuminuria
Prout, W.H. 7
Proximal motor myopathy 624, 626
Pruritus 753–4
Pseudoscleroderma 762
Psychiatric disorders 787–90
   childhood 875
   diagnosis 788
   nature 787–8
   prevalence 787
   prognosis 789–90
   treatment 788–80
      eating disorders 829–30
Psychological problems 784–90
   'brittle' diabetes 890–1
   impotence 780, 782
Psychosexual development, diabetic
   women 776
Puberty
   insulin treatment changes 872
   microvascular disease 548
Public Service Vehicle licences 920
Pumps
   for CSII 417
   implantable 413–6
      brittle diabetes 893–4
      complications 434
      costs 435
      future 435–6
      indications 434–5
      rationale for 431
      technique 432
      types 432, 433
   insulin precipitation in 437–40
      prevention 440
Pupillary responses, autonomic
   neuropathy 640

Pupillary tests, autonomic
   neuropathy 645
Pyelonephritis 817
Pyrophosphate arthropathy 767–8
Pyruvate, gluconeogenesis 304
Pyruvate dehydrogenase activation
   101–2

Quantitative sudimotor axon reflex
   test 645
Quetelet index 182

Rabson–Mendenhall syndrome 278,
   296, 297
Radioreceptor assays, for insulin
   335–6
Rat, BB
   IDDM 114
      spontaneous 155–7
Reagent strips 390–3
Reflectance meters 391–2
Rehydration, ketoacidosis 485–6
Renal abnormalities, correction 665
Renal failure, mortality from 52
Renal haemodynamic changes,
   prognostic significance 665
Renal hypertrophy 671–2
Renal impairment, clinics 945
Renal plasma flow, glomerular
   hyperfiltration 663
Renal replacement therapy 678–9,
   687–93
   causes of death following 693
   complications 692–3
   methods 688, 689
   selection criteria 688–9
   timing 689
   withdrawal from 693
Renin-angiotensin-aldosterone axis,
   glomerular hyperfiltration 665
Respiratory distress syndrome 841
   adult 488
Respiratory sinus arrhythmia 642
Retina, blood flow 567
Retina-derived growth factor, retinal
   neovascularization 569
Retinal detachment
   rhegmatogenous and tractional
      392–4
   tractional 592, 594
Retinal examination, general
   practice 950
Retinal neovascularization 569–70,
   582–4
Retinal screening 945
Retinopathy
   appearances 577, 595–6
   background 590
   capillary dilatation and leakage
      567–8
   clinical classification 590–4

   clinical examination 594–6
   CSII 423
   epidemiology 557–62
   'florid' 582
   and growth hormone 264
   haemodialysis 691
   haemodynamic changes 567
   incidence and progression 521,
      557–62
   lesions 576–84
      non-proliferative (background)
         576–80, 590
      preproliferative 580–2
      proliferative 582–4
   limited joint mobility 763
   natural history 584–7
   nephropathy 682
   new drugs 987
   new vessel formation 569–70,
      582–4
   opthalmological care 560–2
   pathogenesis 564–72
   physical signs 595–6
   pregnancy 837, 857
   preproliferative 580–2, 591
      photocoagulation treatment 598
   prevalence 558–60
      by sex 558
   proliferative 591
      incidence 561
      natural history 587
      photocoagulation treatment 597
      risk profile 521
      somatostatin analogues 983–4
   renal replacement therapy,
      progression 693
   retinal blood flow 567
   risk profiles in IDDM 520–1
   Third World 905–6
   treatment 596–602, 945
   uncomplicated background,
      natural history 584
   vascular occlusion 568–9
   visual symptoms 594–5
   warning signs 581
Rheumatoid arthritis 767
Rhinocerebral mucormycosis
   814–15
RNA synthesis, effects of insulin
   102
Rollo, John 6
Rubella, and IDDM 142–3
   experimental studies 146–7
Rubeosis iridis 587, 593

Saccharomyces cerevisiae, insulin
   biosynthesis 363–4
Sacral agenesis 852, 853
Schmidt's syndrome 267, 268
Scintigraphy
   gastrointestinal problems 745, 746
   gastroparesis 747

Scleroderma diabeticorum 756
Sclermoderma of Bushke 756
Secretin 322
Seip-Berardinelli syndrome 280—1
Self-help groups 937
Sepsis
  after renal replacement therapy
    693
  neuropathic foot 738
Serotonin 208—9
Sex, as determinant of microvascular
    complications 520
Sexual function
  diabetic men 779—83
  diabetic women 775—7
Sexual responsiveness, diabetic
    women 776—7
Shin spots 755
Shoes, for diabetic patient 744
Shoulder, diabetic 765
Shoulder—hand syndrome 766
Simvastatin 987
Single-gene defects 293—4
Skin 753—60
  haemodynamic abnormalities
    547—8
  infections 816—17
Smoking 916
  atherosclerosis 703
  and body weight 459
  hypertension 725
Social services 609—10
Sodium, IDDM 412
Sodium dichloroacetate, lactic
    acidosis 491
Sodium—lithium countertransport
    mechanisms, red blood cells
    661—3
Sodium—potassium-dependent
    adenosine triphosphatase 618
Somatostatin
  actions 318—19
  analogues 982—4
    diabetic complications 983—4
    metabolic effects 982—3
    side-effects and indications 984
  causing hyperglycaemia 805
  and diabetes 319
  production by D cells 64—5
  secretion 317—18
    in NIDDM 203
  source, synthesis and structure
    317
Somatostatinoma syndrome 271, 319
Somatotrophin-release inhibiting
    factor (SRIF) see Somatostatin
Somogyi effect 507, 510—11
  brittle diabetes 887
Sorbinil 768, 985
Sorbitol
  cataract 571
  neuropathy 618—19
  in polyol pathway 537—8

Spine, diabetic 765
SRIF see Somatostatin
Standard meal test, B-cell
    function 351
Starch
  digestion, inhibitors 979—80
  hydrolysis 979
Statins 709, 987
Steatorrhoea 751
  FCPD 252
Sterilization for diabetic women 860
Steroid therapy, withdrawal 805—6
Stevens-Johnson syndrome 758, 759
Stillbirth 838
Streptozotocin 154—5
  low-dose, NIDDM 235
  multiple low-dose 154—5
  neonatal, NIDDM 235—6
  single-dose 154
Stress 784—5
  brittle diabetes 890—1
  insulin absorption 379
  metabolic effects 786—7
  NIDDM 221
Subcutaneous insulin injections see
    Insulin, injection treatment,
    IDDM
Subcutaneous tissues, infection
    816—17
Sucrose, IDDM 411
Sugar intake
  in IDDM 411—12
  in NIDDM 189—90
Sulindac 987
Sulphated insulin 440
Sulphonylurea inadequacy 467
Sulphonylureas 465—9
  choice 468—9
  combined with insulin therapy
    471
  drugs affecting 806, 812
  hypoglycaemia 501—2
  mechanisms of action 465—6
  nephropathy 686
  old age 902
  pharmacokinetics 467, 468
  primary and secondary failure
    466—7
  regulation of insulin secretion 78,
    79
  side-effects 467—8
  skin complications 758—9
Sural nerve biopsy 628—30
Surfen insulins 367
Surgery 820—5
  childhood diabetes 874
  emergency 824—5
  IDDM 822—3
  management during 820—1
  metabolic response to 820
  NIDDM 821
  postoperative management 823
  practicalities of management

    823—4
  preoperative assessment 822
  protocol of management 824
Sustacal test, B-cell function 351
Sweat test, autonomic neuropathy
    645
Sweating disturbances, autonomic
    neuropathy 639
Sweeteners, IDDM 413
Sydenham, Thomas 5
Symmetrical polyneuropathy 623
Syringes
  blind and partially sighted 606—7
  disposable 390
  travel 923

T lymphocytes 123
  T-helper 109—10, 123
  T-suppressor 123
T-cell receptor and IDDM 119
Telephone advice service 947
Temperature
  discrimination threshold 628
  and insulin absorption 378—9
Tenosynoviosclerosis 764
Tenosynovitis 764
Teratogen, identity 853—4
Teratogenesis, mechanisms 851—4
T-helper lymphocytes 123
Thermogenesis
  diet-induced, in obesity 184
  impaired in NIDDM 184—5
  new drugs to increase 981
  substances affecting 213
Thiazide diuretics
  hypertension 721, 726
  inducing hyperglycaemia 804
Third cranial nerve palsy 627
Third World, diabetes 905—8
  complications 905—6
  epidemiological assessments 907
  mortality 906—7
  organization of care 907—8
  problems in management 907
Thirst in diabetes 272
Thromboembolism, ketoacidosis 488
Thrombotic glaucoma 587
Thromboxane A_2, levels 568, 569
Thyroid function, in diabetes 265—7
Thyroid gland and diabetes 265—7
Thyroid-stimulating hormone 266
Tissues, metabolic and functional
    abnormalities 985
Transmucosal absorption of insulin
    447—8
Transplantation
  pancreas 1001—1
    fetal 1010—11
  pancreatic islet 1005—10
  renal 689—90
    criteria for 690
Travel 922—5

Travel (*con't*)
  air 924—5
  extremes of temperature 924
  illness during 924
  information 922
  insurance 923—4
Triacylglycerol lipase 309
Tricyclic drugs 789
  neuropathy 632
Triglyceride, lipolysis 309
  see also Hypertriglyceridaemia,
    Hyperlipidaemia
T-suppressor lymphocytes 123
Tuberculosis 817—18
Tubulin, B cells 74, 75
Tumour necrosis factor, IDDM
  133—4
Turner's syndrome 292—3
Twin studies
  IDDM 116
  NIDDM 172—3
Tyrosine kinase and insulin 102—3

UK Prospective Diabetes Study 474
Ulceration, neuropathic, after renal
  replacement therapy 693
Ulcers
  duodenal 751
  feet 816
  gastric 751
  neuro-ischaemic foot 741
  neuropathic 736—8
    after renal replacement therapy
    693
Ultralente insulins 367
  and surgery 825
University Group Diabetes Program
  474
Uric acid levels 767
Urinary tract infections 817
  diabetic women 776

Urine
  C-peptide determination 350—1
  glucose measurements in NIDDM
    465
  glucose testing 326
Urticaria and insulin antibodies 402

Vacor, diabetes in man 155
Valsalva manoeuvre, heart rate
  response to 641—2
Vascular disease
  epidemiology 703
  nephropathy 680—1
  renal replacement therapy 689
Vascular occlusion, retinopathy
  568—9
Vascular permeability and
  microvascular disease 529—30
Vasoactive intestinal (poly)peptide
  see VIP
Vasodilators 686
  hypertension 729
Vasomotor problems, autonomic
  neuropathy 639
Vasopressin secretion, in diabetes
  272
Vegetable oils 988—9
Venous abnormalities, retinopathy
  581—2
Verapamil 987
Vertebral osteomyelitis 818
Vibration perception threshold
  diabetic foot 743
  measurement 628
VIP, islets of Langerhans 69
VIPoma syndrome 271
Viral infection, diabetogenic
  mechanisms 144
Viruses
  and exocrine pancreatic damage
    143—4
  IDDM

    experimental studies 144—7
    pathogenesis 141—8
  infection of islets and B cells 147
Vision, diabetic drivers 921
Visual acuity, measurement 595
Vitrectomy 601
  indications for 602
Vitreo-retinal surgery 598—602
Vitreous haemorrhages 587, 592, 594
Von Hohenheim 6
Von Mering, Josef 7, 8

Water retention, sulphonylureas 468
Weight
  benefits of loss in NIDDM 454
  gain with sulphonylurea therapy
    468
  ideal 455
  loss
    diabetic neuropathy 620
    predicting rate 455
  and smoking 459
  target 455
Wells, H.G. 965—6
Werner's syndrome 296
Willis, Thomas 5
Wisconsin Epidemiological Study of
  Diabetic Retinopathy
  (WESDR) 557—61
World Health Organization, (WHO)
  diabetes classification 39—40
  justification for 40
  problems with 41
  statistical risk classes 40

Xenon arc photocoagulation 596

Zinc chelators and IDDM 152—3
Zinc deficiency, teratogenesis 852
Zülzer, Georg 8

POLITICAL THEORY

An Introduction to Interpretation

Elizabeth M. James

LANHAM • NEW YORK • LONDON

Copyright © 1976 by
Rand McNally College Publishing Company

University Press of America,® Inc.

4720 Boston Way
Lanham, MD 20706

3 Henrietta Street
London WC2E 8LU England

Printed in the United States of America

Reprinted by arrangement with Houghton Mifflin Company

Library of Congress Cataloging in Publication Data

James, Elizabeth Mathis.
  Political theory.

  Reprint. Originally published: Chicago : Rand
McNally College Pub. Co., c1976.
  Bibliography: p.
  Includes index.
  1. Political science.   I. Title.
JA71.J29   1982   320'.01'1   81-40791
ISBN 0-8191-2008-1 (pbk.)   AACR2

All University Press of America books are produced on acid-free
paper which exceeds the minimum standards set by the National
Historical Publications and Records Commission.

Contents

Preface   vi

Chapter 1.   An Introduction to Interpretation   1

Chapter 2.   The Text   18

Chapter 3.   The Person   30

Chapter 4.   The Environment of Thought   44

Chapter 5.   Meaning and Theory:

Intent v. Effect   64

Chapter 6.   Interpreting the Interpreters   75

Bibliography   87

Index   93

Preface

The idea for this book on interpretation of political thought arose from a need I had recognized in my own teaching experience. When assigning readings in interpretation, even to excellent students, the teacher of political philosophy is often faced with the questions "Why can't we just read Plato?". "Why do we have to read this extra stuff?" Not only is interpretative material seen as "extra stuff," but it is usually labeled as "academic" (approximate translation: irrelevant). While the student attitude sometimes reflects shirking of study responsibility, more often it indicates a lack of understanding of the purpose of interpretation in the discipline of political thought. The problem is frequently compounded by the abundance of different interpretations assigned.

When I sought a reading that would explain my purposes to my political theory classes, I found nothing that met my needs. It was at this point, I began a series of lectures for my students to introduce them to interpretation. These lectures later turned into an essay, then into an article, and finally into this book. My purpose is to help the student who is coming to the discipline for the first time.

I would like to express my appreciation to those who aided directly in the evolution of this project. My students and colleagues at Trinity College were a constant source of encouragement in writing this book. In fact, members of my political theory classes gave me useful criticism through each revision of the manuscript. Mrs. Marguerite Edwards Bach, who has always provided true friendship and an intellectual challenge, read, reviewed, criticized, and edited various versions of this manuscript and encouraged me to continue to sharpen my ideas and present them in readable English.

My former teachers, Professors Wolfgang Kraus and Benjamin Nimer of The George Washington University, Professor Neil A. McDonald of Douglass College, and Professor James N. Rosenau of the University of Southern California have continued their helping roles through their encouragement and/or reading and constructive criticism of this work. In fact, direct lines can be drawn from many of my ideas and attitudes to the lessons conveyed by these excellent teachers. This correlation is especially strong with respect to Drs. Kraus and McDonald whose approaches to political theory are so intertwined with my thoughts that it proves difficult to sort them out for appropriate recognition. The staff of Organizational Development Associates gave me significant help. Beverley J. Graham, Vice President of ODA, helped give continuity and logical flow to many of the ideas developed in the book. Nancy L. Diener of ODA typed the first article. Barbara Vicik Eilts typed the successive versions of the book with care, commitment to perfection, and constructive comments at each stage of the work.

All of the following gave me valuable support during the writing period: Dr. William H. Jackson, Jr., Dr. Timothy D. Mead, Mrs. M. D. Powell, Mr. John Applegath, Mrs. Elizabeth Beasley, Mrs. Lessie Gibson and my parents and parents-in-law. Bob Erhart and Judy Keith of Rand McNally gave me professional editorial assistance and friendly encouragement. They showed an understanding of the person as a writer as well as mastery of their professional craft.

My greatest debt, however, is to Carroll S. James, Jr. He is a husband and friend without peer. His constant support and encouragement, going from hours of discussion and reading of the various drafts through caring for the children on weekends and foregoing visits with friends and family, make the dedication of this book to him and our children but a small token of my gratitude.

While my debts to all of the above are significant, it goes without saying, but must be said in any case, that they share no responsibility for the faults and shortcomings of this book. Whatever value can be found therein, however, they share in its creation.

Elizabeth M. James

Washington, D.C., 1976

To Carroll

Christine Tracy

Lauren Hope

Chapter 1   An Introduction to
           Interpretation

In political theory as an academic discipline the reader is struck, and sometimes bewildered, by the variety of interpretative books written about theory and theorists. Interpretations of the works of any major political philosopher include radically different and often conflicting views about the meaning and significance of the writer and the works under consideration. How is it that the same subject matter elicits such a variety of interpretations from reputable and honest scholars? What are the approaches to theoretical work which produce the abundance of views? And, what are the benefits and the liabilities of each of these various approaches as they seek to comprehend the full meaning of political thought? The goal of this book is to answer these questions.

This chapter will deal with why interpretation of political theory is necessary and what one can hope to gain from the reading of interpretations. It will identify some approaches to interpretation that will be explored relative to political theory in later chapters and will show that these play significant roles in political science and in life in general. And, finally, chapter 1 will emphasize that diversity of interpretation is enriching for the individual and essential for the enhancement of the Western political heritage.

WHY IS INTERPRETATION OF POLITICAL THEORY NECESSARY?

One reason for interpretation is that political theory is not theory in the strict sense of the word as it is used in science. Like scientific theory, political theory *describes and analyzes what is* and tries to *predict what will be,* but in political theory there is no mathematically precise model the merits of which can be proved or disproved in carefully observed experiments. Political theory goes further than scientific theory. It has critical and constructive functions beyond the descriptive and predictive aspects of scientific theory. That is, political theory also *criticizes what is* and *constructs what should be.* These critical and constructive functions make political theory a value-based activity and therefore one in which it is helpful to have many viewpoints.

Another reason that interpretation is necessary is the fact that all the description, prediction, criticism, and construction in political theory is stated in the imprecise language of the author's lifetime. Further, the author's thoughts are colored by the elements of his personality and culture. While imprecision of language and the impact of culture and personality might be viewed as liabilities in scientific theory, in political philosophy they serve as triggers for interpretation and contribute to the development of new, creative political speculation.

Like great works of art, great political theory reflects the complexity of human consciousness. Political theories take on different meanings when viewed from different angles. Their richness is disclosed more fully when filtered through other consciousnesses and examined in the light of various approaches conceived by other minds.

Some of the functions of a good interpreter may be seen by looking at the word *interpretation.* It comes from the Latin word meaning broker or negotiator, and the Latin root is akin to the word for value or price. While it may be hard to envision the similarity of a Wall Street broker, or a labor/management negotiator to an interpreter of political theory, there are some analogies that can be drawn.

When a customer wants to buy stock he calls the broker and places the order in lay language. The brokerage house translates the order into the symbols and actions appropriate to consummate a buy on the floor of the stock exchange. The customer, unused to the traditions of the exchange, would find the language and activity there unintelligible. He would be unable to participate without the skilled "interpretation" of his broker.

Labor/management negotiations also have some functions analogous to those of interpretation in political theory. In a dispute, both sides interpret economic conditions, statutes and prior agreements in terms of their beliefs, judgments, interests, and circumstances. The parties often construe reality differently, and so the disagreement becomes much more fundamental than mere divergence on acceptable solutions. The neutral third party tries to negotiate a settlement based on full consideration of all options possible under the circumstances.

A symphony orchestra also functions as an intermediary. It gives sound to the noiseless notes on the page of a score. In the process of bringing the notes to realization, the orchestra highlights certain relationships within the work and, through its playing, seeks to explain the point or motive of the composer. This phenomenon produces the differences heard by the sophisticated listener when the same composition is performed by different orchestras.

In all of these illustrations, we have been talking about broker or negotiator functions in the sense that one party serves as a mediator between two other parties to an activity: the broker to buyer and seller, the arbitrator to management and labor, the orchestra to composer and listener. In political theory the interpreter mediates between the theorist and the reader.

WHAT CAN THE READER EXPECT TO GAIN FROM INTERPRETATION? Interpretation allows the reader of political philosophy to participate in the discipline's "disinterested search for the principles of the good state and good society."[1] It allows us to carry on a continuing contem-

---

1. Andrew Hacker, *Political Theory: Philosophy, Ideology, Science* (New York: Macmillan Co., 1961), p. 5. Hacker and others have provided substantial help for the student in differentiating political philosophy, political theory political thought and ideology. This book will not duplicate works of differentiation provided by Andrew Hacker; Arnold Brecht, *Political Theory* (Princeton: Princeton University Press, 1959); and Dante Germino, *Modern Western Political Thought* (Chicago: Rand McNally & Co., 1972). Indeed, this book will use the terms political theory, political thought, and political philosophy almost interchangeably, recognizing that useful differentiations can and have been made by others.

Hacker's book also provided a brief typology of interpretative approaches. While some useful insights can be gained from Hacker's discussion he does not identify or meet the needs dealt with in this book.

porary dialogue with the great thinkers as it helps us see more of the meaning of their works.

The search for "meaning" initially involves consideration of the intent of the author of a political theory; however, it also requires exploration of the *implications* of a theoretical position. Some implications of a theory might not have been envisioned by the original theorist. They are, however, part of the study of political theory, regardless of the intent of the philosopher.

Some interpreters find "meaning" not in the intent or theoretical implications of a philosophical product, but in what they themselves impute to be the actual political effects of the theory. These interpreters identify a political philosophy as the cause of subsequent political events or systems and ascribe praise or blame to the philosophy in terms of their own political preferences.

In each of these approaches to the search for meaning—studying the intent of the author, probing the theoretical implications of the author's product, and seeking a link between theoretical cause and imputed political effect—interpretation can be a vehicle for gaining greater insight into the theory and practice of politics. This point rests on the assumption that interpretation of political theory affects politics and that interpretation, in turn, is affected by political practice.[2] A direct line cannot be drawn from a particular interpretation of political thought to specific political programs. However, the variety of approaches can open new ways of looking at the foundation of a system and can thus expand the policy alternatives available within the tradition.

---

2. The issue of "theory and practice" has long concerned the discipline of political thought. For example, today we often hear the terms used as a way of discussing alleged cleavages between that which our founding documents and political values say (the *ought to be*) and the actual, day-by-day expression of this heritage in our society (the *is*).

Aristotle brought our attention to theory and practice when he identified them as two different kinds of *knowledge*. The higher kind *(theorea)* was that which sought to understand the world: knowledge for knowledge's sake. The lesser form *(praxis)* sought applicable, practical knowledge which could be used more readily in a particular situation.

New issues of theory and practice arose from Karl Marx's 19th-century criticism of both Hegelian philosophy (theory) and the reality (practice) it reflected. Marx's critical and constructive thought attempted to provide a "unity of theory and practice" that would transcend what he thought to be the theory/practice, subject/object, individual/society dichotomies of his time.

For more information on these issues see: Shlomo Avineri, *The Social and Political Thought of Karl Marx* (Cambridge: At the University Press, 1968), p. 131; George Lichtheim, *The Concept of Ideology* (New York: Random House, 1967), p. 38; Germino, *Modern Western Political Thought*, pp. 372-373; N. Greenstein and N. Polsby, eds., *Handbook of Political Science* (Reading, Mass: Addison-Wesley, 1975).

The interrelationship between theory and practice makes the definition of political philosophy as a "disinterested search" a desirable yet unattainable objective. No one is devoid of values and policy preferences, divorced from his own time and place. Therefore, the interpreter, like all human beings, has "interests" that will affect his interpretation of theory today just as comparable factors affected earlier philosophers' attempts to deal with theoretical issues.

While we recognize total "disinterest" as an "impossible dream," we see it as worthy of human aspiration. It can inspire each generation to provide the fullest treatment possible for the perennial issues of politics. It can also inspire individual interpreters to try not to allow their "interests" to sway their interpretations.[3]

Some interpreters reject the possibility of a "disinterested search." They study a political philosophy for ideas absorbed from the environment of the writer; that is, the social, political, economic, and philosophical setting of the philosopher. Some call this setting the operative myths of the society.

Still others assert that although one may *try* for a relatively "disinterested search" and full treatment of politics, the goal is not only impossible but misleading. They argue that this goal fails to show that ideas ultimately serve the interests of a dominant group in the social system. They assert that scholars and other groups in a society use prevailing theoretical tools to pose questions and to frame alternative answers without considering the possibility that prevailing approaches may offer an incomplete probing of politics. For example, the existing theoretical modes may not question the differences between values involved in ongoing social practice and those articulated in abstract theoretical statements. They conclude that those who argue for "disinterest" where disinterest is impossible merely rationalize the existing order, including its social class system and its concomitant political system under bourgeois rule. These scholars seek a theory that asks basic questions about the role of the discipline of political theory in society. They seek to reform the discipline to allow it, through critical thought,

---

3. The reader will benefit by understanding the political preferences of those interpreters who genuinely aspire toward a disinterested search for insights into politics. Without impuning the motives of the interpreter, the reader can use knowledge of his "interests" to understand the issues raised, to deal with them more critically, and to evaluate positions with more sophistication.

to offer alternative probes of politics as a means to alternative political values, options and systems.

A brief description of the development of the concept of ideology will give us an example of some controversies about appropriate approaches to interpretation of political life and thought.

The term *ideology* has a long historical development, associated in many minds with the rise of the "isms" of modern times, such as liberalism, Marxism, and conservativism. The historical evolution of the concept and contemporary use of the term in political rhetoric make it hard to understand the meaning implied in a particular instance. The term, *ideology* originated in 18th-century France during the revolution, when it meant a "science of ideas." The label *ideologue* came to be applied to anyone who sought this "science of ideas" and tried to limit autocracy and maximize freedom of thought and expression. Napoleon originally aligned himself with the views of this group but turned against the ideologues once his regime was firmly in power. With his use of the term *ideology* in a disdainful manner began the negative connotation of the word which it continues to bear into our time.[4]

Later, Marx added to the negative tone of the concept when he built on, yet criticized, the Hegelian system of philosophy.[5] He used the term *ideology* to describe ideas that he saw as "justifications or rationalizations for the existing material or economic organization of society."[6] He especially addressed the idea systems through which the bourgeois rationalized capitalism and their ruling position within it.[7] Marx assumed, however, that there must be some thought—scientific thought, objective thought, critical thought—that was not as distorted as the false consciousness of his day. He saw his own "scientific socialism" as a contribution to this more authentic type of thought.[8]

In our time the negative view of ideology has been reinforced by its use in the rhetoric of modern politics. To attack an opponent or label him as dogmatic or fanatical the term ideologue is often employed. The

4. Steven T. Seitz, "Political Ideologies and the Essence of Politics," in *Modern Competing Ideologies,* ed. L. Earl Shaw (Lexington, Mass.: D.C. Heath, 1973), pp. 1-15.

5. Lichtheim, *Ideology,* p. 45, n 1.

6. James A. Gould and Willis H. Truitt, *Political Ideologies* (New York: Macmillan Co., 1973), p. 1.

7. Reo M. Christenson et al., *Ideologies and Modern Politics* (New York: Dodd, Mead, 1971), p. 4.

8. Lichtheim, *Ideology,* p. 45; Seitz, "Essence," p. 4.

negative implication springs in part from the nature of modern systems in which ideologies serve as prescriptive doctrines telling their subscribers "what is, why it is, what ought to be, and (in case of any gaps between the real and the ideal) how to move from what is to what ought to be."[9] Thus, in one modern use of the term, *ideology* describes a system of both belief and action where formulas (for example, ethnic purity in Nazi ideology) serve to interpret the world and to command "active commitment and consensus" among the ideology's followers.[10] As Carl Friedrich, a 20th-century political scientist observed,

> Ideologies are action-related systems of ideas . . . related
> to the existing political and social order and intended either
> to change it or defend it. . . .[11]

In this modern sense, ideologues are not "distinterested" in their interpretation and evaluation of events or ideas. Rather, they explicitly interpret the world in terms of their own ideological formula: labeling that which conforms to it as good and rejecting that which does not conform as bad.

ARE THE INTERPRETERS' APPROACHES TO THEORY CLEAR AND EXPLICIT TO THE READER? Unfortunately for those who read interpretations or wish to judge them, the interpreters frequently fail to make explicit their particular approaches to political philosophy. The interpreter's assumptions about the nature of politics and the nature of knowledge are then unclear to the reader. The purpose may be hidden. The reader may not know what the interpretation sought: the intent of the author, the alternative implications of a theory, or a causal relationship between theory and political events. The interpreter's preference for a particular type of textual analysis, for a biographical or psychological focus, or for a historical context may not be clear. The impact of the interpreter's ideological orientation may also be unclear. Even those seemingly innocent textbooks that contain collections of original source readings with brief introductions by the editors are full of hidden assumptions.

9. Seitz, "Essence," p. 8.
10. Christenson, *Ideologies*, p. 6.
11. Carl Friedrich, *Man and His Government* (New York: McGraw-Hill, 1963), p. 89.

The introductions orient the student toward the original work in a particular manner. The very inclusion of certain passages and the exclusion of others is an interpretation. In their lectures, teachers also draw on interpretations of theorists and mediate between students and the work, frequently without making the assumptions of their approaches clear and sometimes without citing the recognized interpreters who have served as their sources. And, of course, the mind of the student is not a blank sheet. Students often unconsciously apply their own experiences and ideas to a political theory. All of this unexamined interpretation can lead to unchallenged distortions of the original theory or failure to appreciate its full implications. Clarification of an interpreter's approaches to the field and to a particular work can help the student develop a conscious, rational approach to the issues of political theory and political life.

EXAMPLES OF APPROACHES TO INTERPRETATION Inquiry into the issues of interpretation can be of value regardless of one's ideological preference or career orientation. The discussion thus far does not only apply to the discipline of political thought. In fact, all of us face potential interpretative pitfalls as we interact with people whose approaches to the issues of living are not articulated, whose predispositions are unannounced, and whose methods of inquiry are implicit and unexamined either by them or by us. In fact, students, like most people, rarely recognize, let alone examine, their own habitual patterns of sorting out reality and giving meaning to ideas. Let us glance at a few examples of this phenomenon outside political theory before we proceed to examine that field.

Within political science there are many fields in which interpretation is an important factor. Behaviorial scientists recognize that interpretative issues enter their survey work not only at the analytic/interpretative final report stage but also at the points of questionnaire design and subject interviewing.[12] In the case of comparative politics, specialists are faced with the need to minimize distortions that arise from the fact that the

---

12. These issues are discussed in the following: W. G. Runciman, *Social Science and Political Theory* (Cambridge: At the University Press, 1962); Robert Holt, *The Methodology of Comparative Research* (New York: Free Press, 1970); Gabriel A. Almond and G. Bingham Powell, Jr., *Comparative Politics: A Developmental Approach* (Boston: Little, Brown, 1966). Also the *Public Opinion Quarterly* deals with these questions regularly.

questionnaire is designed and the interview conducted by scholars from one background who are studying another culture foreign to them. These problems also arise in interethnic group survey research.

At the interviewing stage the public opinion expert realizes that the interviewers process an interview through the mental filters of the project's goals, their own professional training (or lack thereof), and their life experiences. In addition, project directors recognize that they are dealing with a multiplicity of individual interviewers, each of whom brings his or her own filters to the work. While it is known that these interpretative impacts exist, the impact itself cannot be measured, so it may be neglected in the interpretation of the results in a final report.

Constitutional law is a field rich with illustrations of interpretation. Strict construction of the Constitutional text has not been the exclusive method of judicial decision making. Each justice brings interpretative tools to the basic Constitutional document in order to make decisions. Other contemporaries and, later, scholars bring additional interpretative tools to the study of court decisions. They elaborate the context of judicial deliberations, the intent of the judges, and the effects of the decisions and, perhaps, lay the groundwork for later reinterpretation. Interpretation, then, has been the main vehicle of adapting the 18th-century document to later times and circumstances.

As an illustration, consider how Chief Justice Roger Taney interpreted the meaning of the Constitution concerning individual rights and governmental relationships in his decision in the case of *Dred Scott* v. *Sandford*. Contrast that with a May 1857 speech in which Frederick Douglass, a former slave, interpreted the same U.S. Constitution to reach a conclusion opposite to that reached by the Taney court.[13] A chief issue between these two interpretations was whether a slave was a citizen protected by the U.S. Constitution. Taney argued that regardless of the "justice or injustice, the policy or impolicy" of it, the adopters of the Constitution had not included slaves under their definition of citizenship.[14] On the other hand, Douglass used the rule of interpretation that "requires us to look to the ends for which a law is made and to construe its details in harmony with the ends sought." Douglass thus concluded that, "the

13. Frederick Douglass, "Speech of May 1857," in *Negro Social and Political Thought,* ed. Howard Brotz (New York: Basic Books, 1966), pp. 247-262.

14. Carl B. Swisher, *American Constitutional Development* (Boston: Houghton Mifflin, 1954), pp. 243-257.

Constitution knows all the human inhabitants of this country as 'the peo-ple'"[15] and that the Constitution thus "strikes at the root of slavery."[16]

The *Taney* decision has been interpreted by later scholars in terms of the judicial history of the Supreme Court, the political history of the United States, the biographies and psyches of the judges involved, and the differing ideologies of the North and South prior to the Civil War. Many of these differing interpretations have noted the differences be-tween the intent of some of the judges to put the issue of slavery to rest and the actual effect of their decision in fanning the flames which ultimately broke into the fire of civil war. This is one of the few instances in which a Court interpretation was later set aside formally by a Consti-tutional amendment.

Current controversies about such issues as race relations, obscenity, or freedom of the press reflect academic, legal, and journalistic input into the stuff of Constitutional questions and the ongoing role of the Supreme Court in assessing the meaning of the basic Constitutional document and the American Constitutional heritage.

The "Watergate case" in which a series of illegal and/or unethical acts were allegedly committed by high-ranking members of Richard M. Nixon's White House staff and others,[17] serves as a more extensive example of interpretation as practiced in daily life. Let us look at some of the interpretations that have been presented regarding the ultimate sources of that scandal. All of these approaches have been taken from writers on the Washington scene. As we look at each approach, you should examine yourself to see which of these approaches you are likely to use when presented with a problem. The *content* of the Watergate controversy is not our focus here. Instead, this exercise examines the process by which we sort out the "reality" of an issue to "understand" the "facts" of a controversy. Among the approaches we will consider are the following: close textual analysis, intent v. effect, biography, psy-chology, history, and ideology. Each of these approaches is discussed in a summary fashion here and in greater detail in succeeding chapters.
Close textual analysis On June 27, 1973, John Hanrahan of the *Wash-ington Post* wrote an article headlined "Dean Contradicts Nixon State-

15. Douglass, "Speech," p. 256.
16. Douglass, "Speech," p. 257.
17. U.S. Congress, Senate, Select Committee on Presidential Campaign Activities, *Presi-dential Campaign Activities, 1972: Watergate and Related Activities—Phase I Watergate In-vestigation, Hearings,* 93rd Congress, 1st Session, 1973.

ments: Six Sharp Differences."[18] In that article the reporter reprinted six pieces of text from Nixon's May 22, 1973, Watergate speech.[19] Hanrahan followed each Presidential quote with a statement from the testimony given by former Presidential Counsel John Dean on June 26th as he spoke before the senate committee investigating the Watergate affair. Hanrahan's article highlighted differences between the Nixon and Dean versions of the same events.

Likewise, members of the Watergate committee often engaged in close textual analysis of the testimony of a former witness as they asked succeeding witnesses how the committee could find truth among the contradictory testimonies of different witnesses.[20]

Close textual analysis is a means of highlighting consistency and inconsistency within and between sources. Close textual analysis comes naturally to some people. They enjoy mystery stories in which they can attempt to solve the case through the application of logic to the text at hand. They also may enjoy the process of translating a story from its original language into theirs. They like literature classes in which the focus is on explication of the text. Logic may also be a favorite course for them.

Intent v. effect In the days immediately after Nixon's May 22, 1973 speech, a *Washington Post* editorial[21] engaged in a form of interpretation that played on what it saw as the difference between Nixon's intention in giving the speech and the effect of the speech itself. The editorial concluded that nothing had been so damaging to Nixon's presidency as his May 22nd attempt to defend it. The editorial said, "the President's statement constituted a worse indictment of his performance than has been made by any of the other evidence being invoked against him." Citing Nixon's own version of the emergence of the special White House group headed by Watergate conspirators G. Gordon Liddy and E. Howard Hunt, the editorial asked, "Did Mr. Nixon not understand that he had created a para-police unit that, *at the very least,* required strict supervision by him . . . ? Are we to believe that the President more or less

18. John Hanrahan, "Dean Contradicts Nixon Statements: Six Sharp Differences," *Washington Post,* June 27, 1973, pp. 1, 19.

19. Richard M. Nixon, May 22, 1973, *Text on Watergate,* reprinted in the *Washington Post,* May 23, 1973, p. A-10.

20. Transcript of the Senate Select Committee on Presidential Campaign Activities, especially Summer 1973.

21. "Watergate: Mr. Nixon Makes It Worse," editorial in the *Washington Post,* May 24, 1973, p. A-30.

ignored their activities after he had set them up?" The editorial concluded, "'Trust me' the President says. With every effort of his own to
maintain such trust, he makes it harder."

Certainly, it was not Mr. Nixon's intention to make things worse, but
that was his effect, the editorial concluded. This example brings out an
important issue in interpretation: What is the full meaning of a message?
Is it to be found in the intent of the author or in the effect of the message
on its readers?

Focus on possible differences of intent and effect of communications
comes naturally to some readers or listeners. They tend to point out
the potential differences between what a person thinks he is saying and
what is being heard. They test to make sure that the effect on them
is what the speaker intended, often by asking the speaker, "Did I hear
you say . . . ?" When they lack such direct opportunity, they focus on
the many different potential meanings. Their goal is to come to grips
with what they think was the intention and what they feel will be the
impact of ideas and events.

Biography Several articles and pieces of testimony have attempted to
relate the Watergate scandals to Richard Nixon's life prior to, or simultaneous with, the Watergate affair. For example, columnist Jack Anderson[22] related Nixon's actions during the Watergate year to his experiences as a law student at Duke and as a young man in the Navy. Senator
Barry Goldwater related the Watergate climate to Nixon's long history
as a "loner."[23] The implication of the biographical approach is that the
man's life gives data on which one can interpret events and ideas in
order to establish the full meaning of the episodes under consideration.

Some students understand ideas and events primarily in terms of
the persons involved, their histories and the life styles of the period.
For them the biography of an idea and a person is equivalent to an
"explanation" and leads to "understanding."

Psychology Some writers have gone beyond a biographical approach
and have attempted to apply the methods and concepts of psychology
to the understanding of the ideas and events in which a personality
is involved. For example, *Newsweek* magazine summarized a spate of

22. Jack Anderson, "Nixon Set Style for a Watergate," *Washington Post,* May 16, 1973,
p. B-11.

23. Senator Barry Goldwater on *CBS Special Report,* "The Watergate Year," June 17,
1973. Excerpts reprinted in the *Washington Post,* June 21, 1973, p. A-22.

Watergate-related psychiatric profiles of Richard Nixon which "ranged all the way from an examination of Mr. Nixon's childhood traumas to a treatise on his inner drive for power."[24] One of the books considered by *Newsweek* to be "somewhat more scholarly" was Bruce Mazlish's application of a new discipline called psychohistory,[25] which, according to Mazlish, is a fusion of psychoanalysis and history. He conducted a psychological study of Nixon's family, youth, maturity and personal crises in a historical, political setting. Nixon's character was forged, Mazlish concluded, in the family, especially through the tragic deaths of his brothers and his father's successive business failures. Mazlish argued that Mr. Nixon's campaign of 1968, in which he took the "high road" while using vice-presidential candidate Spiro T. Agnew as a "hatchet man," showed that "Nixon had passed through the 'crisis' of his life . . . an 'identity crisis'—and had finally come to a kind of maturity." That maturity, however, would not go unscathed by the developmental process. Mazlish argued that Nixon remained "ambivalent about aggression, tormented by indecision in crises." While Nixon denied aggressive intent, he glorified fighting and the "hard masculine qualities that necessarily go with it." From this analysis, Mazlish predicted that Nixon would create crises as a means of "testing himself and assuring himself greater public support." Although Mazlish concluded that psychohistory offers "increased understanding of the meaning and significance of its materials," *Newsweek* concluded that each of the psychiatric profiles suffered from being "analysis by long distance."[26]

Current fashion finds many Americans seeking the ultimate source of political ideas and events in the minds of the persons involved. All human efforts are reduced to the psychology of the actors. In the psychological approach, ideas are only the beginning of the data; explanation is provided in terms of a series of psychological forces.

History In attempting to gain the full context of the Watergate case, many writers have put it into a historical context, thus focusing on a time/space orientation. In this approach everything is relevant: the scandals that preceded Watergate serve as an integral part of its understand-

---

24. "Shlock Treatment for the Nixon Psyche," *Newsweek*, December 24, 1973, p. 19.
25. Bruce Mazlish, *In Search of Nixon: A Psychohistorical Inquiry* (Baltimore: Penguin Books, 1973), pp. 96-165.
26. *Newsweek*, "Nixon Psyche," p. 19.

ing; comparisons to Teapot Dome are often drawn.[27] Other aspects of the historical approach can be seen in the attempts to fit Watergate into a context that includes the complexities of post-World War II foreign and domestic relations; the accompanying growth of the presidency; the rise of groups threatening the institutional framework of the U.S. government; and the myriad social, economic, political and cultural changes that have occurred not only in the United States but in the entire world.[28] In the historical approach, Watergate, "the thing itself," is not examined alone; rather, it is seen as only part of a web of reality.

Serving as the group historian by building the context of the issue is a natural approach for many students. They broaden the scope of the conversation to show the complexities within which a more narrow event or idea can be seen "in context." Full meaning can only be seen when the event is taken within its fullest environment of time, space and context.

Ideology Given the historical evolution of the term *ideology*, its meaning is not always clear in use.[29] We will illustrate the ideological approach by looking briefly at the history of the Soviet-Marxist ideology and by showing how some of its current ideologues interpreted the sources of Watergate in terms of their own formula.

In the 19th century, Marx pictured what he considered to be the inevitable transcendence of capitalism through a revolution made by a proletarian political movement. The revolution would end the degradation of all human beings and would erase the class system and the accompanying defective political system. It would create a classless society of Communism.[30]

Some aspects of the Marxian tradition were blended into a Russian setting where, in the name of the "proletariat," Lenin's Bolshevik party took power in 1917 ostensibly to bring about the transition to Marx's Communism. Stalin used the hybrid heritage of the Russian revolutionary tradition and Marxist-Leninist thought to justify authoritarian rule by the

---

27. J. W. Anderson, "Recollections of Teapot Dome," *Washington Post,* May 24, 1973, p. A-30.

28. William Greider, "Watergate: Cause and Effect," *Washington Post,* June 17, 1973, pp. 1-3.

29. The most helpful book on this subject is Lichtheim, *Ideology.* Other helpful books are: Christenson, *Ideologies;* Shaw, *Ideologies;* Hacker, *Theory;* Friedrich, *Man;* Gould and Truitt, *Political Ideologies.* Also see discussions in this chapter and in chapter 4 of this book.

30. For more information on Marx see Avineri, *Marx,* and chapters 4 and 5 of this book.

Communist party and to solidify "socialism in one country." He asserted that internal dissent and external powers were threats that necessitated continual vigilance to maintain the Soviet experiment against the enemies who "encircled" it.

The impact of Stalin's and of his successors' theory and practice of Communism plus a traditional Russian ambivalence about foreigners may help to account for the ideological interpretation placed on Watergate by some Soviet journalists traveling in the United States with Chairman Brezhnev in 1973. In conversations with American reporters, some of the Soviet journalists admitted privately that they were confused by the Watergate scandal. One of the interpretations offered in those conversations illustrates the use of an ideological formula to judge ideas and events. This view held that the Watergate scandal was a "right-wing conspiracy designed to frustrate Mr. Nixon's *detente* policy." In other words, some saw it as a "plot against themselves" as leftists.[31]

When the ideological approach is pushed to the extreme and is not tempered by a desire to engage in a disinterested search for knowledge about politics, meaning and value come more from the categories of analysis in the reader's head than from the data at hand. The data are mere "pieces" to be fit into a pre-existing ideological formula to produce an explanation.

While the content of the incredibly complex Watergate scandal is not the focus of this book, we have used some of the existing interpretations about the source of Watergate to highlight the variety of ways available for approaching reality. The discussion was not intended to show the "right" answer but rather to serve as a brief guide to deepen insight.

ENRICHMENT THROUGH DIVERSITY OF INTERPRETATION The purpose of our discussion of Watergate extended further than just the development of individual insight. It sought to demonstrate the richness that a variety of approaches can give to the contemplation of human experience. Research has shown that group problem-solving tends to produce fuller answers to problems if the differences within the group are wisely and systematically used. One well-known exercise in group

---

31. Robert G. Kaiser, "Watergate Case Bewilders Soviets," *Washington Post,* June 17, 1973, p. A-18.

dynamics by Jay Hall of the University of Texas asks a group of nontechnical people to consider being stranded on the moon seeking survival. First, each member must individually sort out 23 items and arrange them in priority according to their usefulness on a trek to a life-sustaining space station. For example, would water be a higher priority item to take than matches? Second, individuals are asked to join a group and through discussion reach a group consensus about the priorities of items to be taken on the trek. Both the individual and the group answers are then graded relative to the "right" answers developed by experts from NASA. When groups systematically use the radically different and often conflicting views about the meaning and significance of the items under consideration, these differences usually serve as an asset to the group and help it produce better solutions than those found by single individuals. There are essential differences between this type of activity and the discipline of political theory: in the former, differences in the group are used to arrive at correct "facts"; in political theory differences in approaches are used to gain greater insight into the intent and implications of thought. However, both procedures illustrate that variety can enrich human life. Differences in approaches are assets, capable of producing the spice, challenge, and continual stimulation that awaken the capacity for intellectual growth unique to humans.

In succeeding chapters, we will concentrate on making explicit some general assumptions and approaches to knowledge, using the works of the great political thinkers as the starting point, the interpreters as the middle ground, and the student as the final component. Since professional scholars, through their interpretations, hold the middle ground between the creators and the students, they will receive the most attention. In each chapter we will identify an approach to interpretation of political theory. Some of the methods and techniques of the approach will be illustrated and problems encountered in its use will be considered. Attention will be focused on the advantages the approach offers for gaining greater understanding of the meaning of political thought. However, favorable points will be balanced by a consideration of some of the disadvantages involved, that is, the ways in which the single-minded use of the approach can hinder fuller appreciation of political speculation. In the last chapter, points raised in this introduction will be related to ideas about political theory developed in the intervening chapters.

Of necessity, we will take up the general assumptions and approaches singly as in the examples above. This organization runs the risk of creating two misconceptions: that most interpreters use only one method and that any one interpreter always uses the same approach or combination of elements in his or her work. These conclusions are both false. What the reader should take from this study is awareness of the balance and proportion—the emphases—that produce an interpretation and the recognition that it could be radically different if it were based on different combinations and proportions.

Throughout the book we will stress that no single approach has all of the answers for the problems of political theory and political life. We will urge the student to use all approaches in order to gain the fullest possible understanding and appreciation of the meaning of politics. We will argue that the judicious use of all of these, combining them with insight and balance, is the best route to understanding great theory and to maturation of a rational and sophisticated approach to politics. The combination of different approaches is essential to the full performance of the critical and constructive roles of the discipline of political theory and to the enhancement of the Western political heritage.

Chapter 2   The Text

The written work of any great theorist is the departure point for understanding the message of a great mind. Since the political theorist's importance depends upon his or her written work, naturally the interpreter's approach to the text is of fundamental concern. Several basic questions will help us view some of the issues involved in textual interpretation. What factors does the interpreter look for to explain how the text works to achieve the theorist's desired result? What are the advantages and disadvantages of close analysis of a text? What can other approaches to interpretation do to help us maximize the advantages of the textual approach and to minimize its disadvantages? When we interpret texts or judge interpretations of texts, we must be aware of these questions and other subsidiary questions.

Study of textual scholarship shows how we can learn about political thought by means of this approach. We will consider brief examples of the approach as it:

1. looks for meaning through consideration of the definition and connotation of words chosen for use.

2. examines a piece of text in terms of the textual whole: the paragraph in which it was written, the section of which it was a part, and the total work of which it was a component.

3. examines any text as part of the lifetime textual output of the author.

4. provides insight into modern acquisition of a text and works from translations of the original text.

5. analyzes a text in terms of literary form and style.

6. engages in line-by-line analysis of text for internal evidence of the theorist's meaning.

Let us begin by turning to Georg Wilhelm Hegel.[1] One sentence by Hegel is often translated from the original German as follows: "What is rational is actual and what is actual is rational."[2] Rather than becoming involved in puzzling out the meaning of this complex philosophical idea, we will use some interpretative battles waged by others about Hegel's sentence to illustrate elements of the textual approach.

The most famous battles occurred between two groups of Hegel followers, a left-wing and a right-wing. The right-wing saw the statement as a "justification of the powers that be" (that which exists is rational) and they applauded the justification. The left-wing seized the sentence to argue the case for revolutionizing reality to make it more rational.[3]

Neither the left- nor the right-wing interpretation appears to reflect Hegel's intent, if Hegel's intent is judged by the text of *Philosophy of Right* or by the rest of his works. For example, at several points in his writing Hegel was clear in stating that philosophy should comprehend its own era, not offer utopian alternatives to it. So his intent, if judged by Hegel's total works, seems to refute the left-wing.

1. Hegel was born in 1770 and lived until 1831. He was the most prominent philosophical figure of his time, and his influence ultimately extended far beyond any geographic or academic boundaries.

2. Our translation is taken from T. M. Knox, trans., *Hegel's Philosophy of Right* (Oxford: Clarendon Press, 1952), p. 10. For a discussion of Engel's mistranslation of this sentence and amplification on the interpretative battle between the right and the left wings see Shlomo Avineri, *Hegel's Theory of The Modern State* (Cambridge: At the University Press, 1972), pp. 123-131.

3. See Shlomo Avineri, *The Social and Political Thought of Karl Marx* (Cambridge: At the University Press, 1968), pp. 124-150; Robert Tucker, *Philosophy and Myth in Karl Marx* (Cambridge: At the University Press, 1961), pp. 75-77; George Lichtheim, *Marxism* (New York: Praeger Publishers, 1961), p. 6.

The Hegel example illustrates the need to see any part of a text, any single idea, within the context of a whole work and within the whole textual output of a philosopher. For example, consider Hegel's reaction to his right-wing interpreters. Unlike many other political philosophers, Hegel wrote a clarification of his controversial sentence to disavow some judgments about his initial intent. He rejected the view that his sentence served as a "legitimization of everything which exists."[4] He pointed out distinctions between German words he might have used in the sentence and those he actually used.[5] He argued that the words he chose should not be construed as they had been by the right-wing. The exercise proves in Hegel's own hand that the attempt by the Hegelian right-wing to justify themselves by Hegel does not hold up.

Meaning, however, may be found not just in the intent of the author but also in the implications of his thought as filtered through other minds. If this is so, then left- and right-wing interpretations may convey insights into politics beyond the initial ideas that Hegel—or any political philosopher—intended to put forth. Building on the springboard of textual analysis allows us to contemplate and probe the fuller implications of Hegel's thoughts. Such contemplation instructs us that Hegel's descriptions have much to tell us about the nature of modern political life. Interpretation that springs from textual analysis and incorporates other approaches makes Hegel's thought relevant to our understanding of the evolution of contemporary problems and our options for coping with them.

Easier to read than *Philosophy of Right* is *Philosophy of History*.[6] However, the fact that the latter is based on Hegel's students' lecture notes presents interesting problems if we rely solely on close textual analysis in the search for meaning.

First, confusion is encouraged by the fact that various editions of *Philosophy of History* draw on different sets of class notes. For example, the first edition rests solely on notes from the lectures Hegel delivered in 1830-31.[7] A subsequent edition, edited by Hegel's son, incorporates lecture notes from the 1822-23 delivery of the course and from the 1824-

---

4. Avineri, *Hegel*, p. 127.

5. Hegel's distinction between alternative words available to an author to convey his ideas is another interpretative technique often used by textual interpreters. They look at the alternatives to see which ideas the author implicitly or explicitly included or excluded by the choice of available wording. They then impute intent based upon the author's actual choice of phrasing.

6. Georg Wilhelm Friedrich Hegel, *The Philosophy of History*, trans., J. Sibree (New York: Dover Publications, 1956).

7. Hegel, *History*, p. xi.

25 version. Second, Hegel's son asserts that his edition relied primarily on Hegel's own lecture manuscripts and that he used student notes "only for the purpose of rectification and arrangement."[8] All of this confusion leaves the reader with the question: Which is the accurate text to be interpreted? In summarizing the sources used by Hegel's students in their editions of Hegel's works, Walter Kaufmann engages in understatement when he says that few professors would like "to reach posterity by way of their students' notes."[9]

A further difficulty in textual analysis is translation. If the original is in a foreign language that must be translated for the interpreter's use, there may be inaccuracies introduced by the translator. Translation difficulties compound the problems associated with Hegel's *Philosophy of History*.

In early translations of the work the phrase *die germanische Welt* was rendered as "the German world." Later, English readers used this translation of Hegel's phrase to argue that Hegel supported extreme German nationalism. Actually, when the phrase *die germanische Welt* is read in textual context, the early translation proves to be incorrect. Hegel used the phrase to discuss the stage of history within which Christian dominance of Europe developed. Thus, his text included in his concept of *die germanische Welt* all of the people of Western Christianity. The strong textual support for translating the concept in a broader European scope helps refute views that have linked Hegel to Nazi totalitarianism.[10]

We have seen some of the many factors an interpreter must look for as dangers in the textual approach, such as an unreliable text with inaccuracies of translation and/or major changes introduced by someone other than the theorist. Because of these dangers an interpreter must be conscious of the history, the language, and the state of the original sources employed. A text must be judged on the basis of reliability as well as on the basis of availability before its usefulness can be determined.

After acquiring a text, the interpreter attempts to show how the piece works on a number of levels: for example, as literature, as a logical

---

8. Hegel, *History*, pp. xii-xiii.
9. Walter Kaufmann, ed., *Hegel's Political Philosophy* (New York: Atherton Press, 1970), p. 2.
10. Avineri, *Hegel*, p. 228. For other translation issues in Hegel, see Avineri, *Hegel*, pp. 177, 222-229.

approach from analysis of problems to the solution of problems, and as a consistent whole wherein all parts contribute to enhance the meaning. Literary form contributes vitally to the aims of a work. We will examine this point by comparing two literary forms used in political theory: the tract and the utopia.[11]

A tract is inspired by and related to particular political events or crises and is frequently a call for some form of political action. Tom Paine's American revolutionary pamphlet, *Common Sense,* is an example of a tract.[12] In this classic, Paine reacted directly to the events of the moment and made suggestions for changing the situation.[13]

The literary form we call utopia, of which Thomas More was a master, differs in tone and style from a political tract. The inspiration for a utopia may come less from a particular political event or crisis, but it is no less concerned with the real political world. The chief difference is in the literary medium. In a utopia a political model ostensibly beyond the times/pace limitations of current politics is created. Through the model, it seeks to raise fundamental political issues.

Judith Shklar, a contemporary American interpreter of political theory, states that a philosopher's choice of a utopian literary form is related to the aim of the work:

> It [utopia] was designed solely to induce moral recognition in the reader. If one thinks that the only purpose of political philosophy is to provide serviceable guides to action for politicians and political groups, then indeed utopia was a useless enterprise. If critical understanding and judgment, however, are also real ends, then the construction of such models is not only justifiable, it is a perfect instrument.[14]

Difference in aims, then, leads different thinkers to their choices of literary form. Paine, for example, certainly saw his pamphlet as providing

11. This discussion reflects the ideas of Dr. Wolfgang H. Kraus of The George Washington University.

12. Phillip S. Foner, ed., *The Complete Writings of Thomas Paine* (New York: Citadel Press, 1945).

13. In the process of his "this-moment" discussion, Paine also raised some fundamental points about the nature of man, about society, and about the forms of government appropriate to human nature. Paine's ability to move beyond the particular incident to make original contributions about the human political dilemma gave his work universal appeal, well beyond the merit of his argument about the particular political issues which inspired him.

14. Judith N. Shklar, *Men and Citizens* (Cambridge: At the University Press, 1969), p. 225.

"serviceable guides to action for politicians and political groups. . . ."
As we will show in chapter 4, More chose the utopian medium to raise
the sights for contemporary and future political persons by encouraging
critical consideration of all "serviceable guides."

Despite the differences in medium, a tract and a utopia may offer
some of the same fundamental points for our consideration. For example,
Paine rejected the English system of government as unnatural. More
also showed an alternative that he thought more natural than the complex
and corrupt British and European systems. In addition, both Paine and
More saw human vice, especially pride, as having produced governments out of line with human potential.

Tracts and utopias that are valuable bring up basic political issues
of universal concern. Neither form is inherently "better" than the other.
The brilliance of thought and the skill in manipulating a chosen literary
form to achieve goals mark a great political philosopher. A great tract
is distinguished from forgotten propaganda and a worthwhile utopia out-
lives futuristic trash because of the writer's ability to work within the
chosen literary form to move beyond the mundane into the profound.

Verbal expression of the "good life" in political theory is not merely
a description of ideal states. The writer is trying to change people's preferences by altering their cognitions or understandings about the nature
of the political world.[15] To some extent, then, the literary style of theory
writers is limited by their persuasive mission and their desire to appeal
to reason. The work of Jean Jacques Rousseau serves as an excellent
example of the impact of style and form on the product of a political
theorist.

Rousseau,[16] the 18th-century pre-revolutionary French philosopher,
produced insightful political theory. He made a significant impact on the
form, styles, and content of theoretical expression while using various
literary forms to convey political ideas. His *Nouvelle Heloise* is a novel,
in letter format. This form served two purposes: it appealed to a new
audience of women and young people because of its format and subject

15. Neil A. McDonald, *Politics: A Study of Control Behavior* (New Brunswick, New Jersey:
Rutgers University Press, 1965), pp. 42-43. Judith Shklar, *Men and Citizens*, p. 225, takes
much the same view.
16. Jean Jacques Rousseau, *The Social Contract and Discourses*, intro. and trans. G.
D. H. Cole (New York: Dutton, 1950). For a discussion of Rousseau as a person, please
see chapter 3 of this book.

matter (a romantic vision of a new family life) and it allowed "self revelation and dramatic clashes between the characters."[17]

Rousseau's use of form and the originality of his political ideas cannot be disassociated from his highly sophisticated literary style. His style and persuasive mission can be seen clearly in *Social Contract*, in which the introductory sentences set the tone: "Man is born free; and everywhere he is in chains. One thinks himself the master of others, and still remains a greater slave than they."[18] Rousseau's phrasing of the focus of the *Social Contract* further illustrates the unity of his style and content:

> The problem is to find a form of association which will defend and protect with the whole common force the person and goods of each associate, and in which each, while uniting himself with all, may still obey himself alone, and remain as free as before.[19]

In Rousseau's attempt to answer the problem he had identified, he expanded the discipline of political theory by developing and enriching the concepts used in the field. For example, he discussed the "General Will" at varying levels of abstraction as he sought to define the role of the citizen in the state. He moved from the mere recognition of majorities and minorities in politics to the profound identification of an abstract, true, national will beyond the mere particular wills of individuals, minorities, or majorities. Rousseau's discussion of the "General Will" illustrates the unique literary limits of political theory. His manipulation and orchestration of the French language was harnessed to his rational, persuasive mission, that of changing the reader's understanding of the essence of politics and the problems of political life. In the process, Rousseau forced modern thinkers to face the issue of identifying the true political community and devising means for basing government on continuing popular consent. Not all modern thinkers accept Rousseau's solution; some even see his "General Will" as a totalitarian suppression of individual freedom. However, many assert that Rousseau compiled much of the issue agenda on which modern theorists are still working.

17. Shklar, *Men and Citizens*, pp. 222-225.
18. Rousseau, in Cole, *Contract*, pp. 3-4.
19. Rousseau, in Cole, *Contract*, pp. 13-14.

So far, we have used the words "textual approach" in a very general form, showing how the text is acquired and how it becomes the springboard for interpretation. In one type of textual analysis, the text itself is seen as the focus of interpretation and should therefore not be diluted by the effect of any outside information. Internal evidence from the text itself is either exclusively of interest or, at least, the definitive evidence for meaning and intent. Alan Ryan summarized this approach well when he argued, "we usually hold people to what they say rather than to what they may suppose to follow from what they meant to say."[20] As part of an interpretative battle raging about the meaning of John Locke's *Two Treatises,* therefore, Ryan based his work on what Locke *said*.

A strict textual approach can take the form of line-by-line analysis of texts and a search for every clue to meaning. Leo Strauss, a 20th-century interpreter, used a particular form of this approach. The origin of his method can be found in his study of Jewish and Islamic thinkers whose art of writing "hid their intentions from all but a select few."[21] He applied the approach of looking for hidden intention as a vehicle for reading Western political philosophy. He felt that through this method "he had liberated himself and could understand writers as they understood themselves." Thus, his only concern with a writer was with "what is written as opposed to its historical, economic, or psychological background."[22]

Many of the methods Strauss advocated may be seen in his study of Machiavelli.[23] First Strauss said that Machiavelli was himself an interpreter of other political theorists. This is entirely accurate. For example, Machiavelli's *Discourses* were an interpretation of the Roman historian Livy.

20. Alan Ryan, "Locke and the Dictatorship of the Bourgeoisie," in *Locke and Berkeley,* ed. C. B. Martin and D. M. Armstrong (Garden City, N.Y.: Doubleday, 1968), p. 232.

21. Allan Bloom, "Leo Strauss," *Political Theory* 2, no. 4 (November 1974): 380. Also see David Schaefer, "The Legacy of Leo Strauss," *The Intercollegiate Review,* Summer 1974, p. 140.

22. Bloom, "Strauss," p. 385.

23. Machiavelli was born in Florence in 1469. Of all of the theorists mentioned in this book, Machiavelli is one of the most familiar, in name at least. Part of his familiarity springs from popular usage of the word "Machiavellian" to connote lack of scruples. However, the range of his thought was far broader than the coarse axioms usually attributed to him. For a review article which discusses some of the literature on Machiavelli, see: Eric W. Cochrane, "Machiavelli: 1940-1960," *Journal of Modern History* 33, no. 2 (June 1961):113-136. Also see, Leo Strauss, *Thoughts on Machiavelli* (Glencoe, Ill.: Free Press, 1958) for Strauss' interpretation.

Second, Strauss argued that Machiavelli had fundamental rules for reading a text (interpreting it) but that he left these rules unstated. Strauss said that close textual analysis of Machiavelli's works, however, allows the careful scholar to infer these basic rules.

The third point in Strauss's reasoning was that if Machiavelli developed fundamental rules for interpretation he probably intended that his own works be read using these rules. However, neither the creative genius of Strauss nor that of Machiavelli slaved under arbitrary rules. Strauss cautioned against a mechanical application of these rules.[24]

The first of the points in Strauss's argument is not refuted by other interpreters of Machiavelli. The second and the third are the subject of hot debate. Indeed, Machiavelli's works lend themselves to heated dispute. As Benedetto Croce said: "The puzzle of Machiavelli is one that will perhaps never be solved."[25] Strauss thought he had provided a definitive answer through his method.

The basic rule of interpretation, Strauss argued, was that for Machiavelli everything had profound significance! Machiavelli's silence on a commonly held view indicated disagreement; his "manifest blunders" were his way of raising questions about the issue. Other significant clues were found by Strauss in such things as chapter titles and the numbering of chapters, the number of words in chapter titles, mutually exclusive interpretations of the same fact at different points within a book, and digressions from the central point of a chapter. For example, Strauss found a significant relationship between the 26th chapter of the *Discourses* and the fact that the *Prince* has 26 chapters. He used this "clue" as a keystone for understanding the internal relationships of the *Discourses* and the relationships between the two major political works of Machiavelli:

> Since the *Prince* consists of twenty-six chapters and the *Prince* does not give us any information as to the possible meaning of this number, we turn to the twenty-sixth chapter of the *Discourses*. . . . the twenty-sixth chapter of the *Discourses* imitates the *Prince* in such a way as to give us

24. Strauss, *Machiavelli*, pp. 29-30.
25. Benedetto Croce, "Una questione che forse non si chiudera mai; la questione del Machiavelli," *Auaderni di Critica* 5, no. 14 (1949): 1-9 as quoted in Cochrane, "Machiavelli," p. 113 (see footnote 23, above).

a clue to the *Prince*. Since this observation leads to further relevant observations concerning the *Prince,* some of which have been noted before, we gain some confidence that in taking seriously the number 26, we are on the right path.[26]

Strauss used this finding to argue that Machiavelli produced a "concealed blasphemy" in his text when he used a New Testament verse of praise for God to describe David, the tyrant. He concluded that Machiavelli intentionally blasphemed and called God a tyrant.[27] While Machiavelli openly criticized the Church of Rome's contribution to Italian disunity, other interpreters contend that Machiavelli's text did not openly wage war against God Himself. McShea, for example, looks at Strauss's arguments on the chapter 26 dilemma and finds that Strauss left the reader with "unfinished intellectual structures." He argues that Strauss, like a lawyer, creates exhibits for his case (against Machiavelli and modern thought) but fails to show the relevance of his exhibits for the conclusions he draws. McShea concluded:

> Strauss has condemned modernity and the writings of Machiavelli on moral grounds and in terms of the utmost severity. His theoretical basis for doing so seems to be nonexistent, or at best to be so confusing or ambiguous as to put his charges beyond the reach of rational discussion.[28]

Not all share such a damning view of the work. For example, Bloom in a memorial article on Strauss's life work says that Strauss's approach to Machiavelli is such that "suddenly there appears a magic formula which pierces the clouds like the sun to illuminate a gorgeous landscape. The distance between the appearance of this book and its reality is amazing. It is a possession for life."[29]

Strauss's conclusions about Machiavelli are in keeping with his conclusions about "modern" thought in general. Strauss believed that Machia-

26. Strauss, *Machiavelli,* p. 49.

27. Strauss, *Machiavelli,* pp. 49-53.

28. R. J. McShea, "Leo Strauss on Machiavelli," *The Western Political Quarterly* 16 (December 1963):792-796.

29. Bloom, "Strauss," p. 391. See also Harvey Mansfield, "Strauss's Machiavelli," paper presented at the Annual Meeting of the American Political Science Association, Washington, D. C., 1972.

velli was part of the group of "modern" thinkers who have led the way to atheism and to the destruction of the classical heritage of the ancients. Strauss's preference for the state of the classics has been labeled by his critics as "hierarchical or aristocratic, and conservative."[30]

One modern scholar who praises Strauss for his attention to Machiavelli as a serious philosopher disagrees strongly with Strauss's methods and some of his conclusions about Machiavelli and modern thought. Dante Germino rejects Strauss's thesis that Machiavelli was a "knowing and deliberate teacher of evil." Germino bases his views on, among other things, Machiavelli's inconsistencies, his writings on repentance, and some mistranslations of Machiavelli's thoughts on the relationships of means and ends.[31]

Other interpreters have been even more critical of Strauss's methods, and these criticisms are illustrative of charges against some forms of close textual analysis. Frederick Chabod argued against any method which turned the works of Machiavelli into a mere literary exercise.[32] Close textual analysis taken to extremes can become a mechanical game destroying the message of the writer.

Other interpreters object to the way Strauss's method led him to take things out of context and read into them meanings that were not intended. Felix Gilbert criticized Strauss's approach as one "so artificial and arbitrary that it enables anyone to prove anything he wants to." Gilbert argued that once Strauss started with his assumptions, however questionable, his methods plus his assumptions led "to frequently slanted, arbitrary or erroneous" views.[33] As McShea said, "the rules for reading as used by Strauss in the explication of Machiavelli's text seem less a means of finding what that thinker purports to say than for reading preconceived notions into his writings." That is, Strauss "set out to prove that the author of the *Prince* is irreligious and immoral," and his methods produced that conclusion.[34]

30. McShea, "Strauss," p. 787.
31. Dante Germino, "Second Thoughts on Leo Strauss' 'Machiavelli,'" *Journal of Politics* 28 (November 1966): 801-805. Also see Germino, "'Modernity' in Western Political Thought," *New Literary History* 1, no. 2 (Winter 1970): 305. Also see discussion in Dante Germino, *Modern Western Political Thought* (Chicago: Rand McNally, 1972), ch. 1.
32. F. Chabod, quoted by G. L. Mosse in review of *Thoughts on Machiavelli*, by Leo Strauss, in *American Historical Review*, July 1959, p. 955. Mosse criticizes Strauss for failing to put Machiavelli's thought in the context of Florentine history and for including only the history of classical thought which, itself, is viewed by Strauss in a far different light than that of other modern scholars.
33. Felix Gilbert, "Politics and Morality," review of *Thoughts on Machiavelli* by Leo Strauss, *Yale Review*, Spring 1959, p. 468.
34. McShea, "Strauss," pp. 796-797.

These criticisms help support a warning against the possible excesses of close textual analysis without the tempering effect of outside information. In general, when used exclusively, the textual approach strives for an ideal that is false and unattainable for three reasons.

First, a work always presumes a knowledge of the culture that produced it. The philosopher assumes that the readers will understand the framework for his or her effort and that they will use that background to gain meaning from the words. The text, then, must be seen as only part of a complex whole.

Second, when the interpreter rules out any other materials than the text, he becomes the source of meaning for the work rather than the original author: his personal interpretation of the text becomes the only data for understanding meaning. This outcome is certainly not the intention of the approach, but it is indeed the ultimate effect when taken to extremes.

Third, the approach tends to produce the effect of fractioning the work so that, rather than achieving a real understanding of the whole, we dig further and further into bits of text at the loss of fuller understanding of the whole.[35] While detailed analysis can be helpful, its usefulness depends on the ability of the interpreter to reintegrate the materials with broader evidence to produce in the mind of the reader a fuller and deeper understanding than could have been achieved otherwise. *Exclusive* use of the textual approach does not achieve this goal.

None of the above is intended to denigrate the value of careful use of textual analysis and minute primary-source footnoting. Judith Shklar put it well in her work on Rousseau when she said close attention to text eliminated "any self-indulgent speculating and the inaccuracy that mars so much writing on political theory."[36]

Textual analysis is only the first step toward understanding the text as political philosophy, as a product of its time, and as a product of its author. The approaches discussed in the following chapters can add to the understanding of the meaning and significance of the text and can give further insight into the varied potential of politics. That insight, after all, is the purpose of political theory as a discipline.

---

35. D. Daiches, "Fiction and Civilization," in *The Modern Critical Spectrum,* ed. Gerald Jay Goldberg and Nancy Marmer Goldberg (Englewood Cliffs, N. J.: Prentice-Hall, 1962), p. 110.
36. Shklar, *Men and Citizens,* p. 231.

Chapter 3   The Person

THE BIOGRAPHICAL APPROACH The biographical approach relates the works of thinkers to other elements and events of their lives. Many aspects of the author's mental and physical life are relevant, such as places of residence, travel, possessions, friends, loves, and occupation. In some instances, the biographical approach is the dominant one, while in others it provides necessary background for adequate insight into a particular aspect of the work.

This section will illustrate some positive contributions made to interpretation through biographical data and some problems that excesses of the approach can cause. The important point here is to recognize that, regardless of our ability to use biography to identify a source for an idea, it is the idea, itself, that is of primary concern to the reader. While a human being produces a theory and biography can help us understand the intent of the writer, the theory has a life of its own independent from the life of the theorist. Biographical data revealing the philosopher's intent can never relase the reader from the requirement to probe both the theoretical and practical implications of the philosopher's product.

The focus of study will be briefly on a biographical approach to the thought of St. Augustine (354-430), whose work *The City of God* shows much of his political thought.

St. Augustine had "lived" a lot before he was converted to Christianity at the age of 33; therefore, an interpreter cannot overlook the earlier period of his life. However, Karl Jaspers, a 20th-century German scholar, considered Augustine's conversion to be the most important personal fact upon which all interpretation of Augustinian thought must rely. He said:

> Conversion was the foundation of Augustinian thinking. . . . Augustine's development has its one crisis in the conversion, this act of conversion is repeated throughout his life and only thus completed. Consequently, Augustine's baptism is not a fulfillment but a beginning. In his writings we may follow a process by which he grew into the vast totality of Christian, Catholic, ecclesiastical existence, which he helped to make into the spiritual force of a thousand years.[1]

That Jaspers gave the reader his important biographical "key" to the secrets of Augustine's theoretical development helps us understand how Jaspers interpreted Augustine's relationship with classical thought: namely, through the vehicle of Christian belief. While this biographical key is helpful, we cannot dismiss interpretive issues arising from other biographical data: Augustine's early absorption of pagan thought and the impact of his youthful life style on his social and political attitudes. For example, in considering St. Augustine's writings on the relationship of church and state, interpreters have differed on the meanings of his ideas. These differences have focused on Augustine's relationship to a later medieval controversy about the source and scope of state authority, especially as the state related to the church's claims to temporal power. Interpretative differences about Augustine's meaning result par-

---

1. Karl Jaspers, *Plato and Augustine* (New York: Harcourt, Brace, 1962), pp. 66-69, 112-113.

tially from differing views about the *extent* to which Augustine's conversion filtered his earlier learning and experience.

The biographical approach can help an interpreter offer theories about the relationship among works written by the same author at different times during his life. Let us illustrate this point briefly by a discussion of Ernest Barker's 20th-century attempt to provide a biographical linkage between Plato's last major political work, the *Laws*, and his earlier and more famous book the *Republic.*

Plato lived 81 years during a chaotic period of Athenian history which was marked by internal class divisions and external hostilities and wars. He wrote profoundly about the basic questions of political life and left us several models of ideal and practical states in his various works.

Barker argued that Plato wrote the utopia-like *Republic* with the hope that it might be realized in practical politics. He showed that Plato traveled to Sicily three times in an attempt to preach the message of the *Republic* and see it implemented in the policies of the ruling house. He failed. Barker concluded that this failure may have convinced Plato that the *Republic* was "a pattern laid up in heaven, but hardly to be copied on earth." But, Barker continued, "The old practical bent was not extinguished; in extreme old age, in a spirit of kindly tolerance and half-humorous sadness . . . he wrote the *Laws.*" Barker saw the *Laws* as "adhering firmly to the ideal of the *Republic*," but, reflecting Plato's practical disappointment, building a state on a lower, more attainable level.[2] Barker then went on to discuss thoroughly the theoretical relationships between those two works and between those and the rest of Plato's works.

Other scholars have noted the biographical link between Plato's two works and, like Barker, have used additional approaches to encourage the reader not to be satisfied by a biographical explanation alone. For example, Glenn Morrow used Plato's letters as one set of evidence to show both the personal and theoretical link among the ideas of Plato in the *Republic,* his advice to Sicily, and his views in the *Laws.*[3] Morrow emphasized a difference between the young Plato of the *Republic* and the older Plato by citing the advice given to Sicily in Plato's *Seventh Letter:* that Sicily should be returned to its traditional constitution, which

2. Ernest Barker, *The Political Thought of Plato and Aristotle* (New York: Dover Publications, 1959), pp. 63-64.

3. Glenn R. Morrow, "Plato and The Rule of Law" in *Plato,* ed. Gregory Vlastos, (Garden City, N. Y. : Doubleday, 1971), pp. 144-165.

was a government of laws, and not to the philosopher king of the *Republic*.[4] However, Morrow did not stop at the practical advice in Plato's letters, perhaps because he recognized that some authorities question the authenticity of the letters and because he was seeking a solid theoretical link among the major works of Plato. Morrow analyzed the practical procedures supplied by Plato in the *Laws* for insuring the administration and enforcement of rule of law for all members of the polity. He showed similarities and differences between the procedures developed in the *Laws* and the practices of Athens. He contrasted the practical mechanisms of the *Laws* and the ideals of the *Republic* and concluded:

> It may be that the younger Plato did not see, as clearly as the Plato of the *Laws,* the dangers of absolutism, or the difficulty of finding that union of wisdom and integrity required for the exercise of *imperium legibus solutum*.[5]

Morrow quoted from Plato's *Laws* to show that Plato recognized his own youthful failing. Plato wrote:

> A state in which the law is subject and without authority is ripe for destruction; but when the law is sovereign over the rulers, and the rulers servants of the law, then, as I see it, the state is secure.[6]

Plato continued: "a man's vision is at its dullest in his youth and keenest in his old age."[7]

Strauss, however, agreeing that there are questions about the authenticity of Plato's letters and following his individual method of textual interpretation, excludes the biographical link to present his interpretation of the meaning of Plato's works. Strauss stressed the unity of Plato's theoretical contribution: "Plato brings the regime of the *Laws* around by degrees to the regime of the *Republic*. Having arrived at the end of the *Laws,* we must return to the beginning of the *Republic*."[8]

4. L. A. Post, ed., *Thirteen Epistles of Plato,* (Oxford: Clarendon Press, 1965), pp. 56-114.
5. Morrow, "Law," p. 164.
6. Morrow, "Law," pp. 164-165 quoting from Plato, *Laws,* in *The Dialogues of Plato,* vol. V, ed. B. Jowett (Oxford: Oxford University Press, 1892) 715-D, p. 98.
7. Morrow, "Law," p. 165; Plato, *Laws,* 715D.
8. Leo Strauss, "Plato," in Leo Strauss and Joseph Cropsey, *History of Political Philosophy* (Chicago: Rand McNally & Co., 1972), p. 61.

The footnotes for Strauss's interpretation reflect his concept of appropriate data for the interpreter. His notes and suggestions for additional readings include only the works of Plato and, where comparison is drawn to Aristotle, the original works of Aristotle.[9]

While Strauss has produced some interesting findings, other interpretations, whether they share Strauss's thesis of unity in Plato's work or reject it,[10] seem more satisfactory. Works that creatively link a biographical approach to other interpretative approaches, such as Barker's and Morrow's, give additional evidence of the philosopher's intent and thus give the reader a better basis for judging the findings.

Our discussion of the relationship between the *Laws* and the *Republic* illustrates the positive contribution a biographical approach can make when it is incorporated wisely with other approaches to theory.

The autobiography has also been used as a vehicle for interpreting political thought. As in any other biographical approach to theory, autobiography rests to some extent on the assumption that the person and the work are merely two different versions of the same thing: the personality of the writer. There may be some political thinkers whose personal life histories might not lead to a heightened appreciation of their political thought. In most instances, however, autobiographical data will provide an understanding of the mental patterns, the images, and the personality that appear in the written work. Better understanding of the intent of the writer usually can be gained from autobiographical works.[11] In the 18th century, Rousseau used his autobiography, entitled *Confessions*,[12] to reveal much about his personality and its oneness with his work. Perhaps it is this book that has led so many later interpreters to put a heavy emphasis on the biographical approach when dealing with Rousseau's theory.

9. Strauss, "Plato," pp.61-63.

10. For agreement on conclusions but different method, see, Paul Shorey, *The Unity of Plato's Thought* (Chicago: University of Chicago Press, 1903, reproduced 1960).

11. The autobiographical approach has become an important vehicle for development of Black political thought among contemporary Black political writers. Examples are the writings of the nationalist leaders of Africa, for example, Nkrumah and those of recent American Black leaders such as Malcom X. In the 19th century, Frederick Douglass, a freed American slave who became an eminent writer, abolitionist, adviser to presidents, and diplomatic representative of the United States, used the autobiographical vehicle for conveying his political thought. Frederick Douglass, *Life and Times of Frederick Douglass* (New York: Macmillan Co., 1962, reprinted from the revised edition of 1892). St. Augustine also used his autobiography, *Confessions*, as a means of presenting his theoretical positions in the early 5th century. Whitney J. Oates, ed., *Basic Writings of St. Augustine* (New York: Random House, 1948).

12. Jean Jacques Rousseau, *Confessions*, trans. John Grant (New York: Dutton, 1931).

Judith Shklar, who relied heavily on close textual analysis for her contemporary interpretation of Rousseau's thought, also added a judicious handling of a biographical approach. In so doing, she looked into Rousseau's life through many sources, including his *Confessions*. She underlined the link between Rousseau, his life, his work and his autobiography, which is an important part of his work.[13] In her study, Shklar blended her approaches to increase understanding of Rousseau. Her use of biographical data was restrained and prudent. Other interpreters who have attempted to use biographical data to understand Rousseau's thought have not always avoided the biggest pitfall of the approach; they have carried biography to excess, so that biography replaced theoretical study of the issues raised.

A look at the relationship between *Emile* and Rousseau's own life is relevant here. Rousseau admitted to having fathered five illegitimate children and also admitted that he abandoned all of them. And yet he is the author of *Emile,* a great, creative approach to education for children.[14] While Rousseau's behavior toward his children does not affect the logic of *Emile,* some interpreters, seeing personality and theoretical output as inseparably linked, have used such a problematic linkage to assess the value of the theory. One way around the problem is to accept each element—theory and life—as fact and proceed judiciously with the attempt to understand what Rousseau's troubled but creative mind had to convey to us. This approach involves accepting the contribution of biography without allowing it to be a substitute for real consideration of the theory.

Guarding against biography's excesses is neither an excuse nor a call for its exclusion from the approaches used in the discipline. In fact, when an interpreter picks out the important, relevant pieces from the life of the theorist and knows how to use them to gain insight into the meaning of a theoretical text, biography becomes a very valuable aid to interpretation. For example, biography can have the benefit of preventing erroneous interpretations by offering data from life against which

13. Judith N. Shklar, *Men and Citizens* (Cambridge: At the University Press, 1969), p. 219.
14. Jean Jacques Rousseau, *Emile,* trans. Barbara Foxley (New York: Dutton, 1948). LeMaitre says that the position taken by an interpreter on the issue of *Emile* v. Rousseau's conduct toward his own children depends on whether the interpreter is "well-or ill-disposed" toward Rousseau. Jules LeMaitre, *J. J. Rousseau* (Port Washington, New York: Kennikat Press, 1968), p. 220. Addtional information on this controversy can be found in Lester G. Crocker, *Jean Jacques Rousseau: The Quest (1712-1758)* (New York: Macmillan Co., 1968), pp. 178-180.

to check interpretative insights gained through other approaches.[15] Peter Laslett's 20th-century studies of the works of John Locke illustrate this and several other points.

John Locke,[16] who lived in the 17th century, was a political writer and an involved partisan during an era of major English constitutional development. He called for recognition that government rested on the consent of the governed and argued that denial of natural rights would be grounds for sensible revolution to replace the offending administration. "Lockean" arguments provided the climate for revolutionary thought in the American colonies; therefore, they have come down to our generation as truisms. Recently, scholars have turned to serious study of the original Locke to gain greater insight into his contributions to the development of Western constitutionalism.[17]

Laslett depended heavily on close textual analysis for the development of his interpretation of Locke's *Two Treatises*.[18] However, he did not stop with the text. By using knowledge of the personality and life of John Locke, the associations Locke made and kept over the years, the books in Locke's library, the literary and political issues of the day, in addition to the careful study of the texts, Laslett provided new insight into Locke's political thought. For example, knowledge of John Locke's travel, his correspondence, his library holdings, and his notebooks helps refute a common mistake in interpreting his political thought. It had long been held by some that Locke wrote primarily to refute Hobbes' pessimistic theory. By showing that Locke addressed Sir Robert Filmer's divine right, patriarchal theory, not Hobbes' *Leviathan,* Laslett emphasized the actual intellectual and historical impact of Locke's political advice. Specifically, Laslett drew attention to Locke's contribution to consent-based theories of government and to the development of Western constitutionalism.[19]

Further, Laslett's use of multiple approaches showed that, contrary to common opinion, the *Second Treatise* was written in 1679-80, before

15. Robert Orr makes some of the same general points raised here about the assets of intellectual biography in the history of ideas. Orr also warns that the user must avoid telling more about himself than about the ideas under study. Robert R. Orr, "Intellectual Biography as a Form of the History of Ideas," *Interpretation* 4, no. 2 (Winter 1972) : 98-106.

16. Maurice Cranston, *John Locke: A Biography* (New York: Macmillan Co., 1957).

17. John Dunn, "The Politics of Locke in England and America in the Eighteenth Century," in *John Locke: Problems and Perspectives,* ed. John Yolton (Cambridge: At the University Press, 1969), pp. 45-80.

18. Peter Laslett, ed., *John Locke's Two Treatises of Government* (New York: New American Library, 1965).

19. Laslett, *Two Treatises,* pp. 80-105.

the *First Treatise*. It had been held that the treatises were written in the order in which they were numbered: the first written first and the second after the completion of the first. It had also been assumed that the *Second Treatise* was a product of 1689-90, whereas Laslett's research proved that the *Second Treatise* had been written a full decade before its publication.[20]

At first glance, all of the above might appear to be academic paper pushing and date chasing. However, there is real significance in the findings produced by the multiple approaches used by Laslett. Based on these findings, we must revise our judgment about Locke's work and about what he was trying to say and do. A brief review of the highlights of the decade from 1680 to 1690 in England is helpful. Charles II was king. His monarchical style and political positions, pro-French and pro-Roman Catholic, were very unpopular with the party to which Locke and his political friends and mentors subscribed, the Whigs. Further, the fact that Charles lacked a legitimate heir made his Roman Catholic brother, James, heir to the throne. James II came to the throne in 1685 and produced a Roman Catholic son in 1688, a birth that cemented a Catholic dynastic line for formerly Protestant-ruled England. This series of events was exactly what Locke and his fellow believers had feared. They were joined in 1688 by the Tories, former supporters of the king, in offering the throne to James's Protestant, adult daughter, Mary, and her Dutch husband, William of Orange. In 1688, by prior "invitation" from responsible Englishmen, William invaded England and James II fled. William and Mary became rulers over England and Scotland.

Placing Laslett's evidence in that lamentably brief historical sketch allows us to see the significance of his detective work. The 1679 monarchical rule of Charles II clearly violated the principles of natural law and constitutional government outlined by Locke in the *Second Treatise*. Further, the treatise provided for sensible revolution to replace such rulers. For years, the assumption had been that Locke simply jumped on the bandwagon in 1689 and wrote the treatise as a justification for a revolution that had already taken place in 1688. If the *Second Treatise* was written in 1679-80, then it was not a justification for the "revolution" of 1688. It was, indeed, a call for revolution. This knowledge causes a major change in perspective on the work.[21] Laslett's findings

20. Laslett, *Two Treatises*, pp. 60-79.
21. Laslett, *Two Treatises*, p. 60.

give new insights to passages whose meaning or significance we might have taken for granted, given our "understanding" of the history of the work. Indeed, the earlier view of the work may have caused readers to place too great an emphasis on the practical aspect of Locke and on his advice about a revolutionary situation of his own time. While the practical was important to Locke, he also had theoretical interests. Dante Germino built on Laslett's findings to suggest that we can learn much when we move beyond the view that Locke's treatises are a justification for a particular revolution. Rather, if we see Locke's treatises as an attempt "to bring the governments of the world before the bar of reason," we will be able to scrutinize the Lockean tradition, including the Lockean concept of revolution, by Locke's own standards.[22]

Use of Locke's theoretical standard of assessing all governments at the "bar of reason" encourages reconsideration of the American social contract, the current constitutional governmental structure, and contemporary liberal policies. Further, Locke's standards permit citizens to reassert a revolutionary heritage. That heritage insists that government must be rational and just in its actions or face dissolution at the hands of the citizens. Such a reading of Locke allows his writings to be used as critical tools for assessing the worth even of the governments that claim to be based on Lockean theories of consent.[23]

Another contribution of the biographical study of Locke is the insight it gives into the mystery of why he was reluctant to acknowledge the authorship of the two treatises. Laslett showed that only in Locke's final will do we get "direct proof" that he wrote the treatises. Even though it was popularly known among intellectuals that he had written the treatises, he continued to conceal his authorship in a way that Laslett labeled abnormal and obsessive.[24] While recognizing the political reasons for Locke's caution, Laslett also attributed this behavior to a "peculiarity" in Locke's personality, which Laslett terms ambivalence: Locke wanted his books published, but feared criticism. "Criticism always disturbed him deeply, which must be one of the reasons for his refusing to acknowledge books which he knew would be controversial."[25]

22. Dante Germino, *Modern Western Political Thought* (Chicago: Rand McNally & Co., 1972), p. 127.
23. Germino, *Modern Thought*, p. 120.
24. Laslett, *Two Treatises*, pp. 17-18.
25. Laslett, *Two Treatises*, p. 51.

Some interpreters use biographical data on Locke to conclude that he deliberately tried to shield his message in an "inconsistent and obscure" text. Laslett used textual analysis of Locke's various editions and biographical study to conclude that despite Locke's fear of criticism, he was anxious to leave his ideas to posterity accurately and clearly. Laslett showed that Locke wanted his ideas left to the ages under his own name, even if he was, indeed, reluctant to acknowledge his authorship of those controversial views during his lifetime.[26] Laslett supported his conclusions by showing the differences between Locke's manuscript and the first edition printed in 1690 and by citing the pages of corrections, which were written in Locke's own hand, for the 1694 version of the two treatises.[27]

Laslett's use of biographical data, when added to his analysis of Locke's texts and his historical perspective, make his work a good example of the positive values to be gained from a combination of approaches to theory. Laslett's combination allows Locke's thoughts to be related to his actions as a person, an intellectual, and a politican and to the constitutional heritage often identified with his name. Such a combination contributes to the critical and constructive missions of political theory through a better understanding of the theorist's intent and a fuller probing of the theory's implications.

PSYCHOLOGICAL APPROACH Closely related to the biographical approach, in fact really a subcategory of it, is the psychological approach to the political thinker. While the straight biographical approach deals with some aspects of the theorist's psyche, the psychological approach applies the methods of psychology and psychiatry to the thinker. It investigates the life and creative processes to reconstruct the stages in the creation of thought.[28] In some instances, the psychological approach sees the theoretical product as the author's way of working out his mental problems or neuroses: the work is a symptom through which one can understand the illness of the thinker.

26. Laslett, *Two Treatises*, p. 24. For another view, see William Bluhm, *Theories of the Political System* (Englewood Cliffs, N.J.: Prentice Hall, 1965), pp. 302-314.
27. Laslett, *Two Treatises*, pp. 15-17.
28. Sheldon Norman Grebstein, *Perspectives in Contemporary Criticism* (New York: Harper & Row, 1968), p. 239.

Rousseau, who fascinates those with a biographical inclination, also attracts interpreters who use a psychological framework. William H. Blanchard, a contemporary psychological interpreter of Rousseau, said:

> It has seemed more important to show the relationship between his life and his politics than to give further examples of his political ideas. I have attempted to trace the evolution of Rousseau's childhood sado-masochism to the moral foundation for his adult personality. I have taken this particular life as a basis for demonstrating the relationship between personal and political belief.[29]

As is clear in Blanchard's description, the psychological approach rests on the theories about the human psyche found among the various schools of psychiatry and psychology. It uses those theories to gain greater insight into the thought produced by the psyche of the great philosopher.

Erik Erikson, a contemporary scholar, analyst, and writer on human psychological development, has made a tremendous impact on his field through his extension of Freud's ideas. He has presented new ways of looking at man's life pattern, emphasizing that life is a series of stages, all of which contribute toward either a person's mental health or his mental illness. Erikson has also shown that while some people might be debilitated by their inner conflicts, others are actually driven by these conflicts to superhuman efforts.

Using his approach to psychoanalysis, Erikson wrote a book about Martin Luther,[30] the 16th-century Reformation leader.

Erikson on Luther, like the textual analyst on Luther, was looking for what the writer really meant; but the difference lies in the kind of meaning being sought. Erikson was looking for psychological truth which the psychoanalytic method would permit him to approximate. Erikson viewed the climate of Luther's times, using an angle different from that of other approaches. He looked for the "unconscious tendency" which he defined as "ideology":

---

29. William H. Blanchard, *Rousseau and the Spirit of Revolt: A Psychological Study* (Ann Arbor, Michigan: University of Michigan Press, 1967), pp. xi-xii. Blanchard's study cites several other psychological studies of Rousseau which may be of interest to the student.
30. Erik Erikson, *Young Man Luther* (New York: W. W. Norton, 1958), p. 206.

the tendency at a given time to make facts amenable to
ideas, and ideas to facts, in order to create a world image
convincing enough to support the collective and the individual sense of identification.[31]

In *Young Man Luther,* Erikson used primarily psychiatric methods
to answer some questions about the thinker and his thoughts which
no other approaches considered. Erikson pointed out the important psychological crises that mold men. He showed Luther's failure to solve
adequately his personal identity crisis, especially as related to his strong-
willed father, Hans. Erikson argued that Martin's identity crisis was reflected in his theological thought and from there into his social, political
and economic thought and adult leadership role.

Erikson also used Martin Luther's unresolved personality crisis to
explain the peculiarity of Luther's being a revolutionary in religion but
a reactionary in politics. This peculiarity is marked by Luther's extension
of the commandment "Honor thy father" to the relationship between
prince and subject.[32] It can be seen most conspicuously in Luther's reaction to the uprising of peasants in some German states in 1524-25.
When the peasants rebelled, largely over a variety of economic issues,
many of the dissidents thought Luther would support them against the
princes. To their chagrin, Luther wrote a stingingly critical pamphlet in
which he labeled the peasants as a "robbing and murdering horde."
He said a rebel was outside the protection of the law and urged opponents of the insurrection to use any means to put the rebellion down,
assuring reward in heaven for such vigilance. One passage in Luther's
unrestrained diatribe was of particular interest to Erikson:

A rebel is not worth answering with arguments, for he does
not accept them. The answer for such mouths is a fist that
brings blood from the nose.[33]

Erikson said that Martin Luther's reaction to the peasant uprising is identical to that which his father, Hans, had used to put down rebellion in

31. Erikson, *Luther,* p. 22.
32. Erikson, *Luther,* pp. 231-239.
33. Martin Luther, "Against the Robbing and Murdering Horde," in *The Works of Martin Luther,* ed. H. E. Jacobs (Philadelphia: Muhlenberg Press, 1915-1932), 4: 247-254.

his son. Erikson commented about the passage: "Do we hear Hans, beating the residue of a stubborn peasant out of his son?"[34] Erikson concluded that Luther developed a reactionary political theory which reflected his father and was indicative of Martin's unresolved identity crisis.

There are many criticisms of the psychological approach to political theory in general and to Erikson's approach to Luther in particular. Erikson foresaw that one criticism of the psychological approach would be the lack of hard, that is, immediate and personal psychoanalytical evidence and he tried to counter it:

> But a clinician's training permits, and in fact forces, him to recognize major trends even where the facts are not all available . . . and he must be able to sift even questionable sources in such a way that a coherent predictive hypothesis emerges.[35]

Roland Bainton did not accept Erikson's explanation in Luther's case.[36] He questioned the accuracy of Erikson's evidence. He claimed Erikson's sources were "the jottings of inaccurate student note-takers" and material gathered from Luther's contemporary critics. Bainton recognized as more reliable Luther's own texts put into a proper historical and biographical framework.

Bainton's main criticism, however, was leveled against what he felt were the excesses of the psychological approach. Bainton conceded that the approach provided insight into certain aspects of Luther's thought, such as his views on sex and on the Peasant War. But Bainton objected to the fact that:

> Luther's theological development is portrayed in terms of his struggle to achieve independence of his parents that he might be a person in his own right. His theology was sometimes a projection of this struggle upon the cosmos, sometimes a rationalization, and sometimes a device for solving a personal problem.[37]

34. Erikson, *Luther*, p. 236.
35. Erikson, *Luther*, p. 50.
36. R. H. Bainton, "Luther: A Psychiatric Portrait," review of *Young Man Luther* by Erik Erikson, *The Yale Review* (Spring 1959): 409. For Bainton's own approach see his *Here I Stand* (New York: New American Library, 1950).
37. Bainton, "Luther," p. 406.

Bainton felt Luther's theoretical development might have been the same if he had been orphaned in infancy. And the psychological approach could not prove otherwise.

These examples and criticisms, selected to illustrate uses of the psychological approach, lead to the conclusion that if pushed too far, the psychological approach will produce over-simplification and stereotypes of theory rather than a clearer understanding of political thought and the people who produce it.

When used with care and balance, both the psychological and biographical approaches can provide insight into theory and theorists, politics and politicians. They certainly help us understand the intent of the philosopher. Lastly they can help us avoid the pitfall of considering theory in a vacuum as if there were not a human mind and personality as the ultimate source of the work.

Chapter 4   The Environment of Thought

The full environment of thought is approached through two avenues: the historical and the ideological. While these two approaches will be isolated here for analysis, they are, in reality, often closely related and integrated with each other and with the other approaches. The historical approach will be presented first. Then several examples of ideological interpretation will be considered.

THE HISTORICAL APPROACH The historical approach seeks to give a time and space orientation to the political thinker and his or her work; hence it is the most ambitious of all the approaches. Everything is relevant: the text itself, the author's biography, and the cultural, social and economic environment of the time when the work was written. Also relevant is all prior history of thought and events.

Since we have already examined textual, biographical and psychological approaches, we will not repeat them here, even though a historical approach would include them to some extent. Also, we will omit a discussion of the influence of the economic environment because it is treated later, albeit with a particular ideological orientation.

Some facets of the historical approach can be illustrated by a familiar author and a work most students have encountered in some manner: Thomas More's *Utopia*.[1] We will become further acquainted with More through a contemporary, Renaissance scholar, J. H. Hexter. Hexter starts with textual analysis,[2] recognizing all of the problems of the approach. He also makes use of biography but goes much further, adding other elements to produce a historical approach. He tries to discover the chronology of the writing of *Utopia* through careful correlation of the text with the historical events of the day, with the life of More, and in the context of the development of political thought. (For example, he refers to Plato's influence on More.) Hexter acts like a historical detective on the trail of Sir Thomas More to gain fuller meaning of the ideas in *Utopia*.

For example, Hexter studied a section of *Utopia*, referred to as the "Dialogue of Counsel,"[3] in which More used himself as one of the characters involved in the dialogue. Interpreters have found difficulty in unraveling More's beliefs on the issues raised there. It is unclear in the dialogue whether More put his personal views under his own name or in the mouth of Hythloday, the other conversationalist. The issue under discussion was whether a Christian humanist should become involved in the morally ambivalent business of politics. The character "More" said:

> You must not therefore abandon the commonwealth. . . .
> You must strive to guide policy indirectly, so that you make
> the best of things, and what you cannot turn to good, you
> can at least make less bad.[4]

1. J. H. Hexter, *More's Utopia: The Biography of an Idea* (New York: Harper and Row, Harper Torchbooks, 1965). Sir Thomas More was born in 1478 and lived a very full personal, intellectual, religious, and political life until he was beheaded on July 6, 1535, by King Henry VIII. Despite More's criticism of some of the institutional expressions of both church and state in Europe, the basic moral and religious beliefs of Roman Catholicism permeated his thought.

2. Hexter, *Utopia*, pp. 161-165.

3. Hexter, *Utopia*, pp. 98-156.

4. Thomas More, *Utopia*, ed. H. V. S. Ogden (New York: Appleton-Century-Crofts, 1949), p. 23.

Hythloday responded:

> I do not understand what you mean. . . . He [the political
> adviser] will either be corrupted himself by his col-
> leagues, or, if he remains sound and innocent, he will
> be blamed for the folly and knavery of others. He is far
> from being able to mend matters by guiding policy indi-
> rectly![5]

Did More subscribe to the views of Hythloday, the other conversationalist, who opposed political participation? Did More believe, as the
character called More says, that there is an obligation to participate to
make politics less evil? Hexter tried to solve the puzzle about More's
recommendations on political participation.

Hexter observed that the arguments are so well balanced in the text
that it is necessary "to look elsewhere. . . ; we must examine the course
of More's own career around this time."[6] In doing so, Hexter discussed
the politics of the day and related More's own political life to that context.
From all of the biographical and historical evidence he amassed, Hexter
concluded that at the time More wrote the "Dialogue of Counsel" he
did not subscribe to the ideas he put into the mouth of the character
More in *Utopia*. Hexter saw More as playing the devil's advocate while
himself subscribing to the views he had Hythloday express in the book.
Hexter argued that More changed his views in the period between his
writing of the controversial "Dialogue" passages in 1516 and his entry
into royal service in 1518.[7] The historian then showed aspects of the
political scene which changed during the interim that made More's entry
into politics more bearable for him.

Fuller understanding of More's discussion in the dialogue is not just
"historically interesting"; it is helpful to modern students of politics. The

5. More, *Utopia*, p. 24.
6. Hexter, *Utopia*, p. 132.
7. Hexter, *Utopia*, pp. 135-155. Hexter's view is not a universally shared conclusion.
For example contrast W. E. Campbell, *Erasmus, Tyndale and More* (Milwaukee: Bruce Publishing Co., 1930), especially p. 87, and R. W. Chambers, *Thomas More* (New York: Harcourt
Brace, 1935). For example, look at Campbell's textual approach to the chapter. He argued
that More specifically chose the dialogue form becuse it, more than any other literary form,
permitted the author to be forthright about his positions in a published text. Note that Campbell's textual analysis was enriched by a historical perspective to More's text. That is, he
told the reader the uses of various literary forms in the culture of the time and, on the
basis of that historical, as well as textual, knowledge, drew his conclusion.

dialogue permits us to see the timeless problems for moral individuals in the morally ambivalent world of politics. In an age when political cynicism is on the rise, students of politics can profit by looking at political involvement from More's moral perspective. Hexter's findings prod us to identify and pursue changes necessary to reduce cynicism and increase political participation.

Study of changes in the meaning of basic concepts in various eras is one of the valuable contributions made to the discipline of political theory by the historical approach. Ernst Cassirer, a German scholar of the early 20th century, studied the very different meanings that the word "nature" had for persons in different periods. Cassirer contrasted the meaning of "nature" in the medieval era, in the 16th-century Renaissance, and in the 18th-century Enlightenment. Cassirer showed that for the medieval thinker "the extent of natural knowledge is not determined by the object but by its origin. . . ."[8] Nature was seen as a complementary, but secondary, part of reality. For the medieval thinker the supernatural, known through revelation, was superior to nature and was not opposed to the natural but, rather, in harmony with it.

Cassirer contrasted the medieval view with the Renaissance definition of nature to show that change in the basic concept of nature was part of a general cultural change that was essential for the development of science and philosophy as we know them in modern times. Of the Renaissance definition, Cassirer said:

> Its basic tendency can be expressed in the formula that the true essence of nature is not to be sought in the realm of the created, but in that of the creative process. . . . the dualism between creator and creation is thus abolished. . . .[9]

Seeing nature in a new light allowed the emergence of new attitudes about the use of the human mind to discover principles. Changed attitudes and associated cultural developments liberated the human mind, allowing it to follow new paths of discovery in all areas of human experience, including political thought. Cassirer's work makes us aware of the inaccuracies we would introduce if in reading medieval theorists we gave

8. Ernst Cassirer, *Philosophy of the Enlightenment* (Boston: Beacon Press, 1955), pp. 39-40.
9. Cassirer, *Enlightenment,* p. 44.

our definition to their use of the concept of nature. Further, Cassirer's discussion serves as a reminder that some ideas of the past changed over time with a tremendous impact on political thought and practice. Our own world view is also changing. Recognition of concepts that currently *are* changing directs attention to ideas that *should* change in order to produce a desirable world.[10]

Ernst Cassirer has been an important inspiration for those who aspire to good historical interpretation of political thought. Peter Gay, a contemporary interpreter who specializes in the Enlightenment, has acknowledged that he owes his greatest intellectual debt to the writings of Ernst Cassirer in both philosophy and intellectual history.[11] Peter Gay's work is a good example of the historical approach.

In his books on the Enlightenment, he looked at the culture of that era in terms of the broad movements in thought that influenced the political theorist and, in turn, were influenced by him. He attempted to put the thought of that era and the great thinkers of that period into the context of the time and of the prior development of Western culture. His elaborate bibliographic essays add substantially to the usefulness of his works. Gay's historical approach is seen very clearly in his overview of the era, *The Enlightenment: An Interpretation*. A more focused illustration is his study of Voltaire, the 18th-century intellectual who, for some, became "a symbol of his age."[12] In the preface to the 1961 edition of his book on Voltaire, Gay described it as being in the tradition of "the social history of ideas." He elaborated:

> This history aims at comprehending ideas in all their dimensions without reducing them to mere products of circumstance, to track down their intellectual, psychological, social origins, their interplay with other ideas past and present, their logic, their function, their results and their beauty.[13]

10. Consider the evolution of political science from its early civic-training preoccupation to its legalistic, historic, descriptive orientation, to its policy science predisposition, to its behaviorial approach and—perhaps as some suggest—into its current "post behaviorial" stance. See, David Easton, "The New Revolution in Political Science," *The American Political Science Review* 63 (December 1969): 1051-1061.

11. Peter Gay, *The Enlightenment: An Interpretation* (New York: Vintage Books, 1968), p. 423.

12. Peter Gay, *Voltaire's Politics* (New York: Vintage Books, 1965), p. 10.

13. Gay, *Voltaire's Politics*, p. viii.

Gay's approach attempted to correct other interpretations that failed to see Voltaire in the broad framework adopted by Gay. He argued that approaches that were not as complete made Voltaire a "victim of cliches."

Gay asserted that Voltaire was a realist. In accordance with the rules of true historical interpretation, Gay documented his thesis "by anchoring his [Voltaire's] political writings firmly in the ground of his society, his experience, and the history of his century."[14] Gay's work can be seen as more than a mere rescuing of Voltaire's reputation; it also gives the reader insight into the phenomenon of political change through the study of Voltaire's reform program.[15]

Despite the broadness of the historical approach, difficulties arise even in this form of interpretation. One problem is the unattainable ideal toward which it aspires. No scholar can acquire knowledge of the *full* context of the writings of a political philosopher because the facts of such a full context do not exist for the attaining. Obviously, in his *Confessions* Rousseau thought he was giving this background; but Rousseau did not understand his subconscious well enough to grapple fully with some of the unconscious aspects of his life that found their way into his works. Neither was he fully aware of the social assumptions of his own time which he accepted without thought. Interpreters themselves are not fully aware of the socialized values of their times and locations and the impact of these on their own reading of political philosophy.

Another criticism of the historical approach is that knowledge of the environment that produced a work does not help in assessing the value of the theory. David Easton, a contemporary political scientist, criticized traditional political theory for looking too much at the origins of thought. Easton wanted the field to judge critically the fitness of each major political theory as a model for the political future.[16]

The historical approach, then, is inclusive but not perfect.

14. Gay, *Voltaire's Politics*, p. xi.

15. Gay, *Voltaire's Politics*, pp. 334-340.

16. David Easton, *The Political System* (New York: Knopf, 1953), pp. 219-266. Two short articles on the historical approach to ideas are: B. A. Haddock, "The History of Ideas and the Study of Politics," *Political Theory* 2, no. 4 (1974) : 420-432, and J. D. Hubert, "Random Reflections on Literary History and Textual Criticism," *New Literary History* 2, no. 1 (1971): 163-173.

THE IDEOLOGICAL APPROACH This section will provide a separate study of a few interpreters with explicit "ideological" preferences: Marxist, Conservative, New Left, Black Power. This method of presentation will help readers see how different emphases and proportions can emerge when textual, biographical, psychological and historical approaches are combined with an ideological focus.

This section runs the risk of creating two misconceptions. First, it might seem to imply that the works of all of the writers discussed here are of equal profundity. Second, it might appear to label as "ideologues" all of the interpreters used as examples. Neither is the case. Examples were chosen based on their being the clearest and most relevant ways of illustrating the points raised. Also, as the material unfolds, it will be clear that the label "ideologue" would be inappropriate for many of our examples.

The reader must constantly bear in mind that each of the approaches discussed in this book should in use be integrated with the other approaches. As are the other approaches, the ideological is identified and discussed here separately. Such attention highlights the enriching variety of interpretations in political philosophy. Another reason for treating the "ideological approach" as a separate category is the multiplicity of issues involved.

Ideology, as a concept, had a long historical development. As a result of its evolution, there are several meanings for the concept. In its original sense, *ideology* had positive connotations of ridding the world of prejudices and superstitions that were contrary to reason.[17] Later history of the concept—as used by Napoleon, as treated by Marx and Mannheim, and as used by the Americans against the theoretical foundations of Stalin's Russia and Hitler's Germany—gave a negative connotation to the word.[18]

As we said in chapter 1, no human being is totally lacking in political preferences; therefore, political philosophy as the "disinterested search for knowledge about the good state and good society"[19] is a worthy, but impossible, dream. Further, we recalled Marx's view that all non-Marxian philosophy was ideology. Either of these two points could lead

---

17. George Lichtheim, *The Concept of Ideology* (New York: Random House, 1967), p.9.

18. James A. Gould and Willis H. Truitt, eds., *Political Ideologies* (New York: Macmillan Co., 1973).

19. Andrew Hacker, *Political Theory* (New York: Macmillan Co., 1961), p. 5.

to an argument for not treating the ideological approach separately. This argument would hold that the ideology of the interpreter is always intertwined with whatever interpretive approach he chooses, be it textual, biographical, psychological or historical. The argument suggests that the label "ideological interpreter" refers only to someone who is more explicit and consistent in his or her preferred orientation to political ideas than someone who is not so labeled. Self-identified "ideological interpretaters" argue that *all other* students of political theory are also ideological interpreters even though they may be unconscious of the fact or may disavow the label.

The label "ideological interpreter" could also be used to indicate a scholar who asserts that no philosophical text can be divorced from the environment in which the idea system arose. While acknowledging that the philosopher probably intended to be "disinterested," some ideological interpreters will not stop at a philosopher's explicit intent. They will seek further clues to the meaning of a theory through study of ideas implicit in the thought, ideas which are the result of the prevailing social, economic, political, and philosophical environment of the theorist.

In still another sense, the word *ideology* is used to label those doctrines that seek to gain emotive support and commit their followers to political action. In this sense, ideology interprets and evaluates all ideas and events in terms of its own formula in order to structure a view of the world, prescribe beliefs and actions, and give personal identification with a political movement to the follower.[20] In this last sense of the term "ideological approach," the "ideologues" apply their own ideological systems as standards against which to discuss other models of politics, to enshrine ideas with which they agree, and to damn those which challenge their formulas.

Marxist development of the ideas of Karl Marx will illustrate the movement from profound political theory to an ideological approach. The focus will be on the impact of Marxist ideologues as they turned Marx's ideas into formulas, rather than continuing Marx's own profound search for truths about politics. This exercise will illustrate a difference between political philosophy and ideology: the Marxist ideologues' desire for certainty (ideas as formulas) contrasts well with Marx's own desire for answers to basic questions about human behavior. Some would assert,

20. Reo M. Christenson, *Ideologies & Modern Politics* (New York: Dodd, Mead, & Co., 1971), pp. 14-18.

however, that despite Marx's own desire to deal "scientifically" with perennial questions he was, like other theorists, part of a total environment that had an impact on his thought. In other words, some 20th-century interpreters find ideas implicit in Marx's thought that he might not have explicitly intended.

MARXISM Marxism has it roots in the career of the thinker whose name it bears, Karl Marx. Marxism, however, is not the same as Marx's own theoretical output. This section will show some of the sources of the differences between Marx and Marxism.

Marx, the son of a German lawyer, became a landmark as he developed his incisive critical thought, linking, qualifying, and/or rejecting many strains of theory.[21] He was a critic of his contemporary political world and of the philosophical systems that, he thought, gave support to it. His critical system rejected the view that philosophy could not bridge the gap between that which *is* and that which *ought to be*. He sought a unity of theory and practice. He rejected political thought based on atomic, isolated individualism in favor of a view of man as a more social being.[22]

Marx's system was based on his assertion that capitalism would be transcended and classless Communism would emerge through the vehicle of a class-conscious, revolutionary proletariat. The proletarian revolution would produce "true democracy" or Communism, which would involve "the positive abolition of private property, of human alienation . . . the return of man to himself as a social, i.e., really human, being. . . ."[23]

Marx called the idea system of the ruling class and the political thought of the age "ideology." He asserted that ideology was distorted thought or false consciousness. Under capitalism, ideologists rationalized and justified rule by the bourgeoisie. Marx argued that false consciousness could not disappear until "critical," "objective," or "scientific" thinkers/activitists comprehended reality and thereby, given Marx's view about the unity of theory and practice, brought about a new reality.

21. M. Djilas, *The Unperfect Society: Beyond the New Class* (New York: Harcourt, Brace, & World, 1969), pp. 41-43.

22. Shlomo Avineri, *The Social and Political Thought of Karl Marx* (Cambridge: At the University Press, 1971), chap. 1.

23. Karl Marx, *Early Writings*, quoted in Avineri, *Marx*, p. 89.

Many factors contributed to the rise of "Marxism" as an interpretation of Marx. One factor was Marx's own refusal to "recognize the dilemma . . . that though consciousness is conditioned by existence, it can also rise above existence and become a means of transcending alienation. . . ."[24] A second important factor was the failure of the proletariat to emerge as a worldwide revolutionary force.[25] The net result was that "Marxist" interpreters arose within the supporting Marxist social movement. They tried to cope with unresolved issues in Marx's theory. In the process of adapting or defending Marx's thought in a changing world, some Marxist interpreters destroyed the coherence of Marx's thought. They abandoned his assumptions and turned that which remained into an ideology.[26] The Marxist movement was splintered into ideological "schools," each of which sought to apply the proper formula to gain the "correct meaning" of Marx in order to find the truth about politics. The Marxist feuds often took on the climate of a schism within a religion and gave rise to further splits within the supporting social movement. Those who saw their interpretations as "correct" rejected other interpretations and sought to repress them. Such a situation existed historically in the word battles of Lenin, Kautsky, and Bernstein (to mention only a few parties to the Marxist interpretative wars). The battle still rages in the ideological disputes within the Communist world of our own time.

Much attention has been focused on the clash of ideologues within the Marxist system. We should not ignore the significant contribution that Marxian conceptualization has made to the study of our Western heritage when used by scholars who are not Marxist ideologues. Part of that contribution has been the recognition that a political philosophy may be studied as ideology in the sense that the philosophy is reflective of its time, place, and social milieu, that is, its environment. Dolbeare expresses this concept when he says that ideologies are the operative myths people share about the ways governments act and should act.[27] Recognition that even the great philosopher shares, to some extent, in the operative myths of his or her environment allows modern interpreters to read a theorist in the light of the ideological parameters of

24. Lichtheim, *Ideology*, p. 20.
25. Alfred G. Meyer, *Marxism: The Unity of Theory and Practice* (Cambridge: Harvard University Press, 1954).
26. Lichtheim, *Ideology*, p.22.
27. Kenneth Dolbeare, ed., *Directions in American Political Thought* (New York: Wiley, 1969), pp. 5-9.

the philosopher's environment, such as societal expectations about government's purposes, appropriate modes of behavior, or acceptable social, economic, and political relationships. Even though political philosophers were usually harsh critics of aspects of their environments, they were also, to some extent, captives of the social and intellectual systems of their environment—what Erikson called the "unconscious tendency" of any age.[28]

Alban Winspear, who wrote a major book on Plato during the depression of the 1930s,[29] is a good example. His interpretation of Plato has been roundly criticized but is often read for some of the insights it provides.

Plato has been called a conservative, reactionary, or elitist by many, but these interpretations usually rest on textual or historical approaches. Alban Winspear, on the other hand, made his judgments based on the view that all Greek philosophy, including Plato's, was determined by the social revolution of the age. He said all early Greek philosophy reflected the class differences between the landed proprietors on one side and the usurers, merchants, and artisans on the other. The latter group tended to be slave-owning democrats who produced a materialistic-relativistic philosophy. The slave-owning landed class, on the other hand, tended toward a philosophy in which the definition of justice was to "defend inequality and the rule of the few."[30] Winspear put Plato in the latter camp.[31] He then criticized Plato's theory for failing to see the relationship between theoretical arguments about justice and class conflicts in society.

> With all his brilliance and subtle insight, Plato, the architect of the eternal ideas, builds what is after all a magnificent palace of half truths. This even he came to realize in part. As the whole thesis of this book must have made clear—the rift in thought reflects the rift in society. Until that conflict is resolved in actuality, or at least in hope, the troubling doubt

28. See chapter 3 of this book quoting from Erik Erikson, *Young Man Luther* (New York: Norton, 1958), p. 22.
29. Alban Dewes Winspear, *The Genesis of Plato's Thought* (New York: S. A. Russell, 1940).
30. Winspear, *Genesis*, p. 77.
31. Winspear, *Genesis*, p. 270.

that haunted Plato must continue to perplex his philosophical successors.[32]

For Winspear, like Marx, the divisions in society and in thought were intricately interwoven. Winspear criticized Plato for failing to recognize the need for action to overcome social and theoretical divisions resulting from inequality and elite rule. Winspear also criticized our own century, which, he thought, had not resolved those divisions any better than had Plato. Winspear gives us a new way of examining our heritage, which may give us new insights into our world.

C. B. Macpherson, a 20th-century scholar, like Winspear, has used Marxian conceptualization to produce new interpretations. He has placed special emphasis on the 17th century, especially on the theories of John Locke and Thomas Hobbes.

Macpherson brought to our attention the 17th-century social context of the political speculation which contributed to the Western constitutional heritage. He labeled that social system a possessive, individualistic system, based on the primacy of the propertied class. Macpherson built his case by arguing that the 17th-century social system was characterized by a presumption that each human being owned his or her person and that that personhood was reflected, at a minimum, in ownership of personal power to labor. That is, each human being was an independent, isolated economic unit who could compete in the economic marketplace to exchange labor for other commodities needed for living. Since accumulation was permitted in this system, some individuals accumulated stocks of property in the forms of land and other capital goods. Those who had not, for a variety of reasons, accumulated a property stake beyond their own labor had only that labor to sell and were themselves commodities in the market system. They were at a great disadvantage relative to the class of individuals who had greater economic accumulation in the system. This latter class, the bourgeoisie, dominated all political and social relationships as a result of its economic pre-eminence.[33]

Macpherson's view of the social context of 17th-century thought led him to a new view of Hobbes's pessimistic picture of human beings

32. Winspear, *Genesis*, p. 302.
33. C. B. Macpherson, *The Political Theory of Possessive Individualism* (London: Oxford University Press, 1962), pp. 48-49.

in the state of nature. When Hobbes described natural man (human beings stripped of all that society gave to them) existing in a state of nature (no society), he painted a bleak picture.

> In such condition, there is no place for industry; because the fruit thereof is uncertain: and consequently no culture of the earth; no navigation, nor use of the commodities that may be imported by sea; no commodious buildings; no instruments of moving, and removing, such things as require much force; no knowledge of the face of the earth; no account of time; no arts; no letters; no society; and which is worst of all, continual fear, and danger of violent death; and the life of man solitary, poor, nasty, brutish, and short.[34]

Each individual in Hobbes's montage was an isolated, self-seeking atom in fear of violent death. Each individual interacted with others prudently to insure his own survival. This "prudence" produced a condition that had the potential for war by all against all. Macpherson argued that the Hobbesian portrait of human nature and of the social life it produced was not a conjured-up view of "natural man." Macpherson asks us to see Hobbes's bleak picture as an accurate description of Hobbes's time —a dog-eat-dog world of noncommunity. Macpherson argues that the capitalistic organizing of man's material existence had led to a concommitant class structure—"bourgeois," competitive man and the "liberal" political system that excludes the laboring class from political power.

The advantage of Macpherson's unique view of the 17th century is that it raises many questions about the nature of liberalism, which arose from the roots of that social system.[35] He forces contemporary thinkers to assess the assumptions of liberal theory and to reexamine their constitutional theory and practice in terms of possible class biases. Current claims against American liberal democracy by the radical Left and by minorities, such as Blacks, Chicanos, and women, make a theoretical dialogue with Macpherson's view even more relevant. The Macpherson

34. Thomas Hobbes, *Leviathan,* ed. Michael Oakshott (Oxford: Blackwell, 1946), p. 82, or Thomas Hobbes, *Leviathan,* ed. A. D. Lindsay (New York: Dutton Company, 1950), pp. 103-104.
35. Macpherson's interpretation of Locke also raises questions about the liberal heritage. See ch. 5 of Macpherson, *Possessive Individualism.*

interpretation focuses on the issue of whether deficiencies identified by contemporary critics are aberrations of liberal ideals or whether the alleged deficiencies have their source in the theoretical foundation of the polity. For practical purposes, the difference is almost between remaining a reformer within the established system of values or becoming a revolutionary committed to the revision of both the values and practices of American politics.[36]

The use of Marxian conceptualization can point out some implications of political thought which might not be seen readily through the prism of other interpretative approaches. A danger in this approach can develop, however, if the user falls into the trap of arguing that thought is *determined* by material life.

Thought is not only shaped by material life but in turn also shapes it. Thinkers are more than mere reporters of popular myths and operative social systems. They are creative innovators capable of taking on the perennial questions of political life in new surroundings, capable of achieving recommendations for dealing with basic political questions. And their recommendations can have an impact on life independent of the social system from which the ideas sprang.

AMERICAN REVOLUTIONARY THOUGHT: CONSERVATIVE AND NEW LEFT Let us now move away from views grounded in Marxian concepts and consider an example of political theory and practice as interpreted from the conservative stance by Clinton Rossiter.[37] We will compare some of Rossiter's views to those of Jesse Lemisch who comes from the New Left.[38]

Up to this point, our emphasis has been on interpretations of individual political theorists. Here two views about American theory and practice of the Revolutionary War period will be compared. While this move is a shift in emphasis, it serves to illustrate the enriching variety of interpretation produced by different perspectives on a political tradition.

---

36. Kenneth M. Dolbeare and Patricia Dolbeare, *American Ideologies: The Competing Political Beliefs of the 1970's* (Chicago: Markham, 1971).

37. Clinton Rossiter, *Seedtime of the Republic: The Origin of the American Tradition of Political Liberty* (New York: Harcourt, Brace, 1953).

38. Jesse Lemisch, "The American Revolution Seen from the Bottom Up," in *Towards a New Past: Dissenting Essays in American History*, ed. Barton J. Bernstein (New York: Random House Vintage Books, 1967).

An understanding of Clinton Rossiter's basic components of conservativism will help us to understand his interpretation and positive evaluation of the events and thoughts of the American revolutionary era as "consciously conservative."[39] Rossiter emphasized conservativism's reverence for mystery and its view that the whole is greater than its parts. He argued that human nature is a mixture of evil and good and is best developed through inherited institutions, slow, incremental change, and the civilizing power of religion and education; that men are politically unequal, a situation that gives rise to social hierarchy, including a ruling aristocracy; that majority rule must be balanced by a reverence for the community and a constitutional priority on the values of liberty, order, progress and justice; and that rights are earned through the performance of duties.[40]

With these premises Rossiter judged favorably the "consciously conservative" nature he found among the American revolutionary theorists. For example, he praised their limited use of the "confused" theories of Locke[41] and endorsed their conservative limitation of the concept of the "right to resist." Rossiter concluded.

> For all their flirtation with the state of nature, for all their loyalty to the mechanistic explanation of government, Americans could think of man only as a member of a political community.[42]

Rossiter found much to praise in what he unraveled as conservative in the products of the leading theorists and activists of the American political revolution against England. He was delighted with his finding that "the political theory of the American Revolution—a theory of ethical, ordered liberty—remains the political tradition of the American people."[43]

Another scholar who started from different ideological premises produced very different views of American revolutionary thinking. Jesse Lemisch, a contemporary New Left historian, offered his view in *The American Revolution Seen from the Bottom Up.*

39. Rossiter, *Seedtime*, p. 438.
40. Clinton Rossiter, *Conservatism in America* (New York: Knopf, 1955), pp. 60-62.
41. Rossiter, *Seedtime*, pp. 358-359.
42. Rossiter, *Seedtime*, p. 397.
43. Rossiter, *Seedtime*, p. 449.

Lemisch rejected both the liberal interpretation and Rossiter's conservative interpretation of American revolutionary thought and practice. With others of the New Left, he argued that the events and ideas of the "non-elite" provided a fuller understanding of the revolutionary era than the "elitist" sources used by the other schools of thought. He said:

> Leaders like Jefferson and Adams may indeed have shared
> a basic agreement—on a kind of anti-populist consensus. . . .
> thus the conflicts among those within the merely liberal con-
> sensus become less important than those between the
> "mainstream" and those outside it.[44]

Lemisch agreed with Rossiter that Locke was only used selectively by the revolutionary theorists and activists, but he disagreed with the positive value Rossiter placed on the revolutionary leaders' use of Locke. Both of them studied Locke's text on resistance, especially his statement that revolutions happen only when a "long train of Abuses, Prevarications, and Artifices, all tending the same way, make the design visible to the People. . . ."[45]

Both Rossiter and Lemisch noted the similarity of Locke's text to a phrase in the American Declaration of Independence. Lemisch and Rossiter each drew the conclusion that Locke and the writers of the Declaration carefully limited the right to resist. Rossiter liked the revolutionary leaders' reinforcement of the Lockean theory limiting the right of resistance and proclaiming balanced government and ordered liberty. Lemisch found the same interpretation of Locke among American revolutionists, but he disapproved. For Lemisch, the dominant ideas of the revolutionists contributed to elitist government, which has been inherited to our disservice by contemporary America.

Lemisch said:

> Did the people defer to their ruler? Certainly we know that
> their rulers expected them to defer. Obedience was fully
> within the Lockean tradition. Obedience is mandatory until
> the majority concludes that the government has broken its

44. Lemisch, "Bottom Up," p. vii.
45. Peter Laslett, ed., *John Locke's Two Treatises of Government,* (New York: New American Library, Mentor Books, 1965), p. 463. Also see p. 453 and p. 466.

trust. Developing within its tradition, the political theory of the colonial elite saw the people as subordinate to their legislators.[46]

Lemisch argued that the restricted concept of the right to resist worked against the interests of the poor in society.[47]

Further, Lemisch viewed the concept of "equality," which Rossiter so glowingly praised in its limited and "balanced" form, as not really being equality at all. Lemisch agreed with Rossiter that the revolutionary theorists rejected equality as the prime political value, but Lemisch abhored that aspect of the revolutionary theoretical contribution to the American heritage.

Thus, the contemporary New Left critic of American society Jesse Lemisch said that the full context of American revolutionary thought could not be known through sources defined as relevant by liberal and conservative interpreters. He argued that interpretation of American thought must turn to the activities and ideas of the sailors, the Blacks, the workers, and peer farmers as evidence of the political thought outside the elitist "mainstream." Lemisch saw new sources as giving a new understanding to "orthodox" American thought and to the challenges to orthodoxy. He said that these new sources were nothing more than the application of the democratic creed to interpretation of political thought.[48]

The Rossiter/Lemisch example illustrates how important it is to understand the perspective of an interpreter. Understanding of the premises of contemporary New Left thought helps us reflect upon Lemisch's methods and conclusions, just as knowledge of Rossiter's characteristics of conservativism permits us to reflect better upon his interpretation of American thought. This theoretical knowledge, however, is not the sole benefit of our comparison. Contemplation of different perspectives points out that the battles waged in the legislatures, the courts, and even in the streets are not merely differences in perspective on the appropriate means-to-ends in American political life. They are long established conflicts about the appropriate goals for the American experiment. These conflicts have arisen again today not only as a result of modern pressures but also as a result of theoretical issues that were resolved in practice

46. Lemisch, "Bottom Up," p. 10.
47. Lemsich, "Bottom Up," p. 11.
48. Lemisch, "Bottom Up," p. 29.

to the advantage of some—therefore, at the expense of others—at the time of our founding.

BLACK POWER The place of Black people in America was "resolved" at the time of our founding to the disadvantage of the Black citizen. The Black Power ideology of Stokely Carmichael interprets the history of American political thought and practice through the filter of the Black experience.[49] As a way of reviewing the historical approach, let us consider how that approach would study Carmichael's Black Power ideas.

Knowledge of his text is just the beginning of the picture. We must recognize the American Black sub-culture and the African culture from which the Afro-American version was torn. This African context must be added to knowledge of basic American thought and political practice. Further, knowledge and application of the psychology of minoriites and of racism will help produce fuller understanding of the interpretation at hand. The basic point is that history has produced a unique ideology among some Blacks, which influences their interpretation of political thought.

In a historical approach to Carmichael, one would first consider his stated intent. In his works on Black Power, Carmichael stressed the need to set forth a Black perspective to allow Blacks "to reclaim our history and our identity from what must be called cultural terrorism."[50] He argued that no new perspective or interpretation encompassing the Black view could come from White America because of the limitations of White perception, which, in effect, censor Black self-definition.[51]

One would also study the major concepts that he used in historical description and his empirical analysis of the conditions of Blacks in American society and of institutional racism in America. For example, attention would be focused on his argument that integration was negative in its impact upon minorities and their cultures. Carmichael's emphasis on the concept of the uniquely valuable Black community would be studied in depth. He said:

> The racial and cultural personality of the black community
> must be preserved, and that community must win its freedom

49. Stokely Carmichael and Charles V. Hamilton, *Black Power: The Politics of Liberation in America* (New York: Random House, 1967), p. 35.
50. Carmichael and Hamilton, *Black Power,* p. 35.
51. Carmichael and Hamilton, *Black Power,* p. 181.

while preserving its cultural integrity. Integrity includes a pride—in the sense of self-acceptance, not chauvinism—in being black, in the historical attainments and contributions of black people.[52]

A textual analysis of the passage shows that "community" is one of the most important concepts used by Carmichael in developing his ideological position. The unique value of the Black community is a major premise in his thought. In many ways his praise of that community was his most critical comment on American political values and the one most reflective of his Afro-American orientation. He stressed the history of the communal nature of Black human beings and their rejection of the isolated, atomic individualism of American thought and liberal, theoretical interpretation. Carmichael's communal orientation reflected his identification with African thought and life style, as described in some African histories,[53] and in current African state experiments with unique forms of socialism, "African Socialism."[54] The Black community in American history is also seen in the practice of communal life in many forms, such as Black religious communities from the days of slavery to contemporary times.

Another important concept in Carmichael's thinking was his conscious assertion of Pan-Africanism which linked historically the Afro-American population, the former colonial nations of Africa, and the nonliberated peoples of that continent and other areas. The connective tissue among these groups was, he said, their common cultural identity and their shared historical experience of colonial status.[55] The goals of the Black Power ideology were to raise consciousness of this shared plight and to direct positive action by all Black people toward a solution based on the unique value of Black culture.

In seeking to understand Carmichael's interpretation of American value theory, a full historical approach would incorporate biography as well as the other elements cited so far. For example, attention would

52. Carmichael and Hamilton, *Black Power,* p. 55.

53. Igor Kopytoff, "Socialism and Traditional African Societies," in *African Socialism,* ed. William H. Friedland and Carl G. Rosberg, Jr., (Stanford: Stanford University Press, 1964), pp. 53-62. Also see, T. O. Ranger, ed., *Emerging Themes of African History* (Dar es Salaam: East African Publishing House, 1968).

54. See Friedland and Rosberg, *African Socialism,* for excerpts from major African Socialist thinkers from Ghana, Guinea, Mali, Senegal, and Tanzania.

55. Carmichael and Hamilton, *Black Power,* p. xi.

be drawn to his life experiences, from his birth in Trinidad to his youth in New York and Washington, D. C., where he received a B.A. from Howard University. Knowledge of his subsequent marriage to Miriam Makeba, a famous African interpreter of traditional South African music, and their emigration to the African state of Guinea would give further understanding of his interpretation of American life and thought.

The result of combining these approaches in our study would be clearer understanding of Carmichael's position. He rejects White liberal *intentions* and focuses on the *effect* on Blacks of White theoretical and practical interpretations of Western values.

The historical approach pushes the White American interpreter of Black American political thought beyond what might appear to be the "full context." The approach would force some readers beyond the limits of their own preconceptions of "relevance."

Our isolation of the ideological approach has allowed us to focus on a variety of methods used in studying the Western political tradition. Awareness of the method used by an interpreter helps us understand the implications he draws from a theory and allows us to judge the evaluations an interpreter makes about the theory and practice of politics.

Chapter 5   Meaning and Theory: Intent v. Effect

Every interpreter of political theory seeks to find the full meaning of what is being studied. The approaches we have discussed thus far seek the meaning in the author's intent and in the implications of a philosophical product. However, some scholars question the value of that orientation. They ask: Is the author's intention really relevant? Is the search for theoretical implications useful? Shouldn't the real meaning be sought in the results of the theory?

This chapter will deal with intent and effect as two very different approaches to meaning. Whether it is the "intention" or the "effect" that gives meaning is frequently the basic point of departure in debates in interpretation. Clarification of "where we are coming from" in the argument about meaning is the beginning of real dialogue.

CONSISTENCY AND INCONSISTENCY OF INTENT In the preceding chapters, the discussions have been generated by the following questions:

Where is the intention to be found? in the text? through the person of the author? or in the contemporary and/or prior environment of the theory? Another facet of the "intent" issue that can be viewed under any of the approaches is: How can the interpreter deal with the consistency and inconsistency of intention he meets in the works of a philosopher?

One solution might be to choose a single text, such as a writer's best-known work or the one that is most obviously political, and ignore the rest. The problems then are simply those of interpreting any single text. The discipline of political theory does not recommend such a selective approach, although the works of Karl Marx have sometimes met such a fate.

Many students have been introduced to Marx through the *Communist Manifesto* and have concluded that it contains the fullness of Marxian thought. However, the subtle and prolific mind of Marx provides a perfect example of the problems of working with a body of thought produced over a length of time.[1]

Marx's criticism of 19th-century politics and philosophy has many aspects. He envisioned that Communism would transcend capitalism, all that was involved in its system of private property, and the ideology that supported it. The vehicle for the Communist transcendence was a revolutionary proletarian class which would redeem itself and all mankind through revolutionary action. The revolution would, according to Marx, end the degradation of human beings, abolish the class system, and bring about a new history.

At several points during his writing career, Marx discussed the stage of revolutionary development that would occur in the period between the bourgeois state and the transcendence of capitalism by Communism. "The dictatorship of the proletariat" is a concept often associated with Marx's views about this transition era. Actually, Marx himself used the concept only a few times in his work. Examination of some instances in which Marx either used the phrase or otherwise talked about the transition stage will give us a basis for highlighting controversies about consistency and inconsistency and, later, for focusing on intent v. effect in political thought.

In 1844, Marx described "raw" or "crude" Communism which, he said, would precede Communism in its true and positive form. At first it would be:

1. Robert Tucker, ed., *The Marx-Engels Reader* (New York: W. W. Norton & Co., 1972).

> *universal* private property. . . . In its first form [Communism
> is] only a *generalization* and *consummation* of this relation-
> ship. . . . The category of *laborer* is not done away with,
> but extended to all men. . . . In negating the *personality* of
> man in every sphere, this type of communism is really nothing
> but the logical expression of private property, which is its
> negation. General *envy* constituting itself as a power is the
> disguise in which *avarice* re-establishes itself and satisfied
> itself, only in *another* way. . . . crude communism is only
> the consummation of this envy and of this levelling-
> down. . . .[2]

Despite the goal of human emancipation seen in the 1844 manuscripts, Marx noted there the likelihood that the transition would be nothing like true Communism. Indeed, he foretold the awful price that a population would have to pay initially for its revolution.

In 1848 in the *Communist Manifesto* Marx and Engels did not repeat the dreary picture Marx had painted in 1844. The manifesto was written as a policy declaration for the Communist League, which aspired to motivate revolutionary participation, and a description of a harsh, "raw" Communism would hardly entice anyone to join the movement or engage in revolutionary action.[3] Therefore, in the *Communist Manifesto* of 1848, Marx and Engels offered a less wrenching transition:

> We have seen above, that the first step in the revolution
> by the working class is to raise the proletariat to the position
> of ruling class, to win the battle of democracy.
>
> The proletariat will use its political supremacy to wrest,
> by degrees, all capital from the bourgeoisie, to centralize
> all instruments of production in the hands of the State, i.e.,
> of the proletariat organized as the ruling class. . . .[4]

2. Karl Marx, *Economic and Philosophical Manuscripts in Socialist Thought*, ed. Albert Fried and Ronald Sanders (Garden City, New York: Doubleday & Co., Anchor Books, 1964), pp. 288-289.

3. Dante Germino, *Modern Western Political Thought* (Chicago: Rand McNally & Co., 1972), p. 376.

4. Karl Marx and Frederick Engels, *Manifesto of the Communist Party*, in *Karl Marx: The Revolutions of 1848*, ed. David Fernbach (New York: Random House, Vintage Books, 1974), p. 86.

One of the few works in which Marx actually used the concept of "the dictatorship of the proletariat" to describe the transition to Communism was his 1875 *Critique of the Gotha Program* in which he stated:

> Between capitalist and communist society lies the period of the revolutionary transformation of the one into the other. There corresponds to this also a political transition period in which the state can be nothing but the revolutionary dictatorship of the proletariat.[5]

Despite the 1844 manuscripts, the 1848 Manifesto, and his 1875 discussion of the "dictatorship," Marx was sarcastic in his criticism of the work of Bakunin, the anarchist:

> What a wonderful example of barracks-communism! Everything is here: common pots and dormitories, control commissioners and *comptoirs,* the regulation of education, production, consumption—in one word, of all social activity; and at the top *our Committee,* anonymous and unknown, as supreme direction. Surely, this is most pure antiauthoritarianism![6]

Marx added to the potential controversy when he criticized, yet supported, the Paris Commune of 1871.[7] Engels expanded the controversy when he wrote in the introduction to the 1891 edition of *The Civil War in France:*

> Do you want to know what this dictatorship looks like? Look at the Paris Commune. That was the Dictatorship of the Proletariat.[8]

How do we reconcile Marx's criticism of the crude and authoritarian aspects of Bakunin's transition and his criticism of some aspects of the

5. Karl Marx, *Critique of the Gotha Program,* in Tucker, *Marx-Engels Reader,* p. 395.
6. Shlomo Avineri, *The Social and Political Thought of Karl Marx* (Cambridge: At the University Press, 1968), p. 238, quoting from Marx on Bakunin, 1875.
7. Avineri, *Marx,* pp. 239-249.
8. Avineri, *Marx,* p. 240, quoting Engels, *Marx and Engels, Selected Works,* I (London: Lawrence and Wishart, 1968), p. 485.

Commune with his own harsh description of raw Communism and his own discussion of the dictatorship of the proletariat?

There are two possible approaches to interpreting such inconsistencies: one school emphasizes *changes* in the thinker's intent and the other states that the intent remains the same. An example of the former is George Lichtheim, a contemporary scholar who has produced many works on Marxism and has found inconsistencies in Marxian theory.[9] Lichtheim traced the origins of these inconsistencies to historical events in the lives of Marx and his co-author, Frederick Engels. He cited the revolutions which racked Europe in 1848 and the uprising in Paris in 1871. Events of this type had tremendous impact on the writings of the pair, Lichtheim concluded. He found that emphases in their works would change after turning points in history.

Lichtheim also saw inconsistencies in Marxian thought as coming from the variety of theoretical battles in which he engaged. Marx fought with fellow socialists, as well as with other political figures of the day. For example, a piece written to combat "erroneous" views of fellow leftists, such as Bakunin, might differ from an article written to defend leftist movements against bourgeois criticism, such as *The Civil War in France*.

Lichtheim concluded from the inconsistencies that over the years Marx changed his views about the transition to Communism and about many other issues. Lichtheim further concluded that these inconsistencies made Marx the father of both the Soviet experiment and Western reformist socialism.[10]

Not everyone shares Lichtheim's views. Robert Tucker, also a contemporary scholar, belongs to another school of thought, holding that there is a long-term consistency in the works of Marx.[11] He argued that the same concerns infused the works of the older Marx as those which fired the young Marx but that Marx's focus and conceptual presentation differed over the years. Tucker addressed Marx's motivation as the source of consistency. He said that the young Marx of the philosophical manuscripts of the 1840s was concerned with redressing the personal alienation

9. George Lichtheim, *Marxism* (New York: Frederick A. Praeger, 1961). Examples of the writings cited by Lichtheim include the 1859 "Preface to Capital," the 1872 "Amsterdam Address," and the "Inaugural Address" of 1864, all of which differed from the *Communist Manifesto* of 1848. For excerpts of works listed see either Tucker, *Marx-Engels Reader;* Fried and Sanders, *Socialist Thought;* or Fernbach, *Karl Marx.*

10. Lichtheim, *Marxism,* p. 403.

11. Robert Tucker, *Philosophy and Myth in Karl Marx* (Cambridge: At the University Press, 1961).

of the individual, even though the process would entail a period of raw Communism. Tucker believed that the same concern motivated the older Marx but that the method of expression was different. The more mature thought is found in the class-related concepts of his later sociological-economic framework rather than in the philosophical concepts of his youth. Tucker, thus, saw consistency in Marx's views about the transition. Tucker said that the "temporary state of terrible degradation" described as the transition to Communism in the early manuscripts was "the immediate post-revolutionary transitional stage that Marx later designated as the stage of the dictatorship of the proletariat."[12]

Other scholars who do not necessarily share Tucker's particular emphasis share his view that there is an inner consistency in Marxian theory. Some of them read in a different light the works that Lichtheim used as evidence of changes in Marx's intent. Others identify implications in the works of Marx other than the possibilities seen by Lichtheim.[13]

INTENT V. EFFECT There are some interpreters who accept little of what has been stated so far in this chapter. They argue that the theorist's intent is irrelevant in the search for meaning. These interpreters feel that the only factor of importance is the actual effect of the theory in real life. A comparison of two contemporary interpretations of Marx, one by Erich Fromm and the other by Karl Popper, will serve to illustrate the difference in approaches.

Fromm stated his ideas about Marx in terms of Marx's intentions. Popper presented his views in terms of his conclusions about the effects of Marx's thought.

Fromm said:

> Marx's aim was that of the spiritual emancipation of man,
> of his liberation from the chains of economic determination,

12. Tucker, *Philosophy*, p. 154.
13. Differences among interpreters looking for the basic consistency or inconsistency of a thinker's intent can also be observed in studies of Rousseau. Ernst Cassirer, *The Question of Jean Jacques Rousseau* (New York: Columbia University Press, 1954) looks not only at the Rousseau of the *Discourses* but also at the Rousseau of the essays on *Poland* and *Corsica* to show his core consistency. John W. Chapman, *Rousseau—Totalitarian or Liberal?* (New York: AMA Press, 1968) also looks at the career output of Rousseau, but he finds inconsistency. Thus, the route to the "real meaning" of theory via the theorist's intent leads to different conclusions.

> of restituting him in his human wholeness, of enabling him to find unity and harmony with his fellow man and with nature.[14]

Fromm saw consistency of intent:

> [T]he core of the philosophy developed by the young Marx was never changed, and it is impossible to understand his concept of socialism, and his criticism of capitalism as developed in his later years, except on the basis of the concept of man, which he developed in his early writings.[15]

Fromm concluded that Marx would not have seen the Soviet Union as a result of his thought. Thus, Fromm viewed Marx as a consistent humanitarian whose intent was what counted. Popper, on the other hand, didn't care what Marx's intent was. He readily admitted "the humanitarian impulse of Marxism," and stated even more floridly:

> One cannot do justice to Marx without recognizing his sincerity. His open-mindedness, his sense of facts, his distrust of verbiage, and especially of moralizing verbiage, made him one of the world's most influential fighters against hypocrisy and pharisaism. He had a burning desire to help the oppressed, and was fully conscious of the need for proving himself in deeds and not only in words.[16]

But, for Popper, the good intent is worthless; for him, "the final test of a method . . . must be its practical results,"[17] what it causes.

On the basis of his method, Popper rejected Marx as a dangerous historicist, who was a false prophet. Marx's scientific prediction was really value-laden prophecy that misled Marx's followers—with totalitarian consequences, concluded Popper. He argued that Marx had made mistakes in analysis that resulted in a deterministic theory. Marx's predictions told the invariable and inevitable consequences of the causes that he said he had discovered. He led his followers, Popper argued, to be irrational

14. Erich Fromm, *Marx's Concept of Man* (New York: Frederick Ungar Publishing Co., 1961), p. 3.

15. Fromm, *Marx's Man*, p. 79.

16. Karl R. Popper, *The Open Society and Its Enemies*, vol. 2 (New York: Harper & Row, 1963), pp. 81-82.

17. Popper, *Open Society*, p. 134.

and irresponsible, to reject gradualism and democracy, and to see revolution as the invariable and inevitable consequence of the "reality" Marx had identified for them.

Popper was a victim of Nazi totalitarianism. He preferred gradualism and democracy. His preference was based on his desire for rationality and responsibility in human behavior. Therefore, he rejected revolution and those who sought it because totalitarian revolution could not bring forth maximum rationality and quality in human affairs. Popper's mission was to label and then condemn any political philosophy supportive of a closed (totalitarian) society rather than an open (democratic) one. His concern was that thought be evaluated by its results in practice rather than by the author's intent. For him, then, Marx might have had the most beautiful, humane intentions possible, but the totalitarian behavior, which Popper saw as the result of Marx's ideas, was the real meaning of the theory, and on that basis, Popper rejected the theory.

THE LABELING APPROACH A frequent extension of the "effect" approach is the description of the thought of earlier times in terms of popular political labels or categories of the current jargon. For example, attempts are made to answer such questions as, "Was Theorist X a totalitarian?" or, more nebulously, "Was he a forerunner of totalitarianism or a proto-totalitarian?" This approach often fails to recognize that "totalitarianism" is a concept that originated in the 20th-century. It is a problematic concept due to its use both in political theory and in practical political rhetoric. For example, Popper used this 20th-century concept not only in his discussion of totalitarianism-of-the-left (Marx, 19th century) but also in criticism of totalitarianism-of-the-right (Hegel, 19th century, and Plato, 4th century B.C.). Insight into some of the problems and justifications of the labeling approach can be gained by looking at two critics of Popper's methods relative to Hegel and Plato.[18]

18. Some have blamed Martin Luther for the rise of Hitler's regime in 20th-century Germany. This approach to Luther was particularly popular during the 1930s and 1940s. For example, William M. McGovern, *From Luther to Hitler: The History of Fascist-Nazi Political Philosophy* (Boston: Houghton Mifflin, 1941; New York: AMS Press, 1973 reprint of 1941 edition); P.F. Wiener, *Martin Luther: Hitler's Spiritual Ancestor* (London: Hutchison, 1945); L. Brophy, "Luther, Hitler and Chaos," *Catholic Mind* 44 (July, 1946): 389-394; M. Kent, "Propaganda: Past and Present," *Catholic World* 159 (September, 1944): 515-521, among many other books and articles.

Another thinker who is frequently labeled in 20th-century terms as a "totalitarian" is Rousseau, who lived and wrote in the 18th century. Others find elements of both liberalism and totalitarianism in Rousseau's work. J. L. Talmon, *Origins of Totalitarian Democracy* (New York: Norton: 1970), ch. 3, and Chapman, *Rousseau*, ch. 10.

Walter Kaufmann rejected Popper's interpretation of Hegel not only by refuting the "effects" which Popper imputed from Hegel's theory but also by showing Hegel's intent. Kaufmann's approach showed the creative way in which an attack on another interpretation may further the understanding of a political philosopher. Kaufmann used Popper's Hegel chapter in some detail "to explode the popular Hegel legend."[19] Popper's unique interpretation was Kaufmann's central focus. However, Kaufmann used that interpretation as a springboard to criticize many generally held and frequently cited versions of what Hegel is supposed to have said and meant. While recognizing Popper's outspoken opposition to totalitarianism, Kaufmann charged that Popper used many of the same techniques of intellectual dishonesty used by the intelligentsia of totalitarian regimes.[20] Kaufmann's attack was very careful. It was based on Popper's failure to consider basic Hegelian scholarship or to draw on Hegel's complete works. For example, Kaufmann showed that Popper relied on an anthology of Hegel's writings that did not include even one complete work by Hegel.[21]

Further, Kaufmann charged that Popper mishandled Hegel's text, that the materials of quotes were "quilt quotes," often made up of bits and pieces taken out of context, even from different works, and strung together with ellipses.[22] Kaufmann refuted many of Popper's charges that Hegel contributed to the "dark side" (totalitarian) of the Western heritage. For example, Kaufmann disputed Popper's charge that Hegel was partially responsible for the rise of the Nazis and pointed out some of Hegel's ideas that were in direct opposition to Nazi ideology. One obvious example, Kaufmann said, was that Hegel defended equal rights for Jews in his later writings, a view certainly opposed to Nazi theory and practice.[23]

Plato was another "victim" of Popper's method, according to Plato's 20th-century defender, R. B. Levinson. He attempted to refute Popper's charges that Plato of the 4th century B.C. was a forerunner of the

19. Walter Kaufmann, "The Hegel Myth and Its Method," in *Hegel's Political Philosphy*, ed. Walter Kaufmann (New York: Atherton Press, 1970), p. 139. See also, Shlomo Avineri, *Hegel's Theory of the Modern State* (Cambridge: At the University Press, 1972). Avineri's work is discussed in chapter 2 of this book.
20. Kaufmann, *Hegel*, p. 140.
21. Kaufmann, *Hegel*, p. 141.
22. Kaufmann, *Hegel*, pp. 141-143.
23. Kaufmann, *Hegel*, p. 146.
24. R. Levinson, *In Defense of Plato* (New York: Russell and Russell, 1953), p. viii, ch. 2 and Appendix.

20th-century "closed" (totalitarian) society. Levinson[24] used Plato's texts as a starting point and gained additional insight by viewing the culture of Athens and the history of Greece of the era.[25] He used Plato's biography and applied a psychological approach to it to further defend him.[26] Levinson, like Kaufmann, recognized the fact that Popper was a victim of totalitarianism and therefore not very objective. He also rejected Popper's methods and conclusions relative to Plato.[27]

Levinson's judgment was that Popper frequently made incorrect statements or that, while Popper had come up with one possible conclusion, there were others equally or more solidly supported by the data. Levinson, for example, rejected Popper's triangular linking of Plato to Spartan ideals and to Hitlerian goals. Levinson refuted the problematic association of the 4th-century B.C. philosopher to the 20th-century Nazi by showing, among other things, a far broader set of sources for Plato's ideas than the Spartan life style.[28]

The historical approach provided the vehicle through which Levinson attempted to give a "full context" to Plato's intent and his imputed "effects." In this way Levinson defended Plato against charges that he contributed to the rise of totalitarianism. As Levinson said, his approach aimed at correcting interpretations in which,

> Plato's thought is made to revolve around the axis of its least worth. . . . The central aim of this book is to correct these errors of perspective and of fact and, while stopping short of unqualified acceptance of all that Plato was or taught, to restore him to a position of repute and potential influence answering to his actual merit.[29]

Labeling of theory is not very productive for many reasons. First, the categorizing of thought on the basis of labels is vague, at best. That is, there are many elements that go into a great political theory. While an innovative theory might have some elements in common with current political systems, the greatness of its other conceptual contributions may be overwhelmed when a mere label is affixed to the thought. We are

25. Levinson, *Defense*, chs. 6 and 9.
26. Levinson, *Defense*, chs. 5 and 8.
27. Levinson, *Defense*, p. 20.
28. Levinson, *Defense*, p. 564 and pp. 20-21.
29. Levinson, *Defense*, pp. vii-viii.

likely to become so satisfied with having found a niche or a box for a theory that we fail to carry through on the real challenge it presents for us. We may pass up the education the philosopher offers for the security of "categorizing" him. In other words, the label, like any other approach in its extreme, may become a substitute for full study of theory, rather than an aid to understanding great thought.

The first problem becomes even more exaggerated when we apply labels from current times (for example, totalitarian) to theories that were developed decades or centuries before. This second problem contributes to a third problem: namely, the label approach tends to turn into a search for a scapegoat, a search that ignores the complexity of history. At its worst, "labeling," like the whole approach based on imputed "effect," attempts to assert that a particular set of ideas caused later events, such as, that Rousseau's ideas caused the French Revolution of 1789 or that Luther's 16th-century thought gave rise to Hitler several centuries later.

Any single-cause theory of history is usually faulty. Certainly to make a particular political theory the sole cause of later events is to miss the fascinating, multifaceted interaction of ideas and events which is the stuff of history and the meat of political happenings. Study of the possible implications of an idea system, regardless of whether they were intended by the thinker, can add to our understanding of politics and of the options available in our tradition. Such an approach is an alternate position to the assertions that pure meaning is found only in the writer's intent and the polar opposite view that actual effect of theory is true meaning. In the continuing debate about method, the palm branch must go to the method which in each particular case aids the understanding of the political process the most. And of course, the acceptance of one method does not preclude the judicious use of another.

Chapter 6 Interpreting the Interpreters

The main goal of this book has been to help the new student cope with the conflicting interpretations found in political philosophy. The book has shown some reasons that interpretation of political thought is necessary and some of the benefits a reader can gain from interpretation. Different approaches have been identified, and various views about the meaning and significance of political theory have been illustrated. For purposes of clarification the interpretative approaches were treated singly. However, in practice and at their best, they are artfully sorted and combined, manipulated and orchestrated to produce better understanding of political thought.

Unfortunately for the reader, the interpreter frequently fails to identify the approach used and fails to give a rationale for seeing it as the most appropriate one for the subject. For these reasons knowledge of the range of views about the discipline and of the available approaches (with their advantages and liabilities) can be helpful to the student.

INTERPRETATION AND THE DISCIPLINE: POLITICAL SCIENCE AND POLITICAL PHILOSOPHY Political theory is a discipline within a larger field of political studies.[1] The latter, now called political science, had its origins in political philosophy. In recent times, however, contemporary political science has diverged from the historical development and present state of political thought. The label *discipline* then neither describes nor creates a monolithic approach to the political world.

So far in this book we have concentrated on identifying several sources of differences within political theory. Specifically, we have identified differences of approaches: textual, biographical, psychological, historical, ideological. Further, we have noted that differences arise from different views about meaning. Some scholars see meaning in the intent of the author. Others stress the theoretical implications of an idea system. Still others see meaning in a causal relationship between a theory and later events or systems of politics.

Although they have been the source of emphasis in this book, differences about approaches and about the source of meaning are not the only causes of diversity of interpretation. Others are an interpreter's views about the purpose of the discipline, about what constitutes "understanding" of theory, and about the role of the scholar in the world of politics. A brief discussion of these elements of diversity can give additional insights into contemporary interpretation, into the relationship between political science and political philosophy, and into the world of scholarship and politics.

At least three different positions are identifiable and useful for purposes of clarification. However, some cautions are in order. For example, not all interpreters will fit neatly into any one category. Also, we must heed our own warnings about the misuse of labels or categories. That is, the affixing of a label must not obscure the useful differences within a category. The label must not become a substitute for the challenge of the rich differences within and among categories or rule out the possibility of a different system of categories.[2]

---

1. Many books have developed distinctions among political philosophy, political theory, political thought, political science, and ideology. Some of them include: Arnold Brecht, *Political Theory* (Princeton, New Jersey: Princeton University Press, 1959); Dante Germino, *Modern Western Political Thought* (Chicago: Rand McNally & Co., 1972); Andrew Hacker, *Political Theory: Philosophy, Ideology, Science* (New York: Macmillan Co., 1961); Kenneth Dolbeare, *Directions in American Political Thought* (New York: Wiley, 1969).
2. See chapter 5 of this book.

One group identifies itself primarily as behaviorial political scientists. They argue that the purpose of the discipline of political science is *not* to be concerned with "ultimate" questions of political values or goals. Political scientists seek to understand political behavior and relate political means and intermediate values. The purpose of their work may be the achievement of a "value-free" political science (with emphasis on the word *science*) or the development of policy advice for government within the stated societal goals or purposes.[3]

A second category of scholars could be identified as critical and possibly activist intellectuals. They argue that the proper role for the scholar and the purpose of the discipline are not to provide "mere" understanding of political behavior or instrumental means but to seek to change the world in terms of new (read: better) goals or purposes.[4]

For labeling purposes we will call a third group of scholars traditional political theorists, a category made up of many diverse points of view. The traditional political theorists are in agreement among themselves that political philosophy as a rational activity is *not* science and is *not* political activity. In contrast to the other two groups, they argue that the role of the scholar and the purpose of the discipline are to pursue political knowledge in a detached and objective way. They advocate withdrawing from partisan politics to permit the study of questions of ultimate value. The degree of "detachment" considered possible or desirable splits the advocates of this position.[5]

Behaviorial political scientists (group one) emphasize a differentiation between "fact" statements and "value" statements (between political science and political philosophy). They work in the "nonvalue" area of empirical science. Behaviorial political scientists seek scientific theories, which are comparable to theories produced in the natural sciences.

3. For a brief overview, see Rollo Handy and E. C. Harwood, *A Current Appraisal of the Behavioral Sciences* (Great Barrington, Mass.: Behavioral Research Council, 1973). For an earlier but more extensive overview, see Albert Somit and Joseph Tanenhaus, *The Development of American Political Science* (Boston: Allyn and Bacon, 1967).

4. Richard Ashcraft, "On the Problem of Methodology and the Nature of Political Theory," *Political Theory* 3, no. 1 (February 1975): 5-25; William Leiss, "Critical Theory and Its Future," *Political Theory* 2, no. 3 (August 1974): 330-350.

5. See Germino, *Modern Thought*, pp. vii-ix, 2-3, 387-389; D. D. Raphael, *Problems of Political Philosophy* (New York: Praeger Publishers, 1970) among many others. Also see the material on Strauss in chapter 2 of this book. For an overview of political theory in recent years see Dante Germino, "Some Observations on Recent Political Philosophy and Theory," *The Annals of the American Academy*, January 1972, pp. 141-148.

The critical/activist theorists and the traditional political theorists differ on several issues. They agree, however, in their renunciation of the fact/value dichotomy which the behavioral scientists advocate.[6] They argue that advocates of the fact/value dichotomy are: (1) oriented toward the status quo (because they do not question ultimate goals); (2) preoccupied with trivialities (because they deal only with that which can be measured scientifically); (3) uninterested in providing solutions for societal problems (because they have not asked significant questions which challenge the accepted range of problem definitions and available options).[7]

The behaviorial scientists reject the goal of becoming political philosophers and defend themselves as *scientists*. For them, philosophy may have many uses, but since it is not open to scientific study, they will seek theory in the scientific, not philosophical, sense of the term. The natural sciences, not philosophy, provide the behaviorialists' theoretical goal.

The denouncers of strict behaviorial political science differ among themselves on very basic philosophical issues. Critical/activist scholars argue that political theory is not a detached, intellectual exercise and that the role of philosophy is to criticize that which exists and to change the way people see and understand reality: in other words, to change the world. This approach is not a detached approach. Rather, it argues that political science and political philosophy can be analyzed in terms of their development as products of the Western theoretical heritage and social setting. Like the society that produced the heritage and the scholars, the methods of the field are open to renewal as a way of making a better theory and a better world.[8]

Many different scholars fit within the critical/activist category. They have used different routes to reach their conclusions about the mission of political theory. Marx's 11th thesis on Feuerbach expresses a way in which some reached their view: "The philosophers have only interpreted the world, in various ways; the point, however, is to change it."[9]

---

6. Many books discuss this issue. For example, see H. J. Storing, ed., *Essays on the Scientific Study of Politics* (New York: Holt, Rinehart & Winston, 1962). Also see Martin Diamond, "The Dependence of Fact upon 'Value,'" *Interpretation* 2/3 (Spring, 1972): 226-234.

7. Ashcraft, "Methodology," p. 18.

8. Ashcraft, "Methodology," p. 19.

9. Karl Marx, *Theses on Feuerback in The Marx-Engels Reader,* ed. Robert Tucker (New York: Norton, 1972).

The ranks of critical/activist scholars (category two) have swollen in recent times although category three (traditional political theorists) still encompasses a majority of the scholars in the discipline. Among the reasons for the shift toward the critical/activist approach are the impact of the social problems of the 1960s and 1970s and some new insights, for example, those provided by the work of Thomas Kuhn.[10]

Kuhn's *Structure of Scientific Revolutions* gave political scientists and theorists a new view of their discipline. Kuhn emphasized the impact of the historical, social development of a science on the procedures and theories of that science. He showed that the methods of a discipline reflected the social setting of the scholarship. Kuhn's conclusions led some political theorists to question the relationship among political science, political philosophy, and the society at large. Such questioning led some from category three (traditional political theorists) into category two (critical scholars and/or activists). The converts argued that traditional political theory had become a rationale for the status quo. They charged that traditional political theory had become a support for the social structure which produced and supported the scholars, their theoretical discipline, and their methods and procedures. The critical/activist scholars felt that traditional political theory prohibited them from taking a stand intellectually and practically for radical change in the political, economic, and social system. They now demanded that the discipline move toward commitment to a better theory and practice of politics.

Not all traditional political theorists (category three) moved as far as the critical/activist group. While categories two and three are very different from each other and must be considered separately, neither is united internally. Each group is subdivided. Some of the differences are in philosophical orientation (such as, neo-Thomism, existentialism, or anti-essentialist liberalism.)[11] Other differences arise from the variety of approaches to theory and meaning which have been the focus of

10. Thomas Kuhn, *The Structure of Scientific Revolutions* (Chicago: University of Chicago Press, 1962). Kuhn has had a tremendous influence on behavioral political scientists, but that influence lies beyond the scope of this book. For examples and discussion of Kuhn's impact see Martin Landau, *Political Theory and Political Science* (New York: Macmillan Co., 1972), chap. 2, especially pp. 59-60, for Kuhn's impact on anti-establishment activists; Ashcraft, "Methodology," pp. 12-15; Thomas A. Spragens, Jr., *The Dilemma of Contemporary Political Theory: Toward a Postbehavioral Science of Politics* (New York: Dunellen Publishing Co., 1973). Also see reviews of Spragens's work in *American Political Science Review* 69 (March 1975): 260-263.

11. Isaiah Berlin, "Does Political Theory Still Exist?" in *Philosophy, Politics and Society* (2nd Series), ed. Peter Laslett and W. G. Runciman (New York: Barnes & Noble, 1962).

this book. Therefore, among traditional political theorists it is possible to have a textual-analysis school such as Strauss and his followers[12] in the same category with those whose methods Strauss attacked.[13]

Despite the differences within category three, traditional political theorists share some essential features: (1) the view that political philosophy *is not* science and that facts and values are not disassociated and (2) the view that political philosophy *is* a detached activity of the mind. For these scholars, political theory is not a socially involved activity with an agenda for change which the discipline should seek to prove and/or implement. While most traditional political theorists recognize limits on the possiblity for detachment, they all see political philosophy as a rational, and, to some degree, detached study of the perennial questions of politics.[14]

INTERPRETATION: THE DISCIPLINE AND THE STUDENT In this book we have tried to answer the question "Why is interpretation necessary?" We have shown that political theory, unlike scientific theory and, indeed, more like a great artistic masterpiece, is more valuable when seen from many angles or is mediated through the consciousness of different minds with different perspectives. The goal of political theory is not "correct"[15] meaning but understanding of probable meanings which can educate us about politics. The process can provide new adventures into creative political thinking. As readers attempt to interpret great thought, they also engage in criticism of it and develop their own theories of politics. The problems of each age challenge great thought but also allow it to provide fresh insights in new settings. Thus a good interpreter uses prior thought as a vehicle for creative development and carries on the discourse that is political theory.

On the level of factual knowledge alone, interpreters are always adding fresh findings to the discipline. For example, knowledge of Marx, who wrote in the mid-19th century, was increased in 1932 by the publication and subsequent translation of his *Economic and Philosophical*

12. Storing, *Essays*. Also see chapter 2 of this book.
13. See chapter 2 of this text.
14. Germino, *Modern Thought*, pp. vii-ix, 2-3, 387-389, and Hacker, *Political Theory*, pp.1-20.
15. Q. Skinner, "Motives, Intentions and the Interpretation of Texts," *New Literary History* 3, no. 2 (Winter 1972): 396.

Manuscripts.[16] These additions to our holdings of Marx's individual works encouraged us to direct more attention to the writing of Marx as distinct from his collaborative efforts with Engels or Engels's publications of Marx's works after the latter's death. Knowledge of Locke's 17th-century sources has been greatly expanded by Laslett's recent research into Locke's personal library at Oxford.[17]

Interpretation rests on recognition that no interpreter, professional or nonprofessional, is instantaneously and simultaneously an expert in the whole body of a theorist's writings; in manuscript analysis; in translation; in the author's mental and physical life; and in the social, cultural and economic history of the author's era and that of previous eras. A positive assessment of the contribution of interpretation rests on the realization that such "facts" do not have the same significance for various scholars in the discipline. The relevance of "facts" varies with scholars' ideas about the purposes of the discipline, their views about meaning, and their judgments about the best approaches for studying political theory.

The great number of scholars, with a variety of skills, approaches, and outlooks, produces a discipline that polices itself. It provides criticism of critics. An interpretation may present new views, attack or defend existing views, or choose among competing views. This policing function in the discipline helps to account for the variety of interpretations available for readers. The existence of these alternate approaches, each with its own limitations, is part of the discipline's pursuit of the "whole story," which is the understanding of politics.

Sometimes an individual interpretation overreaches the limits of its analytical tools and thus creates some of the disadvantages we have discussed in earlier chapters of this book. However, even when an interpretation overreaches itself, it can make a contribution as long as the discipline of political theory polices itself to provide the "constant intricate shifting and catching of balance" necessary for intellectual health.[18] That is, there is always room for many approaches to an understanding of

16. Karl Marx, *Economic and Philosophical Manuscripts,* trans. T. B. Bottomore in *Marx's Concept of Man,* ed. Erich Fromm (New York: Frederick Ungar Publishing Co., 1966), pp. 87-261.

17. Peter Laslett, ed., *John Locke's Two Treatises of Government* (New York: Mentor Books of the New American Library, 1965).

18. Richard Blackmur, "A Critic's Job of Work," in *Five Approaches to Literary Criticism,* ed. Scott Wilbur (New York: Macmillan Co., 1962), p. 321.

our political heritage. It is only when interpretation becomes doctrinaire in believing that it has achieved complete knowledge that there is potential damage for the discipline and for the nonprofessional reader.

The student can experience some of the self-policing exercised in the discipline. One way to gain policing or critical skills is through study of books of interpretative readings on major thinkers. Books of readings are most helpful when read after the original text of the major philosopher to be interpreted.[19] Another means of honing one's critical skills is through subscription to journals on interpretation. Recognition of the importance of interpretation in the discipline can be seen in the recent emergence of new periodicals in the field.[20] Interpretation of great ideas is also an interdisciplinary search. As such, articles on interpretation of political works now appear in journals of other disciplines and in cross-disciplinary journals.[21]

WHAT CAN THE READER EXPECT TO GAIN FROM INTERPRETATION? What can the nonprofessional reader expect to gain from a keener understanding of interpretation in political theory? One thing that will *not* be found is "a final answer to problems"[22] of politics. However, at the very least, one *can* expect to find help in moving from undisciplined, "common sense" approaches to politics and political ideas. "Common sense" is not a profound, questioning approach to ideas. It often conceals more than it reveals. The very "obviousness" of our common-sense methods and findings often blinds us to basic issues and retards our application of disciplined reasoning to political ideas and events.[23] (For example, everyone knows what democracy is until asked to explain

19. Included are such books as: T. Thorson, ed., *Plato: Totalitarian or Democrat* (Englewood Cliffs, N. J.: Prentice-Hall, 1963); John W. Yolton, ed., *John Locke, Problems and Perspectives* (Cambridge: At the University Press, 1969); Walter Kaufmann, *Hegel's Political Philosophy* (New York: Atherton Press, 1970); K. C. Brown, ed., *Hobbes Studies* (Cambridge: Harvard University Press, 1965). Also see more general books of readings which include different interpretations of a variety of philosophers such as, Isaac Kramnick, ed., *Essays in the History of Political Thought* (Englewood Cliffs, N. J.: Prentice-Hall, 1969); David Hart and James Downton, Jr., eds., *Perspectives on Political Philosophy,* vols. I, II, III (New York: Holt, Rinehart and Winston, 1971); David Thomson, ed., *Political Ideas* (Baltimore: Penguin Books, 1969).

20. *Interpretation* (Martinus Nijoff), The Hague, Netherlands, (and *Political Theory,* California, Sage Publications) among others.

21. *New Literary History,* (Charlottsville, Va.: University of Virginia).

22. D. D. Raphael, *Philosophy,* p. 17.

23. The main ideas herein reflect those of Dr. Neil A. McDonald.

it.) When the reader can understand the rationale behind an author's choice of an interpretative approach, the reader is protected from that author's implicit assumptions. When concentrating on interpretation as a deliberate process, an individual can identify and be enriched by the variety of approaches to profound political ideas.

Nonprofessional readers can facilitate their own learning by recognizing that they, like professional interpreters of theory, favor one approach to political ideas and events over the available alternative approaches. They must also recognize that they are part of their own times and places. For example, recognition that we are *Americans* of the *20th century* gives us a base line for understanding the political ideas of our time and of previous eras.

American culture has not tended to see itself as having an ideological approach to politics. Ideology, however, is not irrelevant in the American context. The "ordinary" American is "guided by ideologically based or derived attitudes and habits" even if they are not the well-differentiated positions of a fascist or Marxist.[24] Some professional political theorist asserted, some years ago, that we were reaching an "end of ideology."[25] With the political movements and events of the 1960s and 1970s, such an end does not appear to be in sight. The elaboration of challenging ideological positions in contemporary America has thrown further doubt on the "end of ideology" thesis. The profusion of different ideological positions today (such as Liberalism, Reform Liberalism, American Marxism, and various approaches to Black Power and Nationalism)[26] refutes the "end of ideology" thesis. Idea systems are not coming closer together in content as the thesis predicted; instead, greater ideological diversity has emerged.

The study of political theory can help you identify your own emotion-supported ideological commitment and to develop a more rational consideration of your political values.[27] This suggested application of the

24. Reo Christenson et al., eds., *Ideologies and Modern Politics* (New York: Dodd, Mead, 1971), p. 10, quoting from and expanding on Robert Lane, *Political Ideology* (New York: Free Press, 1962), pp. 15-16.

25. Daniel Bell, *The End of Ideology* (New York: Free Press, 1960).

26. The categories are those of Kenneth M. Dolbeare and Patricia Dolbeare, *American Ideologies: The Competing Political Beliefs of the 1970's* (Chicago:Markham, 1971). Also see L. Earl Shaw, ed., *Modern Competing Ideologies* (Lexington, Mass: D. C. Heath, 1973) and many other sources cited in our discussion of ideology in chapters 1 and 4.

27. Raphael, *Philosophy*, p. 18. Also see William J. Parente, "Contemporary Liberal Arts Students and Political Science," paper delivered at the Annual Meeting of the American Political Science Association, Washington, D. C., 1972.

discipline in no way implies that you should give up your political values. Rather, this book advises that the study of political theory can contribute to self-knowledge about your own political preconceptions. Further, the study of political theory can produce better understanding of the prevailing ideology of the society, of contemporary political conventions, of the social environment, and of the individual's place within the cultural framework. The individual can also learn how to evaluate critically an argument about political thought and how to grasp what is implied in various interpretations. Through the development of critical thinking, students can improve their insights into politics and into themselves as political thinkers and actors. They can use a critical approach to gain insight into alternative possible political futures produced by theorists and politicians. Based on their own clearer value positions students will be better able to evaluate proposals for a "new political world". They will consider both the ends proffered and the means advocated. All of this mental activity is very helpful as an individual contemplates movement from the arena of thought into the field of political action.[28]

In order to gain the benefits of the discipline of political theory, you might wish to apply to yourself some of the approaches used by professional interpreters in their study of political philosophy. For example, a theoretical self-analysis[29] can show the historical tradition of political speculation from which our own generation has sprung. It can illuminate the unique contributions of our own age to the dialogue of political theory. This historical and sociological perspective will enhance your ability to probe your own beliefs. For some students an ideological self-analysis will illuminate the forces of socialization and the psychological needs which influence their thought. That is, for some individuals the biographical approach and (to the fullest extent possible for the lay reader) the psychological approach can help explain their receptivity to certain ideas and their rejection of other thought. Still other students may recognize themselves as ideologues. Ideologues may find ventures into ideologies with different premises helpful in clarifying their own commitment. Finally, other individuals may find that a combination of approaches, the fullest context possible, may be the best way to mature in political self-knowledge and critical judgment.

28. Ashcraft, "Methodology," p. 19. Also see Dante Germino, "The Relevance of the Classics," paper delivered at the Annual Meeting of the American Political Science Association, Washington, D. C., 1972.

29. Robert E. Lane, *Political Thinking and Consciousness* (Chicago: Markham, 1969).

First, however, the *fact* that each person is a political theorist must be fully realized and accepted by each student.[30] This recognition permits each of us to seek interpretative approaches which help us find full meaning in politics. Realization of our own theoretical natures and abilities will hone our critical faculties and keep us mentally alive to the possibilities involved in politics. Without realization that each of us is a theorist, political thought will appear to be a dead, past-oriented subject matter. The field will appear irrelevant and will be pushed aside as a scholastic exercise to support the "publish or perish" ordeal of college professors. With the realization that we are all political theorists, even if not professional publishers of our findings, we can be future-oriented, self-aware receivers, reviewers, and evaluators of political thoughts. In this way, individuals can arouse their own creative, as well as critical, faculties and add to their enjoyment of political thought and politics.[31]

The stimulation from theorist to reader which produces worthwhile interpretation keeps the discipline of political theory vital and current. Political theories which bring about this progressive process are the great works in political philosophy. In other words, the intelligence and emotional responses of skilled readers, professional or nonprofessional, are the discipline: the court of last resort, the supreme test for the heritage that is political thought.

30. Ashcraft, "Methodology," p. 19.
31. James N. Rosenau, *The Dramas of Politics: An Introduction to the Joys of Inquiry* (Boston: Little, Brown, 1973).

BIBLIOGRAPHY

Ashcraft, Richard. "On the Problem of Methodology and the Nature of Political Theory." *Political Theory* 3, no. 1 (February 1975): 5-25.

Avineri, Shlomo. *Hegel's Theory of the Modern State*. Cambridge: At the University Press, 1972.

———. *The Social and Political Thought of Karl Marx*. Cambridge: At the University Press, 1968.

Bainton, R. H. *Here I Stand*. New York: New American Library, 1950.

Barker, Ernest. *The Political Thought of Plato and Aristotle*. New York: Dover Publications, 1959.

———. *The Social Contract*. New York: Oxford University Press, 1962.

Barney, William L. *The Road to Secession*. New York: Praeger Publishers, 1972.

Beardsley, Philip. "Political Science: Case of the Missing Paradigm." *Political Theory* 2, no. 1 (February 1974): 44-61.

Berlin, Isaiah. "Does Political Theory Still Exist?" In *Philosophy, Politics and Society* (2nd Series), edited by P. Laslett and W. G. Runciman. New York: Barnes and Noble, 1962, pp. 1-33.

Bloom, Allan. "Leo Strauss." *Political Theory* 2, no. 4 (November 1974): 372-393.

Campbell, W. E. *Erasmus, Tyndale and More*. Milwaukee: Bruce Publishing Co., 1930.

Carmichael, Stokely, and Hamilton, Charles V. *Black Power: The Politics of Liberation in America*. New York: Random House, 1967.

Cassirer, Ernst. *The Philosophy of the Enlightenment*. Boston: Beacon Press, 1955.

———. *The Question of Jean-Jacques Rousseau*. New York: Columbia University Press, 1954.

Catton, William, and Catton, Bruce. *Two Roads to Sumter*. New York: McGraw-Hill Book Co., 1963.

Chambers, R. W. *Thomas More*. New York: Harcourt Brace & Co., 1935.

Chambre, Henri. *From Karl Marx to Mao Tse-Tung*. New York: P. J. Kennedy & Sons, 1963.

Chapman, John W. *Rousseau—Totalitarian or Liberal?* New York: AMA Press, 1968.

Christenson, Reo M.; Engel, Alan S.; Jacobs, Dan N.; Rejai, Mostafa; and Waltzer, Herbert, eds. *Ideologies & Modern Politics*. New York: Dodd, Mead & Co., 1971.

Cochrane, E. W. "Machiavelli: 1940-1960." *The Journal of Modern History* 33, no. 2 (June 1961): 113-136.

Craven, Avery. *The Coming of the Civil War*. Chicago: University of Chicago Press, 1957.

Cropsey, Joseph. *Ancients and Moderns: Essays on the Tradition of Political Philosophy in Honor of Leo Strauss*. New York: Basic Books, 1964.

Diamond, Martin. "The Dependence of Fact upon 'Value.'" *Interpretation* 2 (Spring 1972): 226-234.

Djilas, M. *The Unperfect Society: Beyond the New Class*. New York: Harcourt, Brace & World, 1969.

Dolbeare, Kenneth M., and Dolbeare, Patricia. *American Ideologies*. Chicago: Markham Publishing Company, 1971.

Easton, David. *The Political System*. New York: Alfred A. Knopf, 1953.

Erikson, Erik. *Young Man Luther*. New York: W. W. Norton and Co., 1958.

Fernbach, David, ed. *Karl Marx: The Revolutions of 1848*. New York: Vintage Books of Random House, 1974.

Fried, Albert, and Sanders, Ronald. *Socialist Thought*. Garden City, New York: Anchor Books of Doubleday & Co., 1964.

Freidrich, Carl. *Man and His Government*. New York: McGraw-Hill, 1963.

Fromm, Erich. *Marx's Concept of Man*. New York: Frederick Ungar Publishing Co., 1961.

Gay, Peter. *The Enlightenment: An Interpretation*. New York: Vintage Books, 1968.

———. *Voltaire's Politics*. New York: Vintage Books, 1965.

Germino, Dante. *Modern Western Political Thought*. Chicago: Rand McNally & Co., 1972.

————. "The Relevance of the Classics." Paper delivered at the American Political Science Association Annual Meeting, Washington, D. C., 1972.

————. "Second Thoughts on Leo Strauss' Machiavelli." *Journal of Politics* 28 (November 1966): 794-817.

————. "Some Observations on Recent Political Philosophy and Theory." *The Annals of the American Academy*, January 1972, pp. 141-148.

Gould, James A., and Truitt, Willis, H. *Political Ideologies.* New York: Macmillan Co., 1973.

Hacker, Andrew. "Capital and Carbuncles: The 'Great Books' Reappraised." *American Political Science Review* 48 (September 1954): 775-786.

————. *Political Theory: Philosophy, Ideology, Science.* New York: Macmillan, 1961.

Haddock, B. A. "The History of Ideas and the Study of Politics." *Political Theory* 2, no. 4 (November 1974): 420-432.

Hartz, Louis. *The Liberal Tradition in America.* New York: Harcourt, Brace & World, 1955.

Hegel, Georg Wilhelm Friedrich. *The Philosophy of History.* New York: Dover Publications, 1965.

Hexter, J. H. *More's Utopia: The Biography of an Idea.* New York: Harper & Row, Harper Torchbooks, 1965.

Holt, Robert. *The Methodology of Comparative Research.* New York: Free Press, 1970.

Hubert, J. D. "Random Reflections on Literary History and Textual Criticism." *New Literary History* 2, no. 1 (Fall 1971): 163-173.

Jaspers, Karl. *Plato and Augustine.* New York: Harcourt, Brace & World, Harvest Books, 1962.

Jung, H. "Conception of Political Philosophy," *The Review of Politics* 29 (October 1967): 492-517.

Kaufmann, Walter. *Hegel's Political Philosophy.* New York: Atherton Press, 1970.

Landi, Ernesto, "The Political Philosophy of Machiavelli." Translated by Maurice Cranston, *History Today* 14, no. 8 (August 1964): 550-555.

Lane, Robert. *Political Thinking and Consciousness.* Chicago: Markham Publishing Co., 1969.

Leiss, William. "Critical Theory and Its Future." *Political Theory* 2, no. 3 (August 1974): 330-350.

Lemisch, Jesse. "The American Revolution Seen from the Bottom Up." In *Towards a New Past: Dissenting Essays in American History*, edited by Barton J. Bernstein. New York: Random House Vintage Books, 1967.

Levinson, R. *In Defense of Plato*. New York: Russell and Russell, 1953.

Lichtheim, George. *The Concept of Ideology*. New York: Vintage Books, Random House, 1967.

————. *Marxism*. New York: Frederick A. Praeger, 1961.

Locke, John. *Two Treatises of Government*. Edited by Peter Laslett. New York: The New American Library, 1965.

Lothstein, Arthur. *All We Are Saying . . . The Philosophy of the New Left*. New York: Capricorn Books, 1970.

Lowi, T. *The End of Liberalism*. New York: W. W. Norton & Co., 1969.

Machiavelli, Niccolo. *The Prince and the Discourses*. Edited by Max Lerner. New York: Modern Library, Random House, 1950.

Macpherson, C. B. *The Political Theory of Possessive Individualism*. London: Oxford University Press, 1962.

Mazlish, Bruce. *In Search of Nixon: A Psychohistorical Inquiry*. Baltimore, Maryland: Penguin Books, 1973.

McDonald, Lee. *Western Political Theory*. New York: Harcourt, Brace, Jovanovich, 1968.

McDonald, Neil A. *Politics: A Study of Control Behavior*. New Brunswick, New Jersey: Rutgers University Press, 1965.

McGovern, William M. *From Luther to Hitler: The History of Fascist-Nazi Political Philosophy*. Boston: Houghton Mifflin, 1941; New York: AMS Press reprint, 1973.

McShea, R. J. "Leo Strauss on Machiavelli." *The Western Political Quarterly* 16 (December 1963): 782-797.

Meyer, Alfred G. *Marxism*. Cambridge: Harvard University Press, 1954.

More, Thomas. *Utopia*. Edited by H. V. S. Ogden. New York: Appleton-Century-Crofts, Crofts Classics, 1949.

Morrow, Glenn R. "Plato and the Rule of Law." In *Plato*, edited by Gregory Vlastos. Garden City, New York: Doubleday & Co., 1971. Originally a presidential address to the Western Division of the American Philosophical Association, Ohio State University, April 26, 1940, and later published in the *Philosophical Review* 59 (1941).

Orr, Robert R. "Intellectual Biography as a Form of the History of Ideas." *Interpretation* 4, no. 2 (Winter 1974): 98-106.

Paine, Thomas. *The Complete Writings of Thomas Paine.* Edited by Philip S. Fonner. New York: The Citadel Press, 1945.

Parente, William J. "Contemporary Liberal Arts Students and Political Science: Expectations, Activism and Curricular Reform." Paper delivered at the American Political Science Association Annual Meeting, Washington, D. C., 1972.

Popper, Karl R. *The Open Society and its Enemies.* New York: Harper & Row, 1963.

Post, L. A., ed. *Thirteen Epistles of Plato.* Oxford: Clarendon Press, 1925.

Raphael, D. D. *Problems of Political Philosophy.* New York: Praeger Publishers, 1970.

Rosenau, James N. *The Dramas of Politics: An Introduction to the Joys of Inquiry.* Boston: Little, Brown and Co., 1973.

Rossiter, Clinton. *Conservatism in America.* New York: Alfred A. Knopf, 1955.

_____. *Seedtime of the Republic: The Origin of the American Tradition of Political Liberty.* New York: Harcourt, Brace and Co., 1953.

Rousseau, Jean-Jacques. *The Social Contract and Discourses.* Translated and with an Introduction by G. D. H. Cole. New York: E. P. Dutton and Co., 1950.

Rozwenc, Edwin C., ed. *Slavery as a Cause of the Civil War.* Boston: D. C. Health and Co., 1963.

Runciman, W. G. *Social Science and Political Theory.* Cambridge: At the University Press, 1962.

Ryan, Alan. "Locke and the Dictatorship of the Bourgeoisie." In *Locke and Berkeley,* edited by C. B. Martin and D. M. Armstrong. Garden City, New York: Doubleday & Co., 1968.

Sartori, G. "Philosophy, Theory and the Science of Politics." *Political Theory* 2, no. 2 (May 1974): 133-163.

Schaefer, David L. "The Legacy of Leo Strauss: A Bibliographic Introduction." *The Intercollegiate Review* 9, no. 3 (Summer 1974): 139-148.

Shaw, L. Earl, ed. *Modern Competing Ideologies.* Lexington, Massachusetts: D. C. Heath and Co., 1973.

Shklar, Judith N. *Men and Citizens.* Cambridge: At the University Press, 1969.

Shorey, Paul. *The Unity of Plato's Thought.* Chicago: University of Chicago Press, 1903.

Skinner, Quinton, "Interpretation: Motives, Intentions and the Interpretation of Texts." *New Literary History* 3, no. 2 (Winter 1972): 393-408.

Stampp, Kenneth M., ed. *The Causes of the Civil War.* Englewood Cliffs, New Jersey: Prentice-Hall, 1965.

Storing, Herbert J. *What Country Have I?* New York: St. Martin's Press, 1970.

Strauss, Leo. "Note on the Plan of Nietzche's 'Beyond Good and Evil.'" *Interpretation* 3, no. 2, 3, (Winter 1973): 97-113. For complete lists of Strauss's works see Cropsey, Bloom, or Schaefer, above.

―――― "Philosophy as Rigorous Science and Political Philosophy." *Interpretation* 2, no. 1 (Summer 1971): 1-9.

―――― "Plato." In *History of Political Philosphy,* edited by Leo Strauss and Joseph Cropsey. Chicago: Rand McNally & Co., 1972.

―――― *Thoughts on Machiavelli.* Glencoe, Illinois: Free Press, 1958.

Swisher, Carl B. *American Constitutional Development.* Cambridge, Mass.: Houghton Mifflin Co., Riverside Press, 1954.

Talmon, J. L. *Origins of Totalitarian Democracy.* New York: W. W. Norton & Co., 1970.

Tucker, Robert. *The Marx-Engels Reader.* New York: W. W. Norton & Co., 1972.

―――― *Philosophy and Myth in Karl Marx.* Cambridge: At the University Press, 1961.

Waltz, Kenneth. *Man, the State and War.* New York: Columbia University Press, 1965.

Wild, John. *Plato's Modern Enemies and the Theory of Natural Law.* Chicago: University of Chicago Press, 1963.

Winspear, Alban Dewes. *The Genesis of Plato's Thought.* New York: S. A. Russell, 1940.

Wolin, Sheldon. "Political Theory as a Vocation." *American Political Science Review* 63 (December 1969).

Young, Roland. *Approaches to the Study of Politics.* Evanston, Illinois: Northwestern University Press, 1968.

Index

African heritage, 61–63, 34 n. 11
*American Revolution Seen from the
    Bottom Up* (Lemisch), 58–61
American revolutionary heritage,
    57–63. See also 22, 36, 38
anti-essentialist liberalism, 79
approaches, 1, 7, 10–15; 76:
        biography, 12, 30–39; Black
        Power, 61–63; conservative,
        57–61; history, 13–14, 44–49;
        ideology, 14–15, 50–63; intent v.
        effect, 10–12, 64–74; labeling,
        71–74; Marxist, 50–53, New Left,
        57–61; psychology, 12–13,
        39–43; textual analysis, 10–11,
        18–29. See also these specific
        approaches
Aristotle, 4, 34
art, 2, 80
autobiography, 35

Bakunin, Michael, 67–68
Bainton, Roland, 42–43
Barker, Ernest, 32
behavioral political science, 8, 77–80.
    See also political science
Bernstein, Eduard, 53
biography, 30–39; and Supreme
    Court, 10; and Watergate, 12;
    and historical approach, 44–45;
    and ideological approach, 50–51;
    and Black Power, 62–65; and
    Plato, 73; and student, 84
Black Power, 50, 61–63, 83
Black thought, 56, 60–63, 34 n. 11

Blanchard, William, 40
Bloom, Allan, 27–28

Campbell, W. E., 46 n.
Carmichael, Stokely, 61–63
Cassirer, Ernst, 47–49
Chabod, Frederich, 28
City of God (St. Augustine), 31
Civil War in France (Marx), 67–68
Common Sense (Paine), 22–23
common sense, 82–83
Communism, 14–15, 52–53, 65–74
Communist Manifesto (Marx and
    Engels), 65–66
community, 24, 56, 61–62
Confessions (Rousseau), 34, 49
    (St. Augustine), 34
consent, 24, 36
conservative theory 6, 50, 54, 57–61
Critique of the Gotha Program (Marx),
    67
constitutional law, 9–10
critical thought, 2, 6, 17, 39, 51–52,
    77–80, 84–85
Croce, Benedetto, 26
culture, 2, 29, 47–49, 61–62, 81, 83

democracy, 71, 82–83
dictatorship of the proletariat, 65–69
Discourses (Machiavelli), 25–29
Dolbeare, Kenneth, 53
Douglass, Frederick, 9–10, 34

Dred Scott v. Sandford, 9–10

Easton, David, 49
Economic and Philosophical Manuscripts (Marx), 65–67, 80
effect approach, 4, 10–12, 29, 51, 61–63, 64–74, 76
elitist theory, 54, 59
Emile (Rousseau), 35–36
end of ideology, 83
Engels, Frederick, 66–74, 81
Enlightenment, 47–49
The Enlightenment: An Interpretation (Gay), 48
environment of thought, 44–63
equality, 54–61
Erikson, Erik, 40–42; and ideology, 54
existentialism, 79

fact/value, 77–81
false consciousness, 52, 61
Filmer, Robert, 36
Friedrich, Carl, 7
Fromm, Erich, 69–74

Gay, Peter, 48–49
General Will, 24. *See also* Rousseau
Germino, Dante; and Strauss, 28; and Locke, 38
Gilbert, Felix, 28
good life, 23

Hacker, Andrew, 3, f. 1; 77 n.
Hamilton, Charles, 61–63
Hegel, 6, 19–21; and Popper, 71–72; *Philosophy of History,* 20–21; *Philosophy of Right,* 19–20
Hexter, J. H., 45–47
historical approach, 44–50; and Supreme Court, 10; and Watergate, 13–14; and biography/psychology, 39–42;

and Black thought, 61–63; and Popper on Plato, 73; and student, 84
Hitler, Adolf, 50, 73
Hobbes, Thomas, 36; and Macpherson interpretation, 55–57

ideologue, 6–7, 50–51, 84
ideology, ideological approach, 5–7, 14–15, 50–63; and Supreme Court, 10; and Erikson, 40–41; and capitalism, 65; and America, 83–84; and end of ideology, 83; and self analysis, 84
implication of theory, 4, 31, 39, 63–64, 74, 76
intent approach, 4, 64–74; and Supreme Court, 10; and Watergate, 11–12; and textual analysis, 25–29; and biographical approach, 30–39; and psychological approach, 43; and historical approach, 51; and Black thought, 61–63; and political theory, 76
intermediary. *See* interpretation
interpretation, 82 n. 20
interpretation, 1–9, 75–85; and constitutional law, 9–10; and Watergate, 10–15; and Western heritage, 15–17; and student, 75–85. *See also* individual approaches

Jaspers, Karl, 31

Kaufmann, Walter, 21; and Popper on Hegel, 72
Kautsky, Karl, 53
Kraus, Wolfgang, 22 n. 11
Kuhn, Thomas, 79–80

labeling approach, 71–74, 76
language, 2, 11, 20 n. 5
Laslett, Peter, 36–39, 81
Laws (Plato), 32–33
Lemisch, Jesse, 57–61
Lenin, Vladimir, 14, 53
Leviathan (Hobbes), 36
Levinson, R. B., 72–74
liberalism, 6, 56–57, 60, 62, 83
Lichtheim, George, 68
literary form and style, 19; and utopia
    and tract, 22–23; and Rousseau,
    23–25; and More, 22–23, 46
Locke, John, 25, 36–39; and Laslett
    on *Two Treatises*, 38–39, 81;
    and American theory, 36, 58–59;
    and Macpherson interpretation,
    55
Luther, Martin, 40–43; and Nazi
    totalitarianism, 71 n. 18, 74

Machiavelli, Niccolo, 25–29
Macpherson, C. B., 55–57
Mannheim, Karl, 50
Marx, Karl, 4, 6, 14, 78, 80–81; and
    Marxism, 50–53; and intent v.
    effect, 65–71
Marxian conceptualization, 54–57
Marxist thought, 6, 14, 50–53, 65–74,
    83
Mazlish, Bruce, 13
McDonald, Neil, 23 n. 15
McShea, R. J., 27–28
meaning, 1, 4–6, 12; and intent of
    theorist, 4, 25, 64–74, 76; and
    implications of theory, 4, 20, 74;
    and imputed effects of theory, 4,
    7, 64–74; and concepts in textual
    analysis, 19–21; and biography,
    35; and psychology, 40–41; and
    concepts in historical approach,
    14, 47–48; and Black thought,
    61–63; and discipline of political
    theory, 81; and student, 85
mediator *See* interpretation
Medieval theory, 47
More, Thomas, 22–23, 45–47
Morrow, Glenn, 32–33

nationalism, 83
nature, 47–48
Nazi, 7; and Hegel, 21, 72; and
    Luther, 71; and Popper, 71–73
neo-Thomism, 79
New Left, 50, 56–61
New Literary History, 82, n. 21
Nixon, Richard, 10–15
Nouvelle Heloise (Rousseau), 23

Paine, Thomas, 22–23
Pan-Africanism, 62–63
Paris Commune, 67–68
Person approach. *See* biography
Philosophy of History (Hegel), 20–21
Philosophy of Right (Hegel), 19–20
Plato, 32–33; and More, 45; and
    Winspear interpretation, 54–55;
    and totalitarianism, 71–72; and
    Popper, 73–74
political involvement, 45–47
political philosophy. *See* political
    theory
political science, 2, 8, 48 n. 10, 76–80
Political Theory, 82 n. 20
political theory/philosophy, 1–5; and
    discipline 3–7, 29, 50, 74–85;
    and scientific theory, 2, 47,
    76–80; and critical and
    constructive roles, 2, 17, 39; and
    consistency and inconsistency in
    thought, 64–69; and traditional
    theory, 3, 5, 49, 77–80; and role
    of scholar in society, 5–7, 74–80;
    and activist/critical intellectuals,
    52, 77–80. *See also* critical
    thought
political theory/practice, 4–7, 48, 52,
    56–63
Popper, Karl, 69–74
Prince (Machiavelli), 26–29
proletariat, 14, 52–53, 65–74
psychohistory, 13
psychology and psychological
    approach, 39–44; and
    Watergate, 12–13; and Black
    Power, 61; and Plato, 73; and
    student, 84

Renaissance, 45–48
Republic (Plato), 32–33
Rossiter, Clinton, 57–61
Rousseau, Jean Jacques, 23–24; and style, 23–25; and Shklar interpretation, 29; and *Confessions,* 34–35, 49; and *Emile,* 35; and biography, 34–36; and psychology, 40; and totalitarianism, 69–74
Ryan, Alan, 25

St. Augustine, 31–32
science, 2, 47, 77–78, 80
scientific theory, 2, 80; and Marx, 6, 52
Shklar, Judith, 22, 29, 35
Social Contract (Rousseau), 24
Soviet Union, 14–15, 68, 70
Stalin, Joseph, 14, 50
Strauss, Leo, 25–29, 33–34, 80
Structure of Scientific Revolutions (Kuhn), 79–80

Taney, Roger, 9–10
textual analysis, 18–29; and Supreme Court, 10; and Watergate, 11; and Leo Strauss, 25–29; and biography, 36; and historical approach, 45–46; and Black Power, 50, 61–62; and Popper on Hegel, 72; and traditional political theory, 80
theoretical self-analysis, 84–85
Theses on Feuerbach (Marx), 78
totalitarianism, totalitarian theory, 24, 70–74
tract, 22–23
translation, 19–21, 81
Tucker, Robert, 68–69
Two Treatises of Government (Locke), 25, 35–39

utopia, 22–23, 32, 45–47

Voltaire, 48

Washington Post, 10–15
Watergate, 10–15
Winspear, Alban, 54–55

Young Man Luther (Erikson), 40–43

Printed in U.S.A.